Ben. Jonson.
Hector Berlioz
Alexander Graham Bell
Charles Dickens
Louis
Robert Louis Stevenson
Ch. Darwin
Andrew Jackson
Marconi
Keats
Tolstoy
Virginia Woolf
L da Vinci
Robert Fulton
Oliver Cromwell
W. Longfellow
Bernard Buffet
John Adams
Bernard Shaw

The McGraw-Hill
ENCYCLOPEDIA OF
WORLD BIOGRAPHY

Cicero
Enver Pasha

3

AN INTERNATIONAL
REFERENCE WORK
IN TWELVE VOLUMES
INCLUDING AN INDEX

McGRAW-HILL BOOK COMPANY

NEW YORK / SAN FRANCISCO / ST. LOUIS
DUSSELDORF   NEW DELHI
JOHANNESBURG   PANAMA
KUALA LUMPUR   RIO DE JANEIRO
LONDON   SINGAPORE
MEXICO   SYDNEY
MONTREAL   TORONTO

The McGraw-Hill
ENCYCLOPEDIA OF
WORLD BIOGRAPHY

Cicero
———————
Enver Pasha   **3**

The McGraw-Hill
ENCYCLOPEDIA OF
WORLD BIOGRAPHY

Cicero
——————
Enver Pasha

3

Cicero C Cyrus the Great

CICERO / By David W. Reece

Marcus Tullius Cicero (106–43 B.C.) was Rome's greatest orator and a prolific writer of verse, letters, and works on philosophy, politics, and rhetoric that greatly influenced European thought.

Cicero (pronounced sĭs′ə-rō) was born on Jan. 3, 106 B.C., at Arpinum near Rome, the elder son of a wealthy landowner. At an early age Cicero saw military service during the Social War (90–89), but he managed to avoid involvement in the civil wars that followed. He wanted to follow a career in politics and decided first to gain a reputation as an advocate.

Cicero's first appearances in court were made during the dictatorship of Sulla (81–80). In one case, while defending Sextus Roscius of Ameria on a trumped-up charge of murder, he boldly made some outspoken comments on certain aspects of Sulla's regime, and in 79 he left Rome to study in Rhodes. By 76 Cicero was back in Rome, where he married Terentia, whose family was wealthy and perhaps aristocratic. In 75 he held the office of quaestor, which brought him membership in the Senate, and in 70 he scored his first great success, when he prosecuted Caius Verres for gross misgovernment in Sicily. As Verres was defended by the leading advocate of the day, Quintus Hortensius, Cicero's success in this case

Cicero, a Roman bust dating from about 30 B.C., in the Uffizi, Florence. (Alinari)

1

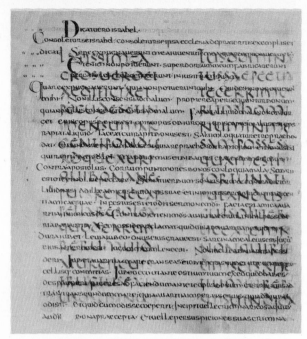

On this palimpsest (a parchment used more than one time) can be seen a two-column fragment of a 4th-century copy of Cicero's De republica. *The text of his treatise was only partially eradicated when the parchment was reused for another manuscript in the 8th century. (Biblioteca Apostolica Vaticana)*

won him great acclaim and considerably helped his political career.

In 69 Cicero held the office of aedile and that of praetor in 66, in which year he made his first major political speech in support of the extension of Pompey's command in the Mediterranean. During the following years he acted as a self-appointed defender of that general's interests. When Cicero stood for the consulship of 63, he reached the highest political office at the earliest legal age, a remarkable achievement for a complete outsider. His consulship involved him in a number of political problems which culminated in the conspiracy of Catiline.

Disillusion and Exile

In the years after his consulship Cicero, politically helpless, watched Caesar, Pompey, and Crassus form the dictatorial First Triumvirate. Cicero refused offers to become a fourth member of this alliance, and his publicly expressed dislike of the violent methods Caesar employed in his consulship (59) led to Cicero's exile to Macedonia. There he lived for 16 months in abject misery, until the efforts of his friends secured his recall in August 57 B.C.

During the next 8 months Cicero tried to separate Pompey from his partners, but early in the summer of 56 Pompey brusquely ordered Cicero to stop his efforts. For the next 4 years he was largely out of politics, devoting himself to writing and occasionally emerging to defend

(inconsistent behavior on his part) various supporters of the Triumvirate.

In 51 Cicero was sent off to govern Cilicia for a year. He was a conscientious and unusually honest administrator, but he was bored by the whole business and hated every moment of his absence from Rome. He finally returned in December 50 B.C., too late to be able to do anything to stop the outbreak of war between Pompey and Caesar. He accepted a commission from Pompey but did little for him, and when Pompey left Italy, Cicero stayed behind.

After Pompey's death Cicero took no part in politics and devoted himself to writing works on philosophy and rhetoric. Apart from his increasing dislike of Caesar's autocratic rule, Cicero's life was made unhappy during these years by domestic sorrows. In the winter of 47/46 he divorced Terentia after 30 years' marriage, and in the following summer he was deeply grieved by the death of his much-loved daughter Tullia.

Second Triumvirate

Cicero was not involved in the conspiracy against Caesar, though he strongly approved of it, and after the assassination he took a prominent part in establishing a compromise between Antony and the conspirators. But before long he concluded that Antony was as great a menace to liberty as Caesar had been. During the winter of 44/43 with a series of vigorous speeches, the "Philippics," he rallied the Senate to oppose Antony in concert with Octavian. But Octavian, having seized power at Rome by force, reached an agreement with Antony and Lepidus to set themselves up as a three-man dictatorship. They started by proscribing many of their enemies, and among the first names on the list was that of Cicero. He could perhaps have escaped, but his efforts were halfhearted, and in December 43 B.C. he met his death at the hands of Antony's agents with courage and dignity.

As a politician, Cicero was ultimately unsuccessful, since he was not able to prevent the overthrow of the republican system of government. Devoted to peace and reason, he lived in an age when political power depended more and more on sheer force. Moreover, he was blind to many of the defects of the republican system and did not realize how much it failed to meet the real needs of the provincials and even of the poorer citizens of Italy and Rome itself.

The Speeches

The texts of 57 speeches have survived, though 2 or 3 are not complete, and Cicero delivered at least 50 more, nearly all of which were published but have since been lost. As Cicero normally edited and polished his speeches before publication, we do not have the text of what he actually said, but in most cases a more or less close approximation.

However, five speeches against Verres were never delivered but were written by Cicero to present material not used in court; the "Second Philippic" is a political pamphlet cast in the form of an imaginary speech; and

Pro Milone represents what Cicero would have said in Milo's defense in 52 if he had not been flustered by a hostile mob into making a poor and ineffective speech.

The corpus of the extant speeches is impressive both for its bulk and its quality. It is hard not to be impressed by their vigor, by their variety of tone, and above all by the lucidity with which Cicero could present a complicated series of facts. Of the forensic speeches, *Pro Cluentio* (66) is the longest and most complicated, but it gives a vivid picture of life in a small Italian town. The much shorter *Pro Archia* (62) is notable for its sincere and eloquent defense of a life devoted to literary pursuits, and *Pro Murena* (63) is an excellent example of Cicero's ability to win a case by disregarding the basic facts and concentrating with charm and wit on such irrelevancies as the Stoic beliefs of one of the prosecutors. Of the political speeches, although the "Catilinarians" are the most famous, the 14 "Philippics" are probably the finest, because in them Cicero was concentrating all his energy and skill with a directness that he did not always achieve.

The Dialogues

Nearly all of Cicero's works on philosophy, politics, or rhetoric are in dialogue form, though Cicero had little of Plato's dramatic instinct for the genre. They are written in that elegant and sonorous Latin prose of which Cicero was such a master. Several are devoted to ethics, religion, or other philosophical subjects, but they cannot be regarded as original contributions to philosophy, for Cicero himself acknowledged, "I provide only the words, of which I have a very large stock." Nevertheless, they are extremely valuable because in them he reproduced the theories of many of the leading Greek philosophers of the post-Aristotelian schools, such as the Stoics and the Epicureans, whose own works have not survived.

Among the more attractive are the short essays on friendship and old age, *De amicitia* and *De senectute* (both 44). Of the longer works, the most important are probably *De finibus* (45), a systematic discussion of ethics; *De natura deorum* (45), a hastily written and disjointed but valuable survey of contemporary religious beliefs; and *De officiis* (winter 44/43), a treatise on moral duties.

Another group is concerned with political theory, especially *De republica* (54–51), of which barely one-third is extant, and *De legibus*, started in 52 but perhaps never completed. These works also are to some extent based on Greek ideas, but the theoretical basis is reinforced by the Roman practical genius for the art of government and Cicero's own considerable experience of politics.

In the works on Cicero's own art of rhetoric there is a similar blend of Greek theory and Roman practical experience. The most important are *De oratore* (55), which is basically a discussion of the training of the ideal orator but takes in many aspects of the art of speaking, such as humor; *Brutus* (45), which contains an account of Roman oratory of great historical importance, with

sketches of nearly 200 speakers; and *Orator* (45), in which Cicero discusses the different styles of oratory and various technical aspects of rhetoric, including a detailed examination of prose rhythms.

The Poetry

In his youth Cicero wrote a quantity of verse, none of which has survived, and he won a considerable reputation as a poet. In later years he composed a short epic on the great soldier Marius and a longer poem on his own consulship. Of such poetry, only a few scattered lines have been preserved, in one or two cases because they are so very bad. We do have, however, several hundred lines of the *Aratea*, a translation of a poem on astronomy by the Alexandrian poet Aratus, and a number of shorter passages also translated from Greek originals. It is clear that Cicero had little real poetic inspiration but was a highly competent craftsman who did much for the development of the dactylic hexameter in Latin, and metrical analysis suggests that in this respect Virgil owed as much to him as to any other poet.

The Letters

The collection of Cicero's letters is undoubtedly the most interesting and valuable part of all his enormous literary output. It includes nearly 800 letters written by him, and nearly another 100 written to him by a wide variety of correspondents. The two major collections are the letters *Ad Atticum* in 16 books, and *Ad familiares*, also in 16 books, published by his freedman secretary Tiro. This latter set includes practically all the letters written to Cicero. There are also two smaller sets, three books of *Ad Quintum fratrem* and two books of *Ad M. Brutum*, both the remains of what were at one time larger collections. Other sets of letters to his son Marcus, to Julius Caesar, to Octavian, and to others have all been lost. The surviving letters belong mainly to his last years; there are only 12 dating before his consulship, while over a quarter of the collection were written in the last 18 months of his life.

Some of the letters are as carefully composed as the speeches or dialogues, but most of them, especially those to his brother or to close friends like Atticus, have a spontaneity which is often lacking in the more calculated prose. In these intimate letters Cicero uses a very colloquial style, with frequent use of slang, ellipse, diminutive forms, and words or phrases in Greek.

But however rapidly they may have been written, Cicero never loses his instinctive sense of style, and their combination of immediacy with stylishness makes them some of the most attractive reading in the whole of Latin literature, quite apart from the fascination of their subject matter, for they cover an immense range of topics. But above all, they give an incredibly vivid picture of Cicero himself: his vanity, his facile optimism and equally exaggerated despair, his timidity and his indecisiveness, but also his energy and industry, his courage, his loyalty, and his basic honesty, kindliness and humanity. Thanks to his letters, we can know Cicero as we know no other Roman, and with all his faults he was a man worth knowing.

Further Reading

Cicero is listed in the Ancient History study guide (III, B, 3). Though a republican, he was very closely involved with the Romans mostly responsible for the fall of the republic: Julius CAESAR, POMPEY, Mark ANTONY, and AUGUSTUS. One of Cicero's less well-known opponents was CLODIUS. The conspiracy of CATILINE provided Cicero with a forum for his views.

Cicero's major works and his correspondence are available in English translation. The best brief account of his career and personality comprises the essays by H. H. Scullard, T. A. Dorey, and J. P. V. D. Balsdon in T. A. Dorey, ed., *Cicero* (1965), a rather uneven collection of studies by various authors. Of the numerous longer accounts, Torsten Petersson, *Cicero: A Biography* (1920), is balanced and reliable, and H. J. Haskell, *This Was Cicero* (1942), is very readable and generally sensible. R. E. Smith, *Cicero the Statesman* (1966), concentrates on the political side of his career and, though generally reliable on facts, is not very profound and is perhaps too favorable to Cicero. David Stockton, *Cicero: A Political Biography* (1971), is a straightforward account of Cicero's public career. Hartvig Frisch, *Cicero's Fight for the Republic* (1946), is an extremely detailed discussion of the last stage of Cicero's career. There is a good brief discussion of Cicero as a philosopher in H. A. K. Hunt, *The Humanism of Cicero* (1954).

For Cicero as an orator and for Roman rhetoric generally, S. F. Bonner, *Roman Declamation in the Late Republic and Early Empire* (1949), and M. L. Clarke, *Rhetoric at Rome* (1953; rev. ed. 1963), should be consulted. The best account of the history of Rome in Cicero's lifetime is in H. H. Scullard, *From the Gracchi to Nero* (1959; 2d ed. 1964), and a more detailed account is in T. Rice Holmes, *The Roman Republic and the Founder of the Empire* (1923).

✳   ✳   ✳

THE CID / By Thomas F. Glick

The Cid (1043–1099), or Cid Campeador, was the greatest Spanish medieval warrior and remains one of Spain's national heroes. At a time when Berber invaders threatened Castile, the Cid alone was able to rally his countrymen and emerge victorious.

R odrigo Diaz, later called the Cid (pronounced sĭd), was born in Vivar, a village north of Burgos. Vivar was the fief of his father, Diego Lainez, a minor nobleman. About 1058 his father died, and Rodrigo went to live in the household of Prince Sancho. When the prince became King Sancho II in 1065, he gave Rodrigo the highest position at court, that of standard bearer or head of the royal armies. Soon after, in order to

Title page of an early edition of Chronicle of the Cid *in the Biblioteca Nacional, Madrid. (MAS)*

settle a jurisdictional dispute between Navarre and Castile, Rodrigo defeated a Navarrese knight in single combat, gaining thereby the epithet of Campeador (from the Latin *campidoctoris*, "one who captures fields").

In 1067 Sancho and Rodrigo besieged the Islamic kingdom of Saragossa. Rodrigo was the outstanding figure in this siege, and it may have been at this time that Christians and Arabs alike began to call him Cidi or Cid (from the Arabic *sayyidi*, "my lord"). In January 1072 Sancho and his brother Alfonso, the king of León, battled at Golpejera. Sancho won the day and forced Alfonso into exile. Their sister Urraca then began to conspire against Sancho at Zamora. Sancho besieged this city and was murdered there in October 1072. After the Cid forced Alfonso to swear that he had no complicity in Sancho's assassination, Alfonso became also king of Castile.

The Cid continued in the royal service and married Alfonso's niece Jimena in 1074. But he was too powerful and popular for Alfonso's taste. The Cid's enemies at

(Opposite) A detail from Cimabue's painted crucifix, in the church of S. Domenico, Arezzo. (Bevilacqua/Pichel)

court declared that he was not a faithful vassal but a traitor, and the King believed them. Thus after a victorious campaign against Toledo, the Cid was exiled from Castile in the summer of 1081. He spent his first decade of exile fighting for various Christian and Moslem rulers. Throughout he remained loyal to Alfonso, despite the King's steadfast refusal to forgive him.

In 1090 the Cid, in coalition with the kings of Saragossa and Aragon, concentrated on repelling the advance of the Berber Almoravids in eastern Spain. In November 1092 he began a siege of Valencia, and the city finally fell in June 1094. As ruler of Valencia, which he captured in the name of Alfonso VI but governed as an autonomous territory, the Cid strove to build up the Christian presence in the largely Moslem town. He ruled there until his death on July 10, 1099. His widow Jimena continued to rule, but in 1102 she was forced to abandon Valencia to the Almoravids.

Further Reading

The Cid is listed in the European History study guide (II, I, 1, b). He served under ALFONSO VI.

The most thorough study of the Cid is by Ramón Menéndez Pidal, Spain's foremost Cid scholar, *The Cid and His Spain* (2 vols., 1929; trans. 1934). A popular account is Stephen Clissold, *In Search of the Cid* (1965).

*   *   *

CIMABUE / By Edmund Eglinski

The Italian painter Cimabue (active last quarter of 13th century) worked in an Italo-Byzantine style characterized by a vigor and vivacity that set it apart from the more conventional art of his times and anticipated the more natural style of the 14th century.

Cimabue (pronounced chē-mä-boo′ā), whose given name was Cenno de' Pepi, was probably born before 1250. The earliest document associated with him dates from June 8, 1272. The only other documented phase of Cimabue's life relates to his apse mosaic, *St. John the Evangelist*, in the Pisa Cathedral, dated 1301–1302. He died sometime after mid-1302.

Some hint of Cimabue's personality comes from literary sources. Dante mentioned Cimabue in the *Divine Comedy* but was more concerned with the moral lesson to be taught about the transitory nature of fame than with Cimabue's character: "Once, Cimabue thought to hold the field/ In painting; Giotto's all the rage today;/ The other's fame lies in the dust concealed" (*Purgatory*, Canto XI, 94–96, trans. Dorothy L. Sayers).

In an early-14th-century commentary on the *Divine Comedy*, Cimabue was described as arrogant and haughty; however, Lorenzo Ghiberti's account of the legend, later repeated by Giorgio Vasari, of how Cimabue discovered Giotto as a shepherd drawing on a flat stone

and offered to train the boy in the artist's craft would suggest that Cimabue's disposition had a charitable side as well.

The majority of extant examples of Cimabue's art consists of frescoes and panel paintings. The most extensive of these are the frescoes in the transept and apse of the Upper Church of S. Francesco in Assisi (ca. 1290). Vasari declared that Cimabue was responsible for all the decorations in the Upper Church except for the series of frescoes given over to the legend of St. Francis. Modern critics have tended to see Cimabue as the guiding spirit behind the decoration of the transept and apse but not necessarily the author of every scene.

The large *Crucifixion* scene in the left transept is the masterpiece among Cimabue's works in Assisi. The fresco, which now has the appearance of a photographic

The Madonna Enthroned with Angels, *completed in 1285 by Cimabue. The work, originally done for the Florentine Church of Sta Trinita, is now in the Uffizi, Florence. (Alinari)*

negative, the result of the blackening of lead pigments, is powerful and evocative. Cimabue took a Byzantine iconographic form, the dead Christ on the cross, and filled it with human drama. From the gentle rhythms among the faithful on the left to the pulsating hysteria of the angels fluttering about the cross, Cimabue related the story of the Crucifixion in direct, humanly comprehensible terms. The firmly rendered figures possess a plasticity and fullness not commonly found in late-13th-century painting and certainly explain why he was cited as the first painter to break away from the "Greek" manner and develop a more natural style of painting.

The Evangelists' portraits in the vaults of the crossing also reveal Cimabue's skill in creating full and plastic forms. Placed in half of the rather awkward triangular format, balanced in the other half with a cityscape, the Evangelists sit on wooden thrones drawn in distorted perspective. Their heads and hands have a volume quite consistent with the three-dimensional rendering of the drapery.

In the Lower Church of S. Francesco is the fresco *Madonna Enthroned with Angels and St. Francis*. It is one of Cimabue's most touching works, although it is in poor condition now.

Two painted wood crucifixes demonstrate the evolution of Cimabue's style. In the earlier work, in S. Domenico, Arezzo, which probably dates from before the frescoes in Assisi (that is, before ca. 1290), the artist retained traditional Italo-Byzantine conventions, especially in the linear definition of muscles, treatment of the hair, gold striations in the opaque loincloth, and two bust-length portraits in the terminals. The later work, formerly in Sta Croce, Florence (destroyed 1966), which probably dates from about the same time as the murals in Assisi, showed a new softness of modeling and abandonment of some Byzantine conventions, like gold striations. The torso of Christ was modeled with broad, widely varied tones which tended to suppress the tortoiseshell appearance seen in the Arezzo crucifix. In the Florence crucifix Cimabue was moving further along the path toward greater naturalism.

The large *Madonna Enthroned* from the Church of Sta Trinita in Florence (1280–1285) is one of the best paintings to study in order to understand Cimabue's art. The artist retained a number of Byzantine motifs but forsook the austere, hieratic remoteness of the typical Byzantine Virgin for a softer, more human warmth. She is more accessible, more loving, more the earthly mother. Cimabue, furthermore, showed a concern for the realistic depiction of space in his arrangement of the angels around the throne and in the perspective of the throne itself. The four busts which appear in openings below the throne are without precedent. They give the panel an architectural stability and importance not found in any other work of the period.

Further Reading

Cimabue is listed in the Art study guide (III, A, 1). Cimabue and his great disciple, GIOTTO, along with Pietro LORENZETTI and Simone MARTINI, were the most renowned artists to execute frescoes in S. Francesco.

The literature on Cimabue is substantial, with most of the work in Italian and German. Among English language works Eugenio Battisti's monograph *Cimabue* (1963; trans. 1967) is the most useful. It includes complete transcriptions of all documents, most of the earliest sources, a *catalogue raisonné*, a good bibliography, and especially fine color and black-and-white reproductions. Alfred Nicholson, *Cimabue: A Critical Study* (1932), is basic for an understanding and appreciation of Cimabue's role in the evolution of Italian painting. It includes very useful appendices, with summaries of documents and sources and lists of authentic and attributed works.

✳   ✳   ✳

CIMAROSA / By Tom R. Ward

The works of the Italian opera composer Domenico Cimarosa (1749–1801) typify the style of Italian opera buffa, or comic opera, in the late 18th century.

Domenico Cimarosa (pronounced chē-mä-rô′zä) was born in Averso near Naples, the son of a very poor family. At the age of 12 he entered the Conservatory of S. Maria di Loreto; he studied composition, voice, and keyboard and sang major parts in conservatory performances.

Cimarosa's first opera, *Le stravaganze del cante*, was produced in Naples in 1772, the year he left the conservatory. From then until 1780 he moved between Rome and Naples, composing 15 operas for the two cities. By the 1780s he was the rival of Giovanni Paisiello, until then the acknowledged leader among opera composers in Italy. Italian companies performed Cimarosa's works in London, Paris, Dresden, and Vienna.

In 1787 Cimarosa went to St. Petersburg, Russia, as chamber composer to Catherine II, joining a long line of Italians who had held posts there beginning in the early 18th century. He composed two operas, *Cleopatra* and *La vergine del sole*, as well as cantatas and vocal and instrumental works during his stay. His constitution was not strong enough to stand St. Petersburg's weather, so he left in 1791 to become conductor to Leopold II in Vienna. It was here that he composed his masterpiece, *Il matrimonio segreto*, in 1792. This, his most popular work, is the only one to remain in the repertory. When Leopold II died that year, Cimarosa lost his position and returned to Naples, where he became conductor to the king and music teacher to the royal children in 1793. In 1799 he was imprisoned for publicly expressing his sympathy for Napoleon. After his release he left Naples for St. Petersburg; on the journey he died in Venice in 1801.

In addition to 61 operas, many with two versions, Cimarosa composed oratorios, cantatas, miscellaneous vocal works, and instrumental works, including 32 one-movement piano sonatas. His melodic gifts so impressed

Domenico Cimarosa. (Alinari-Brogi)

Goethe that he wrote two texts, *Die Spröde* and *Die Bekehrte*, to be sung to Cimarosa's melodies.

Cimarosa's operatic style is similar to that of many of his Italian contemporaries. The speed at which he composed is reflected in his tendency to use conventional procedures. However, he wrote dramatic ensembles very well, both within acts and as finales, to carry forward the dramatic action. Although these ensembles do not show the breadth and depth of a Mozart, they are well above the standard of contemporary practice.

Further Reading

Domenico Cimarosa is listed in the Music study guide (I, F, 3). He continued the tradition of Italian *opera buffa* begun by Giovanni Battista PERGOLESI. Cimarosa's work forms a link with the style of Gioacchino ROSSINI and Gaetano DONIZETTI.

Both Paul Henry Lang, *Music in Western Civilization* (1941), and Donald J. Grout, *A Short History of Opera* (1947; 2d ed. 1965), survey the 18th-century Italian tradition and discuss Cimarosa. See also George T. Ferris, *The Great Italian and French Composers* (1883).

CINQUE / By Maynard W. Swanson

Joseph Cinque (ca. 1813–ca. 1879) was a West African who led a slave mutiny on the Cuban ship "Amistad" in 1839. It led to a celebrated trial in United States courts, which held that slaves escaping from illegal bondage should be treated as free men.

Joseph Cinque (pronounced sĭn′gwā) was born the son of a Mende headman in the village of Mani, in modern Sierra Leone. A rice farmer and trader, he was enslaved for debt and sold to the notorious Spanish slaver Pedro Blanco, on Lomboko Island at the mouth of the Gallinas River, in April 1839. Cinque was then carried to Havana, where he was resold with 51 others, many of them Mendians, and shipped aboard the coasting schooner *Amistad* bound for the Cuban sugar plantations near the port of Guanaja, Puerto Principe.

On June 30 Cinque incited the slaves to revolt at sea, killing the captain and cook and taking prisoner their owners, two merchants named Ruiz and Montez. Cinque tried to force Montez to pilot the vessel to Africa, but Montez reversed the course repeatedly, zigzagging up the North American coast. They were captured off Montauk Point, Long Island, by the U.S. Coast Guard vessel *Washington* and were brought to New London, where the ship, cargo, and rebellious slaves were claimed for salvage money, while Ruiz and Montez sought to regain possession of them.

President Van Buren and Secretary of State John Forsyth, sympathetic to the slaveholders' claims and pressured by the Spanish government, tried to remove the case from the courts and transport the Africans to Cuba. But the Connecticut courts would not release them, and the plight of Cinque and his companions, jailed in New Haven, aroused abolitionist forces led by the New York merchant Lewis Tappan.

Cinque's heroic figure and commanding personality lent itself to the drama, and he was widely lionized as a symbol of the abolitionist cause. The abolitionists argued that the Africans, illegally enslaved, were justified in revolting to regain freedom and were innocent of any true crime in killing their captors to achieve freedom. In a dramatic appeal before the Supreme Court in 1841, the 73-year-old former president John Quincy Adams charged the Federal government with wrongful interference in the courts and obstruction of justice through partiality for slaveholders and antipathy toward blacks. The Court's decision, given on March 9, 1841, went for the abolitionists and set the Africans free.

Tappan and his associates then intended to found an African mission, using Cinque's party as a nucleus. Once in Sierra Leone, however, the not ungrateful but independent-minded Africans clashed with their mentors and soon deserted the enterprise. Cinque established himself as an independent power and became, according to rumors, a successful slave trader himself. Years later, in 1879, he was reported to have reappeared, to die and be buried at the old mission on Sherbro Island.

Further Reading

Joseph Cinque is listed in the Africa study guide (VI, B,

Joseph Cinque. (New Haven Colony Historical Society)

2). Another slave, Olaudah EQUIANO, gained his freedom and wrote a celebrated autobiography.

The fullest account of Cinque is William A. Owens, *Slave Mutiny: The Revolt on the Schooner Amistad* (1953), a dramatized account based on research into the documents of the *Amistad* collection of the New Haven Historical Society, Supreme Court case records, personal papers, and records of the American Missionary Association. Cinque and the *Amistad* mutiny are discussed in the context of the slave trade and the international efforts to suppress it in John R. Spears, "The Story of the Amistad," in *The American Slave Trade: An Account of Its Origin, Growth and Suppression* (1900; reissued 1967 with a new introduction), and in Daniel P. Mannix and Malcolm Cowley, *Black Cargoes* (1962). Contemporary accounts and documentation are found in John W. Barber, *A History of the Amistad Captives . . . with Biographical Sketches . . . also, an Account of the Trials* (1840). The key judicial decisions in the *Amistad* case are contained in Helen Tunnicliff Catterall, ed., *Judicial Cases Concerning American Slavery and the Negro*, vol. 4 (1936).

CLAPHAM / By Reba N. Soffer

The English economic historian Sir John Harold Clapham (1873–1946) established economic history as a significant and independent field of study in Great Britain.

John Harold Clapham was the son of a Wesleyan jeweler in Salford, Lancashire. He attended King's College, Cambridge, on a scholarship, graduating with first-class honors in history in 1895. He received the Lightfoot scholarship in ecclesiastical history the following year and the Prince Consort Prize in 1897 and then was made a fellow of King's. He was influenced most in these early years by the economist Alfred Marshall.

In 1902 Clapham went to the University of Leeds as a professor of economics and a pioneer in economic history. He returned to Cambridge in 1908 as dean of King's and was deeply involved in university affairs until his death. In 1928 the Cambridge chair in economic history was established for him, and he held it for a decade. From 1933 until 1943 he was vice-provost of King's.

Clapham was a member of the Board of Trade on the Cabinet Committee on Priorities (1916–1918), president of the British Academy (1940–1945), editor of *Studies in Economic History*, and joint editor of the first volume of the epochal *Cambridge Economic History of Europe* (1941). He was knighted in 1944.

In 1945 Clement Atlee appointed Clapham chairman of a committee to study economic and social research in England. The committee's recommendations, published after Clapham's death, were accepted and implemented by the government.

Major Efforts and Achievements

Clapham was essentially uninterested in the role of ideas, and in 1922 his famous essay "Of Empty Boxes" attacked theory and analysis which "outran verification." During the 1930s and 1940s, when disagreements on methodology and meaning stirred historians and social scientists, he continued to support narrative histories of institutions based on accumulations of economic data. In his monumental three-volume *Economic History of Modern Britain* (1926–1938), Clapham traced with admiration the achievements of 19th-century free enterprise. Personally sympathetic to the economically displaced, Clapham wrote little about them and even less about the causes for their displacement. His views of economic history as the "story of how men have kept alive and as comfortable as might be" dominated the practice of economic history at Cambridge until recent times.

Although Clapham wrote two studies in political history, his major efforts and achievements were in economic history. Beginning with *The Woolen and Worsted Industries* (1907), his other works of importance are *The Economic Development of France and Germany, 1815–1914* (1921); *The Bank of England: A History* (3 vols., 1944–1958); and *A Concise Economic History of Britain from the Earliest Times to 1750* (published posthumously in 1949 and revised in 1959).

Further Reading

Sir John Harold Clapham is listed in the Social Sciences study guide (VII, A, 1). While a student at Cambridge he was drawn into the study of history by Lord ACTON and Frederic William MAITLAND.

Sir John Harold Clapham. (Radio Times Hulton Picture Library)

Clapperton returned to Scotland on half pay in 1817 and 3 years later met Dr. Walter Oudney, who was preparing an expedition to west-central Africa. Clapperton accepted Oudney's invitation to accompany him, and in 1822, with Maj. Dixon Denham, they set out from Tripoli to cross the Sahara. On Feb. 4, 1823, they reached Lake Chad, being the first Europeans to see it. Thinking it the key to western African river systems, they explored the kingdoms around the lake and discovered the Shari River, which emptied into Lake Chad.

Quarreling over leadership of the party, the three parted, Denham going southeastward and Clapperton and Oudney going west, through the Hausa states, toward the Niger River. Oudney died at Murmur in January 1824, but Clapperton continued, visiting Kano and then Sokoto, where the Fulani sultan Muhammed Bello refused to allow him to continue on to the Niger, only 150 miles away. Bello, however, was friendly to Clapperton and expressed interest in developing trade with Britain. Clapperton and Denham met near Lake Chad and returned to England on June 1, 1825.

Only 3 months later Clapperton left again on a second expedition, this time starting from the Bight of Benin and traveling through Yoruba lands in what is now western Nigeria. He crossed the Niger River near Boussa and reached Kano by July 1826. At Sokoto, Clapperton found that Sultan Bello had become suspicious of British imperialism and refused to enter into agreement with him. Clapperton became ill, and the failure of his expedition

The most complete biographical sketch of Clapham's life and work is G. N. Clark's "Sir John Harold Clapham, 1873–1946" in the *Proceedings of the British Academy,* vol. 32 (1944). A biographical sketch of Clapham by W. H. B. Court is in *Architects and Craftsmen in History,* edited by Joseph T. Lambie (1956). The inaugural address of M. M. Postan as professor of economic history at Cambridge, succeeding Clapham, *The Historical Method in Social Science* (1939), illustrates the continuity of Clapham's influence.

CLAPPERTON / By G. Wesley Johnson

A Scottish explorer of Africa, Hugh Clapperton (1788–1827) extended knowledge of the Fulani empire in what is now northern Nigeria and reached the Niger River in an effort to solve the mystery of that river's course and terminal point.

Hugh Clapperton was born in Annan, the son of a surgeon. He received little formal education and at age 13 went to sea. He joined the Royal Navy and saw service in the Mediterranean, the East Indies, and Canada.

Hugh Clapperton. (Radio Times Hulton Picture Library)

helped destroy him. He died on April 13, 1827, near Sokoto. Clapperton's belief that the Niger emptied into the Atlantic at the Bight of Benin was proved by his servant, Richard Lander, in a later expedition.

Further Reading

Hugh Clapperton is listed in the Africa study guide (VII, A, 1). Later explorers of the lands around the Niger River included William BAIKIE and Heinrich BARTH.

Clapperton and Oudney's role in the first expedition to Lake Chad was minimized by Dixon Denham, who claimed most of the credit for himself in his *Narrative of Travels and Discoveries in Northern and Central Africa, in the Years 1822, 1823, and 1824* (1826). For Clapperton's second journey see his *Journal of a Second Expedition into the Interior of Africa* (1829), edited and commented on by his servant, Richard Lander. See also Lander's *Records of Captain Clapperton's Last Expedition to Africa* (2 vols., 1830). An excellent secondary source that gives an evaluation of Clapperton's accomplishments is E. W. Bovill, *The Niger Explored* (1968).

Lord Clarendon, after a portrait by Adriaen Hanneman. (National Portrait Gallery, London)

CLARENDON / By Walter G. Simon

The English statesman and historian Edward Hyde, 1st Earl of Clarendon (1609–1674), was the first minister of Charles II in exile and then in England until 1666.

The son of Henry Hyde of Dinton, Wiltshire, Edward Hyde was born on Feb. 18, 1609. He attended Oxford University and earned a bachelor of arts degree in 1626, the year after he had begun legal studies at the Middle Temple. Noted for his intellectual abilities, he associated with prominent scholars and writers, and among his friends were the playwright Ben Jonson and the statesman, poet, and literary patron Lord Falkland.

Hyde's first wife died 6 months after their marriage in 1629, and in 1634 he married Frances Aylesbury. Having been called to the bar in 1633, he soon built up a profitable legal practice and was also awarded government posts, owing in part to the influence of his father-in-law, Sir Thomas Aylesbury.

Hyde's political ideals were formed in the period before the English civil war as a member of the Falkland circle. He believed in a balanced sovereignty between Parliament and the monarchy, such as he felt had existed in the time of Queen Elizabeth. It was his tragedy that such a balance was never obtained during his career; he was driven from position to position, never truly leading policy but largely fighting rearguard actions.

In the late 1630s Hyde felt the main violation of this balanced concept of government proceeded from the king. Elected to Parliament in 1640, he was extremely active in the original movements to check royal power and was a leading formulator of the impeachment proceedings against Lord Strafford. But by late 1641 he began to oppose the revolutionary tendencies, particularly in religious matters, among the controlling parliamentary leaders. He successfully obstructed the Root and Branch Bill to destroy the Church and became an adherent of the royal minority in the Lower House.

By 1643 Hyde had become a leading councilor of King Charles I and was among those who proposed the calling of the Parliament at Oxford that opened the civil war. Appointed chief adviser to the heir apparent, Prince Charles, he followed the prince into exile in 1646. During the years of exile, although his advice was not always heeded, he was the principal figure at the prince's court.

Later Career

With the restoration of the monarchy in 1660, Hyde continued as the first minister of the returned prince, who was then styled King Charles II. In 1660 Hyde was created Baron Hyde and in 1661 Earl of Clarendon. For the first year of his ministry he, like the King, favored programs of moderation, amelioration, and toleration, but with the election of the Cavalier Parliament in 1661, Clarendon's position had to change. Since his principal responsibility was to lead Parliament into cooperation with the King, his policy had to be based on accommodation. The new Parliament being rigidly Cavalier royalist and stridently Anglican, Clarendon was forced into a similar posture. Thus the religious laws of the early 1660s, which established persecutive measures against Dissenters, are known as the Clarendon code but were framed largely by those whom Clarendon needed for support in other matters.

Clarendon's position was further complicated by the fact that a number of very ambitious courtiers constantly attacked him on nearly every issue. There were impeachment attempts made upon him as early as 1663. Clarendon was the subject of considerable envy over the marriage in 1660 of his daughter Anne to the heir apparent, James, Duke of York. When the marriage of Charles II and Catherine of Braganza of Portugal proved to be barren, it was rumored that Clarendon had purposely married the King to a barren princess to secure the throne for his own grandchildren. Clarendon was also wrongly blamed for the sale of Dunkirk to the French and for the failure of the English project at Tangier. Finally his obvious disapproval of the manners at court and his increasing high-handedness in council irritated the King.

Clarendon's fall, however, proceeded mainly from the loss of the Dutch War in 1666. Although he had been less than enthusiastic in the pursuit of this war, the defeat did not stem principally from his mishandling of the situation. But the blow to his prestige because of the English loss destroyed his already-weakened influence at court and shattered his party in Parliament. Thus, despite support of Clarendon by the Duke of York's faction and the Anglican bishops, in 1667 Parliament began impeachment proceedings against him. The court party and the King, along with almost every dissident interest in England, including many of the Cavaliers, advocated impeachment. Clarendon was persuaded to flee into exile, and the impeachment was turned into a bill for perpetual banishment.

Clarendon spent the rest of his life in France. He had the satisfaction of seeing many of his enemies shatter themselves in the scramble for office which followed his own fall. During his years in exile he wrote his memoirs and completed his *History of the Rebellion and Civil Wars*. His writings supply historians with some of the best available source material for the period. Clarendon died at Rouen on Dec. 9, 1674.

Further Reading

Lord Clarendon is listed in the European History study guide (V, A, 1, c) and the Social Sciences study guide (IV, A, 1). Among the other ministers of CHARLES II were the 1st Earl of SHAFTESBURY and the 2d Duke of BUCKINGHAM.

The best biographies of Clarendon are T. H. Lister, *Life and Administration of Edward, First Earl of Clarendon* (3 vols., 1837–1838), and B. H. G. Wormald, *Clarendon* (1951), which covers only the civil war period. The serious student of Clarendon or his times should also turn to Clarendon's own writings. The general works on the period, David Ogg, *England in the Reign of Charles II* (2 vols., 1934; 2d ed. 1962), and G. N. Clark, *The Later Stuarts, 1660–1714* (1934; 2d ed. 1955), may be supplemented by such special works as Keith Feiling, *A History*

of the Tory Party, 1640–1714 (1924), which deals extensively with Clarendon's political career.

G. R. **CLARK** / By Don Higginbotham

George Rogers Clark (1752–1818) was an American Revolutionary War soldier. His capture of British posts on the far frontier was of considerable importance, though the idea that Clark "won the Northwest" is an oft-repeated exaggeration.

Standing 6 feet tall, topped by flaming red hair, George Rogers Clark was a true frontiersman. He talked the language of his men and shared in all their hardships. With a flair for the dramatic, he was known to the Indians as "Long Knife" and was skilled in the high-flown, metaphorical oratory of his red "brothers."

Born on a small plantation near Charlottesville, Va., Clark had only a rudimentary education before becoming a surveyor. By the age of 20, he had staked out his own land claims on the Ohio River and obtained "a good deal of cash by surveying." Commissioned a captain in the Virginia militia, Clark saw extensive campaigning in Lord Dunmore's War against the Shawnee Indians in 1774.

George Rogers Clark. (Courtesy of The New-York Historical Society, New York City)

The next year the Ohio Land Company engaged him to lay out its tracts on the Kentucky River. Clark made his home in Harrodsburg, the first settlement in Kentucky. Quickly emerging as a dominant figure, he led the Kentuckians in their successful efforts to be formally annexed as a county of Virginia.

Revolutionary Career

Kentucky's survival against the Indians—who looked upon "the dark and bloody ground" as their own and who were mainly pro-British during the Revolution—was Clark's great concern. Consequently, he went to Williamsburg, the capital of Virginia, to sell the state leaders on a plan for the capture of the British-held villages north of the Ohio and eventually Detroit as well. In January 1778 the Virginia Legislature commissioned Clark a lieutenant colonel, granted him £1,200, and authorized him to take as much of the interior as possible. It was no easy task to get men to leave their thinly populated settlements exposed, but at length, with 175 recruits, he floated down the Ohio and, before its juncture with the Mississippi, set off on foot across southern Illinois. Early in July 1778, Clark took the hamlets of Kaskaskia and Cahokia without bloodshed, and Vincennes a little later. Soon the entire region became known as the county of Illinois in the state of Virginia.

But Clark had to defend his conquests, for Lieutenant Governor Henry Hamilton and a mixed force—Indians, French Canadians, and regulars—swept down from Detroit to restore royal control. Initially, the advantage belonged to Hamilton, who easily wrested Vincennes from the Americans and with superior numbers threatened Clark at Kaskaskia. But Hamilton decided to sit out the winter at Vincennes before attacking and soon saw many of his Frenchmen and Indians return to their northern homes.

Clark, in contrast, would not let adversity bar the door. Believing that "great things have been affected by a few Men well Conducted," he and his "boys" marched 180 miles through torrential rains and other discomforts to recapture Vincennes on Feb. 5, 1779. He also bagged Hamilton himself, who was hated by the Americans for his allegedly indiscriminate use of Indians—"the Famous Hair-Buyer General," boasted Clark of his prize prisoner.

Clark's Significance

Clark's conquest of the Illinois country stood as a dramatic feat accomplished under tremendous physical and material handicaps by a bold and resourceful leader. Unfortunately, he failed to receive the reinforcements that would have enabled him to move against Detroit. Therefore it seems dubious to accept such extreme statements as that Clark "added three—perhaps five—states to the Union"; or that his "rearguard operations" on the frontier "saved the American Revolution from collapse." Moreover, the diplomats who negotiated the Treaty of Paris in 1783 were only very dimly aware of the military events in the back country. In fact, Clark was on the defensive along the Ohio during the last 2 years of the war as the Indians continued to devastate the frontier. In his last important action Clark launched a counteroffensive against the Shawnee tribe, driving it back into central Ohio.

When Clark retired from the Virginia service as a brigadier general, he became chief surveyor of the military lands granted to his soldiers north of the Ohio. In 1784 Congress appointed Clark one of several commissioners to settle outstanding differences, such as land claims, with the Indians of the Old Northwest. His efforts failed, and 2 years later Clark was again in the field with the Kentucky militia. At Vincennes he impressed much-needed supplies owned by Spanish merchants. James Wilkinson, a former Continental general and a paid secret agent of the Madrid government, used the episode to try to destroy Clark's character. Clark also had trouble with Virginia authorities attempting to settle the accounts of his campaign against Henry Hamilton. In the absence of records that had disappeared (they were discovered in the attic of the Virginia Capitol in 1913), Clark was never compensated for heavy personal losses in the public service. Financially ruined and filled with bitterness, he turned increasingly to liquor as an escape.

Visions of glory prompted Clark to join a French-sponsored expedition aimed at taking Spanish Louisiana in 1793, but President Washington prevented its departure and the scheme collapsed. When still another military venture in behalf of France failed in 1798, Clark returned to Louisville. Later, following the loss of one leg and a stroke, he made his home with a nearby sister. Impoverished, crippled, partially paralyzed, and plagued by alcoholism and creditors, he was once heard to say on learning of a friend's passing, "Everybody can die but me." For Clark the pathetic end came none too soon, on Feb. 13, 1818.

Further Reading

George Rogers Clark is listed in the American History study guide (III, D, 1, a). Other Revolutionary War soldiers were Benedict ARNOLD and Daniel MORGAN.

The two standard biographies of Clark are James A. James, *The Life of George Rogers Clark* (1928), and John Bakeless, *Background to Glory: The Life of George Rogers Clark* (1957). Both are factually reliable, and Bakeless is especially interesting. Both, however, tend to exaggerate the importance of Clark's conquests in the Northwest. Recommended for general historical background are Milo M. Quaife, ed., *The Capture of Old Vincennes: The Original Narratives of George Rogers Clark and of His Opponent Gov. Henry Hamilton* (1927); Randolph C. Downes, *Council Fires on the Upper Ohio* (1940); and Francis S. Philbrick, *The Rise of the West, 1754–1830* (1965).

J. B. **CLARK** / By Reba N. Soffer

The American economist John Bates Clark (1847–1938) was the first economic theorist from the United States to achieve an international reputation.

John Bates Clark was born and raised in Providence, R.I. In 1872, after an absence due to his father's illness and death, Clark graduated from Amherst College. Abandoning earlier plans to enter divinity school, he turned to economics. From 1872 to 1875 he studied at the University of Heidelberg under Karl Knies, leader of the German historical school, and at the University of Zurich.

On his return Clark participated actively in the creation of a "new" economics, becoming the third president of the young reformers' American Economic Association. He was professor of history and political economy at Carleton College until 1882. He then taught at Smith College, Amherst, and Johns Hopkins University. From 1895 until his retirement as professor emeritus in 1923, Clark was part of the influential faculty of political science at Columbia University, where he edited the *Political Science Quarterly* (1895–1911). After 1911 he devoted himself to pacifist causes and served as the first director of the Carnegie Endowment for International Peace.

Near the turn of the century, rapid industrial development and serious discontent, especially with the anomalous distribution of wealth, prompted Clark to examine problems of production and distribution. The indisputable influence which he exercised upon at least a generation of economists lay more in his development of analytical tools than in the conclusions he drew from them. Through his marginal utility principle, developed independently of Léon Walras, Carl Menger, and W. S. Jevons, Clark became the leading theorist of a marginal productivity theory of distribution which idealized the relationship between income and an individual's contribution to goods or services.

Clark's first important work, *The Philosophy of Wealth* (1885), attacking the hedonistic and atomistic assumptions of classical economics, attempted to tie economics to social ethics. Clark's major contribution, *The Distribution of Wealth* (1899), discarded his early reformist tendencies to present a deductive system of economic harmony based upon the competition of rational, self-interested men inevitably progressing. Clark began by assuming that society was a biological organism subject to collective moral judgment. Then he divided economics into "static" and "dynamic" analysis, a distinction which continues to characterize American economics. Clark's own analysis was a static description of economic laws in an unchanging society where perfect competition led to economic equilibrium. Static phenomena were not analytical abstractions but real economic forces isolated from dynamic laws of social change so that the mechanics of distribution were revealed. Dynamic laws, to be discovered by future generations using refined empirical techniques, were formulated tentatively by Clark in the last chapters of *Distribution* and in his later *Essentials of Economic Theory* (1907) on the basis of static economics and an optimistic

John Bates Clark. (Library of Congress)

justification of the status quo. To Clark, population growth, improvement in tastes, capital accumulation, technological innovation, and industrial organization were dynamic, necessarily progressive forces.

Clark's other important works included *The Modern Distributive Process* (with Franklin H. Giddings, 1888); *The Control of Trusts* (1901); *The Problem of Monopoly* (1904), influential in the antitrust legislation of 1914; *Social Justice without Socialism* (1914); and *A Tender of Peace.*

Further Reading

John Bates Clark is listed in the Social Sciences study guide (VI, C, 3; VII, C, 3). Thorstein VEBLEN studied under him at Carleton College. Clark's son was the economist John Maurice CLARK.

There is no biography of Clark. The essay on Clark in Paul T. Homan, *Contemporary Economic Thought* (1928), remains the clearest exposition of his economic theory. The discussion by Clark's distinguished economist son, "J. M. Clark on J. B. Clark," in Henry W. Spiegel, ed., *The Development of Economic Thought: Great Economists in Perspective* (1952; abr. ed. 1964), is warm, filial, and defensive but not very useful. John Rutherford Everett, *Religion in Economics: A Study of John Bates Clark, Richard T. Ely, Simon N. Patten* (1946), lifts whole sections from other commentators without adding anything new. Jacob H. Hollander, ed., *Economic Essays Contributed in Honor of J. B. Clark* (1967), which includes a brief memoir by Hollander, shows the development of Clark's thought.

* * *

J. M. CLARK / By Jesse W. Markham

The American economist John Maurice Clark (1884–1963) is perhaps the best-known forerunner of the American economists who are sometimes referred to as the pragmatic school.

John Maurice Clark was born in Northampton, Mass. He graduated from nearby Amherst College in 1905 and did his graduate study in economics at Columbia University, where he received his doctorate in 1910. He instructed at Colorado College (1908–1910) and at Amherst College (1910–1915) until he joined the faculty of political economy at the University of Chicago, where his colleagues included Jacob Viner and Frank Knight. In 1926 he left Chicago to accept a professorship at Columbia, where he remained until he retired in 1957, completing a half century of uninterrupted teaching and productive scholarship.

Clark's works, while primarily theoretical in content, were almost always directed toward clarifying and solving practical economic issues. He skillfully built his own analytical treatises upon the logic underlying the rigorously formulated models of others, first the marginalists and later Edward H. Chamberlin and Joan Robinson. In

John Maurice Clark. (Columbia University, Office of Public Information)

contrast with the methodology of these scholars, and of the younger mathematical economists who rose to prominence during the latter part of his professional life, Clark's methodology relied on the written word rather than geometric and algebraic formulations.

Dynamics of a Market Economy

Clark has been singled out as one of the few economists (John Maynard Keynes was another) born into the profession. He was the son of the distinguished John Bates Clark, a founder and the third president of the American Economic Association. John Maurice Clark, following in his father's footsteps, was the association's thirty-seventh president. The senior Clark had a pronounced influence on Clark's professional and personal life. The father directed the son's doctoral dissertation at Columbia (*Standards of Reasonableness in Local Freight Discriminations*), and in turn the younger Clark was the coauthor of the revised edition of his father's *The Control of Trusts* (1914). Clark dedicated his highly praised *Studies in the Economics of Overhead Costs* to his father, and in his last major work published before his death, *Competition as a Dynamic Process* (1961), he attributed his concern with the dynamics of economics to his father's basic conception that static equilibrium analysis was properly an introduction to the study of dynamics rather than an end in itself.

Virtually all of Clark's works were concerned with the dynamics of a market economy. His article "Towards a Concept of Workable Competition" (1940) greatly influenced the later writings of others concerned with the policy standards applicable to the functioning of a dynamic market economy.

Clark received honorary degrees from Amherst College, Columbia University, the University of Paris, the New School of Social Research, and Yale University. In 1951 Columbia appointed him to the John Bates Clark chair, established in his father's honor. A year later the American Economic Association bestowed on him its highest honor by awarding him the Francis A. Walker Medal for distinguished service in the field of economics.

Further Reading

John Maurice Clark is listed in the Social Sciences study guide (VII, C, 3). His father, John Bates CLARK, was also a famous economist.

Detailed biographies of Clark are in Joseph Dorfman, *The Economic Mind in American Civilization* (5 vols., 1946–1959), and Ben B. Seligman, *Main Currents in Modern Economics: Economic Thought since 1870* (1962). See also T. W. Hutchison, *A Review of Economic Doctrines, 1870–1929* (1953).

M. CLARK / By Stephen E. Ambrose

The American army officer Mark Wayne Clark (born 1896) held important commands in

Europe and Asia and became one of America's leading anti-Communist propagandists.

Mark Clark was born in Madison Barracks, N.Y., on May 1, 1896. After graduating from the U.S. Military Academy in 1917, he fought during World War I as an infantry officer in France, where he was wounded and decorated. He attended the Army's postgraduate schools between the wars and was widely known as a competent, ambitious officer.

In June 1942 Clark became Gen. Dwight Eisenhower's deputy for the invasion of French North Africa that began on Nov. 8, 1942. The next day Clark—whose code name, "Eagle," fitted both his personality and his appearance, since he had a thin but prominent nose—flew into Algiers, where he worked out an armistice with the French. The basis of the deal was American recognition of the French fascist Adm. Jean Darlan as governor of French North Africa. The "Darlan deal" brought a storm of abuse on Clark's and Eisenhower's heads; placing a fascist in charge of the first territory occupied by the Americans in World War II appeared to make a mockery of the principles for which the Allies claimed to be fighting. After Darlan's assassination on Dec. 24, 1942, the indignation faded.

Much to his annoyance, Clark did not hold a combat command in either the Tunisian or Sicilian campaigns. Instead, Eisenhower had him train the U.S. 5th Army for the invasion of Italy that would begin on Sept. 8, 1943.

At the outset Clark's forces just managed to cling to their first beachhead at Salerno south of Naples, and the Italian campaign that followed was one of endless frustration. Clark and the British forces on his right flank were always short of supplies and manpower, and progress up the Italian peninsula was painfully slow. Not until June 5, 1944, did Clark drive the Germans from Rome, a feat almost ignored by the world since the Normandy invasion began the next day. During the remainder of 1944 and the first 4 months of 1945, Clark's troops crept up the peninsula, forgotten by most of the world. For a man of Clark's ambition and keen desire for publicity, it was a trying time.

After the German surrender Clark became commander in chief of the American occupation forces in Austria. He quickly adopted an attitude of extreme hostility toward his Soviet counterparts on the Allied Control Commission for Austria. He was impatient with what he called the "cream puff and feather duster approach to communism" and advocated a get-tough policy with the Russians. He loudly protested against what he considered to be the "appeasement" of the Soviet Union by the United States.

In 1947 Clark served as deputy secretary of state, meeting with the Council of Foreign Ministers to negotiate a peace treaty for Austria. No progress was made at the talks, and late in the year Clark returned to the United States to take command of the 6th Army. Two years later he became chief of Army Field Forces, which made him responsible for the training of the Army. In the spring of 1952 he became commander in chief of the United Na-

Gen. Mark Clark. (Library of Congress)

tions command in Korea, as well as commanding general of the U.S. Army Forces in the Far East. By the time Clark took over in Korea there was a virtual stalemate on the battlefront, and his major concerns were a prisoner-of-war mutiny and the armistice negotiations. On the military front his tactic was to inflict maximum casualties on the Chinese enemy. Fourteen months after he arrived, he signed the armistice agreement and fighting ended. Clark was unhappy with the outcome of the Korean War. He had hoped the United Nations would be able to defeat the North Koreans and Chinese and reunify Korea under Syngman Rhee.

Clark left the Army in 1954 to become president of the Citadel Military College of South Carolina, a position he held until his retirement in 1966. He remained a prominent anti-Communist, especially sensitive to what he considered a serious threat of communism from within the United States.

Further Reading

Mark Clark is listed in the American History study guide (IX, E, 2, b). Omar BRADLEY and George PATTON were other important American military leaders in the European theater during World War II.

Clark wrote two volumes of memoirs: *Calculated Risk* (1950), a full and sprightly account of his World War II career, and *From the Danube to the Yalu* (1954), in which he describes his dealings with the Communists from 1946 to 1953. Kenneth G. Crawford, *Report on North Africa* (1943), and Alan Moorehead, *The End in Africa* (1943), provide information on the North African campaign. For general background on the war in Italy see

Pietro Badoglio, *Italy in the Second World War: Memories and Documents* (trans. 1948), and Chester G. Starr, ed., *From Salerno to the Alps: A History of the Fifth Army* (1948).

✳   ✳   ✳

w. CLARK / By Richard Dillon

The American explorer and soldier William Clark (1770–1838) was second in command of what has been called the American national epic of exploration, the Lewis and Clark expedition of 1804–1806, which traveled from the Missouri River to the Pacific Ocean.

William Clark was born on Aug. 1, 1770, in Caroline County, Va. He joined militia companies fighting Indians in the Ohio country in 1789 and 3 years later won a lieutenant's commission in the U.S. infantry. He was on the Indian and Spanish frontier of the United States and served in Mad Anthony Wayne's successful campaign, terminated by the victory of Fallen Timbers (1794) over the Indians.

Clark resigned his commission in 1796, became a civilian, and tried to straighten out the chaotic financial condition of his famous brother, a hero of the Revolution, George Rogers Clark. However, when Meriwether Lewis offered him a role in what would be known as the Lewis and Clark expedition, he leaped at the opportunity.

In 1801 President Thomas Jefferson had chosen his White House secretary, Capt. Meriwether Lewis, to lead a corps of discovery up the Big Muddy (or Missouri) River and across the Rockies to the Pacific via the Columbia River. He gave Lewis complete freedom to choose his second in command. Without hesitation the Virginian picked his old Army buddy William Clark. When the Army failed to give Clark the promotion he deserved, Lewis ignored the "brass" and addressed Clark as captain, treating him as a virtual co-commander of the expedition.

It was Clark who led the fleet of boats upriver on May 14, 1804, while Lewis was detained in St. Louis by diplomatic and administrative matters. The two officers led their men up the Missouri to the Mandan Indian country of North Dakota, where they wintered before continuing in the spring of 1805. With great difficulty they shifted from canoes to horses and back to canoes as they crossed the unknown Rockies and followed the Columbia River to the sea. Clark was sharing leadership with Lewis in one of the most successful partnerships in the history of the nation.

After wintering at Ft. Clatsop on the Oregon coast, Lewis decided to split the party on its return to Missouri. He sent Clark to explore the Yellowstone River while he reconnoitered the Marias River. Although Lewis never yielded his command to Clark (except when accidentally wounded and incapacitated during a hunting expedi-

William Clark, a painting by Charles Willson Peale. (Independence National Historical Park Collection)

tion), Clark's wilderness and leadership skills contributed to the success of the corps of discovery. While Lewis was more brilliant and intellectual, Clark got along better with the men—and probably the Indians—and was a fine map maker. Both men kept diaries, although spelling was not one of Clark's strong points.

Safe in St. Louis in September 1806, Clark resigned his commission to become brigadier general of militia and superintendent of Indian affairs for Louisiana Territory (later Missouri Territory) under the new governor, Meriwether Lewis. Clark was governor himself from 1813 to 1821, then became an unwilling—and unsuccessful—candidate for governor of the new state of Missouri. He devoted much of his time during the War of 1812 to Indian affairs and kept Missouri Territory almost unharmed by British-inspired Indian raids. He continued in Indian diplomacy after the conflict and by his good sense was able to avert trouble with the Indians, who came to trust him more than any other white man.

Clark died in St. Louis on Sept. 1, 1838. Highly respected as an administrator, soldier, and explorer, for a half century he had served his country well, particularly in keeping the peace on the Indian frontier.

Further Reading

William Clark is listed in the American History study guide (IV, D, 1). He assisted Meriwether LEWIS in western exploration. Zebulon PIKE was a contemporary explorer.

There is no biography of Clark, although one has long been in preparation. The best sources are those on Meriwether Lewis, including John Bakeless, *Lewis and Clark, Partners in Discovery* (1947), and Richard Dillon, *Meriwether Lewis* (1965). An interesting retracing of Lewis and Clark's exploration is Calvin Tomkins, *The Lewis and Clark Trail* (1965). A one-volume abridgment of *The Journals of Lewis and Clark* was edited by Bernard DeVoto (1953).

✳ ✳ ✳

W. A. CLARK / By Herbert H. Lang

The American copper entrepreneur and politician William Andrews Clark (1839–1925) was a key figure in forging statehood for Montana.

William Andrews Clark was born on Jan. 8, 1839, near Connellsville, Pa. He was educated in private academies in Pennsylvania and in Iowa, and after a short stint as a schoolmaster in Missouri, he studied law at Iowa Wesleyan College. At the outbreak of the Civil War, Clark enlisted in an Iowa regiment. Discharged in 1862, he moved to Colorado Territory.

Although Clark's career in Colorado was brief, it was productive, for it was his experience in the mines of the Central City district that brought into focus his lifelong obsession with the accumulation of wealth and political power. In 1863, attracted by the opportunities a new frontier offered an ambitious young man, Clark left Colorado for Montana. From a lucky strike in a claim near Bannack, he extracted $1500 worth of gold, which became the nucleus of an immense fortune.

Over the next few years Clark alternated between mining during the spring and summer and merchandising during the fall and winter. A typical frontier entrepreneur, he operated stores at several mining camps, lent money to men needing a grubstake, sold timbers to the miners, and operated a mail route between Missoula, Mont., and Walla Walla, Wash. In 1867 he formed a partnership to engage in wholesaling. He then established a bank at Deer Lodge in 1870 and at Butte in 1877.

Mining King

In 1872 Clark had set up headquarters in the booming mining town of Butte. He purchased several mines. Realizing that the day of the untrained independent prospector was ending and that the time for scientific mining was dawning, he spent a year at Columbia University School of Mines. Back in Butte he built the Old Dexter mill and organized the Colorado and Montana Smelting Company. But he always sought to diversify his holdings, and soon he founded a newspaper, the *Butte Miner*, and went into lumbering, farming, and ranching. In Butte he established the city waterworks and a streetcar line. He also built, and for a time operated, the San Pedro, Los

Angeles, and Salt Lake Railroad, later sold to the Union Pacific.

Branching out from Montana, Clark established the Los Alamitos Sugar Corporation in Los Angeles and bought the United Verde copper prospect in Arizona. A significant aspect of Clark's business techniques was his refusal to become deeply involved in any commercial enterprise unless he could own it in its entirety.

Political Aspirant

In 1884, when Montanans sought unsuccessfully to win statehood, Clark served as president of an abortive constitutional convention. Four years later he ran as a Democrat for the post of territorial delegate to Congress. To Clark's astonishment he lost by 5,000 votes to Thomas H. Carter, a virtually unknown Republican. Clark had failed to carry either the mining towns or the lumbering districts, both nominally Democratic and areas he had considered safe. With justification Clark attributed his loss to the machinations of Marcus Daly, the founder of the Anaconda Company, a potent rival of Clark's in the copper business. Thus began a political struggle that eventually placed virtually every Montana voter in the camp of either one man or the other.

In 1889, Clark was again chosen as president of a Montana constitutional convention. He was instrumental in incorporating a clause in the constitution fixing the maximum tax rate for mining property at the price paid to the Federal government for a claim. This meant that a claim worth millions could not be assessed at more than $5.

William Andrews Clark. (Library of Congress)

Clark ran unsuccessfully for the U.S. Senate in 1889 and 1893.

Elusive Senatorial Seat

Clark made yet another attempt to capture his long-cherished senatorial post in 1899. The moment seemed auspicious because the Democrats had captured control of the state legislature. After an 18-day contest the legislators chose Clark. Immediately, political foes in and out of his party charged that the election had been won by bribery. Although Clark freely admitted spending several hundred thousand dollars to elect legislators favorable to his political ambitions, he stubbornly denied any involvement in corrupt electoral practices. A grand jury refused to indict him, and he proceeded to Washington, D.C. There Thomas H. Carter, now a senator, introduced petitions from Montana citizens demanding that Clark be denied his seat. After a lengthy hearing, the Senate Committee on Privileges and Elections recommended unanimously that Clark be unseated.

Not yet willing to give up the fight, Clark waited until Governor Robert B. Smith was out of Montana on business and then sent a letter of resignation to Lieutenant Governor A. E. Spriggs, one of Clark's political henchmen. Spriggs immediately appointed Clark to fill the vacancy caused by his own resignation. A travesty of the political process was prevented only by the timely arrival of Governor Smith, who nullified the appointment and sent a replacement for Clark to Washington.

In 1901 Clark was finally elected to the Senate. He served one term (1901–1907) and distinguished himself only in a negative way, by opposing all measures designed to further the conservation of forest and mineral lands.

After leaving the Senate, Clark moved permanently to New York City. He devoted his last years to assembling a fine collection of art, now part of the collection of the Corcoran Gallery in Washington, D.C. Clark died in New York City on March 2, 1925, the last of the West's great copper kings.

Further Reading

William Andrews Clark is listed in the American History study guide (VII, C, 3). Other mining men were Henry COMSTOCK and John William MACKAY.

There is no full-length biography of Clark, but a family history appears in William D. Mangam, *The Clarks: An American Phenomenon* (1941). Other books containing important material on Clark include C. B. Glasscock, *The War of the Copper Kings* (1935); Joseph Kinsey Howard, *Montana: High, Wide, and Handsome* (1943); and K. Ross Toole, *Montana: An Uncommon Land* (1959).

M. CLARKE / By R. M. Younger

Marcus Andrew Hislop Clarke (1846–1881) was an English-born journalist and author who achieved eminence in colonial Australia. He is noted for his novel of early-19th-century convict transportation.

Marcus Clarke was born on April 24, 1846, in Kensington, London. His mother died while he was an infant, and he was brought up by his father, a lawyer with literary interests. When he was 16 his father died and, seeing no future for him in London, relations persuaded the boy to try his fortunes in Australia, where he could be under the eye of an uncle who owned a sheep run and held a judgeship.

After trying and disliking work in a Melbourne bank, Clarke at 19 went into the backcountry to taste the rustic life and gain "colonial experience." He began writing sketches for the *Australian Magazine* and in 1867 returned to Melbourne as a newspaper reporter. Energetic, restless, and unable to settle at any task for long, he found routine tasks intolerable but succeeded as a columnist commenting on people and events. He thus established himself as a leader among the writers and poets who were making Melbourne the literary center of Australia.

At the age of 23 Clarke acquired a magazine which he named the *Colonial Monthly*. In it he serialized his first novel, *Long Odds* (later to be renamed *Heavy Odds*), a lively but unsubstantial story about a young Australian sheep grazier on a visit to England. When the story was complete, Clarke's interest flagged, and the magazine subsequently closed.

"The Great Australian Novel"

Visiting Tasmania, Clarke studied the records of transportation to the island's penal settlements and set about writing a novel recapturing the atmosphere of the old convict days. Under the title *His Natural Life* the story was serialized in the *Australian Journal* (1870–1872). Written mostly a chapter at a time—some portions while the typesetter stood by—it was to rank as Clarke's great achievement. In 1874 a substantially edited version was published in book form; later it appeared as *For the Term of His Natural Life*, the title by which it became established. Meanwhile Clarke was appointed secretary to the trustees of Melbourne's Public Library; later he became the assistant librarian.

Contrasting strongly with his witty and exuberant writings as a columnist, *For the Term of His Natural Life* deals in gloomy and powerful terms with the brutishness of the convict system. As in all his writing, Clarke intensified every phase, making it more striking, if less real. In the story injustice is heaped upon misfortune as Clarke unfolds an agitated drama of bitter human relationships. From melodramatic opening to sentimental conclusion, the story has compelling narrative power and strong human interest. In spite of exaggeration, both action and characterization are extraordinarily vivid. The language is sometimes theatrical; occasionally pathos turns to banality—yet overall the novel manages to outstrip its faults. In its day it was highly regarded and even considered to

Marcus Clarke. (The Mitchell Library, The Library of New South Wales)

be "the great Australian novel." It can more correctly be regarded as representing a landmark of the colonial period—the Anglo-Australian phase—of Australia's literary development. In fact, it is Australian only in subject (and only insofar as Australia can be identified with convictism), and its author was Australian in nothing but residence.

Clarke's third novel, 'Twixt Shadow and Shine (1875), was a light and pleasantly written story; it gained only minor attention. Meanwhile his extravagance had run him into insolvency in 1874. Pressures built up, and he left his public library post. He continued to contribute to newspapers and was active in the theater as an original author and translator, but he remained in hopeless debt. Dispirited, he overworked himself to the point of exhaustion. Early in 1881 he was declared bankrupt for the second time. He died on Aug. 2, 1881. Clarke's fourth novel, Chidiock Tichbourne, or the Catholic Conspiracy, a swashbuckling romance of Elizabethan England, was published in 1893.

Further Reading

Marcus Clarke is listed in the Australia and New Zealand study guide (II, G). Other aspects of life in Australia were described by the chronicler of pioneer life Miles FRANKLIN and by Joseph FURPHY.

A favorable biography of Clarke is A. W. Brazier, Marcus Clarke: His Work and Genius (1902). A concise sketch of Clarke, together with a full listing of his essays, drama, and fiction, is contained in E. Morris Miller and others, Australian Literature (1940). See also Brian Robinson Elliott, Marcus Clarke (1958). For an appreciation of Clarke's For the Term of His Natural Life and comments on his place in the literary development of Australia see H. M. Green, A History of Australian Literature, vol. 1 (1966).

s. CLARKE / By Burnham Terrell

The English theologian and moral philosopher Samuel Clarke (1675–1729) was in his time the foremost exponent of rationalist ethics and a prominent defender of Newtonian physics.

Samuel Clarke was born on Oct. 11, 1675, in Norwich, where his father was alderman and at one time representative in Parliament. He entered Cambridge University at 16. There he discovered Sir Isaac Newton's Principia mathematica and resolved to advance Newton's theories against those of René Descartes, which were then dominant. His translation of Jacques Rohault's popular physics textbook, with notes and comments reflecting Newton's ideas, was used at Cambridge for several decades.

Clarke's ecclesiastical career began as vicar to the bishop of Norwich. In 1704 and 1705 he gave the Boyle Lectures; these were published as A Demonstration of the Being and the Attributes of God (1705–1706) and The Verity and Certitude of Natural and Revealed Religion (1705). They are his chief contributions to philosophy and theology, along with Discourse concerning the Unchangeable Obligation of Natural Religion (1708). He moved to London in 1706 as rector of St. Benet's Church and later served as chaplain at court. In 1709 he became rector of St. James, Westminster, and he held this position, despite charges of heresy provoked by his Scripture Doctrine of the Trinity (1712), until his death.

Clarke became a friend of Newton in London, and his translation of Newton's Opticks into Latin, warmly praised by the author, was published in 1706. Later he was asked by the Princess of Wales to defend Newton against the German philosopher Gottfried Wilhelm von Leibniz. In the controversy with Leibniz, Clarke supported Newton's theory of absolute space and time. The Clarke-Leibniz correspondence, conducted during 1715–1716, appeared in print in 1717. Clarke also wrote numerous treatises on theology, philosophy, and mathematics; an edition of Caesar's Commentaries; and a translation of the first 12 books of the Iliad. He died on May 17, 1729.

Clarke is best known for his ethical theory, which compares moral and mathematical truths. Right and

Samuel Clarke. (Radio Times Hulton Picture Library)

wrong are known self-evidently, like the axioms of mathematics, and depend on "the necessary eternal different relations that different things bear to one another." They express "fitness or suitableness of certain circumstances to certain persons, and unsuitableness of others." He also argued against materialism and atheism and for free will and the immortality and spirituality of the soul.

Further Reading

Samuel Clarke is listed in the Philosophy study guide (IV, E). He carried on an important correspondence with Gottfried Wilhelm von LEIBNIZ on the ideas of Isaac NEWTON.

The Works of Samuel Clarke (4 vols., 1738–1742) was edited, with a biographical preface, by Benjamin Hoadly, Bishop of Salisbury. A modern edition of the Leibniz-Clarke correspondence was prepared by H. G. Alexander, *The Leibniz-Clark Correspondence, together with Extracts from Newton's Principia and Opticks* (1956). William Whiston, *Historical Memoirs of the Life of Dr. S. Clarke* (3d ed. 1748), includes A. A. Sykes's "Elogium" and Thomas Emlyn's "Memoirs of the Life and Sentiments of Dr. Clarke." For Clarke's ethical theory see James Edward LeRossignol, *Ethical Philosophy of Samuel Clarke* (1892). Background studies which discuss Clarke include W. R. Sorley, *A History of English Philosophy* (1920); Gerald R. Cragg, *Reason and Authority in the Eighteenth Century* (1964); and Charles Vereker, *Eighteenth-Century Optimism* (1967).

✳   ✳   ✳

CLAUDE LORRAIN
/ By George V. Gallenkamp

The French landscape painter, draftsman, and etcher Claude Lorrain (1600–1682) was regarded as the prince of landscape painters until the days of impressionism in the mid-19th century.

Claude Lorrain (pronounced klôd lô-răn′) and Nicolas Poussin were the most distinguished exponents of the French classical baroque style, though fulfilling antithetically expressive ends within the theoretical precepts established by the French for painters from the middle of the 17th century. Whereas Poussin was interested in rendering the archeologically precise and imposing monumentality of imperial Rome objectively, Claude preferred to depict the romantic deserted ruins in a rolling countryside. To Claude's admirers, his paintings remain the visual counterpart of the profound sentiment of the beauty of the natural world found in the *Eclogues* and *Georgics* of the ancient Roman poet Virgil. Claude, however, largely deemphasized the role of man in nature in order to enhance the presence and play of cosmic forces, though classical tradition precluded his unbalancing the two to any pronounced degree. If Poussin's art is the last phase of rational formalism in the history of landscape painting, Claude's can be considered the first in the long development of autonomous pictorialism leading to the 19th-century ro-

Claude Lorrain, an engraving by Richard Collin, in the *Bibliothèque Nationale*, Paris. (Photo-Hachette)

The Debarkation of Cleopatra from Tarsus, *a painting by Claude Lorrain, in the Louvre, Paris.*
(H. Roger-Viollet)

mantics and impressionists. A synthesis of the divergent artistic messages of Poussin the scholar and Claude the poet might be said to have been reached in the landscape art of Paul Cézanne, where the poetic content of nature is unified within the formal elements of classical composition.

Claude Lorrain was born Claude Gellée in the village of Chamagne near Nancy. Orphaned at about the age of 12, he moved to Freiburg im Breisgau to live with his brother, who apparently was equipped to teach him engraving. In 1613 he set off with another relative, a dealer in lace, for Rome, where, because of the talent common to many Lorrainers, he found employment as a pastry cook in the house of the landscape painter Agostino Tassi. The position of apprentice soon replaced that of cook, the master teaching the young boy the rudiments of painting.

About 1623 Claude went to Naples, where he studied for a short time with the Flemish artist Goffredo Wals. The impression of the Gulf of Naples from Sorrento to Pozzuoli and the islands of Capri and Ischia was overwhelming and indelibly imprinted upon Claude's memory, for reminiscences of these awesome views of water, earth, sky, and light recurred in his art until the end of his life. In 1625 he returned to Nancy, where he briefly assisted Claude Deruet by executing the architectural backgrounds to the latter's ceiling paintings for the Carmelite church (now destroyed). Claude then made his way back

to Rome—sketching all the way. No record reveals Claude's ever leaving Rome again, and he lived out his life quietly and industriously as a respected member of the colony of foreign artists, though some scholars believe the vividness of the Neapolitan recollections in his paintings implies the necessity of his having returned to Naples and its environs.

After the 1630s Claude's reputation as a landscape painter was firmly established. By the 1640s he counted among his clients the French ambassador Philippe de Béthune, cardinals Bentivoglio and Crescenzio, and Pope Urban VIII. As a clue to the degree of his early success, the French artist Sébastien Bourdon in 1634 imitated Claude's style and passed the work off as an original. Because copyists and imitators of his style abounded, Claude created, to offset this plagiarizing tendency by contemporaries, a catalog of 200 drawings of his original compositions and entitled it *Liber veritatis.*

Artistic Style

This visual record, as well as all other authenticated works by the artist, reveals relatively little change in Claude's style from his early to his late period. The structural formula of composition, transmitted through Tassi, his first teacher, from such late mannerist artists as Paul Brill and Adam Elsheimer, who utilized stage-set structural devices, remains constant in Claude. He sets his scenes consistently as spatial areas receding from picture plane to infinity. The picture plane is established by placing a mass of dark greenish-brown foliage on both sides of the composition, with usually a tall, feathery tree element on one side, as in *The Mill* (1631). When human activity does occur, as in *The Mill*, the action takes place quite animatedly in the front area of the middle distance, set upon or against a barge landing, bridge, or farmhouse. This central focus then is systematically reduced by subtly placed flanking motifs, like stage flats, creating wings, or coulisses, which carry the eye to the far distance of mountains, rivers, or the rolling Roman campagna, as in *Apollo Guarding the Herds of Admetus* (1654).

The real subject of Claude's work is not, however, the forms of nature or the activities of men, but rather the animating power of light, emanating in varied intensities, depending upon the time of day chosen for the theme, playing upon the material realm and transforming it into a peculiar mood impression.

Chiaroscuro, or the play of patterns of dark and light contrasts, is the method Claude generally uses in drawing and painting. Modulation plays down the violence of blindingly dramatic sun and moon effects of such a mannerist precursor as Elsheimer. Claude's drawings, though great in variety, uniformly reveal a preoccupation with values of light and dark rather than with color. As with his paintings, the magic of mood, the veiling of earth and man in an infinite variety of gently controlled radiation and reflection of light which issues from a known but unobtrusive source, is the subject.

Claude's influence was both catalytic and mediating of divergent national talents. In his art he melded the northern emotive response to nature, such as that found in the works of the German Albrecht Altdorfer and the Fleming Joachim Patinir, with the more palpable control of the southern temperament. In this sense Claude's contribution to art is more universal than that of his habitually more formalistic contemporary and countryman Poussin.

Further Reading

Claude Lorrain is listed in the Art study guide (III, F, 1, d). His great contemporary was Nicolas POUSSIN. The scheme of composition Claude followed was begun by GIORGIONE. Claude's paintings were particularly influential on the English landscape artists Richard WILSON and J. M. W. TURNER.

A scholarly and interesting summary in English of all previous studies of Claude is Marcel Röthlisberger, *Claude Lorrain: The Drawings* (2 vols., 1968). Röthlisberger's *Claude Lorrain: The Paintings* (2 vols., 1961) is also valuable. Roger Fry's essay on Claude in his *Vision and Design* (1920) is rich in esthetic and philosophical wisdom and refutes the literary attacks on the artist in John Ruskin's *Modern Painters* (5 vols., 1846–1860). See also Martin Davies's detailed discussion of the *Liber veritatis* in *French School* (1946–1950; 2d ed. 1957), published by the National Gallery in London. There is a discussion of Claude and the general historical period in Anthony Blunt, *Art and Architecture in France, 1500–1700* (1953).

✱ ✱ ✱

CLAUDEL / By Anne P. Jones

The French author and diplomat Paul Louis Charles Claudel (1868–1955) is best known for his plays, in which he explored the relationship between man, the universe, and the divine in a highly poetic and original style.

Paul Claudel (pronounced klō-dĕl′) was one of a group of celebrated writers, all born about 1870, who gave French literature a new orientation. Though quite different from one another, Paul Valéry, Marcel Proust, André Gide, Charles Péguy, Colette, and Claudel all revolted against 19th-century positivism, as well as against the extremes of symbolism which denied reality to the external world. Each, in his own way, experimented with new ways of using the French language and offered new visions of the world and new views of the function of art.

Claudel was born on Aug. 6, 1868, at Villeneuve-sur-Fère-en-Tardenois on the border between the provinces of Champagne and the Ile-de-France. His family, of peasant and petit bourgeois stock, was Roman Catholic but not particularly devout. He received his early education in the various provincial towns where his father worked as a civil servant. In 1882 the family moved to Paris and enrolled young Paul in the famous lycée Louis-le-Grand. As a schoolboy, he was solitary and pessimistic and rebelled against the pervading philosophies of determi-

Paul Claudel. (Radio Times Hulton Picture Library)

nism and positivism, which denied man his free will and made him merely a product of his heredity and environment. He rejected his whole traditional literary education to take refuge in the poetry of Charles Baudelaire, Paul Verlaine, and especially Arthur Rimbaud, who was to be a lifelong source of inspiration. Rimbaud, he wrote later, revealed the supernatural to him and was in part responsible for his return to the Catholic faith, which he had abandoned.

Claudel's Conversion

While studying for a diplomatic career, Claudel underwent on Christmas Day 1886, in the Cathedral of Notre Dame, a profound mystical experience which was to shape his destiny. During the singing of the Magnificat, he suddenly knew that he believed in a living and personal God. His complete conversion and return to the Church were accomplished only after 4 years of study and spiritual struggle to reconcile the opposition between his intuition and his intellect.

This spiritual crisis is evident in Claudel's first works. *Tête d'Or* (1889), his only non-Christian play, is the tragedy of an adventurer who tries to find salvation solely through his own strength and intelligence and ignores an inner voice counseling humility. This play, like all that were to follow it, rejects all the conventions of the French theater, be they classical, romantic, or realistic. It offers a new conception of poetic drama in which psychology and logical dramatic action give way to symbolism and imaginative truth. The play also uses the completely original line of verse, known as the *verset claudélien*, in which Claudel wrote all his poems and plays. The rhythmic pattern of the lines of different lengths is intended to reproduce the natural breathing and heartbeat of the poet or actor in order to indicate the emotional intensity of the passage. In Claudel's second play, *La Ville* (1890), he sees the city, and eventually the entire world, as a single body, a *maison fermée* (closed house) in which each member is responsible for the salvation of the other members.

Diplomatic Career

In February 1893 Claudel received his first diplomatic post, as vice-consul in New York. From then until his retirement in 1935, he lived almost continuously outside France. He served as French ambassador to Japan (1921–1927), the United States (1927–1933), and Belgium (1933–1935).

Claudel's experiences outside France, and especially outside Europe, influenced his work and thought in many ways. His discovery of non-Western conceptions of the theater encouraged him to experiment with revolutionary and, at the time, largely misunderstood dramatic techniques. Most importantly, however, Claudel's travels throughout the world contributed a cosmic dimension to his Catholicism, rendering it often unacceptable to his more orthodox coreligionists.

Major Works

The moving religious drama *Partage de Midi* (1906) is partly based on an episode in Claudel's life that occurred

Tête d'Or (Alain Cluny) kills the king (Jean Louis Barrault) in a production of Claudel's Tête d'Or *at the Odéon, Paris. (French Cultural Services of the French Embassy, New York)*

in 1905, the year before his marriage. Like the hero of this play, after considerable spiritual anguish Claudel had rejected a religious vocation. He also fell in love with a young married woman and learned for the first time the meaning of great love, suffering, and sacrifice.

Claudel's long lyric poems *Cinq Grandes Odes* (1910) and *La Cantate à trois voix* (1931) are meditations on the relationship between the Creator and the created world, on the role of the poet, and on the function of love. These themes reappear in *L'Annonce faite à Marie* (1912; *Tidings Brought to Mary*), Claudel's best-known play. In a medieval setting, the apparent paradox of human relationships is resolved when Violaine, the heroine, reveals how love, separation, suffering, and even evil lead men to understand both their role in the salvation of others and also the divine order of the universe.

Le Soulier de satin (1929; *The Satin Slipper*), considered by many to be his greatest play, is a complicated and gigantic drama of the Renaissance, a period Claudel believed to be the beginning of a new era of Catholicism. Against a background of violence, conquest, and passion, the characters work out their destinies in a plot that reveals Claudel's characteristic themes: man's desire for the infinite, the limitations of human love, and the necessity of human love as an instrument of salvation.

Last Years

Claudel divided the last 20 years of his life between an apartment in Paris and his Château de Brangues. Although he wrote no more poems or plays, he composed lengthy reflections on various scriptural texts. During these years, when his plays were staged, he often attended rehearsals and made changes in his texts for the stage. In 1946 he was elected to the French Academy. He died in Paris on Feb. 23, 1955, and was accorded a state funeral at the Cathedral of Notre Dame before his burial at Brangues. He was survived by his widow, five children, and many grandchildren.

Further Reading

Paul Claudel is listed in the Literature study guide (III, I, 1, b; III, J, 1, a). He was greatly influenced by the poetry of Arthur RIMBAUD. The works of the French authors Georges BERNANOS and François MAURIAC are also profoundly imbued with Catholicism.

Jacques Madaule has made the most comprehensive study of Claudel to date. Especially recommended are three of his volumes, in French: *Le Génie de Paul Claudel* (1933; rev. ed. 1947), *Le Drame de Paul Claudel* (1936; rev. ed. 1964), and *Claudel et le langage* (1968). In English, Wallace Fowlie, *Paul Claudel* (1957), is an excellent short study. Joseph Chiari, *The Poetic Drama of Paul Claudel* (1954), is a sympathetic treatment of his theater. Recommended for general background material on modern French poetry and theater are Marcel Raymond, *From Baudelaire to Surrealism* (1950); Wallace Fowlie, *A Guide to Contemporary French Literature: From Valéry to Sartre* (1957); Roger Shattuck, *The Banquet Years* (1958; rev. ed. 1960); and Jacques Guicharnaud, *Modern French Theatre from Giraudoux to Genet* (1967).

CLAUDIUS I / By Jill N. Claster

Tiberius Claudius Germanicus (10 B.C.–A.D. 54) was the fourth emperor of Rome. Deemed a weak emperor, he nevertheless extended the borders of the empire and reformed its administration.

Born in Lugdunum (modern Lyons) on Aug. 1, 10 B.C., Claudius was the son of Drusus and Antonia and the grandnephew of Augustus. Although Claudius was the sole surviving heir of Augustus after the assassination of Caligula, he was given the throne primarily because of the support shown him by the imperial troops. He assumed the throne unwillingly in 41; indeed, he is said to have been found cowering in a closet after Caligula's death was announced.

Kept in the background and often ignored during the reigns of Augustus, Tiberius, and Caligula, Claudius gained a reputation for stupidity, gluttony, and licentiousness. Although he is pictured by contemporary historians as a man incapable of anything, Claudius seems to have been, in fact, an excellent scholar, linguist, and writer.

Claudius I, a bust in the Uffizi, Florence. (Alinari)

Claudius began his rule with a great deal of enthusiasm and effort. He respected and frequently consulted both the Senate and the magistrates, groups whose prerogatives had been absorbed previously by the emperors. He built many monuments and public works in Rome. He began the campaign that led to the eventual conquest of Britain, and the imperial armies were successful in repelling the threatened German invasions. The Emperor initiated a number of reforms of the Roman legal and administrative systems, and he reestablished sound fiscal policies.

However, Claudius was a man of extremely weak character, easily swayed and led. That same elasticity of nature which had enabled him to survive his predecessor's reign of terror now made him an emperor completely governed by those around him. The aristocracy, which had hoped for a restitution of their former powers and privileges after the death of Caligula, was disappointed and angered when the new emperor surrounded himself with his friends, mainly slaves and freedmen. The middle class was shocked, feeling that Claudius's associates were degrading the dignity of the imperial power. This dissatisfaction led to the first conspiracy against the Emperor, in A.D. 42.

The plot was crushed, but further trouble arose in 48. Claudius's third wife, Messalina, who had previously influenced the Emperor to retaliate against the aristocracy, became involved in a scandal with a Roman senator, Silius. The affair rocked Roman society, and Claudius ordered Messalina to commit suicide.

The Emperor's next wife was Agrippina, his niece and the mother of his successor, Nero. A woman of immense capability and driving ambition, she persuaded Claudius to set aside his own son, Britannicus, and adopt Nero as his heir.

The details surrounding Claudius's death are unclear, although many ancient historians, including Tacitus, say that he may have been poisoned by Agrippina. Claudius died in Rome on Oct. 13, 54.

Further Reading

Claudius I is listed in the Ancient History study guide (III, C, 1). Though he was a more productive emperor than either his predecessor, CALIGULA, or his heir, NERO, they have gained greater fame.

The two ancient sources for the life of Claudius are Tacitus's *Annals* and Suetonius's *The Lives of the Twelve Caesars*. Modern references include Arnaldo Momigliano, *Claudius: The Emperor and His Achievement* (1932; trans. 1934; new ed. 1962), and Vincent M. Scramuzza, *The Emperor Claudius* (1940).

CLAUSIUS / By Stanley L. Jaki

The German physicist Rudolf Julius Emanuel Clausius (1822–1888) was one of the chief architects of thermodynamics and the kinetic theory of gases.

Born on Jan. 2, 1822, in Köslin, Pomerania, R. J. E. Clausius (pronounced klou′zē-o͝os) was the sixth son of the 18 children of the Reverend C. E. G. Clausius, a Lutheran pastor and councilor of the Royal Government School Board in Köslin. Young Clausius received much of his primary and secondary education in the private school which his father established in Uckermünde. After graduating from the gymnasium in Stettin, Clausius enrolled at the University of Berlin, and in 1844 he obtained his teacher's certificate.

During the next 6 years Clausius taught physics at the Friedrich Werder Gymnasium in Berlin. He received his doctoral degree in 1848 from the University of Halle with a dissertation which gave for the first time the explanation of the blue sky and red sunset in terms of the selective reflection of various wavelengths of light by particles present in the atmosphere. In 1850 Clausius became professor of physics at the Royal Artillery and Engineering School in Berlin and also obtained the rank of privatdozent at the University of Berlin.

Theories of Heat

Clausius presented his paper "On the Motive Power of Heat and on the Laws Which Can Be Deduced from It for the Theory of Heat" in 1850. Its significance can best be

gauged by the comments of James Clerk Maxwell, who years later wrote that Clausius "first stated the principle of Carnot in a manner consistent with the true theory of heat." The "true theory" was the consideration of heat as a mechanical process.

Sadi Carnot's explanation of his very successful theory of the efficiency of steam engines seemed, however, to contradict the mechanical theory. In Carnot's words, "no heat was lost" when a steam engine produced work by going through its cycles. Clausius insisted that the "new theory" could only be a mechanical one. More importantly, he showed that it was quite consistent with the mechanical theory to assume that when work was done by heat one part of the heat was "lost," or rather was transformed into work. This part of the heat and the other part which was rejected into the cold reservoir of the engine stood, in Clausius's words, in a "certain definite relation to the quantity of work produced."

Two subsequent papers published in 1851 by Clausius clarified merely some details of his first memoir, but in 1854 he confronted once more the fundamentals. What became known as his fourth memoir carried the title "On a Modified Form of the Second Fundamental Theorem in the Mechanical Theory of Heat." In it Clausius proposed to make Carnot's theorem a particular form of the general proposition, "Heat can never pass from a colder to a warmer body without some other change, connected

R. J. E. Clausius. (The Smithsonian Institution, Washington, D.C.)

therewith, occurring at the same time." With a penetrating analysis, Clausius showed that the Carnot cycle corresponded to the integral $\int (dQ/T)$, the value of which was zero for a reversible, or ideal, process. For an irreversible, or real, process the corresponding value could only be positive.

Herein lay a proposition of utmost importance, but its full meaning was not spelled out by Clausius until about 10 years later. Meanwhile, he moved to Zurich to serve as professor of physics at the Swiss Federal Technical Institute. Two years later he also assumed professorship at the University of Zurich. In Zurich he married Adelheid Rimpau; they had six children.

Kinetic Theory of Gases

The scientific fruits of Clausius's first years in Zurich related to the kinetic theory of gases. Clausius achieved his task in two papers: "On the Kind of Motion Which We Call Warmth" (1857) and "On the Average Length of Paths Which Are Traversed by Single Molecules in the Molecular Motion of Gaseous Bodies" (1858). From the assumption that molecules move in a straight path Clausius calculated the average velocity of hydrogen molecules at normal temperature and pressure. Because the value, about 2,000 meters per second, seemed to contradict the low rate of gaseous diffusion, Clausius offered as explanation the important notion of the free mean path of molecules.

A few years later, in 1862, Clausius published his paper "On the Thermal Conductivity of Gaseous Bodies," in which he successfully derived from theoretical considerations the experimentally known data in question. He deserved indeed the praises heaped on him by Maxwell, who referred to Clausius as the first who "gave us precise ideas about the motion of agitation of molecules." Maxwell also described the adoption of mechanical principles to molecular studies as being "to a great extent the work of Prof. Clausius."

The year 1862 also saw the return of Clausius's full attention to thermodynamics. The results spoke for themselves. In the paper known as his sixth memoir, "On the Application of the Theorem of the Equivalence of Transformations to Interior Work," he concluded that it was "impossible practically to arrive at the absolute zero of temperature by any alteration of the condition of a body."

Concept of Entropy

On April 24, 1865, Clausius read before the Philosophical Society of Zurich his best-remembered paper, or ninth memoir, "On Several Convenient Forms of the Fundamental Equations of the Mechanical Theory of Heat." In it the word "entropy" was used for the first time. The word, as Clausius noted, was coined by him from the Greek τροπη, or transformation: "I have intentionally formed the word *entropy* so as to be as similar as possible to the word *energy*; for the two magnitudes to be denoted by these words are so nearly allied in their physical meanings, that a certain similarity in designation appears to be desirable."

In nontechnical parlance, entropy stands for the inevitable transformation of some part of the energy in any real physical process into a form which is no longer utilizable. Clausius disclosed the far-reaching, cosmic consequences of his analysis of the foundations of thermodynamics: "If for the entire universe we conceive the same magnitude to be determined, consistently and with due regard to all circumstances, which for a single body I have called entropy, and if at the same time we introduce the other and simpler conception of energy, we may express in the following manner the fundamental laws of the universe which correspond to the two fundamental theorems of the mechanical theory of heat. (1) The energy of the universe is constant. (2) The entropy of the universe tends to a maximum."

In 1869 Clausius accepted an invitation to become professor of physics at the University of Bonn after having spent 2 years in the same capacity at the University of Würzburg. The University of Bonn represented the last phase of Clausius's academic career. There he wrote in 1870 his last important paper on thermodynamics, which contained the notion of virial. In 1876 he published a second, considerably enlarged and revised version of what was mainly a collection of his memoirs which had been printed in 1864 under the title *Abhandlungen über die mechanische Wärmetheorie*. The new edition, entitled *Die mechanische Wärmetheorie* (The Mechanical Theory of Heat), was for several decades the standard for textbooks on thermodynamics. The second part of the book deals with the analysis of electrical phenomena on the basis of mechanical principles, a topic which dominated Clausius's attention in Bonn.

Clausius's wife died in 1875. Eleven years later he married Sophie Sack, by whom he had one son. In the summer of 1886 he began to show symptoms of acute anemia. Nevertheless he carried on with the work of seeing to print the third edition of his *Wärmetheorie*, and he even held examinations from his sickbed. He was the embodiment of sincerity and conscientiousness to the end, which came on Aug. 24, 1888.

Further Reading

R. J. E. Clausius is listed in the Science study guide (VI, C, 2). Sadi CARNOT and James Clerk MAXWELL were other pioneers in the field of thermodynamics.

In French, *R. Clausius, sa vie, ses travaux et leur portée métaphysique* (1890), is a booklet by F. Folie, a close friend of the Clausius family and director of the Brussels Observatory. The major documents representing the emergence of thermodynamics as a full-fledged branch of physics are collected in W. F. Magie, ed., *The Second Law of Thermodynamics: Memoirs by Carnot, Clausius and Thomson* (1899). A good critical account of the steps leading to the full formulation of the second law of thermodynamics is given in Frederick O. Koenig's essay, "On the History of Science and of the Second Law of Thermodynamics," in Herbert McLean Evans, ed., *Men and Moments in the History of Science* (1959).

CLAY / By Glenn W. Price

The American political leader and secretary of state Henry Clay (1777–1852) came to national prominence as leader of the "War Hawks," who drove the country into the War of 1812. For the next 40 years he worked for international peace and sought to reconcile warring factions in the nation.

Henry Clay was born on April 12, 1777, in Hanover County, Va., the seventh of nine children of the Reverend John Clay and Elizabeth Hudson Clay. Henry's father died in 1781, the year British and loyalist soldiers raided the area and looted the Clay home. Ten years later his mother remarried and his stepfather moved the family to Richmond, where Henry worked as a clerk in a store and then, from 1793 to 1797, as secretary to George Wythe, chancellor of the High Court of Chancery. Henry had little regular education, but he read in Wythe's library and learned to make the most of scanty information. He moved to Lexington, Ky., in November 1797 and made a reputation as a lawyer. In 1799 he married Lucretia Hart, of a leading family in the community. They had 11 children.

Clay's life-style was that of the frontier South and West; he drank and gambled through the night for high stakes. John Quincy Adams commented, "In politics, as in private life, Clay is essentially a gamester." He fought two duels, one in 1809 and the other in 1826. This did not hinder a public career in young America, and Clay had attributes which served him well in politics. He was tall and slim with an air of nonchalance, and he had a sensitive, expressive face, a warm spirit, much personal charm, and an excellent speaker's voice. Adams, who had observed him closely, said Clay was "half-educated" but added that the world had been his school and that he had "all the virtues indispensable to a popular man."

Early Political Career

In 1803 Clay was elected to the Kentucky Legislature. In 1806 and again in 1810 he was sent to the U.S. Senate to fill out short terms. In 1811 he was elected to the House of Representatives. He was immediately chosen Speaker and was elected six times to that office, making it a position of party leadership.

By 1811 Clay was fanning the war spirit and the aggressive expansionism of the young republic. He said that the "militia of Kentucky are alone competent" to conquer Montreal and Upper Canada, and he organized the war faction in the House of Representatives. Clay was one of five men selected to meet British representatives at Ghent in 1814; there the failure of American arms forced them to a treaty in which no single objective of the war was obtained.

In the House again from 1815 to 1825 (except for the term of 1821–1823, when he declined to be a candidate), Clay developed his "American System," a program designed to unite the propertied, commercial, and manu-

Henry Clay, a daguerreotype portrait. (The Metropolitan Museum of Art, Gift of I. N. Phelps Stokes, Edward S. Hawes, Alice Mary Hawes, Marion Augusta Hawes, 1937)

facturing interests of the East with the agricultural and entrepreneurial interests in the West. It would establish protection for American industries against foreign competition, Federal financing of such internal improvements as highways and canals, and the rechartering of the United States Bank to provide centralized financial control. Clay succeeded for a time in part of his program: the Bank was rechartered and protective tariffs were enacted, reaching a climax in 1828 with the "Tariff of Abominations." But the internal improvements were not carried out in his lifetime (it required the Civil War to nationalize the country sufficiently for such measures), and long before Clay's death the Bank and the protective tariff had fallen at the hands of the Democrats.

Slavery and Politics

Missouri's application for statehood in 1819 raised the issue of slavery and shocked the nation "like a firebell in the night," as the aged Thomas Jefferson said. Clay had advocated gradual emancipation in Kentucky in 1798, asserting that slavery was known to be an enormous evil. Though he came to terms with the institution in practice —owning, buying, and selling slaves—he was never reconciled to it in principle. When he died he owned some 50 slaves. His will distributed them among his family but provided that all children born of these slaves after Jan. 1, 1850, should (at age 25 for females and 28 for males)

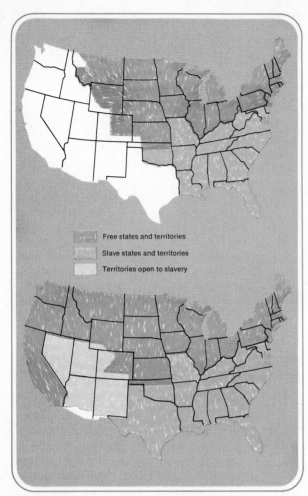

Compromises of 1820 (top) and 1850. Clay's prominent part in working out the Missouri Compromise, in 1820, and the Compromise of 1850, by which sectional controversies over the extension of slavery were temporarily resolved, won him the nickname "Great Compromiser."

be liberated and transported to Liberia. In 1816, Clay was one of the founders of the American Colonization Society, which promoted sending free Negroes to Africa. The racism which he shared with most Americans was an important motivation in the society. (His racism was not restricted to Negroes; he said Indians were "not an improvable breed," and that they were not "as a race worth preserving.")

In the Missouri debate he did not devise the basic compromise—that is, that Missouri be a slave state but that slavery henceforth be prohibited in territory north of 36°30'. But he resolved the second crisis caused by the Missouri constitutional provision that free Negroes could not enter the state; Clay got assurance from the Missouri Legislature that it would pass no law abridging the privileges and immunities of United States citizens. The role which Clay played in the debate was, in fact, as spokesman for the interests of the slave South. In the controversy over the activities of the abolitionists in the 1830s he

defended the right of petition but secured the passage of resolutions in the Senate censuring the abolitionists and asserting that Congress had no power to interfere with the interstate slave trade.

Secretary of State

Clay was a candidate for the presidency in 1824, but three others received more votes, so that his name did not go to the House for election. He defied Kentucky's instruction to cast the state's votes for Jackson, saying he could not support a "military chieftain"; instead, his support elected John Quincy Adams. When Clay subsequently became secretary of state, the traditional steppingstone to the presidency, the cry of "corrupt bargain" was raised. The charge was unwarranted—he had merely supported the man whose views were closest to his own —but the charge lingered for the rest of his life.

Foreign affairs were not particularly important from 1825 to 1829, and most of Clay's diplomatic efforts did not succeed. The United States failed in efforts to purchase Texas from Mexico, nor was progress made toward acquiring Cuba. The State Department was unsuccessful in settling the Maine-Canadian boundary dispute, in securing trade with the British West Indies, and in getting payment from France for losses suffered by Americans during the Napoleonic Wars. Clay had taken a strong position in support of recent Latin American independence movements against Spain, and he tried unsuccessfully to promote active American participation in the Congress of Panama in 1826.

The Adams administration was defeated overwhelmingly in 1828; Clay's own state voted for Andrew Jackson. Adams offered to appoint Clay to the Supreme Court, but he declined and returned to Kentucky. In 1831 he was elected to the Senate and remained in that office until 1842. During these years of Jacksonian democracy Clay fought a losing battle for his American System. In 1833 he devised the compromise on the tariff which brought the nullification threat from John C. Calhoun's South Carolina; his measure provided that duties be lowered gradually until none were higher than 20 percent by 1842. He favored higher duties but said he made the concession to get past the crisis and on to saner times.

Clay correctly estimated that Martin Van Buren was unbeatable in 1837, but he expected the Whig nomination in 1840 and was bitterly disappointed when the aging military hero William Henry Harrison won nomination and election. Clay then anticipated that he would be the actual leader of the administration, but Harrison resisted him for the short time that he lived and Harrison's successor, John Tyler, proved to be opposed in principle to Clay's Whig program. Clay resigned from the Senate in disgust.

Clay was the Whig presidential candidate in 1844, but his equivocation on the expansionist issue of the annexation of Texas cost him the election. He made an abortive effort for the 1848 nomination, which went to the Mexican War general Zachary Taylor. Clay had condemned the initiation of the war but supported it once it got under way.

Compromise of 1850

The fruits of that war brought on another sectional crisis, with threats to dissolve the Union. Clay returned to the Senate in poor health and led in working out the Compromise of 1850. This series of measures admitted California as a free state, organized the new territories without reference to slavery, assumed the public debt of Texas while restricting its area, abolished the slave trade in the District of Columbia, and enacted a fugitive slave law which denied due process and equal protection of the laws to Negroes living in the North. Thus was the rupture of the Union delayed for a decade. Clay died in Washington on June 29, 1852.

Further Reading

Henry Clay is listed in the American History study guide (IV, C, 1; VI, A, 1). He was a member of the Cabinet of John Quincy ADAMS. John C. CALHOUN was another noted War Hawk.

The definitive edition of Clay's writings is James B. Hopkins, ed., *The Papers of Henry Clay* (3 vols., 1959–1963). The best biography of Clay, comprehensive and temperate in interpretation, is Glyndon G. Van Deusen, *The Life of Henry Clay* (1937). An excellent brief study is Clement Eaton, *Henry Clay and the Art of American Politics* (1957), which has a useful bibliographical essay. A fine study of Clay's early life is Bernard Mayo, *Henry Clay: Spokesman of the New West* (1937). The best 19th-century biography, and still very valuable, is Carl Schurz, *Life of Henry Clay* (2 vols., 1887–1889).

CLAYTON / By Kinley J. Brauer

The American lawyer and statesman John Middleton Clayton (1796–1856) served as U.S. secretary of state during 1849–1850.

John M. Clayton was born in Dagsboro, Del., on July 24, 1796. As a young man, he showed exceptional abilities, and in 1815 he graduated from Yale College with highest honors. After studying law in the office of his cousin and at the famous Litchfield Law School in Connecticut, Clayton was admitted to the Delaware bar in 1819. Soon he became one of the state's leading lawyers and orators.

Clayton served Delaware in a number of offices and became active in national politics in 1824 as a partisan of John Quincy Adams in his battle against Andrew Jackson. Conservative in background and outlook, Clayton became a leader of the Delaware Whig party. In 1828 he was elected to the U.S. Senate and became a noted anti-Jacksonian and a confidant of Henry Clay. In 1833 Clayton was effective in securing passage of Clay's compromise tariff. Reelected to the Senate in 1834, he resigned

in 1836. From 1836 to 1839 he was chief justice of Delaware.

In 1839 Clayton supported the presidential candidacy of William Henry Harrison. In 1845, after acquiring a national reputation as a scientific farmer, Clayton returned to the U.S. Senate. He opposed President James Polk's expansionist policies on Oregon and Mexico, although he supported the Mexican War after it began. In 1848 Clayton broke with Clay, supporting the successful presidential candidacy of Zachary Taylor. Taylor appointed Clayton secretary of state in 1849.

As secretary of state, Clayton was intensely nationalistic and an ardent advocate of commercial expansion. But his strict interpretation of international law created unnecessary crises with Spain, Portugal, and France. His interest in commercial expansion was clear in his advocacy of increased trade with the Orient—later implemented by the mission of Matthew Perry to Japan—and his negotiation of the Clayton-Bulwer Treaty in 1850. This treaty won British recognition of an equal American interest in the Central American canal area, and it remained in effect until 1901, when the United States acquired full dominance there.

After Taylor's death in 1850, Clayton resigned his office and returned to his Delaware farm. In 1853 he returned to the Senate, chiefly to defend his treaty with England against attackers who suggested he had yielded unnecessarily to the British. By 1856 declining health rendered him inactive. He died of a kidney disease that year at his home.

John M. Clayton, a photograph by Mathew Brady. (Library of Congress)

Further Reading

John M. Clayton is listed in the American History study guide (VI, A, 4). James GADSDEN and Townsend HARRIS also negotiated important United States treaties prior to the Civil War.

There is no modern biography of Clayton. Mary W. Williams's chapter, "John Middleton Clayton," in volume 6 of Samuel Flagg Bemis, ed., *The American Secretaries of State and Their Diplomacy* (10 vols., 1927–1929; rev. ed., 17 vols., 1963–1967, with vols. 11–17 edited by Robert H. Ferrell), emphasizes Clayton's career as secretary of state but also has other biographical material.

* * *

CLEAVER / By Charles V. Hamilton

Leroy Eldridge Cleaver (born 1935), an American writer and a leader of the Black Panther party, was noted for advocating violent revolution within the United States.

Eldridge Cleaver was born in Wabbaseka, Ark. His family soon moved to Los Angeles. Cleaver dropped out of school after his parents separated. His petty crime record began at the age of 12 with the theft of a bicycle; after 16 he spent the next 15 years in and out of prison.

In the early 1960s, while in jail, Cleaver decided to give up crime. He was influenced by the teachings of the Black Muslims and became a follower of Malcolm X. When Malcolm broke with the Black Muslims, so did Cleaver. Then he became an advocate of "black power," as this position was enunciated by Stokely Carmichael.

In prison Cleaver completed high school and read the works of Karl Marx, Thomas Paine, Richard Wright, W. E. B. Du Bois, and others. He wrote essays, some published in 1962 in the *Negro History Bulletin*, these dealing mainly with race pride and black nationalism. Out of these autobiographical essays came his first book, *Soul on Ice* (1968).

Ramparts magazine, which had brought Cleaver to public attention by publishing some of his prison articles, and Cleaver's lawyer were instrumental in securing his parole in 1966. He immediately began a new life as a writer and political activist. He helped found Black House, a social center for San Francisco youth. In 1967 he met the men who had founded the Black Panther party the year before. He became the party's minister of information, responsible for editing its newspaper. Later that year he married Kathleen Neal. Mrs. Cleaver became the communications secretary of the Black Panther party. The couple had two children.

With *Soul on Ice* Cleaver received national prominence. On April 15, 1968, along with Mrs. Martin Luther

Eldridge Cleaver. (Gerhard E. Gscheidle)

King, Jr., and others, he addressed a mass rally against the Vietnam War in San Francisco.

As he became increasingly outspoken against racial, economic, and political injustices in America, Cleaver's parole officer advised him to discontinue his political activities. But Cleaver was becoming convinced that conditions for black people could not be alleviated without a violent revolution. To effect this, he felt, massive education was required to politicize the people. One method was to utilize a political campaign. In 1968 he urged the Black Panther party to unite with the predominantly white Peace and Freedom party in California to run candidates for local and state offices. Cleaver's wife became a candidate on the Peace and Freedom party ticket for the California State Assembly, along with Black Panthers Huey P. Newton and Bobby Seale.

In April 1968, following the assassination of Martin Luther King, Jr., and after harassment by the police of the Black Panther party, Cleaver was involved in a shoot-out with the Oakland police. One man was killed, and Cleaver was wounded in the foot and arrested. He was accused of violating his parole by possessing a gun, associating with people of bad reputation, and failing to cooperate with his parole agent. He was released on $50,000 bail.

For the next months Cleaver became a prominent spokesman of the radical, revolutionary left. He had moved from cultural, black nationalism to a more Marxist interpretation of revolutionary change. Cleaver believed that blacks should ally with radical whites, and he criticized those black nationalists who refused such coalitions. During this period he toured America as the presidential candidate of the Peace and Freedom party. He lectured on racism at the University of California in the fall of 1968.

Cleaver was scheduled to surrender to prison authorities in November 1968 for hearings on the charge of parole violation. Instead, he disappeared. He went to Cuba and Algiers, visited several Communist countries, and in September 1970 announced the establishment of an international office for the Black Panther party in Algiers.

Cleaver was a brilliant essayist, a cultural and social critic, and above all a political thinker and activist.

Further Reading

Eldridge Cleaver is listed in the American History study guide (X, F, 1). Other black leaders of the period included Martin Luther KING, Jr., and MALCOLM X.

Eldridge Cleaver: Post Prison Writings and Speeches was edited by Robert Scheer in 1968. Lee Lockwood's talks with Cleaver were published as *Conversations with Eldridge Cleaver: Algiers* (1970). Books about the Black Panthers that include Cleaver are Gene Marine, *The Black Panthers* (1969); Ruth Marion Baruch and Pirkle Jones, *The Vanguard: A Photographic Essay on the Black Panthers* (1970); Philip S. Foner, ed., *The Black Panthers Speak* (1970); and Bobby Seale, *Seize the Time* (1970). Two books critical of the Black Panthers are Earl Anthony, *Picking Up the Gun* (1970), and *I Was a Black Panther*, as told to C. J. Moore (1970).

* * *

CLEISTHENES / By N. G. L. Hammond

Cleisthenes (active 6th century B.C.) was an Athenian political leader and constitutional reformer. The first avowed democratic leader, he introduced important changes into the Athenian constitution.

Son of Megacles, leader of the powerful Alcmeonid clan in Athens, and of Agariste, daughter of Cleisthenes, the tyrant of Sicyon, Cleisthenes (pronounced klīs′thə-nēz) was destined for a public career. Accommodating himself to the regime of the tyrants, he was chief magistrate of Athens in 525 B.C., but he and other Alcmeonids were in exile when the tyranny fell in 510.

Cleisthenes ran for leadership of Athens at the head of a noble faction favoring oligarchy; he was defeated by Isagoras, a friend of the Spartan king Cleomenes. Cleisthenes then turned democrat, threatening the position of Isagoras, who asked Cleomenes for help. The Spartan king arrived with troops and tried to disband the Council of 300 and install Isagoras as head of a new council, but the people rose and forced Cleomenes and Isagoras to withdraw. Cleisthenes returned, a committed democrat, to reform the constitution in favor of a moderate democracy.

Constitutional Reforms

Athens had suffered from faction, or tyranny born of faction, for a century, and Cleisthenes aimed at the root of the trouble—clan affiliations in politics. In the past, clans had grouped themselves around a particular clan

Cleisthenes was active in Greece at the time the Andokides Painter did this amphora about 530–510 B.C. The amphora shows two scenes of Herakles banqueting on Olympus, one in red-figure and one in black-figure. (Staatliche Antikensammlungen und Glyptothek, Munich)

leader, such as Isagoras, Megacles, or Peisistratus, and had exerted pressure upon elections and policies by their organized votes. Cleisthenes provided an alternative to clan loyalty by registering the citizens by residence as members of a deme, a small area analogous to an English parish. Moreover, he extended the franchise to vote not only to clansmen but also to members of guilds, who hitherto had inferior rights.

To facilitate central government administration, Cleisthenes brigaded the demes, 170 or so in number, into 10 artificial tribes, allocating to each tribe a number of demes drawn from the three divisions of Attica. In many elections the citizens voted by tribe, returning a tribal official who might also serve the central government.

Since in this democracy the ultimate power was vested in the Assembly of all adult males, Cleisthenes set up a Council of 500 to make government less unwieldy and to steer the Assembly. Each of the 10 tribes selected by lot 50 persons who were councilors for a year (reelection was allowed only once). The council was in permanent session, and each tribal group of 50 served as governing committee in office for a tenth of the year, conducting day-to-day business and presiding over the council and the Assembly.

These reforms lasted as long as democracy in Athens. Cleisthenes is also credited with the invention of ostracism, but this is uncertain.

Further Reading

Cleisthenes is listed in the Ancient History study guide (II, C, 1). He continued the work of SOLON, who is credited with founding Athenian democracy.

Ancient sources on Cleisthenes are Aristotle's *Politics* and the *Athenian Constitution*, translated by John Warrington (1959). Two modern works are Charles Hignett, *A History of the Athenian Constitution to the End of the Fifth Century B.C.* (1952), and N. G. L. Hammond, *A History of Greece to 322 B.C.* (1959; 2d ed. 1967).

CLEMENCEAU / By Charlene M. Leonard

The French statesman Georges Clemenceau (1841–1929) was twice premier of France, in 1906–1909 and 1917–1919. He led France through the critical days of World War I and headed the French delegation to the Paris Peace Conference.

Georges Clemenceau (pronounced klĕ-mäN-sō′) was born on Sept. 28, 1841, at Mouilleron-en-Pareds in the Vendée. Following the family tradition, he studied medicine at Nantes and Paris. In 1865 he traveled to the United States, where he served as correspondent for a Paris newspaper and taught riding and French in a girls' academy at Stamford, Conn. He married one of his pupils, Mary Plummer. They had two daughters and one son but separated after 7 years.

Georges Clemenceau. (National Archives, Washington, D.C.)

Early Political Career

In 1869 Clemenceau returned to France; after the Revolution of 1870 he was appointed mayor of the 18th *arrondissement* of Paris, comprising Montmartre. After being elected as a representative to the National Assembly from Paris in February 1871, he voted against the Treaty of Frankfurt. When the Communard uprising began on Montmartre on March 18, he tried unsuccessfully to prevent bloodshed. Later Clemenceau tried to mediate between the Commune and the Versailles government. Failing again, he resigned his position at Paris and his seat in the Assembly. He was elected in July 1871 to the municipal council of Paris, where he remained until 1876, becoming president in 1875.

In 1876 Clemenceau returned to national politics and was elected to the Chamber of Deputies as representative of the 18th *arrondissement* of Paris. At that time his graying hair was close-cropped, his bushy eyebrows overhung large, black eyes, and his thick, drooping moustache was still black. His highly individual debating style, marked by a caustic wit, soon won him undisputed leadership of the radicals. While he was uncompromisingly atheistic and anticlerical, advocating separation of church and state, Clemenceau believed in human perfectibility through scientific knowledge and moral effort. He firmly upheld liberty and natural rights and was influenced by the ideas of Auguste Comte, J. S. Mill, and Charles Darwin.

Clemenceau possessed a genius for destructive criticism and won the appellation of the "Tiger" for his role in destroying Cabinets. Strongly opposed to imperialism, he brought down the Ferry Cabinet on the Tunisian question in 1881, attacked the Freycinet Cabinet for its desire to intervene in Egypt the following year, and destroyed the Ferry Cabinet of 1885 during the Indochinese crisis.

In 1886 Clemenceau first supported Gen. Boulanger as minister of war in the Freycinet Cabinet but later actively opposed him. Clemenceau also played a prominent role in the Wilson scandal, forcing President Grévy to resign. He subsequently backed Sadi Carnot for the presidency against Jules Ferry and is credited with having said, "I shall vote for the stupidest." This incident contributed to the tradition of a weak presidency that plagued the Third Republic. Clemenceau was denounced as a friend and associate of Cornelius Hertz, a key figure in the Panama scandal, and was also accused of being in the pay of the English. He was greeted with campaign posters showing him juggling English coins, and he failed to win reelection in 1893.

Journalistic Career

Between 1893 and 1903 Clemenceau built a new career in journalism. At first he wrote daily articles for *La Justice*, but in 1897 he began writing for *L'Aurore*, which had a larger circulation. Selections of his articles were published as *Le Mêlée sociale* (1895) and *Le Grand Pan* (1896). In 1898 he published a novel, *Les Plus forts*, and a volume of sketches on Jewish subjects, *Au pied de Sinai*. Another book of articles, *Au fil des jours*, appeared in 1900.

On Jan. 13, 1898, Clemenceau ceded his usual space in *L'Aurore* to Emile Zola's inflammatory article on the Dreyfus Affair, which Clemenceau headlined "J'accuse." Henceforth Clemenceau became a dedicated partisan of the Dreyfus cause. In 1900 he began publishing a weekly, *Le Bloc*, most of which he wrote himself, but he soon returned to *L'Aurore* as editor. Meanwhile, he published his Dreyfusard articles in five volumes.

Senator and Premier

In 1902 Clemenceau was elected senator for the Var, and he accepted the post of minister of interior in the Sarrien ministry in 1906. He used troops to control a strike of miners in the Pas-de-Calais following a mine disaster in that district and employed military engineers to break a strike of electrical workers in Paris.

When the Sarrien ministry resigned in October 1906, Clemenceau became premier. He was confronted with new strikes and used the army to control the most formidable, which involved agricultural workers of the Midi. When Paris postmen struck, Clemenceau denounced strikes by civil servants. Later he created a ministry of labor and negotiated nationalization of the Western Railway. In foreign affairs Clemenceau continued to cultivate close relations with Great Britain and to build up the French alliance system. He refused to apologize to Germany for an incident in Morocco. He was forced out of office in July 1909 in a dispute on naval policy.

After a lecture tour through Brazil and Argentina in 1910, Clemenceau became a member of the senate commissions for foreign affairs and for the army. In 1913 he founded a daily paper, *L'Homme Libre* (The Free Man), to express his views on armaments and the German menace.

World War I

In September 1914 Clemenceau's paper was suppressed because of its criticism of government weaknesses, but it reappeared immediately with the title

The "Big Four" at the Paris Peace Conference in 1919. From left to right: Vittorio Orlando of Italy, David Lloyd George of England, Clemenceau, and President Woodrow Wilson of the United States. (Radio Times Hulton Picture Library)

L'Homme Enchaîné (The Enchained Man). In this journal Clemenceau strove to foster the French will to victory, and to expose all forms of inefficiency in the war effort.

On Nov. 17, 1917, when French morale was near its nadir, President Poincaré asked Clemenceau to form a ministry. He served as minister of war, as well as premier, and summed up his policy: "Je fais la guerre" (I wage war). Clemenceau restored France's self-confidence. He welcomed Marshal Ferdinand Foch's appointment as commander in chief of the Allied armies in April 1918 and gave him unqualified support. When the Germans had advanced to Château Thierry, 18 miles from Paris, Clemenceau proclaimed: "The Germans may take Paris, but that will not prevent me from going on with the war. We will fight on the Loire, we will fight on the Garonne, we will fight even on the Pyrenees. And if at last we are driven off the Pyrenees, we will continue the war at sea. But as for asking for peace, never!" Clemenceau's confidence in his military commanders proved justified, and by June, Foch and Pétain were able to take the offensive. On Nov. 11, 1918, Germany signed the armistice.

Peace Conference

As leader of the French delegation at the Paris Peace Conference, Clemenceau played a major role in drafting the Treaty of Versailles and determining conference policies. He tried to obtain a strong League of Nations backed by military force, and when this failed he proposed other measures to ensure French security: German reparations to pay the whole cost of the war; French annexation of the Saar basin; and creation of a separate Rhineland state under protection of the League of Nations. U.S. president Woodrow Wilson and British prime minister David Lloyd George offered an Anglo-American guarantee of France's frontiers as compensation and forced Clemenceau to compromise all these points. Consequently, the French legislators, who found Clemenceau's rule autocratic and resented being excluded from the peace negotiations, condemned the peace treaty as too lenient and debated 3 months before ratifying it. After the elections of 1919 Clemenceau resigned as premier. An attempt to elect him president in 1920 failed.

Clemenceau retired from parliamentary politics. In 1922 he made a tour of the United States in an attempt to recall that country to its obligations after American rejection of the Versailles Treaty and the Anglo-American guarantee of French security. During the remaining years of his life he divided his time between Paris and the Vendée and devoted himself to writing. In 1927 he had completed a two-volume philosophical testament, *Au soir de la pensée* (*In the Evening of My Thought*). His memoirs of the war and the peace settlement were published after his death as *Grandeurs et misères d'une victoire* (*Grandeur and Misery of Victory*) in 1930. He died in Paris on Nov. 24, 1929.

Further Reading

Georges Clemenceau is listed in the European History study guide (IX, B, 1; X, G, 1). He opposed the policies of Jules FERRY and was a partisan of Alfred DREYFUS. Clemenceau was greatly aided by Marshal Ferdinand FOCH in achieving French victory in World War I.

The most detailed and judicious biography of Clemenceau written in English is Geoffrey Bruun, *Clemenceau* (1943). J. Hampden Jackson, *Clemenceau and the Third Republic* (1946), does a good job of relating Clemenceau's life to the general history of France. Probably the best of the many biographies written at the height of his career is H. M. Hyndman, *Clemenceau: The Man and His Time* (1919). Interesting sidelights are in Clemenceau's *Clemenceau: The Events of His Life as Told by Himself to His Former Secretary, Jean Martet* (trans. 1930). A specialized study of one aspect of Clemenceau's policy is Jere Clemens King, *Foch versus Clemenceau: France and German Dismemberment, 1918–1919* (1960). One of the best works for general historical background is Sir D. W. Brogan, *The Development of Modern France, 1870–1934* (1940; rev. ed. 1966). David Thomson, *Democracy in France* (1946; 4th ed. 1964), provides information on the political and social dynamics of the Third Republic.

✳   ✳   ✳

CLEMENS NON PAPA
/ By Edmond Strainchamps

Jacobus Clemens non Papa (ca. 1510–ca. 1556) was a Flemish composer whose a cappella Masses, motets, and chansons represent high points in the history of Renaissance polyphonic vocal music.

Jacobus Clemens non Papa (pronounced klĕm′ĕnz nŏn pä′pä) was born in Ypres, Flanders. Nothing is known of his education except that he was trained as a priest, and little is known about his career. He seems to have spent his early creative years in Paris, where his first works were published, but he returned to the Low Countries in 1540. It is known that he was in Bruges until 1545, where he served as priest and choirmaster of the children at St. Donatien. In subsequent years Clemens was active as a singer and composer at the cathedrals in Antwerp and 's Hertogenbosch, at Ypres, and finally at Dixmuide, where he died and was buried.

Clemens published under the name Jacques Clément or Jacobus Clemens until 1546, after which he added the appellation "non Papa" to the Latin form of his name. Why he did this is not known, though scholars have suggested it may have been done so that Clemens might distinguish himself from a priest-poet active in Ypres at the time who bore the same name and called himself Jacobus Papa.

The extant works of Clemens—all works for unaccompanied voices—include 15 Masses, 231 motets, a number of songs in French and in Flemish, and 4 books of *Sou-*

terliedekens, or "little psalter songs." These last are simple three-part settings of the Psalms in Flemish that Clemens based on popular melodies of the day. These Psalm settings were intended as devotional pieces for the home, which accounts for their simplicity and easy tunefulness. By contrast, in his Masses and motets, Clemens wrote a rich and varied polyphony, with a seriousness and thoroughness typical of the Renaissance Netherlandish composers. His motets, in which Clemens shows himself ever responsive to the moods and images of his texts, are especially remarkable for both their clarity and expressive power. Many of his motets are remarkable, as well, for their unusual use of chromaticism, much of it notated in the scores, but more of it, many scholars believe, implied and meant to be added to the music only in its performance by the initiate.

Clemens was an outstanding composer in an epoch that produced many composers of genius. His contributions to the genres of the Mass and the motet, in particular, stand as great monuments of the art of polyphony in the Renaissance.

Further Reading

Jacobus Clemens non Papa is listed in the Music study guide (I, C, 1). He was one of the most distinguished Flemish composers of the generation that was active between JOSQUIN DES PREZ and Roland de LASSUS.

Sources in English that contain material on Clemens are Edward E. Lowinsky, *Secret Chromatic Art in the Netherlands Motet* (1946), and Gustave Reese, *Music in the Renaissance* (1954; rev. ed. 1959).

Pope Clement V, detail of a 14th-century fresco by Taddeo Gaddi in S. Maria Novella, Florence. (Alinari)

CLEMENT V / By Norma Erickson

Clement V (1264–1314) reigned as pope from 1305 to 1314. He was the first pope of the "Babylonian Captivity," when the papacy was located in Avignon, France.

Bertrand de Got, who became Pope Clement V, was a nobleman and a native of Gascony, France. He became archbishop of Bordeaux in 1299. His election to the papacy in 1305 followed the pontificate of Boniface VIII (and the brief rule of Benedict XI), during which a long quarrel between France and the papacy culminated in Boniface's capture and mistreatment by henchmen of the French king, Philip IV, at Anagni, Italy, in 1303. France had humiliated the papacy, and the cardinals chose De Got as a compromise candidate who had neither opposed Boniface nor displeased Philip. Although Clement V was not a mere tool of France, throughout his reign he was pressured by Philip IV. At Philip's request Clement was crowned at Lyons; there he suffered a fall from his horse which may have affected his health permanently, for chronic illness contributed to his submission to French demands. Philip IV urged a posthumous heresy trial of Boniface VIII, and it was probably to avoid this that Clement agreed to settle in Avignon in 1309. Further submission is shown by Clement's approval of Philip's bloody suppression of the Knights Templar; his withdrawal of Boniface VIII's bull *Clericis laicos;* and his withdrawal of support for Emperor Henry VII's activities in Italy.

Clement V took important financial and political actions as pope. He introduced the annates, a lucrative papal tax, and thus refilled the papal treasury; but he spent the money unwisely, much of it on his relatives and on loans to France and England. He created 24 cardinals, of whom 23 were French and Gascon, thus producing a French majority. He was condemned for his nepotism, accused of simony, and disliked for his luxurious style of living. But he was also a scholarly man, and he ordered the study of the Hebrew, Syriac, and Arabic languages at the universities of Paris, Bologna, Oxford, and Salamanca. He added to canon law the sixth book of the Decretals, named "Clementines" after him.

Clement's reputation today is predominately unfavorable because of his submission to French domination and his role in creating the Avignon papacy. But much evidence suggests that his intentions were good. It was always his wish to return the papacy to Rome, but poor health and fear of "another Anagni" made him unable to resist Philip IV. Clement died on April 14, 1314.

Further Reading

Clement V is listed in the Religion study guide (I, F, 1, a). Many of the problems that he faced were caused by the conflict between BONIFACE VIII and PHILIP IV of France.

The best source of information about Clement V is Guillaume Mollat, *The Popes at Avignon, 1305–1378* (9th ed. 1949; trans. 1963); translated from the French, this is the classic book on the Avignon papacy and sets Clement's career in the context of his time. The ideology and consequences of the Avignon period are presented in Walter Ullmann, *The Origins of the Great Schism* (1948).

A Gnostic amulet in the Bibliothèque Nationale, Paris, showing a representation of Yahweh, who holds a sword in one hand and the head of Judas Iscariot in the other. Though Clement of Alexandria attacked the Gnostic sects as heretical, his theological writings, like theirs, show an attempt to synthesize Christian teachings with those of the Greek philosophers. (Felici)

CLEMENT OF ALEXANDRIA

/ By Robert F. Evans

The Christian theologian Clement of Alexandria (ca. 150–ca. 215) sought to integrate Greek classical culture with Christian faith.

The date and place of birth of Clement of Alexandria, born Titus Flavius Clemens, are not known, though it is likely that he was born in the decade 150–160, possibly in Athens. Having studied with religious and philosophical teachers in Greece, southern Italy, and Syria, he settled in the Egyptian city of Alexandria. There he was deeply impressed by the teachings of Pantaenus, who had been converted to Christianity from stoicism and who was at the time head of the Christian catechetical school in Alexandria. Clement, remaining a layman, eventually succeeded Pantaenus in this office and held the post for a number of years, probably not more than a decade. In relation to his activities as a Christian teacher Clement produced his three most important writings: *The Exhortation to Conversion, The Tutor,* and *Miscellanies.*

In Alexandria, Clement was at one of the leading intellectual centers of the Hellenistic world. Highly speculative and heretical Gnostic forms of Christian thought had been prominent there for decades among those who professed any form of Christianity. Gnosticism itself represented one way of synthesizing Christian faith with Hellenistic culture. Clement was of the firm conviction that Greek philosophy, particularly Platonic metaphysics and Stoic ethics, represented one of the ways in which God had prepared the world for the coming of Christ. His task, then, was to work toward an orthodox Christian appropriation of Greek thought.

The reader senses in Clement's writings the presence of three groups of critics against whom he constantly defends himself. To the pagan representatives of classical culture he argues the defensibility of any kind of "faith" and of Christian faith in particular. To the heretical Christian Gnostics he shows that the experience of redemption in Christ does not entail a depreciation of the material world created by God. To the simple and orthodox Christians he gives assurance that faith and intellectual sophistication are not incompatible and that philosophy does not inevitably lead to Gnostic heresy.

Clement left Alexandria on the outbreak of persecution against the Christians in 202. There is a fleeting glimpse of him in Syria shortly afterward. Later still he appears in the company of an old pupil, now a bishop in Asia Minor; the bishop sends his old teacher with a letter of congratulation to a newly elected bishop of Antioch. It is generally thought that Clement died about 215.

Further Reading

Clement of Alexandria is listed in the Religion study guide (I, B, 2) and the Social Sciences study guide (I, B, 3). It is thought that ORIGEN studied under him at Alexandria.

The classic study in English, R. B. Tollinton, *Clement of Alexandria: A Study in Christian Liberalism* (2 vols., 1914), is particularly useful for the way in which it synthesizes widely scattered materials, though it is sometimes dull. A splendid treatment of much smaller scope is Henry Chadwick, *Early Christian Thought and the Classical Tradition: Studies in Justin, Clement, and Origen* (1966).

CLEOMENES I / By N. G. L. Hammond

Cleomenes I (active ca. 520–490 B.C.) was a brilliant but unstable Spartan king who attempted to extend his country's influence outside the Peloponnesus.

A son of Anaxandridas, Cleomenes (pronounced klē-ŏm′ə-nēz) first displayed his genius in diplomacy in 519 B.C., when the city of Plataea asked Sparta for help against Thebes. He suggested Plataea ask the assistance of Athens, which accepted and promptly became embroiled with Thebes. Aiming thus to divide and conquer, Cleomenes chose as his next step in central Greece to expel the tyrant Hippias from Athens in 510 and try to bring the city into the Peloponnesian League, of which Sparta held the military command. But Cleomenes, failing to install the pro-Spartan oligarch Isagoras as ruler, was forced to withdraw.

In 508 Cleomenes realized that Athens was an implacable opponent of Spartan power in central Greece. He therefore organized a concerted attack against Athens. In 506 a Boeotian army, led by Thebes, invaded western Attica; the Chalcidians of Euboea invaded northern Attica; and the two Spartan kings, Cleomenes and Demaratus, led the army of the Peloponnesian League into southwestern Attica. When it became known that Cleomenes planned to make Isagoras tyrant of Athens, some Peloponnesians withdrew in protest, and King Demaratus took his force out of the line. The Spartan army disbanded, and Athens defeated Boeotia and Chalcis. Cleomenes proposed in 505 to make Hippias tyrant of Athens but failed. The only rival to Sparta in the Peloponnesus was Argos. Cleomenes led a surprise seaborne attack against it about 495 and won a great victory which disabled Argos for a generation.

Overseas, Cleomenes pursued a cautious policy since Sparta was not a naval power. About 515 he had rejected Samos's plea for help against the Persians. When the Ionians under Aristagoras revolted against the Persians in 499, Cleomenes again refused to lend Sparta's help. But when the Persians threatened to invade Greece in 491, Sparta allied itself with Athens, and Cleomenes went to Sparta's ally Aegina to arrest the leaders of a government which had submitted to Persia. He was rebuffed on the grounds that both Spartan kings were required to make a diplomatic intervention valid. Cleomenes knew that he could not obtain the cooperation of Demaratus, and he therefore plotted to oust him. A potential rival, Leotychidas, disputed the legitimacy of Demaratus, and the case was referred to Delphi, where Cleomenes bribed the priests and obtained the god's verdict against Demaratus. Leotychidas replaced Demaratus and, with Cleomenes, arrested the Aeginatans.

But the bribery became known. Cleomenes fled to Thessaly and then to Arcadia, where he fomented opposition to Sparta. Though Sparta reinstated him late in 491, Cleomenes apparently went insane and committed suicide.

The Dioskouroi, Kastor and Polydeukes, a Spartan relief sculpture executed about the time of Cleomenes I, in the Archeological Museum of Sparta. The mythical heroes, twin sons of Zeus and Leda, are also known as the Gemini, Castor and Pollux. (San-Viollet)

Further Reading

Cleomenes I is listed in the Ancient History study guide (II, D, 1). One of his chief Athenian opponents was CLEISTHENES.

Information on Cleomenes is in W. W. How and J. Wells, *A Commentary on Herodotus*, vol. 2 (1912), and in G. L. Huxley, *Early Sparta* (1962).

✳ ✳ ✳

CLEOMENES III / By N. G. L. Hammond

Cleomenes III (ca. 260–219 B.C.), the king of Sparta from 235 to 219, passed important reforms, revived Sparta's power, and was utterly defeated by Macedon. A vivid personality and dashing leader, he unfortunately lacked vision in politics.

C leomenes was the son of King Leonidas of Sparta. He married Agiatis, the widow of Leonidas's murdered coruler Agis IV, and she influenced Cleomenes deeply in the direction of social change. Since Leonidas was an archconservative, Cleomenes's feelings must have been torn between conservatism and socialism, between father and wife. When Cleomenes succeeded Leonidas in 235 B.C., he inherited policies of

A Laconian cup from the 6th century B.C. picturing Spartan soldiers carrying their dead from the battlefield. Cleomenes III did much to restore Spartan military traditions, which had declined by his time. (Staatliche Museen, Berlin, Photo by Jsolde Luckert)

conservatism and of the king's subordination to the ephors, or magistrates.

Expansion Policies

When the expansion of the Achaeans under Aratus made war inevitable in 229, the ephors authorized Cleomenes to defend the frontiers of Sparta. Not content with defense, he took the offensive with 5,000 men and in 228 forced an Achaean army of 20,000 to withdraw. Cleomenes's reputation soared. Ptolemy III, King of Egypt, now supported Cleomenes instead of Aratus. When Cleomenes hired mercenaries, the ephors scented danger, and after Cleomenes defeated the Achaeans in 227, King Archidamus was recalled to restore Sparta's dual kingship and check Cleomenes. But Archidamus was assassinated, and on winning a decisive victory over the Achaeans, Cleomenes left his citizen troops to occupy Arcadia, slipped back to Sparta with his mercenaries, and seized power. Killing four ephors and banishing 80 opponents, he named his brother successor to Archidamus's throne but from then on was sole military dictator.

Reforms in Sparta

Cleomenes at once introduced the reforms sponsored by Agis and frustrated by Leonidas. Though he may have believed in the socialist doctrines advocated by Agiatis and the Stoic philosopher Sphaerus, Cleomenes's immediate aim was to increase and improve the army. All debts and mortgages were canceled; all land was nationalized; and enough *perioeci*, or noncitizens who served in the forces, and aliens resident in Laconia were enfranchised to raise the number of male citizens to 4,000. Public land was divided into 4,000 equal lots, and each citizen received one. The 4,000 citizens were equipped

in Macedonian style with long pikes, the messes (*syssitia*) were reestablished, and the young were educated in the traditional manner.

With his enlarged army Cleomenes won a decisive victory in Achaea in 226. He offered generous terms if Achaea would enter his revived Peloponnesian League under Spartan leadership. But Achaea opened negotiations with Macedon.

War against Macedon

In 225 city after city—even Argos—joined Cleomenes in the expectation that he would revolutionize their societies as well. The Peloponnesian League was almost complete as a military alliance when, in 224, Achaea accepted Macedon's terms, the cession of Corinth. By now Cleomenes held Corinth but not its fortress, Acrocorinth. The Macedonian king, Antigonus Doson, failed to pierce Cleomenes's defenses at the Isthmus, but his political position was precarious. He had neither spread the socialist revolution nor supported the wealthy; thus the revolutionaries acted on their own, while the wealthy decided to rely on Macedon to reinstate them to their former status of power.

A popular rising at Argos, in concert with Macedonian and Achaean troops, overwhelmed the Spartan garrison in Argos. Abandoning the Isthmus and Corinth, Cleomenes fought his way into Argos and had the upper hand when the Macedonian cavalry appeared. Routed, Cleomenes fled to Tegea, where he heard of Agiatis's death. Antigonus reinstated the wealthy, formed the Hellenic League, condemned Cleomenes as a revolutionary, and declared he had no quarrel with Sparta.

Cleomenes turned to Ptolemy III. In exchange for subsidies he sent his mother and children as hostages to Egypt. In 223 Antigonus captured Tegea, Orchomenus, and Mantinea, entrusting the last to the Achaeans, who sold the population into slavery. Cleomenes captured Megalopolis, but the people escaped. When he offered to return the city if the people would support him, they refused. He sacked Magalopolis, an act of temper which only confirmed his isolation. For the final campaign Cleomenes freed many helots, raising his army to 20,000 men.

In 222 the decisive battle was fought at Sellasia. With 30,000 men Antigonus attacked Cleomenes's prepared position. When his troops overbore the left flank, Cleomenes committed his center to the attack. Charging downhill, the Spartans drove back the Macedonian phalanx but failed to break its formation. Antigonus's forces completed a pincer movement, and the encircled Spartan army was almost annihilated.

Cleomenes escaped, advising Sparta to submit, and sailed to Egypt. Antigonus spared Sparta, but Cleomenes's hopes of return faded. When Ptolemy III died, Ptolemy IV was unsympathetic to the Spartans, and the refugees found themselves virtually interned at Alexandria. In 219 Cleomenes conceived a plan which was as courageous as it was impracticable. Tricking their guards, he and 12 others escaped armed into the streets of Alexandria, called on the people to rise against Ptolemy, and tried to capture the prison of the citadel. Failing, they killed one another, the last committing suicide over the King's body. Ptolemy executed the women and children and had the corpse of Cleomenes flayed and hung on a gibbet.

Further Reading

Cleomenes III is listed in the Ancient History study guide (II, F, 2). One of Cleomenes's misfortunes was that his quest for expansion coincided with the attempt by ARATUS to reconsolidate the empire of ALEXANDER THE GREAT.

Ancient accounts of Cleomenes are in Plutarch and Polybius. A modern discussion is in J. B. Bury and others, eds., *The Cambridge Ancient History*, vol. 7 (1928).

CLEON / By N. G. L. Hammond

Cleon (ca. 475–422 B.C.) was an aggressive Athenian political leader. He was the first member of the nonaristocratic classes to reach a prominent position in Athens's political structure.

From humble origins, Cleon (pronounced klē′ŏn) rose to prominence by attacking the Athenian strong man Pericles and endeavored to succeed him after 429. Exploiting the reaction against Pericles and the angry mood of the people during the Peloponnesian War with Sparta, Cleon advocated in 427 the execution of every adult male and enslavement of the rest of the

population of Mytilene. A nominally free ally of Athens, the city had joined Sparta and had then been forced to capitulate to Athens. Cleon's policy was adopted at first but defeated by a small majority upon reconsideration. The news reached Mytilene just in time to stop the executions. Cleon's proposal to execute the ringleaders— more than 1,000 according to the text of Thucydides— was carried out.

Thus Cleon identified himself with methods which more civilized Athenians, such as Thucydides and Aristophanes, regarded as savage and cruel. When Aristophanes denounced such methods in the comedy *The Babylonians* in 426, it was significant that Cleon prosecuted the producers of the play. Aristophanes retaliated in *The Knights* in 424, pinning on Cleon (whether justly or unjustly, it is not known) all the faults of the bullying demagogue and warmongering agitator.

Between the productions of these two plays, Cleon was very successful in the military field, though he had no experience of command. The opportunity had come in 425, when Athens had a temporary advantage in the war, having isolated a Spartan force on the island of

A Winged Victory commemorating the victory of the Athenians, led by Cleon, over the Spartans at Pylos in 425 B.C. (Deutsches Archäologisches Institut, Athens)

Sphacteria near Pylos. Sparta offered peace and alliance on terms which Thucydides thought favorable. But Cleon persuaded the people to reject the offer. When this temporary advantage seemed to be slipping away, Cleon was criticized, but he turned the criticism against the generals at Pylos. One of them, Nicias, present in the Assembly, offered to resign when Cleon accused the generals at Pylos of incompetence for failing to capture the Spartans at nearby Sphacteria. The Assembly voted the command to Cleon, and with characteristic bluster Cleon said he would return within 20 days with the Spartans. With the help of Demosthenes, the general on the spot, Cleon succeeded.

Cleon now led the state in an aggressive policy, exacting more tribute from allies and attempting to regain lost territory. Sparta replied by opening a new front in Chalcidice, where allies of Athens defected. Cleon tried to deter them by making an example of the Thracian town of Scione. All adult males were executed and the women and children sold into slavery. But defections continued, and the Spartan commander, Brasidas, captured Amphipolis. In an attempt to redeem his prestige, Cleon obtained the command in this theater, was trapped by Brasidas, and perished with 600 Athenians in 422. Cleon's death cleared the way for an inconclusive peace.

Further Reading

Cleon is listed in the Ancient History study guide (II, C, 3, a). PERICLES is the classic example of a strong Athenian political leader.

Ancient sources for Cleon are Aristophanes, in *The Knights*, and Thucydides, both of them hostile. A useful modern study, which includes a discussion of Cleon, is H. D. Westlake, *Individuals in Thucydides* (1968). For background material, including a discussion of Cleon, see N. G. L. Hammond, *A History of Greece to 322 B.C.* (1959; 2d ed. 1967), and Charles A. Robinson, *Athens in the Age of Pericles* (1959).

* * *

CLEOPATRA / By Norman A. Doenges

Cleopatra (69–30 B.C.) was the last of the Ptolemaic rulers of Egypt. She was notorious in antiquity and has been romanticized in modern times as the lover of Julius Caesar and Mark Antony.

Third daughter of Ptolemy XII Auletes, Cleopatra VII Philopator (her full name) learned her political lessons by watching the humiliating efforts of her father to maintain himself on the throne of Egypt by buying the support of powerful Romans. When he died in 51 B.C., the ministers of Cleopatra's brother Ptolemy XIII feared her ambition to rule alone and drove her from Egypt in 48.

Cleopatra. (Trustees of the British Museum)

Cleopatra and Julius Caesar

Cleopatra made preparations to return by force, but when Caesar arrived in Alexandria after the Battle of Pharsalus, she saw the opportunity to use him. She had herself smuggled to him in a rug. Ptolemy XIII died fighting Caesar, who restored Cleopatra to the throne with another brother, Ptolemy XIV, as coregent.

Contrary to legend, Caesar did not dally in Egypt with Cleopatra. Although in 46 she gave birth to a son whom she named Ptolemy Caesarion, Caesar never formally recognized him. That same year Caesar invited her to Rome. Although he spent little time with her, her presence in Rome may have contributed to the resentment against him which led to his assassination.

In April 44 B.C. Cleopatra returned to Alexandria, where Ptolemy XIV had died under mysterious circumstances. She made Caesarion her partner on the throne and awaited the outcome of the political struggle in Rome. When, after the Battle of Philippi, Antony summoned her and other puppet rulers to Tarsus in Cilicia, she responded eagerly. Matching her preparations to the man whose weaknesses she knew, she dazzled Antony and bent him to her will. She easily cleared herself of a charge of helping Brutus and Cassius, and at her request Antony put to death three persons she considered a threat to her throne.

Cleopatra and Mark Antony

In the winter of 41/40 Antony followed Cleopatra to Alexandria, where he reveled in the pleasures of the Ptolemaic court and the company of the Queen. Cleopatra hoped to tie him emotionally to her, but Antony left Egypt in the spring of 40.

In the autumn of 37 Antony sent his wife, Octavia, back to Italy on the excuse that she was pregnant and went to Antioch to make final preparations for his invasion of Parthia. In Antioch he again sent for Cleopatra and with the Queen went through a ritualistic marriage not recognized under Roman law. He also recognized the twins Cleopatra had borne him and made extensive grants of territory to her, including Cyprus, Cyrene, and the coast of Lebanon, all of which had once been part of the Ptolemaic empire.

In 36 Cleopatra returned to Alexandria to await the birth of her third child by him. The failure of the Parthian campaign and Octavian's exploitation of Antony's misadventure drove Antony further into the arms of Cleopatra, who gave him immense financial help in rebuilding his shattered army. When Antony defeated Artavasdes of Armenia in 34, he celebrated his triumph not in Rome but in Alexandria. On the following day he declared Cleopatra and Ptolemy Caesarion joint rulers of Egypt and Cyprus and overlords of all lands west and east of the Euphrates. For Cleopatra this meant the potential union of the Ptolemaic and Seleucid empires under her control, and Antony staked out his claims on the wealth of Egypt for the coming struggle with Octavian.

In Italy, Octavian used the donations at Alexandria and Antony's relations with Cleopatra to turn public opinion against him. The Battle of Actium (Sept. 2, 31), fought for the control of the Roman Empire, led to the final disaster. Because Cleopatra's money built the fleet and supported it, she insisted on fighting at sea. When she fled from the battle with the war chest, Antony had little choice but to follow.

After Actium, Cleopatra tried to negotiate with Octavian for the recognition of her children as her successors in Egypt. But as his price Octavian demanded the death of Antony, and Cleopatra refused. After the final battle outside Alexandria on Aug. 1, 30 B.C., in which his troops deserted him, Antony stabbed himself when he received a false report that Cleopatra was already dead. Antony died in Cleopatra's arms inside her mausoleum, where she had barricaded herself with the treasures of the Ptolemies to keep them from Octavian.

Tricked into surrendering herself, Cleopatra tried again to negotiate with Octavian. Rebuffed, she carefully planned her own death. On August 10, after paying last honors to Antony, she retired to her quarters for a final meal. How Cleopatra died is not known, but on her left arm were found two tiny pricks, presumably from the bite of an asp.

Propaganda taught the Romans to fear and hate Cleopatra. To them she was either a deadly monster who aimed at empire and would destroy Rome or a royal prostitute who seduced Antony to his ruin. But Cleopatra was no slave to her emotions. Strong-willed and ambitious, she sought rule in the East for herself and her descendants and for this purpose used her mind, her body, and her wealth.

Further Reading

Cleopatra is listed in the Ancient History study guide (I, A, 8). Descended from the Macedonian PTOLEMY I, she was one of the political heirs of ALEXANDER THE GREAT.

The principal ancient sources on Cleopatra are Plutarch and Dion Cassius. H. Volkmann, *Cleopatra: A Study in Politics and Propaganda* (1953; trans. 1958), offers a well-balanced and penetrating analysis of the political implications of Cleopatra's relations with Julius Caesar and Antony. Arthur Weigall, *The Life and Times of Cleopatra* (1914; new ed. 1923), and Oskar von Wertheimer, *Cleopatra: A Royal Voluptuary* (trans. 1931), overemphasize Cleopatra's domination of Antony. In S. A. Cook and others, eds., *The Cambridge Ancient History*, vol. 10 (1934), W. W. Tarn views Cleopatra as dominated more by ambition for empire than by love. To Ronald Syme in *The Roman Revolution* (1939), both Antony and Cleopatra were playing a cynical game of politics with each other.

CLEVELAND / By J. Rogers Hollingsworth

Twice elected president of the United States, Stephen Grover Cleveland (1837–1908) owed his early political successes to reformism. His efforts to stem economic depression were unsuccessful, and the conservative means he used to settle internal industrial conflicts were unpopular.

Grover Cleveland's political career developed while the wounds of the Civil War and Reconstruction were healing and just as the serious social and economic problems attendant upon industrialization and urbanization were unclearly emerging. Although a lifelong Democrat, Cleveland was not skilled in party politics; he had emerged from a reform wing of his party and had only a few years of public experience before becoming president. Interested in public issues, he used the presidency to try to shape legislation and public opinion in domestic areas. Yet, by his second term of office, the old, familiar debates over tariffs and currency had been called into question and traditional political alignments began to tear apart. Cleveland, however, was not sensitive to the problems of party harmony; instead, he stood on principle at the price of party unity and personal repudiation. In the depression of the 1890s, his concern for the flow of gold from the Treasury led him to force Congress to repeal the Sherman Silver Purchase Act, and this action caused division of the Democratic

Grover Cleveland. (Library of Congress)

returned to legal practice, concentrating now on corporate law. His legal aspirations (and fees) were modest. His qualities as a lawyer were a good index to the whole of his public service: he was thorough, careful, slow, diligent, serious, severe, and unyielding. His sober approach to his career contrasted sharply with the boisterous humor of his private life, for he was a popular, if corpulent, bachelor.

Quickly Up the Political Ladder

In 1881 Buffalo Democrats, certain that a reform candidate could sweep the mayoralty election, turned to Cleveland. In his one-year term as mayor he stood for honesty and efficiency—exactly the qualities the New York Democrats sought in a candidate for governor in 1882. New York State was alive with calls for reform in politics; a trustworthy candidate was much in demand. Elected governor by a handsome margin, Cleveland favored reform legislation and countered the interests of the New York–based political machine called Tammany Hall and its "boss," John Kelly, to such an extent that it caused a rift between them. After one term as governor, Cleveland was seen as a leading contender for the presidential nomination of 1884. His advantages lay in his having become identified with honesty and uprightness; also, he came from a state with many votes to cast, wealthy contributors, and a strong political organization. Pitted against Republican nominee James G. Blaine, Cleveland even won the support of reform-minded Republican dissidents known as Mugwumps. Several forces favored him: Tammany's eventual decision to support him in New York State, blame for the depression of the 1880s falling on the Republicans, and temperance workers' ire with the Republican party.

Thus, in 4 years, riding a crest of reform movements on municipal, state, and national levels, Cleveland moved from a modest law practice in upstate New York to president-elect. The rapidity of this political success had several implications for the balance of his career—he had not had to make compromises in order to survive, he had not become identified with new programs or different systems, he owed fewer debts to special-interest groups than most new presidents, and he had come to the presidency on the strength of his belief in simple solutions of honesty and reform.

First Term as President

Cleveland's victory margin in 1884 was slim. His Cabinet appointees were men of substance, though not of prominence: Thomas Bayard as secretary of state, Daniel Manning as secretary of the Treasury, and William Endicott as head of the War Department. All shared the conviction that government should be neither paternalistic nor favorable to any special group and that contesting economic groups should settle their differences without government intervention. With little administrative experience and few reasons to think highly of party organization, Cleveland in his first term advocated improved civil service procedures, reform of executive departments, curtailment of largesse in pensions to Civil War

party. The depression worsened, and by his intervention in the Pullman strike of 1894 he alienated the laboring class, thus losing all effectiveness as president. In 1896 Cleveland was rejected by his party.

Cleveland was born in New Jersey but spent most of his life in New York. Despite the early death of his father, a Presbyterian minister, and his consequent family responsibilities, he studied law in a respected Buffalo firm and gained admission to the New York bar in 1859. He joined the Democratic party, acting as ward delegate and ward supervisor before being appointed assistant district attorney for Erie County in 1863. Diligent and devoted, Cleveland set a good, though not brilliant, record. Enactment of the Conscription Act of 1863 caught him in the dilemma of whether to serve in the Army or find a substitute. To continue supporting his mother and sisters, he took the latter option, remaining in Buffalo to practice law. This was a costly decision, for a military record was expected of almost any aspirant to public trust. Though without public office from 1865 to 1870, he steadily enlarged his law practice and gained stature in the community.

Cleveland became sheriff in 1870, a post which promised large fees as well as frustrating experiences with graft and corruption. Although he was respected for his handling of official responsibilities, he made many enemies and won few admirers, for most citizens looked with disfavor on the office of sheriff. After 3 years he veterans, tariff reform, and ending coinage based on silver. He failed to stop silver coinage but achieved at least modest success in the other areas. In one regard Cleveland was an innovative president: he used his office to focus attention on substantive issues, to pressure for legislation, and to define and determine the lines of congressional debate. Previously (and again after Cleveland), U.S. presidents left issues of legislation to Congress, spending most of their efforts on party leadership. Thus, in 1887 Cleveland took a strong position on tariff reform and later supported passage of the Mills Bill of 1888. Although the Mills Bill provided for only moderate tariff reductions, it was viewed as a step in the right direction, a way of reducing the embarrassingly large annual government surpluses.

Private Citizen

The Republicans mobilized to meet tariff reduction head on, stopping the Mills Bill and substituting a protective tariff measure, going into the election of 1888 with the tariff as the key issue. Renominated for the presidency in 1888 without challenge, Democrat Cleveland was opposed by Republican Benjamin Harrison of Indiana, who had the support of businessmen and industrialists favoring protective tariffs. Superior Republican organization, Democratic party feuding, and election fraud lost the 1888 election for Cleveland, although he won a plurality of the popular vote. He moved back to New York to practice law and enjoy his family.

Out of office, Cleveland withdrew from politics for a year but then began again to behave like an interested candidate. Stirred into attacking the McKinley tariff of 1890 and taking a strong position against currency expansion through silver-based coinage, he gained the Democratic presidential nomination in 1892.

Cleveland's campaign against incumbent President Harrison was a quiet one, with the Democrats aided by the 1892 Homestead strike, in which prominent Republicans were involved in the effort to break labor power and to maintain special benefits for the powerful steel magnates. The Democrats scored smashing victories in 1892, not only electing Cleveland but winning control of both House and Senate.

Second Term As President

To his second Cabinet, Cleveland named Walter Gresham as secretary of state, John G. Carlisle as secretary of the Treasury, Daniel S. Lamont as head of the War

A contemporary cartoon lampooning Cleveland during the presidential campaign of 1884. Cleveland, who as mayor of Buffalo had acquired a reputation for honesty and integrity, was accused of being the father of an illegitimate child. Asked to issue a denial, he admitted the story and advised that the public be told the truth. (Library of Congress)

Price   NEW YORK, September 27, 1884.   10 Cents.

Another voice for Cleveland.

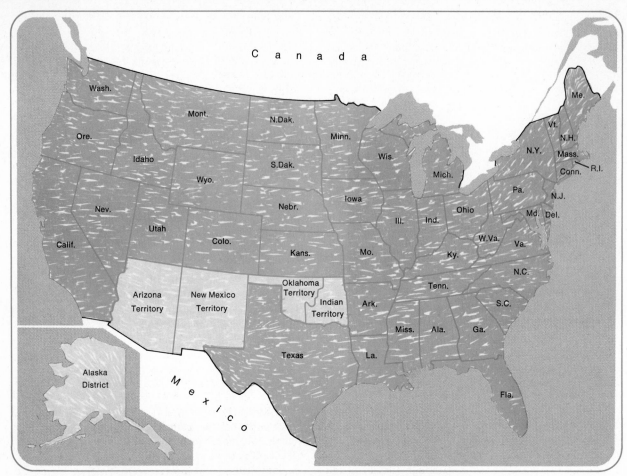

The United States at the close of Cleveland's second administration (March 4, 1897). During his second term of office, Utah was admitted to the Union as the forty-fifth state.

Department, and Richard Olney as attorney general. Like Cleveland's earlier Cabinet, these men agreed on extreme conservatism in handling economic issues. It was to Carlisle, Lamont, and Olney that Cleveland listened most closely, although in the final analysis he made his own decisions.

Policies in Time of Depression

Cleveland had scarcely taken his oath of office when the worst financial panic in years broke across the country. A complex phenomenon, the Panic of 1892–1893 had its roots in overexpansion of United States industry, particularly railroad interests; in the long-term agricultural depression that reached back to the 1880s; and in the withdrawal of European capital from America as a result of hard times overseas. As the panic broadened into depression, the American public tended to focus debate about its cause and cure on one item: the money question. On one side the argument was that businessmen (alarmed by the Sherman Silver Purchase Act requiring a purchase of silver each month) had lost confidence in the monetary system and feared depletion of the gold reserves; to regain their confidence and a return to prosperity, the buying of silver by the Federal government had to be halted. On the opposite side of the argument,

silver exponents maintained that what was needed was more money in circulation, which could be achieved only if more, not less, silver was purchased by the government and used as a basis for coinage.

Cleveland, long afraid of silver as a threat to economic stability, determined that repeal of the Sherman Silver Purchase Act would stem the drain of gold reserves and end the depression by restoring confidence to businessmen; he called a special session of Congress for its repeal. Protracted and bitter debate ensued. The Democratic party divided along sectional lines, with western and southern Democrats standing against repeal. The repeal, however, was voted, but it was ineffective, and gold reserves continued to dwindle. Meanwhile the depression became worse during 1893 and 1894.

Wounds that had opened during the silver-repeal debate were not healed when Cleveland's administration turned to the long-promised issue of tariff reform. Cleveland had been identified for many years with downward revision of tariffs and more equitable distributions. Pressured by sectional interests, the Democrats in Congress were more divided than united over tariff legislation. In addition, the silver battle had virtually torn the party in half, leaving many Democrats with nothing but hatred for the President. The Wilson bill, from the viewpoint of the

President, a fairly satisfactory measure for tariff reduction, was amended almost beyond recognition as it passed through the Senate, emerging with tariff rates only slightly lower than previous ones and carrying a host of provisions for special-interest groups. Highly dissatisfied but unsuccessful in his attempts to improve it, Cleveland allowed the Wilson-Gorman Act to become law without his signature.

To avert what he viewed as financial disaster, Cleveland became involved with four bond issues to draw gold into the Treasury. Not only was this effort to maintain gold reserves unsuccessful, but Cleveland was charged with having catered to Wall Street millionaires when other governmental policies had failed.

Beset by currency and tariff failures and hated by a large segment of the general population and by many in his own party, Cleveland further suffered loss of prestige by his actions in the Pullman strike of 1894. Convinced that the strike of the American Railway Union under Eugene V. Debs against the Pullman Company constituted an intolerable threat to law and order and that local authorities were unwilling to take action, Cleveland and Olney sent Federal troops to Chicago and sought to have Debs and his associates imprisoned. Although Cleveland prevailed and order was enforced, laborers throughout the country were angered by this use of Federal force.

Foreign Policies

The congressional elections of 1894 marked a sharp decline in Democratic power. Bitter at Cleveland and disheartened by worsening depression, American voters turned against the Democrats. Although Cleveland felt betrayed by his party and misunderstood by his constituents, he remained confident that his money policy had been correctly conceived and reasonably executed. Perhaps his party had split, but for him the defense of principle was more important than political harmony. Confronted with possibilities for compromise, Cleveland spurned such options and withdrew into isolation.

More successful in foreign policy, Cleveland exhibited the same determination and toughness. He would not be drawn into the Cuban rebellion against Spain; he would not sanction the Hawaiian revolution engineered by American commercial interests. Yet he took an equally stern posture vis-à-vis the boundary dispute between Venezuela and Great Britain in 1895–1896. Concerned about European influence in the Western Hemisphere, Cleveland and Olney carried the United States to the brink of war by insisting that the dispute be arbitrated. Business interests, clamoring for guarantees of open markets for their products, had considerable influence in shaping Cleveland's policy, which succeeded when Great Britain accepted arbitration.

Again a Private Citizen

Distrusted now and detested, Cleveland was convincingly repudiated by the Democratic Convention of 1896, which nominated William Jennings Bryan on a platform demanding free and unlimited coinage of both silver and gold at the rate of 16 to 1. Cleveland took no role in the campaign. He retired to Princeton, N.J., as soon as his term ended. He occupied himself with writing, occasional legal consultation, the affairs of Princeton University, and very occasional public speaking, but after 1900 he became less reluctant to appear in public. Sympathetic crowds greeted his appearances as the conservative Democratic forces with which he had been identified took party leadership from William Jennings Bryan. Briefly stirred into activity in 1904 to support Alton B. Parker's candidacy for the presidency, Cleveland spent most of his retirement years outside political battles, increasingly honored as a statesman. After offering to assist President Theodore Roosevelt in an investigation of the anthracite coal strike of 1902, he was active in the reorganization of the affairs of the Equitable Life Assurance Society in 1905. His death in 1908 was the occasion for general national mourning.

Further Reading

Grover Cleveland is listed in the American History study guide (VII, A, 3). Richard OLNEY was Cleveland's attorney general during the Pullman strike, in which Eugene V. DEBS was the labor leader pitted against industrialist George PULLMAN. Cleveland's first presidential race was run against James G. BLAINE.

There is an abundant literature on Cleveland. Allan Nevins, *Grover Cleveland: A Study in Courage* (1944), is the best overall treatment. A less sympathetic portrayal of Cleveland is Horace S. Merrill, *Bourbon Leader: Grover Cleveland and the Democratic Party* (1957). Robert Wiebe, *The Search for Order, 1877–1930* (1967), credits Cleveland's efforts to shape legislation, whereas J. Rogers Hollingsworth, *The Whirligig of Politics: The Democracy of Cleveland and Bryan* (1963), criticizes him as a party leader. Cleveland's diplomacy is discussed in Walter LaFeber, *The New Empire: An Interpretation of American Expansion, 1860–1898* (1963). A detailed account of the 1892 campaign is George H. Knoles, *The Presidential Campaign and Election of 1892* (1942), and of the 1896 campaign, Stanley L. Jones, *The Presidential Election of 1896* (1964). Arthur M. Schlesinger, Jr., ed., *History of Presidential Elections* (4 vols., 1971), is valuable as a source on the four campaigns of 1884–1896.

D. CLINTON / By James Morton Smith

The American politician DeWitt Clinton (1769–1828) was mayor of New York City, governor of New York State, and a tenacious sponsor of the state's Erie Canal.

DeWitt Clinton was born in Orange County, N.Y., the son of Gen. James Clinton and Mary DeWitt Clinton. Educated at Kingston Academy and Columbia College, from which he graduated in 1786, he studied law for 3 years. At the age of 18 the precocious youth became an Antifederalist propagandist for his un-

DeWitt Clinton about 1820. (Courtesy of The New-York Historical Society, New York City)

cle, New York governor George Clinton, writing newspaper articles in 1787 and 1788 opposing the ratification of the Federal Constitution. Entering politics in 1789, at the age of 20, he was appointed private secretary to Governor Clinton. He served as a transitional leader between the factional politics of the postrevolutionary period and the party politics of the new professionals which coalesced around New York's U.S. senator Martin Van Buren, who controlled the state political machine.

When John Jay was elected governor in 1795, Clinton aligned himself with the Democratic-Republican party, entering the New York Assembly in 1797, moving to the state Senate in 1798, and joining the Council of Appointment in 1801. In 1802 Clinton was chosen to fill a vacant seat in the U.S. Senate. His chief contribution as senator was the initiation of the 12th Amendment to the Constitution.

In 1803 Clinton resigned his Senate seat to become mayor of New York City, serving until 1815 with the exception of two annual terms. He also served as state senator from 1806 to 1811, lieutenant governor from 1811 to 1813, and political boss of the Democratic-Republicans in New York. But his break with the faction of Robert R. Livingston in 1807 and his opposition to the Embargo Act in 1808 led to strained relations with presidents Thomas Jefferson and James Madison. In 1812 New York Republicans nominated him for the presidency instead of Madison. After Madison's reelection, Clin-

ton failed to be renominated as lieutenant governor and in 1815 was ousted from his position as mayor.

Clinton promptly turned to his favorite project, the promotion of a state canal between the Hudson River and Lake Erie. Since 1810 he had served as one of the canal commissioners; he now organized a campaign advocating state support of the project. In April 1816 the legislature adopted Clinton's plan, which carefully outlined the engineering problems and procedures, the financial necessities, and the commercial potential. In 1817 a Republican caucus nominated Clinton, and he was elected governor by an overwhelming majority. Reelected in 1820 he lost support because of internal dissension in his party. He refused to run again in 1822.

When the group headed by U.S. senator Martin Van Buren overplayed its hand in 1824 and removed Clinton as canal commissioner, the Anti-Regency party nominated Clinton as their gubernatorial candidate. He won easily. Thus Governor Clinton in 1825 presided over the celebration of the opening of both the Champlain Canal and the Erie Canal, the greatest engineering project of its day. Reelected in 1826, he died in office on Feb. 11, 1828.

Clinton had been an active participant in literary, educational, and cultural affairs in New York. He organized the Public School Society in 1805, became the chief patron of the New York City Hospital and the New York Orphan Society, and secured the charter of the New-York Historical Society, serving as its president in 1817. Clinton was a founder of the New York Literary and Philosophical Society, also serving as president of the American Academy of Art and vice president of the American Bible Society.

By his first wife, Maria Franklin, Clinton had 10 children. In 1819 he married Catherine Jones, who survived him.

Further Reading

DeWitt Clinton is listed in the American History study guide (IV, A, 3; IV, E, 2). Aaron BURR and Robert R. LIVINGSTON also were important in New York politics. Clinton's uncle was George CLINTON, also a governor of New York State.

The standard account of Clinton is by Dorthie De Bear Bobbé, *DeWitt Clinton* (1933; rev. ed. 1962). For Clinton's role in the organization of the New York State canal system see Ronald E. Shaw, *Erie Water West: A History of the Erie Canal, 1792–1854* (1966). Specialized studies include Howard L. McBain, *DeWitt Clinton and the Origin of the Spoils System in New York* (1907), and Edward A. Fitzpatrick, *The Educational Views and Influence of DeWitt Clinton* (1911).

G. CLINTON / By Milton M. Klein

The American patriot and statesman George Clinton (1739–1812) was the governor of New

York for 21 years and vice president of the United States for two terms.

George Clinton's father, Charles, was an Ulster County, N.Y., farmer who had emigrated from Ireland in 1729. Charles Clinton achieved modest prominence through military and political office, but it was the marriage of his sons, James to Mary DeWitt in 1765 and George to Cornelia Tappen in 1769, that gave the Clintons status in New York society and future political allies among influential Dutch families.

Revolutionary Radical

Born in Ulster County, on July 26, 1739, George Clinton was educated at home and under a tutor, with the advantage of his father's better-than-average library. After studying law in New York City under William Smith, Jr., one of the famous Whig "triumvirate," he began practice in 1764. His political career was launched in 1768 with his election to the Assembly from Ulster County. There he allied himself with the minority "popular party" of the Livingstons against the DeLancey "court party" which controlled the legislature. For the next 7 years Clinton consistently opposed grants for supporting the king's troops, and he was one of a mere five assemblymen who in 1770 voted against jailing Alexander McDougall, a Whig "firebrand" who had publicly criticized the House for betraying its trust by its military appropriations. In the broader quarrel with Britain, Clinton sided with the radicals, denouncing parliamentary taxation and the Coercive Acts and urging support for the resolves of the First Continental Congress. A delegate to the Second Continental Congress, he was absent when independence was approved, having military obligations in New York, where he had been appointed brigadier general of the Ulster and Orange County militia in December 1775. Despite military shortcomings, the Continental Congress placed him in command of the forts in the Hudson Highlands. However, his energetic efforts did not prevent capture of the forts by the British in late 1777.

War Governor

The new state constitution of 1777 provided for a popularly elected governor. New York's aristocrats, led by Philip Schuyler, John Jay, John Morin Scott, and the Livingstons, expected Schuyler to be chosen. To their consternation the elections brought victory to Clinton—a tribute to his appeal to middle-class and small farmers and his popularity with the soldiers. Schuyler's postelection judgment that neither Clinton's family nor connections entitled him "to so distinguished a predominance" but that he was "virtuous and loves his country, has abilities and is brave" is an apt commentary on Clinton's entire political career. He attracted the majority of New Yorkers by his loyalty to the Revolutionary cause, his honesty, and his devotion to his state. His reputation was enhanced by his able service as war governor, a post which was more often military than political. He organized the defenses of the frontier, procured supplies,

suppressed loyalists, quieted the Indians, and organized campaigns against Tory and British raiders. His universal popularity was attested to by his successive elections to the governorship, often without opposition, until his voluntary retirement in 1795.

Antifederalist and Republican

Conservative in his administration during the Confederation period, committed to the protection of property and a stable financial system, Clinton was equally sensitive to popular liberties and republican government. It was the latter that made him suspicious of the movement for the U.S. Constitution in 1787. Willing to strengthen congressional powers under the Articles of Confederation, he feared the substitution of a "consolidated" for a "federal" government. The acknowledged leader of New York's Antifederalists, he was not so virulent an opponent of the Constitution as Alexander Hamilton made him out to be. He presided over the state's ratifying convention at Poughkeepsie with impartiality and spoke seldom, and then with moderation. There is some doubt that he wrote the Antifederalist essays attributed to him which appeared in the *New York Journal* (September 1787 to January 1788) as "Cato's Letters." Preferring ratification conditional upon amendments, he nevertheless promised to support the new Constitution when New York ratified it 30 to 27, on July 26, 1788, without such conditions.

Vice President

While Clinton continued to be popular personally, his

George Clinton in 1812. (Courtesy of The New-York Historical Society, New York City)

political followers hereafter faced stiff opposition from the Federalists, who in 1789 secured control of the legislature and in 1792 just missed placing John Jay in the governor's chair. Pleading ill health and perhaps sensing defeat, Clinton declined to stand in 1795, and his party was beaten. For the next 6 years his nephew DeWitt Clinton led the newly formed Democratic-Republican party in New York, an alliance of Clintonites, Livingstons, and the followers of Aaron Burr. George Clinton returned as governor for a term in 1801, but his political mantle remained with his nephew. Clinton played out the remainder of his political career on the national scene. In 1792 he was the unsuccessful candidate of Republicans in New York, Virginia, North Carolina, and Georgia for the vice presidency in place of John Adams. In 1804 he replaced Burr for the second place on the Republican ticket and served as vice president during Jefferson's second term. Four years later his followers promoted his candidacy for president on a ticket with James Monroe. When this failed, he settled for another term as vice president under James Madison. His 7 years in Washington (1805–1812) did not enhance his reputation. He had little influence with either administration, presided over the Senate without much skill, and disliked Washington society. Perhaps his most important action was his tie-breaking vote in 1811 to prevent the recharter of the Bank of the United States. He died in office on April 20, 1812.

A moderate reformer who during his governorship promoted road and canal building, lent support for manufactures and reform of the criminal code, and gave aid to libraries and public funds for common schools, Clinton appealed to the middle-class democracy of New York State. He lacked the felicity of language and the talented pen of a Jefferson to extend his influence much beyond his state.

Further Reading

George Clinton is listed in the American History study guide (III, E, 5, b; IV, A, 3). Patrick HENRY and Richard Henry LEE were other ardent Antifederalists. Clinton, Aaron BURR, and Robert R. LIVINGSTON were active in New York State politics.

The standard biography of Clinton is E. Wilder Spaulding, *His Excellency George Clinton: Critic of the Constitution* (1938; 2d ed. 1964). It has been revised in many details by more recent works on early New York political history, most notably Linda Grant De Pauw, *The Eleventh Pillar: New York State and the Federal Constitution* (1966), and Alfred F. Young, *The Democratic Republicans of New York: The Origins, 1763–1797* (1967). *Public Papers of George Clinton* (10 vols., 1899–1914) is an essential source, although the introductory sketch of Clinton's life by the editor, Hugh Hastings, is inaccurate. The Clinton era in New York politics may be traced in Jabez D. Hammond, *History of Political Parties in the State of New York* (2 vols., 1842; 4th ed., 3 vols., 1852), and in De Alva Stanwood Alexander, *A Political History of the State of New York* (4 vols., 1906–1923). Clinton's war governorship is ably analyzed and evaluated in Mar-

garet Burnham Macmillan, *The War Governors in the American Revolution* (1943).

*   *   *

H. CLINTON / By David L. Jacobson

Sir Henry Clinton (1738?–1795) was commander in chief of the British armies during the crucial years of the American Revolution.

Henry Clinton was the only son of George Clinton, governor of colonial New York. He entered the military, serving first in the New York militia and then in 1751 as a regular army lieutenant in the Coldstream Guards. He rose steadily in rank and displayed gallantry and capability during the French and Indian War in America. In the peace that followed 1763 he became colonel of the 12th Regiment and, after May 1772, major general. At this same time he was given a seat in the British Parliament, which he retained for 12 years.

Clinton's most sustained military service occurred during the American Revolution. He fought bravely at Bunker Hill but botched his command in the 1776 expedition

Sir Henry Clinton. (Courtesy of The New-York Historical Society, New York City)

to capture Charleston, S.C. He participated successfully, however, in the Battle of Long Island. Irritation with William Howe led Clinton to consider resigning, a threat he made periodically during his American command. (In 1777, he returned to England, now a lieutenant general, and was made a Knight of the Bath.) In the British battle design of 1777 Clinton was put in command at New York, while Howe moved against Philadelphia and John Burgoyne marched down from Canada. After Burgoyne's defeat and Howe's meaningless capture of Philadelphia, Clinton was the obvious choice to succeed Howe as commander in chief. In mid-1778 Clinton violated orders to evacuate Philadelphia by sea and instead led the British in a land retreat—under difficult conditions and with considerable skill—that included the Battle of Monmouth. For the next 2 years Clinton concentrated his forces around New York, undertaking successful though minor raids against coastal towns.

Clinton's greatest triumph—ironically also the beginning of the end of England's efforts to subdue its former colonies—was his second expedition against Charleston. He captured the city and 6000 American soldiers. This victory encouraged British hopes of conquering the Southern states. However, Charles Cornwallis was left in command when Clinton returned to New York. The relations between Clinton and Cornwallis revealed the same problems earlier apparent in Clinton's disagreements with William Howe. A flurry of orders and counterorders from Clinton in New York and George Germaine in London in effect left Cornwallis free to follow his own inclinations to Yorktown, and the result was his crushing defeat in October 1781. Clinton left his command the following May. While Cornwallis had a friendly reception in England, Clinton—his nominal commander—was blamed, and an acrimonious public debate between the two military leaders ensued.

In and out of Parliament, quarreling with relatives and critics, Clinton was nevertheless promoted to general in 1793 and became governor of Gibraltar the following year. He died at Gibraltar on Dec. 23, 1795. His two sons both rose to the rank of general in the British army.

Clinton was undoubtedly a difficult man. His short, happy marriage—ended by the death of his wife in 1772—was followed by a period of extreme depression. He was unsuccessful as a subordinate to Howe, frequently offering him what was regarded as impertinent advice. He was equally unsuccessful as a commander over Cornwallis, in part because he feared the latter as his chosen successor.

Further Reading

Sir Henry Clinton is listed in the American History study guide (II, D, 2, a). Clinton succeeded William HOWE as British commander in America and was in turn succeeded by Guy CARLETON.

Clinton's own account of his role in America may be found in William B. Willcox, ed., *The American Rebellion: Sir Henry Clinton's Narrative of His Campaigns, 1775–1782* (1954). An interesting biography is William B. Willcox, *Portrait of a General: Sir Henry Clinton in the*

War of Independence (1964). For a careful study of the overall British problems of command see Piers Mackesy, *The War for America, 1775–1783* (1964).

* * *

CLIVE / By Martin Blumenson

The English soldier and statesman Robert Clive, Baron Clive of Plassey (1725–1774), extended British power in India. He checked French aspirations in that area and made possible 200 years of British rule in the Indian subcontinent.

Robert Clive was born of an old and prominent family on Sept. 29, 1725, at Styche in Moreton Say, Shropshire. An unruly youngster, he attended several schools and at 18 was sent to Madras as a clerk and bookkeeper in the East India Company. A moody young man, he once fought a duel and twice attempted suicide.

The rivalry between French and British interests in southern India gave Clive his opportunity for fame and fortune. He volunteered for military service, received an ensign's commission, and participated in several battles

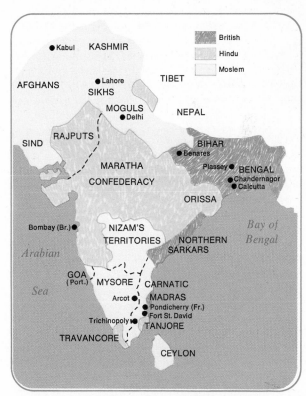

India in 1772. Clive's work in India as soldier and administrator made the British East India Company sovereign ruler over 30 million people and Great Britain the dominant European power in the subcontinent.

Robert Clive. (National Portrait Gallery, London)

against the French; he distinguished himself at Pondicherry in 1748, before the Treaty of Aix-la-Chapelle temporarily ended hostilities. In 1749 he was appointed captain of commissary to supply provisions to the troops, and he began to amass a fortune. But recurring clashes between the French and English East India companies brought him back to active military service.

In 1751 Clive offered to lead an expedition to relieve Trichinopoly (Tiruchirappalli), where Mohammed Ali, the British candidate for nawab, or ruler, was besieged by Chanda Sahib, the French candidate. With only 200 European and 300 Indian troops, plus three fieldpieces, Clive seized Arcot, Chanda Sahib's capital, thereby diverting 10,000 of Chanda Sahib's men from Trichinopoly.

Clive withstood a 50-day siege and, when he received reinforcements, began guerrilla warfare against the French and French-supported troops. The siege of Trichinopoly was finally lifted, and a truce in 1754 recognized Mohammed Ali as nawab. The Treaty of Paris in 1763 confirmed this, and in 1765 the emperor at Delhi admitted British hegemony in southern India.

Clive's brilliant leadership at Arcot gave him an immense reputation in Europe. When he went home in 1753, William Pitt the Elder called him a "heaven-born general." After running unsuccessfully for Parliament, Clive returned to India in 1755 as governor of Fort St. David and as lieutenant colonel in the royal army.

In 1756 Suraja Dowla (Siraj-ud-Daula), the new nawab, seized and plundered Calcutta, the principal city of Bengal and the most valuable trading center in India. Many English fled to ships and escaped, but 146 were imprisoned in a small underground dungeon called the Black Hole. Only 23 would emerge alive. Clive led a relief expedition from Madras in October; he rescued the English prisoners in December, took Calcutta in January, and defeated the nawab's army in February. Peace was made, and the East India Company's privileges were restored.

Displeased with the nawab's friendly attitude toward the French, Clive decided to replace him. In June 1758, at the Battle of Plassey, he defeated Suraja and became company governor and virtual master of Bengal. His position now enabled him to buttress the authority of the new nawab, Mir Jafar, to launch successful military expeditions against the French and to thwart Dutch expansion.

In declining health Clive went to England in 1760. He was given an Irish peerage, knighted, and made a member of Parliament. In 1765, when administrative chaos and fiscal disorder brought the company near disaster in Bengal, he returned to Calcutta as governor and commander in chief.

Clive limited the company to Bengal, Bihar, and Orissa, bringing these states under direct company control. He reformed the company's administrative practices, restored financial discipline while abolishing abuses, and reorganized the army. His efforts made the company sovereign ruler of 30 million people who produced an annual revenue of £4 million sterling.

Clive left India in February 1767. Five years later, in the absence of his strong hand in Bengal, the company appealed to the British government to save it from bankruptcy caused by widespread corruption. Clive's enemies in Parliament claimed that he was responsible for the situation. After a long trial he was exonerated; but continuing attacks on his integrity, together with illness and physical exhaustion, led him to commit suicide in London on Nov. 22, 1774. Somewhat above average height, with a commanding presence though melancholic mien, Clive brought a measure of peace, security, prosperity, and liberty to Indian natives who had been oppressed for many years.

Further Reading

Robert Clive is listed in the European History study guide (VI, A, 2) and the Asia study guide (II, A, 5, b). The French administrator Marquis DUPLEIX represented French interests in India from 1751 to 1754.

There are three standard biographies of Clive: Sir George Forest, *The Life of Lord Clive* (2 vols., 1918); R. J. Minney, *Clive of India* (1931; rev. ed. 1957); and A. Mervyn Davies, *Clive of Plassey* (1939). H. H. Dodwell, *Dupleix and Clive: The Beginning of Empire* (1920), is a classic account of French-British rivalry in India. Lucy Sutherland, *The East India Company in Eighteenth-Century Politics* (1952), clarifies the relationship of government and business.

CLODION / By James L. Connelly

The French sculptor Clodion (1738–1814) is best known for small terra-cotta groups in the rococo style, depicting nymphs and fauns in an erotic and playful manner.

Clodion (pronounced klô-dyôN′), whose real name was Claude Michel, was born in Nancy on Dec. 20, 1738, into a family of sculptors. He studied with his uncle, Lambert Sigisbert Adam, a prominent sculptor whose work was significant in transforming the vigorous and dynamic baroque style into the more delicate rococo. Clodion also worked with the famous rococo sculptor Jean Baptiste Pigalle. In 1759 the Royal Academy awarded Clodion the Grand Prize for Sculpture, and he was in Rome between 1762 and 1771. In 1773 he became a member of the academy. He created his most important works during the 1770s and 1780s.

Clodion possessed great technical virtuosity and executed many types of sculpture in a variety of media. During the 1770s he completed two important commissions for the Cathedral of Rouen: the marble *St. Cecilia* and the bronze *Crucified Christ*. In 1779 the royal government commissioned him to produce a monumental statue of the Baron de Montesquieu, one of the leading philosophers of the Enlightenment. This marble statue

Clodion's Intoxication of Wine (Nymph and Satyr), *a terra-cotta sculpture done about 1775. (The Metropolitan Museum of Art, Bequest of Benjamin Altman, 1913)*

shows the subject seated in a chair and wearing an impressive judge's robe. It is in no way formal or solemn, however, but is a sprightly and vibrant image of one of the most clever intellectuals of the time.

Clodion is most noted for small, intimate terra-cotta sculptures or statuettes of nymphs, fauns, satyrs, and bacchantes, mythological creatures symbolic of erotic pleasure. Such works as the *Intoxication of Wine* (*Nymph and Satyr*) and *Seated Bacchante Playing with a Child* are typical examples and are wholly within the decorative rococo traditions of 18th-century art. These graceful productions convey a mood of exuberant gaiety and depend for their effect upon a delicate play of highly refined textures; the soft medium of terra-cotta allowed Clodion to exploit fully and sensually the contrasting textural values of flesh, hair, fabric, fur, and foliage.

As early as the 1760s, the rococo style was under attack as frivolous and trivial, and during the last half of the century it was gradually replaced by a return to the relative severity of the art of antiquity. Clodion, however, was unaffected by the encroaching neoclassicism, and his statuettes remained popular until the French Revolution. During the Revolutionary and Napoleonic periods neoclassicism triumphed in the arts, and in his later works, such as the reliefs (1806) for the Arc du Carrousel in Paris, Clodion finally accepted the new style. He died in Paris on March 28, 1814.

Further Reading

Clodion is listed in the Art study guide (III, G, 2). He was influenced in his late works by Antonio CANOVA, the leading neoclassic sculptor of the period.

The most important works on Clodion are in French. General background studies in English include Lady Emilia Francis Dilke, *French Architects and Sculptors of the 18th Century* (1900); Chandler R. Post, *A History of European and American Sculpture*, vol. 2 (1921); Germain Bazin, *History of Western Sculpture* (trans. 1968); and Herbert Keutner, *Sculpture: Renaissance to Rococo* (trans. 1969).

CLODIUS / By Stephen L. Dyson

> The Roman politician Publius Clodius Pulcher (died 52 B.C.) was one of the leading demagogues in the 1st century B.C. As tribune, he wielded nearly as much power as Julius Caesar or Pompey.

Clodius (pronounced klō′dĭ-əs) came from one of the most distinguished of Roman families, the Claudii, which later included Roman emperors. His early career showed signs of the turmoil that was a major feature of his later life. In 68 B.C. he preached mutiny to the troops of the aristocratic general Lucullus in Asia Minor. Clodius was also accused of collusion with the revolutionary noble Catiline in 64, although this was

Clodius, a portrait bust in the Vatican Museums, Rome. (Alinari)

which had been prohibited 6 years earlier. From these guilds Clodius could draw gangs of toughs to terrorize Rome. Finally, to hamstring the oligarchic senatorial officials Clodius introduced a law which limited the power of the censors to expel members of the Senate and another which restrained magistrates from using religious omens to block public business, a device much used against Caesar the previous year.

Clodius also settled private grudges. He struck at Cicero by means of a law which outlawed any official who had condemned to death a Roman official without trial. Cicero had done this in the case of supporters of Catiline and was forced to go into exile. Clodius tore down the house of Cicero on the Palatine hill, purchased the property himself, and dedicated a part of it as a shrine to liberty. Clodius also removed Cato, another senator dangerous to him, by securing him a special commission to organize Cyprus as a Roman province.

Clodius now emerged as one of the most powerful men in Rome. Caesar had departed for Gaul, and Clodius's gangs spread terror through the city, so that as prominent a person as Pompey was forced to spend the last period of Clodius's tribunate at home for fear of his life. But Clodius by his attacks united his enemies against him. T. Annius Milo, another demagogic politician of the type of Clodius, began to organize gangs with the support of Pompey and the Senate, and the return of Cicero was engineered.

For 56 Clodius was elected curile aedile, and he used this office to continue his attacks on Cicero, accusing him of sacrilege when Cicero repossessed his property on the Palatine. When Caesar, Pompey, and Crassus renewed their alliance at the conference of Luca, they agreed that Clodius must be controlled.

Clodius was aiming to be praetor when, in 52, his gang met that of Milo on the Appian Way, and in the ensuing brawl Clodius was killed. At his funeral in the forum his supporters started a fire which burned down the senate house.

Further Reading

Clodius is listed in the Ancient History study guide (III, B, 3). Tiberius Sempronius and Gaius Sempronius GRACCHUS exemplified the more idealistic type of plebeian tribune.

Much information on Clodius comes from the writings of his enemy Cicero. Information also appears in Dio Cassius's history of Rome and in the accounts of the lives of Pompey, Cicero, and Lucullus in Plutarch's *Lives*. The best modern account of Clodius and his times is H. Scullard, *From the Gracchi to Nero* (1959). For the political activity of the period see L. R. Taylor, *Party Politics in the Age of Caesar* (1949).

disputed. By these acts he established a reputation as an opponent of the entrenched aristocracy and also built a future power base for himself. In 64–63 he served on the staff of Lucius Murena in Transalpine Gaul but was accused of lining his own pockets at the expense of the provincials.

In 62 Clodius became a source of public scandal when, disguised as a woman, he invaded the exclusively female sacred rites dedicated to Bona Dea (the Good Goddess). Clodius was charged with sacrilege, and although Cicero demolished the alibis of Clodius, the latter managed to win acquittal by the extensive use of bribery. This produced a lifelong enmity between Clodius and Cicero.

In this period when Caesar, Pompey, and Crassus were struggling against the conservatives in the Senate, Clodius's talent as a political organizer and goon became increasingly useful. He was advancing through the usual progression of Roman offices, being quaestor in 61, but he soon saw that his talents and connections could best be used as tribune, a representative of the people. Unfortunately, as an aristocrat he was ineligible for this office. However, Caesar also favored Clodius for tribune and in 59 arranged for Clodius's adoption into a plebeian family, at which time his name was changed from the patrician Claudius to the plebeian Clodius. Thus Clodius was elected tribune for the year 58.

Tribune and Power Broker

As tribune, Clodius rapidly set to work to aid his and his patrons' interests. To curry favor with the people he instituted distribution of free corn. To strengthen his operating base he arranged for the legalization of guilds,

CLOUET / By Robert A. Koch

The French painters Jean (ca. 1485–ca. 1541) and François (ca. 1516–ca. 1572) Clouet were masters of an elegantly mannered, aristocratic style of portrait painting and of colored chalk portrait drawing.

Jean Clouet (pronounced klōō-ě′) was court painter to King Francis I. His son, François, succeeded him as court painter and maintained that position under Henry II, Francis II, and Charles IX.

Jean Clouet

Jean, or Janet, Clouet was the son either of Michel Clouet, known to have painted in Valenciennes, or of the Brussels painter Jan Clouet. In any case, Jean's early training must have exposed him to the formal, cool, and detached Flemish mannerist portrait type as seen in the works of Jan Gossart and Joos van Cleve.

Jean was appointed painter to the court of Francis I in 1516, the year of the monarch's accession to the throne. Though Jean was never naturalized, he became the chief court painter in 1523, a position he held until his death. In France he developed his own courtly style to comply with the French preference for decorative elegance and sophistication. The problem of attribution of his works is difficult, but it seems likely that eight oil portraits and nine miniatures known today are by him. He is recorded as having painted altarpieces at Tours, but these have disappeared, probably destroyed during the religious struggles of the mid-16th century.

Jean's chief claim to fame lies in his establishment as a

A drawing presumed to be a portrait of François Clouet, in the Louvre, Paris. (Giraudon)

François Clouet's Lady in Her Bath, *possibly a portrait of Diane de Poitiers. (National Gallery of Art, Washington, D.C., Samuel H. Kress Collection, 1955)*

medium in its own right of chalk (or hard crayon) drawing in hues of red, white, and black. About 130 examples are attributed to him. Typical is the drawing of Admiral Bonnivet (1516), with its fine feeling for the placement of the head in the usual quarter-turn to the right and the delicate system of shading in diagonal lines that he learned from Leonardo da Vinci, whom Jean would have met at Francis I's château of Amboise, where the great Italian died in 1519.

One of Jean's oils is a half-length portrait of the French humanist Guillaume Budé (ca. 1535). Restrained and nearly monochrome in color, the portrait reflects the drawings in its stress on a patterned silhouette.

Of greatest inherent interest are two portraits of Francis I (both ca. 1525). The one in Florence, which has been questioned as a work by Jean himself, depicts the monarch in monumental fashion, regally erect upon a static, caparisoned horse which fills the space of the tiny panel. The setting is in the Italian mode, with a hint of architecture at the right and a generalized landscape with low horizon to enhance the grandeur of the sitter. The portrait in Paris is a half-length, nearly life-sized presentation of Francis I in dazzling robes, before a tapestried background. There is the trace of a supercilious smile on the

face of this unscrupulous and dissolute Renaissance ruler. It is Jean's best-known painting, not because of its quality, which is not great, but because of the historical importance of the subject.

François Clouet

François Clouet, also called Janet, was born at Tours and was active as a painter by 1536. He succeeded his father as chief court painter and maintained that position until his death in 1572.

More gifted than his father, the son continued the conventions of the international portrait style prevalent throughout the courts of Europe. Under the influence of such supreme Italian mannerist portraitists as Bronzino and of the Netherlander Anthonis Mor van Dahorst (Antonio Moro), François introduced into French court painting a greater naturalism with more emphasis on modeling. This may be seen in the portrait of the apothecary Pierre Quthe (signed and dated 1562). Now posed in the newly fashionable three-quarter-length view, which permits full extension of the arms and a more natural placement of the hands, the sitter's courtly station in life and his calling are indicated by an opened herbal and by a portion of a velvet drape, a space-creating device invented by Titian. François may be fairly said to have surpassed his father in imbuing his subjects with a more natural air; yet they remain restrained and very dignified.

The most interesting painting by François that has survived is ostensibly a genre scene, *Lady in Her Bath* (perhaps painted ca. 1550). It features in outspoken fashion a half-length, bejeweled nude lady seated in her "bath" before a still life of assorted fruits. Immediately behind her are a lad who reaches for the fruit and a nursemaid who suckles a baby swaddled in the Italian fashion. Drapes are drawn to reveal, in a manneristic plunge into deep space, a kitchen maid at a fireplace in an elegant room and, beside her, a pictorial representation of a unicorn, the fabled beast that symbolized virginity. Quite possibly the lady represented is Diane de Poitiers, famous mistress of Henry II. The beautifully rendered nude torso was surely derived from the undraped version of Leonardo's *Mona Lisa* (now lost), but the principal inspiration of the composition was taken from contemporary Flemish interior genre scenes, such as those by Pieter Aertsen, which often have symbolic overtones that are obscure in meaning.

François continued the portrait drawing technique established by his father, with whose works François's are sometimes confused.

Further Reading

Jean and François Clouet are listed in the Art study guide (III, E, 1, c). They were influenced by LEONARDO DA VINCI, and François was also influenced by BRONZINO and TITIAN. The courtly tradition of portraying royal mistresses began with Jean FOUQUET and continued into the 18th century in paintings by François BOUCHER.

The only monograph on the Clouets is in French, but there is a detailed discussion of them in Louis Dimier, *French Painting in the Sixteenth Century* (trans. 1904). See also H. W. Janson, *History of Art* (1962).

CLOUGH / By Glen A. Omans

The English poet Arthur Hugh Clough
(1819–1861) epitomized in his life and poetry
the religious crisis experienced by many
Englishmen of the mid-Victorian period.

Arthur Hugh Clough was born in Liverpool on Jan. 1, 1819. In 1829 he entered Rugby, where he quickly distinguished himself as a scholar and an athlete and became a favorite of Rugby's famous headmaster, Thomas Arnold. In 1837 he entered Balliol College, Oxford, and became friends with Benjamin Jowett and Matthew Arnold, the son of Thomas.

The controversy between members of the conservative Oxford movement and more liberal theologians undermined Clough's faith in orthodox Christianity. He main-

tained his general belief in God; but he became deeply disturbed, and his attempt to keep an open mind on all points of view tended to paralyze his will to act. Thus Clough came to typify his whole generation, which seemed, as Matthew Arnold noted in "Stanzas from the Grande Chartreuse," to be "wandering between two worlds, one dead, the other powerless to be born." Clough himself made this indecision the subject of many poems, such as "Say Not the Struggle Naught Availeth," "Thesis and Antithesis," "Qua Cursum Ventus," and "Easter Day."

In 1842 Clough was granted a fellowship at Oriel College and became a tutor in 1843, but in 1848 he resigned both positions. He then entered into an "after-boyhood" which enabled him to write and publish *The Bothie of Tober-na-Vuolich, a Long Vacation Pastoral*. This long narrative poem reveals the lighter, charming side of his personality.

In 1848, turning his attention from religious to political crises, Clough journeyed to Paris to observe the revolution and was in Rome in June 1849, when the French attacked the city. While in Rome, he wrote *Amours de Voyage*, his second long poem and perhaps his best. This poem explores the indecisive personality of the central character, whose inability to act destroys his love affair. Also in 1849, Clough and Thomas Burbidge published a volume of their shorter poems, entitled *Ambarvalia*. In 1850 Clough began but never finished *Dipsychus*, a long poem modeled after Goethe's *Faust*.

Arthur Hugh Clough about 1860. (National Portrait Gallery, London)

In October 1852 Clough sailed for Boston, where he was befriended by Ralph Waldo Emerson, James Russell Lowell, and Charles Eliot Norton. He returned to England in 1853 and in 1854 married Blanche Smith. Giving up his poetry, he turned to the philanthropic work being done by his wife's cousin Florence Nightingale. But his health began to fail, and in 1861 he left England to tour the Mediterranean. He began another long poem, *Mari Magno*, but never finished it, for he died in Florence on Nov. 13, 1861.

Clough's fame grew after his death. Many of his verses first appeared in a posthumous edition of *Poems* (1862), and a two-volume edition of *Poems and Prose Remains* (1869) was reprinted 14 times before 1900.

Further Reading

Arthur Hugh Clough is listed in the Literature study guide (II, H, 2, b). Matthew ARNOLD wrote his famous elegy "Thyrsis" on Clough.

The best biography of Clough is Katherine Chorley, *Arthur Hugh Clough: The Uncommitted Mind* (1962). Additional insight into Clough's personality can be gained from Frederick L. Mulhauser's edition of Clough's *Correspondence* (2 vols., 1957). An excellent modern critical study is Walter E. Houghton, *The Poetry of Clough* (1963).

CLOVIS I / By William J. Courtenay

The Frankish king Clovis I (465–511) founded the Merovingian kindgom of Gaul, the most successful of the barbarian states of the 5th century. He is widely regarded as the originator of the French nation.

The son of Childeric I and Basina, Clovis (pronounced klō′vĭs) inherited the kingship of the Salian Franks in 481, at the age of 15. In 486 he led his army against Soissons, the last of the Gallo-Roman strongholds, and defeated the Roman governor. He then engaged in a series of campaigns against other barbarian kingdoms, and it was during one of these military ventures that Clovis was converted to non-Arian Christianity. According to Gregory of Tours, Clovis was at a disadvantage in his fight against the Alamans and sought the aid of the God of his Christian wife Clotilde, promising that if he were given victory he would become a Christian. In 506 Clovis inflicted a crushing defeat on the Alamans at Tolbiac (Zülpich).

After the battle Clovis adopted Christianity and by so doing won the support of the Gallo-Roman bishops who controlled a significant portion of the wealth of Gaul and were exceedingly influential with the population. Moreover, his conversion automatically made Clovis's wars into holy wars against heretics and nonbelievers. Many historians have seen Clovis's conversion as a shrewd political move; but it is also likely that the victory of Tolbiac was instrumental in his religious shift and that without a sign of some variety he might never have abandoned his ancestral gods.

Within the Frankish portion of his kingdom Clovis, who was ruthless in his desire for power, gradually eliminated the other kings who had previously been his allies, and by a combination of military expertise and treachery he emerged as the supreme ruler in Gaul.

The period of Frankish expansion, which had begun in 486, ended with the battle against the Visigoths at Vouille (near Poitiers) in 507. Clovis then turned his attention to the government of his newly conquered territories. His reign, which combined elements of Germanic kingship with traditional Roman fiscal and administrative systems, owed much of its success to the cooperation between Clovis and his Germanic followers and the Gallo-Roman episcopate. His policy toward the Church was essentially one of overlordship tempered with consideration for ecclesiastical needs and privileges. In the latter years of his reign, Clovis devoted much energy to the promulgation and codification of the *Lex Salica* (Salic Law), the customary unwritten laws of the Franks, and thus he provided jurisdictional unity for his kingdom.

Clovis died at Paris on Nov. 27, 511, at the age of 45. In keeping with Frankish tradition, his four sons (Chlodomer, Childebert I, Clothar I, and Theuderic) divided his kingdom.

Clovis I, King of the Franks, detail from a 16th-century French tapestry. (Giraudon)

The Frankish kingdom at the death of Clovis. By force and treachery Clovis united the Frankish tribes and founded the most successful of the barbarian states that replaced the Roman Empire in the West. The origins of modern France are traditionally traced to Clovis.

Further Reading

Clovis I is listed in the European History study guide (I, B, 1, a). St. GREGORY OF TOURS wrote a valuable history of this period.

The most important source for the life of Clovis and the character of Merovingian Gaul is the *History of the Franks* by Gregory of Tours, written between 575 and 585 and available in several English translations. The best modern descriptions of the life and times of Clovis are *The Cambridge Medieval History*, vol. 3 (1913), and J. M. Wallace-Hadrill, *The Long-Haired Kings* (1962).

CNUT / By Robert W. Hanning

The Viking Cnut (ca. 995–1035), or Canute, was king of England and Denmark. The first Dane to rule England, he strengthened English law and learning and became a devout supporter of the Church.

Cnut (pronounced kə-no͞ot′) was the second son of Swein, an energetic, barely Christian warrior-king of Denmark who figured prominently in several Danish invasions of England in the late 10th and early 11th centuries. The English under King Ethelred "the Unready" were divided and largely ineffectual. In 1013,

when Cnut went with his father to England, Swein seemed assured of wresting the kingship from Ethelred. But Swein died suddenly in 1014, and Ethelred died 2 years later. Ethelred's son Edmund resisted Cnut's advance across England but died in November 1016, whereupon Cnut became king of England.

As king, Cnut emphasized order throughout England, continuity with the Anglo-Saxon kingship, and the advancement of English culture. To win peace and support, he killed or banished several leading English nobles and sent Edmund's heirs into exile. He also married Ethelred's widow, Aelfgyfu, or Emma (while keeping another Anglo-Saxon gentlewoman as "unofficial" wife), to strengthen his claim as legitimate ruler. He defended the prerogatives of the English Church and issued a code of

King Cnut with his wife Aelfgyfu, from the register of Hyde Abbey written about 1016–1020. (Radio Times Hulton Picture Library)

laws traditional in character and pious in tone. In 1020 and 1027 he issued special proclamations to his subjects, explaining that his policies served the best interests of them all.

Cnut did not neglect his Scandinavian interests. His older brother, King Harold of Denmark, died in 1018 or 1019, and Cnut succeeded him. The Norwegians and Swedes challenged Cnut's ambitions with temporary success, but in 1026 he defeated King Olaf and became the ruler of Norway. By 1027 Cnut was the most powerful monarch in western Europe. His prestige reached its zenith when he traveled to Rome in 1027, in the garb of a pious pilgrim, to attend the coronation of Conrad II as Holy Roman emperor and to discuss with him matters of policy touching on the welfare of his realm and subjects. Cnut was received in Rome with great splendor.

In the latter years of Cnut's reign, Norway again became independent, and Denmark was ruled by Harthacnut, the King's son by his "unofficial" wife. When Cnut died on Nov. 12, 1035, Harthacnut was unable to claim his English inheritance because of Norway's threat to Denmark. So the English nobility turned to Harthacnut's stepbrother Harold to succeed Cnut. Cnut left behind a glowing, double reputation: in England as a just, pious king and in Denmark as a heroic warlord.

Further Reading

Cnut is listed in the European History study guide (I, F, 1; I, J, 1, a and b). He succeeded ETHELRED as king of England.

The main source of facts about Cnut is *The Anglo-Saxon Chronicle,* edited and translated by G. N. Garmonsway (1953). For analyses of Cnut's character, policies, and achievements see F. M. Stenton, *Anglo-Saxon England* (1943; 2d ed. 1947), and C. N. L. Brooke, *The Saxon and Norman Kings* (1963). Laurence Marcellus Larson, *Canute the Great* (1912), is also useful.

COBBETT / By Norbert J. Gossman

The English radical journalist and politician William Cobbett (1763–1835) was an advocate of parliamentary reform and a critic of the new industrial urban age.

William Cobbett was born at Farnham, Surrey, on March 9, 1763. His father, a small farmer, could afford him little schooling. Cobbett worked briefly with a copying clerk in London in 1783; he enlisted in the army in 1784 and served until 1791, mostly in Canada. In 1792 he wrote a pamphlet exposing military corruption but was unable to supply adequate evidence to press his case and fled to France and then to America.

Writing under the name of "Peter Porcupine" in Philadelphia, he attacked the French Revolution and defended England, then at war with France. During his American sojourn Cobbett wrote numerous pamphlets and founded and edited several small periodicals, including the *Political Censor* and *Porcupine's Gazette.* At this stage in his career he was clearly anti-Radical and anti-Jacobin (pro-Federalist and anti-Democrat in American terms). Cobbett savagely criticized the English scientist Joseph Priestley, who had also settled in Philadelphia, for his support of the French Revolution. But criticism of Dr. Benjamin Rush ended Cobbett's American journalistic career; he accused the famous physician and Democrat of killing patients (George Washington, among others) through his bleeding and purging technique. This brought a charge of libel against Cobbett, and he returned to England in 1800.

Britain's Tory government welcomed him as a literary asset in the struggle against republican France. He opened a bookshop in London and in 1802 began his famous *Weekly Political Register.* Gradually moving toward radicalism, he criticized the government's conduct of the long Napoleonic War. He was especially concerned about the war's economic repercussions on the home front. Because of his criticism of the government's handling of an army mutiny, in 1810 Cobbett was convicted of sedition and imprisoned for 2 years. Upon his release in 1812, he emerged as the great popular spokesman for the working classes. In his new, cheaper *Register,* he championed parliamentary reform and attacked the government for the high taxation and widespread unemployment of the postwar period.

Cobbett's newfound radicalism alarmed the government, and he went to America in 1817. On his return to England in 1819 Cobbett discovered a new enemy of the people—industrialism—and he repeatedly attacked this development in his famous *Rural Rides.* These essays, which praise old agricultural England, were first pub-

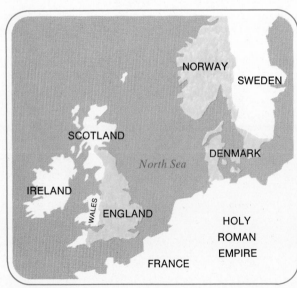

NORWAY

SWEDEN

SCOTLAND

DENMARK

North Sea

IRELAND

WALES

ENGLAND

HOLY ROMAN EMPIRE

FRANCE

Dominions of Cnut in 1027. As ruler of England, Denmark, and Norway, Cnut in 1027 was the most powerful monarch in western Europe. His empire did not survive him.

William Cobbett. (Library of Congress)

The range in the evaluation of Cobbett is suggested by the two standard biographies: G. D. H. Cole, *William Cobbett* (1925), views him as a Radical leader of the working classes, while G. K. Chesterton, *Willaim Cobbett* (1925), considers him a Conservative. More recent biographies of Cobbett are William Baring Pemberton, *William Cobbett* (1949), and John W. Osborne, *William Cobbett: His Thought and His Times* (1966). Osborne more than the earlier biographers minimizes Cobbett's significance, calling him "a failure in politics . . . and of very limited influence in his lifetime." Mary Elizabeth Clark wrote a specialized study, *Peter Porcupine in America* (1939). There is a provocative chapter on Cobbett in Crane Brinton, *English Political Thought in the Nineteenth Century* (1933).

✳   ✳   ✳

COBDEN / By Norbert J. Gossman

The English politician Richard Cobden (1804–1865) was leader of the free-trade movement. He strenuously opposed war and worked unceasingly for the cause of international peace.

T he son of a farmer, Richard Cobden was born on June 3, 1804, near Midhurst, Sussex. There were 11 children in the Cobden family, and poverty was an obstacle in Cobden's youth. His formal education was an unhappy experience. He worked for a time for his uncle in London; then in 1828 he became a calico merchant near Manchester. Prosperity followed, and he soon added Manchester municipal politics to his interests. Repeal of the Corn Laws was the issue that attracted him, and Manchester was the center of the Anti–Corn Law League, which was founded in 1838. This led him to national politics, as he emerged the leader of the free-trade movement.

During these years Cobden visited Europe, America, and Africa, and his travels gave him a perspective in international affairs. Cobden believed that free trade would promote international cooperation. His first attempt at a parliamentary career failed, but he was successful in 1841, when he was elected to Parliament from Stockport. In the same year he persuaded the orator and statesman John Bright to work toward repeal of the Corn Laws. Bright's oratory coupled with Cobden's organizational skills made the Anti–Corn Law League a great success. Prime Minister Peel's conversion to free trade was the final step, and the repeal of the Corn Laws came in 1846.

Opposition to British Policies

Cobden was victorious, but he was also bankrupt; politics and the league had swallowed up his fortune. But a public subscription in 1847 returned him to financial solvency, and his interests turned more to foreign affairs. He became increasingly alarmed by the bellicose policies

lished in the *Register* and in book form in 1830.

Although his grand projects, the *Parliamentary Debates* and the *Parliamentary History of England*, were taken over by others while he was in prison, Cobbett never lost his interest in politics. He ran for Parliament unsuccessfully twice but was elected in 1832 from Oldham, following the acceptance of the Great Reform Bill. The parliamentary reform implemented by the bill fell far short of the demands of Cobbett and the Radicals, since the working class was still denied the vote. He opposed much of the legislation of the new Whig government in the reformed Parliament, especially the New Poor Law of 1834. He died on his farm near Guilford on June 18, 1835.

Cobbett has been praised as the prophet of democracy, but most of his writings look back to the old agrarian England of responsible landlords and contented tenants. He was not a profound thinker; his comments on economic matters were nearly always erroneous. Emotion rather than reason dictated many of his conclusions. But his passion for the interests of the common man and his ability to write in a jargon that was understood by the working class made him the leading English Radical of the early 19th century.

Further Reading

William Cobbett is listed in the Social Sciences study guide (VI, B, 1). As prime minister, Lord GREY secured the passage of the Reform Bill in 1832. In the late 19th century Keir HARDIE was active in organizing workers to prevent their exploitation by an industrialist society.

Richard Cobden. (National Portrait Gallery, London)

regard for basic economic laws; extent of territory, not commercial value, had dictated acquisition. Cobden held that the colonies, if given up, would remain good customers of England but would cease to involve the nation in international difficulties.

America always attracted Cobden's interest. He visited the United States twice and was impressed by the absence of an entrenched landed aristocracy. In contrast to England, the United States was essentially a middle-class nation. The American Civil War deeply disturbed Cobden. He wavered (hating Southern slavery but also disliking Northern protectionism) but finally supported the North. He died in London on April 2, 1865.

Assessment of Political Role

Cobden's outlook was based on an intense internationalism. He firmly believed that free trade would create prosperity at home and introduce a new era of international peace. The main obstacle to both free trade and peace, in Cobden's view, was the aristocracy. He felt that as a class aristocrats were naturally bellicose and believed that the sooner power was transferred from the aristocracy to the middle class, the better for the destiny of all nations.

To the historian Cobden appears as a strange combination of realist and visionary. His work for the Anti–Corn

of Lord Palmerston. Cobden supported a reduction in armaments and suggested a possible trade alliance with Russia in direct opposition to Palmerston's position. Cobden wrote a number of pamphlets condemning the traditional "balance of power" approach in international politics.

At the Great Exhibition of 1851 Cobden's position of "free trade and peace" seemed triumphant; Palmerston was dismissed from office at the end of the year. But the Crimean War (1853–1856) changed all that as the anti-Russian crusade became the order of the day. In 1855 Palmerston returned as prime minister and war leader, and Cobden, who opposed the war, was severely criticized in the press and was defeated in the parliamentary election of 1857. He was, however, returned to Parliament in 1859. He was offered a position in Palmerston's Cabinet but declined. Cobden, partly through William Gladstone's influence, was sent to Paris to prepare an Anglo-French commercial treaty; his efforts led to the signing in 1860 of a 10-year reciprocal "most favored nation" treaty (Cobden-Chevalier Treaty). This was one of his greatest accomplishments.

Britain's colonial policy was also a target of Cobden's criticism. His attacks in this area were closely related to his opposition to British foreign policy. Britain had acquired huge areas of land all over the world without any

COBDEN'S LOGIC.

Punch published this cartoon in 1863 together with two quotes from a Cobden speech: "I don't know, perhaps, any country in the world where the masses of the people are so illiterate as in England. . . . Sound statesmanship requires such an extension of the franchise as shall admit the masses of the people to political power." (Radio Times Hulton Picture Library)

Law League was that of a hard-headed businessman, a man of action. The practical implications for manufacturers (new markets for products) were stressed. But in foreign affairs he was not so well informed; and although his conclusions, dogmatic as they were, may have been correct, he was not able to convince the majority of his countrymen. The bulk of his career in domestic politics, however, must be considered a success. Cobdenite reforms in education as well as in economics were adopted. He was, according to a recent biographer, "the greatest non-party statesman ever to figure in British politics."

Further Reading

Richard Cobden is listed in the European History study guide (VIII, A, 1, b). Like Cobden, John BRIGHT was active in the Anti–Corn Law League. The economists Adam SMITH and David RICARDO were early supporters of the free-trade principle.

The standard biography of Cobden is John Morley, *The Life of Richard Cobden* (1881; 12th ed. 1905). There are newer biographies by Ian Ivor Bowen, *Cobden* (1935), and by Donald Read, *Cobden and Bright: A Victorian Political Partnership* (1967). A specialized study of value is Norman McCord, *The Anti–Corn Law League* (1958; 2d ed. 1968). Recommended for general historical background are E. L. Woodward, *The Age of Reform* (1938; 2d ed. 1962); Norman Gash, *Politics in the Age of Peel* (1953); and George Sidney Roberts Kitson Clark, *The Making of Victorian England* (1962).

✳   ✳   ✳

COCHISE / By Odie B. Faulk

Cochise (ca. 1825–1874) was both hereditary and war chief of the Chiricahua Apache band of American Indians. His ability earned him the designation "the Apache Napoleon."

Born probably in southern Arizona, Cochise (pronounced kō'chēs) grew to imposing manhood. A newspaper correspondent in 1870 described him as 5 feet 9 1/2 inches tall, weighing 164 pounds, with broad shoulders, a stout frame, black eyes, high forehead, hair straight back, large nose, "scarred all over his body with buckshot," and "for an Indian, straight."

As leader of the Chiricahua Apache, Cochise fought the Mexicans relentlessly, as had been his tribe's custom for centuries. Often these raids were conducted in concert with the Warm Springs Apache, who were led by Mangas Coloradas.

Cochise maintained a strong friendship for Americans when they began arriving in numbers in Arizona during the 1850s until the "Bascom affair" of 1861, when Cochise was wrongly accused of kidnapping the stepson of an Arizona rancher, John Ward, and of stealing Ward's cattle. Troops commanded by Lt. G. N. Bascom were sent from nearby Ft. Buchanan to secure the boy's release. Bascom arrested Cochise, who escaped, but hanged his other six prisoners, mainly relatives of Cochise. This sent Cochise on the warpath, determined to kill all white men in Arizona.

In June 1861 Cochise attacked Ft. Buchanan but was driven off. Then, as American troops were withdrawn from Arizona during the Civil War, he led his braves in bloody assaults against the Americans. In 1862 he attacked 700 troops of the California Column at Apache Pass in southeastern Arizona, but howitzer fire drove him off.

Yet Cochise could make exceptions to his hatred of the white man. Thomas J. Jeffords, government superintendent of the mails from Ft. Bowie to Tucson, walked into Cochise's camp to plead for the safety of his mail carriers, which Cochise granted, and thereafter the two men became close friends. In 1869 Henry Clay Hooker, a contract supplier of beef to reservations, was surrounded by Apache warriors and boldly rode into Cochise's camp; there Cochise entertained him and returned his guns, and Hooker was allowed to depart in peace. When he evinced surprise at this treatment, Cochise said he had not been killed because he was supplying beef eaten by Indians.

Jeffords led Gen. Oliver Otis Howard, special Indian commissioner sent by President U. S. Grant to secure peace in the Southwest, to Cochise's camp in October 1872. Cochise signed a peace treaty giving the Chiricahua a reservation some 55 miles square in southeastern Arizona with Jeffords as agent.

Cochise spent his last 2 years in peace, honoring the treaty. He died on June 8, 1874, while visiting Jeffords at the reservation and was buried there.

Further Reading

Cochise is listed in the American History study guide (VII, C, 2). CRAZY HORSE and Chief JOSEPH were other Indian leaders. Gen. Oliver Otis HOWARD made a peace treaty with Cochise.

Two contemporary views of Cochise are offered in Samuel Woodworth Cozzens, *The Marvellous Country, or Three Years in Arizona and New Mexico* (1873; repr. 1967), and James Henry Tevis, *Arizona in the '50's* (1954). A general history of the period that gives an excellent overview is Dan L. Thrapp, *The Conquest of Apacheria* (1967). But the best book for understanding the life of Cochise is a novel: Elliot Arnold, *Blood Brother* (1947).

✳   ✳   ✳

COCKCROFT / By Stanley L. Jaki

John Douglas Cockcroft (1897–1967) was an English physicist. His main contribution to physics consisted in designing a linear accelerator capable of giving such a speed to charged particles as to produce the transmutation of atomic nuclei.

John Cockcroft was born in Todmorden, Lancashire, on May 27, 1897. He attended the University of Manchester, where he studied mathematics under Horace Lamb in 1914–1915. Following service with the Royal Field Artillery in World War I, Cockcroft joined Metropolitan-Vickers, an engineering company, which sent him back to the University of Manchester to study electrical engineering. He transferred to St. John's College, Cambridge, where he took honors in mathematics in 1924.

Cockcroft was one of the gifted young physicists whom Ernest Rutherford gathered at the Cavendish Laboratory. By 1928 Cockcroft was at work on the problem of accelerating protons by high voltages, a task in which he was greatly helped by E. T. S. Walton. At the meeting of the Royal Society on April 28, 1932, it was announced that Cockcroft and Walton "had successfully disintegrated the nuclei of lithium and other light elements by protons entirely artificially generated by high energy potentials." Cockcroft and Walton shared the Nobel Prize in physics for 1951.

Cockcroft's rise in the British scientific establishment was spectacular. In 1934 he became the head of the Royal Society's Mond Laboratory in Cambridge. In 1939 he obtained the coveted Jacksonian chair in experimental physics and that year took charge of the practical implementation of the principle of radar for Britain's coastal and air defense. Following his return in 1940 from the United States as a member of the Tizard Mission, he became head of the Air Defense Research and Development Establishment. By 1944 he was in Canada directing the Canadian Atomic Energy Project, and upon returning to England in 1946 he was appointed director of the Atomic Energy Research Establishment at Harwell. His 12 years there saw the production of the British atomic bomb and also an impressive advance in the peaceful use of atomic energy, exemplified by the construction of the famous nuclear energy power station at Calder Hall.

From 1959 until his death on Sept. 18, 1967, he was master of Churchill College while retaining a part-time membership in the British Atomic Energy Authority. At the last meeting which Cockcroft attended in July 1967, he made interesting predictions about the future of technology and offered the following advice to youth: "Never finish your education. I did not know much about physics when I started to do research. Go on with your reading and going to meetings and continue to work in your spare time on your own subject. It is the only way." Perhaps the finest personal characteristic of Cockcroft was his disarming kindness. It earned him countless friends both within and outside his professional field. The same quality made him also a much admired family man. He married Eunice Elizabeth Crabtree in 1925, and they had four daughters and a son.

Further Reading

John Cockcroft is listed in the Science study guide (VII, C, 1). Eminent British scientists of the same period were Lord RUTHERFORD and Paul DIRAC. At the Cavendish Laboratory, Cockcroft and Peter KAPITSA solved the problem of producing strong magnetic fields.

Biographical material on Cockcroft is in the Nobel Foundation's publication *Nobel Lectures, Physics, 1942–1962: Including Presentation Speeches and Laureates' Biographies* (1964). The voltage multiplier of Cockcroft and Walton is explained in Irving Kaplan, *Nuclear Physics* (1955; 2d ed. 1963). Volume 2 of Henry A. Boorse and Lloyd Motz, eds., *The World of the Atom* (2 vols., 1966), contains a chapter on Cockcroft and describes the Cockcroft-Walton experiments.

John Cockcroft. (Radio Times Hulton Picture Library)

COCTEAU / By Laurent LeSage

The French writer Jean Cocteau (1889–1963) explored nostalgia for childhood and adolescence, frustration in love, and fear of solitude and death.

Jean Cocteau (pronounced kôk-tō′) was born in a suburb of Paris and brought up in a well-to-do home frequented by the artistic notables of the day. As a schoolboy at the Lycée Condorcet, he was anything but a model pupil, but he charmed his teachers by

Jean Cocteau. (French Cultural Services of the French Embassy)

his verve and brilliance. His official debut was at the age of 18, when the renowned actor Édouard de Max gave a lecture on Cocteau's poetry. Cocteau soon visited Edmond de Rostand, Anna de Noailles, and Marcel Proust; everybody and everything fashionable attracted him.

When the Russian ballet performed in Paris, Jean Cocteau was there. Soon he proposed to its director, Sergei Diaghilev, a ballet of his own. The resulting *Blue God*, which was not presented until 1912, was not a success. Nothing daunted, Cocteau started the ballet *David*, for which he hoped Igor Stravinsky would do the music. Although the ballet did not materialize, *Potomak*, a curious prose work of fantasy dedicated to Stravinsky, did get written, and texts composed for both works were finally incorporated in a ballet called *Parade*. Erik Satie and Pablo Picasso collaborated with Cocteau on this production, for which Guillaume Apollinaire, in a program note, coined the word surrealistic.

After World War I, when Dada and surrealism replaced cubism and the "new spirit," Cocteau played about with the new ideas and techniques without adhering strictly to any group. The mime dramas of *The Newlyweds of the Eiffel Tower* and *The Ox on the Roof* as well as the poems of *The Cape of Good Hope* all demonstrate the manner of the day without, however, following any prescribed formula. Subsequently, in verse Cocteau reverted to more conventional prosody, and in fiction, to an uncomplicated narrative style. *The Big Split* and *Thomas the Impostor* present in forthright prose the themes of the author's life and times.

Antigone opened Cocteau's series of neoclassic plays, which enjoyed great success from the late 1920s on with their sophisticated props such as oracular horses, symbolic masks and mirrors, angels, and mannequins. The same trappings would be maintained for his plays of romantic or medieval inspiration and would constitute, as well, recognizable features of Cocteau's films.

In the universe that Cocteau's work evokes, the boundaries between what is real and what is unreal disappear, and none of the conventional oppositions such as life and death or good and bad remains fixed. Enveloping the work is a hallucinatory atmosphere that is characteristic. Cocteau was elected to the French Academy in 1955.

Further Reading

Jean Cocteau is listed in the Literature study guide (III, J, 1, a). Among his contemporaries were André BRETON and André GIDE.

Francis Steegmuller's sympathetic *Cocteau* (1970) is the most comprehensive biography. Margaret Crosland deliberately avoids gossip in her *Jean Cocteau* (1955). Neal Oxenhandler in *Scandal and Parade: The Theater of Jean Cocteau* (1957) expressed indignation at what he considers unfair treatment of Cocteau. Wallace Fowlie is frankly admiring in *Jean Cocteau: The History of a Poet's Age* (1966). Elizabeth Spigge, collaborating with a French biographer (Jean Jacques Kihm) on *Jean Cocteau: The Man and the Mirror* (1968), handles her subject with bland discretion. Not so, however, Frederick Brown, whose hostile treatment of Cocteau has given *An Impersonation of Angels: A Biography of Jean Cocteau* (1968) particular notoriety. Brutal though it is, this is a witty and well-written book.

COEN / By John M. Echols

The Dutch merchant Jan Pieterszoon Coen (ca. 1586–1629) founded Batavia as governor general of the Dutch East India Company. Possessed of great administrative and military ability, he contributed greatly to the expansion of Dutch influence in the East Indies.

Born at Hoorn probably at the end of 1586 (he was baptized on Jan. 8, 1587), Jan Coen (pronounced kōōn) at the age of 13 obtained employment with a firm of former Dutch merchants in Rome, where he remained for almost 7 years and where he learned bookkeeping, other commercial skills, and several languages.

Returning to Holland in 1607, Coen sailed on December 22 of that year for the Dutch East Indies as an employee of the Dutch East India Company. He returned home in 1610, and 2 years later the company dispatched him to the Indies as commander of two ships. At the end of 1614 Coen was named director general, the second highest post, and on April 30, 1618, he was appointed governor general at the age of 31.

Coen had difficulties with the Bantamese and English over the spice trade and transferred the seat of the company in Java from Bantam to Jacatra, where the company storehouse was located. He reinforced this building, making it a reliable fortress. The English, however, concentrated a large fleet off Bantam and seized a heavily laden Dutch ship, *De Swarte Leeuw*. Coen demanded its return, and when this was refused, a fight ensued. Coen's fleet held its own against a superior force until its ammunition was exhausted. He then sailed for the Moluccas, where he obtained reinforcements of 16 ships. Upon his return to Jacatra at the end of May 1619 he found that his garrison had held out, so Coen built a Dutch center which he named Batavia.

In 1621 Coen led a punitive expedition against the Bandanese in East Indonesia, who had been trading with the English. He decimated the population and resettled the survivors. In 1623 he resigned as governor general, but the following year the company persuaded him to take up this post again. British opposition delayed his return, however, until 1627, when he sailed secretly for the Indies and assumed without proper credentials the governor generalship. Shortly after his arrival at Batavia, he was confronted with sieges by the Bantamese and by the kingdom of Mataram. The latter made two unsuccessful attempts to dislodge the Dutch, and during the second attack Coen was suddenly stricken with a tropical disease and died on Sept. 21, 1629.

Jan Coen. (Radio Times Hulton Picture Library)

Further Reading

Jan Coen is listed in the Asia study guide (IV, B, 1). Anthony VAN DIEMEN, a later governor general of the Dutch East India Company, started as clerk under Coen. Sir Stamford RAFFLES conquered Batavia for the British some 100 years after its founding.

There is an extensive bibliography on Coen in Dutch. In English see E. S. De Klerck, *History of the Netherlands East Indies* (2 vols., 1938), and Bernard H. M. Vlekke, *Nusantara: A History of the East Indian Archipelago* (1943; 2d ed. 1959). A valuable background study is J. H. Parry, *The Age of Reconnaissance* (1963).

COFFIN / By Louis Filler

A leading American antislavery reformer and a conductor of the Underground Railroad, Levi Coffin (1789–1877) contributed to the good repute in the North of illegal and contested fugitive slave activities.

Levi Coffin came of an old Nantucket, Mass., family, part of which had settled with a Quaker community in New Garden, N.C. There he was born of farmer parents on Oct. 28, 1789, and raised with little schooling. What he learned came by his own efforts. Coffin aspired at the time to be a teacher and taught a number of seasons in the area. North Carolina still permitted moderate antislavery measures. Coffin, already a friend of Negro runaways, sought means for contributing more openly to Negro opportunity. In 1821 he opened a Sunday school for Negroes. It was successful but stirred the antagonism of white neighbors, who discouraged friendly slaveholders from permitting their Negroes to attend its sessions.

Increasing repression in the state dissatisfied many of Coffin's Quaker associates, and in 1826 they moved to Newport (later Fountain City), Ind., where Negroes resided freely. There Coffin opened a country store, which became a successful enterprise, soon including pork curing and the manufacture of linseed oil. By this time Coffin was wholly dedicated to peaceful measures for opposing the institution of slavery. His home became a center of secret activity for conducting Negro runaways north to freedom on the Underground Railroad, and he gained fame as informal "president" of what was largely a loose federation of people and routes for encouraging fugitive slave enterprises. He also continued his educational efforts in behalf of Negroes.

Coffin was outstanding in his search for alternatives to slave labor and was a major advocate of "free produce," that is, goods produced by free labor. He hoped to persuade Southerners as well as Northerners of its virtues, and he visited the South in his efforts to win partisans for his program. While there he expressed himself freely in

Levi Coffin. (Library of Congress)

most versatile personalities in the American theater. His shows glorified Broadway and patriotism.

criticism of the morals and economics of slavery.

In 1847, with the cooperation of Quaker associates, Coffin moved to Cincinnati, Ohio, to build a business dealing in free produce. Thanks to his commercial abilities, it operated at a profit, though its success did not advance the free-labor movement significantly. He also continued his Underground Railroad and educational work. During the Civil War he gave much thought to the future of slaves who were being freed by military actions or proclamations. He contributed to the work of the Freedmen's Aid Associations set up to ease the free Negroes' plight. In 1864 he visited England to appeal for funds from auxiliary associations there and received more than $100,000 to help feed, clothe, and educate Negroes. The adoption of the 15th Amendment to the Constitution in 1869, giving the vote to Negro men, marked his retirement from active service. He died on Sept. 16, 1877.

Further Reading

Levi Coffin is listed in the American History study guide (V, F, 3, b). Thomas GARRETT also aided fugitive slaves before the Civil War.

Coffin's autobiography, *Reminiscences of Levi Coffin* (1876; 3d ed. 1898), is the major source. See also Wilbur H. Siebert, *The Underground Railroad from Slavery to Freedom* (1898), and Carter G. Woodson, *The Education of the Negro Prior to 1861* (1915).

COHAN / By Milton Plesur

The American actor and playwright George Michael Cohan (1878–1942) was one of the

George M. Cohan was born July 3, 1878 (legend has it as July 4), in Providence, R.I., the son of vaudevillians. He first appeared on stage as a violinist in the family act and then as a "buck and wing" dancer. He was the star of *Peck's Bad Boy* in 1890, and at age 15 he made his Broadway debut. At the concluding curtain call, his words to the audience, "My mother thanks you, my father thanks you, my sister thanks you, and I thank you," became a sentimental trademark of his act. His first wife, Ethel Levey, whom he married in 1899, was his dancing partner after his sister left the act. He married a second time in 1908.

The first Broadway production which he wrote, composed, and directed was *The Governor's Son* (1901). Among the more than 50 plays, comedies, and revues he wrote, produced, or acted in were *Little Johnny Jones* (1904), *Forty-five Minutes from Broadway* (1906), *George Washington, Jr.* (1906), *The Man Who Owns Broadway* (1908), *The Yankee Prince* (1908), *Seven Keys to Baldpate* (1913) (which earned him a reputation as a serious playwright), and *The Cohan Revues* (1916

George M. Cohan, photographed in 1927. (Wide World Photos)

and 1918). He also wrote over 100 vaudeville sketches. The stage style for which he was famous included dapper costumes, a derby or straw hat cocked jauntily over one eye, wisecracks, and lively capers across the stage with a fast swinging cane.

The many popular songs he composed include "Mary's a Grand Old Name," "Give My Regards to Broadway," "So Long Mary," "I'm a Yankee Doodle Dandy," and "You're a Grand Old Flag." His famous World War I song, "Over There" (1917), sold 2 million copies of sheet music and 1 million records. President Woodrow Wilson described it as an inspiration to American manhood, and President Franklin Roosevelt cited the song when presenting Cohan with a congressional medal.

Cohan's role in Eugene O'Neill's *Ah Wilderness* (1933) proved his competence as a serious actor. His impersonation of President Roosevelt in the satire *I'd Rather Be Right* (1937–1938) was also praised.

Cohan made a movie in 1932, *The Phantom President*, but was generally unhappy with Hollywood. In 1942 James Cagney portrayed him in the film biography *Yankee Doodle Dandy* and won the Academy Award. A musical play, *George M!*, featuring his music, was produced on Broadway in 1968.

Cohan died on Nov. 5, 1942. A protean talent, he often wrote his own books and lyrics and sang and danced in, produced, and directed his own shows. Essentially a "song and dance" man, he energized the American musical theater. However uncomplicated and sentimental his works are, they have an important place in theatrical history.

Further Reading

George M. Cohan is listed in the American History study guide (VIII, F, b). Equally renowned impresarios were David BELASCO and Florenz ZIEGFELD.

Cohan's autobiography, *Twenty Years on Broadway and the Years It Took to Get There* (1925), is cheerful and brash but without real insight. A witty, fond, and anecdotal treatment is Ward Morehouse, *George M. Cohan, Prince of the American Theater* (1943).

* * *

H. COHEN / By Ezri Atzmon

The Jewish-German philosopher Hermann Cohen (1842–1918) founded the Marburg Neo-Kantian school of philosophy. His ethical socialism, based on the biblical Jewish moral law, greatly influenced German social democracy.

Hermann Cohen (pronounced kō′ĕn) was born in Coswig, Anhalt, on July 4, 1842. After attending the Jewish Theological Seminary of Breslau, he studied at the universities of Breslau, Berlin, and Halle. In

1873 he became instructor at the Philipps University of Marburg, where he was appointed professor in 1876 and taught until his resignation in 1912. He died in Berlin on April 4, 1918.

Cohen's Thought

Cohen started his philosophical career as an interpreter of the philosophy of Immanuel Kant, and he slowly developed his own system of Neo-Kantianism in three major works: *Logik der Reinen Erkenntnis* (The Logic of Pure Perception), *Ethik des Reinen Willens* (The Ethics of the Pure Will), and *Ästhetik des Reinen Gefühls* (The Esthetics of Pure Feeling). Reacting against materialism and Marxism, Cohen denied the existence of a real external world and interpreted experience as man's subjective creation of objects. Thus, thinking is the source of reality; being is nothing but pure knowledge produced by thought.

Just as the subject of logic is "being" or "whatness," the subject of ethics is "oughtness" or "pure will." Thus, Cohen separated human will from psychologism and ethics from logic, rejecting not only materialism but all monism. The supreme value and measure became the idea of man, who finds his realization in the community of men or the ethical socialistic state.

According to Judaism, God is both the creator of nature and the proponent of moral law, so that the truth of God means a harmonious combination of physical nature with morality. God in Judaism is not a mythological figure but an idea whose essence is revealed in His law.

Hermann Cohen, drypoint engraving by Max Liebermann. (Library of Congress)

Therefore Cohen was not interested in the study of the nature of God but, rather, in the doctrine of the Messiah, which is the Jewish religious expression of the eternity of morality.

In 1880 Cohen announced his renewed belief in Judaism and began to defend the Jewish faith against the anti-Semitic German historian Heinrich von Treitschke. He started lecturing at the Berlin Institute for Jewish Studies and immensely influenced several generations of Jewish thinkers. Although he repudiated Zionism, he took a direct interest in the life of the Jewish people and felt a responsibility for its destiny.

Among Cohen's other major works are *Kants Theorie der Erfahrung* (Kant's Theory of Experience), *Kants Begründung der Ethik* (Kant's Proof of Ethics), and *Kants Begründung der Ästhetik* (Kant's Proof of Esthetics). Among his specifically Jewish works are *Religion und Göttlichkeit* (Religion and Divinity), *Das Gottesreich* (The Kingdom of God), *Der Nächste* (The Fellow Man), and the posthumously published *Die Religion der Vernunft aus den Quellen des Judentums* (The Religion of Reason from the Sources of Judaism).

Further Reading

Hermann Cohen is listed in the Religion study guide (II, F, 1, b). Another member of the Marburg school was Ernst CASSIRER.

The important literature on Cohen is in German. For background material in English see Emile Bréhier, *Contemporary Philosophy since 1850*, vol. 7 (1932; trans. 1969), and Ernst Cassirer, *The Problem of Knowledge* (trans. 1960).

* * *

M. R. COHEN / By Robert W. McAhren

The American philosopher Morris Raphael Cohen (1880–1947) distinguished himself as an expositor of the nature of a liberal society, as a teacher, and as a defender of academic freedom.

Morris R. Cohen was born probably on July 25, 1880, and spent his first years in a Jewish ghetto in Minsk, Russia. He early displayed a preference for the contemplative life. His education was that of an Orthodox Jew. In 1892 the family emigrated to New York, where, during the next 7 years, Cohen drifted away from organized religion and eventually gave up all belief in a personal God.

Cohen entered the College of the City of New York in 1895. His family's penurious, hand-to-mouth existence stimulated Cohen's interest in socialism. From his study of Marx and Hegel developed his earliest preoccupation with the technical aspects of philosophy. In 1898 he met Thomas Davidson, the Scottish scholar whose example would inspire Cohen throughout his life; under his tute-

Morris R. Cohen. (Bibliothèque Nationale, Paris)

lage Cohen read Aristotle, Plato, Hume, and Kant.

After graduating in 1900, Cohen continued his pursuit of philosophy, discovering in Bertrand Russell's *Principles of Mathematics* a "renewed faith" in logic. In 1904 the Ethical Culture Society awarded Cohen a fellowship to do graduate work at Harvard. Two years later, shortly after he completed his doctorate, he married Mary Ryshpan; they had three children.

Ensconced in the philosophy department of the College of the City of New York, Cohen came into his own as a teacher. Demanding of his students and responding sarcastically to careless thinking, he nonetheless drew overflow crowds of students and won great affection and respect. Outside the classroom he led the struggle to uphold academic freedom against authoritarian interference. He was one of the founding members of the American Association of University Professors. As a tide of anti-Semitism rose in the 1930s, he helped organize the Conference on Jewish Relations to study modern Jewry scientifically; he was also editor of its journal, *Jewish Social Studies*.

Meanwhile Cohen was writing scholarly articles and books. In 1923 his edition of C. S. Peirce's essays, *Chance, Love and Logic*, appeared. In 1931 in his most important work, *Reason and Nature: An Essay on the Meaning of Scientific Method*, he developed the concept that characterized all his thought and came closest to representing a metaphysical position. That concept, polarity, held that ideas such as "unity and plurality, similarity and difference, dependence and independence, form and matter, change and permanence" were "equally real," and "the way to get at the nature of things" was to "reason" from such "opposing considerations." Hence the necessity of society's tolerating conflicting points of view.

Ever since he had shared a room with Felix Frankfurter at Harvard, Cohen had indulged a lively interest in jurisprudence, which resulted in *Law and the Social Order: Essays in Legal Philosophy* (1933). He believed that logical reasoning was critically important to all fields of thought. *An Introduction to Logic and Scientific Method* (1934), written with a former student, Ernest Nagel, became a popular college textbook.

In 1938 Cohen left teaching to devote himself to writing. His *Preface to Logic* (1944) elucidated logic's place in the universe. *Faith of a Liberal* (1946) sought to rescue the term "liberal" from connotations of sentimentality. Cohen had already manifested his lifelong fascination with history by helping found the *Journal of the History of Ideas*. He selected the philosophy of history as his topic when the American Philosophical Association chose him to deliver its Carus Lectures, later published as *The Meaning of Human History* (1947).

Cohen died on Jan. 28, 1947. He left many works half finished, which his son Felix, a scholar in his own right, published: *A Source Book in Greek Science* (1948), *A Dreamer's Journey* (1949), *Studies in Philosophy and Science* (1949), *Reflections of a Wondering Jew* (1950), *Reason and Law: Studies in Juristic Philosophy* (1950), *Readings in Jurisprudence and Legal Philosophy* (1951), *King Saul's Daughter: A Biblical Dialogue* (1952), and *American Thought: A Critical Sketch* (1954). Cohen's publications stand as a positive statement of his faith in a liberal civilization and answer those critics who found in him only the sharp tongue of a nihilist.

Further Reading

Morris R. Cohen is listed in the Philosophy study guide (VII, C). One of his students was Ernest NAGEL. Salo BARON commented on Cohen's work.

Cohen's autobiography, *A Dreamer's Journey* (1949), is a candid depiction of the life of a Jewish immigrant. In *Portrait of a Philosopher: Morris R. Cohen in Life and Letters* (1962), Cohen's daughter, Leonora Cohen Rosenfield, supplements lively anecdotes with extensive quotations from his diary and other unpublished manuscripts. For further appreciation and commentary see Salo W. Baron, Ernest Nagel, and Koppel S. Pinson, *Freedom and Reason: Studies in Philosophy and Jewish Culture in Memory of Morris Raphael Cohen* (1951).

* * *

COKE / By Thomas A. Green

The English jurist and parliamentarian Sir Edward Coke (1552–1634) fought to prevent royal interference with the independent common-law courts.

Edward Coke was born at Mileham, Norfolk, and was educated at Trinity College, Cambridge, from 1567 to 1571. Thereafter he rapidly rose in the legal profession from a student at Lincoln's Inn to barrister, reader at Lyon's Inn, and senior member of the Inner Temple. In 1592 Queen Elizabeth I appointed Coke solicitor general, and in the following year he became attorney general. As attorney general, Coke was a forceful prosecutor on behalf of the Crown, and among his most famous prosecutions were those of the Earl of Essex, Sir Walter Raleigh, and the "Gunpowder" plotters. Coke's ascendancy was at the expense of Sir Francis Bacon, whom Essex had supported for the attorney generalship, and the two were rivals throughout their careers.

In 1582 Coke married Bridget Paston, who brought him a fortune. She died in 1598, and Coke then married the beautiful and rich Elizabeth Hatton, who had also been courted by Bacon.

In 1606 James I made Coke chief justice of the Court of Common Pleas. Coke opposed James on the question of the king's right to interpret the common law and to encroach on judicial independence. In accord with his belief in the divine right of kings, James felt that God had endowed him with the wisdom to interpret the traditional English common law. Coke insisted that the interpretation of common law must be left to lawyers. He also opposed James's policy of discussing cases with the judges before they gave judgment. In 1610 he argued that the king could not lawfully create new offenses through his own proclamation. Coke's chief rival during this period, the chancellor, Baron Ellesmere, supported James's view of the royal prerogative.

Coke was appointed chief justice of the King's Bench

Sir Edward Coke. (Radio Times Hulton Picture Library)

in 1613. Both Bacon and Ellesmere favored this shift; though it accorded Coke a higher status and greater wages, it made conflict with the Crown less likely. In the same year Coke was brought into the Privy Council. The battle between Coke and James was not easily avoided, however, and in 1616 the King dismissed his obstreperous judge from both the bench and the government.

Coke returned to favor the following year, when his daughter married the elder brother of George Villiers, the King's favorite courtier and later the powerful Duke of Buckingham. The vain and stubborn Coke again sat in the Privy Council and enjoyed great respect at court for his unrivaled knowledge of the common law. But in 1621 he sat in Commons and was active in the debates against the King's lax enforcement of the anti-Catholic laws and against royal grants of monopoly; as a result he was sent to the Tower for 9 months. Thus 1621 marked the end of his hopes for attaining a high government position and the start of the last phase of his career, as a leader of the parliamentary opposition.

In 1625 Coke was a leader of the attack on the Duke of Buckingham and later supported his impeachment. He held that Commons should withhold further grants of revenue until it was provided with an accounting of government expenditures. In 1628, when Commons sought to place restraints upon royal power, Coke initiated the idea of a Petition of Right. Its principal terms required parliamentary consent for taxation and a statement of charges against those placed under arrest. In 1629 Coke retired to Stoke Poges, where he died in 1634, at the age of 82.

Coke's main writings are the *Reports* and the *Institutes*. Compiled between 1578 and 1615, the former contains cases argued before the royal courts. The four parts of the *Institutes* deal with tenures, statutes, the criminal law, and the jurisdiction of courts. Coke was not above twisting earlier law to the advantage of the 17th-century causes he favored. His holding in Dr. Bonham's case (1610) has attracted the interest of students of American constitutional law, some of whom view it as the first enunciation of the principle of judicial review.

Further Reading

Sir Edward Coke is listed in the European History study guide (V, A, 1, a) and the Social Sciences study guide (IV, B, 1). A later English jurist was Sir William BLACKSTONE.

The sole modern biography of Coke is Catherine Drinker Bowen, *The Lion and the Throne: The Life and Times of Sir Edward Coke, 1552–1634* (1957). This work makes very pleasant reading, while maintaining a high standard of scholarship, and contains a lengthy list of older works and journal articles on Coke.

COLBERT / By Charles Wrong

The French statesman Jean Baptiste Colbert (1619–1683) was one of the greatest ministers of Louis XIV and is generally regarded as the creator of the economic system of prerevolutionary France.

Jean Baptiste Colbert (pronounced kôl-bâr´) was born at Reims on Aug. 29, 1619, of a family of prosperous businessmen and officials. He entered the service of the French monarchy under Michel le Tellier, the father of the Marquis de Louvois. In 1651 he became the agent of Cardinal Mazarin, whom he served so well that the cardinal bequeathed him to King Louis XIV in 1661. Almost immediately Colbert became the most important minister in France. He was made intendant of finances in 1661 and in the next few years assumed responsibility for public buildings, commerce, and the administration of the royal household, the navy, and the merchant marine. His only serious rival was the war minister, Louvois. The two men intrigued against each other for royal favor, with Louvois, especially after 1679, gradually winning the upper hand. Colbert, however, remained immensely powerful until his death.

Colbert's most successful years were from 1661 to 1672. The neglect and corruption of the Mazarin period were replaced by a time of prosperity with expanding industry and mounting employment. The tax system was made slightly fairer and much more efficient, thereby greatly increasing Louis XIV's revenues.

Jean Baptiste Colbert, portrait painted about 1655 by Philippe de Champaigne. (The Metropolitan Museum of Art, Gift of the Wildenstein Foundation, Inc., 1951)

In a mercantilist age Colbert was the supreme mercantilist. His program was to build up the economic strength of France by creating and protecting French industries, encouraging exports, and restricting imports (especially of luxury goods). By endless regulation and supervision, he tried to make French industry, particularly in luxury items, first in Europe; he was partially successful, for the French tradition of high quality in certain fields (for example, tapestry and porcelain) dates from his time.

Colbert organized royal trading companies to compete with the English and the Dutch for the trade of the Far East and the Americas. Although these companies were almost all failures, he was successful in building up one of the strongest European navies and a more than respectable merchant marine. At the same time he laid the foundations of the French overseas empire in Canada, the West Indies, and the Far East. The great expansion of French commerce and industry in the next century was largely due to his groundwork.

Colbert carried through a series of legal codifications of enormous importance, and the Code Napoleon was partly inspired by, and based on, his monumental work. He also made himself responsible for the artistic and cultural life of France. He encouraged, patronized, and regimented artists and writers, and the magnificent building program of Louis XIV was primarily his work.

Colbert was not an innovator. His ideas came from other men, particularly Cardinal Richelieu, and his interpretation of them was often mistaken. But for 22 years he controlled the economic fortunes of France, and he did so with an all-embracing scope and an incredible capacity for work. Some of his projects, however, were unsuccessful. He was unable to unify the diverse systems of weights and measures in France or to secure free trade within the country. His regulation of industry by constant inspection was largely ineffective, as his orders were often disregarded.

The major failure of Colbert stemmed from his determination to end Dutch domination of Far Eastern and European trade. Unable to damage the Dutch by a vindictive tariff war, he supported Louis XIV's unprovoked invasion of Holland in 1672 in the hope that the Dutch would be overrun in a few weeks. But the resultant war lasted until 1679, and the strain on the French economy undid many of the good results of Colbert's work.

Colbert died on Sept. 6, 1683, to the great relief of the general public, with whom he was (for the most part undeservedly) very unpopular. The immense concentration of responsibilities in one minister was never repeated under the monarchy.

Further Reading

Jean Baptiste Colbert is listed in the European History study guide (V, B, 1, b; V, B, 3) and the Social Sciences study guide (IV, B, 2). He was influenced by the policies of Cardinal RICHELIEU. Colbert served Cardinal MAZARIN and then LOUIS XIV.

Most of the work on Colbert is in French. The definitive work in English is Charles Woolsey Cole, *Colbert and a Century of French Mercantilism* (2 vols., 1939). A useful general treatment is in Pierre Goubert, *Louis XIV and Twenty Million Frenchmen* (1966; trans. 1970). Goubert considers that Colbert has been overpraised by French historians and stresses his lack of originality and the elementary nature of his views on economics. However, he does justice to the wide range and great importance of Colbert's work.

✻　　✻　　✻

COLDEN / By Monte A. Calvert

The American botanist and politician Cadwallader Colden (1688–1776), a diverse thinker whose scholarship encompassed natural history, the nature of the universe, and medicine, was also lieutenant governor of New York.

Cadwallader Colden was born on Feb. 7, 1688, in Ireland of Scottish parents; his father was a minister. He received a degree from the University of Edinburgh and then studied medicine in London. He emigrated to Philadelphia in 1710 and went to New York in 1718 at the request of Governor Robert Hunter, who made Colden surveyor general of the colony in 1720. This sinecure allowed him the leisure for a scientific career, although he remained interested in politics, serving as a member of the Governor's Council.

Cadwallader Colden. (Courtesy of The New-York Historical Society, New York City)

In 1739 Colden left New York City to live at his farm, Coldengham, where he spent much of his time in scientific study. He began corresponding with Peter Collinson, the London botanist, who brought Colden into the international natural history circle. Colden became one of the first men in Europe or America to completely master the new Linnaean system of plant classification, which he rigorously applied to the flora surrounding his farm. These descriptions, which he circulated in Europe, drew praise even from Linnaeus himself. Colden criticized the Linnaean reliance on sexual characteristics and suggested a more natural system.

Being located in America had been an advantage for his botanical work, but when Colden turned from natural history to speculations on the nature of the universe, even his finely honed, highly rational mind could not make up for his geographical isolation. *An Explication of the First Causes of Action in Matter* (1745) was his attempt to discover the cause of gravity, postulating a division of the material world into matter, light, and ether. Although it is possible to read an equation of energy with matter in the work, it was in general a rationally deduced system in no way based on the observations of scientists in Europe. He sent copies to European scientists, most of whom refused to comment, but the German scientist Leonhard Euler called it absurd. Colden never accepted the verdict and hoped, by tinkering, to perfect his theory. He consistently produced respectable medical treatises, although his abstract rational tendencies led him to write a dissertation on yellow fever without ever actually having seen a case of the disease.

In 1760 he realized an old ambition to be lieutenant governor of New York. He was a confidant of Governor George Clinton and wrote many speeches and papers for him. In 1764 he declared his intention to enforce the Stamp Act and the following year was burned in effigy by a mob. He tried to balance himself between the radicals and conservatives in the 1770s. After the Battle of Lexington, Colden retired to his Long Island estate, where he died on Sept. 28, 1776.

Colden had married Alice Cristie in 1715 and among their children, a daughter, Jane, became the first woman botanist. Their son David was also a scholar of some standing.

Further Reading

Cadwallader Colden is listed in the American History study guide (II, B, 2, b) and the Science study guide (V, F, 3). Men of colonial times whose interests also spanned politics and science were Benjamin FRANKLIN and David RITTENHOUSE.

There is no up-to-date biography of Colden. Different aspects of his career are treated in Alice M. Keys, *Cadwallader Colden, a Representative Eighteenth Century Official* (1906), and in Isaac Woodbridge Riley, *American Philosophy: The Early Schools* (1907). General background may be found in Brooke Hindle, *The Pursuit of Science in Revolutionary America, 1735–1789* (1956).

✳   ✳   ✳

G. D. H. COLE / By Reba N. Soffer

George Douglas Howard Cole (1889–1959) was an English historian, economist, and guild socialist. His teaching, writing, and commitment to political activism affected three generations of Englishmen.

The son of a builder in West London, G. D. H. Cole went from St. Paul's School to Balliol College, Oxford. He coedited the *Oxford Reformer*, acted in social causes, and joined the Fabian Society. He attempted to reconcile syndicalism and socialism in *World of Labour* (1913), a plea for public ownership of major industries under the democratic control of unions modeled upon medieval guilds. With a first class in classical moderns and greats, he was awarded a fellowship at Magdalen College. Elected to the Fabian executive in 1915, he rebelled against the old guard to head the quasi-independent Fabian Research Bureau.

During the next decade Cole was away from Oxford writing, often with his wife and fellow Fabian rebel, Margaret Postgate Cole; directing tutorial classes at the University of London; and organizing professional trade unions. He returned to Oxford in 1925 as fellow of University College and university reader in economics and was to have compelling influence upon students such as

G. D. H. Cole. (Radio Times Hulton Picture Library)

Hugh Gaitskell. From 1944 until his retirement in 1957 Cole was at All Souls College as first Chichele professor of social and political theory.

Cole was for many years chairman of the Fabian weekly, the *New Statesman*, contributing to almost every issue during his lifetime. In 1931 he formed the Society for Socialist Information and Propaganda but broke with the society when it moved toward communism. That year he formed the New Fabian Research Bureau as a politically neutral agency for accumulating objective information. This group formed the basis for union in 1938 with the older, badly splintered Fabian Society. Collectivization was omitted from the new rules as a concession to Cole.

Cole's prodigious writings (over 130 works) may be divided into five broad and overlapping categories: guild socialism; history; biography; economic, political, and social analysis; and fiction. His strongest treatment of guild socialism, *Self-government in Industry* (1917), was an appeal for the pluralistic and romantic socialism which moved Cole all his life. In *Case for Industrial Partnership* (1957) he tried to adjust the earlier plea to new times.

Cole's historical and biographical work provided the evidence against which he tested his socialist faith and reliance upon the individual. This was especially true in his classic five-volume *History of Socialist Thought* (1953–1960).

Of Cole's perceptive biographies, the two best are *The Life of William Cobbett* (1924) and *The Life of Robert Owen* (1925). The analytical writings, intended to influence or explain, include *Principles of Economic Planning* (1935) and *An Intelligent Man's Guide to the Post-war World* (1947). For recreation he wrote, largely with his wife, more than 15 detective novels.

Further Reading

G. D. H. Cole is listed in the Social Sciences study guide (VII, A, 1; VII, B, 1). Other Fabians were Beatrice WEBB, Sidney WEBB, and Graham WALLAS.

Although there is no biography of Cole, various aspects of his life and thought are discussed in the book by his wife, Margaret Cole, *The Story of Fabian Socialism* (1961). See also Anne Fremantle, *This Little Band of Prophets: The British Fabians* (1959), and Asa Briggs and John Saville, eds., *Essays in Labour History: In Memory of G. D. H. Cole* (1960; rev. ed. 1967), which contains personal recollections of Cole by Ivor Brown, Hugh Gaitskell, Stephen K. Bailey and G. D. N. Worswick. The discussion of Cole's thought in Henry M. Magid, *English Political Pluralism: The Problem of Freedom and Organization* (1941), suffers from an inadequate historical context.

T. COLE / By Frederick A. Sweet

Thomas Cole (1801–1848) was the founder of the Hudson River school of romantic American landscape painting. He treated the idyllic as well as the formidable aspects of nature in great detail and was also noted for his allegorical subjects.

Thomas Cole was born in Bolton-le-Moors, Lancaster, England, and emigrated with his family to Philadelphia in 1818. They soon moved to Steubenville, Ohio, where Thomas, who had studied engraving briefly in England, taught art in his sister's school. He then tried to be an itinerant portrait painter. Seeking better patronage, he returned to Philadelphia in 1823 to paint landscapes and decorate Japan ware. He took drawing lessons at the Pennsylvania Academy and exhibited there for the first time in 1824.

Moving to New York the following year Cole began to receive recognition and may at this time be said to have set in motion the taste for romantic landscape—a genre which would later become known as the Hudson River school. Taking a trip up the Hudson River, he painted three landscapes. Placed in the window of Coleman's Art Store, they were purchased at $25 apiece by three well-known artists of the day: John Trumbull, Asher Durand, and William Dunlap. Cole was now established and able to support himself by his landscapes.

Cole moved up the Hudson in 1826 to Catskill. After seeing the great scenic wonders of the White Mountains and Niagara, he sailed for England in 1829 under the patronage of Robert Gilmore of Baltimore. Although Cole admired the paintings of Claude Lorrain and Gaspard Poussin, he spent little time in European museums, pre-

Thomas Cole, a self-portrait. (Courtesy of The New-York Historical Society, New York City)

ferring to sketch out of doors. After a brief visit to Paris he went down the Rhone River and then to Italy. After 9 weeks in Florence he went to Rome, accomplishing most of the journey on foot.

Returning to New York in 1832, Cole was given a commission by an art patron to execute five panels. Known as the *Course of Empire*, these were considerably influenced by J. M. W. Turner's *Building of Carthage*, which Cole had seen in London.

In November 1836 Cole married Maria Barton, whose family home in Catskill became their permanent residence. Commissions came in from William P. Van Rensselaer for *The Departure* and *The Return*, from P. G. Stuyvesant for *Past and Present*, and from Samuel Ward for four panels, the *Voyage of Life*.

In 1841 Cole went to Europe again. On returning home he visited Mount Desert on the coast of Maine and Niagara. At the time of his death on Feb. 11, 1848, he was at work on a religious allegory, the *Cross of the World*.

With the overland expansion of America, people took great interest in their land and the various aspects of nature. Cole established landscape painting as an accepted form of art. He was a Swedenborgian mystic, and his paintings reflect his intensely religious feelings; never dealing with the trivial, his work has a high moral tone. He had a profound reverence for nature, which he depicted sometimes in a tranquil mood and at other times in a state of violence. He makes the viewer feel man as a helpless creature overwhelmed by the all-powerful forces of nature. He frequently placed a highly detailed tree at the right or left foreground (an inheritance from baroque stage settings), and the landscape beyond unfolds as on a stage. His was a highly romanticized version of nature often overlaid with elements of fantasy and sometimes even including medieval or classical ruins.

Further Reading

Thomas Cole is listed in the Art study guide (IV, C, 1, a). He and Asher DURAND are regarded as cofounders of the Hudson River school of painting. Frederick Edwin CHURCH was another 19th-century American painter.

In the absence of a modern study of Cole, the best source is Louis Legrand Noble, *The Life and Works of Thomas Cole* (1853; edited, with an introduction, by Elliot Vesell, 1964); it includes correspondence and other documents. Howard S. Merritt, *Thomas Cole* (1969), an exhibition catalog, includes a critical introduction. For shorter notices see Frederick A. Sweet, *The Hudson River School and the Early American Landscape Tradition* (1945), and Esther Seaver, ed., *Thomas Cole: One Hundred Years Later* (1949).

✳ ✳ ✳

COLERIDGE / By Albert S. Gérard

The English author Samuel Taylor Coleridge (1772–1834) was a major poet of the romantic movement. He is also noted for his prose works on literature, religion, and the organization of society.

Born on Oct. 21, 1772, Samuel Taylor Coleridge was the tenth and last child of the vicar of Ottery St. Mary near Exeter. In 1782, after his father's death, he was sent as a charity student to Christ's Hospital. His amazing memory and his eagerness to imbibe knowledge of any sort had turned him into a classical scholar of uncommon ability by the time he entered Jesus College, Cambridge, in 1791. Like most young intellectuals of the day, he felt great enthusiasm for the French Revolution and took his modest share in student protest against the war with France (1793). Plagued by debts, Coleridge enlisted in the Light Dragoons in December 1793. Discharged in April 1794, he returned to Cambridge, which he left in December, however, without taking a degree.

The reason for this move, characteristic of Coleridge's erratic and impulsive character, was his budding friendship with Robert Southey. Both young men were eagerly interested in poetry, sharing the same dislike for the neoclassic tradition. They were both radicals in politics, and out of their feverish conversations grew the Pantisocratic scheme—the vision of an ideal communistic community to be founded in America. This juvenile utopia came to nothing, but on Oct. 4, 1795, Coleridge married Sara Fricker, the sister of Southey's wife-to-be. By that time, however, his friendship with Southey had already dissolved.

Poetic Career

In spite of his usually wretched health, the years from 1795 to 1802 were for Coleridge a period of fast poetic

Samuel Taylor Coleridge. (Bibliothèque Nationale, Paris)

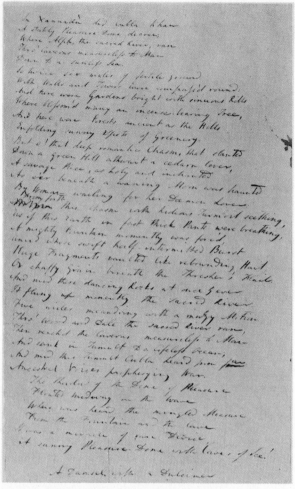

An autograph copy of Coleridge's poem "Kubla Khan." (Trustees of the British Museum)

worth, in whose neighborhood he spent most of his life from 1796 to 1810. This friendship was partly responsible for his *annus mirabilis* (July 1797 to July 1798), which culminated in his joint publication with Wordsworth of the *Lyrical Ballads* in September 1798. As against 19 poems by Wordsworth, the volume contained only 4 by Coleridge, but one of these was "The Ancient Mariner." Coleridge later described the division of labor between the two poets—while Wordsworth was "to give the charm of novelty to things of every day by awakening the mind's attention from the lethargy of custom, and directing it to the loveliness and the wonders of the world before us," it had been agreed that Coleridge's "endeavours should be directed to persons and characters supernatural, or at least romantic." But the underlying world view of the two poets was fundamentally similar. Like Wordsworth's "The Thorn," for example, Coleridge's "The Ancient Mariner" deals with the themes of sin and punishment and of redemption through suffering and a loving apprehension of nature.

A second, enlarged edition of Coleridge's *Poems* also appeared in 1798. It contained further lyrical and symbolic works, such as "This Lime-Tree Bower, My Prison" and "Fears in Solitude." At this time Coleridge also wrote "Kubla Khan," perhaps the most famous of his poems, and began the ambitious narrative piece "Christabel."

In September 1798 Coleridge and the Wordsworths left for Germany, where he stayed until July 1799. In the writings of post-Kantian German philosophers such as J. G. Fichte, F. W. J. von Schelling, and A. W. von Schlegel, Coleridge discovered a world view so congenial that it is almost impossible to disentangle what, in his later thought, is properly his and what may have been derived from German influences. *Sibylline Leaves* (1817) contains lively, humorous accounts of his German experiences.

Personal Difficulties

The dozen years following Coleridge's return to England were the most miserable in his life. In October 1799 he settled near the Wordsworths in the Lake District. The cold, wet climate worsened his many ailments, and turning to laudanum for relief, he soon became an addict. His marriage, which had never been a success, was now disintegrating, especially since Coleridge had fallen in love with Sara Hutchinson, sister of Wordsworth's wife-to-be. Ill health and emotional stress, combined with his intellectual absorption in abstract pursuits, hastened the decline of his poetic power. Awareness of this process inspired the last and most moving of his major poems, "Dejection: An Ode" (1802). After a stay in Malta (1804–1806) which did nothing to restore his health and spirits, he decided to separate from his wife. The only bright point in his life during this period was his friendship with the Wordsworths, but after his return to the Lake District this relationship was subject to increasing strain. Growing estrangement was followed by a breach in 1810, and Coleridge then settled in London.

Meanwhile, however, Coleridge's capacious mind did not stay unemployed; indeed, his major contributions to

growth and intellectual maturation. In August 1795 he began his first major poem, "The Eolian Harp," which was published in his *Poems on Various Subjects* (1796). It announced his unique contribution to the growth of English romanticism: the blending of lyrical and descriptive effusion with philosophical rumination in truly symbolic poetry.

From March to May 1796 Coleridge edited the *Watchman*, a liberal periodical which failed after 10 issues. While this failure made him realize that he was "not *fit* for *public* life," his somewhat turgid "Ode to the Departing Year" shows that he had not abandoned his revolutionary fervor. Yet philosophy and religion were his overriding interests. His voracious reading was mainly directed to one end, which was already apparent in his *Religious Musings* (begun 1794, published 1796)—he aimed to redefine orthodox Christianity so as to rid it of the Newtonian dichotomy between spirit and matter, to account for the unity and wholeness of the universe, and to reassess the relation between God and the created world.

Perhaps the most influential event in Coleridge's career was his intimacy with William and Dorothy Words-the development of English thought were still to come. From June 1809 to March 1810 he published the periodical the *Friend*. Coleridge's poetry and his brilliant conversation had earned him public recognition, and between 1808 and 1819 he gave several series of lectures, mainly on Shakespeare and other literary topics. His only dramatic work, *Osorio*, which was written in 1797, was performed in 1813 under the title *Remorse*. "Christabel" and "Kubla Khan" were published in 1816.

Later Works

In April 1816 Coleridge settled as a patient with Dr. Gillman at Highgate. There he spent most of the last 18 years of his life in comparative peace and in steady literary activity, bringing out several works which were to exert tremendous influence on the future course of English thought in many fields: *Biographia literaria* (1817), *Lay Sermons* (1817), *Aids to Reflection* (1825), and *The Constitution of Church and State* (1829). His apparently rambling style was well suited to a philosophy based on an intuition of wholeness and organic unity.

Although Coleridge's conservative idea of the state may appear both reactionary and utopian, his religious thought led to a revival of Christian philosophy in England. And his psychology of the imagination, conception of the symbol, and definition of organic form in art brought to the English-speaking world the new, romantic psychology and esthetics of literature which had first arisen in Germany at the turn of the century.

When Coleridge died on July 25, 1834, he left bulky manuscript notes, which scholars of the mid-20th century were to exhume and edit. The complete publication of this material will make it possible to realize the extraordinary range and depth of his philosophical preoccupations and to assess his true impact on succeeding generations of poets and thinkers.

Further Reading

Samuel Taylor Coleridge is listed in the Literature study guide (II, G, 1), the Religion study guide (I, P, 1, b), and the Philosophy study guide (VI, A, 2). Among his close associates was William WORDSWORTH. Coleridge's religious thought influenced Frederick Denison MAURICE, Thomas CARLYLE, and Cardinal NEWMAN.

The standard work on Coleridge is E. K. Chambers, *Samuel Taylor Coleridge* (1938; rev. ed. 1950). Norman Fruman, *Coleridge: The Damaged Archangel* (1971), is a comprehensive study of the man and the poet. Two fine works that combine biography with literary criticism are William Walsh, *Coleridge: The Work and the Relevance* (1967), and Walter Jackson Bate, *Coleridge* (1968).

General critical introductions are Humphry House, *Coleridge* (1953); John B. Beer, *Coleridge the Visionary* (1959); Marshall Suther, *The Dark Night of Samuel Taylor Coleridge* (1960); Max F. Schulz, *The Poetic Voices of Coleridge* (1963); Kathleen Coburn, ed., *Coleridge: A Collection of Critical Essays* (1967); and Patricia M. Adair, *The Waking Dream* (1968).

Increasing attention is given to the poet's thought in a great variety of fields. See John H. Muirhead, *Coleridge as Philosopher* (1930). On esthetics see I. A. Richards, *Coleridge on Imagination* (1935; 3d ed. 1962); James V. Baker, *The Sacred River: Coleridge's Theory of the Imagination* (1957); Richard Harter Fogle, *The Idea of Coleridge's Criticism* (1962); and J. A. Appleyard, *Coleridge's Philosophy of Literature: The Development of a Concept of Poetry, 1791–1819* (1965). On religion see Charles Richard Sanders, *Coleridge and the Broad Church Movement* (1942); James D. Boulger, *Coleridge as Religious Thinker* (1961); and J. Robert Barth, *Coleridge and Christian Doctrine* (1969). For general background information the reader is referred to the bibliography in W. L. Renwick, *English Literature, 1789–1815* (1963).

COLET / By Eric McDermott

The English theologian and moral reformer John Colet (ca. 1446–1519) founded St. Paul's School and influenced the humanist Erasmus.

The father of John Colet (pronounced kŏl′ĕt) was Sir Henry Colet, twice mayor of London. He was a wealthy man and the father of 22 children, none of whom survived to maturity except John. After early schooling in London, John went to Oxford, where he spent some 20 years as a scholar and lecturer, eventually receiving a doctorate in divinity about 1504.

After earning a master of arts degree, in 1493 Colet went to Italy and France for 3 years, visiting both Rome and Paris. On Colet's return to Oxford, Erasmus reports: "He publicly and gratuitously expounded all St. Paul's epistles. It was at Oxford that my acquaintance with him began." Moreover, wrote Erasmus, Colet's "opinions differed widely from those commonly received. When I was once praising Aquinas to him as a writer not to be despised among the moderns, since he appeared to me to have studied both the Scriptures and the early Fathers, and had also a certain unction in his writings, he checked himself more than once from replying and did not betray his dislike."

In contrast to the elaborate scriptural exegesis then prevalent, Colet preferred to pay careful attention to the context of St. Paul's letters. Although Colet stressed the importance of the literal meaning of the books of the Bible, he was not a fundamentalist.

Colet received priestly orders in 1498 and left Oxford 6 years later to become dean of St. Paul's Cathedral in London. In 1510 he founded St. Paul's School for boys. The essential moral earnestness that suffused all of Colet's teaching and writing was plainly evident in the great trouble he took over the founding of this establishment, which is still one of the great schools of England. As he said in the statutes he devised for it, "My intent is by this school specially to increase knowledge and worshiping

John Colet, a portrait by Hans Holbein the Younger, in the Royal Art Collection, Windsor Castle. (Copyright Reserved)

of God and our Lord Jesus Christ and good Christian life and manners in the children."

At his death Colet left one published work, his convocation sermon of 1512. A fierce attack on the lives of the clergy, this sermon declared that there "is no need that new laws and constitutions be made, but that those that are made already be kept."

Further Reading

John Colet is listed in the Religion study guide (I, G, 2), the Literature study guide (III, D, 1), and the Social Sciences study guide (III, C). He associated with a group of humanists, among whose members were ERASMUS and Sir Thomas MORE. Like Colet, Hugh LATIMER was an outstanding preacher of this period.

The standard biography of Colet is J. H. Lupton, *A Life of John Colet* (1887; 2d ed. 1961). Among numerous modern studies the most important are Ernest W. Hunt, *Dean Colet and His Theology* (1956), and Sears R. Jayne, *John Colet and Marsilio Ficino* (1963); both works have excellent bibliographies.

COLETTE / By Vinio Rossi

The French author Sidonie Gabrielle Colette (1873–1954) was concerned with feminine independence in experiencing the joys and sorrows of love. She succeeded in translating a delicate sensibility into a vivid, sensual, and highly imagistic prose.

On Jan. 28, 1873, Colette (pronounced kô-lĕt′) was born in a small Burgundian town, Saint-Sauveur-en-Puisaye. In 1893 she married Henri Gauthier-Villars, a Parisian littérateur of doubtful talents and morals. Gauthier-Villars, or Monsieur Willy, as he was known, forced his young wife to produce novels that would satisfy his prurient and financial interests. Her first attempt, *Claudine à l'école* (1900), signed Colette Willy, was quickly a best seller. Three more Claudine novels (*Claudine à Paris, Claudine en ménage, Claudine s'en va*), *Minne*, and *Les Égarements de Minne* were produced in the following 5 years.

The marriage did not fare as well. After divorcing Willy in 1906, Colette became a music hall mime and traveled the circuits with moderate success for 6 years. But the discipline of writing imposed by Willy continued to hold her. Before her divorce she had published *Dialogues des bêtes* (1904) under her maiden name, and she continued to sign in this way her subsequent works, *La Retraite sentimentale* (1907), *Les Vrilles de la vigne* (1908), *L'Ingénue libertine* (1909), and *La Vagabonde* (1911). In 1909 she produced and starred in her first play, *En Camarades*.

From 1910 to 1923 Colette was the literary correspondent for the newspaper *Le Matin*. In 1912 she married her editor in chief, Henri de Jouvenel, and the following year they had a daughter, Colette de Jouvenel, whom Colette called "Bel-Gazou" in her writings. Although the marriage ended after 12 years, these were especially full years for Colette. She published *La Paix chez les bêtes* (1916), a collection of animal stories, and *Les Heures longues* (1917), a collection of her articles and travel notes; with *Mitsou* (1919) and *Chéri* (1920), she entered into her maturity as a novelist and artist, producing a string of masterpieces of the love novel that was to end with *Gigi* (1944). The heroes and heroines of these novels, which include *Le Blé en herbe* (1923), *La Fin de Chéri* (1926), *La Seconde* (1929), *Duo* (1934), *Le Toutounier* (1939), and *Julie de Carneilhan* (1941), resemble in many respects those of Colette's early novels. Her preoccupations are still childhood, adolescent love, jealousy, love rebuked, and the search for absolute happiness in physical love.

In 1925 Colette met Maurice Goudeket, a young businessman turned journalist, with whom she was to have her longest and happiest liaison. They were married on April 3, 1935, and were not separated until Colette's death. During her later years Colette was progressively immobilized by arthritis, but she continued to record her impressions, recollections, and fantasies. She published *De ma fenêtre* (1942), *L'Étoile vesper* (1946), and *Le Fanal bleu* (1949), all semiautobiographical works reflecting the years of World War II in Paris.

Official recognition came soon after the war. In 1945

Colette. (National Archives, Washington, D.C.)

Colette was elected to the Académie Goncourt, over which she presided beginning in 1949, and in 1952 to the Légion d'Honneur. She died in Paris on Aug. 3, 1954.

Further Reading

Colette is listed in the Literature study guide (III, J, 1, a). Her treatment of memory is similar to that of Marcel PROUST.

Two important critical studies of Colette's life and work are Elaine Marks, *Colette* (1960), and Margaret Davies's succinct *Colette* (1961). Also useful are Margaret Crosland, *Madame Colette* (1953), and Maurice Goudeket, *Close to Colette* (1957).

COLIGNY / By Christopher Stocker

The French admiral and statesman Gaspard de Coligny (1519–1572) was the most prominent leader of the French Protestants, or Huguenots, during the first decade of the religious wars in France.

Gaspard de Coligny (pronounced kô-lē-nyē′) was born on Feb. 16, 1519, at his family's château of Châtillon-sur-Loing, the third of four sons of Gaspard de Coligny, Seigneur de Châtillon, and Louise de Montmorency. His mother came from an old and powerful noble house which was headed during Coligny's youth by his uncle, Anne de Montmorency, constable of France and one of the most influential figures in the courts of Francis I and Henry II.

Because of their kinship with Montmorency, Coligny and his brothers Odet and François came into important and lucrative offices and commands. Gaspard was named admiral of France and governor of two major French provinces. As admiral, he became France's first active exponent of colonial expansion in the New World. Between 1555 and 1571 he authorized and supported several colonizing expeditions in an effort to reduce the power of Spain, to find wealth for France, and to provide a haven for French Protestants.

Conversion to Protestantism

Because they belonged to the Montmorency clientage, the Coligny brothers became enmeshed in the bitter rivalry between the constable and the powerful Guise family. This rivalry, originally a political struggle for influence over Henry II, acquired ideological overtones when Gaspard and his brothers converted to Calvinism and the Guises emerged as the foremost defenders of Catholicism. Among the many French nobles to take up the Protestant faith, Coligny stood out because of the sincerity of his conversion and the depth of his attachment to the new faith.

Coligny assumed the role of spokesman for the French Protestants, and his initial hope was to ally with the queen mother, Catherine de Médicis, and work through her to secure toleration for his fellow Huguenots. But the massacre of a Protestant congregation at Vassy in 1562 by the Duke of Guise drove the Protestant nobility, Coligny with them, into armed opposition to the Crown. Three times (1562–1563, 1567, and 1568–1570) Coligny led the Protestants against the armies of the King. After 1562 Catherine de Médicis alternated reprisals against the admiral with attempts to reconcile him to the King and the Catholic party.

Advocate of War with Spain

In 1571 Coligny returned to the royal court armed with a policy that he was determined to have Charles IX adopt. He yearned for a war against Spain, France's traditional enemy, which would be precipitated by French intervention on behalf of the rebelling Spanish Netherlands. He believed that this war would unite Frenchmen in spite of their religious differences and would help the cause of international Protestantism (the leaders of the

Gaspard de Coligny (center) with his two brothers, a print in the Musée Condé, Chantilly. (Giraudon)

revolt in the Netherlands were Calvinists). War against Spain would also allow Coligny to abandon the unwanted role of leader of an opposition faction and would remove the accusation of his enemies that he had been a traitor. This last charge grew out of a treaty with Elizabeth I of England that he had signed in 1562 on behalf of the Protestants of France and which had led to English occupation of Le Havre on the Normandy coast.

Believing that a war with Spain would be disastrous, Catherine de Médicis fought desperately during the summer of 1572 to convince the royal council and her son Charles IX to reject the proposal of war, but Coligny persisted in discussing it with the young king. On August 22 Coligny was fired upon and wounded while walking in Paris. Catherine, the King's brother (later Henry III), and the Duke of Guise were involved in this assassination attempt, which they kept secret from the King.

St. Bartholomew's Night Massacre

When Charles IX initiated an investigation and announced that those involved would be punished severely, Catherine and the others fabricated a supposed Huguenot plot against his life. The overwrought Charles then authorized the assassination of Coligny and other Protestant leaders who had gathered in Paris to celebrate the marriage of the Protestant prince Henry of Navarre to Charles's sister. On the night of Aug. 24, 1572, Coligny was slain in his bed by the attendants of the Duke of Guise and thus became the first of countless victims of the St. Bartholomew's Night massacre.

Further Reading

Gaspard de Coligny is listed in the European History study guide (IV, C, 1) and the Religion study guide (I, I, 3). CATHERINE DE MÉDICIS was involved in the plot to assassinate Coligny.

The best biography of Coligny, sympathetic in tone, is A. W. Whitehead, *Gaspard de Coligny, Admiral of France* (1904). Good for the early years is Eugène Bersier, *Coligny: The Earlier Life of the Great Huguenot* (1884). See also Sir Walter Besant, *Gaspard de Coligny* (2d ed. 1879). Background information is in James Westfall Thompson, *The Wars of Religion in France, 1559–1576* (1909); Paul Van Dyke, *Catherine de Médicis* (2 vols., 1922); and Philippe Erlanger, *St. Bartholomew's Night: The Massacre of Saint Bartholomew* (trans. 1962).

COLLINGWOOD / By Daniel O'Connor

The English historian and philosopher Robin George Collingwood (1889–1943) did important historical research on Roman Britain and made original contributions to esthetics, the philosophy of history, and the philosophy of mind.

B orn at Coniston, Lancashire, R. G. Collingwood received his early education from his father, a painter and a friend and biographer of John Ruskin. Under Ruskin's precepts Collingwood was trained in the arts and crafts in addition to the classical languages. At the age of 14 he went to Rugby to prepare for college. He did brilliant work at Oxford and was elected to a fellowship at Pembroke College in 1912. During World War I he worked in the Admiralty Intelligence Division in London; after the armistice he returned to teaching at Oxford and was elected Waynflete professor of metaphysical philosophy in 1934.

Throughout his teaching career Collingwood spent his summers working on archeological digs in Britain. He regarded this work as a laboratory in which he could test his philosophical theories about the logic of inquiry and about the relationship between history and philosophy. His many publications in this field culminated in his contribution to the *Oxford History of England*.

Collingwood's philosophical work falls into three periods. There was first a youthful period in which he sought to free himself from the realist doctrines of his Oxford teachers. This culminated in his *Speculum mentis*, a comparative study of five forms of experience arranged in an ascending order of truth: art, religion, science, history, and philosophy.

In the middle period of his writing Collingwood produced *Essay on Philosophical Method*. He expanded the insights of this work in *The Idea of Nature* and *The Idea of History*. His overall conclusion was that it is the task of philosophy to explore the presuppositions by which earlier cultures produced their characteristic views on nature and life. The implication is that once the historical part of this task is done, one can raise philosophical questions about the adequacy or truth value of the varying presuppositions. In his last period Collingwood seemed to deny philosophy any independent role—it is absorbed into the history of thought.

Collingwood's work in the last 5 years of his life shows defects and inconsistencies that can be traced in some measure to his rapidly declining health. In 1938 he suffered the first of a series of strokes which finally incapacitated him. He died on Jan. 9, 1943, leaving a number of manuscripts and incompleted works, some of which were published by his literary executors.

Further Reading

R. G. Collingwood is listed in the Philosophy study guide (VII, A) and the Social Sciences study guide (VII, A, 1). His philosophical ideas differed widely from those of his contemporaries G. E. MOORE and Bertrand RUSSELL. Collingwood's *An Autobiography* (1939) follows his maxim that "all history is the history of thought" and describes the development of his ideas with only scattered biographical details. Alan Donagan, *The Later*

R. G. Collingwood. (National Portrait Gallery, London)

Philosophy of R. G. Collingwood (1962), is the best critical work on Collingwood and also contains a bibliography.

E. **COLLINS** / By Patrick Glenn Porter

The American shipowner Edward Knight Collins (1802–1878) operated transatlantic and coastwise packet ships and was the leading figure in America's most ambitious challenge to Great Britain's merchant marine supremacy in the 19th century.

Edward Collins was born on Aug. 5, 1802, in Truro, Mass. He was a member of an old New England family which had emigrated to Massachusetts from England in the 1630s. His father, Israel Gross Collins, was a sailing ship captain, and Edward followed his father's example in choosing a maritime career.

In 1817 Collins moved to New York City, where he was to live for the rest of his life. He worked in a mercantile house for a time and then made several voyages to the West Indies. He later went into business with his father, conducting a general shipping and commission firm. The association with his father brought some profits, which Collins used to begin his lifetime career as a shipowner.

The first venture of Collins was the purchase of a line of packet ships that sailed between New York and Veracruz, Mexico. In 1831 he acquired a similar packet line in the coastwise trade with New Orleans, his ships carrying general merchandise to the South and returning laden with raw cotton. In 1837 he established a sailing line in the transatlantic commerce between New York and Liverpool. The Liverpool line was known as the "Dramatic Line" because the vessels were all named after leading stage actors.

Collins soon became convinced that the future of commercial shipping lay with steam, not sail. Once England awarded Samuel Cunard a subsidy mail contract in 1838 to underwrite expected losses on Cunard's proposed steam line, the age of steamships had begun. Collins became an enthusiastic lobbyist for American subsidies similar to those enjoyed by Cunard. In 1847 Congress agreed to such a plan, authorizing the secretary of the Navy to contract with Collins and his associates for the creation of an Amerian version of the Cunard line.

The venture was ill-starred from the first, poorly advised and poorly managed. Five steamships were to be built, all designed for possible conversion to warships. The Collins line (officially the New York and Liverpool Mail Steamship Company) was to run 20 round-trip passenger voyages annually for 10 years, for which the line was to receive $385,000 a year in Federal funds. But the ships cost almost twice the original estimates, and the

Edward Collins. (New York Chamber of Commerce)

company was in financial difficulties from the first. Although the ships drew many passengers and were very swift vessels (they were superior to their British competition), the firm lost money consistently even after the subsidy was paid. Poor management, higher than anticipated operating costs, and a series of maritime disasters spelled failure for the effort to outdo British merchant marine supremacy. In 1858 Collins dissolved his company. He died in New York City on Jan. 22, 1878.

Further Reading

Edward Collins is listed in the American History study guide (VI, D, 2). Other leading commercial and industrial figures of the 19th century were Donald McKAY and Jay COOKE.

For an account of the Collins shipping line see William E. Bennett (pseudonym of Warren Armstrong), *The Collins Story* (1957). Additional information and good background material are available in William S. Lindsay, *History of Merchant Shipping and Ancient Commerce* (4 vols., 1874–1876); in Robert G. Albion, *The Rise of New York Port* (1939); and in John G. B. Hutchins, *The American Maritime Industries and Public Policy, 1789–1914* (1941).

M. COLLINS / By Joseph M. Curran

The Irish revolutionary leader Michael Collins (1890–1922) was a founder of the Irish Free State.

Michael Collins was born near Clonakilty, County Cork, on Oct. 16, 1890. He was educated at local primary schools and went to London in 1906 to enter the civil service as a postal clerk. For 10 years Collins lived in London, where he became active in various Irish organizations, the most important of which was the Irish Republican Brotherhood (IRB), a secret society dedicated to the overthrow of British rule in Ireland.

Collins returned to Ireland in 1916 to take part in the Easter Rising and after its suppression was interned in North Wales with most of the other rebels. When the internees were released in December 1916, he went to Dublin, where his keen intelligence and dynamic energy soon secured him a position of leadership in the reviving revolutionary movement.

After their victory in the general election of December 1918, the revolutionaries established an Irish Parliament, Dail Eireann, in January 1919. The Dail proclaimed an Irish Republic and set up an executive to take over the government of the country. British attempts to suppress the republican movement were met with guerrilla warfare by the Irish Republican Army (IRA). Collins played the most important role in this struggle. As director of intelligence of the IRA, he crippled the British intelligence system in Ireland and replaced it with an effective Irish network. At the same time he performed other important military functions, headed the IRB, and, as minister of finance in the Republican government, successfully raised and disbursed large sums on behalf of the rebel cause. Despite constant efforts the British were unable to capture Collins or stop his work. The "Big Fellow"

Michael Collins, photographed during the ceremony to launch the Irish Free State in March 1922. (Radio Times Hulton Picture Library)

became an idolized and near-legendary figure in Ireland and won a formidable reputation in Britain and abroad for ruthlessness, resourcefulness, and daring.

After the truce of July 1921, Collins reluctantly agreed to President Eamon De Valera's request to serve on the peace-making delegation headed by Arthur Griffith. During the autumn negotiations in London, the British government firmly rejected any settlement that involved recognition of the republic. Instead its representatives offered Dominion status for Ireland, with the right of exclusion for loyalist Northern Ireland. Collins decided to accept these terms, in the belief that rejection meant renewal of the war and quick defeat for Ireland and that the proposed treaty would soon lead to unity and complete freedom for his country. Using these arguments, he and Griffith persuaded their fellow delegates to sign the treaty on Dec. 6, 1921, and Dail Eireann to approve it on Jan. 7, 1922.

De Valera and many Republicans refused to accept the agreement, however, contending that it constituted a betrayal of the republic and would mean continued subjection to Britain. As the British evacuated southern Ireland, Collins and Griffith did their best to maintain order and implement the treaty but found their efforts frustrated by the opposition of an armed Republican minority. Collins sought desperately to pacify the antitreaty forces without abandoning the treaty but found it impossible to make a workable compromise.

In late June 1922, after the population had endorsed the settlement in an election, Collins agreed to use force against the dissidents. This action precipitated civil war, a bitter conflict in which the forces of the infant Irish Free State eventually overcame the extreme Republicans in May 1923. Collins did not live to see the end of the war; he was killed in ambush in West Cork on Aug. 22, 1922, just 10 days after the death of Arthur Griffith.

Much of Collins's success as a revolutionary leader can be ascribed to his realism and extraordinary efficiency, but there was also a marked strain of idealism and humanity in his character which appealed to friend and foe alike. The treaty that cost him his life did not end partition, as he had hoped, but it did make possible the peaceful attainment of full political freedom for most of Ireland.

Further Reading

Michael Collins is listed in the European History study guide (XI, B, 1). Other leaders in the struggle for Irish independence were Eamon DE VALERA and Patrick H. PEARSE.

Frank O'Connor (pseud. of Michael O'Donovan), *The Big Fellow: Michael Collins and the Irish Revolution* (1937; rev. ed. 1965), offers penetrating insight into Collins's complex personality. Piaras Béaslaí, *Michael Collins and the Making of a New Ireland* (2 vols., 1926), is the most detailed biography. Rex Taylor, *Michael Collins* (1958), fills in important details of the treaty negotiations.

WILKIE COLLINS / By Heinrich H. Stabenau

The English author William Wilkie Collins (1824–1889) wrote intricately plotted novels of sensational intrigue which helped establish the conventions of modern detective fiction.

Wilkie Collins was born in London on Jan. 8, 1824, the son of a successful painter. Leaving school in his sixteenth year, he was apprenticed to a tea importer but had little enthusiasm for business. As a young man, he both wrote and painted. He published a number of articles and stories, exhibited a picture at the Royal Academy, and was an early supporter of the Pre-Raphaelite Brotherhood. His first published novel, *Antonina, or the Fall of Rome* (1850), was modeled on the historical fiction of the popular Edward Bulwer-Lytton.

Collins met Charles Dickens in 1851 and became one of his closest friends. Most of his early stories and novels appeared in Dickens's magazines *Household Words* and *All the Year Round*, and through participation in Dickens's elaborate amateur theatricals he was encouraged to try his hand at drama. However, Collins's melodramas, although popular in their day, are now largely forgotten.

In the novels *Basil* (1852), *Hide and Seek* (1854), and

Wilkie Collins. (Radio Times Hulton Picture Library)

The Dead Secret (1857), Collins placed sensational incident in a realistic contemporary middle-class setting and developed the technique of gradually unfolding a mystery introduced at the beginning of the story.

The Woman in White (1860), based on an incident that had occurred in France some 70 years earlier, marked the maturing of Collins's art and was an immediate popular success on both sides of the Atlantic. In it a scheme to rob a woman of her fortune turns on the existence of a mysterious double who dies and is substituted for the victim. The extraordinarily complex maneuvers of the villain are made even more mystifying by Collins's device of narrating the events through a series of limited observers. Although *Armadale* (1866) contained no mystery, its plot was even more complex and its atmosphere even richer. *The Moonstone* (1868) was Collins's greatest achievement and set a permanent standard for detective fiction. Told, like *The Woman in White*, from a number of limited points of view, it dealt with the recovery by three Brahmins of a diamond stolen from an Indian idol.

After *Man and Wife* (1870), a novel on the problem of the marriage laws, Collins's works concentrate on social issues. But his style was not suited to this type of novel, and he was also becoming deeply addicted to opium after taking laudanum for rheumatic gout.

Collins never married but maintained a rather enigmatic relationship with two women, one of whom lived with him for almost 30 years. He died on Sept. 23, 1889, after prolonged illness.

Further Reading

Wilkie Collins is listed in the Literature study guide (II, H, 1, c). Edgar Allan POE was another pioneer in detective and suspense fiction.

The standard biography of Collins is Kenneth Robinson, *Wilkie Collins* (1952). Also of interest are Stewart Marsh Ellis, *Wilkie Collins, Le Fanu and Others* (1931), and the chapter on Collins in Malcom Elwin, *Victorian Wallflowers: A Panoramic Survey of the Popular Literary Periodicals* (1934).

William Collins, a chalk drawing by his son, C. A. Collins. (National Portrait Gallery, London)

WILLIAM COLLINS / By Anne Doyle

> The English poet William Collins (1721–1759) excelled in the descriptive or allegorical ode. He also wrote classical odes and elegies and lyrics marked by delicate and pensive melody.

William Collins was born on Dec. 25, 1721, in Chichester. His father was a prosperous merchant who was twice elected mayor. In 1733 Collins entered Winchester, intending to study for the clergy. There he began his lifelong friendship with Joseph Warton and his own poetic career. In 1739 his short poem "To a Lady Weeping" was published in the *Gentleman's Magazine*. The following year he entered Queen's College, Oxford, but soon transferred to Magdalene. While at Oxford, he published his *Persian Eclogues* (1742), the only one of his works that was highly regarded during his lifetime.

Having abandoned his plan to enter the clergy, Collins left Oxford. With a small inheritance from his mother, in 1744 he settled in London to become a man of letters. Here he frequented the coffee houses and made friends with David Garrick and Samuel Johnson, who described him as a man "with many projects in his head and little money in his pocket." Among Collins's many projects which came to nothing were a commentary on Aristotle's *Poetics* and a history of the Renaissance.

In 1746 Collins and Joseph Warton planned the joint publication of their odes, but Robert Dodsley, to whom they submitted their manuscript, judged that Collins's work would have little public appeal and published only Warton's. Although Collins's *Odes on Several Descriptive and Allegorical Subjects* was soon undertaken by another publisher, Dodsley's rejection and the subsequent failure of the *Odes* mortified Collins deeply.

Collins continued to write and to practice the pictorial technique announced in the *Odes*. He made literary friendships with James Thomson and with lesser writers such as John Home and Christopher Smart. His most personal poem, the *Ode Occasioned by the Death of Mr. Thomson* (1749), was the last of his works published during his lifetime. Shortly after Thomson's death he sent John Home a manuscript of *An Ode on the Popular Superstitions of the Highlands of Scotland*, a superb poem which anticipates many of the attitudes of the romantic revival.

About this time Collins received a legacy from his uncle and retired to Chichester to carry out some of his ambitious projects. But he became threatened with insanity and sought relief in a trip abroad. When this failed to restore his health, he was committed to an institution. He was later released to the care of his sister, but he never recovered. Collins died on June 12, 1759.

Further Reading

William Collins is listed in the Literature study guide (II, F, 2, b). Among his literary associates was Samuel JOHNSON.

There are two full-length biographies of Collins: H. W. Garrod, *Collins* (1928), and Edward Gay Ainsworth, Jr., *Poor Collins: His Life, His Art, and His Influence* (1937). Chester F. Chapin, *Personification in Eighteenth-Century Poetry* (1955), offers a fine analysis of Collins's poetic technique.

✳   ✳   ✳

COLT / By Carroll Pursell

The American inventor and manufacturer Samuel Colt (1814–1862) first developed and popularized the multishot pistol, or revolver, which found wide use in the last half of the 19th century, especially in the American West.

Samuel Colt was born in Hartford, Conn., the son of a prosperous cotton and woolen manufacturer. In 1824 his father sent him to work in one of his dyeing and bleaching establishments; Colt attended school at the same time. His behavior in school, however, was such that his father sought to discipline him by sending him on a sea voyage as an ordinary seaman. It was a one-year trip to India and the Orient, and it was apparently on this voyage that young Colt began to work on a revolving pistol. On his return he worked for a year in his father's bleachery and then left to travel on his own. Little is known of his activities for the next few years, but for at least a part of that time he billed himself as "Dr. Coult" and gave popular lectures on chemistry and demonstrated the effects of laughing gas.

Colt continued to work on his idea for a pistol and by 1831 had constructed at least two versions of it. By 1833 he had made both a pistol and a rifle on the principles which he later patented in the United States. Just about this time he wandered off to Europe, where he acquired patents in both France and England. He returned to America in 1836 and received an American patent that year. The primary feature of his pistol was a revolving

cartridge cylinder which automatically advanced one chamber when the gun was cocked.

During 1836 Colt built a factory in Paterson, N.J., to make his revolvers, but failing to receive a contract from the government he was unable to produce and sell the gun in quantity. Forced to sell the patent for his revolver, he turned to the problem of submarine warfare, receiving some financial help from the government to build an experimental submarine battery.

In 1846, with the declaration of war against Mexico, the demand for guns rose, and Colt was given a government contract for 1000 of his revolving pistols. Quickly he bought back his patents and opened an armory in New Haven, Conn. This new government patronage, coupled with the growing popularity of the gun in the West (where it was ideally suited to the new kind of horseback warfare being carried out against the Indians) brought Colt financial success at last. His exhibit at the 1851 Crystal Palace international exhibition in London caused widespread comment—for the excellence of his weapons, but most importantly for the example they gave of the mass production of interchangeable parts, which came to be known as the American system of manufactures. In 1855 Colt built his great armory at Hartford, Conn. (the largest private armory of its time), and he lived out his life as a prosperous and respected manufacturer.

Further Reading

Samuel Colt is listed in the Science study guide (VI, H, 3). Other inventors of this period were Elias HOWE and Samuel F. B. MORSE.

Samuel Colt. (Smithsonian Institution, Washington, D.C.)

A good introduction to Colt's life and works is William B. Edwards, *The Story of Colt's Revolver: The Biography of Col. Samuel Colt* (1953). There is a vast literature on guns, written for buffs and collectors, much of which contains references to Colt and his pistol.

* * *

COLUM / By Allen Figgis

The Irish-American author Padraic Colum (1881–1972), best known for his poetry and plays, was active in the Irish Literary Revival.

Padraic Colum was born in County Longford and as a youth met many who had lived through the Great Famine, which ravaged Ireland in the mid-19th century. His father was master of the workhouse (home for the destitute), and thus Padraic saw much of the poverty and land hunger of the people. His uncle was a poultry dealer, and the young Colum traveled with him to fairs and markets. There he met the wandering people of the roads, ballad singers, and storytellers and found inspiration for some of the poems which have become part of Ireland's literary heritage. "She Moves through the Fair" and "The Old Woman of the Roads" are among his numerous simple lyrics which have often been anthologized.

Colum became deeply interested in poetry and theater, and he brought to the great Irish Literary Revival a young man's vision together with an inheritance from the ancient voice of the people. He was one of the founders of the *Irish Review*, and his early poems were published by Arthur Griffith, of whom he later wrote a biography (*Ourselves Alone*, 1959). Among his volumes of poetry were *The Road round Ireland* (1926) and *Images of Departure* (1969). His collected poems were published in 1953.

Colum was a founder-member of the Irish National Theatre Society (forerunner of the Abbey Theatre) and a friend of William Butler Yeats, John Millington Synge, Lady Gregory, AE, and James Stephens. He later celebrated some of these friendships in a book of poems, *Irish Elegies* (1958). His realistic plays—*The Land* (1905), *The Fiddler's House* (1907), and *Thomas Muskerry* (1910)—were an important influence in the development of the modern Irish theater. Their early productions were by the Fay brothers, and it was Frank Fay who taught Colum how to recite verse, an art which he perfected over the years.

Colum was much occupied with contemporary events, especially Ireland's struggle for freedom, and numbered among his friends the Irish patriots Patrick Pearse, Thomas McDonagh, and Roger Casement. In 1912 Colum married the author Mary Maguire, and 2 years later they emigrated to the United States. He retained close ties, however, with literary and political events in Ireland, and his writings continued to derive much of their inspiration from his native country.

The Colums wrote about their long and close friendship with James Joyce and his family many years later in *Our Friend James Joyce* (1958). They cared for Joyce's invalid daughter at a critical period. Colum's fondness for young people is also reflected in his many books for children, best known of which is *The King of Ireland's Son* (1916).

Although a resident of New York, Colum remained something of the traditional wandering Irish poet, traveling widely to give lectures and readings. In 1924 he accepted an invitation from the Hawaii Legislature to make a survey of native myth and folklore; his versions of the Hawaiian tales were published in *The Bright Islands* (1925). He also retold Irish legends in *A Treasury of Irish Folklore* (1954). Colum was always interested in other cultures, from those of classical Greece and Rome to that of the South Sea Islands, which he visited at the age of 86.

After his wife's death in 1957, Colum published the long, semiautobiographical novel *The Flying Swans*, a saga of life in Ireland before the turn of the century. Colum's unfailing kindness in encouraging new poets and writers of talent perhaps contributed to his vitality and the continuing freshness of his ideas throughout his life. He died at Enfield, Conn., on Jan. 11, 1972.

Padraic Colum in 1923. (Library of Congress)

Further Reading

Padraic Colum is listed in the Literature study guide (II, I, 4; II, J, 4). Among his friends were James JOYCE, John Millington SYNGE, and William Butler YEATS.

A comprehensive biographical and critical study of Colum is Zack Bowen, *Padraic Colum* (1970). The autobiography of his wife, Mary Colum, *Life and the Dream: Memories of a Literary Life in Europe and America* (1947; rev. ed. 1966), contains information about their life together. Ernest A. Boyd, *The Contemporary Drama of Ireland* (1917), discusses Colum's early career as an Irish folk dramatist.

St. Columba, drawing from a medieval manuscript. (Stiftsbibliothek, Saint Gall, Switzerland)

ST. **COLUMBA** / By Gerard A. Vanderhaar

The Irish monk St. Columba (ca. 521–597) was a powerful preacher and leader of men. He founded monasteries in Ireland and Scotland, which were influential missionary centers.

The son of a tribal chieftain, Columba was given the name Crimthann when he was baptized shortly after his birth in Gartan, County Donegal. When he was a boy, he was so often found praying in the town church that his friends called him Colm Cille (Dove of the Church), and it was as Colm, or its Latin form Columba, that he was known for the rest of his life.

In his early 20s Columba was strongly influenced by one of his teachers, Finian of Clonard, and asked to be ordained a priest. When a prince cousin gave him some land at Derry, he decided to start a monastery. Because of his love of nature Columba refused to build the church facing east, as was the custom; he wanted to spare the lives of as many oak trees as he could. His foundation of another monastery at Durrow 7 years later was the beginning of an extraordinary decade during which he traveled through northern Ireland teaching about Christianity and inspiring many people by his personal holiness. He founded some 30 monasteries in those 10 years.

Columba's strong personality and forceful preaching aroused considerable antagonism. He was accused in 563 of starting a war between two Irish tribes and was sentenced by the high king never to see Ireland again, to spend the rest of his life in exile. With 12 companions he sailed from the shores he loved, and settled on a bleak island called Iona off the coast of Scotland. The monks made occasional visits to the Scottish mainland, where they preached their kind of Christianity. Soon their community had 150 members.

In 575 Columba was persuaded to visit Ireland to mediate a dispute between the high king and the league of poets. Insisting on remaining faithful to the terms of his exile, that he never see Ireland again, he traveled blindfolded. Although his sympathies were with the po-

ets, his reputation was respected by everyone. He spoke to the assembled nobles and clergy with such force and authority that the king was persuaded to reverse his original decree, and the hostility between the two parties was calmed.

Columba spent the rest of his life on Iona, praying, fasting, and teaching his monks to read and copy the Scriptures. He provided inspiration for their missionary efforts and was influential for a time in the politics of Scotland. Long before his death in 597 he was regarded as a saint by his fellow monks and is today a beloved figure in Irish tradition.

Further Reading

St. Columba is listed in the Religion study guide (I, C, 3). The earlier missionary St. PATRICK brought Christianity to Ireland.

The Life of Saint Columba, written about a hundred years after his death by a monk of his community, Adamnan of Iona, describes him as a poet and miracle worker. It was edited and translated into English by Alan Orr Anderson and Marjorie Ogilvie Anderson (1961). Benedict Fitzpatrick, *Ireland and the Making of Britain* (1922), pays tribute to Columba's influence in shaping the character of the British Isles. There is a charming chapter on Columba (Colm Cille) in Seumas MacManus, *The Story of the Irish Race* (1921).

ST. **COLUMBAN**
/ By Gerard A. Vanderhaar

The Irish missionary St. Columban (ca. 543–615) traveled throughout Europe, preaching a strict, penitential version of Christianity. He founded influential monasteries in France, Switzerland, and Italy.

A s a young student, Columban was so impressed by the dedicated Irish monks who introduced him to religion and literature that he decided to join their ranks. He entered a monastery at Bangor, County Down, not far from his home, and placed himself under the spiritual guidance of its founder, Comgall. For some 30 years he lived quietly in prayer, work, and study. Desiring greater self-sacrifice, Columban asked his abbot if he could go into voluntary exile, leaving his native Ireland to start a monastery on the Continent. Twelve other monks set out with him in 590 for the land of the Franks.

They settled for a while in Burgundy at the invitation of King Childebert, founding three monasteries. So many young men were inspired by their religious zeal that soon more than 200 monasteries were formed, looking to Columban as their spiritual father. The Irish monks with their new, forceful kind of Christianity, stressing self-discipline and purity of life, presented a striking contrast to the complacent churchmen already living among the Franks. Columban spoke out repeatedly against the cruelty and self-indulgence of the kings and royal families, stressing the necessity of penance and introducing a new custom of frequent personal confession.

Columban's Irish brand of Christianity proved so annoying that the local clergy looked for opportunities to discredit him. They seized upon his different method of calculating the date of Easter as an excuse for attacking his orthodoxy and were happy when King Theuderic in 610 expelled him from Burgundy after he had censured the King for living with a mistress.

Other kings welcomed Columban into their territories, and he eventually made his way into what is now Switzerland, founding a monastery near Zurich. Columban refused, however, to settle down into a quiet monastic life and again ran into trouble. He preached so vigorously against the pagan customs of the surrounding Alemani that he was asked to leave their territory. With considerable difficulty Columban and a few faithful followers crossed the Alps and started what was to be their most important monastery in Bobbio in northern Italy. From there the Irish influence spread still further, although in time the harsh personal life of the monks softened as they came in contact with the more moderate ideas of Benedict.

Columban died in his monastery in Bobbio in 615. Many of his letters and sermons were preserved. These, together with his poems and the rules he composed for his monks, influenced European life and culture well into the Middle Ages.

Further Reading

St. Columban is listed in the Religion study guide (I, C, 3 and 4). St. BENEDICT was a major figure in the monastic movement of this period.

Of the several biographies of St. Columban available in English, the one by Francis MacManus, *Saint Columban* (1962), is helpful for its use of contemporary historical scholarship. Most church history studies present the effect of Columban's missionary efforts on the history of Europe, for example, John Ryan, *Irish Monasticism: Origins and Early Development* (1931).

Cloister of the abbey of Luxeuil in eastern France. St. Columban founded the abbey about 590. (Archives Photographiques, Paris)

COLUMBUS / By Charles E. Nowell

The Italian navigator Christopher Columbus (1451–1506) was the discoverer of America. Though he had set out to find a westward route to Asia, his explorations proved to be as important as any alternate way to the riches of Cathay and India.

T he archives of Genoa show that the famous discoverer was born Cristoforo Colombo (Spanish, Cristóbal Colón) there between August and October 1451. His father, Domenico Colombo, followed the weaver's craft, and his mother, Suzanna Fontanarossa, came of equally humble stock. Christopher was the eldest child, and two brothers make some appearance in history under their Hispanicized names, Bartolomé and Diego.

Columbus had a meager education and only later learned to read Latin and write Castilian. He evidently helped Domenico at work when he was a boy and went to sea early in a humble capacity. Since he aged early in appearance and contemporaries commonly took him for older than he really was, he was able to claim to have taken part in events before his time.

In 1475 Columbus made his first considerable voyage to the Aegean island of Chios, and in 1476 he sailed on a Genoese ship through the Strait of Gibraltar. Off Cape St. Vincent they were attacked by a French fleet, and the vessel in which Columbus sailed sank. He swam ashore and went to Lisbon, where his brother Bartolomé already lived. Columbus also visited Galway, in Ireland, and an English port, probably Bristol. If he ever sailed to Iceland, as he afterward claimed to have done, it must have been as a part of this voyage. He made his presumably last visit to Genoa in 1479 and there gave testimony in a lawsuit. Court procedure required him to tell his age, which he gave as "past 27," furnishing reasonable evidence of 1451 as his birth year.

Columbus returned to Portugal, where he married Felipa Perestrelo e Monis, daughter of Bartolomeu Perestrelo, deceased proprietor of the island of Porto Santo. The couple lived first in Lisbon, where Perestrelo's widow showed documents her husband had written or collected regarding possible western lands in the Atlantic, and these probably started Columbus thinking of a voyage of investigation. Later they moved to Porto Santo, where Felipa died soon after the birth of Diego, the discoverer's only legitimate child.

Formation of an Idea

After his wife's death, Columbus turned wholly to discovery plans and theories, among them the hope to discover a westward route to Asia. He learned of the legendary Irish St. Brandan and his marvelous adventures in the Atlantic and of the equally legendary island of Antilia. Seamen venturing west of Madeira and the Azores reported signs of land, and ancient authors, notably Seneca and Pliny, had theorized about the nearness of eastern Asia to western Europe, though it is not known just when Columbus read them. He acquired incunabular editions of Ptolemy, Marco Polo, and Pierre d'Ailly, but again it is uncertain how early he read them. He possibly first depended on what others said of their contents.

From Marco Polo, Columbus learned the names of Cathay (north China) and Cipango (Japan). The Venetian traveler had never visited Japan and erroneously placed it 1,500 miles east of China, thus bringing it closer to Europe. Furthermore, Columbus accepted two bad guesses by Ptolemy: his underestimate of the earth's circumference and his overestimate of Asia's eastward extension. With the earth's sphericity taken for granted, all Columbus's mistaken beliefs combined to make his idea seem feasible.

Christopher Columbus. There are a number of portraits of the great discoverer, all quite different. None was painted during his lifetime. (Italian Cultural Institute)

In 1474 the Florentine scientist Paolo dal Pozzo Toscanelli sent a letter and map to Fernao Martins of Lisbon, telling Martins that a western voyage in the Atlantic would be a shorter way of reaching the Orient than circumnavigation of Africa. Columbus obtained a copy of the letter and used it to clarify his own ideas.

In 1484 Columbus asked John II of Portugal for backing in the proposed voyage. Rejected, Columbus went to Spain with young Diego in 1485, and for nearly 7 years he sought the aid of Isabella of Castile and her Aragonese husband, Ferdinand. The sovereigns took no action but gave Columbus a small annuity that enabled him to live modestly. He found influential friends, including the powerful Duke of Medinaceli and Juan Pérez, prior of La Rábida monastery.

While waiting, the widowed Columbus had an affair with young Beatriz Enriquez de Harana of Cordova, who in 1488 bore his other son, Ferdinand, out of wedlock. He never married Beatriz, though he provided for her in his will and legitimatized the boy, as Castilian law permitted.

Preparations for the First Voyage

In 1492 Columbus resumed negotiations with the rulers. The discussions soon broke down, apparently because of the heavy demands by Columbus, who now prepared to abandon Spain and try Charles VIII of France. Father Pérez saved Columbus from this probably fruitless endeavor by an eloquent appeal to the Queen. Columbus was called back, and in April he and the rulers agreed to the Capitulations of Santa Fe, by which they guaranteed him more than half the future profits and promised his family the hereditary governorship of all lands annexed to Castile.

Financing proved difficult, but three ships were prepared in the harbor of Palos. The largest, the 100-ton *Santa Maria*, was a round-bottomed nao with both square and lateen sails; the caravel *Pinta* was square-rigged; and the small *Niña*, also a caravel, had lateen sails. Recruitment proved hard, and sailing might have been delayed had not the Pinzón brothers, mariners and leading citizens of Palos, come to Columbus's aid and persuaded seamen to enlist. The eldest brother, Martín Alonso, took command of the *Pinta*, and a younger brother, Vicente Yañez, commanded the *Niña*.

The Departure

The fleet left Palos on Aug. 3, 1492, and, visiting the Canaries, followed the parallel of Gomera westward. Weather remained good during the entire crossing, "like April in Andalusia," as Columbus wrote in his diary, and contrary to popular tales, there was no serious threat of mutiny.

By mid-Atlantic, Columbus evidently concluded he

Columbus lands on Hispaniola from a fantastic galley and meets the naked inhabitants of the island paradise in this 1493 print. (Rare Book Division, The New York Public Library, Astor, Lenox and Tilden Foundations)

had missed Antilia, so Cipango became his next goal. Landfall came at dawn of October 12, at the Bahama island of Guanahani, straightway renamed San Salvador by Columbus (probably modern San Salvador, or Watlings Island). Arawak natives flocked to the shore and made friends with the Spaniards as they landed. Believing himself in the East Indies, Columbus called them "Indians," a name ultimately applied to all New World aborigines.

The ships next passed among other Bahamas to Colba (Cuba), where the gold available proved disappointing. Turning eastward, Columbus crossed to Quisqueya, renamed Española (Hispaniola), where on Christmas Eve the *Santa Maria* ran aground near Cap-Haitien. No lives were lost and most of the equipment was salvaged. As relations with the local Taino Arawaks seemed good and Columbus wished to return to Spain immediately, he built a settlement named Navidad for the *Santa Maria*'s crew and left, promising to return in a few months.

The Return

Columbus recrossed the Atlantic by a more northerly route than on his outward passage and reached Europe safely. He had an interview with John II of Portugal, who, by a farfetched interpretation of an old treaty with Castile, claimed the new western islands for himself. Columbus then sailed to Palos and crossed Spain to the court at Barcelona, bearing the artifacts he had brought from Hispaniola and conducting several natives he had induced or forced to accompany him. Strong evidence also suggests that his crew brought syphilis, apparently never reported in Europe before and known to have been endemic in mild form among the Arawaks.

Regarding John II's territorial claims, Isabella and Ferdinand appealed to Pope Alexander VI, an Aragonese Spaniard, for confirmation of their rights, and in 1493 the Pope obliged, granting Castile complete rights west of a line from pole to pole in the Atlantic. But the Treaty of Tordesillas (1494) established a new line, from pole to pole, 370 leagues west of the Cape Verde Islands. Spain was entitled to claim and occupy all non-Christian lands west of the line, and Portugal all those to the east.

Second Voyage

Following an enthusiastic reception by Ferdinand and Isabella, "Admiral" Columbus prepared for a second voyage. He sailed from Cadiz with 17 ships and about 1,200 men in September 1493. Columbus entered the West Indies near Dominica, which he discovered and named. Passing westward and touching Marie Galante, Guadeloupe, and other Lesser Antilles, the fleet came to large Borinquén (modern Puerto Rico).

On reaching the Navidad settlement on Hispaniola, Columbus found the place destroyed. The Spaniards had made themselves so hated in their quest of gold and women that Chief Caonabo, more warlike than the others, had exterminated them. Another settlement, Isabela, proved an equally unfortunate location, and in 1495 or 1496 Bartolomé Columbus founded Santo Domingo on the south side of Hispaniola.

From Isabela the Admiral sent home most of the ships,

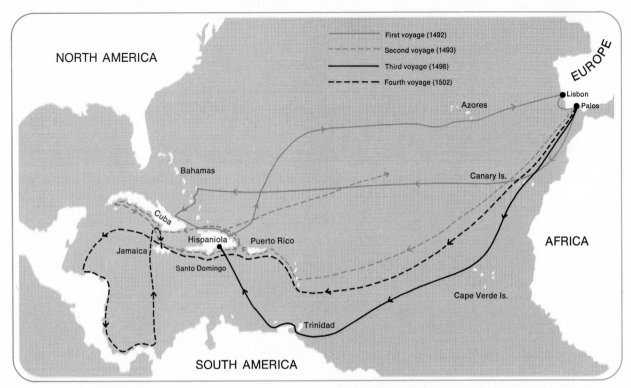

First voyage (1492)
Second voyage (1493)
Third voyage (1498)
Fourth voyage (1502)

NORTH AMERICA

EUROPE

Lisbon
Palos

Azores

Bahamas

Canary Is.

Cuba

Hispaniola

Puerto Rico

AFRICA

Jamaica

Santo Domingo

Cape Verde Is.

Trinidad

SOUTH AMERICA

Columbus's voyages, 1492–1504. Columbus's great dream was to find a sea route to Japan and China. After four voyages to the Caribbean, he died still believing that he had been to Asia. By then, other explorers already guessed that he had, in fact, discovered a "new world."

though retaining the bulk of the men. He dispatched expeditions into the center of the island in search of gold and accompanied one in person. Meanwhile, he installed himself as governor of Hispaniola, intending it to be a trading post for commerce with the rich Oriental empires he expected soon to discover.

Exploration in the Caribbean

Columbus now decided to explore Cuba further by tracing the island's southern coast. With three ships, including his favorite *Niña*, he left Isabela in the spring of 1494 and followed the Cuban coast nearly to its western end. Indians told him of Jamaica not far to the south, and the Admiral turned that way, discovered the island, and had several fights with hostile natives. Returning to the Cuban shore, Columbus sailed to Bahía Cortés, where leaky ships and sailors' complaints forced him to put back.

Back in Hispaniola, Columbus found the Spanish settlers unruly and nearly impossible to govern. Complaints against Columbus reached the Castilian court in such numbers that he at last decided to go to Spain to clear his name. He left in the *Niña* in March 1496 and reached Cadiz in June. Bartolomé, with the rank of *adelantado*, remained to govern the colony in his absence.

Third Voyage

The Admiral's reception at court was visibly cooler, but Vasco da Gama's departure from Portugal for India in 1497 caused the Spanish rulers to dispatch Columbus

again the following year. There were reports of a great continent south of the Admiral's previous discoveries, and Columbus left Sanlúcar de Barrameda with six ships late in May 1498.

The first land sighted had three hills in view, which suggested the Holy Trinity, and Columbus promptly named the island Trinidad. Since it lies by the Gulf of Paria and the Venezuelan mainland, the Admiral became the discoverer of South America on Aug. 1, 1498. The welcome discovery of pearls from oysters in the shallow waters of offshore islands caused the name "Pearl Coast" to be applied for a time to Venezuela, which Columbus even then recognized as a land of continental proportions because of the volume of water flowing from one of its rivers.

Rebellion and Arrest

The Admiral had left Hispaniolan affairs in bad condition 2 years earlier and now hastened to return there and relieve his hard-pressed brother. On arrival he succeeded in partially quieting by compromise a revolt headed by Francisco Roldán, an officeholder, and resumed his governorship. But so many letters of complaint had gone back to Castile regarding the Columbus brothers that the rulers sent out a royal commissioner, Francisco de Bobadilla, with full powers to act as he saw best.

Bobadilla was honest and meant well, but he had already formed a bad opinion of the Columbus family. He put the Admiral and the *adelantado* in chains and sent them to Spain. Andrés Martín, commanding the ship in which they sailed, offered to remove the shackles, but the Admiral refused permission, as he meant to appear fettered before the sovereigns. On arrival in Cadiz in late November 1500, Columbus went to court to receive a kind welcome and assurance by the monarchs that the chains and imprisonment had not been by their orders.

In 1501 the Admiral began preparing for a fourth voyage. The fleet, consisting of four ships, left Cadiz on May 9, 1502, arriving in Santo Domingo on June 29. The Admiral next sailed to Guanaja Island off Honduras, then down the coast of Central America. When Columbus learned from the natives about another saltwater body, the Pacific, not far away, he felt certain that he was coasting the Malay Peninsula, of which he had learned through the writings of Ptolemy. A strait or open water should permit entry to the Indian Ocean. Although Columbus followed the coast nearly to the Gulf of Darien, he found no strait.

In April 1503 the ships left the mainland, but the hulls were thoroughly bored by teredos and had to be abandoned as unseaworthy in Jamaica. The Admiral and his crews were marooned in Jamaica for a year, during which time Diego Mendez and Bartolomeo Fieschi fetched a small caravel from Hispaniola. Columbus finally reached Sanlúcar de Barrameda, Spain, on Nov. 7, 1504.

Columbus had 18 months of life remaining, and they were unhappy. Though only 53 he was physically an aged man, a sufferer from arthritis and the effects of a bout of malaria. But financially his position was good, as he had brought considerable gold from America and had a claim to much more in Hispaniola. He died in Valladolid on May 20, 1506.

Further Reading

Christopher Columbus is listed in the Latin America study guide (I, B, 1). Amerigo VESPUCCI was thought to have discovered the American mainland prior to Columbus, but this is now disputed.

The best works on Columbus are Samuel Eliot Morison, *Admiral of the Ocean Sea: A Life of Christopher Columbus* (2 vols. and 1 vol. condensation, 1942), which concentrates on the nautical aspects, and, in Spanish, Antonio Ballesteros y Beretta, *Cristóbal Colón y el descubrimiento de América* (2 vols., 1945), which discusses all phases of Columbus's career. Invaluable as a source is the 1959 translation by Benjamin Keen of Fernando Colón, *The Life of the Admiral Christopher Columbus by His Son Ferdinand* (1571). Marianne Mahn-Lot, *Columbus* (1960; trans. 1961), gives a brief and accurate account of the discoverer's life.

More specialized works are Samuel Eliot Morison, *The Second Voyage of Christopher Columbus* (1939), which traces this voyage until the arrival at Hispaniola, and George E. Nunn, *The Geographical Conceptions of Columbus: A Critical Consideration of Four Problems* (1924), which has not found general acceptance. A more convincing work by Nunn is *The Columbus and Magellan Concepts of South American Geography* (1932).

Columbus's voyages are discussed in Samuel Eliot Morison, *The European Discovery of America: The Northern Voyages* (1971). Older works that still have considerable value are Washington Irving, *A History of the Life and Voyages of Christopher Columbus* (3- and 4-vol. eds., 1828), and John Boyd Thacher, *Christopher Columbus: His Life, His Work, His Remains* (3 vols., 1903–1904).

Writings devoted to unusual theses are Henry Vignaud, *Toscanelli and Columbus: The Letter and Chart of Toscanelli* (1901; trans. 1902), which maintains that the Toscanelli letters were forgeries; Salvador de Madariaga, *Christopher Columbus* (1939; 2d ed. 1949), which proves to the author's satisfaction that Columbus was a Jew; and Edmundo O'Gorman, *The Invention of America* (1958; trans. 1961), which asserts that Columbus was not a discoverer because he had no intention of making a discovery and never thought he had made one.

COMENIUS / By Jackson Spielvogel

The Moravian theologian and educational reformer John Amos Comenius (1592–1670) is often called the father of modern education.

John Amos Comenius (pronounced kə-mē′nē-əs) was born on Mar. 28, 1592, in southeastern Moravia. His early education was irregular. After deciding to become a priest of the Bohemian Unity of Brethren (a German Baptist sect), he received his higher education in Germany at Herborn, Nassau, and Heidelberg. In 1614 he returned to Bohemia, where he taught in the schools of the Brethren. He was ordained a priest 2 years later and appointed pastor of a parish in Fulneck in 1618.

The sack of Fulneck by the Catholic forces after the outbreak of the Thirty Years War forced Comenius into hiding in Bohemia. Shortly afterward he wrote the allegory *The Labyrinth of the World and the Paradise of the Heart*. In this classic of Czech literature, man finds true happiness in mystical union with Christ.

Because of persecution, the Brethren were forced to leave Bohemia in 1628. Comenius went to Leszno, Poland, where his position as corector of the Brethren's school led him to become interested in educational reform. Many of the educational ideas expressed in his *Didactica magna* (1657; *The Great Didactic*) were developed during this period. Among the reforms that he advocated were gentler discipline; use of the vernacular instead of Latin in the primary schools; and free, universal, compulsory education for both sexes and all social classes. His book *Janua linguarum reserata* (1631; *The Gate of Languages Unlocked*) revolutionized the teaching of Latin and helped establish his reputation throughout Europe as an educational reformer.

John Amos Comenius. (Bildarchiv)

of *Educational Reform* (1900), and John E. Sadler, *Comenius and the Concept of Universal Education* (1966).

COMINES / By Wilson Frescoln

The French chronicler Philippe de Comines (ca. 1445–1511) wrote an extensive memoir of the reigns of Louis XI and Charles VIII.

Born in the château of Renescure in Flanders before 1447, and probably in 1445, Philippe de Comines (pronounced kô-mēn′), or Commynes, was orphaned early. His formal education was limited, but his godfather, Philip V of Burgundy, reared him in his court. In 1464 Comines entered the service of Philip's son Charles the Bold, who became Duke of Burgundy in 1467. As Charles's chamberlain and councilor, he took an important part in the negotiations between the duke and King Louis XI when the latter was held prisoner at Pé-

Elected a bishop of his church in 1632, Comenius expressed his great interest in Christian unity and was conspicuous in the 17th century for his ecumenical beliefs. His development of a universal system of human knowledge among all men and nations, called pansophy, led to his being invited to England. From there he went to Sweden in 1642 and was employed in reforming the nation's school system. In 1650 he established a pansophic school in Hungary as a model for others, but conflicts caused his return to Leszno in 1655. After the sack of the city in 1656, he fled to Amsterdam, where he resided until his death on Nov. 4, 1670.

Further Reading

John Amos Comenius is listed in the European History study guide (V, C, 2) and the Social Sciences study guide (IV, C, 2). Jean Jacques ROUSSEAU, Johann PESTALOZZI, Friedrich FROEBEL, and Maria MONTESSORI shared his belief that the aim of education is the preparation of students for life.

In English, the best biography of Comenius is Matthew Spinka, *John Amos Comenius: That Incomparable Moravian* (1943). The earliest biography is S. S. Laurie, *John Amos Comenius, Bishop of the Moravians: His Life and Educational Works* (1881; new ed. 1892). Otakar Odloziik wrote a brief biographical sketch, *Jan Amos Komensky* (1942). Two books focus on his educational reforms: Will S. Monroe, *Comenius, and the Beginnings*

Philippe de Comines dedicates his Memoirs *to Louis XI in this early-16th-century miniature from the Mémoires de Philippe de Comines. (Giraudon)*

ronne in 1468, and in fact did much to save the King's life.

In 1472 Comines abandoned Charles the Bold to enter the service of Louis XI; he was soon made chamberlain and councilor and was given a generous pension and a confiscated property. In 1473 Louis arranged his marriage with Helen of Chambes, who brought him the lands of Argenton. Comines and the King were in harmony in effecting many a political ruse, but Comines did not approve of Louis's domestic abuses.

After the death of Louis in 1483, Comines engaged in subversive plots against Charles VIII and in 1488 was exiled to one of his own estates. Recalled in 1492, he cooperated with Charles's Italian expedition, even representing the King at the Treaty of Vercelli. After the death of Charles VIII in 1498, Comines received no appointments of importance; he died at Argenton in 1511.

The *Memoirs* of Comines, his only permanent contribution, covers the period from 1464 to 1498. This work is not filled with charming anecdotes but abounds in explanations of the deep-seated and secret causes of political events, and thus Comines is the first French writer to deserve the title of historian in the modern sense. The earlier French chroniclers were content to report events, but Comines was a penetrating observer and a specialist in the secrets of the human mind. He presented some theories that were influential in the 18th century. Both he and his contemporary Niccolò Machiavelli shared the hardheaded view that success alone matters; but, unlike Comines, Machiavelli did not pervert Providence to consecrate reprehensible acts.

Further Reading

Philippe de Comines is listed in the European History study guide (III, A, 1, b; III, A, 2, b) and the Social Sciences study guide (II, A, 5). His *Memoirs* contains striking portraits of CHARLES THE BOLD, LOUIS XI, and CHARLES VIII. His contemporary Niccolò MACHIAVELLI was also a noted historian.

The best French edition of Comines's *Memoirs* is that of Joseph Calmette and Georges Durville (3 vols., 1924–1925). A new translation undertaken by Isabelle Cazeaux, *The Memoirs of Philippe de Commynes*, edited by Samuel Kinser (vol. 1, 1969), promises to replace Sir Andrew Richard Scoble's translation of 1855–1856. The most useful monograph on Comines is in French: Gustave Charlier, *Commynes* (1945). An excellent background study is Joseph Calmette, *Golden Age of Burgundy* (1949; trans. 1963).

COMMONS / By Dwight W. Hoover

The American historian John Rogers Commons (1862–1945) pioneered the study of labor movements in the United States.

John Commons was born on Oct. 13, 1862, in Richmond, Ind. He was educated at Oberlin College and at Johns Hopkins, where he studied under Richard T. Ely. He sat in the same seminars with another fledgling historian, Frederick Jackson Turner. In 1890 Commons married and became an instructor at Wesleyan University. He returned to Oberlin in 1891 and taught at the University of Indiana the next year. He did not complete his doctorate.

Commons's first book, *Distribution of Wealth* (1894), was based on a Turnerian framework. Commons claimed that a turning point had been reached in the economic affairs of the United States because of the disappearance of easily available land. In 1896 Commons went to Syracuse University to fill a chair in sociology, and the following year he published *Proportional Representation*. This work reflected his belief in a democratic, voluntary society and in a system where balance was attained as a result of conflicting pressures.

In 1899 Commons lost his chair in sociology at Syracuse and worked for several nonacademic groups before going to the University of Wisconsin in 1904. The atmosphere was congenial there, as Commons shared faith in adult education and in the "Wisconsin idea"; that is, the state government would utilize the expertise of university professors in reforming and running this same government. His interest at this time had moved toward the study of labor movements. This culminated in two important books: *Trade Unions and Labor Unions* (1905) and his best-known work, *History of Labor in the*

John Commons. (University of Wisconsin)

United States (4 vols., 1918–1935). The latter was written in collaboration with his students. In his study of labor unions, Commons concluded that they had resulted as a reaction to industrial concentration and reflected an American attitude of job rather than class orientation.

Commons's ideas found expression in other books, the most important of which are *Legal Foundations of Capitalism* (1924) and *Institutional Economics* (1934). The former portrayed the law as a necessary link to hold society together; the latter held that unemployment was the greatest hazard of capitalism but that collective action could eliminate it. Historical development, Commons believed, came from the bottom up, and the function of scholars was to aid in the reconstruction of society in a classic, progressive way.

Commons died on May 11, 1945. He was acknowledged as the most significant labor historian of his day, and his ideas were perpetuated by his students, the best-known of whom was Selig Perlman at Columbia.

Further Reading

John Commons is listed in the American History study guide (IX, C, 3, a). Vernon PARRINGTON and Arthur M. SCHLESINGER were contemporary historians. Commons was influenced by Frederick Jackson TURNER.

Commons's autobiography, *Myself* (1934), while pessimistic, catches much of the flavor of the midwestern progressive's character. A discussion of economic ideas may be found in Allen G. Gruchy, *Modern Economic Thought: The American Contribution* (1947), and in volume 3 of Joseph Dorfman, *The Economic Mind in American Civilization* (1949). Commons's *Institutional Economics: Its Place in Political Economy* (1934) presents his mature economic views and contains a complete bibliography of his books and articles published after 1893.

COMPTON / By Roger H. Stuewer

The American physicist Arthur Holly Compton (1892–1962) discovered the "Compton effect" and the proof of the latitude intensity variation. He also played a critical role in the development of the atomic bomb.

Arthur Compton was born in Wooster, Ohio, on Sept. 10, 1892, the youngest child of Elias and Otelia Compton. It was midway during Arthur's early formal education that he became interested in science and carried out his first amateur researches. Although he wrote an intelligent student essay on the mammoth, it was chiefly astronomy and aviation that stimulated him. He purchased a telescope and photographed constellations and (in 1910) Halley's comet. Later he constructed and flew a 27-foot-wingspan glider.

Arthur Compton. (University of Chicago)

During his undergraduate years at the College of Wooster (1909–1913) Compton had to choose a profession. His father encouraged him to devote his life to science. On his graduation from Wooster, therefore, Arthur decided to pursue graduate study, obtaining his master's degree in physics from Princeton University in 1914; in 1916 he obtained his doctoral degree. Immediately after receiving his degree, Compton married Betty Charity McCloskey, a former Wooster classmate; the Comptons had two sons.

Compton Effect

Compton's first position was as an instructor in physics at the University of Minnesota (1916–1917), where he continued his x-ray researches. Leaving Minnesota, he became a research engineer at the newly established Westinghouse laboratory in East Pittsburgh, where he remained from 1917 to 1919, doing original work on the sodium-vapor lamp and developing instrumentation for aircraft. He left Westinghouse because he came to recognize that fundamentally his interest was not in industrial research but in pure research. In particular, he had become intrigued by a recent observation of the English physicist C. G. Barkla, who had scattered hard x-rays from aluminum and found that the total amount of scattered radiation was less than that predicted by a well-known formula of J. J. Thomson. Compton found that he could account for Barkla's observation by assuming that the electrons in the scatterer were very large and therefore diffracting the incident radiation.

Anxious to pursue these studies further, Compton applied for and received a National Research Council fellowship to work with perhaps the foremost experimentalist of the day, Ernest Rutherford, at the Cavendish Laboratory in England. Compton's year in the extremely stimulating intellectual atmosphere at the Cavendish, during which time he carried out gamma-ray scattering experiments and pondered his results, marked a turning point in his career, as he became convinced that he was on the track of a very fundamental physical phenomenon.

Desiring to pursue it further on his own, Compton returned to the United States in 1920 to accept the Wayman Crow professorship of physics at Washington University in St. Louis. There he scattered x-rays from various substances and, eventually, analyzed the scattered radiation by use of a Bragg spectrometer. By the fall of 1922 he had definite experimental proof that x-rays undergo a distinct change in wavelength when scattered, the exact amount depending only on the angle through which they are scattered. Compton published this conclusion in October 1922 and within 2 months correctly accounted for it theoretically. He assumed that an x-ray—a particle of radiation—collides with an electron in the scatterer, conserving both energy and momentum. This process has since become famous as the Compton effect, a discovery for which he was awarded the Nobel Prize of 1927. The historical significance of Compton's discovery was that it forced physicists for the first time to seriously cope with Einstein's long-neglected and revolutionary 1905 light-quantum hypothesis: in the Compton effect an x-ray behaves exactly like any other colliding particle.

Cosmic-ray Work

While the discovery of the Compton effect was undoubtedly Compton's single most important contribution to physics, he made many others, both earlier and later. He proved in 1922 that x-rays can be totally internally reflected from glass and silver mirrors, experiments which eventually led to precise values for the index of refraction and electronic populations of substances, as well as to a new and more precise value for the charge of the electron. After Compton left Washington University for the University of Chicago in 1923 (where he later became Charles H. Swift distinguished service professor in 1929 and chairman of the department of physics and dean of the physical sciences in 1940), he reactivated a very early interest and developed a diffraction method for determining electronic distributions in atoms. Still later he and J. C. Stearns proved that ferromagnetism cannot be due to the tilting of electronic orbital planes.

Perhaps the most important work Compton carried out after going to Chicago was his work on cosmic rays. Realizing the importance of these rays for cosmological theories, Compton developed a greatly improved detector and convinced the Carnegie Institution to fund a world survey between 1931 and 1934. The globe was divided into nine regions, and roughly 100 physicists divided into smaller groups sailed oceans, traversed continents, and scaled mountains, carrying identical detectors to measure cosmic-ray intensities.

The most significant conclusion drawn from Compton's world survey was that the intensity of cosmic rays at the surface of the earth steadily decreases as one goes from either pole to the Equator. This "latitude effect" had been noted earlier by the Dutch physicist J. Clay, but the evidence had not been conclusive. Compton's survey therefore proved that the earth's magnetic field deflects at least most of the incident cosmic rays, which is only possible if they are charged particles. Compton's world survey marked a turning point in knowledge of cosmic rays.

Atomic Bomb and Postwar Endeavors

When World War II broke out, Compton was called upon to assess the chances of producing an atomic bomb. If it were possible to develop an atomic bomb, Compton believed it should be the United States that had possession of it. Detailed calculations on nuclear fission processes proved that the possibility of developing this awesome weapon existed. Compton recommended production, and for 4 years thereafter, as director of the U.S. government's Plutonium Research Project, he devoted all of his administrative, scientific, and inspirational energies to make the bomb a reality.

Compton was under extraordinary pressure as he made arrangements for the purification of uranium and the production of plutonium and many other elements that went into the construction of the atomic bomb. Ultimately, Compton was asked for his personal opinion as to whether the bomb should be dropped on Hiroshima. He gave an affirmative response in the firm conviction that it was the only way to bring the war to a swift conclusion and thereby save many American and Japanese lives.

Between 1945 and 1953 Compton was chancellor of Washington University in St. Louis and strove unceasingly to make that institution a guiding light in higher education. Between 1954 and 1961, as distinguished service professor of natural philosophy, he taught, wrote, and delivered lectures to many groups and, as always, served on numerous boards and committees. In 1961 he became professor-at-large, intending to divide his time between Washington University, the University of California at Berkeley, and Wooster College. His plans were cut short by his sudden death on March 15, 1962, in Berkeley.

Compton was an extraordinarily gifted human being. At the age of 35 he won the Nobel Prize and was also elected to the National Academy of Sciences; later, he was elected to numerous other honorary societies, both foreign and domestic. He received a large number of honorary degrees, medals (including the U.S. government's Medal for Merit), and other honors. In spite of his many achievements and honors, however, he remained a modest and warm human being.

Further Reading

Arthur Compton is listed in the Science study guide (VII, C, 4). Enrico FERMI worked closely with him on the development of the atomic bomb.

The Cosmos of Arthur Holly Compton, edited by Marjorie Johnston (1968), contains Compton's "Personal Reminiscences," a selection of his writings on scientific and nonscientific subjects, and a bibliography of his scientific writings. Compton discusses his role in the development of the atomic bomb in *Atomic Quest* (1956). The early life of the Compton family is the subject of James R. Blackwood, *The House on College Avenue: The Comptons at Wooster, 1891–1913* (1968). General works on modern physics which discuss Compton include Gerald Holton and Duane H. D. Roller, *Foundations of Modern Physical Science* (1958); Henry A. Boorse and Lloyd Motz, eds., *The World of the Atom* (2 vols., 1966); and Ira M. Freeman, *Physics: Principles and Insights* (1968).

Anthony Comstock. (Library of Congress)

A. COMSTOCK / By Louis Filler

The American antivice crusader Anthony Comstock (1844–1915) fought what he personally defined as immoral and obscene acts and publications. Though his crusades were somewhat fanatic, he did help clarify issues in civil liberties relating to art and free speech.

Anthony Comstock was born in New Canaan, Conn., the son of a well-to-do farmer. It has been conjectured that his deep love of his mother, who died when he was 10 years old, contributed to his intense morality. The powerful, stocky young man went to work in a general store. During the Civil War he enlisted and served without incident; he was concerned about moral fitness while in the service.

After the war Comstock became a clerk but found no fit outlet for his energies until 1868. Then, having settled in New York and inspired by activities of the Young Men's Christian Association (YMCA), he secured the arrest of two purveyors of pornographic publications. One of them later attacked him with a bowie knife and inflicted a wound on his face, which Comstock hid under the whiskers that became his trademark.

In 1871 Comstock, with the aid of the YMCA, organized a committee to further his work. Two years later he conducted a successful campaign in Washington, D.C., for a strong Federal law (known popularly as the "Comstock Law") making illegal the transmission of obscene matter through the mails. He was appointed a postal inspector, serving without pay. In 1873 he organized the New York Society for the Prevention of Vice and made it a national symbol of tireless defense of traditional values.

In 1871 Comstock married Margaret Hamilton, a woman 10 years his senior. He was a dedicated husband and citizen. As an agent of the government and secretary of his society, Comstock was fearless and resourceful. He did patently useful work in tracking down, raiding, and prosecuting a wide variety of frauds who advertised false services, including abortions. In 1914 his annual report could note his arraignment over the years in state and Federal courts of some 3,697 persons, of whom 2,740 pleaded guilty or were convicted. Among these were a small number of persons of intelligence and moral fiber concerned for free speech or the right to disseminate knowledge respecting birth control.

But since Comstock's standards remained rigid, they became increasingly impractical. Thus in 1906 his attack, implemented by police, on the Art Students League of New York was not well regarded. Bernard Shaw's denunciation of "Comstockery" evoked considerable agreement. Comstock's 1913 crusade against an innocuous nude painting, Paul Chabas's *September Morn*, did nothing less than make it in reproduction a national sensation.

Comstock's last days were shadowed by reports that he was to lose his post as inspector and by his belief that he was the victim of a conspiracy. He died on Sept. 21, 1915.

Further Reading

Anthony Comstock is listed in the American History study guide (VII, G, 4, f). A woman's-rights leader of the period was Susan B. ANTHONY.

Anthony Comstock, *Traps for the Young* (1883), was edited, with an introduction, by Robert Bremmer in 1967. Charles Gallaudet Trumbull, *Anthony Comstock, Fighter* (1913), is a partisan account. Heywood Broun and Margaret Leech, *Anthony Comstock: Roundsman of the Lord* (1927), treats Comstock with sympathy and good humor.

H. COMSTOCK / By Herbert H. Lang

Henry Tompkins Paige Comstock (1820–1870) was a flamboyant American gold prospector whose name is attached to one of the world's most productive mining districts, the Comstock Lode.

Henry Comstock. (Dictionary of American Portraits, Dover)

Henry Comstock was born in Trenton, Ontario. From a difficult life on the American frontier he developed a rugged body, an independent spirit, an acquisitive nature, and a shrewd way of dealing. He also became a boaster, braggart, and bully.

Trapping for fur in Canada, Michigan, and Indiana, Comstock was later employed by the American Fur Company. After serving in the Black Hawk and the Mexican wars, he guided overland travelers and also engaged in business in Santa Fe and in Mexico.

Though Comstock was attracted back to the United States by the California gold rush, he returned to Mexico. In 1856 he appeared in Nevada tending a flock of sheep. He claimed 160 acres of unoccupied land for a ranch. Although he maintained good relations with the Paiute Indians, they were starving and decimated his flock.

In the late 1850s California prospectors began investigating the Nevada slopes of the Sierra range, locating numerous small but promising claims. Comstock joined them and helped organize the first mining district in the Washoe Valley. In 1859 two prospectors struck a particularly rich body of ore. Comstock appeared on the scene, blustering that the two had "jumped his claim." Although they knew that Comstock had neglected to perfect his claim, to quiet his rage they accepted him as a partner. None of the partners realized that an extremely valuable discovery had been made, a discovery now recognized as the beginning of the fabulous Comstock Lode. Unfortunately, none of the partners kept his claim long enough to greatly profit from it. Comstock sold his share to a California syndicate for $11,000—a fraction of its true worth. He remained in the area just long enough to see his name attached to a mining district he had neither discovered nor developed.

Unsuccessful at merchandising in Carson City, Comstock moved to the Pacific Northwest. He constructed a road in Oregon and prospected in Idaho and Montana. In 1870, after an expedition to the Big Horn Mountains, he returned to the Washoe Valley to testify in one of the numerous court suits over his old mine. On Sept. 27, 1870, during a period of mental depression, he took his own life near Bozeman, Mont.

Further Reading

Henry Comstock is listed in the American History study guide (VII, C, 3). Marcus DALY and Meyer GUGGENHEIM were notable in the gold and silver mining era.

There is no biography of Comstock. Sketches of his life may be found in Dan De Quille, *The Big Bonanza* (1876; enlarged ed. 1947); in Carl B. Glasscock, *The Big Bonanza: The Story of the Comstock Lode* (1931); and in George D. Lyman, *The Saga of the Comstock Lode: Boom Days in Virginia City, Nevada* (1957).

COMTE / By Raymond J. Langley

The French philosopher Auguste Comte (1798–1857) developed a system of positive

philosophy. He held that science and history culminate in a new science of humanity, to which he gave the name "sociology."

Born in Montpellier, Auguste Comte (pronounced kôNt) abandoned the devout Catholicism and royalism of his family while in his teens. He entered the École Polytechnique in 1814 and proved himself a brilliant mathematician and scientist. Comte was expelled in 1816 for participating in a student rebellion. Remaining in Paris, he managed to do immense research in mathematics, science, economics, history, and philosophy.

At 19 Comte met Henri de Rouvroy, Comte de Saint-Simon, and as a "spiritually adopted son," he became secretary and collaborator to the older man until 1824. The relationship between Saint-Simon and Comte grew increasingly strained for both theoretical and personal reasons and finally degenerated into an acrimonious break over disputed authorship. Saint-Simon was an intuitive thinker interested in immediate, albeit utopian, social reform. Comte was a scientific thinker, in the sense of systematically reviewing all available data, with a conviction that only after science was reorganized in its totality could men hope to resolve their social problems.

In 1824 Comte began a common-law marriage with Caroline Massin when she was threatened with arrest because of prostitution, and he later referred to this disastrous 18-year union as "the only error of my life." During this period Comte supported himself as a tutor. In 1826 he proposed to offer a series of 72 lectures on his philosophy to a subscription list of distinguished intellectuals. After the third lecture Comte suffered a complete breakdown, replete with psychotic episodes. At his mother's insistence he was remarried in a religious ceremony and signed the contract "Brutus Napoleon Comte." Despite periodic hospitalization for mental illness during the following 15 years, Comte was able to discipline himself to produce his major work, the six-volume *Course of Positive Philosophy* (1830–1842).

Positivist Thought

Positivism as a term is usually understood as a particular way of thinking. For Comte, additionally, the methodology is a product of a systematic reclassification of the sciences and a general conception of the development of man in history: the law of the three stages. Comte, like the Marquis de Condorcet whom he acknowledged as a predecessor and G. W. F. Hegel whom he met in Paris, was convinced that no data can be adequately understood except in the historical context. Phenomena are intelligible only in terms of their origin, function, and significance in the relative course of human history.

But unlike Hegel, Comte held that there is no *Geist*, or spirit, above and beyond history which objectifies itself through the vagaries of time. Comte represents a radical relativism: "Everything is relative; there is the only absolute thing." Positivism absolutizes relativity as a principle which makes all previous ideas and systems a result of historical conditions. The only unity that the system of positivism affords in its pronounced antimetaphysical bias is the inherent order of human thought. Thus the law of the three stages, which he discovered as early as 1820, attempts to show that the history of the human mind and the development of the sciences follow a determinant pattern which parallels the growth of social and political institutions. According to Comte, the system of positivism is grounded on the natural and historical law that "by the very nature of the human mind, every branch of our knowledge is necessarily obliged to pass successively in its course through three different theoretical states: the theological or fictitious state; the metaphysical or abstract state; finally, the scientific or positive state."

These stages represent different and opposed types of human conception. The most primitive type is theological thinking, which rests on the "empathetic fallacy" of reading subjective experience into the operations of nature. The theological perspective develops dialectically through fetishism, polytheism, and monotheism as events are understood as animated by their own will, that of several deities, or the decree of one supreme being. Politically the theological state provides stability under kings imbued with divine rights and supported by military power. As civilization progresses, the metaphysical stage begins as a criticism of these conceptions in the name of a new order. Supernatural entities are gradually

Auguste Comte. (Radio Times Hulton Picture Library)

transformed into abstract forces just as political rights are codified into systems of law. In the final stage of positive science the search for absolute knowledge is abandoned in favor of a modest but precise inquiry into the relative laws of nature. The absolutist and feudal social orders are replaced gradually by increasing social progress achieved through the application of scientific knowledge.

From this survey of the development of humanity Comte was able to generalize a specific positive methodology. Like René Descartes, Comte acknowledged a unity of the sciences. It was, however, not that of a univocal method of thinking but the successive development of man's ability to deal with the complexities of experience. Each science possesses a specific mode of inquiry. Mathematics and astronomy were sciences that men developed early because of their simplicity, generality, and abstractness. But observation and the framing of hypotheses had to be expanded through the method of experimentation in order to deal with the physical sciences of physics, chemistry, and biology. A comparative method is required also to study the natural sciences, man, and social institutions. Thus even the history of science and methodology supports the law of the three stages by revealing a hierarchy of sciences and methodological direction from general to particular, and simple to complex. Sociology studies particular societies in a complex way since man is both the subject and the object of this discipline. One can consider social groups from the standpoint of "social statics," which comprises the elements of cohesion and order such as family and institutions, or from the perspective of "social dynamics," which analyzes the stage of continuous development that a given society has achieved.

Later Years

By 1842 Comte's marriage had dissolved, and he was supported by contributions from various intellectuals, including the English philosopher J. S. Mill. In 1844 he met Clothilde de Vaux, and they fell deeply in love. Although the affair was never consummated because Madame de Vaux died in the next year, this intense love influenced Comte in his later work toward a new religion of humanity. He proposed replacing priests with a new class of scientists and industrialists and offered a catechism based on the cult of reason and humanity, and a new calendar replete with positivist saints. While this line of thought was implicit in the aim of sociology to synthesize order and progress in the service of humanity, the farcical elements of Comte's mysticism has damaged his philosophical reputation. He died in obscurity in 1857.

Further Reading

Auguste Comte is listed in the Philosophy study guide (VI, F and H) and the Social Sciences study guide (VI, D, 2). Associated with the Comte de SAINT-SIMON, he was influenced by the Marquis de CONDORCET.

Comte's various writings have never been gathered into a critical edition. But Comte personally approved of Harriet Martineau's English redaction of the six volumes

of his main work into *The Positive Philosophy of Auguste Comte* (3 vols., 1896). Secondary studies of Comte include J. S. Mill, *Auguste Comte and Positivism* (2d ed. rev. 1866; 5th ed. 1907); L. Lévy-Bruhl, *The Philosophy of Auguste Comte* (trans. 1903); and a chapter in Frank E. Manuel, *The Prophets of Paris* (1962). For Comte's relationship with Saint-Simon see Manuel's *The New World of Henri Saint-Simon* (1956); and for his relation to the history of positivism see Leszek Kolakowski, *The Alienation of Reason* (trans. 1968). Also useful are the two works of Richmond Laurin Hawkins, *Auguste Comte and the United States, 1816–1853* (1936) and *Positivism in the United States, 1853–1861* (1938), and F. S. Marvin, *Comte: The Founder of Sociology* (1936).

✳   ✳   ✳

CONANT / By Jurgen Herbst

James Bryant Conant (born 1893) was an American chemist, president of Harvard University, and educational critic. He was an effective spokesman for the support of national policies by private and public scientific and educational institutions.

James Conant was born on March 26, 1893, in Dorchester, Mass. Both his father's and his mother's families trace themselves back to 17th-century New England settlers. After graduating *magna cum*

James B. Conant, a charcoal drawing by Enit Kaufman. (Courtesy of The New-York Historical Society, New York City)

laude from Harvard College in 1914, Conant pursued graduate studies in organic chemistry and received his doctorate in 1916. During the next 3 years he served as instructor at Harvard, tried unsuccessfully to set up a private chemistry laboratory, and joined the Army's Chemical Warfare Service. Engaged in the secret production of poison gases, Conant advanced to the rank of major, belonging to the elite group of organic chemists who constituted the nucleus of a growing profession in universities, industry, foundations, and the armed forces.

Returning to Harvard, Conant was appointed assistant professor in 1919, associate professor in 1925, and professor in 1927. He served as chairman of the Division of Chemistry, as consultant to the Du Pont Company, and on the Board of Scientific Advisers of the Rockefeller Institute for Medical Research. In 1933 he became president of Harvard University. Following the policies of Harvard's recent presidents, Conant placed heavy emphasis on bringing talented students and faculty to Harvard. He devised interdisciplinary studies in American civilization and the history of science to improve the liberal education of the undergraduates. He sought to strengthen the graduate school of education by introducing the master of arts in teaching program.

In 1934 Conant joined the Board of Trustees of the Carnegie Foundation for the Advancement of Teaching. During World War II he directed the resources of Harvard in support of the war effort, and he himself became an adviser to the Manhattan Project, which produced the first atomic bomb. He was a member of the General Advisory Committee of the Atomic Energy Commission from 1947 to 1952 and, after his retirement from Harvard in 1953, ambassador to West Germany. From 1957 to 1959 he undertook a study of American secondary education for the Carnegie Foundation and thereafter served in various roles as educational consultant.

Further Reading

James Conant is listed in the Social Sciences study guide (VII, G, 3). John DEWEY and Robert M. HUTCHINS were also renowned educators.

Conant's educational views are contained in the series of books he wrote on secondary education: *The American High School Today* (1959); *The Child, the Parent and the State* (1959); *Slums and Suburbs: A Commentary on Schools in Metropolitan Areas* (1961); and *The Comprehensive High School* (1967). In *On Understanding Science: An Historical Approach* (1947) Conant wrote on the place of science in the general education curriculum of the undergraduate, and in *The Education of American Teachers* (1963) he discussed teacher education.

A more personal account is Conant's autobiography, *My Several Lives: Memoirs of a Social Inventor* (1970). Paul Franklin Douglass, *Six upon the World: Toward an American Culture for an Industrial Age* (1954), examines Conant's achievements in the context of the postwar technological society. See also Lawrence A. Cremin, *The Transformation of the School: Progressivism in American Education, 1876–1957* (1961); Edgar Z. Frie-

denberg, *The Dignity of Youth and Other Atavisms* (1965), which has a chapter critical of Conant; Adolphe E. Meyer, *An Educational History of the American People* (1967); and Robert E. Potter, *The Stream of American Education* (1967).

CONDÉ / By Philip Dawson

The French general Louis de Bourbon, Prince de Condé (1621–1686), became known as the "great Condé" because of his victories in the Low Countries. As the principal French nobleman, he was important in politics but egotistical, imprudent, and stubborn.

Louis de Bourbon was born in Paris on Sept. 8, 1621, to Henri de Bourbon, Prince de Condé (pronounced kôN-dā′), second cousin of Louis XIII, and Charlotte de Montmorency. He was entitled Duc d'Enghien until his father's death in 1646. From 1630 to 1636 he attended the Jesuit school in Bourges, studying Latin classics, Aristotelian philosophy, mathematics, the *Institutes* of Justinian, and political history. He retained intellectual tastes all his life and was long a freethinker on religious matters. His education was completed at the royal military school in Paris.

In accordance with his father's wishes, in 1641 En-

The Prince de Condé. (French Embassy Press and Information Division)

ghien married Claire-Clémence de Maillé-Brézé, daughter of Cardinal Richelieu's younger sister. He lived with his wife infrequently for brief periods. They had a son in late 1643 and a daughter in 1656.

Enghien's military ability was discernible in his first three campaigns (1640–1642). In the spring of 1643 he was put in command of the army in Picardy, and on May 18 he won an overwhelming victory at Rocroy northwest of Sedan. His cavalry turned the flank of the Flemish cavalry and scattered the enemy's rear regiments; he rallied the French infantry and finally overcame the immobile firepower of the veteran Spanish infantry, then the most feared in Europe.

Other victories followed. With his cousin the Vicomte de Turenne, Enghien took the west bank of the Rhine in 1644 and defeated the Bavarian army in 1645. He captured Dunkerque and other northern towns in 1646. Commanding the French forces in Spain in 1647, Condé was unable to take Lerida in Catalonia. But in 1648 he returned north to Hainaut and routed the cavalry of Lorraine and the Spanish infantry at Lens on August 20, a victory that finally brought about the Treaty of Münster.

In the ensuing period of sporadic revolt in France, Louis, now Prince de Condé, aided the queen regent and Cardinal Mazarin by organizing a blockade around rebellious Paris in early 1649. But the queen regent eventually found Condé intolerable and had him arrested with his brother and brother-in-law on Jan. 18, 1650. Finally a realignment of factions in Paris persuaded Mazarin that the princes were more dangerous in prison than at large. He freed them on Feb. 13, 1651. Yet Condé was increasingly dissatisfied.

In September, Condé went to Bordeaux to organize an independent base in the southwest. In 1652, his position there crumbling, he returned to Paris but found his forces locked out of the city. Turenne, now in command of a royal army, tried to pin Condé against the eastern walls of Paris on July 2, 1652. Condé's forces were suddenly let into the city, and cannon were fired from the Bastille on Turenne's troops. Condé's popularity in Paris, however, rapidly declined. He soon departed northward, was named commanding general for Spain, and proceeded to Brussels in March 1653.

While Condé opposed Turenne in a series of inconclusive campaigns in the Low Countries, one of Condé's agents attempted to establish friendly relations with Oliver Cromwell in England. But Cromwell formed an alliance instead with the French king, and in 1658 the allies defeated Condé decisively in the Battle of the Dunes outside Dunkerque. The Spanish negotiators made amnesty for Condé a condition of the peace settlement of 1659 and he returned to France. In 1667 he was again given command of a French army. During February 1668 he captured all the principal towns of Franche-Comté. The province was restored to Spain 3 months later.

In the summer of 1673 the young stadtholder William III was eager to use the imperial, Spanish, and Dutch armies against Condé. On Aug. 11, 1674, they fought an all-day battle near Seneffe south of Brussels, with heavy losses on both sides but no victor.

After 1675 Condé lived at Chantilly. He was reconverted to Catholicism the year before his death in 1686.

Further Reading

The Prince de Condé is listed in the European History study guide (V, B, 1, b). He served under LOUIS XIV. Condé patronized literary and scholarly pursuits and associated with Jacques BOSSUET, Jean de LA BRUYÉRE, Nicolas MALEBRANCHE, MOLIÈRE, Jean RACINE, and Baruch SPINOZA.

The most extensive work on Condé is by King Louis Philippe's second son, Henri d'Orléans, Duc d'Aumale, *Histoire des princes de Condé pendant les XVI et XVII siècles*, vols. 3–7 (1863–1896). It includes hundreds of letters from, to, and about Condé and is generally sympathetic. Material on Condé is also in John B. Wolf, *Louis XV* (1968).

CONDILLAC
By James Dickoff and Patricia James

The French philosopher and educator Étienne Bonnot de Condillac (1715–1780) was a Lockean psychologist and early positivist who greatly influenced economic and political thought in prerevolutionary France.

On Sept. 30, 1715, Étienne Bonnot was born to Gabriel Bonnot, Vicomte de Mably. He later became the Abbé de Condillac (pronounced kôN-dē-yàk′), a territory purchased by his father in 1720. Educated in Paris at the Sorbonne and at St-Suplice, he was ordained a priest in 1740 but chose to become a writer and a tutor. From 1740 to 1758 he frequented the literary salons of Paris and worked at his own education. John Locke's psychology and empiricism and Sir Isaac Newton's search for fundamental principles were strong influences in his reading.

Condillac's *Essai sur l'origine des connaissances humaines* (1746) followed Locke's principles but reduced the operations of human understanding to one principle —sensation—and treated reflection as a sequence and comparison of sensations. The work stated language to be the source of man's superiority to animals and recognized interest as an intimate part of any perception. *Traité des systèmes* (1749) was a study on proper method and the proper use of hypothesis and system.

In the *Traité des sensations* (1754) Condillac showed how ideas originate through sensation. The work stressed the integration of man's senses and stated that the higher forms of understanding develop from mere animal sensation because of man's needs. Condillac's *Traité des animaux* (1755) opposed Buffon's and Descartes's view of animals by declaring that man is like the animals, although more complex because of his more nu-

Étienne Bonnot de Condillac. (Photo-Hachette)

thought in relation to early-20th-century psychology. A less readable but still useful work is Isabel F. Knight, *The Geometric Spirit: The Abbé de Condillac and the French Enlightenment* (1968).

✳   ✳   ✳

CONDORCET / By Paul G. Dobson

The French thinker Marie Jean Antoine Nicolas Caritat, Marquis de Condorcet (1743–1794), expressed the spirit of the Enlightenment in reform proposals and writings on progress. He was the only philosophe to participate in the French Revolution.

Born in Ribemont in Picardy on Sept. 17, 1743, the Marquis de Condorcet (pronounced kôN-dôr-sā′) was educated at the Jesuit college in Reims and later at the College of Navarre in Paris. He excelled in mathematics and in 1765 wrote the *Essay on Integral Calculus.* In 1769 he became a member of the Academy of Science, later becoming its perpetual secretary, and in 1782 was elected to the French Academy. He married Sophie de Grouchy in 1786, and their home became one of the famous salons of the period.

Prior to the French Revolution, Condorcet wrote biographies of A. R. J. Turgot and Voltaire and essays on

merous needs, and that neither man nor animal is mere machine.

In 1758 Condillac went to Parma for 9 years to tutor Louis XV's grandson, Ferdinand de Parma. During this time he composed a 16-volume *Cours d'études pour l'instruction du Prince de Parme.* Opposition from the bishop of Parma delayed publication until 1775, when the volumes appeared in France, under the relaxed censorship of the Turgot ministry.

On returning to France in 1767, Condillac declined an offer to tutor the Dauphin's sons and retired instead to a quiet life of writing at Flux. His 1776 work, *Le Commerce et le gouvernement considerés relativement l'un à l'autre,* considered the consequences of his basic psychological ideas in relation to political economy. Asked to compose an elementary logic for Palatinate schools, Condillac finished *La Logique* in 1779. He died from a fever on Aug. 2, 1780. His unfinished *Langage des calculs* was published posthumously.

In his opposition to obscurantist metaphysics Condillac was an early positivist. He insisted that, although man is ignorant of the thing-in-itself, he need not be in error if he will use a language of analysis, observation with thoroughness, and systems with circumspection.

Further Reading

Étienne Bonnot de Condillac is listed in the Philosophy study guide (V, B, 1) and the Social Sciences study guide (V, C, 2). John LOCKE strongly influenced his thought.

The best introduction to Condillac in English is *Condillac's Treatise on the Sensations,* translated by Geraldine Carr (1930). Zora Schaupp, *The Naturalism of Condillac* (1926), is a fine introduction to Condillac's

The Marquis de Condorcet. (Library of Congress)

the application of the theory of probabilities to popular voting, on the American Revolution and the Constitutional Convention, and on the abolition of the slave trade and slavery. In 1791 he was elected to the Legislative Assembly and later to the National Convention, where he continued to manifest his liberal and egalitarian sentiments.

In the report of the Committee on Public Education, Condorcet advocated universal primary school education and the establishment of a self-regulating educational system under the control of a National Society of Sciences and Arts to protect education from political pressures. However, the Legislative Assembly was hostile to all autonomous corporate structures and ignored Condorcet's plan. His proposal for a new constitution, establishing universal male suffrage, proportional representation, and local self-government, was similarly set aside by the Jacobin-dominated National Convention, which considered it too moderate.

Condorcet's moderate democratic leanings and his vote against the death penalty for Louis XVI led to his being outlawed by the Jacobin government on July 8, 1793. He went into hiding in the home of a close friend, Madame Varnet, where he wrote the *Sketch of an Historical Picture of the Progress of the Human Mind*, his most famous and most optimistic work. This capsulized history of progress presented a set of intellectual and moral goals toward which men ought to work, and it was based on the utilitarian conviction that invention and progressive thought arise out of social need. According to Condorcet, the future progress of reason had become inevitable with the invention of the printing press and the advances in science and criticism. Rather than emphasizing the role of the solitary genius as the agent of progress, the *Sketch* stressed the dissemination of useful knowledge among the masses.

After 8 months of hiding, Condorcet fled Paris but was arrested on March 27, 1794, and imprisoned in Bourg-la-Reine. On March 29 he was found dead in his cell. His identity was unknown, and it is ironic that this critic of classical education was eventually identified by a copy of Horace's *Epistles* that he had been carrying at the time of his arrest.

Further Reading

The Marquis de Condorcet is listed in the European History study guide (VI, B, 3; VII, B, 2) and the Social Sciences study guide (VI, C, 2). Other outstanding *philosophes* were Denis DIDEROT, Jean Jacques ROUSSEAU, and VOLTAIRE.

The best biography of Condorcet is Jacob Salwyn Schapiro, *Condorcet and the Rise of Liberalism* (1934; new ed. 1962). There is an excellent analysis of Condorcet's philosophy in Frank Edward Manuel, *The Prophets of Paris* (1962). Ann Elizabeth Burlingame, *Condorcet: The Torch Bearer of the French Revolution* (1930), is still useful.

CONFUCIUS / By David R. Knechtges

The Chinese teacher and philosopher Confucius (551–479 B.C.) was the founder of the humanistic school of philosophy known as the Ju or Confucianism, which taught the concepts of benevolence, ritual, and propriety.

In the 6th century B.C. China had begun to disintegrate into a loose confederation of city-states. The nominal ruler of China was the King of Chou, who occupied the imperial capital at Loyang in north-central China. The Chou had been the supreme rulers of the entire Chinese Empire 500 years earlier, but now they were simply a pawn of the competing Chinese states. This period is generally depicted as a time of great moral decline, when principles and integrity meant little to the official classes.

Confucius (pronounced kən-fyōō'shəs), an obscure school teacher, found this situation horrifying, and he attempted to seek a remedy by reviving the great moral teachings of the sages of the past. That he failed is unimportant, for his teachings had a profound influence on later Chinese thought and formed the basis for the dominant Chinese ideology, known as Confucianism.

Traditions and Sources on His Life

Confucius is the Latinized name of K'ung Fu-tzu (Great Master K'ung). His original name was K'ung Ch'iu; he is also known by the style name of K'ung Chung-ni. After he died, a large number of myths and legends grew up around his name, making difficult an accurate description of the historical Confucius. Traditionally, Confucius was venerated as a Chinese saint, and for a long time a critical, objective appraisal of his life was impossible. In more recent times both Chinese and Western scholars have ventured to discard some of the legends and myths and to reconstruct a biography from more reliable sources. As a result, a variety of new images of Confucius have emerged, many of them contradicting each other, and the demythologized picture of Confucius is as confusing as the traditional, mythical one.

The most detailed traditional account of Confucius' life is contained in the *Records of the Historian* (*Shih chi*) by Ssu-ma Ch'ien, who lived 145–86 B.C. Many modern scholars have dismissed this biography as a fictionalized, romanticized legend by a Confucian apologist. Nevertheless, in spite of obvious anachronisms, when used with the *Analects* (*Lun yü*), which purports to record actual conversations between Confucius and his disciples, one can reconstruct a satisfactory outline of the philosopher's family background, his career, and the role he played in 6th-century society.

According to the *Records of the Historian*, Confucius was a descendant of a branch of the royal house of Shang, the dynasty that ruled China prior to the Chou. His family, the K'ung, had moved to the small state of Lu, located in the modern province of Shantung in

A Confucian, a Buddhist, and a Taoist discuss the three "ways." (Chinese Classic Art Publishing House, Peking)

northeastern China. There is an early tradition that Confucius' father at an advanced age divorced his first wife because she had borne him only daughters and one deformed son and married a 15-year-old girl from the Yen clan, who gave birth to K'ung Ch'iu. Ssu-ma Ch'ien refers to the relationship as a "wild union," which very possibly indicates that Confucius was an illegitimate child.

Confucius' birth date is given in early sources as either 551 or 552, although the former is more commonly accepted. The exact status of his family at the time of his birth is obscured by later attempts to create for him an illustrious lineage. In the *Analects*, Confucius says that during his youth he was in humble circumstances and forced to acquire many different skills. It is clear that even though the fortunes of his family had declined, he was no commoner. Confucius unquestionably belonged to the aristocratic class known as the *shih*. By the time of Confucius most *shih* served as court officials, scholars, and teachers, and Confucius' first occupation appears to have been as keeper of the Lu granary and later as supervisor of the fields, both low positions but consistent with his *shih* status.

Career as a Teacher

We do not know exactly when Confucius embarked on his teaching career, but it does not appear to have been much before the age of 30. In 518 he may have served as tutor to one of the prominent clans of Lu, the Meng, who wished their sons to be educated in the *li*, or ritual. He is alleged to have journeyed to Loyang that year to instruct himself in the traditional Chou ritual. Here he is said to have met the famous Taoist teacher Lao Tzu, who reportedly bluntly rebuked Confucius for his stuffiness and arrogance. This story is undoubtedly apocryphal and belongs to the corpus of anti-Confucian lore circulated by the Taoist school.

The nominal head of state in Lu at this time was a duke (*kung*), but the actual power lay in the hands of three clans: the Meng, Shu, and Chi. The most powerful of the three in Confucius' time was the Chi, which was frequently in conflict with the ducal house and the other clans. In 517 Duke Chao of Lu took prisoner the prime minister, Chi P'ing-tzu, and was immediately attacked by the other two clans. The duke fled to the neighboring state of Ch'i. Confucius apparently felt a certain loyalty to the duke and fled with him. There are a number of stories about Confucius' adventures in Ch'i, but most of them appear spurious.

Confucius eventually returned to Lu; one suggested date is 515. For several years after his return he does not appear to have accepted a governmental position and instead spent most of his time studying and teaching. He

Confucius advocated moderation in all things. In this work, by the 17th-century Japanese artist Kano Sansetsu, the Chinese sage demonstrates that the vases of his apparatus remain upright and stable if moderately filled but that they become unsteady and may overturn if filled too full. Confucian ideals were influential in Japan during the Tokugawa period. (Courtesy, Museum of Fine Arts, Boston)

gathered around him a large number of students. Although we can only guess at the exact curriculum of the school, it undoubtedly included instruction in ritual, music, history, and poetry.

In 510 Duke Chao died without ever having returned to Lu, and the Chi clan set up another member of the ducal house as Duke Ting. Shortly thereafter, in 505, a swashbuckling adventurer named Yang Hu, who had been a supporter of the Chi family, rebelled and seized power in Lu.

The clans were able to gather enough strength to expel Yang Hu from Lu in 501, but at the same time another military commander, Kung-shan Fu-jao, gained control of the fortified city of Pi, which was the fief of the Chi clan. Kung-shan Fu-jao issued an invitation to Confucius to join his government. The *Analects* records that Confucius was tempted to accept the offer, and only after being rebuked by his disciple Tzu-lu, who was in the employ of the Chi clan, did the master reluctantly decline. The decision to violate his own principles and serve a man in open revolt against the constituted authority of his state is a good indication of Confucius' intense desire to obtain a position, no matter how compromising, from which to implement his ideas.

Political Career

Confucius finally did obtain the post he wanted in 501, this time with the legitimate government of Lu. He first served as magistrate of the city of Chang-tu and later was promoted to the important position of minister of justice (*ssu-k'ou*). There are a number of stories about Confucius' actions in this office, most of which cannot be verified. One of these stories concerns Confucius' role at the Chia-ku convention in the state of Ch'i, a meeting be-

tween the dukes of Ch'i and Lu in 500. At least five sources record that Confucius was responsible for thwarting a plot by Ch'i to kidnap the Duke of Lu and was able to force Ch'i to restore territory it had seized from Lu. Scholars have questioned the historicity of Confucius' participation in this event, but the wide currency of the account must indicate some grain of truth.

Confucius probably owed his position in Lu to the influence of the Chi family, which was still the dominant power. We know from the *Analects* that he was on especially good terms with Chi K'ang-tzu, the son of the head of the Chi clan. Several of Confucius' disciples were employed by the Chi family. Because of his close association with the Chi clan, which in effect was a usurper of the ducal power, it might be supposed that Confucius had compromised his integrity. However, Confucius and his disciples actually seem to have worked to reduce the power of the three clans. For example, in 498 they were able to extract promises from the Chi, Meng, and Shu families to demolish their fortified cities, which were their bases of power. The Chi and Shu actually had begun preparations to dismantle their cities when the Meng reneged and the plan was abandoned. Nevertheless, the episode is a clear example of Confucius' interest in restoring legitimacy in Lu.

His Travels

It must have been shortly after the failure of his plan to dismantle the fortified cities that Confucius decided to leave his home in Lu and embark on a long journey throughout eastern China. The traditional explanation for Confucius' decision to leave is that Ch'i believed that if Confucius continued to advise the Duke of Lu, Lu would become more powerful and eventually dominate the other states around it. Therefore, in order to distract the duke from his political duties, Ch'i sent him 80 beautiful dancers and 30 teams of horses. The duke accepted them and became so engrossed that he did not hold court for 3 days, which so incensed Confucius that he resigned his post. This story clearly is a fabrication designed to disguise a less noble motive for Confucius' departure, namely, pressure from the clans, who must have been alarmed by Confucius' attempt to reduce their power.

Confucius left Lu accompanied by several of his disciples, including the former soldier Chung Yu (Tzu-lu) and Yen Hui, his favorite. They wandered throughout the eastern states of Wei, Sung, and Ch'en and at various times had their lives threatened. Confucius was almost assassinated in Sung by one Huan T'ui. On another occasion he was mistaken for the adventurer Yang Hu and was arrested and held in confinement until his true identity became known.

Confucius was received with great respect by the rulers of the states he visited, and he even seems to have received occasional emoluments. He spent much of his time developing and expounding his ideas on the art of government, as well as continuing his teaching. He acquired a large following, and the solidification of the Confucian school probably occurred during these years of exile. Not all of his disciples followed him on his travels, and several of them actually returned to Lu and assumed positions with the Chi clan. It may have been through their influence that in 484 Confucius was invited back to Lu.

Final Years

Confucius was warmly received in Lu, but there is no indication that he was given a responsible position. Little is known about his last years, although this would have been a logical time for him to work on the many texts and documents he is reputed to have acquired on his journey. Much of his time was devoted to teaching, and he seems to have remained more or less aloof from political affairs.

This was an unhappy period for Confucius. His only son died about this time; his favorite disciple, Yen Hui, died the very year of his return to Lu; and in 480 Tzu-lu was killed in battle. All these losses Confucius felt deeply, and his despair and frustration must have been intensified by the realization that his political ideas had found no sympathetic ear among the rulers of his own state. Confucius died in 479. His disciples conducted his funeral and observed a mourning period for him.

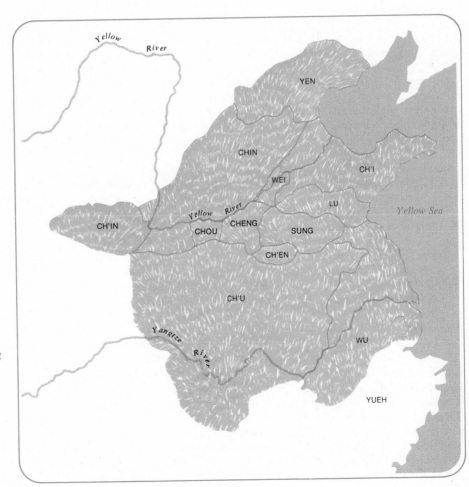

China in the 6th century B.C. China in Confucius' time was a loose confederation of warring states whose rulers were often corrupt and tyrannical. Confucius taught a system of morality, for ruler and ruled alike, that would secure peace and just government.

Confucius' Writings

Confucius has been considered responsible for editing and writing some of the most important works in the Chinese tradition. According to relatively early sources, he arranged the classical anthology of early Chinese poetry, the *Book of Odes* (*Shih ching*), into its present order and discarded spurious material from a historical work known as the *Book of Documents* (*Shu ching*). He is also credited with writing parts of the great divination classic, the *Book of Changes* (*I ching*), and the book of ritual, the *Records of Rites* (*Li chi*). His name is also associated with a work on music, the *Book of Music* (*Yüeh ching*), which is now lost. Few modern scholars accept any of these traditional attributions, and Confucius' connection with these books is simply another aspect of the traditional Confucian myth.

One work that cannot be dismissed so easily, however, is the *Spring and Autumn Annals* (*Ch'un ch'iu*), which is a chronological record of the reigns of the 12 dukes of Lu, beginning with the year 722 and ending in 479 B.C. As early as the philosopher Mencius (ca. 317–289 B.C.), Confucius has been credited with compiling or editing this work, which was claimed to contain hidden criticisms of many of the Lu rulers. Later Confucian scholars tried to discover these hidden criticisms, but most scholars now agree that the *Spring and Autumn Annals* is simply a dry chronicle, containing no hidden meanings, and in spite of Mencius's testimony, Confucius had nothing to do with it.

Confucius' Teachings

Although we cannot be certain that Confucius wrote any of the works attributed to him, it is still possible to know something about the general nature of his philosophy. Shortly after his death his disciples compiled a work known as the *Lun yü*, commonly translated as the *Analects* but more accurately rendered as the *Edited Conversations*. This work consists of conversations between Confucius, his students, and an occasional ruler.

The primary emphasis of the *Lun yü* is on political philosophy. Confucius was concerned about the rampant immorality and amorality of much of the government of his time, and he spent much of his life trying to find a ruler who would accept his teaching that ethical considerations should be the guiding principle of government. Confucius taught that the primary task of the ruler was to achieve the welfare and happiness of the people of his state. To accomplish this aim, the ruler had first to set a moral example by his own conduct, and this example would in turn influence the people's behavior. Confucius rejected the use of a rigid legal system and believed instead that moral custom and voluntary compliance were the best ways of maintaining order in society.

Confucius considered the early years of the Chou dynasty as the embodiment of the perfect form of government. It was not the rulers of this period that he admired so much as the chief minister, Chou Tan, or the Duke of Chou. The Duke of Chou was known in early Chinese tradition as the founder of the state of Lu, and he was probably the chief culture hero in this state. Because Confucius came from Lu, some scholars have claimed that much of Confucius' teachings were simply a revival of this cult. It is certainly true that Confucius himself never claimed to be teaching original ideas but rather termed himself a "transmitter."

Nevertheless, Confucius is the first Chinese thinker to introduce concepts that became fundamental not only to Confucian philosophy but to Chinese philosophy in general. The most important of these are *jen* (benevolence), *yi* (propriety), and *li* (ritual). Confucius believed that the *chün-tzu*, or "gentleman," must set the moral example for others in society to follow. The word *chün-tzu* originally meant "ruler's son," but in the *Lun yü* it refers to the educated "man of virtue," who was not necessarily an aristocrat. The *chün-tzu* was expected to follow a set of ethical principles, of which *jen*, *yi*, and *li* were the most important. *Jen* meant in the *Lun yü* what has been translated as humaneness or benevolence, a quality a *chün-tzu* should cultivate and, once acquired, attempt to transfer to others. *Li* was considered the rules of decorum and ritual that were observed in religious and nonreligious ceremonies and, as applied to the *chün-tzu*, composed his rules of behavior. According to the *Lun yü*, it was through a knowledge of the *li* that *yi*, or propriety, could be attained. *Yi* represents what is right and proper in a given situation, and the *chün-tzu*, by observing the ritual and because of his inclination toward goodness, always knows what is right.

Confucius was basically a humanist and one of the greatest teachers in Chinese history. His influence on his immediate disciples was profound, and they continued to expound his theories until, in the first Han dynasty (206 B.C.–A.D. 8), they became the basis of the state ideology.

Further Reading

Confucius is listed in the Asia study guide (III, A, 3, b). One of his most important disciples was MENCIUS. A different philosophy was espoused by the founder of Taoism, LAO TZU.

The *Lun yü* has been translated many times. There are two acceptable translations: James Legge, *Confucian Analects* (1861), and Arthur Waley, *The Analects of Confucius* (1938).

Because of the nature of the sources, there is no definitive account of Confucius' life. Herrlee Glessner Creel, *Confucius the Man and the Myth* (1949; republished as *Confucius and the Chinese Way*, 1960), is an attempt to discard the Confucian myth and write a biography based on historical material. Creel concludes that Confucius was basically a democrat and revolutionary. At the other extreme is Wu-chi Liu, *Confucius: His Life and Times* (1955), which accepts almost all of the legends rejected by Creel. It is a good example of the traditional Chinese approach to Confucius. A good balance between these two works is Shigeki Kaizuka, *Confucius,* translated from the Japanese by Geoffrey Bownas (1956). Kaizuka critically examines the apocryphal stories but does not dismiss them as readily as Creel.

The significance of Confucius for Chinese thought and society can be studied in any history of Chinese civilization. The best of these are C. P. Fitzgerald, *China: A Short Cultural History* (1938) and *The Horizon History of China* (1969); William Theodore de Bary and others, eds., *Sources of Chinese Tradition* (1960); and Wing-Tsit Chan, *A Source Book in Chinese Philosophy* (1963).

CONGREVE / By Anne Doyle

The English dramatist William Congreve (1670–1729) was the most brilliant of the writers of the Restoration comedy of manners. He possessed the wit and charm of the heroes of his plays and was universally admired by his contemporaries.

William Congreve, painted by Godfrey Kneller in 1709. (National Portrait Gallery, London)

The Restoration comedy of manners was similar to the satiric comedy of Ben Jonson in that it ridiculed violations of moral and social standards, but it centered upon the intrigues of ladies and gentlemen who lived in a highly polished, artificial society, and much of its effectiveness depended upon repartee and brisk and witty dialogue. In 1698 Jeremy Collier attacked the immorality of situation and indecency of dialogue characteristic of Restoration comedy. A change of taste followed, and William Congreve was forced to abandon the stage.

Congreve was born at Bardsey near Leeds on Jan. 24, 1670. His father was a soldier and a descendant of an old English family which owned considerable property in Staffordshire. When Congreve was 4, his father was commissioned to command the garrison at Youghal in Ireland. Later he became agent for the estates of the Earl of Cork, and ultimately the family moved to Lismore. Congreve received all of his education in Ireland. In 1681 he was sent to Kilkenny School, where he met his lifelong friend the satirist Jonathan Swift. In April 1686 Congreve followed Swift to Trinity College, Dublin. While at Trinity, Congreve seems to have written the novel *Incognita; or, Love and Duty Reconciled*, which was published under the assumed name of Cleophil in 1692.

After the Glorious Revolution of 1688 Congreve and his family returned to the family home in Staffordshire, where he seems to have remained for 2 years. It is most probable that it was here that he wrote his first play, *The Old Bachelor*, "to amuse himself in a slow recovery from a fit of sickness." In the spring of 1691 he went to London and enrolled at the Middle Temple to study law, but most of his energy was diverted to literature. Within a year he had made the friendship of John Dryden, the

former poet laureate. In 1692 the two collaborated on a translation of the satires of Juvenal and Persius. That year he also contributed some verses to Charles Gildon's *Miscellany*.

The Dramatist

In 1693 *The Old Bachelor*, which had been revised by Dryden, was produced at the Theatre Royal in Drury Lane with the best actors and actresses of the time taking part in it—including Betterton, Mrs. Barry, and Mrs. Bracegirdle, who was to have the leading role in all of Congreve's plays. The play was a great success and ran for the unprecedented length of a fortnight. Congreve was so encouraged by its reception that he hastened to put forth a second play, *The Double Dealer*, before the end of the year. This play was more complex and better structured than the first, but it was not nearly so well received.

While Congreve was writing his third comedy, *Love for Love*, Betterton and other leading actors rebelled against the management of the Theatre Royal, the only theater in London at the time. They were given permission to build a new theater at Lincoln's Inn Fields, which opened with the production of *Love for Love* in the spring of 1695. Probably Congreve's best acting play, it met with immediate success and placed him among the leading dramatists of the day. He became one of the managers of the new theater and agreed to give the new company a play a year.

At this time he also began to write public occasional verse. He was well established in his literary career, and through Charles Montague, later Earl of Halifax, to whom he had dedicated *The Double Dealer*, he was appointed one of the five commissioners to license hackney coaches at a salary of £100 a year.

Congreve was unable to produce a play a year as promised, but early in 1697 he gave the company the tragedy *The Mourning Bride*. It met with instantaneous success and was the most popular English tragedy for almost a century. The following year he launched an unsuccessful counterattack on Collier's charges against the stage. But by 1700 the taste in comedy had so changed that his next play, *The Way of the World*, failed miserably, and he determined to leave the stage.

Later Career

Although Congreve associated briefly with Sir John Vanbrugh at the Queen's Theatre and wrote librettos for two operas (*The Judgment of Paris* and *Semele*), he spent the rest of his life at leisure. In 1705 he was appointed commissioner for wines and retained this post until 1714, when he received a more lucrative appointment as secretary of Jamaica. In 1710 he published the first collected edition of his works in three volumes. He continued to write poetry and made translations of Homer, Juvenal, Horace, and Ovid. He was highly regarded as a person and colleague by Swift, Pope, Addison, and Gay. Voltaire was annoyed at Congreve's affecting the role of gentleman in preference to that of author, but Congreve's considerateness of his fellow authors was held to be remarkable.

Congreve never married, but he was intimate for many years with Mrs. Bracegirdle, the leading lady of his plays. In later years he was in constant attendance upon the Duchess of Marlborough and is believed to have been the father of the duchess's daughter, Lady Mary Godolphin. His life of pleasure was pursued at the expense of his health, and he suffered greatly from blindness and gout. In the summer of 1728 he went to Bath with the Duchess of Marlborough and John Gay to recover from a long illness. While there his carriage was overturned, and he suffered internal injuries from which he never recovered. He died on Jan. 19, 1729, and was buried in Westminster Abbey. He left the bulk of his fortune to the Duchess of Marlborough, who built a monument to his memory in the abbey.

Further Reading

William Congreve is listed in the Literature study guide (II, E, 3, b). Among his associates were John DRYDEN, Jonathan SWIFT, John GAY, and Sir John VANBRUGH. William WYCHERLEY was another noted Restoration dramatist.

Edmund Gosse, *Life of William Congreve* (1888; rev. ed. 1924), was the first full biography. The fullest and most accurate is John C. Hodges, *William Congreve, the Man: A Biography from New Sources* (1941). Other useful biographical accounts are D. Crane Taylor, *William Congreve* (1931), and Kathleen M. Lynch, *A Con-*

greve Gallery (1951). Studies of the Restoration comedy of manners include John Palmer, *The Comedy of Manners* (1913); Kathleen M. Lynch, *The Social Mode of Restoration Comedy* (1926; rev. ed. 1965); and Norman N. Holland, *The First Modern Comedies: The Significance of Etherege, Wycherley, and Congreve* (1959).

CONKLING / By Joseph R. Conlin

Roscoe Conkling (1829–1888) represented the most unabashed sort of American political partisanship in the 1860s and 1870s. A leader of the "Stalwart" faction of the Republican party, he became a symbol of spoilsmanship in politics.

R oscoe Conkling was born on Oct. 30, 1829, in Albany, N.Y. He attended Mount Washington Collegiate Institute, read law, and became district attorney of Albany. He moved to Utica, where in 1858 he was Whig party mayor. He sat in the House of Representatives from 1859 to 1863 and 1865 to 1867. A staunch supporter of Thaddeus Stevens and the Radical Republicans, Conkling once defended the dying Stevens from physical attack and sat on the "Committee of 15,"

Roscoe Conkling. (Library of Congress)

which drafted the Radical program of reconstruction.

In 1867 Conkling seized effective control of the New York State Republican organization and got himself elected to the Senate. A devoted follower of Ulysses S. Grant, Conkling was at home only in the rough-and-tumble world of "gilded age" politics. Grant offered to make him chief justice of the Supreme Court in 1873, and Chester Arthur offered him a seat on the Court a decade later. But he rejected both.

"I do not know how to belong to a party a little," Conkling said, and he was indeed the sort of partisan that has since vanished from the political scene. He was frank; he insisted loudly where others equivocated; he believed that party workers should receive benefits from winning elections, that is, jobs and other financial rewards; in return he demanded that they support the party as if it were a holy cause. He had a brilliant, quick mind in debate but saved his most scathing remarks for reformers who sought to eliminate political patronage through civil service reform which would distribute political appointments according to merit only.

Conkling battled President Hayes for control of the patronage in New York and hoped in 1880 to reelect Grant to the presidency. But the Republicans nominated James A. Garfield of Ohio. Conkling at once joined battle with President Garfield over patronage. In an attempt to rebuff him Conkling resigned his Senate seat: the idea was to be reelected in the face of Garfield's opposition, thus demonstrating his personal power in New York. But Garfield was killed in the meantime by a madman claiming to be a "Stalwart," and the shocked New York Legislature refused to follow Conkling's will. He effectively retired from politics, noting characteristically, "How can I speak into a grave? How can I battle with a shroud? Silence is a duty and a doom."

Conkling retired to a lucrative legal practice and to the fashionable New York City society that he adorned very well. A large, handsome man with a boxer's physique, he inspired nicknames such as the "Curled Darling of Utica" because of his affectation of gay, fashionably cut clothing. James G. Blaine matched Conkling's invective when he ridiculed Conkling's "haughty disdain, his grandiloquent swell, his majestic, supereminent, overpowering, turkey-gobbler strut." Garfield incisively characterized Conkling as "a singular compound of a very brilliant man and an exceedingly petulant child." For all his arrogance and pomposity, however, Conkling clung to causes such as Negro rights long after better-remembered contemporaries had abandoned them. And one ultimate conclusion about his spoilsmanship must be that he spoke frankly while others were hypocritical. He died in New York City on April 18, 1888.

Further Reading

Roscoe Conkling is listed in the American History study guide (VII, A, 2 and 4). Conkling's hero was Ulysses S. GRANT; his enemy, James A. GARFIELD. Other local "bosses" were William TWEED and Samuel J. TILDEN.

A relative, Alfred R. Conkling, published the customary 19th-century biography upon the death of Conkling, *The*

Life and Letters of Roscoe Conkling: Orator, Statesman, and Advocate (1889). David M. Jordon, *Roscoe Conkling of New York: Voice in the Senate* (1971), is a penetrating and detailed biography. An incisive portrayal of Conkling is contained in H. Wayne Morgan, *From Hayes to McKinley* (1969).

CONRAD / By Robert O'Clair

The Polish-born English novelist Joseph Conrad (1857–1924) was concerned with men under stress, deprived of the ordinary supports of civilized life and forced to confront the mystery of human individuality. He explored the technical possibilities of fiction.

Józef Teodor Konrad Nalecz Korzeniowski (to use the name which Joseph Conrad later drastically simplified for his English readers) was born on Dec. 3, 1857, in Berdyczew. Conrad's childhood was harsh. His parents were both members of families long identified with the movement for Polish independence from Russia. In 1862 Conrad's father, himself a writer and translator, was exiled to Russia for his revolutionary activities, and his wife and child shared the exile. In 1865 Conrad's mother died, and a year later he was entrusted to the care of his uncle Thaddeus Bobrowski.

In 1868 Conrad attended high school in Lemberg, Galicia; the following year he and his father moved to Cracow, where his father died. In early adolescence the future novelist began to dream of going to sea, and in 1873, while on vacation in western Europe, Conrad saw the sea for the first time. In the autumn of 1874 Conrad went to Marseilles, where he entered the French marine service.

For the next 20 years Conrad led a successful career as a ship's officer. In 1877 he probably took part in the illegal shipment of arms from France to Spain in support of the pretender to the Spanish throne, Don Carlos. At about this time Conrad seems to have fallen in love with a girl who was also implicated in the Carlist cause. The affair ended in a duel, which Conrad fought with an American named J. M. K. Blunt. There is evidence that early in 1878 Conrad made an attempt at suicide.

In June 1878 Conrad went for the first time to England. He worked as a seaman on English ships, and in 1880 he began his career as an officer in the British merchant service, rising from third mate to master. His voyages took him to Australia, India, Singapore, Java, Borneo, to those distant and exotic places which would provide the background for much of his fiction. In 1886 he was naturalized as a British citizen. He received his first command in 1888. In 1890 he made the ghastly journey to the Belgian Congo which inspired his great short novel *The Heart of Darkness*.

In the early 1890s Conrad had begun to think about

Joseph Conrad. (Radio Times Hulton Picture Library)

writing fiction based on his experiences in the East, and in 1893 he discussed his work in progress, the novel *Almayer's Folly*, with a passenger, the novelist John Galsworthy. Although Conrad by now had a master's certificate, he was not obtaining the commands that he wanted. *Almayer's Folly* was published in 1895, and its favorable critical reception encouraged Conrad to begin a new career as a writer. He married an Englishwoman, Jessie George, in 1896, and 2 years later, just after the birth of Borys, the first of their two sons, they settled in Kent in the south of England, where Conrad lived for the rest of his life. John Galsworthy was the first of a number of English and American writers who befriended this middle-aged Polish seaman who had come so late to the profession of letters; others were Henry James, Arnold Bennett, Rudyard Kipling, Stephen Crane, and Ford Madox Hueffer (later known as Ford Madox Ford), with whom Conrad collaborated on two novels.

Early Novels

The scene of Conrad's first novel, *Almayer's Folly* (1895), is the Dutch East Indies, and its complicated plot is concerned with intrigues among Europeans, natives, and Arabs. At the center of the novel is Almayer, a trader of Dutch extraction, who is married to a Malay woman and has by her one daughter, Nina. He dreams endlessly of returning to Europe with his daughter, but he is powerless to act. Nina runs away with her young Malay lover, and her father takes refuge in opium and dies pathetically.

An Outcast of the Islands (1896) deals with the same milieu, and in fact Almayer appears again in this work. The main character is a shabby trickster, Willems, who betrays the man who gives him a chance to make something of himself and thus plays a part in Almayer's ruin. The novel ends melodramatically: Willems is shot by the beautiful native woman Aissa, for whom he has abandoned his wife.

In *The Nigger of the "Narcissus"* (1897) Conrad turns to the life of the merchant seaman and to one of his commonest themes, the ambiguities of human sympathy. Just before the *Narcissus* leaves on a long journey, it takes on as one of its crew a huge Negro named James Watt. From the beginning Watt is marked for death, and Conrad studies the effects on the crew of his steady physical deterioration. At first, his fellow seamen are compassionate, but then Watt's recalcitrance and his ingratitude after they have heroically saved his life drive the crew to the brink of mutiny. Watt dies, as the older sailors predict he will, when the ship is finally in sight of land. The novel contains one of Conrad's great set pieces, a wonderfully sustained account of a storm at sea.

The Heart of Darkness (1899) is based on Conrad's voyage up the Congo 9 years before. Narrated by the sympathetic and experienced seaman Marlow, the novel is at once an account of 19th-century imperialist greed and a symbolic voyage into the dark potentialities of civilized man. Marlow is fascinated by the figure of Kurtz, a Belgian whose self-imposed mission is to bring civilization into the Congo. Marlow tracks him down, and he finally finds the dying Kurtz, who has been corrupted by the very natives he has set out to save. Marlow, at the conclusion, visits Kurtz's fiancée, and he cannot find the courage to tell her the truth about her dead lover.

The first phase of Conrad's career culminates in *Lord Jim* (1900). Marlow is again the principal narrator, although Conrad entrusts his complex story to several other voices. Like all of Conrad's mature fiction, *Lord Jim* is a typical work of the 20th century in that a first reading does not begin to exhaust its subtleties of design and meaning. The hero begins as an inexperienced officer on the pilgrim ship *Patna*. In the night the ship, crowded with pilgrims to Mecca, strikes something in the water and seems about to sink. Urged by the other officers and not really aware of what he is doing, Jim deserts the ship. But the *Patna* does not sink, and the officers, Jim among them, are considered cowards. Disgraced, Jim wanders from job to job, moving ever to the East.

Marlow takes a sympathetic interest in the young man and finds him a job in the remote settlement of Patusan. Jim does well and he wins the respect of the natives, who call him Tuan Jim—Lord Jim. But the past catches up with him in the person of Gentleman Brown, a scoundrel who knows about Jim's past and insists that they are brothers in crime. Jim persuades the natives to let Brown go, whereupon Brown murders their chief, Dain Waris.

Jim accepts responsibility for the murder, and he is executed by the natives. Once again, Conrad is concerned with the ways in which sympathy and imagination blur the clear judgment which is essential for the life of action.

Political Novels

Nostromo (1904) is probably Conrad's greatest novel. It is set in Costaguana, an imaginary but vividly realized country on the north coast of South America. Symbolically and realistically the novel is dominated by the silver of the San Tomé mine and its effects on the lives of a large cast of characters. The treasure attracts greedy men, who impose on the country a succession of tyrannies, and it tests and eventually corrupts men who are devoted to high ideals of personal conduct. *Nostromo* is concerned with the relationship between psychology and ideology, between man's deepest needs and his public actions and decisions.

The London of *The Secret Agent* (1907) is a far cry from the exotic settings of Conrad's first fiction. It is a city of mean streets and shabby lives, and in his depiction of these scenes Conrad surely owes something to the works of Charles Dickens. Mr. Verloc is a fat, lazy *agent provocateur* who is paid by a foreign power (probably Russia) to stir up violent incidents which will encourage the British government to take repressive measures against political liberals. His wife, Winnie, married him in the hope that he will provide a safe home for herself and especially for her dim-witted, pathetic brother, Stevie. Verloc plots to blow up the Greenwich Observatory. Stevie is drawn into the plot; he stumbles, carrying an explosive, and is killed. Winnie kills her husband when she learns of Stevie's death—the dying Verloc cannot understand the violence of her reaction—and then kills herself.

Under Western Eyes (1911) is Conrad's study of the Russian temperament. Razumov, who may be the illegitimate son of Prince K———, is a solitary and devoted student. Haldin, another student, bursts into Razumov's apartment after he has assassinated an autocratic politician. Haldin turns to the Prince K——— but is immediately captured by the police. Razumov now goes to Switzerland, where he finds himself in the midst of a group of émigré revolutionaries, among them Haldin's sister, with whom Razumov falls in love. Tortured by his isolation, Razumov finally confesses his responsibility for Haldin's capture and death. He is punished by the revolutionaries and returns to Russia, where he lives out his alienated life.

Later Novels

Thanks to the efforts of his American publisher, Conrad's next novel, *Chance* (1914), was a financial success, and for the rest of his life he was without worries about money. The novel is concerned with a young girl, Flora, and her relationship with her father, an egotistical fraud who spends some time in prison, and with an idealistic sea captain with whom she finds happiness after she has freed herself from her father.

Victory (1915), Conrad's last important novel, is another study in solitude and sympathy. Warned by his father to remain aloof from the world, the hero, Heyst, is twice tempted by sympathy into the active life—with tragic results. The second temptation is offered by the girl Lena, whom Heyst rescues and carries off to his island retreat. Their solitude is invaded by three criminals on the run, and in a melodramatic finale Lena dies saving Heyst's life.

Among Conrad's last novels are *The Shadow Line* (1917), a somber and ultimately triumphant story of another testing sea voyage, and *The Rover* (1923), a historical novel set in France in the years just after the Revolution.

Although there is a valedictory quality about Conrad's last novels—and some evidence of failing powers—he received many honors. In 1923 he visited the United States with great acclaim, and the year after, he declined a knighthood. He died suddenly of a heart attack on Aug. 3, 1924, and he is buried at Canterbury. His gravestone bears these lines from Spenser: Sleep after toyle, port after stormie seas,/ Ease after warre, death after life, does greatly please.

Further Reading

Joseph Conrad is listed in the Literature study guide (II, I, 1, b). His novels, like those of Henry JAMES, are marked by close examination of human motives and moral values. Conrad collaborated with Ford Madox FORD.

Two older major biographical studies, G. Jean-Aubry, *Joseph Conrad: Life and Letters* (2 vols., 1927), and Jessie Conrad, *Joseph Conrad and His Circle* (1935; 2d ed. 1964), have been superseded by a definitive biography, Jocelyn Baines, *Joseph Conrad: A Critical Biography* (1960). Important critical studies of Conrad's work include M. C. Bradbrook, *Joseph Conrad: Poland's English Genius* (1941); F. R. Leavis, *The Great Tradition* (1954); Paul L. Wiley, *Conrad's Measure of Man* (1954); Thomas Moser, *Joseph Conrad: Achievement and Decline* (1957); Albert Joseph Guerard, *Conrad the Novelist* (1958); and Eloise Knapp Hay, *The Political Novels of Joseph Conrad* (1963).

CONSTABLE / By Joseph Burke

John Constable (1776–1837), one of the greatest English landscape painters, represented the naturalistic aspect of romanticism. His calm, deeply poetic response to nature approximated in painting the insights of William Wordsworth in poetry.

John Constable was born in East Bergholt, Suffolk, on June 11, 1776, the son of a well-to-do mill owner. The lush, well-watered Suffolk landscape with its rolling clouds and generally flat, but in parts undulating, terrain made a deep impression on his imagina-

*John Constable, a
self-portrait. (National
Portrait Gallery, London)*

tion, and no painter has referred more frequently to the scenes of his childhood as a recurrent source of inspiration. "Those scenes," he later wrote to a friend, "made me a painter," and again, "The sound of water escaping from mill-dams, etc., willows, old rotten planks, slimy posts and brickwork, I love such things."

Constable was encouraged first by a local amateur and later by his friend Sir George Beaumont, the painter and collector, who advised him to study the watercolors of Thomas Girtin. Constable said that a painting by Claude Lorrain that he saw at this time marked an important epoch in his life. Beaumont's collection later included the *Château de Steen* by Peter Paul Rubens, which Constable studied closely.

On a visit to London in 1796 Constable met the engraver and antiquary J. T. Smith, under whose influence he made sketches of picturesque cottages. In 1799 Constable became a student at the Royal Academy, where he worked diligently at anatomy under a system of instruc-

tion concentrating on the human figure as the basis of history painting.

Nature Paintings

In 1802 Constable exhibited at the Royal Academy for the first time, declaring his intention to become a "natural painter." The following year he sailed from London to Deal, making drawings of ships in the tradition of the English Thames Estuary school. "I saw," Constable wrote to a friend, "all sorts of weather," and what he described as "the natural history of the skies" became a lifelong object of research, culminating in a series of cloud sketches inspired by the cloud classifications of the meteorologist Luke Howard, who published *The Climate of London* in 1818–1820.

In 1806 Constable spent 2 months touring the Lake District, and the following year he exhibited three paintings from the trip at the Royal Academy. After this, however, he broke with the tradition of picturesque travel, preferring to paint the scenes he knew and loved best, notably his native Suffolk; Salisbury, where he stayed with his friend Bishop Fisher and his family; Hampstead Heath; and the Thames Estuary.

A happy marriage to Maria Bicknell, with whom Constable fell in love in 1809, was delayed until 1816 by the opposition of her maternal grandfather, the wealthy rector of East Bergholt. From these 7 years of uncertainty date those attacks of nervous depression which were occasionally to cloud a life of otherwise singular felicity.

In 1824 three of Constable's oil paintings, including *The Hay Wain*, were exhibited at the Paris Salon, where they were acclaimed by Eugène Delacroix and other painters and won a gold medal. The question of their influence on French contemporaries and ultimately on impressionism has been widely discussed. All that can safely be said is that his break with academic convention made a profound impact and was invoked as a sanction by Delacroix not for imitating the English painter but for greater boldness in his own work.

Constable's wife, by whom he had seven children, died in 1828, shortly after he inherited a fortune from her father. Constable had been elected an associate of the Royal Academy in 1819, and 10 years later he became a full member. He died on March 31, 1837, working on the day before his death on *Arundel Mill and Castle*.

Original Contribution

Constable's finished landscapes were always greatly admired. He was revolutionary in painting large canvases consistently as sketches, and he later allowed himself considerable painterly freedom in finished pictures, like the magnificent *Hadleigh Castle*, subtitled *Mouth of the Thames, Morning after a Stormy Night*. Today it is his large sketchlike paintings that are most sought after, particularly those celebrating the themes that had haunted him from childhood: the mill, the lock, and water reflecting sunlight and clouds.

Constable's original contribution was to combine a scientific approach to nature with a romantic intensity of feeling. "Painting," he wrote, "is a science, and should be considered as an enquiry into the laws of nature." But he described his cloud studies as organs of his sentiment, and in a much-quoted passage declared, "painting is with me but another word for feeling."

Further Reading

John Constable is listed in the Art study guide (III, H, 2,

Hadleigh Castle, *painted by Constable about 1828–1829. (From the Collection of Mr. and Mrs. Paul Mellon)*

a). He and J. M. W. TURNER were the two major English romantic landscape artists. Although Constable detested copying, he was profoundly conscious of his debt to the work of his predecessors, notably REMBRANDT, Peter Paul RUBENS, CLAUDE LORRAIN, and Thomas GAINS-BOROUGH.

The best source for information on Constable is still his own writings. *The Letters of John Constable, R. A., to C. R. Leslie, R. A., 1826–1837*, edited by Peter Leslie (1931), contains both the letters, rich in observations on nature and art and illustrating Constable's genius for friendship, and the notes for Constable's critical lectures on the history of landscape painting delivered to the Royal Institution of Great Britain in 1836. Also extremely useful are R. B. Beckett, *John Constable and the Fishers: The Record of a Friendship* (1952), and a six-volume edition of Constable's *Correspondence*, edited by R. B. Beckett (1962–1968). Besides C. R. Leslie's classic, *Memoirs of the Life of John Constable, R. A., Composed Chiefly of His Letters* (1943; new ed. 1951), there is a scholarly literature of distinction on Constable. Preeminent is Graham Reynolds, *Constable: The Natural Painter* (1965). Sydney J. Key, *John Constable: His Life and Work* (1948), is a sound account. One of the best sources of illustrations, reproducing 597 works, is the Victoria and Albert Museum, *Catalogue of the Constable Collection*, written by Graham Reynolds (1960). A masterly specialized study, establishing Constable's relation to both poets and painters, is Kurt Badt, *John Constable's Clouds* (trans. 1950).

Constantine I, a colossal marble head dating from the 4th century. (The Metropolitan Museum of Art, Bequest of Mary Clark Thompson, 1926)

CONSTANTINE I / By Frank C. Bourne

Constantine I (ca. 274–337) was a Roman emperor. He is frequently called "the Great" because of his successes as a general, administrator, and legislator and because of his support of the Christian Church and efforts to maintain Christian unity.

Born Flavius Valerius Constantinus at Naissus (in modern Yugoslavia), Constantine was the son of Constantius Chlorus and his concubine Helena. In 293 his father became the son-in-law and caesar (successor-designate) of Emperor Maximian, who was coruler of the Roman Empire with Emperor Diocletian. In 305 Diocletian and Maximian abdicated, and Chlorus became coruler, having superintendence of the West, while Galerius, Diocletian's son-in-law, superintended the East. The new emperors chose caesars (Maximinus Daia and Falvius Valerius Severus) who were not their relatives. Galerius kept Constantine, who had distinguished himself as a soldier, at his own court, apparently fearing that he might develop imperial ambitions if left with his father. In 306, however, Constantine managed to escape to the West and joined Chlorus in campaigns in northern Britain. Chlorus died at York in July 306, and his troops immediately proclaimed Constantine his successor. Galerius acknowledged Constantine as a caesar, and he raised Severus to the role of emperor (augustus) in the West.

Struggles for Empire

Constantine's dynastic elevation set a bad example. Thereupon Maxentius, old Maximian's son, proclaimed himself augustus in Italy, killed Severus, and obtained Africa as well. He quarreled with his father, however, and Maximian fled to Constantine, gave him his daughter Fausta in marriage, and supported Constantine's pretensions as an augustus. From 307 to 311 five men claimed the rank of augustus: Galerius, Maxentius, Maximinus Daia, Licinius (Severus's successor), and Constantine. But in 310 Maximian entered into a conspiracy against Constantine, and upon its discovery Constantine had his father-in-law strangled. This event was immediately followed by war with Maxentius, who was defeated and drowned at the Battle of the Milvian Bridge in 312. In the East, Galerius had died in 311; and in 313 Maximinus Daia died after being defeated by Licinius.

By 313 Constantine and Licinius were established as corulers of the Roman world. Their relationship was cemented in that year by the marriage of Licinius to Constantine's half sister Constantia; but jealousy and ambition generated friction and suspicion between the emperors, and in 323 war broke out after Constantine had violated Licinius's territory. Licinius was defeated and deposed, but his life was spared at the intercession of Constantia. The following year, however, Constantine found it expedient to execute him.

Constantine and Christianity

Constantine's conversion to Christianity has generated much discussion. In later years he told the historian Eusebius that before his encounter with Maxentius he had seen a cross of light superimposed on the sun with the inscription above it: *in hoc signo vinces* (in this sign you shall conquer). Since the cross was the Christian symbol, he had his troops inscribe the monogram of Christ on their shields before the Battle of the Milvian Bridge, and his subsequent success in battle convinced him that he had the protection of the Christian god. Theretofore Constantine had probably been a worshiper of the Unconquered Sun, and in the beginning he appears to have thought that Christ and the Sun were identical. Constantine's coinage for some time continued to celebrate the Sun, and as late as 321 his order for the observation of Sunday gave as a reason that the day was solemnized "by the veneration of the Sun."

But Constantine's early involvement in the theological disputes of the Christians soon disabused him of any syncretistic notions. Early in his reign a group of puritanical followers of Donatus in Africa charged that the orthodox Catholics were too lenient toward penitent apostates, and their quarrels reached the Emperor. He tried for years to reconcile or suppress the dissidents but ultimately gave up his efforts in despair. More serious were the quarrels concerning the nature of the godhead. A heresy called Arianism, which maintained that Christ was not coeternal with the Father, scandalized many churchmen. Roman emperors, as heads of the state religion, had always been responsible for keeping the gods at peace with men (*pax deorum*). Now it appeared that the Emperor must secure a *pax dei*, lest God be offended at His people's view of His nature. Therefore, in May 325 Constantine convened a council of bishops at Nicaea in Bithynia. This convocation created the Nicene Creed, which established the orthodox view that Christ was of the same substance (*homoousios*) as the Father but was a separate individual. The decisions of the council by no means pleased everyone, and Constantine was engaged in attempts to heal theological schisms right up to his death. Indeed, he was baptized on his deathbed by an Arian.

Constantine's personal religious views have been a puzzle to historians. He continued throughout his life to hold the post of pontifex maximus of the old religion. And he allowed the continued celebration of ancient cults and even the erection of temples in honor of his family, though he specified that worship in them must not include "contagious superstition." The Edict of Milan (313) by Constantine and Licinius conferred toleration on all religious sects but did not establish a state church.

But as time went on, Constantine showed increasing favor to the Christians. He built and endowed magnificent churches at Constantinople and Rome and in the Holy Land, Asia Minor, and Africa. He established allowances of grain for the support of the clergy and the poor. He legalized bequests to churches and gave bishops the right to free slaves as well as the right to judge quarrels between Christians without the right of appeal to civil courts. Many of his favorite officials were Christians, and the education of his sons was put in Christian hands. While the celebration of pagan rites continued, a few

The Arch of Constantine, Rome. Though the arch itself is dated 312–315, it incorporates elements taken from several earlier monuments. To the right of the arch is the Colosseum. (ENIT)

temples were ordered closed, and others were destroyed by Christian mobs without subsequent imperial punishment. Indeed, Constantine himself had some temples plundered, and only the wooden frames of chryselephantine cult statues were left for the worshipers. Here the decisive factor seems to have been the need for the gold and silver sheathing of the statues to help finance the Emperor's elaborate building program.

Constantine's Administration

Constantine continued and elaborated the army reforms begun by Diocletian. He created a large central and mobile army which could be quickly dispatched to any troubled frontier. Civil and military authority in the provinces was carefully divided; and the new army appears to have been under the command of a master of infantry and a master of cavalry. The number of barbarians in the army increased, and Constantine is said to have favored Germans.

Constantine also followed Diocletian in the elaboration of court ritual. He instituted the order of imperial companions (*comites*) and classified them by grades, depending on the offices they held. Grandiloquent titles abounded, and recipients were favored by reduced tax burdens and fewer civic duties. He also gave the ancient title of patrician to close friends and high officials.

Building of Constantinople

After his defeat of Licinius, Constantine was inspired to found a new imperial residence on the Bosporus at the site of ancient Byzantium. Constantinople had a magnificent harbor, the site was easily defensible, and strategically it was more or less equidistant from the dangerous Danubian and Persian frontiers. Constantine ransacked the pagan world for treasures with which to adorn his city, and he spirited a population to it by offering estates in Asia Minor to nobles who would build palaces there and, in an analogy to the Roman dole, by inaugurating rations of food for humbler immigrants.

The founding of Constantinople had far-reaching consequences. Rome was reduced in importance as the capital of the Roman Empire, and the western part of the empire continued to achieve increasing autonomy. The Roman Senate, hitherto a powerful instrument of government, became little more than Rome's city council. The establishment of Constantinople as a de facto second capital hastened the bipartition of the Roman Empire.

Financial Policy

The cost of Constantinople, increased pay for the army and bureaucracy, and lavish grants to the Church and to favorites combined to create multiple financial problems. To meet these Constantine had the accumulated wealth of the parsimonious Licinius and the confiscated treasures of pagan temples. These were supplemented by new taxes on merchants and craftsmen, surtaxes on the land, and a gradual increase of customs dues and other local levies. Constantine's most constructive financial contribution was the creation of the gold solidus, struck at 72 to the pound, which maintained its purity until the 11th century.

But the economy remained weak and the burdens of government heavy. To ensure the performance of essential services, Constantine became more and more authoritarian. As early as 313 he had ordered local senators (*curiales*) bound to their positions because they were liable for the collection and guarantee of taxes. By the end of his reign their duties had become hereditary. Similarly, shipmasters were compelled to remain on their jobs, for the transport of food to cities was not financially attractive. And in 332 tenant farmers were threatened with a reduction to slavery if they left their districts, thus swiftly moving agricultural workers to serfdom. These measures of Constantine rapidly moved the Roman world from a regime of contract to a regime of status, wherein citizens were tied from birth to their places of origin and their professions.

Constantine's relations with his family were not marked by Christian love or charity. He was a calculating and suspicious man, perhaps as a result of his struggle to survive as a youth among the intrigues at the court of Galerius. In any case, during his career he contrived the death of his father-in-law (Maximian) and of two brothers-in-law (Maxentius and Licinius); in 326 he suddenly, and for obscure reasons, executed his eldest and much admired son, the caesar Crispus, and apparently at the same time he killed his nephew Licinianus, who was only 11 years old. It is widely believed that Crispus's fall may have been due to the jealous ambition of his stepmother, Empress Fausta, in behalf of her own three sons. If so, there was an early revulsion of feeling, for she was drowned in her bath in less than a year. By her Constantine had three sons, Constantine II, Constantius, and Constans. They, along with Dalmatius and Hannibalian, sons of Constantine's brother Dalmatius, were made caesars and given the administration of various parts of the empire as though it were Constantine's personal estate. Except for these three sons and two infant nephews (Gallus and Julian) all of Constantine's close relatives, including his half brothers Dalmatius and Julius Constantius, were lynched by the army at Constantine's death, leaving Fausta's brood to fight over the inheritance. The one person that Constantine seems consistently to have trusted was his mother, Helena. Indeed, her grief at her grandson's execution may have been instrumental in Fausta's subsequent fall.

Constantine's effect on subsequent history through his rigorous systemization of society and his foundation of Constantinople was profound, and probably the success of the Christian Church can most reasonably be credited to him. In other lands where Christianity was tolerated but not embraced by the rulers, it remained a minority sect; but Constantine's partiality for Christians during a long reign, and the education of his sons as Christians, gave the Church a half century of such advantages and strengths that the efforts of Julian the Apostate to return to the old ways some 30 years later probably were doomed to failure even had he lived to press his pro-

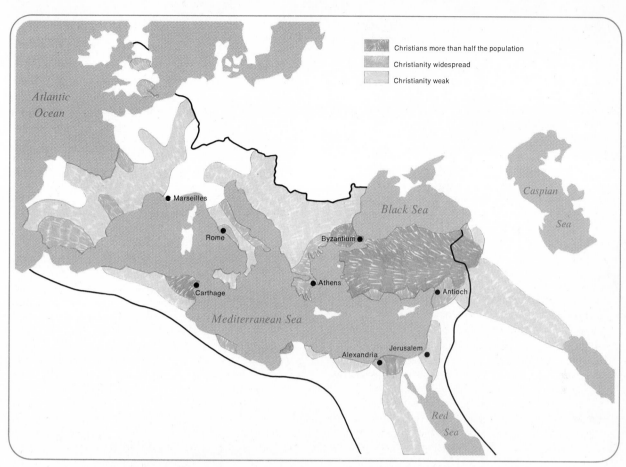

Christianity in the Roman Empire at the time of Constantine I. The Edict of Milan (313), which granted toleration to all religious sects in the empire, ended centuries of persecution of Christians. Despite Constantine's own conversion, the empire was still officially pagan, and Constantine himself held the post of pontifex maximus.

gram. Constantine died near Nicomedia on May 22, 337.

Further Reading

Constantine I is listed in the Ancient History study guide (III, C, 4). One of the later Christian emperors was THEODOSIUS.

There is no continuous ancient account of Constantine and his reign, but material may be found in Eusebius's 4th-century *History of the Church and the Life of the Blessed Emperor Constantine*, a biased panegyric, and in the works of Zosimus, a Greek historian of the late 5th century. Biographies include Lloyd B. Holsapple, *Constantine the Great* (1942), and John Holland Smith, *Constantine the Great* (1971). Discussions of Constantine's Christianity may be found in A. Alföldi, *The Conversion of Constantine and Pagan Rome* (trans. 1948), and A. H. M. Jones, *Constantine and the Conversion of Europe* (1948; new rev. ed. 1962). A good account of the administrative, social, and economic aspects of the reign is in A. H. M. Jones, *The Later Roman Empire, 284–602* (2 vols., 1964).

CONSTANTINE XI/ By John W. Barker

Constantine XI Palaeologus (1405–1453) was the last Byzantine emperor. A gallant prince, he completed the conquest of the Peloponnesus from the Latins and heroically commanded the futile defense of Constantinople against the Turks.

The fourth son of Emperor Manuel II Palaeologus (reigned 1391–1425), Constantine was born on Feb. 8, 1405. Following the Palaeologan custom of apportioning territorial responsibilities to each member of the reigning family, as a young man Constantine was assigned authority in the Black Sea coastal towns. His eldest brother, who had always favored him, became Emperor John VIII in 1425.

In 1427 Manuel's second son, Despot Theodore II of the Morea, announced his decision to resign his power in this important Peloponnesian territory. The Emperor designated Constantine to take Theodore's place. When

Constantine arrived, however, Theodore had changed his mind. It was then agreed that Constantine should renew Byzantine efforts to conquer the areas of the Peloponnesus still in Latin hands, thus making an enclave for himself. He attacked Glarentza and finally won the city in 1428 by marrying the ruler's niece. By 1430 Constantine had conquered Patras and thus controlled the northern Peloponnesus. Two years later his younger brother Thomas annexed the last segments of Achaea, thereby placing all of the Peloponnesus in Byzantine hands for the first time since the Fourth Crusade (1204).

While John VIII attended the Council of Ferrara-Florence from 1437 to 1440, Constantine served as regent in Constantinople. During the following years he presided over what was to be the final flowering of Byzantine unity and prosperity in the Peloponnesus. At John VIII's death at the end of 1448, Constantine succeeded to the imperial throne. He proceeded cautiously regarding the hated agreements for Church union with the Latins, which John had accepted at Florence in hopes of winning Latin aid but which he had never implemented. Finally, under pressure from Rome, Constantine allowed the union to be proclaimed in Hagia Sophia on Dec. 12, 1452. This act greatly antagonized the bulk of his subjects, while it actually won him little effective help from the Latin West.

With only token help from outside, Constantine had to face the empire's last agony, as the Turkish sultan Mohammed II launched his great siege against Constantinople in early April 1453. The Turks finally broke into the

city on May 29, 1453. Constantine died bravely during the ensuing sack.

Further Reading

Constantine XI is listed in the European History study guide (III, K). MOHAMMED II led the Turkish assault on Byzantium.

The only biography of Constantine is Chedomil Mijatovich, *Constantine: The Last Emperor of the Greeks* (1892), which is out of date. For material on Constantine in the Peloponnesus see William Miller, *The Latins in the Levant: A History of Frankish Greece, 1204–1566* (1908). His central role in the final siege is discussed in Edwin Pears's old but still admirable *The Destruction of the Greek Empire and the Story of the Capture of Constantinople by the Turks* (1903); Steven Runciman's newer but less satisfactory *The Fall of Constantinople, 1453* (1965); and David Dereksen, *The Crescent and the Cross: The Fall of Byzantium, May 1453* (1964).

CONTI / By Frank Falcone

> The Venetian merchant-adventurer Niccolò de' Conti (ca. 1396–1469) contributed greatly to Europe's knowledge of the Eastern world.

Niccolò de' Conti (pronounced kōn′tē) was from a noble mercantile family; at an early age he decided to follow in the family tradition by establishing a lucrative trading operation in the East. Unlike most of his fellow Venetians, however, Conti did not concentrate solely on trade with Egypt. In 1419 he began a journey—reminiscent of that of Marco Polo—which lasted nearly a quarter of a century and took him to the Near and Far East. Like Marco Polo, Conti displayed a facility for language and for recording his observations for posterity.

The first phase of Conti's odyssey included a stay in Syria, where he spent enough time to learn to speak the Arabic language. He traveled overland through the desert to Baghdad; from there he moved on to Persia (modern Iran), where he founded a trading company with local merchants. In the course of his business activities, Conti added the Persian language to his repertory. With Persia as his base, Conti extended his operations into India. Sailing extensively in the Indian Ocean, Conti recorded many of his impressions as he landed at various cities. During these years he had an opportunity to experience Indian life personally, since he married an Indian woman and began to raise a family. It was probably at this time that Conti renounced Christianity. It is not clear whether this was done out of conviction or necessity.

Conti eventually extended his visit to the East Indies. His trip there included stops at Sumatra and the Malay Peninsula, a venture that proved extremely profitable. He returned with a shipload of Sumatran spices, gold, and

Constantine XI, last emperor of Eastern Roman Empire. (Harlingue-Viollet)

precious stones. From the Malay Peninsula he sailed northward to Burma, which provided more cargo as well as numerous exotic stories. This part of his long travels included a stop at Java, after which he sailed for Venice.

The trip home was marked by frequent trading stops. He returned via the Red Sea and Suez and finally arrived in Venice in 1444. The reaction to his return was mixed. He was lionized because of the glamour of his long, lucrative trip, while his Indian wife and children were objects of a great deal of curiosity. But Conti's renunciation of Christianity, for whatever reasons, could not be officially condoned. Thus, as Conti's penance, Pope Eugene IV ordered him to provide a detailed, accurate account of what he had done and seen. The result was an account that remains one of the most informative narratives of southeastern Asia to emerge from the early Renaissance period. Like Marco Polo, Conti helped shape Europe's concept of the outside world.

Further Reading

Niccolò de' Conti is listed in the Geography and Exploration study guide (III, A, 2). Marco POLO was an earlier Venetian merchant-traveler.

There is no biography of Conti. Useful background studies are Boies Penrose, *Travel and Discovery in the Renaissance: 1420–1620* (1952), and J. H. Parry, *The Age of Reconnaissance* (1963).

James Cook. (National Portrait Gallery, London)

COOK / By Armin Rappaport

The English explorer, navigator, and cartographer James Cook (1728–1779) is famous for his voyages in the Pacific Ocean and his accurate mapping of it, as well as for his application of scientific methods to exploration.

James Cook was born in Yorkshire on Oct. 27, 1728, into a poor family. At the age of 18 he found employment with a shipowner in his native village of Whitby and made several voyages to the Baltic Sea. When the Anglo-French war broke out in 1755, he enlisted in the Royal Navy and saw service on the *Eagle* as an able-bodied seaman. In a month's time he was promoted to master's mate and 4 years later to master. In 1759 he also received command of a ship and took it to Canada, where he joined the operations in the St. Lawrence River. He performed well enough so that the senior officer of the British fleet put him in command of the flagship.

After the war ended in 1763, Cook was given a schooner, *Grenville*, and was charged with surveying the coasts of Newfoundland, Labrador, and Nova Scotia. For 4 years he sailed up and down these coasts, and when the task was done his findings were of such importance and usefulness that the government had them published.

First Voyage

Upon his return to England in 1767, Cook found the British Admiralty planning to send a ship to the Pacific Ocean to observe the transit of Venus and also to explore new lands in that area. Cook was picked to command the vessel, and on Aug. 26, 1768, in the *Endeavour* he left Plymouth, accompanied by an astronomer, two botanists, a landscape artist, and a painter of natural history. Sailing south and west, he touched the Madeira, Canary, and Cape Verde islands, then went to Rio de Janeiro, rounded Cape Horn into the Pacific, and reached Tahiti on April 13, 1769. On June 3 the transit of Venus was observed, and on July 13 he left the place.

Arriving at New Zealand on October 7, Cook set about at once to make an accurate chart of the waters of the two islands; it took him 6 months. He then sailed along the east coast of Australia, which he named New South Wales and for which he claimed possession in the name of the king. He sailed on through the strait separating Australia from New Guinea, to Java, around the Cape of Good Hope, and reached England on June 12, 1771. In recognition of his achievements—circumnavigating the globe, charting new waters, and discovering new land— he was promoted from lieutenant to commander.

Second Voyage

One year later Cook stood ready for a second voyage, this time to verify the report of the existence of a great southern continent. On July 13, 1772, he left Plymouth in the *Resolution* and, accompanied by another vessel, *Adventure*, sailed southward along the African coast and around the Cape of Good Hope, crossing the Antarctic Circle in January 1773. Finding no great southern continent, he pointed his ship toward New Zealand. This was the starting point for a long cruise in the South Pacific, as he explored the New Hebrides, charted Easter Island and the Marquesas, visited Tahiti and Tonga, and discovered New Caledonia and the islands of Palmerston, Norfolk, and Niue. In January 1775 he was on his way back to England by way of Cape Horn, reaching home on July 29. Thus Cook completed his second Pacific voyage, once again having made a significant contribution by his mapping and charting and his explorations and discoveries.

To those accomplishments Cook added one in nautical medicine, for he had proved that a crew, if properly fed, could make a long voyage without ill effects. He lost only 1 man to disease out of a crew of 118. This feat won him the Copley Gold Medal of the Royal Society and election as a fellow of that distinguished scientific and philosophic association.

Third Voyage

Then came the third and last voyage of Cook's life. Advanced to captain in August 1775, he was now given command of a new expedition to the northern Pacific to search for a passage around North America to the Atlantic Ocean. Once again the great seaman sailed in the *Resolution*, with another vessel, *Discovery*, leaving Plymouth on July 12, 1776. He went down the African coast, around the Cape of Good Hope, across the Indian Ocean to the Pacific, to New Zealand (which he reached in March 1777), northward to Tahiti and to an island sighted on Christmas Eve and named for the occasion, then to the discovery of the Hawaiian Islands, reaching in February 1778 the coast of North America at 44°55′ (present Oregon). He continued northward along the coast to the Bering Sea and through the Bering Strait to the Arctic, but no northern passage could be found. He turned southward to Hawaii for much-needed repairs, fresh supplies, and sunshine in preparation for a return to northern Pacific waters.

But, as fate would have it, Cook did not live to continue the voyage. On Feb. 14, 1779, he was stabbed to death in a skirmish with some natives. Where he fell, an obelisk later would be erected but, as one of his biographers noted, his true monument was the map of the Pacific Ocean.

Further Reading

James Cook is listed in the Geography and Exploration study guide (V, A, 4). The botanist Sir Joseph BANKS accompanied Cook on his first voyage. Another great navigator of this period was Louis Antoine de BOUGAINVILLE.

The Journals of Captain James Cook on His Voyages of Discovery, edited by J. C. Beaglehole (3 vols., 1955–1967), is an invaluable source. The best biography of Cook is Allan Villiers, *Captain Cook, a Seaman's Seaman: A Study of the Great Discoverer* (1967). See also Hugh Carrington, *Life of Captain Cook* (1939); John Reid Muir, *The Life and Achievements of Captain James Cook* (1939); Christopher Lloyd, *Captain Cook* (1952); and R. W. Cameron, *The Golden Haze: With Captain Cook in the South Pacific* (1964). More general works are J. C. Beaglehole, *The Exploration of the Pacific* (1934; 3d ed. 1966); Ian Cameron, *Lodestone and Evening Star: The Epic Voyages of Discovery, 1493 B.C.–1896 A.D.* (1966); and Alan Moorehead, *The Fatal Impact: An Account of the Invasion of the South Pacific, 1767–1840* (1966).

* * *

COOKE / By Louis M. Hacker

From 1862 to 1873 Jay Cooke (1821–1905) was the outstanding merchant banker in the United States. During the Civil War he made possible the sale at par of hundreds of millions of dollars' worth of Union government bonds to the American public.

Born at Sandusky, Ohio, on Aug. 12, 1821, Jay Cooke was the son of a frontier lawyer and politician. He stopped his schooling at 14 and worked as a clerk in his own community and in St. Louis, Mo. He arrived in Philadelphia in 1839; from that time on his activities were virtually always associated with this city,

Jay Cooke. (Library of Congress)

which he made the leading financial center of the country for a brief time. He learned banking in the firm of E. W. Clarke and Company, where he worked until 1857. In 1861 Cooke set up his own banking house, a partnership, Jay Cooke and Company, engaging in the characteristic activities of private or merchant bankers: dealing in gold; buying and selling the notes of state banks; trading in foreign exchange; and acting as "note" broker, that is, the discounting of commercial paper.

Great Financier

The outbreak of the Civil War gave Cooke his great opportunity, and his many fruitful ideas pushed him to the top of the business. Salmon Chase, the secretary of the Treasury and a fellow Ohioan, sought to sell the Treasury's first issues of war bonds and notes through banks and failed (at this time it was customary to dispose of public securities by competitive bidding). Cooke persuaded Chase to appoint him a special "fiscal agent." Using the then unheard-of methods of advertising and personal solicitation by salesmen all over the country, Cooke sold at par (from October 1862 to January 1864) more than $500 million of the 6 percent bonds to as many as 1 million individual investors and country bankers. As fiscal agent, Cooke played another important role: he supported the price of government securities in the New York money market. "Pegging the market" from this time on became a necessary part of such financing. In January 1865 Cooke was called again to handle a large issue of 3-year Treasury notes bearing 7.3 percent interest; in 6 months he sold more than $600 million.

By the end of the war Cooke had three banking houses, each with a separate group of partners, in Philadelphia, New York, and Washington. In 1870 a similar bank was set up in London, and the next year all were brought together as a single partnership. Cooke expanded (and overexpanded) into many fields. He had been friendly to the National Banking Act of 1863 and obtained charters for national banks in Washington and New York; the national banks were the prime source of Cooke's strength.

To these banks and to small investors at home and abroad Cooke, now an investment banker, sold participation in state and railroad loans; the largest loans went to the great land-grant Northern Pacific Railroad, which was chartered to run from Duluth, Minn., to Tacoma, Wash. In this connection Cooke introduced two new ideas into banking: the establishment of banking syndicates as underwriters to handle particular issues, and the active participation by bankers in the affairs of the companies they were helping finance. Thus, Cooke became the banker and fiscal agent of the Northern Pacific in 1869, and he made short-term loans to the railroad out of his own house's resources—a fatal step.

In 1870, although Cooke was responsible for the proposal, he was only one (and a lesser participant) of the investment banking houses taking part in the great refunding operations of the Civil War loans. Congress authorized the sale of $1.5 billion worth of Treasury securities of various types bearing 4 to 5 percent interest in exchange for the higher-priced wartime issues. J. S.

Morgan and Company, and Drexel, Morgan and Company, and their English connections now had their opportunity, and they pushed Cooke into the background.

End of an Empire

Meanwhile, Cooke's troubles with the Northern Pacific Railroad were piling up. In addition to making loans to the railroad, he undertook the underwriting of its initial issue of first-mortgage bonds. But sale of these bonds moved slowly, and the firm of Jay Cooke and Company continued to make advances to the railroad out of the demand liabilities of its customers; this was a risky business. All the western rails required large funds for building and improvements, and when the national economy turned downward in early 1873, investment markets dried up. Cooke's banks and his associated houses were caught in illiquid form—they could not meet the demands of their depositors—with the result that on Sept. 18, 1873, the New York office of Jay Cooke and Company shut its doors, as did the banks with which it was associated.

This started the large-scale Panic of 1873; one of its results was the complete collapse of the Cooke financial empire and the end of Cooke's influence in the money markets; his personal fortune was wiped out. Later in the 1870s he invested a small sum in a silver mine which turned out to be a bonanza, and Cooke was able to sell his holdings for $1,000,000, thus assuring a comfortable old age. He died on Feb. 16, 1905, in Philadelphia.

Further Reading

Jay Cooke is listed in the American History study guide (VII, E, 1). Other American financiers were Jay GOULD, Jacob SCHIFF, and J. P. MORGAN. James J. HILL and E. H. HARRIMAN made their names in railroads.

The best biography of Cooke is Henrietta M. Larson, *Jay Cooke: Private Banker* (1936). An earlier work, drawing extensively on private papers, is Ellis Paxson Oberholtzer, *Jay Cooke: Financier of the Civil War* (2 vols., 1907). Indispensable to an understanding of the role and early development of merchant and investment banking in the United States is Fritz Redlich, *The Molding of American Banking: Men and Ideas* (1951).

COOLEY / By Alvin Boskoff

The American social psychologist, sociologist, and educator Charles Horton Cooley (1864–1929) showed that personality emerges from social influences and that the individual and the group are complementary aspects of human association.

Charles Horton Cooley was born in Ann Arbor, Mich., on Aug. 17, 1864, the son of a well-known jurist, Thomas M. Cooley. After graduating from the University of Michigan (1887), Charles studied mechanical engineering and then economics. In 1889 he entered government work, first with the Civil Service Commission and then with the Census Bureau. He taught political science and economics (1892–1904) and then sociology (1904–1929) at the University of Michigan.

Cooley's first major work, *The Theory of Transportation* (1894), was in economic theory. This book was notable for its conclusion that towns and cities tend to be located at the confluence of transportation routes—the so-called break in transportation. Cooley soon shifted to broader analyses of the interplay of individual and social processes. In *Human Nature and the Social Order* (1902) he foreshadowed George Herbert Mead's discussion of the symbolic ground of the self by detailing the way in which social responses affect the emergence of normal social participation. Cooley greatly extended this conception of the "looking-glass self" in his next book, *Social Organization* (1909), in which he sketched a comprehensive approach to society and its major processes.

The first 60 pages of *Social Organization* were a sociological antidote to Sigmund Freud. In that much-quoted segment Cooley formulated the crucial role of primary groups (family, play groups, and so on) as the source of one's morals, sentiments, and ideals. But the impact of the primary group is so great that individuals cling to primary ideals in more complex associations and even create new primary groupings within formal organizations. Cooley viewed society as a constant experiment in enlarging social experience and in coordinating variety. He therefore analyzed the operation of such complex social forms as formal institutions and social class systems and the subtle controls of public opinion. He concluded that class differences reflect different contributions to society, as well as the phenomena of aggrandizement and exploitation.

Cooley's last major work, *Social Process* (1918), emphasized the nonrational, tentative nature of social organization and the significance of social competition. He interpreted modern difficulties as the clash of primary group values (love, ambition, loyalty) and institutional values (impersonal ideologies such as progress or Protestantism). As societies try to cope with their difficulties, they adjust these two kinds of values to one another as best they can.

Further Reading

Charles Horton Cooley is listed in the Social Sciences study guide (VII, D, 3). George Herbert MEAD studied the development of the mind and the self.

The most detailed biography of Cooley is Edward Jandy, *Charles Horton Cooley: His Life and Social Theory* (1942). A shorter review, by Richard Dewey, appears in Harry Elmer Barnes, ed., *An Introduction to the History of Sociology* (1948). Albert J. Reiss, Jr., ed., *Cooley and Sociological Analysis* (1968), contains a personal account by Robert Cooley Angell.

COOLIDGE / By John Braeman

John Calvin Coolidge (1872–1933) was the thirtieth president of the United States. He has become symbolic of the smug and self-satisfied conservatism that helped bring on the Great Depression.

Charles Horton Cooley. (University of Michigan)

Calvin Coolidge (he dropped the John after college) was born July 14, 1872, at Plymouth Notch, a tiny, isolated village in southern Vermont; he was descended from colonial New England stock. His father was a thrifty, hard-working, self-reliant storekeeper and farmer, active in local politics. Calvin was a shy and frail boy, sober, frugal, industrious, and taciturn. But he acquired from his mother, whom he remembered as having "a touch of mysticism and poetry," a yearning for something better than Plymouth Notch.

Coolidge entered Amherst College in 1891 and graduated *cum laude*. While there he became an effective debater, and his professors imbued him with the ideal of public service. Unable to afford law school, he read law and clerked in a law office in Northampton, Mass. In

Calvin Coolidge (left) signs the Kellogg-Briand antiwar pact; seated next to him is Frank B. Kellogg, secretary of state during the Coolidge administration and, with Aristide Briand of France, the negotiator of the treaty. (Library of Congress)

1897 he was admitted to the bar and the following year opened an office in Northampton. He built a modestly successful local practice. In 1905 he married Grace Goodhue, a charming and vivacious teacher. They had two sons: John, born 1906, and Calvin, born 1908.

Apprentice Politician

Coolidge became active in local Republican politics, serving as a member of the city council, city solicitor, clerk of the Hampshire County courts, and chairman of the Republican city committee. He spent two terms in the Massachusetts House of Representatives and two terms as mayor of Northampton. In 1911 he was elected to the state senate and 2 years later—thanks to luck, hard work, and cautious but skillful political maneuvering—he became president of the state senate. This was a traditional stepping-stone to the lieutenant governorship; he was elected to this post in 1915 and reelected in 1916 and 1917. Meanwhile, he gained a reputation as a loyal party man and follower of the powerful U.S. senator W. Murray Crane, a safe and sound man as regards business and a champion of governmental economy and efficiency. And Coolidge won the friendship of Boston department store owner Frank W. Stearns, who became his enthusiastic political booster.

But Coolidge was no narrow-minded standpatter. His credo was the promotion of stability and harmony through the balancing of all legitimate interests. Thus, he supported woman's suffrage, popular election of U.S. senators, establishment of a public service commission, legislation to prohibit the practice of undercutting competition by charging less than cost, protection of child and woman workers, maternity aid legislation, and the state's savings-bank insurance system.

Governor of Massachusetts

Elected governor in 1918, Coolidge pushed through a far-reaching reorganization of the state government, supported adoption of legislation against profiteering, and won a reputation for fairness as a mediator in labor disputes. But what brought him national fame was the Boston police strike of 1919. He avoided involvement in the dispute on the ground that he had no legal authority to interfere. Even when the police went out on strike, Coolidge failed to act until after Boston's mayor had brought the situation under control. Yet again Coolidge's luck held; and he, not the mayor, received the credit for maintaining law and order. His reply to the plea of the American Federation of Labor president Samuel Gompers for reinstatement of the dismissed strikers—"There is no right to strike against the public safety by anybody, anywhere, any time"—made him a popular hero and won him reelection that fall with the largest vote ever received by a Massachusetts gubernatorial candidate. At the Republican National Convention the following year the rank-and-file delegates rebelled against the party leaders' choice for the vice-presidential nominee and named Coolidge on the first ballot.

Sudden Thrust to the Presidency

Coolidge found the vice presidency frustrating and unrewarding. He presided over the Senate and unobtrusively sat in on Cabinet meetings at President Warren G. Harding's request but took no active role in administration decision making, gaining the nickname "Silent Cal."

Harding's death in 1923 catapulted Coolidge into the

White House. The new president's major problem was the exposure of the corruption that had gone on under his predecessor. But his own reputation for honesty and integrity, his early appointment of special counsel to investigate the Teapot Dome oil-lease scandal and prosecute wrongdoers, and his removal of Attorney General Harry Daugherty when Daugherty refused to open Justice Department files to Senate investigators, effectively defused the corruption issue. Simultaneously, he smoothed the path for his nomination in 1924 through skillful manipulation of patronage. The Republican themes in the 1924 election were prosperity, governmental economy, and "Keep Cool with Coolidge." He won decisively.

Except for legislation regulating and stabilizing the chaotic radio industry, the subsidization and promotion of commercial aviation, and the Railroad Labor Act of 1926 establishing more effective machinery for resolving railway labor disputes, the new Coolidge administration's record in the domestic sphere was largely negative. Coolidge was handicapped by the split in Republican congressional ranks between the insurgents and regulars; furthermore, he was not a strong leader and remained temperamentally averse to making moves that might lead to trouble. He was also handcuffed by his conviction that the executive's duty was simply to administer the laws Congress passed. Most important, he was limited by his devotion to governmental economy, his belief in allowing the widest possible scope for private enterprise, his faith in business self-regulation, his narrow definition of the powers of the national government under the Constitution, and his acceptance of the "trickle-down" theory of prosperity through the encouragement of big business.

Domestic Program

Coolidge's domestic program was in line with this philosophy. He strongly backed Secretary of the Treasury Andrew Mellon's proposals for tax cuts to stimulate investment, and the Revenue Act of 1926 cut the maximum surtax from 40 to 20 percent, abolished the gift tax, and halved the estate tax. He vetoed the World War I veterans' bonus bill (1924), but Congress overrode his veto. He packed the regulatory commissions with appointees sympathetic to business. He twice vetoed the McNary-Haugen bills for the subsidized dumping of agricultural surpluses abroad in hopes of bolstering domestic prices. Coolidge unsuccessfully urged the sale or lease of Muscle Shoals to private enterprise and in 1928 pocket-vetoed a bill providing for government operation. He succeeded in limiting expenditures for flood control and Federal development of water resources. He resisted any reductions in the protective tariff. And he not only failed to restrain, but encouraged, the stock market speculation that was to have such disastrous consequences in 1929.

Foreign Affairs

Coolidge left foreign affairs largely in the hands of his secretaries of state, Charles Evans Hughes and then Frank B. Kellogg. The administration's major achievements in this area were its fostering of a professional civil service, its cautious sympathy toward Chinese demands for revision of the tariff and extraterritoriality treaties, and its efforts to restore friendship with Latin America.

Coolidge had a vague, idealistic desire to promote international stability and peace. But he rejected American membership in the League of Nations as then constituted and, whatever his personal feelings, regarded the League as a dead issue. He felt bound by Harding's prior commitment to support American membership on the World Court, but he never fought for its approval and dropped the issue when other members balked at accepting the reservations added by the Senate anti-internationalists. Although Coolidge did exert his influence to secure ratification of the Kellogg-Briand Pact (1928) outlawing war, his hand was forced by public opinion and he had no illusions about its significance. He supported Hughes's efforts to resolve the reparations tangle; but he was adamant against cancellation of the World War I Allied debts, reportedly saying, "They hired the money, didn't they?" His major effort in behalf of disarmament, the Geneva Conference of 1927, was a failure.

Leaving the White House

Yet Coolidge was popular and could have been reelected in 1928. But on Aug. 2, 1927, he publicly announced, "I do not choose to run for president in 1928." The death of his son Calvin in 1924 had dimmed his interest in politics; both he and his wife felt the physical strain of the presidency, and he had doubts about the continued soundness of the economy. He left the White House to retire to Northampton, where he died on Jan. 5, 1933, of a coronary thrombosis.

Coolidge was not a leader of foresight and vision. But whatever his shortcomings as seen in retrospect, he fitted the popular yearning of his day for stability and normalcy.

Further Reading

Calvin Coolidge is listed in the American History study guide (IX, A, 1). His Cabinet included Andrew MELLON, Charles Evans HUGHES, and Frank B. KELLOGG. He followed Warren G. HARDING into the White House and was in turn succeeded by Herbert HOOVER.

Two illuminating works are *The Autobiography of Calvin Coolidge* (1929) and a record of his press conferences, *The Talkative President: The Off-the-Record Press Conferences of Calvin Coolidge*, edited by Howard H. Quint and Robert H. Ferrell (1964). The most thorough and scholarly biography of Coolidge is Donald R. McCoy, *Calvin Coolidge: The Quiet President* (1967). Two earlier but still useful biographies are Claude M. Fuess's sympathetic *Calvin Coolidge: The Man from Vermont* (1940) and William Allen White's more hostile and less accurate *A Puritan in Babylon: The Story of Calvin Coolidge* (1938).

J. F. COOPER / By Robert E. Spiller

Novelist and social critic James Fenimore
Cooper (1789–1851) was the first major
American writer to deal imaginatively with
American life, notably in his five
"Leather-Stocking Tales." He was also a critic
of the political, social, and religious problems of
the day.

James Cooper (his mother's family name of Fenimore was legally added in 1826) was born in Burlington, N.J., on Sept. 15, 1789, the eleventh of 12 children of William Cooper, a pioneering landowner and developer in New Jersey and New York. When James was 14 months old, his father moved the family to a vast tract of wilderness at the headwaters of the Susquehanna River in New York State where, on a system of small land grants, he had established the village of Cooperstown at the foot of Otsego Lake.

Here, in the "Manor House," later known as Otsego Hall, Cooper grew up, the privileged son of the "squire" of a primitive community. He enjoyed the amenities of a transplanted civilization while reading, in the writings of the wilderness missionary John Gottlieb Heckewelder, about the Indians who had long since retreated westward, and about life in the Old World in the novels of Sir Walter Scott and Jane Austen. Meanwhile, he attended the local school and Episcopal church. The lore of the wilderness learned from excursions into the surrounding forests and from local trappers and hunters, the stories of life in the great estates of neighboring Dutch patroons and English patentees, and the gossip of revolution-torn Europe brought by refugees of all classes furnished him with materials for his later novels, histories, and commentaries.

For the present, however, Cooper was a vigorous and obstreperous young man who was sent away to be educated, first by a clergyman in Albany, and then at Yale, from which he was dismissed for a student prank. His father next arranged for him to go to sea, first in a merchant vessel to England and Spain, and then in the Navy; these experiences stimulated at least a third of his later imaginative writing.

When Cooper returned to civilian life in 1811, he married Susan Augusta DeLancey of a formerly wealthy New York Tory family and established himself in Westchester County overlooking Long Island Sound, a gentleman farmer involved in the local militia, Agricultural Society, and Episcopal church. It was here, at the age of 30, that he published his first novel, written on a challenge from his wife.

First Period of His Literary Career

Precaution was an attempt to outdo the English domestic novels Cooper had been reading, which he imitated in choice of theme, scene, and manner. But he soon realized his mistake, and the next year, in *The Spy*,

James Fenimore Cooper, photographed by Mathew Brady. (Library of Congress)

he deliberately attempted to correct it by choosing the American Revolution for subject, the country around New York City he knew so well for scene, and the historical romance of Scott for model. Thereafter, although many of his novels combined the novel of manners with the historical romance, as well as with other currently popular fictional modes, he never again departed from his concern for American facts and opinions, even though for some of his tales he chose, in the spirit of comparative analysis, scenes in foreign lands and waters.

All of the novels of the first period of Cooper's literary career (1820–1828) were as experimental as the first two. Three dealt with the frontier and Indian life (*The Pioneers, The Last of the Mohicans,* and *The Prairie*), three with the sea (*The Pilot, The Red Rover,* and *The Water-Witch*), and three with American history (*The Spy, Lionel Lincoln,* and *The Wept of Wish-ton-Wish*).

Discovering the "American Problem"

The success of his first America-oriented novel convinced Cooper that he was on the right track, and he decided to turn to his childhood memories for a truthful, if not wholly literal, tale of life on the frontier: *The Pioneers* (1823). Judge Temple in the novel is Judge Cooper, and Templeton is Cooperstown; and originals for most of the characters can be identified, as can the scenes and much of the action, although all of it is given what Cooper called "a poetical view of the subject." Though the traditional novel of manners deals realistically with a group of people in a closed and stable community using an agreed-upon code of social ethics, Cooper tried to adapt this form to a fluid and open society, thereby illuminating the core of the "American problem": how could the original trio of "unalienable rights"—life, liberty, and property (not, as Jefferson had it, the pursuit of happiness)—be applied to a society in which the rights of the Indian possessors of the land were denied by the civilized conqueror who took it from them for his own profit, thus defying the basic Christian ethic of individual integrity and brotherly love?

Natty Bumppo (or Leather-Stocking as he is called in the series as a whole) is neither the "natural man" nor the "civilized man" of European theorists such as John Locke and Jean Jacques Rousseau; he is the American individualist who is creating a new society by a code of personal fulfillment under sound moral self-guidance, improvising as he goes along. In *The Pioneers* Natty is a somewhat crotchety old man whose chief "gift" is his ability to argue his rights with both Indian John and Judge Temple. The central theme which knits this complex web of people and adventures into the cycle of a single year is the emergence of Leather-Stocking as the "American hero."

At this point Cooper was feeling his way toward a definition of his social concern, but in the novel itself the problem is almost submerged in the excitement, action, and vivid description and narrative. In the next of the Leather-Stocking series, *The Last of the Mohicans*, Natty is younger and the romantic story line takes over, making it the most popular of all Cooper's novels. In *The Prairie* Natty in his last days becomes a tragic figure driven west, into the setting sun, in a futile search for his ideal way of life. To most of Cooper's readers these stories are pure

romances of adventure, and their social significance is easily overlooked.

In *The Pilot* (1824) Cooper was drawn to the sea by what he felt was Scott's mishandling of the subject, and he thus discovered a whole second world in which to explore his moral problem. The American hero, John Paul Jones, like other patriots of the time, is in revolt against the authority of the English king, and yet, in his own empire of the ship, he is forced by the dangers of the elements to exert an even more arbitrary authority over his crew. There is a similar problem in *The Red Rover*, the story of a pirate with a Robin Hood complex, and in *The Water-Witch*, a tale of a gentleman-rogue, which is less successful because Cooper turned from the technique of straight romantic narrative to that of symbolism.

Cooper's two historical novels of the period (other than *The Spy*), *Lionel Lincoln* and *The Wept of Wish-ton-Wish*, are set in New England, where Cooper was never at home. The former, although thoroughly researched, is trivial, but in the latter, in spite of lack of sympathy, Cooper made a profound study of the conflict between Puritan morality and integrity and the savage ethic of the frontier.

Second Period

His reputation as a popular novelist established, Cooper went abroad in 1826 to arrange for the translation and foreign publication of his works and to give his family the advantages of European residence and travel. He stayed 7 years, during which he completed two more romances, but thereafter, until 1840, he devoted most of his energy to political and social criticism—both in fiction and in nonfiction. Irritated by the criticisms of English travelers in America, in 1828 he wrote a defense of

Thomas Cole's Landscape Scene from The Last of the Mohicans, *painted in 1827, was inspired by the James Fenimore Cooper novel. (Courtesy New York State Historical Association, Cooperstown, N.Y.)*

American life and institutions in a mock travel book, *Notions of the Americans Picked Up by a Travelling Bachelor*.

Settling his children in a convent school in Paris, he traveled from London to Sorrento, Italy, and also stayed in Switzerland, Germany, France, and England. Europe was astir with reform and revolutionary movements, and the outspoken Cooper was drawn into close friendships with the Marquis de Lafayette and other liberal leaders. One product of this interest was a trio of novels on European political themes (*The Bravo, The Heidenmauer*, and *The Headsman*), but the American press was so hostile to them that Cooper finally declared, in his 1834 *A Letter to His Countrymen*, that he would write no more fiction.

This resolution, however, lasted only long enough to produce five volumes of epistolary travel essay and commentary on Europe (*Gleanings in Europe* and *Sketches of Switzerland*); *The Monikins*, a Swiftean political allegory; and various works on the American Navy, including a definitive two-volume history, a volume of biographies of naval officers, and miscellaneous tracts.

In 1833 Cooper returned to America, renovated Otsego Hall in Cooperstown, and settled his family there for the rest of his life. There is much autobiography in the pair of novels *Homeward Bound* and *Home as Found* (1838), in which he reversed himself to attack the people and institutions of his own land with the same keen critical insight that he had applied to Europe. One reason for this was that a series of libel suits against Whig editors helped personalize his quarrel with the equalitarian and leveling tendencies of the Jacksonian era. He won the suits but lost many friends and much of his reading public. His social and political position is succinctly summed up in *The American Democrat* (1838).

Third Period

The third period of Cooper's literary career began in 1840–1841 with his return to the Leather-Stocking series and two more chapters in the life of Natty Bumppo, *The Pathfinder*, in which Cooper used his own experiences on Lake Ontario during the War of 1812, and *The Deerslayer*, which fills in the young manhood of his hero. These romances were followed by equally vigorous tales of the sea, *The Two Admirals* and *Wing-and-Wing*.

But the most significant development of this period was Cooper's final success in blending the romantic novel of action and the open spaces with the novel of manners and social concern. Returning for subject to the scenes of his first interest, the estates and villages of early upstate New York (with their mixed population of Dutch patroons, English patentees, small farmers and woodsmen, and variegated adventurers carving out civilization in a wilderness peopled by Indians and rife with unexploited wildlife of all kinds), he wrote five novels in two series: *Afloat and Ashore* (1844) and its sequel, *Miles Wallingford*, and the "Littlepage Manuscripts" (1845–1846), depicting in a trilogy (*Satanstoe, The Chainbearer*, and *The Redskins*) the four-generation history of a landed family from their first days of settlement to the

days of the disintegration of their privileged way of life in the face of rampant, classless democracy. Largely unread and unappreciated in their day, these five novels, especially *Satanstoe*, have since become recognized as Cooper's most successful fulfillment of his intention. He had always wished to write a chronicle of his times in fictional form in order to interpret for his countrymen and the world at large the deeper meanings of the "American experiment" in its formative years.

Meanwhile, Cooper's concerns for individual and social integrity and for change had hardened into moral and religious absolutes, and the novels of his last 4 years were less story and more allegory. The best of these, *The Crater* (1847), succeeds where *The Water-Witch* and *The Monikins* failed, in using symbolism to convey a narrative message.

Cooper's Achievement

The power and persistence of this first major American author in attempting a total imaginative redaction of American life, coupled with an equal skill in the description of place and the depiction of action, overcame the liabilities of both the heavy romantic style current in his day and his substitution of the character type for the individual character. Appreciated first in Europe, the most action-packed of his novels survived the eclipse of his reputation as a serious literary artist (brought about through attacks on his stormy personality and unpopular social ideas) and have led to a restudy of the whole of his work in recent years. In this process Cooper has been restored to his rightful place as the first major American man of letters.

Further Reading

James Fenimore Cooper is listed in the Literature study guide (I, B, 4; I, C, 1, a). The self-conscious search for a truly "American" literature began with writers like Cooper, Joel BARLOW, and Noah WEBSTER. Outstanding novelists of the period included Nathaniel HAWTHORNE and Herman MELVILLE.

Probably the most satisfactory short biography of Cooper is James Grossman, *James Fenimore Cooper* (1949), although Donald A. Ringe, *James Fenimore Cooper* (1962), gives fuller critical treatment of Cooper's works, and Robert E. Spiller, *Fenimore Cooper: Critic of His Times* (1931), provides more background analysis of Cooper's social ideas. None of these biographers had the advantage of James F. Beard, who edited *The Letters and Journals of James Fenimore Cooper* (6 vols., 1960–1968), and a new biography is needed.

✳   ✳   ✳

P. COOPER / By Anita Shafer Goodstein

American inventor and manufacturer Peter Cooper (1791–1883) was considered New York City's "first citizen" because of his philanthropy and civic activities. He was a self-made millionaire, and his ideas of government were, for his time, politically radical.

Peter Cooper's father, John, was a craftsman whose restlessness and lack of success resulted in less than a year of formal education for his son, although the boy early became an accomplished mechanic. At 17 Cooper apprenticed himself to a New York City coach maker. Subsequently he was employed by a cloth-shearing factory, where he invented a new shearing device that became the basis for his first independent enterprise. He also bought a grocery store in New York. He married in 1813 and his wife, Sarah, baked the bread sold in the store. In 1827 he bought the glue factory which was the nucleus of his later fortune. Through experimentation he produced a product as good as that imported from Europe and gained a monopoly of the American market. Returns from the glue factory enabled him to participate in the iron and telegraph industries.

Cooper's capital backed the development of a large-scale iron industry centered by 1845 in New Jersey, the Trenton Iron Company, managed by his son-in-law, Abram S. Hewitt, and his son, Edward. Cooper was a dedicated supporter of Cyrus Field in the effort to lay the Atlantic cable, and he was an early sponsor and organizer of the telegraph industry. He was president of the New York, Newfoundland and London Telegraph Company from 1854 to 1874 and, for shorter periods in the 1860s, of the American Telegraph Company and the North American Telegraph Association. His mechanical ingenuity, displayed in inventions as various as a lawn mower and a steam-propelled torpedo, enabled him in 1830 to construct the model locomotive "Tom Thumb," which demonstrated that the Baltimore and Ohio Railroad could be made practicable for sharply curved terrain.

Cooper's philanthropy, however, was more significant than his inventions. The Cooper Union, opened in 1859, reflected Cooper's special desire to provide education for working people. It was a significant contribution to adult education, offering professional and coeducational courses in science, technology, and art at night so that working people could take advantage of them. A well-stocked reading room and weekly public lectures were some of the services offered the public for more than 100 years. Cooper's work provided one model for Andrew Carnegie's later concept of the stewardship of wealth.

Beginning in 1828, when he was elected assistant alderman of the City of New York, Cooper was continuously occupied with civic projects, which included the building of the Croton Reservoir and participation in the Public School Society, which until 1842 oversaw the public schools of the city. His political convictions made him an unusual millionaire in the decades following the Civil War, perhaps America's first "socialist" millionaire. In his 80s he became the presidential candidate of the Greenback party (1876). He sought government management of the currency in the interest of the working classes and proposed government ownership of railroads and public works programs. "Ideas for a Science of Good Government," published in 1883, contained his reform proposals.

Further Reading

Peter Cooper is listed in the American History study guide (VI, D, 3). Other American industrialists were his son-in-law, Abram S. HEWITT, and J. S. MORGAN.

For a biography of Cooper see Edward C. Mack, *Peter Cooper, Citizen of New York* (1949). Allan Nevins, *Abram S. Hewitt* (1935), gives an account of Cooper.

Peter Cooper, a photograph by Mathew Brady.
(Library of Congress)

T. **COOPER** / By George H. Daniels

English-born American scientist and educator Thomas Cooper (1759–1839) was also a controversial political pamphleteer.

Thomas Cooper was born in Westminster, England, on Oct. 22, 1759. He studied at Oxford but failed to take a degree. He then heard anatomical lectures in London, took a clinical course at Middlesex Hospital, and attended patients briefly in Manchester. Having also qualified for the law, he traveled as a barrister, engaged briefly in business, and dabbled in philosophy and chemistry.

Being a materialist in philosophy and a revolutionist by temperament, Cooper believed that the English reaction against the French Revolution proved that freedom of thought and speech was no longer possible in England; in 1794 he emigrated to the United States with the scientist Joseph Priestley. He settled near Priestley at Northumberland, Pa., where he practiced law and medicine and began writing political pamphlets on behalf of the Jeffersonian party. In 1800 Cooper was jailed and fined under the new Alien and Sedition Acts.

After Thomas Jefferson's election to the U.S. presidency, Cooper served as a commissioner and then as a state judge, until in 1811 he was removed on a charge of arbitrary conduct by the Pennsylvania Legislature. Driven from politics, Cooper was elected to the chair of chemistry in Carlisle (now Dickinson) College and then served as professor of applied chemistry and mineralogy at the University of Pennsylvania until 1819. The following year (when clerical opposition denied him the chair Jefferson had created for him at the University of Virginia) Cooper became professor of chemistry in South Carolina College (now University of South Carolina). Elected president of the college, he maintained his connection with it until 1834.

Cooper served mainly as a disseminator of scientific information and as a defender of science against religious encroachments. He edited the *Emporium of Arts and Sciences;* published practical treatises on dyeing and calico printing, gas lights, and tests for arsenic; and edited several European chemistry textbooks for American use. In *Discourse on the Connexion between Chemistry and Medicine* (1818) he upheld the materialist position. In *On the Connection between Geology and the Pentateuch* (1836) Cooper attacked those who sought to correlate geological findings with the biblical account of creation.

A member of the American Philosophical Society, Cooper received an honorary medical degree from the University of New York in 1817. He was twice married: to Alice Greenwood, who bore him three children; and in 1811 to Elizabeth Hemming, by whom he had three children. He died on May 11, 1839.

Further Reading

Thomas Cooper is listed in the Social Sciences study guide (VI, B, 3; VI, G, 3). He was a friend of the scientist Joseph PRIESTLEY. Timothy DWIGHT was a contemporary educator.

The only biography of Cooper is Dumas Malone, *The Public Life of Thomas Cooper, 1783–1839* (1926). Benjamin Fletcher Wright, Jr., *American Interpretations of Natural Law: A Study in the History of Political*

Thomas Cooper, a portrait by Rembrandt Peale. (Courtesy of The New-York Historical Society, New York City)

Thought (1931), analyzes Cooper's political ideas. Bernard Jaffe, *Men of Science in America: The Role of Science in the Growth of Our Country* (1944), includes material on Cooper.

COPERNICUS / By Stanley L. Jaki

The Polish astronomer Nicolaus Copernicus (1473–1543) was the founder of the heliocentric ordering of the planets.

Nicolaus Copernicus (pronounced kō-pûr′nə-kəs) was born on Feb. 19, 1473, in Torun about 100 miles south of Danzig. He belonged to a family of merchants. His uncle, the bishop and ruler of Ermland, was the person to whom Copernicus owed his education, career, and security.

Copernicus studied at the University of Cracow from 1491 to 1494. While he did not attend any classes in astronomy, it was during his student years there that Copernicus began to collect books on astronomy and mathematics. Some of these contain marginal notes by him dating back to that period, but it remains conjectural whether Copernicus had already made at that time a systematic study of the heliocentric theory.

Copernicus returned to Torun in 1494, and in 1496,

through the efforts of his uncle, he became a canon at Frauenburg, remaining in that office for the remainder of his life. Almost immediately Copernicus set out for Bologna to study canon law. In Bologna, Copernicus came under the influence of Domenico Maria de Novara, an astronomer known for his admiration of Pythagorean lore. There Copernicus also recorded some planetary positions, and he did the same in Rome, where he spent the Jubilee Year of 1500.

In 1501 there followed a brief visit at home. His first official act as canon there was to apply for permission to spend 3 more years in Italy, which was granted him on his promise that he would study medicine. Copernicus settled in Padua, but later he moved to the University of Ferrara, where he obtained in 1503 the degree of doctor in canon law. Only then did he take up the study of medicine in Padua, prolonging his leave of absence until 1506.

Upon returning to Ermland, Copernicus stayed in his uncle's castle at Heilsberg as his personal physician and secretary. During that time he translated from Greek into Latin the 85 poems of Theophylactus Simacotta, the 7th-century Byzantine poet. The work, printed in Cracow in 1509, evidenced Copernicus's humanistic leanings. At this time Copernicus was also mulling over the problems of astronomy, and the heliocentric system in particular. The system is outlined in a short manuscript known as the *Commentariolus*, or small commentary, which he completed about 1512. Copies of it circulated among his friends eager to know the "Sketch of Hypotheses Made by Nicolaus Copernicus on the Heavenly Motions," as Copernicus referred to his work. In it, right at the outset, there was a list of seven axioms, all of which stated a feature specific to the heliocentric system. The third stated in particular: "All the spheres revolve about the sun as their midpoint, and therefore the sun is the center of the universe." The rest of the work was devoted to the elaboration of the proposition that in the new system only 34 circles were needed to explain the motion of planets.

The *Commentariolus* produced no reaction, either in print or in letters, but Copernicus's fame began to spread. Two years later he received an invitation to be present as an astronomer at the Lateran Council, which had as one of its aims the reform of the calendar; he did not attend. His secretiveness only seemed to further his reputation. In 1522 the secretary to the King of Poland asked Copernicus to pass an opinion on *De motu octavae spherae* (On the Motion of the Eighth Sphere), just published by Johann Werner, a mathematician of some repute. This time he granted the request in the form of a letter in which he took a rather low opinion of Werner's work. More important was the concluding remark of the letter, in which Copernicus stated that he intended to set forth elsewhere his own opinion about the motion of the sphere of stars. He referred to the extensive study of which parts and drafts were already very likely extant at that time.

Copernicus could pursue his study only in his spare time. As a canon, he was involved in various affairs, including legal and medical, but especially administrative and financial matters. In fact, he composed a booklet in 1522 on the remedies of inflation, which then largely meant the preservation of the same amount of gold and silver in coins. For all his failure to publish anything in astronomy, to have his manuscript studies circulate, or to communicate with other astronomers, more and more was rumored about his theory, still on the basis of the *Commentariolus*.

Not all the comments were flattering. Luther denounced Copernicus as "the fool who will turn the whole science of astronomy upside down." In 1531 a satirical play was produced about him in Elbing, Prussia, by a local schoolmaster. In Rome things went better, for the time being at least. In 1533 John Widmanstad, a papal secretary, lectured on Copernicus's theory before Pope Clement VII and several cardinals. Widmanstad's hand was behind the letter which Cardinal Schönberg sent in 1536 from Rome to Copernicus, urging him to publish his thoughts, or at least to share them with him.

It was a futile request. Probably nobody knew exactly how far Copernicus had progressed with his work until Georg Joachim (Rheticus), a young scholar from Wittenberg, arrived in Frauenburg in the spring of 1539. When he returned to Wittenberg, he had already printed an account, known as the *Narratio prima*, of Copernicus's almost ready book. Rheticus was also instrumental in securing the printing of Copernicus's book in Nuremberg, although the final supervision remained in the care of Andrew Osiander, a Lutheran clergyman. He might

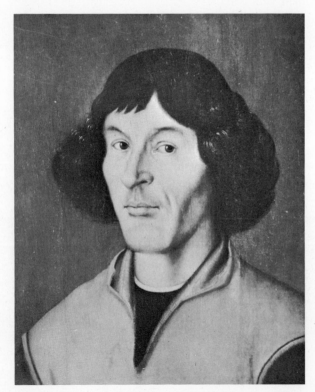

Nicolaus Copernicus, an early-16th-century portrait. (Muzeum Okregowe, Torun)

have been the one who gave the work its title, *De revolutionibus orbium coelestium*, which is not found in the manuscript. But Osiander certainly had written the anonymous preface, in which Copernicus's ideas were claimed to be meant by their author as mere hypotheses, or convenient mathematical formalism, that had nothing to do with the physical reality.

The printed copy of his work, in six books, reached Copernicus only a few hours before his death on May 24, 1543. The physics of Copernicus was still Aristotelian and could not, of course, cope with the twofold motion attributed to the earth. But Copernicus could have done a better job as an observer. He added only 27 observations, an exceedingly meager amount, to the data he took over uncritically from Ptolemy and from more recent astronomical tables. The accuracy of predicting celestial phenomena on the basis of his system did not exceed the accuracy achieved by Ptolemy. Nor could Copernicus provide proof for the phases of Mercury and Venus that had to occur if his theory was true. The telescope was still more than half a century away. Again, Copernicus could only say that the stars were immensely far away to explain the absence of stellar parallax due to the orbital motion of the earth. Here, the observational evidence was not forthcoming for another 300 years. Also, while Ptolemy actually used only 40 epicycles, their total number in Copernicus's system was 84, hardly a convincing proof of its greater simplicity.

Still, the undeniable strength of Copernicus's work lay in its appeal to simplicity. The rotation of the earth made unnecessary the daily revolution of thousands of stars. The orbital motion of the earth fitted perfectly with its period of 365 days into the sequence set by the periods of other planets. Most importantly, the heliocentric ordering of planets eliminated the need to think of the retrograde motion of the planets as a physical reality. In the tenth chapter of the first book Copernicus made the straightforward statement: "In the center rests the sun. For who would place this lamp of a very beautiful temple in another or better place than this wherefrom it can illuminate everything at the same time."

The thousand copies of the first edition of the book did not sell out, and the work was reprinted only three times prior to the 20th century. No "great book" of Western intellectual history circulated less widely and was read by fewer people than Copernicus's *Revolutions*. Still, it not only instructed man about the revolution of the planets but also brought about a revolution in human thought by serving as the cornerstone of modern astronomy.

Further Reading

Nicolaus Copernicus is listed in the Science study guide (III, B). His work prompted the new celestial mechanics of the 17th century, as developed by GALILEO, Johannes KEPLER, and Isaac NEWTON.

A popular modern account of Copernicus's life is A. Armitage, *The World of Copernicus* (1947). In Thomas Kuhn, *The Copernican Revolution* (1957), Copernicus's theory is discussed in the framework of the process lead-

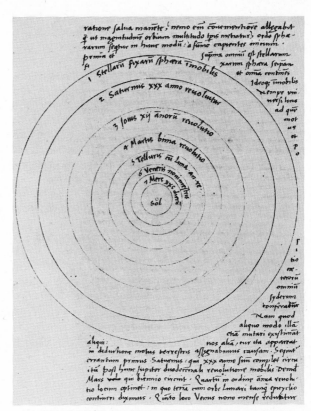

A page from the autograph manuscript of Copernicus's De revolutionibus orbium coelestium, *showing the Copernican concept of the solar system. (Radio Times Hulton Picture Library)*

ing from ancient to modern science through the medieval and Renaissance centuries. For a rigorous discussion of Copernicus's theory the standard modern work is A. Koyré, *The Astronomical Revolution: Copernicus, Kepler, Borelli* (1969).

COPLAND / By David Hamilton

Aaron Copland (born 1900) was one of the most important figures in American music during the second quarter of the 20th century, both as a composer and as a spokesman concerned to make Americans conscious of the importance of their indigenous art music.

Aaron Copland was born on Nov. 14, 1900, in Brooklyn, New York City, where he attended Boys' High School and studied music privately (theory and composition with Rubin Goldmark, beginning in 1917). In 1921 he went to France to study at the American Conservatory in Fontainebleau, where his principal teacher was Nadia Boulanger. During his early studies he had been much attracted by the music of

Scriabin, Debussy, and Ravel; the years in Paris provided an opportunity to hear and absorb all the most recent trends in European music, notably the works of Stravinsky, Bartók, and Schoenberg.

Upon completion of his studies in 1924, Copland returned to America and composed the *Symphony for Organ and Orchestra*, his first major work, which Boulanger played in New York in 1925. *Music for the Theater* (1925) and a Piano Concerto (1926) explored the possibilities of jazz idioms in symphonic music; from this period dates the interest of Serge Koussevitzky, conductor of the Boston Symphony Orchestra, in Copland's music—a sponsorship that proved important in gaining a wider audience for his own and much other American music.

In the late 1920s Copland turned to an increasingly abstract style, characterized by angular melodic lines, spare textures, irregular rhythms, and often abrasive sonorities. The already distinctive idiom of the early works became entirely personal and free of identifiable outside influence in the Piano Variations (1930), *Short Symphony* (1933), and *Statements*, and the basic features of these works remained in one way or another central to his musical style thereafter.

The 1920s and 1930s were a period of intense concern about the limited audience for new (and especially American) music, and Copland was active in many organizations devoted to performance and sponsorship, notably the League of Composers, the Copland-Sessions concerts, and the American Composers' Alliance. His or-

ganizational abilities earned him the sobriquet of "American music's natural president" from his colleague Virgil Thomson.

Beginning in the mid-1930s, Copland made a conscious effort to broaden the audience for American music and took steps to adapt his style when writing works commissioned for various functional occasions. The years between 1935 and 1950 saw his extensive involvement in music for theater, school, ballet, and cinema, as well as for more conventional concert situations. In the ballets *Billy the Kid* (1938), *Rodeo* (1942), and *Appalachian Spring* (1944; Pulitzer Prize, 1945), he made use of folk or folklike melodies and relaxed his previous highly concentrated style, to arrive at an idiom broadly recognized as "American" without sacrifice of craftsmanship or inventiveness. Other well-known works of this period are *El Salón México* (1935) and *A Lincoln Portrait* (1942), while the Piano Sonata (1943) and the Third Symphony (1946) continue the line of development of his concert music. Among his widely acclaimed film scores are those for *Of Mice and Men* (1939), *Our Town* (1940), *The Red Pony* (1948), and *The Heiress* (1949).

Copland's concern for establishing a tradition of music in American life was manifest in his activities as teacher at The New School for Social Research and Harvard and as head of the composition department at the Berkshire Music Center at Tanglewood, Mass., founded by Koussevitzky. His Norton Lectures at Harvard (1951–1952) were published as *Music and Imagination* (1952); earlier books, of similar gracefully didactic intent, are *What to Listen for in Music* (1939) and *Our New Music* (1941).

Beginning with the Quartet for Piano and Strings (1950), Copland made use of the serial methods developed by Arnold Schoenberg, amplifying concerns of linear texture long present in his music. The most important works of these years include the Piano Fantasy (1957), Nonet for Strings (1960), *Connotations* (1962), and *Inscape* (1967); the opera *The Tender Land* (1954) represents an extension of the style of the ballets to the lyric stage.

After his return from France, Copland resided in the New York City area. In addition to many cultural missions, especially to South America, he remained active as a conductor and participated in numerous recordings of his own music.

Further Reading

Aaron Copland is listed in the Music study guide (II, D, 1). Roy HARRIS, Roger SESSIONS, and Virgil THOMSON were contemporary American composers.

An autobiographical sketch is included in Copland's *The New Music, 1900–1960* (titled *Our New Music*, 1941; rev. ed. 1968). Arthur V. Berger, *Aaron Copland* (1953), contains more penetrating observations about Copland's music, but Julia F. Smith, *Aaron Copland: His Work and Contribution to American Music* (1955), is also useful.

Aaron Copland. (Library of Congress)

COPLEY / By Abraham A. Davidson

The portraits of the American painter John
Singleton Copley (1738–1815), outstanding for
their realism and psychological penetration, are
the finest of the colonial period. In England
from 1775, he executed historical paintings as
well as portraits.

John Singleton Copley was born on July 3, 1738,
in Boston. His father died shortly afterward.
When Copley was 10, his mother married the engraver, painter, and schoolmaster Peter Pelham. Copley's
earliest art instruction came from Pelham and from the
leading Boston painter, John Smibert, both of whom
died in 1751. Copley then studied with Joseph Blackburn, an English painter working in Boston.

Boston Period

From about 1760 until 1774 Copley painted the finest
portraits the Colonies had ever known. In these works
Copley's sitters are invariably shown as no more and no
less than what they are. His approach is quite different
from the flattering, contemporary English society portrait.
Yet, for all his directness of observation, Copley never
demeaned his sitters. Instead, an innate nobility, a steadfast, almost heroic quality seems to reside within them.

Copley's Boston portraits include those of Henry Pelham, his half brother (1765), Mrs. Thomas Boylston
(1766), Paul Revere (1768–1770), Mrs. Ezekiel Goldthwaith (1770–1771), and Samuel Adams (1770–1772).
The painting of Henry Pelham (also known as *The Boy
with the Squirrel*), one of Copley's few uncommissioned portraits, shows Henry holding a pet squirrel that
sits beside a half-filled glass of water on a polished table
top. For its time and place the picture is strikingly novel.

Mrs. Boylston's portrait shows a plain but rather handsome woman who looks out of the picture, it seems,
with deeply felt, steadfast convictions. In the portrait of
Paul Revere the famous silversmith sits calmly in shirt
sleeves at a table displaying the tools of his trade. Plump
Mrs. Goldthwaith is fittingly placed beside a bowl of ripe
fruit, whose warm colors are made to cleverly complement the brown tones of her rich satin dress. Copley
showed Samuel Adams, the most uncompromising of
the American revolutionary patriots, standing rigidly, his
face grim and almost masklike.

Departure for England

In the spring of 1774, as America's revolutionary spirit
began to mount, Copley's house was surrounded by a
mob who believed he was sheltering a loyalist. Fearing
for his safety, Copley sailed from America that June. In
1775 he toured Italy. In Naples he painted Mr. and Mrs.
Ralph Izard; this double portrait was Copley's most
elaborate to date. He surrounded the sitters with various
classical artifacts, and in the background he painted the
Colosseum. After a quick tour of Germany and the Low

*John Singleton Copley, a portrait by Gilbert Stuart.
(National Portrait Gallery, London)*

Countries, Copley settled with his family in London in
October 1775.

Haunted by his sense of America's cultural mediocrity,
Copley felt that in Europe he would have a chance to
make his way where it "counted." When, in 1765, he
had sent his portrait of Henry Pelham to London to be
exhibited, Joshua Reynolds, the president of the British
Royal Academy, had replied: "Considering the disadvantages you labored under, it is a very wonderful performance. . . . You would be a valuable acquisition to the art
. . . provided you could receive these aids . . . before
your manner and taste were corrupted or fixed by working in your little way in Boston."

Copley's first English painting was a family portrait that
included his prosperous father-in-law, Richard Clarke
(1776–1777). The figures are placed easily in comfortable
poses, and the tone is one of happy nonchalance.

Historical Paintings

Besides portraits, Copley began painting significant
events of contemporary life as imposing history pieces.
Watson and the Shark (1778) was the first of these.
Copley dramatically painted Brooke Watson, helpless in
the water, perhaps about to be devoured by an enormous
shark, as his friends frantically try to pull him into the
boat. The figures in the boat, grouped in a tight triangular
format, make this one of Copley's greatest compositions.
The brushstrokes, especially in the depiction of the water
in the foreground (as would be true of most of his English work), are handled more loosely than before.

Because of the acclaim accorded *Watson and the*

In his history paintings, such as Watson and the Shark, painted in 1778, Copley depicted current events and emphasized the dramatic aspects of the subject. (Courtesy, Museum of Fine Arts, Boston, Gift of Mrs. George von Lengkerke Meyer)

Shark, in 1779 Copley was elected to full membership in the Royal Academy and, appropriately, devoted much of his time thereafter to painting elaborate history pieces, as such were considered a higher form of painting than portraiture. The *Death of Major Pearson* (1782–1784) celebrates the 1781 defeat of the French at the Isle of Jersey. The *Death of the Earl of Chatham* (1781) depicts William Pitt's death of a stroke in the House of Lords in April 1778, as he rose to debate the war with the Colonies.

The enormous *Siege of Gibraltar* (1791), finished after at least 5 years' work, commemorates the bombardment of Gibraltar by the Spanish and French. Copley employed something of the meticulous realism of his Boston period but on a vast scale. He made models of the fortress and gunboats and even traveled to Germany to get accurate likenesses of the Hanoverian commanders of the siege. But the artistic control of his Boston period was lost in these increasingly grandiose works. Critical reception was lukewarm, and Copley's portrait commissions began to dwindle.

Late Works

Copley never regained his former status. In his late work, parts of paintings are well done, but often the parts do not hang together. In *George IV as Prince of Wales* (1804–1810) the chief figure is brilliantly done in a bright red costume, but the troops in the background look like ants between the legs of his horse.

At the end of his life, criticism of Copley's painting became harsh, and he regretted having left America. Perhaps, had he remained in Boston, he would not have found it necessary to involve himself with elaborate allegories and intricate perspectival schemas. But he simply seems to have declined. Samuel F. B. Morse, who visited Copley in 1811, wrote: "His powers of mind have almost entirely left him; his late paintings are miserable;

it is really a lamentable thing that a man should outlive his faculties." Copley died in London on Sept. 9, 1815.

Further Reading

John Singleton Copley is listed in the Art study guide (III, G, 1, c; IV, A, 1). One of his teachers was John SMIBERT. Copley was encouraged to go to England by Benjamin WEST and Sir Joshua REYNOLDS. Copley's *Watson and the Shark* anticipates the romanticism of Théodore GÉRICAULT and Eugène DELACROIX.

A collection of Copley's work is the Boston Museum of Fine Arts, *John Singleton Copley, 1738–1815: Loan Exhibition* (1938). Jules D. Prown, *John Singleton Copley* (1966), writes more warmly of Copley's English period than previous American writers. For reproductions and biographical sketches see Barbara Neville Parker and Anne Bolling Wheeler, *John Singleton Copley* (1938), and James Thomas Flexner, *America's Old Masters* (1939; 2d ed. 1967).

CORELLI / By Sol Babitz

Arcangelo Corelli (1653–1713) was an Italian composer and violinist. His instrumental works established the chamber music style and form of the late baroque era, and he founded the modern school of violin playing.

Arcangelo Corelli (pronounced kō-rĕl′lē) was born in Fusignano on Feb. 17, 1653. At the age of 13 he went to Bologna, where his main teacher was Leonardo Brugnol, a native of Venice. Corelli studied in Bologna until 1670 and then entered the famous Accademia Filarmonica. In 1671 he left for Rome, where he completed the study of composition under Matteo Simonelli. It has been said that Corelli visited Germany, but this cannot be proved.

In 1689, when Alexander VIII ascended the papal throne, his nephew, Cardinal Pietro Ottoboni, appointed Corelli to conduct weekly concerts at his palace, where Corelli lived for the rest of his life. These concerts helped to establish Corelli as "master of masters."

Corelli's music was published in six opera, each opus containing 12 compositions: Opus 1 (1681), 2 (1685), 3 (1689), and 4 (1694) are trio sonatas; Opus 5 (1700), solo sonatas for violin and continuo; and Opus 6 (1714), concerti grossi for string orchestra.

The trio sonatas of Opus 1 and 3 were intended for church performance (*da chiesa*) with figured bass for organ, and those of Opus 2 and 4 were chamber music (*da camera*) with harpsichord and/or archlute accompaniment. The church sonatas are generally abstract: slowfast-slow-fast, with the first fast movement being fugal. The chamber sonatas begin with a prelude, followed usually by an allemande, a sarabande, and a gigue. A gigue was also occasionally used in a church sonata.

The most influential of Corelli's works was his Opus 5 for violin, containing the *Folia* variations. Like the trio sonatas, the 12 solo sonatas are generally divided between church and chamber sonatas. As is true of much music of the time, the printed page only partially reflects the composer's intent; the performer of these sonatas was expected to improvise elaborate virtuoso ornaments, particularly in slow movements. There are contradictory reports about the ornaments to Corelli's Opus 5, which were published in Amsterdam in 1716 with the "graces" added to the slow movements as the composer "would play them." Later in the century Roger North challenged the authenticity of these graces, but an equally reliable authority, Johann Joachim Quantz, did not. Supporting the latter view is the fact that they are excellent and the germ of them can be found in the first edition in the penultimate measure of the first movement.

Corelli's crowning achievement is his Opus 6, the concerti grossi for string orchestra. In this group is his famous *Christmas* Concerto (No. 8). Although these concerti grossi were not published until the year after his death, Georg Muffat reports that he heard concerti grossi by Corelli in 1682, which could give reason to believe that he, and not Giuseppe Torelli, was the originator of this form. Once again the opus comprises both church and chamber works. Concerti 1–8 are *concerti da chiesa*; 9–12 are *concerti da camera*.

Although famous for the calmness and nobility of his music, Corelli is also known for the "Corelli clash," a bold harmonic suspension. From the standpoint of performing technique his music is less advanced than that of his German contemporaries. That the German violin school was at that time farther advanced than the Italian school might be assumed from the fact that when Corelli heard Nicolas Adam Strungk play he exclaimed, "I am called Arcangelo, but you one might justly call Archidiavolo." But though tamer than the German works, his music when first brought to France was too difficult for the violinists there and was performed by the singers. This would seem to contradict the report by John Mainwaring (1760) that George Frederick Handel found Corelli's playing lacking in fire and demonstrated how he wished to have a passage played, whereupon Corelli said, "This music is the French style, of which I have no experience." Nevertheless, Francesco Geminiani, a pupil of Corelli, reported that Corelli was influenced by Jean Baptiste Lully.

Owing to the modern objective style of playing, Corelli's music sounds very calm today; however, he was noted for his passionate playing, and one observer said that Corelli was so moved that his "eyeballs rolled." Because of the modern smoothly connected bow strokes, his music sounds organlike; however, North reports that Corelli tried to make his violin "speak" and that he said, "Do you not hear it speak?" To obtain this effect today, it would be necessary to follow the instructions of North, Leopold Mozart, and others, who said that every bow stroke must begin with a small softness.

Manfred F. Bukofzer (1947) well states Corelli's historical position: "The decisive step in the development of

Arcangelo Corelli. (Radio Times Hulton Picture Library)

the concerto proper was taken by Corelli and Torelli, both closely associated with the late Bologna school. Corelli can take the credit for the full realization of tonality in the field of instrumental music. His works auspiciously inaugurate the period of late baroque music." Corelli died in Rome on Jan. 8, 1713.

Further Reading

Arcangelo Corelli is listed in the Music study guide (I, D, 1). François COUPERIN greatly admired his music, and in Couperin's ensemble sonata *Le Parnasse, ou L'Apothéose de Corelli* he imitates Corelli's style. Guiseppe TARTINI laid the foundation of the modern school of bowing; his *L'Arte del arco* is a series of variations on a theme by Corelli.

Marc Pincherle, *Corelli: His Life, His Work* (1933; trans. 1956), analyzes Corelli's music and its unique position in the baroque era and discusses Corelli's influence on other composers. A contemporary appraisal of Corelli is in *Roger North on Music*, edited by John Wilson (1959). See also Manfred F. Bukofzer, *Music in the Baroque Era: From Monteverdi to Bach* (1947); William S. Newman, *The Sonata in the Baroque Era* (1959); and David D. Boyden, *The History of Violin Playing: From Its Origins to 1761* (1965).

* * *

CORNEILLE / By Herbert De Ley

The French dramatist Pierre Corneille (1606–1684) wrote more than 30 plays and is often called the father of French tragedy. His tragedies characteristically explore the conflict between heroic love and heroic devotion to duty.

Pierre Corneille (pronounced kôr-nā′y′) was born on June 6, 1606, in Rouen. Educated in the Jesuit school of the city, he completed law studies and became a lawyer there in 1624. In 1628 his father purchased for him, according to the custom of the times, the post of king's advocate in Rouen. Corneille continued for many years to discharge his legal duties as king's advocate, but his real interest was literature. At some time between 1625 and 1629 he wrote the comedy *Mélite*, which was taken up by a traveling theatrical troupe and subsequently presented in Paris, where it was an immense success.

French Classical Drama

In 1629 the French theater was moving away from the exuberant baroque style of the early 17th century toward a dramaturgy based on the theatrical precepts of Aristotle and his commentators since the Renaissance. The general rules included the famous principle of "three unities" (time, place, and action), according to which a play must present a single coherent story, taking place within one day in a single palace or at most a single city. They also included the principles of theatrical verisimilitude (the events presented must be believable) and of *bienséance* (standards of "good taste" must be followed to avoid shocking the audience). These three major precepts structured the great classical theater of the following decades in France.

Corneille apparently first encountered the theatrical mainstream while attending performances of *Mélite* in Paris, and he recalled in later years that his first play was "certainly not written according to the rules, since I didn't know then that there were any." Although Corneille observed the rules more conscientiously in his subsequent plays, he was never completely bound by them. His ambivalent attitude toward the Aristotelian precepts is evident in his highly baroque plays—the extravagant tragicomedy *Clitandre* (1630/1631), the violent tragedy *Médée* (1635), and the fascinating comedy *L'Illusion comique* (1636)—and remains apparent in his first masterpiece, *Le Cid* (1637).

Major Tragedies

Corneille's *Le Cid* is based on traditional stories about the Cid, a medieval warrior and Spanish national hero. In it the young Cid (Don Rodrigue) must avenge his father's honor by fighting a duel with the father of his own fiancée (Dona Chimène). Rodrigue thus finds himself torn between a duty to avenge family honor and a duty to act

Pierre Corneille. (French Cultural Services of the French Embassy)

consistently with the precepts of love. To neglect either would tarnish his *gloire*. The concept of *gloire*, which combines elements of noblesse oblige, virtue, force of will, and self-esteem, seems to have formed the highest ideal of Corneille's world view. In the course of the play Rodrigue fights Chimène's father and kills him, thus forcing Chimène to choose between family honor and her love for Rodrigue. Rodrigue distinguishes himself by defending the city against a Moorish attack, and Chimène distinguishes herself by implacably pursuing vengeance against Rodrigue. In the end the King judges that both have acted according to the most heroic conception of *gloire*; he declares that Chimène has fulfilled her obligation to her father and commands her to marry Rodrigue within a year.

Le Cid was one of the greatest theatrical successes of the 17th century. And although its success was marred by a literary quarrel in which lesser authors attacked its sins against the literary rules, it marked Corneille as a major dramatist and opened the most important epoch of his career. During this period Corneille showed great pride in his literary accomplishments but continued to practice law in Rouen and remained very much a bourgeois provincial who had made good. He was both resentful of, and deferential to, the literary "authorities" who attacked his play. When the newly founded French Academy decided against him, he was genuinely discouraged and apparently abandoned the theater for some time. An academician who remained friendly with Corneille wrote: "I encouraged him as much as I could and told him to avenge himself by writing some new *Cid*. But he talked of nothing but the rules and the things he could have replied to the academicians."

Overcoming his discouragement, Corneille wrote the successful tragedy *Horace* (1640), which was soon followed by *Cinna* (1640) and *Polyeucte* (1642). In these tragedies he continued to explore the concepts of *gloire*, heroism, and moral conflict.

Horace, based on an incident from early Roman history, depicts a young man who with his brothers, the Horatii, is obliged to defend Rome in combat against three brothers (the Curatii) from an enemy town. Horace's wife, however, is a sister of the Curatii, and his own sister is engaged to one of them. In *Cinna* a conspirator hesitates between his fidelity to the state and the desire for vengeance of the woman he loves; and the Roman emperor Auguste, who discovers the conspiracy, must choose between vengeance or clemency for the conspirators. In *Polyeucte* the hero is converted to Christianity during the Roman persecution of the Christians. He openly attacks the pagan religion, and thus he, his wife, his father-in-law (the Roman governor), and a noble Roman envoy must reconcile personal feelings and religious or political duty.

Later Career

In 1644 Corneille returned successfully to comedy with *Le Menteur* and to tragedy with *Pompée*, but thereafter his success as a playwright was less consistent. Although such tragedies as *Nicomède* (1651), *Oedipe* (1659), and *Sertorius* (1662) were favorably received, Corneille wrote a larger number of unsuccessful plays. He tried one formula after another to make a comeback, and courtiers, great ladies, and men of letters took sides for or against him. But the success of each new play became more and more uncertain, and Corneille himself more and more embittered. His last play, *Suréna* (1674), skillfully imitated the style of the playwright who had eclipsed him, Jean Racine, but was less successful than Racine's play of the same year. Although Corneille remained active in the literary world, he wrote nothing more for the theater. He died on Oct. 1, 1684, in Paris.

Critical Judgment

In his tragedies Corneille's treatment of his heroes' moral dilemmas is ambiguous and has inspired divergent views of his meaning. Although his heroes typically possess almost superhuman virtue and courage, each tragedy is resolved by the intervention of superior authority. Some critics have therefore asserted that Corneille's tragic works do not inspire terror or pity, the reactions that Aristotle stated were proper to tragedy. In the 17th century, however, the critic and poet Nicholas Boileau pointed out that in differing from the Aristotelian model Corneille had written "tragedies of admiration."

Such romantics as Victor Hugo, while unfavorable to classical theater in general, admired the heroic and optimistic virtue of Cornelian personages, a characteristic

The title page of the 1641 edition of Corneille's tragedy Horace. (Photo Harlingue-Viollet)

that has also been noted by more recent critics. Others, however, have spoken deprecatingly of the curious innocence or naiveté of even the most admirable of Corneille's heroes and have depicted Rodrigue, Horace, Polyeucte, and the rest as prisoners of a rigid virtue and exaggerated *gloire*. These criticisms possess some validity but also indicate the subtlety of Corneille's tragic vision.

Further Reading

Pierre Corneille is listed in the Literature study guide (III, F, 1). Jean RACINE and MOLIÈRE were the other leading French dramatists of this period.

Some of Corneille's plays were translated into English verse by Lacy Lockert, ed., *Chief Plays* (2d ed., 1957). The best recent work on Corneille in English is Robert J. Nelson, *Corneille: His Heroes and Their Worlds* (1963). Nelson also reprinted selected Cornelian criticism in his excellent *Corneille and Racine: Parallels and Contrasts* (1966). Herbert Fogel surveyed critical opinion, *The Criticism of Cornelian Tragedy* (1967). The best work in English on the baroque esthetic in French literature is Imbrie Buffum, *Studies in the Baroque from Montaigne to Rotrou* (1957), which has chapters on some of Corneille's early plays. E. B. O. Borgerhoff, *The Freedom of French Classicism* (1950), and Will Grayburn Moore, *French Classical Literature* (1961), study the richness of 17th-century literary styles, including Corneille's.

*   *   *

CORNELL / By David A. Williams

American capitalist and philanthropist Ezra Cornell (1807–1874) was the founder of Cornell University, which soon became one of the more advanced educational establishments of the United States.

Ezra Cornell was the son of Elijah and Eunice Barnard Cornell. The family, of New England Quaker stock, settled in De-Ruyter, Madison County, N.Y., in 1819, where Ezra's father farmed and made pottery. Ezra learned something of both, as well as carpentry from his father, a former ship's carpenter. At 18 he set out on his own and in 1828 he settled in Ithaca, N.Y., where he worked as a carpenter and millwright. His employment in building and maintaining flour mills there came to a close when they were converted to textile mills in 1841.

Cornell's interest in promoting a patent plow brought him into contact with the promoters of the Morse magnetic telegraph; from that time on he was involved in the telegraph industry—organizing, building, and operating lines. He constructed lines which connected New York and Washington, Philadelphia and New York, New York

and Albany, then turned to the Midwest to construct a network of lines connecting major points. Cutthroat competition in these early days of the industry led to the combination of many of the leading companies into Western Union Telegraph Company. The concern grew rapidly until it dominated the business in the United States and much of Canada. Cornell's considerable personal fortune was the result of his involvement in such activities during the first 30 years of the industry.

Once he had achieved great personal wealth, Cornell became concerned with public affairs. He financed the construction of a great public library in Ithaca and built and stocked a model farm. His interest in agricultural affairs led to his presidency of the State Agricultural Society. He was a leading member of the New York State Legislature during the 1860s, first as an assemblyman and subsequently as a senator. Here he became concerned with higher education.

Cornell's pledge of his farm as a site plus a half-million-dollar endowment was the essential step that led to the enactment of legislation to found Cornell University. The school opened in 1868. Thereafter Cornell took a keen interest in the university, bestowing sizable gifts and encouraging its adherence to some of his egalitarian ideas of education. The university's freedom from religious ties, interest in the education of women, emphasis upon agricultural and engineering training, and interest in educational opportunities for poor students made it one of the more advanced educational institutions in America. Ezra Cornell, a frequent sight on campus, also carefully administered the disposition of the university's Morrill Act land-grant, husbanding that unique resource and eventually producing substantial returns for the university.

Cornell died in 1874. He was survived by his wife, Mary Anne Wood Cornell, and a son, Alonzo B. Cornell, later governor of New York.

Further Reading

Ezra Cornell is listed in the American History study guide (VII, E, 2). Another industrialist, Cyrus FIELD, promoted the first Atlantic cable. A contemporary American educator was Horace MANN.

There are two full-length biographies of Cornell: Alonzo B. Cornell, *True and Firm: Biography of Ezra Cornell* (1884), and Albert W. Smith, *Ezra Cornell: A Character Study* (1934), which contains an extensive bibliography. There is considerable material relating to Cornell in Andrew Dickson White, *Autobiography*, vol. 1 (1905), and *My Reminiscences of Ezra Cornell* (1890). Histories of Cornell University also contain material of interest.

Ezra Cornell. (Library of Congress)

CORNING / By Saul Engelbourg

American merchant and financier Erastus Corning (1794–1872) was an early leader in the development of railroads in New York State and the first president of the New York Central Railroad. He became a notable political figure in the Democratic party.

Erastus Corning was born on Dec. 14, 1794, in Norwich, Conn. He was an all-round entrepreneur; at one time or another and frequently simultaneously he was a merchant, iron manufacturer, railroad contractor, railroad president, banker, land speculator, and politician. Each phase of his multifaceted career connected with and strengthened the others.

Corning was among those who early recognized the economic growth possibilities inherent in the new railroad. He was already a prominent businessman when he helped organize the Utica and Schenectady Line in 1833. As president, he was paid no salary; instead he sold it iron and steel products. The multiplicity of railroads between Albany and Buffalo, N.Y., reduced efficiency so that it soon became apparent that a new, longer, and continuous railroad joining these two cities was desirable. A convention was held by the various railroads concerned, and the enabling consolidation act was passed by New York State in 1853. Corning was a primary actor in the negotiations which eventuated in the formation of the New York Central Railroad and was chosen the first president. He held that post until he resigned in 1864 for reasons of poor health but remained a director until 1867, when Commodore Cornelius Vanderbilt secured control of the railroad. Corning was also a member of the board of directors of several other major railroads, such as the Chicago, Burlington and Quincy.

Corning pioneered in the practice of making favorable contracts between his own companies, with himself as merchant and manufacturer selling supplies to his railroads; this form of business activity was highly profitable. The relation between Corning and the New York Central, similar to that he had enjoyed with the Utica and Schenectady, finally resulted in an investigation by a stockholders' committee. Even though the committee was composed of his friends, the report criticized Corning. Although the report noted that buying from stockholders was not recommended, the Central continued to buy from Corning. In 1863 the New York newspapers criticized Corning's conflict of interest.

Corning had a reasonably distinguished political life. He supported Andrew Jackson and was elected mayor of Albany, state senator, and member of the House of Representatives as part of the Democratic Albany Regency. Despite his public offices, Corning's political influence came largely behind the scenes. He participated in the peace conference in 1861 in Washington, which was one of several last-ditch efforts to avert the Civil War. Though he had been an antiwar Democrat, he managed to make money in the iron business during the Civil War.

Corning's manifold business activities made him a millionaire. The town of Corning, N.Y., exemplifies his successful land speculation. He had provided the New York Central with superior executive leadership. He made early use of the Bessemer steel process, introducing it in

Erastus Corning, a Mathew Brady photograph. (Library of Congress)

1865. Entrusting his associates with routine matters, he left himself free to expand in the entrepreneurial role. He died on April 9, 1872, in Albany.

Further Reading

Erastus Corning is listed in the American History study guide (VI, D, 2). He was typical of the new entrepreneurial type created by, and in turn creating, industrial America, as were Cornelius VANDERBILT and Ezra CORNELL.

The prime source on Corning is Irene D. Neu, *Erastus Corning, Merchant and Financier, 1794–1872* (1960). A selection of Corning's letters is included in Thomas C. Cochran, *Railroad Leaders, 1845–1890: The Business Mind in Action* (1953). Several railroad studies also contain useful material: Frank Walker Stevens, *The Beginnings of the New York Central Railroad: A History* (1926); Edward Hungerford, *Men and Iron: The History of the New York Central* (1938); Alvin Fay Harlow, *The Road of the Century: The Story of the New York Central* (1947); and John F. Stover, *American Railroads* (1961). George Rogers Taylor, *The Transportation Revolution, 1815–1860* (1951), places Corning's role as a railroad magnate in perspective.

CORNWALLIS / By David L. Jacobson

Charles Cornwallis, 1st Marquess Cornwallis (1738–1805), was a British soldier and statesman. Although remembered best because

of his defeat at Yorktown in the American Revolution, Cornwallis was more often successful in his military activities in India and Ireland.

The Cornwallis family traced its roots to the 14th century in England and its titles back to Stuart times. Charles Cornwallis was educated at Eton, received his ensign's commission in the Grenadier Guards in 1756, then briefly attended a military academy at Turin. During the Seven Years War he participated in many engagements on the Continent. His rise to positions of military and political influence was rapid: he went to the House of Commons from the family borough in 1760, became a lieutenant colonel of the 12th Regiment the following year, and upon the death of his father the next year joined the Lords as the 2d Earl Cornwallis.

In the years of peace Cornwallis was a friend and supporter of Lord Shelburne. Critical of ministerial harshness toward the Colonies, he associated with the Whig peers. Nevertheless, he enjoyed favor at the court: the earl was made constable of the Tower of London in 1770 and promoted to major general 5 years later.

American Revolution

Even though he had opposed Lord North's American policy, Cornwallis was trusted with the command of

Lord Cornwallis, a painting by John Singleton Copley. (Courtesy of The New-York Historical Society, New York City)

reinforcements sent to Gen. William Howe in 1776. He participated in the New York campaign and in the occupation of New Jersey. His failure to catch George Washington at this time and later before the Battle of Princeton led to some criticism by Sir Henry Clinton and a feeling that Cornwallis was too cocksure. In 1777 Cornwallis commanded one of Howe's divisions in the Battle of Brandywine. When Clinton took command in the American theater, Cornwallis rapidly became disgruntled over his limited policy. Relations between the two generals were complicated by the fact that Cornwallis held a dormant commission as Clinton's successor; Clinton regarded this as a threat to his position. Thus the two generals were hardly happy companions in arms, and Cornwallis in pique submitted his resignation just as Clinton tried to do. In 1778 Cornwallis commanded one of the forces in the Battle of Monmouth during Clinton's retreat from Philadelphia. For much of the succeeding year he was in England attending to his dying wife.

In mid-1780 after the siege of Charleston, S.C., Cornwallis received a semi-independent command in the southern states. Nominally still subordinate to Clinton, he was at such a distance from his commander and enjoyed such political favor with George Sackville Germaine (the English secretary of state for the Colonies) in London that he could conduct operations without worrying about restrictions from above. The consequence was Cornwallis's march through the Carolinas—with some real victories, as at Camden, and some Pyrrhic ones—that ultimately led him to Yorktown. His notion was that the best defense of British reconquests in the south was an offensive against Virginia. Lacking sufficient troops, subject to conflicting whims, failing to rally the great loyalist support he had hoped for, and using every loophole in his orders from Clinton and Germaine, he was responsible for the loss of about one-quarter of the British forces in America when he surrendered his command to Washington in October 1781. Cornwallis surrendered in bad grace: he was "sick" and absent from the public ceremonies. While he has had later defenders of his American conduct, Cornwallis undertook far too ambitious a campaign for the means at his disposal and left the British cause in the south in disastrous condition.

In India

Yet Cornwallis's political connections and personal standing were high enough so that he was quickly given new and greater responsibilities. After repeated refusals, he was persuaded to accept the post of governor general of Bengal in early 1786. And in India he was successful enough both as a reform administrator and military leader to acquire a reputation as one of the foremost builders of British rule in Asia. He tried to reduce the corruption endemic in the services of the India Company and to improve the quality of the company's European levies or to reduce English dependence upon them. He was reasonably successful in improving the civil administration, less successful in devising a permanent system for collecting land revenues, and not at all successful in improving the quality of the company's troops. Nonetheless,

The surrender of Lord Cornwallis to George Washington at Yorktown, as depicted by John Trumbull in the rotunda of the Capitol, Washington, D.C. (Library of Congress)

compelled by threats from Tippoo, Sultan of Mysore, to turn away from his avowed policy of nonintervention in the relations of the native states, Cornwallis led a triumphant army in the Third Mysore War (1790–1792). While he stopped short of total victory, Cornwallis compelled the cession of much of Tippoo's territory and payment of a large indemnity and effectively eliminated this threat to the company's power.

Returning to England, Cornwallis was rewarded with the title of marquess. He subsequently was widely used as a diplomatic and military troubleshooter. He served in Flanders trying to coordinate efforts against the French and next in the Cabinet, preparing England against an expected French invasion, and then was ready to set off for India again as governor general. Compromise in India and new threats from Ireland changed his direction. As the Irish troubles deepened, Cornwallis was called to act as viceroy and commander in chief of British forces there. In mid-1798 he disrupted the plans of Irish rebels, compelled the surrender of a small French invading force, and pacified the countryside with—for the time and place—a moderate policy of punishing only the rebel ringleaders. He then sought reforms for Ireland which would prevent future outbreaks. He proposed Catholic emancipation and the abolition of the unrepresentative Irish Parliament in favor of an Act of Union with Great Britain itself. While Cornwallis—with the free

use of bribery—was able to push the Act of Union through the Irish Parliament, he was unable to gain royal acquiescence to Catholic emancipation in Ireland and resigned in protest.

Still Cornwallis continued his services to the government. He was British plenipotentiary during the negotiations at Amiens that led to the brief peace of 1802–1803 with France. Then, in 1805, he was sent off again to Bengal; he died shortly after his arrival. A gentleman born to wealth and influence, he had possessed a sense of duty that led him to serve his country well for many years.

Further Reading

Lord Cornwallis is listed in the American History study guide (III, D, 2, a) and the Asia study guide (II, A, 6, a). Other British officers in the American Revolution were William HOWE and Sir Henry CLINTON. Warren HASTINGS was also active in Indian affairs.

The standard source on Cornwallis's life is Charles Ross, ed., *Correspondence of Charles, First Marquis Cornwallis* (3 vols., 1859). Evaluations of Cornwallis's American activities are found in books dealing with military aspects of the American Revolution. Especially recommended are Piers Mackesy, *The War for America, 1775–1783* (1964), and William B. Willcox, *Portrait of a General: Sir Henry Clinton in the War of Independence* (1964). For another aspect of Cornwallis's career see W. S. Seton-Karr, *The Marquess Cornwallis and the Consolidation of British Rule* (1890), vol. 9 of *Rulers of India.*

CORONADO / By Sandra L. Myres

Francisco Vásquez de Coronado (1510–1554) was a Spanish explorer and colonial official who is credited with one of the first European explorations of Arizona, New Mexico, and the Great Plains of North America.

Francisco Vásquez de Coronado's route, 1540–1542. For 2 years Coronado sought vainly for the fabled riches of Cíbola and Quivira. Disappointed, he nevertheless brought back to Mexico the first real knowledge of the Pueblo Indians and the American Southwest.

Francisco Vásquez de Coronado (pronounced kŏr-ō-nä′dō) was born in Salamanca, the second son of Juan Vásquez de Coronado, a wealthy nobleman. As a younger son, Francisco could not inherit the family estates. He therefore went to the court of Charles I, where he secured a place in the service of Don Antonio de Mendoza, newly appointed viceroy of Mexico.

After his arrival in Mexico in 1535 Coronado rose rapidly in viceregal favor. In 1537 he married the wealthy Doña Beatriz de Estrada, daughter of the former treasurer of New Spain. In 1538 Mendoza appointed the young Coronado governor of the northern province of Nueva Galicia.

These were exciting times. The famous survivor of the Narváez expedition, Alvar Núñez Cabeza de Vaca, arrived at the viceregal court with stories he had heard of seven great cities in "Cíbola," far to the north. Mendoza, anxious to locate and conquer this reputedly golden land, dispatched Father Marcos de Niza and Cabeza de Vaca's companion Estevánico north. When Father de Niza returned in 1539 with a report that he had found the cities, the viceroy immediately outfitted a great expedition and named Coronado to lead it.

In February 1540 the army of more than 230 mounted Spanish gentlemen, 62 foot soldiers, several friars, and nearly 1,000 Indian allies headed north from Compostela. After a long march across northern Mexico and southern Arizona the army reached the Zuñi pueblo of Hawikuh in July. This spot Father de Niza identified as Cíbola, but to the disappointed Spaniards it was only "a little unattractive village" of mud and stone. Although discouraged by the lack of golden cities, Coronado dispatched several small exploring parties. One group marched west to the Colorado River, while another, under Pedro del Tovar, succeeded in reaching the Moqui (Hopi) pueblos north of Zuñi. A third group under García López de Cárdenas pushed northwest to the Grand Canyon. A fourth party under Hernando de Alvarado explored the upper Río Grande. In the winter of 1540 Coronado moved his army to the Río Grande and conquered the Tiguex pueblos near present-day Albuquerque.

At the Tiguex villages the Spaniards heard of a rich land called Quivira somewhere to the north. In the spring of 1541 Coronado set out to try to find this fabled kingdom. Marching eastward across the Pecos River, he turned north onto the Llano Estacado, the great grassland plains of North America; but when he arrived at Quivira on the Arkansas River, he discovered only a poor Indian village. Sickened by his failure to find gold and riches, Coronado left three missionaries to convert the Indians of Quivira and returned to Tiguex, where he gathered the remnants of his army and turned homeward. He arrived in Mexico in 1542, a bitter and disappointed man. For the next 2 decades the Spaniards forgot the northern lands and concentrated on developing their Mexican possessions.

In 1544 Coronado faced charges of neglect of duty and cruelty to the Indians and lost the governorship of Nueva Galicia. He returned to Mexico City, where he managed his estates and served as regidor, or member of the city council, until his death.

Further Reading

Francisco Vásquez de Coronado is listed in the Latin America study guide (I, B, 3). Other explorers in the southwestern region of the present-day United States were Alvar Núñez CABEZA DE VACA and Junípero SERRA.

The diaries and documents pertaining to Coronado's expedition can be found in such collections as George P. Winship, ed., *The Coronado Expedition, 1540–1542* (1896; repr. 1964), and George P. Hammond and Agapito Rey, eds., *Narratives of the Coronado Expedition,*

1540–1542 (1940). The best biography of Coronado is Herbert E. Bolton, *Coronado: Knight of Pueblos and Plains* (1949). Also helpful are Arthur Grove Day, *Coronado's Quest: The Discovery of the Southwestern States* (1940; repr. 1964), and his brief *Coronado and the Discovery of the Southwest* (1967).

COROT / By George Mauner

The fresh and often informal treatment of nature by the French painter Jean Baptiste Camille Corot (1796–1875) marked a significant departure from academic tradition and strongly influenced the development of landscape painting in the 19th century.

On July 16, 1796, Camille Corot (pronounced kô-rō′) was born in Paris, the son of Louis Jacques Corot, a cloth merchant, and Marie Françoise Oberson Corot. At the age of 11 Camille was sent to the Collège de Rouen, and he completed his education at a boarding school in Passy in 1814. He went to work for a draper but announced his wish to become a painter. Although his parents did not approve, they did, upon the death of his youngest sister in 1821, transfer to Corot her annual allowance of 1500 livres, thereby enabling him to lead a carefree if modest existence and pursue his one real ambition.

Corot entered the studio of Achille Etna Michallon and received training in the painting of classical landscapes. When Michallon died, Corot studied with Jean Victor Bertin, who had been Michallon's teacher. During this period (1822–1825) Corot began sketching from nature in the forest of Fontainebleau near Paris and in Rouen.

Italian Sojourns

In 1825 Corot made his first trip to Italy and remained there 3 years. He met the painters Léopold Robert, Edouard Bertin, and Théodore Caruelle d'Aligny and made the first attempts to record his fresh responses to landscape, free from the taste for classical arrangement. Although Corot always spoke of D'Aligny as his true teacher, it was the latter who, while watching Corot paint a view from the Farnese Gardens, exclaimed, "My friends, Corot is our master."

Corot was, indeed, rapidly master of his art, and if there is a weakness in these impressive early works, it lies only in some unconvincing attempts to conform to official expectations by introducing historical or biblical figures into his more ambitious scenes. From Corot's Italian journey dates the *Bridge at Narni* in Paris, a masterpiece that reveals his infallible sense for value and tone relationships. A second version, in Ottawa, more minutely executed and formally arranged, was shown at the Salon of 1827. Corot made two more trips to Italy during the summers of 1834 and 1843.

Growth of His Reputation

In 1830 the tumult of the July Revolution drove the politically indifferent Corot to Chartres, where he painted *Chartres Cathedral*, one of his most originally composed early pictures. In 1831 the Salon accepted several of his Italian and French scenes; although they generally received little notice, the critic Delecluse remarked on their originality. In 1833 Corot's *Ford in the Forest of Fontainebleau* earned a second-class medal; although he also received this award in 1848 and 1867, the first-class medal was always denied him.

Corot's reputation grew steadily if undramatically. In 1840 the state acquired his *Little Shepherd* for the Metz museum, yet in 1843 the Salon jury rejected his *Destruction of Sodom*. In 1845 he was commissioned to paint a *Baptism of Christ* for the church of St-Nicolas du Chardonnet in Paris. He received the cross of the Legion of Honor the following year. At this time Corot found his first private client, Constant Dutilleux, whose future son-in-law, Alfred Robaut, later compiled the standard catalog of the painter's work.

During the liberalized Salon of 1848 Corot was a member of the jury and served again in this capacity the following year, and the state made further purchases of his work for the museums of Douai and Langres. It was only at the Salon of 1855, however, when the Emperor bought

Camille Corot, a self-portrait dating from about 1835. The painting is now in the Uffizi, Florence. (Alinari-Art Reference Bureau)

The Bridge at Narni, *one of two versions painted by Corot. It is in the Louvre, Paris; the second version is in the National Gallery of Canada, Ottawa. (Giraudon)*

his *Souvenir of Marcoussis* that Corot achieved real fame and began to sell his work in quantity.

Characteristics of His Art

Although Corot's art contributed to some aspects of impressionism (and Berthe Morisot received his guidance in 1861), he is appreciated even more for the realization of his poetical vision by means of a subtle and secure handling of his medium than for the historically forward-looking elements in his art. All who met him were impressed by his kindness and generosity as well as his genuine naiveté, which, the poet and critic Charles Baudelaire felt, was the source of the best qualities of his painting. Corot's *Self-Portrait* in Florence is perhaps the best indication of this innocent yet self-assured personality, who observed in one of his notebooks, "Never leave a trace of indecision in anything whatever."

Modern taste tends to prefer Corot's vigorous early and middle-period landscapes to those of his later years which, by contrast, appear somewhat sentimental in their dreamlike, silvery mellowness and suggest reliance on a successful formula. Curiously, it was while Corot was engaged in painting these landscapes (such as *Souvenir of Mortefontaine*) that the force of his early works was now expressed in a group of impressive figure composi-

tions. In these paintings the note of nostalgia and suggestion of allegory (*The Studio*) are often integrated into convincing, technically bold pictorial conceptions (*Young Woman with Rose Scarf* and *Woman with Yellow Sleeve*). Corot exhibited only one of these pictures during his lifetime, the *Woman Reading in a Landscape*, in 1869.

In addition to his landscapes and figure pieces, Corot painted skillful portraits and a number of decorative ensembles. These include a bathroom for Maurice Robert's home at Mantes (1842) with six Italian views (now in the Louvre); the drawing room of the château of Gruyère (1857), and the home of Prince Demidov in Paris (1865).

Corot never married, convinced that family life would be incompatible with his activities as itinerant painter. He died in Paris on Feb. 22, 1875.

Further Reading

Camille Corot is listed in the Art study guide (III, H, 1, d). With John CONSTABLE he is one of the masters of realism tinged with romantic feeling. Corot's work influenced that of Camille PISSARRO.

Of the work done on Corot in English, an excellent recent study is Jean Leymarie, *Corot: Biographical and Critical Study*, translated by Stuart Gilbert (1966). An informative discussion of Corot's relationship to the Barbizon group is in Robert L. Herbert, *Barbizon Revisited* (1962).

CORREGGIO / By Philipp Fehl

The Italian painter Correggio (ca. 1494–1534) is famous for the grace and refinement of his art. He rendered nature with clarity and gentleness, as if it were all music, and he also was a pioneer in executing daringly foreshortened ceiling paintings.

The real name of Correggio (pronounced kōr-rād′jō) was Antonio Allegri, but he is known by the name of his birthplace, Correggio, near Reggio Emilia. He received his early training from fairly indifferent painters in his home town, but his earliest documented works, such as the *Madonna of St. Francis* (1515; Dresden), show him as a master who, much impressed with the monumentality of the works of Andrea Mantegna, knew how to join it to the traditions of the luminous and colorful art of Emilia. An early-17th-century source reports that Correggio worked for a time in Mantua, and several units of the decoration of Mantegna's funerary chapel in S. Andrea have been attributed to his hand.

As was true of most north Italian painters of the time, the art of the great Venetian and Florentine painters was reflected in Correggio's work. Many of his early pictures, such as the *Madonna and Child with the Infant St. John* (ca. 1515; Madrid) and the *Rest on the Flight into Egypt* (ca. 1516; Florence), show that he responded with particular happiness to the inventions and discoveries of Giorgione, Leonardo da Vinci, and Raphael. Another formative influence on his work was the engravings of Albrecht Dürer.

It is established with reasonable certainty that Correggio spent the better part of 1518 or 1519 in Rome. His later work shows that he received immense benefit from studying the works of Raphael and Michelangelo. Correggio was selective in what he adapted from their work, and he succeeded, in his most ambitious paintings, in reconciling and putting to splendid use the often conflicting lessons in the greatness of art that may be drawn from Raphael's Stanza della Segnatura and Michelangelo's Sistine Chapel ceiling.

Mural Paintings

Correggio executed three elaborate fresco commissions in Parma. The first was the decoration of the abbess's drawing room in the Benedictine convent of S. Paolo (ca. 1518–1520). Over the fireplace is a painting of Diana in her chariot. The painted ceiling transforms the chamber into an artful green bower with garlands of fruit hanging down into the room. In the ceiling are simulated niches painted in grisaille with representations of divinities and allegories which look as if they are works of sculpture come to life. Above these niches is a cycle of lunettes in which cupids, painted in flesh color, display various attributes of the hunt.

Correggio's second commission was the decoration of the cupola, apse, and frieze of the church of S. Giovanni Evangelista (1520–1524). Especially in the cupola painting he put to the test the lessons in figure drawing and architectural perspective which only the Roman art of Michelangelo and Raphael can have taught him. Correggio filled the lower rim of the cupola with a majestic array of saints joined by angels. Some of them look down on the viewer; others look up raptly at the figure of Christ, who rises toward a myriad of angels all shining with golden light. Christ not only dominates the figures represented on the cupola but with a great, exhortative, and yet fleeting gesture calls toward himself the worshipers in every part of the church.

Even more ambitious are the frescoes Correggio painted in the Cathedral of Parma (ca. 1524–1530). He transformed the interior of the immense octagonal, funnel-shaped Romanesque cupola into a vision of the heavens opened for the assumption of Mary. A host of music-making and dancing angels, portrayed in the most daring foreshortening, joyfully move about the clouds and, together with a number of saintly figures, surround a core of heavenly light, toward the source of which Mary, her

Correggio, a portrait by Carlo Maratta. (Fonds Albertina, Österreichische Nationalbibliothek)

arms opened in a gesture of bliss and grateful response, is being lifted. The archangel Gabriel, painted very large and almost in the center of the composition, has come to greet Mary and to fly on before her.

Religious Panel Paintings

Correggio, in the period of his maturity, painted five great altarpieces: the *Madonna of St. Sebastian* (ca. 1525), the *Adoration of the Shepherds* (ca. 1530), the *Madonna of St. George* (ca. 1532; all in Dresden), the *Madonna of St. Jerome* (1528), and the *Rest on the Flight into Egypt* (1530; both in Parma). These works, though the presentation of their affecting subject matter is extraordinarily tender and moving, are painted, as befits their size, with a certain splendor of majesty.

In his smaller religious paintings, however, Correggio gave free rein to his lyrical imagination, as can be seen in his *Christ on the Mount of Olives* (ca. 1525; London). The great pathos of the kneeling Christ submitting himself with an open, giving gesture of the arms to the will of his Father is enhanced by the soft darkness of the night surrounding him and the singular gentleness and tearful beauty of his face lit up by a heavenly splendor.

When representing cheerful subjects, such as the *Mystic Marriage of St. Catherine* (ca. 1525; Paris), Correggio bestowed an infinite tenderness upon the scene. The picture shows us not only the happiness of a wonderful moment in the life of the saint but also brings us closer to an understanding of the simplicity and exquisite fineness of the complete and loving surrender of a noble soul to its maker. Among Correggio's other great works in this genre the *Madonna of the Basket* (ca. 1523; London) and the *Madonna Adoring the Christ Child* (ca. 1525; Florence) are especially noted for their lyrical charm.

Mythological and Allegorical Paintings

Correggio brought as much love and gentle understanding to his mythological subjects as to his Christian topics. There are six mythological paintings by Correggio, all commissioned by the Duke of Mantua but not necessarily part of the same decorative project.

The *Education of Cupid* (ca. 1525; London) is a humanistic allegory ostensibly in praise of the love of learning, but the beauty of Venus's fully revealed body, her enigmatic smile, and the splendidly erotic glance of her wide-open and curiously musing eyes directed straight at the beholder triumphantly keep us from paying much attention to the allegorical significance of the story.

The other five paintings represent famous love affairs of Jupiter. In these works Correggio portrayed scenes of sometimes quite absurd encounters, such as that of *Leda and the Swan* (ca. 1532; Berlin), with a literal accuracy

Correggio's Mystic Marriage of St. Catherine, *painted about 1525. The work is in the Louvre, Paris. (H. Roger-Viollet)*

and gentle delight which is, at once, tenderly amused and erotically compassionate. The most artful and affecting among these pictures is surely *Io Approached by Jupiter in the Form of a Cloud* (ca. 1532; Vienna), in which the cloud that softly envelops the enraptured nymph hides and yet reveals a very real physical likeness of the god in the fullness of the beauty of youth.

Correggio also painted two complex and not readily decipherable allegorical compositions for the *studiolo* of Isabella d'Este in Mantua (ca. 1533). One represents the exquisite tortures suffered by the man ruled by passions and vice; the other, the triumph of virtue and statecraft over vice. Characteristically the most impressive and engaging figure in this group is the cupid in the extreme foreground of the picture showing the triumph of the passions. He invitingly holds up a bunch of grapes and looks at us with an irresistibly knowing, sovereign, and vaguely malicious smile.

Influence and Reputation

When Correggio died in 1534 in his native town, he was at the height of his creative life. He left behind no students worthy of his name, and in his immediate neighborhood only Parmigianino profited greatly from the example of his work. Correggio was famous in his lifetime, but since his works, especially the great frescoes in Parma, were in out-of-the-way places, he was at first more readily praised than seriously studied.

At the beginning of the 17th century the Carracci, touched by the facility and grace of Correggio's art, made him one of their greatest heroes. As their influence rose, so did his. Correggio's art of opening up ceilings illusionistically was adapted and, to a considerable extent, vulgarized during the 17th century.

Correggio's influence on 18th-century painting was all-pervasive. When the reputation of 18th-century art declined, the appreciation of Correggio's oeuvre declined with it. And it did not rise again significantly when 18th-century art was restored to critical favor, perhaps because the exquisite grace of Correggio's style demands a greater commitment to gentleness and refinement than does the charming playfulness generally associated with the rococo.

The painter Anton Raphael Mengs was one of the most perceptive and articulate students of the master's work. In his *Memorie sopra il Correggio* (*Opere*, 1783) he wrote that Correggio arrived at a perfection of painting because "he added to the representation of grandness and the imitation of nature a certain lightness which nowadays we are in the habit of calling 'good taste'; but in fact this good taste is simply the ability to delineate the true nature of things and to exclude all extraneous elements as insipid and useless."

Further Reading

Correggio is listed in the Art study guide (III, D, 1, c). He influenced PARMIGIANINO, the CARRACCI, and many other artists. Even an artist of so different a temperament as Gian Lorenzo BERNINI acknowledged his great debt to Correggio. Correggio was in turn influenced by Andrea MANTEGNA, GIORGIONE, LEONARDO DA VINCI, RAPHAEL, MICHELANGELO, and Albrecht DÜRER.

There is no modern appreciation in English of the complete work of Correggio. Arthur E. Popham's magisterial *Correggio's Drawings* (1957) transcends the limited scope indicated by its title and probably will remain one of the best introductions to Correggio's art. It also contains a concise critical review of the most important earlier publications on Correggio. Erwin Panofsky, *The Iconography of Correggio's 'Camera di San Paolo'* (1961), is concerned with the meaning of the allegories in the abbess's drawing room, and it also serves as an introduction to the social and political environment of the time. Works in Italian include A. C. Quintavalle, *L'opera completa del Correggio* (1970), which contains reproductions of all works generally attributed to Correggio, and Roberto Tassi, *Il duomo di Parma* (1966), a splendidly illustrated book on Corregio's ceiling paintings in the the Cathedral.

CORRIGAN / By David O'Brien

American Roman Catholic clergyman Michael Augustine Corrigan (1839–1902) was archbishop of New York during years of rapid change and expansion.

Michael Augustine Corrigan was born in Newark, N.J., the fifth of nine children of Thomas and Mary English Corrigan. His father had emigrated from Ireland in 1828 and was a successful grocer. Michael attended a private school conducted by a relative and spent 2 years at St. Mary's College, Wilmington, Del., graduating from Mount St. Mary's in Emmitsburg, Md., in 1859. Bishop James Roosevelt Bayley sent Corrigan to study for the priesthood as one of the first group of students to attend the new American College in Rome. In 1863 Corrigan was ordained a priest in Rome, and the next year he received his doctorate at the College of the Propaganda Fide.

Returning to New Jersey, Corrigan was named professor of theology and scripture at Seton Hall Seminary, and in 1868 he became the school's president, a post he held until 1876. He served during the same period as vicar general of the Newark diocese. In 1873 he became bishop of Newark, a diocese which covered the state of New Jersey. During his term he successfully systematized parish records and reports and promoted the building of parish schools. In 1880 he was elevated to the post of coadjutor to John McCloskey, Archbishop of New York, whom he succeeded in 1885.

Energetic, though somewhat colorless, and possessed by a passion for order and system, Corrigan developed clear lines of authority in his archdiocese, shored up church finances, adapted parishes to changing ethnic constituencies, sought out foreign-language priests for the hordes of new immigrants, and worked vigorously for the extension of the Catholic school system. Five diocesan synods clarified episcopal authority and clerical responsibility. Archbishop Corrigan completed the building of St. Patrick's Cathedral and constructed a diocesan seminary at Dunwoodie, which he endowed with a chapel from his personal inheritance.

Corrigan's centralization of diocesan affairs was opposed by some priests, whose protests to Rome exposed some of the canonical irregularities in the American system of diocesan management. Most notable was his highly publicized battle with Edward McGlynn, a brilliant priest who questioned the parochial school policy and supported reformer Henry George. Nationally, the archbishop joined other conservative prelates in opposing the more liberal programs advocated by Archbishop John Ireland of St. Paul. Corrigan defended the parochial school and advocated condemnation of secret societies and avoidance of ecumenical contact. He refused to assist the development of the Catholic University of America and staunchly defended the autonomy of his diocese. In later years, when controversy subsided, Corrigan devoted himself to local problems. He died suddenly in 1902.

Archbishop Michael Augustine Corrigan.
(Courtesy of The New-York Historical Society, New York City)

Further Reading

Michael Augustine Corrigan is listed in the Religion study guide (I, Q, 2, d). He succeeded John McCLOSKEY, the second archbishop of New York.

Frederick J. Zwierlein, *Letters of Archbishop Corrigan to Bishop McQuaid* (1946), is the major source for Corrigan's more controversial activities. Diocesan affairs are treated in John Talbot Smith, *The Catholic Church in New York*, vol. 2 (1908). For general background see Thomas T. McAvoy, *A History of the Catholic Church in the United States* (1969).

CORT / By W. James King

The English ironmaster Henry Cort (1740–1800) made possible the large-scale and inexpensive conversion of cast iron into wrought iron, one of the most essential materials of the early industrial revolution.

Henry Cort was born in Lancaster. His father was a mason and brickmaster. Young Cort became a supplier of naval provisions and by the 1770s had accumulated a small fortune.

In 1775, after years of experimenting with improved methods for wrought-iron production, Cort purchased a forge and slitting mill at Fontley. He tried to find an easy way to convert cast iron into wrought iron; traditionally a smith had hammered the iron in a forge. He patented grooved rollers in 1783 which replaced most of the hammering. By 1784 Cort worked out a process of puddling, whereby molten pig iron was stirred in a reverberatory furnace. As the iron was decarbonized by air, it became thicker, and balls of "puddled" iron could be removed as a pasty mass from the more liquid impurities still in the furnace. Puddled iron, like wrought iron, was tougher and more malleable than pig iron and could be hammered and finished with the grooved rollers. He also devised a process whereby red-hot iron was drawn out of the furnace through grooved rollers which shaped the puddled iron into bars, whose dimensions were determined by the shape of the grooves on the rollers. The rollers also helped squeeze out impurities, and preliminary shaping into bars made the iron more readily utilizable for the final product.

There were many advantages to these processes. Puddling used the plentiful coke, instead of the expensive charcoal. The combination of puddling and grooved rollers was a process that could be mechanized, for example, by the steam engine, which had just been introduced. The result was that production of wrought iron was increasingly carried out in a group of coordinated processes in a single economic unit, with reverberation

Henry Cort. (Radio Times Hulton Picture Library)

CORTE REÁL / By Frank Falcone

The Portuguese brothers Gaspar (died 1501) and Miguel (died 1502) Corte Reál were among the early explorers of the northeastern coast of America.

T he Corte Reál (pronounced kōr′tə rē-äl′) brothers were members of a noble Portuguese family. Gaspar was apparently the more aggressive of the two. In 1499 he learned of a grant from King Manoel I to a fellow Portuguese, John Fernandes, to undertake an expedition into the North Atlantic. Manoel sought to establish Portuguese control over a Northwest Passage to India and the Spice Islands. He also wanted someone who would establish Portugal's claims to any new lands that might be discovered in this area. Fernandes did not immediately make use of his grant from the King. Gaspar seized the opportunity to obtain royal permission to undertake his own exploratory expedition in May 1500.

Gaspar Corte Reál left Lisbon in the summer of 1500 in a fleet of three ships, financed by his family. He sailed first to Greenland and spent several months exploring its shoreline. During this time he contacted the natives, whom he compared to the wild natives of Brazil. His ships stayed in Greenland's waters until the winter icebergs forced them to leave. Gaspar and his ships returned to Portugal in late 1500.

The following year Gaspar organized another expedition, this time in conjunction with his brother Miguel. Their expedition departed in May 1501, again bound for unknown lands to the northwest. When they reached land after about 5 weeks, they found themselves on the shores of Labrador. They explored south along the coast, charting approximately 600 miles of shore.

At this point Miguel took two of the ships and returned to Portugal to report their findings. Gaspar, meanwhile, continued south and disappeared. Miguel, now back in Portugal, undertook an expedition to find him. This rescue mission was sanctioned by King Manoel, who also promised Miguel any new islands he might discover. Miguel set out in May 1502 with three ships. The three ships traveled together to Newfoundland, where they decided to divide and meet later. Two of them rendezvoused at the agreed-upon time, but Miguel Corte Reál, like Gaspar, was never seen again, presumably lost in a storm.

King Manoel, a friend of the Corte Reál family, financed a search expedition in 1503. He forbade a third brother, Vasqueanes, an important government official, from undertaking his own rescue attempt.

Further Reading

Gaspar and Miguel Corte Reál are listed in the Geography and Exploration study guide (III, A, 3, d), the American History study guide (I, B, 3, d), and the European History study guide (III, L, 2, f). Among the other 16th-century explorers who searched for the Northwest Pas-

---

processes in a single economic unit, with reverberation and blast furnaces operating side by side. This increased production at a greatly reduced cost, and for the first time iron became one of England's exports.

To obtain more capital, Cort took a partner, Samuel Jellicoe, who put up large sums of money. Jellicoe's father had embezzled these funds from the British government, and when this was discovered, Cort was completely ruined and lost his patent rights. As an acknowledgment of the value of Cort's patents, however, the government granted him a small pension in 1794. Cort died a poor man; he was buried in Hampstead, England.

Further Reading

Henry Cort is listed in the Science study guide (V, H, 1). The iron industry was revolutionized as a result of discoveries by Cort, James WATT, and others, of methods of using coal instead of charcoal in blast furnaces and forges.

There is no biography of Cort. Material on him can be found in T. S. Ashton, *Iron and Steel in the Industrial Revolution* (1924; 2d ed 1951) and *The Industrial Revolution: 1760–1830* (1948; rev. ed. 1964). John C. Hammond and Barbara Hammond, *The Rise of Modern Industry* (1925; 9th ed. 1966), is a classic study that includes information on Cort.

One of the most important navigation instruments available to Gaspar and Miguel Corte Reál was the astrolabe. This drawing, which shows the instrument in use, is from a 1583 manuscript by Jacques de Vaulx. (Bibliothèque Nationale, Paris, Photo Giraudon)

sage were Jacques CARTIER, Sir Martin FROBISHER, and John DAVIS.

Three useful works for the study of Gaspar and Miguel Corte Reál are Edgar Prestage, *The Portuguese Pioneers* (1933); Harold Lamb, *New Found World: How North America Was Discovered and Explored* (1955); and J. H. Parry, *The Age of Reconnaissance* (1963).

CORTÉS / By Lyle N. McAlister

Hernán Cortés (1485?–1547) conquered the Aztec empire in Mexico and became the most famous of the Spanish conquistadores.

Hernán Cortés (pronounced kôr-těz′) was born in Medellín. His parents were of the small landed gentry of the region. As a youth, he studied Latin for 2 years at the University of Salamanca, but lured by tales of new discoveries in America, he abandoned student life and in 1504 sailed for the New World.

Cortés settled initially on the island of Santo Domingo (Hispaniola) but in 1511 joined an expedition to Cuba, where he became a municipal official and an intimate friend of Diego Velázquez, the governor of the island. When Velázquez determined to dispatch an expedition to Mexico, he named Cortés for the command, but Velázquez soon came to suspect Cortés of excessive ambition and determined to relieve him. Cortés, aware of this danger, managed to slip away with part of his followers before the governor could formally confront him. After meeting with other recruits, on Feb. 18, 1519, Cortés departed for Mexico with over 600 Spanish soldiers, sailors,

and captains, some 200 Indian auxiliaries, and 16 horses.

Cortés's route took him first to Yucatán and thence up the Mexican coast to the vicinity of the modern city of Veracruz, where he founded a town, Villa Rica de Veracruz, which became the base for the conquest. There he arranged to have the municipal council—which he had appointed—name him captain general and principal judge, an act which gave him at least quasilegal status. He also negotiated alliances with adjacent Indian tribes and gathered intelligence about the Aztecs.

War with the Aztecs

In August 1519 Cortés struck inland for Tenochtitlán, an island city in Lake Texcoco and the capital of the Aztec confederation ruled by Montezuma II. The most consequential episode in the march was an alliance which Cortés negotiated with the Tlascala, an Indian nation hostile to the Aztecs. In early November the expedition reached the shores of Lake Texcoco. Montezuma, unsure of the intentions of the Spaniards and, indeed, of whether they were gods or men, had offered no overt resistance to their approach and now invited them into Tenochtitlán.

The Spaniards were treated as not entirely welcome guests, and Cortés responded by seizing Montezuma as hostage. At this time Cortés was faced with the arrival of an expedition sent by Governor Velázquez to chastise him. Cortés hastened to the coast to meet the newcomers and, after a surprise attack on them, induced them to join his forces. Upon returning to Tenochtitlán, however, he found the inhabitants in arms and his forces beleaguered in their quarters. Judging the situation to be hopeless, on the night of June 30, 1520, he led his forces from the city to refuge with his Tlascala allies.

In Tlascala, Cortés rebuilt his forces with newly arrived Spaniards and Indian auxiliaries. In May 1521 he began an attack on Tenochtitlán supported by a small navy which had been built in Tlascala, transported to Lake Texcoco, and reassembled. After 75 days of bitter street fighting, on August 13 the city fell to the Spaniards.

Founding of Mexico

Success won legal status for Cortés. On Oct. 15, 1522, Emperor Charles V appointed him governor and captain general of New Spain, the name applied by the Spaniards to the conquered region. It also provided Cortés with an opportunity to display new dimensions of his abilities. He rebuilt Tenochtitlán as the Spanish city of Mexico and dispatched his lieutenants in all directions to subdue other Indian groups. Within a short time most of what is now central and southern Mexico was brought under Spanish rule. Cortés encouraged the introduction of European plants and animals. He vigorously supported the conversion of the native population to Christianity, and his government was marked by consideration for the physical welfare of the Indians.

Cortés's Retirement

The great conqueror's days of glory, however, were short. The Emperor was jealous of powerful and popular captains beyond his immediate control and soon began to withdraw or undermine the governmental powers conceded to Cortés. Royal officials were appointed to oversee the treasury of New Spain, royal judges arrived to dispense justice, and in 1526 he was deprived of the

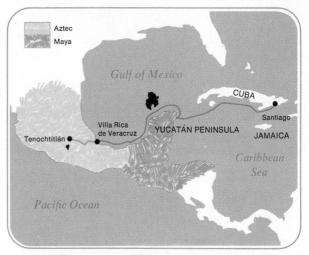

The conquest of Mexico. Cortés sailed from Santiago, Cuba, in February 1519. Two brief stops in the Yucatán Peninsula brought him into contact with the Mayan Indians. Further along the coast, in Aztec territory, he established a base he called Villa Rica de Veracruz. Then, resolutely destroying his fleet, he marched inland toward the Aztec capital, Tenochtitlán.

governorship. Cortés spent 2 years (1528–1530) in Spain defending himself against his enemies and attempting unsuccessfully to recover his administrative authority. He returned, retaining only the honorific military office of captain general but with the title of marquis of the valley of Oaxaca, which conferred on him a vast estate in southern Mexico.

Cortés remained in Mexico for the next. 10 years, managing his estate and undertaking new expeditions which he hoped would recoup his power. His efforts were unsuccessful and in 1540 he returned to Spain, where he lived as a wealthy, honored, but disappointed man until his death in 1547. In compliance with his will, his remains were returned to Mexico, where they repose today in the church of the Hospital of Jesus in Mexico City, an institution which he himself had founded.

Cortés was unquestionably a man of immense abilities. As a conquistador, he displayed an exceptional combination of leadership, audacity, tenacity, diplomacy, and tactical skill. But he was more than a conqueror. He had a vision of a "New Spain" overseas and his statesmanship was instrumental in laying its foundations.

Further Reading

Hernán Cortés is listed in the Latin America study guide (I, B, 4). Bernal DÍAZ DEL CASTILLO accompanied Cortés and recorded his conquests.

The Letters of Cortés was edited by F. A. MacNutt in three volumes in 1908. The best studies of Cortés are F. A. MacNutt, *Fernando Cortés and the Conquest of Mexico* (1909); Salvador de Madariaga, *Hernán Cortés, Conqueror of Mexico* (1942), a fictionalized biography; and H. R. Wagner, *The Rise of Fernando Cortés* (1944). A useful contemporary account is Bernal Díaz del Castil-

Hernán Cortés. (Courtesy of The New-York Historical Society, New York City)

lo, *The True History of the Conquest of New Spain*, translated by A. P. Maudslay (5 vols., 1908–1916). The best single work on the conquest of Mexico is still W. H. Prescott, *History of the Conquest of Mexico* (1843; many later editions). See also R. C. Padden, *The Hummingbird and the Hawk: Conquest and Sovereignty in the Valley of Mexico, 1503–1541* (1967).

CORTONA / By Robert Enggass

The Italian painter and architect Pietro da Cortona (1596–1669) was one of the main representatives of the first full flowering of the high baroque style in Italy.

Pietro Berrettini, known as Pietro da Cortona (pronounced kōr-tō′nä) from his birthplace of Cortona, a little town in Tuscany, was born on Nov. 1, 1596. In Rome, where he went in his teens, the paintings of Annibale Carracci and ancient Roman sculpture especially influenced him. With the encouragement of the learned archeologist Cassiano dal Pozzo he studied, as his contemporary G. B. Passeri tells us, "the statues and bas-reliefs of the ancient Romans, especially various columns, urns, and vases on which were represented sacrifices, bacchic revels, and other pagan ceremonies."

Cortona's Glorification of Pope Urban VIII, *in the Barberini Palace, Rome, is one of the first examples of the mature baroque style in Italian painting. (Alinari)*

Pietro da Cortona, a 1665 self-portrait, in the Uffizi, Florence. (Alinari)

From such ancient sculpture Cortona usually selected those with the most dynamic compositions for his paintings. In his *Rape of the Sabines* (ca. 1629) the figures are arranged on planes parallel to the surface, almost as in a bas-relief, and the Roman architecture and Roman military dress are carefully rendered. But what is most evident is the violence of the individual gestures, the agitation and tumult that fill the whole composition. The highly active figures in Cortona's picture are painted in bright colors that are often laid on rapidly, so that the individual brushstrokes remain visible, much in the manner of the great Venetian artists of the 16th century such as Titian and Veronese.

Cortona's masterpiece of painting is the *Glorification of Pope Urban VIII* (1639), which covers the entire ceiling of the Great Hall of the Barberini Palace in Rome. It is painted to give the illusion that we are looking up into a wide stretch of open sky, partially interrupted by sections of an architectural framework. The sky is filled to overflowing with swarms of human figures who act out endless allegories as they drift back and forth over our heads and under the painted architecture like the last act in some theatrical spectacular in the sky.

Cortona's last major work, the ceiling paintings for the

long gallery in the Pamphili Palace in Rome (1654), depicts the story of Aeneas. The gentler rhythms, the paler colors, and the uncrowded compositions with large stretches of open sky all seem to anticipate the 18th century.

Far less of Cortona's career was devoted to architecture, but here too he demonstrated the highest originality. His facade for the little church of S. Maria della Pace in Rome (1657) spreads across the front of a cloister on one side and an adjacent church on the other. A street runs through what looks like the right aisle. The whole surface of the building seems in motion. Sections of it rise and fall, bulge out or swing back, creating an orchestration as complex as his ceiling paintings and more sophisticated. Cortona died in Rome on May 16, 1669.

Further Reading

Pietro da Cortona is listed in the Art study guide (III, F, 1, a; III, F, 3, a). The style of Cortona, Gian Lorenzo BERNINI, and Francesco BORROMINI is the peak of the high baroque in Italy. As a painter, Cortona was influenced by Annibale CARRACCI, TITIAN, and Paolo VERONESE, and Cortona in turn influenced Giovanni Battista GAULLI.

The standard biography of Cortona is in Italian: Giuliano Briganti, *Pietro da Cortona* (1962). There are good chapters on Cortona in English in Rudolf Wittkower, *Art and Architecture in Italy, 1600–1750* (1958; 2d ed. 1965), and Ellis K. Waterhouse, *Italian Baroque Painting* (1962). The section on Cortona in Robert Enggass and Jonathan Brown, *Italy and Spain, 1600–1750* (1970), gives a detailed explanation of the meaning of Cortona's complicated ceiling painting in the Barberini Palace.

COTTON / By Ola Elizabeth Winslow

John Cotton (1584–1652) was the leading clergyman of New England's first generation, a leader in civil and religious affairs, and a persuasive writer on the theory and practice of Congregationalism.

John Cotton was born in Derby, Derbyshire, England. His father, Roland Cotton, was a lawyer and ardent Puritan; his mother was a deeply religious woman. He entered Trinity College, Cambridge, as a sizar in his thirteenth year, and earned a scholarship to Emmanuel, where he remained for 7 years, taking his bachelor of arts degree in 1603 and his master of arts in 1606. From childhood he had been inclined to the scholar's life, and he remained at Cambridge for 7 more years, taking a bachelor of divinity degree in 1613. Only one other first-generation New Englander held this advanced degree.

During his long experience in the cloistered Cambridge University life, Cotton had learned, in addition to his impressive fund of knowledge—biblical, theological, and ecclesiastical—certain political lessons as well, to be remembered to the last day of his life; among them, how to disagree and yet conform, how to be true to his own convictions and yet at the same time to be safe. He saw both sides of every question in every controversy of his career, and when he took his own position with regard to any one of the issues involved, it would be, in his own words, "a middle way." To approach his mature life with this practical political secret in mind is to find the apparent enigmas about Cotton disappearing.

Aged 29, Cotton became the vicar of the church of St. Botolph in Boston, Lincolnshire. Conscientious Puritan that he was, from the beginning of his 20-year pastorate there, he substituted many simpler forms in the liturgy and succeeded in carrying most of his congregation with him in these changes. He escaped suspicion and remained presumably safe through the employment of a lecturer, a complete conformist, who conducted the more formal services, which would be more closely watched for strict conformity. Under the eye of Archbishop Laud, however, no service would go unwatched, concealment would not be so easy, and suspicion did come.

Escape to America

In the spring of 1632 Cotton received a summons to the Court of High Commission. Knowing what was ahead, he did not appear but went into hiding. On May 7 he sent his resignation from the post of vicar at St. Botolph's to the bishop of London and remained in hiding. Later, with his newly married second wife, he em-

John Cotton. (Library of Congress)

barked in disguise for New England. He was a close friend of John Winthrop, had preached the farewell sermon at Southampton to the vanguard of Winthrop's company in 1630, and had kept in touch with the New England Boston happenings since that date. His first thought for immediate escape had been Holland, but Thomas Hooker's report had changed his plan.

Cotton arrived in Boston on Sept. 4, 1633, and on Sept. 30 was made teacher of the Boston church, a post which he continued to hold for the 19 years he had yet to live. Through these years he was a leading figure in civil as well as religious affairs. Among pulpit men he was the most learned in America, not so eloquent as Thomas Hooker of Hartford and not so persuasive as John Davenport of New Haven, but these two men were his nearest rivals. He stood at the top.

One of Cotton's early civil services was the preparation of an abstract of the laws of New England which was, however, rejected by the colony in favor of one nearer to the Mosaic code. During his first 10 years he had a prominent part in the two controversies which rocked New England to its deepest foundations, the exile of Roger Williams and the heresies of Anne Hutchinson. The Williams controversy unearthed the basic question of the relation between church and state. Magistrates are God's deputies and their power goes as far as life and death, said Cotton. Roger Williams declared that a man's religious loyalties are untouchable by civil power. They were speaking for a future neither man would live to see. In the Anne Hutchinson controversy Cotton was in one of the most uncomfortable situations of his life. At the synod called to list her errors, he split hairs with the accusing brethren over scriptural interpretations to justify his own orthodox preaching; at her trial before the church he strenuously tried to guide her in an orthodox path, only to be obliged to turn against her at the end. This was no doubt a sad moment for him. He had tried to save her and orthodoxy at the same time, but it could not be.

Cotton's Writings

Cotton's printed record is impressive. His exposition of early Congregationalism's purpose and practice is probably his most valuable contribution to American religious history. Among the several titles which illuminate this subject are *The Keyes of the Kingdom of Heaven* (1644), *The Way of the Churches of Christ in New England* (1645), and *The Way of Congregational Churches Cleared* (1645). A statement of his religious views called forth by the Anne Hutchinson controversy in 1636 appears in *Sixteen Questions of Serious and Necessary Consequences Propounded unto Mr. John Cotton with His Answers* (1644). The best volume for the two overlapping debates with Roger Williams is *The Bloudy Tennent Washed and Made White in the Bloud of the Lambe* (1644), together with *The Controversie concerning Liberty of Conscience in Matters of Religion* (1646, 1649). Perhaps the most familiar title in his long list is *Milk for Babes, Drawn out of the Breasts of Both Testaments* (1646), which contains the substance

of 100 sermons and recalls the discipline of uncounted children over three generations.

In his own day Cotton was of great importance. But in the long view of 3 centuries he was not a great man. He belonged to the 17th century and within tight limits. He did not see the changes that were already at work within his own Boston. He had no sympathy with the common man. But the world of willing obedience to authority would not be the world of the future in America. For these reasons his life and thought probably reveal more of what lay behind America's history in its first chapter than those of any other public man of his generation.

Further Reading

John Cotton is listed in the Religion study guide (I, O, 1, b). He was involved in the religious controversies over Roger WILLIAMS and Anne HUTCHINSON.

Two early accounts of Cotton are by his grandson, Cotton Mather, *Magnalia Christi Americana: The Ecclesiastical History of New England* (2 vols., 1702), and by his friend Samuel Whiting, *Concerning the Life of the Famous Mr. Cotton*, which can be found in Alexander Young, *Chronicles of the First Planters of the Colony of Massachusetts Bay from 1623 to 1636* (1846). The best modern study is Larzer Ziff, *The Career of John Cotton* (1962). There is an extensive treatment of Cotton in Perry Miller, *Orthodoxy in Massachusetts, 1630–1650* (1933). Studies devoted to particular aspects of Cotton's life are Emery Battis, *Saints and Sectaries* (1962), which recounts Cotton's involvement in the Anne Hutchinson controversy, and Irwin H. Polishook, *Roger Williams, John Cotton and Religious Freedom* (1967), which attempts a balanced view of the Williams-Cotton controversy.

COUGHLIN / By Charles Alexander

Charles Edward Coughlin (born 1891) was a Canadian-born Roman Catholic priest who became a political organizer in the United States and, during the 1930s, a radical right-wing radio personality.

Born on Oct. 25, 1891, at Hamilton, Ontario, Charles Coughlin received his education in Catholic schools and at St. Michael's College of the University of Toronto. At the age of 20 he began studies for the priesthood, receiving his ordination in 1916. After assisting in several parishes in the Detroit area, Coughlin was formally incardinated into the Detroit diocese in 1923. Three years later Coughlin's bishop assigned him to the new Shrine of the Little Flower Church in the suburban community of Royal Oak, Mich.

In 1926 Coughlin started a weekly broadcast over the local radio station which proved so popular that within 4 years the Columbia Broadcasting System began carrying

Father Charles Coughlin. (Library of Congress)

it nationally. A series of florid denunciations of communism in 1930 gave him a national reputation and occasioned his appearance before the Committee to Investigate Communist Activities, of the U.S. House of Representatives. By the end of the year, however, with the country in the throes of the Great Depression, Father Coughlin had shifted his broadcasts to emphasize the necessity for drastically altering American capitalism under a program keyed to monetary inflation called "social justice," which Coughlin based on the late-19th-century papal encyclical *Rerum novarum.*

In 1931 the network, worried by Coughlin's attacks on the Herbert Hoover administration and by other contentious material in his addresses, discontinued his weekly broadcasts. With contributions from his listeners, Coughlin organized his own radio network, which grew to 26 stations.

During the 1932 presidential campaign Coughlin vigorously championed Franklin D. Roosevelt, proclaiming that America's choice was "Roosevelt or ruin." Roosevelt carefully cultivated Coughlin and benefited substantially from his support in the first year of the New Deal, but he always kept the priest at arm's length. Coughlin, however, saw himself as an unofficial member of the Roosevelt administration and assumed that the President would follow his advice for combating the Depression, particularly his advocacy of massive currency inflation through silver coinage. When Roosevelt refused to accept fully Coughlin's schemes, the priest became a loud critic of the administration.

In 1934 Coughlin formed the National Union for Social Justice to combat communism and to fight for currency inflation and government control of big business. In 1936

Coughlin, determined to stop Roosevelt's reelection, made the National Union the nucleus for the Union party, which also amalgamated much of the following of the late Huey Long and of Francis E. Townsend, crusader for old-age pensions. Roosevelt was overwhelmingly reelected, while the Union party's candidate polled less than 900,000 votes.

After 1936 Father Coughlin's influence declined rapidly. He organized the Christian Front to succeed the National Union and trained his oratorical guns on Roosevelt's foreign policy, which he believed would inevitably involve the country in another war. He also concentrated on the fancied internal menaces of Communists and Jews (who seemed interchangeable in Coughlin's thinking). Fascist Italy and Nazi Germany, he announced, were bulwarks against "Jewish-Communist" power in Europe. Coughlin enunciated a program for an anti-Semitic, fascist-style corporate state, under which established political institutions in the United States would virtually disappear.

Coughlin's anti-Roosevelt oratory became more shrill when World War II broke out in Europe in 1939 and the administration provided more and more assistance to the Allied governments. In 1940 the larger stations in Coughlin's radio network, acting on the basis of a recent National Association of Broadcasters ruling barring "controversial" speakers, refused to renew his broadcasting contracts. When he continued his attacks on the government after Pearl Harbor, his bishop officially silenced him and the Post Office Department banned his weekly newspaper from the mails. After 1942 Father Coughlin confined his activities to those of an ordinary parish priest. He retired from his pastorate in 1966.

Further Reading

Charles Coughlin is listed in the American History study guide (IX, D, 4). Huey LONG of Louisiana was also expert in rabble-rousing.

A biography officially authorized by Father Coughlin and written by a close friend and aide is Louis B. Ward, *Father Charles E. Coughlin* (1933); it must be read with great caution. Charles J. Tull, *Father Coughlin and the New Deal* (1967), is a detached, scholarly study of the radio priest's career during the 1930s. A fuller account of the Union party movement of 1936, in which Coughlin was the central figure, is given in David H. Bennett, *Demagogues in the Depression: American Radicals and the Union Party, 1932–1936* (1969). For information on the upsurge of Catholic social activism in the 1930s, which furnished much of the rationale for Coughlin's activities, see Aaron I. Abell, *American Catholicism and Social Action: A Search for Social Justice, 1865–1950* (1960). There is also information about Coughlin in Arthur M. Schlesinger, Jr., *The Age of Roosevelt* (3 vols., 1957–1960); Rexford G. Tugwell, *The Democratic Roosevelt* (1957); and George Wolfskill and John A. Hudson, *All but the People: Franklin D. Roosevelt and His Critics, 1933–1939* (1969).

COULOMB / By E. Scott Barr

The French physicist Charles Augustin de Coulomb (1736–1806) was famous for establishing the relation for computing the force between electrical charges. He also did pioneering work on sliding and fluid friction.

Charles Augustin de Coulomb (pronounced kōō-lôN′) was born into a distinguished family of Angoulême on June 14, 1736. After being educated in Paris, he spent 9 years in Martinique as an army engineer. Ill health forced him to return to France in 1776, where during the next 13 years his scientific work brought him fame, military advancement, and membership in the Royal Academy of Sciences. He was appointed intendant of France's waters and fountains in 1784. The next 5 years were spent in writing his memoirs on electricity and magnetism. Coulomb had become a noted and influential figure in the academic world but resigned all his positions at the outbreak of the Revolution. He returned to Paris in 1802 for an appointment as one of the inspector generals of public instruction.

Coulomb's 1779 memoir, *The Theory of Simple Machines*, is a compilation of his early experiments on statics and mechanics in which he makes the first formal statement of the laws governing friction. In 1784 he studied torsional elasticity, finding the relationship between the various factors involved in the small oscillations of a body subjected to torsion.

His most notable papers are the seven which Coulomb presented before the academy in 1785 and 1786. In the first he announced the measurement of the electrical forces of repulsion between electrical charges. He extended this work to the forces of attraction in his second memoir. This led to further quantitative work and his famous law of force for electrostatic charges (Coulomb's law). The subsequent papers dealt with the loss of electricity of bodies and the distribution of electricity on conductors. He introduced the "proof plane" and by using it was able to demonstrate the relationship between charge density and the curvature of a conducting surface.

Magnetism was the subject of Coulomb's early studies and the one to which he returned in later years. He noted that magnetism obeyed a relation of attraction and repulsion similar to that for electrical forces. He also established the equation of motion of a magnet in a magnetic field, showing the derivation of the magnetic moment from the period of small oscillations.

In 1801 Coulomb published another important paper, in which he presented the results he obtained by allowing a cylinder to oscillate in a liquid, thus providing a way to find relative liquid viscosities.

Of Coulomb, Thomas Young wrote, "his moral character is said to have been as correct as his mathematical investigations." He remained in Paris until his death on Aug. 23, 1806.

Further Reading

Charles Augustin de Coulomb is listed in the Science study guide (V, C, 2). Henry CAVENDISH was another outstanding physicist of the 18th century.

Most of the information on Coulomb is in French. In English, descriptions of his experiments are in William Francis Magie, *A Source Book in Physics* (1935); Duane Roller and Duane H. D. Roller, *The Development of the Concept of Electric Charge: Electricity from the Greeks to Coulomb* (1954); and Morris H. Shamos, ed., *Great Experiments in Physics* (1960). For general background on the scientific environment of the time see Abraham Wolf, *A History of Science, Technology and Philosophy in the Eighteenth Century* (1939). Brief references also appear in *A History of the Theories of Aether and Electricity: From the Age of Descartes to the Close of the Nineteenth Century* (1910), and Hugh Hildreth Skilling, *Exploring Electricity: Man's Unfinished Quest* (1948).

Charles Augustin de Coulomb. (Photo-Hachette)

COULTON / By Richard C. Clark

The English historian and polemicist George Gordon Coulton (1858–1947) was the leading medievalist of his day. His primary interest was ecclesiastical history.

George Coulton, the son of John James and Sarah Coulton, was born on Oct. 15, 1858, in King's Lynn. In 1877 Coulton entered St. Catharine's College, Cambridge, where he obtained his degree. He then studied for holy orders in the Anglican Church and was ordained deacon in 1883 and priest in 1884. The following year he resigned from the priesthood and began teaching at various private schools. In 1895 he sustained a nervous breakdown; after his recovery he left the academic life to work with a friend who ran a coaching company at Eastbourne. Spending 13 years there in relative financial security gave him the opportunity to pursue his own studies.

During this period Coulton decided to devote his life to the study of medieval life and thought, with special emphasis on the organization and operation of the ecclesiastical system of those centuries. He began to publish works in this field, such as *From St. Francis to Dante* (1906) and *Chaucer and His England* (1908). His developing reputation as a medievalist led to his appointment to the prestigious post of Birkbeck lecturer in ecclesiastical history at Trinity College, Cambridge, in 1910.

In 1919 Coulton was elected to what was then the sole university lectureship in English and later the same year was made a fellow of St. John's College, Cambridge. From that time onward, except during World War II when he was guest lecturer at Toronto, he remained at Cambridge.

Coulton's leading works are considered to be *Five Centuries of Religion* (4 vols., 1923–1950), *The Medieval Village* (1925), *Art and the Reformation* (1928), and *Medieval Panorama* (1938). His depictions in the area of ecclesiastical history, especially of monasticism, have been criticized as being unduly dark and pessimistic.

Throughout his life Coulton supported and vigorously argued in behalf of compulsory military service. He was also an unwavering advocate of what he termed the "moderate Protestant position." In both causes his rather uncompromising attitude was distasteful to many of his antagonists and colleagues. Nevertheless, he felt that his deep moral convictions left him no alternative on this subject. In the cause of compulsory military service he personally investigated conditions in France and Switzerland, spoke and wrote against pacifist views, and published many pamphlets and books, the best-known being *The Case for Compulsory Military Service* (1917). His polemics in religion also embroiled him in controversy throughout his life, particularly with Catholic historians. In fact, in the opinion of several critics his controversies generated more animosity and obfuscation than light.

Further Reading

George Coulton is listed in the Social Sciences study guide (VII, A, 1). Another historian of the Middle Ages was the Belgian scholar Henri PIRENNE.

Coulton's autobiography is *Fourscore Years* (1943). Sarah Campion, *Father* (1948), is a biographical memoir by his daughter.

❋   ❋   ❋

A. S. COUPER / By Lord Todd

The British chemist Archibald Scott Couper (1831–1892) shares with Kekulé the distinction of recognizing the tetravalency of carbon and the capacity of carbon atoms to combine to form chains, thereby providing the basis for structural organic chemistry.

Archibald Scott Couper was born on March 31, 1831, at Kirkintilloch in Dumbartonshire, Scotland, the son of a prosperous cotton weaver. He commenced his university studies at Glasgow mainly in classics, spent the summer semester of 1852 in Berlin, and returned to Scotland to complete his university course in logic and metaphysics at Edinburgh. He spent the period 1854–1856 in Berlin and during this time decided to study chemistry.

Couper entered the laboratory of Charles Wurtz in Paris in the autumn of 1856 and remained there until his return to Scotland in 1858; during these 2 years he made all his contributions to chemistry: two papers containing

George Coulton. (National Portrait Gallery, London)

Archibald Scott Couper. (Library of Congress)

experimental contributions and his now famous memoir "On a New Chemical Theory." A few months after his return to Edinburgh to be assistant to Lyon Playfair, in the autumn of 1858 he suffered a severe nervous breakdown, followed by a general breakdown in health. He retired to Kirkintilloch and lived there incapable of intellectual work and completely lost to chemistry until his death 34 years later.

Work on the Element Carbon

The story of Couper's work, its subsequent disappearance from view, and its later recognition, largely through the efforts of Richard Anschütz, as a major piece of chemical history is one of the most remarkable in science. Early in 1858 Couper, then 27 and after only some 3 years' contact with chemistry, asked Wurtz to present Couper's manuscript "On a New Chemical Theory" to the French Academy. Wurtz, however, delayed taking any steps, and in the interim August Kekulé's paper "On the Constitution and Metamorphoses of Chemical Compounds and on the Chemical Nature of Carbon" appeared, containing essentially similar proposals. Couper protested to Wurtz about his procrastination but was, it is said, shown out of the laboratory.

Couper's paper was, however, finally presented by Jean Baptiste Dumas to the academy on June 14, 1858, and published in the *Comptes rendus;* fuller versions were subsequently published in English and French. After pointing out the inadequacy of current theories, Couper wrote in his paper: "I propose to consider the single element carbon. This body is found to have two highly distinguished characteristics: (1) It combines with equal numbers of equivalents of hydrogen, chlorine, oxygen, sulphur, etc. (2) It enters into chemical combination with itself. These two properties, in my opinion, explain all that is characteristic of organic chemistry. This will be rendered apparent as I advance. This second property is, so far as I am aware, here signalized for the first time."

Valence and Aromatic Compounds

Couper also introduced the use of a line to indicate the valence linkage between two atoms and, had he used 16 rather than 8 for the atomic weight of oxygen, his chemical formulas would have been almost identical with those used today. It is also remarkable that in his paper he represents cyanuric acid by a formula containing a ring of three carbon and three nitrogen atoms joined by valence lines—the first ring formula ever published. The introduction of ring formulas is often ascribed to Kekulé, who in 1865 used this concept to develop his formula for benzene. It is interesting to speculate whether Couper might have anticipated Kekulé's formulation of aromatic compounds had he been able to continue his chemical work. But Couper's paper "On a New Chemical Theory" remains a landmark in the history of organic chemistry.

Further Reading

Archibald Scott Couper is listed in the Science study guide (VI, D, 1). The work of August KEKULÉ on carbon paralleled Couper's.

Alexander Findlay, *A Hundred Years of Chemistry* (1937; 3d ed. 1965), discusses Couper's work and includes a short bibliography. See also Eduard Farber, *The Evolution of Chemistry: A History of Its Ideas, Methods and Materials* (1952; 2d ed. 1969).

J. H. COUPER / By Patrick Glenn Porter

American agriculturist James Hamilton Couper (1794–1866), a leading Southern planter, was among the first to apply scientific research to agricultural operations.

James H. Couper was born on March 4, 1794, in Sunbury, Ga. His father had emigrated from Scotland in 1775. The family moved several times, settling on Georgia's Atlantic coast, where Couper's father bought land on St. Simon Island and formed a plantation partnership with a friend, James Hamilton. Their business was raising long-fibered sea island cotton. In 1804 Couper's father bought another tract of land on the

Altamaha River near Brunswick, Ga. Couper grew up the heir of a wealthy and influential family.

Among Couper's advantages was a college education; he graduated from Yale College in 1814 at the age of 20. He traveled to Holland to study methods of water control for possible use on the Georgia plantations. After his return he became manager of the estate on the Altamaha River. The family fortunes suffered reversals in the 1820s, and Couper's father failed in business in 1826. Hamilton paid off his partner's obligations in exchange for a half interest in the river estate. The younger Couper acquired Hamilton's half interest the following year and remained as manager. When he inherited his father's acres on St. Simon Island, he emerged as a leading Southern planter, supervising some 1,500 slaves.

Couper soon began scientific research and experimentation, setting the pace for his contemporaries and successors in the South. His scientific diking and drainage system at the Altamaha plantation was soon copied by others. Beginning as a cotton planter, he later raised several other commercial crops, including rice and sugarcane. At Altamaha in 1829 he built the most complete, modern sugar mill in the South. He was also the first American to build and operate a cottonseed oil mill; he erected two mills. Although he failed in the cottonseed oil business, his successors in the South found the industry a most prosperous one.

Couper was one of the South's planter aristocrats; he had impeccable manners, a graceful way in conversation, an extensive library, and high social prestige. The Civil War freed his slaves, claimed two of his sons, and destroyed his life. Couper died in 1866; few had better symbolized the meaning of the old, antebellum slavocracy.

Further Reading

James H. Couper is listed in the American History study guide (V, D, 1). Other agriculturists were John DEERE and Edmund RUFFIN.

Couper's associate, Charles Spalding Wylly, wrote *The Seed That Was Sown in the Colony of Georgia: The Harvest and the Aftermath, 1740–1870* (1910), a good source of information on Couper's life. Other helpful works include Frances Butler Leigh, *Ten Years on a Georgian Plantation since the War* (1883); Ralph Betts Flanders, *Plantation Slavery in Georgia* (1933); and Lewis Cecil Gray, *History of Agriculture in the Southern United States to 1860* (2 vols., 1933–1941).

COUPERIN / By Aubrey S. Garlington, Jr.

François Couperin (1668–1733), called Couperin le Grand, was a French composer, organist, and harpsichordist. His harpsichord and organ works are the touchstones of the 18th-century elegant style.

François Couperin (pronounced kōō-prăN′) was born on Nov. 10, 1668, in Paris. The Couperin dynasty was the most famous musical family in France during the 17th and 18th centuries. The first Couperin came to Paris from the region of Brie and became organist for the church of St-Gervais; his brothers soon followed. Couperin's father, Charles, succeeded his brother Louis on the latter's death in 1661. Charles died in 1679, and although François was only 11 years old he was named as Charles's successor at St-Gervais. The post was held open for François both on legal grounds and in the light of his extraordinary talent until he reached the age of 18.

In 1692 Couperin produced his first publications, pieces composed in the Italian manner. While retaining his post at St-Gervais, he entered the service of King Louis XIV in 1693 as one of the organists of the king's chapel at Versailles. Couperin prospered at court, being appointed master of music for the royal children in 1694 and ennobled in 1696.

Couperin composed much church music for use at Versailles. His keyboard and chamber music circulated in aristocratic circles. In 1713 the King granted Couperin the privilege of publishing his own music. He first issued a series of harpsichord suites (which he called *ordres*) written over the preceding 2 decades. In 1714 he published the three surviving sets from a projected group of nine *Leçons des Ténèbres*. *L'Art de toucher le clavecin*, his major theoretical work, appeared in 1716. The

François Couperin. (The Metropolitan Museum of Art, The Crosby Brown Collection, 1901)

second *ordre* of harpsichord pieces came out in 1717, and the following year Couperin succeeded to the post of *ordinaire de la musique* to the King. Encouraged by the success of his publications, Couperin brought out sets and suites of earlier compositions in rapid order, and in 1730 his fourth *ordre* of harpsichord pieces was put together with the assistance of his family. He died on Sept. 12, 1733.

The bulk of Couperin's published work disappeared shortly after his death. Since his only son is presumed to have died in infancy, the post of organist at St-Gervais passed to a nephew. The position remained in the family until the French Revolution, and the dynasty itself died out in the 19th century.

Harpsichord and Church Compositions

Couperin's harpsichord music is marked by a very elegant style and reflects the urbane, sophisticated quality of courtly and intellectual life as it was experienced in the last years of the reign of Louis XIV. Couperin arranged his harpsichord music into dance suites, with faintly suggestive or arcanely humorous titles; these character pieces represent the height of the cultured taste of the 18th-century connoisseur.

The music is not programmatic in the common sense of the term. Instead, Couperin only suggests or hints at the conditions of civilized life in the manner of a memoir. Such titles as *La Diane* and *La Charolaise* from Ordre I or *La Baccaneles* and *Le Réveil-matin* from Ordre II are but intimate suggestions or reminiscences; the titles are not descriptive any more than the music itself pretends to describe the actualities implied in the title.

Couperin's church music is marked by a solemn stateliness. Although not at all pompous it is entirely in keeping with the demands of the court, and in his old age Louis XIV preferred order, serenity, and restraint above all else.

Manual of Performance Practice

L'Art de toucher le clavecin is the most important theoretical work with regard to performance practice surviving from 18th-century France. Here Couperin describes precise articulations for the very complicated style of ornamentation which dominated his harpsichord music. For Couperin ornamentation is not an additive process but one absolutely integral to the construction of the music itself; hence, accuracy is mandatory. This keyboard manual is also very illuminating with regard to such topics as fingering, phrasing, and *notes inégales* (the practice of performing evenly written notes unequally).

The accomplishments of Couperin le Grand are still among the least comprehended and appreciated of major 18th-century composers. Only with careful, scrupulously accurate re-creations in the proper style by the harpsichord can one begin to understand Couperin's supreme compositional gifts.

Further Reading

François Couperin is listed in the Music study guide (I,

D, 2). He and Jean Philippe RAMEAU were the greatest baroque composers of harpsichord music in France. Domenico SCARLATTI also composed many character pieces.

The standard work in English on Couperin's music is Wilfred H. Mellers, *François Couperin and the French Classical Tradition* (1950).

COURBET / By George Mauner

> Jean Desiré Gustave Courbet (1819–1877) was a French painter whose powerful pictures of peasants and scenes of everyday life established him as the leading figure of the realist movement of the mid-19th century.

Gustave Courbet (pronounced kōōr-bĕ′) was born at Ornans on June 10, 1819. He appears to have inherited his vigorous temperament from his father, a landowner and prominent personality in the Franche-Comté region. At the age of 18 Gustave went to the Collège Royal at Besançon. There he openly expressed his dissatisfaction with the traditional classical subjects he was obliged to study, going so far as to lead a revolt among the students. In 1838 he was enrolled as an *externe* and could simultaneously attend the classes of Charles Flajoulot, director of the École des Beaux-Arts. At the college in Besançon, Courbet became fast friends with Max Buchon, whose *Essais poétiques* (1839) he illustrated with four lithographs.

In 1840 Courbet went to Paris to study law, but he decided to become a painter and spent much time copying in the Louvre. In 1844 his *Self-Portrait with Black Dog* was exhibited at the Salon. The following year he submitted five pictures; only one, *Le Guitarrero*, was accepted. After a complete rejection in 1847, the Liberal Jury of 1848 accepted all 10 of his entries, and the critic Champfleury, who was to become Courbet's first staunch apologist, highly praised the *Walpurgis Night*.

Courbet achieved artistic maturity with *After Dinner at Ornans*, which was shown at the Salon of 1849. By 1850 the last traces of sentimentality disappeared from his work as he strove to achieve an honest imagery of the lives of simple people, but the monumentality of the concept in conjunction with the rustic subject matter proved to be widely unacceptable. At this time the notion of Courbet's "vulgarity" became current as the press began to lampoon his pictures and criticize his penchant for the ugly. His nine entries in the Salon of 1850 included the *Portrait of Berlioz*, the *Man with the Pipe*, the *Return from the Fair*, the *Stone Breakers*, and, largest of all, the *Burial at Ornans*, which contains over 40 life-size figures whose rugged features and static poses are reinforced by the somber landscape. A decade later Courbet wrote: "The basis of realism is the negation of the

Gustave Courbet, a self-portrait. (Courtesy Wadsworth Atheneum, Hartford, Conn.)

ideal. . . . *Burial at Ornans* was in reality the burial of romanticism. . . .''

In 1851 the Second Empire was officially proclaimed, and during the next 20 years Courbet remained an uncompromising opponent of Emperor Napoleon III. At the Salon of 1853, where the painter exhibited three works, the Emperor pronounced one of them, *The Bathers*, obscene; nevertheless, it was purchased by a Montpellier innkeeper, Alfred Bruyas, who became the artist's patron and host. While visiting Bruyas in 1854 Courbet painted his first seascapes. Among them is the *Seashore at Palavas*, in which the artist is seen waving his hat at the great expanse of water. In a letter to Jules Vallès written in this period Courbet remarked: "Oh sea! Your voice is tremendous, but it will never succeed in drowning out the voice of Fame shouting my name to the entire world."

Courbet was handsome and flamboyant, naively boast-ful, and aware of his own worth. His extraordinary self-confidence is also evident in another painting of 1854, *The Meeting*, in which Courbet, stick in hand, approaches Bruyas and his servant, who welcome him with reverential attitudes. It has recently been shown that the picture bears a relationship to the theme of the Wandering Jew as it was commonly represented in the naive imagery of the popular Épinal prints.

Of the 14 paintings Courbet submitted to the Paris World Exhibition of 1855, 3 major ones were rejected. In retaliation, he showed 40 of his pictures at a private pavilion he erected opposite the official one. In the preface to his catalog Courbet expressed his intention "to be able to represent the customs, the ideas, the appearance of my own era according to my own valuation; to be not only a painter but a man as well; in short, to create living art."

The Stone Breakers, an 1849 painting by Courbet. The painting was destroyed in 1945 during the bombing of Dresden. (Deutsche Fotothek, Dresden)

One of the rejected works was the enormous painting *The Studio*, the full title of which was *Real Allegory, Representing a Phase of Seven Years of My Life as a Painter*. The work is charged with a symbolism which, in spite of obvious elements, remains obscure. At the center, between the two worlds expressed by the inhabitants of the left and right sides of the picture, is Courbet painting a landscape while a nude looks over his shoulder and a child admires his work. Champfleury found the notion of a "real allegory" ridiculous and concluded that Courbet had lost the conviction and simplicity of the earlier works. *Young Ladies by the Seine* (1856) only served to further convince the critic of Courbet's diminished powers.

But if Courbet had begun to disappoint the members of the old realist circle, his popular reputation, particularly outside France, was growing. He visited Frankfurt in 1858–1859, where he took part in elaborate hunting parties and painted a number of scenes based on direct observation. His *Stag Drinking* was exhibited in Besançon, where Courbet won a medal, and in 1861 his work, as well as a lecture on his artistic principles, met with great success in Antwerp. With the support of the critic Jules Castagnary, Courbet opened a school where students dissatisfied with the training at the École des Beaux-Arts could hear him extol the virtues of independence from authority and dedication to nature.

Courbet's art of the mid-1860s no longer conveyed the democratic principles so clearly embodied in the earlier works. He turned his attention increasingly to landscapes, portraits, and erotic nudes based, in part, on mythological themes. These include the *Venus and Psyche* (1864; and a variant entitled *The Awakening*), *Sleeping Women*, and *Woman with a Parrot* (1866).

In 1870 Courbet was offered the Légion d'Honneur, which, characteristically, he rejected. Now, at the height of his career, he was drawn directly into political activity. During the Franco-Prussian War he was named president of a commission charged with protecting works of art in Paris, and he also served as a member of another commission engaged in a study of the Louvre archives with the intent of discovering frauds traceable to the deposed government of Napoleon III. On March 19, 1871, the Commune was officially established, and a month later Courbet was elected a delegate. On May 8 the column in the Place Vendôme, long associated with Bonapartism, was pulled down, and on June 7, after the abolition of the Commune, Courbet was sentenced to a 6-month prison term for his part in the destruction of the column. He returned to Ornans in 1872, but the following year, when his case was reopened, he fled to Switzerland and settled near Vevey at La Tour de Peilz. In 1874 the government demanded the payment of 320,000 francs toward the reconstruction of the column and the public sale of his possessions. Already seriously ill with dropsy, Courbet was overwhelmed by the hopelessness of his situation. He died at La Tour de Peilz on Dec. 31, 1877.

Further Reading

Gustave Courbet is listed in the Art study guide (III, H, 1, d). He greatly influenced the early work of Paul CÉZANNE, Claude MONET, and Pierre Auguste RENOIR.

The only full biographical study of Courbet in English is Gerstle Mack, *Gustave Courbet* (1951), which is, however, poorly illustrated. Many good illustrations and a concise text are in Robert Fernier, *Gustave Courbet*, translated by Marcus Bullock (1969). *Gustave Courbet*, the catalog to the exhibition held at the Philadelphia Museum of Art and the Boston Museum of Fine Arts in 1959–1960, is noteworthy for its rich documentation of many works, good illustrations, and clear chronology. There is an important discussion of Courbet in John Rewald, *The History of Impressionism* (1946; rev. ed. 1961), and a study of the reception which his works received in "Courbet and His Critics" by George Boas, contained in the anthology edited by Boas, *Courbet and the Naturalistic Movement* (1938).

* * *

COURNOT / By Henri Guitton

The French mathematician, philosopher, and economist Antoine Augustin Cournot (1801–1877) was one of the founders of mathematical economics.

Antoine Augustin Cournot (pronounced kōor-nō′) was born at Gray, Haute-Saône, on Aug. 28, 1801. In 1821 he entered a teachers' training college and in 1829 earned a doctoral degree in mathematics, with mechanics as his main thesis supplemented by astronomy. While studying at the college, he also served (1823–1833) as private secretary to Marshal de Gouvion Saint-Cyr. From 1834 he held successive positions as professor of analysis and mechanics on the science faculty of Lyons, rector of Grenoble Academy, chief examiner for undergraduate students, and, finally, rector of Dijon Academy (1854–1862). He died, nearly blind, in 1877.

Although Cournot was above all a mathematician and a member of the teaching profession, his numerous works show him also to have been a philosopher and economist. In the field of mathematics, in addition to his thesis on the movements of rigid bodies and celestial bodies, he devoted his efforts to two great problems: the theory of functions and the calculus of infinity (1841), and the theory of chance and probability (1843). These theories, above and beyond their mathematical significance, seemed to Cournot to hold an important place in man's general understanding of the world, but more specifically an understanding of the place of economics in man's life.

Cournot was a profound thinker: his advanced ideas

on order and chance, enlightening both for science and mankind in general, are still prophetic. His economic concepts were broad in scope; his theories on monopolies and duopolies are still famous. In the field of economics he wrote few books or treatises. One book, however, has had an immense bearing on modern economic thought: *Recherches sur les principes mathématiques de la théorie des richesses* (*Researches on the Mathematical Principles of the Theory of Wealth*) was published in 1838 and reedited in 1938 with an introduction by Georges Lutfalla.

Unfortunately, this book met with no success during Cournot's lifetime because the application of the formulas and symbols of mathematics to economic analysis was considered audacious. In an attempt to improve the comprehensiveness of this work, Cournot rewrote it twice: in 1863 under the title *Principes de la théorie des richesses*, and in 1877 in *Revue sommaire des doctrines économiques*. These last two works are oversimplified and less informative versions of the original, since they were stripped of the mathematical language. *Researches* can, however, be thought of as the point of departure for modern economic analysis.

Having introduced the ideas of function and probability into economic analysis, Cournot derived the first formula for the rule of supply and demand as a function of price $[D = f(p)]$. He made clear the fact that the practical uses of mathematics in economics do not necessarily involve strict numerical precision; economists must utilize the tools of mathematics only to establish probable limits

Antoine Augustin Cournot.

and to express seemingly inaccessible facts in more absolute terms. Cournot's work is recognized today in the discipline called econometrics.

Further Reading

Antoine Augustin Cournot is listed in the Social Sciences study guide (VI, C, 2). As a student, Cournot was a disciple of the mathematicians Joseph Louis LAGRANGE and Pierre Simon de LAPLACE.

S. W. Floss, *An Outline of the Philosophy of Antoine-Augustine Cournot* (1941), is a detailed, comprehensive study of Cournot's philosophic writings. Jacob Oser, *The Evolution of Economic Thought* (1963), includes a discussion of Cournot's theories.

✳   ✳   ✳

COUSIN / By Walter V. Brewer

> The French educator and philosopher Victor Cousin (1792–1867) helped to reorganize the French primary school system. He also established the study of philosophy as a major intellectual pursuit of the French secondary and higher schools.

Victor Cousin (pronounced kōō-zăN′) was born in Paris in the midst of the Revolution on Nov. 28, 1792, the son of a poor watchmaker. Like most boys of humble birth at that time, Cousin languished in the streets awaiting the appropriate age to enter an apprenticeship. When he was 11, a fateful event altered the course of his life: in a street fight between schoolboys Cousin came to the rescue of the underdog, whose mother was looking on. A woman of means, she gratefully paid for Cousin's schooling at the Lycée Charlemagne, where he became one of the most brilliant students in the school's history. He continued his successful scholarly career first as a student at the prestigious École Normale, where he decided on a career in philosophy, and then as a teacher of philosophy in several schools, and finally as a professor at the Sorbonne.

Development of Eclecticism

In 1817 and again in 1818 Cousin traveled to Germany to meet the leading lights of German letters, J. W. von Goethe, Friedrich Schleiermacher, Friedrich von Schelling, and, most important of all, G. W. F. Hegel. According to Cousin's "eclecticism," as he called his approach, the human mind can accept all carefully thought-out and moderate interpretations of the world. No system of thought is seen to be false, merely incomplete. By studying the history of philosophy, Cousin directed his students to choose from each system what is true in it and in so doing to arrive at a complete philosophy. The introduction of the history of philosophy as a major discipline in higher schools in France is a lasting accomplishment of Cousin. He organized the history of philosophy in two major works: *Cours de l'histoire de la philosophie* (Course of the History of Philosophy), written and revised between 1815 and 1841, portions of which have been translated into English; and the widely read *Du vrai, du beau, et du bien* (1836), which has been translated into English under the title *Lectures on the True, the Beautiful, and the Good*, and which came out in 31 editions over 90 years.

Political Pressures

During the repressive years of the Bourbon restoration (1820–1830), Cousin, considered too liberal, was fired from the Sorbonne. While traveling in Germany during that time, he was jailed for 6 months for being a liberal agitator, a charge that was wholly unfounded.

In the government of the July Monarchy (1830–1848) Cousin rose to the heights of power and success as an educator and statesman. As a member of the Council of State and later as a peer, he exercised the major influence over French schools and universities. Because of his knowledge of Germany, Cousin was sent to study the successful primary school systems of several German states, especially Prussia. His book *Report of the State of Public Instruction in Prussia* (1833), recommending reforms to the French, was read abroad and stirred many Americans, Horace Mann and Calvin Stowe among other, to visit Prussia to learn how the budding American common school could best be guided in its development. The Guizot Law of 1833, which was a constitution for the French primary school system, was written by Cousin and based on his *Report*.

The Revolution of 1848 left Cousin without a job. Yet

Victor Cousin. (Giraudon)

his influence continued to be felt into the next two generations, since the leaders of the French nation were the graduates of the schools that for 18 years had felt the imprint of Cousin's dynamic style, thought, and personality. Cousin never married. His voluminous correspondence, which continued steadily until his death, attests to close friendships with many leaders in Europe and North America.

Further Reading

Victor Cousin is listed in the Social Sciences study guide (VI, C, 2). In his philosophy he sought to combine the idealism of G. W. F. HEGEL with the merits of John LOCKE, Thomas REID, and Immanuel KANT into a system that would be in the tradition of René DESCARTES and other French thinkers.

The best book in English on Cousin, an affectionate and colorful biography, is Jules Simon, *Victor Cousin* (2d ed. 1882; trans. 1888). See also George Boas, *French Philosophies of the Romantic Period* (1925).

✻   ✻   ✻

COVERDALE

/ By Eric McDermott

The English Puritan Miles Coverdale (1488–1569) was the first to translate the complete Bible into English.

Miles Coverdale. (Radio Times Hulton Picture Library)

Miles Coverdale was a Yorkshireman of whose early education nothing is known. He joined the Augustinian friars at their great Barnwell Priory at Cambridge and became a priest, probably in 1514. He was very much influenced by his prior, Robert Barnes, an early and very active Lutheran, who was ultimately put to death under Henry VIII for his heretical opinions. Coverdale's increasingly heretical views caused him first to abandon his religious profession and then to leave England. By 1529 he had settled at Hamburg, Germany, and was engaged in assisting William Tyndale with his English translation of various parts of the Holy Scriptures.

By 1534 Coverdale was in Antwerp, where a merchant commissioned him to render the whole Bible in English. The printing of Coverdale's translation was completed by October 1535. This Bible, although allowed to circulate in England, lacked official approval because of its heretical tendentiousness and its inadequacy as a translation. Accordingly, Thomas Cromwell engaged Coverdale to work in England on a new version, using a revised edition of Tyndale's work known as Matthew's Bible. Coverdale's renewed efforts resulted in the publication in 1539 of the widely accepted Great Bible.

Meanwhile, Coverdale had taken a Scottish wife and with her went to Strassburg in 1540, when Henry VIII's approval of various executions made a longer stay in En-

gland dangerous. He returned to England, however, after Henry's death in 1547; he won favor, especially as a preacher, from the Privy Council and was rewarded with the bishopric of Exeter in 1551. As bishop, he earned a good reputation both from the fine example of his life and from his pastoral solicitude. But Coverdale was deposed soon after Mary I's accession to the throne in 1553. He would probably have been executed for heresy had not the king of Denmark successfully pleaded with Mary to allow him to depart for Copenhagen in 1555.

During his 4-year sojourn on the Continent, Coverdale visited various cities and worked on the Puritan version of the Bible, which appeared at Geneva in 1560. Then he returned to England. He was never restored to Exeter, probably because of his Puritanism, but he continued to preach and was warmly esteemed by his Puritan associates. He died in London on Jan. 20, 1569. His second wife, whom he married after his first wife's death in 1565, administered his estate. Of the two children by his first marriage, nothing seems to be known.

Further Reading

Miles Coverdale is listed in the Religion study guide (I, J, 1) and the Literature study guide (II, D, 1, b). He worked with William TYNDALE, and his patron was Thomas CROMWELL.

The most recent study of Coverdale is James F. Mozley, *Coverdale and His Bibles* (1953), which outlines his life in the first chapter and has useful bibliographical appendices. An earlier study is Henry Guppy, *Miles Coverdale and the English Bible, 1488–1568* (1935).

* * *

COVILHÃO / By Frank Falcone

The Portuguese adventurer Pedro de Covilhão (ca. 1455–ca. 1530) was an explorer and diplomat, notably in eastern Africa.

In 1487 King John II commissioned Pedro de Covilhão (pronounced kōo-vē-lyouN′) to undertake an exploratory-diplomatic venture as part of Portugal's effort to break the Venetian hold on commerce with the East. Covilhão's specific assignment was to gather information about trade routes and friendly ports throughout the Arabic world. He was also instructed to find out more about the mysterious kingdom of Prester John, the legendary priest-king, which was reputed to be somewhere in Africa, India, or China. Contact with a Christian king in the Moslem world would have been extremely valuable to Portugal.

Covilhão's background made him a likely candidate for the dual mission. Not only had he served John II as a spy, but he was one of the few Portuguese diplomats fluent in Arabic. He traveled to Alexandria and Cairo successfully disguised as a Moslem. Joining a caravan, he worked his way down the eastern coast of Africa, gathering information about the size and condition of facilities along the way. In 1490 Covilhão returned along the coast to Cairo. There he met messengers from King John and sent back with them a detailed report of his reconnaissance trip. His firsthand account of trade routes and ports, previously known only to Moorish traders, now made it possible for Portuguese expeditions to begin trading incursions along the eastern coast of Africa. His reports coincided with the discovery of a sea route around the Cape of Good Hope, thus further facilitating direct Portuguese contact with the Eastern world.

In order to pursue the legend of Prester John, Covilhão unilaterally decided to journey further east. He left Cairo in 1491 headed first for Mecca, this time disguising himself as a Moslem pilgrim. By so doing, he placed himself in grave danger, because discovery as an infidel meant certain death. He traced the legend of Prester John to Abyssinia (Ethiopia). While he did not find Prester John —who purportedly died years before his arrival in 1493 —he did receive a warm welcome from the Abyssinian king. The king apparently recognized the value of this imaginative and bold foreigner, for he did not allow Covilhão to return to Portugal. Covilhão proved to be a valuable and useful servant; he was rewarded with titles and a substantial settlement of land, and he even married an Abyssinian.

Covilhão died sometime between 1527 and 1530. Before his death, however, he was able to be of further service to Portugal. When that government sent a diplomatic mission to Abyssinia in 1520, Covilhão served as interpreter and also informed the Portuguese envoys about the customs and traditions of his host's nation.

Further Reading

Pedro de Covilhão is listed in the Geography and Exploration study guide (III, A, 2). Niccolò de' CONTI was another outstanding European traveler of this period.

Three useful works for the study of Covilhão are Arthur Percival Newton, *Travel and Travellers of the Middle Ages* (1926); Edgar Prestage, *The Portuguese Pioneers* (1933); and J. H. Parry, *The Age of Reconnaissance* (1963).

* * *

Pedro de Covilhão's journeys to Abyssinia (Ethiopia) and other parts of Africa were motivated in part by his king's desire to find the legendary Christian kingdom of Prester John, which was thought to be somewhere in Africa. This 1558 map is from an atlas by Diego Homem. (Trustees of the British Museum)

COWARD / By Frederick R. Benson

The English playwright, actor, and composer Noel Coward (born 1899) was known for his genial urbanity and frequently acerbic wit.

oel Coward was born in Teddingham, Middlesex, and studied intermittently at the Royal Chapel School in London. A restless and extroverted youth, he made his acting debut at the age of 12 and a year later won praise for his portrayal of Slightly in *Peter Pan.*

Coward's first play, *Rat Trap,* an exercise in psychological realism, was written in 1917 but not published until 1926. He played the leading role in his next play, *The Last Track* (1918). His first drama to be noted by the critics was *The Vortex* (1924), a serious play about narcotics addiction. During this period he was regarded as the spokesman for the younger generation, although his works were often condemned as immoral.

In 1929 Coward starred in the Broadway production of his *Bitter Sweet,* a romantic musical that was popular in both Great Britain and the United States. This play's popular song, "I'll See You Again," is one of his notable efforts as a composer; among his other songs are "Mad Dogs and Englishmen" and "I'll Follow My Secret Heart."

Coward's important plays of the next decade or so included *Private Lives* (1930), a sophisticated marital comedy; *Cavalcade* (1931), a patriotic depiction of British Victorian tradition; *Design for Living* (1937), a stylish comedy; and *Blithe Spirit* (1941), a fantasy concerning spiritualism. During World War II Coward entertained troops on the major battlefronts and later detailed his experiences in *Middle East Diary* (1945). In 1942 he wrote, codirected with David Lean, and acted in the motion picture *In Which We Serve,* which presented life aboard a British naval destroyer. He continued his collaboration with Lean on the filming of *Blithe Spirit* (1945) and on the scenario for *Brief Encounter* (1946), one of the screen's most tender love stories.

Although Coward's dramas of succeeding years—*Peace in Our Time* (1947), *Quadrille* (1952), *Nude with Violin* (1956), and *Sail Away* (1961)—lacked the freshness of his earlier works, he compensated for his eclipse as a writer by embarking on a career as an entertainer and raconteur. In 1960 he gave his finest performance as the secret agent in the Carol Reed–Graham Greene film, *Our Man in Havana.* Coward also wrote two volumes of autobiographical reminiscences, *Present Indicative* (1937) and *Future Indefinite* (1954); two collections of short stories, *To Step Aside* (1939) and *Star Quality* (1951); and a novel, *Pomp and Circumstance* (1960), portraying British life on a South Seas island. He was knighted by Queen Elizabeth in 1970.

Further Reading

Noel Coward is listed in the Literature study guide (II, J, 3). He was the outstanding modern creator of drawing-room comedy in the tradition of William CONGREVE and Oscar WILDE.

In addition to Coward's autobiographical works, see Robert Greacen, *The Art of Noël Coward* (1953), a brief biographical and critical study; James Agee, *Agee on Film* (1958); and Kenneth Tynan, *Curtains: Selections from Drama Criticism and Related Writings* (1961) and *Tynan Right and Left: Plays, Films, People, Places and Events* (1967).

COWELL / By Edward E. Cole, Jr.

Henry Dixon Cowell (1897–1965) was an inventive and productive American composer, pianist, teacher, and author.

enry Cowell was born in Menlo Park, Calif. A precocious pianist and violinist, he began composing by the age of 8. He received his first systematic training under Charles Seeger at the University of California, prior to Army service in World War I.

During the 1930s Cowell, already established in America as a sort of maverick composer, pursued musicological studies in Europe, meanwhile touring as a pianist-composer. He often caused near-riots with audiences when playing works including "tone clusters"—a term and technique he originated that is used by many avant-garde composers. A tone cluster is produced by placing the

Noel Coward. (Radio Times Hulton Picture Library)

Henry Cowell. (National Archives, Washington, D.C.)

"hymn and fuguing tune." He was also an early experimenter with electronic instruments, such as the theremin, and pioneered in writing "serious" music for bands. His music, too prolific to list here, covers, often in depth, almost every thinkable musical combination. He was frequently disguisedly conservative in his compositions. For example, his invocation of "Americana" in certain works, except for certain subtle creative techniques employed, could sound "apple-pie American." Yet, especially in later years, traveling the world widely (especially Asia), he could dig deeply into the ancient musical lores of, for example, Iran or Japan, and produce an effective work sounding part Persian or part Japanese, part cosmopolitan-modern. He had set out to shock audiences, especially as a performing pianist-composer; later, he composed intricate, but somehow very accessible, music disturbing to practically no one.

Cowell once stated: "As a creator of music I contribute my religious, philosophical, and ethical beliefs in terms of creative sound: that sound which flows through the mind of the composer with a concentrated intensity that baffles description, the sound which is the very life of the composer, and which is the sum and substance of his faith and feeling." Virgil Thomson summed up: "Cowell's music covers a wider range in both expression and technic than any other living composer.... Add to this massive production his long and influential career as pedagog, and Cowell's achievement in music becomes impressive indeed. There is no other quite like it. To be fecund and right is given to few."

Further Reading

Henry Cowell is listed in the Music study guide (II, D, 1). Charles IVES and John CAGE were other modern American composers.

Information about Cowell is available in John T. Howard, *Our Contemporary Composers: American Music in the Twentieth Century* (1941); William W. Austin, *Music in the Twentieth Century* (1966); Peter Yates, *Twentieth Century Music* (1967); and David Ewen, *The World of Twentieth Century Music* (1968).

fist, full hand, or full forearm over a section of the keyboard, while usually the other hand continues to play normally. Occasionally, Cowell rose and sat a moment on the keyboard. He sometimes delved into the innards of the piano, using fingers or plectra to stroke or pluck strings, playing while standing, his other hand on the keyboard, with pedal effects produced by a foot. Meanwhile, he was experimenting with new effects that could be produced on orchestral instruments. However, he was also composing comparatively simple pieces reflective of his Irish parentage and his love of American folklore.

Cowell became one of the most vocal champions of new and of older, neglected American composers. He founded the *New Musical Quarterly*, contributed to many musical magazines, and edited *American Composers on American Music* (1933). He and his wife wrote *Charles Ives and His Music*. He was cofounder and often president or board member of the American Composers Alliance, an organization that made unpublished scores by both noted and younger composers available. Cowell even raised money during the 1930s and 1940s to sponsor recordings featuring the works of younger American composers. He later was a director-member of Composers' Recordings, Inc. Meanwhile, teaching in a number of colleges and universities, he influenced many American and some foreign composers, who have since achieved success.

Cowell conjured a special American musical form of his own in which one will find some of his most significant music, aside from his many symphonies. He called it

COWLEY / By Norman Rabkin

The English writer Abraham Cowley (1618–1667) was among the first to use the Pindaric ode form in English poetry. He contributed importantly to the development of the familiar essay in English.

The posthumous son of a merchant, Abraham Cowley was born in London and educated at Westminster and Trinity College, Cambridge, where he became a fellow in 1640. Like Richard Crashaw, he left Cambridge in 1643, when Oliver Cromwell's occupation of the city threatened the continuance of his fellowship, and joined the court at Oxford. He served the English court in Paris in 1646 and spent the next years on royal business. Returning to England in 1654, he was arrested the following year but after his release made his peace with Cromwell. He returned to Oxford to study medicine and earned a doctor of medicine degree in 1657.

With the Restoration in 1660 Cowley regained his fellowship together with some land whose rent provided a livelihood somewhat less than what he had hoped for from the court. For the rest of his life he lived in retirement studying botany and writing essays. He was one of the first to be nominated for membership in the Royal Society. His contemporary reputation as a poet was greater than it has been since, and his funeral at Westminster Abbey in 1667 was the most magnificent that had yet been afforded a poet.

Cowley's earliest volume, *Poetical Blossoms* (1633), published when he was only 15, comprises a schoolboy's imitations of Edmund Spenser and other Elizabethans. At Cambridge he wrote some plays, including *The Guardian* (1642), which was produced after the Restoration as *The Cutter of Coleman Street*. In 1647 he published *The Mistress*, a collection of poems, included with revisions in the *Poems* of 1656, which contained other poems as well, including his odes and the unfinished *Davideis*, a biblical epic. His odes made this form the vehicle for grandiose invention and influenced poetry for the next century. More verses appeared in 1663, and

in 1668 his posthumous *Works* made additional poetry and his essays available.

The lyrics of *The Mistress* were influenced by metaphysical and cavalier traditions. They lack the virtues of the poetry they imitate, however, and thus served Dr. Johnson well in the next century when he chose them to illustrate the shortcomings of the metaphysical school. Cowley's religious epic, however, is the work of a man of common sense and rationality.

Further Reading

Abraham Cowley is listed in the Literature study guide (II, E, 2, c). Much of his poetry shows the influence of John DONNE.

The famous life of Cowley in Samuel Johnson's *Lives of the English Poets* appeared in 1779. A modern biography is Arthur H. Nethercot, *Abraham Cowley, the Muse's Hannibal* (1931). Studies of his poetry and its background are in George Williamson, *The Donne Tradition* (1930), and Douglas Bush, *English Literature in the Earlier Seventeenth Century* (1945; 2d ed. 1962).

COWPER / By Brian Wilkie

> The most characteristic work of the English poet William Cowper (1731–1800) is gentle and pious in mood and deals with retired rural life. He often anticipated the attitudes and subjects of romantic and Victorian authors.

William Cowper was born on Nov. 26, 1731; his mother was a descendant of the poet John Donne. He studied law and was admitted to the bar in 1754. A love affair with his cousin ended unhappily in 1756, largely because the girl's father was concerned over Cowper's mental stability. In 1763 Cowper suffered a complete nervous breakdown as a consequence of worry about an examination he was to take for a clerkship in the House of Lords. After several attempts at suicide he was committed to a madhouse.

After recuperating, Cowper spent his life under the care of several friends and patrons, notably Mrs. Mary Unwin (a clergyman's widow), the evangelical clergyman John Newton (whose religious zeal probably did not aid Cowper's troubled mind), and Cowper's cousin Lady Hesketh. In collaboration with Newton, Cowper wrote numerous hymns. His life after 1765 was one of rustic retirement, punctuated by severe breakdowns in 1773, 1787, and 1794. His intermittent attacks of madness were generally characterized by severe religious gloom and often by a sense that he was irrevocably damned.

Cowper's most significant literary work was done in the last 2 decades of his life. In 1780–1781 he wrote a series of reflective essays in couplets; in 1782 he composed the immensely popular "John Gilpin's Ride," in which he burlesques the heroic ballad. In 1783 Cowper

Abraham Cowley, a portrait by Sir Peter Lely.
(National Portrait Gallery, London)

William Cowper, a portrait painted in 1792.
(National Portrait Gallery, London)

began his curious long poem *The Task* (published 1785), which begins with a mock-elevated disquisition on the historical evolution of the sofa from the humble three-legged stool (a lady had suggested the topic in response to Cowper's complaint that he lacked a subject for blank verse). It then treats a multitude of descriptive and reflective subjects and is probably Cowper's most typical poem. In it quiet meditation is mingled with atmospheric description of simple rural life and placid natural scenes.

Cowper's translation of Homer (1784–1791) demonstrated his opposition to what he considered the artificial elevatedness of Alexander Pope's version. In 1799 Cowper wrote the somber poem "The Castaway"; like the earlier "Lines Supposed to Be Written by Alexander Selkirk" (published 1782), it is a study of human isolation and has poignant religious overtones.

Cowper was one of the best and most prolific English letter writers. He also composed the texts of many well-known hymns, including "There Is a Fountain Filled with Blood," "God Moves in a Mysterious Way," and "Oh for a Closer Walk with God." He died on April 25, 1800.

Further Reading

William Cowper is listed in the Literature study guide (II, F, 2, b). In its treatment of nature, understated blank verse, and simple diction, Cowper's *The Task* anticipates the poetry of William WORDSWORTH.

For Cowper's life see Maurice J. Quinlan, *William Cowper* (1953), and William N. Free, *William Cowper* (1970), which also contains a fine discussion of Cowper's poetry. Charles Ryskamp, *William Cowper of the Inner*

Temple (1959), deals with the poet's early years. For critical comment see Morris Golden, *In Search of Stability: The Poetry of William Cowper* (1960), and Patricia A. Spacks, *The Insistence of Horror: Aspects of the Supernatural in Eighteenth-Century Poetry* (1962).

COXE / By Richard T. Farrell

American political economist and businessman Tench Coxe (1755–1824) vigorously defended the development of a balanced national economy in which agriculture, manufacturing, and commerce would all contribute to the general prosperity of the country.

Tench Coxe was born in Philadelphia on May 22, 1755. His father, a respected merchant, was active in local politics. At the age of 16 Tench entered the College of Philadelphia (now the University of Pennsylvania) to study law. He was more interested in business than law, however, and when he came of age, he became a partner in his father's firm.

Coxe faced a dilemma during the American Revolution, as did many other established merchants. When the British invaded Philadelphia, he decided to remain neutral rather than declare his support for the Colonies. Some of his critics have claimed that Coxe was actually a royalist sympathizer and that he joined Gen. William Howe's army against the patriots. Considering his later career, however, this seems doubtful. More likely, the decision was based on economic rather than political motives. After the British withdrew from Philadelphia, his name was listed among those persons accused of treason. But the charges were dropped when no one appeared against him.

Following the Treaty of Paris (1783), Coxe turned his attentions to economic and social problems facing the new nation. In addition to serving on several local committees which attempted to restore order to both state and interstate commercial relations, he was a delegate to the Annapolis Convention (1786) and served briefly in the Continental Congress (1788). He also worked for banking reforms and served as secretary for an organization that promoted the abolition of slavery and relief for free Negroes held in bondage unlawfully.

Coxe began to consider national politics seriously after 1787. Although not a delegate to the Constitutional Convention, he worked enthusiastically for the adoption of the Constitution. He believed the new government would create a sound basis for establishing a national economy and would facilitate orderly economic growth. In 1790 he was appointed assistant to the treasurer, Alexander Hamilton. He supported assumption of state debts, full payment of the national debt, and creation of a national bank. His most influential contributions were made in Hamilton's *Report on Manufactures*. In 1792 he

Tench Coxe at 40. (Courtesy of The New-York Historical Society, New York City)

became commissioner of revenue. Although Coxe split with the Federalist party, he remained active in the government until 1797, when he was removed from office by John Adams. Having supported Thomas Jefferson in the election of 1800, he was appointed purveyor of public supplies and held this position until 1812.

Coxe played an important role in the development of American manufacturing. Called by some the father of the American cotton industry, he urged large-scale cultivation of cotton and in 1786 unsuccessfully attempted to import copies of Richard Arkwright's cotton-processing machinery. He died in Philadephia in 1824.

Further Reading

Tench Coxe is listed in the American History study guide (IV, E, 1). Wade HAMPTON and Elkanah WATSON were agriculturists of the period.

Harold Hutcheson, *Tench Coxe: A Study in American Economic Development* (1938), is a thorough study of Coxe's economic philosophy. For Coxe's views on cotton production see George S. White, *Memoir of Samuel Slater: The Father of American Manufactures* (1836).

✳   ✳   ✳

COXEY / By Joseph R. Conlin

The American reformer and eccentric Jacob Sechler Coxey (1854–1951) was a well-to-do businessman who, distressed by the economic depression of the 1890s and impelled by the era's reform ideas, led a march of unemployed workers to Washington, D.C., in 1894.

Born in Selinsgrove, Pa., on April 16, 1854, Jacob Coxey quit school at 15 and went to work in the rolling mills of Danville. Ten years later he was an operator of a stationary engine. He briefly ran a scrap iron business, then moved to Massillon, Ohio, and in 1881 purchased a sandstone quarry supplying steel and glass factories. Business prospered and Coxey expanded his interests into agricultural holdings. By 1894 he was the wealthiest man in Massillon, his reputed fortune $200,-000.

Like many men of his time, Coxey was interested in reform, especially in currency questions. He had been a Greenback Democrat and a member of the Greenback party. He was an unsuccessful candidate for the Ohio Senate in 1885. By the 1890s he was a Populist. In 1894, when he burst into national prominence, Coxey was 40 years old, of medium height, had a neatly trimmed mustache, and presented the general appearance of a prosperous, conservative citizen of the middle class. He was no outstanding orator but impressed people with his simple earnestness and sincerity.

This was the age of the "tramp problem"—tens of thousands of unemployed men on the road in search of work. Along with a colorful colleague, Carl Browne, Coxey conceived the idea of a march on Washington by a "Commonweal of Christ" to dramatize the plight of the country's unemployed. The object was to pressure Congress to adopt Coxey's two pet schemes, designed to relieve the distress of the unemployed while waging war on the interest-based wealth he despised. His Good Roads Bill called for the issuance of $500,000,000 to be expended on the construction of rural roads for wages of $1.50 for an 8-hour day. His Bond Bill authorized the Federal government to purchase bonds from local governments with fiat money, which the latter would use to employ men in constructing various public works, again paying Coxey's minimum wage.

The marchers left Massillon in late March 1894, traveled on foot about 15 miles a day through bad weather, and arrived in Washington on May 1. Coxey had predicted he would arrive with 100,000 men, but his band never numbered more than 300 on the road and his following in Washington was about 1000. (Other "armies" patterned after Coxey's sometimes numbered 2000.) The expedition ended in fiasco with Coxey and Browne arrested and sentenced to 20 days in jail for walking on the grass.

Coxey stuck to his ideas. He testified in Washington several times (including as late as 1946) and ran for innumerable offices for almost every political party. He was Republican mayor of Massillon (1931–1934). In 1932 he received 7,000 votes as the presidential nominee of his Farmer-Labor party. In 1944 he delivered the speech on the Capitol steps in Washington that he had begun exactly 50 years earlier. He died in Massillon on Jan. 14, 1951.

Jacob Coxey. *(Library of Congress)*

Coxey was an eccentric, but much of the substance of his 1894 proposals was subsequently adopted in government measures. The ideas which he propagandized were in the air during the 1890s. Coxey's contribution was to synthesize and promote them in a coherent program.

Further Reading

Jacob Coxey is listed in the American History study guide (VII, E, 4). "True" labor leaders in America included Eugene V. DEBS and Samuel GOMPERS.

The lack of a recent comprehensive study of Coxey must be attributed to the excellence of the standard work on the subject: Donald L. McMurry, *Coxey's Army: A Study of the Industrial Army Movement of 1894* (1929; rev. ed. 1968). The revised edition contains an excellent introduction by John D. Hicks that traces Coxey's career after the publication of McMurry's book. See also John D. Hicks, *The Populist Revolt* (1931).

COYSEVOX / By James L. Connelly

The work of the French sculptor Antoine Coysevox (1640–1720) reflected a shift in official French taste from the relatively severe classicism of the 1660s and 1670s to the more expressive and Italianate baroque style and foreshadowed the rococo.

Antoine Coysevox (pronounced kwȧz-vôks′) was born in Lyons on Sept. 29, 1640. He studied at the Royal Academy in Paris (1657–1663). By the late 1670s he was employed at Versailles with many other sculptors engaged in the task of creating fountains and statues for the vast gardens. The artists working on this project were required to conform to the demand by the Royal Academy for a restrained, classical version of the baroque style. Although Coysevox never visited Italy, his personal taste tended to the more fluid, dramatic Italian baroque, and the garden sculpture he executed in the French classical manner is generally dull and uninspired.

During the 1680s the classicism which had dominated the Royal Academy became less constricting, and by the 1690s Louis XIV was himself inclined toward a more specifically Italian baroque style. These developments freed Coysevox's expressive talent, and he gradually began to overshadow François Girardon, his most important rival and the sculptor whose work most clearly reflected the earlier French taste for baroque classicism.

A brilliant example of Coysevox's fully developed personal style is the great stucco relief sculpture (1683–1685) of Louis XIV, which he executed for the Salon de la Guerre (Hall of War) at Versailles. In keeping with the name of this magnificently pompous reception room,

Antoine Coysevox, a portrait by Hyacinthe Rigaud. *(Giraudon)*

Coysevox's relief presents the King on horseback as a conquering emperor riding victoriously over his fallen enemies. The bursting composition, the dramatic use of space, the boldly vigorous high relief, and the lively surface of this work are stylistic characteristics which constitute a break with French classicism.

Coysevox executed over 200 pieces of sculpture, including garden statues, religious works, portrait busts, reliefs, and tombs. His important tomb for Cardinal Mazarin (1689–1693; now in the Louvre, Paris) is surrounded by three richly draped bronze female figures personifying virtues and depicts Mazarin, in marble, kneeling on top of the tomb; the cardinal's gesture is lively and vibrant, and the long train of his vestment flows behind him in dramatic twists and folds and overlaps the edges of the tomb.

Coysevox's later works reveal marked tendencies toward the rococo, the light, delicate, intimate style which was to dominate the arts during the first half of the 18th century. These tendencies are especially to be seen in Coysevox's late portrait busts and in works such as the *Duchesse de Bourgogne as Diana* (1710) at Versailles. The duchess is shown as a lighthearted goddess of the hunt, her pose animated, her draperies gently agitated by her movement; the composition is pierced with space, and the surface presents a refined contrast of delicate textures. Coysevox died in Paris on Oct. 10, 1720.

Further Reading

Antoine Coysevox is listed in the Art study guide (III, F, 2; III, G, 2). His chief rival was François GIRARDON.

The most important works on Coysevox are in French and include Georges Keller-Dorian, *Antoine Coysevox* (2 vols., 1920), and Luc Benoist, *Coysevox* (1930). For a brief but thorough and excellent analysis of Coysevox's place in 17th-century French art see Sir Anthony Blunt, *Art and Architecture in France, 1500–1700* (1953; rev. ed. 1957).

CRABBE / By Patricia Craddock

The English poet George Crabbe (1754–1832) is noted for his unsentimental realism in portraying people and events and his precision in describing visible nature.

George Crabbe was born on Dec. 24, 1754, in Aldeburgh, a poor fishing village in Suffolk. His father, part owner of a fishing boat and a customs master, had had some education. Therefore when George proved to have no promise as a seaman, his father sent him to schools at Bungay and Stow Market.

In 1768 Crabbe was apprenticed to a surgeon. But this master taught him little, and in 1771 he changed masters and moved to Woodbridge. There he met his future

George Crabbe. (National Portrait Gallery, London)

wife, Sarah Elmy, who accepted his proposal and had the faith and patience not only to wait for Crabbe but to encourage his verse writing.

In 1772 Crabbe had his first literary success; his poem on hope won a prize offered by *Wheble's Lady's Magazine*. Two years later his "Inebriety" was published. During the next years he completed his apprenticeship, studied midwifery in London, and attempted to practice in Aldeburgh. Then, in April 1780, Crabbe borrowed £5 and set off for London to try his literary fortunes. A poem, "The Candidate," was accepted, but the publisher's bankruptcy deprived Crabbe of any possible profit. In March 1781 he appealed in desperation to Edmund Burke, who recognized the merits of the man and his poems.

With Burke's aid Crabbe published three long poems: *The Library* (1781), *The Village* (1782), and *The Newspaper* (1785). *The Village* was much the best, the first example of Crabbe's special talent for telling with literal and compelling truth the often sordid stories of rural and village folk. In 1781 Crabbe took orders, and the following year he became the Duke of Rutland's chaplain.

In December 1783 Crabbe was at last able to marry. Although the duke died in 1787, Crabbe's life continued to be marked by happy domesticity and moderate advancement as a clergyman. A second period of publication, with much critical and some popular success, produced *The Parish Register* (1807), *The Borough* (1810), and *Tales in Verse* (1812), all in the vein of *The Village*. In 1813 his wife died, and in 1814 Crabbe moved to his last home and parish, in Trowbridge, Wiltshire. *Tales of the Hall*, his last volume of poems, was published in 1817. Crabbe died on Feb. 3, 1832, in Trowbridge.

Further Reading

George Crabbe is listed in the Literature study guide (II, F, 2, b). Last of the line of Alexander POPE in that he wrote satirically in heroic couplets, Crabbe anticipated the directness and concern with nature of the romantics, among them William WORDSWORTH.

The first and fullest life of Crabbe is by his son, George Crabbe, Jr., *The Life of the Rev. George Crabbe, LLB* (1834). The best bibliography is in Frederick Clark's translation of René L. Huchon, *George Crabbe and His Times* (1907). Recent critical studies are those of Robert L. Chamberlain, *George Crabbe* (1965), intended for general readers, and Oliver F. Sigworth, *Nature's Sternest Painter: Five Essays on the Poetry of George Crabbe* (1965), intended for specialists. A good brief critical biography is Thomas E. Kebbel, *Life of George Crabbe* (1888), in the "Great Writers" series.

CRANACH THE ELDER

/ **By Dario A. Covi**

The German painter, engraver, and designer of woodcuts Lucas Cranach the Elder (1472–1553) is best known for the delightfully mannered style he practiced as court painter to the electors of Saxony.

Lucas Cranach the Elder, a self-portrait, in the Uffizi, Florence. (Alinari)

Lucas Cranach (pronounced krăn′ək) the Elder was born at Kronach, Franconia. He was apparently trained by his father, Hans, a painter, and from 1495 to 1498 undertook work at Kronach for Coburg and Gotha. There is evidence that Cranach resided in Vienna between about 1500 and 1504. In 1504 he married Barbara Brengbier of Gotha, who bore him three daughters and two sons, Hans (died 1537) and Lucas the Younger (1515–1586), both of whom were painters.

In 1505 Cranach established residence at Wittenberg, where he was court painter to three successive electors: Frederick the Wise, John the Constant, and John Frederick the Magnanimous. Cranach was a prosperous and respected citizen. He owned several houses and land, held the office of councilor, and was a burgomaster. He also worked for other princely patrons and was a follower and lifelong friend of Martin Luther.

In 1550 Cranach followed John Frederick the Magnanimous to Augsburg, where the elector was in exile, and in 1552 accompanied him to Weimar. Cranach died in Weimar on Oct. 16, 1553.

Early Works

Cranach's earliest known works belong to the period of his Vienna residence and are strongly expressive in style, with figures and landscape dramatically united in movement; an interest in picturesque landscape manifests itself, anticipating tendencies peculiar to the so-called Danube school. Characteristic examples are *St. Jerome in Penitence* (1502), the half-length portraits of Dr. Johannes Cuspinian and his wife Anna (ca. 1502–1503), and the *Crucifixion* in Munich (1503). In the composition of the *Crucifixion* Cranach broke sharply with iconographic tradition and employed bold foreshortening and other spatial devices that reflect a knowledge of the art of Michael Pacher and, through it, of Andrea Mantegna. In Cranach's first signed painting, *Rest on the Flight into Egypt* (1504), the spirit is idyllic and the actions of the figures are lively.

Change in Style

Cranach's work became less emotional after he moved to Wittenberg in 1505, although the change was slower in the woodcuts than in the paintings. His woodcuts were technically inspired by Albrecht Dürer's but less finely cut and less clearly organized. In Cranach's woodcuts a dramatic emphasis prevailed, and a preference for tone led, by 1509, to the use of the chiaroscuro technique, as in the *St. Christopher* of 1506, reused or recut and printed with a color block in 1509. The change in style in the paintings may be seen in the *Martyrdom of St. Catherine* in Dresden (1506), in which the emphatic rendering of the garment patterns, the falling tongues of fire, and the crowding of the figures result in a loss of compositional unity and spatial clarity; and in the *Holy*

Kinship Altarpiece (1509), painted soon after Cranach's trip to the Netherlands, in which Flemish influence accounts for the general disposition and costumes of the figures.

Thereafter Cranach's painting was increasingly distinguished by minimal modeling, stress on linear detail, clean contours, and, in the portraits and most pictures of one or two figures, unmodeled backgrounds. This may be observed in works of such diverse subject matter as the *Madonna and Child* in Breslau (ca. 1510), the model for many variants to issue from his workshop; *Cardinal Albrecht of Brandenburg as St. Jerome in His Study* (1525), based on Dürer's engraving *St. Jerome in His Study;* the *Judgment of Paris* (1530) and *Venus* (1532), in which the subjects are classical but the interpretation is pervaded by a naive charm due in large part to Cranach's curvaceous, gently erotic female nudes; the full-length portraits of Duke Henry the Pious and his wife Catherine (1514); the *Fountain of Youth* (1546); and Reformation pictures like the *Fall and Salvation* (1529) and *Christ Blessing the Little Children* (1538). Cranach also painted hunting scenes for the lodges of his princely patrons.

Cranach's drawings include eight pages of marginal illustrations for the Prayer Book of Maximilian (1515) and magnificent animal and portrait studies, like the head of Martin Luther's father (ca. 1527). His best-known engraving is the *Penance of St. John Chrysostom* (1509).

Further Reading

Lucas Cranach the Elder is listed in the Art study guide (III, E, 1, b). The Danube school derives from the painting of Michael PACHER. The Danube style found its purest expression in the works of Albrecht ALTDORFER. Cranach often used motifs from the woodcuts of Albrecht DÜRER.

A good summary of Cranach's life and art, with reproductions of his most characteristic work, is in Eberhard Ruhmer, *Cranach,* translated from the German by Joan Spencer (1963). For Cranach's drawings see Jakob Rosenberg, *Die Zeichnungen Lucas Cranach d. A.* (1960); and for the prints see F. W. H. Hollstein, *German Engravings, Etchings and Woodcuts, ca. 1400–1700,* vol. 6 (1954).

CRANDALL / By Frederick C. Schult, Jr.

American educator Prudence Crandall (1803–1890) made one of the early experiments in providing educational facilities for Negro girls.

In painting his 1503 Crucifixion *Cranach broke with pictorial tradition, placing Christ's cross on the extreme right rather than in the center of the picture. The picture is also unusual in that Christ is not seen frontally but is turned in space. (Bayerische Staatsgemäldesammlungen, Munich)*

Prudence Crandall was born on Sept. 3, 1803, in Hopkinton, R.I., to a Quaker family. Her father moved to a farm at Canterbury, Conn., in 1813. She attended the Friends' Boarding School at Providence, R.I., and later taught in a school for girls at Plainfield, Conn. In 1831 she returned to Canterbury to run the newly established Canterbury Female Boarding School. When Sarah Harris, daughter of a free Negro farmer in the vicinity, asked to be admitted to the school in order to prepare for teaching members of her race, she was accepted. Immediately, the townspeople objected and pressured to have Sarah dismissed.

Miss Crandall was familiar with the abolitionist movement and had read William Lloyd Garrison's *Liberator.* Faced with the town's resolutions of disapproval, she met with abolitionists in Boston, Providence, and New York to enlist support for the transformation of the Canterbury school into a school for Negro girls. The *Liberator* advertised for new pupils. In February 1833 the white pupils were dismissed, and by April, 20 Negro girls took up studies. A trade boycott and other harassments of the school ensued. Warnings, threats, and acts of violence against the school replaced disapproving town-meeting resolutions.

Abolitionists came to Miss Crandall's defense, using

Prudence Crandall. (Cornell University Libraries, Ithaca, N.Y.)

until her death on Jan. 28, 1890. In 1886 the Connecticut Legislature had voted her an annual pension of $400.

Further Reading

Prudence Crandall is listed in the Social Sciences study guide (VI, G, 3). Other American educators included Horace MANN and G. Stanley HALL.

Wendell P. and Francis J. Garrison, *William Lloyd Garrison, 1805–1879: The Story of His Life Told by His Children* (4 vols., 1885–1889), and John C. Kimball, *Connecticut's Canterbury Tale: Its Heroine Prudence Crandall and Its Moral for Today* (1886), are informative accounts of Prudence Crandall's work. See also Thomas E. Drake, *Quakers and Slavery in America* (1950), and Dwight L. Dumond, *Antislavery: The Crusade for Freedom in America* (1961).

H. CRANE / By Hyatt H. Waggoner

Hart Crane (1899–1932) was an American poet in the mystical tradition who attempted through the visionary affirmations of his richly imagistic, metaphysically intense poetry to counter the naturalistic despair of the 1920s.

the issue as a stand against opposition to furthering the education of the freed Negro. Despite attacks the school continued operation. On May 24, 1833, the Connecticut Legislature passed a law prohibiting such a school with Negroes from outside the state unless it had the town's permission, and under this law Miss Crandall was arrested in July. She was placed in the county jail for one night and then released under bond.

A prominent abolitionist, Arthur Tappan of New York, provided money to hire the ablest lawyers to defend the Quaker school teacher at her trial, which opened at the Windham County Court on Aug. 23, 1833. The case centered on the constitutionality of the Connecticut law about Negro education. The defense held that the Negroes were citizens in other states, were so therefore in Connecticut, and could not be deprived of their rights under the Federal Constitution. The prosecution denied that freed Negroes were citizens. The county court jury failed to reach a decision. Although a new trial in Superior Court decided against the school, when the decision reached the Supreme Court of Errors on appeal, the case was dismissed for lack of evidence.

The judicial process had not stopped the operation of the Canterbury school, but the townspeople's violence against it increased and finally closed it on Sept. 10, 1834. The Quaker lady had married a Baptist preacher, Calvin Philleo, on Sept. 4, 1834. He took her to Ithaca, N.Y., and from there they went to Illinois and finally to Elk Falls, Kans., where Prudence Crandall Philleo lived

Hart Crane was born on July 21, 1899, in Garrettsville, Ohio, the son of the successful Cleveland manufacturer of "Crane's Chocolates," and was raised in Cleveland. He violently repudiated the business values of his father and attached himself to his more cultivated mother. Crane's life was permeated with severe psychic disturbances perhaps originating in this nearly classic Oedipal situation; he eventually became an avowed homosexual and a severe alcoholic.

Apprentice Poet

In 1916 Crane went to New York, where he held odd jobs to support himself while writing poetry. Later he worked in several midwestern cities before returning to New York in the early 1920s to align himself with the literary avant-garde. Immersing himself in the study of his American literary ancestors, particularly Herman Melville, Walt Whitman, and Emily Dickinson, Crane also managed to become familiar with the experimental verse being published in the "little magazines" of the period and to read the latest works of T. S. Eliot and Ezra Pound.

From 1925 until the end of his life Crane received financial assistance from the New York banker and art patron Otto Kahn. Thus he was able to prepare for publication his first volume of poetry, *White Buildings* (1926).

Earlier, in 1922, a reading of the *Tertium Organum*, written by the Russian mystic P. D. Ouspensky, had affected Crane profoundly, for it provided what seemed a cogent defense of Crane's own belief in the validity of mystical knowledge based on ecstasy and direct illumination. Ouspensky used Whitman as the chief example of a modern man possessed of mystic awareness, further enhancing Crane's interest in Whitman's poetry. This interest eventually resulted in Crane's most ambitious project, *The Bridge* (1930), a series of closely related long poems (inspired by Whitman's example) on the transcendent meaning of the United States, in which the Brooklyn Bridge symbolized the spiritual evolution of civilization. Crane attempted to build a metaphysical "bridge" between the individual and the race, the temporal and the eternal, and the physical and the transcendent.

The tortuous spiritual affirmations of Crane's poetry, with its illumination and exaltation, represented the positive side of an intense lifelong struggle against despair and self-disgust. On April 26, 1932, after a year in Mexico on a Guggenheim fellowship, Crane committed suicide by leaping into the Gulf of Mexico from the ship that was returning him to the United States. Thus the poet united himself with the sea that had so often served him as symbol of both the universal creative life-force and the threat of annihilation.

Analysis of the Writings

Allen Tate's foreword to his friend's first volume, *White Buildings*, remains perhaps the best brief introduction to Crane's difficult and intense poetic vision. Tate wrote: "The poetry of Hart Crane is ambitious.... It is an American poetry. Crane's themes are abstractly, metaphysically conceived, but they are definitely confined to an experience of the American scene.... Crane's poems are a fresh vision of the world, so intensely personalized in a new creative language that only the strictest and most unprepossessed effort of attention can take it in.... Melville and Whitman are his avowed masters. In his sea poems ... there is something of Melville's intense, transcendental brooding on the mystery of the 'high interiors of the sea.' ... Crane's poetry is a concentration of certain phases of the Whitman substance, the fragments of the myth."

The best of *White Buildings*, "Repose of Rivers" and most of the "Voyages," are conceivably the greatest mystical poems in America since early Whitman.

Crane's "General Aims and Theories" (1926) is a rather tortured attempt to explain the terms of his mystical "way up" toward illumination and discovery through the creative adventure of art: "It is my hope to go *through* the combined materials of the poem, using our 'real' world somewhat as a spring-board.... Its evocation will not be toward decoration or amusement, but rather toward a state of consciousness, an 'innocence' (Blake) or absolute beauty. In this condition there may be discoverable under new forms certain spiritual illuminations, shining with a morality essentialized from experience directly, and not from previous precepts or preconceptions. It is as though a poem gave the reader as he left it a single, new *word*, never before spoken and impossible to actually enunciate ..." [Crane's italics].

But the best illustrations of Crane's poetic aims are found in the poetry itself. These poems are notoriously

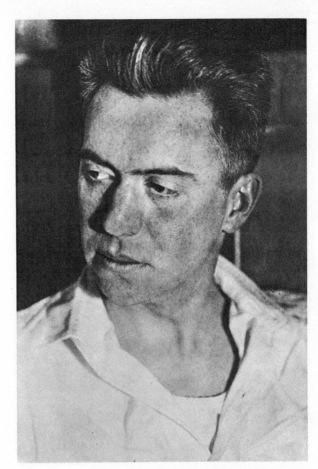

Hart Crane. (National Archives, Washington, D.C.)

difficult to paraphrase, precisely because, when Crane is most successful, the mystical experience "described" in the poetry is actually simulated for the reader in the actual reading of the poem itself. In "At Melville's Tomb" Crane moves toward the achievement of religious illuminations by what he termed the "logic of metaphor." Often, as in "The Broken Tower," a late poem, the avenue to mystic vision is paved with erotic images similar to those employed by Whitman.

Although "The Proem" to *The Bridge* is surely one of Crane's greatest achievements, the work as a whole is disappointing in comparison with the best of *White Buildings*. Attempting no less than an esthetic distillation of the "Myth of America" while plunging ever deeper into personal despair and doubt, psychic disturbance, and alcoholism, Crane was unable to realize his enormous intentions.

The intent of the book, which grew out of Crane's devotion to Whitman and his desire to refute the spiritual desolation of Eliot's *Waste Land*, was to provide a defense of mystical experience in the age of modern science. Ouspensky's scientifically learned book had provided Crane with an invaluable weapon in the struggle, but the indispensable ally was Whitman. At the center of *The Bridge* is the poem "Cape Hatteras," which Crane himself described as "a kind of ode to Whitman." Within it, Crane echoes several of Whitman's works. For both poets, science and technology do not destroy faith based on mystical awareness but enlarge and promote it.

The Achievement

But it was in "The Proem" that Crane had fully repaid his debt to Whitman. Affirmation and denial, dream and fact, in their paradoxical fusion and conflict, manage to incorporate both Whitman's vision and the materialistic temper of the 1920s that seemed to invalidate that vision. The parabolic curve of the actual bridge, which never closes in on itself, suggests the "inviolate curve" of the perfect circle of infinity and the upward movement of the spirit, while at the same time seeming to tend toward the finite closing of the arc in the intensely real steel girders of the span. The final line of the poem resolves its profound ambiguity in a plea for illumination which will "of the curveship lend a myth to God."

But Crane's attempt to demonstrate the possibility of spiritual experience in the modern wasteland through the creation of an "intrinsic," "secular" myth exacted a severe toll on the poet's already-strained psychological resources. Unable to trust completely in mystic intuitions derived largely secondhand from Whitman, and unsure of the validity of the supporting metaphysics supplied by Ouspensky but not fully corroborated in his own speculations, the poet sustained his fragile equilibrium mainly by strength of will. The excesses of Crane's personal life were probably as much the result of his tortured consciousness as of any purely clinical disorder. The failure of *The Bridge* to live up to its universal implications represented a collapse of will rather than a failure of the poet's art. The times were out of joint for the fulfillment of Crane's quest for transcendent certainty.

Although Crane published only two volumes of poetry in his brief career, he is regarded as one of the five or six greatest American poets of the 20th century. (Crane's *Complete Poems* and *Selected Letters and Prose* were published in New York in 1966.)

Further Reading

Hart Crane is listed in the Literature study guide (I, E, 2, b). He and E. E. CUMMINGS were the only poets of their time wholly committed to a transcendental faith. Crane's literary ancestors in the American tradition were Walt WHITMAN, Herman MELVILLE, and Ralph Waldo EMERSON.

The Letters of Hart Crane, 1916–1932, edited by Brom Weber (1952), is an invaluable source for the turbulent events of Crane's life. There are two excellent biographies of Crane: Philip Horton, *Hart Crane: The Life of an American Poet* (1937), and John Unterecker, *Voyager: A Life of Hart Crane* (1969), which introduces previously unpublished material. See also Brom Weber, *Hart Crane: A Biographical and Critical Study* (1948). A standard critical work is R. W. B. Lewis, *The Poetry of Hart Crane: A Critical Study* (1967).

* * *

s. CRANE / By Robert Regan

Stephen Crane (1871–1900), an American fiction writer and poet, was also a newspaper reporter. His novel "The Red Badge of Courage" stands high among the world's books depicting warfare.

After the Civil War, William Dean Howells, Henry James, and others established realism as the standard mode of American fiction. In the 1890s younger writers tried to enlarge the territory of realism with impressionist, symbolist, and even new romantic approaches. Of these pioneers, Stephen Crane was the most influential.

Crane was born on Nov. 1, 1871, the fourteenth and last child of Mary Helen Crane and the Reverend Doctor Jonathan Townley Crane, presiding elder of the Newark, N.J., district of the Methodist Church. A frail child, Stephen moved with his family from one parsonage to another during his first 8 years. In 1880, with the death of Dr. Crane, Mrs. Crane moved her family to Asbury Park, N.J. Stephen was exposed early to writing as a career: his mother wrote on religious topics and lectured for the Women's Christian Temperance Union, and his brother Townley worked as a newspaper reporter.

In 1888 Crane entered military school, where he made

Stephen Crane. (Syracuse University Library)

an impressive record on the drill field and the baseball diamond but not in the classroom. Without graduating he went to Lafayette College, then to Syracuse University. He flunked out, but whatever his academic record, his time had not been wasted: in his fraternity house Crane, aged 20, had written the first draft of *Maggie: A Girl of the Streets*. Returning to Asbury Park as a reporter under his brother for the *New York Tribune*, Crane attended Hamlin Garland's lectures on the realistic writers. Garland was interested in the young writer, read his manuscripts, and guided his reading.

In 1891 Mrs. Crane died. Crane spent much of the next year in Sullivan County, N.Y., where another brother practiced law. Five "Sullivan County Sketches" were published in the *Tribune* and *Cosmopolitan* (his first magazine appearance). He went frequently to New York City, haunting the Bowery in search of experience and literary material. When he returned to Asbury Park, he lost his job on the *Tribune* (and his brother's too) by writing an accurate description of a labor parade that undermined his Republican publisher's standing in an election campaign. This year also brought unhappy endings to two romances.

Career as Novelist

In autumn 1892 Crane moved to New York City. By spring he submitted a second version of *Maggie* to a family friend, Richard Gilder, editor of the *Century*. Gilder tried to explain his rejection of the manuscript, but Crane interrupted bluntly, "You mean that the story's too honest?" Honest the story is, and blunt and brutal. It shows Maggie as a simple, ignorant girl bullied by her drunken mother, delivered to a seducer by her brother, driven by the seducer into prostitution and, finally, to suicide. In approach the novel is akin to the "veritism" of Garland and the realism of Howells, but it differs stylistically in its ironic tone, striking imagery (especially color imagery), and its compression. "Impressionism" is the term often applied to the very personal style Crane was developing. Convinced that no publisher would dare touch his "shocking" novel, Crane printed it at his own expense, using the pseudonym Johnston Smith. The book went unnoticed and unpurchased, except for two copies. Garland, however, admired it and called it to the attention of Howells, then America's most influential man of letters, who recognized Crane's achievement and tried unsuccessfully to get the novel reissued.

By summer 1893 Crane was well into what was to be a Civil War novel. As research he read *Century* magazine's series "Battles and Leaders of the Civil War" and, it is believed, traveled in Virginia to interview Confederate veterans. What he found missing from the history books was the actual sensation any single individual experiences in battle; this is what *The Red Badge of Courage* conveys. Just as Maggie represents every girl victimized by a slum environment, so Henry Fleming represents every recruit who reels through the noise and glare of war. Neither character had a name in Crane's first drafts: they are "every woman," "every man," buffeted by

A young Union soldier as sketched by Winslow Homer, typifying the characters in Stephen Crane's The Red Badge of Courage. (Cooper Union Museum for the Arts of Decoration, New York City)

forces they neither control nor understand. Though there were delays—painful ones for the penniless author—this book was destined for early success. A shortened version was serialized in the *Philadelphia Press* and hundreds of other newspapers in 1894. The instant critical and popular enthusiasm spread to England when the complete book was published the following year. A revised version of *Maggie* was issued along with an earlier novel about slum life, *George's Mother*, in 1896. The syndicate that had arranged newspaper publication of *Red Badge of*

Courage sent Crane to the West and Mexico to sketch whatever struck his fancy.

Poet and Journalist

Crane's first book of poems, *The Black Riders*, was on the press before his departure. "A condensed Whitman," the *Nation* aptly called him. His "lines," as he called his poems, are terse, natural, and forceful; ironic and unsentimental. Their language is in the best sense journalistic, just as Crane's reportage had been from the beginning poetic.

The excursion west and to Mexico produced sensitive sketches and materials for a number of Crane's finest stories. Back in New York, he published newspaper articles critical of the city's corrupt police. The police made New York uncomfortable for Crane, so he departed for Cuba to report the anti-Spanish insurrection there. En route he stopped in Jacksonville, Fla., where he met Cora Stewart, a handsome New England woman in her late 20s, separated from her husband, the son of a British baronet. Cora, owner of the Hotel de Dream, an elegant boardinghouse–cum nightclub–cum brothel, gave it all up to become (quite without clerical or legal formalities) "Mrs. Stephen Crane."

In spite of this "marriage," Crane left for Cuba aboard a small steamer. It sank on its first day out. Crane's heroic role in the disaster—he barely escaped with the captain and two other men—evoked his best short story, "The Open Boat."

War Correspondent

For the Hearst newspapers Crane covered the war between Greece and Turkey. Crane, it appears, wanted to see if war was really as he had depicted it in *Red Badge of Courage*: it was. But the trip yielded mediocre war reportage and a bad novel, *Active Service* (1899). Cora had followed Crane to Greece; they next went to England, where Crane finished his powerful novella *The Monster* and three of his finest short stories, "The Bride Comes to Yellow Sky," "Death and the Child," and "The Blue Hotel."

The Spanish-American War in 1898 provided new employment. Crane sent distinguished reports to the *New York World*. He was with Cora in England when his second volume of poems, *War Is Kind*, appeared in 1899. Sick and aware of nearing death, he wrote furiously. That spring Cora took him to the Continent, where he died on June 5, 1900, in Badenweiler, Germany, of tuberculosis. His haunting tales of childhood, *Whilomville Stories*, and Cuban tales, *Wounds in the Rain*, appeared later that year.

Further Reading

Stephen Crane is listed in the Literature study guide (I, D, 2). His mentors were Hamlin GARLAND and William Dean HOWELLS.

Robert W. Stallman, *Stephen Crane: A Biography* (1968), is the authoritative source on Crane's life. The two most interesting studies—one biographical, the other critical—are by poets: John Berryman, *Stephen Crane*

(1950), and Daniel G. Hoffman, *The Poetry of Stephen Crane* (1956). Also recommended are Maurice Bassan, ed., *Stephen Crane: A Collection of Critical Essays* (1967), and, for views of Crane in the context of his period, Warner Berthoff, *The Ferment of Realism* (1965), and Larzer Ziff, *The American 1890s* (1966).

CRANMER / By Eric McDermott

The English ecclesiastic Thomas Cranmer (1489–1556) was the first Protestant archbishop of Canterbury.

Thomas Cranmer was born in Aslacton, Nottinghamshire, on July 2, 1489, the son of a village squire. He went to Cambridge University at the age of 14; though of indifferent scholarship, he received a bachelor's degree in 1511 and a master's degree in 1514. He also received a fellowship at Jesus College and seemed well on the way to an ecclesiastical career when, at 25, he abandoned his fellowship and married Black Joan of the Dolphin Inn at Cambridge. Very little is known of this girl, who died, as did his child by her, within a year of their marriage. Cranmer then returned to his former way of life. His fellowship was restored, and by 1520 he had been ordained a priest and become a university preacher. Five years later he received the degree of doctor of divinity.

A chance meeting in August 1529 with two members of King Henry VIII's administration led to Cranmer's employment in the royal service; he worked toward obtaining the annulment of Henry's marriage with Catherine of Aragon. In January 1532 he was sent as ambassador to the court of Emperor Charles V at Ratisbon and at Nuremberg. At the latter town he made two acquisitions: Lutheran sympathies, if not convictions, and a young German wife, Margaret, a Lutheran and a niece of the prominent Lutheran scholar Andreas Osiander.

Protestant Archbishop

Within a year of his appointment as ambassador, Cranmer was recalled and nominated for the office of archbishop of Canterbury. He knew that this appointment was given him in return for his future annulment of the King's marriage. The bulls of his appointment to the See of Canterbury were obtained, under compulsion and with great speed, from Pope Clement VII by March 1533, and Cranmer was consecrated archbishop on March 30. On May 23 he concluded the trial of Henry's marriage to Catherine of Aragon by declaring the marriage to have been invalid. On May 28 Cranmer publicly adjudged Henry's marriage to Anne Boleyn in the previous January to have been lawful; and on June 1, Whitsunday, he anointed and crowned her as queen of England in Westminster Abbey.

For the rest of his life Cranmer was a major instrument

Thomas Cranmer, a portrait painted in 1546 by Gerlach Flicke. (National Portrait Gallery, London)

in establishing royal supremacy in spiritual matters as in temporal affairs and thus destroying the independence of the English Church. In 1536 he presided over a commission of bishops and divines which met at Lambeth Palace, his London home. This commission published the Ten Articles, a statement of the beliefs of the Henrician Church, which it was hoped could be accepted by Lutherans as well as Catholics.

On May 15, 1536, Anne Boleyn was condemned to death for treason by reason of her adultery. Her execution was postponed for 2 days, however, in order that Cranmer might declare her marriage to Henry invalid and thus bastardize their daughter, Elizabeth. On the day Anne died, Cranmer granted Henry a dispensation to marry Jane Seymour despite their consanguinity.

Disputes and negotiations over religious beliefs and practices filled these years. In 1539 Cranmer opposed the Act of the Six Articles; he believed the act was too Catholic despite the fact that Henry VIII himself had drawn up the final text. He helped, however, to put together the religious work known as the King's Book, although much of its content was contrary to his beliefs. His overwhelming Erastianism stifled his opposition to this book and allowed him to approve its use in his diocese.

Liturgical Plans

In the last years of Henry's reign Cranmer's beliefs gradually became more Protestant, and his enemies at court sought to have him deposed, if not condemned, for heresy. Nevertheless, Henry, apparently well aware of all this, protected him and allowed him to develop the liturgical plans that were to bear such famous fruit. Cranmer published the English Litany in 1544 and the

First Book of Common Prayer in 1549 during the reign of King Edward VI. A more Protestant version of the latter work, the Second Book of Common Prayer, was issued in 1552, and it proved to be the foundation of, and the most lasting formative influence in, the Church of England. A. G. Dickens (1964) calls it "a devotional asset ranking second after the English Bible," and it exerted a most powerful influence on the development of the English language. Finally came the Forty-two Articles of Religion, which received royal approval a month before Edward's death in 1553. Cranmer and others had worked on these articles for many years, and they were the prototypes of the famous Thirty-nine Articles established in Queen Elizabeth's reign.

With the accession of Queen Mary, there remained for Cranmer, who had so injured her and her mother and had been so prominent in promoting the destruction of the Catholic Church, only imprisonment and death for heresy. Despite his recantations of his heretical views he vigorously affirmed his Protestantism as he was burned at the stake on March 21, 1556.

Further Reading

Thomas Cranmer is listed in the Religion study guide (I, J, 1). HENRY VIII, Cardinal WOLSEY, and Thomas CROMWELL played large roles in the establishment of the Church of England.

A thorough biography is Jasper Ridley, *Thomas Cranmer* (1962). See also Francis E. Hutchinson, *Cranmer and the English Reformation* (1951), and Theodore Maynard, *The Life of Thomas Cranmer* (1956). For background material A. G. Dickens, *The English Reformation* (1964; rev. ed. 1967), and J. J. Scarisbrick, *Henry VIII* (1968), are useful.

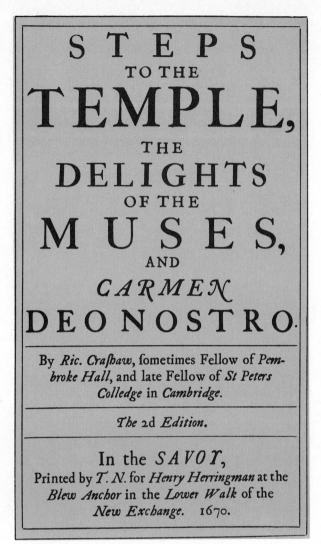

The title page of a 1670 edition of Richard Crashaw's Steps to the Temple, The Delights of the Muses, and Carmen Deo Nostro.

CRASHAW / By Norman Rabkin

The English poet Richard Crashaw (1612/1613–1649) was Roman Catholic in sensibility and ultimately in allegiance. His poetry is the single major body of work in English that can be called baroque.

Richard Crashaw was born in London. His father, a stern Puritan who hated the Church of Rome as much as he did worldly pleasures—his son was to share the latter of his prejudices but not the former—was preacher at the Temple Church. Crashaw was educated at the Charterhouse, where he received a rigorous classical education under the tutelage of a royalist master. He had already indicated his poetic talent and religious sensibility in poems in Latin and Greek before he entered Pembroke College, Cambridge, in 1631.

At the university Crashaw found himself in the matrix of an extraordinary number of the period's best poets: John Donne, George Herbert, Andrew Marvell, Sir John Suckling, Abraham Cowley, and John Milton, to name some of the most important. His own college was High Church in ritual and spiritual allegiance. In 1634 Crashaw received a bachelor of arts degree, and in 1635 he was elected a fellow of Peterhouse, which was strongly influenced by the conservative, High Church archbishop William Laud. In fact, the religious atmosphere of this college was scarcely distinguishable from Roman Catholicism. During the years that followed, Crashaw participated often in the life of the religious establishment at Little Gidding, a village near Cambridge. By 1639 he was an ordained preacher.

The civil war, however, changed his life. Cromwell seized Cambridge in 1643 and efficiently rooted out all traces of "popery." Crashaw did not wait to be ejected from his fellowship by the Puritans but left at the beginning of the occupation and spent the rest of his life in exile at Little Gidding and Oxford and on the Continent.

The civil war deprived him of a successful career as preacher and probably of continued participation in the Anglican Church. His years of exile were dogged by poverty, ill health, and neglect by his patrons. Crashaw became a Roman Catholic in 1645. He died in 1649 in Loreto, Italy, where he was in the service of Cardinal Palota.

Crashaw's major poetry appeared in *Steps to the Temple* in 1646 (enlarged in 1648). Though the title suggests the dominance of George Herbert, the major influences in fact are the spirit and esthetic techniques of the Continental Counter Reformation, which produced the arts known as baroque. The major poetic influence was the Italian Giambattista Marino, some of whose work Crashaw translated. Crashaw's baroque poetry, exemplified in "The Weeper," thrives on paradox, imagery flamboyant to the point of grotesquerie, stock religious symbols, and concern with martyrdom and mysticism.

Further Reading

Richard Crashaw is listed in the Literature study guide (II, E, 2, c). The works of his contemporaries John DONNE, Abraham COWLEY, George HERBERT, and John MILTON also demonstrate a strong concern with religious matters.

The standard work on Crashaw, equally useful for historical and literary backgrounds, biography, and critical interpretation, is Austin Warren, *Richard Crashaw: A Study in Baroque Sensibility* (1939).

CRASSUS / By Norman A. Doenges

Marcus Licinius Crassus Dives (ca. 115–53 B.C.) was a Roman politician and member of the First Triumvirate, for which he provided financial backing. He spent much of his political career in frustrated rivalry with Pompey.

Crassus (pronounced krăs′əs) was descended from a long line of distinguished senators. When, during the uprising of Cornelius Cinna in 87 B.C., his father committed suicide and his brother was murdered by the forces of Gaius Marius, Crassus fled to Spain. After the death of Cinna he came out of hiding, gathered a small military force, and eventually joined Sulla when he returned to Italy from the East. In command of the right wing at the battle of the Colline Gate in 82, Crassus was mainly responsible for the final victory of Sulla over the Marians. During the subsequent Sullan proscriptions he began to amass his enormous fortune by buying the property of the proscribed. Later he continued his speculations in real estate by buying fire-damaged properties. But in spite of his wealth, which he used for political purposes, he lived modestly, was temperate in his personal habits, and cultivated people in all walks of life.

Through careful training he also became one of the most effective orators of his day.

Early Public Career

Praetor in 73, Crassus was chosen by the Senate, after the defeat of both consuls in 72, to take over command in the war against Spartacus although he held no public office at the time. He drove Spartacus into Bruttium and there cut him off by building a wall across the toe of Italy. Although Spartacus broke through the wall during the winter, Crassus defeated him in two decisive engagements, but not until he had asked the Senate to summon for help M. Lucullus from Thrace and Pompey from Spain. Pompey caught a few stragglers from the final battle and characteristically claimed a share of Crassus' victory.

Pompey returned to Rome to run for the consulship of 70 B.C. with a program of reform in mind. Unwilling to be outdone, Crassus decided to run with him, but the rivalry of the two men was so great that they almost came to blows during their year in office, and Pompey captured the support of the people with his legislation to remove the restrictions on the tribunate and to open the jury courts again to the equestrians. As a result, Crassus had to stand by while Pompey was voted his great commands in the 60s.

While Pompey was absent in the East, Crassus sought to outmaneuver him politically in Rome. He used his money and his affability to support candidates for high political office, but apart from Julius Caesar, whom Crassus supported for aedileship in 65, all of his candidates failed because of Pompeian and senatorial opposition. In 65 Crassus was himself elected censor with Q. Lutatius Catulus. But his attempts to purge the Senate and win the support of Cisalpine Gaul with a grant of citizenship were vetoed by his colleague, and both men resigned from office prematurely. There is no concrete evidence that Crassus played an active part in the conspiracies of Autronius and Sulla in 66 or of Catiline in 63, although he may have hoped to profit from the unrest they caused.

First Triumvirate

When Pompey returned and found himself checked politically by Cato and the senatorial leaders, Crassus' maneuvers finally paid off in the formation of the First Triumvirate and the election of Julius Caesar to the consulship of 59 B.C. Pompey had been forced to turn to Crassus and Caesar for help. They tended to cooperate during Caesar's year in office to offset Pompey's enormous prestige and power.

In the years after 59 when Caesar was absent in Gaul, the rivalry between Pompey and Crassus broke out anew as Crassus used P. Clodius to harass Pompey and the two men competed for honors and commands. At one point Pompey complained to the Senate that Crassus was trying to assassinate him. Finally, in 56, the triumvirs met at Luca to compose their differences and make more realistic arrangements for sharing their power. Pompey and Crassus were to hold the consulship together for the second time in 55. Thereafter all three men would have coordinated commands for a period of 5 years, Caesar in Gaul, Pompey in Spain, and Crassus in Syria for a campaign against the Parthians.

As consuls in 55, Crassus and Pompey quelled opposition against the triumvirate. Toward the end of the year Crassus left for the East. In 54 he conducted a successful campaign across the Euphrates and was hailed by his troops. In the following year he again attacked, but he allowed himself to be drawn into the Mesopotamian desert, where his whole army of seven legions and 4,000 cavalry was surrounded and cut off by the Parthian mounted archers near the city of Carrhae. After losing his son, Crassus led the remnants of his legions to the city. To save themselves, his troops then forced Crassus to meet with the Parthian commander Surena. Crassus was treacherously slain at the conference on June 6, 53 B.C.

Plutarch says that in Crassus many virtues were obscured by one vice, avarice. In politics he was the spokesman for Roman financial interests. His failure was that he had no political goals beyond his own personal advancement or protection. The baton he briefly carried rightly passed to Caesar, a man of wider vision.

Further Reading

Crassus is listed in the Ancient History study guide (III, B, 3). He provided the financial backbone for the First Triumvirate, which also included Julius CAESAR and POMPEY.

The main ancient sources for Crassus are Plutarch's *Lives*, Cicero's speeches and letters, and Appian's *Roman History*. See also *The Cambridge Ancient History* (12 vols., 1922–1939) and H. H. Scullard, *From the Gracchi to Nero* (1959; 2d ed. 1963).

CRAWFORD / By John R. Howe, Jr.

American politician William Harris Crawford (1772–1834) was a leader of the Old Republican wing of the Jeffersonian-Republican party.

William H. Crawford was born in western Virginia on Feb. 24, 1772. At the end of the American Revolution, William's family moved to South Carolina but by 1786 settled near Augusta, Ga. For several years Crawford worked on the family farm and acquired the rudiments of an education. By 1804, having built a respectable law practice, he married and established a homestead (later expanded into a plantation) near Lexington, Ga.

Politics rather than law, however, was to be the focus of Crawford's considerable ambitions. Large in stature, handsome, magnanimous and affable though somewhat coarse, and with a limitless store of entertaining anecdotes, Crawford quickly became a popular figure. Build-

William H. Crawford. (Library of Congress)

ing his career as the upland leader of a powerful coalition of well-to-do and conservative merchant and planter interests, Crawford secured election to the Georgia Legislature in 1803. Within 4 years he succeeded to the U.S. Senate. By 1808 he had emerged as the single most powerful political figure in the state. In the Senate, Crawford spoke for the Old Republican section of the Jeffersonian party, emphasizing states' rights, governmental economy, and simplicity.

The pragmatic search for office rather than ideological consistency was, however, Crawford's main characteristic. In 1807 he opposed Thomas Jefferson's embargo and by 1811 had become not only an apologist for federally controlled internal improvements but one of the most enthusiastic advocates of rechartering the Bank of the United States. After a brief turn as U.S. minister to France, Crawford resigned and was appointed secretary of war and then secretary of the Treasury by President James Madison (a post Crawford held through both of James Monroe's administrations). In 1816, though publicly disavowing his candidacy, Crawford secured within the Jeffersonian-Republican caucus 54 votes to Monroe's 65 for the party's presidential nomination. During the next years Crawford worked vigorously to strengthen his national political base, using the patronage and influence provided by his control of the Treasury.

After Monroe's reelection in 1820, sparring for the election of 1824 began among the leading candidates—Crawford, John Quincy Adams, John Calhoun, Andrew Jackson, and Henry Clay. By 1823 Crawford had patched together an impressive, if motley, following of Southern

Old Republicans and certain Northern commercial interests. For a while Crawford seemed the leading candidate. In 1823, however, he was stricken with paralysis. His followers vainly attempted to sustain his candidacy. In the final election Crawford ran a poor third.

With Crawford's physical condition permanently impaired and his political strength dissipated, his national career was at an end. He spent the rest of his life in Georgia, serving as judge of the state's Northern Judicial Circuit from 1827 until his death.

Further Reading

William H. Crawford is listed in the American History study guide (V, A, 1). He competed with Andrew JACKSON and John Quincy ADAMS for the presidential nomination in 1824.

Crawford's personal papers were lost shortly after his death; consequently, there can be no definitive biography. The best is Phillip Jackson Green's sympathetic *The Life of William Harris Crawford* (1965), although Green does not incorporate recent scholarship. Still useful is J. E. D. Shipp, *Giant Days: or, The Life and Times of William H. Crawford* (1909).

Crazy Horse. (Bibliothèque Nationale, Paris)

CRAZY HORSE / By Odie B. Faulk

The American Indian Crazy Horse (ca. 1842–1877), Oglala Sioux war chief, is best known as the leader of the Sioux and Cheyenne renegades who won the Battle of the Little Bighorn, where Gen. Custer died.

Born on Rapid Creek, S.Dak., near the present Rapid City, Crazy Horse (Tashunca-Uitco) was a strange, quiet Sioux youth, serious and thoughtful. His skin and hair were so light that he was mistaken for a captive white child, and he was called "Light-Haired Boy" and "Curly."

Crazy Horse grew to manhood wild and adventurous, implacably hating the reservations and the encroaching whites. He married a Cheyenne girl and thus had close ties with that tribe. After he came to prominence as a warrior, many Cheyenne followed him.

Crazy Horse probably participated in the Sioux wars of 1865–1868 but as a warrior, not a leader. By the last of these wars, in 1876, however, he had risen to prominence. He and his followers refused to return to the reservation by Jan. 1, 1876, as had been ordered by the U.S. Army following the outbreak occasioned by the Black Hills gold rush. Crazy Horse and his followers bore the first burden of this campaign. Their village of 105 lodges was destroyed by Col. J. J. Reynolds on March 17. The Indians' horses were captured, but Crazy Horse rallied his braves, trailed the soldiers 20 miles, and recaptured most of the horses. On June 17 he and 1,200 warriors defeated Gen. George Crook and 1,300 soldiers,

turning them away from a rendezvous with the forces of Gen. Alfred Terry.

Crazy Horse next moved north, where he joined with Sitting Bull's followers on the Little Bighorn River. On June 25 he was in command of the warriors who massacred Gen. George Custer and 264 soldiers. Then, with 800 warriors he went into winter quarters in the Wolf Mountains near the headwaters of the Rosebud River. On Jan. 8, 1877, the village was destroyed in an attack led by Col. N. A. Miles. Crazy Horse continued to fight for 4 months before surrendering on May 6 with 1,100 men, women, and children at Red Cloud Agency near Camp Robinson, Nebr. An army officer there described Crazy Horse as 5 feet 8 inches tall, lithe and sinewy, with a weathered visage; wrote Capt. John G. Bourke: "The expression of his countenance was one of great dignity, but morose, dogged, tenacious and melancholy. . . . He was one of the great soldiers of his day and generation."

On Sept. 5, 1877, the officers at the post, convinced that Crazy Horse was plotting an outbreak, ordered him locked up. Crazy Horse drew his knife and began fighting. In the struggle he was mortally wounded in the abdomen, either by a soldier's bayonet or his own knife. His death deprived the Oglala Sioux of one of their most able leaders.

Further Reading

Crazy Horse is listed in the American History study guide (VII, C, 2). SITTING BULL was his compatriot, and generals George CROOK and George CUSTER were his U.S. Army opponents.

Details on Crazy Horse's life are in Mari Sandoz, *Crazy Horse: The Strange Man of the Oglalas* (1942), and Earl

A. Brininstool, *Crazy Horse* (1949). A good, condensed version of his life is in Alvin M. Josephy, *The Patriot Chiefs* (1961). John G. Bourke, *On the Border with Crook* (1891), gives a contemporary assessment.

* * *

CREEL / By Daniel R. Beaver

George Creel (1876–1953), American writer and journalist, was the first propaganda minister in American history.

George Creel was born on Dec. 1, 1876, on a farm in Lafayette County, Mo. His father, Henry Clay Creel, was a former Confederate officer. George spent his boyhood in Missouri, where he attended what public schools were available.

Creel's real education began at 20, when he secured a job as a reporter on the *Kansas City World*. In 1899 he became editor of the *Kansas City Independent*. After joining the Progressive wing of the Democratic party, he enjoyed considerable influence in Missouri politics. In 1909 he moved to Denver, Colo., where he edited the *Denver Post* (1909–1911) and the *Rocky Mountain News* (1911–1913). His pamphlets for the Democratic

George Creel. (Library of Congress)

National Committee in 1916 brought him to the attention of President Woodrow Wilson, who named Creel chairman of the Committee on Public Information at the outbreak of World War I.

Creel directed the flow of government propaganda on the war and faced, for the first time in the 20th century, the issues of censorship, news manipulation, and the public's "right to know," so important to the freedom of the press in a democratic society. His task was to convince a divided country of the wisdom of Wilson's decision to join the war against Germany. Creel established a system of voluntary press censorship. He refused to distribute information on most of the cruder Allied atrocity stories; instead he blanketed the nation with official information which portrayed the United States as crusading for freedom and democracy to save European civilization from Germany's brutish despoliation. Private American organizations such as the National Security League and the American Protective Association were far less careful in their publications than the Creel committee. Whoever was at fault, the result was an outbreak of war madness unparalleled in American history.

Creel always insisted that private groups rather than the Committee on Public Information were responsible for the wartime hysteria. In three books, *How We Advertised America* (1920), *The War, the World and Wilson* (1920), and his autobiography, *Rebel at Large* (1947), he defended his committee. But he never fully escaped the cloud that World War I cast over his name.

In 1920 Creel retired to private life. In the 1930s he helped moderate Democrats defeat Upton Sinclair's abortive EPIC (End Poverty in California) campaign in California. Creel remained active as a writer, newsman, and national commentator until his death on Oct. 3, 1953.

Further Reading

George Creel is listed in the American History study guide (VIII, C, 2). Others on the American home front during World War I included Bernard BARUCH and William Gibbs McADOO.

Creel's autobiography, *Rebel at Large: Recollections of Fifty Crowded Years* (1947), is the best source for his life. For the Committee on Public Information see James P. Mock and Cedric Larson, *Words That Won the War: The Story of the Committee on Public Information, 1917–1919* (1939), and Horace C. Peterson, *Propaganda for War: The Campaign against American Neutrality, 1914–1917* (1939). For Creel and the New Deal see Arthur M. Schlesinger, Jr., *The Age of Roosevelt*, especially volume 3, *The Politics of Upheaval* (1960).

* * *

CRÉMAZIE / By Jack Warwick

Octave Crémazie (1827–1879) was a Canadian poet who was closely linked to the emergence of French-Canadian literature.

Known as Octave, Claude-Joseph-Olivier Crémazie (pronounced krā-má-zē′) was born on Nov. 8, 1827, and educated in Quebec. He became the business associate of his brother Joseph in 1844. Octave used their bookshop as a base for his literary interests, buying, reading, and discussing recent works from France, particularly Victor Hugo's. A group around Crémazie formed what became known as the *École Patriotique* or the *École de Québec*. Nationally self-conscious and grandiloquently romantic, it created the first characteristic body of French-Canadian literature about 1860. Meanwhile, Crémazie's own affairs went badly, and in 1862 he fled to France to avoid pursuit for forging guarantors' signatures in order to gain credit for his failing business.

Crémazie's writings include occasional verse, more personal poems, various letters, and a diary. The poems which made his name commemorate events in Canadian history. Thus *Le Vieux soldat canadien* celebrated the arrival in Quebec of the first French naval vessel (1855) since the British conquest in 1760, and *Le Drapeau de Carillon* celebrated the centenary of Montcalm's victory of 1758 at Carillon (now Ticonderoga, N.Y.). The latter poem also mentions the theme of *l'abandon*, the feeling that France failed its valiant Canadian colony, in spite of which, in Crémazie's opinion, the cult of France must be maintained.

Prolonged exile in France made Crémazie aware of his own outmoded, rhetorical style, and he expressed a preference for his lyrical poems, especially *La Promenade des trois morts*, which, however, he was too discouraged to complete.

Although direct contact with French literary circles crushed Crémazie as a poet, it stimulated him to write some valuable critical comments in his letters to Canada. He blamed the low standard of Canadian taste for his former success and felt that this had led him away from developing his finer talents. Canadian literature, he felt, could never excel either as a French or as an American creation.

These contradictions in Crémazie's attitude to his cultural context are indicative of French Canada's grave doubts about its cultural survival. In politics Crémazie supported right-wing positions generally and French im-perialism in particular, but he was a liberal patriot at home. A similar deep contradiction is found in his poetic diction, for his attempts to imitate Hugo are overshadowed by his obvious affinity to the older style of the neoclassicists.

Crémazie was in Paris during the siege of 1870 and kept a diary containing details on living conditions and expressing anti-Communard sentiments. He died on Jan. 18, 1879, in Le Havre, where he had found modest employment.

Further Reading

Octave Crémazie is listed in the Canada study guide (III, C, 1, b). His influence parallels that of François-Xavier GARNEAU and is seen in such poets as Louis-Honoré FRÉCHETTE, but not in the later movement represented by Paul MORIN.

Crémazie's works were collected and published in 1883 as *Oeuvres complètes*, although there are many omissions. Maurice Dassonville, *Crémazie* (1956), contains useful biographical and bibliographical information. For background information see Ian Forbes Fraser, *The Spirit of French Canada: A Study of the Literature* (1939).

*   *   *

CRERAR/ By J. L. Granatstein

Thomas Alexander Crerar (born 1876) was a Canadian political leader who, using farmers' organizations as a power base, represented the Western point of view in Canada's government.

Thomas Alexander Crerar (pronounced krē′rär) was born at Molesworth, Ontario, on June 17, 1876. The family moved west to Portage la Prairie, Manitoba, where Crerar was educated. After a stint of teaching in small rural schools, he turned to wheat farming and eventually to grain buying.

In 1907 Crerar became president of the Grain Growers Grain Company, a farmers' organization that had been established to fight the railway monopolies and the Eastern-controlled elevator companies. The Grain Growers quickly established a position of power, and Crerar, who was president until 1929, acquired a reputation as an articulate spokesman for the Western point of view.

Inevitably he was drawn into politics. During World War I Sir Robert Borden formed a Union government to ram conscription through Parliament. Crerar was one of several outsiders brought into the government by the Conservative leader, and he was minister of agriculture from 1917 to 1919. As such, he played a part in directing the war effort in its closing stages. But he also found himself part of a government that was dedicated to the maintenance of the high tariff and to the conscription of farmers' sons, both concepts that were anathema to

Octave Crémazie. (The Public Archives of Canada)

Thomas Alexander Crerar. (The Public Archives of Canada)

Western farmers, who wanted cheap agricultural implements and a sure labor supply.

Crerar resigned in 1919 and turned to bolstering the farmers' organizations. In 1921 he led the newly formed Progressive party to the polls in the general election. The Progressives were a loose coalition of provincial farmers' groups, divided in aims and ideology, disparate in composition, and burdened with a startling naiveté about the workings of the political system. Despite their success in the election, Crerar did not find it easy trying to shepherd his party through the intricacies of parliamentary procedure, for most of his followers distrusted all political parties, including their own.

Crerar's desire was to link up with the governing Liberal party, using his farm support as a bludgeon to win real concessions for the West. But after his supporters balked and after a series of frustrating incidents, he resigned as leader in 1923. The party hung on for a few years, but its strength was broken.

Returning to Parliament as a Liberal in 1935, Crerar entered the Cabinet of Mackenzie King as minister of immigration and minister of the interior. In 1936 he became minister of mines and resources, a portfolio he held until 1945. In this department Crerar played an important part in mobilizing Canadian industry for war, and he was always the leading spokesman for Manitoba in the government. Just before the end of World War II, Crerar was appointed to the Senate, where he remained as vigorous and outspoken as ever until his retirement in 1966 at the age of 90.

Further Reading

Thomas Alexander Crerar is listed in the Canada study guide (IV, A, 1). Western Canada also produced William ABERHART, the leader of the Social Credit movement.

There is no biography of Crerar. The best book on the Progressive party is W. L. Morton, *The Progressive Party in Canada* (1950). Also important are Ramsay Cook, ed., *The Dafoe-Sifton Correspondence, 1919–1927* (1966) and his *The Politics of John W. Dafoe and the Free Press* (1963).

CRÈVECOEUR / By Everett H. Emerson

Hector St. John de Crèvecoeur (1735–1813), a French-American farmer and writer, was one of the most perceptive observers of American life in the late 18th century.

Michel Guillaume Jean de Crèvecoeur (pronounced krĕv-kœr′) was born in Caen, France, on Jan. 31, 1735. (Later he would sign his first book J. Hector St. John.) After a Jesuit education and a visit in England, where he learned English, he served as a map maker with Louis Montcalm's army in Canada from about 1755 to 1759. He left the army but stayed in the New World, where after a good deal of traveling, working as a surveyor, and note-taking, he became a farmer, first in Ulster County, then in Orange County, N.Y.

In 1769 Crèvecoeur married Mehitable Tippet, by whom he had three children, the eldest being named America-Francés. For a time his life was idyllic, but the American Revolution interrupted it. Unwilling to commit himself to either side at the time, he tried to visit France, which led to his imprisonment by the British for 3 months. Finally, in 1780 he returned to his old home in France via Dublin and London. While in London he arranged for publication of his most famous work, *Letters from an American Farmer* (1782). The book provides a comprehensive picture of American life, from Nantucket to Charleston: manners, customs, education, plant and animal life. Crèvecoeur posed as a provincial who sought to answer typical European questions about America. The most memorable portion is Letter Three, "What is an American?"

The book made Crèvecoeur famous. It was published in Philadelphia, as well as in Ireland, Holland, and Germany. He prepared a second edition, in French, much enlarged and more literary: *Lettres d'un cultivateur américain* (1784). The original English versions of some of these letters were not published until 1925 (*Sketches of Eighteenth Century America*). In 1783, returning to America as French consul to New York, Connecticut, and

New Jersey, he found that his wife had died and two children were missing. He located the children in Boston, then established a home in New York City. He developed packet-boat service between France and New York.

In time ill health largely incapacitated Crèvecoeur. In June 1785 he returned to France, seeking to improve commercial relations between France and America. He prepared a three-volume version of the French *Lettres*, published in 1789, the year of his return to America and to his position as consul. He was honored by election to the American Philosophical Society. Under the pen name of Agricola, his letters on potato culture, sheep feeding, sunflower oil, and other topics were published in various American journals.

In 1790 Crèvecoeur left America for the last time. For a while he lived quietly in his father's home in Normandy, for his health was poor and the French Revolution was in progress. He kept in touch with America through a son farming in New Jersey, and he wrote his longest work. It appeared in 1801 as *Le Voyage dans la Haute Pennsylvanie et dans l'état de New-York* (available in English as *Eighteenth-Century Travels in Pennsylvania and New York*, 1961). It has never been as popular as the *Lettres*. Crèvecoeur spent 3 of his last years in Munich, where his son-in-law was minister plenipotentiary. He died in France in 1813.

Hector St. John de Crèvecoeur in 1786. (Courtesy of The New-York Historical Society, New York City)

Further Reading

Hector St. John de Crèvecoeur is listed in the Literature study guide (I, B, 2) and the American History study guide (II, C, 1, c). The colonial diarist William BYRD II also contributed to early American literature with his *History of the Dividing Line*. An example of the patroon landowner in the Dutch-influenced colony of New York was Kiliaen VAN RENSSELAER.

Two valuable studies of Crèvecoeur in English are Julia Post Mitchell, *St. Jean de Crèvecoeur* (1916), and Thomas Philbrick, *St. John de Crèvecoeur* (1970).

CRICK / By George Basalla

The English molecular biologist Francis Harry Compton Crick (born 1916) contributed to the establishment of the double-helical model of the DNA molecule.

Francis Crick was born June 8, 1916, in Northampton. At University College, London, he studied physics and mathematics and obtained his degree in 1937. Work on an advanced degree was halted by the coming of World War II, when Crick had to shift his interest from pure science to the design and production of magnetic mines. By the time the war ended, he had decided to pursue a career in biology, not physics. His decision was influenced by a reading of the book *What Is Life?* by physicist Erwin Schrödinger, with its message that an intensive investigation of the gene was likely to reveal the nature of life.

Crick began his study of biology at Strangeways Laboratory, Cambridge, in 1947, but within 2 years he left to join the Medical Research Council Unit for Molecular Biology at Cavendish Laboratory and to enroll as a doctoral student at Caius College, Cambridge. While at Cavendish he met (1951) the young American biologist James D. Watson, who shared his interest in the gene and the genetic material, deoxyribonucleic acid (DNA). In 1953 Crick and Watson jointly proposed their double-helical model of the DNA molecule, which brought them the Nobel Prize in 1962, an honor they shared with English biophysicist Maurice Wilkins. In addition to the prize, Crick received distinguished lectureships, awards from scientific organizations, and membership in honorary societies, including the Royal Society of London (1959).

The discovery of the structure of DNA is considered to be one of the greatest events in 20th-century biology. Genes are responsible for transferring hereditary information from one generation to the next, and since they are DNA molecules, or segments of them, the structure of DNA provides the key to understanding the physical basis of heredity. The giant DNA molecule is a complex

Francis Crick. (Cambridge Newspapers Ltd.)

CRISPI / By Leon T. Blaszczyk

The Italian statesman Francesco Crispi (1819–1901) fought for Italian unification and twice served as premier of Italy.

Francesco Crispi (pronounced krēs′pē) was born on Oct. 4, 1819, in Ribera, Sicily. After studying law at the University of Palermo, in 1846 he became an attorney in Naples. He took an active part in the revolutionary struggle of 1848–1849, and after its failure he fled to Piedmont, where he engaged in radical journalism. Implicated in Giuseppe Mazzini's attempt to foment revolt in Milan in 1853, Crispi was expelled from Piedmont. In the following years he lived in Malta, London, and Paris and traveled throughout Europe.

In 1859 Crispi returned to Sicily and rejoined the independence movement. The following year he participated in Giuseppe Garibaldi's campaign in Sicily. When the kingdom of Italy was proclaimed in 1862, Crispi was elected deputy to the first Italian Parliament and became a leader of the left opposition to the premier, the Conte di Cavour. Although a zealous republican, in 1865 he became a supporter of King Victor Emmanuel II, after deciding that the monarchy could accelerate national unification.

In 1876 Crispi was elected president of the Chamber of Deputies. In December 1877 he became minister of the interior, but in March 1878 he resigned after being

one, and Crick and Watson faced the difficult task of determining the exact arrangement of its molecular subunits. While Wilkins and others attempted to discover this arrangement by concentrating exclusively upon x-ray diffraction techniques, Crick and Watson approached the problem by conceiving and building large-scale models that would account for all the known physical and chemical properties of DNA. Watson first suggested the double helix as the basic feature of DNA, but it was Crick, with his background in physics, who supplied the theoretical and mathematical knowledge so important to the team's success.

Upon completion of the work on the structure of DNA, Crick began an investigation of the genetic code, that is, the precise manner in which the gene controls the synthesis of proteins.

Further Reading

Francis Crick is listed in the Science study guide (VII, D, 1). He shared the Nobel Prize in physiology or medicine with James D. WATSON.

The personal and intellectual story of the discovery of the structure of DNA is told in James D. Watson's candid book *The Double Helix* (1968), in which Crick is depicted as a genius who exasperated many of his English colleagues but delighted his unconventional American friend. For Crick's statement of his philosophy of biology see his book *Of Molecules and Men* (1966).

* * *

Francesco Crispi. (Alinari)

accused of bigamy. Although acquitted, he withdrew from political life for several years.

In 1887, after again serving briefly as minister of the interior, Crispi became premier. He broadened communal and provincial self-government, bettered public health conditions, and approved a more liberal penal code. However, he introduced severe regulations concerning public order and gave civil authorities the power to prohibit meetings and restrain freedom of association.

In the area of foreign policy Crispi supported Italian colonialism in Africa. He extended and unified Italian acquisitions in Africa and imposed an Italian protectorate on Ethiopia. He sought support of this policy from Germany and Austria-Hungary, Italy's allies in the Triple Alliance. Angered at French expansion in Africa, in 1887 Crispi influenced Parliament to refuse to renew the Italian commercial treaty with France. There then began a 10-year tariff war which greatly damaged the Italian economy.

In 1891, because of the unpopularity of his tariff and tax policy, Crispi was forced to resign. But in 1893, in an atmosphere of internal strife resulting from peasant riots and the growing worker movement, he again became premier. He outlawed all Socialist societies and associations of peasants and workers and disfranchised hundreds of thousands of Italians. He did not convoke Parliament in 1895 but ruled for 6 months as dictator.

Crispi continued his aggressive policy in Africa. But in 1896, following the crushing defeat of the Italian army at Adowa, Ethiopia, he was again forced to resign. He then lived in poverty and oblivion in Naples until his death on Aug. 11, 1901.

Further Reading

Francesco Crispi is listed in the European History study guide (IX, F, 1). Benito MUSSOLINI later shared his dream of an Italian empire in Africa.

Rich material on Crispi's life is in *The Memoirs of Francesco Crispi*, translated by Mary Prichard-Agnetti and edited by Thomas Palamenghi-Crispi (3 vols., 1912–1914). There is one biography of Crispi in English, W. J. Stillman, *Francesco Crispi: Insurgent, Exile, Revolutionist and Statesman* (1899).

CROCE / By David Hershberg

The Italian philosopher, critic, and educator Benedetto Croce (1866–1952) dominated Italian intellectual life in the first half of the 20th century. His many critical and philosophical writings brought Italian letters well into the mainstream of European thought.

Born to a prosperous middle-class family, at the age of 9 Benedetto Croce (pronounced krō′chā) began a rigorous Catholic education in Naples. When his parents and sister were killed in an earthquake

Benedetto Croce. (Popperfoto)

in 1883, Croce went to Rome. While he never completed his law degree at the University of Rome, he reacted enthusiastically to the lectures on moral philosophy by Professor Antonio Labriola. Returning to Naples in 1886, Croce began a period of dedicated research, enriched by journeys to Spain, England, Germany, and France. Although his early works were largely historical, Croce transcended Positivistic scholarship and soon began inquiry into the nature of art and history and their relationship. He pursued this path relentlessly after his close study of G. W. F. Hegel and Giambattista Vico. With Labriola's encouragement, Croce briefly (1895–1899) cultivated Marxism but refuted this doctrine in *Historical Materialism and Marxist Economics* (1900).

A long and fruitful collaboration with the philosopher Giovanni Gentile began in 1896. Working with Gentile, Croce edited *Classics of World Philosophy, Writers of Italy*, and *The Library of Modern Culture*. In 1903 Croce founded the bimonthly *La critica*, an international cultural review. For his contributions to Italian letters, in 1910 Croce was made a life member of the Italian Senate. Later, as minister of education (1920–1921), he conceived educational reforms implemented by Gentile, who subsequently occupied that office.

Croce's opposition to fascism, however, severed his

association with Gentile. Through his "Manifesto of the Anti-Fascist Intellectuals" (1925), his denunciation of the Lateran Pact (1929), and his open criticism of Mussolini, Croce became the symbol of Italian intellectual freedom. After the fall of fascist Italy, he was a liaison between the Allies and the Italian monarchy but declined public office. In 1947 Croce established the Italian Institute for Historical Studies, to which he donated a large part of his house and extensive library.

His Thought

The essence of Croce's thought may be found in his four-part *Filosofia dello spirito* (1902–1917; *Philosophy of the Spirit*), amplified and clarified in many subsequent writings. For Croce, philosophy is the science of the mind, or spirit, wherein all reality resides. The mind's activity takes two distinct, interrelated but not opposite forms, the theoretical and the practical (or cognition and volition). The former perceives and understands reality, the latter creates and changes it. Within the sphere of theory, Croce distinguishes between intuition and logical thought. Similarly, in the realm of the practical, he separates the particular (utilitarian or economic) from the universal (ethical). These four interrelated divisions, none of which has primacy over the others, give rise to man's spiritual activities, which Croce treats in the four volumes of the *Filosofia: Aesthetics, Logic, Philosophy of Conduct (Economics and Ethics),* and *Theory and History of Historiography.*

In *Aesthetics* Croce declared that art is intuition. Realizing that intuition requires communication through language, he later spoke of "lyrical intuition" as creatively expressed impression. Still pursuing the theme in *La poesia* (1936), Croce distinguished between poetry ("achieved expression") and literature (which bears an external resemblance to poetry but fulfills another function).

As spokesman for an antimystical and antiutopian humanism which maintains that the goal of philosophy is an understanding of the course of human events, Croce has been criticized for not accepting an all-embracing belief, such as Catholicism or communism. He held, however, that there exists no final system or any eternally valid philosophy. Instead, Croce espoused "Historicism," a term by which he characterized the inherently evolutionary nature of his thought.

Further Reading

Benedetto Croce is listed in the Philosophy study guide (VII, A), the Literature study guide (III, I, 3), and the Social Sciences study guide (VII, A, 2). He was influenced by G. W. F. HEGEL and Giambattista VICO and worked closely with Giovanni GENTILE.

In general, the most reliable translations of Croce's work are by Arthur Livingston and R. G. Collingwood. For a capsule portrait of Croce see Cecil J. S. Sprigge, *Benedetto Croce: Man and Thinker* (1952). A more complete study is Gian N. G. Orsini, *Benedetto Croce: Philosopher of Art and Literary Critic* (1961). There is a chapter on Croce in William Kurtz Wimsatt, Jr., and Cleanth

Brooks, *Literary Criticism: A Short History* (1957). Henry Stuart Hughes, *Consciousness and Society: The Reorientation of European Social Thought, 1890–1930* (1958), includes a discussion of Croce.

CROCKETT / By Roger L. Nichols

David Crockett (1786–1836), American frontiersman and politician, became during his own lifetime a celebrity and folk hero, particularly to Americans living in the newly settled midwestern regions of the country.

D avy Crockett grew to manhood in a backwoods area. He experienced the crudeness and poverty of the frontier squatter and later used this knowledge in his political campaigns. A master storyteller, the semiliterate Crockett proved a formidable political campaigner, as well as the personification of the characters in the frontiersmen's "tall tales" of that day. Although he is known chiefly for his exploits as a hunter and soldier, Crockett's major contributions included political efforts to get free land for frontier settlers, relief for debtors, and an expanded state banking system for Tennessee.

Davy Crocket, a lithograph acknowledged by him to be his "only correct likeness." (National Portrait Gallery, Smithsonian Institution, Washington, D.C.)

Davy Crockett, the son of John and Rebecca Crockett, was born on Aug. 17, 1786, in Hawkings County, East Tennessee. John Crockett failed as a farmer, mill operator, and storekeeper. In fact, he remained in debt, as did Davy, all his life. Because of continuing poverty, Davy's father put him to work driving cattle to Virginia when he was 12 years old. Returning to Tennessee in the winter of 1798, Davy spent 5 days in school. After a fight there, he played hookey until his father found out and then, to escape punishment, ran away.

Crockett worked and traveled throughout Virginia and did not return home for nearly 3 years. Several years later he decided that his lack of education limited his marriage possibilities, and he arranged to work 6 months for a nearby Quaker teacher. In return Crockett received 4 days a week of instruction. He learned to read, to write a little, and to "cypher some in the first three rules of figures."

In 1806 Crockett married Mary Finley; the young couple began their life together on a rented farm with two cows, two calves, and a loan of $15. Frontier farming proved difficult and unrewarding to Crockett, who enjoyed hunting more than work. After five years he decided to move farther west. By 1813 he had located his family in Franklin County, Tenn.

Life on the Frontier

Shortly afterward the so-called Creek War began. During the summer of 1813 a party of frontiersmen ambushed a band of Creek Indian warriors in southern Alabama. Settlers in the area gathered at a stockade called Ft. Mims. The Indians attacked on Aug. 30, 1813, found the garrison undefended, and killed over 500 people. Within 2 weeks frontier militia units gathered for revenge, and Crockett volunteered for 3 months' duty that year. In September and October he served as a scout. During the famous mutiny against Andrew Jackson in December, Crockett was on leave, and reports that he deserted the militia during the Creek War are unfounded. He served again from September 1814 to February 1815. During this campaign Crockett was a mounted scout and hunter; apparently his unit encountered little fighting.

In 1815 Mary Crockett died. Within a year Crockett remarried. While traveling with neighbors in Alabama to examine the newly opened Creek lands during 1816, he contracted malaria and was left along the road to die. But he recovered and returned to Tennessee, pale and sickly, much to the surprise of his family and neighbors who thought he was dead. He has been quoted as remarking about his reported death, "I know'd this was a whopper of a lie, as soon as I heard it."

Local and State Politics

In 1817 Crockett was a justice of the peace and the next year was serving also as a county court referee. In 1818 his neighbors elected him lieutenant colonel of the local militia regiment, and that same year he became one of the Lawrenceburg town commissioners. He held this position until 1821, when he resigned to campaign for a seat in the state legislature. During the campaign Crock-

ett first displayed his shrewd ability to judge the needs of the frontiersmen. He realized that their isolation and need for recreation outweighed other desires. Therefore, he gave short speeches laced with stories, followed by a trip to the ever present liquor stand—a tactic well received by his audience, who elected him. Crockett appears to have been a quiet legislator, but his first-term actions demonstrate the areas of his future legislative interest. Having grown to manhood among the debt-ridden and often propertyless squatters, Crockett served as their spokesman. He proposed bills to reduce taxes, to settle land claim disputes, and in general to protect the economic interests of the western settlers.

When the legislative session ended in 1821, Davy went west again, this time to Gibson County, Tenn., where he built a cabin near the Obion River. Two years later he was elected to the Tennessee Legislature. This victory demonstrates his improved campaign techniques and his realization that antiaristocratic rhetoric was popular. Again he worked for debtor relief and equitable land laws.

Congressional Career

During 1825 Crockett ran for Congress; he campaigned as an antitariff man, however, and the incumbent easily defeated him. Two years later Crockett won the election. Throughout his congressional terms he worked for the Tennessee Vacant Land Bill, which he introduced during his first term. This proposal would have offered free land to frontier settlers in return for the increase in value which they would bring about because of their improvements.

In 1829, although he opposed several of President Andrew Jackson's measures, Crockett's campaign for reelection as a Jacksonian was successful. But during his second term in Congress, Crockett grew increasingly hostile to Jackson. He opposed the President on the issues of Indian removal, land policy, and the Second National Bank. In the election of 1831 Crockett was defeated. Two years later he regained his congressional seat by a narrow margin. By 1834 he had become such an outspoken critic of Jackson that Whig party leaders used Crockett as a popular symbol in their anti-Jackson campaigns. It was during these activities that several purported biographies and autobiographies of Crockett appeared. Their purpose was to popularize him and to show that not all frontiersmen supported the Jackson administration. These literary efforts failed to sway most of the voters, and Crockett was defeated in 1835, ending his congressional career.

During his three terms in Washington, Crockett tried to represent the interests of his frontier district. In doing so, he became enmeshed in a dispute with the Tennessee Jackson forces. The continuing fight with this group not only prevented him from making any lasting legislative contributions but also ended his political career.

Death at the Alamo

In 1835 Crockett and four neighbors headed into Texas looking for new land. By January 1836 he had joined the

Texas Volunteers, and within a month he reached San Antonio. In the first week of March he and the other defenders of the Alamo died during the siege and capture of that fort. Popular tradition places Crockett as one of the last defenders who died protecting the bedridden Col. William Travis during the final assault. The fact is, however, that Crockett was one of the first defenders to die, alone and unarmed.

Crockett's death at the Alamo engendered a notoriety and a lasting fame which his political activities would never have earned him. Through the newspaper accounts and other writings—fact and fiction—Crockett came to represent the typical westerner of that day. With the passage of time, tales and legends concerning his exploits grew. As a result, the popular image bears less relationship to the actual person than may be said about almost any other prominent figure.

Descriptions of Crockett are varied, but it is generally conceded that he was about 5 feet 8 inches tall, of medium weight, and with brown hair, blue eyes, and rosy cheeks. He was noted for a fine sense of humor, honesty, and ability as an entertaining public speaker. Although he occasionally posed as a backwoods bumpkin, those who knew him realized that he was a man of ability and character.

Further Reading

Davy Crockett is listed in the American History study guide (V, C, 1). Other frontiersmen were James BRIDGER and Kit CARSON. In a later period, frontier characters BUFFALO BILL and Annie OAKLEY are interesting.

A lack of source material has limited the scholarly studies of Crockett but has not prevented numerous popular accounts. Beginning with Matthew St. Clair Clarke's anonymously published *Life and Adventures of Col. David Crockett of West Tennessee* (1833), such accounts have continued to appear. Of the 19th-century books only *A Narrative of the Life of David Crockett, of the State of Tennessee* (1834), written by Crockett himself, is at all reliable.

The best work on Crockett is James A. Shackford, *David Crockett: The Man and the Legend* (1956), which separates the myths surrounding him from the historical person. Crockett's position in folklore is examined in Franklin J. Meine, ed., *Tall Tales of the Southwest: An Anthology of Southern and Southwestern Humor, 1830–1860* (1930), and Richard M. Dorson, ed., *Davy Crockett: American Comic Legend* (1939). For an understanding of politics in the Old Southwest see Thomas P. Abernethy, *From Frontier to Plantation in Tennessee: A Study in Frontier Democracy* (1932); Arthur M. Schlesinger, Jr., *The Age of Jackson* (1945); and Charles G. Sellers, *James K. Polk, Jacksonian: 1795–1843* (1957).

*   *   *

CROLY / By Thomas W. Wood, Jr.

An American editor and author, Herbert David Croly (1869–1930) created the political philosophy known as "new nationalism" and was a founder of the magazine "New Republic."

Herbert Croly was born on Jan. 23, 1869, into an immigrant but middle-class family. Croly's father was editor of the *New York World* and the *New York Graphic*, and his mother wrote under the nom de plume Jennie June. Both parents were civic reformers.

Croly studied a year at the College of the City of New York and off and on for 11 years at Harvard before quitting academia in 1899 without taking a degree. A rather homely man, he had a high bulging forehead and a heavy nose on which rimless glasses rested. So soft-spoken that he seemed to whisper, he was inordinately shy among strangers; according to his biographer his shyness approached the pathological. Croly's written words were as laborious as his spoken ones.

In 1892 Croly married Louise Emory of Baltimore, a wealthy socialite. He was editor of the *Architectural Record* from 1900 to 1913, when he quit to write books.

Croly wrote four books: *The Promise of American Life* (1909), *Marcus Alonzo Hanna: His Life and Work* (1913), *Progressive Democracy* (1914), and *Willard Straight* (1924), the biography of the banker who helped underwrite the *New Republic*, a magazine founded by Croly and two other journalists.

The Promise of American Life is the foundation of Croly's reputation. Despite the tortuous sentences, which often left readers confused, it attracted a follow-

Herbert Croly. (New Republic)

ing, and *American Magazine,* at the height of the 1912 presidential campaign, hailed Croly as the "man from whom Colonel [Theodore] Roosevelt got his 'new nationalism.' " Croly first was attracted to his subject by the "dilemma of the artist or intellectual in an industrial society." He felt "empty individualism had run riot," that merit was measured by cash, and that industrial society was too mechanical. With the frontier gone, "automatic progress" was an end. He theorized that liberty and equality might actually conflict—despite America's heritage and the views of Jeffersonian Democrats. He pointed out that 19th-century "robber barons" cited slogans of individualism while forming monopolies.

Croly wanted "constructive discrimination" that would favor the weak. Equal rights for all, he argued, "merely left the great mass of people at the mercy of strong political and economic interests." He asserted that big government should control big business and big unions and that small businesses and nonunion people should be sacrificed as inefficient or failing parts of his system. Elite saint-heroes, or uncommon common men (like Abraham Lincoln), were to assure honesty of the system that Croly looked upon as "nationalized democracy."

Though he had suffered a paralytic stroke in 1928, Croly was still editor of the *New Republic* when he died on May 17, 1930.

Further Reading

Herbert Croly is listed in the American History study guide (VIII, F, S). H. L. MENCKEN and Oswald Garrison VILLARD were other outspoken editors of important magazines.

Charles Forcey, *The Crossroads of Liberalism: Croly, Weyl, Lippmann, and the Progressive Era, 1900–1925* (1961), is the best study of Croly. See also Richard Hofstadter, *The Age of Reform: From Bryan to F. D. R.* (1955).

CROMER / By John E. Flint

The English statesman Evelyn Baring, 1st Earl of Cromer (1841–1917), ruled Egypt from 1883 to 1907.

Evelyn Baring was born on Feb. 26, 1841, at Cromer Hall in Norfolk. He entered Woolwich in 1855 to train for the Royal Artillery and in 1858 went with his battery to the Ionian Isles. After service in Malta and Jamaica he entered staff college in 1867, later moving into intelligence work for the War Office. In 1872 he was appointed private secretary to his cousin Lord Northbrook, the viceroy of India.

Baring returned to England in 1876, and the next year he was sent as commissioner to Egypt to represent British bondholders. But Khedive Ismail was attempting to rid himself of Anglo-French financial control, and in 1878

Lord Cromer, painted in 1902 by John Singer Sargent. (National Portrait Gallery, London)

Baring resigned. When Ismael was deposed and Khedive Tewfik enthroned, Anglo-French control was reestablished, and in September 1879 Baring became British controller. Six months later, however, he returned to India as finance member on the viceroy's council.

In September 1883 Baring, now knighted, went to Egypt as British agent and consul general. Britain had occupied Egypt in the previous year and crushed the nationalists under Urabi. The country was bankrupt, and the Sudan in full rebellion under the Mahdists. To limit costs, Baring wished Egypt to evacuate the Sudan. His Egyptian ministers were opposed to his plan, but Baring forced them to obey, thus establishing British colonial control over theoretically independent Egypt.

By 1888 Baring had balanced Egypt's budget, which went into surplus in 1889. In the following years he abolished forced labor, reformed the systems of justice and administration, and extended direct British control over all aspects of interior government. Baring (who had already earned the nickname of "Overbaring" in India) became an almost viceregal figure.

In 1901 Baring was created Earl of Cromer. He opposed the growing Egyptian nationalist movement, which demanded that Britain's promises of withdrawal be fulfilled. The 1906 Denshwai incident, in which several Egyptian peasants were executed, incensed the Egyptian nationalists and gained them sympathy in Britain, where Henry Campbell-Bannerman's Liberal government insisted on progress toward self-government in Egypt. But Cromer could not adjust to these new policies and, his health failing, he resigned in March 1907.

Cromer took his seat in the House of Lords as a Liberal in 1908 but devoted most of his time to his writing. He died on Jan. 29, 1917.

Further Reading

Lord Cromer is listed in the European History study guide (IX, A, 2) and the Africa study guide (VIII, A, 2). Charles George GORDON and Lord KITCHENER were British military leaders in Egypt and the Sudan during this period.

Cromer's *Modern Egypt* (2 vols., 1908) is a history of Egypt in the 19th century, culminating in an account of his own accomplishments there. His other works include *Abbas II* (1915), a study of his relations with the Khedive of Egypt, and *Political and Literary Essays* (3d series, 1916). Cromer's authorized biography is by the Marquess of Zetland, *Lord Cromer: Being the Authorized Life of Evelyn Baring, First Earl of Cromer* (1932). The most interesting and definitive modern scholarly study is by an Egyptian, Afaf L. al-Sayyid, *Egypt and Cromer: A Study in Anglo-Egyptian Relations* (1968).

Oliver Cromwell, a painting by Robert Walker. (National Portrait Gallery, London)

O. CROMWELL / By J. H. Plumb

The English statesman and general Oliver Cromwell (1599–1658) won decisive battles in the English civil war. He then established himself and his army as the ruling force in England and later took the title Lord Protector of Great Britain and Ireland.

Oliver Cromwell was born on April 25, 1599, at Huntingdon. His father, Richard Cromwell, was a younger son of one of the richest men in the district, Sir Henry Cromwell of Hinchinbrook, known as the "Golden Knight." Cromwell's mother was the daughter of Sir William Steward, who managed the tithe revenues of Ely Cathedral. Little is known of Cromwell's childhood, except that his circumstances were modest and he was sent to the local school. His schoolmaster, Dr. Beard, was a devout Calvinist; most of Cromwell's intense religious convictions were derived from Beard, whom he venerated throughout his life.

In 1616 Cromwell entered Sidney Sussex College, Cambridge. He left the following year on the death of his father. For the next few years he lived in London, where in 1620 he married Elizabeth, the daughter of Sir James Bourchier, a wealthy leather merchant. Cromwell then returned to his small estate in Huntingdon, where he farmed his land and played a modest part in local affairs, acquiring a reputation as a champion of the poor and dispossessed. During these years Cromwell experienced periods of deep melancholy, suffused with religious doubt, but after much spiritual torment he became convinced that he was the instrument of God.

Political Situation in 1640

When Cromwell entered Parliament for Cambridge in 1640, England had been ruled personally by Charles I for 11 years. The King had pursued an authoritarian policy in religion and finance which had distressed many country gentlemen, including Cromwell. Furthermore Charles had plunged into war with Scotland, which had risen in revolt when Archbishop William Laud had persuaded him to impose the English Prayer Book on the Scottish Church. The Scots rapidly defeated the King; destitute of money and at the mercy of the Scots, Charles I was forced to call Parliament.

The mood of Parliament was highly critical, and there was a closely knit body of Puritan country gentlemen and lawyers who were determined that the power of the King and the Anglican Church should be limited by Parliament. Several of Cromwell's relatives, particularly the influential John Hampden and Oliver St. John, belonged to this group, which was led by John Pym. Cromwell threw in his lot with these men. A middle-aged man without parliamentary experience, he spoke rarely, but when he did it was usually in support of extreme measures. Cromwell soon established his reputation as a firm upholder of the parliamentary cause; he was dedicated to the reform of the Church and of the court and was highly critical of the King.

Civil War

By 1642 the King and Parliament had become so antagonistic that armed conflict was inevitable. At the outbreak of war in August 1642, Cromwell headed a regiment whose prime duty was to defend East Anglia. He rapidly demonstrated not only his skill as a military leader by rapid raids into royalist territory combined with skillful retreat, but also his capacity to mold an effective army from his force of raw recruits.

Under the leadership of the Earl of Manchester, Cromwell's commander, regiments from other counties were brought together in a formidable body, known as the Eastern Association. In 1643 Cromwell's cavalry worsted the royalists in a number of sharp engagements—Grantham (May 13), Gainsborough (July 18), and Wincaby (October 13). These successes helped to create parliamentary supremacy in East Anglia and the Midlands. Cromwell's reputation as Parliament's most forceful general was made the next year, however, at the battle of Marston Moor (July 2, 1644), when his Ironsides routed the cavalry of Prince Rupert, the most successful royalist general. To Cromwell, whose religious convictions strengthened with every victory that he won, Marston Moor was God's work, and he wrote, "God made them stubble to our swords."

The victories in eastern England, however, were not matched by success elsewhere. After 2 years of war the King was still in the field, and there was a growing rift between Parliament and the army. Many disliked the price paid for alliance with the Scots (acceptance of the Presbyterian form of church government), and most longed for peace. Cromwell, however, yearned for victory. He bitterly attacked the Earl of Manchester, and after complex political maneuvering he emerged as the effective leader of the parliamentary armies. He proved his exceptional capacities as a general on June 14, 1645, when he smashed the royalists' army at Naseby in Northamptonshire. Within 12 months the royalist armies had capitulated.

In 5 years Cromwell had risen from obscurity to renown. A large man with a long, red face studded with warts, he nevertheless possessed considerable presence. His mood was usually somber, thoughtful, and deeply religious. His soldiers sang psalms as they went into battle, and every regiment had its preacher.

The next 3 years taxed Cromwell's skill and faith. His army became riddled with Levellers, whose radical doctrines called for a far more democratic social structure than Cromwell and his fellow generals would tolerate. Parliament and the Scots inclined not only to peace with the King but also to a rigid form of Presbyterianism, which Cromwell disliked. He believed passionately in toleration, excepting always papists and atheists.

In 1648 the royalists rose again, sided by the Scots, but in a lightning campaign Cromwell smashed both. The republicans were then determined to bring Charles I to trial, and Cromwell did nothing to stop them. At last agreeing that the King was "a man of blood" and should be executed, he signed Charles I's death warrant.

Further Campaigns

The execution of the King settled nothing. Legally, the House of Commons, purged to such an extent that it was called the Rump, ruled. But the army, Scotland, and Ireland were soon in rebellion. The Scottish Presbyterians proclaimed Charles II (Charles I's son) their lawful monarch, and the Irish Catholics did likewise. In England the radicals were a rampant minority, the royalists a stunned majority, but neither had any respect for the Rump.

Cromwell suppressed the Levellers by force and then set about subduing first Ireland and then Scotland. In the former Cromwell fought a tough, bloody campaign in which the butchery of thousands of soldiers at Drogheda (Sept. 11, 1649) and hundreds of civilians at Wexford (Oct. 11) caused his name to be execrated in Ireland for centuries.

On June 26, 1650, Cromwell finally became commander in chief of the parliamentary armies. He moved against the Scots and got into grievous difficulties. At Dunbar in August 1650 he was pressed between the hills and the sea and was surrounded by an army of 20,000 men. But the folly of the Scottish commander, Leslie, enabled Cromwell to snatch a victory, he thought by divine help, on September 3. The next year Charles II and his Scottish army made a spirited dash into England, but Cromwell smashed them at Worcester on Sept. 3, 1651. At long last the war was over and Cromwell realized that God's humble instrument had been given, for better or worse, supreme power.

Cromwell's Rule: 1653–1658

For 5 years after the execution of the King, Parliament tried to formulate a new constitution. Its failure to do this so exasperated Cromwell that on April 20, 1653, he went with a handful of soldiers to the House of Commons, where he shouted at the members, "The Lord be done with you," and ordered them out.

Until his death Cromwell tried to create a firm new constitutional base for his power. His first attempt to establish a constitution by means of a nominated Parliament in 1653 ended in disaster, so the Council of Army Officers promulgated the Instrument of Government, by which Cromwell became Protector in December 1653. He was assisted by a Council of State on whose advice he acted, for Cromwell believed sincerely in the delegation and sharing of power. For 8 months Cromwell and his Council ruled most effectively, sweeping away ancient feudal jurisdictions in Scotland and Ireland and uniting those countries with England under one Parliament, which was itself reformed. When the Parliament met in 1654, however, it soon quarreled with Cromwell over the constitution. He once more took power into his own hands and dissolved Parliament on June 22, 1655.

Cromwell's government became more authoritarian. Local government was brought under major generals, soldiers whom he could trust. This infuriated the radical left as well as the traditionalists. Again attempting to give his authority a formal parliamentary base and also needing additional revenue, Cromwell reconvened Parliament. His successes abroad and his suppression of revolts at home had greatly increased his popularity; thus when Parliament met, he was pressed to accept the crown, but after much soul-searching he refused. He took instead the title Lord Protector under a new constitution—the Humble Petition and Advice (May 25, 1657). This constitution also reestablished the House of Lords and made Cromwell king in all but name. But Cromwell was no Napoleon; there were definite limits to his personal ambition. He did not train his son Richard to be his successor, nor did he try to establish his family as a ruling dynasty. And at the height of his power he retained his deep religious conviction that he was merely an instrument of God's purpose.

Cromwell pursued an effective foreign policy. His navy enjoyed substantial success, and the foundation of British power in the West Indies was laid by its capture of Jamaica (1655). He allied himself with France against Spain, and his army carried the day at the battles of the Dunes in 1658. These victories, combined with his dexterous handling of Scotland and brutal suppression of Ireland, made his personal ascendancy unassailable, in spite of failures in his domestic policy. But shortly after his death on Sept. 3, 1658, Cromwell's regime collapsed, and the restoration of the monarchy followed in 1660.

Critical Assessment

Cromwell's greatness will always be questioned. As a general, he was gifted yet lucky; as a statesman, he had some success but was unable to bring his plans to complete fruition. Although his religious conviction often appears to be a hypocritical cloak for personal ambition, his positive qualities are unmistakable. He believed passionately both in religious toleration and in representative government (limited to men of property, however). He encouraged reform, and much of it was humane. He brought to the executive side of government a great degree of professionalism, particularly in the army and navy. Britain emerged from the Commonwealth stronger, more efficient, and more secure. Perhaps the most remarkable qualities of Cromwell were his sobriety and his self-control. Few men have enjoyed such supreme power and abused it less.

Further Reading

Oliver Cromwell is listed in the European History study guide (V, A, 1, b) and the Religion study guide (I, N, 1, b). Unlike him, Sir Henry VANE opposed the execution of

A satiric print depicts Oliver Cromwell dissolving the Rump Parliament with the order, "Be gone you rogues; you have sate long enough." The artist inscribed on the walls of the House of Commons, in English and in Dutch, "This House is to lett." (The Mansell Collection)

CHARLES I. John LILBURNE led the Levellers, a radical Puritan sect whose activities Cromwell suppressed. Although George MONCK served ably under Cromwell, he later worked for the restoration of CHARLES II to the English throne.

Cromwell's letters and speeches are collected by Wilbur C. Abbott in *The Writings and Speeches of Oliver Cromwell* (4 vols., 1937–1947). The literature on Cromwell is enormous. The best and most complete biography of him is Sir Charles Firth, *Oliver Cromwell and the Rule of the Puritans in England* (1900; repr. 1961). An excellent brief biography is C. V. Wedgwood, *Oliver Cromwell* (1939). Maurice Ashley, *Oliver Cromwell and the Puritan Revolution* (1958), is also valuable. The problems of Cromwell's character and policies are well explored in Richard E. Boyer, ed., *Oliver Cromwell and the Puritan Revolt* (1966). Equally valuable is Maurice P. Ashley, ed., *Cromwell* (1969). Cromwell's career as a general is best studied in C. V. Wedgwood, *The King's War* (1958); Alfred H. Burne and Peter Young, *The Great Civil War: A Military History of the First Civil War, 1642–1646* (1959); and Austin H. Woolrych, *The Battles of the English Civil War* (1961). The best bibliographical guide is Wilbur C. Abbott, *Bibliography of Oliver Cromwell* (1929).

T. **CROMWELL** / By Stanford E. Lehmberg

The English statesman Thomas Cromwell, Earl of Essex (ca. 1485–1540), was the chief minister of Henry VIII from 1532 to 1540 and was largely responsible for revolutionary reforms in the English Church and in administration of the state.

Thomas Cromwell was born in Putney, near London. His father, Walter Cromwell, was a fuller and shearer of cloth who also worked as a blacksmith, innkeeper, and brewer. Perhaps an unruly youth, Thomas received little formal education. About 1504 he traveled to Flanders and Italy, where he served as a mercenary soldier. While abroad he had an opportunity to learn French and Italian and to observe something of the diplomatic maneuvers of the European powers. When he returned to England about 1513, he married Elizabeth Wykes, whose father was also a shearer. Their only son, Gregory, proved dull and despite an elaborate education never achieved prominence.

In 1514 Cromwell entered the service of Thomas Wolsey, the great cardinal who dominated both Church and state. Cromwell's administrative abilities were soon recognized, and he became involved in all of Wolsey's business, especially the suppression of certain small monasteries and the application of their revenues to new colleges founded in Ipswich and Oxford. During this period Cromwell evidently studied law; in 1524 he was admitted to Gray's Inn, one of the Inns of Court. He also

entered Parliament and in 1523 may have delivered a famous speech denouncing Henry VIII's war in France and its accompanying taxation.

When Wolsey fell from power, Cromwell attached himself directly to the court. In 1529 he was elected to the Reformation Parliament, the later sessions of which he helped manage for the King. In 1532 he began to accumulate government offices, and he so gained the confidence of Henry VIII that he became the King's chief minister. He drafted the act in restraint of appeals, passed by Parliament in 1533 to allow Henry's divorce to be granted in England without interference from the Pope, and subsequent legislation which affirmed royal supremacy in religion and provided for a Church of England independent of Rome. His great ideal was the establishment of England as an "empire," completely self-contained and owing no allegiance to any external power.

Although he was not a priest, Cromwell was now named the King's vice-gerent, or deputy, in spiritual affairs. He was largely responsible for legislation which authorized the dissolution of the monasteries and the confiscation of their property by the King. Although more interested in politics than theology, he was probably a sincere Protestant and certainly a supporter of Archbishop Thomas Cranmer.

In secular affairs Cromwell sought efficiency above all. He instituted revolutionary reforms, especially in financial administration. His multiplicity of offices—the King's principal secretary, lord privy seal, master of the jewels, clerk of the hanaper, master of the rolls, chancellor of the Exchequer, and master of the court of wards—gave him control over virtually every aspect of government. Unlike Wolsey and his predecessors, Cromwell was never lord chancellor; he can be regarded as the first chief minister of a new type, a layman basing his influence on the office of principal secretary. In 1536 he was ennobled as Baron Cromwell of Oakham, in the county of Rutland, and in 1540 he was created Earl of Essex. Although his magnificence never approached Wolsey's, he enjoyed the considerable wealth which he acquired. He had four houses, all in or near London; friends and foreign ambassadors later recalled their pleasant walks in his gardens.

Cromwell always had his enemies, mainly religious conservatives like Stephen Gardiner, Bishop of Winchester, or members of the old aristocracy like Thomas Howard, Duke of Norfolk. After Cromwell arranged the King's disastrous marriage to Anne of Cleves, these foes combined to topple him, charging that he was an overmighty subject and a heretic. He was not given a trial but was condemned by a bill of attainder. On July 28, 1540, he was beheaded on Tower Hill. A clumsy executioner made the scene more than usually horrible, even by Tudor standards.

Although often criticized for his ambition, political ruthlessness, and plunder of the Church, Cromwell was a genuinely affable man, an administrative genius, and a loyal adviser to the King. It is doubtful that Henry VIII could have secured his divorce or devised his great scheme of ecclesiastical nationalization without Cromwell.

Thomas Cromwell, Earl of Essex, painted in 1533 by Hans Holbein the Younger. (Copyright The Frick Collection, New York)

Further Reading

Thomas Cromwell is listed in the European History study guide (IV, A, 1, a) and the Religion study guide (I, J, 1). He served first Cardinal WOLSEY and then HENRY VIII.

Most of Cromwell's extant letters are printed in Roger B. Merriman, *Life and Letters of Thomas Cromwell* (2 vols., 1902). There is no satisfactory biography of Cromwell. His work in secular administration is best described in Geoffrey R. Elton, *The Tudor Revolution in Government* (1953), while his influence in the English Church is discussed in Arthur G. Dickens, *Thomas Cromwell and the English Reformation* (1959).

CROOK / By Odie B. Faulk

The American army officer George Crook (1828–1890) campaigned against Indians in the southwestern and northwestern United States, but he was also an outspoken champion of Indian rights.

Born on Sept. 8, 1828, on a farm near Taylorsville, Ohio, George Crook was appointed to the U.S. Military Academy in 1848. Four years later he graduated thirty-eighth in a class of 56 and was commissioned a lieutenant of infantry. Assigned to the Pacific Northwest, he spent the next 9 years exploring the area and fighting Indians.

During the Civil War, Crook was appointed colonel of the 38th Ohio Infantry, in command of the Department of West Virginia. By 1865, having distinguished himself in numerous battles, he was commissioned a major general of volunteers.

At the end of the Civil War, Crook reverted to the rank of lieutenant colonel and commanded the 23d Infantry, which was headquartered at Boise, Idaho. He campaigned against Indians until 1871, when President Grant sent him to command the Department of Arizona. By this time he usually wore a weather-beaten canvas suit and a Japanese summer hat but no military trappings of any type, not even a symbol of his rank. Because of his manner of dress and his peculiar whiskers, the Apache dubbed him "Gray Fox."

Using unorthodox techniques, such as the enlistment of Apache scouts to guide his troops, Crook quickly brought peace to Arizona. For this feat he received a spectacular promotion in 1873, from lieutenant colonel to brigadier general.

In 1875 Crook was transferred to command the Department of the Platte, where he had to contend with the Sioux. His success on the northern plains was not so great as it had been in the Southwest, and in 1882 he returned to quell disorders in the Department of Arizona. He quickly restored order, forcing renegade Apache to return to their reservation. He also conducted the final Geronimo campaign of May 1885 through March 1886, which brought Geronimo to the conference table, where surrender terms were arranged. Geronimo returned to the Sierra Madre of Mexico, however, and Crook was pressured into asking for a transfer. Politics dictated a military solution to the Apache wars, while Crook believed in diplomacy.

In 1886 Crook resumed command of the Department of the Platte; then, in 1888, upon his promotion to major general, he was assigned the Division of the Missouri, with headquarters in Chicago. He died there on March 21, 1890.

Crook was a model soldier—fearless, modest, a good listener. He did not drink or use strong language. In his years in the West he fought corrupt Indian agents and spoke and wrote in favor of granting the Indians full citizenship and the right to vote. His wife, Mary, supported him throughout his long and colorful career.

Further Reading

George Crook is listed in the American History study guide (VII, C, 2). Crook campaigned successfully against the Apache and their leader GERONIMO, but victory over the Sioux and their fabled chiefs—CRAZY HORSE, RED CLOUD, and SITTING BULL—eluded both Crook and Gen. George CUSTER.

Martin F. Schmitt, ed., *General George Crook: His Autobiography* (1946), is the standard account of Crook's life; Schmitt pieced this work together from Crook's diary and letters and gave an excellent picture of the man. John G. Bourke, *On the Border with Crook* (1891; repr. 1962), is the account of Crook's adjutant during many of his military years, while Crook's own work, *Résumé of Operations against Apache Indians, 1882–1886* (1887), indicates his attitude toward the Indians.

CROOKES / By E. Scott Barr

The English chemist and physicist Sir William Crookes (1832–1919) discovered the element thallium and invented the radiometer, the spinthariscope, and the Crookes tube.

William Crookes was born in London on June 17, 1832. His education was limited, and despite his father's wish that he become an architect, he chose industrial chemistry as a career. He entered the Royal College of Chemistry in London, where he began his researches in chemistry. In 1859 he founded the *Chemical News*, which made him widely known, and remained its editor and owner all his life.

Most notable among Crookes's chemical studies is that one which led to his 1861 discovery of thallium. Using spectrographic methods, he had observed a green line in the spectrum of selenium, and he was thus led to announce the existence of a new element, thallium. While determining the atomic weight of thallium, using a delicate vacuum balance, he noticed several irregularities in weighing, which he attributed to the method. His investigation of this phenomenon led to the construction in 1875 of an instrument that he named the radiometer.

In 1869 J. W. Hittorf first studied the phenomena associated with electrical discharges in vacuum tubes. Not knowing of this, Crookes, 10 years later, made a parallel but more extensive investigation. In his 1878 report he pointed out the significant properties of electrons in a vacuum, including the fact that a magnetic field causes a deflection of the emission. He suggested that the tube was filled with matter in what he called the "fourth

George Crook. (Library of Congress)

William Crookes. (Radio Times Hulton Picture Library)

state"; that is, the mean free path of the molecules is so large that collisions between them can be ignored. Tubes such as this are still called "Crookes tubes," and his work was honored by naming the space near the cathode in low pressure "Crookes dark space."

Crookes also made useful contributions to the study of radioactivity in 1903 by developing the spinthariscope, a device for studying alpha particles. He foresaw the urgent need for nitrogenous fertilizers, which would be used to cultivate crops to meet the demands of a rapidly expanding population. Crookes did much to popularize phenol (carbolic acid) as an antiseptic; in fact, he became an expert on sanitation. Mention should also be made of the serious and active interest he took in psychic phenomena, to which he devoted most of 4 years.

Crookes was knighted in 1897. His marriage lasted from 1856 until the death of his wife in 1917; they had 10 children. He died in London on April 4, 1919.

Further Reading

William Crookes is listed in the Science study guide (VI, C, 1). Other British physicists of the 19th century included James Clerk MAXWELL and Michael FARADAY. While at the Royal College of Chemistry, Crookes became assistant to August Wilhelm von HOFMANN, one of the major chemists and most influential teachers of the century.

A biography of Crookes is Edmund E. Fournier d'Albe,

The Life of Sir Wm. Crookes (1923). For background information see Alexander Findlay, A Hundred Years of Chemistry (1937; 3d ed. 1965), and Eduard Farber, The Evolution of Chemistry: A History of Its Ideas, Methods and Materials (1952; 2d ed. 1969).

✳   ✳   ✳

CROWTHER / By Per Hassing

The Anglican bishop Samuel Adjai Crowther (ca. 1806–1891) was a pioneer African missionary and the first African Anglican bishop in Nigeria.

Samuel Crowther, of the Yoruba tribe, was enslaved in 1821 and put aboard a ship which was captured by the British navy. The freed slaves were sent to Freetown, Sierra Leone, where Crowther was baptized and, in 1827, became the first teacher to graduate from the Church Missionary Society's Teacher Training College at Fourah Bay. He joined the 1841 Niger expedition, sent out by England to explore the Niger River, combat the slave trade, and open the country for legitimate trade. Climatic conditions prevented success, but Crowther distinguished himself. He was invited to England for further training and ordained in the Church of England in 1843.

Crowther worked as a priest in Sierra Leone but soon became a member of the Anglican Mission in Nigeria,

Samuel Crowther. (Radio Times Hulton Picture Library)

first at Badgray and later at Abeokuta. There, by accident, he recognized his mother after 25 years of separation and baptized her in 1848.

Crowther preached in Yoruba, translated parts of the New Testament and the Book of Common Prayer and also published a *Vocabulary of the Yoruba Language* (1852). He believed that evangelization and trade should go together in order to bring peace and prosperity to the country.

In 1854 and 1857 Crowther was a member of two further Niger expeditions. The second suffered shipwreck, and Crowther did not return to Lagos until 1859. In 1855 he published *Journal of an Expedition up the Niger and Tshadda Rivers*, and in 1859, with J. C. Taylor, *The Gospel on the Banks of the Niger, 1857–1859*.

Crowther made frequent visits to England. In 1857 he was made head of the Niger Mission, and as the work prospered he was consecrated a bishop of the Church of England in West Africa in 1864 and also awarded an honorary doctor of divinity degree by Oxford University.

As a bishop, Crowther faced many difficulties. There was local opposition, both African and European; his duties and rights were not easily defined, and he was short of African helpers. Many of his African staff came from Sierra Leone and found it difficult to live in Nigeria. But the work prospered, and soon there were more than 600 Christians, with 10 priests and 14 teachers and catechists. His task was hard, but the fact that he was an African bishop inspired many African Christians in the years that followed. He died on Dec. 31, 1891, and was buried in Lagos.

Further Reading

Samuel Crowther is listed in the Africa study guide (VII, C, 4, c). Other explorers of the Niger were William BAIKIE and Hugh CLAPPERTON.

A full-length biography of Crowther is Jesse Page, *The Black Bishop: Samuel Adjai Crowther* (1908). Two more recent evaluations are in J. F. Ade Ajayi, *Christian Missions in Nigeria, 1841–1891* (1965), and E. A. Ayandele, *The Missionary Impact on Modern Nigeria, 1842–1914* (1966).

* * *

CRUZ / By Richard Graham

Oswaldo Gonçalves Cruz (1872–1917) was a Brazilian microbiologist, epidemiologist, and public health officer who founded experimental medicine in Brazil and directed controversial programs to eradicate yellow fever and smallpox from Rio de Janeiro.

Oswaldo Cruz (pronounced kro͞os) was born in the province of São Paulo, the son of a doctor. He completed medical school at the age of 20, perhaps as much because of the elementary nature of medi-

Oswaldo Cruz in 1903. (Organization of American States)

cal instruction then provided in Brazil as because of his brilliance. In 1896 he went to Paris, where he worked at the Pasteur Institute for 3 years. Cruz returned to Brazil as the bearer of an entirely new outlook on medical problems. His understanding of modern principles regarding contagion was perhaps not unique even in Brazil, but he was exceptional in his ability to surmount the political obstacles to the application of this understanding to public health. He almost immediately demonstrated these abilities in the coastal city of Santos, where he stopped an epidemic of bubonic plague in mid-course in 1899.

In 1902 Cruz became the Brazilian director general of public health. Brazil's progress and effort to secure international respect had so far been severely hampered by the frequent epidemics that ravaged the population, discouraged immigration, upset the normal patterns of trade, and debilitated both workers and managers. With the President's backing, Cruz launched a vigorous campaign aimed at imposing sanitary standards first of all upon the capital city. He especially worked to eradicate the mosquito responsible for the transmission of yellow fever. Simultaneously he pushed through the Brazilian congress a law requiring compulsory smallpox vaccination of all citizens.

These programs encountered the resistance of a superstitious and conservative population. Alarmed by these newfangled ideas and the invasion of their privacy and individual freedom, the people were easily manipulated by opponents of the regime: urban riots and even an unsuccessful military revolt were the result. The President, however, continued to give Cruz his full support, and the campaign was successful. As of that time Rio de Janeiro ceased to be a synonym for epidemic disease.

Meanwhile, Cruz also became director of the newly formed Institute of Experimental Pathology. His energetic and progressive leadership soon made it world-famous in the field of tropical medicine. He personally conducted field experiments in the upper Amazon and began the long process by which malaria was effectively restricted in Brazil. His career was cut short by Bright's disease.

Further Reading

Oswaldo Cruz is listed in the Latin America study guide (IV, C, 2, b). In his efforts to eradicate yellow fever Cruz employed methods made famous in Cuba by Carlos Juan FINLAY and Walter REED.

Very little has been written in any language on Cruz. He is discussed briefly in Fielding H. Garrison, *An Introduction to the History of Medicine* (1913; 4th rev. ed. 1929), and in Arturo Castiglioni, *A History of Medicine* (trans. 1941; 2d rev. ed. 1947).

CUAUHTEMOC / By Jaime Suchlicki

Cuauhtemoc (ca. 1496–1525) was the last of the Aztec rulers and a heroic defender of his empire against the Spanish conquistadores. Cuauhtemoc is revered by many Mexicans as the symbol of the Indians and as the representative of Mexican nationality.

Aztecs flee the approaching Spanish after Cuauhtemoc's unsuccessful defense against Hernán Cortés, an illustration from an account of the ceremonies of the Indians of Michoacán Province, in the Biblioteca Nacional, Madrid. (MAS)

Cuauhtemoc (pronounced kwou-tĕm′ōk) was born in Tenochtitlán (modern Mexico City), capital of the Aztec empire, the son of the Aztec emperor Ahuitzótl and the princess Tlilalcapatl. When he was 15, he entered the *calmecac*, or school for the nobility, devoted primarily to the study of religion, science, and art. Then he participated in a number of military expeditions to bring neighboring peoples under Aztec rule. Because of his military exploits he was appointed *techutli*, a term indicating an upper military and administrative position. In 1515 he was also appointed lordship of the region of Tlaltelolco.

In 1519 the Spanish conquistadores, led by Hernán Cortés, began the conquest of Mexico. Cortés captured the Aztec emperor Montezuma and ruled the empire from behind the throne. In 1520, however, the Indians under the leadership of Cuauhtemoc's uncle Cuitlahuac, who had succeeded Montezuma as Aztec emperor, rebelled and expelled the Spaniards. Cortés regrouped his men and prepared to recapture Tenochtitlán.

By this time Cuitlahuac had died, and Cuauhtemoc had inherited the throne. Cortés now faced a determined and courageous Indian leader. In May 1521 the

Spaniards began the siege of the city. The Aztecs fought valiantly, but the water supply dwindled when the Spaniards cut the aqueduct, and by August, with most of the city in ruins, the Aztec defense finally collapsed. Cuauhtemoc attempted to escape but was captured by Cortés's men. Cuauhtemoc asked to be killed, but Cortés refused, taking him to his headquarters in Coyoacán and keeping him under house arrest.

Cuauhtemoc remained in captivity for a long time. On one occasion he was subjected to brutal torture because the Spaniards, believing that he knew where Aztec treasures were hidden, decided to force Cuauhtemoc to reveal the locations of the gold. Cuauhtemoc endured the suffering and revealed no secrets.

During his captivity Cuauhtemoc accompanied Cortés on several expeditions, including one to Honduras in October 1524. For months Spaniards and Indians traveled through Central America, and many of Cortés's Indian allies died of starvation. Cortés became convinced by his men that Cuauhtemoc was urging Indians to rebel. Although Cuauhtemoc protested that he was innocent, Cortés insisted that he and several other Indian leaders must die. Cuauhtemoc was hanged near the town of Itzancanal on Feb. 26, 1525.

Further Reading

Cuauhtemoc is listed in the Latin America study guide (I, A, 1). His death, like that of other Indian chiefs in South America, such as ATAHUALPA of Peru's Incas and LAUTARO of Chile's Araucanian Indians, marked the beginning of his people's domination by the Spaniards.

There is much written on Cuauhtemoc but mostly in Spanish. In English, Cora Walker, *Cuatemo: Last of the Aztec Emperors* (1934), is of dubious value. Some information on Cuauhtemoc as well as on the Aztecs in general is in J. Eric Thompson, *Mexico before Cortez: An Account of the Daily Life, Religion, and Ritual of the Aztecs and Kindred Peoples* (1933); George C. Vaillant, *Aztecs of Mexico: Origin, Rise, and Fall of the Aztec Nation* (1941; rev. ed. 1962); and Eric R. Wolf, *Sons of the Shaking Earth* (1959).

CUDWORTH / By Burnham Terrell

The English philosopher and theologian Ralph Cudworth (1617–1688) was the most important of the Cambridge Platonists, a 17th-century circle which expounded rationalistic theology and ethics.

Ralph Cudworth, engraving by George Vertue. (Department of Prints & Drawings, British Museum)

Ralph Cudworth was born in Aller, Somerset, where his father was rector. His father, who had also been a fellow of Emmanuel College, Cambridge, and chaplain to James I, died in 1624, and Cudworth therefore had his early education from his stepfather, Dr. Stoughton. He entered Emmanuel College in 1632 and received a bachelor of arts degree in 1635, a master of arts degree in 1639, and a bachelor of divinity degree in 1646. In 1645 he was appointed master of Clare College and regius professor of Hebrew. He served as rector of North Cadbury, Somerset, from 1650 to 1654, then returned to Cambridge as master of Christ's College. In 1654 he also married and subsequently had two sons, John and Charles, and a daughter, Damaris (later Lady Masham). His daughter's philosophical writing and her friendship with John Locke helped spread Cudworth's ideas. The rest of his career was at Christ's College; he was involved in the political events of the time and served on and advised parliamentary committees.

Cudworth opposed excessive dogmatism in religion and advocated a predominantly moral conception of Christianity, with latitude in matters of ritual and organization. His earliest public statement of his position was a sermon preached before the House of Commons in 1647 and published later that year.

In *A Treatise on Eternal and Immutable Morality* Cudworth wrote, "It is universally true that things are what they are not by will but by nature." Thus truth, in morals, religion, and metaphysics, is discoverable by the use of reason. Those who set God's will or the will of a human sovereign above reason—Thomas Hobbes, the nominalists and Calvinists, even the rationalist René Descartes—were Cudworth's targets. Against Hobbes's alleged atheism, materialism, determinism, individualism, and ethical relativism, Cudworth defended theism, dualism, free will, organic political theory, and ethical absolutism.

Cudworth's metaphysical dualism asserts a distinction between active and passive powers, not the Cartesian distinction between thought and extension. Active powers, comprising unconscious "spiritual plastic powers" and deliberative operations, prudential and moral, are teleological. The passive powers are mechanical. In making reason active, Cudworth avoids the usual problems of moral psychology by reaffirming the Socratic identification: to know the good is to love it.

Cudworth's principal philosophical works are *The True Intellectual System of the Universe* (1678) and *A Treatise on Eternal and Immutable Morality* (1731). He died on June 26, 1688, and was buried in the chapel of Christ's College.

Further Reading

Ralph Cudworth is listed in the Philosophy study guide (IV, E). He opposed the philosophy of Thomas HOBBES. His works influenced 18th-century ethical theory, particularly that of Richard PRICE.

For discussions of Cudworth the philosopher see John H. Muirhead, *The Platonic Tradition in Anglo-Saxon Philosophy* (1931), and Lydia Gysi, *Platonism and Cartesianism in the Philosophy of Cudworth* (1962).

John Arthur Passmore, *Ralph Cudworth: An Interpretation* (1951), contains the most comprehensive bibliography.

✳   ✳   ✳

CUFFE / By Edwin S. Redkey

The Afro-American ship captain, merchant, and philanthropist Paul Cuffe (1759–1817) was active in the campaign for civil rights for blacks and Indians in Massachusetts. He is best known for his pioneering efforts to settle free Afro-Americans in West Africa.

Paul Cuffe was born on Jan. 17, 1759, near New Bedford, Mass., of an Indian mother and an African father, Cuffe Slocum, who had purchased his own freedom. Paul was the youngest of 10 children. His father died when Paul was a teenager, leaving the family to find its own means of support. Cuffe's education consisted of basic reading and writing, plus enough mathematics to permit him to navigate a ship. At the age of 16 he began his career as a common seaman on whaling and fishing boats. During the Revolutionary War he was held prisoner by the British for a time but managed afterward to start small-scale coastal trading. Despite attacks by pirates, he eventually prospered. He built larger vessels and successfully traded south as far as Virginia and north to Labrador. In later life he owned several ships which engaged in trading and whaling around the world.

Cuffe was a vigorous, pious, and independent man. He refused to use the name of his father's owner, Slocum, and adopted his father's given name, Cuffe (or Cuffee). In 1780 he and his brother John petitioned the Massachusetts government either to give blacks and Indians the right to vote or to stop taxing them. The petition was denied, but the case helped pave the way for the 1783 Massachusetts Constitution, which gave equal rights and privileges to all citizens of the state.

Cuffe was a devout and evangelical Quaker. He married at the age of 25. At his home in Westport, Mass., he donated a town school and helped support the teacher. Later he helped build a new meetinghouse. Through his connections with Quakers in other cities he became involved in efforts to improve the conditions of Afro-Americans. Strongly opposed to slavery and the slave trade, he joined other free blacks in the Northern states in their abolitionist campaigns.

When Cuffe learned of the Sierra Leone Colony in West Africa, which had been founded by English philanthropists in 1787, he began corresponding with English Quakers active in the movement to settle Afro-Americans there. In 1811 he sailed with his all-black crew to investigate the colony. Impressed and eager to start settling American blacks there who could evangelize the Africans, establish business enterprises, and work to stop the slave trade at its source, Cuffe returned to the United States after conferring with his allies in England. He planned to take a ship loaded with settlers and merchandise to Sierra Leone annually, but the War of 1812, between the United States and Britain, delayed him. Meanwhile, he petitioned the American government for aid and actively recruited future settlers among the free blacks of Baltimore, Philadelphia, New York, and Boston.

In 1815 Cuffe sailed with 38 settlers for Sierra Leone, where he helped them establish new homes with the cooperation of colonial authorities. Enthusiastic over his success, despite the heavy personal expense, he found increased interest in the project among American blacks. Soon, however, the newly formed American Colonization Society, which operated with support of Southern slave owners and advocated settlement of former slaves in Africa, began to frighten free blacks, who feared forced deportation. Before Cuffe could pursue his own settlement project, his health failed.

On Sept. 9, 1817, Cuffe died, mourned by all who knew him.

Further Reading

Paul Cuffe is listed in the American History study guide (IV, G, 3). Other free blacks of the early national period included Richard ALLEN and Benjamin BANNEKER.

The only biography of Cuffe is Henry N. Sherwood, *Paul Cuffe* (1923). Recent scholarship has added little to this fine study. Cuffe is also discussed in Benjamin G. Brawley, *Negro Builders and Heroes* (1937); Langston Hughes, *Famous Negro Heroes of America* (1954); Wil-

Paul Cuffe, an 1812 engraving by Mason and Maas. (Library of Congress)

liam C. Nell, *The Colored Patriots of the American Revolution* (1968); and William J. Simmons, *Men of Mark: Eminent, Progressive and Rising* (1968).

*　　*　　*

CUGOANO / By Maynard W. Swanson

> Ottobah Cugoano (ca. 1757–after 1803) was an African of Fanti origin from the Gold Coast in present-day Ghana. He became a prominent figure among the free blacks of late-18th-century London and in 1787 published an attack on slavery and the slave trade.

Ottobah Cugoano (pronounced (coō-gō-än′ō) was born near Ajumako and grew up in the household of the Fanti chief Ambro Accasa, ruler of Ajumako and Assinie. Cugoano was enslaved as a youth, taken to Grenada in the West Indies, and from there brought to England, where he was freed.

Educated while a slave and converted to Christianity, Cugoano soon emerged as a leader of opinion among the free blacks of London, where he corresponded under the adopted name of John Stewart, or Stuart, and became familiar with the abolitionist leaders Granville Sharp and Thomas Clarkson. Cugoano was a friend of Olaudah Equiano, with whom he collaborated in representing African interests.

Cugoano's book, *Thoughts and Sentiments on the Evil of Slavery*, was an impressively sustained intellectual assault which demolished the popular theological and biblical justifications for slavery and invoked the universality of the Christian God and His ethic, the equality of all men. It appealed to the humanitarian ideals of Enlightenment Europe and asserted the human right of Africans to freedom and dignity in the pursuit of their own destiny. Following the ideas of Adam Smith, Cugoano argued the economic insanity of slavery, previewing the later popular views of a "legitimate" commerce to replace the "illegitimate" slave trade. He proposed the outright manumission of all slaves 7 years or more in the colonies, the instruction of the rest in preparation for freedom, and a naval blockade in West Africa.

Several authorities believe that Cugoano's theological arguments were coached by Clarkson or Sharp, while his friend Equiano may have helped revise his book's first draft. Nevertheless, the work probably remains essentially a product of Cugoano's own thoughts and feelings, an articulate African's response to the impact of European expansion.

Very little is known of Cugoano's later career. In 1791 he was involved in Clarkson's scheme for recruiting Nova Scotia and New Brunswick Negroes to Sierra Leone. The same year he published a shorter version of *Thoughts and Sentiments*, in which he gave notice of intent to establish an African school in London. The Italian-Polish patriot Scipione Piattoli knew Cugoano during his London years (ca. 1800–1803), and the French writer

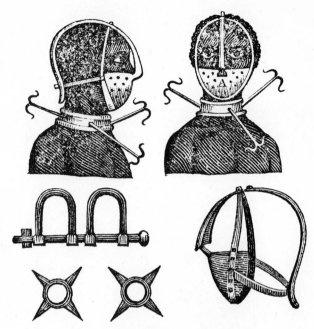

Iron mask, collar, and shackles used by slave traders in Ottobah Cugoano's time. (Library of Congress)

Henri Grégoire says Cugoano married an English woman. Beyond this, Ottobah Cugoano left no further record.

Further Reading

Ottobah Cugoano is listed in the Africa study guide (VI, D, 2). Olaudah EQUIANO and Joseph CINQUE also became well known in the struggle against slavery.

Cugoano's work, *Thoughts and Sentiments on the Evil and Wicked Traffic of the Slavery and Commerce of the Human Species* (1787), was reissued in a second edition by Paul Edwards, entitled *Thoughts and Sentiments on the Evil of Slavery* (1969). Edwards added an informative introduction and appended five previously unpublished manuscript letters by Cugoano that are helpful in determining the authorship of *Thoughts and Sentiments*. The most useful and informative modern treatment of Cugoano is by Robert July, *The Origins of Modern African Thought: Its Development in West Africa during the Nineteenth and Twentieth Centuries* (1967), who considers Cugoano an important precursor of 19th- and 20th-century African thought. Prince Hoare, *Memoirs of Granville Sharp, Esq.* (1820), contains some letters from Cugoano and references to his relationship with Sharp. Christopher Fyfe, in *A History of Sierra Leone* (1962), agrees with Paul Edwards and doubts that Cugoano is the sole author of *Thoughts and Sentiments*.

c. CULLEN / By Saunders Redding

> The American Countee Cullen (1903–1946) was one of the most widely heralded black poets of the Harlem renaissance, though he was less

concerned with social and political problems than were his black contemporaries. He is noted for his lyricism and his artful use of imagery.

Countee Cullen, whose real surname was Porter, was born May 30, 1903. Nothing is known about where he was born, and little is known of his parents. An orphan in New York City, he was adopted by the Reverend Frederick A. and Mrs. Carolyn Cullen, whose name he took. Following graduation from DeWitt Clinton High School, where he won a high school poetry contest, he attended New York University. In 1925 he took a baccalaureate degree, and his first book of poems, *Color,* was published. His metrical skill reminded many readers of the English poet Algernon Swinburne. He earned a master's degree at Harvard and then became assistant editor of *Opportunity: Journal of Negro Life,* which printed the fugitive pieces of black writers and gave publicity to the black artists who contributed so much to the cultural awakening of the 1920s.

Cullen knew what was going on in Negro life, but he was not deeply involved. *Ballad of the Brown Girl* and *Copper Sun,* both published in 1927, contain mostly personal Keatsian lyrics, which, generally speaking, show no advance and no development from the poems in his first volume. The piece entitled "Heritage" is a noteworthy exception. In a critical preface to the collection of Negro poetry, *Caroling Dusk* (1927), which he edited, Cullen argues that "Negro poetry . . . must emanate from some country other than this in some language other than our own." Though he later claimed that his poetry "treated of the heights and depths of emotion which I feel as a Negro," he did not want to be known as a "Negro" poet.

Even after his marriage in 1928 to Yolande, the only daughter of the Negro radical and activist W. E. B. Du Bois, Cullen stayed aloof from action and affirmative argument about race. His marriage lasted only through the first year of a 2-year visit to France, where he completed the long, narrative, parabolic poem "The Black Christ," which became the title poem of his fourth volume. *The Medea and Some Poems* (1935) was his last book of verse. From 1934 to 1945 he taught French in a New York public school.

Cullen's poetry is traditional in structure. His output in prose suffers from an absence of genuine commitment and is undistinguished. His novel, *One Way to Heaven,* satirizes upper-class Negro life. *The Lost Zoo* and *My Nine Lives and How I Lost Them* are children's books. Cullen collaborated on a musical play, *St. Louis Woman* (1946), but whatever emotional power and integrity it had was supplied by Arna Bontemps. The play opened on March 31, 1949. Cullen had died earlier, on Jan. 9, 1946. *On These I Stand,* his own selection of his best poems, was published in 1947.

Further Reading

Countee Cullen is listed in the Literature study guide (I, E, 2, b). Other black American poets included Paul Lau-

Countee Cullen in 1941. (Library of Congress, Carl Van Vechten Collection, Courtesy of Saul Mauriber)

rence DUNBAR, Phillis WHEATLEY, Claude McKAY, and Imamu Amiri BARAKA.

The only full-length work on Cullen is Blanche E. Ferguson, *Countee Cullen and the Negro Renaissance* (1966). Stephen H. Bronz, *Roots of Negro Racial Consciousness, the 1920's: Three Harlem Renaissance Authors* (1964), discusses Countee Cullen, James Weldon Johnson, and Claude McKay. Cullen is appraised in such anthologies and critical works as James Weldon Johnson, ed., *The Book of American Negro Poetry* (1922; rev. ed. 1931); Alain L. Locke, ed., *The New Negro: An Interpretation* (1925); J. Saunders Redding, *To Make a Poet Black* (1939); Margaret Just Butcher, *The Negro in American Culture: Based on Materials Left by Alain Locke* (1956); and Herbert Hill, ed., *Soon, One Morning: New Writings by American Negroes, 1940–62* (1963).

M. CULLEN / By William S. A. Dale

The Canadian painter Maurice Galbraith Cullen (1866–1934) was a pioneer of impressionism in

Canadian art and is particularly noted for his winter landscapes.

Maurice Cullen was born at St. John's, Newfoundland, and brought up in Montreal. He began his training as a sculptor under Philippe Hébert, and with a legacy from his mother he went to Paris in 1887 for further study at the École des Beaux-Arts. Once he saw the works of Claude Monet, however, he turned to painting and for the next few years sought out the favorite haunts of the French impressionists: Moret, Giverny, and Brittany. He exhibited at the Salon and was elected a member of the Société Nationale des Beaux-Arts.

With an established European reputation, Cullen returned to Montreal in 1895 and began to paint the winter landscapes along the St. Lawrence River in the vicinity of Quebec City and the night scenes of Montreal, for which he is best known. By 1897 he was a regular exhibitor with the Royal Canadian Academy, and he became a full member in 1907. In spite of this, his work was not immediately accepted by a public devoted to 19th-century European art, and he would have starved without the support of a few patrons, like Sir William Van Horne.

In 1900 Cullen managed to finance a second stay in Europe, this time for 2 years, and besides visiting familiar haunts in France with his old friend James Wilson Morrice, he ventured as far as North Africa. Between 1910 and 1912 he painted on the rugged coast of Newfoundland, and one of his larger canvases shows his native town of St. John's.

Maurice Cullen in 1898. (The National Gallery of Canada, Ottawa)

After World War I, in which Cullen served as a war artist, his reputation in Canada grew steadily. By the time he died in 1934 at his country retreat in Chambly, he was revered not only by the young rebels he had inspired in his lean years but by the wider Canadian public as well.

Unlike his friend Morrice, with whom he sometimes sketched on the Ile d'Orléans below Quebec, Cullen preferred to paint out of doors, even in the coldest weather, in order to capture the effect of sunlight on snow. He was one of the first Canadian artists to recognize the fact that snow shadows reflect the blue of the sky, and he did not hesitate to abandon the gentle haze of the French impressionists for the sharp clarity of the Canadian atmosphere. In his uncompromising honesty of subject and style, he was a true pioneer of the national school of landscape painting.

Further Reading

Maurice Cullen is listed in the Canada study guide (IV, C, 2). Like artists Emily CARR and David MILNE, he sought his subjects mostly out of doors.

The authoritative biography of Cullen is by his dealer in Montreal, William R. Watson, *Maurice Cullen* (1931). For general background see J. Russell Harper, *Painting in Canada: A History* (1966).

* * *

CUMMINGS / By Hyatt H. Waggoner

The American poet Edward Estlin Cummings (1894–1962) presented romantic attitudes in technically experimental verse. His poems are not only ideas but crafted physical objects which, in their nonlogical structure, grant fresh perspectives into reality.

In his publications E. E. Cummings always gave his name in lowercase letters without punctuation (e e cummings); this was part of his concern for the typography, syntax, and visual form of his poetry. He worked in the Emersonian tradition of romantic transcendentalism, which encouraged experimentation, and may have been influenced also by Walt Whitman, the poet that Ralph Waldo Emerson had personally encouraged.

Born in Cambridge, Mass., on Oct. 14, 1894, of a prominent academic and ministerial family, E. E. Cummings grew up in the company of such family friends as the philosophers William James and Josiah Royce. Had he lived in Emerson's time, he too might have been described as a "Boston Brahmin." His father, Edward Cummings, after teaching at Harvard, became the nationally known Congregational minister of the Old South Church in Boston, preaching a Christian-transcendentalist theology. Eventually Cummings came to espouse a positive position similar to that of his father, but not before an early period of rebellion against the stuffiness of Cambridge ladies, the repressiveness of conventional moralism, and the hypocrisy of the churches.

E. E. Cummings. (Library of Congress, Photo by DeGaston)

After receiving his bachelor of arts degree (1915) and master's degree (1916) from Harvard, Cummings became an ambulance driver in France just before America entered World War I. He was imprisoned for 3 months on suspicion of holding views critical of the French war effort, and this experience provided the material for his first book, *The Enormous Room* (1922), an experiment in blending autobiographical prose reporting with poetic techniques of symbolism.

Early Career

Cummings's transcendentalism, which stressed individual feeling over "objective" truth in a period when critical canons of impersonal, rationalistic, and formalistic poetry were being articulated, resulted in early rejection of his work. For several decades he had to pay for the publication of his books, and reviewers revealed very little understanding of his intentions. His first volume of verse, *Tulips and Chimneys* (1923), was followed by a second book of poems 2 years later. Though Cummings received the Dial Award for poetry in 1925, he continued to have difficulty in finding a publisher.

In the 10 years following 1925 only two volumes of Cummings's poems were published, both at his own expense: *is 5* (1926) and *W* (*ViVa*; 1931). In that decade Cummings also arranged for the publication of one experimental play, *Him* (1927), and a diarylike account of a trip to the U.S.S.R., *Eimi* (1933). With characteristic sarcasm Cummings named the 14 publishers who had rejected the manuscript of *No Thanks* (1935) in the

volume itself and said "Thanks" to his mother, who had financed its publication.

Poetic Techniques

Despite his dedication to growth and movement, and in contrast to his reputation as an experimenter in verse forms, Cummings actually tended to lack fresh invention. Especially in the 1930s, when he felt most alienated from his culture and his fellow poets, he repeated himself endlessly, writing many versions of essentially the same poem. He tended to rely too much on simple tricks to force the reader to participate in the poems, and his private typography, although originally expressive and amusing, became somewhat tiresome. Cummings's other stylistic devices—the use of low dialect to create satire and the visual "shaping" of poems—often seem self-indulgent substitutes for original inspiration.

However, Cummings's most characteristic device, the dislocation of syntax and the breaking up and reconstituting of words, was more than just another trick when it operated organically within the context of a poem's meaning. When he wrote, in one of his own favorite poems, "i thank You God for most this amazing," he emphasized the nonlogical quality of the statement by its syntactical ambiguity. "Most" intensifies the entire line in its displaced position and indicates why he thanks God; it moves "this amazing" toward "most amazing" in an authentic recreation of the miraculous process of the natural world. In general, Cummings's best dislocations expressed his belief in that miraculousness of the ordinary which logical syntax could not convey, bringing the reader to a freshness of perception that was Cummings's way toward illumination.

Poetic Achievement

The love poems and religious poems represent Cummings's greatest achievements; usually the two subjects are interrelated in his work. For example, "somewhere i have never travelled, gladly beyond" is one of the finest love lyrics in the English language, and Cummings's elegy on the death of his beloved father, "my father moved through dooms of love," is a profoundly moving tribute. Often he used a dislocated sonnet form in these poems, but what makes them memorable is not their formal experimentalism but their unique combination of sensuality with a sense of transcendent spirit. Cummings wrote some of the finest celebrations of sexual love and the religious experience of awe and natural piety produced in the 20th century, precisely at a time when it was highly unfashionable to write such poems.

Early in his career Cummings had divided his time between New York and Paris (where he studied painting); later, between New York and the family home in North Conway, N.H. He was always interested in the visual arts, and his paintings and drawings, late impressionist in style, were exhibited in several one-man shows in the 1940s and 1950s.

Ripening into Honor

After World War II a new generation of poets in rebellion against their immediate predecessors began to find in Cummings an echo of their own distinctly Emersonian ideas about poetry, and Cummings began to receive the recognition that had eluded him so long. In 1950 the Academy of American Poets awarded this self-described "failure" a fellowship for "great achievement," and his collected *Poems, 1923–1954* (1954) won praise in critical quarters which earlier had tended to downgrade Cummings for his unfashionable lyric romanticism.

Harvard University honored its distinguished alumnus by asking Cummings to deliver the Charles Eliot Norton Lectures in 1952–1953, his only attempt at formal artistic autobiography, later published as *i: six nonlectures* (1953). In the lectures Cummings said that perhaps 15 poems were faithful expressions of his stance as artist and man. The total number of truly memorable short poems is certainly higher than this modest figure but still only a fraction of the nearly 1,000 poems published in his lifetime.

Although Cummings did not "develop" as a poet either in terms of ideas or of characteristic style between the publication of *Tulips and Chimneys* and his final volume, *73 Poems* (1963), his work does show a deepening awareness and mastery of his special lyrical gift as poet of the mysteries of "death and forever with each breathing," with a corresponding abandonment of earlier defensive-offensive sallies into ideology and criticism. His finest single volume, *95 Poems* (1958), illustrates Cummings's increasing ability toward the end of his life to give content to his abstractions through the artifact of the poem-object itself, rather than depending entirely on pure rhetoric. If only a tenth of his poems should be thought worthwhile by the end of the century, Cummings will have been established as one of the lasting poets America has produced.

Late Works and Influence

Cummings's *Collected Poems* was published in 1960. In addition to the works mentioned, Cummings published several other experimental plays, a ballet, and some 15 volumes of verse. Shortly before his death at North Conway on Sept. 3, 1962, Cummings wrote the texts to accompany photographs taken by his third wife, Marion Morehouse. Titled *Adventures in Value* (1962), this work exemplifies his lifelong effort to *see* intensely and deeply enough to confront the miraculousness of the natural. Today's young poets of neoromantic inclinations consider him, along with William Carlos Williams, one of their artistic ancestors, although Cummings produced no significant stylistic followers.

Further Reading

E. E. Cummings is listed in the Literature study guide (I, E, 2, b). He can be considered part of the transcendental tradition of Ralph Waldo EMERSON and Walt WHITMAN. The other transcendentalist of Cummings's period was Hart CRANE.

Good discussions of Cummings and his work include Charles Norman, *The Magic-Maker: E. E. Cummings* (1958); Norman Friedman, *E. E. Cummings: The Growth of a Writer* (1964); Barry A. Marks, *E. E. Cummings* (1964); and Robert E. Wegner, *The Poetry and Prose of E. E. Cummings* (1965). There is a section on Cummings in Hyatt H. Waggoner, *American Poets: From the Puritans to the Present* (1968).

CUNHA / By Richard Graham

Euclides Rodrigues Pimenta da Cunha (1866–1909) was a Brazilian writer whose account of the clash between the Brazilian army and fanatic followers of a backwoods mystic became a national classic.

Euclides da Cunha (pronounced kōō′nyə) was born in the province of Rio de Janeiro on Jan. 20, 1866. Orphaned at the age of 3, he was raised by aunts, interned in various boarding schools, and shuffled around a great deal. He was always moody, reserved, lonely, and unpredictable. At 18 he enrolled in the military academy, where he specialized in military engineering. Two years later he apparently suffered a nervous breakdown that led to a court-martial and dismissal for insubordination, but he was reinstated. The incident may already have reflected an abhorrence for war. In 1896 he resigned from the army as a first lieutenant and subse-

Euclides da Cunha. (Bibliothèque Nationale, Paris)

quently took up civil engineering while writing occasional newspaper articles.

When, in 1897, the army was forced to dispatch a fifth expedition into the backlands to crush a small messianic cult, Cunha accompanied the troops as a war correspondent for a leading Brazilian newspaper. Fighting in the searing heat of the drought-stricken region of northeast Brazil, the army proceeded to systematically exterminate the last of the sectarians, partially because they refused to surrender. Cunha not only wrote the commissioned articles but gathered the material for his broadly conceived, great book. In the next 5 years he directed engineering works by day and wrote at night. The result was *Os sertões* (1902), translated as *Rebellion in the Backlands.*

Because of its vivid portrayal of the agony and bitterness of warfare, its anticipation of the technique of the documentary novel, its philosophical insights, and its perceptive interpretation of Brazil, the book was an immediate success. In it Cunha probed Brazil's developmental problems and drew attention to the misery and ignorance that still characterize Brazil's interior. Although he was grudgingly persuaded by the then current "scientific" ideas on racial superiority, his social Darwinism was tempered with admiration for the mestizos, who had been so brutally treated by the allegedly more civilized representatives of the coastal cities. In some ways it was an antimilitary tract, certainly a denunciation of man's inhumanity. At the same time, the book portrayed flesh-and-blood men caught up in a drama that moved inevitably to a tragic conclusion.

Cunha subsequently wrote several less important historical, biographical, geographical, and anthropological pieces, several of them dealing with the Amazon. A dispute over a woman led to his assassination at the age of 43 on Aug. 15, 1909.

Further Reading

Euclides da Cunha is listed in the Latin America study guide (IV, C, 2, b). Much of Brazilian literature is concerned with the country's social problems. Typical examples are the writings of Joaquim Maria MACHADO DE ASSIS and Jorge AMADO.

The introduction by Samuel Putnam to Cunha's *Rebellion in the Backlands* (1902; trans. 1944), briefly surveys his life. See also Putnam's *Marvelous Journey: A Survey of Four Centuries of Brazilian Writing* (1948), and Erico Verissimo, *Brazilian Literature: An Outline* (1945). There are numerous works in Portuguese about Cunha.

CUNNINGHAM / By Edward E. Cole, Jr.

The American Merce Cunningham (born 1919) was a solo dancer of commanding presence, a controversial choreographer, an influential teacher, and an organizer of an internationally acclaimed avant-garde dance company.

Born in Centralia, Wash., on April 19, 1919, Merce Cunningham studied modern dance under Bonnie Bird in Seattle. Here he met the composer John Cage. From 1940 to 1945 Cunningham was a soloist with the Martha Graham Company, creating such roles as the Christ Figure in *El Penitente*, the Acrobat in *Every Soul Is a Circus*, March in *Letter to the World*, and the Revivalist in *Appalachian Spring*.

While still with the Graham Company, Cunningham began independent work, at first in solo concerts. His first important large creation was *The Seasons* (1947), with music by Cage. For the next quarter century, Cage acted as Cunningham's chief composer and musical adviser.

Cunningham's first substantial success came in 1952 (also the year he formed his own company-school) with his setting of Igor Stravinsky's "dance episodes with song," *Les Noces*. He continued working with music by experimentalist composers such as Erik Satie, Pierre Schaeffer, and Alan Hovhaness, as well as with Cage. Cunningham also danced to sounds produced solely by his own voice: grunts, shrieks, squeals, and howls.

Cunningham's personal dance style, reflected in his choreography, was usually athletic in forcefulness. But he could also effect a slow, nearly suspended motion which, when opposed sharply to the cross rhythms of accompaniments—either musical, or antimusical—produced unique effects. Cunningham never used such "tricks" as facial expressions to reach an audience, relying solely upon pure body movement to produce effects.

Cunningham experimented with Cage and others of futuristic thought from fields of dance, music, theater, visual arts, and even the technical sciences in combining abstract dance elements with *musique concrète*, electronic music, random sounds, lighting effects, action films or photo slides superimposed upon or backlighting stage action, pure noise, and even silence. But, though he worked frequently with "chance" methods, Cunningham remained a deadly serious creator who never really

Merce Cunningham. (The Cunningham Dance Foundation, Inc.)

left anything to uncertainty. For example, in the late 1960s he worked on dances using body-attached cybersonic consoles which could increase, reduce, distort, unbalance, and then rebalance sounds by stage movements, according to the dimensions of different spatial areas; and on the control of stage lighting as affected by the dancers moving within range of electronic devices that changed hues and densities of illuminations.

In 1958 Cunningham's company began tours which took them to nearly every continent. Cunningham gave lecture-demonstrations or participated in symposiums at universities and museums around the world. By 1970 he had created nearly 100 ensemble dance works and dozens of solos for himself, had made significant documentary films on modern dance, and had authored a book.

Further Reading

Merce Cunningham is listed in the American History study guide (X, F, 4). His longtime collaborator was composer John CAGE.

Cunningham's partly autobiographical *Changes* (1968) mainly relates his ideas on dance. Pictures of his company's work are in Jack Mitchell, *Dance Scene U.S.A.* (1967), with commentary by Clive Barnes. Walter Sorell, ed., *The Dance Has Many Faces* (1951; 2d ed. 1966), includes good essays on modern dance and Cunningham's place in it.

CURIE / By Stanley L. Jaki

> The Polish-born French physicist Marie Sklodowska Curie (1867–1934) pioneered radioactive research by her part in the discovery of radium and polonium and in the determination of their chemical properties.

Marie Curie (pronounced kyŏŏ-rē′) was born in Warsaw on Nov. 7, 1867, the youngest of the five children of Wladislaw and Bronislava Boguska Sklodowska. Marie was a brilliant student, gaining a gold medal upon completing her secondary education in 1883. As girls could not attend universities in Russian-dominated Poland, Marie at her father's suggestion spent a year in the country with friends. On returning to her father's house in Warsaw the next summer, Marie had to begin to earn her living through private tutoring, and she also became associated with the "Floating University," a group of young men and women who tried to quench their thirst for knowledge in semiclandestine sessions. In early 1886 she accepted a job as governess with a family living in Szczuki, but the intellectual loneliness she experienced there only stiffened her determination to achieve somehow her dream to become a university student. One of her sisters, Bronya, was already in Paris, successfully passing the examinations in medicine. In March 1890 she offered hospitality to Marie whose

acceptance was a foregone conclusion, but it was not until September 1891 that Marie could leave for Paris.

When classes began at the Sorbonne in Paris in early November 1891, Marie Sklodowska enrolled as a student of physics. By 1894 she was desperately looking for a laboratory where she could work on her research project, the measurement of the magnetic properties of various steel alloys, and it was suggested that she see Pierre Curie at the School of Physics and Chemistry of the University of Paris. Their first meeting was movingly recorded in the future Madame Curie's recollections: "He seemed very young to me although he was then age thirty-five. I was struck by the expression of his clear gaze and by a slight appearance of carelessness in his lofty stature. His rather slow, reflective words, his simplicity, and his smile, at once grave and young, inspired confidence. A conversation began between us and became friendly; its object was some questions of science upon which I was happy to ask his opinion."

Although Marie Sklodowska was insistent from the very start that she would go back to Poland in half a year to assist her subjugated country in whatever way she could, Pierre Curie was most intent to see her more and more often. The result was that she returned to Paris in October 1894 after spending the summer months in Poland. The next summer witnessed their wedding and the beginning of a most extraordinary partnership in scientific work. By mid-1897 Madame Curie could list as her scientific achievements two university degrees, a fellowship, and a monograph on the magnetization of tempered steel. Their first daughter, Irène, had just been born, and it was in that euphoric atmosphere that the Curies' attention turned to the mysterious radiation from uranium recently discovered by Antoine Henri Becquerel. It was Madame Curie's hunch that the radiation was an atomic property and therefore had to be present in some other elements as well. Her search soon established the fact of a similar radiation from thorium, and the historic word "radioactivity" was coined by Madame Curie.

While searching for other sources of radioactivity, the Curies had before long to turn their attention to pitchblende, a mineral well known for its uranium content. To their immense surprise the radioactivity of pitchblende far exceeded the combined radioactivity of the uranium and thorium contained in it. From their laboratory two papers reached the Academy of Sciences within 6 months. The first, read at the meeting of July 18, 1898, announced the discovery of a new radioactive element, which the Curies named polonium after Madame Curie's native country. The other paper, announcing the discovery of radium, was read at the December 26 meeting.

To substantiate the existence of the new elements and to establish their properties, the Curies had to have sufficiently large quantities. Fortunately, the Austrian government was willing to give the Curies a ton of pitchblende, but to process it a laboratory was needed. After long search, the Curies had to settle for a shed occupying part of a courtyard in the School of Physics and Chemistry. From 1898 to 1902 the Curies processed several tons of pitchblende, but it was not only the extremely precious centigrams of radium that rewarded their superhuman labors. The Curies also published, jointly or separately, during those years a total of 32 scientific papers. Among them was the one which announced that diseased, tumor-forming cells were destroyed faster than healthy cells when exposed to radium.

From abroad came the full measure of recognition which the French Academy of Sciences refused to give in 1902, when Pierre Curie presented himself as candidate for membership. In November 1903 the Royal Society in

Marie and Pierre Curie. (H. Roger-Viollet)

London gave the Curies one of its highest awards, the Davy Medal; and a month later followed the announcement from Stockholm that three French scientists, A. H. Becquerel and the Curies, were the joint recipients of the Nobel Prize in physics for 1903. Finally even the academics in Paris began to stir and a chair in physics was created at the University of Paris, and a few months later Madame Curie was appointed director of research associated with the new chair. In December 1904 their second daughter Ève, was born; while the next year brought the election of Pierre Curie to the Academy of Sciences and their travel to Stockholm, where he delivered on June 6 the Nobel lecture, which was in fact their joint address. Its concluding paragraph evoked in prophetic words the double-edged impact on mankind of every major scientific advance. Still Curie asserted his conviction that "mankind will derive more good than harm from the new discoveries."

The illustrious husband-and-wife team, now installed in more appropriate academic positions, had, however, their happy days numbered. The first academic year of Pierre Curie in his new professorship was not over when, on the rainy mid-afternoon of April 19, 1906, he was run down by a heavy carriage and killed instantly. Two weeks later the widow was asked to take over her late husband's post. Honors began to pour in from scientific societies all over the world on a woman left alone with two small children and with the gigantic task of leadership in radioactivity. In 1908 she began to give as titular professor at the Sorbonne the first, and then the only, course on radioactivity in the world. In the same year she edited the collected works of her late husband, and in 1910 she published her massive *Traité de radioactivité*. The next year the Academy of Sciences showed once more its true colors by denying with a one-vote majority the membership to the person who 11 months later became the first to receive twice the Nobel Prize, this time in chemistry.

In addition to the Nobel Prize the two finest honors that came to Madame Curie in 1911 were her election as permanent member of the Solvay Conferences in physics and the erection in Warsaw of the Institute of Radioactivity, whose directorship was offered to her by a most distinguished group of Polish intellectuals. The first of these honors reflected on her stature as a scientist. The second honor was more of an emotional satisfaction and represented some temptation for Madame Curie to turn her back on the unappreciative scientific establishment of her adopted country. But she decided to stay in France, though she did her best to assist the new institute in Warsaw in every possible way. A most important factor in Madame Curie's decision to stay was the future of the laboratory which Dr. P. P. E. Roux, the director of the Pasteur Institute, proposed to build for her. The plan finally jolted the Sorbonne to join hands with the Pasteur Institute in establishing the famous Radium Institute. Its dedication took place in July 1914, a year after the institute in Warsaw had been dedicated in Madame Curie's presence.

Madame Curie devoted much of her time during the 4 years of World War I to equipping automobiles in her own laboratory with x-ray (Roentgen) apparatus to assist the sick. It was these cars that became known in the war zone as "little Curies." By the end of the war Madame Curie was past her fiftieth year with much of her physical energy already spent, together with her savings, which she had patriotically invested in war bonds. But her dedication seemed to be inexhaustible. The year 1919 witnessed her installation at the Radium Institute, and 2 years later her book *La Radiologie et la guerre* was published. In it she gave a most informative account of the scientific and human experiences gained for radiology during the war. With the end of the war also came the appointment of her daughter Irène, a physicist, as an assistant in her mother's laboratory.

Shortly afterward, a momentous visit took place in the Radium Institute. The visitor was Mrs. William B. Meloney, editor of a leading magazine in New York and representative of those countless women who for years had found in Madame Curie their ideal and inspiration. A year later Mrs. Meloney returned to tell Madame Curie that a nationwide subscription in America had produced the sum of $100,000 needed to purchase a gram of radium for her institute. She was also asked to visit the United States with her daughters and collect in person the precious gift. Her trip was a triumph in the finest sense of the word. In the White House, President Warren G. Harding presented Madame Curie with the golden key to the little metal box containing the radium.

On questions other than scientific, Madame Curie rarely uttered public comment of any length. One of the exceptions was her statement at a conference in 1933 on "The Future of Culture." There she rallied to the defense of science, which several panelists held responsible for the dehumanization of modern life. "I am among those," she emphasized, "who think that science has great beauty. A scientist in his laboratory is not only a technician; he is also a child placed before natural phenomena which impress him like a fairy tale. We should not allow it to be believed that all scientific progress can be reduced to mechanism, machines, gearings, even though such machinery also has its own beauty."

The most heartwarming experience of the last phase of Madame Curie's life was probably the marriage of Irène in 1926 to Frédéric Joliot (later Joliot-Curie), the most gifted assistant at the Radium Institute. Before long it was evident to her that their union would be a close replica of her own marvelously creative partnership with Pierre Curie.

She worked almost to the very end and succeeded in completing the manuscript of her last book, *Radioactivité*. In the last years her great support was her younger daughter, Ève. She was also her mother's faithful companion when, on July 4, 1934, death claimed the one of whom Albert Einstein aptly said, "Marie Curie is, of all celebrated beings, the only one whom fame has not corrupted."

Further Reading

Marie Curie is listed in the Science study guide (VII, C, 2). Another notable physicist was Frédéric JOLIOT-CURIE, her son-in-law. Antoine Henri BECQUEREL discovered radioactivity in uranium.

The classic biography of Marie Curie, written by her daughter, is Ève Curie, *Madame Curie* (trans. 1937), a work which emphasizes the human element. *Nobel Lectures: Physics, 1901–1921* (1967), published by the Nobel Foundation, includes a biographical sketch. General background works which discuss Madame Curie include Gerald Holton and Duane H. D. Roller, *Foundations of Modern Physical Science* (1958), and Henry A. Boorse and Lloyd Motz, eds., *The World of the Atom* (2 vols., 1966).

✳   ✳   ✳

CURLEY / By Philip J. Funigiello

The American politician James Michael Curley (1874–1958) was a magnetic political figure, particularly as mayor of Boston.

James Curley was born on Nov. 20, 1874, in Boston, a city whose upper-class Yankee Protestant families despised Irish Catholics socially and discriminated against them politically. He became a symbol of the emergence of the Irish from their proletarian status to political dominance. Reared in politics, alienated from

James Curley in 1943. (Library of Congress)

any sense of community, Curley formed a hard, unwavering, egocentric determination to succeed.

Curley overcame handicaps of birth and poor education, and his political ascendancy was meteoric. Elected to the Common Council in 1900, he then progressed to the Board of Aldermen and the Massachusetts Legislature. His Irish slum constituency elected him in 1911 to the first of four undistinguished terms in Congress. In 1928 he was a firm supporter of Governor Alfred E. Smith for president. Denied a place in the Massachusetts delegation to the 1932 Democratic convention, Curley managed to be chosen a delegate from Puerto Rico. His support was instrumental in winning the presidential nomination for Franklin D. Roosevelt, but he broke with Roosevelt after the President refused to appoint him ambassador to Ireland.

As governor of Massachusetts in 1935, Curley was criticized for his spending, job trading, and high-speed motorcades across the Commonwealth. In 1936 he was an unsuccessful candidate for the U.S. Senate.

Of his many political posts, Curley best enjoyed being mayor of Boston. He was elected in 1913, 1921, 1929, and 1945. In an age of such figures as Tom Pendergast of Kansas City and Frank Hague of Jersey City, Curley enjoyed his self-described role as political "boss." But whereas the others had powerful political machines, Curley's greatest strength lay in his personal magnetism. The core of his political support always came from the slums. Curley lacked a political philosophy beyond that of taking care of himself and his own.

Politics was a game he took as he found it; his only desire was to win, not to change or reform. He fabricated a Ku Klux Klan scare during his first gubernatorial campaign, and he regularly blackmailed Boston's propertied classes and social elite to subsidize his huge public works projects and padded city payrolls. He served two terms in prison: in 1904 for impersonating a friend in a civil service examination, and in 1947 for graft in connection with Federal contracts while serving as a member of Congress. His conduct frequently brought him into conflict with the Catholic hierarchy of Boston.

A political legend in Boston for more than half a century, Curley lived to see himself perpetuated as a literary legend. He was the prototype for Frank Skeffington, the principal figure in Edwin O'Connor's novel *The Last Hurrah*. Curley died on Nov. 12, 1958.

Further Reading

James Curley is listed in the American History study guide (IX, A, 3). Another political boss was Frank HAGUE.

Curley's autobiography, *I'd Do It Again: A Record of All My Uproarious Years* (1957), is a rambling and uneven document enlivened by the candidly brazen quality of the author's confessions. The beginning of the Curley legend and the first attempt to put his career in perspective is Joseph F. Dinneen, *The Purple Shamrock: The Honorable James Michael Curley of Boston* (1949). A frankly hostile account of Curley's governorship is Wendell D. Howie, *The Reign of James the First: A Histori-* *cal Record of the Administration of James M. Curley as Governor of Massachusetts* (1936).

CURRIE / By J. L. Granatstein

Sir Arthur William Currie (1875–1933) was the leader of the Canadian Corps during World War I, the first native Canadian to head his country's forces in France and Flanders.

Arthur Currie was born at Napperton, Ontario, on Dec. 5, 1875, and he was educated in the public schools of Strathroy. In 1894 he moved to British Columbia and taught in the public schools of Sidney and Victoria for 5 years. He then became involved with insurance and real estate, businesses which he practiced with little success and through which he became heavily indebted.

Currie's metier, however, was soldiering. He joined the 5th Regiment of Canadian Garrison Artillery in 1897 and received his commission in 1900. His rise through

Sir Arthur Currie. (United Press International Photo)

the ranks was swift, and in 1909 he was given command of the regiment. His command was one of the most efficient in Canada, and Currie's personal reputation was high with the minister of militia in Ottawa.

As a result, when war broke out in 1914, Currie was offered the command of a brigade in the 1st Canadian Division. After training in England, Currie led his troops to France in February 1915. Very shortly thereafter he and his untried men faced the first German gas attack at Ypres but stood their ground with incredible fortitude. In September 1915 Currie took charge of the 1st Canadian Division, and he led the troops through a series of terrific battles—Mont-Sorrel, the Somme, Fresnoy, and Vimy.

As a commander, Currie was not a brilliant strategist. But he was an excellent tactician, skillful in the use of artillery, meticulous in his planning. Most important, he was careful of the lives of his men, something for which World War I generals were not renowned. When the command of the Canadian Corps fell vacant in June 1917, Currie was the logical choice for the post. As with his previous commands, he did extraordinarily well, and he led the corps through the horror of Passchendaele and through Arras and Amiens. The record of the corps was second to none, and Currie received and merited enormous praise.

After the war Currie was made general and named the inspector general of the military forces of Canada, a position he held until 1920, when he resigned to become principal of McGill University in Montreal. Often mentioned as a possible leader of the Conservative party, Currie decided to remain in academic life. He died on Nov. 30, 1933.

Further Reading

Sir Arthur Currie is listed in the Canada study guide (IV, A, 1). Canada's wartime leader was Sir Robert BORDEN.

There is a biography of Currie by Hugh M. Urquhart, *Arthur Currie* (1950), that is very discreet. The best study on the Canadian Corps and its commander, however, is John Swettenham, *To Seize the Victory: The Canadian Corps in World War I* (1965).

* * *

CURRIER AND IVES

/ **By Abraham A. Davidson**

Nathaniel Currier (1813–1888) and James Merritt Ives (1824–1895) were partners in the firm of Currier and Ives, the most important 19th-century lithographic company in America. Their prints were widely sold across the nation.

Nathaniel Currier, born in Roxbury, Mass., was apprenticed in his teens to a Boston lithographic firm. He established his own lithography business in New York City in 1835. The lithographer James Ives,

Nathaniel Currier. (Courtesy, Free Library of Philadelphia)

born in New York City, entered into partnership with Currier in 1857. Currier retired in 1888, Ives a few years later; but the firm was carried on by their sons and flourished until 1907.

Lithography had begun in America in the 1820s. It was quicker and less expensive than engraving, hence the remarkable success of the firm of Currier and Ives. Soon after setting up business they produced extensive folios, usually based on paintings. Some of the work was crude, but the quality varied considerably. The star artists of the firm were Arthur F. Tait, who specialized in sporting scenes; Louis Maurer, who executed genre scenes; Fanny Palmer, who liked to do picturesque panoramas of the American landscape; and George H. Durrie, who supplied winter scenes.

So well known did Currier and Ives become that it was common to refer to any large mixed batch of prints as Currier and Ives prints. The firm was astoundingly prolific and produced prints on practically every aspect of the American scene. In the 1870s they issued four catalogs featuring 2800 subject titles.

Currier and Ives sometimes focused on current events. (In 1840 Currier produced what may have been the first illustrated "extra" in history when he depicted scenes of the fire that had broken out that year aboard the steamship *Lexington* in Long Island Sound.) Political cartoons and banners were commonly produced, like the *Presidential Fishing Party of 1848*, showing the candidates

James Ives. (Courtesy, Free Library of Philadelphia)

with fishing poles trying to hook fish on which names of various states are inscribed.

Historical prints were another field, and copies from the historical paintings of John Trumbull were especially popular. The Civil War print *Battle of Fair Oaks, Va., May 31, 1862* shows the first balloon ever used for warfare observation. Sentimental prints included one showing a married couple walking along a riverbank and another showing a girl taking care of her little sister. There were also prints for children, such as *Robinson Crusoe and His Pets* and *Noah's Ark*; country and pioneer home scenes, which included *Early Winter*, a beautiful scene of people skating on a frozen pond before a snow-covered country cottage; and lithographed sheet music. Still other categories were Mississippi River prints, including *On the Mississippi Loading Cotton* and *Midnight Race on the Mississippi*; railroad prints that sometimes featured minute descriptions of trains, as in *"Lightning Express" Trains Leaving the Junction*; and home prints, which were produced in especially large quantities.

Currier and Ives avoided controversial subjects, although there was at least one print showing the branding of slaves prior to embarkation from Africa. Prints of sporting events focused on prize fights (like the 1835 match between John C. Heeman and the English champion Tom Sayers), boat races, and even, in the early stages of its development, baseball.

As America expanded, so did the demand for Currier and Ives prints. Today they provide a vivid picture of daily life in 19th-century America.

Further Reading

Nathaniel Currier and James Ives are listed in the Art study guide (IV, C, 2). The first paintings of Grandma MOSES were copies of Currier and Ives prints. The master of 19th-century American photography was Mathew BRADY.

Harry T. Peters, *Currier and Ives: Printmakers to the American People* (1942), is the authoritative work, containing 192 plates and an excellent introduction. Both Colin Simkin, *Currier and Ives' America* (1952), and Roy King and Burke Davis, *The World of Currier & Ives* (1968), contain useful introductions and reproductions. See also Currier's own *Currier & Ives Chronicles of America*, edited by John Lowell Pratt and with an introduction by A. K. Baragwanath (1968).

CURRY / By James I. Robertson, Jr.

The American politician Jabez Lamar Monroe Curry (1815–1903) was the main force behind improved education in the South in the latter half of the 19th century.

Born on June 5, 1815, in Lincoln County, Ga., J. L. M. Curry was the son of a slaveholding family that ultimately moved to Alabama. He graduated from the University of Georgia and the Harvard University Law School. While at Harvard, Curry heard a lecture by Horace Mann that awakened his zealous interest in universal education.

In 1845 Curry was admitted to the Alabama bar, and he quickly gained prominence as a lawyer. Three terms in the Alabama Legislature preceded 4 years as a member of the U.S. House of Representatives. During the Civil War he served first in the Confederate Congress and then as a colonel on the staffs of generals Joseph E. Johnston and Joseph Wheeler.

Shortly after his 1866 ordination as a Baptist minister, Curry accepted the presidency of Howard College in Alabama. He left that post in 1868 to become a professor of English, philosophy, and law at Richmond College, Va. Meanwhile, New England philanthropist George Peabody had donated $2,000,000 as a fund for the improvement of Southern schools. When the directorship of the Peabody Fund became vacant, Curry was immediately nominated. As one endorser stated: "He is so many-sided, so clear in his views, so judicious and knows so well how to deal with all classes of men. His whole being is wrapped up in general education, and he is the best lecturer or speaker on the subject in all the South." In 1881 Curry received the appointment. He later became special agent for a similar educational endowment, the Slater Fund.

His supreme goal, Curry stated, was to "preach a crusade against ignorance." He practiced as well as preached, for he was the inspiration behind the establishment of normal schools in 12 Southern states; he was the chief organizer of elementary schools in a number of major cities; and he constantly prodded state legislatures to create more and better rural schools. His 40 reports and 10 addresses on education at this time dominated the subject. Two historians, Thomas D. Clark and Albert D. Kirwan, wrote: "Scarcely a major educational advance was to be made in the South between 1881 and 1902 that was not influenced in some way by J. L. M. Curry; in fact his name became synonymous with public education."

In his last years Curry served as special minister to Spain, president of the Board of Foreign Missions of the Southern Baptist Convention, and president of the Southern Historical Association. He died on Feb. 12, 1903, in Asheville, N.C., and is buried in Richmond, Va. His statue is one of two memorials placed by Alabama in the U.S. Capitol's "Hall of Statuary."

Curry's writings included *Constitutional Government in Spain* (1889), *William Ewart Gladstone* (1891), *The*

Southern States of the American Union (1895), The Civil History of the Government of the Confederate States (1901), and a number of religious tracts.

Further Reading

J. L. M. Curry is listed in the American History study guide (VII, B, 2, a; VII, F, 3, c). Booker T. WASHINGTON and L. Q. C. LAMAR were other important figures in the social and educational revitalization of the South after the Civil War.

The best work on Curry is Jessie P. Rice, *J. L. M. Curry: Southerner, Statesman and Educator* (1949). An older study, still reliable and based in great part on Curry's writings, is Edwin A. Alderman and Armistead C. Gordon, *J. L. M. Curry: A Biography* (1911). Curry's *Civil History of the Government of the Confederate States* (1901) contains many personal reminiscences.

A. G. CURTIN / By James I. Robertson, Jr.

The American politician Andrew Gregg Curtin (1815–1894) was the influential governor of Pennsylvania during the Civil War and one of Abraham Lincoln's most powerful supporters.

Andrew Gregg Curtin's father was an Irish immigrant who settled in Pennsylvania in 1793 and became one of the first manufacturers of iron in that state. Curtin was born on April 23, 1815, at Bellefonte in Center County. Following an excellent tutorial education, he read law and was admitted to the bar in 1839. He promptly formed a partnership with John Blanchard, later a member of Congress. From the beginning, Curtin was a success. Magnetic, honest, and popular, he possessed a congenial manner, ready wit, and extraordinary power of speech.

Curtin entered Pennsylvania politics at the age of 25. As a Whig, he campaigned actively on behalf of the presidential candidacies of William Henry Harrison, Henry Clay, Zachary Taylor, and Winfield Scott. In 1854 he declined the nomination for governor and threw his support to the successful candidacy of James Pollock, who repaid Curtin with the high post of secretary of the commonwealth. Curtin's most notable achievement in that position was in fostering the cause of public education.

In 1860 Curtin was instrumental in securing the Republican presidential nomination for Abraham Lincoln. He himself agreed to run for governor against strong Democratic opposition. He won the election by a wide margin, and his victory was instrumental in swinging Pennsylvania to Lincoln in the national election a month later.

An ardent unionist, Curtin had an untarnished record as Pennsylvania's Civil War governor. He aroused such early and enthusiastic support for the North that five companies of Pennsylvania troops were the first soldiers

J. L. M. Curry, an engraving after a photograph by Mathew Brady. (Library of Congress)

Andrew Gregg Curtin. (Library of Congress)

to arrive in Washington for the capital's defense. When the state raised double its initial quota of 14,000 volunteers, Curtin organized the extra force into the Pennsylvania Reserve Corps. Throughout the war Curtin was "ceaseless in his devotion to the wants and needs" of Pennsylvania soldiers. He ensured that his regiments had the most up-to-date arms and equipment; he went to unparalleled lengths to care for the wounded; and he fathered a law providing for the education of war orphans in the state. These and similar endeavors earned him the sobriquet "Soldier's Friend."

Following a second term as governor, Curtin in 1869 accepted the ambassadorship to Russia. He returned to America in 1872 and supported the presidential candidacy of Horace Greeley, an action which alienated leading Republicans. Curtin then joined the Democratic party. Defeated in an 1878 bid for Congress, he ran again in 1880 and won the first of three consecutive terms in the national legislature. Thereafter he retired to his mountain home, where he died Oct. 7, 1894.

Further Reading

Andrew Gregg Curtin is listed in the American History study guide (VI, B, 1, c). He and Horatio SEYMOUR were influential governors during the Civil War. Horace GREE-

LEY was a candidate for the presidency, with Curtin's support.

Curtin's messages and proclamations as governor of Pennsylvania were published by the state. No adequate biography of him exists. William H. Egle edited a series of laudatory sketches *Andrew Gregg Curtin: His Life and Services* (1895). For an analysis of Curtin's Civil War career see William B. Hesseltine, *Lincoln and the War Governors* (1948).

J. CURTIN / By R. M. Younger

John Joseph Curtin (1885–1945) was an Australian political leader who rose from trade union official and journalist to prime minister. His forthright approach to Australia's wartime difficulties and his rousing leadership gained him his countrymen's respect.

John Curtin was born in Creswick, Victoria, on Jan. 8, 1885. He attended public schools and at the age of 13 took a job in a Melbourne printery while continuing his studies. The oratory of Tom Mann, Britain's "new unionism" figure, deeply influenced Curtin during Mann's Australian sojourn from 1902 to 1908.

Attending the Labour party's "college" for speakers and running unsuccessfully for a parliamentary seat, Curtin gained skill in public speaking and insight into campaign methods. From 1911 he was a union secretary, and in 1916 he also became secretary of the Anti-Conscription League, which opposed the plans of Prime Minister William Morris Hughes to make overseas service compulsory. Charged with failure to enlist for military service, Curtin was set free when the proclamation under which he had been detained was withdrawn. Separate proceedings against him on a sedition charge were dropped later.

In 1916 Curtin moved to Perth to become editor of the *Westralian Worker*. Between 1918 and 1934 he was elected several, but not consecutive, times to the House of Representatives, and he was Australian delegate to the International Labor Conference in Geneva in 1924.

By 1934 Curtin was stressing the dangers of impending war, and he urged greater defense preparedness while others in his party were speaking of disarmament. He also demonstrated a grasp of financial and economic issues. Elected as Labour's parliamentary leader in 1935, Curtin showed skill in healing a serious schism which had been weakening the party in New South Wales.

Wartime Leader

In 1939 Curtin refused the invitation of the Liberal prime minister Robert Gordon Menzies to include Labour in an all-party wartime administration. Instead, in 1940, Curtin joined the interparty Advisory War Council and awaited a situation favorable for a Labour government. It came in September 1941, when two uncommitted members pledged their support, giving him a slim majority in the House.

After Pearl Harbor, with Australia directly threatened, Curtin called for an all-out war effort built around United States help. He quickly instituted a succession of measures designed to eliminate all activities absorbing manpower and resources that might be diverted to the war effort. Early in 1942 he successfully urged the U.S. government to send Gen. Douglas MacArthur to Australia as commander of a combined force capable of defending the country and ultimately converting it into a base for a northward drive against the Japanese. At the same time Curtin refused the British Cabinet's request to divert Australian ground forces—then returning from the Middle East—for the reinforcement of the Burma front, deciding that they should return to Australia to stave off any invasion. By his vigorous leadership Curtin gained national acceptance for his austerity measures designed to intensify all phases of the war effort.

Labour won the 1943 elections with majorities in both House and Senate. As the danger of invasion receded, Curtin decided to remove the long-standing ban on use of military conscripts beyond Australian territory. Labour had traditionally held firmly to the rule against overseas service for conscripts, but Curtin persuaded the party to update the law so that Australian land forces could ac-

company U.S. forces and Australian air and naval units in the northward drive.

Preparations for the Postwar Era

Curtin constantly expressed his belief that the sacrifices being asked of fighting men should be honored by the creation of a postwar world with greater social justice and enhanced opportunity for the individual, and a world in which causes of war were eliminated. As well as introducing progressive legislation to pave the way for general reconstruction and national advancement after the war, he began immediately to plan for the reintegration of armed services personnel into civilian life when peace was restored, and he mapped arrangements for a long-range immigration program. The government adopted full employment as a basic objective and, in international discussions on postwar economic planning, stressed this concept as the centerpiece of national policies.

In 1944 Curtin called for greater awareness of the regional significance of Australia and New Zealand—by now linked in the "Anzac" pact, which he and his external affairs minister, Dr. Herbert Vere Evatt, had been instrumental in developing. Curtin also gave the fullest support to the creation of the United Nations, sending a large and influential Australian delegation to the formulative meeting in San Francisco in June 1945, and encouraged the U.S. government to maintain an active role in the security of the Pacific. He died in Canberra on July 1, 1945.

Further Reading

John Curtin is listed in the Australia and New Zealand study guide (II, E). One of his coworkers, Joseph Benedict CHIFLEY, later became prime minister.

A useful biography of Curtin is Alan Chester, *John Curtin* (1943). Curtin's role in Labour party affairs is discussed in Louise Overacker, *The Australian Party System* (1952), and Leslie Finlay Crisp, *The Australian Federal Labour Party: 1901–1951* (1955). Comprehensive coverage of Australia's war role is contained in *Australia in the War of 1939–1945*, Series I to V (22 vols., 1952——). An economic analysis of Curtin's administration is E. Ronald Walker, *The Australian Economy in War and Reconstruction* (1947). The planning for a postwar immigration flow is outlined in Arthur A. Calwell, *How Many Australians Tomorrow?* (1945). The Curtin government's approach to international affairs is indicated in H. V. Evatt, *Foreign Policy of Australia: Speeches* (1945).

John Curtin. *(Australian News & Information Bureau)*

B. R. CURTIS / By Donald M. Roper

Benjamin Robbins Curtis (1809–1874) was one of the most able lawyers on the U.S. Supreme Court in the 19th century.

Benjamin Robbins Curtis was born into an old New England family in Watertown, Mass., on Nov. 4, 1809. He graduated second in his class at Harvard in 1829, then took a degree from Harvard Law School. In 1833 he married Eliza Maria Woodward, with whom he had five children. When she died in 1844, he married again and had three more children.

Through the influence of a prominent uncle, Curtis became a partner in a Boston law firm in 1834, remaining until 1851 and becoming one of the leading commercial lawyers in the United States. He was elected to the Massachusetts General Court in 1849 and 1851 and was largely responsible for the Massachusetts Practice Act of 1851, which eliminated many legal abuses. When what was then the New England seat on the U.S. Supreme Court became vacant in 1851, President Millard Fillmore appointed Curtis.

In his first term Curtis's ability to cut to the heart of a problem led to establishing a commonsense interpretation of the commerce clause in *Cooley v. Board of Wardens*, which allowed states to regulate local commercial matters while not diminishing Congress's power. Another precedent-setting case enabled administrative officers to determine and collect debts without a court order. He was also highly effective in conference, "educating" by persuasion his fellow justices.

Riding the New England circuit, Curtis continued to show concern for law and order and preservation of the Union. Though labeled a "slave-catcher judge" because of his strict enforcement of the Fugitive Slave Act, he dissented on the precedent-setting Dred Scott case (1852) and wrote a long minority opinion demonstrating that Negroes were U.S. citizens in 1787, that residence in free territory made a man free, and that Congress had complete authority to legislate for the territories, including prohibiting slavery. Misunderstandings with Chief Justice Roger B. Taney over dissemination of these opinions were partly responsible for Curtis's resignation from the Court.

Returning to a lucrative private practice, Curtis argued several important cases before the U.S. Supreme Court. When his second wife died in 1860, he married again. He supported the North in the Civil War but raised important questions about presidential power in a pamphlet critical of Abraham Lincoln's Emancipation Proclamation and of suspension of the writ of habeas corpus. He opposed Lincoln's reelection in 1864. When President Andrew Johnson was impeached, Curtis and William M. Evarts defended him before the Senate.

In 1874 Curtis suffered a brain hemorrhage and died at Newport, R.I., on September 15. His course of lectures at Harvard for 1872–1873, *Jurisdiction, Practice and Peculiar Jurisprudence of the Courts of the United States*, was published in 1880.

Further Reading

Benjamin Robbins Curtis is listed in the American History study guide (VI, A, 3). Roger B. TANEY was chief justice during Curtis's service on the Supreme Court.

There is no modern biography of Curtis. A eulogistic memoir by his brother and a volume of his writings edited by his son were published as *A Memoir of Benjamin Robbins Curtis, L.L.D., with Some of His Professional and Miscellaneous Writings* (2 vols., 1879; repr. 1969). Vincent C. Hopkins, *Dred Scott's Case* (1951), details Curtis's role in that case. His Court career appears in Leo Pfeffer, *This Honorable Court: A History of the United States Supreme Court* (1965).

✳ ✳ ✳

Benjamin Robbins Curtis. (Library of Congress)

G. W. **CURTIS** / By Joseph R. Conlin

American writer, orator, and, especially, civil service reformer, George William Curtis (1824–1892) was a patrician whose ideals and causes are blurred in historical retrospect by a personal elitism that bordered on priggishness and was out of step even in his own time.

George William Curtis was born into a very old New England family in Providence, R.I. After attending school in Massachusetts, he spent several years in New York City, where he worked as a clerk. Already a disciple of Ralph Waldo Emerson, Curtis lived for 2 years at the transcendentalist utopian colony, Brook Farm. He returned to New York City, then in 1846 left on

George William Curtis. (Library of Congress)

sight I ever knew," Curtis noted in the patronizing tone that characterized much of his writing, "that man glaring at me in a fury of hate, and storming out his foolish blackguardism. I was all pity. I had not thought him great, but I had not suspected how small he was."

Curtis's personal life was exemplary and refined. To his admirers, of whom there were many, he was remembered—as one eulogist put it—as the "firm and sweet-souled leader of the public conscience." He died on Aug. 31, 1892.

Further Reading

George William Curtis is listed in the American History study guide (VII, G, 4, a). Another civil servicer reformer was Carl SCHURZ. Curtis objected to the presidential candidacy of James G. BLAINE and found New York State machine politician Roscoe CONKLING particularly repugnant.

There is no recently published biography of Curtis. All standard accounts of the "gilded age" discuss his important role in the civil service reform movement, for example, Matthew Josephson, *The Politicos, 1865–1896* (1938), and H. Wayne Morgan, *From Hayes to McKinley* (1969).

CURTISS / By Carroll Pursell

The American aviation pioneer Glenn Hammond Curtiss (1878–1930) developed the first successful seaplane and manufactured the famous World War I Jenny training plane.

Glenn Curtiss was born in Hammondsport, N.Y. After finishing grade school, he moved to Rochester, working for the telegraph company and later for the Kodak Company. But having acquired a taste for mechanics and a passion for speed, he returned to Hammondsport and opened a bicycle shop. He raced bicycles and won many prizes locally and statewide. When motorcycles became available, he began to race them as well, and in 1902 he started to make and sell first the motors, then the entire motorcycles, at his shop. He became famous as a racer and in 1906, riding an eight-cylinder cycle of his own construction, set a speed record of 137 miles per hour, which stood for 20 years.

After the dirigible balloonist Thomas Scott Baldwin ordered an engine for one of his balloons from Curtiss, Curtiss concentrated on the problems of flight. A balloon powered by a Curtiss engine won a major race at the St. Louis International Exposition in 1904. Baldwin moved to Hammondsport, and the two men manufactured the first dirigible adopted by the U.S. Army.

The successful flight of the Wright brothers in 1903 had demonstrated the potential of heavier-than-air craft, and Curtiss now turned in this direction. Alexander Graham Bell, the inventor of the telephone, for some years

---

the grand tour of Europe fashionable for well-to-do New Englanders. However, he added to this an unusual side trip to the Near East and wrote two books on his impressions of Egypt and Syria.

Curtis also published a satire of New York City life but in 1856 virtually abandoned "high" literature for journalism and politics. Curtis's New England sense of propriety showed clearly when, that same year, he assumed the debts run up by a magazine of which he was an editor, debts for which he was not legally liable. This sense of duty and rectitude characterized his whole career, as editor of *Harper's Weekly* during the Civil War and as a professional reformer.

Most of the well-known reforms of the century attracted Curtis. He was an abolitionist and a spokesman for woman's suffrage, and he spoke frequently on the need for reconciliation between industrial capitalists and laborers according to his concept of social justice. But he was best known and most active as an advocate of civil service reform in an age when politics seemed to mean little more than a scuffle for spoils.

Curtis was the classic "Mugwump," the name given to those Republicans who bolted the party in 1884 because its candidate, James G. Blaine, had some financial irregularities in his career. Curtis was genteel, hobnobbing with the prominent literati of his day, and more than a little condescending in his political dealings. In 1877, for example, the leading New York Republican spoilsman, Roscoe Conkling, denounced Curtis and other "snivel service" reformers in a vitriolic speech before the New York State Republican Convention. "It was the saddest

Glenn Curtiss, photographed in 1909. (Library of Congress)

had been an enthusiastic supporter of airplane development, and in 1907 established the Aerial Experiment Association at Hammondsport, placing Curtiss in charge of experiments. A year later Curtiss won the *Scientific American* trophy flying his famous *June Bug*. During the next several years he won many air races in the United States and abroad. He barnstormed across the country, popularizing the idea of flying, and also established a number of flying schools, which benefited from the publicity his racing victories brought to him.

In 1908 Curtiss began to work on the problems of seaplanes and 3 years later successfully took off from, and landed again on, the water off San Diego, Calif. In 1912 he developed his famous flying boat; and in 1919 his NC4, developed for the U.S. Navy, became the first airplane to cross the Atlantic Ocean.

After the outbreak of World War I Curtiss moved his manufacturing facilities to Buffalo and built, by 1919, more than 5,000 Jennies. Although he had become wealthy, these years were marred by a court fight with the Wright brothers over the invention of the aileron, a wing device to maintain vertical stability, which Curtiss had developed for Bell's association.

After the war Curtiss worked on automobiles and other devices as well as airplanes and was active in the Curtiss-Wright Corporation, but his real period of pioneering in aviation had ended by 1920.

Further Reading

Glenn Curtiss is listed in the Science study guide (VII, H, 3). Wilbur and Orville WRIGHT also contributed to early aviation. Curtiss conducted aerial experiments for Alexander Graham BELL.

A standard biography of Curtiss is Alden Hatch, *Glenn Curtiss: Pioneer of Naval Aviation* (1942). His exploits are placed in a larger context in the contemporary account of Howard Mingos, *The Birth of an Industry* (1930), and in Welman A. Shrader, *Fifty Years of Flight: A Chronicle of the Aviation Industry in America, 1903–1953* (1953). The years after World War I are well covered by John B. Rae, *Climb to Greatness: The American Aircraft Industry, 1920–1960* (1968).

CURZON / By Lyle A. McGeoch

The English statesman George Nathaniel Curzon, 1st Marquess Curzon of Kedleston (1859–1925), served as viceroy of India and as a member of several Cabinets.

High offices in the British political and imperial structure at the end of the 19th century and the beginning of the 20th century were generally held by men chosen on the basis of highly restrictive family and educational connections. George Curzon was the epitome of this system, and it was useful to his political and social ambitions before World War I. Afterward, however, he was hurt by his connection with it and by his inconsistent actions that bordered on opportunism in his late drive for government leadership.

George Curzon was born on Jan. 11, 1859, at Kedleston Hall, Derbyshire. His early life was dominated by the influence of a governess and a schoolmaster who were both strict disciplinarians; those years were not very happy ones for him, but he did exceptionally well at school. He was a leader and an outstanding student at Eton from 1872 to 1878 and at Balliol College, Oxford, from 1878 to 1882, although he was disappointed when he missed getting every honor. With an aristocratic appearance and a bearing that commanded attention, he put unrestrained energy into his work and was not satisfied unless he was in the center of every situation.

In the 3 years after leaving Oxford, Curzon traveled extensively in the Mediterranean world and used the knowledge he acquired to write articles on important issues. In 1885 Lord Salisbury, the prime minister, chose him as his assistant private secretary. Curzon lost his first election that year, but he won a seat the next year in the House of Commons. From 1887 to 1894 he continued to travel widely, choosing Asia as his particular interest and writing three outstanding books on Asian affairs: *Russia in Central Asia* (1889), *Persia and the Persian Question* (1892), and *Problems of the Far East* (1894).

Curzon began his government service in 1891 as undersecretary in the India office in Salisbury's government. The government fell from power in 1892, but when the Conservatives came in again in 1895, Curzon was named parliamentary undersecretary in the Foreign Office, directly under Salisbury, who was both prime minister and foreign secretary. Curzon was the principal government spokesman on foreign affairs in the House of Commons.

Viceroy of India

Curzon was chosen viceroy of India in 1898. This position was perfectly suited to his desire for public attention, since he was in charge of the entire British administration of the Indian empire. He stayed in India for 7 years, ruling firmly in matters of domestic policy and making strong appeals in matters of foreign policy. In the latter, Curzon was particularly involved in the problem of defense along India's frontiers and in those areas of possible danger from Russian expansion and competition —Persia, Afghanistan, and Tibet.

Military matters were Curzon's undoing. He and Lord Kitchener, the commander in chief of the Indian army after 1902, became locked in a dispute over military organization; the government in England, then under Prime Minister Arthur Balfour, chose to sacrifice Curzon in favor of Kitchener, who was a more popular figure. Curzon returned to Britain in late 1905, out of favor with his own Conservative party leadership and, since the Liberals were coming into power, with no opportunity of remaking his reputation in another government assignment.

War Cabinet and Foreign Office

Curzon was out of politics except as a member of the House of Lords, until he was included in the wartime coalition government formed in May 1915. When David Lloyd George became prime minister in December 1916, Curzon was brought into the five-man War Cabinet, and he participated in all the major decisions of the latter part of World War I. He was given the task of running the Foreign Office through most of 1919, while Lloyd George and the foreign secretary, Lord Balfour, were at the Paris peace conference, and in late 1919 he was named as Balfour's successor in the Foreign Office.

Curzon's service in the War Cabinet and as foreign secretary was the second peak in his career. But his role in the Foreign Office in the postwar era was not so satisfactory to Curzon as it would have been in an earlier era. British government was changing, and concentration of authority in the prime minister's hands had increased tremendously under Lloyd George's personal control and the emergency of wartime government. Curzon was a leading candidate for prime minister in May 1923; he was disappointed at the last moment, however, and Stanley Baldwin was chosen instead. Curzon was dismayed, but he stayed on to serve under Baldwin in the same post until the government fell in January 1924. Curzon's public service ended then, and he died on March 20, 1925.

Further Reading

Lord Curzon is listed in the European History study guide (IX, A, 2) and the Asia study guide (II, A, 6, b). He disagreed with Lord KITCHENER on military policies in India. He later served under David LLOYD GEORGE and Stanley BALDWIN.

The most complete work on Curzon is the Earl of Ronaldshay, *The Life of Lord Curzon* (3 vols., 1928). Two studies which are old but still worthwhile are Harold Nicolson, *Curzon, the Last Phase, 1919–1925: A Study in Post-war Diplomacy* (1934), and Arthur Anthony Baumann's sketch in Humbert Wolfe, ed., *Personalities: A Selection from the Writings of A. A. Baumann* (1936). Two other books essential to a full understanding of Curzon as a man are Leonard Mosley, *The Glorious Fault: The Life of Lord Curzon* (1960; published in England as *Curzon: The End of an Epoch*), and Kenneth Rose, *Superior Person* (1969). Michael Edwardes, *High Noon of Empire: India under Curzon* (1965), deals with India while Curzon was viceroy. Recommended for general historical background are R. C. K. Ensor, *England, 1870–1914* (1936); Gordon A. Craig and Felix Gilbert, eds., *The Diplomats, 1919–1939* (1953); *The Cambridge History of the British Empire*, vol. 3: E. A. Benians and others, eds., *The Empire-Commonwealth, 1870–1919* (1959); and A. J. P. Taylor, *English History, 1914–1945* (1965).

Lord Curzon. (Popperfoto)

CUSHING / By Patsy A. Gerstner

The American neurosurgeon Harvey Williams Cushing (1869–1939) developed operative techniques that made brain surgery feasible.

Harvey Cushing was born on April 8, 1869, in Cleveland, Ohio. He graduated from Yale University in 1891 and received a medical degree in 1895 from Harvard Medical School. After a year's internship at Massachusetts General Hospital he went to Johns Hopkins, where he was William Halsted's resident in surgery. From Halsted he learned meticulous surgical technique.

During a trip to Europe in 1900 Cushing worked with some of Europe's leading surgeons and physiologists, including Charles Scott Sherrington, Theodore Kocher, and Hugo Kronecker. They directed his attention to neurosurgery, to which he devoted the rest of his life. Shortly after his return to Johns Hopkins he was made associate professor of surgery. In 1902 he married Katharine Crowell.

In 1907 Cushing began studies of the pituitary gland. He unraveled many of the disorders affecting the gland and showed that a surgical approach to the pituitary was possible. In 1912 *The Pituitary Body and Its Disorders* was published. In that same year he accepted the Moseley professorship of surgery at Harvard and an appointment as surgeon in chief at Peter Bent Brigham Hospital in Boston. During World War I he served in France as

Harvey Cushing. (Library of Congress)

director of Base Hospital No. 5. His wartime experiences formed the basis of a book, *From a Surgeon's Journal* (1936). Cushing's active affiliation with Harvard continued until 1932, when he was named professor emeritus. The following year he accepted the Sterling professorship of neurology at Yale.

Throughout his career Cushing studied brain tumors and published many important books on the subject, including: *Tumours of the Nervus Acusticus and the Syndrome of the Cerebellopontile* (1917); *A Classification of the Tumours of the Glioma* (1926), with P. Bailey; *Tumours Arising from the Blood Vessels of the Brain: Angiomatous Malformations and Hemangioblastomas* (1928), with Bailey; *Intracranial Tumours* (1932); and *Meningiomas: Their Classification, Regional Behavior, Life History, and Surgical End Results* (1938). He published numerous historical essays, and his biography of Sir William Osler (1925) received the Pulitzer Prize in 1926.

Cushing's use of local anesthesia in brain surgery was an outstanding achievement, as were his many special surgical techniques. In 1911 he introduced special sutures to control the severe bleeding that accompanies brain surgery and often made it impossible.

In 1937 Cushing accepted a position as director of studies in the history of medicine at Yale. He guided the development of a historical library to which he left his own excellent collection of historical books. He was especially interested in Andreas Vesalius, the 16th-century anatomist, and was at work on the *Bio-Bibliography of Vesalius* at the time of his death, on Oct. 7, 1939. The work was completed by his friends and published in 1943.

Further Reading

Harvey Cushing is listed in the Science study guide (VII, G, 4). His contemporary Alexis CARREL helped develop surgical medicine.

The definitive biography of Cushing is John F. Fulton, *Harvey Cushing* (1946). A shorter biography for the general reader is Elizabeth Harriet Thomson, *Harvey Cushing: Surgeon, Author, Artist* (1950). On the occasion of Cushing's seventieth birthday, in 1939, *A Bibliography of the Writings of Harvey Cushing* was published by the Harvey Cushing Society.

CUSHMAN / By John Reardon

The actress Charlotte Cushman (1816–1876) was the first great American-born tragedienne, in a career spanning 4 decades.

Charlotte Cushman, who was descended from one of the original Pilgrim families, was born in Boston in 1816. Faced with poverty in her late teens, she determined to become an opera singer, a career for which her remarkable voice—a full contralto and almost full soprano—well suited her. But while performing in New Orleans, she strained her voice by reaching too high, and at the age of 19 her singing career ended.

Undaunted, Miss Cushman decided to become an actress. Her debut as Lady Macbeth in New Orleans in 1835 began a career that lasted for 40 years and encompassed almost 200 roles. After her first success Miss Cushman joined New York theater companies, where at least two plays were performed each evening and the bill was changed each day. Here she served a diligent apprenticeship; yet, after 8 years, she was still in "miserable, frightful uncertainty" about her career.

Then in 1843, William Macready, the great English actor, played Macbeth to her Lady Macbeth. He was so impressed by Miss Cushman's undisciplined talent that he urged her to go to London for training. In appreciation for this fortuitous advice, she later said she had "groped in darkness until she met Mr. Macready and learned his method." By 1845 she was hailed in London as an actress with the "godlike gift" of genius. Three years later she played a command performance before Queen Victoria as Katherine in *Henry VIII*.

When Miss Cushman returned to the United States in 1849, she found herself not only a celebrated actress but a symbol of the achievement of American culture. She sustained her reputation as the greatest American tragedienne until her retirement in 1875.

Charlotte Cushman was not beautiful or even particularly feminine. Her talent lay in portraying women of great passion and pathos; in such roles her muscular frame and powerful yet controlled voice could overwhelm and sometimes frighten the audience. The mysterious old gypsy Meg Merrilies in *Guy Mannering* was her most famous role, followed by Lady Macbeth, Queen Katherine, and Nancy in the dramatization of *Oliver Twist*. So strong was her presence that she won praise in men's roles, playing Romeo, Cardinal Wolsey, and Hamlet.

As early as 1852 Miss Cushman made the first of many farewell appearances. She knew that she was suffering from cancer; the disease plagued her for the next 24 years and was finally the indirect cause of her death from pneumonia in Boston in 1876. Yet until the end she continued to act, and when her strength failed, she gave dramatic readings. Both on and off the stage she was a lady of dignity, passion, and majesty.

Further Reading

Charlotte Cushman is listed in the American History study guide (V, F, 6). Edwin FORREST was another illustrious Shakespearean actor of the mid-19th century. Later in the century Edwin BOOTH became important.

The most intimate portrait of Charlotte Cushman was done by her friend Emma Stebbins, *Charlotte Cushman, Her Letters and Memories of Her Life* (1878). It is extremely sympathetic and somewhat sentimental but provides evidence of Miss Cushman's strength and sensitivity in private and public life. William Winters includes private recollections and accounts of her performances

Charlotte Cushman. (Courtesy of The New-York Historical Society, New York City)

in *Other Days* (1908) and *The Wallet of Time*, vol. 1 (1913). Two excellent if brief analyses of Miss Cushman's talent and place appear in Lloyd Morris, *Curtain Time* (1953), and Garff Wilson, *A History of American Acting* (1966).

CUSTER / By Odie B. Faulk

No figure of the Indian wars in America so typifies that era as George Armstrong Custer (1839–1876). He is known universally for the massacre that bears his name and for the blundering that brought it about.

George Custer was born in New Rumley, Harrison County, Ohio, on Dec. 5, 1839. His ambition from youth was to be a soldier, and he secured an appointment to West Point in 1857. A poor, mischievous student, he graduated at the bottom of his class in 1861, but was commissioned a second lieutenant in the 2d Cavalry.

The Civil War was in progress, and Custer fought on the Union side. For gallant conduct at the engagement at Aldie on June 16, 1863, he was breveted a brigadier general and given command of a brigade from Michigan. By the end of the war, at the age of only 25, he had been promoted to brevet major general. During the war he had married his childhood sweetheart, Elizabeth Bacon.

The conflict over, Custer reverted to his permanent rank of captain in the 5th Cavalry but soon was promoted to lieutenant colonel of the 7th Cavalry; he would actively hold this command until his death. In 1867 he was charged with absence from duty and suspended for a year but was reinstated by Gen. Philip H. Sheridan in 1868. On November 27 of that year he achieved a startling victory over Chief Black Kettle and the Cheyenne Indians at the battle of the Washita. His regiment was then fragmented, and he spent 2 years in Kentucky. In 1873 the regiment was reunited in the Dakota Territory. He was described at this time as tall, slender, energetic, and dashing, with blue eyes and long golden hair and mustache. At the post he wore velveteen uniforms decorated with gold braid, but in the field he affected buckskins. He rarely drank or used tobacco and spent his spare hours reading military history and studying tactics.

Rumors of gold in the Black Hills led to a government expedition in 1874, which Custer commanded. Scientists from the Smithsonian Institution confirmed the rumors, and the swarm of gold seekers to the area caused the Sioux Indians to go on the warpath. Custer was to lead the campaign against the Sioux and Cheyenne in early 1876, but instead he was summoned to Washington to testify before a congressional committee investigating fraud in the Indian Bureau. Custer's testimony, unfavorable to Secretary of War W. W. Belknap, so angered President Grant that he removed Custer from command of the expedition to punish the Indians. Public outcry at the President's act, along with the request of Gen. Alfred Terry that Custer accompany the campaign, caused Grant to restore Custer to command of the 7th Cavalry, which then took the field.

On the Yellowstone River, Terry's scouts reported Indians in the vicinity, and Custer was sent to investigate, with orders to exercise caution. On the morning of June 25, 1876, he came upon a village later estimated to have contained from 2,500 to 4,000 Sioux and Cheyenne warriors under Chief Crazy Horse. Splitting his command into three parts, Custer personally led 264 men into battle. His force was surrounded on the hill that now bears his name, overlooking the valley of the Little Bighorn River. He and all the men under his personal command were massacred there, while Maj. Marcus Reno and Capt. Frederick Benteen took refuge on the bluffs overlooking the river and escaped.

The Custer massacre electrified the nation, although it had little effect on the outcome of the Sioux wars. Reno and Benteen were accused of cowardice by admirers of Custer, while Custer's detractors bemoaned the death of the troops under his command due to his rash order to charge so superior an Indian force. This controversy continues, for Custer was a man so paradoxical that he could fight corruption in the Indian Bureau to the disservice of his own carrer, yet also order a charge to kill Indians.

Further Reading

George Custer is listed in the American History study guide (VII, C, 2). The Sioux chief who led the massacre was CRAZY HORSE. Custer was a favorite of U.S. Army general Philip H. SHERIDAN.

So many books have been written about Custer that no one book can be singled out as best. Custer's autobiography, *My Life on the Plains: or, Personal Experiences with Indians* (1874), gives insights into his character, as do the books by his wife, Elizabeth Bacon Custer, *Boots and Saddle: or, Life in Dakota with General Custer* (1885) and *Tenting on the Plains: or, General Custer in Kansas and Texas* (1887). See also Marguerite Merington, ed., *The Custer Story: The Life and Intimate Letters of George A. Custer and His Wife Elizabeth* (1950).

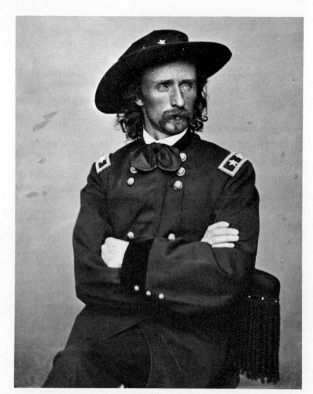

George Custer. (Library of Congress)

CUTLER / By Roger L. Nichols

American clergyman, scientist, and politician
Manasseh Cutler (1742–1823) was a member of
the Ohio Company of Associates and coauthor
of the Northwest Ordinance of 1787.

Manasseh Cutler, the third child and eldest son of Hezekiah and Susanna Cutler, was born on May 13, 1742, in Killingly, Conn. He grew to manhood on his parents' farm. After graduating from Yale in 1765, he taught school in Dedham, Mass. The following year he married Mary Balch, and the couple moved to Martha's Vineyard, where Cutler ran a store. Cutler studied law, and by 1767 he was practicing in the Court of Common Pleas. The following year he returned to Yale to receive a master of arts degree and then began his study for the ministry. In September 1771 he was ordained and installed as pastor in the Congregational Church at Ipswich (later Hamilton), Mass.

Cutler's first church was to be his lifelong parish, although he frequently left Ipswich for business or for political activity. During the early years of the Revolutionary War he served as a chaplain.

Because of continuing financial difficulties, Cutler turned to studying medicine under the tutelage of a member of his congregation, and by 1779 he began practice. From medicine he turned to a study of the physical and biological sciences and began working with such varied instruments as sextants, telescopes, and microscopes, in addition to experimenting with an "electrical machine" and carrying out a widespread program of smallpox vaccination.

Among his widely varied scientific activities, botany became Cutler's particular interest. He examined and classified at least 350 species of plants found in New England, and during the 1780s he published an article, "An Account of Some of the Vegetable Productions Naturally Growing in This Part of America." In recognition of his untiring scientific activity, Cutler received membership in the American Academy of Arts and Sciences, the American Philosophical Society, the Philadelphia Linnaean Society, and the American Antiquarian Society. Yale gave him an honorary degree in 1789.

On March 1, 1786, Cutler joined a group of New England speculators who formed the Ohio Company of Associates. Hoping to take advantage of the Federal government's desperate need for funds, the company proposed buying Federal land with depreciated government securities issued during the Revolutionary War. The company sent Cutler to negotiate, and he suggested that Congress table its plan to sell land in small amounts to individual citizens and, instead, sell a vast tract at the confluence of the Muskingum and Ohio rivers to his company.

Finally, during July 1787, the secretary of the Board of Treasury, whose office handled land sales, intimated that Congress would accept Cutler's plan if members of the government could share in the profits. The result was a complex scheme under which the Ohio Company got its 1,000,000 acres of land, and a second group, the Scioto Company, got an option on several million acres more. On July 27, 1787, the Board of Treasury agreed to sell the land to the Ohio Company of Associates at a true cost of about 8 cents an acre.

Next, Cutler reminded Congress that few citizens would migrate to the new territory until Congress pro-

Manasseh Cutler, an engraving by J. C. Buttre. (Library of Congress)

vided a system of orderly government there. This was no new idea. Congress had argued about the question for years. But Cutler's demand for a workable plan, coupled with the expectations of profits from increasing land sales, caused Congress to act. In early July 1787 Cutler helped to rewrite a proposal for establishing government in the West, and on July 13 the Ordinance of 1787, or the Northwest Ordinance, was adopted.

The ordinance established the territory northwest of the Ohio and provided for a series of steps through which the government of the region would move toward eventual statehood on an equal footing with the original 13 states. It created an American colonial system for the new territories and assured continuing political rights to citizens who wished to move to the frontier. For Cutler and the Ohio Company of Associates, the land sale and pattern for later government opened the area for settlement.

After visiting Ohio for a year, Cutler returned to Massachusetts, where he served a single term in the General Court and then represented his district for two terms in the U.S. House of Representatives. In 1804 he retired to private life. He continued his scientific activities and participated in the scholarly organizations to which he belonged. A tall, portly man with gracious manners, he was a striking figure in his black velvet suit, black knee stockings, and silver shoe buckles. Cutler died on July 28, 1823.

Further Reading

Manasseh Cutler is listed in the American History study guide (IV, D, 3). He, Andrew JACKSON, and Robert LIV-

INGSTON all played important roles in the westward expansion of the United States.

There is no modern biography of Cutler, and historians have to depend on William P. and Julia P. Cutler, *The Life, Journals and Correspondence of Rev. Manasseh Cutler* (2 vols., 1888), for the basic factual information about his career. Cutler's activity in the Ohio Company may be traced in both the introduction and documents of Archer B. Hulbert, ed., *Ohio in the Time of the Confederation* (4 vols., 1918), and in Frazer E. Wilson, *Advancing the Ohio Frontier* (1953). Francis S. Philbrick, *The Rise of the West, 1754–1830* (1965), provides a balanced discussion of the era and its major developments.

CUVIER / By Lyndsay A. Farrall

The French zoologist and biologist Baron Georges Léopold Cuvier (1769–1832) made significant contributions in the fields of paleontology, comparative anatomy, and taxonomy and was one of the chief spokesmen for science in postrevolutionary France.

Baron Cuvier. (Bulloz)

Georges Léopold Cuvier (pronounced kü-vyā′) was born on Aug. 23, 1769, in Montbéliard, a small, French-speaking town in the duchy of Württemberg, where his father was commandant of the local artillery. Cuvier was christened Jean Léopold Nicolas Frédéric, but after the death of his elder brother, Georges, in 1769, he was known as Georges. His parents hoped that he would keep up the family tradition of one son from each generation training for the Lutheran ministry, but instead Cuvier attended the Académie Caroline in Stuttgart (1784–1788), studying commerce and economics, police and public administration, law, and chemistry, mineralogy, botany, and zoology. He was active in the school's natural-history society and studied privately under K. F. Kielmeyer, one of the early German *Naturphilosophes*.

Soon after graduation, Cuvier became tutor to the D'Hericys family, Protestant nobles who lived in Normandy, with whom he remained until 1793. When his home district was absorbed into France that year, Cuvier became a French citizen. He served as secretary of Becaux-Cauchois until 1795 and then moved to Paris. He obtained a position as assistant to the professor of comparative anatomy at the Jardin des Plantes (later the National Museum of Natural History) and began his first course of lectures in comparative anatomy there in December. At the same time, he was elected a member of the anatomy and zoology section of the Institut de France. In 1800 Cuvier was appointed secretary for the physical sciences section of the Institut and professor of general natural history at the Collège de France.

From 1800 until his death Cuvier was very active both as a research scientist and as a scientific educationalist and administrator. Moreover, under successive French governments he held various offices of state and investigated and reported on state problems. These concerned not only science but also religion, as Cuvier remained a devout Lutheran throughout his life. In 1802 Napoleon appointed him inspector general of higher schools; later he was responsible for reorganizing education in Italy, the Netherlands, and other conquered territory beyond the borders of France. Also in 1802, he became professor of comparative anatomy at the Jardin des Plantes. The following year Cuvier was appointed one of the two permanent secretaries of the Académie des Sciences of the Institut de France. In 1807–1808 he prepared a special report for Napoleon on the development of science since the French Revolution.

Cuvier married Anne Marie Coquet de Trazaille, a widow with four children, in 1804. Of their own four children, only one daughter survived infancy.

In the 15 years after his arrival in Paris, Cuvier was at his most active in scientific research. He published major works on animal classification, fossils, theoretical paleontology, natural history, and comparative anatomy. His later life was taken up more and more by administrative and state matters, so that although he continued to publish much scientific work it did not have the originality of his earlier publications.

Cuvier was appointed a councilor of the Napoleonic University of France in 1808. He was a member of the Council of State from 1813 until his death. In 1817 he became vice president of the Ministry of the Interior; the following year he was elected a member of the Académie Française. In 1820 he was made a baron. From 1821 to 1827 Cuvier was chancellor of the University of France. In 1822 he was appointed grand master of the Faculties of Protestant Theology in the University of Paris, and in 1826 he was made a grand officer of the Legion of Honor. In 1828 he became director of all non-Catholic churches in France. In 1831 Louis Philippe raised Cuvier to the peerage. He died on May 13, 1832.

In public life Cuvier was, above all, concerned for good order. His generally conservative attitudes were at least partly a response to the chaos and breakdown of social order which he had experienced in the years of the French Revolution. As a scientist who did not depend on his political activities for recognition or status, Cuvier was more concerned with the good working of the various institutions of French life than with party and personality politics. As an adviser to the state on education, he strongly opposed the influence of the Roman Catholic Church and particularly that of the Society of Jesus. He supported secular education and tried to see that it included a fair proportion of natural science.

Contributions to Science

Cuvier's life spanned the period during which it became possible in France, for virtually the first time, to make a profession of science. He was not trained to be a scientist, as professional training in the sciences was virtually unknown when he went through college. He and his colleagues took part in setting up the first such courses in France.

Soon after Cuvier arrived in Paris in 1795, he took up the problem of the classification of animals and together with a colleague published a very important paper on the classification of mammals. Cuvier was concerned with the practical question of which features of an animal should be used to distinguish it from other species. Underlying the need for a practical system of classification was his search for a theoretical justification for the taxonomic system he advocated. Throughout his life he continued to be concerned with the problem of classification.

In 1798 Cuvier published an introductory textbook in natural history, *Tableau élémentaire de l'histoire naturelle des animaux*, which became the standard text for French colleges. He was also aware of the need for a comprehensive reference book and manual in zoology, and in 1817 he published the four-volume *Le Règne animal . . .*, whose full title, "The Animal Kingdom, arranged according to structure, in order to form a basis for zoology, and as an introduction to comparative anatomy," well describes the functions he hoped it would serve. The work was revised and reissued in five volumes in 1829–1830; by then it had been translated into many languages and had become a standard zoological reference throughout the world.

Cuvier's lectures in comparative anatomy were collected and edited by two of his assistants and published in five volumes between 1800 and 1805 under the title *Leçons d'anatomie comparée*. His concern for classifi-

cation led him to pay special attention to the anatomy of the various systems of organs as he developed his own theories about which systems should be used for purposes of classification.

Another area in which Cuvier carried out major research was the study of fossils. He believed that a study of fossil animals would clarify geological theories about the development and history of the earth. From 1796 until 1812 he published a series of papers on the fossil remains of animals and their significance for geology; they were collected in four volumes in 1812 as *Recherches sur les ossements fossiles de quadrupèdes*.

Appended to this collection was a summary of Cuvier's views about the formation of the different surface layers of the earth, which was later revised and entitled *Discours sur les révolutions de la surface du globe*. In this work he put forward the view that the earth had suffered successive catastrophes in the form of floods which had swamped all but the highest mountains. This view of geological history became known as catastrophism; it was opposed by the uniformitarians, who believed that the surface structure of the earth was due to ordinary everyday causes, which continued to be active up to the present, and not just catastrophic events.

Cuvier and Classification

By the end of the 18th century biologists were faced with an enormous problem of classification because of the large number of new animal and plant specimens collected from different parts of the world. The ideas and practices which had been developed from the time of Carl Linnaeus were no longer satisfactory. One aspect of the problem of classification was its philosophical basis. For some naturalists a system of classification was merely an arbitrary but practical way to distinguish between and learn about different animals. Others, however, argued that there was a "natural" system of classification which indicated some sort of real relationship between the animals in the different parts of the system.

Cuvier believed that animals could be classified into

The "English Garden" and the greenhouse at the Jardin des Plantes, Paris; Cuvier was a professor at the Jardin from 1802. (Library of Congress)

different kinds and that each kind of animal could be represented for classification purposes by an ideal "type." The animal type would include all the characteristics distinguishing it from other types. According to Cuvier, types would not change from generation to generation. He arrived at the mature statement of his view on classification in 1812. He classified all animals into four main branches (*embranchements*) according to the construction of their nervous system; he used the nervous system because he considered it the most important system physiologically or functionally. Less important, or subordinate, systems of characteristics were used to create classificatory subdivisions within the four branches. He called this method of classification the principle of the subordination of characters.

Cuvier justified his system of classification philosophically by arguing along Aristotelian lines that animals were distinguished from other orders of creation by their ability to sense and perceive things. Hence, he argued, the most important, or the most "animalistic," physiological system was that responsible for sensation, namely, the nervous system. He then based his system of classification of animals on the differences of their nervous system. "In considering the animal kingdom from this point of view," he said, ". . . I have found that there exist four principal forms, four general plans, upon which all of the animals seem to have been modeled . . ." (quoted in William Coleman, 1964). These four models, or branches, of the animal kingdom were the Vertebrata, the Mollusca, the Articulata, and the Radiata.

This new system of classification, together with the encyclopedic works which Cuvier based on it, greatly helped the naturalists of his day to assimilate and understand all the new information about animals. Despite its success, however, his system was immediately challenged by those whose philosophy of biology differed considerably from his own.

Theory of Evolution

Cuvier did not live to see Charles Darwin propound his theory of evolution by natural selection, yet he is frequently portrayed as one of the most important antievolutionary figures in the history of biology. This reputation arose largely from the clash with his contemporaries Jean Baptiste de Lamarck and Étienne Geoffroy Saint-Hilaire, who supported evolutionary ideas.

Lamarck taught that there was no such thing as a constant species. He held that the more individual animals he examined, the less certain he became about saying that there were definite boundaries between the forms of different species. Moreover, he put forward the view that the form of species changed from generation to generation through the effects of use or disuse on the various parts of animals. The usage of different organs would change because of changes in the environment. Lamarck pointed to the fossil remains of animals as evidence supporting his theory. Among the fossils were animal forms no longer existing on earth. These, he claimed, were ancestor to the present array of animals.

Cuvier agreed with Lamarck that there was much variation among animals. But he held that most of the variation was among the secondary, or subordinate, characters of animals and that these were not important for the functional integrity of the animals. Organs such as the heart and lungs and the nervous and digestive systems—which were important for the functional integrity of an animal—varied slightly and within very definite limits in the one species, according to Cuvier. However, his strongest argument was that Lamarck could produce no evidence of the transformation of species, whereas Cuvier could show, from evidence recently brought back to France by Napoleon's army, that domestic animals had not changed since the time of the ancient Egyptians. Furthermore, he showed that the disappearance of various fossil animals was due to their becoming extinct rather than transforming into new species.

Both Lamarck and Geoffroy Saint-Hilaire supported the idea that all animals could be arranged into a "great chain of being" from the simplest to the most complex and that this was shown by certain similarities in the structures of all the species. Cuvier also strongly opposed this idea, which was used by some evolutionists. For him the four branches of the animal kingdom which he had postulated could in no way be likened to each other.

Cuvier's arguments against evolution fitted very well into his own conservative philosophy of biology and with his Christian faith, which supported the view that all present species must have descended from a common pair of ancestors created by God at the beginning of the world. Because his brilliant biological system fitted so well with the conservative point of view in both science and theology, his arguments against the evolution theory have been used countless times since his death.

Further Reading

Baron Cuvier is listed in the Science study guide (VI, E, 2; VI, F, 2). James HUTTON first propounded the doctrine of uniformitarianism in the late 18th century. It was overshadowed by Cuvier's doctrine of catastrophism, but uniformitarianism was later widely accepted owing to the efforts of Charles LYELL.

The best biography of Cuvier is William R. Coleman, *Georges Cuvier, Zoologist* (1964). Alexander B. Adams, *Eternal Quest: The Story of the Great Naturalists* (1969), has an excellent chapter devoted to Cuvier.

CUVILLIÉS / By Edward A. Maser

François Cuvilliés (1695–1768) was a Flemish-born, French-trained architect, interior decorator, and ornament designer who brought to Munich the new rococo style and produced there, particularly in the Amalienburg and the court theater, masterpieces of the Bavarian rococo.

rançois Cuvilliés (pronounced kü-vē-yā′) was born a dwarf in Soignies, Hainaut, on Oct. 23, 1695. Discovered about 1706 by Prince Elector Maximilian Emmanuel of Bavaria, who was in exile in Flanders, Cuvilliés was educated with the court pages, although he was officially the court dwarf. He returned with Maximilian Emmanuel from exile to Munich in 1715 and was allowed to work with the court architect, Joseph Effner.

Maximilian Emmanuel then sent Cuvilliés to Paris in 1720 to study under François Blondel the Younger, where he remained until 1724. On his return to Munich, Cuvilliés was appointed court architect in 1725, thus beginning his long career in the service of the house of Wittelsbach, the rulers of Bavaria. For them he produced such works as Schloss Brühl and the so-called Reiche Zimmer (the ''rich rooms'') and the Green Gallery of the Residenz in Munich between 1730 and 1737.

Cuvilliés's masterpiece, and one of the finest creations of the Bavarian rococo, is the famous Amalienburg, a hunting lodge built for the electress Maria Amalia on the grounds of the summer palace at Nymphenburg outside of Munich. This small palace, single-storied and with only six main rooms, is, in its exterior, very plain, but its interior, particularly the central round mirrored hall, decorated in pale blue and silver, and the flanking bedroom and sitting room, decorated in deep yellow and silver, are the masterpieces of Cuvilliés and Johann Baptist Zimmermann, who produced the stucco decoration after Cuvilliés's designs. The simplicity of the layout of the main rooms forms a suitable foil for the rich and fantastic ornament of the walls, the mirrors, and the doors, and even some of the furniture, especially the console tables of the central hall, all designed by Cuvilliés.

Cuvilliés repeated his triumph in the small court theater he built in the Residenz at Munich (1751–1753). Although the theater was destroyed during World War II, all the furnishings, the paneling, and carved decoration were saved; they were fully restored and are now installed inside the Residenz. The court theater is known as the Cuvilliés Theater, in honor of the architect. Cuvilliés's other works in Munich are the Hohnstein Palace, now the Archbishop's Palace (1733–1737), the Preysing Palace (1740), and the facade of the Theatine church (1765–1768). Outside of Munich, the churches of Berg am Laim, Diessen, Schäftlarn, and Benediktbeuren all have altars or rooms decorated by Cuvilliés.

During the last 30 years of his life Cuvilliés also produced many designs for decorations and ornament, which, engraved and sold as pattern books, served to spread his personal mixture of French and German rococo throughout central Europe. His son, François Cuvilliés the Younger (1731–1777), assisted his father, engraved his designs, and, after the elder Cuvilliés's death on April 14, 1768, completed many of his works.

Further Reading

François Cuvilliés is listed in the Art study guide (III, G, 3, c). The Bavarian rococo style is also exemplified in the

The Amalienburg on the grounds of the Nymphenburg palace near Munich. Designed by François Cuvilliés, the Amalienburg was built between 1734 and 1739. (Library of Congress)

work of Johann Baptist and Domenikus ZIMMERMANN and Cosmas Damian and Egid Quirin ASAM.

In English, the following surveys deal with Cuvilliés: John Bourke, *Baroque Churches of Central Europe* (1958; 2d ed. 1962); Nicholas Powell, *From Baroque to Rococo* (1959); Eberhard Hempel, *Baroque Art and Architecture in Central Europe* (1965); and Henry-Russell Hitchcock, *Rococo Architecture in Southern Germany* (1968).

CUYP / By Madlyn Kahr

The landscapes of the Dutch painter Aelbert Cuyp (1620–1691) are famous for their golden light and alluring color. He painted Dutch rural life in its full variety.

orn in Dordrecht, Aelbert Cuyp (pronounced koip) was probably first taught by his father, the painter Jacob Gerritsz Cuyp, known mainly for his portraits. Between 1640 and 1645 Aelbert painted skillful monochromatic dune and river landscapes with diagonal compositions, much in the manner of Jan van Goyen.

Because of the scarcity of dated works it is impossible to say precisely when Cuyp introduced the misty golden light that is the hallmark of his mature style, but it was certainly in the 1640s. This innovation was based in part on his observations of the optical effects of moist atmosphere; this was a time when optical experimentation attracted widespread interest among the Dutch. The many drawings and paintings Cuyp made of activities on

Young Herdsmen with Cows, a painting by Aelbert Cuyp. (The Metropolitan Museum of Art, Bequest of Benjamin Altman, 1913)

the rivers that made Dordrecht a busy port in his day give evidence of his scrutiny of subtle variations in light effects. The major impetus for this interest, however, probably came from Jan Both, who returned from Italy to Utrecht in 1641 and painted there until his death in 1652. To Claude Lorrain's unprecedented demonstration of the unifying power of light in landscape painting, Both added a new specificity through attentive study of appearances at different times of day. This approach was central to Cuyp's mature achievement. The particular light of a given moment became part of his subject. In his ability to translate specific light effects into paint, he surpassed his models and created landscape paintings of unique poetic sensibility.

As is clear from his *Young Herdsmen with Cows* (ca. 1655) Cuyp ensconced his soft, golden luminosity in firmly structured compositions. The monumental cattle, silhouetted against the sky, emphasize the aerial perspective and create the illusion of a visual field of vast depth. Considered relationships and classical restraint likewise contribute to the calm perfection of his matchless scenes of moonlight on the water, for example, *Sailing Boats and Mill*. As Cuyp apparently never went to Italy, it seems that his Italianate scenes, such as *Travelers in a Hilly Landscape*, depend on works by Both and other Italianizing Dutch artists.

Having achieved sudden affluence through marriage in 1658, Cuyp painted little thereafter. There are no dated pictures after 1655.

Further Reading

Aelbert Cuyp is listed in the Art study guide (III, F, 1, b). He has been called the Dutch CLAUDE LORRAIN. Cuyp's earliest works reflect the landscape style of Jan van GOYEN.

Wolfgang Stechow, *Dutch Landscape Painting of the*

Seventeenth Century (1966), deals perceptively with Cuyp's development and his place within the Dutch landscape tradition. See also Jakob Rosenberg, Seymour Slive, and E. H. Ter Kuile, *Dutch Art and Architecture, 1600–1800* (1966). Two older works which include chapters on Cuyp are Eugène Fromentin, *The Masters of Past Time: Dutch and Flemish Painting from Van Eyck to Rembrandt* (1876; trans. 1913; new ed. 1948), and W. Bode, *Great Masters of Dutch and Flemish Painting* (1906; trans. 1909; rep. 1967).

ST. **CYPRIAN** / By Robert F. Evans

Thascius Caecilianus Cyprianus (died 258) is known as St. Cyprian. As bishop of Carthage, he was the most prominent leader of Western, or Latin, Christianity in his time. He contributed to the development of thought on the nature and unity of the Church.

Born to a high-ranking pagan family in Roman Africa probably during 200–210, Cyprian (pronounced sĭp′rē-ən) was converted to Christianity about 246. He was bishop of Carthage no more than 3 years later. Within months of his becoming bishop, the Roman imperial government inaugurated its first empire-wide persecution of the Church. Cyprian retreated to an unknown spot in the country and directed Church affairs by letter and messenger.

During his exile and in the years following his return in 251, Cyprian faced a serious pastoral problem. Under torture and threat of death many Christians had either performed the required pagan sacrifices or so far complied with the government as to acquire papers certifying that they had performed them. These "lapsed" Christians penitently wished, however, to be readmitted to communion in the Church. Breaking with the traditional rigorism of the Church, Cyprian gradually moved to the position that all lapsed Christians could be fully readmitted after clear evidence of penitence. He differed crucially from dissident elements in Carthage and Rome, however, in his insistence that only the duly appointed bishop had authority to adjudicate the matter.

In arriving at his solution to this problem, Cyprian developed his constitutional theory of the Church. He believed that the "episcopate" was a single, divinely appointed, governing office shared by the many bishops, each of whom possessed the full authority of the office in his own locale. Christ's Apostles were the first bishops, and their plenary authority had continued in the duly elected and consecrated bishops who were their successors. To act apart from the bishop was to place oneself outside the Church and to lose the hope of salvation. Cyprian expressed these concepts in the treatise *De unitate ecclesiae*.

The last 3 years of Cyprian's life were marked by con-

St. Cyprian before the proconsul Paternus, a panel from a 12th-century Catalonian altarpiece now in the Museo Arqueologico Episcopal, Vich, Spain. (MAS)

ST. CYRIL OF ALEXANDRIA
/ By Robert F. Evans

St. Cyril (died 444) was bishop of Alexandria. A Doctor of the Church, he played a leading role in the controversies over the correct understanding of the person of Jesus Christ.

Nothing certain is known concerning Cyril's early years except that he was born in Alexandria and was the nephew of Theophilus, his predecessor as bishop of that city. He was a member of his uncle's entourage at the infamous Synod of the Oak, where Theophilus was successful in bringing about the deposition of John Chrysostom from his post as bishop of Constantinople. Having become bishop in 412, Cyril soon brought about the seizure of property belonging to the Novatianists, an austere Christian sect. He also instigated the virtual dissolution of the Jewish community in his city.

About 430 Cyril began his campaign to bring about the downfall of Nestorius, the bishop of Constantinople. The bishops of Alexandria generally had tended to resent the new and rising prestige of the See of Constantinople. More particularly, Cyril had a deep and quite sincere conviction that the theology of Nestorius represented a serious threat to authentic Christian confession of faith in Christ. Nestorius represented the suspect theological traditions of another great and rival Christian metropolis, Antioch, whence he had been called to Constantinople.

According to Cyril, the Church's traditional belief in the Incarnation requires the acknowledgment that God the Word, the second "person" of the Trinity, is himself the one and only subject, or agent, in every deed and word acted and spoken by Jesus Christ; this implies for him that Mary, the mother of Jesus, is to be called *theotokos* (she who bears God). Nestorius dissented from such teachings, fearing that they destroyed the full humanity of Jesus and detracted from the dignity of God.

The Emperor summoned a general council of bishops to adjudicate the matter at Ephesus in 431. Once there, Cyril himself convened the council and swiftly accomplished the condemnation of Nestorius before Eastern bishops friendly to the latter had arrived. After these irregular proceedings, Nestorius resigned voluntarily, and Cyril thereby accomplished one of his chief goals. Under government pressure in 433, however, Cyril made surprising concessions in reaching reconciliation with the more moderate of Nestorius's allies through a famous document, the Formulary of Reunion. Cyril's other writings include letters, theological and apologetic treatises, and commentaries on books of the Bible.

Further Reading

St. Cyril of Alexandria is listed in the Religion study guide (I, B, 2). His younger contemporary EUTYCHES also opposed the teachings of NESTORIUS.

There is no book-length general treatment of St. Cyril, though there are works in foreign languages on special

---

troversy with Stephen, the bishop of Rome. Disagreements among Christians over the problem of the lapsed had resulted in the emergence of dissident sects in Rome and Carthage. The question then arose whether persons baptized in a sect should be "rebaptized" if and when they decided to enter the Catholic Church. Cyprian, consistent with his principles, taught that baptism outside the Catholic Church was no Christian baptism at all; but Stephen, whose position ultimately prevailed in the Western Church, defended the traditional Roman policy of recognizing sectarian baptism and requiring that persons coming to Catholicism from the sects receive only the laying on of the bishop's hand.

When persecution of the Church was renewed, Cyprian went calmly and with dignity to his death as a martyr on Sept. 14, 258.

Further Reading

St. Cyprian is listed in the Religion study guide (I, B, 3). In the 4th century DONATUS expressed the rigorous attitude toward lapsed Christians.

The classic study of St. Cyprian is Edward White Benson, *Cyprian* (1897), which is still of great value as a comprehensive account of the man's life and times. See also G. S. Walker, *The Churchmanship of St. Cyprian* (1969).

St. Cyril of Alexandria. (Bibliothèque Nationale, Paris)

aspects of his thought. In English, good general essays on him can be found in G. L. Prestige, *Fathers and Heretics: Six Studies in Dogmatic Faith* (1940), and Hans von Campenhausen, *The Fathers of the Greek Church*, translated by Stanley Godman (1959; rev. ed. 1962).

SAINTS **CYRIL** AND **METHODIUS**
/ **By Gerard A. Vanderhaar**

The Greek missionaries Saints Cyril (827–869) and Methodius (825–885) were the apostles of the Slavic peoples. Preaching Christianity in the native language, they brought the Slavic countries firmly into the sphere of the Christian Church.

Methodius was 2 years old when his brother, Cyril, was born in Thessalonica in northeastern Greece in 827. Cyril was given the name Constantine at his baptism. Methodius entered the service of the Byzantine emperor and worked faithfully, if without distinction, for a number of years. Constantine studied at the imperial university in Constantinople but refused the offer of a governor's post and asked instead to be or-

dained a priest. He was more intellectually inclined than Methodius and spent some years as the official librarian of the most important church in eastern Europe, Hagia Sophia in Constantinople. He taught philosophy for a time at the imperial university and was sent by Patriarch Ignatius on one occasion to the Arabian caliph's court as a member of a delegation to discuss theology with the Moslems.

In the meantime Methodius had left government service and entered a monastery in Bithynia east of Constantinople. In 856 Constantine also decided to withdraw from the active life of a scholar-churchman and joined Methodius in the same monastery. The brothers' solitude lasted only 4 years. In 860 they were sent by Patriarch Ignatius to assure the Christian faith of the Khazars in Russia, who were wavering in the face of strong Jewish and Moslem influence. When they were on their return journey, Constantine discovered what he believed to be the bones of an early Christian pope, St. Clement of Rome, and carried them with him for the rest of his life.

From the time they were boys in Thessalonica, the brothers could speak Slavic. When the Moravian king Ratislav, unhappy with the Latin Christianity preached in his Slavic country by Charlemagne's German missionaries, turned to Constantinople for help, Constantine and Methodius were again summoned from their monastery and sent by Emperor Michael II to Moravia. This mission was to be their lifetime concern. In 863 the brothers reached the country (today Czechoslovakia) and immediately began teaching and preaching in the Slavic language of the people. They started a school to train young men for the priesthood. They conducted the liturgical services in Slavic and eventually developed a special Slavic alphabet in order to put the Bible and the liturgy in writing.

For 5 years Constantine and Methodius worked steadily to establish Christian worship according to the forms

Saints Cyril and Methodius, at Christ's side, are guarded by angels in this 9th-century fresco in the church of S. Clemente, Rome. (Alinari)

and language of the Moravian people. They inevitably clashed with the German missionaries, who were committed to the Latin form of Christianity. The two brothers were invited to Rome in 868 by Pope Nicholas I to explain their work. The Pope was so impressed by their success that he made them both bishops and, contrary to expectation, authorized them to carry on their ministry in Slavic. Constantine, however, had no further desire for the active missionary life. He entered a monastery in Rome in 869 and took a new name, Cyril, as a sign of his new life. Fifty days later he died.

Methodius returned to Moravia and continued his efforts for 16 years more. An incident in 871 extended his influence still further. The visiting king of Bohemia was invited to dine with the Moravian king. The guest found that he and his entourage were considered heathens and were expected to sit on the floor, while the host and Bishop Methodius, as Christians, were being served at a raised table. He asked what he could expect to gain by becoming a Christian. Bishop Methodius said, "A place higher than all kings and princes." That was enough. The king asked to be baptized, along with his wife and entire retinue, and returned to Bohemia to encourage many of his people to accept the Christian faith.

Methodius's difficulties with the Latin clergy continued to plague his later years. He was summoned to Rome again in 878 by Pope John VIII. This time the influence of the Latinists was stronger. The Pope decreed that Methodius must first read the Mass in Latin, then translate it into Slavic. The bishop returned, subdued. He died in 885. Cyril and Methodius were considered heroes by the people and were formally recognized as saints of the Roman Catholic Church in 1881.

Further Reading

Saints Cyril and Methodius are listed in the Religion study guide (I, C, 3; I, D, 1). The earlier missionary St. BONIFACE preached Christianity to the Germans.

Most of the works on Cyril and Methodius are in Slavic or Russian. There are several helpful books in English, however. Francis Dvornik, *The Slavs: Their Early History and Civilization* (1956), describes the brothers' influence on the life and language of the people among whom they worked. Zdenek Radslav Dittrich, *Christianity in Great-Moravia* (1962), is a scholarly study of the history of the churches they helped found, and Matthew Spinka, *A History of Christianity in the Balkans* (1968), places their missionary results in the context of the history of eastern Europe.

CYRUS THE GREAT

/ By Eugene W. Davis

Cyrus the Great (reigned 550–530 B.C.) was the founder of the Persian Empire. His reign witnessed the first serious contacts between Persians and Greeks and the permanent loss of political power by the peoples of the old centers of power in Mesopotamia.

In the new Median Empire, which shared with Babylon the spoils of the fallen Assyrian power, the Persians were a subordinate group, though closely related to the Medes and speaking a similar Indo-European language. They were ruled by their own local kings, and one of these married a daughter of the Median king Astyages; their son was Cyrus. Astyages seems not to have been popular, and when, in 550 B.C., Cyrus revolted, Astyages's own troops went over to Cyrus. The Median Empire thus became the Persian Empire. It is worth noting that Cyrus treated his defeated grandfather with honor and that instead of sacking Ecbatana, the Median capital, he kept it as one of his own because Pasargadae, the Persian center, was too remote for use as a capital. Cyrus also continued to keep Medes in high office.

War with the Greeks

The Medes and the Persians were so similar that foreigners tended to see only a change of dynasty (the Greeks still called the whole group Medes), but any such upset implied to the other powers a tempting weakness, and Cyrus soon found himself embroiled in new wars. The first was with Croesus, King of Lydia, a wealthy state in western Asia Minor whose subjects included the Greek cities along its coast. Croesus tried to find allies, including, with the aid of the Delphic oracle, the states of mainland Greece. But Cyrus moved too quickly. In a winter campaign he surprised and took Croesus' "impregnable" capital of Sardis. The Greek Herodotus says that Cyrus spared Croesus, though this has been questioned; Croesus may have committed suicide to avoid capture.

Cyrus then returned to the east, but he left Harpagus, a Mede, to complete the conquest. Over the next years Harpagus subdued the local peoples, including the Greek cities of the coast. The importance of this first serious contact between Greeks and Persians was doubtless unrecognized by either people, yet each was to become and remain for 2 centuries the main foreign preoccupation of the other.

Conquest of Babylon

Nabonidus (Nabu-Naid) of Babylon had originally favored Cyrus, but border conflicts led to war, and in 539 Cyrus captured Babylon. Here again his victory was made easy by the aid of Nabonidus's own subjects, for Nabonidus had alienated many powerful interests, especially the priesthood of Marduk, Babylon's chief god. Cyrus posed as both a liberator and a supporter of the local gods and once in power pursued a careful policy of religious toleration. The most important example of this was his allowing the Jews to return to their homeland.

Not only the civilized states to the west but also the steppe peoples to the east engaged Cyrus's attention,

The Cylinder of Cyrus the Great, about 536 B.C. This cuneiform cylinder refers to Cyrus's capture of Babylon and lists the measures he took to repair wrongs done by previous rulers of the city. (Trustees of the British Museum)

and during his remaining years he pushed his frontiers to the Indus and the Jaxartes (modern Syr Darya). He died in 530 somewhere east of the Caspian Sea, fighting a tribe called the Massagetae.

Cyrus's right to be called "the Great" can hardly be questioned, and not only because his conquests were vastly larger than any before him anywhere on earth. The sudden emergence of Persia as the dominant power in the Near East is the most striking political fact of the 6th century B.C., while the conquest of Mesopotamia (Egypt was left for Cyrus's son Cambyses) marks the first time that a true Indo-European-speaking people had gained control of the old centers of civilization. Further, Cyrus's policy of generosity toward the conquered became standard Persian practice; among the imperial peoples of history, the Persians remain outstanding in their ready toleration of local customs and religions.

Further Reading

Cyrus the Great is listed in the Ancient History study guide (I, D, 1). He was the first of the Achaemenid dynasty, which included DARIUS I and XERXES.

Though business and government documents from the Persian Empire are extant, knowledge of the personal lives of the Persian kings comes almost entirely from Greek sources. Herodotus's *Histories* ranks first; Xenophon's *Cyropedia* is mainly a propaganda piece. Good recent treatments are in A. T. Olmstead, *History of the Persian Empire, Achaemenid Period* (1948); Roman Ghirshman, *Iran: From the Earliest Times to the Islamic Conquest* (1954); and Richard N. Frye, *The Heritage of Persia* (1962).

Daguerre D Dzerzhinsky

DAGUERRE / By William N. Slatcher

Louis Jacques Mandé Daguerre (1787–1851), a French painter and stage designer, invented the daguerreotype, the first practical and commercially successful photographic process.

Louis Daguerre, from a daguerreotype. (Courtesy of The New-York Historical Society, New York City)

Louis Daguerre (pronounced də-gâr′) was born on Nov. 18, 1787, at Cormeilles-en-Parisis. Abandoning his architectural training in 1804, he turned to scene painting and became a pupil of I. E. M. Degotti at the Paris Opéra. In 1822 Daguerre and Charles Bouton developed the diorama, a large-scale peep show in which a painting on a large translucent screen was seemingly animated by the skillful play of light on each side. Daguerre made dioramas for 17 years.

Daguerre used the camera obscura to make sketches for his stage designs and, like so many others, wished to avoid the tedious tracing and fix the image chemically. After several unsuccessful efforts he learned in 1826 that J. N. Niépce was working toward the same end and had made some progress. A cautious correspondence followed, in which Niépce revealed his heliograph process, and in 1829 Daguerre and Niépce formed a partnership to develop the method.

Heliography depended on the hardening action of sunlight on bitumen and the subsequent dissolution of the soft shadow parts of the image. Using this method on a glass plate, Niépce had obtained and fixed a photograph from the camera obscura in 1826. But his aspirations went beyond a visible image to a photoengraved plate from which he could pull prints. This goal led to his using bitumen on silver-coated copperplates and then iodizing the silver revealed after dissolving the unexposed bitumen. The removal of the hardened bitumen produced a silver–silver iodide image. But Niépce went no further.

Building on his partner's foundation, Daguerre discovered the light sensitivity of silver iodide in 1831 but was unable to obtain a visible image. His discovery in 1835 that the latent image present on a silver iodide plate exposed for so short a time as 20 minutes could be developed with mercury vapor marked a major advance. Fixing was achieved in 1837, when he removed the unreduced silver iodide with a solution of common salt. Having improved Niépce's process beyond recognition, Daguerre felt justified in calling it the daguerreotype. He ceded the process to the French government. He revealed his discovery on Aug. 19, 1839.

Daguerre retired to Bry-sur-Marne in 1840 and died there on July 10, 1851. He had little more to do with the daguerreotype, leaving its improvement to others. It was perhaps the invention which most caught popular fancy in the mid-19th century, but it proved to be a blind alley in the development of modern photography.

Further Reading

Louis Daguerre is listed in the Science study guide (VI, H, 2). Samuel F. B. MORSE introduced the daguerreotype to America, and Mathew BRADY took many daguerreotypes. George EASTMAN stimulated the development of photography.

Daguerre's life is fully documented in Helmut and Alison Gernsheim, *L. J. M. Daguerre: The History of the Diorama and the Daguerreotype* (1956). Their *The History of Photography* (1955) is an excellent overall discussion of photography.

DAIGO II / By H. Paul Varley

> The Japanese emperor Daigo II (1288–1339) attempted to restore the power of the throne upon the destruction of the country's first military government, or shogunate, in 1333.

Since the establishment of a centralized state in Japan under the influence of Chinese civilization in the 7th century, the Japanese sovereigns had gradually lost power. During most of the 10th and 11th centuries the Fujiwara family dominated the court at Kyoto as imperial regents. At the end of the 11th century and during the first half of the 12th, retired (or cloistered) emperors reasserted the authority of the imperial family in court politics. Yet, even as they did so, real power in Japan was shifting from the courtier class of Kyoto to an emergent warrior class in the provinces. This shift was climaxed by the founding of a shogunate by the

Daigo II. (International Society for Educational Information, Tokyo, Inc.)

warrior clan of Minamoto at Kamakura in the eastern provinces in 1185.

Kamakura Shogunate

The founder of the Kamakura shogunate was Minamoto Yoritomo, who received the title of shogun, or "generalissimo," from the imperial court. But in the early 13th century actual control of the regime at Kamakura was seized by members of the Hojo clan, who established the office of shogunate regent. The Hojo regents allowed the imperial court little voice in the governing of the country. Emperors continued to reign but they did not rule.

The Hojo regents proved to be among the most effective administrators of medieval Japan, but by the end of the 13th century the Kamakura shogunate had nevertheless begun to decline. One of the chief reasons for this decline was the expense and effort required to repulse two attempts by forces of the Mongol dynasty of China to invade Japan in 1274 and 1281.

Dispute over Succession to the Throne

After the Mongol invasions there arose a dispute over succession to the throne in Kyoto. At first the dispute was of little concern to the Hojo, since the throne exercised no political power. As Hojo rule continued to weaken in the early 14th century, however, discontented members of both the courtier and warrior classes began to turn to the court in opposition to the Kamakura shogunate.

Meanwhile, the contending branches of the imperial family had temporarily agreed to the practice of alternately providing successors to the throne. But when Daigo II of the so-called junior branch became emperor in 1318, he objected strongly to this procedure and determined to hold the throne permanently for himself and his line of descendants. In response to attempts by the

Hojo to force continuance of alternate succession with the senior branch of the imperial family, Daigo II began to scheme to overthrow the Kamakura shogunate and to restore imperial rule.

Daigo II was apparently privy to an anti-Hojo plot that was uncovered in Kyoto in 1324, and in 1331 he actively encouraged an armed rising in the region of Kyoto that had to be put down by forces of the shogunate. The Hojo attempted to settle this second incident by exiling the Emperor to an island in the Japan Sea. Nevertheless, sporadic, guerrilla-type fighting continued in the central provinces around Kyoto, and in 1333 several great warrior chieftains, who had previously been the vassals of Kamakura, defected to the loyalist cause of Daigo II and helped bring about the sudden overthrow of the shogunate.

Imperial Restoration

Upon his triumphal return to Kyoto in 1333, Daigo II sought to take the administrative powers of the country directly into his own hands and to launch an "imperial restoration." But this restoration, which was an anachronistic attempt to reverse the course of several centuries of history, lasted only a brief 3 years. The warrior class was in the ascendancy in Japan, and the imperial court, which was imbued with the governing techniques of an earlier age, was ill-equipped to meet its demands or to fulfill its needs.

As dissatisfaction with the restoration government grew, warriors throughout the land began to look for leadership elsewhere. The chieftain who came to the fore and who increasingly gave indications of his wish to open a new shogunate was Ashikaga Takauji. However, Daigo II, who opposed the sharing of national powers with anyone, steadfastly refused to appoint Takauji as the new shogun. And when, in 1335, Takauji showed signs of assuming shogunlike authority even without imperial approval, the Emperor commissioned Nitta Yoshisada, a keen rival of Takauji, to chastise the Ashikaga.

War between the Courts

The effort to check the Ashikaga plunged Japan into a civil war that lasted for more than half a century. In 1336 Takauji occupied Kyoto and forced Daigo II to abdicate in favor of a member of the senior branch of the imperial family. But in the final month of the year Daigo II fled to Yoshino in the mountainous region to the south of Kyoto and proclaimed that he was still the legitimate sovereign.

The government that Daigo II opened at Yoshino is known in history as the Southern court to distinguish it from the Northern court in Kyoto, and the period of opposition between the two, which lasted until 1392, is called the age of war between the courts. Daigo II died in 1339, and the last spark of his movement to restore the throne to power was extinguished in 1392, when the Southern court abandoned its resistance.

Further Reading

Daigo II is listed in the Asia study guide (III, B, 4, a). His attempts at restoration of imperial power were the last until the restoration of Emperor MEIJI in 1868.

ASHIKAGA Takauji, TOKUGAWA Ieyasu, and MINAMOTO Yoritomo were the most powerful shoguns during the 5 centuries of military rule.

H. Paul Varley, *Imperial Restoration in Medieval Japan* (1971), provides a detailed analysis of Daigo II's attempt to restore imperial rule in the 14th century. For a good historical account of the country, and also Daigo's activities, see Sir George B. Sansom, *A History of Japan* (3 vols., 1958–1963).

✳   ✳   ✳

DAIMLER / By William N. Slatcher

> The German mechanical engineer Gottlieb Daimler (1834–1900) was a pioneer in the development of the internal combustion engine and the automobile.

Gottlieb Daimler (pronounced dīm′lər) was born on March 17, 1834, at Schorndorf near Stuttgart. He attended a technical school (1848–1852) in Stuttgart while serving as a gunsmith's apprentice. After 4 years (1853–1857) at a Strassburg steam engine factory, he completed his training as a mechanical engineer at the Stuttgart Polytechnic. He returned to Strassburg in 1859, but 2 years later, having recognized the need for a small, low-power engine capable of economic intermit-

Gottlieb Daimler. (Bildarchiv)

tent operation, he left to tour France and England. In Paris he saw E. Lenoir's new gas engine.

Daimler spent the next decade in heavy engineering. He joined Bruderhaus Maschinen-Fabrik in Reutlingen as manager in 1863 and there met Wilhelm Maybach, with whom he was to collaborate closely for the rest of his life. Daimler went to Maschinenbau Gesellschaft in Karlsruhe as director in 1869. When he joined Gasmotoren-Fabrik in Deutz as chief engineer in 1872, Daimler, N. A. Otto, and Eugen Langen perfected the Otto atmospheric (oil) engine. Daimler was asked by the Deutz board in 1875 to develop a gasoline-powered version, but this idea was dropped in favor of commercial exploitation of the four-cycle Otto engine.

Daimler Motor Company

In 1882 Daimler and Maybach set up a factory in Stuttgart to develop light, high-speed, gasoline-powered internal combustion engines. Their aim from the start appears to have been to apply these engines to vehicles. During their early trials it seemed that ignition troubles were insurmountable, but in 1883 Daimler developed and patented a reliable self-firing ignition system using an incandescent tube in the cylinder head. Maybach worked to reduce the size while increasing the economy, and by 1885 their first gasoline-powered engine was fitted to a motorcycle. That year a more powerful, water-cooled unit was fitted into a carriage. They then developed a two-cylinder V engine, applied it to a motor car, and exhibited it at the 1889 Paris Exhibition. Though the public took little notice of the vehicle, it did attract R. Panhard and E. Lavassor, who developed the engine in France and began automobile manufacture in 1891.

In Germany the need for more capital led to the creation of Daimler-Motoren-Gesellschaft mbH (1890), but business disagreements led Daimler and Maybach to break away in 1893 and continue experimental development alone. They entered endurance trials and road races to establish the utility of the automobile and showed the way so clearly that Daimler returned to his company in full control in 1895. He died in Stuttgart on March 6, 1900.

Further Reading

Gottlieb Daimler is listed in the Science study guide (VI, H, 2). Among the other pioneers of the automobile industry was Henry FORD, founder of the Ford Motor Company. Rudolf DIESEL developed another type of internal combustion engine.

Perhaps the best recent study of Daimler is in Eugen Diesel and others, *From Engines to Autos: Five Pioneers in Engine Development* (1960).

*   *   *

DALADIER / By Jack E. Reece

The French statesman Édouard Daladier (1884–1970) represented his country at the Munich Conference in September 1938.

The son of a baker, Édouard Daladier (pronounced dà-là-dyā′) was born on June 18, 1884, at Carpentras. An ardent Dreyfusard schoolteacher and member of the Radical Socialist party, he was elected to Parliament in 1919. He attained ministerial rank under his former teacher Édouard Herriot in 1924 and served in most cabinets until 1940.

During his first premiership, from January to October 1933, Daladier signed the Four-Power Peace Pact with Great Britain, Germany, and Italy. Widely considered a "strong man," he was recalled to power in January 1934 to deal with disorders provoked by right-wing extremists. Undeterred, they rioted in Paris on Feb. 6, 1934, and forced Daladier to resign after only 11 days in office. A rival of Herriot and leader of the progressive Radicals, Daladier led his party into Léon Blum's left-wing Popular Front coalition, which won the parliamentary elections of May 1936. He then became minister of national defense.

As international tension mounted following Hitler's annexation of Austria, France once more turned to a "strong man," and Daladier resumed the premiership in April 1938. With France the prisoner of British foreign policy, Daladier was forced to support the appeasement policy of Neville Chamberlain. Consequently, he was compelled to acquiesce in the dismembering of Czechoslovakia at Munich in 1938. This act destroyed the security system of France in eastern Europe and encouraged Adolf Hitler in his policy of aggression and violence.

Daladier declared war on Germany after Hitler's inva-

Édouard Daladier. (French Embassy Press & Information Division)

sion of Poland in September 1939. He continued in office until March 20, 1940, when he yielded to another "strong man," Paul Reynaud. He remained in the government, however, as minister of war and then as foreign minister until June 16, 1940. Arrested in September by Vichy authorities, he was sent to Riom for trial in 1942. Daladier defended himself with such courage and vigor that the proceedings were suspended. In 1943 he was deported to Germany, where he remained until his liberation in April 1945.

After the war Daladier sought to resume his political career but with little success. Although returned to Parliament, he was too much identified with the events which led to the fall of France to regain his prewar position of leadership. Even his tenure as president of the Radical party after the death of Herriot in 1957 was brief and inglorious. After his electoral defeat in the parliamentary elections of November 1958, he retired. Daladier died in Paris on Oct. 10, 1970.

Further Reading

Édouard Daladier is listed in the European History study guide (XI, C, 1). Other prominent French politicians of this period included Léon BLUM and Édouard HERRIOT. Neville CHAMBERLAIN was closely associated with the policy of appeasement.

As with most French political leaders, Daladier has no biographer. His career before 1940, however, is intelligently discussed in Alexander Werth, *The Twilight of France, 1933–1940* (1942); D. W. Brogan, *The Development of Modern France, 1870–1939* (1947; rev. ed. 1966); and Peter J. Larmour, *The French Radical Party in the 1930's* (1964).

DALAI LAMA / By Hugh Richardson

The Dalai Lama was the spiritual and temporal ruler of Tibet. In 1959 Tendzin Gyatso (born 1935), fourteenth holder of the office, escaped from Chinese-occupied Tibet to India, where he continued to be regarded as the spiritual leader of all Tibetans.

Tibetans regard Tendzin Gyatso, who became the Dalai Lama (pronounced dä′li lä′mə) in 1939, as the fourteenth in a succession of embodiments of the bodhisattva Chenrezi. The succession began with a disciple of the 14th-century reformer Tsongkhapa who instituted the dGe-lugs-pa sect of Tibetan Buddhism, popularly known as the Yellow Hats. A bodhisattva, having attained enlightenment, is exempt from the cycle of existence in this world of suffering but may return, out of compassion, in the body of a Lama to help others to deliverance. When such a Lama dies, his successor is sought in a child born not long after, in whom the spirit is once more reincarnated.

The title Dalai (Ocean-wide) was not used until the

third embodiment, Sonam Gyatso (1543–1588), who received it from the Mongol ruler Altan Khan, whom he converted together with his people. Mongol adherence greatly strengthened the Yellow Hats against jealous opposition by the earlier sects, which had provided the rulers of Tibet. In 1642 the Mongol prince Gusri Khan invaded Tibet, defeated its king, and installed the fifth Dalai Lama, Ngawang Gyatso (1617–1682), as spiritual head and temporal ruler. Gusri assumed the title of king but regarded himself as military protector of the Lama. With Gusri's support and by combining energetic firmness with diplomatic conciliation, the Dalai Lama consolidated his position so effectively that after Gusri's death, in 1655, the Mongol kingship dwindled into a subordinate role.

Justly known as the Great Fifth and lastingly commemorated by his superb Potala Palace, Ngawang Gyatso increased the prestige and wealth of the Yellow Hats, whom he transformed from a religious sect into a dominant political power. From his day the mystique of a ruler combining in his person supreme spiritual and temporal authority was reverently accepted by all Tibetans. Temporal power was no mere formality. In a small, leisurely administration, delegation of authority was unknown, and the Dalai Lama personally decided even trivial business.

Chinese Overlordship

A risk inherent in the reincarnation system appeared with Ngawang's successor, Tshangyang Gyatso (1683–1707), who grew up a pleasure-loving, poetically inclined youth—an engaging personality but not suitable for a Dalai Lama. Dissension centering on his unusual character gave the Chinese emperor, mindful of the religious influence of the Yellow Hats over Mongolia, an opportunity to intervene in Tibetan affairs and to establish in 1720 a loose overlordship that lasted until 1911.

Since Dalai Lamas were celibate and their families customarily debarred from political activity, power during the long interregnum between the death of one Lama and the majority of the next reverted to the Yellow Hat church, which supplied a regent. The unquestioned dominance won by the Great Fifth tempted some ambitious regents to find ways of holding on to that power. Indeed, until the accession of the thirteenth Dalai Lama in 1879, no figure comparable to the Fifth emerged; and as several reincarnations died young, for about 150 years Tibet was ruled by monk regents.

Thirteenth Dalai Lama

Thupten Gyatso (1876–1933), having survived a perilous minority, proved an autocratic and strong-willed ruler. His immature flirting with Russia and rejection of overtures from the Indian government led to his flight to China from the Younghusband expedition, which reached Lhasa in 1904. Six years later he was in flight again, this time from a Chinese invasion and to India. An honored and observant guest there, he decided that Tibet, for its survival, needed some modernization. Returning to Lhasa in 1913, after the fall of the Ch'ing dynasty had removed all trace of Chinese overlordship, he stout-

The fourteenth Dalai Lama. (Keystone Press, London)

ly defended Tibet's independence and maintained good relations with the British government in India through Sir Charles Bell, the resident in Sikkim, with whom he had formed a close friendship. But the Dalai Lama's attempted innovations in education, military training, and other areas were mostly frustrated by conservative monastic opposition.

Discovery of the Fourteenth Dalai Lama

Two years after the death of the thirteenth Dalai Lama in 1933, search parties set out, following the customary guidance of oracles, visions, and omens, to look for the child in whom his spirit had chosen to return. Unmistakable signs were eventually found in 2-year-old Lamo Dondup, the fifth surviving child of a small farmer and his wife, Tibetan by race but living under the jurisdiction of the Moslem governor of the Chinese border province of Chinghai. The boy penetrated the disguise assumed, for secrecy, by the searchers and chose unerringly from an assortment of objects those that had belonged to the late Dalai Lama.

The story became known to the governor and the Chinese central government, which saw the prospect of recovering through this child some of the influence lost in 1911. Correspondence with distant Lhasa dragged on for 2 years before the Tibetans secured the release of the child on payment of a large sum of money. Late in 1939 he reached Tibetan territory and was at once formally acknowledged by a delegation of high lamas and officials. They escorted him to Lhasa, where the boy, in his fifth year, was duly initiated as a monk, given the name Tendzin Gyatso, and enthroned as Dalai Lama.

Early Childhood

From the first, his dignified self-possession and strength of will beyond his years inspired faith and devotion in his people. There followed intensive religious education and training for his high office. In his autobiography, *My Land and My People*, the Dalai Lama wrote of his religious studies and of his interest in everything mechanical. His striking intellectual powers, concentration, seriousness, and sense of duty were described by Heinrich Harrer, who met him when he was 12.

The promising youth would normally have been given ruling powers at the age of 18, but in 1950, in his sixteenth year, the Communists who had seized control in China invaded eastern Tibet. The Tibetan government in alarm prematurely conferred full powers upon Tendzin Gyatso and, as a precaution, he moved to Chumbi, near the Indian border.

An appeal to the United Nations having failed to win support against Chinese aggression, there was no alternative to acceptance of a treaty signed on behalf of Tibet in Peking in 1951 by a virtually captive Tibetan delegation. The Dalai Lama then returned to Lhasa to head his government under the shadow of Chinese military occupation.

Difficulties with the Chinese

The Chinese interpreted their undertaking to retain an autonomous Tibetan government very differently from the Tibetans, and the young Dalai Lama found himself struggling to maintain his rights and those of his church and people against efforts to introduce the ideas and methods of Communist China. He was compelled to dismiss two ministers and to accept as an equal colleague a youth educated in China, whom the Chinese, without Tibetan agreement, established as the reincarnation of the Panchen Lama, the second Yellow Hat dignitary. In these unprecedented difficulties the Dalai Lama showed great self-control and diplomatic skill, embarrassing the Communists by a program of social and agricultural reform which they obstructed in favor of their own unwelcome measures.

In 1955 he went to China and met Mao Tse-tung, whose personality impressed him so much that he did not regard Mao as responsible for Chinese excesses. But he also saw with foreboding the oppression inflicted on the people of the borderland known as Amdo and Kham, Tibetans by race but since the 18th century under nominal Chinese control. In 1956 they rose in revolt with widespread fighting which evoked cruel reprisals.

Fear that similar bloodshed and devastation might affect all Tibet distressed the Dalai Lama so much that when, in 1956, with reluctant Chinese consent he visited India, he discussed with Jawaharlal Nehru the possibility of seeking asylum there. It was no coincidence that the Chinese premier, Chou En-lai, was in India too; and, with Nehru as intermediary, he persuaded the Dalai Lama to return to Lhasa with the assurance that Chinese reforms would be discontinued. Mao announced the postponement publicly, and some troops and officials were withdrawn, but enough remained to cause resentment by their continuous pressure.

The 1959 Rising

Tension rose sharply when armed refugees from Amdo and Kham, no longer able to hold their ground, directed well-organized guerrilla activities against Chinese camps and convoys in central Tibet. When the Dalai Lama refused a demand to use Tibetan troops against them, rumors spread that he would be taken to China as a hostage. In March 1959, when it became known that the Chinese commander had invited the Dalai Lama to an entertainment, insisting that he come without his usual escort, the Lhasa populace, in fear and anger, massed at

the Summer Palace to prevent his leaving. The Dalai Lama, striving to calm the wild excitement and avert a violent explosion that could end only in disaster, exchanged letters with the Chinese commander which gave the impression that he was almost held prisoner. The people were supported by Tibetan troops, who moved into position against the heavily armed Chinese forces. In face of growing threats the Chinese fired warning shots toward the palace, and the Dalai Lama, seeing no hope of restoring order, agreed to leave Lhasa secretly.

A seemingly miraculous dust storm covered the escape through encircling Chinese troops, who knew nothing for 3 days. After 2 weeks' dangerous and strenuous journeying the Dalai Lama reached the Assam frontier of India. Nehru, warned in advance, readily offered asylum.

Refuge in India

The Dalai Lama, who was quite composed, issued immediately on arrival a denial that he had been under duress; not long after, he held a press conference marked by thoughtful serenity and absence of bitterness. So long as Nehru hoped for an understanding with China, public activity by the Dalai Lama was discouraged, but Indian sympathy took the practical form of sheltering and feeding some 50,000 Tibetans who streamed after him. About 20,000 more were similarly received by Nepal, Bhutan, and Sikkim. After the breach between India and China in 1962 the Dalai Lama traveled extensively in India, Japan, and Thailand, encouraging the education and resettlement of the refugees. At his remote headquarters at Dharamsala in northern India he also met, with simple informality, many foreign visitors.

While Tibetan culture, religion, and national identity were being destroyed in Tibet itself, the Dalai Lama attempted to keep them alive in India. Nonetheless, recognizing that the past could never be re-created, he drafted a constitution with a strongly democratic character; and, while reminding Tibetans of the generous hospitality and help they were receiving as refugees, he emphasized that they must look ahead and work with faith and perseverance to learn useful skills for the hoped-for return to Tibet.

Further Reading

The Dalai Lama is listed in the Asia study guide (III, A, 17). Sir Francis YOUNGHUSBAND led an expedition to Tibet in 1904 to secure a treaty of cooperation with India.

The successive Dalai Lamas and their place in the Tibetan polity are outlined in Sir Charles Bell's two works, *Tibet, Past and Present* (1924; trans. 1930) and *Portrait of the Dalai Lama* (1946), and in Hugh Richardson, *A Short History of Tibet* (1962). W. D. Shakabpa, *Tibet: A Political History* (1967), is specially interesting as the first political history written in a Western style by a Tibetan. The fourteenth Dalai Lama's autobiography, *My Land and My People* (1962), is of primary importance; and fascinating glimpses of his early days may be seen in Heinrich Harrer, *Seven Years in Tibet* (1953; trans.

The palace of the Dalai Lama in Lhasa, Tibet.

1954). See also Nöel Barber, *From the Land of Lost Content: The Dalai Lama's Fight for Tibet* (1969).

* * *

DALE / By E. Ashworth Underwood

The English pharmacologist and neurophysiologist Sir Henry Hallett Dale (1875–1968) shared the Nobel Prize in Physiology or Medicine for discoveries relating to the chemical transmission of nerve impulses.

Henry Dale, son of C. J. Dale, a businessman, was born in London on June 9, 1875. He entered Trinity College, Cambridge, in 1894 with a scholarship, read physiology and zoology, and graduated bachelor of arts in 1898. During 2 years of postgraduate work at Cambridge he worked under W. H. Gaskell, J. N. Langley, and (Sir) F. Gowland Hopkins. In 1900 Dale started the clinical work at St. Bartholomew's Hospital, London, that was necessary for his Cambridge medical degree, which he took in 1903. After research at University College, London, and a period in Paul Ehrlich's research institute at Frankfurt am Main, Dale was invited by (Sir) Henry S. Wellcome in 1904 to accept the post of pharmacologist to the Wellcome Physiological Research Laboratories. Two years later he became director of the laboratories, a post which he held until 1914. He graduated as a doctor of medicine at Cambridge in 1909.

In 1914 Dale was appointed the first pharmacologist to

Sir Henry Dale. (Keystone)

the National Institute for Medical Research, newly established under the Medical Research Committee (later Council). He became its first director in 1928, a post from which he retired in 1942. Dale's work embraced important researches in four different subjects, all initiated while he was at the Wellcome Laboratories and continued at the National Institute.

Problem of Ergot

A liquid extract of the fungus ergot had been used for centuries in obstetrics to stimulate the contractions of the pregnant uterus. Several alkaloids had already been isolated from this extract, and one of these was claimed to be the active principle. But this alkaloid, ergotine, was not nearly so powerful as the liquid extract, and, on Dale's appointment to the Wellcome Laboratories, Wellcome asked him to try to clear up the problem. Just before that the chemist George Barger, who was also working in the laboratories, had prepared other substances from ergot, and in 1906 Dale carried out a detailed pharmacological investigation of their activity. In succeeding years Barger and others isolated several more supposed "active principles," but Dale could not satisfy himself that any of these was the substance that made the watery extract so potent. It was not until 1935 that the real active principle, ergometrine, was isolated by Dale's former coworker Harold Ward Dudley. But the work that Dale carried out for some years on ergot was to give him pointers to nearly all his future work.

Action of Pituitary Extracts

In 1909 Dale showed that an extract of the posterior lobe of the pituitary gland produced powerful contractions of the uterus of a pregnant cat. As a result, pituitary extract (pituitrin) was soon extensively used in obstetrics. He also showed that this effect was caused by an active principle of the extract different from that which produced a rise of blood pressure. In 1920–1921, with Dudley, he isolated and studied the active principle, oxytocin, that produced the powerful contractions.

Histamine and Its Effects

In 1910 Barger and Dale, working on an ergot extract, discovered that a substance in it, later called histamine, had a direct stimulant effect on plain (smooth) muscle, especially that of the uterus and bronchioles. (Histamine had previously been synthesized, but it was not known to occur naturally, in the animal body or elsewhere.) They also showed that it caused a general fall in blood pressure and that its injection produced most of the features of anaphylactic shock. In 1911 they were the first to show that it could be present in animal tissues, as they had isolated it from the wall of the intestine.

No further work was done on histamine until the later years of World War I, when the problem of "secondary" surgical and traumatic shock had become of great practical importance. In 1918 Dale, working with Alfred Newton Richards, showed that small doses of histamine caused constriction of the arteries along with a general dilatation of the capillaries. In 1919 Dale, working with

(Sir) Patrick Playfair Laidlaw, showed that massive doses of histamine produced a general dilatation of the blood vessels and capillaries, together with an exudation of plasma from the capillaries, a fall in body temperature, and respiratory depression. These features were almost identical with those found in surgical shock, and in a subsequent study Dale found that the dose of histamine necessary to produce the condition was much smaller if there had been previous hemorrhage. These discoveries were of great practical importance in surgery. Theoretically, they indicated that, in the case of injury to the tissues, histamine was produced by the body cells. But in 1919 there was no evidence that histamine was produced by the body cells, and it was not until 1927 that Dale and his coworkers showed that histamine is normally present in significant amounts in the lung and in the liver.

Meanwhile Dale had carried out various researches that were to lead to another aspect of the histamine problem. In 1913 he noticed the extreme sensitivity of the isolated uterus of a particular guinea pig when treated with a normally quite innocuous dose of horse serum. He later discovered that this particular guinea pig had already been used for the assay of diphtheria antitoxin and was therefore already sensitized to horse serum. By following up this chance observation Dale was able to produce in guinea pig plain muscle all the essential features of anaphylaxis, thus greatly advancing knowledge of the cause of this condition. In 1922 Dale and Charles Halliley Kellaway showed that anaphylactic phenomena are probably due to the location of the antibody in the cell substance. Ten years later other workers showed that in anaphylaxis histamine is actually released by the injured cells. The modern use of antihistaminic drugs stems essentially from Dale's work on histamine.

Chemical Transmission of the Nerve Impulse

Even as late as the first 2 decades of the 19th century the manner in which an impulse, passing down a nerve to a muscle, causes the latter to contract was quite unknown. In 1904 Dale's friend Thomas Renton Elliott, then working in the same laboratory as Dale at Cambridge, suggested as a result of his research on adrenaline that sympathetic nerve fibers might act on plain muscle and glands by liberating this substance at their endings. But this suggestion was never actively followed up by anyone, though it profoundly influenced Dale's later research.

In 1914 Dale found unusual activities in a certain ergot extract, and the active principle responsible for these unusual effects was isolated by Dale's chemical coworker, Arthur James Ewins. It proved to be acetylcholine, the acetyl ester of choline. This work led to an important paper by Dale (1914), in which he showed that the action of acetylcholine on plain muscle and glands was very similar to the action of parasympathetic fibers, and that acetylcholine reproduces those effects of autonomic nerves that are absent from the action of adrenaline. These observations had no direct sequel at that time, because there was then no evidence that acetylcholine was normally present in the animal body. Nevertheless, this paper foreshadowed an understanding of the chemical transmission of the nerve impulse.

In 1921 one specialized form of chemical transmission was proved by Otto Loewi, who showed that the slowing of the frog's heart that occurred when the vagus nerve was stimulated was due to the liberation of a chemical substance. He suspected that this substance might be acetylcholine, but he cautiously called it the "vagus substance" because even then acetylcholine was not known to be present in the animal body. Indeed, it was not until 1933 that two of Dale's coworkers proved that Loewi's vagus substance was acetylcholine.

In 1929 Dale and Dudley found acetylcholine in the spleens of horses and oxen—the first occasion on which it had ever been found in the animal body—and the experiments of Dale and John Henry Gaddum (1930) strongly suggested that the effects produced by stimulation of parasympathetic nerves were due to the liberation of acetylcholine. But about this time Dale became convinced that, in laboratory animals, if acetylcholine was present at all, it must either be in very much smaller quantities than was found in the spleens of oxen, or alternatively it must be destroyed very rapidly.

In 1933 and 1934 the mode of action of impulses in sympathetic nerves was cleared up by Dale and his coworkers, (Sir) George Lindor Brown, Wilhelm Siegmund Feldberg, Gaddum, and others. It was known that, when fibers leading to a sympathetic ganglion were stimulated, a minute amount of a substance suspected to be acetylcholine was produced in the ganglion, but this substance was immediately destroyed by an esterase. But the action of this esterase was inhibited by eserine, so that, by adding eserine to the fluid used to wash out the ganglion, sufficient of the substance was collected for it to be tested. The substance was thus shown to be acetylcholine. They then showed that even a single nerve impulse in a single nerve fiber passing to a sympathetic ganglion released an incredibly minute amount of acetylcholine, and this amount was approximately measured (10^{-15} gram). It was shown that, having acted as a trigger at the synapse, the acetylcholine was immediately destroyed.

Dale and his coworkers then turned to the problem of a chemical transmitter in the case of voluntary muscle. This problem, which had eluded all others who had worked on it, was technically more difficult. But in 1936 they showed that the amount of acetylcholine liberated when a single impulse in one motor fiber reached the end plate of that fiber was also of the order of 10^{-15} gram. In 1936, also Dale, with Brown and Feldberg, showed that the direct injection—under certain conditions—of acetylcholine into the drained vessels in a muscle produced a contraction. The chemical transmission of the nerve impulse, in both parasympathetic and motor nerves, was now conclusively proved and its mode of action elucidated. For these researches Dale shared the Nobel Prize with Loewi in 1936.

Later Life

From 1940 to 1947 Dale was a member of the Scientific Advisory Committee to the War Cabinet, and he was its chairman from 1942. When he retired from the directorship of the National Institute in 1942, he became Fullerian Professor and director of the Davy-Faraday Laboratory at the Royal Institution. From this post he retired in 1946. He had been chairman of the Wellcome Trust since its establishment in 1936, and he now devoted more and more of his time to the work of this scientific trust, of which he remained chairman until 1960.

Dale received very many honors. He was elected a Fellow of the Royal Society in 1914. He was its Croonian Lecturer in 1919; he received its Royal Medal in 1924 and the Copley Medal—its highest honor—in 1937. He was its Secretary from 1925 to 1935 and its President from 1940 to 1945. In 1947 he was President of the British Association and from 1948 to 1950 President of the Royal Society of Medicine. In 1922 he was elected a Fellow of the Royal College of Physicians, and he gave its Croonian Lecture in 1929.

Dale was knighted in 1932 and created Knight Grand Cross of the Order of the British Empire in 1943. In 1944 he was appointed to the Order of Merit. He received honorary degrees from 25 universities, and he was an honorary or corresponding member of over 30 foreign learned societies. He died at Cambridge on July 23, 1968.

Further Reading

Sir Henry Dale is listed in the Science study guide (VII, F, 1; VII, G, 1). He and Otto LOEWI shared the Nobel Prize. Among the many distinguished scientists who worked with Dale in his laboratory was Charles H. BEST.

There is a short biography of Dale in *Nobel Lectures, Physiology or Medicine, 1922–1941* (1965); it also contains his Nobel Lecture, which deals solely with his work on the chemical transmission of the nerve impulse. Dale's work as a whole is discussed in some detail in C. Singer and E. A. Underwood, *A Short History of Medicine* (1962). More important, but more difficult, is Dale's own *Adventures in Physiology* (1953), in which he reprinted 30 of his most important scientific papers, with his later comments on each paper.

DALHOUSIE / By Ian K. Steele

The British statesman James Andrew Broun Ramsay, lst Marquess of Dalhousie (1812–1860), served as governor general of India from 1848 to 1856. He is noted for his vigorous, often ruthless, expansion and westernization of British India.

James Ramsay, the third and youngest son of the 9th Earl of Dalhousie, was born in the ancestral Dalhousie castle in Midlothian, Scotland, on April 22, 1812. He graduated from Christ Church, Oxford, in 1833 and married in 1836. He was elected to Parliament in 1837. As his brothers had both died, he succeeded to the title upon his father's death in 1838 and entered the House of Lords. Dalhousie served as vice president of the Board of Trade in 1843 and as president in 1845 and early 1846. The following year he accepted the governor generalship of India.

Within 3 months of Dalhousie's assuming office in January 1848, the Punjab was aflame with renewed fighting between the British and the Sikhs. This hard-fought second Sikh war did not end until February 1849, when a British victory in Gujarat forced surrender upon the Sikhs. Dalhousie annexed the Punjab and helped make it the example of reformed imperial administration.

Although military conquest also served as a preliminary to the annexation of lower Burma in 1852, most of Dalhousie's extensions of British-controlled territory resulted from his strict application of the doctrine of lapse. Hindu princes under British influence needed British permission to adopt a male heir, and failure to obtain such permission meant forfeiture of the government, though not the private estate, of the ruler. Applying this policy, Dalhousie annexed Satara, Jaitpur, and Sambalpur in 1849, adding Jhansi and the major Maratha state of Nagpur in 1853.

While adding nearly 250,000 square miles to his gov-

Lord Dalhousie. (National Portrait Gallery, London)

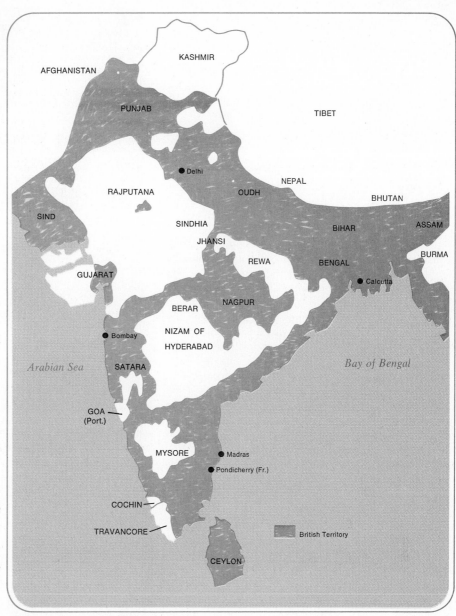

India in 1856. By military conquest and strict application of the doctrine of lapse, Dalhousie vigorously expanded British territory in India during his 8-year administration as governor general.

ernment, Dalhousie also made important contributions to the integration and economic development of British India. In 1854 he freed himself and his successors from the minutiae of local government in Bengal by creating the post of lieutenant governor there. He gave real impetus to railway and canal construction, initiated telegraph services, and overhauled the postal services to provide a uniform and inexpensive rate of postage within India.

Though in failing health, Dalhousie supervised the annexation of Oudh in February 1856. The following month he returned home to receive the thanks of Queen Victoria and a generous pension from the East India Company. The outbreak of the Indian Mutiny in 1857 brought bitter attacks upon him, but he was not well enough to reply to his critics. He died in Dalhousie castle on Dec. 19, 1860.

Further Reading

Lord Dalhousie is listed in the European History study guide (VIII, A, 2) and the Asia study guide (II, A, 6, a). Warren HASTINGS was the first governor general of India.

J. G. A. Baird edited *Private Letters of the Marquess of Dalhousie* (1910). The standard biography is Sir William Lee-Warner, *The Life of the Marquis of Dalhousie* (2 vols., 1904). Manindra N. Das, *Studies in the Economic and Social Development of Modern India: 1848–56* (1959), is a thorough and favorable investigation of Dalhousie's policies. Aspects of Dalhousie's contribution are also assessed in R. J. Moore, *Sir Charles Wood's Indian Policy, 1853–1866* (1966).

✳ ✳ ✳

DALI / By Moira Roth

The Spanish painter Salvador Dali (born 1904) was one of the best-known and most flamboyant surrealist artists. Possessed with an enormous facility for drawing, he painted in a precise illusionistic fashion his dreams and bizarre moods and imagery.

Salvador Dali (left) and Man Ray in 1934. (Library of Congress, Carl Van Vechten Collection, Courtesy of Saul Mauriber)

Salvador Dali (pronounced dä′lē) was born near Barcelona. According to his autobiography, his childhood was characterized by fits of anger against his parents and schoolmates and resultant acts of cruelty. He was a precocious child, producing highly sophisticated drawings at an early age. He studied painting in Madrid, responding to various influences, especially the metaphysical school of painting founded by Giorgio de Chirico, and at the same time dabbling in cubism.

Gradually Dali began to evolve his own style, which was to execute in an extremely precise manner the strange subjects of his fantasy world. Each object was drawn with painstaking exactness, yet it existed in weird juxtaposition with other objects and was engulfed in an oppressive perspectival space which often appeared to recede too rapidly and tilt sharply upward. He used bright colors applied to small objects set off against large patches of dull color. His personal style was evolved from a combination of influences, but increasingly from his contact with surrealism. The contact was at first through paintings and then through personal acquaintance with the surrealists when he visited Paris in 1928. In 1929 Dali painted some of his finest canvases, when he

was still young and excited over his surrealist ideas and had not yet developed so extensively his elaborate personal facade. He began to build up a whole repertoire of symbols, mainly drawn from handbooks of abnormal psychology, stressing sexual fantasies and fetishes.

Paranoic-Critical Method

The surrealists saw in Dali the promise of a breakthrough of the surrealist dilemma about 1930. Many of the surrealists had broken away from the movement, feeling that direct political action had to come before any mental revolutions. Dali put forth his "paranoic-critical method" as an alternative to having to politically conquer the world. He felt that his own vision could be imposed on and color the world to his liking so that it

Dali painted the Persistence of Memory in 1931. (Collection, The Museum of Modern Art, New York)

became unnecessary to change it objectively. Specifically, the paranoic-critical method meant that Dali had trained himself to possess the hallucinatory power to look at one object and "see" another. On the nonvisual level, it meant that Dali could take a myth which had a generally accepted interpretation and impose upon it his own personal and bizarre interpretation. For example, the story of William Tell is generally considered to symbolize filial trust, but Dali's version had it as a story of castration. This way he had of viewing the world began early when he was told in art school to copy a Gothic virgin and instead drew a pair of scales. It meant that although Dali assumed many of the attitudes of madness this was, at least in part, consciously done.

A key event in Dali's life was his meeting with his wife, Gala, who was at that time married to another surrealist. She became his deliberately cultivated main influence, both in his personal life and in many of his paintings.

Break with the Surrealists

Toward the end of the 1930s Dali's romantic and flamboyant view of himself began to antagonize the surrealists. There was a final break on political grounds, and André Breton angrily excommunicated Dali from the surrealist movement. Dali continued to be extremely successful commercially, but his seriousness as an artist began to be questioned. He took a violent stand against abstract art, mixed with the fashionable world, and began to paint Catholic subjects in the same tight illusionistic style which had previously described his personal hallucinations.

Further Reading

Salvador Dali is listed in the Art study guide (III, J, 1, e). He was influenced by the metaphysical school of painting propounded by Giorgio de CHIRICO.

Dali presents a fascinating though exaggerated vision of himself in his autobiographical writings, the best of which is *The Secret Life of Salvador Dali* (1942; rev. ed. 1961). A sober but admiring study is James Thrall Soby, *Salvador Dali* (1941; 2d rev. ed. 1946). Robert Descharnes, *The World of Salvador Dali* (trans. 1962), is lavishly illustrated.

✻   ✻   ✻

DALLAPICCOLA / By Dika Newlin

The Italian composer Luigi Dallapiccola (born 1904) is best known for his twelve-tone compositions, often of highly lyrical and expressive nature.

Luigi Dallapiccola (pronounced däl-lä-pēk′kō-lä) was born on Feb. 3, 1904, at Pisino in Istria. The town (now Pazin, Yugoslavia; after World War I, part of Italy) belonged to the Austro-Hungarian Empire during his childhood. In 1917 the Dallapiccolas and oth-

er Italian families of that community were deported to Graz, Austria, for political reasons. There Dallapiccola had his first opportunity to hear major operas, such as Wolfgang Amadeus Mozart's *Don Giovanni* and Richard Wagner's *Die Meistersinger* and *The Flying Dutchman*. At this time he decided definitely to become a musician, although his father, a professor of classical languages, insisted that he complete a classical education also.

In 1921 Dallapiccola graduated from high school. The next year he went to Florence, where he entered the harmony class of the conservatory in 1923. Two years later he composed three songs *Fiuri de Tapo* (texts by Biagio Marin); these remained unpublished and unperformed. In 1931 he became a professor at the Florence Conservatory. Dallapiccola's first major commission came in 1934: *Divertimento in quattro essercizi* for soprano and five instruments (on a 12th-century text), written for the group Le Carillon in Geneva.

In his early works Dallapiccola did not follow twelve-tone principles. However, he came to feel that the consistent use of the twelve tones would enable him to write richer and more expressive melodies. A fine example of such a melody occurs at the beginning of his opera *Volo di notte* (1937–1939; Night Flight; text after Saint-Exupéry). The *Canti di prigionia* (1939–1941; Prison Songs; texts by Mary, Queen of Scots, Boethius, and Savonarola) are united by a single twelve-tone row but still contain many free passages. His first work to use the strict twelve-tone method throughout is the *Cinque*

Luigi Dallapiccola. (Library of Congress)

frammenti di Saffo (1942). Dallapiccola was the first Italian composer to study and apply twelve-tone principles systematically. In applying them he also found his personal style. While he learned much from the example of Arnold Schoenberg, Alban Berg, and Anton Webern, Dallapiccola's expressiveness is his own.

Most of Dallapiccola's important works are vocal. He often chose texts which glorified the idea of liberty. Three of his major compositions on this theme are the *Canti di prigionia; Il Prigioniero*, a one-act opera with prologue (1949; text after Villiers de l'Isle-Adam and Charles de Coster); and *Canti de liberazione* for choir and orchestra (1955; Songs of Liberation; texts from Castillio, St. Augustine, and the Book of Exodus). His opera *Ulysses* (1967) deals with Ulysses' quest for himself and his final delivery into the hands of God.

Further Reading

Luigi Dallapiccola is listed in the Music study guide (I, J, 4; I, K, 4). Other modern Italian composers are Luciano BERIO and Luigi NONO. The twelve-tone system begun by Arnold SCHOENBERG was continued by Alban BERG and Anton WEBERN.

The only biography available in English on Dallapiccola is Roman Vlad's brief study, *Luigi Dallapiccola* (trans. 1957).

DALTON / By E. Scott Barr

> **The English chemist John Dalton (1766–1844) provided the beginnings of the development of a scientific atomic theory, thus facilitating the development of chemistry as a separate science. His contributions to physics, particularly to meteorology, were also significant.**

John Dalton was the youngest of three surviving children of a Quaker handloom weaver. He was born about Sept. 6, 1766 (no exact record exists), in Eaglesfield. Until he was 11, he attended school, then at the age of 12 became a teacher. For about a year he next worked as a farm helper, but at 15 he returned to teaching, privately for the most part, pursuing it as a career for the remainder of his life.

In his work Dalton used relatively simple equipment and has been accused of being "a very coarse experimenter." However, he had a gift for reasoning and for drawing correct conclusions from imperfect experiments. He himself attributed his success primarily to simple persistence.

Studies in Meteorology

Dalton's lifelong interest in meteorology did much to make that study a science. He began keeping records of the local weather conditions—atmospheric pressure, temperature, wind, and humidity—in 1787 and maintained them for 57 years until his death. During this time

John Dalton. (National Library of Medicine, Bethesda, Md.)

he recorded more than 200,000 values, using equipment which for the most part was made by him.

Dalton's interest in the weather gave him a special interest in mixtures of gases, and his earliest studies were concerned with atmospheric physics. The formulation of his law of partial pressures (Dalton's law) was announced in 1803. It defined the pressure of a mixture of gases as the sum of the pressures exerted by each component solely occupying the same space. In 1800 he studied the heating and cooling of gases resulting from compression and expansion, and in 1801 he formulated a law of the thermal expansion of gases. His work on water vapor concentration in the atmosphere, using a homemade dew-point hygrometer, and his 1804 study of the effect of temperature on the pressure of a vapor brought him international fame.

Developing the Atomic Theory

The formulation of the atomic theory, Dalton's greatest achievement, was developed gradually, almost inadvertently, through a series of observations resulting from his preoccupation with gases. It began with an attempt to explain why the constituents of a gaseous mixture remain homogeneously mixed instead of forming layers according to their density. The theory was first alluded to in a paper presented before the Manchester Literary and Philosophical Society in 1803 on the absorption of gases by water and other liquids. In the last section of the paper was the first table of atomic weights. The acceptance of his theory prompted Dalton to expand it further, and finally he published it in his *New System of Chemical Philosophy* (1808). Although William Higgins claimed priority over Dalton, the consensus is that Dalton conceived the idea that the atoms of different elements are distinguished by differences in their weight. As contrasted to others who may have vaguely glimpsed the principle, Dalton presented it as a universal and consistent fact and applied it to the explanation of chemical phenomena.

Other, less significant contributions were his pioneering investigation of thermal conductivity in liquids and his 1794 paper in which he discussed color blindness.

Later Life

Dalton lived a simple life, kept to the doctrines of his Quaker faith, and never married. During most of his life he had little money and was almost excessively economical; however, by tutoring and doing routine chemical work at low pay his few wants were met. He had no flair for lecturing: his voice was rather harsh, and he was inclined to be rather stiff and awkward in manner. He is said to have had no grace in conversation or in writing. Despite his lack of these social assets, he apparently lived a quite happy life and had many friends.

In 1810 Dalton refused an invitation to join the Royal Society but was finally elected in 1822 without his knowledge. As his fame grew, he received many honors, including a doctor's degree from Oxford in 1832, at which time he was presented to King William IV. For this occasion he had to wear the famous scarlet regalia of Oxford, which fortunately looked gray to his color-blind eyes and therefore was acceptable to him as an orthodox Quaker.

In 1837 he suffered a damaging stroke; the following year another left him with impaired speech. A final stroke came on the night of July 26, 1844.

Further Reading

John Dalton is listed in the Science study guide (VI, D, 1). From the time of the ancient Greeks until Dalton postulated his theory, an atomistic theory, held by EMPEDOCLES, DEMOCRITUS, and others, prevailed. This theory, however, was a philosophic rather than a scientific doctrine.

The most recent biography of Dalton is Frank Greenaway, *John Dalton and the Atom* (1966). See also L. J. Neville-Polley, *John Dalton* (1920), and Bernard Jaffe, *Crucibles* (1930). The background for Dalton's work, its influence, and biographical and historical material are contained in David Stephen L. Cardwell, ed., *John Dalton and the Progress of Science* (1968), which comprises essays presented by Dalton scholars at a conference marking the bicentenary of Dalton's birth. Dalton's scientific achievements are summarized in James R. Partington, *History of Chemistry*, vol. 3 (1962). A. L. Smyth, *John Dalton, 1766–1844: A Bibliography of Works by and about Him*, was published in 1966.

* * *

DALY / By Herbert H. Lang

American miner and business leader Marcus Daly (1841–1900) founded the Anaconda  Copper Mining Company and was a power in Montana politics.

Marcus Daly was born on Dec. 5, 1841, at Ballyjamesduff in County Cavan, Ireland. In 1856 he emigrated, settling first in New York City, where he found work as an errand boy and hostler. Five years later he moved to California and got a job as a mucker (clean-up man) in a gold mine. Despite his lack of education, Daly was intelligent and ambitious and soon had learned enough about good mining practice to become foreman of a mine on the Comstock Lode in Nevada. He remained in the Virginia City area from 1862 to 1868 and then moved to Utah, where he operated several silver mines for a firm of Salt Lake City bankers and mine owners.

Daly's big opportunity came when this firm sent him to Butte, Mont., to examine their mining claims. Deciding to remain in Montana, Daly purchased the Alice silver prospect from his employers. He sold the mine at a large profit, which he then used in 1880 to purchase a small silver deposit known as the Anaconda from a prospector named Michael Hickey. Historians have speculated whether Daly actually knew that the mine contained a huge body of copper or was just lucky in his investment. Daly soon acquired adjoining claims, then entered into a partnership with three other men who provided the capital to develop the Anaconda.

Marcus Daly. (Library of Congress)

Western mining centers. The hope of quick wealth attracted hordes of prospectors to western mining camps and towns after the discovery of gold in California in 1848. With luck and a minimum of equipment, a miner could "strike it rich," and many did. But when mining came to require large capital investment, the independent miner gave way to companies like Daly's Anaconda Copper.

Daly's partners were not enthusiastic about a copper mine in Montana. It was too far from the copper market, the market was limited, and what there was of a market was already monopolized by Michigan miners. But Daly, anticipating a great expansion in the use of copper, gambled that—with large-scale production—he could compete successfully with eastern mining interests. The rapid, phenomenal growth of Anaconda attests to Daly's business acumen.

From copper mining Daly branched out into related enterprises—banking, lumbering, and coal mining. He founded the town of Anaconda, constructed water and power facilities, went into ranching, bred racehorses, developed fruit orchards, built the largest smelter in the world, and constructed a railroad from Anaconda to Butte.

Daly also established a newspaper, the *Anaconda Standard*, which he used to further his political objectives. Although he personally sought no public office, he did finance the campaigns of Democrats for seats in the state and national legislatures. He also waged an expensive but unsuccessful fight to make Anaconda the state capital; Helena won the coveted prize by a margin of only a few thousand votes. But above all, Daly's political activities were directed toward frustrating the political ambitions of his archrival in copper mining, William Andrews Clark.

Until 1894 the Anaconda was operated as a partnership. Then the partners incorporated as the Anaconda Mining Company. When a Rothschild syndicate bought one partner's share of the property in 1895, the company reorganized as the Anaconda Copper Mining Company. In 1899 Standard Oil purchased Anaconda. Through all these changes Daly continued to serve as president of the company.

On Nov. 12, 1900, after a lengthy illness, Daly died in New York City. He was remembered as charitable, generous, and fair. His memory of his beginnings as an immigrant and a humble miner enabled him to maintain good relations with his workers. Anaconda had no labor disturbances so long as Daly remained at the helm.

Further Reading

Marcus Daly is listed in the American History study guide (VII, C, 3). His competitor was William Andrews CLARK. The man who gave his name to the famous Comstock Lode was Henry COMSTOCK.

There is no biography of Daly, but material on his career may be found in Federal Writer's Program, *Copper Camp, Stories of the World's Greatest Mining Town: Butte, Montana* (1943); Isaac F. Marcosson, *Anaconda* (1957); and K. Ross Toole, *Montana: An Uncommon Land* (1959).

DALZEL / By Maynard W. Swanson

The Scottish slave trader Archibald Dalzel (1740–1811) was the author of the famous and authoritative "History of Dahomy," which, though written in defense of the slave trade, dealt seriously with the traditions of that country.

Archibald Dalzel (Dalziel until 1778) was born at Kirkilston on Oct. 23, 1740, the oldest of four brothers and one sister. Trained as a surgeon, he saw medical service in the Royal Navy during the Seven Years War but failed to enter private practice afterward. After several false starts he became a surgeon for the Committee of Merchants Trading to Africa (the African Committee). Sent to Anomabu in 1763, he was soon slave-trading on his own account, suppressing his initial qualms with the lucrative prospects of his new career.

From 1763 to 1778 Dalzel enjoyed steadily increasing success. In 1767 he was made director of the English fort at Whydah on the Slave Coast, main port of the kingdom of Dahomey, where he prospered, netting up to £1,000 a year, until he decided to retire to England. He arrived in London in 1771; his profits, however, had been inadequate, and he turned again to slaving, at first in partnership and then independently as the owner of three ships and a budding plantation in Florida. By 1778 Dalzel fancied himself ready to become a gentleman planter at Kingston, Jamaica, when he and practically his entire

wealth were seized by a privateer while en route to England, where he arrived bankrupt.

Out of humiliation he changed his family name to Dalzel. He spent the next 13 years in irregular and often bizarre employments, by turns a candidate for the civil service, a pirate, a bookseller, and a Spanish wine merchant, failing in all and never, it seems, considering seriously the medical profession for which he was at least indifferently qualified. He then became a lobbyist for the slave-trading interests against the abolitionist movement in the 1780s. This brought him once more to the favorable notice of the African Committee, who in 1791 appointed him governor of their West African headquarters at Cape Coast Castle.

From 1792 until 1802 Dalzel labored energetically, yet in the end unsuccessfully, to restore the revenues of a declining company. Dalzel's governorship was a personal failure, as all his ventures had been, and he was still a poor man upon his retirement in 1802.

"History of Dahomy"

Archibald Dalzel died bankrupt in 1811, but the events and circumstances of his disappointed life were lightened by a conspicuous achievement: his great book, *History of Dahomy*. Recognized since his time as a work of literary merit and intellectual power, it appeared in 1793 and was an unusual event for the 18th century, given the Enlightenment's scorn for the non-European past.

Dalzel conceived and wrote his book as an intellectual and moral defense of the slave trade. Notwithstanding this aspect of the work, his history continues to receive

Archibald Dalzel. (Bulloz)

respect for its general accuracy, and recognition for its value as a colorful supplement to African traditions, because it deals seriously and with acute observation with the one state of the West African interior with which Europeans had direct contact over the entire course of its history.

Further Reading

Archibald Dalzel is listed in the Africa study guide (VI, B, 1). Another slave trader with literary ambitions was Theodore CANOT.

Elizabeth Donnan's classic *Documents Illustrative of the History of the Slave Trade to America* (4 vols., 1930–1935; repr. 1965) prints Dalzel's testimony on the slave trade to the Committee of the Privy Council in 1789. Dalzel's *History of Dahomy* (1793; new imp. 1967) contains an introduction by John D. Fage, who reviews Dalzel's career and gives him credit, despite Dalzel's antiabolitionist intent, as a historian of that African kingdom. The best account of the rise of Dahomey is I. A. Akinjogbin, *Dahomey and Its Neighbors, 1708–1818* (1967). Akinjogbin disagrees with Dalzel's and Robert Norris's theories of Dahomean motives for expansion. Dalzel gave, nonetheless, as Akinjogbin himself asserts, the best single account of Dahomey in the 18th century. Further mention of Dalzel's career is in John D. Hargreaves, *West Africa: The Former French States* (1967).

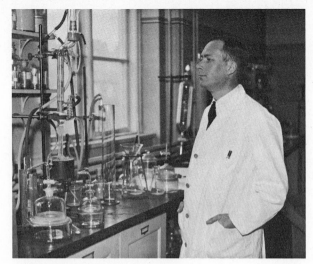

Henrik Dam in his laboratory. (Royal Danish Ministry of Foreign Affairs, Copenhagen)

DAM / By E. Ashworth Underwood

The Danish biochemist Carl Peter Henrik Dam (born 1895) shared the Nobel Prize in Physiology or Medicine for his discovery of vitamin K.

Henrik Dam (pronounced däm), the son of Emil Dam, an apothecary, was born in Copenhagen on Feb. 21, 1895. He graduated in chemistry at the Polytechnic Institute, Copenhagen, in 1920 and then held two instructor's posts in chemistry and biochemistry. In 1928 he was appointed assistant professor of biochemistry in the University of Copenhagen. In 1929 he was appointed associate professor, and in 1941 professor. In 1934 he graduated as a doctor of science of that university. While holding a Rockefeller Fellowship he worked at Freiburg (1932–1933) and at Zurich (1935).

In 1928 Dam started to work on the cholesterol metabolism of chicks. He fed them a practically sterol-free artificial diet to which vitamins A and D had been added. He proved that, contrary to the current view, chicks could synthesize cholesterol. But he also found that some chicks developed internal hemorrhages and delayed blood coagulation. In 1932 scientists in California claimed that this disease was due to the absence of vitamin C from the diet, but Dam showed that it was not

cured by the addition of ascorbic acid (that is, pure vitamin C) to the diet. He also demonstrated that a diet rich in cereals and seeds prevented the disease, and in 1934 he announced that it was due to the absence from the diet of a hitherto unrecognized factor. He then found this factor to be fat-soluble, and in 1935 he announced that it was a new vitamin, which he designated vitamin K. The Californian workers rapidly confirmed his findings.

In 1939 pure vitamin K was first synthesized—from green leaves—by Dam, Paul Karrer, and their coworkers, and independently by E. A. Doisy and L. F. Fieser. In 1940 Doisy prepared from putrefied fish meal a similar vitamin, which he called K_2, and the original vitamin was thereafter called K_1. By 1939 Dam had shown that the blood of chicks fed on a vitamin K–free diet was very deficient in prothrombin, which is normally present and essential to clotting. He established a method of estimation, defined the vitamin K unit, and found the best sources to be green leaves and tomatoes.

In 1938 Dam and Glavind found that persons showing the cholemic bleeding tendency, which can cause complications in operations for obstructive jaundice, had vitamin K deficiency. In 1939–1940 Dam and his coworkers demonstrated that a prothrombin deficiency in newborn babies, causing them to bleed easily, could be effectively treated by administering vitamin K to the infant or to the mother before the birth.

In 1940, while Dam was lecturing in the United States, Germany invaded Denmark. As he was unable to return home until after the war, he worked during the war years at the Woods Hole Marine Biological Laboratories, at the University of Rochester, and at the Rockefeller Institute. During his absence he was appointed to the Copenhagen chair of biochemistry (1941), and shared the Nobel Prize with Doisy in 1943.

In 1937 Dam showed that the absence of vitamin E from the diet of chicks caused excessive exudation of plasma from the capillaries. He subsequently showed that the diet had also to be deficient in certain fatty acids. Much of his later work dealt with fatty acids, and he was for a period (1956–1963) director of the division of biochemistry of the Danish Fat Research Institute.

In addition to his Nobel Prize, Dam's many other honors included the Honorary Fellowship of the Royal Society of Edinburgh.

Further Reading

Henrik Dam is listed in the Science study guide (VII, G, 2). The composition of vitamin C was discovered by Albert von SZENT-GYÖRGYI.

A biography of Dam is in *Nobel Lectures, Physiology or Medicine, 1942–1962* (1964), which also contains his Nobel Lecture. A discussion of his work is in Theodore Sourkes, *Nobel Prize Winners in Medicine and Physiology, 1901–1965* (1966).

*   *   *

FATHER DAMIEN / By Hans Hoekendijk

The Belgian missionary Father Damien (1840–1889) is known for his work among the lepers on Molokai in the Hawaiian Islands.

Father Damien at 33. (Library of Congress)

Father Damien (pronounced dà-myäN′) was born Joseph de Veuster in Tremeloo, Belgium, on Jan. 3, 1840, of pious and sturdy Flemish peasant stock. In 1860 he joined his brother in the Contemplative Congregation of the Sacred Heart of Jesus and Mary. After he experienced a vision of St. Francis Xavier, he was convinced that he had a missionary vocation. Without special preparation he substituted for his brother in a missionary party sailing for Hawaii in 1863. After arrival there he was ordained a priest and was then known as Father Damien.

After regular work in a parish, where he proved to be a true priest-workman, the great challenge of Father Damien's life came. He heard about the island of Molokai with its leprosarium, where incurable lepers were sent. He decided that these people "in darkness" needed a resident priest and volunteered for this service. "I am bent on devoting my life to the lepers," he said.

With his creative imagination the apostle brought new breath of hope to these people without hope. His down-to-earth Christian humanism led him to attempt the remaking of man's life even in the despair of Molokai, and he worked with the lepers to build houses, schools, and meeting places. At the same time he studied new ways of treating lepers. He also offered a context of celebration; he encouraged festivity to provide hope in the experience of decay and frustration. One of Father Damien's key words was participation. He had only intermittent coworkers from outside, and instead he recruited and trained coworkers from the lepers. The "prayer leaders" were the members of his team ministry, and his "model parish" eventually grew to become a sign of hope.

Father Damien received the highest Hawaiian decoration for his pioneering work with lepers, and his work received great publicity. He also earned a number of enemies because of his stubbornness and lack of organizational ability. In spite of many obstacles he persisted in his work even after 1878, when he was sure that he himself had leprosy. In one of his last letters he wrote, "My face and my hands are already decomposing, but the good Lord is calling me to keep Easter with Himself." He died on April 15, 1889. Above his grave on Molokai his friends set a black marble cross with the inscription, "Damien de Veuster, Died a Martyr of Charity." His body was reburied in Louvain in 1936.

Further Reading

Father Damien is listed in the Religion study guide (I, P, 2, k). He was influenced by the earlier missionary activities of St. FRANCIS XAVIER.

Of the many biographies of Father Damien, a popular, although eulogistic, one is Omer Englebert, *The Hero of Molokai: Father Damien, Apostle of the Lepers* (1955). See also John Farrow, *Damien the Leper* (1937).

*   *   *

DAMPIER / By Gordon Rimmer

The English privateer and author William Dampier (1652–1715) explored the Western

Australian coastline and stimulated interest in the Pacific through popular travel books.

William Dampier was born the son of a Somerset farmer in June 1652. He sailed to Newfoundland and the East Indies while still a boy and took part in the Third Dutch War (1672–1674). After a brief sojourn in Jamaica as undermanager of a plantation, he joined the buccaneers of the Caribbean in Capt. Morgan's heyday. In 1686 Capt. Swan of the *Cygnet*, in which Dampier was sailing, decided to seek prizes in the Pacific before returning to England. After spending 6 months in the Philippines, Swan's crew seized the ship and cruised in Far Eastern waters between China and Australia. Dampier accordingly spent the summer of 1688 at King Sound in Western Australia. After being marooned on one of the Nicobar Islands, he traveled by native canoe to Sumatra and served as a gunner at Bencoelen before returning to England.

Dampier recorded details of his amazing adventures along with navigational data in a diary on which he based *A New Voyage round the World* (1697) and *Voyages and Descriptions* (1699). Impressed with his work, the English Admiralty commissioned him with the rank of captain to command an expedition to explore the Australian coastline. He reached Shark Bay, Western Australia, in August 1699, and using Tasman's charts, he sailed up the coast for a month seeking an estuary. After revictualing at Timor, he proceeded along the north coast of New Guinea and discovered New Britain but abandoned plans to explore the east coast of Australia because his ship, the H.M.S. *Roebuck*, was in poor condition. On the way home, the *Roebuck* was lost off Ascension Island, and the crew were rescued by returning East India men.

A court-martial in 1702 found Dampier unfit to command a naval vessel. During the next 4 years he led an unsuccessful privateering expedition in the South Seas. Between 1708 and 1711 he again sailed around the world as pilot for Capt. Woodes Rogers, a privateer sponsored by Bristol merchants. It was on this voyage that Alexander Selkirk, who had previously been marooned by the crew of a ship under Dampier's command, was picked up at one of the Juan Fernández Islands in the South Pacific. Dampier died in London in March 1715 before receiving his share of the expedition's spoils.

Further Reading

William Dampier is listed in the Australia and New Zealand study guide (I). Other explorers of Australian waters were Abel TASMAN and James COOK.

An account of Dampier which notes both his achievements and defects is Christopher Lloyd, *William Dampier* (1966). See also Clennell Wilkinson, *Dampier: Explorer and Buccaneer* (1929). There is an exciting account of buccaneers in the Caribbean and Pacific in P. K. Kemp and Christopher Lloyd, *The Brethren of the Coast* (1960).

C. A. **DANA** / By Harvey Levenstein

The American journalist Charles Anderson Dana (1819–1897), as editor of the "New York Sun" in the late 19th century, created the first modern newspaper.

Charles A. Dana was born on Aug. 8, 1819, in the small country town of Hinsdale, N.H., the son of an unsuccessful country storekeeper. When the family moved to upstate New York, Charles went to work in an uncle's general store in Buffalo. During the Panic of 1837, the store failed, and at the age of 18 Dana found himself with $200 saved but without a job. Luckily, he had spent much of his youth educating himself and had learned enough Greek and Latin to pass the entrance exams for Harvard College.

Dana attended Harvard for 2 years but was forced to leave because of failing eyesight and lack of money. An interest in the ideas of Charles Fourier, the French utopian socialist, led Dana to join the major Fourierist experi-

William Dampier, painted about 1697. (National Portrait Gallery, London)

Charles A. Dana. (Courtesy of the American Museum of Natural History)

mental community in the United States, Brook Farm in West Roxbury, Mass. Dana lived and worked there happily for 5 years until the community was disbanded after a fire. Because he had done some writing at Brook Farm, Dana gravitated toward journalism and in 1847 became city editor of Horace Greeley's *New York Tribune.*

In 1862, after a 15-year association, Dana and Greeley had a major falling-out and Dana was fired. The Civil War was raging, and Dana went to work for the Union government in various capacities, rising to assistant secretary of war under Edwin Stanton. He left the government in 1865 to become editor of a short-lived Chicago paper and then raised enough money among prominent Republicans in New York City to buy the failing *New York Sun.*

As editor, Dana rapidly transformed the *Sun.* Before the Civil War the prime "news" function of a newspaper had been to promulgate the editor's political opinions, but the dramatic firsthand accounts of battles during the Civil War had brought the news correspondent to prominence. In the *Sun* this trend was reinforced. Although Dana continued to expound his political beliefs on the editorial page, the emphasis in the paper became accurate, lively news stories. This approach contrasted with that of most American newspapers, which continued to imitate the turgid, third-person, literary style of the *London Times.* Dana also began running "human-interest" stories, which focused on the pathos or humor in the lives of ordinary people. Because of their popularity,

human-interest stories became a hallmark of modern journalism throughout much of the world.

Dana's *Sun* was an immediate success, and it dominated New York journalism for about 15 years. However, his erratic political views worked against the newspaper. He was generally a Republican and continually attacked the New York City Democratic machine, but in national politics he frequently could not bring himself to support the Republican candidate. His failure to support either presidential candidate in 1880 cost him considerable circulation and prestige. Shortly thereafter, the founding of Joseph Pulitzer's popular *New York World* cost even more in circulation. When Dana died in 1897, the *Sun* remained "a newspaperman's newspaper," but it had been displaced for the man in the street by the more sensational representatives of the new "yellow journalism," the Hearst and Pulitzer papers.

Further Reading

Charles A. Dana is listed in the American History study guide (VII, G, 5). Horace GREELEY and Edwin Lawrence GODKIN were other New York journalists.

James Harrison Wilson, *The Life of Charles A. Dana* (1907), is a sympathetic biography, but Charles J. Rosebault, *When Dana Was the Sun* (1931), is livelier and more colorful. The best serious study of Dana's ideas is Candace Stone, *Dana and the Sun* (1938). There are interesting sections on Dana in Frank M. O'Brien, *The Story of the Sun, New York, 1833–1928* (1918; new ed. 1928); Willard Grosvenor Bleyer, *Main Currents in the History of American Journalism* (1927); and Kenneth Stewart and John Tebbel, *Makers of Modern Journalism* (1952).

R. H. DANA, JR. / By Robert F. Lucid

American author and lawyer Richard Henry Dana, Jr. (1815–1882), wrote one of the most persistently popular nonfiction narratives in American letters, "Two Years before the Mast." He was also an adviser in the formation and direction of the Free Soil party.

Son of Richard Henry Dana, Sr. (1787–1879), the Massachusetts poet and editor, the younger Dana distinguished himself in 1834, when he abruptly left the security of Harvard undergraduate life and shipped round Cape Horn to California on a tiny hide-trading brig. He returned 2 years later, completed his studies, and in 1840 was admitted to the bar. In the same year *Two Years before the Mast* was published by Harper and Brothers, and though the publisher had deftly lifted the copyright (paying Dana just $250), the author hoped that the book would at least bring him some law practice.

Richard Henry Dana, Jr. (Library of Congress)

Dana's hopes were realized—indeed his office filled with sailors and he became known as the "Seaman's Champion"—and he eventually shaped an impressive legal career. Still, the fact that his publisher realized $50,000 from the book did at times move Dana to complaint. He comforted himself with the knowledge that if he had lost money he had gained fame. The book was embraced by all factions—reformers, temperance crusaders, and romantic lovers of the sea, who saw the oceans as at least comparable to the prairies when it came to charting a frontier to explore. Since the day of its publication the book has never been out of print.

Years later, however, Dana wrote to his son: "My life has been a failure compared with what I might and ought to have done. My great success—my book—was a boy's work, done before I came to the Bar." There were other books: *The Seaman's Friend* (1841), a manual and handbook for sailors; and *To Cuba and Back* (1859), an interesting account of a vacation voyage.

But Dana's real commitments were to the law, where he finally prospered, and to politics, where he finally failed. Celebrated as the legal champion of fugitive black slaves, Dana consistently missed opportunities for high public office, even within the Free Soil party he had helped create. In 1878 he packed up and left for Europe, furious that his appointment as minister to England had failed of approval in the Senate.

In Europe Dana joined some of the brilliant expatriate circles then dominating Rome and seemed to find some peace. He called it "a dream of life," but even the dream ended, in January 1882, and he was buried in the same Italian graveyard that contained the remains of John Keats and Percy Bysshe Shelley.

Further Reading

Richard Henry Dana, Jr., is listed in the Literature study guide (I, C, 1, f). The most powerful American writer about the sea was of this era, too—Herman MELVILLE.

Charles Francis Adams, Jr., *Richard Henry Dana* (1890), and Samuel Shapiro, *Richard Henry Dana, Jr., 1815–1882* (1961), are recommended studies. Of interest also are two editions of *Two Years before the Mast*, one edited by Dana's son, R. H. Dana III (1911), and the other by John H. Kemble (1964). See also *The Journal of Richard Henry Dana* (3 vols., 1968). Background information is in D. H. Lawrence, *Studies in Classic American Literature* (1923; repr. 1964).

DANDOLO / By John H. Geerken

The Venetian doge Enrico Dandolo (ca. 1107–1205) made Venice the largest colonial power in all of Christendom.

Although Enrico Dandolo (pronounced dän′dō-lō) held a number of public offices throughout his life, it was not until he became doge in 1192 at the age of 85 that his career acquired historical impor-

Enrico Dandolo, a painting by the school of Tintoretto in the Doges' Palace, Venice. (Anderson-Alinari)

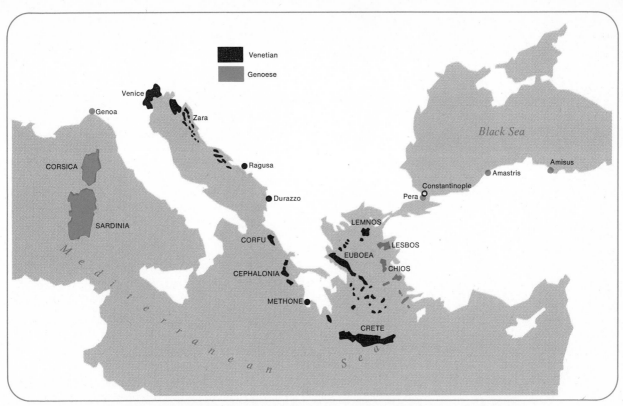

The commercial empires of Venice and Genoa in the 13th century. Venice and Genoa long struggled for control of the seaborne trade between the East and Europe. After its defeat of Genoa in 1380, Venice was indisputably mistress of the Mediterranean.

tance. In his first years as doge he defeated an armada from Pisa. He subsequently sent a powerful squadron to the canal of Otranto to break a blockade which the Pisans, aided by the king of Sicily, had set up to injure Venetian commerce.

Dandolo's most significant political achievement was his contriving to have Venetian ships hired for the Fourth Crusade (1202). Venice's direct participation with a powerful fleet was contingent upon its receiving half of the spoils of victory. But since the doge had not received full payment in advance for transporting the French cavalry, he refused to put them aboard, and the crusade did not take place. Instead, Dandolo induced the forces to attack the city of Zara, then in rebellion against Venice. And for thus turning Christian against Christian, he and all Venetians were excommunicated by the Pope.

After the bloody defeat of Zara the French crusaders wintered there, thus providing Dandolo with a ready body of men. These he employed in alliance with Alexis Angelus, son of Isaac II, the emperor of Constantinople, against Isaac's brother Alexis III, who had deposed and blinded the Emperor. In return, Alexis Angelus promised both the assistance of Byzantine forces in the crusade and the unification of the Greek and Latin churches. Dandolo moved with the crusaders against Constantinople. The siege of the city provoked an internal revolution which ousted Alexis III and effected the return of the Emperor and his son Alexis Angelus. But when the crusaders sought the union of the Greek and Latin churches, a second revolution took place which led to the imprisonment of the aged emperor and the death of his son.

In the face of this impasse Dandolo encouraged the crusaders to reconquer the city for themselves; and in April 1204 Constantinople fell to the Latins, who established a Latin empire on the ruins of the Greek one. Although Dandolo, who had personally directed all operations, was offered the crown of the new empire, he resolutely declined it, contenting himself with the enormous advantages which the conquest had brought to his city. From April 1204 until his death little is recorded of Dandolo's activities. He died on June 14, 1205.

Further Reading

Enrico Dandolo is listed in the European History study guide (II, H, 1, b; II, M, 4). Pope INNOCENT III launched the Fourth Crusade.

Margaret Oliphant devotes a colorful and sympathetic chapter to Dandolo in *The Makers of Venice: Doges, Conquerors, Painters and Men of Letters* (1887). Also useful are Steven Runciman, *A History of the Crusades* (3 vols., 1951–1954), and Ernle Bradford, *The Sundered Cross: The Story of the Fourth Crusade* (1967).

✻   ✻   ✻

DANIELS / By Harvey Levenstein

The American journalist and statesman Josephus Daniels (1862–1948) was secretary of the Navy in Woodrow Wilson's Cabinet and served as Franklin D. Roosevelt's ambassador to Mexico.

Josephus Daniels was born in Washington, N.C., on May 18, 1862. After his father was killed in the Civil War, his mother moved to Wilson, where he was raised and sent to school. In his early teens he developed an interest in journalism and upon graduating from high school became a partner in, and then the owner-editor of, the local weekly newspaper. He studied law at the University of North Carolina and eventually moved to Raleigh, where he edited two papers.

A dedicated and active Democrat, Daniels worked in Washington, D.C., in 1893 as chief clerk in the Department of the Interior. Upon returning to Raleigh, he bought the *News and Observer* and soon established himself as an influential man in the state. In national politics Daniels supported William Jennings Bryan, and during Bryan's three unsuccessful bids for the presidency Daniels stumped throughout the country on his behalf.

In 1911 Daniels supported Woodrow Wilson and was appointed the new president's secretary of the Navy. As his assistant secretary, Daniels chose an aristocratic young New York politician named Franklin D. Roosevelt.

Daniels had little previous experience with the Navy, but he did have some set beliefs about how American institutions should be run. He ran afoul of the officer corps by trying to abolish some of their traditional privileges and institute more humane and democratic treatment of enlisted men. A devout Methodist and a teetotaler, he is perhaps most famous in the Navy for having banned alcoholic beverages from ships. He served as secretary of the Navy until 1921, when the defeat of the Democrats sent him back to North Carolina to his lifelong love, journalism.

Roosevelt and Daniels had had some differences in the Navy Department (Roosevelt tended to sympathize much more with the Navy brass), but they had ended their association in Washington with deep mutual respect. Thus, when Roosevelt became president in 1933, he rewarded Daniels with the ambassadorship to Mexico. This aroused considerable consternation in Mexico, for Daniels had supervised the occupation of Veracruz during the Mexican Revolution in 1914.

Daniels however, turned out to be an ambassador with charm, good sense, and, above all, a deep concern for the Mexican people. In 1938, when the Mexican government nationalized the foreign-owned oil industry, Daniels argued for U.S. government restraint against Secretary of State Cordell Hull and the spokesmen for the oil interests, who demanded drastic retaliatory action. Daniels believed that the nationalization was an act of nationalism, not of communism, and that the long-run economic benefits to the United States, in terms of a higher Mexican standard of living and increased purchases from the United States, would far outweigh the short-run losses.

In 1941 Daniels retired to Raleigh and from there, even at an advanced age, continued to keep in touch with Mexican affairs and Mexican friends. He died in Raleigh on Jan. 15, 1948.

Further Reading

Josephus Daniels is listed in the American History study guide (VIII, A, 2; VIII, F, 5). During his long tenure in the Cabinet of Woodrow WILSON, Daniels served with Newton D. BAKER, Robert LANSING, and A. Mitchell PALMER.

In his later years Daniels wrote a long, rambling autobiography; the three volumes are *Tar Heel Editor* (1939), *The Wilson Era: Years of War and After, 1917–1923* (1946), and *Shirt-sleeve Diplomat* (1947). *The Cabinet Diaries of Josephus Daniels: 1913–1921*, edited by E. David Cronon (1963), is a useful source on both Daniels and the Wilson administration. The best single book on Daniels is Cronon's *Josephus Daniels in Mexico* (1960), which concentrates on his time as ambassador. Jonathan Daniels, *The End of Innocence* (1954), and Joseph L. Morrison, *Josephus Daniels: The Small-d democrat* (1966), are flattering portraits.

Josephus Daniels. (Library of Congress)

D'ANNUNZIO / By Oscar Büdel

The Italian poet and patriot Gabriele D'Annunzio (1863–1938) was one of the last major representatives of fin-de-siècle decadence in European literature.

Gabriele D'Annunzio (pronounced dän-nōōn′tsyō) was born on March 12, 1863, at Pescara of well-to-do parents. He was educated at the Convitto Cicognini of Prato; he then attended the University of Rome but did not take a degree. Of small physique, bald at an early age, he nevertheless lived in Rome the life of a dandy and ladies' man. In 1883 he married the duchess Maria Hardouin di Gallese, with whom he had three sons. His daughter Renata (the Sirenetta of the novel *Notturno*) was born out of wedlock by a married woman, Maria Gravina Cruyllas, one of his many companions.

In 1910 D'Annunzio was forced to sell La Capponcina, a sumptuous villa near Florence, where he had lived since 1899. He moved to France, settling finally in Arcachon. In 1915 he returned to Italy to campaign for its entry into World War I. He made famous speeches at Quarto dei Mille and from the steps of Rome's Capitoline Hill. An active participant in the war, he flew over Trieste (1915) and Vienna (1918) and lost the sight of an eye after a bad landing. In 1919 he and his legionnaires occupied Fiume, thus anticipating its later union with It-

aly. D'Annunzio's rightist leanings made him sympathetic to the Fascist regime, which in 1924 conferred on him the title of Principe di Montenevoso. The government also gave him a villa, Il Vittoriale, on the Lake of Garda, where he resided until his death on March 1, 1938.

Literary Works

One of the most prolific writers of modern Italian literature, D'Annunzio tried all genres with varying success. His accomplished virtuosity in technical matters is evident primarily in his poetry, where the search for new sensual experiences is one of his prime concerns. He also glorified heroic deeds in his patriotic poetry (*Odi navali*, 1892–1893). A synthesis and symphonic repetition of his earlier poetry is evident in the cycle *Laudi del cielo, del mare, della terra e degli eroi* (1903–1904; Hymns of the Sky, Sea, Earth and Heroes).

D'Annunzio collected the best of his short stories in the volume *Novelle della Pescara* (1902). As a story teller, he owes much to Gustave Flaubert and Guy de Maupassant. His novels are of an extreme autobiographical nature. He is Andrea Sperelli in *Il piacere* (1889; *The Child of Pleasure*), Tullio Hermil in *L'innocente* (1892; *The Intruder*), and Giorgio Aurispa in *Trionfo della morte* (1894; *Triumph of Death*). *Il fuoco* (1900; *The Flame of Life*) depicts his relationship to Eleonora Duse. Among D'Annunzio's numerous plays the best are *Francesca da Rimini* (1902) and *La figlia di Jorio* (1904; *The Daughter of Jorio*).

Further Reading

Gabriele D'Annunzio is listed in the Literature study guide (III, I, 3). He was strongly influenced by the philosophy of Friedrich NIETZSCHE.

Two major critical biographies of D'Annunzio in English are Tom Antongini, *D'Annunzio* (1938), and Anthony R. E. Rhodes, *The Poet as Superman: A Life of Gabriele D'Annunzio* (1959). On D'Annunzio's relationship with Eleonora Duse see Bertita L. Harding, *Age Cannot Wither: The Story of Duse and D'Annunzio* (1947), and Frances Winwar, *Wingless Victory: A Biography of Gabriele D'Annunzio and Eleonora Duse* (1956).

Gabriele D'Annunzio. (Italian Cultural Institute)

DANQUAH / By W. Scott Thompson

Joseph B. Danquah (1895–1965) was a Ghanaian political leader and a principal founder of the Gold Coast nationalist movement. As a scholar, he sought to accommodate the best of his country's tribal past to modernity.

Joseph B. Danquah (pronounced dän′kwä) was born in December 1895 into the most prominent family in Ghana, the Ofori-Attas. In 1915 Danquah became secretary to his elder brother, Nana Sir

Ofori-Atta, the paramount chief of Akim Abuakwa. In 1921 Danquah went to London for a higher education and by 1927 he had finished his doctorate with the thesis *The Moral End as Moral Excellence*. He also studied law, which became his principal mainstay and led him to politics in opposition to the British rulers.

Independence and Opposition

After World War II, nationalist sentiment grew. Danquah was instrumental in founding the United Gold Coast Convention (UGCC), the elite party from which sprang all successive independence movements, until Kwame Nkrumah broke with Danquah in 1949 to found his own party. Danquah spent the rest of his life fighting Nkrumah and providing defense for Nkrumah's opponents. But Danquah won neither in the 1954 or 1956 parliamentary elections nor in the presidential election of 1960, in which he polled only 10 percent of the vote.

Danquah's last 5 years is a story of personal courage with few parallels in modern African history. He had neither the inclination nor the ability to rally his countrymen against the growing tyranny, but always he spoke out and encouraged the younger opposition members. After a railroad strike in 1961, which very nearly toppled Nkrumah's regime, Danquah was detained without charges. He was released in June 1962, but like few others the experience did not silence him. He hung onto his one semiofficial position as president of the Bar Association, and when Nkrumah tried to intimidate—and threatened

to overthrow—the popular government of Sylvanus Olympio in Togo, Danquah characteristically protested both the legality and morality of the Ghanaian moves.

After an attempt on Nkrumah's life in January 1964, Danquah was again detained. The notion that Danquah was implicated in the assassination plot was nowhere taken seriously. But Danquah, and all he symbolized, did indeed threaten Nkrumah; and, no doubt, Nkrumah's insecurity explains the isolation and near-starvation diet of Danquah's last year. His only card left was his life, which he unwittingly played perfectly. In response to appeals from Bertrand Russell, Nkrumah planned to release Danquah dramatically to increase support, but before he could do so, Danquah died of heart failure on Feb. 8, 1965. No event did more to silence Nkrumah's remaining defenders or to isolate the regime internationally. A year after Danquah's death Nkrumah's regime was overthrown.

Literary Output

Danquah's scholarly contributions spread throughout his life, and his political career must be seen in terms of his self-identification as a scholar proud of his past. Danquah's preoccupation with Christianity and the need to adapt it to local tradition led to his book *The Akan Doctrine of God* (1944). His historical research in the 1930s led him to propose that on independence the Gold Coast be renamed Ghana, after the early African empire. Earlier research led to *Gold Coast: Akan Laws and Customs and the Akim Abuakwa Constitution* (1928). His play, *The Third Woman*, appeared in 1943.

Further Reading

Joseph B. Danquah is listed in the African study guide (IX, B, 3). George PADMORE, the most prominent ideologist of African nationalism, called Danquah the doyen of Gold Coast politicians, even though Padmore was the mentor of Kwame NKRUMAH.

Danquah's career may be traced in David Kimble, *A Political History of Ghana: The Rise of Gold Coast Nationalism, 1850–1928* (1963; rev. ed. 1965), and Dennis Austin, *Politics in Ghana, 1946–1960* (1964).

Joseph B. Danquah. (Ghana Information Service, Accra)

DANTE / By Mark Musa

The Italian poet Dante Alighieri (1265–1321) wrote "The Divine Comedy," the greatest poetic composition of the Christian Middle Ages and the first masterpiece of world literature written in a modern European vernacular.

Dante (pronounced dän′tā) lived in a restless age of political conflict between popes and emperors and of strife within the Italian city-states, particularly Florence, which was torn between rival factions. Spiritually and culturally too, there were signs of change.

With the diffusion of Aristotle's physical and metaphysical works, there came the need for harmonizing his philosophy with the truth of Christianity, and Dante's mind was attracted to philosophical speculation. In Italy, Giotto, who had freed himself from the Byzantine tradition, was reshaping the art of painting, while the Tuscan poets were beginning to experiment with new forms of expression. Dante may be considered the greatest and last medieval poet, at least in Italy, where barely a generation later the first humanists were to spring up.

Dante was born in Florence, the son of Bellincione d'Alighiero. His family descended, he tells us, from "the noble seed" of the Roman founders of Florence and was noble also by virtue of honors bestowed on it later. His great-grandfather Cacciaguida had been knighted by Emperor Conrad III and died about 1147 while fighting in the Second Crusade. As was usual for the minor nobility, Dante's family was Guelph, in opposition to the Ghibelline party of the feudal nobility which strove to dominate the communes under the protection of the emperor.

Although his family was reduced to modest circumstances, Dante was able to live as a gentleman and to pursue his studies. It is probable that he attended the Franciscan school of Sta Croce and the Dominican school of S. Maria Novella in Florence, where he gained the knowledge of Thomistic doctrine and of the mysticism that was to become the foundation of his philosophical culture. It is known from his own testimony that in order to perfect his literary style he also studied with Brunetto Latini, the Florentine poet and master of rhetoric. Perhaps encouraged by Brunetto in his pursuit of learning, Dante traveled to Bologna, where he probably attended the well-known schools of rhetoric.

A famous portrait of the young Dante done by Giotto hangs in the Palazzo del Podestà in Florence. We also have the following description of him left us by the author Giovanni Boccaccio: "Our poet was of medium height, and his face was long and his nose aquiline and his jaws were big, and his lower lip stood out in such a way that it somewhat protruded beyond the upper one; his shoulders were somewhat curved, and his eyes large rather than small and of brown color, and his hair and beard were curled and black, and he was always melancholy and pensive."

Dante does not write of his family or marriage, but before 1283 his father died, and soon afterward, in accordance with his father's previous arrangements, he married the gentlewoman Gemma di Manetto Donati. She bore him several children, of whom two sons, Jacopo and Pietro, and a daughter, Antonia, are known.

Lyric Poetry

Dante began early in life to compose poetry, an art, he tells us, which he taught himself as a young man (*Vita nuova*, III, 9). Through his love lyrics he became known to other poets of Florence, and most important to him was his friendship with Guido Cavalcanti, which resulted from an exchange of sonnets.

Both Dante and Guido were concerned with the effects of love on the mind, particularly from a philosoph-

Dante, a portrait by Andrea del Castagno, in the Cenacolo di S. Apollonia, Florence. (Italian Cultural Institute, New York)

ical point of view; only Dante, however, began gradually to develop the idea that love could become the means of spiritual perfection. And while Guido was more interested in natural philosophy, Dante assiduously cultivated his knowledge of the Latin poets, particularly Virgil, whom he later called his guide and authority in the art of poetry.

During his youth Dante had known a young and noble Florentine woman whose grace and beauty so impressed him that in his poetry she became the idealized Beatrice, the "bringer of blessings," who seemed "a creature come from heaven to earth, A miracle manifest in reality" (*Vita nuova*, XXVI). She is believed to have been Bice, the daughter of Folco Portinari, and later the wife of Simone dei Bardi. Dante had seen her for the first time when both were in their ninth year; he had named her in a ballad among the 60 fairest women of Florence. But it was only later that Beatrice became the guide of his thoughts and emotions "toward that ideal perfection which is the goal of every noble mind," and the praise of her virtue and grace became the subject of his poetry.

When the young Beatrice died on June 8, 1290, Dante was overcome with grief but found consolation in thoughts of her glory in heaven. Although another woman succeeded briefly in winning Dante's love through her compassion, the memory of Beatrice soon aroused in him feelings of remorse and renewed his fidelity to her.

He was prompted to gather from among all his poems those which had been written in her honor or had some bearing on his love for her. This plan resulted in the small volume of poetry and prose, the *Vita nuova* (New Life), in which he copied from his "book of memory" only those past experiences belonging to his "new life"—a life made new through Beatrice. It follows Dante's own youthful life through three movements or stages in love, in which Beatrice's religious and spiritual significance becomes increasingly clear. At the same time it traces his poetic development from an early phase reminiscent of the Cavalcantian manner to a foreshadowing of *The Divine Comedy*. In the last prose chapter, which tells of a "miraculous vision," the poet speaks of the major work that he intends to write and the important role Beatrice will have in it: "If it be the wish of Him in whom all things flourish that my life continue for a few years, I hope to write of her that which has never been written of any other lady."

The *Vita nuova*, written between 1292 and 1294, is one of the first important examples of Italian literary prose. Its 31 poems, most of them sonnets symmetrically grouped around three canzoni, are only a small selection of Dante's lyric production. He wrote many other lyrics inspired by Beatrice which are not included in the *Vita nuova*; in addition there are verses written to other women and poems composed at different times in his life, representing a variety of forms and stylistic experiences.

Political Activities

Dante's literary interests did not isolate him from the events of his times. On the contrary, he was involved in the political life of Florence and deeply concerned about the state of Europe as a whole. In 1289 he had fought with the Florentine cavalry at the battle of Campaldino. In 1295 he inscribed himself in the guild of physicians and pharmacists (membership in a guild being a precondition for holding public office in Florence). He became a member of the people's council and served in various other capacities. For 2 months in 1300 he was one of the six priors of Florence, and in 1301 he was a member of the Council of the One Hundred.

In October 1301 Dante was sent in a delegation from the commune to Pope Boniface VIII, whose policies he openly opposed as constituting a threat to Florentine independence. During his absence the Blacks (one of the two opposing factions within the Guelph party) gained control of Florence. In the resulting banishment of the Whites, Dante was sentenced to exile in absentia (January 1302). Despite various attempts to regain admission to Florence—at first in an alliance of other exiles whose company he soon abandoned and later through his writing—he was never to enter his native city again.

Dante led the life of an exile, taking refuge first with Bartolommeo della Scala in Verona, and after a time of travel—to Bologna, through northern Italy, possibly also to Paris between 1307 and 1309—with Can Grande della Scala in Verona (1314). During this time his highest hopes were placed in Emperor Henry VII, who descend-

ed into Italy in 1310 to restore justice and order among the cities and to reunite church and state. When Henry VII, whose efforts proved fruitless, died in Siena in 1313, Dante lost every hope of restoring himself to an honorable position in Florence.

Minor Works

During these years of wandering Dante's studies were not interrupted. Indeed, he had hoped that in acquiring fame as a poet and philosopher he might also regain the favor of his fellow citizens. His study of Boethius and Cicero in Florence had already widened his philosophical horizons. After 1290 he had turned to the study of philosophy with such fervor that "in a short time, perhaps 30 months" he had begun "to be so keenly aware of her sweetness that the love of her drove away and destroyed every other thought." He read so much, it seems, that his eyes were weakened.

Two uncompleted treatises, *De vulgari eloquentia* (1303–1304) and the *Convivio* (1304–1307), belong to the early period of exile. At the same time, about 1306, he probably began to compose *The Divine Comedy*.

In *De vulgari eloquentia*, a theoretical treatise in Latin on the Italian vernacular, Dante intended to treat of all aspects of the spoken language, from the highest poetic expression to the most humble familiar speech. The first book is devoted to a discussion of dialects and the principles of poetic composition in the vulgar tongue; the second book treats specifically of the "illustrious" vulgar tongue used by certain excellent poets and declares that this noble form of expression is suitable only for the most elevated subjects, such as love, virtue, and war, and must be used in the form of the canzone.

The *Convivio* was intended to consist of 15 chapters: an introduction and 14 canzoni, with prose commentaries in Italian; but only 4 chapters were completed. The canzoni, which are the "meat" of the philosophical banquet while the prose commentaries are the "bread," appear to be written to a beautiful woman. But the prose commentaries interpret these poems as an allegorical exaltation of philosophy, inspired by the love of wisdom. Dante wished to glorify philosophy as the "mistress of his mind" and to treat subjects of moral philosophy, such as love and virtue. The *Convivio* is in a sense a connecting link between the *Vita nuova* and *The Divine Comedy*. Thus in the latter work reason in the pursuit of knowledge and wisdom becomes man's sole guide on earth, except for the intervention of Divine Grace, in his striving for virtue and God. In the *Convivio* Dante also defends the use of the vernacular as a suitable medium for ethical and scientific subjects, as well as amorous ones.

The Latin treatise *De monarchia*, of uncertain date but possibly attributable to the time of Henry VII's descent into Italy (1310–1313), is a statement of Dante's political theories. At the same time it is intended as a practical guide toward the restoration of peace in Europe under a temporal monarch in Rome, whose authority proceeds directly from God.

During his exile Dante also wrote various Latin epistles

*Dante and Virgil are unable to enter the city of Dis without the help of an angel (*Inferno, *Canto IX). The drawing is from Sandro Botticelli's series to illustrate* The Divine Comedy; *the drawings were executed between 1490 and 1497. (Biblioteca Vaticana, Rome)*

and letters of political nature to Italian princes and cardinals. Belonging to a late period are two Latin eclogues and the scientific essay *Quaestio de aqua et terra* (1320). *Il fiore*, a long sonnet sequence, is of doubtful attribution.

In 1315 Dante twice refused pardons offered him by the citizens of Florence under humiliating conditions. He and his children were consequently condemned to death as rebels. He spent his last years in Tuscany, in Verona, and finally in Ravenna. There, under the patronage of Guido da Polenta and joined by his children (possibly also his wife), Dante was greatly esteemed and spent a happy and peaceful period until his death on Sept. 13 or 14, 1321.

"The Divine Comedy"

The original title of Dante's masterpiece, which he completed shortly before his death, was *Commedia*; the epithet *Divina* was added by posterity. The purpose of this work, as Dante writes in his letter to Can Grande, is "to remove those living in this life from the state of misery and lead them to the state of felicity." The *Commedia* is divided into three parts: *Inferno* (Hell), *Purgatorio* (Purgatory), and *Paradiso* (Heaven). The second and third sections contain 33 cantos apiece; the *Inferno* has 34, since its opening canto is an introduction to the entire work. The measure throughout the poem is terza rima, consisting of lines in sets of 3, rhyming aba, bcb, cdc, and so on.

The main action of the literal narrative centers on Dante's journey to God through the agency of Beatrice; the moral or allegorical meaning that Dante wishes the reader to keep in mind is that God will do for everyman what he has done for one man, if everyman is willing to make this journey. Dante constructs an allegory of a double journey: his experience in the supernatural world points to the journey of everyman through this life. The poet finds himself in a dark wood (sin); he tries to escape by climbing a mountain illuminated by the sun (God). Impeded by the sudden appearance of three beasts, which symbolize the major divisions of sin in the *Inferno*, he is about to be driven back when Virgil (human reason) appears, sent to his aid by Beatrice. Virgil becomes Dante's guide through Hell, in a descent which is the first stage in his ascent to God in humility. The pilgrim learns all there is to know about sin and confronts the very foundation of sin, which is pride, personified in Lucifer frozen at the very center of the universe. Only now is he spiritually prepared to begin his ascent through the realm of purification.

The mountain of the *Purgatorio* is a place of repentance, regeneration, and conversion. The penitents endure severe punishments, but all are pilgrims directed to God, in an atmosphere of love, hope, and an eager willingness in suffering. On the mountain's summit Beatrice (divine revelation) comes to take Virgil's place as Dante's guide—for the final ascent to God, human reason is insufficient.

The *Paradiso* depicts souls contemplating God; they are in a state of perfect happiness in the knowledge of His divine truths. The dominant image in this realm is light. God is light, and the pilgrim's goal from the start was to reach the light. His spiritual growth toward the attainment of this end is the main theme of the entire poem.

Further Reading

Dante is listed in the Literature study guide (III, D, 1 and 4), the Religion study guide (I, F, 2), and the Philosophy study guide (II, D, 3). PETRARCH also helped to establish the vernacular as the language of literature. Giovanni BOCCACCIO wrote the first biography of Dante.

For an understanding of how little scholars know of Dante's life, see Michele Barbi, *Life of Dante,* edited and translated by Paul Ruggiers (1954). Recommended as important guides to the study of Dante are Charles A. Dinsmore, *Aids to the Study of Dante* (1903); Umberto Cosmo, *A Handbook to Dante Studies* (trans. 1947); and Thornes G. Bergin, *Dante* (1965). A variety of critical approaches to Dante are offered in Bernard Stambler, *Dante's Other World: The Purgatorio as Guide to the Divine Comedy* (1957); Charles S. Singleton, *Dante Studies I and II* (1958); Irma Brandeis, *The Ladder of Vision: A Study of Dante's Comedy* (1960); Mark Musa, *Essays on Dante* (1964); Jefferson B. Fletcher, *Dante* (1965); and Francis Fergusson, *Dante* (1966).

DANTON / By Paul G. Dobson

> The French statesman Georges Jacques Danton (1759–1794) was a leader during the French Revolution. Called the "orator of the streets," he was the most prominent early defender of popular liberties and the republican spirit.

Born in Arcis-sur-Aube in Champagne on Oct. 26, 1759, Georges Jacques Danton (pronounced däN-tôN′) was the son of a lawyer and minor court official. He was educated by the Oratorians at Troyes and in 1785 earned a degree in law at the University of Reims. He was employed in the office of public prosecutor in Paris and in 1787 purchased the office of advocate to the King's Council.

His Character

Danton's massive stature, ready wit (which did much to overcome his physical ugliness), stentorious voice, and impromptu and fiery speeches made the public accept him as its champion of liberty. Danton was a pragmatist who believed that the Revolution could only succeed if it limited its program to the possible, which meant upholding the rights of property, ending the war as quickly as possible by negotiation, and restoring order through a strong central government.

Danton had tendencies toward laziness and the dissolute life, which often blunted the force of his actions and made him appear capricious and unreliable to many of his contemporaries. There seems to be little doubt that he was implicated in financial corruption, but this appears more the result of thoughtlessness than a deliberate attempt to profit from the Revolution. At heart Danton appears to have been less a radical than an energetic and undisciplined individualist whose personality and the force of circumstances enabled him to become a great popular leader.

Revolutionary Activities

Danton's part in founding the Cordeliers Club, which became the advance guard of popular revolutionary activity, suggests that from the beginning of the Revolution he inclined toward the "people's cause." He was involved in the fall of the Bastille on July 14, 1789, and was the most outspoken critic of the commune and the Marquis de Lafayette. Following King Louis XVI's unsuccessful flight in June 1791, Danton was among those who called for the creation of a republic, and his speeches were considered responsible for the popular agitation that culminated in the massacre of the Champ de Mars.

In December 1791 Danton was elected first deputy prosecutor of the Paris Commune. Following the invasion of the Tuileries on June 20, 1792, he was elected president of the Théâtre Française Electoral District. He spoke out against the distinction between active and passive citizens and thus became one of the first to espouse the modern conception of the legal equality of all citizens. At the same time he began to play the primary role in the conspiracy that led to the overthrow of the monarchy on Aug. 10, 1792. He had become convinced, as had others, that as long as the monarchy continued to exist the Revolution would be endangered.

Danton was subsequently named minister of justice and became the predominant member of the Executive Committee. In this capacity he rallied the nation against the invading Prussians. It appears that he could have done little to prevent the September Massacres (1792), but his silent complicity in them deepened the split between himself and the Rolandists, which did much to force the trial of the King. Although Danton opposed this trial since it would make a negotiated peace impossible, he eventually voted in favor of execution of the King.

During this period Danton delivered his famous speech to the National Convention, which stated that to protect the Revolution it was necessary for France to secure its natural boundaries, although this might mean a perpetuation of the war. On April 6, 1793, he was elected to the newly established Committee of Public Safety and to the Revolutionary Tribunal; he was thus enabled to act as an emergency dictator. Although Danton be-

Georges Jacques Danton.
(Giraudon)

lieved that it was necessary to destroy internal dissent, his diplomatic policies continued to be moderate. He thus alienated the Commune, which began to look to Robespierre and more radical Jacobins for leadership. Setbacks in the Vandée and his attempted protection of the Girondists, even after their exclusion from the National Convention, resulted in Danton's not being re-elected to the Committee on July 10, 1793. The leadership of the Revolution passed to Robespierre.

In October Danton retired to his home in Arcis; he returned to Paris the following month at the insistence of his friends, who feared Robespierre's terrorist policies. The increasingly radical demands of the Hébertists, however, were more frightening to Danton, and he lent his support to Robespierre. After the Hébertists had been suppressed, Robespierre moved against Danton, who had called for an end to the Terror. Danton and his followers were arrested and tried for antirevolutionary activity. On April 5, 1794, Danton went to the guillotine,

which he had vowed to either pull down or die beneath.

Further Reading

Georges Jacques Danton is listed in the European History study guide (VII, B, 1, b). He opposed the extremism of Jacques René HÉBERT.

Danton has been the subject of a controversial literature. His great supporter was Alphonse Aulard, who unfortunately never wrote a biography of his hero. However, Aulard's *The French Revolution: A Political History, 1789–1804* (1901; trans., 4 vols., 1910) clearly indicates his admiration for Danton as the greatest example of revolutionary spirit. Louis Madelin, *Danton* (1914; trans. 1921), and his vignette of Danton in *Figures of the Revolution* (1928; trans. 1929) offer a more moderate but still favorable interpretation in which Danton's realism is praised. On the other side of the ledger are the works of Albert Mathiez, which condemn Danton as corrupt, vacillating in his diplomacy, insensitive to popular needs, and the tool of Orléans. Unfortunately, none of these works is in translation. Something of Mathiez's approach permeates Robert Christophe, *Danton: A Biography* (trans. 1967). Probably the best biography is Hermann Wendel, *Danton* (1930; trans. 1935), which provides an even and thoughtful approach.

DARÍO / By Donald A. Yates

Rubén Darío (1867–1916) was a Nicaraguan poet whose work is considered to have given the major impetus to the late-19th-century literary movement in Spanish America called modernism.

R ubén Darío (pronounced dä-rē′ō) was born Félix Rubén García y Sarmiento on Jan. 18, 1867, in Metapa. Raised as an orphan in the home of an aunt, he showed at an early age an astonishing ability for versification. His early Jesuit training appears to have had little influence on his subsequent behavior, except perhaps to intensify his mystical inclinations. At 13, he published the first poem he was to sign as Rubén Darío, adopting the more euphonious last name of a paternal great-grandfather.

Rubén Darío. (Organization of American States)

Early Career

An intelligent, nervous, superstitious boy, Darío was taken by friends to the capital city of Managua in 1881. But in an effort to frustrate his announced plan to marry at age 14, he was sent to El Salvador. There he met the poet Francisco Gavidia, who introduced him to French literature and instructed him in new styles of versification. In 1884 Darío returned to Managua, took a job at the National Library, learned French, and set out on an intensive program of literary study.

In Darío's first volume of poetry, *Primeras notas* (1885), his liberal attitudes were clearly manifested. In 1886, hoping to find a more stimulating literary environment, he traveled to Valparaiso, Chile, where he wrote for the newspaper *La Epoca*. He began to read the French Parnassian and symbolist poets, whose influence on what he wrote in the next few years was fundamental.

Darío's *Azul* (1888) was a collection of the prose and poetry he had been writing in Chile. The elegance and refinement of his style were strikingly fresh in the Spanish language. *Azul* is generally considered to be the first book of the Spanish American literary tendency designated as modernism, which introduced new forms and standards of expression and effected a virtual renovation of Spanish American literary style.

His Travels

Darío's subsequent travels were almost as influential as his writings in publicizing the new trend. He returned to Central America in 1889 and founded a newspaper in El Salvador, and another in Guatemala in 1890. He was mar-

ried for the first time in 1890 and in 1891 settled in Costa Rica. In 1892 and 1893 he made his first visits to Europe, returning from the second trip directly to Buenos Aires, where he had been appointed the Colombian consul. Although he soon lost that appointment, he remained in Argentina until 1898, publishing his important works, *Los raros* (1896), a collection of essays dealing with writers Darío admired, and *Prosas profanas* (1896), the book with which the ground gained by the modernist tendency—now being cultivated by poets throughout Spanish America—was consolidated.

In 1898 the Buenos Aires newspaper *La Nación*, with which Darío had been associated since 1889, sent him to Spain as a correspondent. He was soon transferred to Paris, which became the center of his activities for nearly 5 years. In his most mature collection of poetry, *Cantos de vida y esperanza* (1906), much of the surface brilliance of his earlier work is replaced by a more serious, human, meditative tone. Some of the elegance is missing, but it is replaced by the conscience of a man now aware of the world around him and the social and political circumstances of Spanish America at the turn of the century.

Late Work

Between 1907 and 1915 Darío's life was complicated by continuous travel between Europe and Spanish America, the consequences of his chronic intemperance, and persistent marital troubles involving his second wife, from whom he had long been separated, and Francisca Sánchez, a Spanish woman who had borne him three children. He continued to write and publish his poetry, but these later volumes reveal a decline in his creative powers: *El canto errante* (1907), *El viaje a Nicaragua* (principally prose; 1909), and *Poema del otoño* (1910). He died in León, Nicaragua, on Feb. 6, 1916.

Further Reading

Rubén Darío is listed in the Latin America study guide (IV, D, 2). Equally well-known literary figures of Latin America are Miguel Angel ASTURIAS and Gabriela MISTRAL.

The best source on Darío's life is Charles Dunton Watland, *Poet-Errant: A Biography of Rubén Darío* (1965). Much new Darío criticism appeared in commemoration of the centennial celebration of the poet's birth in 1967. Of the works in English, especially useful is George D. Schade and Miguel González-Gerth, eds., *Rubén Darío: Centennial Studies* (1970). Two excellent studies of distinct aspects of the poet's work are Donald F. Fogelquist, ed., *The Literary Collaboration and the Personal Correspondence of Rubén Darío and Juan Ramón Jiménez* (1956), and Dolores Ackel Fiore, *Rubén Darío in Search of Inspiration: Greco-Roman Mythology in His Stories and Plays* (1963).

DARIUS I / By Eugene W. Davis

> Darius I (522–486 B.C.), called "the Great," was a Persian king. A great conqueror and the chief organizer of the Persian Empire, he is best known for the unsuccessful attack on Greece which ended at Marathon.

A member of a collateral branch of the Achaemenidian royal family, Darius (pronounced dəriʹəs) apparently was not close to the throne when Cambyses died in 522 B.C. The story of Darius's accession is told most fully by the Greek Herodotus, whose version clearly reflects the official account set up by Darius's own order in the famous rock inscription at Behistun.

According to Herodotus, Cambyses had had his brother Smerdis (Bardiya) executed, but while Cambyses was absent in Egypt, a Magian priest named Gaumata, trusting in a chance resemblance, put himself forward as Smerdis and seized the throne. Cambyses started back but died en route, and the false Smerdis was generally accepted. Darius, with the aid of a few who knew that Smerdis was dead, murdered Gaumata and in his own person restored the royal line.

Organization of the Empire

Though Darius was an excellent soldier and extended his empire east, north, and into Europe, he saw himself as an organizer and lawgiver rather than as a mere conqueror. Little of his work was startlingly original, but the blending of the old and new and the interlocked order-

ing of the whole gave his work importance. He divided the empire into 20 huge provinces called satrapies, each under a royally appointed governor called a satrap who had administrative, military, financial, and judicial control in his province. To check on such powerful subordinates, Darius also appointed the satrap's second-in-command, having him report to the King separately. Standing garrisons under commanders independent of the satrap were stationed strategically. However, since all these officials were more or less permanent, there remained the possibility that all three might conspire to plot revolt. Accordingly, a further set of royal officials—inspectors called the King's "eyes" or "ears"—were frequently sent out.

Since in so huge an empire—it covered some 1 million square miles—there was always the problem of communication and transportation, Darius established a system of well-maintained all-weather roads and a royal courier system with posthouses and regular relays of horses and riders. The trip from Sardis in western Asia Minor to Susa in Persia normally took 3 months; a royal message could cover it in a week.

Darius also regulated the tribute, hitherto collected irregularly as needed, on a fixed annual basis according to the wealth of each satrapy. Though hardly low, this tribute does not appear to have been burdensome. He also instituted the first official Persian coinage.

Military Organization

Militarily the empire was organized on the satrap system, but the results were less happy. Aside from the resident garrisons and the royal bodyguard there was no standing army. At need, satraps involved were ordered to raise a quota of men and bring them, armed and ready, to an appointed assembly point. Inescapably, a Persian army was thus long on numbers but short on uniformity; each contingent was armed and trained in its local fashion and spoke its native tongue. Persian infantry was usually of

Darius I kills a lion in this impression of a contemporary cylinder seal, in the British Musem. Above the King's chariot is the winged god Ahura Mazda. The two palms are the conventional way of depicting the southern Mesopotamian landscape. At left is an inscription, "Darius the Great King," in Old Persian, Elamite, and Babylonian cuneiform. (The Mansell collection)

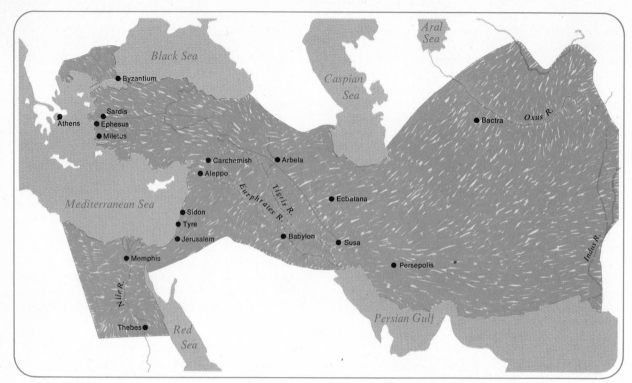

The Persian Empire under Darius I. Darius organized his vast empire into 20 provinces, or satrapies, each governed by a satrap possessing viceregal authority. To check these powerful subordinates, Darius surrounded them with other officials and inspectors who reported directly to him. (The King's Highway runs from Sardis to Susa.)

very poor quality; the cavalry, provided by the Persians themselves, the Medes, and the eastern steppe dwellers, was generally quite good. The Persian fleet was levied in the same manner as the army, but since the Mediterranean maritime peoples all copied from each other, there was little problem of diversity. The fleet's weakness was that, being raised entirely from among subject peoples, it had no real loyalty.

Darius's Religion

Darius, himself a firm supporter of Ahura Mazda, the Zoroastrian god, said in the Behistun inscription that Ahura Mazda "gave" him his kingdoms, and with him Zoroastrianism became something like the national religion of the Persians. For the empire, however, he continued Cyrus's policy of toleration of local cults, and this mildness became and remained, except perhaps under Xerxes, a distinctive feature of Persian rule.

War with the Greeks

Darius's first European campaign, about 513, was aimed not at Greece but north toward the Danube. Herodotus recorded that Darius intended to conquer the complete circuit of the Black Sea and that he was turned back north of the Danube by the native Scythians' scorched-earth policy. This may be, or it may be that Darius never intended any permanent conquest north of the Danube and that Herodotus turned a limited success into a grandiose failure in order to make all Persian operations in Europe at least partly unsuccessful. Darius did secure the approaches to Greece and the control of the grain route through the Bosporus.

The next act in the Greco-Persian drama was the so-called Ionian Revolt (499–494), an uprising against Persia of most of the Greeks of Asia Minor headed by the Ionians, and particularly by the city of Miletus. Though the revolt was put down by Darius's generals, its seriousness is indicated by its length and by the fact that the Ionians' appeal to the Greek homeland was answered, at least in part, by Athens and Eretria.

Darius had to take the Greek matter seriously. Not only did he have the duty of avenging the burning of his city of Sardis during the revolt, but he must have become convinced that to ensure the quiet of his Greek subjects in Asia Minor he would have to extend his rule also over their brothers across the Aegean. After the collapse of the revolt, the attempt of Darius's son-in-law, Mandonius, to carry the war into Greece itself ended when the Persian fleet was wrecked in a storm off Mt. Athos (492).

Battle of Marathon

Perhaps Mardonius's ill-fated venture was really an attempt to conquer all Greece; the next effort certainly was not. Darius sent a naval expedition—he himself never set eyes on Greece—against only Athens and Eretria (490). The attack was perfectly well known to be coming, but the Greeks had their customary difficulties of cooperation, and Eretria, unsupported, fell and was burned in revenge for Sardis. Athens appealed to the Grecian states, but only 1,000 men from little Plataea reached Athens.

The Persians landed on the small plain of Marathon northeast of Athens, and the Greeks took up station in easily defendable nearby hills out of reach of the Persian cavalry. After some days' waiting, the Persians began to reembark, perhaps for a dash on Athens. The Greeks, led by Miltiades, were forced to attack, which they did with a lengthened front to avoid encirclement by the more numerous Persians. In this first major encounter between European and Asian infantry, the Greek closely knit, heavily armed phalanx won decisively. The Persian survivors sailed at once for Athens, but Miltiades rushed his forces back, and the Persians arrived to see the Greeks lined up before the city. Abandoning action, they sailed home, and the campaign of Marathon was over.

Though to the Western world Marathon was a victory of enormous significance, to the Persians it was only a moderately serious border setback. Yet this defeat and peace in Asia Minor called for the conquest of all Greece, and Darius began the mighty preparations. A revolt in Egypt, however, distracted him, and he died in 486, leaving the next attack for his son Xerxes.

Further Reading

Darius I is listed in the Asia study guide (I, A, 4, a). Other great Persian kings were CYRUS THE GREAT and XERXES. Two of the best Greek military commanders during the Greco-Persian wars were MILTIADES and THEMISTOCLES.

Herodotus's *History* is the principal source of information on Darius. Aeschylus's *Persae* is also important. The Behistun inscription is Darius's official account; it is contained in Roland G. Kent, *Old Persian: Grammar, Texts, Lexicon* (1950; 2d ed. rev. 1953). The fullest recent treatment of Darius is in A. T. Olmstead, *History of the Persian Empire* (1948; rev. ed. 1959), which asserts that Darius was a usurper. Roman Ghirshman, *Iran from the Earliest Times to the Islamic Conquest* (1954), is more traditional. Richard Frye, *The Heritage of Persia* (1963), is also of interest.

❋   ❋   ❋

DARROW / By Sanford Levinson

As an American labor lawyer and as a criminal lawyer, Clarence Seward Darrow (1857–1938) helped sharpen debate about the path of American industrialism and about the treatment of individuals in conflict with the law.

Clarence Darrow was born on April 18, 1857, in Farmdale, Ohio, to Amirus and Emily Darrow. He was introduced early to the life of the dissenter, for his father, after completing studies at a Unitarian seminary, had lost his faith and had become an agnostic

living within a community of religious believers. Furthermore, the Darrows were Democrats in a Republican locale.

After completing his secondary schooling near Farmdale, Darrow spent a year at Allegheny College in Meadville, Pa., and another year at the University of Michigan Law School. Like almost all lawyers of the time, he delayed his admission to the bar until after he had read law with a local lawyer; he became a member of the Ohio bar in 1878. For the next 9 years he was a typical small-town lawyer, practicing in Kinsman, Andover, and Ashtabula, Ohio.

Seeking more interesting paths, however, Darrow moved to Chicago in 1887. In Ohio he had been impressed with the book *Our Penal Machinery and Its Victims* by Judge John Peter Altgeld. Darrow became a close friend of Altgeld, who was elected governor of Illinois in 1892. Altgeld not only raised questions about the process of criminal justice but, when he pardoned several men who had been convicted in the aftermath of the Haymarket riot of 1886, also questioned the treatment of those who were trying to organize workers into unions. Both of these themes played great roles in Darrow's life.

Labor Lawyer

Darrow had begun as a conventional civil lawyer. Even in Chicago his first jobs included appointment as the city's corporation counsel in 1890 and then as general

Clarence Darrow about 1922. (Library of Congress)

attorney to the Chicago and North Western Railway. In 1894, however, he began what would be his primary career for the next 20 years—labor law. During that year he defended the Socialist Eugene V. Debs against an injunction trying to break the workers' strike Debs was leading against the Pullman Sleeping Car Company. Darrow was unsuccessful, though; the injunction against Debs was finally upheld by the Supreme Court.

In 1906–1907 Darrow successfully defended William D. "Big Bill" Haywood, the leader of the newly formed Industrial Workers of the World, against a charge of conspiring to murder former governor Steunenberg of Idaho. But in 1911 disaster struck as Darrow, defending the McNamara brothers against a charge of blowing up the Los Angeles Times Building, was suddenly faced with his clients' reversing their previous plea of innocence to one of guilt. In turn, Darrow was indicted for misconduct but was not convicted. With this his career as a labor lawyer came to an end.

Criminal Lawyer

Darrow had always been interested in criminal law, in part because of his acceptance of new, psychological theories stressing the role of determinism in human behavior. He viewed criminals as people led by circumstance into committing antisocial acts rather than as free-willing monsters. For this reason he was a bitter opponent of capital punishment, viewing it as a barbaric practice. Now he embarked on a new major career as a criminal lawyer.

Without a doubt Darrow's most famous criminal trial was the 1924 Leopold-Loeb case, in which two Chicago boys had wantonly murdered a youngster. For the only time in his career Darrow insisted that his clients plead guilty, then turned his attention to saving them from the death penalty. He was successful in this, partly because he was able to introduce a great deal of psychiatric testimony supporting his theories of the determining influences upon individual acts.

Scopes Trial

During this period Darrow also participated in another great American case, the Scopes trial of 1925 in Dayton, Tenn. The issue was the right of a state legislature to prohibit the teaching of Darwinian theories of evolution in the public schools. Darrow, as an agnostic and as an evolutionist, was doubly contemptuous of the motives behind the fundamentalist law that had been passed, and he sought to defend the young schoolteacher who had raised the issue of evolution in his class. Technically, he was unsuccessful, for Scopes was convicted and fined $100 for his crime. But Darrow's defense, and particularly his cross-examination of William Jennings Bryan (the three-time Democratic candidate for president who spoke for the biblical, antiscientific, fundamentalist side) served to discredit religious fundamentalism and won national attention.

Two books among Darrow's many writings typify his concerns toward the end of his life. In 1922 he wrote *Crime: Its Cause and Treatment*; in 1929 appeared *Infi-*

dels and Heretics, coedited with Wallace Rice, in which he presented the case for freethinking. To these two issue-oriented books he added in 1932 his autobiography, *The Story of My Life*.

Darrow's last important public service was as chairman of a commission appointed by President Franklin D. Roosevelt to analyze the operation of the National Recovery Administration. He died on March 13, 1938.

Further Reading

Clarence Darrow is listed in the American History study guide (VIII, A, 4). He was a friend and spiritual ally of Illinois governor John Peter ALTGELD; in the Scopes trial he was pitted in debate against William Jennings BRYAN. Darrow defended Eugene V. DEBS in the labor strike he was leading against the company owned by George PULLMAN.

The standard popular biography of Darrow is Irving Stone, *Clarence Darrow for the Defense* (1941). A more recent work is Miriam Gurko, *Clarence Darrow* (1965). A specialized, scholarly study is Abe C. Ravitz, *Clarence Darrow and the American Literary Tradition* (1962), which takes note of Darrow's participation in some of the literary controversies of his time.

DARWIN / By Sydney Smith

The English naturalist Charles Robert Darwin (1809–1882) discovered that natural selection was the agent for the transmutation of organisms during evolution, as did Alfred Russel Wallace independently. Darwin presented his theory in "Origin of Species."

The concept of evolution by descent dates at least from classical Greek philosophers. In the 18th century Carl Linnaeus postulated limited mutability of species by descent and hybridization. Charles Darwin's grandfather, Erasmus Darwin, and the Chevalier de Lamarck were the chief proponents of evolution about 1800. Such advocacy had little impact on the majority of naturalists, concerned to identify species, the stability of which was considered essential for their work. Natural theology regarded the perfection of adaptation between structure and mode of life in organisms as evidence for a beneficent, all-seeing, all-planning Creator. Organic structure, planned in advance for a preordained niche, was unchanged from the moment of creation. Variations in structure in these earthly imperfect versions of the Creator's idea were minor and impermanent.

In 1815 William Smith had demonstrated a sequence of fossil populations in time. Charles Lyell, adopting James Hutton's uniformitarian view that present conditions and processes were clues to the past history of the earth, wrote his *Principles of Geology* (1830–1833), which Darwin on his *Beagle* circumnavigation found most apt for his own geological observations. Fossils in South America and apparent anomalies of animal distribution triggered the task for Darwin of assembling a vast range of material. A reading of Thomas Malthus's *Essay on the Principle of Population* in 1838 completed Darwin's conceptual scheme.

Critics, for whom the *Origin* is paramount among Darwin's considerable output, have accused him of vacillation and procrastination. But recent study of unpublished manuscripts and his entire works reveal a continuity of purpose and integrity of effort to establish the high probability of the genetic relationship through descent in all forms of life. Man is dethroned as the summit of creation and as the especial concern of the Creator. This revolution in thought has had an effect on every kind of human activity.

Darwin was born on Feb. 12, 1809, at Shrewsbury, the fifth child of Robert and Susannah Darwin. His mother, who was the daughter of the famous potter Josiah Wedgwood, died when Charles was 8, and he was reared by his sisters. At the age of 9 Charles entered Shrewsbury School. His record was not outstanding, but he did learn to use English with precision and to delight in Shakespeare and Milton.

In 1825 Darwin went to Edinburgh University to study medicine. He found anatomy and *materia medica* dull and surgery unendurable. In 1828 he entered Christ's College, Cambridge, with the idea of taking Anglican orders. He attended John Stevens Henslow's course in botany, started a collection of beetles that became famous, and read widely. William Paley's *Natural Theology* (1802) delighted Darwin by its clear logical presentation, and he later regarded this study as the most worthwhile benefit from Cambridge. He received his bachelor's degree in 1831.

Voyage of the "Beagle"

On Henslow's recommendation Darwin was offered the position of naturalist for the second voyage of H.M.S. *Beagle* to survey the coast of Patagonia and Tierra del Fuego and complete observations of longitude by circumnavigation with a formidable array of chronometers. The *Beagle* left on Dec. 27, 1831, and returned on Oct. 2, 1836. During the voyage Darwin spent 535 days at sea and roughly 1200 on land. Enough identification of strata could be done on the spot, but sufficiently accurate identification of living organisms required systematists accessible only in London and Paris.

Darwin kept his field observations in notebooks with the specimens listed serially and their place and time of collection documented. On July 24, 1834, he wrote: "My notes are becoming bulky. I have about 600 small quarto pages full; about half of this is Geology the other imperfect descriptions of animals; with the latter I make it a rule to describe those parts which cannot be seen in specimens in spirits. I keep my private Journal distinct from the above." Toward the end of the voyage, when sea passages were long, he copied his notes and arranged them to accord with systematics, concentrating on range and habits. Geology was prepared with fewer

Charles Darwin, the last photograph taken of the naturalist. (Courtesy of the American Museum of Natural History)

inhibitions; he wrote from Mauritius in April 1836: "It is a rare piece of good fortune for me that of the many errant (in ships) Naturalists there have been few, or rather no, Geologists. I shall enter the field unopposed."

During the trip Darwin discovered the relevance of Lyell's uniformitarian views to the structure of St. Jago (Cape Verde Islands). He found that small locally living forms closely resembled large terrestrial fossil mammals embedded between marine shell layers and that the local sea was populated with living occupants of similar shells. He also observed the overlapping distribution on the continuous Patagonian plain of two closely related but distinct species of ostrich. An excursion along the Santa Cruz river revealed a section of strata across South America. He observed the differences between species of birds and animals on the Galápagos Islands.

Publications Resulting from Voyage

Darwin's *Journal of Researches* was published in 1839. With the help of a government grant toward the cost of the illustrations, the *Zoology of the Voyage of the Beagle* was published, in five quarto volumes, from 1839 to 1843. Specialist systematists wrote on fossil and living mammals, birds, fish, and reptiles. Darwin edited the work and contributed habits and ranges of the animals and geological notes on the fossils. Two themes run through his valuable and mostly neglected notes: distribution in space and time and observations of behavior as an aid to species diagnosis. He also published *The Struc-*

ture and Distribution of Coral Reefs (1842); he had studied the coral reefs in the Cocos Islands during the *Beagle* voyage.

Darwin abandoned the idea of fixity of species in 1837 while writing his *Journal*. A second edition, in 1845, had a stronger tinge of transmutation, but there was still no public avowal of the new faith. This delightful volume is his most popular and accessible work.

Darwin's Transmutation (Species) Notebooks (1837–1839) have recently been reconstructed. The notion of "selection owing to struggle" derived from his reading of Malthus in 1838. Earlier Darwin had read Pyrame de Candolle's works on plant geography, so his mind was receptive. The breadth of interest and profusion of hypotheses characteristic of Darwin, who could carry several topics in his mind at the same time, inform the whole. From this medley of facts allegedly assembled on Baconian principles all his later works derive.

It was not until Darwin's geological observations of South America were published in 1846 that he started a paper on his "first Cirripede," a shell-boring aberrant barnacle, no bigger than a pin's head, he had found at Chonos Island in 1835. This was watched while living, then dissected, and drawn while the *Beagle* sheltered

Darwin's microscope and part of his study in his home at Down, Sussex. After returning from the voyage of the Beagle, Darwin was almost continually in poor health. He often worked no more than 4 hours a day and spent the remainder of his time reading, resting, or walking. (With the kind permission of the President and the Council of the Royal College of Surgeons)

from a week of severe storms. The working out of the relationship to other barnacles forced him to study all barnacles, a task that occupied him until 1854 and resulted in two volumes on living forms and two on fossil forms.

Darwin married Emma Wedgwood, his first cousin, in 1839. They lived in London until 1842, when ill health drove him to Down House, where he passed the rest of his life in seclusion. Four of their sons became prominent scientists: George was an astronomer and mathematician, Francis a botanist, Leonard a eugenist, and Horace a civil engineer.

Development of Ideas on Evolution

In 1842 and 1844 Darwin wrote short accounts of his transmutation views. The 1844 sketch in corrected fair copy was a testament accompanied by a letter to his wife to secure publication should he die. Late in 1844 Robert Chambers's *Vestiges of Creation* appeared advocating universal development by descent. A great scandal ensued, and criticism of the amateur pretensions of the author was savage. Darwin decided to bide his time and become more proficient as a biologist.

In 1855 Darwin began to study the practices of poultry and pigeon fanciers and worldwide domesticated breeds, conducted experiments on plant and animal variation and its hereditary transmission, and worried about the problem of plant and animal transport across land and water barriers, for he was persuaded of the importance of isolation for speciation. The last step in his conceptual scheme had already occurred to him in 1852 while pondering Henri Milne-Edwards's concept of diversification into specialized organs for separation of physiological functions in higher organisms and the relevance of these considerations for classification when related to the facts of embryological development. Darwin's "principle of divergence" recognizes that the dominant species must make more effective use of the territory it invades than a competing species and accordingly it becomes adapted to more diversified environments.

In May 1856 Lyell heard of Darwin's transmutation hypothesis and urged him to write an account with full references. Darwin sent the chapter on distribution to Lyell and Sir Joseph Hooker, who were deeply impressed. Darwin continued his writing, and on June 14, 1858, when he was halfway through, he received an essay from Alfred Russel Wallace containing the theory of evolution by natural selection—the same theory Darwin was working on. Lyell and Hooker arranged for a reading of a joint paper by Wallace and Darwin, and it was presented at a meeting of the Linnaean Society on July 1. The paper had little effect.

"Origin of Species"

On Nov. 24, 1859, Darwin published *On the Origin of Species by Means of Natural Selection, or the Preservation of Favoured Races in the Struggle for Life*. The analogy of natural selection was prone to misunderstanding by readers, since it carried for them an implied pur-

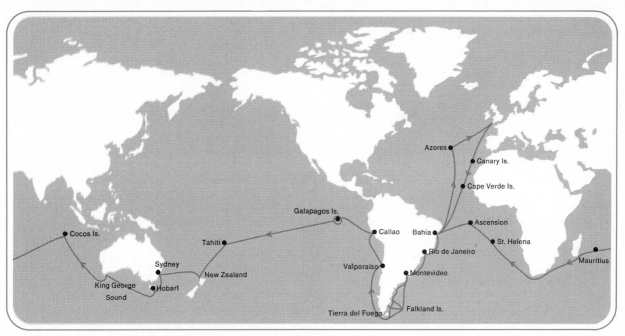

The voyage of the Beagle, 1831–1836. The 5-year voyage around the world was the turning point of Darwin's life. An inexperienced amateur at its start, he returned with the facts and ideas that led ultimately to his Origin of Species.

pose on the part of a "deified" Nature. Herbert Spencer's phrase "survival of the fittest" was equally misleading because the essence of Darwin's theory is that, unlike natural theology, adaptation must not be too perfect and rigid. A mutable store of variation must be available to any viable population in nature.

The publication of Darwin's book secured worldwide attention for his hypothesis and aroused impassioned controversy. His main champion was T. H. Huxley. Darwin, remote in his retreat at Down House, took painstaking note of criticism and endeavored to answer points of detail in the five more editions of *Origin* produced during his lifetime. He avoided trouble and made several unfortunate concessions which weakened his presentation and made his views seem vague and hesitant. The first edition is easily the best.

Later Works

In *On the Various Contrivances by Which British and Foreign Orchids Are Fertilised by Insects* (1862) Darwin showed how the welfare of an organism may be hidden in apparently unimportant peculiarities. It became hard to say what is "useless" in nature. His *The Variation of Animals and Plants under Domestication* (1868; rev. ed. 1875) expanded on a topic he had introduced in *Origin*. A chapter in *Origin* on man as the most domesticated of animals grew into the book *The Descent of Man and Selection in Relation to Sex* (1871). *The Expression of the Emotions in Man and Animals* (1872) developed from material squeezed out of the *Descent*.

Plants became an increasing preoccupation, the more so since Darwin had his son Francis as collaborator and amanuensis. Papers Darwin had published in 1864 were collected into *The Movements and Habits of Climbing Plants* (1875), and these ideas were further generalized on uniformitarian lines and published as *The Power of Movement in Plants* (1880). All plants, not merely climbing ones, were shown to execute to some degree exploratory "circumnutation" movements. Studies on fertilization of plants by insects recorded as early as 1840 led to *The Effects of Cross and Self-Fertilisation in the Vegetable Kingdom* (1876) and *The Different Forms of Flowers on Plants of the Same Species* (1877). *Insectivorous Plants* (1873) pursued the reactions of plants to stimuli. Darwin's last work returned to observations he had made in 1837: *The Formation of Vegetable Mould through the Action of Worms, with Observations on Their Habits* (1881). He died on April 19, 1882, and was buried in Westminster Abbey.

Further Reading

Charles Darwin is listed in the Science study guide (VI, E, 1). He was influenced by the views of Thomas MALTHUS, William PALEY, and Charles LYELL. Darwin and Alfred Russel WALLACE arrived at the same theory independently and simultaneously. T. H. HUXLEY was a leading advocate of Darwin's views.

Primary sources on Darwin include *The Life and Letters of Charles Darwin*, edited by Francis Darwin (3 vols., 1887), which has an autobiographical chapter; *More Letters of Charles Darwin*, edited by Francis Darwin and A. C. Seward (1903); and his *Autobiography*, edited with appendix and notes by his granddaughter, Nora Barlow (1958; repr. 1969). An excellent, nontechnical account of Darwin's life and work is Sir Gavin de

Beer, *Charles Darwin: Evolution by Natural Selection* (1964). Other biographical studies are Paul B. Sears, *Charles Darwin: The Naturalist as a Cultural Force* (1950), and Gerhard Wichler, *Charles Darwin: The Founder of the Theory of Evolution and Natural Selection* (1961). Gertrude Himmelfarb, *Darwin and the Darwinian Revolution* (1959), offers a provocative reinterpretation of the man and his impact.

A dramatic pictorial account of Darwin's trip around the world in the *Beagle* is Alan Moorehead, *Darwin and the Beagle* (1969), which incorporates excerpts from Darwin's autobiography, journal, and letters. Parts of Darwin's work are examined in P. R. Bell, ed., *Darwin's Biological Work: Some Aspects Reconsidered* (1959), and Darwin's vast influence is assessed in Michael T. Ghiselin, *The Triumph of the Darwinian Method* (1969). A good, succinct presentation of the essence of Darwin's ideas is Benjamin Farrington, *What Darwin Really Said* (1967), which can serve as a review of the major problems raised by Darwin's theories.

* * *

DAS / By Amalendu Chakraborty

Chitta Ranjan Das (1870–1925) was an Indian lawyer and poet who became a nationalist leader. His main aim was swaraj, or self-rule, for India.

Chitta Ranjan Das. (A. Chakraborty)

Chitta Ranjan Das (pronounced däs) was born in Calcutta on Nov. 5, 1870, into a progressive Brahmo family. His father, Bhuvan Mohan, was a solicitor and a journalist who edited the English church weekly, *The Brahmo Public Opinion*. Das graduated from Presidency College in Calcutta in 1890 and went to England to compete in the Indian civil service examination. He failed the exams but joined the Inner Temple and was called to the bar in 1892.

Das returned to India in 1893 and started law practice in the Calcutta High Court. Following his successful defense of Aurobindo Ghose in the 1908 Alipur bomb conspiracy case, Das rose steadily and built a lucrative profession.

From his early youth Das was a nationalist. He was an active member of the Students' Association (1886), where Surendranath Banerjee had lectured on patriotism. At Presidency College, Das organized an undergraduate association and moved for permitting the use of Bengali in university examinations. He came in close contact with Bipin Chandra Pal and Aurobindo Ghose and helped them in publishing the *Bande Mataram*, an English weekly for propagating the ideals of *swaraj*.

Das was politically most active between 1917 and 1925. In 1917 he presided over the Bengal Provincial Conference and put forward a plan for village reconstruction through the establishment of local self-government, cooperative credit societies, and the regeneration of cottage industry. The same year he began to attend the Indian National Congress sessions regularly and was elected to all important committees. His powerful oratory, political foresight, and tact gave him a leading position in the Congress. He denounced the Montagu-Chelmsford Reform, which established a dyarchy for India, and joined Gandhi's noncooperation movement in 1920. He toured the whole country, carrying the new creed to every door. In 1921 he was arrested with his wife and son and sentenced to 6 months' imprisonment. The same year he was elected president of the Ahmedabad Congress.

On the failure of Gandhi's noncooperation movement, Das devised a new strategy. As president of the Gaya Congress (1922), he advocated an obstructionist policy inside the legislative councils with a view to mending or ending the dyarchy. But the majority in the Congress rejected his proposal. Thereupon, Das formed the Swarajya party with Motilal Nehru.

The Swarajya party gained tremendous success in Bengal and the central provinces and won majority seats in the legislative councils (1924). In Bengal the party inflicted repeated defeats upon the government, and the British bureaucracy in its earlier form met its doom in Bengal. In 1924 the Swarajists captured power in the Calcutta Corporation, and Das became the first popularly elected mayor of Calcutta.

Das realized that Hindu-Moslem unity was essential for the attainment of *swaraj*. In 1924 he formulated his famous Communal Pact to promote permanent peace between India's two major communities. He also wanted an assimilation of Eastern spirit and Western technique. He envisioned a pan-Asiatic federation of the oppressed nations and advocated India's participation in it. For his devotion to the cause of self-rule he gained the title Deshabandhu (friend of the country).

Das's genius was also revealed in the field of literature. He founded and published a literary magazine, *Narayan* (1914), and composed a number of poetical works. His first collection of poetry, *Malancha* (1895), raised a storm of protest among Brahmos. He was branded as an atheist, and in 1897 the Brahmo leaders boycotted his marriage. His successive works, *Mala* (1904), *Sagar Sangit* (1913), and *Kishore-Kishoree* and *Antaryami* (both 1915), reveal a Vaishnava devotionalism. Das died in Darjeeling on June 16, 1925.

Further Reading

Chitta Ranjan Das is listed in the Asia study guide (II, A, 6, c). Das strongly influenced Subhas Chandra BOSE.

There are two major biographies of Das: Prithwis Chandra Roy, *Life and Times of C. R. Das* (1927), and Hemendra Nath Das Gupta, *Deshbandhu Chittaranjan Das* (1960). Critical treatments of Das's political, economic, and religious ideas are in Sukumar Ranjan Das, *Chitta Ranjan* (1922); Dilip Kumar Chatterjee, *C. R. Das and Indian National Movement* (1965); and Stephen N. Hay, *Asian Ideas of East and West* (1970).

* * *

DAUBIGNY / By Francis E. Hyslop, Jr.

The French painter and etcher Charles François Daubigny (1817–1878), a member of the Barbizon school, was one of the first landscape painters to work out of doors in a systematic way.

Charles Daubigny (pronounced dō-bē-nyē′) was born in Paris on Feb. 15, 1817. His father, Edmé François Daubigny, was a landscape painter, and his uncle and aunt were miniaturists. Daubigny made the customary trip to Italy (1835–1836) and did some ideal landscapes, but his eventual direction was more decisively shaped by Dutch landscape painting. In 1838 he enrolled as a student of the academic painter Paul Delaroche.

Although Daubigny enjoyed a reasonable success at the Salons, where he exhibited from 1838 on, graphic art in the form of etchings, woodcuts, lithographs, and illustrations contributed substantially to his income. *Pond with Storks* (ca. 1851), with its painstaking analytical detail, is a representative Barbizon school work; it also echoes Dutch art of the 17th century. Some of Daubigny's rarely seen drawings, such as *River Landscape*

(ca. 1860), have an astonishingly light, airy, and evocative touch.

Daubigny painted in the forest of Fontainebleau near Barbizon, along the rivers of northern France, and on the coast. He assimilated many sources and worked in many different manners. The *Pond of Gylieu* (1853), balanced, meticulous in execution, and suffused with soft light, was a particularly popular picture. The *Lock at Optevoz* (1859), done in blocky masses and heavier impasto, is reminiscent of Gustave Courbet. Daubigny's *Banks of the Oise* (ca. 1860), which is more delicate and luminous, gives a foretaste of Alfred Sisley. In contrast, the heaviness and dark greens of *Landscape near Pontoise* (1866) call to mind the work of Camille Pissarro. Intimate forest pictures such as *Landscape* (ca. 1877), executed in softer greens with a fluttery touch, illustrate the persistence of Camille Corot's influence.

Daubigny, whose work was considered to be too much a matter of "impressions," gave help and encouragement to Claude Monet, who followed him even in the practice of using a houseboat as a floating studio. Daubigny visited England and the Netherlands in 1870–1872. He died at Auvers-sur-Oise on Feb. 21, 1878.

Lacking the boldness and imagination to be a major artist, Daubigny was a hardworking, conscientious craftsman who never stopped looking at art and nature and who never stopped producing fresh and appealing pic-

Charles Daubigny. (New York Public Library, Picture Collection)

tures—along with some that were dull, flat, and routine. Historically, his role was to bridge the gap between the popular but fading Barbizon school and the more audacious and original impressionist school.

Further Reading

Charles Daubigny is listed in the Art study guide (III, H, 1, b). In 1846 Théodore ROUSSEAU established his studio at Barbizon, and Jean François MILLET settled there after 1848. Daubigny had a decisive influence on Claude MONET.

Most of the literature on Daubigny dates from the 19th and early 20th centuries. David Croal Thomson, *The Barbizon School of Painters* (1902), is a representative work. Almost the only up-to-date publication is Robert L. Herbert, *Barbizon Revisited* (1962), a catalog of an important exhibition organized in part by the Boston Museum, and a thorough account of the whole movement. John Rewald includes some useful material in *History of Impressionism* (1946; rev. ed. 1961).

DAUDET / By Patricia Zele Gossen

The French novelist, dramatist, and short-story writer Alphonse Daudet (1840–1897) is remembered chiefly for his regionalist sketches of Provence and for his transitional role in the evolution of 19th-century theater.

Alphonse Daudet. (New York Public Library, Picture Collection)

Born in Nîmes, as a child Alphonse Daudet (pronounced dō-dā′) experienced the heady delights of a sun-drenched Provence and the darkening contrasts of his family's steadily worsening financial condition. His father, a silk manufacturer, had to abandon business there in 1849, moving the family north to Lyons; never fully recovering from the depression which followed the Revolution of 1848, the Daudets finally lost everything in 1857. The family became scattered, and Alphonse—never an enthusiastic student—found himself miserably placed as a *pion*, or monitor, in a provincial *collège*. After a few months he was rescued by his elder brother Ernest, who brought him to Paris and generously encouraged the boy's already evident literary talents. A collection of undistinguished love verses, *Les Amoureuses*, represented a most traditional debut for Alphonse, but again through his brother's influence he was directed by the opportunities of journalism to contribute prose *chroniques*, stylish social sketches, which won him entry to the prestigious *Figaro* (1859); already in these early compositions, a mixture of what critics have called "rose-water fantasy" and often sharp satire reveals Daudet's most characteristic modes: sentimentality and imaginative flight.

Early Career

Until 1865 the young Daudet enjoyed financial security as a comfortable undersecretary to the Duc de Morny —a position accorded, in almost fairy tale manner, by a chance notice of the Empress Eugénie. In these years he collaborated in writing a number of one-act plays (*La Dernière idole*, 1862; *Les Absents*, 1864; *L'Oeillet blanc*, 1865), helped toward the stage by the Duc de Morny's influence. Daudet decided to live solely by his pen after the duke's death, and in 1866 the first of his regionalist sketches, or *Lettres de mon moulin* (*Letters from My Mill*), based on Provençal folklore began appearing in Paris papers.

Two years later Daudet's first long work, *Le Petit chose* (*The Little Good-for-nothing*), was completed; largely autobiographical, this early novel speaks of boyhood joys and travails but in the end leads its hero to the failure and obscurity which Daudet's recent successes were to forestall. The serial publication of his *Aventures prodigieuses de Tartarin de Tarascon* (1869) assured Daudet a place in Parisian literary circles, and today—with *Lettres* and *Le Petit chose*—it represents his most lasting contribution to French letters. Full of boisterous good humor and the vitality of southern climes, Daudet's picaro Tartarin nevertheless stands in sharp contrast to the young hero of *L'Arlésienne*, originally one of the Provençal tales related in *Lettres*, and adapted for the stage as Daudet's most serious dramatic effort in 1872. Here somber passion and jealousy lead to suicide—a thematic shift typical of Daudet's search for personal and artistic maturity in these years. *L'Arlésienne* failed miserably before the theatergoers of 1872, and this reversal of fortune turned Daudet resolutely back to novel writing. The play remains important, however, for the transformation Daudet there attempted in established theatrical formulas. Augustin Scribe's "well-made play" and the "comedy of manners" fostered by Alexandre Dumas *fils* and Émile Augier had for 20 years held dominion over the French stage. The seemingly plotless, moody, sequential arrangement of *L'Arlésienne* (with incidental music by Georges Bizet) produced shock and laughter, reactions of a prejudiced public erased only by a second, successful production in 1885, when Émile Zola's campaign for naturalistic reform in the theater as well as the novel had begun to condition audiences to a genre less dependent on formal contrivance, closer to the unconnected sequences of life.

Later Works

Married in 1867, a father the following year, Daudet felt that the press of family responsibilities made success imperative; the shock of defeat and occupation after the Franco-Prussian War (1870) turned his imagination to a more serious vein, and it was at this time as well that he met regularly with Gustave Flaubert, Ivan Turgenev, Edmond de Goncourt, and Zola—all diversely arguing for an art expressive of nature in all its determinisms, of man in his natural milieu. Zola's formulation of "naturalism," weighted with scientific analogies, would not come until 1880, but Daudet followed the author of *Les Rougon-Macquart* as closely as his temperament permitted and over the next 20 years produced 10 long novels of his own (*Froment jeune et Risler aîné,* 1874; *Jack,* 1876; *Le Nabab,* 1877; *Les Rois en exil,* 1879; *Numa Roumestan,* 1881; *L'Évangéliste,* 1883; *Sapho,* 1884; *L'Immortel,* 1887; *La Lutte pour la vie,* 1889; *Le Soutien de famille,* 1896). Perhaps the most accomplished of the early, more determinedly objective works is *Jack,* the story of an illegitimate son reared below his station, forced to become a laborer, and eventually destroyed by the brutalizing world of industrial society. The novel contains one of the first protests heard in France against the dehumanizing effects of child labor.

As in all these realistic novels of manners, however, Daudet undermines both the force of *Jack's* social protest and the novel's very artistic integrity with lacrimonious appeals to reader sentiment and verbose developments. Sentimentality is perhaps the hallmark of Daudet's fictional world. Daudet died after an apoplectic attack on Dec. 16, 1897.

Further Reading

Alphonse Daudet is listed in the Literature study guide (III, H, 1, b). He achieved wide popular success with a distinctly sentimental realism, while Émile ZOLA and the naturalist school advocated depiction of contemporary life in all its brutality.

Daudet's works, particularly his novels, have found many translators; a recent version of *Letters from My Mill* is by John P. Macgregor (1966). Studies of Daudet in English include the early but still valuable book by R. H. Sherard, *Alphonse Daudet: A Biographical and Critical Study* (1894), and the recent general treatment by Murray Sachs, *The Career of Alphonse Daudet: A Critical Study* (1965). Daudet's theatrical works are studied by

Guy Rufus Saylor in *Alphonse Daudet as a Dramatist* (1940).

DAUMIER / By Francis E. Hyslop, Jr.

Honoré Victorin Daumier (1808–1879) was a French lithographer, painter, and sculptor. A romantic realist in style, he produced caricatures that are abiding commentaries on politics and social manners.

In some 40 years of political and social commentary Honoré Daumier (pronounced dō-myā´) created an enormously rich and varied record of Parisian middle-class life in the form of nearly 4,000 lithographs, about 1,000 wood engravings, and several hundred drawings and paintings. In them the comic spir-

Honoré Daumier, a bronze self-portrait sculpture, in the Bibliothèque Nationale, Paris. (Giraudon)

The Laundress, a painting by Daumier, in the Louvre, Paris. Another version is in the Metropolitan Museum, New York City. (Giraudon)

Early Works

Under the sponsorship of Charles Philipon, publisher of *Caricature* and *Charivari,* Daumier drew political cartoons in the early 1830s until press censorship in 1835 forced him to do satiric pictures of bourgeois manners. Among his best-known early lithographs are *Lafayette Buried,* portraying the fat king as a hypocritical mourner, although the dark black shape of Louis Philippe is esthetically attractive; the *Legislative Belly,* depicting a group of potbellied legislators and organized in a broad light and shade pattern; and *Rue Transnonain,* concerned with police brutality and showing a family murdered in a bedroom, which is dramatically effective in its restraint.

In order to give a forceful character to his images of legislators, Daumier modeled busts of his targets in clay before executing his drawings. He was on friendly terms with several sculptors and periodically returned to the use of sculptured forms; some of them were later carried out in terra-cotta or cast in bronze.

Between 1836 and 1838 Daumier did a notable series of 100 lithographs about an imaginary swindler named Robert Macaire, who symbolized the get-rich-quick philosophy of the times. His character is tellingly suggested in a famous print entitled *The Public Is Stupid.*

In the early 1830s Daumier published a series of 50 devastatingly anticlassical lithographs entitled *Ancient History.* Delightfully comic in effect, they also effectively exploit the rich blacks possible in the lithographic technique. The *Abduction of Helen of Troy* and *Narcissus* are good examples: Paris, gleefully smoking a cigar, is riding in triumph on the shoulders of Helen; Narcissus, admiring his reflection, is hideously scrawny.

Later Work

The Revolution of 1848 gave Daumier another opportunity to do political cartoons, among them The *Last Meeting of the Council* and *Victor Hugo and Émile Girardin* (as supporters of Louis Napoleon). At this time he also began his serious work as a painter with a competition picture, heroic in conception, *The Republic;* an unfinished *We Want Barabbas;* and a revolutionary street scene, *The Uprising,* whose authenticity some scholars question.

In 1850, as Louis Napoleon seemed to be an increasing threat to the republic, Daumier fashioned a sculptured caricature, *Ratapoil* ("Ratskin"), which symbolized the whole class of Bonapartist followers and Napoleon himself. It is a strikingly novel pictorial conception of sculpture and seems almost to have been "painted" with some fluid material.

A decade later *The Laundress* (ca. 1863; two versions) reflects Daumier's deep interest in ordinary people and, in subject at least, belongs to the mid-century development of realism. *The Drama* (ca. 1860) is one of the few paintings directly related to a lithograph. A rather ambitious work for Daumier, it has a twofold psychological character: the amused detachment of the artist observing a melodrama and the excited absorption of the audience.

it of Molière comes to life once again. After having been the scourge of Louis Philippe and the July Monarchy (1830–1848), Daumier continued as a satirist of Louis Napoleon and the Second Empire (1851–1870). Poor himself, the artist sympathized with the struggling bourgeois and proletarian citizens of Paris. As a man of the left, he battled for the establishment of a republic, which finally came in 1870. Liberals have always applauded Daumier; some conservatives, however, have been inclined to consider him woolly-minded.

Honoré Daumier, born on Feb. 26, 1808, in Marseilles, was the son of a glazier. When Honoré was 6, the family moved to Paris, where the elder Daumier hoped to win success as a poet. Honoré grew up in a home in which humanistic concerns had some importance. A born draftsman and designer who was largely self-taught, he received some formal instruction from Alexandre Lenoir, one of Jacques Louis David's students. An obscure artist named Ramelet taught Daumier the elements of the new, inexpensive, and popular technique of lithography. Daumier's style is so much his own that it is not easy to disentangle influences from other artists. Rembrandt and Francisco Goya are usually mentioned, along with Peter Paul Rubens, the Venetian school, and photography.

In the early 1860s, when Daumier had no regular employment, he did many small canvases, watercolors, and drawings. His persistent interest in the arts comes out delightfully in a little watercolor picture, *The Connoisseurs*, in which his skill in expressing human responses by silhouettes and physical attitudes is perfectly realized.

In the late 1860s Daumier gave a great deal of attention to the European scene, especially to the development of Prussia as a military threat. The menace of militarism is summed up in *European Equilibrium* (1867) and the devastation of the Franco-Prussian War in *Peace—an Idyl* (1871). The late lithographs are conceived in a new, open, and sketchily linear style.

Although Daumier, like Gustave Courbet, maintained that it was necessary to be of one's own time, he sometimes turned to literary sources, as in the long series of interpretations of Don Quixote, painted at the end of his career. *Don Quixote and Sancho Panza,* with its balancing of two eternal human types, reflects the balance in his own temperament of opposed romantic and realistic impulses.

During his own time Daumier was not widely recognized as a painter, and his only one-man show of paintings was held in 1878. He died the following year on February 11 in Valmondois.

Daumier's Influence

Caricaturists and social critics have been keenly aware of Daumier's contribution for well over a century. In the field of painting his mark has been less considerable. Daumier was a draftsman and an almost monochromatic tonalist. Later artists put less emphasis on drawing and created their pictures primarily with touches of color. If Daumier's effective use of flat "stains" and abstract shapes in wash drawings and lithographs remind us of Édouard Manet, we cannot be sure that the parallelism is more than fortuitous. On the other hand, realistic café scenes such as *Absinthe* (1863) were followed by a whole line of similar works by Manet, Edgar Degas, and Henri de Toulouse-Lautrec.

Further Reading

Honoré Daumier is listed in the Art study guide (III, H, 1, d). Other artists who were famous for their caricatures were William HOGARTH, Franciso GOYA, and George GROSZ.

Bernard Lemann, *Honoré Daumier* (1946), is a carefully chosen selection of 240 lithographs, well reproduced, with a good introduction and notes. K. E. Maison, *Honoré Daumier* (1968), is a two-volume *catalogue raisonné* of the paintings, watercolors, and drawings; it is the most up-to-date study, with the main emphasis on authenticity and dating rather than on the interpretation of Daumier's work. Maison's *Daumier Drawings* (1960) is also a useful book in spite of its rather gray plates. Jacques Lassaigne's general survey, *Daumier* (1938; trans. 1939), remains a good introduction. Oliver W. Larkin, *Daumier: Man of His Time* (1966), is a solid and well-illustrated study. Howard P. Vincent, *Daumier and His World* (1968), is freshly researched and well written.

Jeanne L. Wasserman's catalog of Daumier's sculptural works, *Daumier Sculpture* (1969), is very thorough.

DAVENPORT / By Jesper Rosenmeier

English Puritan clergyman and author John Davenport (1597–1670) founded the New Haven colony in America and was its theological ruler for its first 30 years.

Of a distinguished English family, John Davenport was the fifth son of the mayor of Coventry. He attended the free grammar school at Coventry, then entered Oxford but had to withdraw for lack of money. Made vicar of St. Stephen's in London when he was 19, he became widely known as a pulpit orator. He returned to Oxford to take a bachelor of divinity degree. All this time he seems to have remained loyal to the Church of England, although he knew members of the Puritan party. Prior to his election to St. Stephen's he had written letters professing his conformity in order to allay suspicion and silence his opposition.

Davenport's Nonconformism evidently developed gradually. In 1629 he was one of the group actively work-

John Davenport, a painting done in 1670 and attributed to John Foster. (Yale University Art Gallery)

ing for a charter for the America-bound Massachusetts Bay Company, and he was a friend of John Cotton. Davenport's was a strictly orthodox Puritanism; in Holland (as later in New England) he opposed the baptism of the children of the unregenerate. His views brought him into conflict with the Dutch Classis, and he was denied the right to preach. Thus, on John Cotton's invitation, Davenport sailed for Boston in 1637, with his wife and his lifelong friend, the merchant Theophilus Eaton. In Boston, Davenport took part in the Antinomian crisis, which involved Anne Hutchinson's heretical idea of "grace." He founded the colony of New Haven in 1638 and became its pastor, while Theophilus Eaton became its governor.

Devoted to the life of the colony, Davenport also authored many tracts, including *The Knowledge of Christ* (1653) and *The Saints Anchor-hold in All Storms and Tempests* (1701). In *A Discourse about Civil Government in a New Plantation Whose Design Is Religion* (1633) he defended theocracy, which he defined as making "the Lord God our Governor." Davenport's political and theological positions were expressed with the intensity of one who acts in constant expectation of the Messiah. He preached sermons in support of the regicide judges Edward Whalley and William Goffe, who fled to America and were said to have found refuge in his house.

Davenport opposed assimilating New Haven into the larger Connecticut colony. When efforts against this union failed, Davenport in 1667, feeling Christ's interests "miserably lost," accepted the pastorate of the First Church in Boston. He died in Boston on May 30, 1670.

Further Reading

John Davenport is listed in the Religion study guide (I, O, 1, c). He was invited to America by John COTTON. Thomas HOOKER and John WINTHROP were early settlers of Connecticut.

Letters of John Davenport, Puritan Divine, edited by Isabel MacBeath Calder, was published in 1937. For information on Davenport see A. W. M'Clure, *The Lives of John Wilson, John Norton, and John Davenport* (1846), and Cotton Mather, *Magnalia Christi Americana: or, The Ecclesiastical History of New-England* (1702; rev. ed., 2 vols., 1853–1855; repr. 1967). Robert G. Pope, *The Half-way Covenant: Church Membership in Puritan New England* (1969), includes an extensive chapter on Davenport. He is also discussed in Perry Miller, *The New England Mind: From Colony to Province* (1953).

DAVID / By David Rudavsky

David, the second king of the Israelites (reigned ca. 1010–ca. 970 B.C.), was regarded as a model king and founded a permanent dynasty.

D avid was born in Bethlehem, the youngest son of Jesse of the tribe of Judah. The prophet Samuel, after revoking Saul's designation as king, secretly anointed David as Saul's successor. David attained great popularity by killing the Philistine giant Goliath in combat (1 Samuel 17:49), although another biblical source attributes this feat to one named Elhanan (2 Samuel 21:19). A skilled harpist, David was brought to the royal

Donatello's bronze David, done for the Medici, in the Museo Nazionale, Florence. (Alinari-Anderson)

court to divert Saul with music and alleviate the depression that Saul had succumbed to under the strain of his responsibilities. At court David won the undying friendship of the crown prince, Jonathan, whose sister Michal he married.

After Saul's jealousy had forced David to flee for his life, he had two opportunities to slay the King but magnanimously spared him. Saul eventually met his end at Gilboa, together with three of his sons, including Jonathan. After a period of mourning, David proceeded to Hebron, where he was chosen king by the elders of Judah. Saul's general Abner, however, proclaimed Ishbaal (Ishbosheth), a surviving son of the dead king, as the sovereign. In the civil war that ensued, Ishbaal and Abner were slain. Their deaths removed the last obstacles from David's path to the throne, and about 1010 B.C. he was crowned king of all the Israelites.

After numerous battles David liberated Israel from the yoke of the Philistines and ushered in a golden era for his people. He captured Jerusalem and made it his capital because of its strategic military position and its location outside the boundaries of any tribe. He placed the Ark of the Covenant in a tent near his residence, thereby making Jerusalem the religious, as well as the national, center of all of Israel and preparing the way for his son and successor, Solomon, to erect the Holy Temple there.

David expanded his kingdom to Phoenicia in the west, the Arabian Desert in the east, the Orontes River in the north, and Etzion Geber (Elath) in the south. But internal political troubles overtook David. His son Absalom led a rebellion which was finally suppressed when Joab, David's general, killed him, although the King had ordered that he be spared. David also had to quash an uprising of Saul's tribe, the Benjaminites.

The Bible idealizes David as a warrior, statesman, loyal friend, and gifted poet, yet it does not fail to mention his faults and moral lapses. At one time David callously plotted the death in battle of one of his officers, Uriah the Hittite, so that he could marry Uriah's beautiful wife, Bathsheba. For this he was denounced by the prophet Nathan, and, recognizing that he had committed a great moral wrong, the King fasted and prayed in repentance.

Jewish tradition ascribes to David the authorship of the Book of Psalms and refers to him as the "sweet singer of Israel." The Messiah, too, was to come forth from "the stock of Jesse" (Isaiah 9:5, 11:10), and indeed the New Testament speaks of Jesus as a descendant of the House of David (Matthew 1:16). David's tomb, traditionally assumed to be on Mt. Zion, has become a venerated place of pilgrimage.

Further Reading

David is listed in the Religion study guide (II, A, 5). He succeeded SAUL and was succeeded by SOLOMON.

The Bible portrays the life and achievements of David in 1 Samuel 16 through 2 Samuel 5, 2 Samuel 19–20, 1 Kings 1–2, and 1 Chronicles 10–29. The chapter on King David in Harry Meyer Orlinsky, *Ancient Israel* (1954), is recommended. See also Martin North, *The History of*

Israel (1953; 2d ed. 1960); John Bright, *A History of Israel* (1959); and Mortimer J. Cohen, "David the King," in Simon Noveck, ed., *Great Jewish Personalities in Ancient and Medieval Times* (1959).

DAVID I / By Coburn V. Graves

David I (1084–1153) reigned as king of Scotland from 1124 to 1153. He is noted for his introduction of Norman institutions into Scotland.

David I came to the Scottish throne when his brother King Alexander I died in 1124 without an heir. David's two wars with England failed to bring northern English lands into his realm. He first marched south on the pretext of protecting the interests of his niece Matilda, daughter of Henry I, against Stephen, who had claimed the English throne. The Scottish army was routed at the Battle of the Standard, fought at Cutton Moor in 1138. David, however, was able to secure recognition of his son, Henry, as holder of Northumberland and Huntingdon, to which David's wife had been heiress. When a second invasion of England in 1140 proved as futile as the first, David gave up his program of expansion and devoted himself to internal Scottish affairs.

David brought a number of Norman nobles and churchmen with him when he traveled from England to take the Scottish crown. Norman nobles displaced Celtic leaders in the north, and their castles began to rise to symbolize the shift of political power. Landholdings based on Scottish customary rights were made subject to Norman charters, and Norman practices in law and administration were introduced. For the man in the field, however, it was a quiet revolution; no one was displaced, and the new system was grafted onto the old in a peaceful way.

Norman influences were especially apparent in the Church. David increased the number of dioceses from four to nine and named Normans as bishops of the new ones. He also founded 10 monasteries, welcoming to Scotland new orders that were popular south of the border, the Cistercians and the Augustinian canons regular. His active patronage of the Church won for David an enduring reputation for piety.

David was truly the father of the city, or burgh, in Scotland. He himself chartered only four or five burghs, but he allowed the development of private burghs under the aegis of his ecclesiastical and lay nobles. The rise of cities was related to a developing commerce, and to help the growing trade David broke new ground by issuing a silver penny, the first Scottish coinage. Within the cities a new class developed, the townsmen.

For Scotland, David was a constructive revolutionary:

King David I of Scotland (left) with his grandson Malcolm, from the 14th-century Kelso Charter. The charter pertains to an abbey, now in ruins, which was established by David at Kelso, Roxburghshire, about 1128. (Courtesy Duchess of Roxburghe; Photo, National Library of Scotland)

the language and customs of the Scots gave way to English speech and manners; the Church was organized on patterns akin to those of England and Rome; and the rise of burghs saw the emergence of the Scottish middle class.

Further Reading

David I is listed in the European History study guide (II, D, 1, b; II, E, 1). He was the son of MALCOLM III and St. MARGARET OF SCOTLAND.

David's Normanizing work is covered in R. L. Graeme Ritchie, *The Normans in Scotland* (1954). A judicious appraisal of David's contributions is in *A New History of Scotland*, vol. 4: *Scotland from the Earliest Times to 1603*, written by William Croft Dickinson and George S. Pryde (1962; rev. ed. 1965). An interesting summary of the epoch is provided by Eric Linklater, *The Survival of Scotland: A New History of Scotland from Roman Times to the Present Day* (1968).

＊　　＊　　＊

J. L. DAVID / By F. Hamilton Hazlehurst

The French painter Jacques Louis David (1748–1825) was the leader of the neoclassic movement. His style set the artistic standards for many of his contemporaries and determined the direction of numerous 19th-century painters.

Jacques Louis David (pronounced dä-vēd′) early turned his back on the frivolous rococo manner, looking instead to antiquity for inspiration. Following the ideals of Nicolas Poussin, to whom the artist candidly admitted he owed everything, David sought to reduce classical principles to their barest, unencumbered essentials. In this endeavor he observed with avid interest the neoclassicism propounded by Johann Winckelmann and the illustrations of antiquity found in the paintings of Anton Raphael Mengs. An outspoken political firebrand, David espoused the cause of the French Revolution and under the Convention held sway as the virtual dictator of the arts; later when Napoleon came to power, he acted willingly as his artistic spokesman.

Jacques Louis David, a self-portrait, in the Louvre, Paris. (Giraudon)

The Rape of the Sabine Women, *painted by Jacques Louis David. The work, completed in 1799, hangs in the Louvre, Paris. (Giraudon)*

David was born in Paris on Aug. 30, 1748. His well-to-do bourgeois family placed him in the studio of that arch-practitioner of the rococo manner, the eminent painter François Boucher, to whom David was apparently distantly related. Perhaps because of his own advanced years, Boucher encouraged David to study under Joseph Marie Vien, a painter who had been attracted by the new wave of interest in antiquity while studying in Rome. In 1771 David won second prize in the Prix de Rome competition, but it was not until 3 years later and after severe mental frustration that he won the first prize with his painting *Antiochus Dying for the Love of Stratonice.*

Early Works

David went to Rome in 1775 in the company of Vien, who had just been named the director of the French Academy there. David studied the ancient architectural monuments, marble reliefs, and freestanding statues. In addition, he strove for a clearer understanding of the classical principles underlying the styles of the Renaissance and baroque masters Raphael, the Carracci, Domenichino, and Guido Reni. The effects of David's Romanization were first witnessed in his *Belisarius Asking for Alms,* exhibited in Paris in 1781. When he returned to Paris in 1780, he was an artist already thoroughly imbued with the tenets of classicism. He was admitted to the French Academy in 1783 with his painting *Andromache by the Body of Hector.*

The following year David returned to Rome in order to paint the *Oath of the Horatii,* a work which was immediately acclaimed a masterpiece both in Italy and in France at its showing at the Parisian Salon of 1785. The painting reflected a strong interest in archeological exactitude in the depiction of figures and settings. Its careful-

ly calculated severity of composition and its emphasis on a sculptural hardness of precise drawing, which David saw as more important than color, contributed to the forceful moralistic tone of the subject: the oath being administered to the Horatii by their father, who demanded their sacrifice for the good of the state. In this single work, with its strong republican implications, those aspiring to do so could find a call to revolution, a revolution which was in fact only 5 years distant. The *Oath* was followed by other moralizing canvases such as the *Death of Socrates* (1787) and *Brutus and the Lictors Bringing Home to Brutus the Bodies of His Sons* (1789), both extolling the classical virtues.

French Revolution

With the Revolution in full swing, David for a time abandoned his classical approach and began to paint scenes describing contemporary events, among them the unfinished *Oath of the Tennis Court* (1791), glorifying the first challenge to royal authority by the parliamentarians of the period. He also concentrated on portraits of the martyred heroes of the fight for freedom, including the *Death of Marat* (1793), the *Death of Lepeletier de Saint-Fargeau* (1793) and the *Death of Joseph Bara* (1794), all executed with an unvarnished realism. The artist was deeply involved with the political scene; elected to the National Convention in 1792, he served as a deputy to that all-powerful body and was one of those who voted for the execution of King Louis XVI.

David had apparently long harbored great animosity toward the French Academy, perhaps because it had failed to fully recognize his talents when he had first submitted works for the Grand Prix competition. Though an honored member by the time of the Revolution, in 1793 he hastened its dissolution, forming a group called the Commune of the Arts; this group was almost immediately supplanted by the Popular and Republican Society of the Arts, from whose ranks the Institute ultimately would be formed.

A friend of Robespierre, David nearly accompanied him to the guillotine when the Jacobin fell from power in 1794. Imprisoned for 7 months, first at Fresnes and then in the Luxembourg, the artist emerged a politically wiser man. It was while in prison that David executed one of his rare landscapes: the *Gardens of the Luxembourg* (1794), a view from his prison window. By 1798 he was busy on what he proclaimed his masterpiece, the *Rape of the Sabine Women*. The subject matter, derived from the classical legend described by Livy in which the Sabine women intervened in the battle between their fathers and brothers and their Roman husbands, represented a calculated appeal by David to end the internecine conflict that had ripped France asunder; further, the vast canvas was planned as a sort of manifesto proclaiming the validity of the antique.

David and Napoleon

It was at this time that David met Napoleon Bonaparte, in whose person he recognized a worthy new hero whom he promptly proceeded to glorify. The Emperor in turn realized the rich potential of David as a propagandist born to champion his imperial regime, and it was probably with this in mind that he invited the artist to accompany him on his Egyptian campaign; that David declined to go was surely due only to the fact that he was then deeply absorbed in the creation of his avowed masterpiece, the *Sabine Women*. Named "first painter," David executed a number of portraits of the Emperor, the most notable of which is probably that entitled *Bonaparte Crossing the St. Bernard Pass* (1800), in which the subject was idealized in physical stature and romanticized as the effortless man of action. Among the major commissions granted David by the Emperor were the colossal scenes treating specific episodes of his reign. The best-known of these are the *Coronation of Napoleon and Josephine* (1805–1807), containing over 100 portraits, and the *Distribution of the Eagles* (1810).

Though David would have preferred to be remembered for his history painting, he was at his best as a portraitist. Certain of his portraits, such as *Madame Sériziat and Her Daughter* and *Monsieur Sériziat* (1795), are done with an incredible directness and thus retain a freshness and vivacity not often encountered in David's more serious works. His unfinished portrait *Madame Récamier* (1800), with the subject shown in long, loosely flowing robes, vaguely reminiscent of the antique, summarizes the studied elegance of the neoclassic age.

With Bonaparte's defeat at Waterloo and the subsequent restoration of the Bourbons, David tried to retreat into quiet seclusion, but his earlier political affiliation and, more particularly, his actions during the heat of the Revolution were not calculated to warm his relations with the new rulers. He was declared persona non grata and fled to Switzerland. A short time later he settled in

Brussels, where he continued to paint until his death on Dec. 29, 1825. His family's urgent request that his ashes be returned to France was denied. He was buried amidst great pomp and circumstance in the church of Ste-Gudule in Brussels.

David's Influence

There was scarcely a young painter of the following generation who was not influenced by David's style, a style which had within it such diverse aspects as classicism, realism, and romanticism. Among his foremost pupils, each of whom developed various different facets of his style, were Antoine Jean, Baron Gros; Pierre Narcisse Guérin; François Gérard; Girodet de Roucy-Trioson; and perhaps most important, J. A. D. Ingres.

Further Reading

Jacques Louis David is listed in the Art study guide (III, G, 1, b; III, H, 1, a). He studied briefly with François BOUCHER and was influenced by RAPHAEL, the CARRACCI, Guido RENI, and most importantly, Nicolas POUSSIN. David's followers included Baron GROS and J. A. D. INGRES.

Most of the vast literature on David is in French. In English, the best studies are W. R. Valentiner, *Jacques Louis David and the French Revolution* (1929), and David L. Dowd, *Pageant Master of the Republic: Jacques-Louis David and the French Revolution* (1948). David is also discussed in the following general studies of the period: Lionello Venturi, *Modern Painters* (2 vols., 1947–1950); Walter Friedlaender, *David to Delacroix* (1952); and Jack Lindsay, *Death of the Hero: French Painting from David to Delacroix* (1961).

DAVIES / By Allen S. Weller

American painter Arthur Bowen Davies (1862–1928) introduced a contemporary quality in a basically romantic style and was a pioneer in bringing American art into the mainstream of progressive Western painting.

Arthur B. Davies was born in Utica, N.Y., on Sept. 26, 1862. He was sketching and painting scenes of the Mohawk Valley before he was 16, when his family moved to Chicago. He studied at the Art Institute there, worked for the board of trade, and went on an engineering expedition to Mexico. In 1887 he went to New York City and studied at the Art Students League, where Robert Henri and George Luks became his friends. Davies's earliest professional work (1888–1891) was magazine illustration. He married in 1890 and moved to a farm near Congers, N.Y.; soon afterward he competed unsuccessfully for the mural decorations of the Appellate Court in New York City. In 1894 the New York art dealer

*Arthur B. Davies, photographed about 1910.
(Library of Congress)*

William Macbeth provided him with a studio over his gallery, gave him a one-man show, and introduced him to industrialist Benjamin Altman, who provided funds for his first trip abroad. In Europe he was impressed by the Venetians and by Delacroix, Puvis de Chavannes, and Whistler.

By 1900 Davies had found his characteristic theme: the female nude in a landscape setting, romantic, nostalgic, frequently with a mysterious ritualistic quality. The figures, small in scale, are often arranged in a friezelike procession against dark and forbidding backgrounds. The mood is poetic, with a peculiarly personal symbolism that is suggested by mythological themes or by obscure symbolic titles. A new grandeur was introduced in his work as the result of a trip to California in 1905 during which he made studies of mountains.

Davies was one of "The Eight" whose 1908 exhibition at the Macbeth Gallery challenged the authority and conservatism of the National Academy of Design. Five of the exhibiting artists stressed urban realism in subject matter; Davies and Maurice Prendergast established notes of fantasy and charm which were wholly personal. Davies was a master of many media—oil, watercolor, pastel, lithograph, etching, sculpture, murals, and tapestry designs.

From 1912 to 1914 Davies was president of the Society of Independent Artists, which had been formed to organize the Armory Show of 1913. This celebrated exhibition first introduced American artists and the American public to the European pioneers of 20th-century style.

Davies's work for a period reflected a new cubist influence but returned eventually to the idyllic fantasies that were his natural language.

Though Davies was a habitual recluse and worked in considerable secrecy, he attracted devoted admirers and was generous in his admiration of progressive artists. During the 1920s he executed a series of murals and designed tapestries. He also became obsessed with the act of inhalation and believed that the character and quality of Greek art was due to the fact that it represented figures consciously controlling their breathing. It has even been said that his personal experiments in breathing led to his heart attack in 1923. After that he went again to Europe, where he painted a series of romantic landscapes in northern Italy. He died in Florence, alone in his studio, on Oct. 24, 1928.

Further Reading

Arthur B. Davies is listed in the Art study guide (IV, E, 7). He had been impressed by the painting of James McNeill WHISTLER.

There is no comprehensive study of Davies. Royal Cortissoz, *Arthur B. Davies* (1931), is a brief but useful picture book. Davies's important role in formation of the Armory Show is documented in Milton W. Brown, *The Story of the Armory Show* (1963). There are interesting personal sidelights in Bennard B. Perlman, *The Immortal Eight: American Painting from Eakins to the Armory Show, 1870–1913* (1962).

A. J. **DAVIS** / **By Alan Gowans**

> Alexander Jackson Davis (1803–1892) was a leading figure of the 19th-century Gothic revival in American architecture.

Alexander Jackson Davis began as an apprentice architectural draftsman to Josiah Brady of New York in 1826, though his early painting ambitions remained evident in his lifelong picturesque approach to architectural design. In 1829 Davis joined Ithiel Town in what became the first architectural firm of a modern sort in the United States, lasting until Town's death in 1844.

Davis specialized in domestic architecture, leaving more public or monumental commissions to Town. Hundreds of houses were built directly or indirectly from Davis's designs; he was also among the first architects to design furniture for his larger houses. He claimed to have been first to introduce to America "the English Gothic Villa with Barge Boards, Bracketts, Oriels, Tracery in Windows . . . in 1832" and also the Italianate villa, with a drawing exhibited about 1835. In the early 1840s Davis began moving into the orbit of A. J. Downing, illustrating Downing's book, *Country Houses*, in 1850. After Downing's death Davis designed and supervised all buildings in Llewellyn Park in West Orange, N.J., conceived by

The William J. Rotch house, New Bedford, Mass., designed by Alexander Jackson Davis. (Library of Congress, Photo by Ned Goode, 1961)

Downing and financed by Llewellyn P. Haskell as America's first "garden suburb" (1852–1869).

Picturesqueness was predominant in all Davis's works. Yet in his last major project, an unsuccessful submission in the 1867 competition for the New York City Post Office, he designed a metal and glass structure which clearly presaged 20th-century "functional" concepts. Far from being contradictory, however, both picturesqueness and functionalism were from the first inherent in the American—as distinct from English or French—Gothic revival.

In America, Gothic revival architecture never challenged the Roman or Greek revival in mass popularity; indeed, its associations were fundamentally "antiestablishment." Gothic was an "arty" style, associated with the idea of the "natural man." There was always something eccentric about it: a typical example was the exaggerated asymmetry and anticlassical proportions of Davis's H. K. Harral house in Bridgeport, Conn. (ca. 1846; demolished). Such stylistic self-consciousness inevitably encouraged self-conscious formalism—emphasis on the "naturalness" of Gothic forms and structure as an end in itself—and thence to the kind of "functionalism" exhibited in Davis's 1867 Post Office design. For historical reasons, however, the picturesque side of Gothic revival architecture predominated in America so that its chief legacy was the Arts and Crafts movement of about 1890 to about 1910, prefaced by the Romanesque of H. H. Richardson and climaxed by the early work of Louis Sullivan and Frank Lloyd Wright. Combining something of both trends, Davis has claim to be the most representative of all American Gothic revivalists.

Further Reading

Alexander Jackson Davis is listed in the Art study guide (IV, C, 4). His works prefigured some of those of Louis SULLIVAN and Frank Lloyd WRIGHT.

Though many articles have appeared in recent years on various aspects of Davis's life and career, the only book-length biography is Roger H. Newton, *Town & Davis, Architects: Pioneers in American Revivalist Architec-*

ture, 1812–1870 (1942), which has serious limitations. Davis's influence and career are discussed in Alan Gowans, *Images of American Living: Four Centuries of Architecture and Furniture as Cultural Expression* (1964).

✳   ✳   ✳

H. W. DAVIS / By Joel H. Silbey

The American congressman Henry Winter Davis (1817–1865) was a leading advocate of Radical Republican policies during the Civil War and a violent opponent of President Lincoln's more conservative course.

Henry Winter Davis was born Aug. 16, 1817, in Annapolis, Md. He attended Kenyon College, studied law at the University of Virginia, and in 1840 established practice in Alexandria, Va. In 1850 he moved to Baltimore, where he became active in Whig politics, absorbing much of the strong nationalist perspective of that party.

Alarmed by the influx of Catholic immigrants in the early 1850s, Davis joined the Whigs and Democrats in the nativist Know-Nothing movement. He was elected to Congress three times as a Know-Nothing between 1855 and 1859. In 1860, as the Know-Nothing movement declined, Davis cooperated with the Republican party in Congress but maintained a measure of political independence by supporting the former Whig John Bell, the Constitutional Union candidate, for president. Davis was defeated for reelection in 1861.

Maryland's secession from the Union appeared to be a real possibility in 1861. Davis took the lead in rallying the unionist forces there in the fight to keep the state loyal. His militant unionism and dislike for the Democrats and conservative Republicans made him increasingly sympathetic to the Radical Republicans' crusade to crush secession and the slave power. Reelected to Congress as an unconditional unionist in 1863, Davis cooperated with the Radicals in attacking Lincoln's moderate policies on slavery and his conciliatory attitude toward the South and in seeking to wrench the initiative in policy making away from the President in favor of Congress.

In 1863 Lincoln issued a relatively mild Reconstruction plan permitting 10 percent of a seceded state's voters as of 1860 to form a new state government once they took a loyalty oath to the Union. Angered by the plan's moderation and restoral of a status quo in the seceded states, Davis and Senator Benjamin Franklin Wade of Ohio introduced a counterproposal (Wade-Davis Bill, 1864) which politically proscribed many Confederate sympathizers, required immediate emancipation, compelled repudiation of the Confederate war debt, and insisted that a majority of loyal electors, rather than 10 percent, set up any new government. When Lincoln pocket-vetoed the measure, the two congressmen issued the

Wade-Davis Manifesto, bitterly castigating the President for his "rash and fatal act" in defying Congress and Radical policies. But despite some initial support, they had overreached themselves. Most Republicans drew back from such violent assaults on the President in an election year. Davis, swallowing his disgust, even worked for Lincoln's reelection rather than chance a Democratic victory.

Davis's always precarious political position in conservative Maryland was weakened by his opposition to the President, and he was not renominated in 1864. He continued active in the lame-duck session of Congress in 1864–1865 as a critic of the administration and an advocate of further radical proposals, including Negro suffrage. In December 1865 he contracted pneumonia and died on the 30th in Baltimore.

Further Reading

Henry Winter Davis is listed in the American History study guide (VI, B, 1, b). Benjamin Franklin WADE was his ally in Congress.

The only biography of Davis is a poor one by Bernard C. Steiner, *Life of Henry Winter Davis* (1916). Charles Wagandt, *The Mighty Revolution: Negro Emancipation in Maryland, 1862–1864* (1964), is an excellent analysis of the fight for Negro equality in Civil War Maryland and puts Davis's activities in useful perspective, as does Hans

L. Trefousse, *The Radical Republicans: Lincoln's Vanguard for Racial Justice* (1969).

JEFFERSON DAVIS / By Frank E. Vandiver

Jefferson Davis (1808–1889) was president of the Confederate States of America during the Civil War. His honesty, character, and devotion elevated his cause above a quest for the perpetuation of slavery to a crusade for independence.

History has served Jefferson Davis badly by placing him opposite Abraham Lincoln. Davis is grudged even the loser's mite, for Fate chose Robert E. Lee to embody the "Lost Cause." Yet Davis led the Confederacy and suffered its defeat with great dignity, and he deserves a better recollection.

Davis was born on June 3, 1808, in what is now Todd County, Ky. The family soon moved to Mississippi. After attending Transylvania University for 3 years, he entered the U.S. Military Academy at West Point, from which he graduated in 1828. He served in the infantry for 7 years. At Ft. Crawford, Wis., he fell in love with Sarah Knox Taylor, daughter of post commandant Zachary Taylor. Col. Taylor disapproved of the proposed match. Davis resigned his commission in 1835, married Sarah, and took her to Mississippi; within 3 months she died of malaria. Davis contracted a light case of it, which, combined with grief, permanently weakened his health. From 1835 to 1845 he lived in seclusion at Brierfield, a plantation given him by his brother, Joseph. He and Joseph were close, shared reading habits, argued, and sharpened each other's wits and prejudices.

During these quiet years Davis developed a Southerner's fascination for politics and love for the land. In December 1845 Davis and Varina Howell, his new bride, went to Washington, where Davis took a Democratic seat in the House of Representatives. The Davises made a swift impression. Varina entertained well; Jefferson earned notice for his eloquence and the "charm of his voice."

War with Mexico interrupted Davis's congressional service. He resigned in 1846 to command a volunteer regiment attached to Zachary Taylor's army. Col. Davis and his men won quick approval from the crotchety old general, and the earlier hostilities between the two men were forgotten. Distinguished service by Davis's outfit at Monterey, Mexico, was followed by real heroism at Buena Vista (Feb. 22, 1847). Wounded, Davis returned to Mississippi and received a hero's laurels. In 1847, elected to the U.S. Senate, Davis became chairman of the Military Affairs Committee. But in 1851 Mississippi Democrats called him back to replace their gubernatorial candidate, thinking that Davis's reputation might cover the party's shift from an extreme secessionist position to one

Henry Winter Davis. (Library of Congress)

of "cooperationist" moderation. This almost succeeded; Davis lost to Henry S. Foote by less than 1,000 votes.

U.S. Secretary of War

When President Franklin Pierce appointed Davis secretary of war in 1853, Davis found his happiest niche. He enlarged the Army, modernized military procedures, boosted soldiers' pay (and morale), directed important Western land surveys for future railroad construction, and masterminded the Gadsden Purchase.

At the close of Pierce's term Davis reentered the Senate and became a major Southern spokesman. Ever mindful of the Union's purposes, he worked to preserve the Compromise of 1850. Yet throughout the 1850s Davis was moving toward a Southern nationalist point of view. He opposed Stephen A. Douglas's "squatter sovereignty" doctrine in the Kansas question. Congress, Davis argued, had no power to limit slavery's extension.

At the 1860 Democratic convention Davis cautioned against secession. However, he accepted Mississippi's decision, and on Jan. 21, 1861, in perhaps his most eloquent senatorial address, announced his state's secession from the Union and his own resignation from the Senate and called for understanding.

Confederate President

Davis only reluctantly accepted the presidency of the Confederate States of America. He began his superhuman task with very human doubts. But once in office he

Jefferson Davis. (Courtesy of the New-York Historical Society, New York City)

became the foremost Confederate. His special virtues were revealed by challenge—honesty, devotion, dedication, the zeal of a passionate patriot.

As president, Davis quickly grasped his problems: 9 million citizens (including at least 3 million slaves) of sovereign Southern states pitted against 22 million Yankees; 9,000 miles of usable railroad track against 22,000; no large factories, warships, or shipyards; little money; no credit, save in the guise of cotton; scant arms and no manufacturing arsenals to replenish losses; miniscule powder works; undeveloped lead, saltpeter, copper, and iron resources; and almost no knowledge of steelmaking. Assets could be counted only as optimism, confidence, cotton, and courage. Davis would have to conjure a cause, anneal a new nation, and make a war.

With sure grasp Davis built an army out of state volunteers sworn into Confederate service—and thus won his first round against state rights. Officers came from the "Old Army" and from Southern military schools. Supplies, arms, munitions, clothes, and transportation came from often reluctant governors, from citizens, and, finally, by means of crafty legerdemain worked by staff officials.

When supplies dwindled drastically, Davis resorted to impressing private property. When military manpower shrank, Davis had to ask the Confederate Congress for the greatest military innovation a democracy could dare —conscription. In April 1862 Congress authorized the draft.

Confederate Strategy

Nor was Davis timid in using his armies. Relying usually on leaders he knew, he put such men as Albert Sidney Johnston, Joseph E. Johnston, P. G. T. Beauregard, Braxton Bragg, James Longstreet, Thomas J. Jackson, Nathan Bedford Forrest, and Robert E. Lee in various commands. He developed a strategy to fit Confederate circumstances. Realizing that the weaker side must husband and hoard yet dare desperately when the chance came, Davis divided the Confederate military map into departments, each under a general with wide powers. He sought only to repel invaders. This strategy had political as well as military implications: the Confederacy was not aggressive, sought nothing save independence, and would fight in the North only when pressed. Davis's plan brought impressive results—First Manassas, the Seven Days, Second Manassas, and the clearing of Virginia by September 1862. Western results seemed equally promising. Shiloh, while not a victory, stabilized the middle border; Bragg's following campaign maneuvered a Union army out of Tennessee and almost out of Kentucky.

These successes led Davis to a general offensive in the summer and fall of 1862 designed to terrify Northerners, themselves yet untouched by war; to separate other, uncertain states from the Union; and to convince the outside world of Southern strength. Though it failed, the strategy had merit and remained in effect. Checks at Fredericksburg, Holly Springs, and Chancellorsville stung the North. When Union general U. S. Grant moved against Vicksburg in spring 1863, it looked as though he might be lost in Mississippi, with Gen. Joseph Hooker snared in Virginia's Wilderness.

But Grant's relentless pressure on Vicksburg forced Davis to a desperate gamble that resulted in the Battle of Gettysburg, the loss of Vicksburg, and a cost to the South of over 50,000 men and 60,000 stands of arms. Men and arms were irreplaceable, and Davis huddled deeper in the defensive.

Davis had tried perhaps the most notable innovation in the history of American command when he adopted the "theater" idea as an expansion of departmental control. Joseph E. Johnston became commander of the Department of the West, taking absolute power over all forces from the Chattahoochee River to the Mississippi River, and from the Gulf of Mexico to Tennessee. It was a great scheme for running a remote war and might have worked, save for Johnston's hesitancy in exercising his authority. Davis lost faith in his general but not in his plan.

In 1864, after Atlanta's fall, Davis approved Gen. John Bell Hood's plan of striking along William T. Sherman's communications into Tennessee, with the hope of capturing Nashville. Logistical support for this bold venture was coordinated by P. G. T. Beauregard, the new commander of the Department of the West. But Beauregard also distrusted his own authority. Hood failed before Nashville; but by then things had so deteriorated that the blame could hardly be fixed on any one in particular.

Wartime Innovations

Innovation was essential: the armies had to be supported—and in this quest Davis himself changed. Ever an advocate of state rights, he became an uncompromising Confederate nationalist, warring with state governors for federal rights and urging centralist policies on his reluctant Congress. Conscription and impressment were two pillars of his program; others included harsh tax laws, government regulation of railroads and blockade running, and diplomacy aimed at winning recognition of Confederate independence and establishing commercial relations with England and France. Davis came to advocate wide application of martial law. Finally he suggested drafting slaves, with freedom as the reward for valor. These measures were essential to avoid defeat; many were beyond the daring of the Confederate Congress.

Congress's inability to face necessity finally infuriated Davis. Though warm and winning in personal relations, he saw no need for politicking in relations with Congress. He believed that reasonable men did what crisis demanded and anything less was treason. Intolerant of laxity in himself or in others, he sometimes alienated supporters.

Southern Defeat

As Confederate chances dwindled, Davis became increasingly demanding. He eventually won congressional support for most of his measures but at high personal cost. By the summer of 1864 most Southern newspapers were sniping at his administration, state governors were quarreling with him, and he had become the focus of

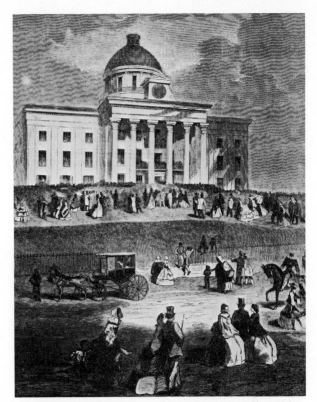

The inauguration of Jefferson Davis as president of the Confederate States of America in Montgomery, Ala., on Feb. 18, 1861. In May the government transferred to Richmond, Va. (Library of Congress)

Southern discontent. The South was losing; Davis's plan must be wrong, the rebels reasoned. Peace sentiments arose in disaffected areas of several states, as did demands to negotiate with the enemy. Davis knew the enemy's price: union. But he tried negotiation. Yet when the Hampton Roads Conference in February 1865 proved fruitless and Davis called for renewed Confederate dedication, the Confederacy was falling apart, and there was almost nothing to rededicate. Confederate money had so declined in value that Southerners were avoiding it; soldiers deserted; invaders stalked the land with almost no opposition. Lee surrendered on April 9, 1865; Johnston surrendered on April 26. Davis and a small party were captured at Irwinville, Ga., on May 10.

Years of Decline

Accused of complicity in Lincoln's assassination, and the object of intense hatred in both North and South, Davis spent 2 years as a state prisoner. He was harshly treated, and his already feeble health broke dangerously. When Federal authorities decided not to try him for treason, he traveled abroad to recuperate, then returned to Mississippi and vainly sought to rebuild his fortune.

Through a friend's generosity Davis and his family received a stately home on Mississippi's Gulf Coast. Here from 1878 to 1881 Davis wrote *Rise and Fall of the Confederate Government*. And here, at last, he basked in a kind of fame that eased his final years. He died in New Orleans on Dec. 6, 1889, survived by Varina and two of their six children.

Further Reading

Jefferson Davis is listed in the American History study guide (VI, B, 2, a). Judah BENJAMIN was in his Cabinet. Confederate generals included Joseph E. JOHNSTON and Robert E. LEE.

A primary source is Dunbar Rowland, ed., *Jefferson Davis, Constitutionalist: His Letters, Papers and Speeches* (10 vols., 1923), which includes an autobiography in volume 1. Biographies include Varina H. Davis, *Jefferson Davis: A Memoir* (1890); William E. Dodd, *Jefferson Davis* (1907); Allen Tate, *Jefferson Davis, His Rise and Fall* (1929); Robert W. Winston, *High Stakes and Hair Trigger: The Life of Jefferson Davis* (1930); Robert McElroy, *Jefferson Davis: The Unreal and the Real* (2 vols., 1937); and Hudson Strode, *Jefferson Davis* (3 vols., 1955–1964). See also Burton J. Hendrick, *Statesmen of the Lost Cause* (1939); Robert W. Patrick, *Jefferson Davis and His Cabinet* (1944); Frank E. Vandiver, *Jefferson Davis and the Confederate State* (1964) and *Their Tattered Flags* (1970).

JOHN DAVIS / By Charles E. Nowell

English navigator John Davis (ca. 1550–1605), though remembered chiefly as a northern explorer, sailed many seas, took part in naval fighting, and invented a nautical instrument.

John Davis, a Devonshire man, was friendly with the Gilbert and Raleigh families and at times sailed with members of both. One of the most proficient seamen of his day, he published both a practical and a theoretical work on navigation. The backstaff he invented for finding altitudes of heavenly bodies at sea (so named because the pilot using it turned his back to the sun) held the field for a century and a half.

Davis made his first exploration voyage in 1585 in search of the Northwest Passage to the Orient. He rounded Cape Farewell in Greenland and went north to Godthaab (64°N) before crossing Davis Strait to Cumberland Gulf in Baffin Island, where the lateness of the season compelled his return to England. The next year he persuaded merchants, mostly in Devon, to send a larger expedition. He detached two vessels to explore Gilbert Sound and with a third continued investigation of Davis Strait without making a substantial discovery. Codfish caught and salted off Labrador helped defray costs of the expedition, but Davis found the Devon merchants unwilling to risk money for a new voyage.

Davis nevertheless acquired backing in London and in 1587 went again with three ships, though the pinnace *Ellen*, in which he sailed, made the only explorations.

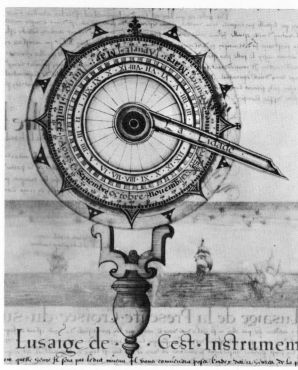

An astrolabe. By measuring the angle between the horizon and the North Star with this instrument, navigators in the Age of Exploration could determine their latitude. A quadrant invented by John Davis marked an improvement over the ancient astrolabe.

The result was no profit but considerable discovery, as Davis reached a point about 73°N on the west Greenland coast before turning across Davis Strait to explore Baffin Island further. Homeward bound, the *Ellen* visited the mouth of Hudson's Strait but did not penetrate it. When Davis reached England on Sept. 15, 1587, he had at least demonstrated the unlikelihood of anyone's pushing through to the Pacific in a single voyage.

This ended Davis's career as an explorer. He received unfair criticism for not having accomplished more; meanwhile, the great Spanish Armada was nearly ready to attack England. In the channel fighting against the Spaniards, Davis appears to have commanded the ship *Black Dog*, but his combat record is unknown.

Following the Armada's defeat, Davis took part in several voyages, but none involved discovery. He sailed with Thomas Cavendish in 1591 on an expedition intended to penetrate the Strait of Magellan, carry operations into the Pacific, and find the western outlet of the Northwest Passage. This came to nothing because of the bad condition of the ships; Davis did sight the Falkland Islands, though some historians believe these were earlier discovered by Amerigo Vespucci. His last expedition, to the East Indies under the orders of Sir Edward Michelborne, resulted in his death at the hands of Japanese pirates in 1605.

Davis was married to Faith Fulford in 1582, but Faith proved faithless and with her paramour, a counterfeiter, brought false and unavailing charges against her accomplished husband, whom she had borne several sons.

Further Reading

John Davis is listed in the Geography and Exploration study guide (III, A, 3, d). Other explorers of the Northwest Passage were Sebastian CABOT and Sir Martin FROBISHER.

Source accounts of Davis's voyages and excerpts from his writings are contained in *The Voyages and Works of John Davis,* published by the Hakluyt Society (2 vols., 1880). Convenient summaries of the voyages are available in Edward Heawood, *A History of Geographical Discovery in the Seventeenth and Eighteenth Centuries* (1912). James A. Williamson, *Age of Drake* (1938; 5th ed. 1965), summarizes the explorer's career. Davis is also discussed in Samuel Eliot Morison, *The European Discovery of America: The Northern Voyages* (1971).

O. **DAVIS** / By Margaret Walker Alexander

Ossie Davis (born 1917) was a leading black American playwright, actor, director, and television and movie star.

Ossie Davis as Gabriel in a 1951 production of Marc Connelly's play The Green Pastures. *(Library of Congress, Carl Van Vechten Collection, Courtesy of Saul Mauriber)*

Ossie Davis was born in Cogdell, Ga., on Dec. 18, 1917. He grew up in Waycross. At Howard University in Washington, D.C., he was encouraged to pursue an acting career. He joined an acting group in Harlem in New York City and took part in the American Negro Theater, founded there in 1940.

Davis made his debut in the play *Joy Exceeding Glory* (1941). During Army service in World War II he wrote and produced shows. While playing his first Broadway role in *Jeb* (1946), he met actress Ruby Dee, and they were married 2 years later.

Davis's first movie role was in *No Way Out* (1950). This was followed by Broadway performances in *No Time for Sergeants, Raisin in the Sun,* and *Jamaica.* Other movie roles included *The Cardinal, Shock Treatment,* and *Slaves.* An important achievement was his pioneer work as a black actor in television, appearing in dramas and on such regular series as *The Defenders* and *The Nurses.* He also wrote television scripts.

Equally talented, Davis and Ruby Dee played together many times on the stage, in television, cabaret, and movies. They starred in Davis's own play *Purlie Victorious* (1961) and in the movie based on it, *Gone Are the Days. Purlie Victorious* was published and reprinted in anthologies. Davis coauthored the musical version of this hilarious satire, *Purlie* (1970), which enjoyed great success during its Broadway run.

In the late 1960s Davis pioneered in Hollywood as a black film director with *Cotton Comes to Harlem,* among other films. With Ruby Dee he appeared on stage and television, reading the poetry of famous black Americans, and he made recordings of black literature. Perhaps one of his most memorable endeavors was his eulogy on Malcolm X in 1965, when he called the slain leader "Our Shining Black Prince." Davis frequently lectured and read at universities and schools.

Davis's published essays include "The Wonderful World of Law and Order," "The Flight from Broadway," and "Plays of Insight Are Needed to Make the Stage Vital in Our Lives." He also wrote the play *Last Dance for Sybil* and the musical adaptation of Mark Twain's *Pudd'nhead Wilson.*

Davis had a deep love for his people and his heritage. He was an example of black identity and pride, and he devoted much time and talent to the civil rights movement in America. He received a number of awards, including the Mississippi Democratic Party Citation, the Howard University Alumni Achievement Award in dramatics, and the Frederick A. Douglass Award (with Ruby Dee) from the N.Y. Urban League. The Davises had three children and made their home in New Rochelle, N.Y.

Further Reading

Ossie Davis is listed in the American History study

guide (X, F, 4). Other black writers of this time included James BALDWIN and Imamu Amiri BARAKA.

Lindsay Patterson, ed., *Anthology of the American Negro in the Theatre: A Critical Approach* (2d ed. 1968), includes a short article by Davis. Other works which discuss him are Harry A. Ploski and Roscoe C. Brown, Jr., *The Negro Almanac* (1967); Mitchell Loften, *Black Drama: The Story of the American Negro in the Theatre* (1967); and Doris E. Abramson, *Negro Playwrights in the American Theatre, 1925–1959* (1969).

* * *

R. H. DAVIS / By Walter Blair

The American journalist Richard Harding Davis (1864–1916) was also a fiction writer and dramatist whose swashbuckling adventures were popular with the American public.

Richard Harding Davis was born into a well-to-do and rather pious Episcopalian family in Philadelphia. His father, an editorial writer, and his mother, a well-known fiction writer, often entertained Philadelphia artists and visiting actors and actresses, and the boy from the start was completely at ease with celebrities. After graduating from Episcopal Academy and Lehigh University, he studied political economy during a postgraduate year at Johns Hopkins University. In 1886 Davis became a reporter for the *Philadelphia Press*. The

editor and other reporters confidently expected the cocky young dandy to fall on his face, but he shortly proved to be a superb reporter and a talented writer. From 1888 to 1890 he was in New York writing special stories for the *Sun*. He also published two volumes of short stories, *Gallegher and Other Stories* (1891) and *Van Bibber and Others* (1892). At the age of 26 he became the managing editor of *Harper's Weekly* and soon was writing accounts of his worldwide travels, which were collected in books such as *Rulers of the Mediterranean* (1894), *About Paris* (1895), and *Three Gringos in Venezuela and Central America* (1896).

As a picturesque and alert correspondent for New York and London newspapers, always appropriately attired for each adventure, Davis covered the Spanish War and the Spanish-American War in Cuba, the Greco-Turkish War, the Boer War, and—toward the end of his life—World War I. He based a number of books upon his experiences. More short stories filled 10 volumes, including *The Lion and the Unicorn* (1899), *Ranson's Folly* (1902), and *The Scarlet Car* (1907). A number of Davis's novels covered the international scene; notable were *Soldiers of Fortune* (1897), *The King's Jackal* (1898), *Captain Macklin* (1902), and *The White Mice* (1909). In addition, Davis wrote about two dozen plays, of which dramatizations of *Ranson's Folly* (1904), *The Dictator* (1904), and *Miss Civilization* (1906) were the most successful.

The critic Larzer Ziff in *The American 1890's* admirably summarized Davis's significance: "He demonstrated to those ... who would listen that their capacity for excitement was matched by the doings in the wide world. But he also demonstrated to an uneasy plutocracy ... that their gospel of wealth coming to the virtuous and their public dedication to genteel manners and gentlemanly Christian behavior were indeed justified."

Further Reading

Richard Harding Davis is listed in the Literature study guide (I, D, 3). Among the outstanding journalists working in New York City in the early 20th century were Herbert CROLY, Walter LIPPMANN, and H. L. MENCKEN.

For a complete list of Davis's writings consult Henry Cole Quinby, *Richard Harding Davis: A Bibliography* (1924). Two studies relate the author to his background admirably: Fairfax D. Downey, *Richard Harding Davis: His Day* (1933), and Gerald Langford, *The Richard Harding Davis Years: A Biography of a Mother and Son* (1961).

* * *

Richard Harding Davis. (Courtesy of The New-York Historical Society, New York City)

S. DAVIS / By William C. Lipke

Stuart Davis (1894–1964) was an American cubist painter whose colorful compositions, with their internal logic and structure, often camouflage the American flavor of his themes.

tuart Davis was born in Philadelphia on Dec. 7, 1894. His father was the art editor of the *Philadelphia Press*. At the age of 16 Davis began studying art with Robert Henri, leader of "The Eight," a group of artists also known as the "Ashcan school." In the famous 1913 Armory Show, Davis exhibited five watercolors. His works of this period are close to the realistic style of "The Eight," but Davis soon began moving toward the more lively, Fauve manner, visible in *Gloucester Street* (1916).

Davis's new interest in cubism is partly explained by his statement that "a painting . . . is a two-dimensional plane surface and the process of making a painting is the act of defining two-dimensional space on that surface." He experimented with the geometric visual language of Dutch painter Piet Mondrian in his own painting *The President* (1917) and tried synthetic cubist devices in the more pictorially ordered *Lucky Strike* (1921).

Davis's trip to New Mexico in 1923 manifested itself in more simply conceived, flatter paintings. *Still Life* and *Supper Table* (both 1925) reflect a move toward minimal pictorial elements, with a bold outline accentuating objects. The resolution of these earlier abstract tendencies can be found in the *Eggbeater Series* (1927–1930), still-life paintings in which Davis sought to "focus on the logical elements" of the composition instead of establishing a "self-sufficient system" that worked apart from

Blips and Ifs, a painting by Stuart Davis. (Courtesy Amon Carter Museum, Fort Worth, Tex.)

the objects. The late paintings in this series show a less abstract approach and an increased clarity of form and color.

In 1928 Davis traveled to Paris. In general, the work that followed reveals not only a greater interest in urban landscape but a move toward more lively, linear composition, often using sets of words within the picture to carry the rhythm. *Places des Vosges Number 2* (1928) juxtaposes line and color on a lightly textured surface, showing Davis's skill at rendering rhythmical equivalents of visual phenomena.

During the Great Depression, Davis became art editor of the Artists' Congress magazine, *Art Front*. Like many contemporary painters, he executed public murals: *Men without Women* (1932) at the Radio City Music Hall in New York City; *Swing Landscape* (1938), now at the University of Indiana; a mural for WNYC radio station in New York City; and the now-destroyed *History of Communication* (1939) for the New York World's Fair. But unlike many artists working under government auspices, Davis did not alter his esthetic outlook to accommodate public taste.

Davis's paintings during his last 2 decades show continued preoccupation with the lyrical order of visual experience. They draw on the tradition of Henri Matisse and Joan Miró, yet their content is indigenous to America. *Hot Stillscape for Six Colors* (1940), explosive with color and rhythm; *Visa* (1951); and *The Paris Bit* (1959) all integrate the visual feel of words with related color schemes and shapes.

Davis published a number of writings and taught in New York City at the Art Students League and the New School for Social Research.

Further Reading

Stuart Davis is listed in the Art study guide (IV, E, 3). He was influenced by Henri MATISSE and Joan MIRÓ.

The most lively interpretation of Davis is E. C. Goossen, *Stuart Davis* (1959), which includes a useful bibliography and numerous illustrations. Autobiographical

Stuart Davis. (Library of Congress)

material can be found in James Johnson Sweeney, *Stuart Davis* (1945), and the exhibition catalog to the Museum of Modern Art show of the same year edited by Sweeney. A recent assessment of Davis's work is by H. H. Arnason in his *History of Modern Art* (1968).

* * *

W. M. DAVIS / By T. W. Freeman

The American geographer and geologist William Morris Davis (1850–1934) formulated a concept of the cycle of erosion, but his theories of landscape evolution are now sharply contested.

Of Quaker stock, William M. Davis was born in Philadelphia, Pa., on Feb. 12, 1850. He graduated from Harvard in 1869. From 1870 to 1873 he was a meteorological assistant at the Córdoba observatory in Argentina. In 1878 he returned to Harvard to teach geology and geography. Warned by senior colleagues that it would be difficult to gain promotion without publication, Davis soon became known for his contributions to journals. In all he wrote some 500 papers, chiefly on physical geography but also on the teaching of geography in schools and universities. These included 42 papers on meteorology and a textbook, *Elementary Meteorology* (1894).

In 1890 Davis became professor of physical geography at Harvard, and 9 years later he was appointed professor of geology. He retired from Harvard in 1912.

In 1889, in the first volume of the *National Geographic Magazine,* Davis published a notable paper on the rivers and valleys of Pennsylvania, followed in 1890 by a study of the rivers of northern New Jersey. For 10 years he published papers in this journal, which was then austerely academic; his work also appeared in numerous American and European journals. Steadily he developed his theory of the cycle of erosion under humid, arid, glacial, and other conditions. It provided a wonderful framework for teaching and research, profitably used by his disciples, notably the geologist Douglas W. Johnson. Block diagrams and sketches of unique clarity helped readers to visualize landscapes in three dimensions. For a time Davis's ideas on the evolution of landscapes were the basis of most geomorphological teaching. But there were always dissenting voices that called attention to the large assumptions on which some of the Davisian views were based, and at present some geomorphologists regard his views as interesting period pieces.

Davis was always anxious to bring geographers together, and through his enterprise the Association of American Geographers was founded in 1904. In 1911 he ran a 9-week "geographical pilgrimage" from Wales to Italy. He also organized the 8-week transcontinental expedition of the American Geographical Society in 1912 for European and American geographers. He was an enthusiastic fieldworker, and several of his papers were

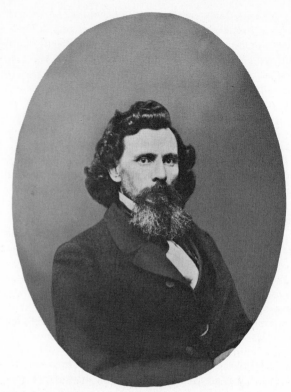

William M. Davis. (Library of Congress)

based on his careful fieldwork in Europe.

Davis was professor of physiographic geology at the California Institute of Technology from 1930 to 1934. He died in Pasadena on Feb. 5, 1934.

Further Reading

William M. Davis is listed in the Geography and Exploration study guide (VII, B). Isaiah BOWMAN was the director of the American Geographical Society from 1916 to 1935.

Davis's *Geographical Essays,* edited by Douglas Wilson Johnson (1909), gives his most important papers. His work is discussed in Preston E. James and Clarence F. Jones, eds., *American Geography: Inventory and Prospect* (1954).

* * *

DAVY / By June Z. Fullmer

The English chemist and natural philosopher Sir Humphry Davy (1778–1829) isolated and named the elements of the alkaline-earth and alkali metals and showed that chlorine and iodine were elements.

Humphry Davy was born on Dec. 17, 1778, in Penzance, Cornwall. He was apprenticed when he was 16 to an apothecary in Penzance, where he evinced a great interest in chemistry and experimentation, using as his guide Lavoisier's famous work, *Traité élémentaire de chimie*. His obvious talents attracted the attention of Gregory Watt and Davies Giddy (later Gilbert), both of whom recommended him to Dr. Thomas Beddoes for the position of superintendent of the newly founded Pneumatic Institution in Bristol. He worked there from October 1799 to March 1801.

The Pneumatic Institution was investigating the idea that certain diseases might be cured by the inhalation of gases. Davy, sometimes perilously, inhaled many gases and found that the respiration of nitrous oxide produced surprising results. Inhalation of "laughing gas," as it was soon called, became a novel form of entertainment, although nearly 50 years passed before it was actually used as an anesthetic. Davy also experimented with the newly invented voltaic pile, or battery.

Davy left Bristol to become the lecturer in chemistry at the Royal Institution in London. Sir Joseph Banks and Count Rumford had founded the Royal Institution in 1799 as a research institute and as a place for educating young men in science and mechanics. Here Davy's genius emerged full-blown. Not only did his brilliant lectures attract a fashionable and intellectual audience, but he also continued his electrical research. In 1806 he showed that there was a real connection between electrical and chemical behavior; for this achievement Napoleon I awarded him a prize. In 1807 he electrolyzed molten potash and soda and announced the isolation of two new elements, naming them potassium and sodium. In 1808 he isolated and named calcium, barium, strontium, and magnesium. Later he showed that boron, aluminum, beryllium, and fluorine existed, although he was not able to isolate them.

Lavoisier had claimed that a substance was an acid because it contained oxygen. Davy doubted the validity of this claim and in 1810 showed that "oxymuriatic acid gas" was not the oxide of an unknown element, murium, but a true element, which he named chlorine.

In 1812 Davy married a wealthy widow, Jane Apreece, and was knighted by the King for his great discoveries. Napoleon I invited him to visit France, even though the two countries were at war. Sir Humphry and his wife went to France in 1813, taking with them as valet and chemical assistant the 22-year-old Michael Faraday. The French presented them with a curious substance isolated from seaweed, and Davy, working in his hotel room, was able to show that this was another new element, iodine. When he returned to England, he was asked by a group of clergymen to study the problem of providing illumination in coal mines without exploding the methane there. Davy devised the miner's safety lamp and gave the invention to the world without attempting to patent or otherwise exploit it. Working in another area, he demonstrated how electrochemical corrosion could be prevented.

In 1820, after Sir Joseph Banks had died, Sir Humphry was made president of the Royal Society. He began the needed internal reform of the society, but bad health forced him to resign in 1827. The remaining years of his life he spent wandering about the Continent in search of a cure for the strokes from which he suffered. He died

Humphry Davy. (National Portrait Gallery, London)

on May 29, 1829, in Geneva, Switzerland, where he was buried.

Further Reading

Humphry Davy is listed in the Science study guide (VI, D, 1). Robert BUNSEN and Michael FARADAY were other 19th-century chemists.

Davy's own writings are the best source of information about his scientific work. They were edited in nine volumes by his brother, John Davy, *The Collected Works of Sir Humphry Davy* (1839–1840). A complete listing of all his writings is in June Z. Fullmer, *Sir Humphry Davy's Published Works* (1969). John Davy wrote a biography, *Memoirs of the Life of Sir Humphry Davy* (2 vols., 1839), to correct the excesses of John Ayrton Paris's biography, *The Life of Sir Humphry Davy* (2 vols., 1831). Recent biographies are Anne Treneer, *The Mercurial Chemist: A Life of Sir Humphry Davy* (1963), which discusses Davy's relationship to the romantic poets, and Sir Harold Hartley, *Humphry Davy* (1966), which concentrates on his life and importance as a scientist.

* * *

DAWES / By Odie B. Faulk

As a U.S. senator, Henry Laurens Dawes (1816–1903) sponsored important legislation designed to assimilate American Indians into the mainstream of national life.

Henry Dawes was born near Cummington, Mass., on Oct. 30, 1816. After completing grade school and the academy at Cummington, he graduated from Yale College. He taught school for a few months, then began writing for local newspapers, read law, and was admitted to the Massachusetts bar in 1842. His first office was at North Adams, but he soon moved to Pittsfield. He served in the lower house of the Massachusetts Legislature in 1848–1849 and 1852, was elected to one term in the state senate in 1850, and became a member of the state constitutional convention of 1853.

In 1857, running as a Republican, Dawes was elected to the U.S. House of Representatives, a position he held until 1875. His seniority in the House brought him considerable power, which he used to write antislavery legislation. He was chairman for 10 years of the Committee on Elections, chairman of the House Committee on Appropriations in 1869, and chairman of the House Ways and Means Committee after 1871. He was a staunch believer in protective tariffs, especially for textiles, and he introduced the legislation to provide for daily weather reports that led eventually to the establishment of the U.S. Weather Bureau.

Dawes entered the U.S. Senate in 1875. A New England Yankee with high cheekbones and a gray beard, Dawes never achieved national prominence, but he was able to influence legislation to help the American Indians. As chairman of the Senate Committee on Indian Affairs, he secured funds for educational facilities on the reservations and also brought the Indians under Federal criminal laws.

Dawes is best remembered as author of the Dawes Severalty Act (1887). Originating in his belief that Indians should be brought into the American political and economic system instead of clinging to their tribal ways, the act was aimed at breaking up the reservation system. It provided 160 acres to each head of family (and smaller amounts of land to others) who would leave the reservation. After a probationary period of 25 years, the Indians would be granted full title to the land and United States citizenship. At the time, this legislation was considered visionary.

After three terms in the Senate, Dawes retired to Pittsfield in 1892. He was consulted on national problems until his death on Feb. 5, 1903.

Further Reading

Henry Dawes is listed in the American History study guide (VII, C, 2). He succeeded Charles SUMNER in the U.S. Senate.

George F. Hoar, *Autobiography of Seventy Years* (2 vols., 1903), contains excellent material on Dawes's service in Congress. His efforts on behalf of the Indians are recounted in Loring Benson Priest, *Uncle Sam's Stepchildren: The Reformation of United States Indian Policy, 1865–1887* (1942). He is briefly discussed in J. P. Kinney, *A Continent Lost—A Continent Won: Indian Land Tenure in America* (1937); Harold E. Fey and D'Arcy McNickle, *Indians and Other Americans: Two Ways of Life Meet* (1959); and George H. Mayer, *The Republican Party, 1854–1964* (1964).

DAWSON / By Vivian F. McBrier

Black American composer, performer, and music educator William Levi Dawson (born 1899) used the rich vitality of the Negro musical heritage as a basis for all types of music, including arrangements of folk songs and original compositions.

Henry Dawes, a Mathew Brady photograph. (Library of Congress)

William Dawson was born on Sept. 26, 1899, at Anniston, Ala. At the age of 13 he entered Tuskegee Institute and graduated in 1921 with first honors. He received the bachelor of music degree from the Horner Institute of Fine Arts in Kansas City, Mo., in 1925. He studied composition under Felix Borowski at the Chicago Musical College and under Adolph Weidig at the American Conservatory of Music. In 1927 he received the master of music degree from the American Conservatory of Music in Chicago.

Dawson's membership in the band and orchestra at

William Dawson in 1943. (Library of Congress)

D, 1). Robert DETT and William Grant STILL were contemporary black composers.

Dawson is discussed briefly in Maud Cuney-Hare, *Negro Musicians and Their Music* (1936), and the *International Library of Negro Life*, vol. 5: *The Negro in Music and Art*, compiled by Lindsay Patterson (1967; 2d ed. 1968).

DAYAN / By Ezri Atzmon

The Israeli general and statesman Moshe Dayan (born 1915) served as minister of defense of Israel, beginning in 1967.

Tuskegee had been excellent professional preparation for serving as first trombonist with the Chicago Civic Orchestra from 1926 to 1930. In 1929 he won the *Chicago Daily News* contest for band directors, and in 1930 Wanamaker Contest prizes for the song "Jump Back, Honey, Jump Back" and the orchestral composition "Scherzo."

In 1931 Dawson became director of the School of Music at Tuskegee. In 1932–1933 Dawson conducted the institute's 100-voice a cappella choir in a month's engagement at the opening of the International Music Hall of Radio City and in a concert at Carnegie Hall, New York City; in a concert at the White House and another at Constitution Hall, Washington, D.C.; and in a series of national and international broadcasts. In 1934, under the sponsorship of the President of the United States and the State Department, the Tuskegee Choir made a concert tour of international and interracial good will to the British Isles, Europe, and the U.S.S.R. Leading critics in America and abroad praised the choir highly.

Dawson had wide experience as a director and consultant to festival groups. In 1956 Tuskegee Institute conferred upon him the honorary degree of doctor of music and he was sent by the U.S. State Department to conduct various choral groups in Spain.

Although Dawson's choral arrangements are popular, he is best known for his *Negro Folk Symphony*, which had its world premiere by the Philadelphia Symphony Orchestra under Leopold Stokowski (1934). In this work the composer used melodic and rhythmic language borrowed from Negro spirituals, along with original material in the same idiom. The symphony is imaginative, dramatic, and colorfully orchestrated.

In 1952 Dawson visited seven countries in West Africa to study indigenous African music. He later revised the *Negro Folk Symphony*, infusing it with a rhythmic foundation inspired by African influences.

Further Reading

William Dawson is listed in the Music study guide (II,

Moshe Dayan (pronounced dă-yän´) was born in the kibbutz of Degania, Palestine. His father Samuel, a farmer, was a founder of Degania and Nahalal and a leader of the cooperative settlement (*moshavim*) movement. During the riots of 1936–1939 Dayan joined the Supplementary Police Force of Palestine under the British. Later he joined the first mobile

Gen. Moshe Dayan (center) with generals Itzhak Rabin and Uzi Narkiss at the Lions' Gate, near the wall of the Old City of Jerusalem, in June 1967. (Israel Information Services, New York)

commando platoons (*palmakh*) of the Haganah. In 1940 Dayan was arrested by the British because of his participation in the underground Haganah organization. After his release from prison in 1941, however, he joined the British army in order to fight against Nazi Germany. On a foray into Vichy-controlled Syria, he was wounded and lost his left eye.

During the struggle between the Palestine Jewish community and the British mandatory government in 1947, Dayan again served in the underground Haganah. During the War of Independence in 1948 he participated in the campaign against the Egyptian army. In 1949 he led the Israeli forces in the final battles around Jerusalem, and after the war he represented Israel at the Rhodes Armistice Conference. He was acclaimed a national hero for his part in the Sinai campaign against Egypt in 1956.

After retiring from the army in 1958, Dayan entered politics as a leading member of the ''Young Mapai'' and was appointed minister of agriculture in 1959, a post he occupied until 1964. Shortly after David Ben Gurion's resignation as prime minister in 1963, Dayan also withdrew from government. But he soon returned to politics as a member of the Rafi opposition party, which Ben Gurion formed in 1965.

In May 1967 Dayan became minister of defense. Under his command and with the close collaboration of the chief of staff, Gen. Itzhak Rabin, the Israeli armed forces won an unprecedented victory over the combined Arab military forces of Egypt (United Arab Republic), Jordan, Syria, Iraq, and Saudi Arabia in the Six Day War of June 1967. As a result of its victory, Israel occupied vast Arab territories and blocked the Suez Canal to international navigation. After this conflict Dayan continued to strengthen Israel's military forces in order to ensure the state's survival in the troubled Middle East. Dayan had a deep concern for the soldiers in the field and always paid meticulous attention to their safety and comfort. He became upset when, during retaliatory actions, lives were lost without territorial gains.

Dayan vigorously denied the allegation that he saw the problem of Arab-Israeli relations ''through the sights of a gun.'' As minister of agriculture, he met frequently with Arab farmers and tried to give them every assistance. He always held that the Arabs of Israel should have equal rights and bear equal responsibilities with the other citizens of Israel.

Dayan's attitude toward prisoners of war and Arab civilians in the territories occupied after the Six Day War attested to his strong sense of justice. While energetically combating terrorist activities, he maintained a liberal policy toward the people of the occupied areas, giving them as much freedom as possible to run their own affairs and allowing commercial and social relations with Jordan.

Dayan had sides to his character that belied his image as a tough, unemotional fighter. He was passionately attached to the land and in particular to his farm in Nahalal. He had a great interest in archeology, which he pursued through digging in his spare time and reading extensively on the subject. Dayan was also an author, and among his publications are *Israel's Border and Security Problems* (1955), *Diary of the Sinai Campaign* (1966), and *A New Map, New Relationships* (1969).

Further Reading

Moshe Dayan is listed in the Asia study guide (I, H, 2). He worked closely with David BEN GURION and Golda MEIR.

Naphtali Lau-Lavie, *Moshe Dayan* (1968), is a full-length biography. Moshe Ben Shaul, ed., *Generals of Israel* (trans. 1968), contains a succinct portrayal of Dayan by Doris Lankin. Two works that rely primarily on pictures are David Curtis and Stephen G. Crane, *Dayan: A Pictorial Biography* (1967), and Pinchas Jurman, ed., *Moshe Dayan: A Portrait* (1969).

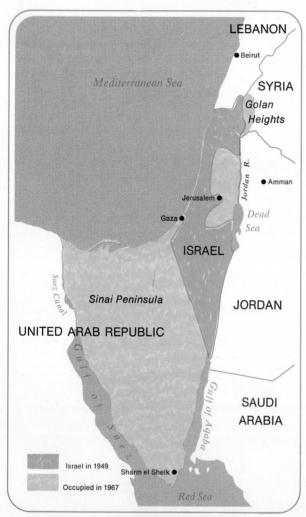

Israel and occupied territories, 1967. Under Dayan's command, the Israeli armed forces in June 1967 launched an attack against the menacing Arab states that surrounded it. The Six Day War gave the Israelis control of the Sinai Peninsula, the west bank of the Jordan River, and the Golan Heights in Syria.

DAYANANDA / By Peter A. Pardue

The Indian religious leader Swami Dayananda Saraswati (1824–1883) founded the Arya Samaj, or Society of Nobles, and epitomized the aggressive Hindu religious reformer.

Dayananda Saraswati. (Bibliothèque Nationale, Paris)

Dayananda Saraswati (pronounced dä-yə-nän′də sär′əs-wə-tē) was born into a wealthy Brahmin family in Gujarat, a part of western India somewhat isolated from British colonial influence. He was raised in the orthodox Hindu tradition but soon found himself unsatisfied with the archaic teachings and practices, especially idol worship and other primitivisms imposed on him. At the age of 19 he left his family and undertook a long period of rigorous, ascetic study of the ancient Vedas—the oldest core of Hindu religion.

Dayananda concluded that current religious beliefs and social institutions were hopelessly corrupt. With this conviction he began to preach an aggressive reforming doctrine which urged a return to the pristine Vedic tradition. While his commitments seemed basically "fundamentalist" and somewhat orthodox, in fact, he advocated radical reforms such as the abolition of idol worship, of child marriages, of the inequality of women, and of hereditary caste privileges. He praised the way of the Europeans and named as the causes of their advancement their representative assemblies, education, active lives, and the fact that they "help their countrymen in trade."

In his religious teaching he accepted the old doctrine of *karma* and transmigration, but he developed a highly sophisticated monistic philosophy which stressed ideals of self-perfection and ethical universalism: "I believe in a religion based on universal and all-embracing principles which have always been accepted as true by mankind— the *primeval eternal religion,* which means that it is above the hostility of all human creeds whatsoever." In 1875 Dayananda founded the Arya Samaj in Bombay as the institutional medium for the propagation of his teaching. He preached in vernacular Hindi in an effort to break through the elitist Sanskrit culture and to reach the masses. His society was open to all men and women on the basis of personal interest and commitment. His disciples perused the Vedas in minute detail, finding there the essential precursors of Western science and technology, including electricity, microbiology, and other modern inventions.

His outspoken criticism of Hindu tradition and his reforming interests provoked the hatred of many orthodox and conservative circles, and he argued abrasively with Moslem and Christian sectarians in favor of the universal philosophy of his own interpretation of the Vedas. Numerous attempts were made on his life, and he was finally poisoned.

The Arya Samaj was one of the most influential movements of the early modern period in India. It contributed to the rise of Indian nationalism by instilling a sense of pride in the integrity of the most unique and ancient traditions of Indian heritage while simultaneously undercutting the great bulk of conservative Hindu interpretation and law. Dayananda's personality and purifying reforms earned him the epithet "the Luther of India."

Further Reading

Dayananda Saraswati is listed in the Asia study guide (II, A, 6, b). A contemporary mystic and religious leader was RAMAKRISHNA.

Dayananda's *Light of Truth* was translated into English in 1906. A biography of Dayananda is Har Bilas Sarda, *Life of Dayanand Saraswati, World Teacher* (1946).

DEÁK / By Steven Bela Vardy

The Hungarian statesman Francis Deák (1803–1876) was one of the creators of Austria-Hungary. Called the "Sage of the Nation," he was the architect of the Austro-Hungarian Compromise of 1867.

The son of a nontitled nobleman and estate owner, Francis Deák (pronounced dĕ′äk) was born at Söjtör on Oct. 17, 1803. After studying law, he joined the administration of his native Zala County. In 1833 he became one of his county's representatives at the national Diet at Pozsony (Pressburg, Bratislava), and from then on his activities became irrevocably linked with Hungarian national politics. At this time Hungary was under the control of the Austrian Hapsburgs, who, during the past 3 centuries, had made repeated efforts to integrate the country into their dynastic state. With the rise of 19th-century Magyar nationalism, however, the politically conscious Hungarian leading classes reacted and demanded the reestablishment of the original "personal union" relationship (partnership under a common ruler) with Austria, while also calling for liberal social and political reforms.

During the 1830s Deák championed such causes as the liberation of serfs, Polish liberties, religious freedom, and freedom of speech. During 1841–1842 he chaired the commission that recommended the elimination of corporal punishment, the death sentence, and the feudal courts and called for the introduction of a new court and jury system. However, the commission's proposals were defeated at the next Diet (1843–1844).

By this time Deák's unquestioned integrity, good judgment, and dedication to progressive goals had made him a most respected national leader, and in 1847 the factionalized liberals turned to him to draw up the program of the "united opposition." By combining Louis Kossuth's radical views and Baron Joseph Eötvös's centralist ones with his own, he formed the basis of the "March-April Compromise" of 1848, which transformed Hungary into a near-independent parliamentary state under its own responsible government.

Deák became the minister of justice in the new Batthyány government. In this post he devoted his attention both to the liquidation of the remnants of feudalism and to the prevention of a final break between Hungary and the dynasty. Following the Batthyány government's resignation (Sept. 28, 1848), Deák continued his parliamentary work. But in December he was unsuccessful in negotiating a compromise with Prince Alfred Windischgrätz, the commander in chief of the Austrian imperial forces sent to put down the Hungarian revolution. Deák then withdrew from politics and retired to his estate at Kehida.

Deák did not return to politics until 1854. In that year he moved to Pest, and thereafter his home became the center of Hungarian national politics. It was there that he worked out his successful policy of passive resistance and noncollaboration.

When Francis Joseph of Austria appeared willing to negotiate following the Italian defeat in 1859, Deák assumed the leadership in the negotiations and formulated specific conditions in parliamentary addresses to the throne. Aided by Eötvös and Count Julius Andrássy, Deák began serious negotiations in 1865, although they were interrupted by the Austro-Prussian War of 1866. Deák's partial retreat in accepting the idea of common foreign, military, and financial affairs, together with his refusal to raise his demands after Austria's defeat, helped result in the Compromise (*Ausgleich*) of 1867, which transformed the Hapsburg Empire into the dual state of Austria-Hungary.

Having attained his goal, Deák declined to head the

Francis Deák. (Library of Congress)

new government or to serve in the Cabinet headed by his protégé Andrássy. Nor did he accept any titles or honors for his achievement, although he remained the acknowledged leader of the ruling political party, which bore his name. But age, infirmity, and increasing dissatisfaction with Hungarian liberalism as it developed during the 1870s gradually caused him to withdraw from active politics. A confirmed bachelor, Deák died in Budapest on Jan. 28, 1876.

Further Reading

Francis Deák is listed in the European History study guide (VIII, D, 1). Other prominent Hungarian leaders of this period were Count Julius ANDRÁSSY and Louis KOSSUTH.

Anglo-American scholarship has been very remiss on Deák, and aside from Florence M. Arnold-Forster's slight and out-of-date account, *Francis Deák, Hungarian Statesman: A Memoir* (1880), there is virtually nothing available in English. Imre Lukinich, *A History of Hungary in Biographical Sketches* (1937), contains only a brief popular account. Those who read French can consult Louis Eisenmann, *Le Compromis Austro-Hongrois de 1867* (1904), which has much to say about Deák. Others must rely on general works on 19th-century Hungary and the Hapsburg Empire. The most recent and detailed one-volume work on Hungary is Dominic G. Kosáry and Steven Bela Vardy, *History of the Hungarian Nation* (1969). On the empire, C. A. Macartney's monumental *The Habsburg Empire, 1790–1918* (1968) supersedes all previous works.

✳   ✳   ✳

DEAKIN / By R. M. Younger

Alfred Deakin (1856–1919) was an Australian
political leader who established a remarkable
record in colonial and federal politics in
constructive and progressive causes.

*Alfred Deakin. (Australian News & Information
Bureau)*

A lfred Deakin was born in the gold-boom city of
Melbourne on Aug. 3, 1856. He studied law at the
University of Melbourne, became a writer for the
progressive newspaper *Age,* and in 1879 was elected to
the legislative assembly of Victoria.

Deakin served in a succession of ministries. An ardent
advocate of irrigation (then untried in Australia), he visited California in 1884–1885 and induced George and
Benjamin Chaffey to develop an irrigation settlement on
arid land along the Murray River in Australia. In 1886 he
secured passage of the Irrigation Act to seal the arrangement.

When the proposals for federation of the Australian
territories at the Federal Convention of 1891 lapsed in
the colonial legislatures, he supported public calls for a
popularly elected convention, and his powerful oratory
warmed thousands to the federal cause; and in 1900 he
was a member of the group which visited London to
support the Constitution Bill.

A tall, slight man with a black beard and a plentiful
crop of hair, Deakin was usually likened more to an academic than to an active politician. Some considered that
he suffered from "mental remoteness," but others saw in
him "an attractively refined and intellectual man."

Attorney general in the first federal ministry (1901–
1903), Deakin succeeded Edmund Barton as prime minister. Refusing to accede to Labour party demands, he
soon resigned, but in 1905, after Labour had made electoral gains, he formed a new Liberal ministry and stayed
in office with Labour support until 1908. During this
period, curbs on alien immigration were eased somewhat, pensions provided for the aged, and important
commercial laws adopted. After a commission (set up in
1906) proposed that only factories paying "fair and reasonable" wages should be given the benefit of tariff protection, Deakin affirmed his New Protection doctrine of
a benefit to the worker from tariffs; in 1907 a minimum,
or "basic," wage was established.

Deakin lost support in 1908 but became prime minister for a third term (1909–1910) in a "fusion" with erst-
while opponents on the non-Labour side. A significant
defense measure was the creation of an Australian naval
squadron. When Labour (under Andrew Fisher) replaced
Deakin, many liberal measures advocated earlier by him
were adopted. Deakin remained in the House of Representatives until 1913. He died in Melbourne, in retirement, on Oct. 7, 1919.

Further Reading

Alfred Deakin is listed in the Australia and New Zealand study guide (II, D). One of his close associates was
Sir Edmund BARTON.

Deakin's comments on the events leading to federation are contained in his *The Federal Story: The Inner
History of the Federal Cause, 1880–1900* (1944; 2d ed.
1963). A biography by an admirer of Deakin's policies is
Walter Murdoch, *Alfred Deakin: A Sketch* (1923). A fuller biography is J. A. La Nauze, *Alfred Deakin* (2 vols.,
1965). Background on federation is provided in John
Quick and Robert Garran, *The Annotated Constitution
of the Australian Commonwealth* (1901); Bernhard
Ringrose Wise, *The Making of the Australian Commonwealth: 1889–1900* (1913); and John Quick, *Sir John
Quick's Notebook,* edited by L. E. Freedman (1965). The
record of the Deakin administrations is covered in H. G.
Turner, *The First Decade of the Australian Commonwealth . . . 1901–1910* (1911), and Arthur Norman
Smith, *Thirty Years: The Commonwealth of Australia,
1901–1931* (1933).

DEANE / By Ralph Ketcham

Silas Deane (1737–1789), a leading merchant
and advocate of American independence, was a
highly controversial commissioner to France
from 1776 to 1778.

Silas Deane is introduced to the Marquis de Lafayette by Baron de Kalb. As an American diplomatic agent in France, Deane helped recruit a number of foreign officers for the American Revolutionary Army. (Library of Congress)

Silas Deane was born Dec. 24, 1737, into a family long resident in Connecticut. He took his bachelor and master of arts degrees from Yale College and was admitted to the bar in 1761. He consolidated his standing among the commercial and political leaders of the colony by two marriages, first to Mehitabel Webb, and after her death to Elizabeth Saltonstall. After 10 years as a prosperous merchant and lawyer he was elected to his state's General Assembly in 1772, where he soon stood among the active foes of British measures.

In the first and second Continental Congresses, Deane worked to establish and equip colonial armed forces and personally supplied the expedition that captured Ft. Ticonderoga in 1775. Though for unknown reasons he was not reappointed delegate to Congress in 1776, he had earned national standing as one of the most energetic, resourceful leaders of the Revolution.

Commissioner to France

In March 1776 Congress sent Deane to France, authorized to hasten war supplies to America and to gain French recognition of the soon-to-be-independent Colonies. Deane found France (and its ally Spain) eager to aid the Colonies against England, the ancient enemy of both

countries. Yet, the French were unwilling to make open opposition, and he was confronted by numerous informal, clandestine arrangements. Authorized to extend credit for war material, Deane could never be sure what persons or groups in America stood behind his negotiations. Equally uncertain was the status of the French—were they giving, lending, or selling supplies? And were they private businessmen, agents of Louis XVI, or perhaps joint stock operators backed by both France and Spain? Opportunities for misunderstanding, fraud, and profiteering abounded.

The only certainties are that France, under the guidance of the foreign minister Comte de Vergennes, made funds and material available, and that Deane did get quantities of guns and uniforms that sustained American armies in the 1777 campaigns, including the vital victory at Saratoga. Deane also encouraged many European military officers to join the American army.

Deane's Actions under Attack

In late 1776, when Benjamin Franklin came to France as a second commissioner, he endorsed Deane's arrangements without probing details, finding him generally "sincere and hearty in our cause." Less trustful was the third American commissioner, Arthur Lee, who suspected that Deane, and by acquiescence at least, Franklin, were in collusion with French profiteers who were billing Congress huge sums for worthless goods, materials never sent, or supplies meant to be gifts. Lee's charges led to Deane's recall soon after he signed (with Lee and Franklin) the French Alliance in February 1778.

Unsolved Mystery

Called to account by Congress, Deane began appearances before that body in August 1778 to defend himself against charges brought by Lee's powerful friends. Lacking adequate records to prove either guilt or innocence, the hearings degenerated into personal bickerings and factional disputes, eventually leaving those disposed to trust and welcome French aid on Deane's side, and those deeply suspicious of it on Lee's. The acrimonious affair led to the resignation of Henry Laurens (who was against Deane) as president of Congress and his replacement by the more friendly John Jay. Deane published a vigorous self-defense, hurling countercharges at Lee; the ensuing "paper war" became fierce. Lacking reliable evidence, Congress postponed any decision.

After fretting, half-disgraced, for 2 years, Deane returned to Europe to seek evidence to clear himself. The necessary documents were lost, hidden, or nonexistent. Feeling ill-treated and worn down by poor health, Deane wrote despondently to American friends, advising them, in view of the disarray in the patriot cause, to reconcile with England. These letters, intercepted and printed in the loyalist press in New York, added to the cloud already hanging over Deane and seemed to prove him maliciously disloyal.

Sick and bankrupt, Deane spent his last years in England, where his only apparent friend was the notorious "double spy" Dr. Edward Bancroft, who during 1776–1777 had presented himself to Deane and Franklin to spy for them but was actually reporting every detail of the clandestine American negotiations to the British ministers.

Deane died mysteriously while on a ship about to leave for Canada. Recent material presented by historian Julian Boyd strongly implies that Bancroft poisoned Deane to silence incriminating testimony of further double-dealing.

Though in 1842 Congress awarded Deane's heirs $37,000 (a small fraction of their claim) in payment for losses Deane had incurred during the Revolution, no evidence has yet appeared to clarify the charges against him.

Further Reading

Silas Deane is listed in the American History study guide (III, C, 1 and 4). He worked with Benjamin FRANKLIN and Arthur LEE as ministers to France during the American Revolution.

No satisfactory, recent biography of Deane exists. Of the older accounts, George L. Clark, *Silas Deane: a Connecticut Leader in the American Revolution* (1913), is useful, as is a biographical notice by Charles Isham in volume 1 of *The Deane Papers, 1774–1790* in the *New York Historical Society Collections* (3 vols., 1887–1890). Further letters are in *The Deane Papers: Correspondence between Silas Deane, His Brothers and Their Business and Political Associates, 1771–1795* in the collections of the Connecticut Historical Society (1930). Samuel F. Bemis, *The Diplomacy of the American Revolution* (1935), discusses Deane's diplomatic activity in France. Edmund C. Burnett, *The Continental Congress* (1941), describes disputes over Deane in Congress. Carl C. Van Doren, *The Secret History of the American Revolution: An Account of the Conspiracies of Benedict Arnold* (1941), divulges as much as is known of the intrigues surrounding Deane's career.

DEB / By David Kopf

> Radhakant Deb (1783–1867) was a Bengali reformer and cultural nationalist who dedicated his life to the preservation of orthodox Hinduism.

Historians have generally looked upon Radhakant Deb (pronounced rä′də-kənt dĕb) with disfavor, chiefly because he defended sati (suttee), the immolation of widows on funeral pyres of their dead husbands. Recent studies which focus on the psychology of Indian nationalism in opposition to British cultural imperialism have prompted a reevaluation of figures like Radhakant, Vivekananda, and Dayananda who, while ambivalent to forms of Westernization, were nevertheless modernizers of the Indian traditions.

Radhakant was a member of the Calcutta Hindu elite, which owed both its wealth and social status to profitable relations with Europeans. In the sophisticated atmosphere of the metropolis, Radhakant learned Arabic, Persian, Urdu, Sanskrit, Bengali, and English.

In 1816 Radhakant's father, Gopi Mohun Deb, contributed a large sum of money toward the establishment of Hindu College, the earliest institution of higher learning in Asia organized along European lines, and served on its first managing committee with members of the prominent Tagore and Mullick families. Some years later, Radhakant took his father's place on the committee.

Radhakant's intellectual development with respect to Western learning seems to have begun when he joined the newly formed Calcutta School Book Society and School Society in 1817–1818. He took an active role in the institutional operations of the School Society by becoming its "native" secretary and by personally supervising the reform of Calcutta primary schools.

His new cultural attitudes, intellectual development, and deepening social consciousness in the 1820s are best reflected in his publications for the School Book Society. His *Bangla siksa-grantha* (1821) was a small encyclopedia for student use and included an elementary analysis of language structure, spelling rules, geographical terms, and basic arithmetic. Also in 1821, Radhakant collaborated with J. D. Pearson in bringing out the first edition of the *Nitikatha* (Moral Tales), which drew on both Christian and Hindu traditions and was designed to inculcate a feeling of morality without sectarian bias. In 1822 Radhakant was coauthor of a book called *Stri-sikhar bidya,* which advocated female education. He also translated Western textbooks on the natural sciences, such as *Jyotibidya* (Astronomy), and on history, such as *Pracin itihaser sammacchay* (Essence of Ancient History).

Radhakant's dubious image as orthodox leader of Bengali Hindus began in 1830, when he and his followers founded the Dharma Sabha (Association in Defense of Hindu Culture) in opposition to Lord Bentinck's decree abolishing sati. Since the Sabha organized its defense of the indigenous culture against alien intrusion and used collective political means to articulate its position, it became modern India's first protonationalist movement. The founding of the Sabha proved to be the turning point in Radhakant's life, and for the next 30 years until his death, he increasingly sought ways and means of reconciling reformism with the demands of cultural nationalism.

Further Reading

Radhakant Deb is listed in the Asia study guide (II, A, 6, a). He has been pictured as the conservative adversary of Ram Mohun ROY. Other modernizers of Indian tradition were DAYANANDA and VIVEKANANDA.

There is no biography of Radhakant Deb in English. He is briefly referred to in most surveys of modern Indian history, and there is abundant material on his activities in articles on the Calcutta School Society, the British Indian Association, and the history of printing in Bengal. An evaluation of Radhakant's role in the 19th-century Bengal renaissance is in David Kopf, *British Orientalism and the Bengal Renaissance: The Dynamics of Indian Modernization, 1773–1835* (1969). See also Nemai Sadhan Bose, *The Indian Awakening and Bengal* (1960), and Ramesh C. Majumdar, *Glimpses of Bengal in the Nineteenth Century* (1960).

DᴇBAKEY / By Patsy A. Gerstner

The American surgeon Michael Ellis DeBakey (born 1908) devised procedures for replacing diseased portions of the aorta, the artery from the heart, and was a leader in the development of the artificial heart.

Michael DeBakey was born in Lake Charles, La., on Sept. 7, 1908. From Tulane University he received a bachelor of science degree in 1930, a medical degree in 1932, and a master of science degree for research on peptic ulcers in 1935. He then served as a

Michael DeBakey. (Baylor College of Medicine)

medical resident in Europe at the universities of Strasbourg and Heidelberg. He married Diana Cooper on Oct. 15, 1936.

In 1937 DeBakey became a member of the Tulane faculty, remaining until 1948, with service during World War II in the Surgeon General's Office. DeBakey had already become expert in blood transfusion and had developed a roller-type pump for use in transfusions; it became an important component of the heart-lung machine.

In 1948 DeBakey was appointed professor of surgery at Baylor University College of Medicine in Houston, Tex. A year later he assumed responsibilities as surgeon in chief at Houston's Ben Taub General Hospital. In the 1950s DeBakey originated complex surgical procedures for the correction of aneurysms and blockages of the aorta that involve replacing the diseased part with Dacron tubing.

The work for which DeBakey is best known concerns the artificial heart. He initially concentrated on developing a left ventricular bypass (half an artificial heart) and in 1967 successfully implanted his device. He worked toward the development of a completely artificial heart and believed that such a heart was the ultimate answer to human heart replacement in spite of others' interest in heart transplantation.

In 1969 a former colleague, Dr. Denton Cooley, implanted a completely artificial heart in a human. Since Cooley had worked closely with DeBakey and because he was assisted by Dr. Domingo Liotta, who had worked with DeBakey on the artificial heart, DeBakey claimed priority of development. Cooley's artificial heart was not successful, and DeBakey held that much more work was needed to perfect the device.

DeBakey received numerous awards and honors and in 1964 served on the President's Commission on Heart Disease, Cancer and Stroke. This Commission recommended, among other things, the establishment of intensive-care centers for these diseases and community centers for diagnosis. DeBakey authored several hundred scientific articles. His books include *Battle Casualties, Incidence, Mortality, and Logistic Considerations* (1952) with G. W. Beebe and *Cold Injury, Ground Type* (1958) with T. F. Whayne. In addition to his other positions DeBakey was chairman of the Department of Medicine at Methodist Hospital in Houston and physician in chief at the Fondren-Brown Cardiovascular Research Center.

Further Reading

Michael DeBakey is listed in the Science study guide (VII, G, 4). Another American surgeon was Harvey CUSHING.

DeBakey's work is briefly discussed in Richard Hardaway Meade, *An Introduction to the History of General Surgery* (1968), and Robert G. Richardson, *Surgery: Old and New Frontiers* (1969), which is a revised and enlarged edition of *The Surgeon's Tale* (1958).

DE BOW / By Arthur W. Coats

An American business journalist, statistician, and protectionist, James Dunwoody Brownson De Bow (1820–1867) was a proslavery propagandist for Southern sectionalism.

James D. B. De Bow, who was born in Charleston, S.C., on July 20, 1820, became an almost penniless orphan on the death of his father, a once prosperous merchant. After limited schooling and severe privations, he saved enough to enter the College of Charleston, graduating as valedictorian in 1843. Unsuccessful as a lawyer, he took up journalism in an effort to supplement his income. He contributed political and philosophical articles to the *Southern Quarterly Review* and became its editor in 1845.

De Bow was also actively involved in the campaign to promote Southern economic development, and at the 1845 commercial convention in Memphis he was a delegate and secretary for South Carolina. To further the cause of Southern commerce, he founded the *Commercial Review of the South and Southwest,* based in New Orleans. At first this monthly magazine was unsuccessful, and it was suspended in 1847. But it was revived with the aid of Maunsel White, a wealthy sugar planter, and eventually acquired a larger circulation than any other Southern magazine. In 1848 De Bow became professor of public economy, commerce, and statistics at the University of Louisiana, occupying a chair White founded for him, and he held a similar appointment at the Kentucky Collegiate and Military Institute.

Advocating Sectional Bias

During the 1850s De Bow was an increasingly influential and partisan spokesman for the Southern viewpoint, and his writing undoubtedly helped to widen the breach in the country. He defended slavery, declaring that the South suffered neither competition between slave and free labor nor the conflict between immigrant and native workers which occurred in the North. He advocated the reopening of the slave trade and favored tariff protection.

Predicting gloomy prospects for agriculture, De Bow called on Southerners to emulate the North by developing trade and manufactures and by providing state land grants for railroads. He believed railroads would enhance the region's strength and prosperity but, like John C. Calhoun, he regarded Federal internal improvements as corrupt and unconstitutional. De Bow strongly advocated the compilation of statistics to reveal and mobilize Southern economic resources, and in 1848–1849 he was head of the newly established Louisiana state government statistical bureau. Despite De Bow's strong sectional bias, President Franklin Pierce appointed him superintendent of the U.S. Census in 1850, a post he held until 1855. In addition to issuing the Seventh Census, he published *Industrial Resources of the South and Western*

James D. B. De Bow. (Library of Congress)

States (3 vols., 1853) and a compendium based on the census, entitled *Statistical View of the United States* (1854).

In the late 1850s De Bow was involved in plans to construct a Southern transcontinental railroad and to promote direct trade between the South and Europe. Although few of his schemes bore fruit, his importance was recognized by his presidency of the Knoxville Commercial Convention of 1857.

During the Civil War, De Bow was chief Confederate agent for the purchase and sale of cotton, and after the war he revived the *Review*. He died on Feb. 27, 1867.

Further Reading

James D. B. De Bow is listed in the Social Sciences study guide (VI, C, 3). Henry Charles CAREY also advocated a policy of tariff protection. Southern proponents of slavery were John C. CALHOUN and Thomas R. DEW.

The two major sources are W. D. Weatherford, *James Dunwoody Brownson De Bow* (1935), and James A. McMillen, *The Works of James D. B. De Bow* (1940). The latter work contains a bibliography of De Bow's *Review*, a check list of his miscellaneous writings, and a list of references relating to him. See also the brief account in Joseph Dorfman, *The Economic Mind in American Civilization, 1606–1865*, vol. 2 (1947).

DEBS / By Gerald W. McFarland

> Eugene Victor Debs (1855–1926), a leading American union organizer and, after 1896, a prominent Socialist, ran five times as the Socialist party nominee for president.

E ugene V. Debs was born on Nov. 5, 1855, in Terre Haute, Ind., where his French immigrant parents, after considerable hardship, had settled. Debs began work in the town's railroad shops at the age of 15, soon becoming a locomotive fireman. Thrown out of work by the depression of the 1870s, he left Terre Haute briefly to find a railroad job but soon returned to work as a clerk in a wholesale grocery company. Even though he was no longer a fireman, he joined the Brotherhood of Locomotive Firemen in 1874 and rose rapidly in the union. In 1878 he became an associate editor of the *Firemen's Magazine*. Two years later he was appointed editor of the magazine and secretary-treasurer of the brotherhood.

Debs also pursued a political career in the early 1880s. A popular and earnest young man, he was elected city clerk of Terre Haute as a Democrat in 1879 and reelected in 1881. Soon after his second term ended in January 1884, he was elected to the Indiana Legislature, serving one term.

Eugene V. Debs about 1909. (Library of Congress)

Changing Concept of Unionism

During the 1880s Debs remained a craft unionist, devoted to "orthodox" ideals of work, thrift, and respectable unionism. With the Firemen's Brotherhood as his base, he sought to develop cooperation among the various railroad brotherhoods. A weak federation was achieved in 1889, but it soon collapsed due to internal rivalries. Tired and discouraged, Debs resigned his positions in the Firemen's Brotherhood in 1892, only to be reelected over his protest.

Debs's new project was an industrial union, one which would unite *all* railroad men, whatever their specific craft, in one union. By mid-1893, the American Railway Union (ARU) was established, with Debs as its first president. Labor discontent and the severe national depression beginning in 1893 swelled the union's ranks. The ARU won a major strike against the Great Northern Railroad early in the spring of 1894. Nevertheless, when the Pullman Company works near Chicago were struck in May, Debs was reluctant to endorse a sympathetic strike of all railroad men. His union took a militant stance, however, refusing to move Pullman railroad cars nationally. By July, Debs felt the boycott was succeeding, but a sweeping legal injunction against the union leadership and the use of Federal troops broke the strike. Debs was sentenced to 6 months in jail for contempt of court, and his lawyer, Clarence Darrow, appealed unsuccessfully to the U.S. Supreme Court.

Conversion to Socialism

Having moved from craft to industrial unionism, Debs now converted to socialism. Convinced that capitalism and competition inevitably led to class strife, Debs argued that the profit system should be replaced by a cooperative commonwealth. Although he advocated radical change, he rejected revolutionary violence and chose to bring his case to the public through political means. He participated in the establishment of the Social Democratic party in 1898 and its successor, the Socialist Party of America, in 1901.

Debs was the Socialist candidate for president five

times. His role was that of a spokesman for radical reform rather than that of a party theorist. A unifying agent, he tried to remain aloof from the persistent factional struggle between the evolutionary Socialists and the party's more revolutionary western wing. As the party's presidential candidate in 1900 and 1904, he led the Socialists to a fourfold increase in national voting strength, from about 97,000 to more than 400,000 votes. While the party's vote did not increase significantly in 1908, Debs drew attention to the Socialist case by a dramatic national tour in the "Red Special," a campaign train. The year 1912 proved to be the high point for Debs and his party. He won 897,011 votes, 6 percent of the total.

Imprisonment for Sedition

When World War I began in 1914, the party met with hard times. The Socialists were the only party to oppose economic assistance to the Allies and the preparedness movement. Debs, while refusing the Socialist nomination for president in 1916, endorsed the party view that President Woodrow Wilson's neutrality policies would lead to war. In 1917 America's entrance into war resulted in widespread antagonism toward the Socialists. When Debs spoke out in 1918 against the war and Federal harassment of Socialists, he was arrested and convicted of sedition under the wartime Espionage Act. He ran for the last time as the Socialist presidential candidate while in prison, receiving nearly a million votes, more actual votes (but a smaller percentage of the total) than in 1912.

On Christmas Day 1921, President Warren G. Harding pardoned Debs, but Debs could do little to restore life to the Socialist party, battered by the war years and split over the Russian Revolution. Debs had welcomed the Revolution; yet he became very critical of the dictatorial aspects of the Soviet regime, refusing to ally himself with the American Communist party. Debs died on Oct. 20, 1926, having won wide respect as a resourceful evangelist for a more humane, cooperative society.

Further Reading

Eugene V. Debs is listed in the American History study guide (VII, G, 4, c; VIII, F, 4, e). Other early proponents of American socialism were Morris HILLQUIT and Daniel DE LEON. Before he became a Socialist, Debs was an important labor organizer, as were Samuel GOMPERS and Terence V. POWDERLY.

The most recent edition of Debs's writings is *Writings and Speeches of Eugene V. Debs,* with an introduction by Arthur M. Schlesinger, Jr. (1948). There are two excellent modern studies of Debs's career: Ray Ginger, *The Bending Cross: A Biography of Eugene Victor Debs* (1949), and H. Wayne Morgan, *Eugene V. Debs: Socialist for President* (1962). McAlister Coleman, *Eugene V. Debs: A Man Unafraid* (1930), is the best of the older biographies. Ira Kipnis, *The American Socialist Movement, 1897–1912* (1952), and David A. Shannon, *The Socialist Party of America* (1955), are invaluable sources on the Socialist party.

DEBUSSY / By Laurence D. Berman

The French composer Achille Claude Debussy (1862–1918) developed a strongly individual style and also created a language that broke definitively with the procedures of classical tonality.

The world having made peace with his innovations by the time of his death, Claude Debussy (pronounced də-bü-sēʹ) subsequently came to be regarded as the impressionist composer par excellence—a creator of poetic tone pictures, a master colorist, and the author of many charming miniatures (including *Clair de lune, Golliwog's Cake Walk,* and *Girl with the Flaxen Hair*). Only a handful of critics between World Wars I and II were concerned with the historical impact of his accomplishment, the scope of which is gradually coming to be recognized. It is generally accepted today that his coloristic harmonies do not simply "float" but "function" in terms of a structure analogous to the classical tonal structure and are governed by equally lucid concepts of tension and repose.

Claude Debussy was born on Aug. 22, 1862, at St-Germain-en-Laye into an impoverished family. Thanks to his godparents, he was able to enter the Paris Conservatory 10 years later. Although he worked hard to gain a solid grounding, the archaic and mechanical nature of much of what he studied there did not escape him. Still, certain aspects of his training were exciting, notably his introduction to the operas of Richard Wagner.

Attitude to Wagner

In 1884 Debussy won the Prix de Rome for his cantata *L'Enfant prodigue.* In Rome the following year he was homesick for Paris, and he wrote that one of his few solaces was the study of Wagner's opera *Tristan und Isolde.* Not many years later Debussy harshly criticized Wagner, but his scorn seems directed more toward Wagner's dramaturgy than toward his music. Although Debussy could ridicule the *dramatis personae* of *Parsifal,* he did not neglect to add that the opera was "one of the finest monuments of sound that have been raised to the imperturbable glory of music." Throughout his life Debussy was fascinated by the chromatic richness of the Wagnerian style, but in keeping with Verlaine's epigram, "One must take eloquence and wring its neck," he would categorically reject Wagnerian rhetoric. His inclinations were toward conciseness and understatement.

Influence of the Gamelan Orchestra

At the height of his enthusiasm for Wagner, Debussy had an experience as important for his later development as Wagner had been for his beginnings: the revelation of the Javanese gamelan at the Paris World Exposition of 1889. This exotic orchestra, with its variety of bells, xylophones, and gongs, produced a succession of softly percussive effects and cross rhythms that Debussy was later to describe as a "counterpoint by comparison with

Claude Debussy about 1907. (French Cultural Services)

which that of Palestrina is child's play." What has come to be regarded as the typical impressionist texture—an atmosphere of melodic and harmonic shapes in which dissonant tones are placed so as to reduce their "shock" value to a minimum and heighten their "overtone" value to a maximum—was a logical conclusion to the explorations in sonority of 19th-century European composers. Yet without the specific influence of the gamelan Debussy might never have realized this texture in all its complexity.

The effect of the experience at the Exposition of 1889 was not immediately manifested in Debussy's work. It was the process of growth in the years 1890–1900 that brought the elements of the exotic music of the gamelan into play with others already discernible in his style and produced a new tonal language. The completion of this process toward the end of the decade can thus serve as a line of demarcation dividing the earlier years, not without their masterpieces—*Ariettes oubliées* (1888), *Prélude à l'après-midi d'un faune* (1892; *Afternoon of a Faun*), and the String Quartet (1893)—from the period of maturity.

Mature Works

Debussy's first large-scale piece of his mature period, the *Nocturnes* for orchestra (1893–1899), is contemporaneous with the work on his only completed opera, *Pelléas et Mélisande* (1894–1902), based on a play by Maurice Maeterlinck. The notoriety surrounding the premiere of *Pelléas* in 1902 made Debussy the most controversial

figure in musical France and divided Paris into two strongly partisan camps.

Two years later Debussy abandoned his wife of 5 years, Rosalie Texier, to live with and eventually marry Emma Bardac, a woman of some means. The first taste of existence free from material worry seems to have had a beneficial effect on his productivity. During these years he wrote some of his most enduring works: *La Mer* (1905) and *Ibéria* (1908), both for orchestra; *Images* (1905), *Children's Corner Suite* (1908), and two books of *Préludes* (1910–1912), all for piano solo.

Debussy's pieces of the following years show certain marked changes in style. Not as well known as his works of the preceding years but in no way inferior, they have less surface appeal and are therefore more difficult to approach. It is ironic that just when he was exploring new avenues of thought he was in a sense relegated to the shadows by a "radicalism" more sensational than anything connected with *Pelléas* 10 years earlier. Debussy's ballet *Jeux*, his last and most sophisticated orchestral score, which had its premiere on May 15, 1913, was virtually eclipsed by the scandal of Igor Stravinsky's ballet *Sacre du printemps* (*Rite of Spring*) on May 29. Debussy's ambivalent attitude toward Stravinsky's music may reflect a certain resentment of the younger composer's noisy arrival on the scene. Debussy evinced a genuine, if limited, admiration for Stravinsky's work and even incorporated certain Stravinsky-like effects in *En blanc et noir* (1915) and the *Études* (1915). Whether or not Debussy's general tendency in his late pieces to achieve a drier, less "impressionistic" sound is the direct result of Stravinsky's influence is difficult to say.

When Debussy composed these last-mentioned works, he was already suffering from a fatal cancer. He completed only three of a projected group of six sonatas "for various instruments" (1915–1917). He died in Paris on March 25, 1918.

Characteristics of Debussy's Music

A notable characteristic of Debussy's music is its finesse, but it is a characteristic applicable to almost every other aspect of his artistic behavior as well. His choice of texts to set to music (from Verlaine, Stéphane Mallarmé, and Maeterlinck), his own efforts in verse for the song set *Proses lyriques* (1894), and his fine prose essays (posthumously compiled under the title *Monsieur Croche, the Dilletante-Hater*) all attest to a culture that must have been mostly innate, since there is so little evidence of it in his early family life or formal education.

Finesse and understatement would seem to reinforce the mysterious and dreamlike elements in Debussy's music. In this respect his opera *Pelléas* is the key work of his creative life, because through it he not only achieved the synthesis of his mature style, but also in the art of allusion of Maeterlinck's play found the substance of what he could express in music more tellingly than anyone else. The words and actions of the opera pass as if in a dream, but the dream is suffused with an inescapable feeling of dread. Debussy brings to this feeling a disquieting intensity through music of pervasive quiet, broken rarely and only momentarily by outbursts revealing the underlying terror.

Similarly, in *Nuages* (*Clouds*), the first movement of the *Nocturnes,* the clouds are not cheerful billows in a sunlit sky but ominous signs—of what we cannot be sure. Characteristically, Debussy leaves us with a mystery: he presents us with the imminence of disaster but not disaster itself. Premonition is a force capable of disrupting the amiable surface of Debussy's music and is also one of the music's chief emotional strengths. What is more, it is a symbol of Debussy's position vis-à-vis European music at the turn of the century.

Further Reading

Claude Debussy is listed in the Music study guide (I, I, 9). He was drawn to some of the music of Richard WAGNER. Maurice RAVEL was the leading exponent of impressionism after Debussy. In his late music Debussy showed some influence of the work of Igor STRAVINSKY.

Afternoon of a Faun, a painting by Leon Bakst inspired by Vladimir Nijinsky's performance in that ballet, for which the dancer had choreographed Debussy's tone poem Prélude à l'après-midi d'un faune. *Debussy's music was, in turn, an impression of Stéphane Mallarmé's poem. (Courtesy Wadsworth Atheneum, Hartford, Ella Gallup Sumner and Mary Catlin Sumner Collection)*

The standard biography for many years was Léon Vallas, *Claude Debussy: His Life and Works* (trans. 1933). Its scholarliness and serious approach give it lasting value. It has been joined in recent years by Edward Lockspeiser's indispensable *Debussy: His Life and Mind* (2 vols., 1962–1965). This study places Debussy in the context of Paris at the turn of the century and gives a vivid picture of an extraordinary moment in France's cultural life. See also Oscar Thompson, *Debussy: Man and Artist* (1937); Rollo H. Myers, *Debussy* (1948); and Victor I. Seroff, *Debussy: Musician of France* (1956). "The Adventure and Achievement of Debussy" in William W. Austin, *Music in the 20th Century* (1966), is a valuable combination of biography and analysis.

DEBYE / By Stanley L. Jaki

> The main contribution of the Dutch-born American physical chemist Peter Joseph William Debye (1884–1966) was the development of methods based on induced dipole moments and x-ray diffraction for the investigation of molecular structures.

Peter Debye was born on March 24, 1884, in Maastricht, Netherlands, the son of William and Maria Reumkens Debije. At the age of 17 Debye entered the Technical Institute of Aachen and earned his diploma in electrical engineering in 1905. He immediately obtained the position of assistant in technical mechanics at the institute. At the same time his interest in physics received strong promptings from Arthur Sommerfeld, then serving on the faculty. Debye followed Sommerfeld to the University of Munich and obtained his doctorate in physics by a mathematical analysis of the pressure of radiation on spheres of arbitrary electrical properties.

The dissertation and a 1907 paper on Foucault currents in rectangular conductors gave clear evidence of Debye's ability to produce the mathematical tools demanded by his topics. A fitting recognition of Debye's youthful excellence was his succession in 1911, at the age of 27, to Albert Einstein in the chair of theoretical physics at the University of Zurich. While in Zurich he worked out, on the basis of Max Planck's and Einstein's ideas, the first complete theory of the specific heat of solids and the equally important theory of polar molecules. Debye was professor of theoretical physics at the University of Utrecht from 1912 until 1914, when he received the prestigious post of director of the theoretical branch of the Institute of Physics at the University of Göttingen. In 1915 he became editor of the famed *Physikalische Zeitschrift* and served in that capacity for 25 years.

X-ray Research

In Göttingen, Debye started a most fruitful collaboration with P. Scherrer. Their first paper, "X-ray Interference Patterns of Particles Oriented at Random" (1916), gave immediate evidence of the enormous potentialities of their powder method to explore the structure of crystals with very high symmetry. It also proved very useful in work with polycrystalline metals and colloidal systems. Two years later Debye and Scherrer extended the method from the study of the coordination of atoms to the arrangement of electrons inside the atom. It was in this connection that they formulated the important concept of "atomic form factor." Debye and Scherrer formed such a close team that when, in 1920, Debye became professor of experimental physics and director of the physics laboratory at the Swiss Federal Technical Institute in Zurich, Scherrer followed him there. The two inaugurated a most influential x-ray research center which attracted students from all over the world.

In the field of x-ray research Debye's signal success in Zurich was his demonstration in early 1923 that in the collision between x-rays and electrons, energy and momentum are conserved; he also suggested that the interaction between electromagnetic radiation and electrons must therefore be considered as a collision between photons and electrons. But Debye's principal achievement in Zurich consisted in the formulation of his theories of magnetic cooling and of interionic attraction in electrolyte solutions. The latter work, in which he collaborated with E. Hückel, was closely related to Debye's pioneering research on dipole moments. Debye had already been for 2 years the director of the Physical Institute at the University of Leipzig when his classic monograph, *Polar Molecules,* was published in 1928.

War and Postwar Years

Debye's rather rapid moves from one university to another were motivated by his eagerness to work with the best available experimental apparatus. Thus in 1934 he readily accepted the invitation of the University of Berlin to serve both as professor at the university and as director of the Kaiser Wilhelm Institute. The latter establishment, now known as Max Planck Institute, was just completing, with the help of the Rockefeller Foundation, a new laboratory which was to represent the best of its kind on the Continent. During his stay in Berlin, Debye became the recipient of the Nobel Prize in chemistry for 1936. It was awarded to him "for his contributions to our knowledge of molecular structure through his investigations on dipole moments and on the diffraction of x-rays and electrons in gases."

Meanwhile, the Nazi government began to renege on its original promise that Debye would not be asked to renounce his Dutch citizenship while serving as director of the Kaiser Wilhelm Institute, a post with a lifetime tenure. Shortly after World War II broke out, he was informed that he could no longer enter the laboratory of the institute unless he assumed German citizenship. As Debye refused, he was told to stay home and keep busy writing books. But he succeeded in making his way to Italy and from there to Cornell University, which invited him to give the Baker Lectures in 1940.

Debye made Cornell his permanent home. He served there as head of the chemistry department for the next 10 years. His wartime service to his adopted country (he became a citizen in 1946) concerned the synthetic rubber program. In pure research he further investigated, in collaboration with his son, Peter P. Debye, the light-scattering properties of polymers, on which he based the now generally accepted absolute determination of their molecular weights. He was a member of all leading scientific societies and the recipient of all major awards in chemistry. His outgoing personality kept generating enthusiasm and goodwill throughout his long life, which came to an end on Nov. 2, 1966. Since 1913 he had been married to Mathilde Alberer, who shared his lively interest in gardening and fishing.

Further Reading

Peter Debye is listed in the Science study guide (VII, D, 2). The demonstration of the conservation of energy and momentum was achieved independently in 1923 by Arthur COMPTON in the United States.

The best sources available on Debye's life and on the various aspects of his scientific work are the introductory essays in *The Collected Papers of Peter J. W. Debye* (1954). A detailed biographical profile of Debye is in the Royal Society, *Biographical Memoirs of Fellows of the Royal Society,* vol. 16 (1970). Debye is discussed in Eduard Farber, *Nobel Prize Winners in Chemistry, 1901–1961* (1953; rev. ed. 1963); Aaron I. Ihde, *The Development of Modern Chemistry* (1964); and *Chemistry: Nobel Lectures, Including Presentation Speeches and*

Peter Debye. (Süddeutscher Verlag)

Laureates' Biographies, 1922–41, published by the Nobel Foundation (1966).

✳   ✳   ✳

DECATUR / By Marvin R. Zahniser

The American naval officer Stephen Decatur (1779–1820) is best known for his daring exploits in the Tripolitan War and as a successful commander in the War of 1812.

Stephen Decatur was born on Jan. 5, 1779, at Sinepuxent, Md. He studied at the Episcopal Academy and then at the University of Pennsylvania. After working briefly in Philadelphia, Decatur accepted a midshipman's commission at the outset of the naval war with France (1798–1800). He won quick promotion to lieutenant in May 1799.

Decatur saw action in the war with Tripoli and, under Commodore Edward Preble, commanded the 12-gun schooner *Enterprise.* On Feb. 16, 1804, Decatur led the daring evening expedition that destroyed the captured frigate *Philadelphia* in the Tripoli harbor. He was quickly promoted to captain, and as such he commanded a division of gunboats in each of Preble's bombardments of Tripoli. In the first attack, on August 3, Decatur and his crew boarded and captured two Tripolitan gunboats;

Stephen Decatur, a portrait by Rembrandt Peale. (Courtesy of The New-York Historical Society, New York City)

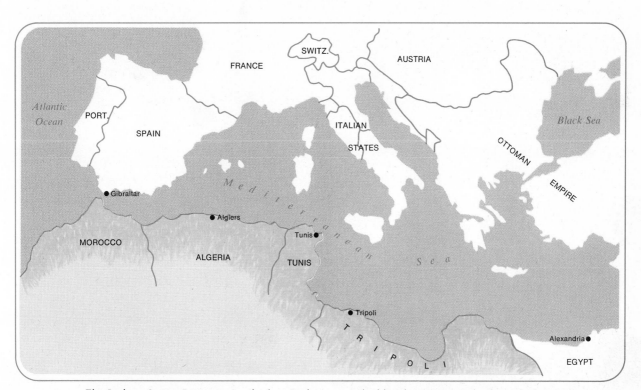

The Barbary States. For centuries the four Barbary states had lived on piracy and tribute. In the Tripolitan War (1801–1805) the United States compelled Tripoli to renounce all rights to halt and levy tribute on American ships. Stephen Decatur was the most conspicuous hero in this generally inept and inglorious conflict.

such feats made Decatur the most dashing figure of the war.

In 1806 Decatur married Susan Wheeler, daughter of a wealthy Virginia merchant. Two years later he was made commander of the southeastern naval forces. He also sat on the court-martial board in 1808 that suspended Capt. James Barron after the *Chesapeake-Leopard* affair. In 1811 he served as president of the court of inquiry following the *President–Little-Belt* affair.

In the War of 1812 Decatur was in command when the *United States* scored a victory over the British frigate *Macedonian* on Oct. 25, 1812, near Madeira off the Moroccan coast. When the *United States* was blockaded in New London, Conn., in 1814, Decatur and his crew were transferred to the *President*. In a violent storm on the night of Jan. 14, 1815, the *President* tried to run the British blockade but was grounded on a sandbar for 2 hours and somewhat damaged; the next morning it was sighted by the blockading fleet. After a lengthy chase and moderate casualties suffered in a brisk fight with the *Endymion,* the American ship surrendered. A court of inquiry credited Decatur's capture to unforeseeable ship damage and praised him highly.

Following the War of 1812, Decatur led an expedition to the Mediterranean that successfully exacted payment from Algiers for damages inflicted on Americans during the war by the Barbary pirates. Fetes and dinners followed his return. Decatur gave the much-repeated patriotic response to one toast: "Our Country! In her intercourse with foreign nations may she always be in the right; but our country, right or wrong." From 1815 until his death Decatur served on the Board of Navy Commissioners. He died on March 22, 1820, in a duel near Bladensburg, Md., with Capt. James Barron, who held Decatur responsible for his own failure to be reinstated to command. First buried near Washington, D.C., Decatur's remains were transferred in 1846 to St. Peter's Churchyard, Philadelphia, beside his parents' grave.

Further Reading

Stephen Decatur is listed in the American History study guide (IV, B; IV, C, 3). Other naval heroes of the War of 1812 were James LAWRENCE and Oliver Hazard PERRY.

A competent biography is Charles Lee Lewis, *The Romantic Decatur* (1937). The source materials for Decatur's participation in the Barbary Wars are available in *Naval Documents Related to the United States Wars with the Barbary Powers* (7 vols., 1939–1944). A critical evaluation of Decatur's participation in the War of 1812 is Alfred Thayer Mahan, *Sea Power in Its Relation to the War of 1812* (2 vols., 1905).

* * *

DEERE / By David A. Williams

The American inventor and manufacturer John Deere (1804–1886) was one of the first to design agricultural tools and machines to meet the specific needs of midwestern farmers.

John Deere was born in modest circumstances in Rutland, Vt., the third son of William Rinold and Sarah Yates Deere. After receiving the limited education available to a country boy, Deere was apprenticed at 17 to a blacksmith in Middleburn, Vt. He completed his apprenticeship in 4 years and became a master craftsman.

In 1836 Deere left Vermont for Grand Detour, Ill., where he found ready employment in his trade. He prospered, for the farmers kept him fully occupied supplying their customary needs. They also presented him with an unusual problem posed by the local soil. The soil of Illinois and other prairie areas not only was difficult to plow because of its thick sod covering but also tended to clog the moldboards of plows. Deere tried covering the moldboard and cutting a plowshare from salvaged steel. Steel surfaces tended to shed the thick soil and were burnished by the abrasive action of the soil. Deere's new plows, introduced in 1839, sold readily, and within a decade the production of plows by Deere and his new associate, Leonard Andrus, exceeded 1,000 per year. Deere parted company with his partners to move to Moline, Ill., which was better situated for a market, transportation, and raw materials.

Repeated experiments produced an excellent moldboard and demonstrated that further improvements in the plow were dependent on using better-quality steel. Deere imported such steel from an English firm until a

John Deere. (Library of Congress)

Pittsburgh firm cast the first plow steel in the United States for him. Deere's production of plows soared to 10,000 by 1857 as agriculture in the Midwest grew to meet the unprecedented demands of the growing home and export market.

The business was incorporated in 1868 with Deere and his son, Charles, in the executive positions. During the Civil War the company prospered as it diversified its output to include wagons, carriages, and a full line of agricultural equipment. It also adopted modern administrative practices and built an efficient sales, distribution, and service organization which reached into all parts of America. Deere remained active in the management of the company until his fatal illness in 1886. He was succeeded by his son.

John Deere married twice. His first wife, Demarius Lamb, died in 1865. Two years later he married her younger sister, Lucinda Lamb.

Further Reading

John Deere is listed in the American History study guide (VI, D, 1). Another agricultural inventor was Cyrus McCORMICK.

Full-length studies of Deere are Neil M. Clark, *John Deere: He Gave to the World the Steel Plow* (1937), and Darragh Aldrich, *The Story of John Deere: A Saga of American Industry* (1942). See also Stewart H. Holbrook, *Machines of Plenty: Pioneering in American Agriculture* (1955), and Wayne D. Rasmussen, *Readings in the History of American Agriculture* (1960).

✻ ✻ ✻

DEERING / By Elisha P. Douglass

American manufacturer William Deering (1826–1913) made improvements in the grain harvester that greatly increased production of grain throughout the world.

Born in South Paris, Maine, William Deering intended to study medicine but, because of his father's need for help in his woolen mill, went to work there instead. During the next 20 years he made a considerable fortune selling woolen goods and speculating in western lands. In 1870 he lent $40,000 to E. H. Gammon, who was manufacturing the Marsh grain harvester in Illinois. When Gammon's health failed in 1873, Deering moved to Illinois to manage the company.

With the rapid expansion of wheat-growing in the Midwest during the 1870s and the efficient design of his machine, Deering's sales soared. His harvester had a mechanical grain lift that saved the labor of four men on ordinary reapers. To further improve his harvester, Deering experimented with an automatic wire binder. He finally purchased the rights to the still experimental Appleby twine binder.

In 1879 Deering became sole owner of the company and took a gamble by building 3,000 twine binders for

William Deering. (Library of Congress)

the next harvest. Although the machines did not work perfectly, they represented a major technological breakthrough and established a standard design for harvesters throughout the world. Competition among the manufacturers of agricultural machinery grew fierce, and litigation over patents mounted to unprecedented levels. Between 1880 and 1885 the number of machines manufactured in a year rose from 60,000 to 250,000, while the number of manufacturers dropped from over 100 to about 20. The Deering Harvester Company, largely on the worth of its twine binder and Deering's business talent, swept ahead of most competitors. By 1890 the company's Chicago plant, with 9,000 employees, had a daily capacity of 1,200 machines of various kinds, which it sold all over the world.

During the 1890s the intense competition between Deering's company and his principal competitor, the McCormick Harvester Company, became damaging to both. As a result, when Deering retired, the two companies merged in 1902, thus forming the nucleus of the International Harvester Company.

A simple, unaffected man of complete integrity, Deering achieved success based on the huge demand for agricultural machinery at the time plus his own good business judgment and unremitting efforts to improve his products.

Further Reading

William Deering is listed in the American History study guide (VII, E, 5). Cyrus McCORMICK was his competitor.

The best source of information about Deering is a privately printed volume, *William Deering* (no author, 1914), containing biographical sketches, testimonials, and reprints of newspaper obituaries. Accounts of his company and its bitter competition with the McCormick Harvester Company can be found in Herbert N. Casson, *Cyrus Hall McCormick: His Life and Work* (1909); William T. Hutchinson, *Cyrus Hall McCormick* (2 vols., 1930–1935); and Cyrus McCormick, *The Century of the Reaper: An Account of Cyrus Hall McCormick* (1931).

✳   ✳   ✳

DEFOE / By Michael Shugrue

The English novelist, journalist, poet, and government agent Daniel Defoe (1660–1731) wrote more than 500 books, pamphlets, articles, and poems. Among the most productive authors of the Augustan Age, he was the first of the great 18th-century English novelists.

Daniel Defoe was the son of a dissenting London tallow chandler or butcher. He early thought of becoming a Presbyterian minister, and in the 1670s he attended the Reverend Charles Morton's famous academy near London. In 1684 he married Mary Tuffley, who brought him the handsome dowry of

Daniel Defoe. (National Portrait Gallery, London)

£3,700 and bore him seven children. Defoe participated briefly in the abortive Monmouth Rebellion of 1685 but escaped capture and punishment. From 1685 through 1692 he engaged in trade in London as a wholesale hosier, importer of wine and tobacco, and part owner and insurer of ships. In later life he also dealt in real estate and manufactured bricks.

Defoe evidently knew King William III; indeed, his bankruptcy in 1692 for the enormous sum of £17,000 was primarily because of losses suffered from underwriting marine insurance for the King. Although he settled with his creditors in 1693, he was plagued by the threat of bankruptcy throughout his life and faced imprisonment for debt and libel seven times.

Arrested in 1703 for having published *The Shortest Way with the Dissenters* in 1702, Defoe was tried and sentenced to stand in the pillory for 3 days in July. He languished in Newgate Prison, however, until Robert Walpole released him in November and offered him a post as a government agent. Defoe continued to serve the government as journalist, pamphleteer, and secret agent for the remainder of his life. The most long-lived of his 27 periodicals, the *Review* (1704–1713), was especially influential in promoting the union between England and Scotland in 1706–1707 and in supporting the controversial Peace of Utrecht (1713).

Defoe published hundreds of political and social tracts between 1704 and 1719. During the 1720s he contributed to such weekly journals as *Mist's* and *Applebee's*, wrote criminal biographies, and studied economics and geography as well as producing his major works of fiction. He died in a comatose lethargy in Ropemaker's Alley on April 24, 1731, while hiding from a creditor who had commenced proceedings against him.

Defoe's interests and activities reflect the major social, political, economic, and literary trends of his age. He supported the policies of William III and Mary after the Glorious Revolution of 1688–1689, and analyzed England's emergence as the major sea and mercantile power in the Western world. He pleaded for leniency for debtors and bankrupts and defended the rights of Protestant dissenters. Effectively utilizing newspapers and journals to make his points, he also experimented with the novel form, which was still in its infancy.

His Nonfiction

No brief account of Defoe's works can do more than hint at the range, variety, and scope of his hundreds of publications. His first major work, *An Essay upon Projects* (1697), which introduced many topics that would reappear in his later works, proposed ways of providing better roads, insurance, and education, and even planned a house for fools to be supported by "a Tax upon Learning, to be paid by the Authors of Books."

In 1701 Defoe published *The True-Born Englishman*, the most widely sold poem in English up to that time. He estimated that more than 80,000 copies of this defense of William III against the attacks of John Tutchin were sold. Although Defoe's prose satire against the tyranny of the Church of England, *The Shortest Way with the Dis-*

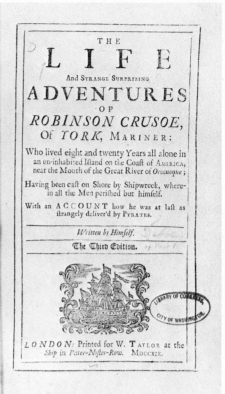

Title page and frontispiece from the third edition of Defoe's Robinson Crusoe. *The book went through four editions in its first 4 months. The situation of a civilized man confronting nature absolutely alone has had permanent appeal. (Library of Congress)*

senters (1702), led to his arrest, the popularity of his *Hymn to the Pillory* (1703) indicated the favor that he had found with the London public. From 1704 to 1713 in his monumental *Review*, Defoe discussed almost every aspect of the political, economic, and social life of Augustan England.

Defoe's allegorical moon voyage, *The Consolidator: Or Memoirs of Sundry Transactions from the World in the Moon* (1705), reviews the political history of the previous century, defends his political activities, and describes the ingenious machine which lifts the narrator to Terra Luna: a chariot powered by 513 feathers, one for each member of the British Parliament. His *Appeal to Honour and Justice* (1715) is perhaps his most moving and personal account of his services to the English crown.

"Robinson Crusoe"

At the age of 59, after a full career as businessman, government servant, political pamphleteer, and journalist, Defoe embarked upon a career as novelist and within 6 years produced the half-dozen novels which have given him his greatest fame.

In April 1719 Defoe published his most enduring work, *The Life and Strange Surprizing Adventures of Robinson Crusoe*. The immediate success of the story of the shipwrecked Crusoe's solitary existence on a desert island for more than 20 years, of his encounter with the native Friday, and of his eventual rescue inspired Defoe to write *The Farther Adventures of Robinson Crusoe* later in 1719 and *Serious Reflections during the Life*

and Surprizing Adventures in 1720. That year he published another travel novel, *The Life, Adventures, and Pyracies of the Famous Captain Singleton*.

The greatness of *Robinson Crusoe* lies not only in Defoe's marvelously realistic descriptive passages but in the fact that the novel recounts one of the great myths of Western civilization—man's ability to endure, survive, and conquer a hostile environment. As a fictional adaptation of the story of Alexander Selkirk, who had been stranded on an island near Chile early in the century, the novel shows Augustan England's interest in travel literature, religious allegory, and mercantilist economics.

Other Major Fiction

Defoe published comparatively little in 1721 because he was hard at work on the three major books that were to appear the following year. In January 1722 he published *The Fortunes and Misfortunes of the Famous Moll Flanders*, probably the most successful of his novels. Its irony, vivid details, and psychologically valid individual scenes more than compensate for its structural weaknesses. The elderly Moll writes of her early life, of her five husbands, of her life as a prostitute, and of her adventures as a thief.

A Journal of the Plague Year, issued in March 1722, presents a stunning picture of life in London during the Great Plague of 1665, and it was thought to be history rather than fiction for more than a hundred years. The third important novel to appear in 1722, *The History and Remarkable Life of the Truly Honourable Col. Jacque*, was published in December. In this study of a young man's rise to gentility, Defoe characteristically combined a brilliant command of detail and individual scene with an interesting but awkwardly plotted story.

Defoe published *The Fortunate Mistress; or, ... Roxana* early in 1724. Though Roxana moves in a more fashionable world than did Moll Flanders, she shares with Moll native cunning and an instinct for self-preservation. Like *Moll Flanders*, *Roxana* juxtaposes moral homilies with titillating narrative passages. In 1724 Defoe also published *A Tour Thro' the Whole Island of Great Britain,* one of the most thorough and fascinating guidebooks of the period.

The History of the Remarkable Life of John Sheppard (1724), one of Defoe's finest criminal biographies, was followed in 1725 by *The True and Genuine Account of the Life and Actions of the Late Jonathan Wild*. Defoe's intimate knowledge of London's underworld and of its prisons explains the vitality and accuracy of these hastily written criminal lives. These works also display his characteristically clear, strong, idiomatic English prose.

Although he continued to write until his death, only a few of Defoe's later works are worthy of note: *The Complete English Tradesman* (1725), *The Political History of the Devil* (1726), *A New Family Instructor* (1727), and *Augusta Triumphans* (1728), which was Defoe's plan to make "London the most flourishing City in the Universe."

Further Reading

Daniel Defoe is listed in the Literature study guide (II, F, 1, c). Although Defoe's fiction was and is widely read, the works of his younger contemporaries Samuel RICHARDSON and Henry FIELDING exerted a greater influence on the development of the novel as a literary form.

The standard bibliography of Defoe is John Robert Moore, *A Checklist of the Writings of Daniel Defoe* (1960). There are two major critical biographies: James R. Sutherland, *Defoe* (1937; 2d ed. 1950), and John Robert Moore, *Daniel Defoe: Citizen of the Modern World* (1958). Important critical studies of Defoe's works include Arthur W. Secord, *Studies in the Narrative Method of Defoe* (1924); Maximillian E. Novak, *Economics and the Fiction of Daniel Defoe* (1962) and *Defoe and the Nature of Man* (1963); and J. Paul Hunter, *The Reluctant Pilgrim* (1966). Recommended for general historical and social background are J. H. Plumb, *England in the Eighteenth Century* (1950); A. R. Humphreys, *The Augustan World: Life and Letters in Eighteenth-Century England* (1954); Ian P. Watt, *The Rise of the Novel: Studies in Defoe, Richardson and Fielding* (1957); and Ian P. Watt, ed., *The Augustan Age* (1968).

DE FOREST / By Carroll Pursell

The American inventor Lee De Forest (1873–1961) pioneered in radio, both in developing broadcasting and in inventing the audion. He is considered one of the fathers of radio.

Lee De Forest was born in Council Bluffs, Iowa, where his father was a minister. While Lee was still a boy, his father became the president of the College for the Colored in Talladega, Ala. Because of his father's association with Negroes, young Lee was shunned by playmates and sought relief from his loneliness in invention and mechanics. He took bachelor of science and doctor of philosophy degrees from Yale in 1896 and 1899. He then went to work for the Western Electric Company in Chicago.

During the 1890s Guglielmo Marconi transmitted radio waves over increasing distances; his work culminated in 1901 with a transatlantic message. The new field of radio attracted many inventors, among them De Forest. In 1910 he literally electrified the musical world by broadcasting the voice of Enrico Caruso by radio. In 1916 De Forest made what he believed to be the first news broadcast by radio.

The greatest single contribution of De Forest to the field, however, was his invention of the triode, or audion, as he called it, for which he received a patent in

Lee De Forest holding his audion amplifier about 1915. (New York Public Library, Picture Collection)

1908. One of the major goals of inventors was to come up with a more powerful and sensitive detector, or receiver. In 1904 John Ambrose Fleming, a consultant to the Edison Electric Light Company, patented a two-electrode vacuum tube which he called a thermionic valve. Acting between the two electrodes, one of which was heated, the oscillating radio waves were made unidirectional. De Forest's contribution, which he claimed was made in ignorance of Fleming's earlier work, was to add a third element, thus converting the diode to a triode. This new element was a grid (or zigzag piece of wire) placed between the other two. Although no one, including the inventor himself, realized the importance or the exact action of the audion, it proved to be the basis of all subsequent radio development because it could be used to send, receive, or amplify radio signals better than any other device.

In 1902 De Forest became vice president of the De Forest Wireless Telegraph Company and in 1913 vice president of the Radio Telephone Company and the De Forest Radio Company. He worked on other electrical problems, including talking motion pictures and television, and eventually received over 300 domestic and foreign patents. He made and lost four fortunes during his lifetime and was extensively engaged in court litigation with such formidable foes as Irving Langmuir of the General Electric Company and Edwin Armstrong, with whom he disputed invention of the feedback circuit. This last dispute was decided in favor of De Forest in 1934. He retired to a private research laboratory in Hollywood, Calif.

Further Reading

Lee De Forest is listed in the Science study guide (VII, H, 3). He had legal patent struggles with Irving LANGMUIR and Edwin ARMSTRONG.

De Forest's autobiography is *Father of Radio* (1950). A more balanced account of his contributions is the standard history of radio, William R. Maclaurin, *Invention and Innovation in the Radio Industry* (1949). The business side of radio is covered in Erik Barnouw, *A History of Broadcasting in the United States* (1966).

DEGAS / By Abraham A. Davidson

The French painter and sculptor Hilaire Germain Edgar Degas (1834–1917) is classed with the impressionists because of his concentration on scenes of contemporary life and his desire to capture the transitory moment, but he surpassed them in compositional sense.

Edgar Degas (pronounced də-gä′) was born on July 19, 1834, in Paris, the son of a well-to-do banker. From an early age Edgar loved books, especially the classics, and was a serious student in high

Edgar Degas, a self-portrait etching. (Metropolitan Museum of Art, Bequest of Mrs. H. O. Havemeyer, 1929; The H. O. Havemeyer Collection)

school. His father hoped his son would study law, but Edgar enrolled at the École des Beaux-Arts in 1855, where he studied under Louis Lamothe, a pupil of J. A. D. Ingres. Degas always valued his early classical training and had a great and enduring admiration for Ingres, a painter with a decisively linear orientation.

In 1856 Degas went to Naples, where his sister lived, and eventually he settled in Rome for 3 years. He admired the Early Christian and medieval masterpieces of Italy, as well as the frescoes, panel paintings, and drawings of the Renaissance masters, many of which he copied. Back in Paris in 1861, he executed a few history paintings (then regarded as the highest branch of painting). Among these was the *Daughter of Jephthah* (1861), which is based on a melodramatic episode from the Old Testament. He copied the works of the old masters in the Louvre, a practice he kept up for many years.

From 1862 until 1870 Degas painted portraits of his friends and family. In 1870, during the Franco-Prussian War, he served in the artillery of the national guard. Two years later he went to New Orleans to visit members of his family, who were in the cotton business. Between 1873 and 1883 Degas produced many of his paintings and pastels of the racecourse, music hall, café, and ballet. He had no financial problems, and even prior to the 1870s he had established his reputation as a painter. Degas stopped exhibiting at the respected Salon in 1874 and displayed his works with those of the less well-established impressionists until 1886. Although he was associated with the impressionists, his preoccupation with draftsmanship and composition was not characteristic of the group.

Beginning in the mid-1870s Degas suffered from failing eyesight. From the 1890s on he became increasingly miserly and more and more of a recluse. In the last years of his life he was almost totally blind and wandered aim-lessly through the Parisian streets. He died on Sept. 27, 1917, in Paris.

His Portraiture

Portraiture was more important for Degas than for any of the other impressionists. Some of his portraits are among the best produced in Western art since the Renaissance, and many reveal his profound understanding of human nature. In the *Belleli Family* (1859), a group portrait executed in Naples of his aunt, her husband, and their two daughters, Degas caught the divisions within a family. Belleli's emotional separation from his wife is suggested by his pose and by his physical isolation within the room, as he sits cramped at a fireplace, with his back to the viewer. One of the daughters

Absinthe, an 1876 painting by Degas, in the Louvre, Paris. (Giraudon)

repeats the triangular form of her mother, who shields her, while the other, shown in a more unstable pose, seems to be divided in her loyalties. Among Degas's other portraits are the very soft *Head of a Young Woman* (1867), *Diego Martelli* (1879), and *Estelle Musson* (1872–1873), the blind wife of Degas's brother René, in which the silver and rose tones bring into relief the remote tenderness of the sitter.

Depiction of the Modern Scene

By 1870 Degas had abandoned his desire to become a history painter, and he drew his characters instead from the contemporary Parisian scene. While the bourgeois fashionable world of the ballet, theater, and racetrack interested him considerably, he sometimes depicted squalid scenes of dissipation, as in *Absinthe* (1876). Degas was especially attracted by the spectacle of the ballet with its elegance of costume and scenery, its movement which was at once spontaneous and restrained, its artificial lighting, and its unusual viewpoints. Usually he depicted the ballerinas off guard, showing them backstage at an awkward moment as they fasten a slipper or droop exhausted after a difficult practice session. He seems to have tried deliberately to strip his dancers of their glamour, to show them without artifice.

On the surface Degas, operating in this candid-camera fashion, fits easily within the confines of impressionism as an art of immediacy and spontaneity. But these scenes of contemporary Parisian life are not at all haphazardly composed: the placement of each detail is calculated in terms of every other to establish balances which are remarkably clever and subtle and which are frequently grasped by the viewer only after considerable study. In *Dancers Practicing at the Bar* (1877) the perspective of the floorboards is so adjusted and the angle of vision so calculated that a resin shaker at the left of the canvas is able to balance in interest and compositional force the two dancers almost completely to the right of center.

Degas conceived of the human figure as operating within an environmental context, to be manipulated as a prop according to the dictates of greater compositional interest. Eccentricities of poses and cuttings of the figures, which were inspired to a degree by Japanese prints, do not occur accidently in his paintings. In *A Carriage at the Races* (1873) the figure in the carriage to the left is cut nearly down the middle. Had Degas shown more of this figure, an obvious and uninteresting symmetry would have been set up with the larger carriage in the right foreground.

Degas's Techniques

In copying the Old Masters, Degas sometimes attempted to uncover their techniques. For example, when he copied Andrea Mantegna and some of the Venetians, Degas tried to simulate the Venetian method of building up the canvas with layers of cool and warm tones by a series of glazes. From the mid-1870s he worked increasingly in pastel; and in his last years, when his sight was failing, he abandoned oil completely in favor of pastel, which he handled more broadly and with greater freedom than before.

Pastel, for the most part an 18th-century medium, helped Degas produce qualities of airiness and lightness, as in the *Ballerina and Lady with Fan* (1885). However, Degas would endlessly experiment with unusual techniques. He would sometimes mix his pastel so heavily with liquid fixative that it became amalgamated into a sort of paste. He would do a drawing in charcoal and use layers of pastel to cover part of this. He would combine pastels and oil in a single work. He would even pass through a press a heavily pigmented charcoal drawing in order to transfer the excess of pigment onto a new sheet so as to make an inverse proof of the original. In his monotypes he used etching in a new way: he inked the unetched plate and drew with a brush in this layer of ink; then he removed all the ink in places to obtain strong contrasts of light and dark or painterly effects in this printing medium. Thus, in a variety of ways Degas succeeded in obtaining a richness of surface effects.

Bronze Sculptures

After 1866 Degas executed bronze statues of horses and dancers, up to 3 or 4 feet high, which complemented his interest in these subjects in his paintings. His bronze and painted wax figures of dancers, like the *Little Dancer of Fourteen Years* (1880–1881), are often clothed in real costumes, an innovation that gives them a remarkable immediacy. In the statues of dancers, Degas catches the figures in a transitory moment, as they are about to change position. As in the paintings, Degas strips the dancers of glamour and sometimes reveals them as scrawny adolescents. The surfaces of Degas's bronzes are not smooth but retain the rich articulations of the wax and thereby complement the expressive surfaces of the impressionist painting.

Further Reading

Edgar Degas is listed in the Art study guide (III, H, 1, e). He greatly admired the work of J. A. D. INGRES and Eugène DELACROIX. Degas's work influenced many of his contemporaries, particularly Édouard MANET, Paul GAUGUIN, Pierre BONNARD, and Pablo PICASSO.

Jean Sutherland Boggs, *Portraits by Degas* (1962), is the definitive work on Degas and is thoroughly documented. John Rewald, *Degas: Works in Sculpture* (1944), shows a little-known aspect of Degas and contains 112 plates. Lillian Browse, *Degas Dancers* (1949), contains a fair text and over 150 good black-and-white illustrations of Degas's ballet dancers done in pastel, oil, and sculpture. Daniel Catton Rich, *Edgar Hilaire Germain Degas* (1951), glosses over Degas's debt to the art before him.

DE GASPERI / By Joseph N. Scionti

The Italian statesman Alcide De Gasperi (1881–1954) was one of the founders of Italian democracy after World War II.

Alcide De Gasperi (pronounced dä gäs'pä-rē) was born on April 3, 1881, at Pieve Tesino in Trentino, then controlled by Austria. As a young man, he became active in the Irredentist movement to bring Italian-speaking people still under Austrian jurisdiction into the kingdom of Italy. In 1906 he began publication of the polemical journal *Il Trentino*. This brought him a good deal of attention, and in 1911 he was elected to the Austrian Parliament as deputy for Trentino, a post he held for 6 years.

De Gasperi then joined the new Catholic People's party (Partito Popolare Italiano), founded by the Catholic political leader Don Luigi Sturzo. Trentino became part of Italy following World War I, and De Gasperi served as a deputy in the Italian Parliament from 1921 to 1924. Hard work brought him a position of eminence, and when Don Sturzo was forced into exile in 1924, De Gasperi became general secretary of the party.

As Mussolini's hold on the Italian government grew stronger, the position of the party became ever more precarious, and in 1926 it was dissolved. De Gasperi was imprisoned but was released 3 years later when, amid the atmosphere of good feeling between Mussolini and the Vatican, the archbishop of Trent intervened on his behalf. De Gasperi found asylum and temporary peace in the Vatican, where he studied Catholic social doctrine.

During World War II De Gasperi became active in the underground and was one of the founders of the illegal Christian Democratic party (Democrazia Christiana). He also founded the newspaper *Popolo*. After the liberation of Italy in June 1944, he served as minister without portfolio and then as foreign minister; in December 1945 he became premier, a post he held until 1953. As chief of the Italian delegation at the World War II peace conference, he elicited concessions from the Allies that guaranteed Italian sovereignty.

After the formal end of the monarchy in June 1946, De Gasperi functioned as head of the Christian Democrats, the party that dominated Parliament for the next 8 years. As premier, he gave moderate guidance that kept a precarious balance, during this critical postwar period, between disparate elements within the party and the nation. By avoiding conflicts with the numerous Socialists and Communists, he managed with great delicacy to put Italian democracy on a firm foundation. Besides his successful negotiations with the Allied Powers, his most striking achievement in foreign policy was the agreement with Austria (September 1946) to establish the southern Tirol as an autonomous region.

When the Christian Democrats did not gain a majority in the elections of 1953, De Gasperi was unable to establish a workable Cabinet and was forced to resign as premier. The following year he also had to forgo the leadership of his party, and 2 months later, on Aug. 19, 1954, he died.

Further Reading

Alcide De Gasperi is listed in the European History study guide (XII, D, 1). He opposed the policies of Benito MUSSOLINI.

Alcide De Gasperi. (Library of Congress)

Sources on De Gasperi in English are scarce. Elisa A. Carrillo, *Alcide de Gasperi: The Long Apprenticeship* (1965), covers his early life through his entry into the Quirinale as premier. Consult Denis Mack Smith, *Italy: A Modern History* (1959), for the political picture. English translations of the works by Luigi Sturzo that are helpful are *Church and State* (1939), *Italy and the Coming World* (1945), and *Italy and Fascism* (1967).

DE GAULLE / By David Schoenbrun

The French general and statesman Charles André Joseph Marie De Gaulle (1890–1970) led the Free French forces during World War II. A talented writer and eloquent orator, he served as president of France from 1958 to 1969.

Charles De Gaulle (pronounced də gōl') was born on Nov. 23, 1890, in the northern industrial city of Lille. His father, Henri, was a teacher of philosophy and mathematics and a veteran of the Franco-Prussian War of 1870, in which the Prussians humiliatingly defeated what the French thought was the greatest army in the world. This loss colored the life of the elder De Gaulle, a patriot who vowed he would live to avenge the defeat and win back the provinces of Alsace and Lorraine. His attitude deeply influenced the lives of his sons, whom he raised to be the instruments of his revenge and of the restoration of France as the greatest European power.

From his earliest years Charles De Gaulle was immersed in French history by both his father and mother. For many centuries De Gaulle's forebears had played a role in French history, almost always as patriots defending France from invaders. In the 14th century a Chevalier de Gaulle defeated an invading English army in defense of the city of Vire, and Jean de Gaulle is cited in the Battle of Agincourt (1415).

Charles's great-great-grandfather, Jean Baptiste de Gaulle, was a king's counselor. His grandfather, Julien Philippe de Gaulle, wrote a popular history of Paris; Charles received this book on his tenth birthday and, as a young boy, read and reread it. He was also devoted to the literary works of his gifted grandmother, Julien Philippe's wife, Josephine Marie, whose name gave him two of his baptismal names. One of her greatest influences upon him was her impassioned, romantic history, *The Liberator of Ireland, or the Life of Daniel O'Connell*. It always remained for him an illustration of man's resistance to persecution, religious or political, and an inspiring example he emulated in his own life.

Perhaps the major influence on De Gaulle's formation came from his uncle, also named Charles de Gaulle, who wrote a book about the Celts which called for union of the Breton, Scots, Irish, and Welsh peoples. The young De Gaulle wrote in his copybook a sentence from his uncle's book, which proved to be a prophecy of his own life: "In a camp, surprised by enemy attack under cover of night, where each man is fighting alone, in dark confusion, no one asks for the grade or rank of the man who lifts up the standard and makes the first call to rally for resistance."

Military Career

Charles De Gaulle's career as defender of France began in the summer of 1909, when he was admitted to the elite military academy of Saint-Cyr. Among his classmates was the future marshal of France Alphonse Juin, who later recalled De Gaulle's nicknames in school— "The Grand Constable," "The Fighting Cock," and "The Big Asparagus."

After graduation Second Lieutenant De Gaulle reported in October 1912 to Henri Philippe Pétain, who first became his idol and then his most hated enemy. (In World War I Pétain was the hero of Verdun, but during World War II he capitulated to Hitler and collaborated with the Germans while De Gaulle was leading the French forces of liberation.) De Gaulle led a frontline company as captain in World War I and was cited three times for valor. Severely wounded, he was left for dead on the battlefield of Verdun and then imprisoned by the Germans when he revived in a graveyard cart. After he had escaped and been recaptured several times, the Germans put him in a maximum security prison-fortress.

After the war De Gaulle went to general-staff school, where he hurt his career by constant criticism of his superiors. He denounced the static concept of trench war-

fare and wrote a series of essays calling for a strategy of movement with armored tanks and planes. The French hierarchy ignored his works, but the Germans read him and adapted his theories to develop their triumphant strategy of blitzkrieg, or lightning war, with which they defeated the French in 1940.

When France fell, De Gaulle, then an obscure brigadier general, refused to capitulate. He fled to London, convinced that the British would never surrender and that American power, once committed, would win the war. On June 18, 1940, on BBC radio, he insisted that France had only lost a battle, not the war, and called upon patriotic Frenchmen to resist the Germans. This inspiring broadcast won him worldwide acclaim.

Early Political Activity

When the Germans were driven back, De Gaulle had no rivals for leadership in France. Therefore in the fall of 1944 the French Parliament unanimously elected him premier. De Gaulle had fiercely opposed the German enemy, and now he vigorously defended France against the influence of his powerful allies Joseph Stalin, Winston Churchill, and Franklin Roosevelt. De Gaulle once stated that he never feared Adolf Hitler, who, he knew, was doomed to defeat, but did fear that his allies would dominate France and Europe in the postwar period.

By the fall of 1945, only a year after assuming power, De Gaulle was quarreling with all the political leaders of

Charles De Gaulle, photographed in 1969. (French Embassy Press and Information Division)

France. He saw himself as the unique savior of France, the only disinterested champion of French honor, grandeur, and independence. He despised all politicians as petty, corrupt, and self-interested muddlers, and, chafing under his autocratic rule, they banded against him. In January 1946, disgusted by politics, he resigned and retreated into a sulking silence to brood upon the future of France.

In 1947 De Gaulle reemerged as leader of the opposition. He headed what he termed "The Rally of the French People," which he insisted was not a political party but a national movement. The Rally became the largest single political force in France but never achieved majority status. Although De Gaulle continued to despise the political system, he refused to lead a coup d'etat, as some of his followers urged, and again retired in 1955.

Years as President

In May 1958 a combination of French colonials and militarists seized power in Algeria and threatened to invade France. The weakened Fourth Republic collapsed, and the victorious rebels called De Gaulle back to power as president of the Fifth Republic of France. From June 1958 to April 1969 he reigned as the dominant force in France. But he was not a dictator, as many have charged; he was elected first by Parliament and then in a direct election by the people.

As president, De Gaulle fought every plan to involve France deeply in alliances. He opposed the formation of a United States of Europe and British entry into the Common Market. He stopped paying part of France's dues to the United Nations, forced the NATO headquarters to leave France, and pulled French forces out of the Atlantic Alliance integrated armies. Denouncing Soviet oppression of Eastern Europe, he also warned of the Chinese threat to the world. He liberated France's colonies, supported the Vietnamese "liberation movement" against the United States, and called for a "free Quebec" in Canada.

De Gaulle had an early success in stimulating pride in Frenchmen and in increasing French gold reserves and strengthening the economy. By the end of his reign, however, France was almost friendless, and his economic gains had been all but wiped out by the student and workers protest movement in spring 1968.

De Gaulle ruled supreme for 11 years, but his firm hand began to choke and then to infuriate many citizens. In April 1969 the French voted against his program for reorganizing the Senate and the regions of France. He had threatened to resign if his plan was rejected and, true to his word, he promptly renounced all power. Thereafter De Gaulle remained silent on political issues. Georges Pompidou, one of his favorite lieutenants, was elected to succeed him as president. Charles De Gaulle died at Colombey-les-Deux-Églises on Nov. 9, 1970.

Further Reading

Charles De Gaulle is listed in the European History study guide (XI, P, 2, a; XII, B, 1) and the International Law study guide (V, A, 3, a). His isolationist policies were opposed by Jean MONNET and Robert SCHUMAN.

De Gaulle's *War Memoirs* (3 vols., 1954–1959; trans. 1955–1960) is available in a single volume as *The Complete War Memoirs of Charles de Gaulle* (1964). The first volume of his postwar memoirs is *Memoirs of Hope* (trans. 1971). His *The Edge of the Sword* (1959; trans. 1960) is a personal credo on the qualities of leadership. Jean Lacouture, *De Gaulle* (1964; trans. 1966), is one of the best biographies, written by an astute French observer. Jean R. Tournoux, *Pétain and De Gaulle* (1964; trans. 1966), is a study of the relationship of the two men from World War I. A biography in three parts, examining De Gaulle's roles as soldier, savior of his nation, and statesman, is David Schoenbrun, *The Three Lives of Charles de Gaulle* (1966). Other more specialized studies include Jacques de Launay, *De Gaulle and His France: A Psychopolitical and Historical Portrait* (trans. 1968); Anton W. DePorte, *De Gaulle's Foreign Policy, 1944–46* (1968); and Raymond Aron, *De Gaulle, Israel, and the Jews* (1968; trans. 1969).

Gen. De Gaulle marches past the Arc de Triomphe at the liberation of Paris in 1944. (Harlingue-Viollet)

DEKKER / By Barry B. Adams

The English playwright and pamphleteer Thomas Dekker (ca. 1572–ca. 1632) is noted for his vivid portrayals of London life and his genial sympathy for the lower classes.

Nothing is known of Thomas Dekker's parentage or education. Throughout his life he remained closely identified with London, where he was probably born about 1572. He acquired some knowledge of Latin, French, and Dutch, and he may have seen military service in his early years.

The first evidence of Dekker's association with the stage appears in the records of Philip Henslowe, the theatrical manager whose diary provides much valuable information about the more practical side of Elizabethan drama. Henslowe also reveals that Dekker was imprisoned for debt—a not uncommon fate for dramatists of the period.

Early in his career Dekker produced his most popular play, *The Shoemaker's Holiday* (1599). This engaging mixture of sentimental romance and homely urban realism shows Dekker's modest talents to best advantage. The principal focus of interest is the honest, convivial shoemaker Simon Eyre, who by virtue of industry and good luck rises to become lord mayor of London. Always mindful of his humble origins, the madcap lord mayor holds a grand feast for the apprentices of London and decrees that Shrove Tuesday be set aside as a holiday for shoemakers. Simon also plays a part in bringing together the wellborn lovers Rowland Lacy and Rose Otely and in restoring Rafe Damport to his wife, Joan. The play is seasoned with the diverting good humor of Dame Margery, Simon's talkative, down-to-earth wife, and the shoemakers Hodge and Firk.

About 1603 Dekker turned his hand to the writing of popular prose pamphlets. By 1610 he had produced at least 13 of these, *The Gull's Hornbook* (1609) being the best-known. While these works have little merit as literature, they do provide a fascinating picture of the seamier side of London life in the early 17th century.

During this period Dekker continued his dramatic work, usually as a collaborator. *The Honest Whore* (Part 1, 1604; Part 2, ca. 1605) and *The Roaring Girl* (ca. 1610, written with Thomas Middleton) are among the six or seven plays from this period of Dekker's career. From 1613 to 1619 he evidently wrote nothing; these years may have been spent in prison, but the evidence on this point is not conclusive. In 1620 he reappears as a pamphleteer and playwright. His later dramatic works (done in collaboration with such playwrights as Philip Massinger, William Rowley, and John Ford) reveal his abiding interest in London life, with his earlier sunny realism occasionally qualified by a note of bitterness.

Dekker composed the annual lord mayor's pageant in 1628 and 1629. He died shortly afterward, probably in 1632, heavily in debt.

Further Reading

Thomas Dekker is listed in the Literature study guide (II, E, 3, a). Among his collaborators were John FORD, Philip MASSINGER, and Thomas MIDDLETON.

Thomas Dekker, from the woodcut on the title page of his Dekker His Dreame *(1620). (Radio Times Hulton Picture Library)*

The basic biography is M. L. Hunt, *Thomas Dekker* (1911; repr. 1964). Critical studies include K. L. Gregg, *Thomas Dekker: A Study in Economic and Social Backgrounds* (1924); J. H. Conover, *Thomas Dekker: An Analysis of Dramatic Structure* (1969); and G. R. Price, *Thomas Dekker* (1969).

DE KOONING / By Carl Belz

The Dutch-born American painter Willem de Kooning (born 1904) was a leader of the abstract expressionist movement of the 1940s and 1950s.

Before the 1940s the major advances in modern painting were forged on English and European soil. American artists, although aware of these advances, had not generally participated in their origin. After World War II, however, the United States, and in particular New York City, became a focal point for modernist developments. The most celebrated of these is known as abstract expressionism—abstract, because most of the new art eschewed all traces of visible reality; and expressionism, because it appeared to have been created through uncontrolled and sometimes violent painterly gestures. Known also as action painting or painterly ab-

Willem de Kooning in 1971. (M. Knoedler & Co., Inc., New York)

straction (historians have yet to agree on the most appropriate designation), abstract expressionism reached international scope and influence during the 1950s.

Willem de Kooning and Jackson Pollock are the best-known exponents of this new American style. Although their works inspired public ridicule at first, both artists are now recognized as major figures within the broader tradition of art history. For De Kooning this recognition is especially significant, because he always viewed himself as a link in the great tradition of painterly art that runs from the Renaissance to the present day.

De Kooning was born in Rotterdam, Holland, on April 24, 1904. In 1916 he left school to work as a commercial artist, and he enrolled in evening classes at the Academy of Fine Arts in his native city, where he studied for 8 years. During this period he became aware of the group called de Stijl, whose membership included Piet Mondrian and Theo van Doesburg, two of the most influential abstractionists of the early 20th century.

Early Career

In 1926 De Kooning emigrated to the United States. He took a studio in New York City and supported himself by doing commercial art and house painting. In his own painting he began to experiment with abstraction but, like many artists during the Depression, was unable to devote full time to his work. The opportunity to do so came in 1935, when he worked for a year on the Federal Art Project of the Works Project Administration.

In the 1940s De Kooning's career as a painter began to accelerate. He participated in several group shows and in 1946 had his first one-man exhibition in New York City. Among sophisticated patrons and dealers this show established De Kooning as a major figure in contemporary American painting. In the same year he married Elaine Fried, and 2 years later he taught at the experimental Black Mountain College, which was then under the direction of the influential color abstractionist Josef Albers.

De Kooning's paintings from the 1930s and 1940s reveal many of the same stylistic vacillations that characterize his better-known productions of the period after 1950. In the early work De Kooning approached the problems of abstraction cautiously. *Bill-Lee's Delight* (1946), for instance, is ostensibly devoid of subject matter from the visible world. Roughhewn masses sweep toward the center of the composition, where they collide, overlap, and twist into painterly space. However, many of the planes, particularly those on the periphery of the painting, appear to be remnants of the human body; their undulating contours loosely recall arms, legs, and torsos that have been distilled into pictorial entities. In other words, the painting retains figurative allusions in spite of its apparent abstractness.

Retaining the Human Image

Bill-Lee's Delight indirectly reveals De Kooning's deep commitment to the image of the human body. Even earlier works show the character of this commitment more explicitly. *Queen of Hearts* (1943–1946) presents the three-quarter image of a seated woman whose head, breasts, and arms are drawn with loosely flowing contours. The figure is freely distorted and somewhat unsettling: the head is twisted, the facial anatomy is askew, and the limbs and breasts appear ready to twist off and float into space. In overall style the painting recalls European surrealism with its eerie interpretations of figurative content. It is also similar to the abstract, quasi-surrealist style of Arshile Gorky, with whom De Kooning had once shared a studio.

Some of De Kooning's finest paintings were executed in the period that ended in 1950; these include *Ashville* (1949) and *Excavation* (1950). Both works retain some figurative allusions, but they achieve a powerful, abstract flatness, thereby insisting upon their identity as paintings. Moreover, both canvases achieve this identity within a relatively restricted color range; this lends tautness to the compelling presence of each painting.

De Kooning since 1950

In spite of the achievement marked by paintings like *Ashville* and *Excavation*, De Kooning was evidently uncomfortable with the problems of abstraction. In 1950 he returned to the human figure, embarking upon his famous "Woman" series. *Woman I* (1950–1952) is probably the most famous of the series. The figure is executed in a tortured, aggressive manner and emerges like some demonic presence. Paint itself is likewise assaulted—dragged, pushed, and scraped—with a technique that, for many viewers, is the summa of abstract expressionist style.

When the "Woman" paintings were shown in 1953 in New York City, they catapulted De Kooning to fame and notoriety. Although he was honored with numerous awards and retrospective exhibitions after that, his work periodically revealed doubts and uncertainties about its direction.

During the late 1950s De Kooning again abandoned the human figure in favor of abstraction. The paintings from these years are sometimes called "landscapes" because their open, expansive space is suggestive of the space of the natural environment. In *Suburb in Havana* (1958), for instance, broad, earth-colored diagonals reach into space and extend toward a blue mass that resembles both sky and water. Because of the explosiveness with which they open pictorial space, these landscapes must count among De Kooning's most spontaneous and exhilarating achievements.

From the early 1960s De Kooning's development seemed problematic and uncertain. Once again he returned to the human figure and a second "Woman" series. These works display the master's characteristic blend of technical gusto and emotional fervor, but they evoked mixed opinions among his critics. Perhaps more historical perspective is needed before these paintings can be viewed objectively.

De Kooning's first retrospective took place in 1953 in Boston. In 1954 he enjoyed a second, at the Venice Biennale. The largest retrospective was held in New York City

De Kooning painted Woman I *between 1950 and 1952. (Collection, The Museum of Modern Art, New York)*

in 1969. He was elected to the National Institute of Arts and Letters in 1960, and he received the Freedom Award Medal in 1964.

Further Reading

Willem de Kooning is listed in the Art study guide (IV, E, 9). He, Jackson POLLOCK, and Franz KLINE were the major postwar American abstract expressionists. Arshile GORKY was a pioneer at abstract expressionism in his late works.

Several monographs on De Kooning have been written, among them, Thomas B. Hess, *Willem de Kooning* (1959), and Harriet Janis and Rudi Blesh, *De Kooning* (1960). Also important is Hess's *Willem de Kooning* (1969), the catalog for the Museum of Modern Art's De Kooning retrospective of 1969. For a more general picture of De Kooning's relation to postwar American art see Barbara Rose, *American Art since 1900* (1967).

DELACROIX / By Francis E. Hyslop, Jr.

The French painter Ferdinand Victor Eugène Delacroix (1798–1863) repudiated the neoclassic manner and developed a freer and more romantic style with a particular emphasis on color.

For 40 years Eugène Delacroix (pronounced də-lå-krwä′) was one of the most prominent and controversial painters in France. Although the intense emotional expressiveness of his work placed the artist squarely in the midst of the general romantic outpouring of European art, he always remained an individual phenomenon and did not create a school. As a personality and as a painter, he was admired by the impressionists, postimpressionists, and symbolists who came after him.

Born on April 28, 1798, at Charenton-Saint-Maurice, the son of an important public official, Delacroix grew up in comfortable upper-middle-class circumstances in spite of the troubled times. He received a good classical education at the Lycée Impérial. He entered the studio of Pierre Narcisse Guérin in 1815, where he met Théodore Géricault.

Early Style

Delacroix's public career was launched with a flourish at the Salon of 1822, in which he exhibited *Dante and Virgil in Hell*. Large, somewhat hastily painted, still traditional in its bas-relief type of design, it was nevertheless novel in subject matter and in the emotional intensity conveyed by powerful, contorted forms and smoldering, vibrant tones.

Delacroix shared the new Anglophilia of French culture, played the role of a dandy, read Shakespeare, Byron, and Scott, visited England, and was impressed by English artists such as Richard Bonington and John Constable. Indeed, Constable's landscapes are supposed to have influenced Delacroix's *Massacre at Chios*, shown in 1824. An immense canvas, almost 14 feet high, it was obviously designed to create an impression at the Salon. Although Baron Gros called it "the massacre of painting," the government purchased it. Based on an incident in the Greek war of independence, the painting is as exotic as Delacroix's later North African pictures and is filled with a romantic taste for violence.

Among the dozen paintings Delacroix submitted to the Salon of 1827–1828, the immense, baroque *Death of Sardanapalus*, based on a theme by Byron, is remarkable for its theatrical fervor and luxuriant color. *Liberty Leading the People*, inspired by the Revolution of 1830, closed the first phase of Delacroix's career. It is almost the only important work, except for the *Massacre at Chios*, that had any connection with contemporary history: the scene was Parisian but the interpretation was allegorical.

Mature Style

The stimulus of a fortuitous 6-month trip to Morocco in 1832 had a lifelong effect on Delacroix's development and gave him an inexhaustible store of pictorial materials. The most immediate result was *Women of Algiers in Their Apartment* (1834), in which an Oriental subject allowed for the kind of "visual feast" and poetic effect that he always considered the proper aims of painting.

Also notable among the pictures of the 1830s and 1840s by Delacroix were historical scenes painted on commission, such as the *Battle of Taillebourg* (1837)

Eugène Delacroix, a self-portrait, in the Louvre, Paris. (Giraudon)

and the *Entry of the Crusaders into Constantinople* (1840). They reflect his natural taste for the grand manner and for large-scale compositions, as well as his persistent enthusiasm for the dynamic style of Peter Paul Rubens and the mundane splendor of Paolo Veronese.

Those who believe that Delacroix turned back to classicism in the 1830s could point to his painting *Medea* (1838), a picture that could almost have been painted by Jacques Louis David. "I am a pure classic," Delacroix insisted at this time, only to confess in a paradoxical counterstatement, "If by romanticism they mean the free manifestation of my personal impressions . . . then I am a romantic and have been one since I was fifteen."

In 1833 Delacroix began his career as a mural painter, and in the next 28 years he executed paintings in Paris in the Chamber of Deputies (Palais-Bourbon), the Senate (Luxembourg Palace), the church of St-Denis-du-St-Sacrement, the Louvre, the City Hall, and St-Sulpice. Drawing heavily on classical and biblical themes and aided by assistants, he employed a technique in which the colors were mixed with wax. Although many of the subjects were traditional, the style in which they were carried out was full of romantic fire and excitement (*Attila Hemicycle*, finished 1847, Palais-Bourbon). In the ceiling panel of the Louvre, the *Triumph of Apollo* (1851), Delacroix achieved a highly successful baroque manner of his own. The murals are among the finest French decorative paintings.

Late Style

In the 1850s Delacroix's natural tendency toward freedom in the treatment of form and looseness of touch became more marked: *Marphise* (1852) and the sketch for *Eurydice* (1856) are good examples. Such works are reminiscent of the boldness of the late Titian—and of the late Auguste Renoir. Brilliance and luminosity of color increase; all forms are fused together in a dense pictorial whole.

There is an appreciable increase in Christian themes in the final period of Delacroix's career. "I was much impressed by the Requiem Mass," he wrote in his *Journal* (Nov. 2, 1854). "I thought of all that religion has to offer the imagination, and at the same time of its appeal to man's deepest feelings." The *Christ on the Lake of Genesareth* (1854) in Baltimore illustrates the rough-textured, agitated, and tumultuous style that often appeared in his final years of painting. This theme, which seems to have had a broad symbolic significance for the artist, must have become truly obsessive, for there are seven different versions of it.

In the last 10 or 12 years of his life Delacroix showed a renewed interest in the "pagan" North African subjects of his Moroccan experience of 1832. Among the most striking are the tiger and lion hunts and scenes of animal violence, which were created as much from imagination and from Rubens as from direct observation of animal behavior in Africa or Paris. Perhaps the sketch *Lion Hunt* (1854), done in preparation for a large painting in Bordeaux, is the most astonishing of these works. The wild, explosive design, created by fluid patches of warm color,

Death of Sardanapalus, a painting by Delacroix that was exhibited in the Salon of 1827–1828.
The theme is based on a poem by Lord Byron. The work is in the Louvre, Paris. (Giraudon)

has very properly been considered an anticipation of Fauvism.

Charles Baudelaire's enthusiastic praise of Delacroix's contribution to the Salon of 1859 was not enough to outweigh the bitter criticism. In any case, the painter decided not to exhibit at the Salon again. In 1861, disappointed by the poor response to his new mural paintings in St-Sulpice (*Jacob Wrestling with the Angel*), Delacroix wrote that he did not see much point in continuing with work that interested only 30 people in Paris. And yet, if he had been offered other commissions and had had the strength to do them, he would have gone on. By that time artistic work had become his only passion, his only solace. Two years later failing health overcame his determined will, and Delacroix died in Paris on Aug. 13, 1863.

Delacroix's Influence

In the early years of his career Delacroix found black a valuable "color." Later he said, "Gray is the enemy of all paintings"; and finally he wrote, "Banish all earth colors." Although he does not seem to have used a fully spectral palette, he moved in that direction, exploited

complementary contrasts, and demonstrated the usefulness of separate touches and the possibility of constructing a picture by means of individual, interlacing brushstrokes and patches of color. These devices were developed further by the impressionists and postimpressionists. On the other hand, the symbolists followed Delacroix in the pictorial projection of inner, imaginative fantasies and in the abstractly expressive use of color.

Further Reading

Eugène Delacroix is listed in the Art study guide (III, H, 1, c). He was influenced by Peter Paul RUBENS, Paolo VERONESE, Théodore GÉRICAULT, Richard BONINGTON, and John CONSTABLE. Delacroix's color had a strong influence on Paul CÉZANNE and Vincent VAN GOGH.

Delacroix's *Journal* was translated by Walter Pach in 1937. Lucy Norton did another translation of the greater part of the *Journal* in 1951. The most comprehensive study of Delacroix is René Huyghe, *Delacroix* (trans. 1963). The best short account is Lee Johnson, *Delacroix* (1963). Independent in outlook, and with many unfamiliar comparative illustrations, is Frank A. Trapp, *The Attainment of Delacroix* (1970). Two excellent but more specialized books are George P. Mras, *Eugène Delacroix's Theory of Art* (1966), and Jack J. Spector, *The Murals of Eugène Delacroix at Saint-Sulpice* (1967).

* * *

DeLANCEY / By Carl E. Prince

The American merchant Stephen DeLancey (1663–1741) founded an elite New York family and was an important colonial politician and entrepreneur.

During the first half of the 18th century, when family connections meant everything in the commercial and political life of the American colonies and in New York particularly, Stephen DeLancey moved in the highest echelons of both spheres. He was born in Caen, France, offspring of a notable Huguenot family that was forced out of France in 1685 with other Huguenots by the Edict of Nantes. Shortly after his arrival in New York, DeLancey married into the well-to-do Van Cortlandt family, thus taking a place in the colony's aristocratic structure. By 1702 DeLancey was described as one of the "most distinguished" and active members of the New York legislative assembly. He remained so for more than a quarter century.

His given name in French, Étienne, long since dropped by DeLancey, was introduced anew in 1725 as a derisive reference to his French birth by New York's royal governor William Burnet. For political reasons Burnet was trying to remove DeLancey from the Assembly on the spurious grounds that, being foreign-born, he was ineligible to sit in that body. DeLancey not only survived this assault but also apparently improved his political position as a result. He epitomized the kind of "placeman" (elite representative of a key family) that dominated colonial American politics.

DeLancey also typified the enterprising and freewheeling trader who moved so successfully across the colonial landscape. He was, at various times, a commercial agent for several European merchant houses, a supplier of English troops quartered in different parts of the New World during successive colonial wars, merchant to English interests in Canada and to settlements in the New York wilderness, and moneylender to sundry enterprises sponsored by New York's colonial government. He was a shrewd, well-connected dealer at a time of wide-open economic opportunities. His efforts anchored the DeLancey fortune for future generations of the family.

Stephen's son, James DeLancey, born in New York in 1703, studied law in London and then returned to practice in his hometown. Becoming a judge of the New York State Supreme Court in 1731, he was its chief justice until his death in 1760. James and his son (also named James) took their place among New York's

colonial elite. That they remained loyal to England during the American Revolution curtailed, but did not entirely end, the political and economic power the family wielded for nearly a century.

Further Reading

Stephen DeLancey is listed in the American History study guide (II, C, 2). Other important colonial merchants were Peter FANEUIL and Edward SHIPPEN.

While much has been written about later DeLanceys, there is almost nothing about the founder of the dynasty. The best secondary source for Stephen DeLancey's activities is Lawrence H. Leder, *Robert Livingston, 1654–1728, and the Politics of Colonial New York* (1961). See also Stanley Nider Katz, *Newcastle's New York: Anglo-American Politics, 1732–1753* (1968).

* * *

DELANY / By Edwin S. Redkey

Afro-American intellectual Martin Robinson Delany (1812–1885), a journalist, physician, army officer, politician, and judge, is best known for his promotion before the Civil War of a national home in Africa for Afro-Americans.

Martin Delany was born free in Charlestown, Va., on May 6, 1812. His parents traced their ancestry to West African royalty. In 1822 the family moved to Chambersburg, Pa., to find a better racial cli-

Martin Delany. (Schomberg Collection, New York Public Library)

mate. At the age of 19 Martin attended an Afro-American school in Pittsburgh. He married Kate Richards there in 1843; they had 11 children.

In 1843 Delany also founded one of the earliest Afro-American newspapers, the *Mystery*, devoted particularly to the abolition of slavery. Proud of his black skin and African ancestry, Delany advocated unrestricted equality for blacks, and he participated in conventions to protest slavery. Frederick Douglass, the leading black abolitionist, made him coeditor of his newspaper, the *North Star*, in 1847. But Delany left in 1849 to study medicine at Harvard.

At the age of 40 Delany began the practice of medicine, which he would continue on and off for the rest of his life. But with the publication of his book *The Condition, Elevation, Emigration, and Destiny of the Colored People of the United States, Politically Considered* (1852; repr. 1968), he began to agitate for a separate nation, trying to get blacks to settle outside the United States, possibly in Africa, but more probably in Canada or Latin America. In 1854 he led a National Emigration Convention. For a time he lived in Ontario. Despite his bitter opposition to the American Colonization Society and its colony, Liberia, Delany kept open the possibility of settling elsewhere in Africa. His 1859–1860 visit to the country of the Yorubas (now part of Nigeria) to negotiate with local kings for settling Afro-Americans there is summarized in *The Official Report of the Niger Valley Exploring Party* (1861; repr. 1969).

When Delany returned to the United States, however, the Civil War was in progress and prospects of freedom for blacks were brighter. He got President Abraham Lincoln to appoint him as a major in the infantry in charge of recruiting all-black Union units.

After the war Delany went to South Carolina to participate in the Reconstruction. In the Freedmen's Bureau and as a Republican politican, he was influential among the state's black and white population. In 1874 he narrowly missed election as lieutenant governor. In 1876, as the Republicans began losing control of the state, Delany switched to the conservative Democrats. Newly elected governor Wade Hampton rewarded him with an important judgeship in Charleston. As a judge, Delany won the respect of blacks and whites alike. In 1878 he helped sponsor the Liberian Exodus Joint Stock Steamship Company, which sent one ill-fated emigration ship to Africa. The next year his *The Principia of Ethnology* argued for pride and purity of the races and for Africa's self-regeneration.

When his political base collapsed in 1879, Delany returned to practicing medicine and later became a businessman in Boston. He died on Jan. 24, 1885.

Further Reading

Martin Delany is listed in the American History study guide (VI, F, 4). He worked with Frederick DOUGLASS and was made a judge in South Carolina by Governor Wade HAMPTON.

A recent biography of Delany is Victor Ullman, *Martin R. Delany: The Beginnings of Black Nationalism* (1971).

A contemporary account is Frank A. Rollin, *Life and Public Services of Martin R. Delany* (1868; repr. 1969). William J. Simmons, *Men of Mark* (1968), includes a biographical sketch. For the significance of Delany's black nationalist thought before the Civil War see Howard H. Bell, *A Survey of the Negro Convention Movement, 1830–1861* (1970).

DE LA ROCHE / By Michael Gnarowski

Mazo Louise de la Roche (1879–1961) was a Canadian author whose masterful and dramatic description of a family of Canadian country squires gained her international recognition.

Mazo de la Roche was born on Jan. 15, 1879, in the town of Newmarket near Toronto into a middle-class family. She was educated in suburban schools in and near Toronto and had firsthand experience with farm life when her family rented a homestead outside the town of Bronte, Ontario. Here the author, who had been writing stories for a number of years with little success, underwent formative experiences which helped to crystallize important ideas of a

Mazo de la Roche. (*Radio Times Hulton Picture Library*)

country squirearchy which would be central to her best-known work.

Her Work

Beginning her career as a writer of short stories, Mazo de la Roche published her first novel, *Possession*, in 1923 and had several plays produced in the 1920s. International popularity came with the publication of *Jalna* (1927), which won the $10,000 Atlantic–Little Brown Award that year and which launched the Whiteoak family and the story of its dynastic ups and downs through a series of widely published and much-translated novels.

Mazo de la Roche spent all of her creative life in Canada except for the years 1929–1939, when she lived abroad, mainly in England. Her published work includes 22 novels written between 1923 and 1960; a novella, *A Boy in the House* (1952); four works with an autobiographical background, of which *Ringing the Changes* (1957) is an important if misleading autobiography; five produced plays, from *Low Life* (1925) to *The Mistress of Jalna* (1951), and an adaptation of *Whiteoaks of Jalna* which was created for the stage in London and New York; short stories, many of which have been anthologized; a history of Quebec; and two books for children. She died in Toronto on July 13, 1961.

Whiteoak Family

The story of the Whiteoak family and of its ancestral seat of Jalna spans a period of a century; it is a masterful and imaginative portrayal of a large family of characters—often seen as a rich gallery of eccentrics—allowed to work out their lives against the backdrop of a genteel and idealized Ontario countryside. While the personages of the Whiteoak family are romantically conceived, they are, in the main, compelling characterizations of individuals, whose carefully constructed roles and situations are evoked by means of meticulous stage setting, psychological manipulation, and skillful and accurate description. Several of these in the Jalna gallery are real and memorable figures, and even the less significant characters benefit from the author's skill at allowing the nature of each individual to develop and grow while retaining a set of identifiable and basic qualities.

The major thrust of the Jalna series was to stave off the all-embracing sweep of a vulgar, democratized, and materialistic way of North American life and to celebrate and advance a set of low-key, aristocratic, but practical values. The sense of a spiritual connection with England is a strong and profoundly significant if latent motif.

There is some indication that while the novels of Mazo de la Roche enjoyed a favorable review press well into the 1930s, she was ultimately disappointed by what has been described as a lack of serious critical response to her writing. Another source of annoyance was that whenever an extended appraisal of the Jalna novels was attempted, it was usually developed in terms of a comparison with John Galsworthy's saga of the Forsyte family, an approach not borne out by the profound but readily apparent differences in the intentions, backgrounds,

personalities, and social attitudes of the two writers.

Further Reading

Mazo de la Roche is listed in the Canada study guide (IV, C, 1, a). Other Canadian writers were Morley CALLAGHAN and Hugh MacLENNAN.

The most satisfying study is Ronald Hambleton, *Mazo de la Roche of Jalna* (1966), a sympathetic and balanced assessment.

DELCASSÉ / By Charlene M. Leonard

The French statesman and journalist Théophile Delcassé (1852–1923) was the chief architect of the Triple Entente between France, Britain, and Russia.

Théophile Delcassé (pronounced děl-kå-sā′) was born on March 1, 1852, in Palmiers. After graduating from the University of Toulouse in 1874, he went to Paris and in 1879 began to write for Léon Gambetta's journal, *La République française*. He continued his association with that paper until 1888 and also contributed to the *Paris* from 1881 to 1889.

In 1889 Delcassé was elected to the Chamber of Deputies. He was undersecretary for the colonies from January to December 1893 and served as second minister of colonies from May 1894 to January 1895. His policies were governed by his belief that colonial strength would enhance France's position as a European power.

In June 1898 Delcassé was appointed minister of foreign affairs, and he retained this position until June 1905. His policies aimed to strengthen French interests and achieve the diplomatic isolation of Germany. He won both Spanish and American friendship by his successful mediation in the Spanish-American War of 1898. This opened the way for subsequent rapprochements with both the United States and Spain. Meanwhile, during the Fashoda crisis of 1898, Delcassé won a measure of respect from the British by withstanding their pressure for 6 weeks.

Between 1899 and 1903 Delcassé transformed the Franco-Russian alliance into an active instrument of policy by broadening its scope to include defense of the European balance of power. He achieved understanding with Italy, based on settlement of differences in Africa. This culminated in 1902 in mutual guarantees of neutrality. Three agreements of April 8, 1904, settled British and French colonial differences and became the foundation of the Entente Cordiale between Britain and France. Meanwhile, Delcassé also encouraged cooperation between Russia and Britain, which led in 1907 to the formation of the Triple Entente. Italian, British, and Spanish agreements guaranteed France a free hand in Morocco, but Delcassé was forced to resign in 1905 during the first

Théophile Delcassé. (French Embassy Press and Information Division)

Moroccan crisis, when the Cabinet refused to support his policy.

As minister of marine from March 1911 to January 1913, Delcassé reorganized and strengthened the French navy and engaged in joint naval planning with Britain. As ambassador to Russia between March 1913 and January 1914, he improved the joint military planning of France and Russia and accelerated development of Russia's strategic railroads. Early in World War I Delcassé was named minister of foreign affairs, but he resigned after 14 months, when Bulgaria joined the Central Powers, proving the failure of his Balkan policy. Delcassé refused to vote for the Treaty of Versailles, which he felt gave France "neither reparations nor security," and retired from public life after 1919. He died at Nice on Feb. 22, 1923.

Further Reading

Théophile Delcassé is listed in the European History study guide (IX, B, 2) and the Africa study guide (VIII, B, 1). EDWARD VII also played an important role in establishing the Entente Cordiale.

The best study of Delcassé in English is Charles W. Porter, *The Career of Théophile Delcassé* (1936), which concentrates on his writings, speeches, and political acts and implies that he must bear a considerable responsibility for developments leading to World War I. See also John Francis Parr, *Théophile Delcassé and the Practice of the Franco-Russian Alliance: 1898–1905* (1952), and

Christopher Andrew, *Théophile Delcassé and the Making of the Entente Cordiale* (1968).

DE LEON / By Joseph R. Conlin

The American Socialist theoretician and political leader Daniel De Leon (1852–1914) was, according to Lenin, "the greatest of modern Socialists—the only one who has added anything to Socialist thought since Marx." However, De Leon's Socialist Labor party remained a tiny sect.

According to his own testimony, Daniel De Leon was born into a wealthy family on the island of Curaçao near Venezuela, but it is possible that he was American-born. He was also said to have studied languages, history, philosophy, and mathematics at Dutch and German universities between 1865 and 1871. In 1872 he came to New York City and briefly assisted Cuban revolutionaries editing a Spanish-language newspaper. De Leon taught at a preparatory school and in 1876 entered Columbia University Law School. He graduated in a year and in 1883 was appointed to an international law lectureship at Columbia. He left Columbia in 1889, when he was denied a promised promotion.

De Leon's career at Columbia apparently declined because of his support of Henry George's third-party mayoralty candidacy in 1886 and his interest in the Nationalist movement of Edward Bellamy. At any rate, De Leon joined a tiny, almost moribund German organization in New York, the Socialist Labor party (SLP), and within a few years became the acknowledged master of the organization. In 1891 he became editor of the party's paper

Daniel De Leon. (New York Public Library, Picture Collection)

and was never seriously shaken in his leadership of the SLP until his death, in 1914.

The stormy, radical career of De Leon caused him to be resented as a disrupter by most of the Socialists in the United States. Personally, he was arrogant, inflexible, and intolerant of dissent; he even expelled his favorite son, Solon, from the SLP for questioning one of his theses. His unsuccessful attempts to control labor unions earned him further enmity, and his dictatorship within the SLP caused the secession of many former followers.

De Leon's attempt to align the Knights of Labor as an auxiliary to the SLP in the early 1890s only hastened the decline of that union. After an unsuccessful attempt to "bore from within" the American Federation of Labor, he organized the Socialist Trades and Labor Alliance (STLA) in 1895. It grew no faster than the parent SLP, and in 1905 he merged it into the Industrial Workers of the World (IWW). Again, his collaborators suspected his intentions, and in 1908 he and the STLA were tacitly expelled from the IWW. De Leon claimed that his followers were the true IWW, and the fiction was maintained until his death.

A prolific and brilliant writer, De Leon turned out dozens of pungent pamphlets and essays on topics facing the revolutionary movement of his day. Like his writings, his speeches were models of clarity and logic, studded with vivid metaphors and aphorisms. But his insistence on a hard-and-fast ideology did not prosper, and the leadership of American socialism passed to the more flexible Socialist Party of America even during his lifetime.

Further Reading

Daniel De Leon is listed in the American History study guide (VII, G, 4, c). Other, more moderate Socialists were Edward BELLAMY and Eugene V. DEBS.

There is no biography of De Leon, an incredible oversight considering his importance. Most accounts of his career in histories of the American Socialist movement are essentially hostile to him. These include Ira Kipnis, *The American Socialist Movement, 1897–1912* (1952); Howard H. Quint, *The Forging of American Socialism* (1953); David A. Shannon, *The Socialist Party of America* (1955); and Melvyn Dubofsky, *We Shall Be All: A History of the Industrial Workers of the World* (1969). A helpful study is *Daniel De Leon, the Man and His Work: A Symposium* (1920), published by the Socialist Labor party. There is also an essay on De Leon in Charles A. Madison, *Critics and Crusaders: A Century of American Protest* (1947; 2d ed. 1959).

DE L'ORME / By George V. Gallenkamp

The French architect Philibert de l'Orme (1510/1515–1570), or Delorme, established on French soil true classical standards in architecture.

Philibert de l'Orme (pronounced də lôrm′) was born in Lyons, the son of a master mason. He went to Rome about 1533 to measure and excavate ancient Roman buildings. In the humanist circle he frequented, he met Cardinal Jean du Bellay and François Rabelais, the cardinal's secretary, who became his friend. De l'Orme returned to Lyons in 1536, where he built the house of Antoine Bullioud.

Du Bellay called De l'Orme to Paris in 1540 to design his château at St-Maur-lès-Foussés, of which De l'Orme boasted that it was the first building in France "to show how the proportions and measures of architecture should be observed." This single-story structure, reminiscent of Giulio Romano's Palazzo del Tè in Mantua, was the first building in France to have a horseshoe staircase and to use a single columnar order, the Corinthian, in all elements of its decoration.

Henry II in 1547 appointed De l'Orme superintendent of buildings. For Henry II the architect built the tomb of Francis I at St-Denis (1547–1557).

Diane de Poitiers, mistress of Henry II, commissioned De l'Orme to build her château at Anet (1547–1552), which was remarkable not only for its new monumentality and correct classicism but also for its brilliant originality. Only the chapel, entrance gate, and *avant-corps* (frontispiece at the house entrance) remain, the last element, however, now standing in the courtyard of the École des Beaux-Arts in Paris. The chapel was unique in France for the use of the circle as the figure of design;

Philibert de l'Orme, an engraving in the Bibliothèque des Arts Décoratifs, Paris. (Photo-Hachette)

the entrance for the interaction of block forms discreetly ornamented with Doric columns; and the *avant-corps*, De l'Orme's adaptation of the medieval château entrance bay, for the massive proportions of its orders.

When Henry II died in 1559, his widow, Catherine de Médicis, immediately dismissed De l'Orme and replaced him with her countryman Primaticcio. During his period of disgrace De l'Orme wrote two treatises: *Nouvelles inventions pour bien bastir et à petits frais* (1561), on the practical engineering of vaults and roofs, and *Architecture* (1567). The latter work, though exceedingly entertaining reading because of its many anecdotes, is very sound in practical advice to patrons and builders. About 1563 Catherine recalled De l'Orme to enlarge St-Maur for her son, Charles IX, and to build her new palace of the Tuileries in Paris. Only the lower section of the central pavilion of the Tuileries was complete at the time of De l'Orme's death.

Further Reading

Philibert de l'Orme is listed in the Art study guide (III, E, 3). The other great architect of the period was Pierre LESCOT. CATHERINE DE MÉDICIS temporarily replaced De l'Orme with PRIMATICCIO.

There are two excellent works in English that provide information on De l'Orme, both by Anthony Blunt: *Philibert de l'Orme* (1958) is a lucid monograph deficient only in the wasted opportunity to make vivid both the artist and his times by developing the rich personalities of De l'Orme and his contemporary associates. Blunt wisely avoids the issue of latent mannerism in the architect's style in order to establish positively his classical contributions. *Art and Architecture in France, 1500–1700* (1953; 2d rearranged impression 1957) includes an incisive summary of De l'Orme's works and is especially instructive because of the clarity of Blunt's stylistic analyses.

* * *

DEL PILAR / By Epifanio San Juan, Jr.

Marcelo H. Del Pilar (1850–1896) was a Philippine revolutionary propagandist and satirist. He tried to marshal the nationalist sentiment of the enlightened Filipino ilustrados, or bourgeoisie, against Spanish imperialism.

Marcelo Del Pilar (pronounced dĕl pē-lär′) was born in Kupang, Bulacan, on Aug. 30, 1850, to cultured parents. He studied at the Colegio de San José and later at the University of Santo Tomas, where he finished his law course in 1880. Fired by a sense of justice against the abuses of the clergy, Del Pilar attacked bigotry and hypocrisy and defended in court the impoverished victims of racial discrimination. He preached the gospel of work, self-respect, and human

Marcelo Del Pilar.

dignity. His mastery of Tagalog, his native language, enabled him to arouse the consciousness of the masses to the need for unity and sustained resistance against the Spanish tyrants.

In 1882 Del Pilar founded the newspaper *Diariong Tagalog* to propagate democratic liberal ideas among the farmers and peasants. In 1888 he defended José Rizal's polemical writings by issuing a pamphlet against a priest's attack, exhibiting his deadly wit and savage ridicule of clerical follies.

In 1888, fleeing from clerical persecution, Del Pilar went to Spain, leaving his family behind. In December 1889 he succeeded Graciano Lopez Jaena as editor of the Filipino reformist periodical *La solidaridad* in Madrid. He promoted the objectives of the paper by contacting liberal Spaniards who would side with the Filipino cause. Under Del Pilar, the aims of the newspaper were expanded to include removal of the friars and the secularization of the parishes; active Filipino participation in the affairs of the government; freedom of speech, of the press, and of assembly; wider social and political freedoms; equality before the law; assimilation; and representation in the Spanish Cortes, or Parliament.

Del Pilar's difficulties increased when the money to support the paper was exhausted and there still appeared no sign of any immediate response from the Spanish ruling class. Before he died of tuberculosis caused by hunger and enormous privations, Del Pilar rejected the assimilationist stand and began planning an armed revolt. He vigorously affirmed this conviction: "Insurrection is the last remedy, especially when the people have acquired the belief that peaceful means to secure the remedies for evils prove futile." This idea inspired Andres Bonifacio's Katipunan, a secret revolutionary organization. Del Pilar died in Barcelona on July 4, 1896.

Del Pilar's militant and progressive outlook derived from the classic Enlightenment tradition of the French *philosophes* and the scientific empiricism of the European bourgeoisie. Part of this outlook was transmitted by Freemasonry, to which Del Pilar subscribed.

Further Reading

Marcelo Del Pilar is listed in the Asia study guide (IV, C, 2). Other Filipinos important in the struggle against the Spanish were Emilio AGUINALDO, Andres BONI-FACIO, and José RIZAL.

An important source of information about Del Pilar is Magno S. Gatmaitan, *Marcelo H. Del Pilar, 1850–1896: A Documented Biography* (1966).

✳ ✳ ✳

DEMOCRITUS / By Edward Rosen

The Greek natural philosopher Democritus (ca. 494–ca. 404 B.C.) promulgated the atomic theory, which asserted that the universe is composed of two elements: the atoms and the void in which they exist and move.

Democritus. This bronze head—a Roman copy of an original sculpture executed about 250 B.C.—is in the Museo Nazionale, Naples. (Alinari)

Democritus (pronounced dĭ-mŏk′rə-təs) was born in Abdera, the leading Greek city on the northern coast of the Aegean Sea. Although the ancient accounts of Democritus's career differ widely, they all agree that he lived to a ripe old age, 90 being the lowest figure. During that long career Democritus wrote many books. *Little Cosmology*, a veritable encyclopedia, has perished because its contents displeased those, such as the reactionary philosopher Plato, whose decisions determined which works should be preserved. Of all of Democritus's many-sided interests, his espousal of the atomic theory accounts for his renown and also for the disappearance of the treatises which won him that renown.

Atomic Theory

Democritus did not originate the atomic theory; he learned it from its founder, Leucippus, the author of the *Big Cosmology*. While this work too has vanished, some conception of its contents may be obtained from Aristotle. He opposed the atomic theory, but in doing so he summarized its principal doctrines. Thus he attributed to Leucippus the ideas that the atoms are "infinite in number and imperceptible because of the minuteness of their size. They move about in empty space (for there is empty space) and by joining together they produce perceptible objects, which are destroyed when the atoms separate." The point at which Leucippus's elaboration of the atomic theory stopped and Democritus's contributions to it began can no longer be identified. In antiquity the theory's major features were sometimes ascribed to Leucippus and Democritus jointly and sometimes to Democritus alone.

Perhaps according to both of them and certainly according to Democritus, the atom was the irreducibly minimal quantity of matter. The concept of the infinite divisibility of matter was flatly contradicted by the atomic theory, since within the interior of the atom there could be no physical parts or unoccupied space. Every atom was exactly like every other atom as a piece of corporeal stuff. But the atoms differed in shape, and since their contours showed an infinite variety and could be orient-

ed in any direction and arranged in any order, the atoms could enter into countless combinations. In their solid interior there was no motion, while they themselves could move about in empty space. Thus, for the atomic theory, the physical universe had two basic ingredients: impenetrable atoms and penetrable space. For Democritus, space was infinite in extent, and the atoms were infinite in number.

By their very nature the atoms were endowed with a motion that was eternal and not initiated by any outside force. Since the atoms were not created at any time in the past and would never disintegrate at any time in the future, the total quantity of matter in the universe remained constant: this fundamental principle of Democritus's atomic theory implies the conservation of matter, the sum total of which in the universe neither increases nor diminishes. Though Democritus's conception of the atom has been modified in several essential respects in modern times, his atomic theory remains the foundation of modern science.

For Democritus, "time was uncreated." His atomic universe was temporally everlasting and spatially boundless, without beginning and without end in either space or time. Just as no special act of creation brought Democritus's universe into being, so the operations of his cosmos did not serve any particular purpose. Consequently Democritus's atomic theory was irreconcilable with the teleological view, which regarded the world as having been planned to fulfill some inscrutable destiny.

As the founder of the atomic theory declared in his only surviving statement, "Nothing occurs at random, but everything happens for a reason and by necessity."

Moral Teachings

Just as Democritus's cosmogony invoked no creator-god, so his moral teachings appealed to no supernatural judge of human conduct. He attributed the popular belief in Zeus and other deities to primitive man's incomprehension of meteorological and astronomical phenomena. To support his theory about the origin of worship of the various divinities, Democritus assailed the widespread notion that rewards for righteous actions and punishments for wrongdoing were administered in an afterlife. In the long history of Greek speculation Democritus was the first thinker who had the courage to deny that every human being has an individual soul which survives the death of the body.

Democritus sought to diminish pain during life, of which "the goal is cheerfulness." Cheerfulness is identical not with pleasure, as he was misinterpreted by some people, but "with a calm and steady mind, undisturbed by any fear or superstition or other irrational feeling." Yet Democritus did not advocate a quiet life of repose. His was not the outlook of the retired citizen, drowsing in his rocking chair on the front porch and idly watching the world go by. Democritus taught a naturalistic morality, avoiding ascetic renunciation as well as excessive indulgence, and urging energetic participation in beneficial activities. In particular, "Democritus recommends mastering the art of politics as most important, and undertaking its tasks, from which significant and magnificent benefits are obtained for the people." Perhaps from his governmental experience in Abdera, Democritus learned that "good conduct seems to be procured better by the use of encouraging and convincing words than by statute and coercion. For he who is restrained by law from wrongdoing is likely to commit crime covertly. On the other hand, he who is attracted to uprightness by persuasion is unlikely to transgress either secretly or openly."

Probing the Infinitesimal

Archimedes, the most brilliant mathematician of antiquity, gave Democritus credit for the discovery that the volume of a cone is one-third that of a cylinder having the same base and altitude. Archimedes added, however, that this theorem was enunciated by Democritus "without proof." In Democritus's time Greek geometry had not yet reached the stage at which it demanded rigorous proofs of its theorems. Democritus stated: "If a cone is cut by a plane parallel to its base, shall we regard the surfaces forming the sections as equal or unequal? If unequal, they make the cone uneven, having numerous indentations and protrusions, like a flight of stairs. But if the surfaces are equal, the sections will be equal and the cone comes to look like a cylinder, consisting of equal circles." Democritus's conception of the cylinder as being made up of an indefinite number of minutely thin circular layers shows him beginning to probe the momentous question of the infinitesimal, the starting point of a most valuable branch of modern mathematics.

Further Reading

Democritus is listed in the Science study guide (I, B, 3), the Philosophy study guide (I, A, 4), and the Social Sciences study guide (I, C, 1). EPICURUS modified his atomic theory. PROTAGORAS is said to have been Democritus's secretary.

A comprehensive study of Democritus is Cyril Bailey, *The Greek Atomists and Epicurus* (1928). More recent discussions can be found in William Keith Chambers Guthrie, *A History of Greek Philosophy* (3 vols., 1962–1969); Andrew Thomas Cole, *Democritus and the Sources of Greek Anthropology* (1967); David J. Furley, *Two Studies in the Greek Atomists* (1967); and G. F. Parker, *A Short Account of Greek Philosophy from Thales to Epicurus* (1967).

✳　✳　✳

DEMOIVRE / By John D. North

The Franco-English mathematician Abraham Demoivre (1667–1754) was a successful exponent of the calculus of Newton and Leibniz and an early writer on the mathematics of life insurance.

Abraham Demoivre (pronounced də-moi′vər), the son of a surgeon living at Vitry, Champagne, was born May 26, 1667. He was given a Protestant schooling and at the age of 11 went to the Protestant

Abraham Demoivres, a mezzotint by J. Faber, after a 1736 painting by Joseph Highmore. (Trustees of the British Museum, Department of Prints and Drawings)

University of Sedan. He studied logic at Saumur, and at the Collège d'Harcourt in Paris he learned the physics of the day, mainly according to the system of René Descartes. When Demoivre was 18, Louis XIV revoked the Edict of Nantes, which had granted toleration to Protestants, and the youth was forced to flee Paris, eventually settling in London.

Once in London, Demoivre earned a meager living as a private teacher and lecturer in mathematics and natural science. He obtained a copy of Isaac Newton's recently published *Principia* (1687) and studied it assiduously. It is said that he tore the book into sheets, carrying a few around at a time in his pocket to master it in his spare time. Demoivre made the acquaintance of Newton, Edmund Halley, and other members of the Royal Society. His mathematical talents were recognized, and in 1695 he presented his first paper to the society, "Method of Fluxions," on Newton's calculus. By 1697 he had been elected a fellow of the Royal Society.

Demoivre published a number of papers, but his most original work was a book on the subject of probability, *Doctrine of Chances* (1718). It contained several innovations, including methods for approximating to functions of large numbers. Isaac Todhunter, historian of theories of probability, contended that the subject owed more to Demoivre than any other mathematician, except possibly Pierre Simon de Laplace. It was as a natural extension of his writings on probability that Demoivre wrote *Annuities on Lives* (1725), the first mathematical work on this subject. It is based on a law of mortality that differs little from one devised by John Hudd in 1671. Though Demoivre's principles have since been modified, his work was still being defended by eminent actuarial mathematicians of the 19th century. Demoivre accused Thomas Simpson, a younger pioneer of the same subject, of plagiarism but later dropped the charge.

Demoivre was honored by many European societies. One important theorem applying complex or "imaginary" numbers to trigonometry bears his name. He died in London on Nov. 27, 1754.

Further Reading

Abraham Demoivre is listed in the Science study guide (V, A, 1). He was an intimate friend of Isaac NEWTON and was acquainted with Edmund HALLEY and Daniel BERNOULLI. Leonhard EULER eventually enlarged upon Demoivre's trigonometry and helped thereby to shift the subject from the realm of geometry to that of analysis.

There is no biography of Demoivre. For background and a brief biographical sketch see David Eugene Smith, *History of Mathematics*, vol. 1 (1923).

✳   ✳   ✳

DEMOSTHENES / By John E. Rexine

Demosthenes (384–322 B.C.) is regarded as the greatest of Greek orators and perhaps the greatest orator of all times. He saw clearly the significance of the rise of an autocratic Macedonia and its implications for traditional Athenian and Greek political freedom.

Demosthenes (pronounced dǐ-mǒs′thə-nēz) was the son of a wealthy manufacturer of weapons named Demosthenes of the deme of Paeania in Attica. The orator's father died when Demosthenes was 7 years old, and his estate was turned over to his two brothers, Aphobus and Demophon, and a friend, Therippides, who sorely mismanaged it.

Early Career

Though a sickly child, Demosthenes was determined to obtain redress from his guardians. In order to prepare himself, he studied rhetoric and law under Isaeaus, and though by age 20 only about one-tenth of the capital remained for him, he successfully prosecuted his guardians. The four speeches dealing with this business are preserved in "Against Aphobus" and "Against Onetor."

Though the legend about his declaiming with pebbles in his mouth and practicing by the seashore midst the thunder of the waves may be apocryphal, there is no doubt that Demosthenes rigorously prepared himself to overcome any physical disabilities; and though apparently not a good improviser, he was closely familiar with the writings of Thucydides, Plato, and Isocrates. Demosthenes spent 15 years as a professional speech writer (*logographos*) and ranged over a wide variety of subjects with a mastery of oratorical form and of technical legal details. Thirty-two of these private orations are preserved, though only a third of these are generally considered genuine.

In 355 B.C. Demosthenes found himself employed as

Demosthenes, an ancient portrait bust in the Louvre, Paris. (Giraudon)

an assistant to the public prosecutors in the assembly, in the courts, and in other public places. The speeches against Androtion, Timocrates, and Aristocrates show evidence of a mind of considerable ability. His first public appearance in 354 in "Against Leptines" defends the policy of exempting from special taxation citizens who had performed outstanding services to the state. "Against Aristocrates" (352) shows him dealing with foreign policy, while "On the Navy Boards" (354), "For Megalopolis" (352), and "For the Rhodians" (351) show a Demosthenes keenly interested in foreign affairs and pushing hard for administrative reforms.

Opponent of Macedon

The year 351 marks a turning point in Demosthenes's career since in a series of nine orations he began his famous "Philippics" (351–340), warning Athens of the threatening danger of an ever expanding Macedon and an ever imperialistically encroaching Philip. The "First Philippic" was succeeded by three "Olynthiac" speeches, centering on Olynthus, the strongest Greek city in the north, which was threatened by Philip. Demosthenes pleaded that the Athenians dispatch forces to help Olynthus out of its plight, but the Athenians were not convinced of the gravity of the situation and Olynthus fell in 348. Philip was not to be stopped as his attention was now directed southward. Once he became admitted to the Amphictyonic League in 346, Macedon became a Greek power with support in Athens itself.

Though Demosthenes supported the peace treaty with Philip in 346 in his oration "On the Peace," he soon saw that Philip had other plans. So in 344 in the "Second Philippic," in "On the Chersonese," and in the "Third Philippic" (341) he renewed his attack on Philip and his designs, while in "On the Embassy" (343) he attacked Aeschines, whom he accused of having betrayed the best interests of Athens. Gradually Demosthenes assumed the leadership of the opposition to the growing military and political aggrandizement of Philip, an opposition that developed into armed conflict and resulted in the crushing defeat of the Athenians and their allies at Chaeronea in 338. Demosthenes himself was among the defeated refugees.

Though defeated, Demosthenes was not broken in spirit. He continued to fight Philip, and for his services Ctesiphon proposed a golden crown be presented to him at the city Dionysia, a proposal that motivated Aeschines, Demosthenes's chief competitor, to bring charges against Ctesiphon on the grounds that an illegal proposal had been preferred. The trial took place in 330, and Demosthenes brilliantly defended Ctesiphon and himself in what is considered his masterpiece "On the Crown."

Decline of Leadership

Thereafter Demosthenes's leadership waned. He was charged with having received money from Harpalus, the governor of Babylon and the treasurer of Alexander the Great, who had absconded with funds to Athens on the basis of a false rumor that Alexander was dead. Harpalus

Manuscript of an oration by Demosthenes. This manuscript, dating from the 1st century A.D., is the earliest extant Greek literary document written on parchment. (Trustees of the British Museum)

was refused admission to Athens because of an army of 6,000 that he had with him.

Upon demand Harpalus dismissed his troops and was admitted, but Alexander demanded his surrender. Demosthenes retorted by proposing that Harpalus be kept in custody and that the funds he had be deposited in the Parthenon. When Harpalus escaped there was a shortage of 370 talents, and Demosthenes was accused of having accepted a bribe of 20 talents to assist in the escape. Charged and brought to trial, Demosthenes was fined 50 talents, but because he was unable to pay he went into exile.

It is still not clear whether Demosthenes was actually guilty of misconduct in the Harpalus incident or not. At any rate, Demosthenes tried to organize support against Macedon in the Peloponnesus; was recalled to Athens, which was subsequently occupied by Macedon; and was condemned to death but escaped to the Temple of Poseidon in Calauria, where he committed suicide in 322.

His Works

Sixty-one orations, six letters, and a book of 54 proems have been attributed to Demosthenes, though all are certainly not genuine. Private law court speeches include those against Aphobus and Onetor (363–362), "Against Dionysodorus" (323–322), "For Phormio" (350), and the first "Against Stephanus" (349). The subjects cover guardianship, inheritance, loans, mining rights, and forgery, among others.

The political law court speeches include "Against Androtion" (355), "Against Leptines" (354), "Against Timocrates" (353), "Against Aristocrates" (352), "Against Midias" (347), "On the Embassy" (343), "On the Crown" (330), and "Against Aristogeiton" (325–324). Topics covered include abolition of immunity from taxation for public-spirited citizens, embezzlement, assaulting a public official, bribery, and the private lives of Demosthenes and Aeschines.

Political speeches include "On the Navy Boards" (354), "For Megalopolis" (352), "For the Rhodians" (351), "First Philippic" (351), three "Olynthiacs" (349), "On the Peace" (346), "Second Philippic" (344), "On the Chersonese" (341), "Third Philippic" (341), "Fourth Philippic" (composite), "On the Halonnese" (342), and "On the Treaty with Alexander" (probably not by Demosthenes). The six "Letters" have been reinvestigated recently and the majority of them may be genuine. Both domestic Greek history and politics and foreign affairs are involved.

His Significance

Demosthenes is generally acknowledged to be Greece's greatest orator, though he never lacked for rivals in his lifetime. It has been said that he united in himself the excellences of his contemporaries and predecessors. More than a master of rhetorical form, Demosthenes was a man of superior moral and intellectual qualities who knew how to use language for its best effects.

Perhaps most significant of all was Demosthenes's ability to see the implications of the rise of Macedonian political and military power and to become the staunchest and most persistent defender of individual Greek freedom against the new power; but he was not farsighted enough to see that the Greek city-state was no longer a viable political unit and that it would be replaced by the Hellenistic imperial state.

Further Reading

Demosthenes is listed in the Ancient History study guide (II, C, 5, a). Another great Greek orator was ISOCRATES. Of the Roman orators, CATO THE ELDER and CICERO were the best known.

Books on Demosthenes appear less frequently than they did in the past. A number of older works are still worth consulting: Samuel H. Butcher, *Demosthenes* (1881); Arthur W. Pickard-Cambridge, *Demosthenes* (1914); Charles D. Adams, *Demosthenes and His Influence* (1927); and Werner W. Jaeger, *Demosthenes: The Origin and Growth of His Policy* (1938). Jonathan Goldstein, *The Letters of Demosthenes* (1968), provides a fascinating investigation into the question of the historical value and authenticity of the six letters attributed to Demosthenes.

DEMPSEY / By Arthur Daley

One of the world's greatest heavyweight boxers, the American William Harrison "Jack" Dempsey (born 1895) was so popular that he drew more million-dollar gates than any prizefighter in history.

Jack Dempsey was born in Manassa, Colo., on June 24, 1895, the ninth child of Hyrum and Cecilia Dempsey. The family was so poor that Jack began farming at the age of 8. From age 16 to 19 he lived in hobo jungles.

Dempsey's early boxing often took place in back rooms of frontier saloons. His first fight of record was in 1915 against "One-Punch" Hancock. Dempsey's one-punch win earned him $2.50; his highest purse, 11 years later, was $711,000 for his first match with Gene Tunney. Called the "Manassa Mauler," Dempsey earned more than $3,500,000 in all in the ring.

Dempsey's appeal lay in his punching ability: he was a ruthless tiger stalking his prey, fast as any big cat and deadly with either paw. He won the world's heavyweight title on July 4, 1919, against Jess Willard. With his first real punch Dempsey shattered Willard's cheekbone and knocked him down seven times in the first round. Willard was unable to answer the bell for the start of the fourth.

Jack Dempsey about 1921. (Library of Congress)

Two years later Dempsey drew the world's first million-dollar gate against Georges Carpentier of France, scoring a fourth-round knockout. Another million-dollar bout was in 1923 against Luis Angel Firpo of Argentina; few bouts have packed such unbridled fury and spectacular savagery. Dempsey was knocked down twice, once through the ropes and out of the ring; 10 times Firpo went down, the tenth time for keeps—all within the span of 3 minutes 57 seconds. The Mauler was dethroned in Philadelphia in 1926, when Gene Tunney outpointed him before the largest crowd ever to witness a championship: 120,757 spectators.

Dempsey knocked out Jack Sharkey before the second Dempsey-Tunney fight a year later in Chicago. This last bout became the focus of an enduring controversy. Dempsey floored Tunney in the seventh round but refused to go to a neutral corner according to the rules. The countdown was delayed, and Tunney, given this extra respite, recovered sufficiently to outbox Dempsey the rest of the way.

Dempsey went on to become a highly respected restauranteur in New York City. He enjoyed a fantastic popularity, revered as one of the true titans of American sports.

Further Reading

Jack Dempsey is listed in the American History study guide (IX, D, 6). Other American sports heroes were Joe LOUIS and Babe RUTH.

The most authoritative book on Dempsey is his autobiography, *Dempsey*, written with Bob Considine and Bill Slocum (1960). The best statistical background is in *Nat Fleischer's Ring Record Book* (1970). Dempsey's manager, Jack "Doc" Kearns, appraises him in *The Million Dollar Gate*, written with Oscar Fraley (1966). The second Dempsey-Tunney fight is in Mel Heimer, *The Long Count* (1969).

DEMUTH / By Martin Friedman

American painter Charles Demuth
(1883–1935), distinguished for intimate
watercolors and geometrized urban scenes, was
one of the leading artists of precisionism, an
American idiom of cubism in the 1920s.

Charles Demuth was born in Lancaster, Pa., on Nov. 8, 1883. A childhood leg injury left him lame, and at an early age he began to draw and paint. After studying at the School of Industrial Art in Philadelphia, he entered the Pennsylvania Academy of Fine Arts in 1905 and took classes with William Merritt Chase and Thomas Anschutz.

In 1907 Demuth went to Paris, where Fauve painting with its expressive form and color affected his early

I Saw the Figure 5 in Gold, *Charles Demuth's "poster portrait" of the poet William Carlos Williams, was executed in 1928. (The Metropolitan Museum of Art, Alfred Stieglitz Collection)*

work. *Studio Interior* (ca. 1907), one of the few surviving works of this period, is a watercolor whose roughly outlined, loosely painted figures are reminiscent of those of Henri Matisse and Georges Rouault. It foreshadows the illustrational style Demuth employed, in refined form, later. He continued his studies at the Pennsylvania Academy (1908–1910), and his interest in figure drawing increased. As he refined his focus, the personages depicted became vehicles for acute psychological expression. In Paris again in 1912, he attended classes at the academies Julian, Colarossi, and Moderne. One of the few American artists of the period with firsthand understanding of the new European movements of cubism and Dada, Demuth evolved an art that transcended their literal and localized themes. In fact, he always remained receptive to a wide range of influences, and various styles found intelligent transmutation in his work.

Demuth's early watercolors, shown at the Pennsylvania Academy in 1912 and 1913, revealed a fragile, understated style; his landscapes, executed in delicate washes, evoked a gamut of European associations. Fauve references remained, but a new concern with formalism was evident, and there are parallels to Paul Cézanne's prismatic vistas in such paintings as *New Hope, Pennsylvania* (1911/1912). But even when Demuth employed the analytic approach of Cézanne or the cubist planes of Pablo Picasso, his art remained concerned with surface quality, not internal structure.

By 1915 Demuth was established as a major American

artist through his landscapes, flower studies, and small-scale paintings of cabaret and circus performers. His figures have a weightless and phantomlike quality; in *Two Acrobats* (1918), entertainers dressed in tuxedoes float surrealistically through a vague landscape. Demuth's sensitive linear style was eminently suited to illustrating plays and novels such as Émile Zola's *Nana*, Henry James's *The Turn of the Screw*, Frank Wedekind's *Pandora's Box*, and Edgar Allan Poe's *The Mask of the Red Death*. These illustrations, not meant for publication, reflect Demuth's taste for the psychologically distorted and depict sexual conflict and social decadence.

In *White Architecture* (1917) Demuth used the cubist technique with delicacy and individuality and employed color sparingly to modify a complex of overlaid and intersecting structural planes derived from the building itself. He developed this style in his paintings of factories and industrial sites, beginning in 1918, and thus was a pioneer of the precisionist movement.

Demuth did a unique group of "poster portraits" (symbolic still-life paintings) that reflected the interests and attributes of friends, including painters Georgia O'Keeffe, Marsden Hartley, and Arthur Dove and poet William Carlos Williams. The best-known of these, *I Saw the Figure 5 in Gold* (1928), a "portrait" of Williams, whose title derives from a Williams poem, is a direct ancestor of pop art, using the numeral 5 in a repeated abstract arrangement. Demuth died in Lancaster on Oct. 25, 1935.

Further Reading

Charles Demuth is listed in the Art study guide (IV, E, 4). Other precisionists were Georgia O'KEEFFE and Charles SHEELER.

The life and artistic development of Demuth are covered in A. C. Ritchie, *Charles Demuth* (1950), and Emily Farnham, *Charles Demuth: Behind a Laughing Mask* (1971). There is an essay on Demuth by Martin Friedman in the Walker Art Center Catalog *The Precisionist View in American Art* (1960). Older monographs include A. E. Gallatin, *Charles Demuth* (1927), and William Murrell, *Charles Demuth* (1931).

DEODORO DA FONSECA

/ By Michael M. Smith

Manoel Deodoro da Fonseca (1827–1892) was the first president of Brazil. Perhaps his greatest contribution was the assumption of authority in the last days of the empire and his leading role in the establishment of the republic.

Manoel Deodoro da Fonseca. (Organization of American States)

Manoel Deodoro da Fonseca (pronounced dā-ō-dō′rō də fōN-sā′kə) was born on Aug. 5, 1827, in Alagoas. In 1843 he entered the Military School in Rio de Janeiro and after graduation in 1847 began a series of assignments that took him to all parts of the empire. In 1864 he participated in military campaigns in Uruguay and later against Francisco Solano López in the Paraguayan War. He later rose to field marshal.

Militarism, nurtured during the Paraguayan War, became reality in the late 1870s. The army looked upon itself as the savior of the nation, and the Military School was the center of positivist propaganda. Deodoro's prestige had grown to such stature that when the Duque de Caxias died in 1880 the Conservative party hoped that Deodoro would assume the duke's role of pacifying the restive army. But Deodoro also had the admiration of the young officers, who were increasingly attracted to republicanism and positivism. Promoted to quartermaster general of the army, he was assigned to an office in Rio, where he became the military strongman around whom the officers and their sympathizers rallied.

As the military-civilian crisis intensified, Deodoro was first transferred to Mato Grosso and then returned to Rio in June 1889. Rumors of cutbacks in military personnel and troop transfers to the frontier to diminish the army's strength in Rio aggravated the growing conflict.

Pressed by militants to lead a coup and proclaim a republic, Deodoro believed that the military's honor could be maintained by merely overthrowing the ministry. After repeated entreaties he agreed to lead the revolt. Yet his real goal is still unclear. Even during the actual coup, led by Floriano Peixoto on Nov. 15, 1889, when Deodoro became ill, he seems to have thought it was simply a move against an antagonistic ministry. Emperor Pedro II was sent into exile the next day.

On November 17 the provisional government was formed with Deodoro as the chief executive. Unfortunately, he was ill-suited for the position. Accustomed to instant obedience, he had little patience or administrative ability. Receiving minimal cooperation from his ministers and daily attacks in the press, he became increasingly bewildered by his new responsibilities. On Jan. 20, 1891, his Cabinet resigned en masse. On February 24, however, the constitution was proclaimed, and the Constituent Congress elected Deodoro president and Peixoto his vice president.

Unpopular and frequently seriously ill, Deodoro faced chronic disorder within the country and fiscal chaos. He was in constant conflict with Congress, and Peixoto plotted against him. On Nov. 3, 1891, Deodoro dissolved Congress, proclaimed a state of siege in Rio and its environs, and ruled by decree. His dictatorial regime was short-lived, however, as he faced the rebellious disaffection of the army and continuing poor health. On November 22 he suffered a serious heart attack. Two days later he resigned and was succeeded by Peixoto.

Peixoto effectively crushed a revolt to restore Deodoro in January 1892, but by then Deodoro was suffering serious physical and mental decline. He died in Petrópolis on Aug. 22, 1892.

Further Reading

Manoel Deodoro da Fonseca is listed in the Latin America study guide (IV, C, 1, a). The establishment of a republican Brazil was facilitated by the liberalized regime of PEDRO II.

The standard work in English on Deodoro is Charles Willis Simmons, *Marshal Deodoro and the Fall of Dom Pedro II* (1966). It provides a sympathetic treatment of a man thrust into a position of responsibility far beyond his own ambition and ability. For background see João Pandiá Calógeras, *A History of Brazil* (trans. 1939).

✳   ✳   ✳

DERAIN / By J. P. Hodin

André Derain (1880–1954) was considered by leading critics in the 1920s to be the most outstanding French avant-garde painter and at the same time the upholder of the classical spirit of French tradition.

A ndré Derain (pronounced də-răN′) was born on June 10, 1880, in Chatou. He began to paint when he was about 15. He studied at the Academy Carrière in Paris (1898–1899), where he met Henri Matisse. Derain was a close friend of Maurice Vlaminck, with whom he shared a studio in 1900 and also his radical views on painting, literature, and politics. Derain was drawn, through Vlaminck and Matisse, into the art movement known as Fauvism.

Derain's first artistic attempts were interrupted by mili-

tary service (1901–1904), after which he devoted himself exclusively to art. He experienced impressionism, divisionism, the style of Paul Gauguin and Vincent Van Gogh, and Vlaminck's and Matisse's techniques by applying them to his own work. He copied in the Louvre and traveled a great deal in France to paint its various landscapes. He spent the summer of 1905 at Collioure with Matisse and that fall exhibited with the Fauves.

The art dealer Ambrose Vollard signed a contract with Derain in 1905, and the following year the artist went to London to paint some scenes of the city commissioned by Vollard. Derain's *Westminster Bridge* is one of his Fauve masterpieces.

About 1908 Derain became interested in African sculpture and at the same time explored the work of Paul Cézanne and early cubism. He became a friend of Pablo Picasso and worked with him in Catalonia in 1910.

In Derain's work, which comprises landscapes, figure compositions (sometimes religious), portraits, still lifes, sculptures, decors for ballets, and book illustrations, we can discern various periods, all of which are distinguished by masterpieces. About 1911 he was attracted by Italian and French primitive masters; he also admired the "primitive" art of Henri Rousseau. After World War I, during which Derain served at the front, he studied the masters of the early Renaissance and then Pompeian art. All these left traces in his work. Finally he emerged as a realist and intensified his contact with nature. In rejecting the cerebral art of cubism and abstraction, he defended the return of the human figure to painting. His development as an artist was dramatic, and although Picasso called him a *guide de musées*, in other words, not an innovator but a traditionalist, Derain's best work will survive many of the experimental attempts of his contemporaries because of its inherent painterly qualities.

Toward the end of his life Derain lived, practically forgotten, in his country home at Chambourcy. The retrospective exhibition in Paris in 1937 was the climax of his fame. He died in Garches on Sept. 2, 1954. The large retrospective exhibitions organized from 1955 to 1959 established a new appreciation of Derain as a major artist.

André Derain, a self-portrait. (French Cultural Services of the French Embassy)

Further Reading

André Derain is listed in the Art study guide (III, J, 1, b). He was associated with Henri MATISSE and Maurice VLAMINCK during his Fauve period and with Pablo PICASSO in his cubist phase.

Denys Sutton, *André Derain* (1959), gives an objective picture of Derain's development and the attitude of critics to his work. Other monographs are Malcolm Vaughan, *Derain* (1941), and Gaston Diehl, *Derain* (trans. 1964).

DE SANCTIS / By David Hershberg

The Italian critic, educator, and legislator Francesco De Sanctis (1817–1883) was the foremost Italian literary historian of the 19th century.

Francesco De Sanctis. (Italian Cultural Institute)

Francesco De Sanctis (pronounced dā săngk′tēs) was born in Morra Irpina near Naples. His early inclination toward learning suggested a career in the priesthood. But his interest in pedagogy and his loss of religious faith after 1834 altered his course, and he turned toward education. Trained by the literary scholar and philologist Basilio Puoti, he founded an academy under Puoti's leadership.

De Sanctis supported the short-lived Neapolitan revolution of 1848 and proposed a series of scholastic reforms calling for free compulsory education, improved teacher training, and greater uniformity and continuity in schools. But the tide of reaction in 1849 annulled these proposals and forced De Sanctis to leave Naples. In December 1850 he was imprisoned on a fabricated charge of plotting to kill the King. When released 2 years later, De Sanctis traveled to Turin, the Piedmontese capital, where, consistent with his lifelong conviction, he advocated Italian unification under the house of Savoy. There he also delivered a series of distinguished lectures on Dante, for which he was invited to be professor of Italian literature at Zurich, a post he held from January 1856 to August 1860.

Returning to Italy and to political activity, De Sanctis worked to reform the University of Naples and was elected to Parliament. Appointed minister of education, he championed quality education as a matter of civic responsibility, though he realized the difficulty of carrying out such a program in a largely illiterate and tradition-bound nation. During the later stages of his legislative career, De Sanctis also served as professor of comparative literature at the University of Naples (1871–1878).

Although after 1865 De Sanctis continued to hold public office, his literary pursuits assumed greater importance. *Critical Essays* (1866), the revised *Essay on Petrarch* (1869), and the monumental *History of Italian Literature* (written in 1868–1871 as a teaching manual) represent his major contributions to literary criticism and historiography. Among the basic tenets of his critical approach are: art is the product of the fantasy of great men; the work of art is absolutely independent of science, morals, history, or philosophy; and art is the appropriate synthesis of content and form.

De Sanctis accepted the Positivists' demand for rigorous scholarship but maintained that minutiae are not a critic's central concern. Faulted by some for apparent inattention to detail and for focusing only on major figures, De Sanctis was defended eloquently by Benedetto Croce, who oversaw the posthumous publication of De Sanctis's other works. Later, elaborating on De Sanctis's esthetics, Croce recognized the lack of systematic theories and the consequent imprecision of terminology, but he praised De Sanctis's critical acumen and wide range of interests.

Further Reading

Francesco De Sanctis is listed in the Literature study guide (III, G, 3). His esthetic theories contrast sharply with those of Alessandro MANZONI and the other Italian romantics. Benedetto CROCE stressed the importance of De Sanctis's work.

In addition to numerous studies in Italian by Croce and others, one may profitably consult Louis A. Breglio, *Life and Criticism of Francesco De Sanctis* (1941).

DESCARTES / By Raymond J. Langley

The French thinker René Descartes (1596–1650) is called the father of modern philosophy. He initiated the movement generally termed rationalism, and his "Discourse on Method" and "Meditations" defined the basic problems of philosophy for at least a century.

To appreciate the novelty of the thought of René Descartes (pronounced dā-kärt′), one must understand what modern philosophy, or rationalism, means in contrast to medieval, or scholastic, philosophy. The great European thinkers of the 9th to 14th century were not incapable of logical reasoning, but they differed in philosophic interests and aims from the rationalists. Just as the moderns, from Descartes on, usually identified philosophy with the natural and pure sciences, so the medievals made little distinction between philosophical and theological concerns.

The medieval doctors, like St. Thomas Aquinas, wanted to demonstrate that the revelations of faith and the dictates of reason were not incompatible. Their universe was that outlined by Aristotle in his *Physics*—a universe in which everything was ordered and classified according to the end that it served. During the Renaissance, however, men began exploring scientific alternatives to Aristotle's hierarchical universe. Further, new instruments, especially Galileo's telescope, added precision to scientific generalizations.

By the beginning of the 17th century the medieval tradition had lost its creative impetus. But the schoolmen, so called because they dominated the European universities, continued to adhere dogmatically to the traditional philosophy because of its association with Catholic theology. The rationalists, however, persistently refused professorships in order to preserve their intellectual integrity or to avoid persecution. They rejected the medieval practice of composing commentaries on standard works in favor of writing original, usually anonymous, treatises on topics suggested by their own scientific or speculative interests. Thus the contrast is between a moribund tradition of professorial disputes over trivialities and a new philosophy inspired by original, scientific research.

René Descartes, a portrait by the Dutch painter Frans Hals, in the Louvre, Paris. (Giraudon)

Descartes participated in this conflict between the scholastic and rationalist approaches. He spent a great part of his intellectual effort—even to the extent of suppressing some of his writings—attempting to convince ecclesiastical authorities of the compatibility of the new science with theology and of its superiority as a foundation for philosophy.

Early Life

René Descartes was born on March 31, 1596, in La Haye, in the Touraine region, between the cities of Tours and Poitiers. His father, Joachim, a member of the minor nobility, served in the Parliament of Brittany. Jeanne Brochard Descartes, his mother, died in May 1597. Although his father remarried, René and his older brother and sister were raised by their maternal grandmother and by a nurse for whom he retained a deep affection.

In 1606 Descartes entered La Flèche, a Jesuit college established by the King for the instruction of the young nobility. In the *Discourse* Descartes tells of the 8-year course of studies at La Flèche, which he considered "one of the most celebrated schools in Europe." According to his account, which is one of the best contemporary descriptions of 17th-century education, his studies left him feeling embarrassed at the extent of his own ignorance.

The young Descartes came to feel that languages, literature, and history relate only fables which incline man to imaginative exaggerations. Poetry and eloquence persuade man, but they do not tell the truth. Mathematics does grasp the truth, but the certainty and evidence of its reasoning seemed to Descartes to have only practical applications. Upon examination, the revelations of religion and morals seem as mysterious to the learned as to the ignorant. Philosophy had been studied by the best minds throughout the centuries, and yet "no single thing is to be found in it which is not subject to dispute." Descartes says that he came to suspect that even science, which depends upon philosophy for its principles, "could have built nothing solid on foundations so far from firm."

Travel and First Writings

The 18-year-old Descartes left college with a reputation for extreme brilliance. In the next years he rounded out the education befitting a young noble. He learned fencing, horsemanship, and dancing and took a law degree from Poitiers.

From 1618 to 1628 Descartes traveled extensively throughout Europe while attached to various military units. Although a devout Catholic, he served in the army of the Protestant prince Maurice of Nassau but later enlisted in the Catholic army of Maximilian I of Bavaria. Living on income from inherited properties, Descartes served without pay and seems to have seen little action; he was present, however, at the Battle of Prague, one of the major engagements of the Thirty Years War. Descartes was reticent about this period of his life, saying only that he left the study of letters in order to travel in "the great book of the world." Something of the man of the world is caught in the remark attributed to Descartes that there are three things impossible to find: "a beautiful woman, a good book, and a perfect preacher."

This period of travel was not without intellectual effort. Descartes sought out eminent mathematicians, scientists, and philosophers wherever he traveled. The most significant of these friendships was with Isaac Beeckman, the Dutch mathematician, at whose suggestion Descartes began writing scientific treatises on mathematics and music. He perfected a means of describing geometrical figures in algebraic formulas, a process that served as the foundation for his invention of analytic geometry. He became increasingly impressed with the extent to which material reality could be understood mathematically.

During this period Descartes was profoundly influenced by three dreams which he had on Nov. 10, 1619, in Ulm, Germany. He interpreted their symbols as a divine sign that all science is one and that its mastery is universal wisdom. This notion of the unity of all science was a revolutionary concept which contradicted the Aristotelian notion that the sciences were distinguished by their different objects of study. Descartes did not deny the multiplicity of objects, but rather he emphasized that only one mind could know all these diverse things. He felt that if one could generalize man's correct method of knowing, then one would be able to know everything. Descartes devoted the majority of his effort and work to proving that he had, in fact, discovered this correct method of reasoning.

From 1626 to 1629 Descartes resided mainly in Paris. He acquired a wide and notable set of friends but soon felt that the pressures of social life kept him from his work. He then moved to Holland, where he lived, primarily near Amsterdam, for the next 20 years. Descartes cherished the solitude of his life in Holland, and he described himself to a friend as awakening happily after 10 hours of sleep with the memory of charming dreams. He said his life in Holland was peaceful because he was "the only man not engaged in merchandise." There Descartes studied and wrote. He carried on an enormous correspondence throughout Europe, and in Holland he acquired a small, but dedicated, set of friends and disciples. Although he never married, Descartes fathered a natural daughter who was baptized Francine. She died in 1640, when she was 5.

First Works

Descartes's research in mathematics and physics led him to see the need for a new methodology, or way of thinking. His first major work, *Rules for the Direction of the Mind*, was written by 1629. Although circulated widely in manuscript form, this incomplete treatise was not published until 1701. The work begins with the assumption that man's knowledge has been limited by the erroneous belief that science is determined by the various objects of experience. The first rule therefore states that all true judgment depends on reason alone for its validity. For example, the truths of mathematics are valid independently of observation and experiment. Thus the second rule argues that the standard for any true knowledge should be the certitude demanded of demonstrations in arithmetic and geometry. The third rule begins to specify what this standard of true knowledge entails. The mind should be directed not by tradition, authority, or the history of the problem, but only by what can clearly be observed and deduced.

There are only two mental operations that are permissible in the pure use of reason. The first is intuition, which Descartes defines as "the undoubting conception of an unclouded and attentive mind"; the second is deduction, which consists of "all necessary inference from other facts that are known with certainty." The basic assumption underlying these definitions is that all first principles are known by way of self-evident intuitions and that the conclusions of this "seeing into" are derived by deduction. The clarity and distinctness of ideas are for Descartes the conceptual counterpart of human vision. (For example, man can know the geometry of a square just as distinctly as he can see a square table in front of him.)

Many philosophers recognized the ideal character of mathematical reasoning, but no one before Descartes had abstracted the conditions of such thinking and applied it generally to all knowledge. If all science is unified by man's reason and if the proper functioning of the mind is identified with mathematical thinking, then the problem of knowledge is reduced to a question of methodology. The end of knowledge is true judgment, but true judgment is equivalent to mathematical demonstrations that are based on intuition and deduction. Thus the method for finding truth in all matters is merely to restrict oneself to these two operations.

According to the fourth rule, "By method I mean certain and simple rules, such that if a man observe them accurately, he shall never assume what is false as true . . . but will always gradually increase his knowledge and so arrive at a true understanding of all that does not surpass his powers." The remaining sixteen rules are devoted to the elaboration of these principles or to showing their application to mathematical problems. In Descartes's later works he refines these methodological principles, and in the *Meditations* he attempts a metaphysical justification of this type of reasoning.

By 1634 Descartes had written his speculative physics in a work entitled *The World*. Unfortunately, only fragments survive because he suppressed the book when he heard that Galileo's *Dialogue on the Two Great Systems of the Universe* had been condemned by the Catholic Church because of its advocacy of Copernican rather than Ptolemaic astronomy. Descartes also espoused the Copernican theory that the earth is not the center of the universe but revolves about the sun. His fear of censure, however, led him to withdraw his work. In 1634 he also wrote the brief *Treatise on Man*, which attempted to explain human physiology on mechanistic principles.

"Discourse" and "Meditations"

In 1637 Descartes finished *Discourse on Method*, which was published together with three minor works on geometry, dioptrics, and meteors. This work is significant for several reasons. It is written in French and directed to men of good sense rather than professional philosophers. It is autobiographical and begins with a personal account of his education as an example of the

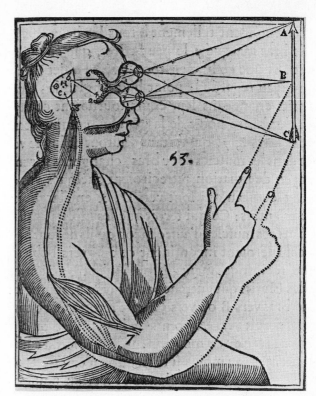

Diagram illustrating perception of movement, a woodcut from a 1664 edition of Descartes's Treatise on Man. *Descartes attempted to describe all physical activity in purely mechanistic terms. (National Library of Medicine, Bethesda, Md.)*

need for a new method of conducting inquiry.

The work contains Descartes's vision of a unity of science based on a common methodology, and it shows that this method can be applied to general philosophic questions. In brief, the method is a sophistication of the earlier *Rules for the Direction of the Mind*. In the *Discourse* Descartes presents four general rules for reducing any problem to its fundamentals by analysis and then constructing solutions by general synthesis.

Meditations on First Philosophy appeared in 1641–1642 together with six (later seven) sets of objections by distinguished thinkers including Thomas Hobbes, Antoine Arnauld, and Pierre Gassendi and the author's replies. The *Meditations* is Descartes's major work and is one of the seminal books in the history of philosophy. While his former works were concerned with elaborating a methodology, this work represents the systematic application of those rules to the principal problems of philosophy: the refutation of skepticism, the existence of the human soul, the nature of God, the metaphysical basis of truth, the extent of man's knowledge of the external world, and the relation between body and soul.

The first meditation is an exercise in methodological skepticism. Descartes states that doubt is a positive means of ascertaining whether there is any certain foundation for knowledge. All knowledge originates either from the senses or from the mind. Examples of color blindness, objects seen in perspective, and so on testify to the distortions inherent in vague sense perception. The recognition of these phenomena as distorted suggests a class of clear perceptions which are more difficult to doubt. But Descartes then points out that such images appear as clear to man in dreams as in an awakened state. Therefore all sensory experience is doubtful because sense data in itself does not indicate whether an object is seen or imagined, true or false.

What about the realm of pure ideas? Descartes simplifies the argument by asking whether it is possible to doubt the fundamental propositions of arithmetic and geometry. Man cannot doubt that two plus two equals four, but he may suspect that this statement has no reality apart from his mind. The standard of truth is the self-evidence of clear and distinct ideas, but the question remains of the correspondence of such ideas to reality. Descartes imagines the existence of an all-powerful "evil genius" who deceives man as to the content of his ideas, so that in reality two plus two equals five.

The second meditation resolves these skeptical issues in a deceptively simple manner by arguing that even if it is doubtful whether sense images or ideas have objects, it is absolutely true that man's mind exists. The famous formula "I think, therefore, I am" is true even if everything else is false. Descartes's solution is known as subjectivism, and it is a radical reversal of previous theories of knowledge. Whereas nature had been assumed to be the cause of man's images and ideas, Descartes states that man is a "thinking thing" whose subjective images and ideas are the sole evidence for the existence of a world.

The third meditation demonstrates that God is "no deceiver," and hence clear and distinct ideas must have objects that exactly and actually correspond to them. Descartes argues that the idea of God is an effect. But an effect gets its reality from its cause, and a cause can only produce what it possesses. Hence either Descartes is a perfect being or God exists as the cause of the idea of God.

The fourth meditation deals with the problem of human error: insofar as man restricts himself to clear and distinct ideas, he will never err. With this connection between ideas and objects Descartes can emerge from his doubts about knowledge. The external world can be known with absolute certainty insofar as it is reducible to clear and distinct ideas. Thus the fifth meditation shows the application of methodology to material reality in its quantifiable dimensions, that is, to the extent to which material reality can be "the object of pure mathematics."

The sixth, and final, meditation attempts to explain the relation between the human soul and the body. Since Descartes believed in mechanism, there could be no absolute connection between a free soul and a bodily machine. After considerable hesitation he expresses the relation between mind and matter as a "felt union." The body is the active faculty that produces the passive images and imaginings man finds in his mind. Actually Descartes's explanation is logically impossible in terms of the "subjective" separation of mind; similarly, the unresolved dualism of the "felt union" violates the principle of assenting only to clear and distinct ideas.

The remainder of Descartes's career was spent in defending his controversial positions. In 1644 he published the *Principles of Philosophy*, which breaks down the arguments of the *Meditations* into propositional form and presents extra arguments dealing with their scientific application. In 1649 Descartes accepted an invitation from Queen Christina of Sweden to become her teacher. There he wrote *The Passions of the Soul*, which is a defense of the mind-body dualism and a mechanistic explanation of the passions. But Descartes's health was undermined by the severity of the northern climate, and after a brief illness he died in Stockholm in 1650.

Further Reading

René Descartes is listed in the Philosophy study guide (IV, A), the Science study guide (IV, A, 2), and the Social Sciences study guide (IV, C, 2). Other 17th-century rationalists were Gottfried Wilhelm von LEIBNIZ and Baruch SPINOZA.

The most complete edition of Descartes's works in English is *The Philosophical Works of Descartes*, translated by Elizabeth S. Haldane and G. T. R. Ross (2 vols., 1955), although many editions of individual works in new translations are available in paperback. The standard biography is Haldane's *Descartes: His Life and Times* (1905; repr. 1966). The best general introductions to Descartes's philosophy are A. Boyce Gibson, *The Philosophy of Descartes* (1932); Stanley V. Keeling, *Descartes* (1934; 2d ed. 1968); and Albert G. A. Balz, *Descartes and the Modern Mind* (1952). Works on specialized topics of an analytic or critical nature include Norman Kemp Smith, *Studies in the Cartesian Philosophy* (1902) and *New Studies in the Philosophy of Descartes: Descartes as Pioneer* (1952); Jacques Maritain, *Three Reformers: Luther, Descartes, Rousseau* (trans. 1928) and *The Dream of Descartes* (trans. 1944); and Leslie J. Beck, *The Method of Descartes: A Study of the Regulae* (1952).

DESIDERIO DA SETTIGNANO
/ By Eleanor Dodge Barton

The short working career of the Italian sculptor Desiderio da Settignano (1428/1431–1464) was entirely centered in Florence. He was one of the most sensitive carvers of marble, especially in his images of children, in the history of this medium.

Desiderio da Settignano (pronounced dā-sē-dâ′ryō dä sät-tē-nyä′nō) was born in Settignano, the youngest of three sons of a mason, Bartolommeo di Francesco. All three sons joined the sculptors' guild in Florence; Desiderio matriculated in 1453. In 1456 Desiderio and his older brother, Gero, rented a studio in Florence. There are few certain details recorded of Desiderio's earlier training and later life. He must have been

Bust of a Lady by Desiderio da Settignano. The marble bust is believed to be a portrait of Isotta da Rimini. (National Gallery of Art, Washington, D.C., Samuel H. Kress Collection)

subtle variations of expression, type, and design give such traditional themes as the Madonna and Child or youthful angels a new grace and humanity.

Further Reading

Desiderio da Settignano is listed in the Art study guide (III, B, 2). The influence of DONATELLO on him was significant.

The quality of Desiderio's sculpture can be appreciated in Clarence Kennedy's sensitive photographs in *Studies in the History and Criticism of Sculpture*, vol. 5: *The Tabernacle of the Sacrament*, by Desiderio da Settignano (1929). Both John Pope-Hennessy, *Introduction to Italian Sculpture*, vol. 2: *Italian Renaissance Sculpture* (1958); and Charles Seymour, Jr., *Sculpture in Italy: 1400–1500* (1966), include important critical estimates of Desiderio's work.

DE SMET / By Donald K. Gorrell

The Belgian Jesuit priest Pierre Jean De Smet (1801–1873) was a pioneer Roman Catholic missionary among the American Indians west of the Mississippi River.

influenced by Donatello, but scholars now believe that Desiderio's actual training was under Bernardo Rossellino, with whom he may have worked on the tomb of Beata Villana in S. Maria Novella before 1451.

Desiderio must have had an established reputation by 1453, since he was then awarded the important commission for the tomb of the humanist scholar and state chancellor of Florence, Carlo Marsuppini, in Sta Croce. The date of completion of this monument is not known, nor is it certain when Desiderio began his second major project, the *Tabernacle of the Sacrament* in S. Lorenzo, but this was surely in place by 1461. The charming frieze of *putti* heads on the exterior of the Pazzi Chapel was probably completed in 1461. According to Giorgio Vasari, Desiderio's last work was the painted wooden statue of St. Mary Magdalene, left unfinished and completed by Benedetto da Maiano after Desiderio's death in 1464.

From the outset Desiderio's talent was distinct, assured, and very rare. His Marsuppini tomb, planned to balance Bernardo Rossellino's tomb of Leonardo Bruni on the opposite wall of Sta Croce, is at once a harmonious counterpart to its model and an independent achievement, animating and enriching the sober, dignified characterization of the deceased with the grace notes of an ornamental setting in which every detail is chiseled with an incomparable combination of featherlike delicacy and prismatic precision and strength.

The same seemingly effortless ease controls the astonishing inventions of Desiderio's *Tabernacle of the Sacrament* and invests his smaller separate reliefs and images, whether of the infant Christ Child or the aged St. Jerome, with a serene radiance that never degenerates into sentimentality and is never reduced to a formula. His

Pierre Jean De Smet (pronounced də smĕt′) was born at Termonde on Jan. 30, 1801. At the age of 14 he entered the seminary at Malines. On Sept. 21, 1821, he arrived in the United States to enter the novitiate of the Jesuit order at White Marsh in Maryland. Two years later he was a member of a group that traveled overland to St. Louis whose purpose was to establish a new novitiate in the West. At his ordination as priest in 1827 he expected assignment as missionary among the Indians, but other pastoral assignments and serious illness delayed his dream for another decade.

Father De Smet's long missionary work among the American Indians began in 1838, when he was sent among the Potawatomi Indians to found a mission. On this journey he began to keep the journals and write the long letters that were published later in book form and became the literary basis for his reputation. In 1840 he set out on the first of several long expeditions across the Northwest to evaluate the possibilities for missions among the Flathead and Nez Percé Indians in the Oregon country.

During 1841–1842 Father De Smet returned to Oregon, explored more of the territory, and established several missions. Finding that Canadian priests had already begun work in the Willamette Valley, he agreed to collaborate with them in extending the system of Catholic missions. He traveled to New Orleans and eastern cities and then went to six countries in Europe to solicit badly needed funds and personnel in 1843. Father De Smet returned directly to Oregon with several priests, nuns, and supplies the next year by sailing around Cape Horn. In future years he made many journeys through the

Pierre Jean De Smet. (Library of Congress)

West; he eventually crossed the Atlantic 19 times.

The entire region from St. Louis to the Pacific Northwest became his domain. Father De Smet was the leading "black robe" (Jesuit) to the Indians, and he was so respected that he was the only white man trusted by them. In turn, he loved the Indians and sought to keep white traders, settlers, or government agents from abusing them. Both the U.S. government and Indian tribes used him as mediator. He was especially important in this regard in 1851 at Ft. Laramie and in the Yakima War (1858–1859); he also undertook a number of peace missions to the Sioux. Eventually, he came to distrust government dealings with the Indians as much as he had earlier deplored Protestant missionary efforts among them.

Father De Smet's superiors increasingly recognized his appeal and thrust him into the work of propagandist and fund raiser for the Indian missionary work. Not as happy doing this as when working among the Indians, he nevertheless served faithfully until his health failed. He died at St. Louis on May 23, 1873.

Further Reading

Pierre Jean De Smet is listed in the Religion study guide (I, Q, 2, b). Like him, Isaac Thomas HECKER helped to forge a strong Roman Catholic movement in the United States.

The best biography of De Smet is John Upton Terrell's well-written *Black Robe: The Life of Pierre-Jean De Smet: Missionary, Explorer, and Pioneer* (1964). *Life, Letters and Travels of Father Pierre-Jean De Smet*, edited by Hiram Martin Chittenden and Alfred Talbot Richardson (4 vols., 1905), is the basic source, containing nearly all the missionary's published materials.

✳　　✳　　✳

DE SOTO / By William R. Gillaspie

The Spanish conqueror and explorer Hernando de Soto (1500–1542) participated in the conquest of Peru, explored the southeastern part of the United States, and was the first white man to cross the Mississippi River.

Hernando de Soto (pronounced dĕ sō′tō) was born at Jerez de los Caballeros in the province of Estremadura. Although of noble lineage, he was without wealth. "With only a sword and shield" he accompanied Pedrarias when the latter assumed his post as governor of Darien (Caribbean side of the Isthmus of Panama and Colombia). As Pedrarias's lieutenant, De Soto explored the area encompassing modern Costa Rica, Nicaragua, and Honduras in the 1520s.

Sailing from Nicaragua in 1531, De Soto joined Francisco Pizarro in the conquest of Peru, emerging from the conquest with a reputation as a skilled horseman and "one of the four bravest captains who had gone to the West Indies." With a fortune of 100,000 pesos in gold, De Soto returned to Spain in 1536, where Emperor Charles V rewarded his exploits by appointing him governor of Cuba and *adelantado* of Florida. As *adelantado*, he was commissioned to conquer and colonize, at his own expense, the entire region which is now the southern part of the United States.

De Soto returned to Cuba in 1538, where he assumed the governorship and prepared for his expedition to Florida. Hoping to find another Peru, De Soto and 620 men

Hernando de Soto. (Cifra Grafica)

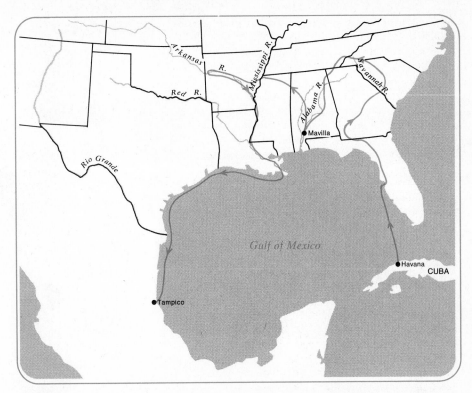

De Soto's expedition, 1539–1542. Hoping to duplicate Francisco Pizarro's exploits in Peru, De Soto wandered for 3 years through what is now the southeastern United States without finding an advanced Indian civilization. He and his men were probably the first white men to see the Mississippi River.

landed south of Tampa Bay on May 30, 1539. A reconnaissance party returned with Juan Ortiz, a survivor of the earlier ill-fated Narváez expedition, who had lived among the Indians for 12 years. With Ortiz acting as interpreter, De Soto began a 3-year journey in search of treasure and an advanced Indian population. Marching up the west coast of Florida, he wintered near the present site of Tallahassee. In the spring of 1540 De Soto resumed the march through Georgia. At the Savannah River he met an Indian chieftainess who offered him a long string of pearls and told him more could be found in nearby burial grounds. After collecting 350 pounds of pearls, the expedition continued northward into what is present-day South and North Carolina, across the Smoky Mountains into Tennessee, and southward into Georgia and Alabama. Their severest battle with Indians, which resulted in heavy casualties and loss of the pearls, occurred in southeastern Alabama at a large town called Mavilla.

De Soto set out once again to the northwest into northern Mississippi. In May 1541 he sighted the Mississippi River south of Memphis. After crossing the Mississippi he explored Arkansas and established his winter quarters near the present site of Fort Smith. Now resolved to return to the sea, he reached the mouth of the Arkansas River, where he died of fever on May 21, 1542.

De Soto's men wrapped his body in mantles packed with sand and cast it into the river. The 311 survivors, under Luis de Moscoso, built seven brigantines, floated down the Mississippi, and coasted along the Gulf shore until they reached Tampico, Mexico, on Sept. 10, 1543.

Further Reading

Hernando de Soto is listed in the Geography and Ex-

ploration study guide (III, A, 4, c). Pánfilo de NARVÁEZ preceded him in the exploration of much of the American Southeast.

The most recent sources on De Soto are Garcilaso de la Vega, *The Florida of the Inca*, edited by John G. and Jeannette J. Varner (trans. 1951), and James A. Robertson, ed., *True Relation of the Hardships Suffered by Governor Fernando de Soto and Certain Portuguese Gentlemen during the Discovery of the Province of Florida* (trans., 2 vols., 1932–1933). Accounts of De Soto's career can be found in Woodbury Lowery, *The Spanish Settlements within the Present Limits of the United States, 1513–1561* (1901); Edward G. Bourne, *Spain in America, 1450–1580* (1904); and Herbert E. Bolton, *The Spanish Borderlands: A Chronicle of Old Florida and the Southwest* (1921).

✳ ✳ ✳

DESSALINES / By Bleecker Dee

Jean Jacques Dessalines (1758–1806) was a Haitian nationalist and the first ruler of a free Haiti. Although he was a courageous military leader during the war of independence, he failed as administrator and statesman.

There is little detailed information on the exact origins of Jean Jacques Dessalines (pronounced dā-sà-lēn′). Like the first great Haitian leader, Pierre Dominique Toussaint L'Ouverture, Dessalines was black and born into slavery in northern Haiti. Unlike Toussaint, he remained illiterate all his life.

In the turbulent decade between the great slave revolt of 1791 and final independence on Jan. 1, 1804, Dessalines was one of Toussaint's principal lieutenants. During the period when Toussaint was operating against the mulattoes in southern Saint Domingue (later Haiti), Dessalines captured Jacmel, one of their main strongpoints, and followed up his campaign by exterminating the survivors. This ferociousness marked Dessalines throughout his career.

When Napoleon sent his brother-in-law, Captain General Charles Leclerc, to return the colony to slavery, Dessalines was the commander of the important port city of Saint-Marc. Many generals defected but not Dessalines. He and Toussaint retreated into the interior, where in March 1802 Dessalines was finally overwhelmed in the battle of Crête-à-Pierrot.

After Toussaint was captured and spirited away to France, Dessalines emerged as the principal figure of the Haitian war of independence. Gen. Leclerc's forces had taken heavy casualties in the campaigns against the armies of ex-slaves and were now trying to cope with guerrilla tactics and, at the same time, with yellow fever. Leclerc died of the disease in November 1802. A year later Dessalines defeated Leclerc's successor, Governor General Rochambeau, in the battle of Vertieres, near the present city of Cap-Haitien.

Haitian Independence

On Jan. 1, 1804, Dessalines proclaimed Haitian independence at Gonaïves. Unfortunately for Haiti, Dessalines's qualities of personal courage were not matched by desperately needed tolerance, statesmanship, and magnanimity. He had himself named governor general for life, with the right to choose a successor, following this by crowning himself Emperor Jean Jacques I, but without creating a nobility. In his own words: "Moi seul, je suis noble" (Only I am noble).

His hatred of whites continued after Haitian independence, and he methodically butchered any white Frenchman he could find. Obsessed with fear of French reconquest, he drained off great amounts of energy and money to maintain a large standing army and to build a series of forts.

Dessalines faced the task of rebuilding a shattered agricultural, labor-intensive economy the only way he knew—by order and discipline. A citizen was either a laborer or a soldier. Prosperity of a sort was restored but at the price of personal freedom and without the superb administration which Henri Christophe's regime would soon have in the north. Though the lower classes grudgingly accepted his decrees, the mulattoes, many of whom were longtime landholders and people of education and position, refused to bow to his increasingly harsh demands. Jean Jacques I was assassinated in an ambush near Port-au-Prince on Oct. 17, 1806.

Further Reading

Jean Jacques Dessalines is listed in the Latin America

Jean Jacques Dessalines, an engraving in the Bibliothèque Nationale, Paris. (Photo-Hachette)

study guide (III, A). Also instrumental in the winning of independence for Haiti were Henri CHRISTOPHE and Pierre Dominique TOUSSAINT L'OUVERTURE.

An excellent source on Haitian history and personalities is James G. Leyburn, *The Haitian People* (1941; rev. ed 1966). Other useful works include C. L. R. James, *The Black Jacobins* (1938; 2d ed. 1963); Ludwell Lee Montague, *Haiti and the United States, 1714–1938* (1940); Selden Rodman, *Haiti: The Black Republic* (1954); and Charles Moran, *Black Triumvirate* (1957).

DETT / By Vivian F. McBrier

A black American composer, conductor, and music educator, Robert Nathaniel Dett (1882–1943) elevated the Negro folk spiritual into an art form.

Robert Dett was born in Ontario, Canada, on Oct. 11, 1882, the youngest of four children of educated and musically talented parents. In 1893 the family moved to Niagara Falls, N.Y., where they operated a tourist home.

Dett studied piano in childhood and composed several pieces, but his serious music training began in 1901 on entering Halstead Conservatory, Brockport, N.Y. In 1903 he enrolled at the Oberlin Conservatory of Music, graduating in 1908 with a bachelor of music degree.

Dett began teaching in 1908 at Lane College, Jackson, Tenn. From 1911 he taught in Lincoln Institute, Jefferson City, Mo. But it was at Hampton Institute, Va., that he made his most significant creative contributions (1913–1932). He organized the Hampton Choral Union to bring the people of the community and Hampton Institute closer together, and the Musical Art Society, which presented one of the country's outstanding college concert programs; and he directed the famous Hampton Institute Choir. He also organized and directed the school of music.

In 1920 Dett studied at Harvard University, winning one prize for his essay, "The Emancipation of Negro Music," and another for the best composition in concerted vocal music, *Don't Be Weary Traveler*. Other honors included an honorary doctor of music degree from Howard University, Washington, D.C., in 1924; an honorary doctor of music degree from Oberlin College in 1926; and the Harmon Award for creative achievement in 1928.

Dett was an idealist who loved humanity and was dedicated to uplifting his race through education. As a teacher, he sought to inspire rather than to dictate. As a choral conductor, he received national and international fame. Critics highly praised the concerts given by the Hampton Institute Choir in New York City, Boston, and Philadelphia. In a 1930 goodwill tour the choir gave concerts in the capitals of seven European countries.

As a composer, Dett was a skillful craftsman in the language and style of the romanticists. He achieved his goal —to give the Negro pride by creating something which would be musically his own yet would bear comparison with other peoples' artistic utterances. His published compositions include 5 piano suites and 12 piano solos, 23 vocal solos, 46 choral works, 2 collections of spirituals (one collection comprising four volumes), an oratorio with orchestral accompaniment, and a violin selection.

Further Reading

Robert Dett is listed in the Music study guide (II, D, 1). William DAWSON was a contemporary black composer.

There is a brief biography of Dett in Wilhelmena S. Robinson, *Historical Negro Biographies* (1968). He is discussed in Maud Cuney-Hare, *Negro Musicians and Their Music* (1936); John P. Davis, ed., *The American Negro Reference Book* (1966); and the *International Library of Negro Life and History*, vol. 5: *The Negro in Music and Art*, compiled by Lindsay Patterson (1967; 2d ed. 1968).

DE VALERA / By Joseph M. Curran

The Irish revolutionary leader and statesman Eamon De Valera (born 1882) served as prime minister and later president of Ireland.

Eamon De Valera (pronounced dĕv-ə-lâr′ə) was born in New York City on Oct. 14, 1882. In 1885, after the death of his Spanish father, he was sent to live with his Irish mother's family in County Limerick. He graduated from the Royal University of Ireland in 1904 and became a mathematics teacher.

De Valera was an ardent supporter of the Irish language revival movement and also became a member of Sinn Fein and the Irish Volunteers. After the failure of the 1916 insurrection, he became the senior surviving rebel leader when his death sentence was commuted because of his American birth. Released by the British government in 1917, he was acclaimed in Ireland as the leader of the revolutionary independence movement. He became president of the Irish Republic established by the separatists after their victory in the election of December 1918. In June 1919 De Valera traveled to the United States, where he won much sympathy and financial support for the Irish cause. He returned to Ireland in December 1920 as the guerrilla war with Britain was moving into its final phase.

De Valera accepted British proposals for a truce in July 1921 and sent a delegation to London to negotiate a peace settlement. The British refused to accept his compromise plan for an Irish republic in external association with the British Empire and offered instead dominion status for Ireland, with the right of exclusion for loyalist Northern Ireland. In December 1921 the Irish delegates accepted these terms, believing them to be the best obtainable without further war. De Valera, however, denounced the treaty as a betrayal of the republic which would mean continued subjection to Britain. Despite his protests the Republican Parliament, Dail Eireann, approved the treaty by a small majority in January 1922. Continued dispute over the settlement led to civil war in June 1922, and supporters of the new Irish Free State defeated the Republicans in May 1923.

Prime Minister

After the civil war De Valera led the Republican opposition to the pro-treaty government of William T. Cos-

Eamon De Valera in 1932. (United Press International Photo)

grave. In 1926 he broke with the extreme Republicans and founded a constitutional opposition party, Fianna Fail, which entered the Dail in 1927. Fianna Fail won the 1932 election, and De Valera formed a government which lasted for 16 years.

As prime minister, he removed the last remaining restrictions on Irish sovereignty imposed by the treaty. His refusal to continue payment of land-purchase annuities to Britain led to an economic war between the two countries, which enabled him to pursue plans to make Ireland more self-sufficient economically. His government also extended social services, suppressed extremist threats to the state, and introduced a constitution in 1937 which made the Free State a republic in all but name. In 1938 agreements made with Britain ended the economic war and British occupation of Irish naval bases retained under the treaty. De Valera was unable, however, to end the partition of Ireland.

De Valera had been a strong supporter of collective security through the League of Nations, but he maintained a policy of neutrality, with overwhelming popular support, throughout World War II. In the postwar period Fianna Fail alternated in power with two interparty governments, the first of which formally established the Irish Republic in 1949. Returned to office with a decisive majority in 1957, De Valera retired from active politics in 1959, when he was elected president of the republic. He was reelected in 1966, the fiftieth anniversary of his entry into Irish political life. Failing eyesight troubled him from the 1930s onward and left him almost blind before his retirement from active politics.

The wisdom of De Valera's policies has been widely disputed but not his unequaled impact on Irish life in the 20th century. The charismatic appeal of "Dev" was firmly based on his understanding of the outlook and way of life of a large section of the Irish people and on his countrymen's great respect for his ability, austere dignity, and idealism.

Further Reading

Eamon De Valera is listed in the European History study guide (XI, B, 1). Among his colleagues was Michael COLLINS.

The most complete biography is *Eamon de Valera* (1970) by the Earl of Longford and Thomas P. O'Neill, written with the full cooperation of the subject. A three-volume biography in the Irish language by O'Neill and others is in process of completion. Background histories of Ireland include Timothy Patrick Coogan, *Ireland since the Rising* (1966); Desmond Williams, ed., *The Irish Struggle, 1916–1926* (1966); and T. W. Moody and F. K. Martin, eds., *The Course of Irish History* (1967).

DEW / By Thomas Wagstaff

Thomas Roderick Dew (1802–1846), one of the earliest and ablest defenders in America of Negro slavery, articulated the proslavery argument that dominated the Southern mind during the 30 years before the Civil War.

Thomas Dew, the son of a wealthy planter, was born in King and Queen County, Va., on Dec. 5, 1802. He graduated from William and Mary College, and, after traveling in Europe and studying in Germany, he took the chair of political law at William and Mary in 1827. His major scholarly interest was political economy, and most of his published writings were in that field. In 1832 he became president of William and Mary, a post he held until his death in 1846.

In 1831 the bloody Nat Turner slave rebellion in Southampton County, Va., sparked the most intense critical discussion of slavery in the antebellum South. The Virginia Legislature vigorously debated the subject of slavery for a year, and motions for its abolition were only narrowly defeated. Prior to this, Southern intellectuals, following the lead of Thomas Jefferson, had generally treated slavery as a necessary evil, to be tolerated only until the problem of dealing with an unassimilable free black population could be resolved. Many Southerners were adherents of the American Colonization Society, which advocated gradual emancipation and colonization of freed blacks in Africa; this proposal figured prominently in the Virginia debate.

Dew had first contributed to the sectional controversy by publishing *Lectures on the Restrictive System* (1829), attacking the protective tariff. Now, in his *Review of the Debate in the Virginia Legislature of 1831–1832* he argued that colonization was economically impossible. He stated that the South's only alternatives were abolition, with the free blacks remaining and becoming "the most worthless and indolent of . . . citizens," or a continuation of slavery. He advocated the second course, strongly defending slavery on historical, economic, and theological grounds. He concluded, "It is the order of nature and of God that the being of superior faculties and knowledge should control and dispose of those who are inferior."

Dew's theories, developed and expanded, became staples of the proslavery argument that dominated the South politically for the following decades, finally generating the secession movement and the Civil War. Dew contracted pneumonia while on a trip and died in Paris on Aug. 6, 1846.

Further Reading

Thomas Dew is listed in the American History study guide (V, F, 3, h; VI, F, 3, d). John C. CALHOUN was the South's other prominent defender of slavery.

There is no biography of Dew. Most general works on the history of the South and the Civil War note his work. The most useful treatments are in William E. Dodd, *The Cotton Kingdom* (1919), and William Sumner Jenkins, *Pro-slavery Thought in the Old South* (1935). His college career is treated in Herbert B. Adams, *The College of William and Mary* (1887).

G. **DEWEY** / By Graham A. Cosmas

American naval officer George Dewey (1837–1917) was the celebrated victor of the Battle of Manila Bay in the Philippines during the Spanish-American War.

George Dewey was born on Dec. 26, 1837, in Montpelier, Vt. After attending the local public schools and a private military academy, he entered the U.S. Naval Academy at Annapolis, graduating third in his class in 1858. He entered active service with the rank of lieutenant.

During the Civil War, Dewey saw hard combat at New Orleans, the opening of the Mississippi River, and the capture of Ft. Fisher. At war's end he had the rank of lieutenant commander and the respect of superiors who controlled his professional destiny.

During the 1870s and the early 1880s Dewey held routine assignments. As chief of the Bureau of Equipment and then as president of the Board of Inspection and Survey, between 1889 and 1897 Dewey played an important part in the construction of the new fleet of armored, steam-propelled steel warships.

In October 1897 with the backing of Assistant Secretary of the Navy Theodore Roosevelt, Dewey, now a commodore, was assigned to command the fleet's Asiatic squadron. Anticipating war with Spain, Roosevelt wanted an able officer who could aggressively carry out a plan for an attack on Manila, capital of the Spanish-held Philippines.

George Dewey. (Library of Congress)

When Congress declared war in late April 1898, Dewey sailed for Manila with six light cruisers and an assortment of auxiliary vessels. On May 1, after a daring night run past the batteries guarding the harbor entrance, he attacked a Spanish squadron in Manila Bay that was similar in strength and composition to his own. When the firing ended, Dewey's force, without losing one man or ship, had sunk or set afire every Spanish vessel. This one-sided victory paved the way for the American conquest of the Philippines, and it transformed the obscure naval officer into a popular hero who was rewarded with parades, banquets, and triumphal arches upon his return to the United States.

Dewey's first wife had died in childbirth in 1872, and in 1899 he married Mrs. Mildred McLean Hazen, a longtime friend. A brief Dewey presidential boom flared and fizzled. Promoted to admiral of the Navy, Dewey assumed the presidency of the newly created General Board of the Navy in 1900. During the next 15 years under Dewey's aggressive leadership, the Board became the nation's most influential military planning agency, working out basic war strategy and guiding the enlargement of the fleet. A few weeks before the outbreak of World War I in 1914, Dewey suffered a stroke that removed him from active duty. He died in Washington, D.C., on Jan. 16, 1917.

Further Reading

George Dewey is listed in the American History study guide (VII, D, 3, b). Theodore ROOSEVELT was assistant secretary of the Navy during the Spanish-American war.

The Autobiography of George Dewey covers his career to 1899. The most thorough biography is in Richard S. West, Jr., *Admirals of American Empire* (1948). A full-length study is Laurin Hall Healy and Luis Kutner, *The Admiral* (1944). For the Manila campaign see French Ensor Chadwick, *The Relations of the United States and Spain: The Spanish-American War* (2 vols., 1911). John A. S. Grenville and George Berkeley Young, *Politics, Strategy, and American Diplomacy* (1966), contains new information on Manila and on Dewey's work with the General Board.

J. **DEWEY** / By Robert W. McAhren

During the first half of the 20th century, John Dewey (1859–1952) was America's most famous exponent of a pragmatic philosophy that celebrated the traditional values of democracy and the efficacy of reason and universal education.

Born on Oct. 20, 1859, in Burlington, Vt., John Dewey came of old New England stock. His father was a local merchant who loved literature. His mother, swayed by revivals to convert to Congrega-

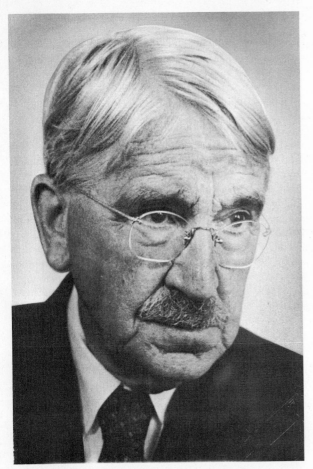

John Dewey. (Columbia University, Office of Public Information)

tionalism, possessed a stern moral sense. The community, situated at the economic crossroads of the state, was the home of the state university and possessed a cosmopolitan atmosphere unusual for northern New England. Nearby Irish and French-Canadian settlements acquainted John with other cultures. Boyhood jobs delivering newspapers and working at a lumberyard further extended his knowledge. In 1864, on a visit to see his father in the Union Army in Virginia, he viewed firsthand the devastating effects of the Civil War.

Educational Career

Dewey's career in Vermont public schools was unremarkable. At the age of 15 he entered the University of Vermont. He found little of interest in academic work; his best grades were in science, and later he would regard science as the highest manifestation of human intellect. Dewey himself attributed his "intellectual awakening" to T. H. Huxley's college textbook on physiology, which shaped his vision of man as entirely the product of natural evolutionary processes.

Dewey later remembered coming in touch with the world of ideas during his senior year. Courses on psychology, religion, ethics, logic, and economics supplanted his earlier training in languages and science. His

teacher, H. A. P. Torrey, introduced him to Immanuel Kant, but Dewey found it difficult to accept the Kantian idea that there was a realm of knowledge transcending empirical demonstration. Dewey also absorbed Auguste Comte's emphasis on the disintegrative effects of extreme individualism. The quality of his academic work improved and, at the age of 19, he graduated Phi Beta Kappa and second in his class of 18.

Dewey hoped to teach high school. After a frustrating summer of job hunting, his cousin, principal of a seminary in Pennsylvania, came to his rescue. For 2 years Dewey taught the classics, algebra, and science, meanwhile reading philosophy. When his cousin resigned, however, Dewey's employment ended. He returned to Vermont to become the sole teacher in a private school in Charlotte, near his alma mater. He renewed acquaintance with Torrey, and the two discussed the fruits of Dewey's reading in ancient and modern philosophy.

Intellectual Development

At this time most American teachers of philosophy were ordained clergymen who tended to subordinate philosophical speculation to theological orthodoxy. Philosophy was in the hands of laymen in only a few schools. One such school was in St. Louis, where William T. Harris established the *Journal of Speculative Philosophy*. Here Dewey published his first scholarly effort. Finally, Dewey decided to pursue a career in philosophy and applied for admission to the newly founded Johns Hopkins University, another haven for lay philosophers.

At Johns Hopkins in 1882 Dewey studied with George S. Morris, who was on leave as chairman of the philosophy department at the University of Michigan. Under Morris's direction Dewey studied Hegel, whose all-encompassing philosophical system temporarily satisfied Dewey's longing to escape from the dualisms of traditional philosophy. In 1884 Dewey completed his doctorate and, at Morris's invitation, went to teach at Michigan.

In Ann Arbor, Dewey met and married Alice Chipman. His interests turned toward problems of education as he traveled about the state to evaluate college preparatory courses. His concern for social problems deepened, and he adopted a vague brand of socialism, although he was unacquainted with Marxism. He still taught Sunday school, but he was drifting away from religious orthodoxy. In 1888 he accepted an appointment at the University of Minnesota, only to return to Michigan a year later to the post left vacant by Morris's death.

The next stage in Dewey's intellectual development came with his reading of William James's *Principles of Psychology*. Dewey rapidly shed Hegelianism in favor of "instrumentalism," a position that holds that thinking is an activity which, at its best, is directed toward resolving problems rather than creating abstract metaphysical systems.

In 1894 Dewey moved to the University of Chicago as head of a new department of philosophy, psychology, and pedagogy. Outside the academic world he became friends with the social reformers at Hull House. He also admired Henry George's analysis of the problems of poverty. To test his educational theories, he started an experimental school, with his wife as principal. The "Dewey school," however, caused a struggle between its founder and the university's president, William R. Harper. In 1904, when Harper tried to remove Mrs. Dewey, her husband resigned in protest. An old friend of Dewey's engineered an offer from Columbia University, where Dewey spent the rest of his teaching years. His colleagues, some of the most fertile minds in modern America, included Charles A. Beard and James Harvey Robinson.

Peak of His Influence

Living in New York City placed the Deweys at the center of America's cultural and political life. Dewey pursued his scholarship, actively supported the Progressive party, and, in 1929, helped organize the League for Independent Political Action to further the cause of a new party. He also served as a contributing editor of the *New Republic* magazine and helped found both the American Civil Liberties Union and the American Association of University Professors. After World War I, reaching the peak of his influence, he became a worldwide traveler, lecturing in Japan at the Imperial Institute and spending 2 years teaching at the Chinese universities of Peking and Nanking. In 1924 he went to study the schools in Turkey and 2 years later visited the University of Mexico. His praise for the Russian educational system he inspected on a 1928 trip to the Soviet Union earned him much criticism.

As a teacher, Dewey exhibited the distracted air of a man who had learned to concentrate in a home inhabited by five young children. Careless about his appearance, shy and quiet in manner, he sometimes put his students to sleep, but those who managed to focus their attention could watch a man fascinated with ideas actually creating a philosophy in his classroom.

In 1930 Dewey retired from teaching. A year earlier, national luminaries had used the occasion of his seventieth birthday to hail his accomplishments; such celebrations would be repeated on his eightieth and ninetieth birthdays. He continued to publish works clarifying his philosophy. In public affairs he was one of the first to warn of the dangers from Hitler's Germany and of the Japanese threat in the Far East. In 1937 he traveled to Mexico as chairman of the commission to determine the validity of Soviet charges against Trotsky. His first wife having died in 1927, Dewey, at the ripe age of 87, married a widow, Mrs. Roberta Grant. In the early years of the cold war Dewey's support of American intervention in Korea earned him criticism from the U.S.S.R. newspaper *Pravda*. He died on June 1, 1952.

Dewey's Philosophy

In his philosophy Dewey sought to transcend what he considered the misleading distinctions made by other philosophers. By focusing on experience, he bridged the gulf between the organism and its environment to emphasize their interaction. He rejected the dualism of spirit versus matter, insisting that the mind was a product of

evolution, not some infusion from a superior being. Yet he avoided the materialist conclusion which made thought seem accidental and irrelevant. While he saw most of man's behavior as shaped by habit, he believed that the unceasing processes of change often produced conditions which customary mental activity could not explain. The resulting tension led to creative thinking in which man tried to reestablish control of the unstable environment. Thought was never, for Dewey, merely introspection; rather, it was part of a process whereby man related to his surroundings. Dewey believed that universal education could train men to break through habit into creative thought.

Dewey was convinced that democracy was the best form of government. He saw contemporary American democracy challenged by the effects of the industrial revolution, which had produced an overconcentration of wealth in the hands of a few men. This threat, he believed, could be met by the right kind of education.

The "progressive education" movement of the 1920s was an effort to implement Dewey's pedagogical ideas. Because his educational theory emphasized the classroom as a place for students to encounter the "present," his interpreters tended to play down traditional curricular concerns with the "irrelevant" past or occupational future. His influence on American schools was so pervasive that many critics (then and later) assailed his ideas as the cause of all that they found wrong with American education.

Philosophical Works

To the year of his death Dewey remained a prolific writer. Couched in a difficult prose style, his published works number over 300. Some of the most important works include *Outlines of a Critical Theory of Ethics* (1891), *The Study of Ethics* (1894), *The School and Society* (1899), *Studies in Logical Theory* (1903), *How We Think* (1910), *The Influence of Darwin on Philosophy and Other Essays in Contemporary Thought* (1910), *German Philosophy and Politics* (1915), *Democracy and Education* (1916), *Reconstruction in Philosophy* (1920), *Human Nature and Conduct* (1922), *Experience and Nature* (1925), *The Public and Its Problems* (1927), *The Quest for Certainty* (1929), *Individualism Old and New* (1930), *Philosophy and Civilization* (1931), *Art as Experience* (1934), *Liberalism and Social Action* (1935), *Logic: The Theory of Inquiry* (1938), *Freedom and Culture* (1939), *Problems of Men* (1946), and *Knowing and the Known* (1949).

Further Reading

John Dewey is listed in the Social Sciences study guide (VII, F, 3). William JAMES influenced him. A contemporary educational innovator was Robert M. HUTCHINS.

Surprisingly there is no book-length biography of Dewey. The student must rely on articles, including Dewey's autobiographical fragment, "From Absolutism to Experimentalism," in George P. Adams and William Pepperell Montague, eds., *Contemporary American Philosophy: Personal Statements* (1930). His daughters compiled an authoritative sketch of his life in Paul Arthur Schilpp, ed., *The Philosophy of John Dewey* (1939), which also contains valuable summaries of aspects of his philosophy.

Indispensable for any examination of Dewey's thought is Sidney Hook, *John Dewey: An Intellectual Portrait* (1939). John E. Smith presents an excellent chapter on Dewey in *The Spirit of American Philosophy* (1963). Paul K. Conkin in *Puritans and Pragmatists: Eight Eminent American Thinkers* (1968) attempts an evaluation of Dewey's place in the context of American ideas. Morton G. White, *Social Thought in America* (1949), considers assumptions common to Dewey and his colleagues in other disciplines. Longer, more challenging treatments of Dewey's ideas are in George R. Geiger, *John Dewey in Perspective* (1958); Robert J. Roth, *John Dewey and Self Realization* (1962); and Richard J. Bernstein, *John Dewey* (1966). See also Jerome Nathanson, *John Dewey: The Reconstruction of the Democratic Life* (1951).

M. DEWEY / By Milton Berman

The American librarian and reformer Melvil Dewey (1851–1931) established the Dewey decimal system of classifying books and played a prominent role in developing professional institutions for librarians.

Melvil Dewey was born in Adams Center, N.Y., on Dec. 10, 1851, the youngest of five children of impoverished parents. His father, a boot maker and keeper of a general store, and his sternly religious mother inculcated principles of hard work and economy in the youth, along with a sense of self-righteousness that marked him throughout his life. He early demonstrated strong mathematical ability and a fascination with systems and classifications. His education was

Melvil Dewey in 1896.
(Library of Congress)

slowed by the need to earn money, and he did not enter Amherst College until he was 19, graduating in 1874.

Dewey worked in the college library during his last 2 years as a student and for the 2 years following his graduation. Although then still attracted to a missionary career, he carried out intensive investigations of other libraries and began to develop his own ideas. His work culminated in 1876, when he published *A Classification and Subject Index for Cataloguing and Arranging the Books and Pamphlets of a Library*. This system, still in use today in most public and some college libraries, was his major contribution to his profession.

Arranging the various fields of knowledge into a logical order and using a decimal system of notation to indicate the arrangement of books, Dewey's system proved easy both for librarians and users to understand, capable of expansion to suit the needs of large as well as small libraries, and applicable to a wide variety of books and ideas. Although he was not the first to come up with the basic idea, his version was both logical and workable. Pushed by Dewey and his students with missionary zeal, it triumphed over its competitors.

In 1876 Dewey left Amherst for Boston, where he founded the Library Bureau and worked for a number of reform movements, including the metric system, temperance, tobacco, and spelling. The spelling of his first name (he was baptized Melville) demonstrates his devotion to the last-mentioned cause. He played a major role in founding the American Library Association in 1876 and served as its secretary (1876–1890) and president (1890–1891, 1892–1893). He edited *Library Journal* (1876–1880) and all through his life contributed to it.

In 1883 Dewey accepted an offer to become librarian of Columbia College and vigorously proceeded to put his ideas into effect, reclassifying and recataloging the library and starting a library school. The zeal with which he applied his ideas was accompanied by a spirit of intolerance of disagreement and tactlessness toward others that aroused controversy and bitter opposition, climaxing in his suspension by the Columbia trustees in 1888. Although exonerated of the charges brought against him, he resigned later that year.

In 1888 Dewey was chosen director of the New York State Library and moved to Albany the following year, taking his library school with him. Again, he plunged into his work, expanding the scope and usefulness of his institution by enlarging its collections and establishing or improving the home education department, the extension division, and the traveling libraries. He helped found the Association of State Libraries in 1890 and was active in its deliberations. Again, his professional competence was counterbalanced by his inability to manage human relationships. Charges of profiting from financial transactions with his students were dismissed, but after he was rebuked by the board for his role in organizing a club at Lake Placid, N.Y., that discriminated against Jews, he resigned as of Jan. 1, 1906.

After leaving Albany, Dewey concentrated on the affairs of his club and a similar venture he began in Florida in 1927. He died of a cerebral hemorrhage on Dec. 26, 1931, in his Florida home.

Further Reading

Melvil Dewey is listed in the Social Sciences study guide (VI, G, 3). Other educators were Booker T. WASH-INGTON, Nicholas Murray BUTLER, and Abbott Lawrence LOWELL.

George Grosvenor Dawe, *Melvil Dewey: Seer, Inspir-er, Doer* (1932), is an uncritical, family-sponsored biography that has many quotations from Dewey's letters and essays. Fremont Rider, *Melvil Dewey* (1944), is shorter and more critical though still favorable to its subject. No convenient collection of Dewey's writings, which are mostly periodical contributions, exists.

T. E. DEWEY / By Norman A. Graebner

Thomas Edmund Dewey (1902–1971) was governor of New York State from 1942 to 1954 and a Republican presidential candidate.

Thomas E. Dewey, photographed during his 1944 presidential campaign. (Library of Congress)

Thomas E. Dewey was born on March 24, 1902, at Owosso, Mich. In 1923 he received his bachelor of arts degree from the University of Michigan. After briefly studying music and law in Chicago, he entered Columbia University Law School. After his graduation in 1925, he toured England and France. Returning to New York, he entered the state bar, accepted a clerkship in a law office, and became active in the Young Republican Club. In 1928 Dewey married Frances E. Hutt; they had two children.

In 1931 the U.S. attorney for the Southern District of New York appointed Dewey his chief assistant. In addition to fundamental honesty and natural courage, Dewey possessed a capacity for careful and deliberate case preparation and an amazing self-control that enabled him to remain cool under pressure. With the resignation of the U.S. attorney in November 1933, Dewey took that position—at 31 the youngest U.S. attorney ever. When President Franklin D. Roosevelt appointed a Democrat to the position 5 weeks later, Dewey returned to private law practice. In 1935 he was appointed special prosecutor for the Investigation of Organized Crime in New York. His campaign against narcotics and vice racketeers obtained 72 convictions in 73 prosecutions. In 1937 he was elected district attorney for New York County.

In 1942 Dewey was elected governor of New York. He quickly established a reputation for political moderation and administrative efficiency, enjoying cordial relations with the legislature. Success as governor, added to his reputation in fighting New York racketeers, sent Dewey's political stature soaring. In 1944 he was the Republican party's presidential nominee. He ran well, despite Roosevelt's record as a war leader and Dewey's lack of experience in international affairs. Reelected governor of New York in 1946, he proceeded to ram a series of liberal laws through the legislature.

As the acknowledged front-runner in his second presidential campaign—against Democrat Harry Truman in 1948—Dewey refused to tax himself, made only a few speeches, avoided controversial issues, and scarcely recognized the opposition. He lost to Truman by a narrow margin. In 1950 he was elected to his third successive term as New York's governor.

At the suggestion of State Department adviser John Foster Dulles, Dewey visited 17 countries in the Pacific in 1951. In 1955 he reentered private practice with the New York firm of Dewey, Ballantine, Bushby, Palmer, and Wood. By 1957 Dewey had been awarded 16 honorary degrees. His books include *The Case against the New Deal* (1940), *Journey to the Far Pacific* (1952), and *Thomas E. Dewey on the Two Party System* (1966). He died on March 16, 1971, at Bal Harbour, Fla.

Further Reading

Thomas E. Dewey is listed in the American History study guide (X, A, 5). He ran for president against Harry TRUMAN.

Writings on Dewey remain limited. Stanley Walker, *Dewey: An American of This Century* (1944), was prepared for Dewey's first presidential campaign. Several good chapters on Dewey's race against Truman are in

Irwin Ross, *The Loneliest Campaign: The Truman Victory of 1948* (1968).

✳   ✳   ✳

DIAGNE / By Irving Leonard Markovitz

Blaise Diagne (1872–1934) was a Senegalese political leader. He was the first black African deputy elected to the French National Assembly and a pioneer of modern African and pan-African politics.

Blaise Diagne (pronounced dē-ä′nyə) was born on the small island of Gorée off the coast of Dakar into a well-to-do Senegalese middle-class family. His family had the political rights of French citizens and were among the Africans who could elect a deputy to the French National Assembly.

In 1914 Diagne was elected to the National Assembly in Paris, defeating six European candidates. On Sept. 29, 1916, he achieved the enactment of a law that bears his name and which reaffirmed the rights of Franco-African citizens at a time when there was a movement in France for their curtailment. In 1917 Diagne was appointed commissioner of the republic and placed in charge of conscription in West Africa. In this post he helped recruit over 180,000 men to fight for France in World War I.

Blaise Diagne. (H. Roger-Viollet)

Reelected deputy by large majorities in 1920 and 1924, Diagne also served as president of the 1919 international Pan-African Congress and cooperated with prominent Americans like W. E. B. Du Bois and Marcus Garvey.

In his first election manifesto Diagne told his followers that "your adversaries tremble at the idea of your political and social awakening." However, he sought his alliances with the various traditional elites and sought to reach the "masses" only indirectly. Diagne also bettered the status of Senegalese troops, giving them a sense of self-importance that persisted to independent Senegal's army.

Yet, as time passed, Diagne increasingly not only explicitly cast aside independence and even self-government as legitimate goals but defended every major aspect of the colonial system, including forced labor. By completely assimilating the cultural and political values of France and by acquiring positions of wealth and eminence, Diagne considered himself to be the personification and justification of French colonialism. He went on to become the first African to hold a high ministerial position in the French government. From June 26, 1931, until Feb. 19, 1932, he was undersecretary of state for the colonies.

While Diagne's first successes marked an important stage in the political evolution of Francophone Africa, new leaders, especially Léopold Senghor, soon rejected the legitimacy of French cultural hegemony.

Further Reading

Blaise Diagne is listed in the Africa study guide (VIII, B, 3). While he was essentially a political conservative, Léopold SENGHOR and Lamine GUEYE represented the nationalistic, anticolonialist Africans. Other pan-Africanists, in English-speaking Africa, were Jomo KENYATTA, Kwame NKRUMAH, and George PADMORE.

The best general background reading available in English on Diagne is Michael Crowder, *Senegal: A Study of French Assimilation Policy* (1962; rev. ed. 1967). See also Ruth S. Morgenthau, *Political Parties in French-Speaking West Africa* (1964), for a history of political development. See also S. O. Mezo and Ram Desai, eds., *Black Leaders of the Centuries* (1970).

✳   ✳   ✳

DIAS / By Eric Axelson

Bartolomeu Dias de Novais (died 1500) was a Portuguese explorer who discovered the Cape of Good Hope and opened the sea route to the Indian Ocean.

It is not known when or where Bartolomeu Dias (pronounced dē′əs) was born, and no information has survived about his early life. He emerged from obscurity only in 1487, when he sailed from Portugal with orders from King John II to continue exploration

The Cape of Good Hope, rounded by Bartolomeu Dias in 1488. (Roger-Viollet)

beyond a landmark raised by Diogo Cão in 1486 on the coast of South-West Africa. The King instructed Dias to discover a sea route to India which bypassed Moslem-dominated routes between the East and Europe and to seek information about the Christian empire of Abyssinia.

Journey of Discovery

In command of two caravels, each of about 100 modern tons, and of a storeship of about double that size, Dias left the Tagus River in August 1487. Beyond the farthest point reached by Cão, Dias made a close coasting. On Jan. 6, 1488, off the Serra dos Reis, in modern South Africa, Dias left the coast and was out of sight of land for 13 days. He steered eastward and found no land so altered course to the north. He closed the coast again opposite a river, the Gouritz of today. The coast ran eastward, and on February 3 he entered and named the bay of São Bras (modern Mossel Bay). Here he took in fresh water and bartered livestock from the local inhabitants, the Khoi-Khoi (Hottentots).

Continuing east, Dias came to a bay which he called Golfo da Roca; it was soon to be known as the Baia da Lagoa, a name subsequently corrupted to Algoa Bay. In this bay the crews verged on mutiny: they protested their shortage of provisions, pointed out that they had reached the extremity of the continent, and urged Dias to turn for home. A council agreed to this course, but Dias won consent to continue for a few more days.

At the end of the stipulated term the caravels reached a river which Dias called the Infante (probably modern Keiskama) after the captain of the second caravel. The coast was running decisively to the northeast, the sea became warmer, and it was clear that the expedition had indeed rounded Africa and reached the Indian Ocean. At the earliest conjunction of suitable site and favorable

weather, at what came later to be called Kwaaihoek, 4 miles west of the Bushman's River, Dias landed and supervised the erection of a *padrão*, a square limestone pillar cut and inscribed in Portugal and surmounted by a block with the Portuguese coat of arms and a cross. It was a landmark, an assertion of Portuguese sovereignty, and a symbol of Christianity. Dedicated to St. Gregory, it was raised on March 12, 1488.

On May 16 Dias gave the name St. Brandon to a cape which soon became known as Agulhas. Dias discovered and named the Cape of Good Hope because, a contemporary recorded, "it gave indication and expectation of the discovery of India." There, on June 6, 1488, he probably raised another *padrão*, dedicated to St. Philip. On Dias Point, west of Lüderitz, on July 25 he raised another *padrão*, dedicated to St. James. The caravels returned to the Tagus in December 1488. Dias had proved the sea route into the Indian Ocean.

Later Career

Dias helped administer the Guinea gold trade until 1494, when King Manuel I appointed him to supervise the construction of two square-rigged ships for Vasco da Gama's expedition. Dias kept the squadron company as far as the Cape Verde Islands, when he turned off to Guinea.

On the return of Vasco da Gama, Manuel dispatched a fleet of 13 vessels under Pedro Álvares Cabral to the Indian Ocean to profit by the discoveries. In the fleet were 4 caravels under Bartolomeu Dias, who was instructed to found a trading station and fortress at the gold-exporting port of Sofala. The expedition left Brazil on May 2, 1500. On May 12 a comet came into view, "a prognostication of the sad event that was to take place," the Portuguese chronicler João de Barros remarked. The comet disappeared on May 23. The next day a sudden storm overwhelmed 4 ships, which sank with all hands; among those lost was Dias.

Further Reading

Bartolomeu Dias is listed in the Geography and Exploration study guide (III, A, 3, a). Vasco da GAMA and Pedro Álvares CABRAL later used the information gathered by Dias to reach India.

Biographical information in English on Dias is scant. Boies Penrose, *Travel and Discovery in the Renaissance* (1955), and J. H. Parry, *The Age of Reconnaisance* (1963), are excellent surveys of European overseas expansion that include mention of Dias. Useful background is provided in Eric Axelson, *South-East Africa, 1488–1530* (1940).

DÍAZ / By Albert L. Michaels

José de la Cruz Porfirio Díaz (1830–1915) was a Mexican general and political leader. During his 34-year, virtually unchallenged rule of Mexico the economy grew and the country remained at peace despite its anachronistic social system.

Latin American countries in the 19th century remained chained to a colonial past with few exceptions. Mexico, one of the Western Hemisphere's most poorly governed states, had suffered more than most. After half a century of independence its economy lay ruined, its people were exhausted by civil war, and over half its territory had been lost to the United States. The autocratic government of Porfirio Díaz (pronounced dē′äs) sought to bring order out of this chaos and to make Mexico into a modern industrialized state. A charismatic and capable leader, he almost succeeded in this protean task, yet finally failed because he gave economic development far too high a priority over social justice.

Porfirio Díaz was born in the southern Mexican state of Oaxaca into a middle-class urban family of mixed Spanish-Indian ancestry. His father, a moderately well-to-do veterinarian and innkeeper, died when Porfirio was only 3 years old. Though as a child he learned carpentry and shoemaking to help support his family, his mother sent him to study in a seminary in hope of his attaining the priesthood. But Díaz did not want to enter the

clergy; he left the school and entered the Institute of Arts and Sciences in the city of Oaxaca, where he studied law under Benito Juárez. Díaz's legal training left him a convinced liberal determined to break the stranglehold that the professional army, the Church, and large landholders held over contemporary Mexico.

Military Career

In 1846 Díaz had enlisted in the national guard to combat the North American invaders, but he did not participate in the fighting. He later attributed his anticlericalism to his witnessing priests distributing tracts favoring the foreign invasion. In the 1850s he served as a guerrilla officer against the conservative clerical forces seeking to prevent liberal reforms. In 1861 the victorious liberals appointed him a brigadier general.

The conservative defeat was rapidly followed by the French intervention, and Díaz again fought but this time to keep the Austrian Archduke Maximilian off the throne of Mexico. In 1862 he participated in the successful Mexican defense of Puebla but was later captured when the city surrendered. He escaped, raised another liberal army, and laid siege to the city of Oaxaca. Again he was captured only to escape once more. By 1865 he had established a reputation as a brilliant guerrilla fighter and as a man able to overcome great odds despite adversity. Juárez, the liberal president, appointed Díaz commander of his eastern forces. Díaz governed eight states and commanded some 20,000 troops. In June 1867 Díaz took the city of Mexico from the conservatives, who had been abandoned by the French. He ruled the city as governor until July, when he presented it to Juárez, who welcomed him coldly. Díaz also handed over the eastern army's large treasury to the national government. At this time he was one of Mexico's most famous men and a threat to the determined Juárez, who believed himself the only one capable of governing Mexico.

Politician and Rebel

In 1867 Díaz ran against Juárez for the presidency but was heavily defeated. In 1868 he retired from the army to his native state of Oaxaca, where the grateful citizens had given him a large farm, La Noria. Hoping to increase his prestige by a short retirement, Díaz devoted himself to the raising of sugarcane. In 1871 he again opposed Juárez for the presidency in an election marked by much bitterness over Juárez's decision to seek a fourth term. The election ended in a tie between Díaz, Juárez, and Sebastián Lerdo de Tejada, and the Mexican Congress made Juárez president and Lerdo vice president.

The disappointed Díaz retired to Oaxaca, where he staged a revolt whose program promised effective suffrage and no reelection. Juárez acted quickly by sending troops to Oaxaca to crush the rebellion, which cost Felix Díaz, Porfirio's brother, his life. Porfirio fled to the coastal state of Nayarit, but Juárez's victory was soon followed by his death in 1872, bringing Lerdo the presidency. Díaz accepted a general amnesty and opened a furniture factory in Veracruz, while he prepared for another try at the presidency. In 1876, after Lerdo announced plans to

Porfirio Díaz. (Organization of American States)

succeed himself, Díaz again revolted. Lerdo's regime, plagued by popular apathy and a querulous military, soon collapsed and Lerdo fled into exile. Díaz then ran unopposed and was elected to fill Lerdo's unexpired term.

Ruler of Mexico

Díaz's 34-year rule is known as the *Porfiriato*; it was a period of relative peace and economic growth. During his first term Díaz began to reestablish the federal government's power over the diverse Mexican states. He enlarged and gave great power to a constabulary, the Rurales. They destroyed many of the bandit gangs which had proliferated during the civil wars and later crushed all political opposition to Díaz's rule. He also formed a compromise with the Catholic Church, by which the federal government would not harass the Church if the latter would not interfere in Mexican politics.

In 1880 Díaz left the presidency to Gen. Manuel González, a longtime supporter and friend. Díaz became governor of Oaxaca and watched while González ran the country into bankruptcy. Friends of the government made huge fortunes in public-land speculation, and foreign companies bought up huge tracts of Mexican land. The government reversed the old Spanish mining laws and allowed foreigners to purchase subsoil rights, or ownership of all oils and metals contained in the ground. The mining industry entered a boom period in which Mexico produced more gold and silver in 20 years than it had in the previous 4 centuries. Díaz, a widower, meanwhile had contracted his second marriage, to Carmen Romero Rubio, the daughter of a rich supporter of Lerdo. This marriage, sometimes called the "aristocratization of Porfirio Díaz," marked the rough mestizo general's entrance into the best Creole society. Carmen, a devout Catholic, not only made Díaz socially respectable but also helped form a tacit alliance between the government and the Mexican Catholic Church.

In 1884 Díaz abandoned his "no reelection" policy and again assumed the Mexican presidency. Continually reelected until his violent overthrow, Díaz was then free to pursue further the policies begun in 1876. Political peace was maintained through the Rurales and the policy known as "bread or club." Outstanding opponents were given government jobs or rich concessions; those who refused such bribes faced death, exile, or prison. Political power lay with Díaz, his old military cronies, and a small group of wealthy Creoles, known as the Científicos.

Economic Progress

The Científicos, most prominent in the 1890s, cleverly adopted the positivism of the French philosopher Auguste Comte as a justification for their increasing monopoly over the nation's wealth. Defining their program as one of "freedom, order, and progress," they tried to establish a religion of science based on the cold indexes of Mexico's expanding economy. The Científicos saw Mexico's future best served by massive white European immigration, which would relegate the Mexican Indian and mixed breeds to a permanently inferior role. The army launched campaigns against the Yaquí

tribes in the north and the Mayas in the south, while the government press defined the Indians as a "national burden."

In 1893 the prominent Científico José Ives Limantour became minister of finance, and Mexico became one of Latin America's most prosperous nations. By cutting the military budget, the astute banker gave Mexico its first budgetary surplus in years; railroad trackage increased to 16,000 miles as foreign trade quadrupled over the 1870 level. The new transportation system allowed domestic industries such as beer, pulque, and textile mills to develop along railroad lines. In 1903 Mexico built its first steel mill in Monterrey. By 1910 Mexico was producing some 800 million barrels of oil per year. Limantour also abolished the sales tax and put Mexico on the gold standard.

Tides of Discontent

For most of rural Mexico the *Porfiriato* vaunted "order and progress" had meant economic and social disaster. In 1910 most rural workers earned about the same wage that they had earned in 1810. At the same time the cost of living had increased alarmingly. A rising population and a decreasing productivity of land resulted in many Mexican peasants' existing beneath subsistence level, while the fortunes of the Porfirian aristocracy grew yearly. Only a few peasants were able to find jobs on the railroads or in the growing industries, and many migrated to the United States seeking employment. Despite many promises illiteracy stood at about 87 percent.

The underdevelopment of rural Mexico was heightened by the government's actions. Laws requiring clear land title, surveying, and the dissolution of communal holdings led to the creation of huge estates at the expense of smallholders. The government sold off public lands to foreigners and cronies at bargain prices. Only the large estates could get improvement loans from the banking system. The government's policy of creating large efficient estates to produce export crops caused growing concern among those who held small ranches and farms. Later, those rural middle classes were to compose the backbone of the revolutionary forces. From 84 to 95 percent of the rural families had no land at all, while wealthy families often had estates running into millions of acres. The Terrazas family had 13.5 million acres in Chihuahua, while the Escandón estate in Hidalgo stretched for 90 miles.

The Revolution

In 1910 the Porfirian elite prepared to celebrate a century of Mexican independence. Confident after 34 years of peaceful rule, they were unaware that their carefully contrived system stood on the verge of collapse. The young were impatient with foreign economic control, the destruction of the indigenous peoples, and the hoarding of political power by the Porfirian elite. The ranchers of the north and the communities of the south, still independent and armed, feared that they would become rapidly submerged into large haciendas, and labor in mining and textiles was becoming restive.

In 1907 Díaz made a critical political error. The aging president told James Creelman, a North American journalist, that Mexico was ready for democracy and that he was about to retire. The interview, published in English and intended for foreign consumption, soon reached Mexico. Opposition parties began to form throughout the nation as both the ambitious and the sincerely critical sought to find a form of government better able to reconcile development and social justice. After some confusion most opposition coalesced around Francisco Madero, the wealthy scion of a prominent Mexican family from the northern state of Coahuila.

Too late Díaz tried to correct his error. In 1910 he reelected himself and jailed Madero. The latter, now a national hero, escaped and called for revolution. As the country rose, the weak army collapsed. Díaz, deserted by many of his followers and without effective armed forces, resigned office on May 25, 1911. He fled to France, where he died in relative poverty on July 2, 1915.

Further Reading

Porfirio Díaz is listed in the Latin America study guide (IV, K, 1, a). His downfall prompted the power struggle between Francisco MADERO, Victoriano HUERTA, and Venustiano CARRANZA. Auguste COMTE held that the perfect state should be governed by a coalition of scientists, industrialists, and intellectuals.

There is very little written in English on Díaz. The best biography is probably Carleton Beals, *Porfirio Díaz: Dictator of Mexico* (1932). Useful information may also be found in John Kenneth Turner, *Barbarous Mexico* (1911; 4th ed. 1914); Henry Bamford Parkes, *A History of Mexico* (1938; 3d ed. 1960); Daniel Cosío Villegas, *The United States versus Porfirio Díaz* (1956; trans. 1963); and James D. Cockcroft, *Intellectual Precursors of the Mexican Revolution* (1969). An excellent popular history of the revolution that began with the overthrow of Díaz is Ronald Atkin, *Revolution! Mexico, 1910–1920* (1970).

* * *

DÍAZ DEL CASTILLO

/ By Lyle N. McAlister

The Spanish soldier Bernal Díaz del Castillo (ca. 1496–ca. 1584) was a member of the expedition that conquered the Aztec empire. His "A True History of the Conquest of New Spain" is the most complete contemporary chronicle of that event.

Bernal Díaz del Castillo (pronounced dē′äth *th*ĕl käs-tē′lyō) was born in Medina del Campo of a respectable although not distinguished family. He was enchanted by tales of the fortunes to be found in newly discovered America, and in 1514 he left for the New World in the entourage of Pedrarias, who had been appointed governor of Castilla del Oro (the Isthmus of Panama and adjacent mainland of South America). Díaz was soon disenchanted with the prospects in this area and moved on to Cuba. While based there, he participated in two expeditions which explored the coasts of the Gulf of Mexico in 1517 and 1518, respectively.

In 1519 Díaz joined the expedition organized by Hernán Cortés for the conquest of Mexico and participated in the campaigns which led in 1521 to the fall of Tenochtitlán, the Aztec capital. His exact status in the enterprise is not clear. He intimates that he exercised some authority and enjoyed the confidence of Cortés, but other evidence indicates that he was little more than a common foot soldier.

After the conquest of the Aztecs, Díaz settled in the province of Coatzacoalcos, southeast of Veracruz, where he had been awarded grants of land and Indian labor. These properties, however, provided him with only a modest livelihood, so in 1540 he went to Spain to plead for more substantial recognition of his merits and services. He was rewarded by a somewhat better allocation of lands and Indians in the province of Guatemala. Here he settled, probably in 1541, and became a respected citizen, a municipal official, and the father of a numerous progeny, legitimate and illegitimate. But until his death about 1584, he complained of poverty and bemoaned the inconspicuous rewards he had received for his services to the King.

History of the Conquest

Possibly while still in Mexico, Díaz conceived the idea of recording his memories of the Conquest, but it was not until the early 1550s that he really began to write. The project progressed slowly. Then in the 1560s he read a book entitled *The History of the Conquest of Mexico* (1552), written by Francisco López de Gómara, a former chaplain of the Cortés family. Gómara's account appeared to glorify the role of Cortés at the expense of the common soldier, an interpretation that Díaz resented; it provided him with an incentive to complete his own account, which he entitled *A True History of the Conquest of New Spain*. In 1568, about age 72, he completed his task and in the mid-1570s sent a copy of the manuscript to Spain for publication. It did not appear in print, however, until 1632 and then only after the editor, Friar Alonzo Remón, had considerably altered the text. It was not until 1904–1905 that a true edition appeared, prepared by the Mexican historian Genaro García from the original manuscript, which had survived in Guatemala.

The *True History* begins in 1517 and terminates in 1568, but the bulk of it concentrates on the epic years 1519–1521. Díaz admitted and deplored his unpolished style, and it is in fact that of a common soldier. The narrative is prolix and digressive; events are sometimes transposed and observations and interpretations often naive. Yet he possessed a deep honesty and remarkable memory. For the most part his account is factually correct. He was also a superlative raconteur with a deep sense of personal involvement and a flair for the dramatic. The *True History* is not only a major historical docu-

Cortés's expedition landing in Mexico, in an illustration from the 16th-century Codex Azcatitlán. *Bernal Díaz del Castillo was a member of this expedition and later its historian.*

ment but also one of the greatest adventure stories of all time.

Further Reading

Bernal Díaz del Castillo is listed in the Latin America study guide (I, B, 4). Álvar Núñez CABEZA DE VACA was a contemporary chronicler of Spanish conquests in the New World.

Genaro García's edition of Díaz's history was translated into English by Alfred Percival Maudslay and published by the Hakluyt Society as *The True History of the Conquest of New Spain* (5 vols., 1908–1916). Volume 1 contains useful notes on Díaz and his work. Several abridged English editions appeared subsequently. A good, recent biography of the chronicler is Herbert Cerwin, *Bernal Díaz: Historian of the Conquest* (1963).

* * *

DICKENS / By Avrom Fleishman

The English author Charles John Huffam Dickens (1812–1870) was, and probably still is, the most widely read Victorian novelist. He is now appreciated more for his "dark" novels than for his humorous works.

Charles Dickens was born on Feb. 7, 1812, at Portsea (later part of Portsmouth) on the southern coast of England. He was the son of a lower-middle-class but impecunious father whose improvidence he was later to satirize in the character of Micawber in *David Copperfield*. The family's financial difficulties caused them to move about until they settled in Camden Town, a poor neighborhood of London. At the age of 12 Charles was set to work in a warehouse that handled "blacking," or shoe polish; there he mingled with men and boys of the working class. For a period of months he was also forced to live apart from his family when they moved in with his father, who had been imprisoned in the Marshalsea debtors' prison. This experience of lonely hardship was the most significant formative event of his life; it colored his view of the world in profound and varied ways and is directly or indirectly described in a number of his novels, including *The Pickwick Papers*,

Charles Dickens in 1867. (Library of Congress)

Oliver Twist, and *Little Dorrit*, as well as *David Copperfield*.

These early events of Dicken's life left both psychological and sociological effects. In a fragmentary autobiography Dickens wrote, "It is wonderful to me how I could have been so easily cast away at such an age.... My father and mother were quite satisfied.... My whole nature was so penetrated with grief and humiliation of such considerations, that even now, famous and caressed and happy, I often forget in my dreams that I have a dear wife and children; even that I am a man; and wander desolately back to that time of my life."

The sociological effect of the blacking factory on Dickens was to give him a firsthand acquaintance with poverty and to make him the most vigorous and influential voice of the lower classes in his age. Despite the fact that many of England's legal and social abuses were in the process of being removed by the time Dickens published his exposés of them, it remains true that he was the most widely heard spokesman of the need to alleviate the miseries of the poor.

Dickens returned to school after an inheritance (as in the fairy-tale endings of some of his novels) relieved his father from debt, but he was forced to become an office boy at the age of 15. In the following year he became a free-lance reporter or stenographer at the law courts of London. By 1832 he had become a reporter for two London newspapers and, in the following year, began to contribute a series of impressions and sketches to other newspapers and magazines, signing some of them "Boz." These scenes of London life went far to establish his reputation and were published in 1836 as *Sketches by Boz*, his first book. On the strength of this success he married; his wife, Catherine Hogarth, was eventually to bear him 10 children.

Early Works

In 1836 Dickens also began to publish in monthly installments *The Posthumous Papers of the Pickwick Club*. This form of serial publication became a standard method of writing and producing fiction in the Victorian period and affected the literary methods of Dickens and other novelists. So great was Dickens's success with the procedure—summed up in the formula, "Make them laugh; make them cry; make them wait"—that *Pickwick* became one of the most popular works of the time, continuing to be so after it was published in book form in 1837. The comic heroes of the novel, the antiquarian members of the Pickwick Club, scour the English countryside for local points of interest and are involved in a variety of humorous adventures which reveal the characteristics of English social life. At a later stage of the novel, the chairman of the club, Samuel Pickwick, is involved in a lawsuit which lands him in the Fleet debtors' prison. Here the lighthearted atmosphere of the novel changes, and the reader is given intimations of the gloom and sympathy with which Dickens was to imbue his later works.

During the years of *Pickwick*'s serialization, Dickens became editor of a new monthly, *Bentley's Miscellany*.

When *Pickwick* was completed, he began publishing his new novel, *Oliver Twist*, in this magazine—a practice he continued in his later magazines, *Household Words* and *All the Year Round*. *Oliver* expresses Dickens's interest in the life of the slums to the fullest, as it traces the fortunes of an innocent orphan through the London streets. It seems remarkable today that this novel's fairly frank treatment of criminals like Bill Sikes, prostitutes like Nancy, and "fences" like Fagin could have been acceptable to the Victorian reading public. But so powerful was Dickens's portrayal of the "little boy lost" amid the low-life of the East End that the limits of his audience's tolerance were gradually stretched.

Dickens was now embarked on the most consistently successful career of any 19th-century author after Sir Walter Scott. He could do no wrong as far as his faithful readership was concerned; yet his books for the next decade were not to achieve the standard of his early triumphs. These works include: *Nicholas Nickleby* (1838–1839), still cited for its exposé of brutality at an English boys' school, Dotheboys Hall; *The Old Curiosity Shop* (1840–1841), still remembered for reaching a high (or low) point of sentimentality in its portrayal of the sufferings of Little Nell; and *Barnaby Rudge* (1841), still read for its interest as a historical novel, set amid the anti-Catholic Gordon Riots of 1780.

In 1842 Dickens, who was as popular in America as he was in England, went on a 5-month lecture tour of the United States, speaking out strongly for the abolition of slavery and other reforms. On his return he wrote *American Notes*, sharply critical of the cultural backwardness and aggressive materialism of American life. He made further capital of these observations in his next novel, *Martin Chuzzlewit* (1843–1844), in which the hero retreats from the difficulties of making his way in England only to find that survival is even more trying on the American frontier. During the years in which *Chuzzlewit* appeared, Dickens also published two Christmas stories, *A Christmas Carol* and *The Chimes*, which became as much part of the season as plum pudding.

First Major Novels

After a year abroad in Italy, in response to which he wrote *Pictures from Italy* (1846), Dickens began to publish *Dombey and Son*, which continued till 1848. This novel established a new standard in the Dickensian novel and may be said to mark the turning point in his career. If Dickens had remained the author of *Pickwick*, *Oliver Twist*, and *The Old Curiosity Shop*, he might have deserved a lasting reputation only as an author of cheerful comedy and bathetic sentiment. But *Dombey*, while it includes these elements, is a realistic novel of human life in a society which had assumed more or less its modern form. As its full title indicates, *Dealings with the Firm of Dombey and Son* is a study of the influence of the values of a business society on the personal fortunes of the members of the Dombey family and those with whom they come in contact. It takes a somber view of England at mid-century, and its elegiac tone becomes characteristic of Dickens's novels for the rest of his life.

Mr. Pickwick and Sam Weller, an illustration for Dickens's The Pickwick Papers *by Hablot K. Browne, better known by his pseudonym "Phiz." Chosen by Dickens in 1836 to illustrate* Pickwick, *"Phiz" also illustrated nine of the author's later works, including* David Copperfield, Bleak House, *and* A Tale of Two Cities. *(Berg Collection, New York Public Library)*

Dickens's next novel, *David Copperfield* (1849–1850), combined broad social perspective with a very strenuous effort to take stock of himself at the midpoint of his literary career. This autobiographical novel fictionalized elements of Dickens's childhood degradation, pursuit of a journalistic and literary vocation, and love life. Its achievement is to offer the first comprehensive record of the typical course of a young man's life in Victorian England. *Copperfield* is not Dickens's greatest novel, but it was his own favorite among his works, probably because of his personal engagement with the subject matter.

In 1850 Dickens began to "conduct" (his word for edit) a new periodical, *Household Words*. His editorials and articles for this magazine, running to two volumes, cover the entire span of English politics, social institutions, and family life and are an invaluable complement to the fictional treatment of these subjects in Dickens's novels. The weekly magazine was a great success and ran to 1859, when Dickens began to conduct a new weekly, *All the Year Round*. In both these periodicals he published some of his major novels.

"Dark" Novels

In 1851 Dickens was struck by the death of his father and one of his daughters within 2 weeks. Partly in response to these losses, he embarked on a series of works which have come to be called his "dark" novels and which rank among the greatest triumphs of the art of fiction. The first of these, *Bleak House* (1852–1853), has perhaps the most complicated plot of any English novel, but the narrative twists serve to create a sense of the interrelationship of all segments of English society. Indeed, it has been maintained that this network of interrelations is the true subject of the novel, designed to express Thomas Carlyle's view that "organic filaments" connect every member of society with every other member of whatever class. The novel provides, then, a chastening lesson to social snobbery and personal selfishness.

Dickens's next novel is even more didactic in its moral indictment of selfishness. *Hard Times* (1854) was written specifically to challenge the prevailing view of his society that practicality and facts were of greater importance and value than feelings and persons. In his indignation at callousness in business and public educational systems, Dickens laid part of the charge for the heartlessness of Englishmen at the door of the utilitarian philosophy then much in vogue. But the lasting applicability of the novel lies in its intensely focused picture of an English industrial town in the heyday of capitalist expansion and in its keen view of the limitations of both employers and reformers.

Little Dorrit (1855–1857) has some claim to be regarded as Dickens's greatest novel. In it he provides the same range of social observation that he had developed in previous major works. But the outstanding feature of this novel is the creation of two striking symbols of his views, which operate throughout the story as the focal points of all the characters' lives. The condition of England, as he saw it, Dickens sums up in the symbol of the prison: specifically the Marshalsea debtors' prison, in which the heroine's father is entombed, but generally the many forms of personal bondage and confinement that are exhibited in the course of the plot. For his counterweight, Dickens raises to symbolic stature his traditional figure of the child as innocent sufferer of the world's abuses. By making his heroine not a child but a childlike figure of Christian loving-kindness, Dickens poses the central burden of his work—the conflict between the world's harshness and human values—in its most impressive artistic form.

The year 1857 saw the beginnings of a personal crisis for Dickens when he fell in love with an actress named Ellen Ternan. He separated from his wife in the following year, after many years of marital incompatibility. In this period Dickens also began to give much of his time and energies to public readings from his novels, which became even more popular than his lectures on topical questions.

Later Works

In 1859 Dickens published *A Tale of Two Cities*, a historical novel of the French Revolution, which is read today most often as a school text. It is, while below the standard of the long and comprehensive "dark" novels, a fine evocation of the historical period and a moving tale of a surprisingly modern hero's self-sacrifice. Besides publishing this novel in the newly founded *All the Year Round*, Dickens also published 17 articles, which appeared as a book in 1860 entitled *The Uncommercial Traveller*.

Dickens's next novel, *Great Expectations* (1860–1861), must rank as his most perfectly executed work of art. It tells the story of a young man's moral development in the course of his life—from childhood in the provinces to gentleman's status in London. Not an autobiographical novel like *David Copperfield, Great Expectations* belongs to the type of fiction called, in German, *Bildungsroman* (the novel of a man's education or formation by experience) and is one of the finest examples of the type.

The next work in the Dickens canon had to wait for the (for him) unusual time of 3 years, but in 1864–1865 he produced *Our Mutual Friend*, which challenges *Little Dorrit* and *Bleak House* for consideration as his masterpiece. Here the vision of English society in all its classes and institutions is presented most thoroughly and devastatingly, while two symbols are developed which resemble those of *Little Dorrit* in credibility and interest. These symbols are the mounds of rubbish which rose to become features of the landscape in rapidly expanding London, and the river which flows through the city and provides a point of contact for all its members besides suggesting the course of human life from birth to death.

In the closing years of his life Dickens worsened his declining health by giving numerous readings from his works. He never fully recovered from a railroad accident in which he had been involved in 1865 and yet insisted on traveling throughout the British Isles and America to read before tumultuous audiences. He broke down in 1869 and gave only a final series of readings in London in the following year. He also began *The Mystery of Edwin Drood* but died in 1870, leaving it unfinished. His burial in Westminster Abbey was an occasion of national mourning.

Further Reading

Charles Dickens is listed in the Literature study guide (II, H, 1, b). He admired and was influenced by Henry FIELDING and Tobias SMOLLETT. His social thought owes much to that of Thomas CARLYLE. The novels of Elizabeth GASKELL also examine the problems of industrialization in England.

The definitive biography of Dickens is Edgar Johnson, *Charles Dickens: His Tragedy and Triumph* (2 vols., 1952). This supersedes but does not render obsolete the long-standing "official" biography by John Forster, *The Life of Charles Dickens* (3 vols., 1872–1873; new ed., 2 vols., 1966). The most interesting psychological study is Edmund Wilson, "Dickens: The Two Scrooges," in *The Wound and the Bow: Seven Studies in Literature* (1941). The best critical interpretation is J. Hillis Miller, *Charles Dickens: The World of His Novels* (1958). F. R. and Q. D. Leavis, *Dickens the Novelist* (1970), contains essays on Dickens's major novels. For the earlier novels the most informative reading is Steven Marcus, *Dickens: From Pickwick to Dombey* (1965). The most useful book on the social and historical background of the novels is Humphry House, *The Dickens World* (1941; 2d ed. 1950).

*   *   *

EMILY **DICKINSON**

/ By Richard M. Ludwig

One of the finest lyric poets in the English language, the American poet Emily Dickinson (1830–1886) was a keen observer of nature and a wise interpreter of human passion. Her family and friends published most of her work posthumously.

American poetry in the 19th century was rich and varied, ranging from the symbolic fantasies of Edgar Allan Poe through the moralistic quatrains of Henry Wadsworth Longfellow to the revolutionary free verse of Walt Whitman. In the privacy of her study Emily Dickinson developed her own forms and pursued her own visions, oblivious of literary fashions and unconcerned with the changing national literature. If she was influenced at all by other writers, they were John Keats, Ralph Waldo Emerson, Robert and Elizabeth Barrett Browning, Isaac Watts (his hymns), and the biblical prophets.

Emily Dickinson was born on Dec. 10, 1830, in Amherst, Mass., the eldest daughter of Edward Dickinson, a successful lawyer, member of Congress, and for many years treasurer of Amherst College, and of Emily Norcross Dickinson, a submissive, timid woman. The Dickinsons' only son, William Austin, also a lawyer, succeeded his father as treasurer of the college. Their youngest child, Lavinia, was the chief housekeeper and, like her sister Emily, remained at home, unmarried, all her life. The sixth member of this tightly knit group was Susan Gilbert, an ambitious and witty schoolmate of Emily's, who married Austin in 1856 and moved into the house next door to the Dickinsons. At first she was Emily's confidante and a valued critic of her poetry, but by 1879 Emily was speaking of her "pseudo-sister" and had long since ceased exchanging notes and poems.

Early Education

Amherst in the 1840s was a sleepy village in the lush Connecticut Valley, dominated by the Church and the college. Emily Dickinson was reared in Trinitarian Congregationalism, but she never joined the Church and probably chafed at the austerity of the town. Concerts were rare; card games, dancing, and theater were unheard of. For relaxation she walked the hills with her dog, visited friends, and read. But it is also obvious that Puritan New England bred in her a sharp eye for local color, a love of introspection and self-analysis, and a fortitude that sustained her through years of intense loneliness.

Miss Dickinson graduated from Amherst Academy in 1847. The following year (the longest time she was ever to spend away from home) she attended Mount Holyoke Female Seminary at South Hadley, but because of her fragile health she did not return. At the age of 17 she settled into the Dickinson home and turned herself into a competent housekeeper and a more than ordinary ob-

Emily Dickinson, a daguerreotype portrait. (Courtesy of the Amherst College Library, Emily Dickinson Collection)

server of Amherst life.

Early Work

It is not known when Miss Dickinson began to write poetry or what happened to the poems of her early youth. Only five poems can be dated prior to 1858, the year in which she began gathering her work into handwritten fair copies bound loosely with looped thread to make small packets. She sent these five early poems to friends in letters or as valentines, and one of them was published anonymously without her permission in the *Springfield Republican* (Feb. 20, 1852). After 1858 she apparently convinced herself she had a genuine talent, for now the packets were carefully stored in an ebony box, awaiting inspection by future readers or even by a publisher.

Publication, however, was not easily arranged. After Miss Dickinson besieged her friend Samuel Bowles, editor of the *Republican*, with poems and letters for 4 years, he published two poems, both anonymously: "I taste a liquor never brewed" (May 4, 1861) and "Safe in their Alabaster Chambers" (March 1, 1862). And the first of these was edited, probably by Bowles, to regularize (and thus, flatten) the rhymes and the punctuation. Emily Dickinson began the poem: "I taste a liquor never brewed—/ From Tankards scooped in Pearl—/ Not all the Frankfort Berries/ Yield such an Alcohol." But Bowles printed: "I taste a liquor never brewed,/ From tankards scooped in pearl;/ Not Frankfort berries yield the sense/ Such a delicious whirl." She used no title; Bowles titled it "The May-Wine." (Only seven poems were published

Emily Dickinson's bedroom, in the Dickinson House, Amherst, Mass. (Courtesy of the Amherst College Library, Emily Dickinson Collection)

during her lifetime, and all had been altered by editors.)

Friendship with T. W. Higginson

In 1862 Emily Dickinson turned to the literary critic Thomas Wentworth Higginson for advice about her poems. She had known him only through his essays in the *Atlantic Monthly*, but in time he became, in her words, her "preceptor" and eventually her "safest friend." She began her first letter to him by asking, "Are you too deeply occupied to say if my verse is alive?" Six years later she was bold enough to say, "You were not aware that you saved my life." They did not meet until 1870, at her urging, surprisingly, and only once more after that. Higginson told his wife, after the first meeting, "I was never with anyone who drained my nerve power so much. Without touching her she drew from me. I am glad not to live near her."

What Emily Dickinson was seeking was assurance as well as advice, and Higginson apparently gave it without knowing it, through a correspondence that lasted the rest of her life. He advised against publishing, but he also kept her abreast of the literary world (indeed, of the outside world, since as early as 1868, she was writing him, "I do not cross my father's ground to any house or town"). He helped her not at all with what mattered most to her—establishing her own private poetic method—but he was a friendly ear and a congenial mentor during the most troubled years of her life. Out of her inner turmoil came rare lyrics in a form that Higginson never really understood—if he had, he would not have tried to "edit" them, either in the 1860s or after her death. Emily Dickinson could not take his "surgery," as she called it, but she took his friendship willingly.

Years of Emotional Crisis

Between 1858 and 1866 Miss Dickinson wrote more than 1100 poems, full of aphorisms, paradoxes, off rhymes, and eccentric grammar. Few are more than 16 lines long, composed in meters based on English hymnology. The major subjects are love and separation, death, nature, and God—but especially love. When she writes "My life closed twice before its close," one can only guess who her real or fancied lovers might have been. Higginson was not one of them. It is more than likely that her first "dear friend" was Benjamin Newton, a young man too poor to marry, who had worked for a few years in her father's law office. He left Amherst for Worcester and died there in 1853.

During a visit to Philadelphia a year later Emily Dickinson met the Reverend Charles Wadsworth. Sixteen years her senior, a brilliant preacher, already married, he was hardly more than a mental image of a lover for the Amherst spinster. There is no doubt she made him this, but nothing more. He visited her once in 1860. When he moved to San Francisco in May 1862, she was in despair. Only a month before, Samuel Bowles had sailed for Europe to recover his health. Little wonder that in her first letter to Higginson she said, "I had a terror . . . — and so I sing as the Boy does by the Burying Ground—because I am afraid." She needed love, but she had to indulge this need through her poems, perhaps because she felt she could cope with it no other way.

When Bowles returned to Amherst in November, Miss Dickinson was so overwhelmed she remained in her bedroom and sent a note down, ". . . That you return to us alive is better than a summer, and more to hear your voice below than news of any bird." By the time Wadsworth returned from California in 1870 and resettled in Philadelphia, the crisis was over. His second visit, in 1880, was anticlimax. Higginson had not saved her life; her life was never in danger. What had been in danger was her emotional equilibrium and her control over a talent that was so intense it longed for the eruptions that might have destroyed it.

Last Years

In the last 2 decades of her life Emily Dickinson wrote fewer than 50 poems a year, perhaps because of continuing eye trouble, more probably because she had to take increasing responsibility in running the household. Her father died in 1874, and a year later her mother suffered a paralyzing stroke that left her an invalid until her death. There was little time for poetry, not even for serious consideration of marriage (if it was actually proffered) with a widower and old family friend, Judge Otis Lord. Their love was genuine, but once again the timing was wrong. It was too late to recast her life completely. Her mother died in 1882, Judge Lord 2 years later. Miss Dickinson's health failed noticeably after a nervous collapse in 1884, and on May 15, 1886, she died of nephritis.

Posthumous Publication

How the complete poems of Emily Dickinson were finally gathered is a publishing saga almost too complicated for brief summary. Lavinia Dickinson inherited the ebony box; she asked Mabel Loomis Todd, the wife of an

Amherst astronomy professor, to join Higginson in editing the manuscripts. Unfortunately, they felt even then that they had to alter the syntax, smooth the rhymes, cut some lines, and create titles for each poem. Three volumes appeared in quick succession: 1890, 1891, and 1896. In 1914 Emily Dickinson's niece, Martha Dickinson Bianchi, published some of the poems her mother, Susan, had saved. In the next 3 decades four more volumes appeared, the most important being *Bolts of Melody* (1945), edited by Mrs. Todd and her daughter, Millicent Todd Bingham, from the manuscripts the Todds had never returned to Lavinia Dickinson. In 1955 Thomas H. Johnson prepared for Harvard University Press a three-volume edition, chronologically arranged, of "variant readings critically compared with all known manuscripts." Here, for the first time, the reader saw the poems as Emily Dickinson had left them. The Johnson text of the 1,775 extant poems is now the standard one.

It is clear that Emily Dickinson could not have written to please publishers, who were not ready to risk her striking aphoristic style and original metaphors. She had the right to educate the public, as Poe and Whitman eventually did, but she never had the invitation. Had she published during her lifetime, adverse public criticism might have driven her into deeper solitude, even silence. "If fame belonged to me," she told Higginson, "I could not escape her; if she did not, the longest day would pass me on the chase. . . . My barefoot rank is better." The 20th century has lifted her without doubt to the first rank among poets.

Further Reading

Emily Dickinson is listed in the Literature study guide (I, D, 4). She was a contemporary of Walt WHITMAN, Herman MELVILLE, and Mark TWAIN.

Thomas H. Johnson edited *The Letters of Emily Dickinson* (3 vols., 1958). His three-volume variorum edition of her poems (1955) was followed by a one-volume *The Complete Poems of Emily Dickinson* (1960) and a selection of 575 poems, *Final Harvest* (1961).

The best of the early biographies of Emily Dickinson is George Whicher, *This Was a Poet: A Critical Biography of Emily Dickinson* (1938). It has been superseded by Richard Chase, *Emily Dickinson* (1951); Thomas H. Johnson, *Emily Dickinson: An Interpretive Biography* (1955); and David Higgins, *Portrait of Emily Dickinson: The Poet and Her Prose* (1967). Jay Leyda, *The Years and Hours of Emily Dickinson* (2 vols., 1960), is a valuable source book.

There are numerous critical studies. The best general appreciation is Charles R. Anderson, *Emily Dickinson's Poetry: Stairway of Surprise* (1960). More recent studies are Clark Griffith, *The Long Shadow: Emily Dickinson's Tragic Poetry* (1964); Albert J. Gelpi, *Emily Dickinson: The Mind of the Poet* (1965); Ruth Miller, *The Poetry of Emily Dickinson* (1968); and William R. Sherwood, *Circumference and Circumstance: Stages in the Mind and Art of Emily Dickinson* (1968). Richard B. Sewall edited *Emily Dickinson: A Collection of Critical Essays* (1963).

Equally useful is Cesar R. Blake and Carlton F. Wells, eds., *The Recognition of Emily Dickinson: Selected Criticism since 1890* (1964).

Emily Dickinson's place in the history of American poetry is well established in Roy Harvey Pearce, *The Continuity of American Poetry* (1961), and Hyatt H. Waggoner, *American Poets from the Puritans to the Present* (1968).

J. DICKINSON / By Robert A. Rutland

John Dickinson (1732–1808), American lawyer, pamphleteer, and politician, helped guide public opinion during the clash between colonial and British interests prior to the American Revolution. Although he had opposed American independence, he worked to strengthen the new nation.

A fter 1769 John Dickinson was without peer in the pamphlet war for colonial rights, which the moderates preferred to a shooting war. He was not a "man of the people," but he shared with most American Whigs the aspiration for self-government. He was cautious but not an obstructionist.

John Dickinson, a painting by Charles Willson Peale. (Independence National Historical Park Collection, Philadelphia)

John Dickinson was born Nov. 13, 1732, in Talbot County, Md., the son of a judge. Dickinson began his legal studies in 1750 in Philadelphia, but 3 years later he went to London and became a reader at the Middle Temple.

In England, Dickinson studied the authorities, heard cases argued, and visited the theater and the family of Pennsylvania proprietor Thomas Penn. He took his law degree in 1757 and returned to America with the disillusioned view that Parliament was a school for corrupt bargainers of meager talents.

Dickinson was admitted to the Philadelphia bar, and after 1760, when his father died, he divided his time between Kent County, Del., and the thriving Pennsylvania capital. Elected to the colonial legislature in 1762, he showed little awe for the Penn family's proprietary interests but displayed a lifelong tendency to see both sides of an issue and then lean toward the middle ground. When the antiproprietary leaders insisted that the colony should be wrested from the Penns and converted into a royal province, Dickinson warned that the transition might exact a heavy price. The colony was torn between the Quaker party and the Scotch-Irish faction, and Dickinson insisted that a change of masters was in itself no solution to their deep-rooted problems.

Debating American Independence

No one could foresee the rapid deterioration of British-American relations set off by the Stamp Act in 1765, when local concerns finally gave way to larger problems. Whereas Benjamin Franklin at first saw no harm in the stamped paper, Dickinson sensed the dreaded implications it carried. As a delegate to the Stamp Act Congress, he met leaders of active antiparliamentary parties from other colonies. His "Declaration of Rights and Privileges" adopted by the Congress denounced taxes voted in England and collected in America. Regulation of trade was one thing, but levying taxes struck at the main artery of colonial government. Dickinson wrote several pamphlets which suggested that Britain would, if necessary, bleed the Colonies into obedience. In common with James Otis, the foremost pamphleteer of the day, Dickinson argued that "immutable maxims of reason and justice" supported the American discontent.

Repeal of the Stamp Act temporarily relaxed tensions, but the Townshend Acts of 1767 gave Dickinson renewed opportunity to serve as a moderate spokesman. In the maelstrom of American discontent, Dickinson's *Letters from a Pennsylvanian Farmer* capitalized on the shifting grounds of argument. The new duties were contrary to natural law, he argued, and clearly unconstitutional. Dickinson denied the sophistry that claimed there were internal and external duties and that Parliament might legally enact only the latter. Levying taxes, he argued, was the precious prerogative of the colonial assemblies alone but Parliament might enact regulatory duties on trade. Dickinson insisted that the point of tightened British controls was to keep Americans obedient rather than happy. Widely published in newspapers and as a pamphlet, his *Letters* (as Franklin said) echoed

"the general sentiments" of the colonists. The tone was neither humble nor belligerent.

Dickinson tried to rouse the lethargic Philadelphia merchants into a more active stand and corresponded with James Otis and other resistance leaders. In 1770 he was elected to the Pennsylvania Assembly. He married Mary Norris the same year. In the backlash of the Boston Tea Party, Philadelphians debated both their role in aiding a sister city and their position in the imperial argument. Dickinson helped clarify matters in his pamphlet *An Essay on the Constitutional Power of Great Britain*, which granted Parliament power to regulate foreign trade but little else in American life. In the First Continental Congress he drafted both the cogent "Address to the Inhabitants of Quebec," a summary of the rights of Americans, and the petition to George III seeking reconciliation.

Dickinson's attitude characterized the Second Continental Congress, which John Adams saw as holding "the Sword in one Hand [and] the Olive Branch in the other." Dickinson's "Olive Branch" petition to the King boomeranged. By ignoring it, George III slammed the door on moderate Americans and placed Dickinson in a difficult position.

Dickinson's Approach Too Moderate

By 1776 Dickinson was arguing against the inevitable; his opposition to the Declaration of Independence left him a conscientious but marked man. His proposed "Articles of Confederation" proved useful as Congress patched together a national government, but in state politics his ideas were rejected, and he was dropped from the congressional delegation. Exasperated, Dickinson challenged supporters of the ultrademocratic Pennsylvania Constitution by calling for an immediate revision of their work. Frustrated and convinced he was ill, he temporarily retired.

Gradually, Dickinson regained his old political form. In 1779 Delaware sent him back to Congress and in 1781 elected him its chief executive. A year later Pennsylvania also chose him as its president, and he briefly held both offices. Soon, however, he returned to Pennsylvania to serve 3 years as its president. Dickinson was sent to the Annapolis Convention and was a Delaware delegate to the Federal Convention in 1787. Age and health excused him from an active role in debate, but in the ratification campaign he wrote the "Fabius" letters in support of the United States Constitution.

Thereafter, Dickinson appeared rarely in public bodies. He helped draft the 1792 Delaware Constitution but took no part in a similar work for Pennsylvania. He veered away from the Federalists to attack Jay's Treaty. He supported the rising Republican party and Jefferson in 1800 but refused to become politically active himself. Dickinson died on Feb. 14, 1808, at Wilmington, Del.

Further Reading

John Dickinson is listed in the American History study guide (III, C, 1 and 2; III, E, 1) and the Literature study guide (I, B, 3). Other members of the Continental Congress were John ADAMS and John JAY. Dickinson and James OTIS were leading pamphleteers.

There is no satisfactory comprehensive biography of Dickinson. Charles J. Stillé, *The Life and Times of John Dickinson* (1891), is inadequate. David L. Jacobson, *John Dickinson and the Revolution in Pennsylvania, 1764– 1776* (1965), is excellent for its analysis of a significant period. Dickinson's papers in the several leading Philadelphia archives have not yet been collected and edited by a competent scholar. *The Political Writings of John Dickinson*, edited by himself (1801), and Paul L. Ford, ed., *The Writings of John Dickinson* (1895), leave gaps.

✳ ✳ ✳

DIDEROT / By Paul G. Dobson

The French philosopher, playwright, and novelist Denis Diderot (1713–1784) is best known as the editor of the "Encyclopédie."

Denis Diderot. (Giraudon)

On Oct. 15, 1713, Denis Diderot (pronounced dēd-rō′) was born in Langres, Compagne, into a family of cutlers, whose bourgeois traditions went back to the late Middle Ages. As a child, Denis was considered a brilliant student by his Jesuit teachers, and it was decided that he should enter the clergy. In 1726 he enrolled in the Jesuit college of Louis-le-Grand and probably later attended the Jansenist Collège d'Harcourt. In 1732 he earned a master of arts degree in philosophy. He then abandoned the clergy as a career and decided to study law. His legal training, however, was short-lived. In 1734 Diderot decided to seek his fortune by writing. He broke with his family and for the next 10 years lived a rather bohemian existence. He earned his living by translating English works and tutoring the children of wealthy families and spent his leisure time studying. In 1743 he further alienated his father by marrying Anne Toinette Champion.

The "Encyclopédie"

On Jan. 21, 1746, André François le Breton and his partners were granted permission to publish a 10-volume encyclopedia. On the advice of the distinguished mathematician Jean d'Alembert and with the consent of Chancellor D'Aguesseau, Diderot was named general editor of the project.

For more than 26 years Diderot devoted the bulk of his energies and his genius to the writing, editing, and publishing of the *Encyclopédie*. For Diderot, the aim of the work was "to assemble the knowledge scattered over the face of the earth; to explain its general plan to the men with whom we live . . . so that we may not die without having deserved well of the human race." Such was the plan and the purpose of the *Encyclopédie*, and it was also the credo of the Enlightenment. But the project was more than just the compilation of all available knowledge; it was also a learning experience for all those regu-

larly connected with it. It introduced Diderot to technology, the crafts, the fine arts, and many other areas of learning. It was an outlet for his curiosity, his scholarly interests, and his creativity.

In 1751 D'Alembert's *Preliminary Discourse* and the first volume were published. In January 1752 the second volume appeared, but the opposition of the Jesuits and other orthodox critics forced a temporary suspension. Publication was soon resumed and continued at the rate of one volume a year until 1759, when the Royal Council forbade further operations. Diderot and Le Breton, however, continued to write and publish the *Encyclopédie* secretly until 1765, when official sanction was resumed. In 1772 the completed work was published in 17 volumes of text and 11 volumes of plates under the title *Encyclopédie, ou Dictionnaire raisonné des sciences, des arts, et des métiers.*

Other Writings

Throughout the period of his association with the *Encyclopédie*, Diderot continued to devote himself to other writing. In 1746 he published *Philosophical Thoughts*, which was concerned with the question of the relationship between nature and religion. He viewed life as self-sufficient and held that virtue could be sustained without religious beliefs. In *Sceptics Walk* (1747) and *Letters on the Blind* (1749) Diderot slowly turned from theism to atheism. Religion became a central theme in his writings, and he aroused the hostility of public officials who considered him a leader of the radicals, "a clever fellow, but extremely dangerous."

In 1749 Diderot was imprisoned for 3 months because of his opinions in *Philosophical Thoughts*. Although he had stated, "If you impose silence on me about religion and government, I shall have nothing to talk about," after his release he reduced the controversial character of his published works. Therefore most of his materialistic and antireligious works and several of his novels were not published during his lifetime.

During his long literary career Diderot moved away from the mechanical approach to nature, which was characteristic of the Enlightenment's use of the discoveries of Sir Isaac Newton. Such works as *D'Alembert's Dream, Conversation between D'Alembert and Diderot, Thoughts on the Interpretation of Nature, Elements of Physiology,* and *Essay on Seneca* vividly point to the evolution of his thought and to its modernity.

In his mature writings Diderot tends to see man as an integral part of an organic and vitalistic nature, governed by laws that are incomprehensible to him. Nature, according to Diderot, is a continually unfolding process, which reveals itself, rather than being revealed by man. Forms in nature develop from earlier forms in a continually evolving process, in which all elements, animate and inanimate, are related to one another. Man can know nature only through experience; thus rationalistic speculation is useless to him in understanding nature.

Diderot is one of the pre-19th-century leaders in the movement away from mathematics and physics, as a source of certain knowledge, to biological probability and historical insight. As one modern scholar has stated, Diderot's approach to nature and philosophy was that of mystical naturalism.

Later Years

Following the completion of the *Encyclopédie,* Diderot went into semiretirement; he wrote but infrequently published his works. His earnings as editor of the *Encyclopédie* guaranteed him a modest income, which he supplemented by writing literary criticism. In addition, he sold his library to Empress Catherine of Russia, who allowed him to keep it while he lived and paid him an annual salary as its librarian. On July 30, 1784, Diderot died in the home of his daughter, only 5 months after the death of his beloved mistress and intellectual companion, Sophie Voland.

The great paradox of Diderot's life is found in the tensions that existed between his basically bourgeois nature and his bohemian tendencies. This struggle was mirrored in his novel *Rameau's Nephew,* in which the staid Rameau and his bohemian nephew represent aspects of Diderot's personality. Fittingly, Diderot's last words, "The first step toward philosophy is incredulity," are an adequate measure of the man.

Further Reading

Denis Diderot is listed in the Social Sciences study guide (V, B, 2) and the Literature study guide (III, F, 1; III, G, 1). Among others associated with the *Encyclopédie* were Jean d'ALEMBERT, Jean Jacques ROUSSEAU, and VOLTAIRE.

Two biographies of Diderot are outstanding: Lester G. Crocker, *Diderot: The Embattled Philosopher* (1952), an accurate and penetrating work, but with a tinge of romanticism; and Arthur M. Wilson, *Diderot: The Testing Years, 1713–1759* (1957), apparently a more scholarly work, but in reality lacking only the romanticism of Crocker. Both works show notable scholarship in the area of Diderot studies. Among the shorter works, George R. Havens, *The Age of Ideas* (1955), contains four excellent and highly original chapters on Diderot.

DIEFENBAKER / By J. L. Granatstein

John George Diefenbaker (born 1895) was prime minister of Canada and leader of the Progressive Conservative party. Though his government had some remarkable successes, he left a legacy of bitterness and disunion for his party.

John Diefenbaker was born at Neustadt, Ontario, on Sept. 18, 1895. In 1903 his family moved west to the prairies. After war service in England, he was invalided home. He then took a law degree at the University of Saskatchewan. His law career was successful from the outset, and Diefenbaker won a reputation as a fierce cross-examiner.

Politics was clearly his first love, however, although his first attempts were unsuccessful. He was defeated in five elections before he won a seat in Parliament in 1940. There he quickly established a reputation, and in 1942 and 1948 he tried and failed to win the party leadership. In 1956, however, Diefenbaker was the overwhelming choice of a leadership convention, becoming at age 61 the leader of the Opposition.

In a stunning upset in the 1957 election, Diefenbaker won a minority victory and formed a remarkably successful government. New legislation flooded the statute books, helping pensioners and farmers and cutting taxes. Early in 1958 Diefenbaker dissolved Parliament and scored a devastating victory, winning 208 of 265 seats.

The Conservative leader could only go downhill from the heights of 1958. Unemployment soon began to climb, Quebec was restive, there were difficulties with the United States, and the Liberals were recovering. The forceful image that had propelled Diefenbaker to victory was replaced with one of bumbling indecisiveness. An election in 1962 saw Diefenbaker returned to office with a minority government, and early in 1963 the administration was defeated in Parliament. The defeat was caused by the Prime Minister's inability to decide if Canada should accept nuclear warheads for the country's NORAD defense systems. His defense minister resigned, the U.S. State Department intervened, and the Conservatives were soon in a state of collapse. It was a tribute to Diefenbaker's campaigning skills that, although his party lost the election of 1963, it survived at all.

The last 4 years of Diefenbaker's party leadership were stormy. Bolstered by the support of loyal westerners, he

John Diefenbaker.

was still a force to be reckoned with, but to urbanites the "Chief" was electoral poison. An attempt to challenge him in 1964 was crushed, and although the party came together to fight the 1965 election, the final attack came in 1966, when Diefenbaker was discredited. For a year more he hung on, but at a leadership convention in 1967 he was trounced.

Further Reading

John Diefenbaker is listed in the Canada study guide (IV, A, 3). He succeeded the Liberal Louis ST. LAURENT as prime minister.

There are as yet no scholarly studies of Diefenbaker, although an official biography has been in preparation. The best sources are Peter Newman, *Renegade in Power: The Diefenbaker Years* (1964) and *The Distemper of Our Times: Canadian Politics in Transition, 1963–1968* (1968).

DIELS / By Robert F. Erickson

The German organic chemist Otto Paul Hermann Diels (1876–1954) discovered a technique of atomic combination which led to the synthesis of an important group of organic compounds.

ermann Diels (pronounced dēls) was born in Hamburg on Jan. 23, 1876. After studying chemistry at the University of Berlin he was awarded a doctoral degree in 1899. In that year he joined the faculty as assistant professor and became associate professor in 1914. He became professor of chemistry at the University of Kiel in 1916 and held this position until his retirement in 1948.

In his early work at Berlin, Diels discovered carbon suboxide (1906) and investigated its properties. The compound was important because of its high degree of reactivity and because its chemical structure provided important information as to the composition of other oxides of the carbon atom. However, Diels's most important work was done at Kiel, where he was assisted by Kurt Alder. Together they were able to work out the technique of a new atomic combination.

The now famous Diels-Alder reaction involved a diene synthesis. In this reaction there appeared a new molecular structure, one which hitherto had not been recognized. It consisted of what came to be identified as a conjugated diene, that is, an organic substance containing two double-bonded carbon atoms in a ring compound. The first experiments showed that the compound butadiene would react vigorously with maleic anhydride to produce a six-membered ring compound, and further experimentation showed that the simple dienes, such as butadiene, could be changed into cyclic dienes, which, in turn, could be used as the bases for a new group of organic compounds.

One of the most remarkable aspects of the Diels-Alder reaction was the lack of a need for reagents, catalysts, or high temperatures and pressures. The process proceeded at a relatively slow pace at temperatures usually associated with animal organisms. The potentiality of the reaction was profound. Diels went on to one synthesis after another, among the most notable being that of the polymerization of the diene isoprene into synthetic rubber. Other investigators produced a whole family of plastics, alkaloids, and polymers from the technique of the Diels-Alder reaction. The synthesis of cortisone was an outcome of this technique. In addition to this work, Diels also investigated cholesterol and bile acids, and

Hermann Diels. (German Information Center, New York)

the degradation products involved in dehydrogenation brought about by the use of the metal selenium.

Although the new organic products for which Diels was so much responsible may have produced benefits for mankind, it should not be forgotten that one of the most important parts of his research was a new insight into chemical combination and molecular structure. In 1950, in recognition of his many contributions to chemical science, Diels, together with Alder, was awarded the Nobel Prize. Diels died at Kiel on March 7, 1954.

Further Reading

Hermann Diels is listed in the Science study guide (VII, D, 2). Among his teachers was the great German organic chemist Emil FISCHER.

There is virtually nothing in English on the life of Diels. However, for discussions of his scientific achievements, the reader should consult Eduard Farber, *Nobel Prize Winners in Chemistry, 1901–1961* (1953; rev. ed. 1963); Aaron J. Ihde, *The Development of Modern Chemistry* (1964); Nobel Foundation, *Chemistry: Nobel Lectures, Including Presentation Speeches and Laureates' Biographies*, vol. 3 (1964); and James R. Partington, *A History of Chemistry*, vol. 4 (1964).

Ngo Dinh Diem in 1955. (Wide World Photos)

DIEM / By Richard Butwell

Ngo Dinh Diem (1901–1963) was South Vietnam's first premier and president. Leader of South Vietnam after the 1954 partition, he initially provided inspiring leadership but later became dictatorial when pressed by the Vietcong assault against his government.

The son of a minister and councilor to a former Vietnamese emperor, Ngo Dinh Diem (pronounced n'gō dĭn dyĕm) was born Jan. 3, 1901, near Hue. In the 17th century his ancestors had been converted to Catholicism by missionaries to their Buddhist homeland, subsequently suffering much persecution.

Graduating from the government's school of administration at Hue, Diem rose to be governor of Phan Thiet province at the age of 28. Four years later he was named minister of interior in Emperor Bao Dai's central administration of the protectorate of Annam at Hue. Diem soon resigned his post, however, because neither the French nor Bao Dai would support reforms he advocated. For 21 years, from 1933 to 1954, Diem played no role of importance in Vietnam. His reputation as a nationalist grew nonetheless, largely based on his abandonment of high position in protest of French colonial rule.

Twice during the wartime Japanese occupation, Diem refused invitations to serve as premier. Held captive by Ho Chi Minh's Communist Viet Minh at the war's end, he was offered the post of interior minister in Ho's government but refused. He also declined to participate in Bao Dai's pro-French government of limited "independence" in 1949.

Diem traveled to the United States in 1950, the first year of American aid to still French-ruled Vietnam. He returned after a brief stay in France and lobbied for American support of full independence for Vietnam. He left the United States a year later and took up residence in a Belgian monastery.

Following the fall of Dien Bien Phu in 1954, Diem returned to Vietnam to accept the premiership, which he assumed on July 7, two weeks before the Geneva Accords divided the country. Long opposed to Emperor Bao Dai, Diem defeated him in a noncontested election in 1955, declaring South Vietnam a republic and becoming its first president.

Diem at first displayed outstanding leadership, building new schools and roads and surprisingly quickly rehabilitating a badly shattered economy. He refused to acquiesce in the 1956 reunification elections set by the Geneva Accords, however. The Communists subsequently inaugurated a strategy of armed revolt.

Diem became more autocratic as the war years progressed. His family had always been clannish, and he became increasingly dependent on the advice of his brother, Ngo Dinh Nhu, whose attractive and assertive wife also played a major role in his government. Diem's lack of judgment was particularly evident in 1963, when government forces fired on Buddhist demonstrators in Hue, killing eight and precipitating a crisis in which several monks subsequently burned themselves to death. The Americans, who had heretofore strongly supported Diem, gave evidence of wavering, and this was all that a group of soldiers needed to depose him. Diem was overthrown and murdered on Nov. 2, 1963.

Further Reading

Ngo Dinh Diem is listed in the Asia study guide (IV, A, 3, d). Among his Communist Vietnamese opponents were HO Chi Minh and Vo Nguyen GIAP.

Probably the most accurate, although unsympathetic, portrait of Diem is in Willard A. Hanna, *Eight Nation Makers* (1964), which is a volume of portraits of major Southeast Asian leaders of the late 1950s and early 1960s. A longer and too laudatory treatment is Anthony T. Bouscaren, *The Last of the Mandarins: Diem of Vietnam* (1965). A more balanced account is in Denis Warner, *The Last Confucian* (1963; rev. ed. 1964). Robert Shaplen's excellent *The Lost Revolution: The U.S. in Vietnam, 1946–1966* (1965; rev. ed. 1966) contains a perceptive study of Diem.

DIESEL / By William N. Slatcher

> The German mechanical engineer Rudolf Diesel (1858–1913) is remembered for the compression-ignition internal combustion engine which bears his name.

Rudolf Diesel (pronounced dē′zəl) was born March 18, 1858, in Paris. His interest in mechanics was early roused by frequent visits to the Conservatoire des Arts et Métiers. Early in the Franco-Prussian War (1870) all Germans had to leave Paris, and the Diesels went to England in poverty. After a brief stay there, Rudolf went to an uncle in Augsburg, Germany, where he received a thorough scientific schooling. From 1875 he attended the Munich Polytechnikum (later the Technische Hochschule) and graduated with highest honors. He studied thermodynamics under Carl von Linde and resolved—given the opportunity—to design a heat engine with a thermodynamic cycle approximating to the ideal described by Sadi Carnot in 1824. Great fuel economy could be expected from such a machine. But the opportunity was a long time coming. Meanwhile, in 1880 he returned to Paris to assist in the construction of a refrigeration plant for Linde and then became manager of it. During this period (1881–1890) he put much effort into an abortive design for an expansion engine using ammonia as working fluid (ammonia was also the working fluid in the refrigerator). From Paris, Diesel moved to Berlin in 1890 and continued to work for Linde's refrigeration concern.

About 1890 Diesel saw that air could be used as the working fluid and worked out the elements of his engine cycle. Air, highly compressed in a cylinder, would rise in temperature; fuel injected into this hot gas would burn spontaneously. Ideally, combustion would occur at constant temperature and pressure, and expansion of the gases would drive the piston. Thus the conversion of heat to work would reach an optimum. Diesel's design was sufficiently advanced for him to patent it in 1892, and he described it in the paper "The Theory and Design of a Rational Heat Engine" (1893). With Linde's support two outstanding German concerns, Maschinenfabrik, Augsburg, and Friedrich Krupp, Essen, agreed to finance its development. From 1893 Diesel worked on the engine at Augsburg. By 1897 the engine was perfected to Diesel's satisfaction, and it was displayed in the Munich Exhibition of 1898. It used a heavier fuel oil than the then relatively explosive gasoline engines with which it was to compete. Its fuel economy was remarkable, and it ran quietly.

With success came worldwide interest, and manufacturers were licensed to build the engine. In 1897 Adolphus Busch acquired the United States license for $1 million cash. In 1899 a new company was established in Augsburg to make the engine, but Diesel's illness and rife speculation in the shares made the venture a failure. However, development work forged ahead elsewhere. Illness, stemming from overwork in the development period, crippled Diesel, and though he continued lecture tours, his direct involvement in the engine declined. He died at sea after falling from the Antwerp-Harwich steamer *Dresden* on the night of Sept. 29/30, 1913.

Further Reading

Rudolf Diesel is listed in the Science study guide (VI, H, 2). Sadi CARNOT wrote a famous book on the motive

Rudolf Diesel. (German Information Center, New York)

power of heat which stimulated Diesel's work. Gottlieb DAIMLER made another type of internal combustion engine.

The chapter on Diesel in Eugen Diesel and others, *From Engines to Autos: Five Pioneers in Engine Development* (1960), provides valuable information. A laudatory biography of Diesel, written in a journalistic style, is Robert W. Nitske and Charles Morrow Wilson, *Rudolf Diesel: Pioneer of the Age of Power* (1965).

* * *

DILLINGER / By Joel Goldfarb

John Dillinger (1903–1934) was the most famous modern American criminal. During the Depression of the 1930s his bank robberies were generally regarded as revenge on society's financial institutions that were unfairly exploiting the economically distressed.

John Dillinger was born on June 22, 1903, in Indianapolis, Ind. His mother died when he was quite young; he was raised by an older sister and eventually, when his father remarried, by his stepmother. At 16 he quit school and began to work intermittently. A year later his father moved the family to a farm near Mooresville, Ind. Dillinger rejected rural life and spent most of his time in the surrounding cities.

In 1923 Dillinger fell in love, but the girl's father ended the romance. Embittered, Dillinger stole a car which he later abandoned. Afraid of being prosecuted, he joined the Navy but deserted a few months later. In 1924 he was arrested for assault and attempted robbery. On the advice of his father he pled guilty; not only did he receive a more severe sentence than his accomplice, who pled not guilty, but also the accomplice secured parole after 2 years, while Dillinger languished in prison.

A difficult prisoner, Dillinger served much of his time in solitary confinement. As is frequently the case, Dillinger's confinement, instead of reforming and rehabilitating him, only trained him to be a criminal. When he left prison in 1933, he carried a map, supplied by inmates, of prospective robbery sites.

Released during the worst of the Depression, as an ex-convict it is unlikely that Dillinger could have secured legitimate employment. He quickly found employment robbing banks, however, and almost overnight became a kind of Robin Hood national hero. The fact that people were killed during his holdups was overlooked; instead the national press played him up as a brilliant, daring, likeable individual, beating the banks which had been inhumanely foreclosing mortgages on helpless debtors.

Dillinger became a challenge for law enforcement officials, for he often made them look like fools; conflicts between police jurisdictions made him difficult to capture. When he was captured, he was able to escape. His most famous exploit was when he broke out of heavily guarded Crown Point County Jail armed only with a wooden gun. Eventually, however, the members of his gang were killed or caught. Dillinger moved to Chicago, disguised himself, and attempted to disappear. But he was recognized by Anna Sage, a woman who lived with his girl friend, Polly.

On July 22, 1934, Anna Sage went to a movie with Dillinger and Polly; she wore an orange skirt to identify herself, and Dillinger, to waiting Federal agents. They gunned him down. Even in death Dillinger remained a thorn in the side of the establishment. Anna Sage ("the lady in red") became a hated figure, like most informers, and the image of law enforcement suffered through what was regarded as too little willingness to take Dillinger, then almost a national hero, alive.

Further Reading

John Dillinger is listed in the American History study guide (IX, D, 7). Another notorious criminal was Al CAPONE. The leader of the Federal Bureau of Investigation was J. Edgar HOOVER.

Interesting popularized accounts of Dillinger are contained in Robert Cromie and Joseph Pinkston, *Dillinger: A Short and Violent Life* (1962), and in John Toland, *The Dillinger Days* (1963). For a perspective on Dillinger in the context of his times consult Don Congdon, ed., *The Thirties: A Time to Remember* (1962). The law enforcement viewpoint is presented in Andrew Tully, *The FBI's Most Famous Cases* (1965). See also Jay R. Nash and Ron Offen, *Dillinger: Dead or Alive* (1970).

* * *

John Dillinger. (Underwood & Underwood News Photos)

DILTHEY / By Daniel O'Connor

The German historian and philosopher Wilhelm Christian Ludwig Dilthey (1833–1911) held that psychological principles should form the basis of historical and sociological research.

Wilhelm Dilthey (pronounced dĭl'tī) was born in Biebrich, a village in the Rhineland, on Nov. 19, 1833. His family was intimately connected with the dukes of Nassau, serving for generations as chaplains and councilors. His early education was at a local gymnasium, from which he graduated in 1852. Following family tradition, Dilthey entered the University of Heidelberg to study theology. After three semesters he moved to Berlin for historical studies under Friedrich Trendelenburg. To please his father, he took the examination in theology and preached his first sermon in 1856. His preferred occupation was secondary teaching, but after 2 happy years he was forced to give this up as a result of persistent ill health. The next half-dozen years were spent in historical research and philosophical study at Berlin.

In 1864, with an essay on the ethics of Friedrich Schleiermacher, Dilthey entered university teaching. In 1866 he was called to Basel; in 1882, after brief tours in Kiel and Breslau, he returned to Berlin as professor of theology, a post he held until 1905. In 1874 Dilthey married Katherine Puttmann, and the couple had one son and two daughters. He died on Oct. 3, 1911, in Seis.

Dilthey published little during his lifetime, but since his death 14 volumes of collected writings have appeared. These include profound essays in intellectual history and original work on the philosophy of the mind. He made repeated efforts to arrive at general categories for interpreting comparative *Weltanschauungen* (philosophies of life). In imitation of Immanuel Kant's opus, Dilthey aspired to write a "Critique of Historical Reason," tracing the emergence and evolution of the great systems of thought. Dilthey concluded that no overall synthesis of these varying outlooks was possible but that an awareness of a certain historical relativity was the condition for intellectual liberation and creative work.

Dilthey argued convincingly for historical interpretation in all inquiries into man and his culture. Human life and creativity cannot be understood abstractly but only as part of a historical process. The historian must sympathetically enter into the alien cultures he seeks to understand. Much of Dilthey's work was an effort to describe the characteristic differences between this approach in historical subjects and the approach of the natural scientist toward his subject matter.

Further Reading

Wilhelm Dilthey is listed in the Philosophy study guide (VI, H). Although his work had considerable influence on such thinkers as Martin HEIDEGGER, José ORTEGA Y GASSET, and Max WEBER of Germany, it has had

Wilhelm Dilthey. (Bildarchiv)

relatively little impact on Anglo-American thought.

Fragmentary biographical information on Dilthey is contained in William Kluback, *Wilhelm Dilthey's Philosophy of History* (1956). H. A. Hodges, *Wilhelm Dilthey: An Introduction* (1944), contains a good bibliography, and his *The Philosophy of Wilhelm Dilthey* (1952) is the most comprehensive treatment.

DINESEN / By Allen Simpson

Isak Dinesen was the pseudonym used by the Danish author Karen Dinesen Blixen-Finecke (1885–1962). Her stories place her among Denmark's greatest authors.

Isak Dinesen (pronounced dĭn'ə-sən) was born on April 17, 1885, the daughter of a wealthy landowner, adventurer, and author. In 1914 she went to Africa, married, and bought a coffee plantation. After her divorce in 1921 she managed the plantation alone until economic disaster forced her to return to Denmark in 1931, where she lived the rest of her life on the family estate, Rungstedlund, near Copenhagen.

The years in Africa were the happiest of Isak Dinesen's life, for she felt, from the first, that she belonged there.

Isak Dinesen. (Nordisk Pressefoto, Copenhagen)

Had she not been forced to leave, she wrote later, she would not have become an author. In the dark days just before leaving, she began to write down some of the stories she had told to her friends among the colonists and natives. She wrote in English, the language she used in Africa. Her books usually appeared simultaneously in America, England, and Denmark, written in English and then rewritten in Danish.

Isak Dinesen's first collection, *Seven Gothic Tales*, appeared in America in 1934, where it was a literary sensation, immediately popular with both critics and public. The Danish critical reaction was cool. Danish literature was still dominated by naturalism, as it had been for the past 60 years, and her work was a reaction against this sober, realistic fiction of analysis.

Isak Dinesen's second book, *Out of Africa* (1937), a brilliant recreation of her African years, was a critical and popular success wherever it appeared. Although it has little in common, stylistically and formally, with her stories, it describes the experiences which formed her views about life and art. The third central work in her authorship, *Winter's Tales*, appeared in 1942.

A characteristic of Isak Dinesen's works is the sense that the reader is listening to a storyteller. She wanted to revive in her "listeners" the primitive love of mystery that she found in her African audience, which she felt was like the audiences that listened to Homer, the Old Testament stories, the *Arabian Nights*, and the sagas (elements from all of which she skillfully wove into her stories). She attempted to reawaken the sense of myth

and, with myth, the sense of man's tragic grandeur, which she felt had been lost.

Fifteen years after *Winter's Tales*, Isak Dinesen published *Last Tales* (1957), containing some of her finest stories. This volume includes "The Cardinal's First Tale," an excellent defense of her art and a critique of naturalism. In 1958 appeared *Anecdotes of Destiny*. Her last book, *Shadows on the Grass* (1961), is a pendant to *Out of Africa*.

Isak Dinesen was the first Danish author to achieve world fame since Hans Christian Andersen and Søren Kierkegaard. Her influence on Danish literature was especially strong in the 1950s when, through her stories and personal contact, she was an inspiration to younger authors searching for new means of expression. She died on Sept. 6, 1962.

Further Reading

Isak Dinesen is listed in the Literature study guide (III, J, 5). Her contemporary Martin Andersen NEXØ was also an outstanding Danish author.

Useful studies of Dinesen in English are Eric O. Johannesson, *The World of Isak Dinesen* (1961), and Robert Langbaum, *The Gayety of Vision: A Study of Isak Dinesen's Art* (1964).

DINGANE / By Colin Webb

Dingane (ca. 1795–1840) was a Zulu king whose reign was blighted by domestic and external difficulties which culminated in fierce conflict with his white neighbors.

Dingane (pronounced dēn-gän′ə) was a younger son of the Zulu chieftain Senzangakona. Little is known of Dingane's career until 1828, when he successfully conspired to assassinate his half brother Shaka who, after Senzangakona's death, had expanded the petty Zulu chieftainship into a powerful warrior kingdom at the expense of neighboring chiefs.

Although many welcomed Dingane's accession for the relief it offered from the fierce militarism of Shaka's reign, it is doubtful whether Dingane ever felt secure on the throne he had seized. His position was that of a usurper who owed his rise from obscurity to the achievements of the brother he had murdered. His kingdom, not yet 12 years old, was a forced creation in which national spirit had still not effectively submerged older political loyalties. And, among his subjects, assassination and social fission were established techniques for dealing with political difficulties. In 1829 the Qwabe subchief, Nqetho, led his followers south in a major secessionist movement, and defections continued during the years that followed.

Dingane lacked the qualities of the warrior leader. Indolent and inconstant, jealous and untrusting, he failed to arouse loyalty and affection in his subjects. To preserve his hold over his kingdom, he resorted to the methods of terrorism and extermination that Shaka had used; but he was unable to inject into his warriors the fierce fighting spirit that had once made them the terror of southeastern Africa, and his campaigns were either inconclusive or ended in humiliating defeat.

Probably because he valued trade and feared that injury to the interests of British subjects might bring retribution from the Cape, Dingane tolerated the small settlement of English traders and hunters that Shaka had permitted at the port of Natal, but he did so with diminishing enthusiasm. The traders possessed firearms that gave them a power disproportionate to their numbers. They defied his commands yet lacked law-enforcing authorities of their own. And their settlement became a place of refuge for thousands of deserters from Zululand.

In 1830 Dingane had sent an embassy to the Cape, but the expedition was tactlessly managed and relations with the whites deteriorated. For a while after 1835 Dingane seems to have hoped that the missionary Capt. A. F. Gardiner would serve as a "subchief" and control the Natal settlement, but again he was disappointed for Gardiner was unable to establish his authority.

Dingane's most serious difficulties began toward the end of 1837, when he was confronted by the leader of a large party of Trekkers (Afrikaner emigrants) from the Cape, seeking to establish a republic on his southern borderlands. These were rebels against British rule, injury to whose interests was unlikely to bring retaliation from the Cape. But Dingane seems to have feared that an outright refusal of their request might precipitate a conflict in which Zulu armies with a record of failure would be forced into open conflict with men whose firearms had already dispersed the great Ndebele kingdom of Mzilikazi. He therefore appeared to assent to their demands, but in February 1838 he trapped and massacred a large deputation headed by Piet Retief and then sent out his armies to fall upon the unsuspecting Trekker camps under cover of night.

This attempt to rid himself of the intruders by treachery and surprise failed in its purpose. The Trekkers rallied and in December at Blood River inflicted on the Zulu armies the heavy slaughter that Dingane seems to have anticipated from open conflict. Fission followed within the Zulu body politic. Dingane's half brother Mpande defected south with thousands of followers, entered into a client relationship with the Trekkers, and in February 1840 routed Dingane's troops at the battle of Magongo. Dingane, a refugee from his own people, sought his escape northward but was murdered in the Ubombo Mountains later in the year.

His efforts to preserve his throne and insulate his kingdom from the disturbing presence of white neighbors profoundly influenced the attitudes of the emergent Afrikaner people, amongst whom the conflict was commemorated as one between "civilization" and "barbarism."

Further Reading

Dingane is listed in the Africa study guide (VII, F, 2, b). His half brother SHAKA created the first Zulu military monarchy.

Peter Becker, *Rule of Fear* (1964), is a popular account of the life and times of Dingane based on oral tradition and documentary sources. It should be read with Alfred T. Bryant, *Olden Times in Zululand and Natal* (1929); Donald R. Morris, *The Washing of the Spears* (1965); and John D. Omer-Cooper, *The Zulu Aftermath* (1966). Also helpful is Monica Wilson and Leonard Thompson, eds., *The Oxford History of South Africa* (1969).

Dingane in 1838.

DINWIDDIE / By Irwin H. Polishook

The Scottish merchant Robert Dinwiddie (1693–1770) rose through colonial administrative ranks to the lieutenant governorship of Virginia.

Robert Dinwiddie was born of an old Scottish family. His father was a prosperous merchant, and his mother also came from a commercial family. Robert was educated at the University of Glasgow

Robert Dinwiddie. (The New York Public Library, Picture Collection)

and entered his father's countinghouse. He later carried on a successful career as a merchant.

Dinwiddie's role as a colonial administrator began in 1721, when he was appointed British representative in Bermuda. After 16 years of service in Bermuda he received the important position of surveyor general, which included jurisdiction over Pennsylvania and the southern colonies of British North America. By tradition the surveyor general was entitled to a seat on the Virginia Council, a post Dinwiddie insisted on assuming. Characteristic of Dinwiddie's service in the Colonies was his zealous attention to the offices under his authority and a tendency to maximize his position by emphasizing the royal prerogative. In recognition of these qualities, he was appointed lieutenant governor of Virginia, England's largest colony, and took office on July 4, 1751.

As lieutenant governor, Dinwiddie saw the beginnings of the conflict on Virginia's frontiers that led to the French and Indian War. He was a firm advocate of British expansion into the west. He sought the help of the Indians and the other British colonies in the struggle against the French, pressed the legislature for defense funds, and favored the use of regular armed forces in place of the less reliable militia. Dinwiddie made George Washington a lieutenant colonel in 1754.

Generally, Dinwiddie was able to work in harmony with the Virginia Legislature. He did, however, prompt a serious conflict with the House of Burgesses shortly after he took office. In hope of increasing the British king's revenues, Dinwiddie tried to levy a fee for land patents, which would also require landholders to pay quitrents to the Crown. This precipitated the famous "Pistole Fee" controversy, in which the lower house charged that the governor had imposed an unlawful tax that endangered colonial liberty—a precursor of the arguments of the American Revolution.

The pressures of office and the war badly taxed Dinwiddie's health. At his own request he was relieved of office in 1758 and with his wife and two daughters returned to Britain. He died in London on July 27, 1770.

Further Reading

Robert Dinwiddie is listed in the American History study guide (II, B, 3, b). Other colonial governors of Virginia were Sir William BERKELEY and Lord DUNMORE.

The most comprehensive study of Dinwiddie is the occasionally laudatory work by Louis Knott Koontz, *Robert Dinwiddie: His Career in American Colonial Government and Western Expansion* (1941). Also valuable are Douglas Freeman, *George Washington: A Biography* (7 vols., 1948–1957), and Richard L. Morton, *Colonial Virginia* (2 vols., 1960). The "Pistole Fee" controversy is best examined in Jack P. Greene, *The Quest for Power: The Lower House of Assembly in the Southern Royal Colonies, 1689–1776* (1963).

DIOCLETIAN / By Frank C. Bourne

> **Diocletian (245–ca. 313), in full Gaius Aurelius Valerius Diocletianus, was a Roman emperor. He established the characteristic form of government for the later empire, the Dominate.**

Diocletian (pronounced dī-ə-klē′shən), whose name before he became emperor was simply Diocles, was a Dalmatian of humble birth. He became commander of Emperor Numerian's bodyguard. When the Emperor was murdered by his praetorian prefect, the troops chose Diocletian in November 284 to succeed and avenge his master.

By early 285 Diocletian had circumvented all opposition and determined to take immediate steps to bring to an end the 50 years of military anarchy (235–284) that had seen 26 emperors gain the throne, and scores of unsuccessful pretenders. He therefore decided to appoint as his caesar (successor-designate) a man of his own age, his old fellow soldier Maximian. The wisdom of this policy was immediately demonstrated by Maximian's military successes in Gaul, Germany, and North Africa between 286 and 290. Diocletian, meanwhile, controlled the Danubian and eastern frontiers. His satisfaction with the arrangement led him in 286 to raise Maximian to the rank of augustus, or coemperor.

Consolidation of the Empire

In 293 Diocletian extended and formalized the system

of joint leadership by the establishment of the so-called tetrarchy. He and Maximian adopted as their caesars and aides Galerius and Constantius (I) Chlorus, respectively, and each young man was prevailed upon to divorce his wife and become the son-in-law of his augustus. Maximian assumed the general supervision of the West (prefecture of Italy) with headquarters in Milan; Constantius had special responsibility in Gaul and Britain and Galerius in the Balkans (Illyrium). Diocletian was in general control of the East with headquarters at Nicomedia (modern Izmir, Turkey), but the others also regarded him as their superior and guide.

Diocletian's innovation proved a military success: in 296 Constantius returned Britain, which had split away nearly a decade before, to the empire; Maximian triumphed over Moorish revolts in 297; and Diocletian suppressed insurrections in Egypt in 295 and 297. Galerius held the Danubian frontier successfully, and in 297 he so thoroughly defeated Narses I of Persia that more than 50 years of peace was achieved for that area.

Roman Administration and Army

During the 3d century governors of the larger provinces of the empire had repeatedly become rival claimants for the throne. Diocletian sought to correct this danger by splitting up the provinces into far smaller units—the number rose from less than 50 to well over 100—and within these units civil and military administrations were carefully separated. The smaller units fostered more careful and personal administrative and judicial work by governors and promoted imperial stability, but

Roman legions battling Germanic tribesmen along the northeastern boundary of the Roman Empire, a relief from the Column of Marcus Aurelius, Rome. (Archiv für Kunst und Geschichte, Berlin)

resultant proliferation of bureaucratic machinery effected a severe strain on the economy.

Diocletian also began to systematize a new organization of the army, formalizing tendencies that constant 3d-century warfare had brought about. The old legions, now sedentary and in effect a militia of farmers, were stationed along the frontiers to absorb the first shock of external attack. New, mobile, and much smaller legions (1,000 to 1,500 men, as opposed to the old 6,000) were stationed in garrison cities to back up the frontier troops. Diocletian also developed the use of mounted troops and began the organization of special crack troops, the *comitatenses,* or friends of the emperor, to serve as an imperial bodyguard. All this raised the size of the army from about 400,000 to about 500,000 men. It also increased the financial burdens of the state, though the frontier troops undoubtedly largely supported themselves from the land.

Finance Reforms

Diocletian undertook an ambitious building program, which included the enormous Baths of Diocletian at Rome and his palace for retirement at Spalato (modern Split) in Dalmatia, and he also encouraged his colleagues to sponsor public works. This program, with the demands of the bureaucracy and the army, severely strained the empire's finances, and Diocletian undertook a complete reform of the tax structure to meet these needs. His new system was based on the establishment of units of approximately equal value of land or of living things: that is, the unit of land (a *jugum*) could equal 20 acres of first-class plowland, 5 acres of vineyard, or 225 olive trees; or the head unit (*caput*) could equal the labor of one man, two women, or the sale value of a given number of animals. The value of the nation's resources was to be reviewed periodically; and the emperor and his advisers, after determining the national budget, each year could then set the tax rate per *jugum* and *caput*.

Diocletian, an ancient Roman portrait bust in the Capitoline Museum, Rome. (Alinari)

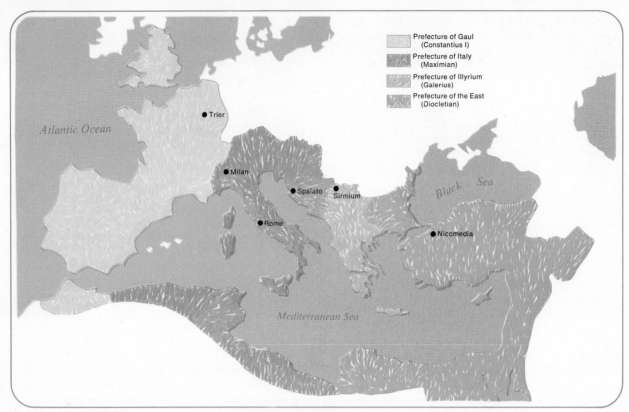

The Roman Empire under Diocletian. Diocletian's reorganization of the empire briefly revived the vigor and efficiency of its government. He and his coemperor and their two caesars each presided over a prefecture, although his colleagues continued to regard Diocletian as their superior.

A steady debasement of the coinage during the 3d century had undermined all public confidence in the monetary system. Diocletian instituted a complete currency reform, and a uniform currency for the whole empire was devised. It appears, though the details are obscure, that this reform sent prices skyrocketing, probably because much of the old coinage was still in circulation and was now suspect. In any case, the desperate plight of soldiers and bureaucrats, who were on a fixed salary, forced Diocletian in 301 to issue an edict setting maximum prices for almost every conceivable article and service throughout the empire. The penalty for nonobservance was death. The efficacy of the measure appears to have been disappointing and the need brief. The extant fragments of the edict are of immense value in calculating the standard of living in the Roman world.

The Court

Diocletian had lived and fought for many years in the East, and he had observed that the secluded Oriental potentates were victimized by their subjects far less frequently than the more democratic Romans. Therefore, though himself a man of simple tastes, he determined to surround the throne with all the trappings of Oriental monarchy. He seldom appeared in public, but when he did it was with diadem, royal purple, and robes embroidered with gold. This was supported by an appeal to

religion. Diocletian was considered the special spokesman on earth for Jupiter, the king of the gods, and he assumed the epithet "Jovius"; Maximian became "Herculius" as the representative of Hercules, the industrious son and helper of Jupiter, and who, as the benefactor of mankind, was running a close race with Christ for the allegiance of the Roman masses.

Relations with Christians

For most of his reign Diocletian was tolerant of dissident religious sects, including the Christians. But some Romans, especially Galerius, felt that the Christians were subverting Diocletian's attempt to emphasize the religious basis of his government to strengthen the state. In 303 Diocletian finally was prevailed upon to issue an edict banning Christian churches, assemblies, and sacred books. This ban was soon followed by two fires of mysterious origin in the Emperor's own palace in Nicomedia, which probably suggested the need for three further and progressively more severe edicts. These edicts were observed in a very uneven fashion, however, being strictly enforced only in Galerius's domain.

Diocletian's Retirement

In 303 Diocletian visited Rome for the first time to observe his twentieth anniversary as emperor. The following year he suffered from a very severe illness, probably a stroke, which seems to have convinced him that it was high time to turn over the reins of government to the caesars. On May 1, 305, therefore, he abdicated at Nicomedia, and by prearrangement Maximian performed the same act simultaneously at Milan. Galerius and Constantius Chlorus were elevated to the rank of augusti, while Flavius Valerius Severus became caesar in the West and Maximin Daia in the East.

Diocletian retired to the palace that he had prepared for himself in Spalato. There he busied himself with his vegetable garden, refusing to return to the political scene except for one brief peacemaking conference in 308 between his squabbling successors. He died at Spalato, probably in 313.

Further Reading

Diocletian is listed in the Ancient History study guide (III, C, 4). Among the most illustrious of his successors were CONSTANTINE I and THEODOSIUS.

The most comprehensive and thorough account of Diocletian and his government is in French. In English, there are adequate accounts in the *Cambridge Ancient History*, vol. 12 (1939), and in A. H. M. Jones, *The Later Roman Empire, 284–602* (2 vols., 1964).

✳ ✳ ✳

DIOGENES / By Donald A. Ross

Diogenes (ca. 400–ca. 325 B.C.), a Greek philosopher, was the most famous exponent of Cynicism, which called for a closer imitation of nature, the repudiation of most human conventions, and complete independence of mind and spirit.

The son of Hicesias, Diogenes (pronounced dī-ŏj′ə-nēz) was born in Sinope. He arrived in Athens after he and his father had been exiled from their native city for debasing the coinage in some way. His life in Athens was one of great poverty, but it was there that he adopted Antisthenes's teachings and became the chief exponent of Cynicism.

Although late authors attribute many works to Diogenes, none survives. One persistent tradition is that he wrote tragedies, perhaps to show that the misfortunes celebrated in the works of that genre could have been averted through the way of life which he taught. Because of his great notoriety and because many people in antiquity considered him the founder of Cynicism, a body of legend soon grew up about him and obscured the true accounts of his life. One certainty is that he developed a caustic wit which he used unsparingly on his contemporaries to show them the utter disregard in which he held their conventions and beliefs. The date and place of his death are uncertain, although it is unlikely that he lived later than 325 B.C.

Diogenes was not famous for developing a strong theoretical argument for his way of life. Antisthenes, the pupil of Socrates, was his inspiration, and he put into practice his master's teachings in a way which made a striking impression upon his contemporaries. Indeed, it was Diogenes's application of Antisthenes's principles which gained for him the notoriety he enjoyed. His goals were self-sufficiency, a tough and ascetic way of life, and *anaideia*, or shamelessness.

The first was the ultimate goal at which the Cynic life aimed. It involved a search for true happiness through the realization that wealth, rank, honors, success, and other such worldly aims were as nothing compared with complete independence of mind. The second and third aims supported the first.

Diogenes held that through a rigorous denial of all but the barest necessities of life one could train the body to be free of the world and its delusions. Through *anaideia* one could show the rest of humanity the contempt in which their conventions were held.

It was perhaps this last characteristic of Diogenes and his followers which gave the sect its name, since *anaideia* involved carrying out acts in public which most men usually do in private. Other accounts hold that the name Cynic (doglike) derives from the Gymnasium Kynosarges in Athens, where Antisthenes taught.

Crates, Diogenes's pupil, propagated the master's teachings after his death. In addition to the influence which Diogenes had on numbers of his contemporaries,

Diogenes, portrait bust in the Vatican Museums, Rome. (Alinari-Giraudon)

he also served as a source for the development of Stoicism.

Further Reading

Diogenes is listed in the Philosophy study guide (I, C, 1). The Stoics were fond of ascribing to him some of their own ideas in an attempt to link the development of their school with SOCRATES through ANTISTHENES and ZENO OF CITIUM.

Excellent accounts of the life of Diogenes, as it can be pieced together from various ancient traditions, may be found in D. R. Dudley, *A History of Cynicism* (1937), and Farrand Sayre, *Diogenes of Sinope* (1938). Also good, although more for the Cynics as a group than for Diogenes, is Eduard Zeller, *Outlines of the History of Greek Philosophy* (1881; trans. 1931).

DIOP / By Irving Leonard Markovitz

Cheikh Anta Diop (born 1923) was an African historian who, in a series of studies, dramatically and controversially maintained that the scope of Africa's contribution to world civilization was considerably larger than hitherto acknowledged.

Cheikh Anta Diop. (Courtesy of the Senegalese Ministry of Foreign Affairs, Paris)

Cheikh Anta Diop (pronounced dē-ŏp′) was born at the end of 1923 in Diourbel, Senegal. He received a higher education in France, where he earned a doctorate of letters and was active in African student politics. Upon returning to Senegal, he joined what is today the Institut Fondamentale d'Afrique Noire, where he began, and became the head of, the only carbon-14-dating laboratory in Africa. He also led and founded two political parties in Senegal: the Bloc des Masses Senegalaises in 1961 and a few years later the Front Nationale Senegalaise, both of which were outlawed by the government on the grounds that they threatened destruction of the existing order.

Diop, however, left his mark in the realm of the reassessment of the role of the black man in history and culture. He brought together African culture and politics, a significant development, because people who feel they possess no past of their own tend to be absorbed and assimilated into the governing system.

Diop's argumentative thesis stresses the great contributions of Egypt to the origins of culture and science and then asserts that Egyptian civilization was of black origin. Diop also challenged the prevailing view that the flow of cultural influence was from the north, the European or "Hamitic" areas, southward to the more primitive areas. He argued that the beginnings of civilization arose below the Sahara. The center of a storm of controversy, Diop has nevertheless opened up new paths of exploration, given a new generation redemptive faith in its roots, and presented, if nothing else, a poetic image of greatness that in its daring may come closer to truth than the prosaic rebuttal of its critics, as discovery is piled upon discovery in the unfolding of a new renaissance.

Among Diop's books is *Anteriorité des civilisations nègres: Mythe ou vérité historique* (1967; Anteriority of Black Civilizations: Myth or Historical Verity). In 1966 at Dakar the World Festival of Negro Arts honored Diop as "the black intellectual who has exercised the most fruitful influence in the twentieth century."

Further Reading

Cheikh Anta Diop is listed in the Africa study guide (IX, C, 5). Another African who extolled pride in being African and in African heritage was Léopold SENGHOR.

The best summaries of Diop's work can be found in Claude Wauthier, *The Literature and Thought of Modern Africa* (1964; trans. 1966). An important selection from Diop's *Nations, nègres, et cultures*, in which he accounts for the myths of Negro inferiority, can be found in Irving Leonard Markovitz, ed., *African Politics and Society* (1970).

DIRAC / By Stanley L. Jaki

The English physicist Paul Adrien Maurice Dirac (born 1902) formulated a most general type of quantum mechanics and a relativistic wave equation for the electron which led to the prediction of positive electrons, the first known forms of antimatter.

P aul Dirac was born on Aug. 8, 1902, at Monk Royal in Bristol, the son of Charles Adrien Ladislas Dirac and Florence Hannah Holten Dirac. Paul received his secondary education at the old Merchant Venturers' College and, at the age of 16, entered Bristol University. He graduated 3 years later in electrical engineering. Unable to find employment, he studied mathematics for 2 years before moving to Cambridge as research student and recipient of an 1851 Exhibition scholarship award. His student years (1923–1926) at Cambridge saw the emergence of the mathematical formulation of modern atomic physics in the hands of Louis de Broglie, Werner Heisenberg, Erwin Schrödinger, and Max Born. It was therefore natural that Dirac's attention should turn to a cultivation of mathematics most directly concerned with atomic physics.

Negative Kinetic Energy

Dirac's first remarkable contribution along these lines came before he earned his doctorate in 1926. In his paper "The Fundamental Equations of Quantum Mechanics" (1925), Dirac decided to extricate the fundamental point in Heisenberg's now famous paper. Before Heisenberg, computation of energy levels of optical and x-ray spectra consisted in a somewhat empirical extension of rules provided by Niels Bohr's theory of the atom. Heisenberg succeeded in grouping terms connnected with energy levels in columns forming large squares and also indicated the marvelously simple ways in which any desired energy level could be readily calculated. Dirac found that what Heisenberg really wanted to achieve consisted in a most general type of operation on a "quantum variable" x which was done by "taking the difference of its Heisenberg products with some other quantum variable."

At that time neither Heisenberg nor Dirac had realized that the "Heisenberg products" corresponded to operations in matrix calculus, a fact which was meanwhile being proved by Born and Pascual Jordan in Göttingen. They showed that the noncommutative multiplication of the "Heisenberg quantities" could be summed up in the formula $(p \times q) - (q \times p) = h/(2\pi\sqrt{-1})$, where h is Planck's constant and p and q some canonically conjugate variables. Independently of them, Dirac also obtained the same formula, but through a more fundamental approach to the problem. Dirac's crucial insight consisted in finding that a very simple operation formed the basis of the formula in question. What had to be done was to calculate the value of the classical Poisson bracket $[p,q]$ for p and q and multiply it by a modified form of Planck's constant.

That such a procedure yielded the proper values to be assigned to the difference of $p \times q$ and $q \times p$ was only one aspect of the success. The procedure also provided an outstanding justification of the principle of correspondence, tying into one logical whole the classical and modern aspects of physics. Dirac once remarked that the moment of that insight represented perhaps the most enthralling experience in his life.

But the most startling result of Dirac's equation for the electron was the recognition of the possibility of negative kinetic energy. In other words, his equations implied for the electron an entirely novel type of motion whereby energy had to be put into the electron in order to bring it to rest. The novelty was both conceptual and experimental and received a remarkably quick elucidation.

The experimental clarification came when C. D. Anderson, doing cosmic-ray research in R. A. Millikan's laboratory in Pasadena, Calif., obtained on Aug. 2, 1932, the photograph of an electron path, the curvature of which could be accounted for only if the electron had a positive charge. The positively charged electron, or positron, was, however, still unconnected with the negative energy states implied in Dirac's theory of the electron. The work needed in this respect was largely done by Dirac, though not without some promptings from others. A most lucid summary of the results was given by Dirac in the lecture which he delivered on Dec. 12, 1933, in

Paul Dirac. (H. Roger-Viollet)

Stockholm, when he received the Nobel Prize in physics jointly with Schrödinger.

World of Antimatter

The most startling consequences of Dirac's theory of the electron consisted in the opening up of the world of antimatter. Clearly, if negative electrons had their counterparts in positrons, it was natural to assume that protons had their counterparts as well. Here Dirac argued on the basis of the perfect symmetry that according to him had to prevail in nature. As a matter of fact, it was a lack of symmetry in Schrödinger's equation for the electron that Dirac tried to remedy by giving it a form satisfactory from the viewpoint of relativity.

All this should forcefully indicate that Dirac was a thinker of most powerful penetration who reached the most tangible conclusions from carrying to their logical extremes some utterly abstract principles and postulates. Thus by postulating the identity of all electrons, he was able to show that they had to obey one specific statistics. This fact in turn provided the long-sought clue for the particular features of the conduction of electricity in metals, a problem with which late classical physics and early quantum theory grappled in vain. This attainment of Dirac paralleled a similar, though less fundamental, work by Enrico Fermi, so that the statistics is now known as the Fermi-Dirac statistics.

This contribution of Dirac came during a marvelously creative period in his life, from 1925 to 1930. Its crowning conclusion was the publication of his *Principles of Quantum Mechanics*, a work still unsurpassed for its logical compactness and boldness. The latter quality is clearly motivated by Dirac's unlimited faith in the mathematical structuring of nature. The book is indeed a monument to his confidence that future developments will provide the exact physical counterparts that some of his mathematical symbols still lack.

A telling measure of Dirac's main achievements in physics was the recognition that greeted his work immediately. In 1932 he was elected a fellow of the Royal Society and given the most prestigious post in British science, the Lucasian chair of mathematics at Cambridge. He received the Royal Society's Royal Medal in 1939 and its Copley Medal in 1952. He was a member of many academies, held numerous honorary degrees, and was a guest lecturer in universities all over the world. He married Margaret Wigner, sister of Nobel laureate Eugene P. Wigner, in 1937.

Further Reading

Paul Dirac is listed in the Science study guide (VII, C, 1). Modern atomic physics was formulated by Niels BOHR, Louis de BROGLIE, Erwin SCHRÖDINGER, Werner HEISENBERG, Max BORN, and Dirac. Enrico FERMI and Dirac developed quantum statistics.

Humorous details on Dirac's life can be found in George Gamow, *Biography of Physics* (1961), together with a not too technical discussion of Dirac's theory of holes. See also Niels H. de V. Heathcote, *Nobel Prize Winners in Physics, 1901–1950* (1954). For a rigorous

account of Dirac's role in quantum mechanics, the standard work is Max Jammer, *The Conceptual Development of Quantum Mechanics* (1966). Background works which discuss Dirac include James Jeans, *Physics and Philosophy* (1942), and Barbara Lovett Cline, *The Questioners: Physicists and the Quantum Theory* (1965).

DISNEY / By John F. Matthews

An American film maker and entrepreneur, Walter Elias Disney (1901–1966) created a new kind of popular culture in feature-length animated cartoons and live-action "family" films.

Walt Disney was born in Chicago on Dec. 5, 1901, the son of a hard-bitten, rootless jack-of-all-trades. He was raised partly on a midwestern farm, partly in Kansas City, and was able to acquire some rudimentary art instruction from correspondence courses and Saturday museum classes. He became a World War I high school dropout at 17.

Briefly overseas as an ambulance driver, Disney returned in 1919 to Kansas City for apprenticeship as a commercial illustrator and later made primitive animated advertising cartoons. By 1922 he had set up his own shop in association with Ub Iwerks, whose drawing ability and technical inventiveness were prime factors in Disney's eventual success.

Initial failure sent Disney to Hollywood in 1923, where in partnership with his loyal elder brother Roy he managed to resume cartoon production. Living frugally, he reinvested profits to make better pictures. His insistence on technical perfection and his unsurpassed gifts as story editor quickly pushed his firm ahead. The invention of such cartoon characters as Mickey Mouse and Donald Duck, combined with the daring and innovative use of music, sound, and folk material (as in *The Three Little Pigs*) made the Disney shorts of the 1930s a phenomenon of worldwide significance. This success led to the establishment of immensely profitable, Disney-controlled sidelines in advertising, publishing, and franchised goods, which helped shape popular taste for nearly 40 years.

Disney's rapid expansion of studio facilities to include a training school developed a whole new generation of animators and made possible the production of the first feature-length cartoon, *Snow White* (1938). Other costly animated features followed, including *Pinocchio, Bambi*, and the celebrated musical experiment *Fantasia*. With *Seal Island* (1948), wildlife films became an additional source of income, and in 1950 his use of blocked funds in England to make pictures like *Treasure Island* led to what became the studio's major product—live-action films, which practically cornered the traditional

Walt Disney in 1936. On the board are his famous cartoon characters Minnie Mouse and Mickey Mouse. (Disney Productions)

"family" market. Eventually the Disney formula emphasized slick production techniques. It included, as in his biggest hit, *Mary Poppins,* occasional animation to project wholesome, exciting stories heavily laced with sentiment and, often, music.

In 1954 Disney successfully invaded television, and in 1957 he opened Disneyland, a gigantic projection of his personal fantasies, which has proved the most successful amusement park in history. Happily married for 41 years, this moody, deliberately "ordinary" man was moving ahead with plans for gigantic new outdoor recreational facilities at the time of his death on Dec. 15, 1966.

Further Reading

Walt Disney is listed in the American History study guide (IX, D, 6). Samuel GOLDWYN was another maverick of the motion picture industry who put his personal stamp on film making.

The best book on Disney is Richard Schickel, *The Disney Version: The Life, Times, Art, and Commerce of Walt Disney* (1968). A useful source of technical information is Robert D. Feild, *The Art of Walt Disney* (1942). The most intimate portrait of Disney is by his daughter, Diane Disney Miller, *The Story of Walt Disney* (1957).

DISRAELI / By Anne Fremantle

The English statesman Benjamin Disraeli, 1st Earl of Beaconsfield (1804–1881), supported imperialism while opposing free trade. The leader of the Conservative party, he served as prime minister in 1868 and from 1874 to 1880.

Benjamin Disraeli was born on Dec. 21, 1804, in London, the second child and first son of Isaac D'Israeli, a Sephardic Jew whose father, Benjamin, had come from Cento near Ferrara, Italy. (The family had originally gone to Italy from the Levant.) Disraeli's mother, whom he appears to have disliked, was a Basevi, from a Jewish family that fled Spain after 1492, settling first in Italy and at the end of the 17th century in England. Disraeli's maternal grandfather was president of the Jewish Board of Deputies in London.

Isaac D'Israeli, when elected warden of the Bevis Marks Synagogue, resigned from the congregation rather than pay the fee of £40 entailed upon refusal of office. He had his four children baptized in the Church of England in 1817. Benjamin went first to a Nonconformist, later to a Unitarian school. At 18 he left school and studied for a year at home in his father's excellent library of 25,000 books. His father was a literary man who had published *The Curiosities of Literature* (1791), a collection of anecdotes and character sketches about writers, with notes and commentary in excellent English. Though the book was published anonymously, its authorship soon became known, and Isaac achieved fame.

In November 1821 Benjamin was articled for 400 guineas by his father for 2 years to a firm of solicitors. He later held this against his father, who, he declared, had "never understood him, neither in early life, when he failed to see his utter unfitness to be a solicitor, nor in latter days when he had got into Parliament." However, Benjamin did not consider he had wasted his time, since working

Benjamin Disraeli about 1860. (Radio Times Hulton Picture Library)

in the solicitor's office "gave me great facility with my pen and no inconsiderable knowledge of human nature."

In 1824, encouraged by John Murray, Disraeli wrote his first novel, the crude and jejune political satire *Aylmer Papillon*. The same year he started reading for the bar. He also speculated wildly on the stock exchange and lost heavily. He next became involved in a project sponsored by John Murray to publish a daily paper. Its failure was complete. His next novel, *Vivian Grey*, published anonymously, gave great offense to Murray, who was pilloried in it. Fifty years later this novel was still quoted against Disraeli; although he declared that it described his "active and real ambition," it was full of blunders that clearly showed he did not move in the social circles to which he pretended. It was attacked by the powerful *Blackwood's Magazine*, and in a later novel, *Contarini Fleming* (1832), Disraeli wrote, "I was ridiculous. It was time to die." But instead of dying, he had a nervous breakdown and traveled for 3 years (1828–1831).

Political Career

On his return to England in 1832, Disraeli twice contested and lost High Wycombe in parliamentary elections. He also continued writing: *The Young Duke* (1831), *The Present Crisis Examined* (1831), and *What Is He?* (1833). He sent a copy of his *Vindication of the British Constitution* (1835) to Sir Robert Peel and received an acknowledgment. In 1835 he again ran unsuccessfully for Parliament; that year, however, he told Lord Melbourne that his ambition was to be prime minister. Disraeli at this time was a thin, dark-complexioned young man with long black ringlets; he dressed extravagantly, in black velvet suits with ruffles and black silk stockings with red clocks. His eccentric speeches were received with shouts of derision.

After failing in five elections in 5 years, Disraeli was elected to Parliament in 1837 for Maidstone in Kent, sharing a double seat with Wyndham Lewis. His maiden speech occasioned much laughter in Parliament, but he sat down shouting, "The time will come when you will hear me." In 1837 he published the novels *Venetia* and *Henrietta Temple*. In 1839 he spoke on the Chartist petition and declared "the rights of labour" to be "as sacred as the rights of property." The same year he married Mrs. Wyndham Lewis, 12 years his senior, his parliamentary colleague's widow. He often declared jokingly that he had married for money; however, when his wife said he would do it again for love, he agreed. She made him an admirable wife. (Once, when he was on his way to make an important speech and had shut the carriage door on her hand, she never uttered a word until he got out, then she fainted.)

Disraeli was always financially incompetent. In 1840 he bought the estate of Hughenden; a year later he was £40,000 in debt, although his father had paid his debts on three occasions. In 1841 he won Shrewsbury and in 1842 wrote his wife that he found himself "without effort the leader of a party chiefly of youth." This party was called Young England and consisted basically of Disraeli

and three of his friends, who openly revolted against Peel.

In 1842 more than 70 Tories voted with Disraeli against Peel, and the government was defeated by 73 votes. Peel resigned 4 days later, and Queen Victoria sent for Lord John Russell. In bringing down Peel, Disraeli nearly wrecked his party and his own career. He was in power for only 6 years out of a parliamentary life of more than 40 and spent longer in opposition than any other great British statesman.

In *Coningsby* (1844) and *Sybil* (1845), his two great political and social novels, Disraeli attacked Peel. In *Tancred* (1845), his last novel for 25 years, Disraeli wrote that the Anglican Church was one of the "few great things left in England." These three novels "have a gaiety, a sparkle, a cheerful vivacity" which carry the reader over their "improbabilities and occasional absurdities."

In 1848 Disraeli became leader of the Tories (Conservatives) in the House of Commons. In 1851, on Lord John Russell's resignation, the Queen sent for Lord Derby, who dissolved Parliament and gained 30 seats. In February 1851 Derby offered Disraeli the chancellorship of the Exchequer. Disraeli demurred, stating that the Exchequer was a "branch of which I had not knowledge"; Derby replied, "They give you the figures." Disraeli then accepted. The Cabinet was known as the "Who? Who?" from the deaf old Duke of Wellington's repeated questions to Lord Derby. Disraeli lowered the tax on tea in his 1852 budget and changed the income tax. In December 1852 the government was beaten, and Derby and his Cabinet resigned.

Disraeli commented that the Crimean War (1854–1856) was "a just but unnecessary war." During the outcry over the Indian mutiny (1857) he protested "against meeting atrocities by atrocities" and said, "You can only act upon the opinion of Eastern nations through their imaginations." In February 1858 he voted against the second reading of the Conspiracy to Murder Bill, when Lord Palmerston was defeated and resigned. Disraeli became chancellor of the Exchequer once more, and on March 26 brought in his India Bill, which "laid down the principles on which the great subcontinent was to be governed for 60 years." The following year his Reform Bill, redolent of what John Bright called "fancy franchises," was defeated. Palmerston then came in again for 6 years. In June 1865, however, Lord Derby came back as prime minister, and Disraeli once more became chancellor. When his Reform Bill passed in 1867, he went home to his wife, ate half a pie, and drank a bottle of champagne, paying his wife the compliment, "My dear, you are more like a mistress than a wife."

Prime Minister

In 1868 Lord Derby resigned, and on February 16 the Queen wrote, "Mr. Disraeli is Prime Minister. A proud thing for a man risen from the people." A minority premier, he passed the Corrupt Practices Bill, abolished public executions, and had his wife, who was dying of cancer, made a peeress. But in autumn 1868 the Liberals under William Gladstone came to power, and Disraeli

An 1868 illustration from a French periodical shows Disraeli (standing, left) speaking in the House of Commons. Because his reputation as a novelist and speaker preceded his leadership of the government, Disraeli attracted more than usual attention in the capitals of Europe. (Photo-Hachette)

became leader of the opposition. In 1870 he published *Lothair*. In 1872 his wife died.

In 1874 the Liberals and Home Rulers were defeated by the Conservatives, and "that Jew," as Mrs. Gladstone called him, became prime minister. "Power! It has come to me too late," Disraeli was heard to say. He was patient and formal with his colleagues, did not talk much, was a debater rather than an orator, but seldom relinquished his purpose. He was an intimate of the Queen and called her "the Faery." He became her favorite politician, although she began their association with reservations about his exotic appearance, dress, and style.

Although devoted to Disraeli, Victoria threatened to abdicate over the Eastern question, as she was violently pro-Turk. Constantinople was "the key to India," and Disraeli was determined not to let Russia get there. In 1875 he purchased the Egyptian khedive's interest in the Suez Canal Company and in 1876 made Victoria the empress of India. Disraeli and Salisbury represented England at the Congress of Berlin (1878), from which they returned bringing "peace with honour." (His phrase was used by Neville Chamberlain in another context in 1938.) Among the acts passed during Disraeli's premiership were the 1874 and 1878 Factory Acts and the Poor Law Amendment Act of 1878. In 1876 Disraeli became a member of the House of Lords as the 1st (and only) Earl of Beaconsfield.

In 1880 Gladstone and the Liberals returned to power. Disraeli retired to Hughenden, where he wrote *Endymion* and began another novel, *Falconet*. He died of bronchitis on April 19, 1881, and was buried next to his wife. His last recorded words were, "I had rather live but am not afraid to die."

Further Reading

Benjamin Disraeli is listed in the European History study guide (VIII, A, 1, b; IX, A, 1, a) and the Literature study guide (II, H, 1, c). He opposed Sir Robert PEEL. Disraeli's great rival William GLADSTONE also served under VICTORIA.

The standard biography of Disraeli is William Flavelle Monypenny and George Earle Buckle, *The Life of Disraeli* (6 vols., 1911–1920; rev. ed., 2 vols., 1929). Robert Blake, *Disraeli* (1966), is also recommended. Cecil Roth, *Benjamin Disraeli, Earl of Beaconsfield* (1952), covers well the Jewish aspects of his life. B. R. Jerman, *The Young Disraeli* (1960), is a study of his career until 1837. See also C. C. Somervell, *Disraeli and Gladstone* (1925).

DIX / By Charles and Joyce Crowe

Dorothea Lynde Dix (1802–1887) was an American reformer whose pioneer efforts to improve treatment of mental patients stimulated broad reforms in hospitals, jails, and asylums in the United States and abroad.

Dorothea Dix. (Library of Congress)

On April 4, 1802, Dorothea Dix, the daughter of Joseph and Mary Dix, was born in Hampden, Maine. When Joseph failed at farming, he became an itinerant preacher and wrote, printed, and sold tracts, which his wife and daughter laboriously sewed together. Dorothea remembered her childhood in that bleak, poverty-stricken household as a time of loneliness and despair. At the age of 12 she ran away from home and made her way to Boston, where she persuaded her grandmother to take her in. Two years later Dorothea went to Worcester to live with a great aunt and opened a school, which she maintained for 3 years. She returned to Boston in 1819 to attend public school and to study with private tutors.

Teaching Career

In 1821 Miss Dix opened an academy for wealthy young ladies in her grandmother's house. She also conducted a free school for poor children. As a teacher, she was a strict disciplinarian, a rigorous moralist, and a passionate explorer of many fields of knowledge, including the natural sciences. Her contagious joy in teaching made her schools highly successful. During convalescent periods from attacks of chronic lung disease, she wrote children's books.

In 1835 ill health forced Miss Dix to abandon teaching; she went abroad for 2 years. When she returned to America, she was in better health but irresolute about her future. Four years of indecision ended when she volunteered to teach a Sunday school class for young women in the East Cambridge, Mass., jail. She discovered that the quarters for the insane had no heat, even in the coldest weather. When the jailer explained that insane people did not feel the cold, and ignored her pleas for heat, she boldly took the case to court and won.

Mental Institution Reforms

For 2 years Miss Dix traveled throughout Massachusetts, visiting jails, workhouses, almshouses, and hospitals, taking notes on the deplorable conditions she observed. In 1845 Dr. Samuel Gridley Howe presented her "Memorial to the Massachusetts Legislature." The address began, "I proceed, gentlemen, briefly to call your attention to the *present* state of insane persons confined within the Commonwealth, in *cages, closets, cellars, pens; chained, naked, beaten with rods,* and *lashed into obedience.*" This dramatic presentation caused a public controversy which won the support of Charles Sumner and other public figures in the resulting newspaper debate. Despite bitter opposition, the reform bill passed by a large majority.

Miss Dix went on to other northeastern states and then throughout the country, state by state, visiting jails, almshouses, and hospitals, studying their needs, and eliciting help from philanthropists, charitable organizations, and state legislatures for building and renovating facilities and for improving treatment. During these years she founded new hospitals or additions in Massachusetts, Rhode Island, New York, New Jersey, Pennsylvania, and Canada and received approval to found state hospitals by the legislatures of Indiana, Illinois, Kentucky, Tennessee, Missouri, Maryland, Louisiana, Alabama, South Carolina, and North Carolina.

European Crusade

In 1848 Miss Dix took her fight to Congress in an attempt to win appropriation of 12,500,000 acres of land, which would provide tax revenue for asylums. The bill finally passed both houses only to be vetoed by President Franklin Pierce. The discouraged reformer then traveled through England, Ireland, and Scotland, inspecting mental hospitals. English and Irish institutions were not bad, but Scottish facilities were appalling, and Miss Dix set about to improve them, taking her case finally to the lord advocate of Scotland.

Perhaps Dorothea Dix's most significant European accomplishment was in Rome, where she discovered that "6,000 priests, 300 monks, 3,000 nuns, and a spiritual sovereignty, joined with the temporal powers, had not assured for the miserable insane a decent, much less an intelligent care." She negotiated an audience with Pius IX, who was moved by her appeal and personally verified her reports. He ordered construction of a new hospital and a thorough revision of the rules for the care of mental patients. Before her return to the United States, Miss Dix evaluated hospitals and prisons in Turkey, Greece, Italy, France, Austria, Russia, Scandinavia, Holland, Belgium, and Germany and recommended reforms.

Civil War Nurse

In 1861, at the age of 59, Miss Dix volunteered her services for wartime duty in the Civil War. Appointed "superintendent of women nurses," she set up emergency training programs, established temporary hospitals, distributed supplies, and processed and deployed nurses. Despite wartime hardships she never relaxed her standards of efficient service, proper procedure, and immaculate hospital conditions. Her inspections of army hospitals did not make her popular with authorities, and her stringent ideas of duty and discipline were not shared by the relatively untrained nurses and jealous officials, who resented her autocratic manner. Although she was often discouraged by petty political opposition and the ever present problems of inadequate facilities, supplies, and staff, she carried out her duties until the end of the war.

Dorothea Dix resumed her reform efforts until age forced her to retire. Until her death in 1887 she made her home in the Trenton, N.J., hospital, which she had often referred to affectionately as her "first child."

Further Reading

Dorothea Dix is listed in the American History study guide (V, F, 4, c; VI, F, 5). Clara BARTON and Henry BELLOWS were among the other reformers at work during the Civil War.

The most commonly cited biographies of Dorothea Dix are early ones. Francis Tiffany, *The Life of Dorothea Lynde Dix* (1890), is a standard work which contains copious quotations from letters and reports. More recent is Helen E. Marshall, *Dorothea Dix: Forgotten Samaritan* (1937). Additional details are provided in Gladys Brooks's concise and popular *Three Wise Virgins* (1957). See also Albert Deutsch, *The Mentally Ill in America: A History of Their Care and Treatment from Colonial Times* (1937; 2d ed. 1949), and Norman Dain's brief but scholarly *Concepts of Insanity in the United States, 1789–1865* (1964).

DJILAS / By T. C. W. Blanning

The Yugoslavian writer and political prisoner Milovan Djilas (born 1911) was the most celebrated of the Eastern European intellectuals who supported communism in the 1930s but were disillusioned by the practices of Communist regimes after 1945.

Milovan Djilas (pronounced jē′läs) was born in the Kingdom of Montenegro, which after World War I became part of Yugoslavia. He joined the Yugoslavian Communist party in 1932 and in the same year was sent to prison for 3 years. His progress through the ranks of the party was rapid; in 1938 he was elected to the Central Committee and in 1940 to the Politburo.

After World War II, during which he organized guerrilla warfare against the Germans, Djilas resumed his political career. In 1945 he was appointed minister for the province of Montenegro and in 1948 minister without portfolio and secretary of the Politburo. In 1953 he became vice president of the Yugoslavian Republic.

Although by this time Djilas was third in the party hierarchy, his political career was almost over. He had become increasingly disillusioned even with Tito's brand of "national" communism, and at the beginning of 1954 he published a number of newspaper articles critical of the regime. He was stripped of his various offices and given a suspended sentence. In November 1956, after the publication of similar criticisms in the American journal *New Leader,* he was sentenced to 3 years' hard labor.

Djilas was still in prison when his book *The New Class* was published in September 1957 in the United States. This acute analysis of the Communist system sought to show that communism did not lead to a "withering away" of the state, as Karl Marx had predicted, but rather to the formation of a new ruling class just as selfish as any previous oligarchy. One month after the publication of *The New Class* he was sentenced to a further 7-year term of imprisonment.

In January 1961 Djilas was released on condition that he abstain from all political activity, but his freedom was short-lived. He was rearrested in April 1962, charged with providing material for foreign newspaper articles critical of Yugoslavia, and was sentenced to 5 years in prison, to which was added 3 1/2 years (the unserved balance of the previous sentence). Shortly afterward his book *Conversations with Stalin,* which developed further the arguments first expressed in *The New Class,* was published abroad.

Djilas was not released from prison until 1966. Two

Milovan Djilas. (National Archives, Washington, D.C.)

years later his confiscated manuscripts were returned, together with a passport for foreign travel. His relations with the government remained tense, however, and early in 1970 his passport was removed again.

Further Reading

Milovan Djilas is listed in the European History study guide (XII, H, 1). His imprisonment for criticizing the regime of TITO exposed the limitations of this type of communism.

There is no satisfactory biography of Djilas. The most revealing books about him are his own writings: *The New Class* (1957); *Land without Justice* (1958); and *Conversations with Stalin* (trans. 1962). The best and most recent work on Yugoslavia is Phyllis Auty, *Tito: A Biography* (1970), which has a full bibliography.

DOBELL / By R. M. Younger

The Australian artist Sir William Dobell (1899–1970) was one of the world's leading modern portraitists. His best portraits revealed extraordinary psychological insight.

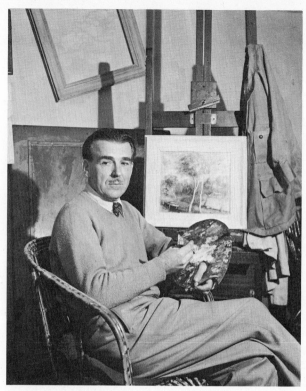

William Dobell in 1960. (Australian News & Information Bureau)

William Dobell was born in Newcastle, New South Wales, on Sept. 24, 1899. He moved to Sydney in 1925 to study at the Julian Ashton Art School. In 1929 he went to London on a traveling scholarship to study at the Slade School, where he won prizes for draftsmanship and painting. Later he exhibited at the Royal Academy and before the New English Group.

Dobell returned to Sydney in 1939. He maintained a subjective approach to painting, and his work was very different from that of current Australian styles. In 1943 he won the Archibald Prize, Australia's principal award for portraiture, for a painting of fellow-artist Joshua Smith. The award was immediately challenged on the grounds that Dobell's entry showed a degree of distortion which made it a caricature rather than a true portrait, but the court upheld the judging panel's decision. Resultant newspaper publicity greatly expanded interest in Dobell's work, but as a result of the controversy Dobell withdrew to Wangi, a small coastal town north of Sydney, and became a shy and enigmatic figure.

Gentle by nature, Dobell was also shrewd, warm, and strong in feeling, and these characteristics shone through his work. He was intensely interested in his fellowman. He achieved some of his effects by deft underscoring of aspects that typified the subject's character, and others by sharp delineation of exciting and unusual features of the subject.

Dobell was also a notable landscapist. He painted local scenes, views of Southeast Asia, and a series of cameos capturing the strangeness of New Guinea. He belonged to no school but acknowledged inspiration from Rembrandt, William Hogarth, Pierre Auguste Renoir, and Chaim Soutine.

Dobell gained numerous significant awards and received many commissions, among them four for portraits for use as *Time* magazine cover subjects, including one of Australian prime minister Robert Menzies in 1960. Exhibitions of his work attracted exceptionally widespread attendance; and a sale in Sydney in 1962 realized record prices for an Australian artist. He was knighted in 1966 and died in Wangi on May 14, 1970.

Further Reading

Sir William Dobell is listed in the Australia and New Zealand study guide (II, G). Contemporary painters were Sir Russell DRYSDALE and Sidney NOLAN.

A good general reference work on Dobell is *The Art of William Dobell*, edited by Sydney Ure Smith (1946). Dobell's place in Australia's art history is analyzed in several publications giving concise coverage of the work of various painters. Two of the most useful are a catalog produced by the Australian Government, Commonwealth Art Advisory Board, with commentaries by leading critics, for the 1962 Exhibition, *Australian Painting: Colonial, Impressionist, Contemporary;* and Bernard W. Smith, *Australian Painting 1788–1960* (1962). An illuminating outline of Dobell and his work is contained in James Gleeson's elaborately illustrated review, *Masterpieces of Australian Painting* (1969).

DOESBURG / By Moira Roth

The Dutch artist Theo van Doesburg (1883–1931) was one of the founders of the modern art movement called de Stijl and the chief promoter of its ideas.

Theo van Doesburg (pronounced dōōs′bûrKH), whose real name was C. E. M. Kupper, was born on Aug. 30, 1883, in Utrecht. He was involved in painting and interior decorating and writing on art, but it was only in 1917 after he had met the painter Piet Mondrian that Van Doesburg formulated his ideas clearly. The two painters founded the group de Stijl (the Style) and the avant-garde review of the same name when they and several other artists established a number of common aspirations which formed the basis of the movement.

Van Doesburg's temperament made him the public leader of the group. He was an impulsive and vigorous man, with strong likes and dislikes, in contrast to the far more reticent and cautious Mondrian. De Stijl esthetic was based on geometric abstractions and applied not only to painting but to other arts, especially architecture. Unlike many art movements in the 20th century, de Stijl aimed at social and spiritual reforms rather than purely artistic concerns. The leaders believed that a purified geometric esthetic would exert a strong and calming influence on those who saw a de Stijl painting or lived in a de Stijl house.

Van Doesburg traveled extensively from 1919 on, visiting the active centers of progressive art in Germany and France. He gave lectures, wrote numerous articles, and made many personal contacts with the avant-garde leaders in those countries. His contacts and interests were wider than those of Mondrian, who left de Stijl in 1925 because he disagreed with Van Doesburg on esthetic grounds.

In 1922 Van Doesburg became briefly involved with Dadaism and traveled on a wild lecture tour with the German Dadaist Kurt Schwitters. Van Doesburg worked at the same time with the constructivists and became

interested in the Bauhaus, which had recently been founded in Germany. In the 1920s his interests progressively widened, and he wrote about these new interests in his articles for the *De Stijl* review; these articles helped to change the direction of the movement. Finally, he formulated a more dynamic version of de Stijl and published this as a manifesto of what he called elementarism. He continued to experiment with novel ideas, both in writing and painting, and collaborated with the painter Jean Arp. Just before his death on March 7, 1931, in Davos, Switzerland, Van Doesburg helped found the Abstraction-Création group in Paris.

Further Reading

Theo van Doesburg is listed in the Art study guide (III, J, 5). Other members of de Stijl were Piet MONDRIAN, J. J. P. OUD, and Gerrit T. RIETVELD.

Most of the writing on Van Doesburg is in Dutch. Two useful discussions of de Stijl and Van Doesburg's role in the movement are in Reyner Banham, *Theory and Design in the First Machine Age* (1960; 2d ed. 1967), and H. L. C. Jaffé, *De Stijl* (1964).

DOLE / By Jacob Adler

The American statesman Sanford Ballard Dole (1844–1926) was president of the Republic of Hawaii and, after its annexation to the United States in 1898, first governor of the Territory of Hawaii.

Sanford Dole was born in Honolulu, Hawaii, on April 23, 1844, the son of Protestant missionaries from New England. He grew up on the Hawaiian islands of Oahu and Kauai and went to missionary schools run by his father. He left the islands to attend Williams College in Williamstown, Mass., where he spent a year. After another year in a Boston law office, he was admitted in 1868 to the Massachusetts bar. But that same year he returned to Honolulu to practice law. He showed a good deal of interest in community affairs and often wrote for newspapers. In 1873 he married Anna P. Cate of Maine.

Dole was elected to the Hawaiian Legislature in 1884 and 1886 as a reform party member. In 1887 he became a leader in the movement that wrested a new constitution from King David Kalakaua, reducing his power. The King, under pressure from his ministers, appointed Dole associate justice of the Supreme Court. Dole's legal decisions were marked by clarity and grace of style, and his dissents were noted for their vigor.

Dole served as a justice until 1893, when he reluctantly accepted leadership of a revolutionary movement that overthrew Queen Liliuokalani, who had succeeded her brother Kalakaua. She had tried to proclaim a new constitution that would return personal power to the throne.

Composition (The Cow), a 1916 work by Theo van Doesburg. (Collection, The Museum of Modern Art, New York)

Dole became president of a provisional government that sought annexation to the United States. When President Grover Cleveland tried to restore the Queen (after charges that the United States had helped overthrow her), Dole wrote one of his most important state papers eloquently denying Cleveland's right to interfere. With no prospect of quick annexation, the Republic of Hawaii was formed on July 4, 1894. The constitution named Dole president to serve until 1900.

Hawaii's support of the United States in the war with Spain in 1898 turned the balance in favor of renewed annexation efforts already under way. In 1898 President William McKinley signed a joint congressional resolution of annexation and appointed Dole a member of the commission to draft laws governing Hawaii. In 1900 McKinley appointed Dole as first governor under the Organic Act for the Territory of Hawaii. Dole served until 1903, when he resigned to become judge for the U.S. District Court for Hawaii. In 1916 he retired to private practice.

Dole is generally credited with a deep, sympathetic understanding of the native Hawaiians, although some persons might consider his attitude toward the Hawaiians slightly patronizing and paternalistic.

Further Reading

Sanford Dole is listed in the American History study guide (VII, D, 2, b; VIII, B, 4). Dole led the struggle against Queen LILIUOKALANI, who sought a return to strong monarchical government.

E. M. Damon, *Sanford Ballard Dole and His Hawaii* (1957), based on primary sources, is sympathetic and uncritical. The account was undertaken at Dole's express

Sanford Dole in 1902. (Library of Congress)

wish. Dole tells his own story of the dramatic last years of the kingdom in his *Memoirs of the Hawaiian Revolution* (1936), edited by Andrew Farrell.

DOLLFUSS / By Wayne S. Vucinich

The Austrian statesman Engelbert Dollfuss (1892–1934) served as chancellor of Austria from 1932 to 1934.

Engelbert Dollfuss (pronounced dôl′fōos) was born on Oct. 4, 1892, near Texing, Lower Austria. Trained in law at the University of Vienna and in economics at the University of Berlin, he served as an officer in World War I. After the war he was secretary of the Peasant's Association of Lower Austria and became director of the Lower Austrian Chamber of Agriculture in 1927. In 1930 he was appointed president of the Austrian Federal Railways system because of his association with the Christian Socialist party, and in 1931 he was named minister of agriculture and forests.

On May 20, 1932, Dollfuss became chancellor of Austria, although his government possessed only a one-vote majority in the Nationalrat (lower house of Parliament) and a minority in the Bundesrat (upper house). To strengthen Austria's financial position, Dollfuss obtained a loan of £9 million sterling from the League of Nations in return for an agreement not to enter a customs union with Germany for 20 years, a stipulation which angered pan-German, Nationalist, and Socialist elements in Austria.

Subject to bitter attacks from all sides, Dollfuss suspended Parliament when its three presidents resigned on March 4, 1933, and thereafter ruled by decree. In May he founded the Vaterländische Front to mobilize support for his rule, and it was with this organization that the notorious Heimwehr merged in 1934. The latter was a defense force formed after World War I; it later espoused Italian Fascist principles, became a political party in 1930, and perpetrated acts of terror and violence against its opponents.

To bolster his foreign position and prevent Austria from uniting with Nazi Germany, Dollfuss met Mussolini at Riccione in August 1933 and received a guarantee of Austrian independence at the cost of abolishing all political parties and revising the Austrian constitution along Fascist-corporatist lines. On the prompting of Mussolini, he utilized an outbreak of rioting by leftist elements in February 1934 to destroy the Social Democratic party organization, thus removing Austria's most strongly anti-Nazi force from the scene.

Announcing his wish to order the state according to the encyclical *Quadragesimo Anno* of Pope Pius XI, Dollfuss proclaimed a new constitution on May 1, 1934, providing for state organization through professional corporations like those in Fascist Italy. The opposition of

represented the Catholic wing of the great German historical movement of the 19th century.

Engelbert Dollfuss, photographed in 1933. (National Archives, Washington, D.C.)

German and Austrian Nazis to his government only increased, however, as he evidenced his determination to oppose the surrender of Austrian independence. Finally, during an abortive Nazi putsch on July 25, 1934, Nazi agents entered the Chancellery in Vienna and during their brief occupation of the building assassinated Dollfuss.

While Dollfuss's dogged determination to maintain the integrity of Austria made him a martyr, the weakness of his political position coupled with that of his small state forced him to implement the very authoritarian principles antithetical to the Christian ideals articulated in his 1934 constitution and to the continued independence of Austria.

Further Reading

Engelbert Dollfuss is listed in the European History study guide (XI, E, 1). He was succeeded by Kurt von SCHUSCHNIGG.

There is not much information on Dollfuss in English. Perhaps the most useful work is Paul R. Sweet, "Mussolini and Dollfuss: An Episode in Fascist Diplomacy," in Julius Braunthal, *The Tragedy of Austria* (1948).

DÖLLINGER / By Daniel O'Connor

The German historian and theologian Johannes Josef Ignaz von Döllinger (1799–1890)

O n Feb. 28, 1799, J. J. I. von Döllinger (pronounced dûl/ĭng-ər) was born in Bamberg. His father was professor of physiology and anatomy at Bamberg and later at Würzburg and, though Catholic, markedly anticlerical. This influence was offset by the piety of Döllinger's mother, and the boy's interest turned to theology after a few semesters in Würzburg studying philosophy and philology. He entered the seminary at Bamberg and was ordained a priest in 1822. Disillusioned with academic studies, he desired only a country pastorate but, after serving as curate for barely a year, he was prevailed upon by his father to return to academic life.

Döllinger then taught canon law and Church history at the gymnasium in Aschaffenburg. His interests turned to patristic studies, and he published the first of many books on Church history, for which he achieved wide recognition. In 1827 he accepted the chair of Church history at the University of Munich, a post he held until 1872. In Munich he joined the circle of F. X. von Baader and J. von Görres. This group was monarchist in politics, strongly influenced by German romanticism, and inclined toward strengthening Church ties with Rome. Thereafter Döllinger became increasingly active in public life, always working to spread the influence of religion. He represented Lower Bavaria at the Congress of Frankfurt in 1848–1849.

In his historical studies Döllinger stressed historical continuity and organic development. Arguing that the Reformation represented a breach in this continuity, he led a counterattack against the influential school of Leopold von Ranke and other Protestant or liberal historians.

J. J. I. von Döllinger. (Library of Congress)

Döllinger's efforts to revive German Catholicism gradually led him to minimize dependence on Rome, and increasingly after 1850 he argued for a German national church. He also insisted on the right of scholars to be free from ecclesiastical censorship. Just prior to the opening of the Vatican Council in 1869, his book *The Pope and the Council,* which argued the supremacy of a general council, was condemned in Rome. During the proceedings he corresponded with the minority who opposed the infallibility decree. But his publication of *Roman Letters from the Council* (1870) injured the cause by its intemperate and sarcastic tone. In 1871 he was excommunicated for refusing to subscribe to the Council decrees on papal prerogatives and a year later was forced out of his professorship.

Döllinger was friendly with leaders of the schismatic group called the "Old Catholics" but refused to join their movement. In later years he worked to promote reunion among the churches. Accepting the last rites from an Old Catholic priest, he died in Munich on Jan. 10, 1890.

Further Reading

J. J. I. von Döllinger is listed in the Religion study guide (I, P, 2, e). He opposed the historical thought of Leopold von RANKE. The English historian Lord ACTON was tutored by Döllinger for 5 years.

Louise von Kobell, *Conversations of Dr. Döllinger* (1891; trans. 1892), provides personal reminiscences. Lord Acton gives a lengthy estimate of Döllinger's historical work in his *History of Freedom, and Other Essays* (1907).

DOMAGK / By E. Ashworth Underwood

The German bacteriologist and experimental pathologist Gerhard Johannes Paul Domagk (1895–1964) was awarded the Nobel Prize in Physiology or Medicine for his discovery of the antibacterial effects of prontosil.

Gerhard Domagk (pronounced dō′mäk) was born at Lagow, Brandenburg, on Oct. 30, 1895. He began the study of medicine at the University of Kiel in 1913. After World War I, throughout which he served in the army, he graduated in medicine at Kiel in 1921. In 1924–1925 he was a lecturer in pathology in the universities of Greifswald and Münster. He became director of research in experimental pathology and bacteriology on the staff of the I. G. Farbenindustrie at Wuppertal-Elberfeld in 1927.

Beginnings of Chemotherapy

Early in the 1900s a synthetic organic arsenic compound was used to treat experimental trypanosomiasis. Paul Ehrlich confirmed this and then began to search for a similar compound for the treatment of syphilis. Succes-

Gerhard Domagk. (German Information Center, New York)

sive organic compounds were synthesized and tested. In 1910 he found that his 606th compound was very effective; he called it salvarsan. During the next 20 years efficient antimalarial remedies were synthesized, but there were no such remedies against the common bacterial and streptococcal infections of temperate climates, despite many attempts to solve this problem.

Chemotherapy of Bacterial Infections

Shortly after his appointment to the I. G. Farbenindustrie, Domagk was made responsible for another massive attempt to achieve chemotherapy of the bacterial infections. His chief chemists, Fritz Mietzsch and Joseph Klarer, synthesized organic compounds, and Domagk tested the activity of these compounds against various organisms, in cultures and in laboratory animals. For a long time they were unsuccessful. But some years earlier the two chemists had synthesized a red azo dye combined with a sulfonamide radical. Intended for treating leather, it was already on the market under the name Prontosil Rubrum. Their tests had shown that it had little activity against bacteria in cultures, but in 1932 preliminary tests suggested that it might be protective against streptococcal infections in mice. In December a crucial experiment was carried out, which showed conclusively that prontosil was very effective in protecting mice against a highly virulent streptococcus. These very satisfactory laboratory results were not published for over 2 years, partly because of doubt whether prontosil would be tolerated by human subjects. But Domagk personally had no doubt, because he had as a last resort given his daughter, who was near death as a result of a streptococcal infection, a dose of prontosil. She had miraculously recovered.

When Domagk published his laboratory results in 1935 he did not mention his daughter's case, but work on prontosil was at once started in several countries. It was shown that the action of prontosil was due to its sulfonamide radical, which alone was active, and that sulfanilamide, a similar sulfonamide compound, was as active as prontosil and cheaper to manufacture. This was the first of the many similar drugs synthesized and tested. These sulfonamides were shown to be effective in many diseases in addition to streptococcal infections, such as puerperal fever, pneumonia, and cerebrospinal fever.

For his work in this field Domagk was awarded the Nobel Prize in Physiology or Medicine for 1939, but he was forced by the Nazis to decline the award, which he had already accepted. After the war he was presented with the medal and the diploma, but the prize money had meanwhile reverted to the Nobel Foundation.

Chemotherapy of Tuberculosis

The effective discovery of the method of concentrating penicillin, the first of the antibiotics, in 1940 stimulated a search for other antibiotics and chemotherapeutic remedies that might be effective in treating tuberculosis. Domagk's chemical coworkers supplied him with the first of the thiosemicarbazones, and in 1946 he showed their power to inhibit the growth of the tubercle bacillus in culture. But as they caused liver damage they had later to be given up. Meanwhile, in 1944, the antibiotic streptomycin had been discovered, but its undoubted effectiveness in treating tuberculosis was found to be limited by its tendency to produce resistant strains of the bacillus. A little later the effectiveness of *para*-aminosalicylic acid (PAS) was discovered and also its value in delaying the appearance of resistant strains. But the thiosemicarbazones led to the discovery in 1951, by Domagk and others, of the activity of isonicotinic acid hydrazide (isoniazid). It was found that in man isoniazid was most efficient when combined with streptomycin and PAS.

Chemotherapy of Cancer

For 30 years, beginning in 1925, Domagk wrote numerous papers on experimental tumor formation. In 1955 he turned to the chemotherapy of malignant tumors. In 1958 he published his results obtained with ethyleneimino quinones and their derivative Trenimon. Although then promising, these results later remained unconfirmed.

Later Life

In 1958 the University of Münster conferred on Domagk the title of professor, and on his retirement from the I. G. Farbenindustrie he worked on cancer research at that university. His many honors included honorary degrees from six universities. In 1959 he was elected a Foreign Member of the Royal Society, and he was the recipient of the Paul Ehrlich Gold Medal and of the Cameron Prize of the University of Edinburgh. He died at Burberg, Baden-Württemberg, on April 24, 1964.

Further Reading

Gerhard Domagk is listed in the Science study guide (VII, G, 2). Paul EHRLICH did early work on chemotherapy. Penicillin was first effectively concentrated and made available for manufacture by Howard W. FLOREY (later Lord Florey) and his coworkers. Streptomycin was discovered by Selman A. WAKSMAN.

There is a biography of Domagk in *Nobel Lectures: Physiology or Medicine, 1922–1941* (1965), which also contains his Nobel Lecture, not delivered until 1947. For the background of Domagk's discovery see I. Galdston, *Behind the Sulfa Drugs* (1943). For further developments see G. M. Findlay, *Recent Advances in Chemotherapy* (1930), especially the second (1939) and third (vol. 1, 1950) editions.

DOMENICO VENEZIANO
/ By Curtis Shell

The major contribution of the Italian painter Domenico Veneziano (1410?–1461) to early Renaissance painting was his subtle observation of the reaction of colors to conditions of natural light.

Domenico Veneziano (pronounced dō-mä′nē-kō vä-nä-tsyä′nō), whose real name was Domenico di Bartolomeo da Venezia, was originally from Venice, but he worked in Florence for most of his life. His date of birth is uncertain but can be approximated through stylistic comparisons with his better-documented contemporaries, such as Fra Filippo Lippi and Andrea del Castagno.

Much uncertainty remains among scholars about the beginnings and the chronology of Domenico's art. In 1438 he wrote a letter to Piero de' Medici asking for work and mentioning Fra Angelico and Filippo Lippi. This shows that Domenico was well versed in Florentine artistic affairs and leads to the assumption that he might have been in Florence before 1439, when he settled there. Only minute fragments remain of the important series of frescoes he painted intermittently from 1439 to 1445 for the church of S. Egidio in Florence, in which he was assisted by Piero della Francesca. In the surviving fragment of the fresco from the so-called Carnesecchi Tabernacle one sees traces of Domenico's Venetian background in the construction and ornamentation of the marble throne on which the Madonna sits. This fragment also demonstrates Domenico's awareness of the art of his Florentine contemporaries Fra Angelico, Masolino, and Lorenzo Ghiberti, as well as the principles of linear perspective only recently discovered by the architect Filippo Brunelleschi and applied in relief sculpture by Donatello and in painting by Masaccio.

Dated about 1445 is Domenico's well-preserved altarpiece from the church of S. Lucia dei Magnoli in Florence and the five fragments of its predella. The elaborate architectural settings in bright, light greens, pinks, and grays, as well as the simulated marble inlay patterns, are reminiscent of the colors of Giotto's bell tower of the Florence Cathedral and the ornamentation found in Tuscan proto-Renaissance buildings, such as the 12th-cen-

Domenico Veneziano's altarpiece Virgin and Child with Saints Francis, John the Baptist, Zenobius, and Lucy. *The work, painted about 1445 for the church of S. Lucia dei Magnoli, Florence, is now in the Uffizi in that city. (Alinari)*

tury Baptistery in Florence. The figures, well rendered with a sense of weight and volume, are plausibly situated in space. This is made especially eloquent through Domenico's strict observance of the natural flow of light and of the shadows cast by objects.

Other examples of Domenico's art are the fine *Madonna against a Rose Hedge* in Washington and the exquisite *Madonna and Child* in Florence (Berenson Collection). In his large tondo *Adoration of the Magi* there is a sumptuous display of ornament, and the figures clothed in fanciful garments are placed in a deeply receding and realistic landscape.

Further Reading

Domenico Veneziano is listed in the Art study guide (III, B, 1, a). His chromatic and luministic inventions paved the way for the art of PIERO DELLA FRANCESCA.

In English there is a fine article on Domenico Veneziano by Luciano Berti in the *Encyclopedia of World Art*, vol. 4 (1961). See also Lionello Venturi and Rosabianca Skira-Venturi, *Italian Painting: The Creators of the Renaissance* (1950), and Frederick Hartt, *History of Italian Renaissance Art* (1970).

ST. DOMINIC / By Gerard A. Vanderhaar

The Spanish churchman St. Dominic (ca. 1170–1221) founded the Dominican order, a religious community officially called the Order of Preachers.

Dominic was born to the well-to-do Guzmán family in the town of Caleruega in northern Spain. As a young man, he studied the liberal arts and theology at Palencia. After he was ordained a priest, he joined the cathedral canons of the city of Osma, who lived a community life under the rule of St. Augustine.

When he was about 30, Dominic accompanied his bishop on several diplomatic missions in northern Europe. In the course of these travels he became aware of the religious ideas of the Albigensians, a Manichaean movement in southern France. This sect believed that the soul is good and the body is evil and that man must be purified and must not indulge in any physical pleasures. The Pope had sent legates to counteract the movement, but with their sumptuous clothes, fine horses, and numerous attendants they only succeeded in reinforcing the Albigensians' beliefs. Dominic saw that the only way to preach orthodox doctrine effectively to these people was to be as poor as they were and to be thoroughly knowledgable in Christian theology. He stayed in southern France for several years and, together with a small group of like-minded men, tried to put his ideas into practice by preaching, studying, praying, and living in poverty.

After a papal crusade crushed the heretics, in 1215 Dominic and his group of 16 were welcomed by the bishop of Toulouse and established as the official preachers of that diocese. Dominic then went to Rome, where he obtained Pope Innocent III's approval for the establishment of a religious order dedicated to preaching and based on a deep knowledge of the Scriptures and Christian truth. Until this time religious orders had been

St. Dominic, a portrait painted within a generation of his death and attributed to Guido da Siena. (Fogg Art Museum, Harvard University, Bequest of Hervey E. Wetzel, 1911)

associated with monasteries, where men lived apart from the world and spent their time in prayer and physical work. But Dominic conceived of a group of men who would be dedicated primarily to preaching and thus to helping people in the mainstream of life. Living together in a city house, where they would pray and study, these men would be able to go wherever they were needed and would substitute study for the traditional manual labor of monks.

In 1217 Dominic showed his confidence in the men who shared his ideal and scattered the little group of 16 around Europe. He sent some to Paris to study theology, some to Bologna to study law, and others to Rome and Madrid. Two stayed behind in Toulouse and two more in nearby Prouille. Wherever they went, these men attracted others, and soon there were hundreds of followers of Dominic's ideal, many of them students and masters at universities.

During the next 2 years Dominic traveled over 3,000 miles on foot, visiting and encouraging his men in Toulouse, Paris, Milan, and Rome and in Spain. In 1220 the first meeting or general chapter of the friars took place in Bologna, and there it was decided that the order would have a representational system of government, with the friars in each house electing their superiors for fixed terms. These representatives met again in 1221 and divided the order geographically into provinces. Shortly after this meeting Dominic died in Bologna in 1221; he was canonized in 1234.

Dominic's genius had several ingredients. He was a charismatic leader, able to evaluate a situation and act decisively. He had confidence in his own ideals and in the people who shared them. His mind was sharpened by study, but before he wrote, lectured, or preached, he turned to God in prayer. It was said of Dominic that "he loved everyone, so everyone loved him." By 1256 the group he had founded had over 13,000 members, and it continues to flourish today.

Further Reading

St. Dominic is listed in the Religion study guide (I, E, 3). His contemporary St. FRANCIS OF ASSISI shared many of his ideals.

Marie Humbert Vicaire, *Saint Dominic and His Times* (2 vols., 1957; trans., 1 vol., 1964), is the most complete and accurate biography of St. Dominic in English. Pierre Mandonnet, *Saint Dominic and His Work* (2 vols., 1938; trans., 1 vol., 1944), contains a thorough study of the historical and religious background of Dominic's life. Bede Jarrett, *Life of Saint Dominic* (1924; 2d ed. 1934), presents the personal warmth and genius of the saint.

DOMITIAN / By Eugene W. Davis

The Roman emperor Domitian (51–96), in full Titus Flavius Domitianus Augustus, though reputed to be a complete tyrant, modernized Rome's fiscal administration and secured the empire's frontiers.

Born in Rome on Oct. 24, 51, the younger son of Vespasian, Domitian (pronounced də-mǐsh′ən) came to the throne when his brother Titus died young after only 2 years of rule. From the start Domitian reigned as a complete autocrat, partly perhaps because of his lack of political skills, but partly certainly because of his own nature. Domitian was personally suspicious and unlovable, and the relations between him and those around him began ill and ended worse.

Domitian's reign can be considered under two main heads: his administration, which was excellent, and his frontier policy, which was generally successful. Provincial government was so carefully supervised that the Roman biographer Suetonius admits that the empire enjoyed a period of unusually good government and security. Domitian's policy of employing members of the equestrian class rather than his own freedmen for some important posts was also a step forward. The finances, which Titus's fecklessness had plunged into confusion, were restored despite building projects and foreign wars.

Religion was a special concern of Domitian, and he vigorously strove to breathe life again into the ancient Roman faith; he built temples and established ceremonies and even tried to enforce morality by law. This zeal

for religion may explain the hostility of the Christian writers, for though he was not a persecutor of Christians, he was an ardent propagator of paganism.

Frontier Policy

The northern frontiers needed Domitian's special attention. His governor Agricola pushed the conquest of Britain into Scotland, invaded the Highlands, and even proposed to add all Ireland to the empire after subduing Scotland. Tacitus, Agricola's son-in-law, writes that Agricola's recall in 84 was due to Domitian's jealousy, but more probably it reflected increasing concern with dangers on the Rhine-Danube frontier.

In Germany, Domitian himself took the field, continuing and extending his father's policy of shortening the frontier by annexing the triangle between the Rhine and Danube. The latter part of the reign saw increasing trouble on the lower Danube from the Dacians, a tribe occupying approximately what is now Romania. Led by an able king, Decebalus, the Dacians in 85 invaded the empire. The war ended in 88 in a compromise peace which left Decebalus as king and gave him Roman "foreign aid" in return for his promise to help protect the frontier (chiefly against himself).

One of the reasons Domitian failed to crush the Dacians was a revolt in Germany by the governor Antonius Saturninus. The revolt was quickly suppressed, but henceforth Domitian's always suspicious temper grew steadily worse. It was, of course, the people nearest him who suffered, and after a reign of terror at court Domitian was murdered on Sept. 18, 96, in a plot to which even his own wife, Domitia Longina, was a party. The Senate, which had always hated him, hastened to condemn his memory and repeal his acts, and Domitian joined the ranks of the tyrants of considerable accomplishments but evil memory. He was the last of the Flavian emperors, and his murder marked the beginning of the period of the so-called Five Good Emperors.

Further Reading

Domitian is listed in the Ancient History study guide (III, C, 2). The other Flavian emperors were VESPASIAN and TITUS.

Among the ancient sources, Tacitus's *Agricola* and Pliny the Younger's *Panegyric* are viciously hostile; Suetonius's *Lives of the Twelve Caesars* is scandalous but less rancorous. Among modern works, M. I. Rostovtzeff, *Social and Economic History of the Roman Empire* (1926; 2d rev. ed. 1957), and B. W. Henderson, *Five Roman Emperors* (1927), are the fullest and fairest.

Domitian, portrait bust in the Capitoline Museum, Rome. (Alinari)

DONATELLO / By Robert A. Koch

The Italian sculptor Donatello (1386–1466) was the greatest Florentine sculptor before Michelangelo and certainly the most influential individual artist of the 15th century in Italy. Nearly every later sculptor and numerous Florentine and Paduan painters were indebted to him.

Donatello's St. George, *in the Bargello, Florence. (Alinari-Anderson)*

Though Donatello (pronounced dŏn-ə-tĕl′ō) was a descendant of a branch of the important Bardi family, he was brought up in a more plebeian tradition than his older contemporary Lorenzo Ghiberti. Gifted with humanistic insight and a quality of will that were highly prized in the early Renaissance, Donatello revealed the inner life of his heroic subjects, memorable images which have conditioned our very conception of 15th-century Florence. Sharing neither Ghiberti's feeling for line nor Filippo Brunelleschi's interest in proportion, Donatello worked creatively with bronze, stone, and wood, impatient with surface refinements and anxious to explore the optical qualities he observed in the world about him. His later art, saturated with the spirit of Roman antiquity, is frequently disturbing in its immediacy as it attains a level of dramatic force hitherto unknown in Italian sculpture.

Donato di Niccolò Bardi, called Donatello, was born in 1386 in Florence. Little precise biographical information has come down to us, although many anecdotes are recorded by Giorgio Vasari in his *Lives*. Donatello was apprenticed to Ghiberti, and in 1403, at the age of 17, Donatello was working for the master on the bronze reliefs of the First Doors of the Baptistery. By 1407 he had left Ghiberti for the workshops of the Cathedral.

Early Works

One of Donatello's earliest known works is the life-sized marble *David* (1408; reworked 1416; now in the Bargello, Florence). Intended to adorn a buttress of the Cathedral, in 1414 it was set up in the Palazzo Vecchio as a symbol of the Florentine republic, which was then engaged in a struggle with the king of Naples. Dramatic in posture and full of youthful energy, the *David* possesses something of the graceful late Gothic feeling of a figure by Ghiberti, though Donatello now admits us to a world of psychological tensions.

Rapidly maturing, Donatello produced a strong, original, dynamic style in two works: the large marble figure *St. Mark* in a niche on the exterior of Orsanmichele, completed between 1411 and 1413, and the seated *St. John the Evangelist* for the facade of the Cathedral (now in the Museo dell'Opera), finished in 1415. These powerful, over-life-sized figures established the sculptor's reputation. The *St. Mark* broke with tradition in its classical stance, realistically modeled drapery, and concentrated face with such optical subtleties as a detailed analysis of the eye. It became a stunning symbolic portrait of a noble Florentine hero in the embattled republic of Donatello's day.

Donatello's new style was confirmed in the famous *St. George*, carved in marble about 1416–1417 for the exterior of Orsanmichele (later replaced by a bronze copy; the original is in the Bargello). Resolute in stance, the

Christian saint has the face not of an ideal hero but of a real one. Even more significant is the little marble relief *St. George and the Dragon*, that decorates the base of the niche. The marble was ordered in 1417, and the relief was completed shortly afterward. This is an important date, for the relief is the earliest example in art of the new science of perspective used to create a measurable space for the figures. Up to this time artists had conceived of a flat background in front of which, or in which, the figures were placed; now the low, pictorial forms seem to emerge from atmosphere and light. Donatello was probably influenced by the contemporary theoretical studies in perspective of the architect Brunelleschi.

Between 1415 and 1435 Donatello and his pupils completed eight life-sized marble prophets for niches in the Campanile of the Cathedral (now in the Museo dell'Opera). The most impressive of the group are the so-called *Zuccone* ("big squash" or "baldy"), perhaps representing Habakkuk, and the *Jeremiah*, in both of which there is great psychological tension and a convincing, deliberate ugliness.

Middle Period

Donatello received many commissions, which he often executed in collaboration with other artists. An unusual work is the *Marzocco*, the emblematic lion of the Florentines, carved in sandstone and imbued with a

Detail of the statue Jeremiah *by Donatello. The statue, originally done for the Campanile of the Cathedral in Florence, is now in the Museo dell'Opera del Duomo. (Alinari)*

grand contrapuntal vigor; it was ordered in 1418 for the papal apartments in S. Maria Novella (now in the Museo Nazionale). Donatello's optical principles and his vigorous style in relief sculpture reached a climax in the gilded bronze *Feast of Herod,* completed in 1427 for the font in the Baptistery, Siena; Ghiberti, Jacopo della Quercia, and other sculptors also executed reliefs for the baptismal font. In Donatello's very low relief composition he approximated, but deliberately avoided the accurate construction of, one-point architectural perspective.

About 1425 Donatello entered into partnership with Michelozzo, sculptor and architect, with whom he made a trip to Rome after 1429. (Vasari states that Donatello went to Rome with Brunelleschi. This would have been much earlier, perhaps in 1409; but there is no document to confirm such a trip.) With Michelozzo he produced a series of works, including the tomb of Pope John XXIII in the Baptistery, Florence, and the tomb of Cardinal Brancacci in S. Angelo a Nilo, Naples, both of which were in progress in 1427. The first of these established a type of wall tomb that was decisive for many later Florentine examples.

Probably just after the trip to Rome, Donatello created the well-known gilded limestone *Annunciation* tabernacle in Sta Croce, Florence, enclosing a lyrical pair of Gabriel and the Virgin Mary. He was also commissioned to carve for the Cathedral a *Singing Gallery* to match the

one already begun by Luca della Robbia (both now in the Museo dell'Opera). Using marble and mosaic, Donatello presented a classically inspired frieze of wildly dancing *putti.* It was begun in 1433, completed 6 years later, and installed in 1450.

Later Works

Much of Donatello's later work manifests his understanding of classical art, for example, the bronze *David* in the Bargello, a preadolescent boy clothed only in boots and a pointed hat. This enigmatic figure is in all probability the earliest existing freestanding nude since antiquity.

From 1443 to 1453 Donatello was in Padua, where he created the colossal bronze equestrian monument to the Venetian *condottiere* called Gattamelata in the Piazza del Santo. It was the first important sculptural repetition of the 2d-century equestrian statue of Marcus Aurelius in Rome. Donatello portrayed Gattamelata as the ideal man of the Renaissance. Another major commission in Padua was the high altar of S. Antonio, decorated with four large narrative reliefs representing the life of St. Anthony, smaller reliefs, and seven life-sized statues in bronze, including a seated Madonna and Child and a bronze Crucifixion. Donatello had earlier made remarkable experiments with illusionistic space in his large stucco medallions for the Old Sacristy of S. Lorenzo in Florence; now his major bronze Paduan reliefs present an explosive conception of space with sketchy figures and a very excited continuous surface. The influence of these scenes on painters in northern Italy was to prove enormous and long lasting.

Back in Florence, the aged Donatello carved a haunting, emaciated *Mary Magdalen* from poplar wood for the Baptistery (1454–1455). Romantically distorted in extreme ugliness, the figure of the penitent saint in the wilderness originally had sun-tanned skin and gilding on her monstrous hair. In 1456 Donatello made an equally disturbing group in bronze of Judith cutting off the head of Holofernes. Now in the Piazza della Signoria, Florence, it was originally commissioned, apparently as a fountain, for the courtyard of the Medici Palace.

At his death on Dec. 13, 1466, Donatello left two unfinished bronze pulpits in S. Lorenzo, Florence. On one are relief panels, showing the torture and murder of Christ by means of distorted forms and wildly emotional actions. Finished by his pupil Bertoldo di Giovanni, the pulpit scenes reveal the great master's insight into human suffering and his pioneering exploration of the dark realms of man's experience.

Further Reading

Donatello is listed in the Art study guide (III, B, 2). He trained under Lorenzo GHIBERTI. Donatello collaborated on various works with MICHELOZZO. Donatello's equestrian monument of Gattamelata provided the model for the Colleoni statue by Andrea del VERROCCHIO. Donatello's influence can be seen in the paintings and sculpture of ANDREA DEL CASTAGNO, Filippo LIPPI, Antonio POLLAIUOLO, Andrea MANTEGNA, Luca della ROBBIA, and DESIDERIO DA SETTIGNANO. Not until the time of MICHELANGELO was there another such giant in sculpture.

The best scholarly study of Donatello in English is H. W. Janson, *The Sculpture of Donatello* (2 vols., 1957; 1 vol., 1963). Recommended for the reproduction of wonderful photographic details of selected sculptures are Ludwig Goldscheider, *Donatello* (1941), and the small but compendious book by Luigi Grassi, *All the Sculpture of Donatello* (1958; trans., 2 vols., 1964), which includes many works of debatable authenticity.

DONATUS / By Donald F. Winslow

Donatus (died ca. 355) was the schismatic bishop of Carthage during the first decades of the Donatist movement.

Little is known of Donatus (pronounced dô-nā′tŭs) before 311, when the Christian Church in North Africa was torn by schism. He is reported to have come from Casae Nigrae in Numidia, southwest of Carthage. He may also have engaged in some quasi-schismatic activity of an "anti-Catholic" sort before coming to Carthage.

The cause of the schism may be said to lie in the persecution of the Church in 303 by the emperor Diocletian. As in the Decian persecution and the Novatian schism that had swept Rome 50 years before, the Church was divided into two camps concerning those who had apostatized under threat of torture or death. The "laxists" sought easy and quick rehabilitation for the lapsed; the "rigorists" held that any act of compromise, even the handing over of the Scriptures to the state (those who did so were called *traditores*), deprived the lapsed Christian of the right to receive the Sacraments and, if he was a clergyman, of the right to administer the Sacraments.

In North Africa the rigorists tended to be the rural Berbers, given to a hatred of apostasy and a sometimes extreme veneration of martyrs. Donatus was a member of this faction. The more urban and urbane "Catholics" were laxist in discipline and politically and sociologically oriented more toward Rome and the empire than toward the surrounding countryside.

Some 10 years after the Diocletian persecution, the episcopal office in Carthage fell vacant upon the death of Bishop Mensurius. Amid rival factions and behind-the-scenes maneuvering, a hastily called and peremptorily administered group of Catholics met and elected Caecilian as their new bishop. Because of his severe antirigorist views, Caecilian had many enemies, not least of whom was Lucilla, a wealthy Spanish lady residing in Carthage. Caecilian, when a deacon, had alienated her by harshly criticizing her practices of martyr worship.

The opposition, consisting mostly of Lucilla and the Numidian clergy, was quick to move. They claimed that Caecilian was in fact not a bishop because one of his coconsecrators, Felix of Aptunga, had been a *traditor* during the persecution and therefore the consecration was invalid. They elected and consecrated their own bishop, Majorinus, claiming him to be the true bishop. Thus began in 312 the great schism that was to rend North Africa for the next century. "Bishop was set up

Figure from an early Christian tomb found in Carthage. (Musée National du Bardo, Tunis)

against Bishop," wrote Optatus, "and altar against altar." This was the same year in which Constantine was converted to Christianity; the persecution of the Church by the state was now at an end, but the persecution of the Donatists was just beginning.

Majorinus lived only a year after his consecration as rival bishop. It was Donatus who took his place, and because of his long and powerful episcopacy, the schism was named after him. During the first year of his reign the Roman Church formally condemned Donatism at the Council of Arles in 314. But the Donatists became increasingly intransigent in their views and in their anti-Catholic activity. "Under the hot Numidian sun," one historian wrote, "nothing was forgiven or forgotten." Donatus proved an able and enthusiastic leader of his fellow schismatics; they swore by his "white hairs," wrote St. Augustine later. Finally Donatus was driven from Carthage by force in the proconsular Macarian persecution of 347. He died in exile less than 10 years later.

The schism persisted, but the Donatists were never as strong as they had been under Donatus. At the turn of the century the Donatists, with their militant activists (known as the *circumcelliones*), were to test the intellectual skills of the great Catholic bishop of Hippo, Augustine, as well as sorely to try his patience. Violence and futile attempts at reconciliation continued well into the 5th century, and not until the onslaught of Islam did the Donatists (and Catholics) of a divided and weakened Christian North Africa finally disappear.

Further Reading

Donatus is listed in the Religion study guide (I, B, 1). St. AUGUSTINE was a major opponent of Donatism. Primary sources for the life of Donatus and the history of Donatism are found chiefly in the works of Optatus, Bishop of Milevis, and in the anti-Donatist writings of St. Augustine. Modern studies in English are few, but W. H. C. Frend, *The Donatist Church: A Movement of Protest in Roman North Africa* (1952), and Stanley L. Greenslade, *Schism in the Early Church* (1953; 2d ed. 1964), are important.

DONIZETTI / By Tom R. Ward

The Italian opera composer Gaetano Donizetti (1797–1848) was one of the first composers of the romantic movement in Italy.

Gaetano Donizetti (pronounced dŏn-ə-zĕt′ē) was born in Bergamo on Nov. 29, 1797. He received his first instruction in music from an uncle, but the beginning of his formation as a composer came in 1806, when he was accepted as a free student in the Lezione Caritatevoli, a school supported by the church of S. Maria Maggiore for the training of musicians and choristers for its services. The director was Simon Mayr, a

Gaetano Donizetti. (Alinari-Brogi)

German who had settled in Bergamo in 1805. Although not known today, his music was held in high esteem in his lifetime. Mayr's influence seems to have been decisive. He kept young Donizetti in the school although his voice was not of the necessary quality, even writing works for student performances in which these vocal defects could be avoided.

Following this training, Donizetti went to Bologna in 1815 to study with Padre Mattei, a student of Padre Martini and a teacher of Gioacchino Rossini. Mayr gave Donizetti financial support as well as letters of introduction. Donizetti's first publication, a set of variations on a theme by Mayr, appeared in 1815.

Donizetti's first three operas date from 1816 and 1817 and were not performed during his lifetime. His first opera to be performed was *Enrico di Borgogna*, given in Venice in 1818. From this time until 1844 he produced operas of all types at a fantastic pace. In 1827 he agreed to compose 12 operas for Venice within a 3-year period. This speed in production shows in many works that perfunctorily filled the established forms of the day. His works all allow the singer ample opportunity for display with cadenzas and brilliant coloratura writing. Many of his librettos deal with violent passions that are not always turned to best dramatic effect. However, works like *L'elisir d'amore* (1832), *Lucia di Lammermoor* (1835), *La*

Fille du régiment (1840), and *Don Pasquale* (1843) have gained a place in the repertory for themselves and an important historical position for their composer.

Although now known primarily for his operas, Donizetti produced a large number of compositions in other genres. In addition to 71 operas, he composed cantatas, sacred works, symphonies, string quartets and quintets, and numerous works for piano solo, voice and piano, and piano and other instruments.

Donizetti's fame quickly spread throughout Italy; he went to Paris, where we wrote five operas, and to Vienna, where he became principal court conductor in 1842. His last years, 1844–1848, were spent in rather severe circumstances because of the progressive deterioration of his health, both physical and mental.

Further Reading

Gaetano Donizetti is listed in the Music study guide (I, G, 3). The other contemporary Italian composers of romantic opera were Gioacchino ROSSINI and Vincenzo BELLINI.

Two recent biographies of Donizetti are Herbert Weinstock, *Donizetti and the World of Opera* (1963), and William Ashbrook, *Donizetti* (1965), both containing numerous documents, lists of works, and librettos. Donizetti's place in early-19th-century music is discussed in Alfred Einstein, *Music in the Romantic Era* (1947), and Donald J. Grout, *A Short History of Opera* (2 vols., 1947; 2d ed. 1965).

DONNE / By J. Max Patrick

John Donne (1572–1631), English metaphysical poet, Anglican divine, and pulpit orator, is ranked with Milton as one of the greatest English poets. He is also a supreme artist in sermons and devotional prose.

John Donne's masculine, ingenious style is characterized by abrupt openings, paradoxes, dislocations, argumentative structure, and "conceits"—images which yoke things seemingly unlike. These features in combination with his frequent dramatic or everyday speech rhythms, his tense syntax, and his tough eloquence were both a reaction against the smoothness of conventional Elizabethan poetry and an adaptation into English of European baroque and mannerist techniques. Since Donne's times such poetry has been unaptly called "metaphysical"—a term more appropriate for the philosophical verse of Lucretius.

Son of a prosperous ironmonger of Welsh ancestry, Donne was born between Jan. 4 and June 19, 1572, and was bred a Londoner and a Roman Catholic. His mother, a great niece of Sir (later St.) Thomas More, came from a cultured, devout family: her father, John Heywood, wrote interludes; her brother Jasper was a Jesuit; and her

son Henry, John's brother, died in 1593 of a fever caught in Newgate Prison, where he was incarcerated for harboring a Roman Catholic priest. Donne's father died when John was 4, and his mother married a prominent physician.

His Poetry

After some years at Oxford (from 1584) and possibly Cambridge, Donne studied law at Lincoln's Inn (1592–1594) and became one of the first to write in English formal verse satires in the classical mode. It was also in the 1590s that he wrote many of his amatory poems. Most of them are dramatic monologues expressive of attitudes toward love, ranging from cynical fleshly realism to platonic idealism. It is sounder to see them not as autobiographical but as exposing the extremes of carnal and spiritual love and as putting in a favorable light love in which they are complementary. He also composed verse letters, elegies, epithalamia, and epigrams; they were published after his death as *Songs and Sonnets*.

Donne partook in the Earl of Essex's expeditions against the Spanish in Cadiz and the Azores in 1596–1597 and reflected this military experience in his poems "The Storm" and "The Calm." By 1597–1598, when he became secretary to Sir Thomas Egerton, the lord keeper, he had dissociated himself from Roman Catholicism. In 1601 he blasted the promise of a successful career by secretly marrying Lady Egerton's niece, Ann More. He was dismissed from his post and temporarily imprisoned,

John Donne, after an original portrait by Donne's contemporary, the miniaturist Isaac Oliver the Elder. (National Portrait Gallery, London)

A 17th-century view of London, showing the old St. Paul's Cathedral, of which Donne was dean.

and for about a decade he and his ever-increasing family were largely dependent on relatives and patrons.

During this middle period Donne wrote *Biathanatos,* a treatise on instances of justifiable suicide which may have been intended as a satire on casuistry; it was published by his son in 1646. His *Pseudo-Martyr* (1610) accused Roman Catholics of fostering false martyrdom for secular ends. *Ignatius His Conclave* (1611) was popular in both English and Latin versions: it brilliantly satirized the Jesuits but is interesting today because it reflects the then new astronomy of Galileo and toys with the notion of colonizing the moon.

Donne continued to write secular poems and, about 1609–1610, a powerful series of "Holy Sonnets," in which he meditated on sickness, death, sin, and the love of God. In 1611 he composed two companion poems, *The Anniversaries,* on the Idea of woman, the decay of the physical universe, the vanity of this world, and, in contrast, the permanence of God and spiritual values. These commemorated the death of little Elizabeth Drury and won him the patronage of her father, with whom Donne traveled to France and Germany. He briefly served as a member of Parliament in 1601 and again in 1614.

Church Career

About 1606 Thomas Morton offered Donne a benefice if he would take Anglican orders. But it was not until 1615, after long pious and practical hesitations, that he was ordained a priest. Appointed a royal chaplain in the same year, he also received a doctor of divinity degree from Cambridge. In 1616–1622 he was reader in divinity at Lincoln's Inn, where he preached regularly. He was desolated in 1617 by the death of his wife: she had borne him 12 children, 5 of whom died. He preached frequently at court and in 1619 was an embassy chaplain in Germany. In 1621, on James I's nomination, he became dean of St. Paul's Cathedral, attracting huge congregations with his brilliant oratory. A serious illness in 1623 gave rise to his *Devotions,* those moving meditations on sickness, death, and salvation from which Ernest Hemingway derived the title *For Whom the Bell Tolls.*

On Feb. 25, 1631, Donne left his sickbed to preach his last and most famous sermon, "Death's Duel." On March 31 he died. An effigy of him wrapped in funeral shrouds survived the burning of St. Paul's in the Great Fire of 1666 and is preserved in the present cathedral, built by Sir Christopher Wren. The effigy is that of an old, seasoned man who has thought and suffered greatly but has achieved some peace of soul. His youthful portraits show black hair, clear skin, intense eyes, an ample brow, and a pointed, bearded chin. His later pictures reveal the same intensity and alertness.

His Character

Donne's was a complex personality, an unusual blend of passion, zeal, and brilliance; God and women were his favorite themes, but his subject matter otherwise ranged over the pagan and the pious, the familiar and the esoteric, the cynical and the sincere, the wittily bright and the theologically profound.

Largely because of Izaak Walton's charming but somewhat unreliable *Life of Dr. John Donne* (1681) and because of the risqué elements in Donne's secular poetry, a myth grew up contrasting a youthful Jack Donne the rake with a pious and repentant Dr. John Donne, Dean of St. Paul's. That in his younger days he was an attractive conversationalist, socialite, and courtier is undeniable, but his works reveal that he was always a serious student and a seeker after truth; and there is no sound evidence to support the myth. Certainly after his ordination he dedicated his remarkable genius wholeheartedly to the service of God and thus became one of the most brilliant stars in that hierarchy of extraordinary Anglican priests—among them, Robert Herrick, George Herbert, and Robert Burton—whose exceptional literary genius was dedicated to the glory of God and the welfare of man.

Further Reading

John Donne is listed in the Literature study guide (II, E, 2, c). He is credited with inspiring a metaphysical school of poets which included George HERBERT, Richard CRASHAW, and Henry VAUGHAN.

Biographies of Donne written before 1960 are unreliable. Robert C. Bald's definitive *John Donne: A Life* (1970) supersedes all previous biographies. The frequently reprinted work by Izaak Walton, *Life of Dr. John Donne* (many editions) should be read as great literature, more imaginative than accurate. Edward LeComte, *Grace to a Witty Sinner: A Life of Donne* (1964), is written for the general reader.

Among the studies of Donne's work, K. W. Gransden's concise *John Donne* (1954; rev. ed. 1969) and Frank Kermode, *John Donne* (1957), are introductions for beginners. James B. Leishman, *The Monarch of Wit* (1951; 6th ed. 1962), and Clay Hunt, *Donne's Poetry* (1954), provide solid foundations for interpreting the poems. Arnold Stein, *John Donne's Lyrics* (1962), emphasizes Donne's style and wit. Varied approaches are collected in Helen Gardner, ed., *John Donne* (1962), and Leonard Unger further illuminates such approaches in *Donne's Poetry and Modern Criticism* (1950). Judah Stampfer, *John Donne and the Metaphysical Gesture* (1970), is impressionistic but stimulating. Far more reliable is Donald L. Guss, *John Donne, Petrarchist* (1966), which relates *Songs and Sonnets* to their Italian influences; N. J. C. Andreasen, *John Donne, Conservative Revolutionary* (1967), also relates the poetry to tradition.

Evelyn M. Simpson, *A Study of the Prose Works* (1924; 2d ed. 1948), is fundamental. Also excellent are William R. Mueller, *John Donne, Preacher* (1962), and Joan Webber, *Contrary Music: The Prose Style of John Donne* (1963). For the scientific background, Charles M. Coffin, *John Donne and the New Philosophy* (1937), and Marjorie Hope Nicolson, *The Breaking of the Circle* (1950; rev. ed. 1960), still have value. Wilbur Sanders, *John Donne's Poetry* (1971), is a judicious survey. Among the more general works relating to Donne are George Williamson, *The Donne Tradition* (1930); Helen C. White, *The Metaphysical Poets* (1936); Joseph E. Duncan, *The Revival of Metaphysical Poetry* (1959); and, of outstanding importance, Douglas Bush, *English Literature in the Earlier Seventeenth Century* (1945; rev. ed. 1962), and Louis L. Martz, *The Poetry of Meditation* (1954; rev. ed. 1962).

＊　＊　＊

DONNELLY / By W. Turrentine Jackson

Ignatius Donnelly (1831–1901) was an American politician, reformer, and author. He was an outstanding spokesman for the political reform movements of the second half of the 19th century that culminated in the Populist revolt.

Born in Pennsylvania of Irish parents, Ignatius Donnelly attended the free public schools and read law in Philadelphia. Interested in real estate promotion, he moved to Minnesota in 1856 and established the *Emigrant Aid Journal* to promote settlement. The Panic of 1857 destroyed his projected ideal community and his fortune but not his optimism. He returned to practicing law and entered politics to help promote the organization of the Republican party.

Elected lieutenant governor of Minnesota in 1859, Donnelly was a tireless and fighting politician. He served three terms in the House of Representatives (1863–1869), where he strongly supported the Civil War and Reconstruction programs of the Republican party. In advocating the interests of the Northwest, chiefly land grants for railroad construction, he evoked the ire of economy-minded congressmen.

As the Republican party moved toward conservatism, Donnelly joined the protesters in the Liberal Republi-

Ignatius Donnelly. (Library of Congress)

cans, the Grangers, and the Greenbackers successively. Serving in the Minnesota Senate (1874–1879), he crusaded for reforms to aid the underprivileged and published a weekly newspaper, the *Anti-Monopolist*. When his attempt to return to Congress was blocked in 1878 he abandoned politics for writing.

Capitalizing on the popular interest in science fiction, Donnelly's first book, *Atlantis: The Antediluvian World* (1882), attempted to demonstrate the existence of Plato's fabled island Atlantis. *Ragnarok: The Age of Fire and Gravel* (1883) followed. *The Great Cryptogram* (1888) tried to prove that Francis Bacon was the author of Shakespeare's plays.

After another unsuccessful bid for Congress in 1884, Donnelly became active in the Farmers' Alliance and was returned to the Minnesota Senate in 1887. In 1890 he wrote *Caesar's Column: A Story of the Twentieth Century,* painting a graphic picture of the potential horrors of life in the United States in the coming century, yet closing with a statement of what might be achieved through reform. The book was widely read. As president of the Farmers' Alliance in Minnesota, Donnelly was actively involved in the establishment of the Populist, or People's, Party. Presiding officer in caucus and conventions and author of the challenging preamble to the party's 1892 platform, he was among the Populists' foremost leaders.

Four years later Donnelly reluctantly followed the leadership of William Jennings Bryan, but he soon concluded that the fusion of the Populists with the Democrats on the free-silver issue was a betrayal of broader reforms. Donnelly ran for the vice presidency on the Populist ticket in 1900.

Late in life Donnelly married his second wife, his 21-year-old stenographer, who assisted him in publishing a newspaper, the *Representative*. He died on Jan. 1, 1901. His biographer rightly asserts that Donnelly was the hero of the Populist movement, his name synonymous with reform, a true rebel who was never without a feeling of alienation.

Further Reading

Ignatius Donnelly is listed in the American History study guide (VII, G, 4, d). He was associated in the Populist cause with Benjamin Ryan TILLMAN and Thomas E. WATSON. At one point Donnelly reluctantly joined forces with William Jennings BRYAN.

The only full-length biography of Donnelly is the excellent volume by Martin Ridge, *Ignatius Donnelly: The Portrait of a Politician* (1962). John D. Hicks published scholarly interpretations of Donnelly's life in *The Populist Revolt: A History of the Farmers' Alliance and the People's Party* (1931) and in numerous articles, the last of which is in John A. Garraty, ed., *The Unforgettable Americans* (1960). Popular interpretations of Donnelly's career are numerous and include those of Stewart H. Holbrook in *Dreamers of the American Dream* (1957) and Gerald W. Johnson in *The Lunatic Fringe* (1957).

DONNER / By Edward A. Maser

The Austrian sculptor Georg Raphael Donner (1693–1741) was the first exponent of classicism in 18th-century Austria and the greatest sculptor of the period.

Georg Raphael Donner (pronounced dôn′ər) was born in Esslingen, Lower Austria, on May 24, 1693, the son of a carpenter. After studying with Johann Kaspar Prenner, a goldsmith to the imperial court in Vienna, Donner was apprenticed at the age of 13 to the sculptor Giovanni Giuliani to assist on statuary for the Liechtenstein Palace in Vienna. Donner worked mainly in Vienna and Pressburg (modern Bratislava, Czechoslovakia). His sculptures are largely in marble and bronze, but he early developed a fondness for lead; the soft sheen of the material was well suited to his characteristic smooth modeling, firm outlines, and gracefully elongated figures, based on his obvious study of 16th-century Italian sculpture, whose manneristic qualities he blended with classical ideals in a highly individual harmony.

In 1725 Donner worked with his assistants in Salzburg on sculpture for the famous staircase in Mirabell Palace. Donner personally executed the figure *Paris* (1726). While in Salzburg he also did some work for the local mint, producing ducats with portraits and coats of arms of the prince-bishop. In 1728 the primate of Hungary, Prince-Bishop Emre Esterhazy, called Donner to his court in Pressburg, where in the Cathedral, he carved the sculpture of the high altar of the chapel of St. Elemosynarius (1732). This chapel also contains the prelate's tomb, for which Donner carved the highly expressive kneeling figure of the primate. He also made the equestrian statue *St. Martin and the Beggar* for the high altar of the Cathedral (1735), an over-life-sized lead

Georg Raphael Donner's Reclining Nymph, *executed about 1739. (Busch-Reisinger Museum, Harvard)*

sculpture combining classicistic clarity with touches of realism, for the warrior saint wears an 18th-century hussar's uniform rather than classical dress. The marble statue *Emperor Charles VI* (1734) reveals the baroque qualities underlying Donner's classicism in the momentary pose of the Emperor.

Donner's most famous work is the Providentia Fountain on the Neue Markt in Vienna. Unveiled in 1739, the lead figures were replaced by bronze copies in 1873, and the originals are now in the Baroque Museum, Vienna. The figures of the four rivers on the fountain are prime examples of his debt to the late Renaissance and of his naturalistic tendencies. He also carved reliefs for the Viennese mint and cast in bronze the Andromeda Fountain in the courtyard of the Vienna city hall (now Altes Rathaus). His last important work is the moving *Pietà* in the Cathedral of Gurk (1741). Donner died on Feb. 15, 1741, in Vienna, where his pupils and his brother Mathias continued to work in his style until late in the century.

Further Reading

Georg Raphael Donner is listed in the Art study guide (III, G, 2). Contemporary Austrian artists were the painter Paul TROGER and the architect Johann Lucas von HILDE-BRANDT.

Donner's work is discussed in Nicolas Powell, *From Baroque to Rococo* (1959), and Eberhard Hempel, *Baroque Art and Architecture in Central Europe* (1965). The only monograph on Donner is in German, C. Blauensteiner, *Georg Raphael Donner* (1947); it contains excellent photographs.

DOOLITTLE / By Francis W. Warlow

The American poet, translator, and novelist Hilda Doolittle (1886–1961), generally called H.D., was an imagist whose lyric art conveys intense feelings through sharp images and "free" forms.

Hilda Doolittle was born on Sept. 10, 1886, in Bethlehem, Pa.; her father was a professor. She entered Bryn Mawr College in 1904. She had met Ezra Pound in 1901, and in 1905, while he was studying at the University of Pennsylvania, he introduced her to William Carlos Williams, then a medical school student at the university. Hilda quit school in 1906 because of ill health. During the next 5 years she studied Greek and Latin literature, tried Latin translation, and wrote a few poems. By 1911 the apprenticeship of this tall young woman, attractive in a long-faced, large-eyed way, was nearly over.

Miss Doolittle toured Europe and stayed on in London, where Pound took her under his wing. She and Richard Aldington found a common interest in carrying over into

Hilda Doolittle. (Copyright The H. W. Wilson Company, New York)

English the spare beauty of Greek art and literature. Pound called them *Imagistes*, thus creating a new literary movement based on common speech, the exact word, new rhythms, absolute freedom in choosing subjects, clarity, and concentration. Pound helped both poets get published, persuading Miss Doolittle in 1913 to sign herself "H.D., Imagiste." (H.D. remained perhaps the only faithful imagist, less out of decision than because her natural way of writing simply coincided with Pound's program.)

H.D. married Aldington in 1913. In 1916 he left for World War I front lines, and she issued her first volume, *Sea Garden*, also succeeding him as literary editor of the *Egoist*. A year later she resigned because of poor health and was replaced by T. S. Eliot. The anxieties of the war, a miscarriage, and her husband's infidelity overwhelmed her. In 1919, pregnant, ill with pneumonia, and saddened by the death of her father, she separated from Aldington and later bore a daughter, Perdita.

Winifred Ellerman, a wealthy novelist-to-be known as "Bryher," became H.D.'s friend and benefactor. They settled in neighboring houses in a Swiss village in 1923. Thereafter H.D. lived either in Switzerland or in London. Meanwhile she issued *Hymen* (1921) and *Heliodora* (1924). *Collected Poems* (1925) established her place in modern poetry. "Helen" and the more sustained lament "Islands" are representative selections.

H.D.'s first novel, *Palimpsest* (1926), deals with the trials of sensitive women and artists in a harsh world. Her second novel was *Hedylus* (1928). In 1927 she published a verse play, *Hippolytus Temporizes*. A new volume of poems, *Red Roses from Bronze* (1931), and *The Hedgehog* (1936), prose fiction, like her early volumes contained choruses translated from Greek plays. Her most ambitious translation was *Euripides' Ion* (1937). The following year she divorced Aldington.

H.D. was in London during World War II. *By Avon River* (1949) deals with Shakespeare and Elizabethan and Jacobean writers. *Tribute to Freud* (1956) records her gratitude for her psychoanalysis. Her novel *Bid Me to Live* (1960) is an account of a situation that approximates her marital breakup. Her most ambitious work, *Helen in Egypt* (1961), concludes that perfect love can be found only in death. She died that year in Switzerland.

In all of H.D.'s poetry, discrete colors and forms, frugal rhythms, focused emotions, and clarity of thought suggest a Greek miniaturist or, in longer works, a Japanese scroll painter.

Further Reading

Hilda Doolittle is listed in the Literature study guide (I, E, 2, b). Her mentor was Ezra POUND, and her fellow poet in the imagist movement was William Carlos WILLIAMS.

There are two full-length studies of Hilda Doolittle: Thomas B. Swann, *The Classical World of H.D.* (1962), and Vincent Quinn, *H.D.* (1968). Biographical material is also available in the autobiographies of Richard Aldington, *Life for Life's Sake* (1941), and Bryher (pseudonym of Winifred Ellerman), *The Heart to Artemis: A Writer's Memoirs* (1962). Stanley K. Coffman, *Imagism: A Chapter for the History of Modern Poetry* (1951), discusses the movement of which H.D. seems the best representative.

DOS PASSOS / By Robert S. Gold

The reputation of the American novelist John Roderigo Dos Passos (1896–1970) is based chiefly on his early work, especially the trilogy "U.S.A."

John Dos Passos was born in Chicago on Jan. 14, 1896, the illegitimate son of a noted New York lawyer, John Randolph Dos Passos, and a wealthy Virginian, Lucy Addison Sprigg. His father did not acknowledge paternity until a year before his death, when the young Dos Passos was 20. As a boy, Dos Passos lived principally on the Virginia farm of his mother's family, and he also traveled frequently with his mother to Mexico, Belgium, and England.

Dos Passos attended Choate School under the name John Roderigo Madison. He graduated from Harvard in 1916, meanwhile publishing stories, verse, and reviews in the Harvard *Monthly*.

In 1917 Dos Passos was in Spain, studying Spanish culture. During World War I he enlisted in the Norton-Harjes Ambulance Unit and served in Spain and Italy. In 1918 he became a private in the U.S. Medical Corps, serving in France. Demobilized in 1919, he remained in Europe to finish two novels: *One Man's Initiation— 1917* (1920) and *Three Soldiers* (1921). During the 1920s Dos Passos worked as a newspaper correspondent and traveled extensively but, as an increasingly successful author, he lived chiefly in New York.

First Novels

One Man's Initiation—1917, based on Dos Passos' experiences as an ambulance corpsman, is poignantly antiwar. It also foreshadows a more pervasive theme of his work: contemporary technological society's crippling effects on its inhabitants.

Dos Passos' first significant novel, *Three Soldiers,* is a bitterly ironic commentary on the professed ideals for which World War I was fought and, more deeply, on the "values" by which modern, mechanized man lives. Dos Passos sees the real enemy as the army itself, which by exacerbating the ordinary weaknesses and inner conflicts of its members causes irreparable harm. His three major characters are entirely broken by army life. *Three Soldiers* is part of an anti–World War I literary tradition that includes works by Ernest Hemingway, Robert Graves, E. E. Cummings, William Faulkner, and Erich Maria Remarque.

Literary Experiment

Manhattan Transfer (1925) is Dos Passos' first major experimental novel. Set in New York, it is a panoramic view of the frustrations and defeats of contemporary urban life. Frequently shifting focus among its marginally related characters, the novel details an oppressive picture of human calamity and defeat; fires, accidents, brawls, crimes, and suicides abound, and unhappiness is pervasive. The novel is uneven; it is contrived in its plotting and confusing in its use of time but interesting and especially noteworthy for its development of formal devices that would be better employed in *U.S.A.*

Dos Passos' 1920s output also included a volume of free verse, *A Pushcart at the Curb* (1922); two impressionistic travel books, *Rosinante to the Road Again* (1922) and *Orient Express* (1927); a novel, *Streets of Night* (1923); two plays; and a tract in defense of the anarchists Sacco and Vanzetti, *Facing the Chair* (1927).

Politics and Reportage

The political implications of Dos Passos' early writings are clearly socialist, and in 1926 he helped found the *New Masses,* a Marxist political and cultural journal, to

John Dos Passos. (United Press International Photo)

which he contributed until the early 1930s. In 1927 he was jailed in Boston for picketing on behalf of Sacco and Vanzetti. In 1928 he visited the Soviet Union. Returning to the United States in 1929, he married Katherine F. Smith.

As a political reporter for the *New Republic* and other journals during the early 1930s, Dos Passos covered labor flareups, political conventions, the Depression, and the New Deal. His fundamental distrust of organized society extended to organizations as well, and despite his sympathy with many Communist causes he was always a maverick rather than a party radical. In 1934 an overt rift developed between Dos Passos and the Communist movement, and it marked the beginning of a long shift to the right in his political sympathies.

After a one-man show of his sketches in 1937, Dos Passos went to Spain to help Hemingway and Joris Ivens make a film documentary of the Spanish Civil War, *The Spanish Earth*. Dos Passos and Hemingway, who had earlier survived an auto accident together, were good friends until Dos Passos' sympathies with the anarchist faction estranged Hemingway, who was partial to the main Loyalist forces.

In 1940 Dos Passos became active in behalf of political refugees, and during World War II did a good deal of war writing, principally for *Harper's* and *Life* magazines, for whom he later covered the postwar Nuremberg trials.

Major Work

U.S.A. (1937), Dos Passos' masterpiece, is a trilogy made up of *The 42nd Parallel* (1930), *Nineteen-Nineteen* (1932), and *The Big Money* (1936). To solve the time problem that flawed *Manhattan Transfer*, Dos Passos employed three unusual devices: "The Camera Eye," autobiographical episodes rendered in a Joycean stream of consciousness; "Newsreel," a Dada-like pastiche of mass culture, combining fragments of pop songs, newspaper headlines, and political speeches; and short biographies, impressionistic sketches of some of the prominent figures of the 1900–1930 time span—Henry Ford, William Randolph Hearst, Thomas A. Edison, Charles Steinmetz, and others. These sections serve as time guides and also as markers separating the narrative chapters that constitute the bulk of the trilogy and are concerned with a cross section of American social types. Among these are Mac McCreary, a poor boy who grows to a class consciousness and revolutionary commitment so strong that he deserts his family to serve the revolution in Mexico; Eleanor Stoddard, a New York interior decorator, whose gentility and estheticism are pitiably empty responses to her sordid childhood; Evaline Hutchins, an aspiring artist with little talent whose boredom with her habit of failure leads her to suicide; J. Ward Morehouse, a self-made millionaire publicist and labor politician and a prototype of the ruthless opportunist; Richard Savage, a Harvard esthete and idealist who ultimately succumbs to the enticements of big business and becomes a Morehouse employee; Mary French, an idealistic union official who becomes disillusioned with the radical movement when her Communist fiancé marries someone of the party's choice; and Charley Anderson, a likable inventor who makes a fortune in the airplane business.

The characters' lives cross briefly and futilely. All are seen in dual perspective: publicly, as they relate to the class struggle between labor and industry; and privately, as they suffer frustration and a gnawing sense of unfulfillment. Though they are closely observed, the characters rarely get beyond social typology, so that the predominant narrative sections, ironically, are less compelling than the "device" sections. However, its scope and daring give *U.S.A.* distinction, and it had a powerful impact on the social novel in America.

Later Life and Work

In a 1947 auto accident Dos Passos lost an eye and his wife was killed. In 1950 he married Elizabeth H. Holdridge; their daughter was Dos Passos' only child. After 1949 he lived principally on his family farm in Westmoreland, Va. Dos Passos died on Sept. 28, 1970, in Baltimore.

Always prolific, after the war Dos Passos divided his writing between reportage and fiction. His later novels tend toward moodiness and romantic despair. *District of Columbia* (1952) is a trilogy consisting of *Adventures of a Young Man* (1939), *Number One* (1943), and *The Grand Design* (1949). A chronicle of the Spotswood family, it takes as its theme the destruction of individuals by a complex, mechanistic, industrial society. Critics were generally displeased with the trilogy.

Chosen Country (1951), an autobiographical novel; *Most Likely to Succeed* (1954), a novel of leftist infighting; and *The Great Days* (1958), a semiautobiographical novel, add up to little more than an anti-Communist warning to the effect that the end never justifies the means. This is also the substance and weakness of *State of the Nation* (1944), *Tour of Duty* (1946), the General Mills–commissioned *The Prospect before Us* (1950), and *The Theme Is Freedom* (1956).

Among Dos Passos' other nonfiction titles are *The Ground We Stand On* (1941), a historical survey of Anglo-American democracy; *The Head and Heart of Thomas Jefferson* (1954), a biography; *Prospects of a Golden Age* (1959), a composite biographical account of early American culture; and *The Portugal Story* (1969), a historical study.

Further Reading

John Dos Passos is listed in the Literature study guide (I, E, 2, a). He was a friend of Ernest HEMINGWAY and influenced the work of Norman MAILER.

Dos Passos' *The Best Times* (1966) is a fragmentary autobiography, ranging from 1896 to 1936 but focused mainly on the 1920s; it offers an especially interesting account of his literary friendships. John H. Wrenn, *John Dos Passos* (1962), is a good critical biography. A complete biography by Melvin Landsberg is now in progress. Excellent critical evaluations of Dos Passos may be found in Malcolm Cowley, *Exile's Return* (1934; new ed. 1951); Joseph Warren Beach, *American Fiction, 1920–1940* (1941); Maxwell Geismar, *Writers in Crisis: The American Novel between Two Wars* (1942); Alfred Kazin, *On Native Grounds: An Interpretation of Modern American Prose Literature* (1942; abr. ed. 1956); and Jean-Paul Sartre, *Literary and Philosophical Essays* (1955).

DOSTOEVSKY / By Edward Wasiolek

The Russian novelist Fyodor Dostoevsky (1821–1881) mixed social, Gothic, and sentimental elements with psychological irrationalism and visionary religion. The form of the novel vastly increased in scope and flexibility as a result of his works.

Fyodor Dostoevsky (pronounced dôs-tô-yěf′skē) was born in Moscow in 1821, the son of a staff doctor of a Moscow hospital. His father, a cruel man, was murdered by his serfs in 1839, when Dostoevsky was 18 and attending school in St. Petersburg. Sigmund Freud and other psychoanalysts believed that throughout his life Dostoevsky felt a secret guilt about his father's murder. Dostoevsky was trained to be a military engineer, but he disliked school and loved literature. When he finished school, he abandoned the career he was trained for and devoted himself to writing. His earliest letters show him to be a passionate, enthusiastic, and somewhat unstable young man.

Fyodor Dostoevsky. (Photo Harlingue-Viollet)

Early Works

Dostoevsky began his writing career in the tradition of the "social tale" of the early 1840s, but he transformed the fiction about poor people in abject circumstances into a powerful philosophical and psychological instrument. His entry on the literary stage was brilliant. In 1843 he finished his first novel, *Poor Folk,* a social tale about an abject civil servant. The novel was praised profusely by the reigning critic, Vissarion Belinsky. Dostoevsky's second novel, *The Double* (1846), was received less warmly; his subsequent works in the 1840s were received coldly and antagonistically by Belinsky and others, and Dostoevsky's literary star sank quickly. *The Double* has emerged, however, as his most significant early work, and in many respects it was a work far in advance of its time.

Dostoevsky was always sensitive to critical opinion, and the indifferent reception of *The Double* caused him to back off from the exciting originality of the novel. From 1846 to 1849 his life and work are characterized by some aimlessness and confusion. The short stories and novels he wrote in this period are for the most part experiments in different forms and different subject matters. He continued to write about civil servants in such tales as *Mr. Prokharchin* (1846) and *The Faint Heart* (1847). *The Landlady* (1847) is an experiment with the Gothic form; *A Jealous Husband, an Unusual Event* (1848) and *Nine Letters* (1847) are burlesques; *White Nights* (1848) is a sentimental romance; and the unfinished novel *Netochka Nezvanova* (1847) is a mixture of Gothic, social, and sentimental elements. Despite the variety and lack of formal and thematic continuity, one may pick out themes and devices that reappear in the mature work of Dostoevsky.

Dostoevsky's life showed some of the same pattern of uncertain experimentation. Although he had already shown the religious and conservative traits that were to become a fixed part of his character in his mature years, he was also attracted at this time to current revolutionary thought. In 1847 he began to associate with a mildly subversive group called the "Petrashevsky Circle." In 1849, however, the members were arrested and the circle was disbanded. After 8 months of imprisonment, Dostoevsky was sentenced to death. This sentence was actually a hoax designed to impress the prisoners with the Czar's mercy, when he commuted the death penalty. At one point, however, Dostoevsky believed he had only moments to live, and he was never to forget the sensation and feelings of that experience. He was sentenced to 4 years of imprisonment and 4 years of forced service in the Siberian army.

Years of Transition (1859–1864)

Dostoevsky returned to St. Petersburg in 1859 with a consumptive wife, Maria Issaeva, a widow whom he had married in Siberia. Their marriage was not happy; Dostoevsky and his wife reinforced each other's unhealthy tendencies. To support himself, Dostoevsky edited the journal *Time* with his brother Mikhail and wrote a number of fictional works. His first published works after returning from Siberia were the comic stories *The Uncle's Dream* (1859) and *The Village Stepanchikovo* (1859). In 1861 he published *Memoirs from the House of the Dead,* a fictionalized account of his experiences in prison. That year he also published *The Insulted and the Injured,* a poorly structured novel characterized by improbable events and situations. By and large his work during this period showed no great artistic advance over his early work and gave no hint of the greatness that was to issue forth in 1864 with the publication of *Notes from the Underground.*

Dostoevsky's life during this period was characterized by poor health, poverty, and complicated emotional situations. He fell in love with the young student Polina Suslova, a girl of complicated and difficult temperament, and carried on a frustrating and torturous affair with her for several years. He went abroad in 1862 and 1863 to get away from his creditors, to repair his health, and to engage in his passion for gambling. His impressions of Europe were unfavorable; he considered European civilization to be dominated by rationalism and rampant with rapacious individualism. His views on Europe are contained in *Winter Notes and Summer Impressions* (1863).

Thus, at the point when his great talent was to become evident, Dostoevsky was pursued by creditors, his wife was dying, and he was carrying on a love affair with a young girl. His journal had been closed down by the censors, and he was fatally pursuing his self-destructive passion for gambling.

Notes from the Underground (1864) is a short novel, written partly as a philosophical monologue and partly as a narrative. In this work Dostoevsky attempts to justify the existence of individual freedom as a necessary and inevitable attribute of man. He argues against the view that man is a rational creature and that society may be so organized as to assure his happiness. He insists that man desires freedom more than happiness, but he also perceives that unqualified freedom is a destructive force since there is no guarantee that man will use his freedom constructively. Indeed, the evidence of history suggests that man seeks the destruction of others and of himself.

"Crime and Punishment"

Dostoevsky's first wife died in 1864, and in the following year he married Anna Grigorievna Snitkina. She was efficient, practical, and serene and therefore the very opposite of his first wife and his mistress. There is very little doubt that she was largely responsible for introducing better conditions for his work by taking over many of the practical tasks that he loathed and handled badly.

In 1866 Dostoevsky published *Crime and Punishment,* which is the most popular of his great novels, perhaps because it appeals to various levels of sophistication. It can be read as a serious and complex work of art, but it can also be enjoyed as an engrossing detective story. The novel is concerned with the murder of an old pawnbroker by a student, Raskolnikov, while he is committing robbery, ostensibly to help his family and his

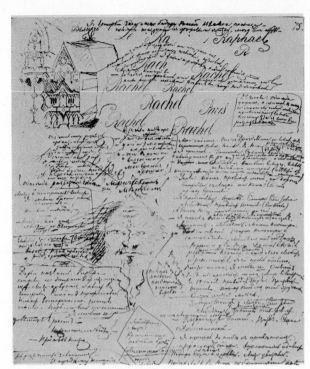

A page from the autograph manuscript of Dostoevsky's novel The Possessed, *in Dostoevsky House, Moscow. (Photo Harlingue-Viollet)*

own career. The murder occurs at the very beginning of the novel, and the rest of the book has to do with the pursuit of Raskolnikov by the detective Porfiry and by his own conscience. In the end he gives himself up and decides to accept the punishment for his act.

Raskolnikov's intentions in committing the murder share something of the complexity and impenetrability of Hamlet's motives. One can, however, dismiss some of the aims that Raskolnikov consciously gives. The humanitarian motive of murdering a useless old woman to save the careers of many useful young men is clearly a rationalization, since Raskolnikov never makes use of, or even appears interested in, the money he has stolen. The "superman" theory divides mankind into extraordinary and ordinary people, and the extraordinary people are permitted to cross the boundaries of normal morality. This theory appears to be a more accurate representation of Raskolnikov's thoughts. But some critics consider this too a rationalization of something deeper in his nature. There is some evidence that Raskolnikov suffered from a deep sense of guilt and committed the murder to provoke punishment and thus alleviate his guilt.

"The Idiot"

The Dostoevskys went abroad in 1867 and remained away from Russia for more than 4 years. Their economic condition was very difficult, and Dostoevsky repeatedly lost what little they had at the gaming tables. *The Idiot* was written between 1867 and 1869, and Dostoevsky stated that in this work he intended to depict "the wholly beautiful man."

The hero of the novel is Prince Myshkin, a kind of modern Christ. He is a good man who attempts to live in a corrupt society, and it is uncertain whether he succeeds or not, since he leaves the pages of the novel with the world about him worse than when he entered. Nastasya Fillipovna, one of Dostoevsky's great female characters, shares the stage with Prince Myshkin. When she was a young girl, her honor had been violated, and she lives to wreak vengeance on the world for the hurt she had suffered. While Prince Myshkin preaches forgiveness, Nastasya Fillipovna burns with the desire to pay others back. Nastasya Fillipovna is nevertheless attracted to Prince Myshkin, and throughout the novel she vacillates between Myshkin, the prince of light, and Rogozhin, an apostle of passion and destruction. In the end Rogozhin kills Nastasya Fillipovna, and Prince Myshkin is powerless to prevent this crime.

Some readers view *The Idiot* as Dostoevsky's finest creation, while others see it as the weakest of his great novels. It is certainly a less tidy work than *Crime and Punishment,* but it is perhaps a more challenging novel.

"The Possessed"

Dostoevsky began *The Possessed* (also translated as *The Devils*) in 1870 and published it in 1871–1872. The novel began as a political pamphlet and was based on a political murder that took place in Moscow on Nov. 21, 1869. A radical named Nechaev had a member of his conspiratorial group murdered because the member would not obey him unquestioningly. Nechaev escaped to Switzerland but was arrested and returned to Russia, where he died in prison. Nechaev's actual influence on revolutionary movements in Russia was small, but his bravado and his friendship with Mikhail Bakunin worked to increase his reputation. Dostoevsky saw Nechaev as the end product of pernicious tendencies in liberalism and radicalism.

In *The Possessed* Dostoevsky raises a minor contemporary event to dimensions of great political and philosophical importance. The novel is a satire of liberalism and radicalism; it is set in a small provincial town and concerns the contrasting influence of father and son. The father, Stepan Trofimovich Verkhovensky, represents the liberalism of the 1840s, and the son, Peter Verkhovensky, represents the radicalism of the 1860s. Dostoevsky believed that the earlier liberalism was responsible for the later radicalism. Nicholas Stavrogin, a mysterious and compelling figure, stands apart from the political and ideological struggle, but it is clear that Dostoevsky sees in him the ultimate principle from which the disastrous consequences stem. Stavrogin represents the totally free will, attached to nothing and responsible for nothing. In Stavrogin, Dostoevsky reconfronted the problem of free will.

Many readers see *The Possessed* not only as an accurate portrayal of certain tendencies of the politics of the time but also as a prophetic commentary on the future of politics in Russia and elsewhere.

"The Brothers Karamazov"

During the 1870s Dostoevsky became increasingly interested in contemporary social and political events and increasingly concerned about liberal and radical trends among the youth. Except for his brief flirtation with liberal movements in the 1840s, Dostoevsky was a staunch conservative. The novel *A Raw Youth* (1875) grew out of his interest and concern about the youth of Russia, and the theme of the novel may be described as a son in search of his father. The novel is something of a proving ground for *The Brothers Karamazov* but is not generally considered to be on the same level as the four great novels.

The Brothers Karamazov (1879–1880) is the greatest of Dostoevsky's novels and the culmination of his lifework. Sigmund Freud ranked it with *Oedipus Rex* and *Hamlet* as one of the greatest artistic achievments of all time. The novel is about four sons and and their guilt in the murder of their father, Fyodor. Each of the sons may be characterized by a dominant trait: Dmitri by passion, Ivan by reason, Alyosha by spirit, and Smerdyakov by everything that is ugly in human nature. Smerdyakov kills his father, but in varying degrees the other three brothers are guilty in thought and intention.

The greatest section of the novel is "The Legend of the Grand Inquisitor," in which Ivan narrates a meeting between Christ and the Grand Inquisitor, a devil surrogate. The Grand Inquisitor presents man as slavish, cowardly, and incapable of freedom; Christ sees him as potentially capable of true freedom. The novel, however, does not confirm the validity of either view.

Dostoevsky sent the epilogue to the *The Brothers Karamazov* to his publisher on Nov. 8, 1880, and he died soon afterward, on Jan. 28, 1881. At his death he was at the height of his career in Russia, and mourning was widespread. His reputation was beginning to penetrate into Europe, and interest in him has continued to increase.

Further Reading

Fyodor Dostoevsky is listed in the Literature study guide (III, H, 7). His early works were influenced by Nikolai GOGOL. Dostoevsky and his contemporary Leo TOLSTOY are usually considered the two greatest Russian novelists.

Translations of Dostoevsky's works are available in many editions; those by Constance Garnett and David Magarshack are recommended.

There are many biographies of Dostoevsky. Two competent ones which differ in approach are Edward Hallett Carr, *Dostoevsky* (1821–1881): A New Biography (1931), and Henry Troyat, *Firebrand: The Life of Dostoevsky* (trans. 1946). Useful, more recent biographical data may be found in Robert Payne, *Dostoyevsky: A Human Portrait* (1961), which treats Dostoevsky's life and work. An intimate view of Dostoevsky the man is presented in the reminiscences of his daughter, Aimée Dostoyevsky, *Fyodor Dostoyevsky: A Study* (1921). See also A. Steinberg, *Dostoievsky* (1966).

Ernest J. Simmons, *Dostoevski: The Making of a Novelist* (1940), is a detailed and objective account of the circumstances surrounding the production of Dostoevsky's novels, as well as a consideration of their substance. Konstantin Vasilevich Mochulskii, *Dostoevsky: His Life and Work,* translated by Michael A. Minihan (1967), is the most detailed analysis of Dostoevsky's work. A critical analysis of the individual works may be found in Edward Wasiolek, *Dostoevsky: The Major Fiction* (1964). For a philosophical and theological consideration of Dostoevsky's work, Nikolai A. Berdiaev, *Dostoevsky,* translated by Donald Attwater (1957), is a classic. For a psychological approach, Sigmund Freud's widely anthologized essay "Dostoevsky and Parricide" is recommended. It may be found in William Phillips, ed., *Art and Psychoanalysis* (1957). For general historical and literary background, Prince D. S. Mirsky, *A History of Russian Literature* (2 vols., 1927), is recommended; it is also available in an abridged volume, edited by Francis J. Whitfield (1958).

D. **DOUGLAS** / By Carroll Pursell

The American aeronautical engineer Donald Wills Douglas (born 1892) developed and manufactured aircraft that dominated the world market for many years.

D onald Douglas was born in Brooklyn, N.Y. After high school he was appointed to the U.S. Naval Academy at Annapolis, where he became enthusiastic about the infant field of aviation. In 1912 he entered the Massachusetts Institute of Technology; two years later he became the first man to receive a degree in aeronautical engineering from that school.

Douglas joined Glenn L. Martin's aircraft firm as chief engineer in 1915. The following year he went to Washington as chief civilian aeronautical engineer for the U.S. Army Signal Corps. Within a few months he resigned over a dispute with the War Production Board and returned to the Martin Company.

In 1920 Douglas quit the Martin Company to set up his own firm in Los Angeles. He was president of the Douglas Company until 1957. He was the first of many manufacturers to go into production permanently in Los Angeles, where the availability of capital, skilled labor, and flying weather for most of the year made an attractive package for the aeronautical industry.

Douglas's first effort was to produce a single-engine airplane capable of flying nonstop across the country. When this failed, he successfully sought a contract from the U.S. Navy for airplanes and eventually became the leading manufacturer of naval aircraft. In 1932 Douglas and other firms were asked by Transcontinental and Western airlines to design a craft capable of traveling 1,080 miles with 12 passengers at a speed of up to 185 miles per hour (mph). Douglas accepted the challenge and produced the DC-1 (for Douglas Commercial), which was first flown on July 1, 1933, and was able to carry 12 passengers at a cruising speed of 170 mph. An

Donald Douglas (right) is seated next to President Franklin D. Roosevelt in this 1942 photograph. (U.S. Army)

all-metal, twin-engine plane, it was one of the first to establish the usefulness of wing flaps in commercial planes. This aircraft (only one was built) was a prototype for the succeeding members of the DC family.

The most famous Douglas plane was the DC-3, which carried 21 passengers at a cruising speed of 190 mph. It was so successful that within 2 years after it first appeared, it was carrying 95 percent of the nation's civil air traffic. During the late 1930s Douglas worked on designs for a four-engine transport, eventually designated the DC-4. In 1955 Douglas, whose planes were flying over half the world's passenger-miles, began to develop the jet-propelled DC-8. The merger of the firm in 1967 with McDonnell Aircraft, to make the McDonnell Douglas Corporation, strengthened its position in the aerospace industry.

Further Reading

Donald Douglas is listed in the Science study guide (VII, H, 3). Glenn CURTISS and Igor SIKORSKY also made important contributions to the development and manufacture of aircraft.

The standard biography of Douglas is Frank Cunningham, *Sky Master: The Story of Donald Douglas* (1943). Douglas's most famous airplane, the DC-3, is covered in Charles J. Kelly, *The Sky's the Limit: The History of the Airlines* (1963). The best history of the industry generally is John B. Rae, *Climb to Greatness: The American Aircraft Industry, 1920–1960* (1968).

G. DOUGLAS / By D. W. Robertson, Jr.

The Scottish poet, prelate, and courtier Gavin Douglas (ca. 1475–1522) is best known for his vigorous translation of Virgil's "Aeneid" into Scots, the English of the lowlands of Scotland. He is sometimes listed among the Scottish Chaucerians.

Gavin Douglas was the third son of Archibald "Bell-the-Cat" Douglas, 5th Earl of Angus, a man of distinguished family, very active in court affairs. Little is known about Gavin's early life, but he entered the University of St. Andrews in 1490 and earned a master of arts degree in 1494. He may have studied law at Paris under the distinguished Scottish theologian John Major (or Mair).

Douglas soon rose in ecclesiastical preferment and was appointed provost of St. Giles Church, Edinburgh, about 1501. About this time he wrote *The Palace of Honor,* a poem in the form of a dream vision; in it he emphasizes the difference between worldly honor and true honor before God. He probably spent some time abroad, in England, France, and Italy, during the early years of the 16th century.

Douglas completed his translation of Virgil in July 1513. It includes not only the original 12 books of the *Aeneid* but also the thirteenth book, composed by Mapheus Vegius in 1428. Douglas wrote a prologue for each book, and these prologues contain interesting material reflecting the critical, philosophical, and moral commonplaces of the time. Rather than translating "word for word," Douglas followed the advice of St. Gregory the Great and translated "meaning for meaning." Moreover, he made Virgil's characters act and speak like his own contemporaries. There are frequent turns of phrase reminiscent of Geoffrey Chaucer. The result is an extremely lively and effective poem that has won high praise from modern critics.

After the disastrous Battle of Flodden in 1513, in which James IV and much of the Scottish nobility, including the elder brothers of Gavin Douglas, perished, Douglas ceased writing poetry and devoted himself to court affairs. The widowed Queen Margaret, who married Douglas's nephew Alexander, assisted him considerably. He was made bishop of Dunkeld but was imprisoned for a time in 1515–1516 and could occupy his see only by making a show of force to dislodge another contender for the office. He died in London in 1522.

Further Reading

Gavin Douglas is listed in the Literature study guide (II, C, 1, b). Both he and the English poet John SKELTON were influenced by Geoffrey CHAUCER.

The Poetical Works of Gavin Douglas was edited by John Small (4 vols., 1874). A new edition of Douglas's translation of Virgil's *Aeneid,* with a full introduction, notes, and a glossary, was prepared by David F. C. Coldwell for the Scottish Text Society (4 vols. 1957–1964). The society also issued *The Shorter Poems of Gavin Douglas,* edited by Priscilla J. Bawcutt (1967). Brief selections are available in *Gavin Douglas: A Selection from His Poetry,* edited by Sydney Goodsir Smith (1959), and in *Selections from Gavin Douglas,* edited by David F. C. Coldwell (1964). There is a stimulating discussion of Douglas in C. S. Lewis, *English Literature in the Sixteenth Century: Excluding Drama* (1954).

* * *

J. DOUGLAS / By R. W. Pfaff

The Scottish patriot Sir James Douglas (1286?–1330) supported Robert Bruce, later King Robert I, in the Scottish struggle for independence from England.

James Douglas was the eldest son of a notable Scottish patriot, Sir William Douglas, called "the Hardy." Sir William had been among the early leaders of resistance to the ambitions of Edward I of England to dominate Scotland. Edward imprisoned Sir William in the Tower of London and, on the latter's death in 1297, confiscated the Douglas estates.

It is not surprising, therefore, that the young James appears to have grown up with passionate anti-English feelings. He reached manhood just as Robert Bruce laid claim to the crown of Scotland (1306) and from that time was one of Bruce's most faithful and important lieutenants.

Douglas's career may be divided into two phases. The

Gavin Douglas, as represented on the seal he used as bishop of Dunkeld. (Public Record Office, London)

The ruins of Castle Douglas in Kirkcudbrightshire near Dumfries, Scotland. Twice Douglas burned his castle to drive out English garrisons. (H. Roger-Viollet)

first was the 8 years of Bruce's struggle to claim the Scottish crown. This was a period of virtual guerrilla warfare, with Douglas emerging from his hiding places for a daring raid or the capture of a strategic castle. At the decisive Scottish victory at Bannockburn in 1314, Douglas commanded one of the four divisions of the Scots and, for his skillful leadership, was knighted on the battlefield by Bruce, now firmly established on the throne.

After Bannockburn, in the second phase of his public career, Douglas served as Warden of the Marches (the disputed frontier area between England and Scotland). In 1317 he diverted an English threat to the borders by staging a raid deep into English territory. Ten years later he dispersed the danger of an English invasion by an audacious attack in which he surprised the enemy forces by night and nearly captured the young Edward III in his bed.

Bruce's reliance on, and affection for, Sir James never ceased. When the King was dying in 1329, he apparently asked Sir James to carry out the spirit of an unfulfilled crusading vow by bearing Bruce's heart to the Holy Land. During the subsequent journey Douglas joined the King of Castile in a "crusade" against the Moslems in Spain and died there in battle in 1330.

It is as a hero of Scottish romance and legend that Douglas's real fame lies. Two sobriquets, "the Good" and "the Black Douglas," indicate his differing reputations in Scotland and in England (though "black" probably referred originally to the color of his hair). His name lives on, especially through the works of Sir Walter Scott, *Castle Dangerous* and *Tales of a Grandfather*.

Further Reading

Sir James Douglas is listed in the European History study guide (III, E, 1, a). He was a loyal and effective aide of ROBERT I.

There is no modern biography of Douglas. The fullest treatment is in Sir Herbert E. Maxwell, *A History of the House of Douglas* ... (2 vols., 1902). The principal near-contemporary source is John Barbour's long poem *The Bruce* (ca. 1375; trans. by W. M. MacKenzie, 1909, and by Archibald A. H. Douglas, 1964).

S. A. DOUGLAS / By Fawn M. Brodie

U.S. senator Stephen Arnold Douglas (1813–1861), the foremost leader of the Democratic party in the decade preceding the Civil War, was Lincoln's political rival for the presidency.

Stephen A. Douglas was born in Brandon, Vt., on April 23, 1813. His father's early death meant Stephen's dependence on a bachelor uncle and later a detested apprenticeship as a cabinetmaker. When his mother remarried and went to Canandaigua, N.Y., Stephen followed. He attended the academy there, developed a formidable talent as a debater, and became an ardent follower of Andrew Jackson.

Douglas made up for his short stature (5 feet 4 inches) in aggressiveness, audacity, and consuming political ambition. When he said farewell to his mother at 20, he promised to return "on his way to Congress," a prediction he made good 10 years later. He settled in Illinois, where he became a teacher. He taught himself law with borrowed books, became active in the Democratic party, and at 27 was a member of the Illinois State Supreme Court, the youngest ever to attain that office. He was called Judge Douglas thereafter.

Career in Congress

Elected to the House of Representatives in 1843 and to the Senate in 1847, Douglas became a power in all legislation having to do with territories in the West. Known as the "Little Giant" because of his massive head, heavy brown hair, broad shoulders, and booming voice, he soon won the reputation of being the most formidable legislative pugilist in Washington. His enemies called him ruthless; his admirers strove to make him president.

In 1847 Douglas married Martha Denny Martin. The following year she inherited a Mississippi plantation with 150 slaves; by the terms of his father-in-law's will, Douglas was made manager. Though he always denied ownership of any slaves himself, he did manage the plantation up to his death, and there is little doubt that he looked upon his own marriage as symbolic of a successful bridging of North and South. When his wife, after bearing two sons, died in childbirth, he became depressed and turned for a time to liquor. A tour abroad rejuvenated his spirits, and in 1856 he married the beautiful Adèle Cutts, another Southern woman.

Though privately Douglas held slavery to be "a curse beyond computation," publicly he pronounced it a matter "of climate, of political economy, of self-interest, not

Stephen A. Douglas about 1860. (Library of Congress)

a question of legislation." It was good for Louisiana, he said, but bad for Illinois. Essentially proslavery in his legislation, he voted against abolition petitions, favored the annexation of Texas, helped Henry Clay push through the Compromise of 1850, and encouraged the purchase of Cuba to make a new slave state.

Doctrine of "Squatter Sovereignty"

Douglas's failure to reckon with the enormity of the slavery evil, and the growing Northern resentment against it, led him to devise in 1854 what modern historian Allan Nevins called "the worst Pandora's box in our history." In planning for two new states, Kansas and Nebraska, he insisted that the slavery issue be resolved by the settlers themselves rather than by Congress, thus repudiating the 20-year-old Missouri Compromise. Southern extremists saw in this "squatter sovereignty" doctrine an opportunity to make Kansas a slave state, though a majority of the actual settlers were against slavery. Missourians crossed the border at election time to overwhelm the polls and vote in a proslavery government. The antislavery majority set up a rival government in Topeka, and soon there was a small but bloody civil war in Kansas. Douglas was denounced by the abolitionists. Charles Sumner in the Senate called him the squire of slavery, "ready to do all its humiliating offices."

When President James Buchanan recognized the pro-

slavery government in Kansas, Douglas, angered by the misuse of his popular-sovereignty doctrine, denounced the President in 1857, thereby alienating his friends in the South and damaging his presidential chances. But his Kansas-Nebraska Bill had also alienated his antislavery followers in Illinois, who charged him with conniving with railroad speculators. In 1858 he went home to face a difficult reelection battle, with Abraham Lincoln as his opponent.

Debates with Lincoln

In his famous debates with Lincoln, Douglas opposed Negro citizenship in any form and attacked as "monstrous heresy" Lincoln's insistence that "the Negro and the white man are made equal by the Declaration of Independence and by Divine Providence." Douglas held that Negroes "belong to an inferior race and must always occupy an inferior position." Lincoln denounced Douglas's popular-sovereignty idea as "a mere deceitful pretense for the benefit of slavery" and emphasized the callousness of Douglas's statement: "When the struggle is between the white man and the Negro, I am for the white man; when it is between the Negro and the crocodile, I am for the Negro."

Douglas barely won the senatorial election, but the debates won national recognition for his rival. In 1860, when Lincoln was nominated for president on the Republican ticket, Douglas said of him to Republicans, "Gentlemen, you have nominated a very able and a very honest man."

Presidential Candidate

Douglas expected to be nominated for president in the Democratic convention in Charleston, but a bloc of Southerners bolted the party, nominating instead John C. Breckinridge. The remaining Democrats nominated Douglas at a second convention in Baltimore. A fourth convention, organized by the Constitutional Union party, nominated John Bell. Douglas suspected that the four-candidate election would ensure Lincoln's victory but nevertheless campaigned vigorously, urging support for the Union he loved. "I wish to God," he said in New York City, "that we had an Old Hickory now alive in order that he might hang Northern and Southern traitors on the same gallows." In the South he deplored secession, which he said would make it necessary for his children to obtain a passport to visit the graves of their ancestors.

As Douglas feared, Lincoln's victory brought the immediate secession of South Carolina from the Union, and other states quickly followed. Douglas still labored for compromises to restore the Union, and he urged Lincoln to support a projected 13th Amendment which would guarantee that slavery would never be tampered with in the slave states. The firing on Ft. Sumter on Jan. 9, 1861, by Confederate forces ended his compromise efforts. He now swung behind Lincoln, urging a vigorous war effort and rallying Northern Democrats to the cause of the Union.

Douglas contracted typhoid fever and died June 3,

1861. Thus Lincoln lost his ablest rival at precisely the moment in history when he was most needed.

Further Reading

Stephen A. Douglas is listed in the American History study guide (VI, A, 1). Another senatorial titan of the period was Henry CLAY. Douglas opposed Abraham LINCOLN for the presidency in 1860.

The bulk of Douglas's papers are at the University of Chicago, with additional letters in the Illinois State Historical Society Library and the Chicago Historical Society. The brief *Autobiography of Stephen A. Douglas* (1913) and a volume of his letters, *The Letters of Stephen A. Douglas,* edited by Robert W. Johannsen (1961), are good source materials. The earliest good biography is Allen Johnson, *Stephen A. Douglas: A Study in American Politics* (1908). George Fort Milton in *The Eve of Conflict: Stephen A. Douglas and the Needless War* (1934) proves to be the most sympathetic of all the biographers and contends that, had Douglas been elected president in 1860, he would have prevented the Civil War. The same thesis is echoed in Gerald M. Capers, *Stephen A. Douglas: Defender of the Union,* edited by Oscar Handlin (1959). Historians are more critical of Douglas than these laudatory biographers.

W. O. **DOUGLAS** / By Max Lerner

William Orville Douglas (born 1898) was one of the most liberal and activist justices of the U.S. Supreme Court and a vigorous and controversial writer.

William O. Douglas was born on Oct. 16, 1898, at Yakima, Wash., where his father, a Scotsman from Nova Scotia, had moved as an itinerant preacher. At the age of 4 William was stricken with polio; to strengthen his spindly legs he began the hiking and later the mountain climbing that became one of his characteristic signatures. When he was 6 his father died, leaving the mother and the three children to make their way on very little. William worked his way through school at Yakima, got a scholarship to Whitman College, and on graduating spent 2 years teaching high school English.

But Douglas's aim was the law. He arrived at Columbia Law School in 1922 almost penniless. He was befriended by Dean Harlan Stone and deeply influenced by Professor Underhill Moore, who had a new approach to the legal sociology of corporate business. This was also the period of the creative jurisprudence on the U.S. Supreme Court of Justice Louis D. Brandeis, and this "People's Attorney" and iconoclastic judge became one of Douglas's heroes. After working for a big New York City law firm and practicing for a year in Yakima, Douglas joined the faculty at Columbia Law School but resigned in protest against the appointment of a new dean without faculty consultation. A chance meeting with Dean Robert M. Hutchins of the Yale Law School led to Douglas's appointment to a professorship there at the age of 32.

New Deal Days

Douglas's life was transformed by President Franklin Roosevelt's New Deal, with its sense of social urgency and unparalleled opportunity for reform. In 1934 the newly created Securities and Exchange Commission asked the young law professor for a memorandum on the abuses of corporate reorganization and how these could be remedied. Douglas's reply was an eight-volume report that led to his appointment in 1936 as a member of the Commission and in 1937 as chairman. He prodded the stock exchanges into reorganizing themselves and also developed the Commission's surveillance of the prospectuses for new security issues, which did much to stabilize the exchanges.

When Justice Brandeis retired from the Supreme Court, President Franklin Roosevelt turned to Douglas, despite his youth. Justice Douglas took his seat on April 17, 1939. There was talk of Douglas's resigning for high political office on two occasions during the intervening years. One time was in 1944, when Roosevelt sent two names to the Democratic Convention managers as his preferences for vice-presidential running mate—Douglas and Harry Truman. The choice fell to Truman, partly because political moguls mistrusted Douglas just as busi-

William O. Douglas. (National Archives, Washington, D.C.)

ness moguls did. The second occasion was in 1948, when President Truman, needing a strong, liberal running mate, offered the place to Douglas, who turned it down.

Justice Douglas

As a justice, Douglas was one of the hardcore liberal "activists," in the sense that he believed that judicial neutrality was a myth and that judges could not rely on constitutional precedent or hard-and-fast constitutional texts to give them the judicial answers. Douglas believed that judicial statesmanship must keep up with social change and that a judge has the duty actively to shape the law in the desired social direction. Placed for a time in a dissenting minority with Justice Hugo Black, he later found himself part of a liberal majority, as Roosevelt's appointees gradually took over the Court. He went on the defensive again in the conservative Frederick Vinson Court of the cold war period but again was part of the liberal majority of the Earl Warren Court.

Douglas took a strong role in the Negro desegregation cases, in the assurance of fair governmental procedures for the accused, in the freedom of religion cases, and in the cases concerning the right of access to birth-control information. In the obscenity cases he took a firm stand for the absolute freedoms guaranteed against censorship of any sort by the 1st Amendment.

Douglas's continuous record of militant judicial liberalism was bound to awaken hostility. There were rumblings about impeaching Douglas when he granted a brief stay of execution to Julius and Ethel Rosenberg, who had been convicted of spying on American atomic bomb technology. Anti-Douglas sentiments were fed by his three divorces and by his judicial opinions in the religion-in-the-schools and the obscenity cases: to a growing number of people he had offended God, the home, and the purity of the printed word. He gave his enemies an opening by serving as director of the Parvin Fund, whose purposes were impeccable but whose money (it turned out) came from sources tainted with gambling. His book, *Points of Revolution* (1970), compared the current American Establishment with George III's, saying that unless it accepted the pressures for nonviolent revolutionary change, it would be overthrown by violence; this also stirred ire. The impeachment movement this time gained considerable strength in the House of Representatives, fed mainly by tensions of the era and partisan politics.

Renaissance Man

An indomitable traveler, naturalist, mountain climber, lecturer, and writer, as well as teacher, administrator, and judge, Douglas reasserted the possibility of a many-faceted Renaissance existence as against a specialized, limited life. His career covered 4 decades of stormy American experience, from the early New Deal days to the tensions of the Vietnam War and the student confrontations of the late 1960s and early 1970s. He brought to these years of turmoil legal and financial skills, a passion for individual freedom, and a plain-spoken brusqueness. He will be remembered as one of the few public figures who dared challenge convention and the Establishment during the middle of the 20th century.

Further Reading

William O. Douglas is listed in the American History study guide (X, A, 6). His liberal companions on the Supreme Court included Hugo BLACK and Earl WARREN.

A biographical sketch and a selection of Douglas's judicial opinions are in Vern Countryman, ed., *Douglas of the Supreme Court: A Selection of His Opinions* (1959). Douglas and the Supreme Court are also discussed in John Paul Frank, *The Warren Court* (1964); Leo Pfeffer, *This Honorable Court: A History of the United States Supreme Court* (1965); and Henry Julian Abraham, *Freedom and the Court: Civil Rights and Liberties in the United States* (1967). See also the chapter "William O. Douglas: Diogenes on Wall Street" in Max Lerner, *Ideas Are Weapons: The History and Uses of Ideas* (1939).

DOUGLASS

/ By Arna Alexander Bontemps

The foremost black abolitionist in antebellum America, Frederick Douglass (ca. 1817–1895) was the first Negro leader of national stature in United States history.

Frederick Douglass was born, as can best be determined, in February 1817 (he took the 14th as his birthday) on the eastern shore of Maryland. His mother, from whom he was separated at an early age, was a slave named Harriet Bailey. She named her son Frederick Augustus Washington Bailey; he never knew or saw his father. (Frederick adopted the name Douglass much later.) Douglass's childhood, though he judged it in his autobiography as being no more cruel than that of scores of others caught in similar conditions, appears to have been extraordinarily deprived of personal warmth. The lack of familial attachments, hard work, and sights of incredible inhumanity fill the text of his early remembrances of the main plantation of Col. Edward Lloyd. In 1825 his masters decided to send him to Baltimore to live with Mr. Hugh Auld.

Mrs. Auld, Douglass's new mistress and a Northerner unacquainted with the disciplinary techniques Southern slaveholders used to preserve docility in their slaves, treated young Douglass well. She taught him the rudiments of reading and writing until her husband stopped her. With this basic background he began his self-education.

Escape to Freedom

After numerous ownership disputes and after attempting to escape from a professional slave breaker, Douglass was put to work in the Baltimore shipyards. There in

1838 he borrowed a Negro sailor's protection papers and by impersonating him escaped to New York. He adopted the name Douglass and married a free black woman from the South. They settled in New Bedford, Mass., where several of their children were born.

Douglass quickly became involved in the antislavery movement, which was gaining impetus in the North. In 1841, at an abolitionist meeting in Nantucket, Mass., he delivered a moving speech about his experiences as a slave and was immediately hired as a lecturer by the Massachusetts Antislavery Society. By all accounts he was a forceful and even eloquent speaker. His self-taught prose and manner of speaking so inspired some Harvard students that they persuaded him to write his autobiography. The *Narrative of the Life of Frederick Douglass* was published in 1845. (Ten years later an enlarged autobiography, *My Bondage and My Freedom,* appeared. His third autobiography, *Life and Times of Frederick Douglass,* was published in 1881 and enlarged in 1892.) The 1845 publication, of course, meant exile for Douglass, a fugitive slave.

Fearing capture, Douglass fled to Britain, staying from 1845 to 1847 to speak on behalf of abolition and to earn enough money to purchase his freedom when he returned to America. Upon his return Douglass settled in Rochester, N.Y., and started publishing his newspaper, *North Star* (which continued to be published under various names until 1863).

In 1858, as a consequence of his fame and as unofficial spokesman for American blacks, Douglass was sought out by John Brown as a recruit for his planned attack on the Harpers Ferry arsenal. But Douglass could see no benefit from what he considered a futile plan and refused to lend his support.

Civil War and Reconstruction

The Civil War, beginning in 1861, raised several issues, not the least of which was what role the black man would play in his own liberation—since one of the main objectives of the war was emancipation of the slaves. Douglass kept this issue alive. In 1863, as a result of his continued insistence (as well as of political and military expediency), President Abraham Lincoln asked him to recruit Negro soldiers for the Union Army. As the war proceeded, Douglass had two meetings with Lincoln to discuss the use and treatment of Negro soldiers by the Union forces. In consequence, the role of Negro soldiers was upgraded each time and their military effectiveness thereby increased.

The Reconstruction period laid serious responsibilities on Douglass. Politicians differed on the question of race and its corresponding problems, and as legislative battles were waged to establish the constitutional integrity of the slaves' emancipation, Douglass was the one black man with stature enough to make suggestions.

In 1870 Douglass and his sons began publishing the *New National Era* newspaper in Washington, D.C. In 1877 he was appointed by President Rutherford B. Hayes to the post of U.S. marshal for the District of Columbia. From this time until approximately 2 years before his

Frederick Douglass. (Library of Congress)

death Douglass held a succession of offices, including that of recorder of deeds for the District of Columbia and minister-resident and consul-general to the Republic of Haiti, as well as chargé d'affaires to Santo Domingo. He resigned his assignments in Haiti and Santo Domingo when he discovered that American businessmen were taking advantage of his position in their dealings with the Haitian government. He died in Washington, D.C., on Feb. 20, 1895.

Further Reading

Frederick Douglass is listed in the American History study guide (V, F, 3, b and e). Other fugitive slaves were Josiah HENSON and Anthony BURNS. Harriet TUBMAN and James FORTEN were black abolitionists.

Douglass's writings can be found in *The Life and Writings of Frederick Douglass,* edited by Philip S. Foner (4 vols., 1950–1955). *Frederick Douglass,* edited by Benjamin Quarles (1968), contains excerpts from Douglass's writings, portrayals of him by his contemporaries, and appraisals by later historians.

Benjamin Quarles, *Frederick Douglass* (1948), is a well-written, scholarly biography. See also Philip S. Foner, *Frederick Douglass: A Biography* (1964), and Arna Bontemps, *Free at Last: The Life of Frederick Douglass* (1971). There is a biographical sketch of Douglass in William J. Simmons, *Men of Mark: Eminent, Progressive and Rising* (1887; repr. 1968). Works that discuss Douglass at length are John Hope Franklin, *From Slavery to*

Freedom: A History of American Negroes (1947; 3d ed. 1967); Louis Filler, *The Crusade against Slavery, 1830–1860* (1960); and Martin Duberman, ed., *The Antislavery Vanguard: New Essays on the Abolitionists* (1965).

DOVE / By Robert Reiff

Arthur Garfield Dove (1880–1946) was a pioneer of modern art in America. As early as 1910 he was abstracting forms in nature to suggest landscape situations.

Arthur G. Dove was born in Canandaigua, N.Y., on Aug. 2, 1880. When he graduated from Cornell University in 1903, he became a magazine illustrator, an occupation that would supply his livelihood until 1930, when, with the assistance of Duncan Phillips, he was able to devote all of his time to painting.

In 1907 Dove joined the painters Alfred Maurer and

Portrait of Ralph Dusenberry, a collage by Arthur G. Dove, executed in 1924. (The Metropolitan Museum of Art, The Alfred Stieglitz Collection, 1949)

Arthur G. Dove. (William Dove)

Arthur B. Carles, Jr., on a trip to Europe. Dove spent most of his time in Paris, where he saw the art of the Fauves and was particularly impressed by the work of Henri Matisse. Dove exhibited in the Salon d'Automne in 1908 and 1909.

Dove returned to America in 1910 and continued to paint in an essentially impressionistic manner, though moving more and more toward abstraction. These works closely resemble Wassily Kandinsky's first abstractions, although there is no possibility of an influence since both artists were working along the same lines at about the same time. In his paintings Dove sought to project the essence of nature by ridding forms of extraneous detail and emphasizing rhythms. He replaced bulk with pattern, heightened and modified color, and simplified contours. In 1911 Dove exhibited his Parisian works in a group show at Alfred Stieglitz's gallery in New York City. The following year Dove had his first one-man show there, exhibiting 10 of his abstract canvases.

Dove's most original and striking works are his collages, such as the *Portrait of Ralph Dusenberry* (1924). Here he assembled shingles, a page from a hymnbook, a carpenter's folding rule, and an American flag. The work is a form of pictorial biography of a man whom Dove had actually known. In his collage *Goin' Fishin'* (1925) he evoked the spirit of rural America by combining pieces of a bamboo fishing pole with a denim shirt. Dove's later painting is more and more abstract. *Fog Horns* (1929) suggests piercing but distant blasts penetrating a thick fog through fuzzy-edged, concentric forms against a solid, heavy gray sky.

Dove exhibited annually at An American Place, the new Stieglitz gallery. He was a virtual recluse for the last decade of his life, first at Geneva, N.Y., and then at Centerport, N.Y., where he died on Nov. 23, 1946.

Further Reading

Arthur G. Dove is listed in the Art study guide (IV, E, 3). His early abstract paintings are like the first abstractions of Wassily KANDINSKY. Alfred STIEGLITZ gave first one-man shows to many modern artists.

A good book on Dove has not yet been written. The best available work is Frederick S. Wight, *Arthur G. Dove* (1958). It has a fine selection of plates, some in color, and includes a bibliography of Dove's catalogs and exhibitions. Background works include two works edited by Alfred H. Barr, Jr., *Fantastic Art: Dada, Surrealism* (1936; 3d ed. 1947) and *Masters of Modern Art* (1954; 3d ed. 1958); and Oliver W. Larkin, *Art and Life in America* (1949; rev. ed. 1960).

DOW / By Louis Filler

Neal Dow (1804–1897) was an American temperance reformer. His long, successful career, together with his reputation as father of the "Maine Law," made him a national figure.

Born in Portland, Maine, on March 20, 1804, Dow was raised in a well-to-do and highly moral Quaker household. Although he read widely and had a good mind, his father was skeptical of the conduct of and influences among college students and was unwilling to send him to college. Accordingly, Dow entered his father's tannery, rose to a partnership, and expanded his business interests in several directions; these accomplishments did not, however, satisfy his need for civic participation.

Dow next entered into temperance activities. He became unusually well informed about the subject in a state which consumed large amounts of liquor, and he became an outstanding speaker against its use. Dow and others in the Maine Temperance Union developed a program aimed at total abolition of liquor sales; since a substantial number of the members were also antislavery advocates, they doubly antagonized the conservative proliquor forces.

In 1846 a measure intended to prohibit liquor sales in Maine was enacted but was so ineffective that it doubled Dow's determination to impose a better-drawn measure. In 1851 Dow became mayor of Portland and applied himself to influencing the state legislature and governor to pass the measure. Despite bitter recriminations it became law, and its passage made Dow famous. He applied the "Maine Law" firmly in Portland and accepted

engagements throughout the North to express his sentiments against liquor and slavery. Opposition to the Maine Law consolidated and grew aggressive. Elected mayor again in 1855, Dow continued his fight for full enforcement. Later that year a riot was instigated by proliquor forces in which a rioter was killed and several others wounded by police defending a legally administered liquor supply. Rumor and antiprohibition propaganda accused Dow of murder, but though the Maine Law itself became subject to shifting public sentiment, Dow's good repute held firm. In 1857 he took the first of three lecture trips to England.

Despite his Quaker heritage Dow volunteered for service in the Civil War and was awarded a colonelcy of volunteers. He was active in the Gulf command, was promoted to brigadier general, and served later in Florida. Wounded in 1863, Dow was taken prisoner and spent 8 months at Libby Prison, Richmond, Va., and at Mobile, Ala., before being exchanged.

After the war Dow resumed his temperance work. Dissatisfied with the conduct of the Republican party and its chieftains, in 1880 he joined with other prohibitionists and became their candidate for president, receiving 10,-305 votes. He died in Portland on Oct. 2, 1897.

Further Reading

Neal Dow is listed in the American History study guide (VII, G, 4, f). Another temperance reformer of the period following the Civil War was Frances WILLARD.

Dow's autobiography, published posthumously, *The*

Neal Dow. (Library of Congress)

Reminiscences of Neal Dow (1898), is clearly and circumstantially presented. Dow's early temperance career receives brief but authoritative treatment in John A. Krout, *The Origins of Prohibition* (1925).

✳ ✳ ✳

DOWLAND / By Franklin B. Zimmerman

The British composer and lute virtuoso John Dowland (1562–1626) was the leading English lutanist composer of his time. A sensitive, original melodist, he found his forte in pensive song-soliloquys.

According to recent research, John Dowland was born in December 1562 near Dublin. Nothing is known of his early training. From about 1580 until sometime before July 1584 he served as a musician to Sir Henry Cobham, the English ambassador in Paris, and his successor, Sir Edward Stafford. In 1588 Dowland received his bachelor of arts degree at Christ Church, Oxford. Unable to obtain employment in England, possibly because he had been converted to Roman Catholicism in Paris, he visited the courts of Brunswick and Hesse and then traveled to Venice and Florence.

In 1597 Dowland received a degree from Cambridge. He still could find no employment in England, so he took a position at the court of Christian IV of Denmark, whom he served from 1598 until 1607. Apparently released for unsatisfactory service, he returned to England, where it seems that his renunciation of Catholicism opened doors formerly closed to him. He entered the service of Lord Walden. At last, in 1612, he was appointed a King's Musician for the Lutes at the court of James I. He held this position until his death in 1626 and was succeeded by his son, Robert.

Dowland's reputation as a composer rests chiefly on his four books of lute songs. These works may be performed as solo ayres with lute accompaniment or as part songs for four voices. In either arrangement the chief melodic interest lies in the top voice, a feature that gives the songs considerable historical significance.

The four song collections show Dowland's mastery of a new musical idiom, with a harmonic directness that cuts through the old polyphonic complexities. His handling of the lyrics was very sensitive, and he had a remarkable gift for beautiful and expressive melody. Such songs as "Come again, sweet love" and "Lady if you so spite me" exhibit his skill in the merry vein. A diametrically opposite character is to be found in the pathetic melancholy songs for which he is better known. The most expressive of these, such as "Sorrow stay," "I saw my lady weep," and "Flow my tears," relate in literary content as in melodic substance to Dowland's instrumental collection, *Lachrimae, or Seaven Teares Figured in Seaven Passionate Pavans* (1605). The gently descending "Lachrimae" motive established its own tradition and was imitated not only by Dowland's contemporaries, but also by composers in the late 17th century.

Further Reading

John Dowland is listed in the Music study guide (I, C, 6). His "Lachrimae" motive inspired many composers, including William BYRD and Henry PURCELL.

A monograph on Dowland is badly needed. Peter Warlock, *The English Ayre* (1926), discusses him. Background material can be found in Paul Henry Lang, *Music in Western Civilization* (1941); Gustave Reese, *Music in the Renaissance* (1954; rev. ed. 1959); Jack A. Westrup, *An Introduction to Musical History* (1955); and Donald J. Grout, *A History of Western Music* (1960).

✳ ✳ ✳

Autograph manuscript of John Dowland's "Lachrimae" motive. (Department of Manuscripts, British Museum)

DOWNING / By Paul F. Norton

American horticulturist and landscape architect Andrew Jackson Downing (1815–1852) was interested in all aspects of nature and how man might gain pleasure and benefit from it.

Andrew Jackson Downing was born at Newburgh, N.Y., on Oct. 31, 1815; he remained a lifelong resident there. His father was a wheelwright and later a nurseryman. Andrew had little formal education

Andrew Jackson Downing.
(Library of Congress)

partner in landscape and architectural commissions. In 1851 they worked on the U.S. Capitol and the White House grounds and on estates on Long Island and in the Hudson River valley.

Downing's death on July 28, 1852, while escorting his wife and others on a boat ride down the Hudson River, is a story of heroism and tragedy. The boat caught fire from engines overheated by its negligent captain, who was attempting to outrace another boat to New York City. As people jumped overboard, Downing threw chairs to them as life preservers, and he was evidently swallowed by the river as he tried to save those unable to swim.

Further Reading

Andrew Jackson Downing is listed in the Art study guide (IV, C, 4). He influenced the landscape architect Frederick Law OLMSTED. Generations later Frank Lloyd WRIGHT insisted upon the integral relationship of house to site.

There is no biography of Downing or critical catalog of his work. The memoir by George W. Curtis in Downing's posthumously published *Rural Essays* (1853) is a fine but typically 19th-century character sketch. George B. Tatum's introduction to a recent edition of Downing's *Architecture of Country Houses* (1968) gives additional information. Downing's work is also discussed in Marie Luise Gothein, *A History of Garden Art*, vol. 2 (trans. 1928).

but learned a good deal from reading, corresponding with innumerable professional horticulturists in America and abroad, and his own keen observation. When the father died in 1822, the eldest son took over the nursery business, later joined by Andrew. In 1837 Andrew bought his brother's share of the business. The following year he married Caroline E. DeWint, a grandniece of President John Quincy Adams.

For the next 14 years Downing improved his knowledge of horticulture by study and long, observant walks in the nearby hills. He published the results of his research in the horticultural magazines of Europe and the United States and in his several books. The *Treatise on the Theory and Practice of Landscape Gardening* (1841) introduced him to the American public, which gradually came to consider Downing the leading authority on the subject. He frequently received commissions for landscape projects, even from the Federal government. When his book reached England, it was highly praised.

Downing's interest in the art of landscaping led him to inquire into the relationship of the countryside to the country house and vice versa, so that several of his later books are important for their theories on architectural style. Always deeply concerned with nature, Downing thought of houses as a part of nature, and he designed them to fit their surroundings. *Cottage Residences* (1842) was the first of Downing's writings to assert that the house must fit its site.

In 1845 Downing returned to a strictly horticultural work, *The Fruits and Fruit Trees of America*, a popular book that went through many editions and contributed to his prestige as a pomologist. The next year he became editor of a newly founded magazine, *Horticulturist*. Returning to architecture again, he published *Additional Notes and Hints to Persons about Building in This Country* (1849). His most important book on architecture, *Architecture of Country Houses*, was published in 1850. In that same year Downing traveled to England, where he saw the great gardens and country landscapes he had known only from books. On his return to America he enlisted the services of Calvert Vaux as his business

DOYLE / By Glen A. Omans

The British author Sir Arthur Conan Doyle (1859–1930) is best remembered as the creator of the famous detective Sherlock Holmes.

Arthur Conan Doyle was born in Edinburgh, Scotland, on May 22, 1859, into an Irish Roman Catholic family of noted artistic achievement. After attending Stonyhurst College, he entered Edinburgh University as a medical student in 1876. He received a doctor of medicine degree in 1885. In his spare time, however, he began to write stories, which were published anonymously in various magazines from 1878 to 1880.

After two long sea voyages as a ship's doctor, Doyle practiced medicine at Southsea, England, from 1882 to 1890. In 1885 he married Louise Hawkins and in March 1891 moved his young family to London, where he began to specialize in ophthalmology. His practice remained small, however, and since one of his anonymous stories, "Habakuk Jephson's Statement," had enjoyed considerable success when it appeared in the *Cornhill Magazine* in 1884, he began to devote himself seriously to writing. The result was his first novel, *A Study in Scarlet*, which introduced Sherlock Holmes, the detective, to the reading public in *Beeton's Christmas Annual* for

1887. This was followed by two historical novels in the tradition of Sir Walter Scott, *Micah Clarke* in 1889 and *The White Company* in 1891. The immediate and prolonged success of these works led Doyle to abandon medicine and launch his career as a man of letters.

The second Sherlock Holmes novel, *The Sign of the Four* (1890), was followed by the first Holmes short story, "A Scandal in Bohemia" (1891). The instant popularity of these tales made others like them a regular monthly feature of the *Strand Magazine,* and the famous *Adventures of Sherlock Holmes* series was begun. In subsequent stories Doyle developed Holmes into a highly individualized and eccentric character, together with his companion, Doctor Watson, the ostensible narrator of the stories, and the pair came to be readily accepted as living persons by readers in England and America. But Doyle seems to have considered these stories a distraction from his more serious writing, eventually grew tired of them, and in "The Final Problem," published in December 1893, plunged Holmes and his archenemy, Moriarty, to their apparent deaths in the falls of Reichenbach. Nine years later, however, he published a third Sherlock Holmes novel, *The Hound of the Baskervilles,* but dated the action before Holmes's "death." Then, in October 1903, Holmes effected his mysterious resurrection in "The Empty House" and thereafter appeared intermittently until 1927, 3 years before Doyle's own death. All told, Doyle wrote 56 Sherlock Holmes stories and 4 novels (*The Valley of Fear,* 1914, was the last).

Among the other works published early in his career, which Doyle felt were more representative of his true artistry, were *Beyond the City* (1892), a short novel of contemporary urban life; *The Great Shadow* (1892), a historical novel of the Napoleonic period; *The Refugees* (1893), a historical novel about French Huguenots; and *The Stark Munro Letters* (1894), an autobiographical novel. In 1896 he issued one of his best-known historical novels, *Rodney Stone,* which was followed by another historical novel, *Uncle Bernac* (1897); a collection of poems, *Songs of Action* (1898); and two less popular novels, *The Tragedy of Korosko* (1898) and *A Duet* (1899).

After the outbreak of the Boer War, Doyle's energy and patriotic zeal led him to serve as chief surgeon of a field hospital at Bloemfontein, South Africa, in 1900. His *The Great Boer War* (1900) was widely read and praised for its fairness to both sides. In 1902 he wrote a long pamphlet, *The War in South Africa: Its Cause and Conduct,* to defend the British action in South Africa against widespread criticism by pacifist groups. In August 1902 Doyle was knighted for his service to England.

After being twice defeated, in 1900 and 1906, in a bid for a seat in Parliament, Sir Arthur published *Sir Nigel* (1906), a popular historical novel of the Middle Ages. The following year he married his second wife, Jean Leckie. The two first met in 1897 but apparently resisted the growing attraction between them successfully until after the death of Louise Doyle, in 1906, of tuberculosis. Doyle now took up a number of political and humanitarian causes. In 1909 he wrote *Divorce Law Reform,* championing equal rights for women in British law, and *The Crime of the Congo,* attacking the exploitation of that colony by Belgium. In 1911 he published a second collection of poems, *Songs of the Road,* and in 1912 began a series of science fiction stories with the novel *The Lost World,* featuring another of his famous characters, Professor Challenger.

After the outbreak of World War I, Doyle organized the Civilian National Reserve against the threat of German invasion. In 1916 he published *A Visit to Three Fronts* and in 1918 again toured the front lines. These tours, plus extensive correspondence with a number of high-ranking officers, enabled him to write his famous account *The British Campaigns in France and Flanders,* published in six volumes (1916–1919).

Doyle had been interested in spiritualism since he rejected his Roman Catholic faith in 1880. In 1915 he apparently experienced a "conversion" to "psychic religion," so that after the war he devoted the rest of his life and career to propagating his new faith in a series of works: *The New Revelation* (1918), *The Vital Message* (1919), *The Wanderings of a Spiritualist* (1921), and *History of Spiritualism* (1926). From 1917 to 1925 he lectured on spiritualism throughout Europe, Australia, the

Sir Arthur Conan Doyle, photographed in 1922 by Pirie MacDonald. (Courtesy of The New-York Historical Society, New York City)

United States, and Canada. The same cause led him to South Africa in 1928 and brought him home exhausted, from Sweden, in 1929. He died on July 6, 1930, of a heart attack, at his home in Crowborough, Sussex.

Further Reading

Sir Arthur Conan Doyle is listed in the Literature study guide (II, I, 1, b). The works of Edgar Allan POE and Wilkie COLLINS were also important in the development of the detective story.

An intimate view of Doyle emerges from his autobiography, *Memories and Adventures* (1924), and from his autobiographical novel, *The Stark Munro Letters* (1894). The best biographical and critical study of Doyle is Pierre Nordon, *Conan Doyle: A Biography,* translated by Frances Partridge (1966), although Nordon is sometimes careless about dates and bibliographical data. John Dickson Carr's "novelized" biography, *The Life of Sir Arthur Conan Doyle* (1949), is entertaining but incomplete. Two useful shorter biographies are Hesketh Pearson, *Conan Doyle: His Life and Art* (1943), and Michael and Mollie Hardwick, *The Man Who Was Sherlock Holmes* (1964). A. E. Murch, *The Development of the Detective Novel* (1958; rev. ed. 1968), gives important insight into the literary significance of the Sherlock Holmes stories.

✳   ✳   ✳

Luis María Drago. (Library of Congress)

DRAGO / By Victor C. Dahl

The Argentine international jurist and diplomat Luis María Drago (1859–1921) is known for the "Drago Doctrine," which held that international law did not authorize European powers to use armed intervention to force American republics to pay public debts.

Luis María Drago (pronounced drä′gō), the son of Luis María Drago and Estela Sánchez Drago, was born on May 6, 1859, in Buenos Aires. After being educated by tutors and in private schools, he began to work for newspapers and to study at the university in 1875. In 1882 he completed a doctorate of laws, served briefly in the provincial legislature, and became a judge in the Buenos Aires civil and criminal courts. Later he published a pioneer study of penal problems.

In 1902 Drago was elected to the Chamber of Deputies, but almost immediately President Julio Roca appointed him minister of foreign relations. British and German fleets at that time were blockading Venezuela's coast to force payment of debts to their nationals. Drago's instructions to Argentina's representative in Washington declared that international law did not sanction intervention to compel sovereign republics to repay public indebtedness. This "Drago Doctrine" stemmed from an 1868 pronouncement by another Argentine jurist, Carlos Calvo, who had maintained that foreign creditors must seek recourse through domestic courts of countries where they lend money.

Elected again to the Chamber of Deputies in 1906, Drago soon resigned to serve on the International Court of Justice at The Hague. The next year the Court ratified a modified version of the Drago Doctrine, which had already been adopted by the 1906 Pan-American Conference. This doctrine has been credited with developing Pan-American unity against European intervention, thereby forestalling territorial acquisitions in the Western Hemisphere like those in Asia and Africa. However, the United States' increasing strength constituted the major bulwark against European imperialism.

Drago's minor role in the Venezuelan debt crisis and his significant International Court service earned worldwide respect. In 1909 the United States and Venezuela asked him to arbitrate a claims dispute. From 1910 to 1912 Drago, at the behest of Britain and the United States, arbitrated the North Atlantic fisheries dispute, and neither side questioned his decisions. In 1912 Columbia University awarded him an honorary doctorate for contributions to international peace; and the Carnegie Endowment for International Peace acclaimed him as "the highest exponent of the intellectual culture of South America." He served again in Argentina's Chamber of Deputies from 1912 to 1916. He died in Buenos Aires on June 9, 1921.

Further Reading

Luis María Drago is listed in the International Law

study guide (III, B). He was the grandson of former Argentine president Bartolomé MITRE. Another Argentine working for international cooperation was the Nobel Peace Prize winner Carlos SAAVEDRA LAMAS.

The only extensive account of Drago's life is in Spanish. A brief sketch of his career appears in William Belmont Parker, ed., *Argentines of Today* (2 vols. in 1, 1920). For thorough examinations of the Drago Doctrine see Dexter Perkins, *The Monroe Doctrine, 1867–1907* (1937), and Harold F. Peterson, *Argentina and the United States, 1810–1960* (1964).

D. **DRAKE** / By Richard T. Farrell

> The American physician Daniel Drake
> (1785–1852) was one of the founders of the
> medical school in Cincinnati, Ohio. He also
> participated in social, political, and economic
> movements in the Ohio Valley.

Daniel Drake was born on Oct. 20, 1785, near Plainfield, N.J. His family soon moved to Kentucky. At the age of 15 he began to study medicine with a Cincinnati doctor, later graduating from the University of Pennsylvania. Returning to the Ohio Valley in 1805, he devoted the remainder of his life to science and the development of the West.

Drake played a major role in establishing a medical school in Cincinnati. He also wrote extensively on medical subjects, his most important work being *Principal Diseases of the Interior Valley of North America,* and was cofounder in 1826 of the *Ohio Medical Repository,* a medical journal designed to improve medical standards in the West. Another project that took up his time was the establishment of adequate hospital facilities in the Ohio Valley. In his *Natural and Statistical View, or Pictures of Cincinnati,* published in 1815, Drake recorded valuable data on the geology, botany, and meteorology of this region.

Drake crusaded against the "quack" doctors who invaded the frontier. He attacked the laws which allowed such unscrupulous men to practice and the politicians who refused to pass legislation to prevent them from taking advantage of the frontier's need for doctors.

Drake also supported social reform movements. Although an active crusader against the intemperate use of alcohol, he was not for total abstinence. As a doctor, he stressed the adverse effects of alcohol on the body; as a reformer, he stressed the social implications of overindulgence. He made speeches in behalf of the temperance movement and in 1841 helped organize the Physiological Temperance Society of Louisville.

Politically, Drake advocated national unity. He violently condemned the nullification crisis of 1832–1833. On the slavery question he condemned both Northern abolitionists and Southern "fire-eaters" as disruptive forces.

Daniel Drake. (National Library of Medicine, Bethesda, Md.)

Firmly opposed to slavery and to its extension into the territories, he also opposed extremism. To solve the slavery problem he strongly supported a national colonization policy.

In the words of his best biographer, Daniel Drake was "a man possessing commanding talents. By some he has been called a genius. He had an unusual, almost prophetic vision, a philanthropic outlook, an abiding philosophy, as well as a scientific and inquisitive mind."

Further Reading

Daniel Drake is listed in the American History study guide (V, E, 6, b). Other doctors of the period were Horace WELLS and William BEAUMONT.

The most complete biography of Drake is Emmet F. Horine, *Daniel Drake, 1785–1852: Pioneer Physician of the Midwest* (1961). A description of his early life is included in Charles D. Drake, ed., *Pioneer Letters in Kentucky: A Series of Reminiscential Letters from Daniel Drake . . . to His Children* (1870). For a contemporary view of Drake and life in the Ohio Valley see Edward D. Mansfield, *Memoirs of the Life and Services of Daniel Drake, M.D.: Physician, Professor, and Author* (1855).

F. **DRAKE** / By Charles E. Nowell

> The English navigator Sir Francis Drake (ca.
> 1541–1596) was the first of his countrymen to
> circumnavigate the globe. His daring exploits at

sea helped to establish England's naval supremacy over Spain and other European nations.

Francis Drake, the eldest son of a yeoman farmer, was born near Tavistock, Devonshire. His father later became a Calvinist lay preacher and raised his children as staunch Protestants. Young Drake received some education; he learned the rudiments of navigation and seamanship early and did some sailing near his home. The Drakes were related to the Hawkins family of Plymouth, well-to-do seamen and shipowners. The Hawkins connection got Drake a place on a 1566 slave-trading expedition to the Cape Verde Islands and the Spanish Main.

First Command

In 1567 John Hawkins made Drake an officer in a larger slave-trading expedition. Drake ultimately received command of one of Hawkins's ships, the *Judith*, and accompanied his relative to Africa, Río de la Hacha, and Santa Marta, where Hawkins disposed of the slaves. The English were caught, however, in the harbor of San Juan de Ulúa by a Spanish fleet that opened fire without warning and destroyed most of their ships. Only Drake's *Judith* and Hawkins's small vessel escaped to England. Embittered by this, Drake resolved to devote his life to war against Spain.

Elizabeth I of England and Philip II of Spain were not at war then, but grievances were steadily mounting. The Queen declined to offend Philip and would not allow Hawkins to go to sea again immediately, but she had no objections to a voyage by the obscure Drake. In 1569 Drake had married Mary Newman of Plymouth, but finding domesticity dull, he departed in 1570 for the Spanish Main with a small crew aboard the 25-ton *Susan*. He hoped to learn how the Spaniards arranged for shipping Peruvian treasure home, and he felt that the ports of Panama City and Nombre de Dios on the Isthmus of Panama were the key. His 1570 voyage was largely one of reconnaissance during which he made friends with the Cimaroons, who were escaped Negro slaves dwelling out of Spanish reach on the Isthmus and stood ready to help him. During a 1571 expedition he captured Nombre de Dios with Cimaroon help but lost it immediately when, wounded, he had to be carried to safety. After depredations off Cartagena, he intercepted a Spanish gold train near Nombre de Dios and returned to England with the bounty.

His arrival embarrassed the Queen, who still hoped for peace with Spain, and Drake evidently received a broad hint to leave the country temporarily. He is known to have served in Ireland with the Earl of Essex, who was trying to crush a rebellion in Ulster. By 1576 relations with Spain had worsened, and Drake returned to England, where a new expedition was being planned in which Elizabeth had a financial share. Drake's main instructions were to sail through the Strait of Magellan and probe for the shores of Terra Australis Incognita, the

great southern continent that many thought began with Tierra del Fuego. Drake received five ships, the largest being the *Pelican* (later named the *Golden Hind*), and a crew of about 160.

Adventures on the "Golden Hind"

The fleet left Plymouth in December 1577 for the southern Atlantic, stopping at Port San Julián for the Southern Hemisphere winter. Ferdinand Magellan had once crushed a mutiny there, and Drake did the same. He tried and executed Thomas Doughty, an aristocratic member of the expedition, who had intrigued against him in an attempt to foment a rebellion.

When Drake passed through the strait and entered the Pacific, only the *Golden Hind* remained; the other ships had been lost or had parted company. Contrary winds forced him southward, and he perhaps sighted Cape Horn; in any event, he realized that the two oceans came together and that Terra Australis would not be found there. He traveled along the coasts of Chile and Peru, capturing and destroying Spanish ships but sparing Spanish lives.

Between Callao and Panama Drake took an unarmed treasure ship, bearing gold, emeralds, and all the silver the *Golden Hind* could carry. Knowing that Spaniards would try to waylay him in the strait, Drake bypassed Panama and, near Guatalco, Nicaragua, captured charts and directions to guide him across the Pacific. Perhaps seeking the Strait of Anian, he sailed nearly 48°N, and then descended to a point at or near Drake's Bay, in Cali-

Sir Francis Drake at age 43, a portrait by Jodocus Hondius. (National Portrait Gallery, London)

The *Spanish Armada,*
destined for defeat by Sir
Francis Drake and his
fellow commanders,
moves through the English
Channel in this
contemporary print. At the
lower left, English ships
attack and set fire to a
large galleon. (The Mansell
Collection)

fornia, where he made friends with the Indians and over-hauled the ship. He left a brass plate naming the country Nova Albion and claiming it for Elizabeth. (In 1936 a plate fitting the description was found near Drake's Bay.)

Drake then crossed the Pacific to the Moluccas and near there almost came to grief when the ship struck a reef. Skilled handling freed it, and his circumnavigation of the globe continued via the Indian Ocean and the Cape of Good Hope. Drake arrived in Plymouth in 1580, acclaimed by the public and his monarch. In April 1581 he was knighted on the deck of the *Golden Hind.*

Drake did not immediately go to sea again and in 1581 became mayor of Plymouth. After his wife died, he married a young aristocrat, Elizabeth Sydenham. Sir Francis, now a wealthy man, made the bride a substantial settlement. He had no children by either wife.

Expedition against Spain

By 1585 Elizabeth, after new provocations by Philip, felt ready to unleash Drake again. A large fleet was outfitted, including two of her own vessels. Drake, aboard his command ship, the *Elizabeth Bonaventure,* had instructions to release English vessels impounded by Philip, though Elizabeth certainly knew he would exceed orders.

Drake fulfilled the Queen's expectations. He sacked Vigo in Spanish Galicia and then sailed to Santo Domingo and Cartagena, capturing and holding both for ransom. He would have tried to cross the Isthmus and take Panama, a project he had cherished for years, but an epidemic so reduced his crews that he abandoned the idea. On the way to England he destroyed the Spanish settlement at St. Augustine, in Florida, and farther north, took home the last remaining settlers at Sir Walter Raleigh's unfortunate North Carolina colony.

The expedition, which reached Portsmouth in July 1586, had acquired little treasure but had inflicted great physical and moral damage on Spain, enormously raising English prestige in the bargain. Formal war was now inevitable, and Philip started plans to invade England. In February 1587 the Queen beheaded Mary of Scotland who had been connected with plots to dethrone or mur-

der Elizabeth, to the outrage of Catholic Europe and many English Catholics. Philip began assembling his Armada in Portugal, which had been in his possession since 1580.

Spanish Armada

Elizabeth appointed Lord Charles Howard of Effingham commander of her fleet and gave Drake, Hawkins, and Martin Frobisher immediately subordinate posts. Drake advocated a strong preventive blow at Philip's unprepared Armada and received permission to strike. In April 1587 he recklessly sailed into Cadiz and destroyed or captured 37 enemy ships. He then occupied the Portuguese town of Sagres for a time and finally, in the Azores, seized a large Portuguese carrack bound homeward from Goa with a rich cargo.

The Cadiz raid damaged but did not cripple the Armada, which, under Alonso de Guzmán, Duke of Medina Sidonia, sailed in May 1588. It was alleged that Lord Howard was a figurehead and that the "sea dogs" Drake, Hawkins, and Frobisher won the victory in the July encounters. Recent evidence refutes this and shows Howard to have been in effective command. Drake took a conspicuous part in the channel fighting and captured a galleon, but he does not seem to have distinguished himself above other English commanders.

The Armada was defeated, and Drake's career thereafter proved anticlimactic. He met with his first formidable defeat in 1589, when he commanded the naval expedition sent to take Lisbon. He seemed to have lost some of his old daring, and his cautious refusal to ascend the Tagus River for a naval bombardment partly accounted for the failure. Drake did not go to sea again for 5 years. He concerned himself mainly with Plymouth matters. He sat in Parliament, but nothing of note marked his presence there.

Final Voyage

In 1595 Elizabeth thought she saw a chance of ending the war victoriously by cutting off the Spanish treasure supply from the Isthmus of Panama. For this she selected

Hawkins, then 63, and Drake, in his 50s. The cautious Hawkins and the impetuous Drake could never work well together, and the Queen further complicated the situation by giving them equal authority; in effect, each commanded his own fleet. The Queen's order that they must be back in 6 months scarcely allowed time to capture Panama, and when they learned of a crippled Spanish treasure ship in San Juan, Puerto Rico, they decided to go there. Through Drake's insistence on first going to the Canary Islands, their destination was revealed, and the Spaniards sent word ahead to Puerto Rico. Hawkins died as they reached the island, leaving Drake in sole command. The Spaniards had strengthened their San Juan defenses, and Drake failed to capture the city.

Ignoring the Queen's 6-month time limit, the aging Drake, still trying to repeat his earlier successes, made for the Isthmus to capture Nombre de Dios and then Panama. He easily took the former, not knowing that it had been superseded by Puerto Bello as the Caribbean terminus of the Plate fleets. His landing party, which soon realized it was following a path long out of use, was ambushed by Spaniards and forced to retreat.

Drake knew the expedition was a failure; he cruised aimlessly to Honduras and back and then fell ill of fever and dysentery. He died off Puerto Bello on Jan. 28, 1596, and was buried at sea. Sir Thomas Baskerville, second in command, took the expedition home to England.

Further Reading

Sir Francis Drake is listed in the Geography and Exploration study guide (III, A, 4, e; III, A, 5). Another famous British "sea dog," Sir Martin FROBISHER, commanded one of Drake's ships in the West Indies expedition of 1585.

The most complete account of Drake's circumnavigation is provided by his nephew, Sir Francis Drake, in *The World Encompassed by Sir Francis Drake,* published by the Hakluyt Society (1854). Primary material can be found in John Barrow, *Life, Voyages, and Exploits of Sir Francis Drake, with Numerous Original Letters* (1844). Julian S. Corbett, *Drake and the Tudor Navy* (2 vols., 1898; rev. ed. 1899), can be supplemented with more recent studies such as James A. Williamson, *Age of Drake* (1938; 4th ed. 1960) and *Sir Francis Drake* (1966), and

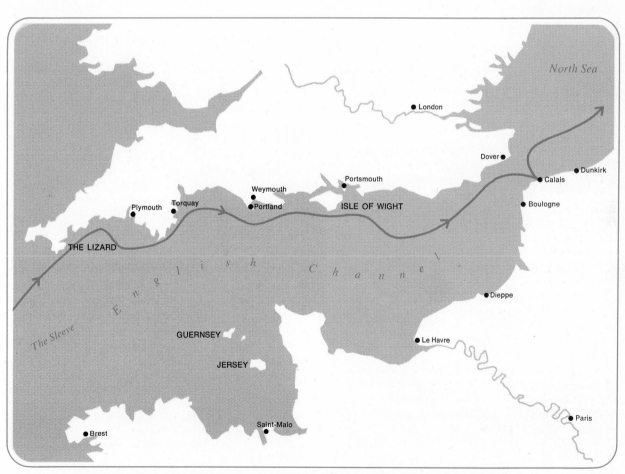

The Spanish Armada in the English Channel. From Lisbon, in May 1588, the Armada sailed for Flanders to pick up a Spanish army for the invasion of England. In the English Channel it survived the daring attacks of the English fleet under Admiral Charles Howard and captains Drake, Hawkins, and Frobisher. At Calais the English attacked again with fire ships. Unable to reach the Spanish army in Flanders or to obtain fresh supplies there, the Armada returned to Spain by a disastrous voyage around the British Isles.

Kenneth R. Andrews, *Drake's Voyages: A Reassessment of Their Place in Elizabethan Maritime Expansion* (1967). For general background see J. H. Parry, *The Age of Reconnaissance* (1963).

* * *

DRAPER / By Gerald J. Goodwin

The Anglo-American scientist and historian John William Draper (1811–1882) pioneered in scientific applications of photography and popularized a "scientific" approach to social and intellectual history.

John William Draper was born near Liverpool, England, on May 5, 1811. He did premedical studies at University College, London. In 1832 Draper, his wife, mother, and sisters sailed to America.

Settling in Mecklenburg County, Va., Draper began scientific research in his own laboratory. He experimented in capillary attraction and published on a variety of scientific subjects. He completed his medical studies at the University of Pennsylvania in 1836, then returned to Virginia to become professor of chemistry and natural philosophy at Hampden-Sidney College. He contributed to British and American scholarly journals. In 1838 he was appointed professor of chemistry and botany at the University of the City of New York.

Draper's career as a research scientist flowered from 1839 to 1856. His earliest important project involved him in a race with Samuel F. B. Morse to be the first in America to apply the photographic technique of the French inventor Louis Daguerre to portraiture. In solving these problems Draper developed expansive notions about the uses of photography in scientific investigation. A brilliant experimentalist, he was especially important for outlining the scientific applications of photography. He pioneered in expanding beyond both extremes of the visible spectrum with photographic techniques and was a founder of the theory of photochemical absorption.

Draper helped establish the medical school of the University of the City of New York and became its president in 1850. His *Human Physiology* (1856) marked the end of his scientific career.

Draper's second career—in history and social analysis—grew out of his first. He believed in the possibility of progress through science and technology and wrote about history and society with the conviction that a "scientific" approach to society was desirable. His *History of the Intellectual Development of Europe* (1863) traced the history of Western thought. *Thoughts on the Future Civil Policy of America* (1865) and a three-volume *History of the American Civil War* (1867–1870), the first serious history of the war, followed. His last major work, *History of the Conflict between Religion and Science* (1874), was a condensation of his 1863 book.

Convinced that nature was the compulsive force behind history, Draper in his version of environmental determinism emphasized climate. Although his histories are seriously defective, he was a pioneer in the history of ideas. After his death on Jan. 4, 1882, Draper's reputation as a scientist diminished while his fame as a historian flourished.

Further Reading

John William Draper is listed in the Science study guide (VI, B, 3; VI, D, 3) and the Social Sciences study guide (VI, A, 3). Both Draper and the inventor Samuel F. B. MORSE were instrumental in introducing the daguerreotype, developed by Louis DAGUERRE, into the United States.

Donald H. Fleming, *John William Draper and the Religion of Science* (1950), is an excellent biography. For background material see Nathan Reingold, ed., *Science in Nineteenth-Century America* (1964), and Howard S. Miller, *Pursuit of Science in Nineteenth Century America* (1969).

* * *

John William Draper. (Library of Congress)

DRAYTON / By David A. Fleming

The English poet Michael Drayton (1563–1631) attempted to create a strong national culture by

turning for inspiration to English history rather than to foreign sources.

Like his contemporary William Shakespeare, Michael Drayton was the son of a prosperous Warwickshire tradesman. He received a good education as a page in the house of Sir Henry Goodere, but there is no record of his ever having studied at a university.

Drayton's first publication, *The Harmony of the Church,* a somewhat clumsy paraphrase of the Bible, appeared in 1591, when he was 28. Succeeding publications exemplify a wide variety of genres. *Idea, the Shepherd's Garland* (1593) is a collection of nine pastoral poems, celebrating ideal beauty, in imitation of Edmund Spenser. *Idea's Mirror* (1594), a sonnet sequence, also portrays the poet's beloved (probably Anne Goodere, the daughter of his patron), under the Platonic name of "Idea."

By 1593 Drayton had also written his first historical romance in verse, *Piers Gaveston.* Two heroic poems followed, drawing on incidents in English history: *Robert, Duke of Normandy* and *Mortimeriados,* both published in 1596. The latter, which portrays the evils of civil strife, was considerably revised and republished as *The Baron's Wars* (1603). The most popular of Drayton's early works, *England's Heroical Epistles,* was published in 1597. Written in imitation of Ovid's *Heroides,* it consists of a series of verse letters between lovers famous in English history.

Drayton turned to the fashionable genre of satirical verse in two rather obscure works, *The Owl* (1604) and *The Man in the Moon* (1606). Some of his most famous shorter works were published in *Poems Lyric and Pastoral* (1606), including the patriotic "Battle of Agincourt" and the "Ode to the Virginian Voyage," which celebrates English discoveries in America. Drayton's ambitious *Polyolbion* (1612–1622), a long topographical poem, describes region by region the beauties and traditions of England and attempts to provide a legendary basis for the Stuart claim to the English throne. The most important of the poems of Drayton's later years, his *Nymphidia* (1627), is a delicate mock-heroic tale of the fairy kingdom, peopled with characters like those that appear in Shakespeare's *Midsummer Night's Dream.*

Although Drayton often lacks dramatic power and intellectual depth, he has been rightly praised for his versatility, narrative skill, and insight into character. He died in London in 1631 and was buried in Westminster Abbey.

Further Reading

Michael Drayton is listed in the Literature study guide (II, E, 2, a). He was influenced by Edmund SPENSER.

The Works of Michael Drayton was edited by J. William Hebel (5 vols., 1931–1941; rev. ed. 1961). A more recent edition of Drayton's *Poems* was edited by John Buxton (2 vols., 1953). Biographical and critical studies of Drayton's life and works include Oliver Elton, *Michael Drayton* (1905); Glenn P. Haskell, *Drayton's Secondary*

Michael Drayton in 1599. The painting, by an unknown artist, is in the National Portrait Gallery, London. (Radio Times Hulton Picture Library)

Modes (1936); Bernard H. Newdigate, *Michael Drayton and His Circle* (1941; rev. ed. 1961); and Joseph A. Berthelot, *Michael Drayton* (1967). Recommended for general background are Lisle C. John, *The Elizabethan Sonnet Sequences* (1938); Hallett D. Smith, *Elizabethan Poetry* (1952); and Clive S. Lewis, *English Literature in the Sixteenth Century, Excluding Drama* (1954).

DREISER / By Robert Regan

American novelist Herman Theodore Dreiser (1871–1945) projected a vitality and an honesty that established several of his novels as classics of world literature.

Like other naturalistic novelists of the 1890s Theodore Dreiser believed in evolutionary and materialistic determinism and gave these ideas powerful expression. Preoccupied with sex, he demanded the freedom to write about it as he saw fit. His hard-won victories over narrow-minded censorship marked a turning point in the history of the American novel.

Dreiser was born Aug. 27, 1871, in Terre Haute, Ind., one of 12 children of a German Catholic immigrant and

Theodore Dreiser. (Photo Harlingue-Viollet)

an Ohio woman who gave up her Mennonite religion and her family's good opinion to marry him. Theodore was a sickly child with an almost sightless right eye; he seemed at first to have less chance of survival than the three brothers who had died before him in infancy.

Growing Up Poor

For the elder Dreiser, making a living for his large family was difficult. In 1867 he had moved them to Sullivan, Ind., where, by going deeply into debt, he bought a woolen mill that seemed promising. But in 1869 fire destroyed Dreiser's mill, leaving him even more deeply in debt. This burden was to weigh heavily upon all members of the family for years. Theodore was 7 in 1878, when his parents decided that breaking up their home was necessary for economic survival. The older children followed their father in search of jobs. The younger three, including Theodore, moved with their mother to Vincennes and then back to Sullivan. There one of the older daughters rejoined them; she was pregnant by a man who refused to marry her. When the baby was stillborn in April 1878, they buried it secretly.

The family's years in Sullivan were hard for young Dreiser. He was sent home from parochial school because he had no shoes. The family was so poor that Mrs. Dreiser took in washing (Dreiser was to remember having to deliver the bundles to affluent homes), and the boys gathered coal from the railroad tracks to keep the fire going. Dreiser's father descended upon the household occasionally to rail about the children's failings in religion and morality.

The year 1881, however, brought a melodramatic reversal for the family. Paul, one of the older brothers,

unexpectedly appeared, beaming with good humor and opulence. He had begun to establish his reputation as a songwriter (he would later win fame with such songs as "My Gal Sal" and "On the Banks of the Wabash"; for the latter Theodore supplied the words of the first stanza and chorus). Paul settled his mother with the younger children in a cozy home in Evansville and himself in the town's most spendid brothel, which was kept by Sallie Walker—his "Gal Sal." Food, clothing, and coal were now no problem, but Paul's flagrant life of sin troubled the religious Theodore. Paul's turbulent romance with the beautiful madam ended in 1884; he left town to seek work elsewhere. Mrs. Dreiser took her family to Chicago, where Theodore got a job in a dry goods store, but he was miserable and soon quit. His father rejoined the family, also out of work. Without Paul's help the Dreisers ran quickly into debt again, and soon they fled the bill collectors to Warsaw, Ind.

The nuns who had been Dreiser's teachers up to that time had made him fear school. In Warsaw he entered the public schools. A young woman teacher encouraged the shy boy to read: he fell in love with her and with the books she recommended. Again older sisters stirred town gossip: one ran off with a bar cashier who had stolen $3,500 from the bar's safe, and another had an affair with the son of a wealthy family that ended in pregnancy. These events would later provide materials for Dreiser's fiction, but at 15 he felt them only as humiliating. He left school and went to Chicago to work as a dishwasher and then a stock clerk.

In 1888 one of Dreiser's Warsaw teachers found him in Chicago and sent him to the University of Indiana the next year. College lasted only a year for him, but it was an important year. As a result of his exposure to college girls, his consciousness of the power of sex, the great theme of his fiction, became acute—and acutely painful. He returned home in 1890 to work and help care for his mother, who died that November. When a Bavarian priest refused her a funeral Mass because she had not received the last rites of the Church, Dreiser lost whatever remained of his father's religion.

Journalistic Career

Before his twenty-first birthday Dreiser had found a job on the staff of the *Chicago Globe*. Progressing rapidly in newspaper work, he moved to the *St. Louis Globe-Democrat*. In 1893 the *St. Louis Republic* sent him to the World's Columbian Exposition in Chicago as leader of a group of schoolteachers, one of whom was a pretty redhead named Sara Osborne White, called "Jug." Dreiser was then having an affair with his landlady and was romantically involved with some other women, but Jug would 6 years later become his wife. To fulfill his dream of quick success, and perhaps also to try to escape Jug, Dreiser quit his job and traveled east, taking a job on the *Pittsburgh Dispatch*. There he saw the injustices of industrial society in sharp focus, yet his editors stopped his stories about them, explaining, "The big steel men just about own the place."

If he could not write, Dreiser could read: Honoré de

Balzac shaped his conception of the novel, and T. H. Huxley and Herbert Spencer gave him a new philosophy. Spencer, Dreiser reported later, "took every shred of belief away from me; showed me that I was a chemical atom in a whirl of unknown forces. . . ." In that frame of mind he moved to New York in 1894 and found work on the *World*. But the shy young man, very tall, very thin, his bad eye partially hidden by his gold-rimmed glasses, neither looked nor acted the part of the brash metropolitan reporter. If he had not quit, he would surely have been fired.

Almost destitute, Dreiser convinced his brother Paul and two other songwriters to let him edit a magazine that would give their work wider audience. Dreiser titled it *Ev'ry Month*, and filled it with popular poetry, stories, and essays, as well as the songs; he also published Stephen Crane's "A Mystery of Heroism," some other pieces of literary interest, and many of his own serious articles. He left this magazine in 1897 but found work on other magazines, for which he interviewed Thomas A. Edison, Andrew Carnegie, William Dean Howells, Marshall Field, and other celebrities, writing of their rise to success. For the first time he had money—and no further excuse for postponing marriage to the eager Jug; it took place in December 1898.

For more than a dozen years Dreiser continued his successful journalistic career in New York. He wrote features for the *Daily News*; edited dime novels; and served as editor of *Smith's Magazine, Broadway Magazine*, and three magazines published to encourage women to buy Butterick dress patterns, including the *Delineator*. He raised the *Delineator's* circulation dramatically by anticipating the responses of its female readers. (In 1908 he secured H. L. Mencken as a contributor— the beginning of a long, important friendship.) Dreiser was one of the best-paid editors in the country in 1910, when the enraged mother of an 18-year-old girl with whom he was in love got him fired by threatening to make public the sordid history of his philandering. His marriage also suffered: Jug went home to her family in Missouri. She returned now and again, but in 1914 their separation became permanent, although neither sought a divorce.

Career as Novelist

Dreiser had begun experimenting with fiction in 1899. His first important novel, *Sister Carrie*, occupied him for about 4 months in 1899–1900. Jug helped with the grammar, and literary friends reduced the manuscript by 40,-000 words after Dreiser had finished it; although Dreiser required help in polishing the surface of his work, the profundities of the novel's conceptions and characterizations prove that he was from the beginning a master of the essentials of fiction. The novel's heroine, Carrie Meeber, goes to Chicago to live with her sister and seek work but finds working conditions terrible and pay small. She becomes the mistress of a salesman but turns subsequently to Hurstwood, manager of an elegant bar. Hurstwood, whose marriage is breaking up, is tempted to steal money from the bar's safe, which he finds open. He

removes the money, then decides to return it to the safe, but the safe door accidently closes and locks: chance has made him a thief. Chance operates again and again in the lives of Hurstwood and Carrie (with whom he runs away), bringing one to suicide and the other to an ungratifying success as a musical comedy star. The novel is far from explicit in its treatment of sex, but in its failure to give virtue and vice their appropriate rewards it constituted an affront to the official moral standards of the day. One publisher turned it down; but at Doubleday, Page and Company, it received a warm reception from Frank Norris, who was reader for the firm. Doubleday contracted to publish *Carrie*, but when Frank Doubleday and his wife read it, they had second thoughts. Dreiser held the firm to their contract, however, and they published the book in 1901 but did not advertise it. Norris tried hard to publicize it, but the final tally showed 456 copies sold, giving the author a royalty of $68.40. Not until 1907, when another publisher reissued it, did *Sister Carrie* attract notice and sell.

The initial failure of *Sister Carrie* drove Dreiser to a nervous and physical breakdown, but with Paul's help he recovered and turned back to his editorial work. When he lost his job at Butterick in 1910, he went to work on the other novels he had begun after *Sister Carrie*. Now he finished *Jennie Gerhardt*. Published in 1911, it received critical acclaim and sales success, in part because, without compromising his principles, Dreiser avoided affronting public morals this time: Jennie, also drawn from Dreiser's wayward sisters, does not prosper from her sins. Encouraged by the novel's success, Dreiser pressed ahead on *The Financier*, which was based on the sensational career of Charles T. Yerkes (named Frank Algernon Cowperwood in the novel), who made a fortune in Philadelphia, went to prison for embezzlement, and made another fortune after his release, while scoring almost as many romantic triumphs as business coups. *The Titan* (1914) and *The Stoic* (1947) continue with the same character.

A trip to Europe in 1911 provided material for *A Traveler at Forty* (1913), but Dreiser devoted his best efforts to fiction. *The Genius* (1915) is his most autobiographical novel. The romance with the young girl that had ended Dreiser's career at Butterick constitutes a principal incident, but the artist-hero's philosophic calm at the story's end is more wish-fulfillment fantasy than autobiography. Some critics expressed moral outrage. The New York Society for the Suppression of Vice got the book banned for over a year; yet out of the storm a critical consensus was emerging: whatever the moral or literary failings of *The Genius*, it was the work of an artist who possessed elements of genius himself.

"An American Tragedy"

In the following year Dreiser published several volumes of nonfiction, notably *Twelve Men* (1919). That same year he met his charming 25-year-old cousin Helen Richardson, who was fleeing an unhappy marriage. They moved to Los Angeles together, where she contributed to their household expenses by taking supporting parts in films. In nearly 3 years in California, Dreiser wrote several volumes of sketches, some bad poetry, and the first 20 chapters of his greatest novel. Based on the highly publicized 1906 murder trial of a young New York man, *An American Tragedy* (2 vols., 1925) shows Clyde Griffiths, impoverished son of a street evangelist, working in his rich uncle's shirt factory and falling in love with a girl of beauty, wealth, and position. Only one thing blocks their marriage: Clyde has made a factory girl pregnant. Alone with the pregnant girl in a boat on a lake, he plots to murder her but loses his nerve; nevertheless, there is an accident, she drowns, and he later pays with his life. The book is genuinely tragic: Clyde is not villain but victim. If there is a villain, it is society with its conventionalism, its economic injustice, and its hypocrisy about sex. The book was a triumph: Joseph Wood Krutch spoke for most critics when he called it "the greatest American novel of our generation." The first 2 weeks' royalty check was for $11,872.02.

That splendid success was the last of Dreiser's novels to appear in his lifetime (two inferior pieces, *The Bulwark,* 1946, and *The Stoic,* 1947, appeared after his death). In 1926 he traveled with Helen to Europe; in 1927 his trip to the Soviet Union resulted in *Dreiser Looks at Russia* (1928). In 1929 he and Helen settled near Mount Kisco, N.Y. In 1942 Dreiser's wife died, and in 1944 he married Helen. Travel, political activity, and a surprising turn toward mysticism occupied his late years. When he died of a heart attack in Hollywood, Calif., on Dec. 28, 1945, he was already well established in the history of world literature. Distinguished films were made in 1951 of *An American Tragedy* (under the title *A Place in the Sun*) and *Sister Carrie.*

Further Reading

Theodore Dreiser is listed in the Literature study guide (I, E, 1, a). Frank NORRIS, Jack LONDON, and Upton SINCLAIR were also realistic writers of the period.

Dreiser's autobiographical works include *A Hoosier Holiday* (1916), *A Book about Myself* (1922), and *Dawn* (1931). W. A. Swanberg's admirable *Dreiser* (1965) is the standard biography, but Robert H. Elias, *Theodore Dreiser: Apostle of Nature* (1949), remains valuable for its critical emphasis. Charles Shapiro, *Theodore Dreiser: Our Bitter Patriot* (1962); John J. McAleer, *Theodore Dreiser: An Introduction and Interpretation* (1968); and Ellen Moers, *Two Dreisers* (1969), are full-length discussions of the novels. Larzer Ziff, *The American 1890s: Life and Times of a Lost Generation* (1966), contains a brilliant assessment of Dreiser's accomplishments and relation to his period.

* * *

C. R. DREW / By William Montague Cobb

American Negro surgeon Charles Richard Drew (1904–1950) pioneered in developing the blood bank and was an outstanding leader in the training of surgeons.

Charles R. Drew was born in Washington, D.C., on June 3, 1904, the eldest of five children. The close-knit family lived in modest circumstances and was highly respected.

Drew was educated in the Washington public schools. He earned a bachelor of arts degree from Amherst College (1926) and his doctor of medicine and master of surgery degrees from McGill University in Canada (1933). Having decided upon a career in surgery, he went to Howard University in Washington, D.C., in 1935. After the next year as a surgical resident, he was sent by Howard for 2 years of advanced study under a General Education Board fellowship to Columbia University, which awarded him the doctor of medical science degree (1940).

At Columbia, under the direction of John Scudder, Drew completed his pioneering and definitive thesis *Banked Blood* (1940). The Blood Transfusion Betterment Association in New York funded various programs of research; one of these, on blood plasma, was conducted by Scudder and Drew. In 1940, during World War II, Scudder suggested that the association ship dried plasma to France and England. The association appointed Drew director of its "Blood for Britain" project in September 1940.

In 1941 Drew was appointed director of the first American Red Cross Bank and assistant director of blood procurement for the National Research Council, in charge of blood for use by the U.S. Army and Navy. He criticized the policy of segregating blood racially as having no scientific basis.

In October 1941 Drew returned to Howard as head of the department of surgery and was made an examiner for the American Board of Surgery. Chief of staff of Freedmen's Hospital from 1944 to 1946, he was appointed medical director of the hospital for 1946–1947. At Howard, Drew firmly established a progressive modern surgery program. He was a dynamic and inspirational teacher. While he was still alive, eight of his residents became diplomates of the American Board of Surgery, and many more who started their training under him became board-certified and did significant work all over the world.

Drew published 19 papers, the first 13 dealing with blood therapy. The last 6 reflected broadening interests, one posthumous title being "Negro Scholars in Scientific Research."

During 6 years as chairman of the surgical section of the National Medical Association, Drew brought new vigor and standards to the group. He was in demand as a speaker, and he served on numerous boards with a wide spectrum of interests, including the 12th Street Branch of the YMCA in Washington.

Most of Drew's achievements were promptly recognized. He received the Spingarn Medal of the NAACP (1943) and honorary doctor of science degrees from Virginia State College (1945) and Amherst College (1947). In 1946 he became a fellow of the International College of Surgeons and served in 1949 as surgical consultant to the surgeon general, U.S. Army. Drew's radiant geniality and warm sense of humor endeared him to patients. He mar-

Charles R. Drew. *(National Library of Medicine, Bethesda, Md.)*

ried Minnie Lenore Robbins on Sept. 23, 1939, and the couple had four children. He was killed in an automobile accident on April 1, 1950.

In 1959 the Sigma Pi Phi fraternity presented an oil portrait of Dr. Drew to the American National Red Cross. In Los Angeles the Charles R. Drew Medical Society and the Charles R. Drew Postgraduate Medical School of the Martin Luther King Jr. Hospital perpetuate his name. A health center in Brooklyn and the Harlem Hospital Center blood bank in New York City are named for him. The surgical section of the National Medical Association has an annual Charles R. Drew Forum for the presentation of original surgical research, and about 20 public schools in America have been named for him.

Further Reading

Charles R. Drew is listed in the Science study guide (VII, G, 4). Another black American doctor of the period was Daniel Hale WILLIAMS.

Three full-length studies of Drew are Richard Hardwick, *Charles Richard Drew: Pioneer in Blood Research* (1967); Robert Lichello, *Pioneer in Blood Plasma: Dr. Charles Richard Drew* (1968); and Roland Bertol, *Charles Drew* (1970). There are sections devoted to Drew in Ben Richardson, *Great American Negroes*

(1945; rev. ed. 1956); Emma Gelders Sterne, *Blood Brothers: Four Men of Science* (1959); and Louis Haber, *Black Pioneers of Science and Invention* (1970).

D. **DREW** / By Louis M. Hacker

Daniel Drew (1797–1879) was one of America's sensational stock manipulators, speculating particularly in Erie Railroad securities.

Born July 29, 1797, at Carmel, N.Y., Daniel Drew grew up on the family farm. His career began as a cattle drover and horse trader: he drove cattle from the countryside into New York City. Successful, he extended activity into Ohio and Illinois, bringing livestock back to his own New York stockyard.

Drew was said to have watered his beeves heavily before bringing them to market, thus increasing their weight (hence the origin of the term "stock-watering" in connection with the issuance of fraudulent corporate securities). By 1834 he was a New York City resident, operating steamboats on the Hudson River, Lake Champlain, and Long Island Sound. A bold competitor, he made money and in 1844 set up the Wall Street brokerage firm of Drew, Robinson and Company.

In 1853 Drew entered the life of the Erie Railroad and in 1857 became a director. He was soon notorious as a bold manipulator of Erie securities. He sold its stock short in 1866 and made a killing.

During 1866–1868, along with Jay Gould and James Fisk (Drew was really their "front"), Drew entered into a war with Cornelius Vanderbilt for control of the Erie. Vanderbilt had put together three railroads that gave him a direct line from Buffalo to New York City; he wanted the Erie in order to monopolize entry into New York and to prevent it from becoming a serious competitor on the Lake Shore route to Chicago he was contemplating.

Meanwhile the Erie management, with Drew as treasurer, had authorized issuance of convertible bonds for improvements. In order to check Vanderbilt, Drew (with Gould and Fisk on the sidelines) sold the bonds in 1868 in defiance of a court order and issued 100,000 new shares of Erie, thus creating a wild market, with Vanderbilt buying and the manipulators selling short. Drew, Gould, and Fisk fled to Jersey City to avoid court action; then Gould bribed state legislators to get conversion of the bonds into stock legalized. Vanderbilt was frustrated, but Gould settled with him and compensated him for his losses. In the end Gould owned the Erie, and Drew was forced off the board of directors.

Drew's star sank in 1870, when Gould and Fisk sold Erie stock in England to force up its price: Drew, selling short, lost $1,500,000. During the depression of 1873–1879 Drew was finished; his banking firm failed, and in 1876 he filed for bankruptcy. He died on Sept. 18, 1879, in New York, wholly dependent upon his son. In his heyday Drew played the philanthropist, building Methodist

Daniel Drew, engraving after a photograph by Mathew Brady. (Library of Congress)

churches at Carmel and Brewster, N.Y., and spending $250,000 to set up the Drew Theological Seminary at Madison, N.J.

Further Reading

Daniel Drew is listed in the American History study guide (VII, E, 1). His partners were Jay GOULD and James FISK.

Bouck White, *The Book of Daniel Drew* (1910), is a semifictional biography. The early story of the "Erie War" is in Charles F. Adams, Jr., and Henry Adams, *Chapters of Erie and Other Essays* (1871). A more sophisticated account is in Julius Grodinsky, *Jay Gould: His Business Career, 1867–1892* (1957).

✳   ✳   ✳

DREYFUS/ By William H. Logue

The French army officer Alfred Dreyfus (1859–1935) was unjustly convicted of treason. The effort, eventually successful, to clear his name divided French society and had important political repercussions.

Alfred Dreyfus (pronounced drā′fəs) was born at Mulhouse on Oct. 9, 1859, into a Jewish textile-manufacturing family. After the Franco-Prussian War his family left Alsace in order to remain French citizens. Choosing a military career, Dreyfus entered the École Polytechnique in 1878. After further study, during which he attained the rank of captain in 1889, he was assigned as a trainee to the general staff. Dreyfus was a competent and hardworking, though not brilliant or popular, young officer. His ordeal was to prove that he was a man of great courage but limited vision: his whole life was devoted to the army, and he never lost confidence that it would recognize and remedy the wrong done him.

Arrest and Conviction

The Dreyfus case began in September 1894, when French Army Intelligence found among some papers taken from the office of the German military attaché in Paris, a list (bordereau) of secret documents given to the Germans by someone in the French army. A hasty and inadequate investigation convinced the anti-Semitic Intelligence chief, Col. Sandherr, that Dreyfus was the traitor. Apart from a certain resemblance between his handwriting and that of the bordereau, no very convincing evidence against Dreyfus could be discovered. He was arrested, however, on October 15.

Dreyfus's court-martial was held behind closed doors during December 19–21. A unanimous court found him guilty and imposed the highest legal penalty: perpetual imprisonment, loss of rank, and degradation. He was sent to the infamous Devil's Island, where he was to spend almost 5 years under the most inhumane conditions. Still protesting his innocence, Dreyfus was unaware that he had been convicted with the aid of a secret dossier prepared by Army Intelligence. Communication of the dossier to the judges without the knowledge of the defense violated due process and was the first of many actions that would bring discredit on the army and ruin the careers of the officers involved.

Convinced of his innocence, the Dreyfus family, led by his brother Mathieu, sought new evidence which would persuade the army to reopen its investigation. Aside from a few individuals such as the brilliant young writer Bernard Lazare and the respected Alsatian life-senator Scheurer-Kestner, they found few supporters, and their efforts stirred the anti-Semitic press to raise the bogey of a "Jewish syndicate" trying to corrupt the army.

Fortune came to Dreyfus's aid for the first time in July 1895, when the new Intelligence chief, Lt. Col. Marie Georges Picquart, became convinced of Dreyfus's innocence and discovered a Maj. Walsin-Esterhazy to be the real author of the bordereau. Although Picquart was unable to convince his superiors to reexamine the verdict, he remained determined to help free Dreyfus.

Still unable to persuade the government to act, the supporters of Dreyfus—the Dreyfusards—now took their case to the public, charging Esterhazy with the crime for which Dreyfus was being punished. The anti-Semitic press counterattacked, and the Dreyfus case began to turn into the Dreyfus Affair, as public passions were raised against the few who dared to challenge the verdict of the court-martial. Supported by friends within the command, Esterhazy demanded a court-martial to prove his innocence; he received a triumphant acquittal in January 1898. The evidence against Esterhazy was little better than that which had convicted Dreyfus, but his acquittal dashed the hopes of the Dreyfusards, who had expected his conviction to prove Dreyfus innocent.

Retrial and Exoneration

The controversial novelist Émile Zola, however, found a way to reopen the case: he charged in an open letter to the President of the Republic entitled *J'accuse* that the military court had acquitted Esterhazy although they knew him to be guilty. Zola hoped to bring the facts of Dreyfus's case before a civil court, where it would be more difficult for the army to conceal what had happened; he was only partially successful, but increased public concern and violence in the streets forced the authorities to take further action.

The minister of war, Godefroy Cavaignac, aiming to quiet criticism, publicly revealed much of the evidence against Dreyfus. But the Dreyfusards, headed by socialist leader Jean Jaurès, charged that forgery was obvious. Cavaignac's further investigation led to the confession and suicide (Aug. 31, 1898) of an Intelligence officer, Lt. Col. Joseph Henry, who had been manufacturing evidence to strengthen the case against Dreyfus. This was the turning point of the Affair. The government brought the case before the highest appeals court, which declared (June 3, 1899) Dreyfus entitled to a new trial.

Dreyfus was brought back to France to face a new court-martial at Rennes in September 1899. It returned, by a vote of 5 to 2, the incredible verdict of guilty with extenuating circumstances and sentenced him to 10 years' imprisonment. The honor of the army had been made such an issue by the anti-Dreyfusards that no military court could ever find him innocent. No one believed in the honor of the army more than Dreyfus, and only with difficulty could he be persuaded to accept the pardon offered by President Émile Loubet.

Dreyfus continued to seek exoneration, and his record was finally cleared by the civil courts in July 1906. He was returned to service, promoted, and decorated, but he soon retired. Returning to active duty during World War I, he then spent his retirement in complete obscurity, and his death on July 11, 1935, passed almost unnoticed.

Political Consequences

Dreyfus understood little of the battle that raged in his name. The question of his innocence became a secondary matter beside the public issue of individual human rights versus the demands of state policy. Political issues also played a part in the Affair: to many conservatives the army and the Church seemed the last bulwarks of social stability; both would be undermined by the victory of the Dreyfusards. On the left many welcomed the opportunity to strike at the monarchist and clerical forces, which they saw as enemies of the Republic. Last but not least was the question of anti-Semitism. The Affair saw the first outpouring of modern political anti-Semitism, which proved a harbinger of the Nazi terror.

Alfred Dreyfus (center) after his pardon and restoration to the French army. (National Archives, Washington, D.C.)

The immediate political consequence of the Affair was to bring the Radicals to power; they made the Church the scapegoat for the sins of the anti-Dreyfusards, taking a number of anticlerical measures culminating in the separation of Church and state in 1905. The passions exposed by the Affair were submerged in World War I but reappeared in the defeat of 1940 and under the Vichy regime.

Further Reading

Alfred Dreyfus is listed in the European History study guide (IX, B, 1). Among his supporters were Georges CLEMENCEAU, Jean JAURÈS, and Émile ZOLA.

There are hundreds of books dealing with the Dreyfus Affair. A well-balanced introduction is Douglas Johnson, *France and the Dreyfus Affair* (1966). The detailed study by Guy Chapman, *The Dreyfus Case: A Reassessment* (1955), upsets much of the standard Dreyfusard version but underestimates the importance of anti-Semitism. The role of crowd psychology is explored by Nicholas Halasz, *Captain Dreyfus: The Story of a Mass Hysteria* (1955). For something of the man see Dreyfus's prison memoirs, *Five Years of My Life, 1894–1899* (trans. 1901).

✳ ✳ ✳

DRIESCH / By Daniel O'Connor

The German biologist and philosopher Hans Adolf Eduard Driesch (1867–1941) was a leading representative of vitalism in the 20th century.

Hans Driesch (pronounced drēsh) was born at Bad Kreuznach on Oct. 28, 1867, into a prosperous middle-class family. After studying zoology at the University of Freiburg, he spent some semesters at Munich and then finished his degree at Jena in 1889 under the direction of Ernst Haeckel. Haeckel had apparently established mechanism as the dominant theory in biology and zoology, and Driesch's early work was a series of experimental efforts to confirm this theory. Contrary to his expectations, the experiments seemed to cast doubt on the hypothesis that living beings can be understood on purely mechanist principles.

From 1891 to 1900 Driesch worked at the Marine Biological Station in Naples, continuing his experiments and groping for a theoretical formulation of his results. At this point in his career, he began to read the classical modern philosophers, looking for an adequate philosophical theory of the organism. At the end of a long series of publications in which he explored tentative hypotheses and halfway theories, he finally presented an account of the life processes in genuinely teleological and dynamic terms in the book *The Localization of Morphogenetic Processes* (1894).

Thereafter Driesch's interests shifted from experimental work to conceptual analysis. He sought to explain the relationship between the concepts of life and the concepts of matter. In 1908 he published his Gifford Lectures, *The Science and Philosophy of the Organism,* the first full-length presentation of his ideas. At this point Driesch determined to take up a career in academic philosophy and became a lecturer at Heidelberg. Before a decade had elapsed, he had published a complete system of philosophy in three volumes, of which the most basic is his *Theory of Order* (1912).

In 1919 Driesch took a chair of systematic philosophy at Cologne and 2 years later accepted a similar post at Leipzig. In later years he was a visiting professor in China, the United States, and South America. After Hitler's assumption of power, Driesch was forced out of his position. He became interested in parapsychology and published on such phenomena as telepathy, clairvoyance, and telekinesis. Driesch was married to Margarete Reifferschneidt, and the couple had two children. He died on April 17, 1941.

Further Reading

Hans Driesch is listed in the Philosophy study guide (VI, D). Henri BERGSON was another leading vitalist of this period.

In spite of his unusually large output of books and articles, Driesch's work has evoked little response. Ruth Moore, *The Coil of Life: The Story of the Great Discoveries in the Life Sciences* (1961), includes a biographical chapter on Driesch. His theories are discussed in Joseph Needham, *Order and Life* (1936); Rainer Schubert-Soldern, *Mechanism and Vitalism: Philosophical Aspects of Biology,* edited by Philip G. Fothergill (trans. 1962); and Jane M. Oppenheimer, *Essays in the History of Embryology and Biology* (1967). A classic critique of vitalism is Moritz Schlick, *Philosophy of Nature* (trans. 1949).

Hans Driesch. (Süddeutscher Verlag)

DRUSUS / By Robert Dale Sweeney

Marcus Livius Drusus (ca. 124–91 B.C.) was a Roman statesman who attempted to unite the nobility with the equestrian order and to reconcile the cities of Italy to the rule of Rome.

Drusus (pronounced drŏŏ′səs) was a member of a great plebeian family, the son and grandson of consuls. Drusus' mother belonged to the great patrician family of the Cornelii; his wife was Servilia, daughter of the Optimate leader Q. Servilius Caepio; and his sister Livia was married to Servilia's brother, also named Q. Servilius Caepio.

Drusus, a Roman portrait statue. (Vatican Museums, Rome)

Political Career

It was inevitable that a man of Drusus' wealth and family connections should enter politics. He was elected a military tribune (ca. 105 B.C.), became one of the *decemviri stilitibus iudicandis*, a court of 10 which decided cases as to whether a man was free or a slave (ca. 104), and was chosen a quaestor (ca. 102), the first step on the ladder of public office for aspiring Roman politicians. He was aedile in 94 and became a pontifex at some unknown time, an office which he held until his death.

Domestic Reforms

On Dec. 10, 92, Drusus became a plebeian tribune and used his own influence and the powers of this office to propose an extraordinary series of reforms designed to solve the major domestic problems of the day. He proposed to placate the poor citizens by suggesting the establishment of 12 colonies in Italy to which they could migrate, with a free distribution of land. To smooth relations between the Senate and the equestrian order (*equites*), Drusus wanted to restore to the senators the

right, taken from them by C. Gracchus and given to the *equites*, of sitting on the juries which decided cases of alleged corruption in office. Equestrian opposition was to be overcome by doubling the size of the Senate by adding 300 *equites* to it. The restive cities of Italy Drusus wanted to conciliate by extending Roman citizenship to all Italians.

These proposals were adopted into law by the assembly of all citizens, but they violated Roman law providing that one bill of proposals could not contain several unrelated topics; force had been used as well. This gave an opportunity to Drusus' opponents to reopen the question. His brother-in-law Caepio, who had quarreled with him and had divorced his sister Livia, and the consul Marcus Philippus led the opposition. After violent agitation and threats of mass movements in support of Drusus by the Italians, Drusus' enemies persuaded a majority of the Senate to declare all of these laws invalid. The results were tragic: Drusus was murdered in his home, his supporters were subjected to prosecution in the law courts, and the Italians rose in open rebellion in the Social War (91–87).

Further Reading

Drusus is listed in the Ancient History study guide (III, B, 3). He was one of a number of social reformers that included Gaius MARIUS and Tiberius Sempronius and Gaius Sempronius GRACCHUS. His ideas influenced CICERO and bore fruit in the policies of AUGUSTUS.

There is no book-length work on Drusus. The best summary of his career is that by Hugh Last in the *Cambridge Ancient History*, vol. 9 (1932; corrected repr. 1951). For general background see Matthias Gelzer, *The Roman Nobility* (1912; trans. 1969); A. N. Sherwin-White, *The Roman Citizenship* (1939); and H. H. Scullard, *From the Gracchi to Nero* (1959).

DRYDEN / By Anne Doyle

The English author John Dryden (1631–1700) is best known as a poet and critic. He also wrote almost 30 plays and was one of the great dramatists of his time.

John Dryden was born on Aug. 9, 1631, in Aldwinckle, Northamptonshire, in the parsonage of All Saints Church, where his maternal grandfather was rector. His family were supporters of Oliver Cromwell and comfortably situated. When Dryden was 15, he was sent to London to Westminster School to study under the celebrated headmaster, Dr. Richard Busby, who was known both for his rigorous discipline and for his ability to instill in his students a knowledge of Latin and Greek.

In 1649 while still at Westminster, Dryden published his first poem, "Upon the Death of Lord Hastings." The

John Dryden, a 1693 portrait by Sir Godfrey Kneller. (National Portrait Gallery, London)

next year he was admitted to Trinity College, Cambridge. While at Trinity he published a poem in honor of a friend, John Hoddesdon, but there is no evidence that his university career was especially dedicated to poetry. In 1654, the year he earned a bachelor of arts degree, his father died, leaving him family property that yielded an income of about £40 a year. After his father's death Dryden seems to have settled in London as secretary to his cousin Sir Gilbert Pickering, but there is no record of his activities until 1659, when his third poem, "Heroic Stanzas to the Glorious Memory of Cromwell," was published.

Shortly after the death of Cromwell, Charles II was restored to the throne. Although Dryden had been brought up to support the parliamentary party, he was evidently weary of the chaos and disorder that followed upon Cromwell's death, for in 1660 he welcomed the King with his poem "Astraea redux." The following year he offered a second tribute, "To his Sacred Majesty," to celebrate Charles II's coronation. He was criticized for changing his political allegiance, but he never withdrew the loyalty proclaimed in these two poems, although it would have been advantageous for him to do so in 1688, when William III came to the throne.

Early Career

After the Restoration, Dryden settled into the business of playwriting. In the early months of 1663 his first play, *The Wild Gallant*, was produced, but it proved a failure.

Late in that year he married Lady Elizabeth Howard, the sister of his friend Sir Robert Howard. The Howard family were of considerable means and had long supported the royalist cause.

Some of Dryden's most successful plays belong to a type peculiar to his own age called the heroic play. These were spectacular productions featuring exotic characters who defended their honor and proclaimed their love in rhyming couplets. Although the heroic themes of these plays were similar to those of Pierre Corneille, the sensational plots generally were derived from earlier English dramatists such as Francis Beaumont and John Fletcher. In 1665 Dryden collaborated with his brother-in-law, Sir Robert, on a heroic play, *The Indian Queen*. It was such a success that Dryden immediately wrote a sequel called *The Indian Emperor*.

In the summer of 1665 the plague hit London, and the theaters were closed. Dryden and his wife moved to the Howards' country estate at Charleton, Wiltshire. Here Dryden occupied himself with the writing of a long poem on the Dutch War and the London fire, *Annus mirabilis*, and a critical essay in prose, *An Essay of Dramatic Poesy*. He also wrote a play, *Secret Love*.

The years following the plague proved prosperous for Dryden. Both *Secret Love* and *The Indian Emperor*, whose performance had been delayed by the closing of the theaters, enjoyed great popularity. Dryden came to be regarded as the leading dramatist of the age. In 1667 he brought forth *Sir Martin Mar-All*, a new comedy adapted from Molière. He also accepted Sir William Davenant's invitation to collaborate on an operatic version of Shakespeare's *Tempest*. In 1668 the King's Company made him a shareholder in return for his promise to give them three plays a year. When Davenant died in the spring of 1668, Dryden was designated poet laureate and historiographer royal.

Heroic Plays

The years following Dryden's appointment as laureate brought his greatest heroic plays. In 1669 he produced *Tyrannic Love*, a play based on the life of St. Catherine. The next year saw the production of *The Conquest of Granada*, his most famous heroic play. Dryden continued to write dramas of this type, but it soon became apparent that he was weary of writing for the stage and tastes other than his own. He had, in fact, been eager for some time to undertake the writing of an epic poem. He had worked with epic materials in *Annus mirabilis* and the heroic plays and had even turned John Milton's *Paradise Lost* into an opera called *The State of Innocence* (1674); but the necessity of supporting himself by writing what would prove popular for the stage had deprived him of leisure to pursue his private poetical interests.

In 1676, in his dedication of his final heroic play, *Aureng-Zebe*, to the Earl of Mulgrave, Dryden expressed his discontent with the stage and begged the earl for the financial support necessary to pursue epic poetry. In 1677 he received a warrant for an additional £100 to his salary as poet laureate. This would have provided a reasonable income, but Charles's treasury was low, and Dryden was forced to abandon his epic dream because he was able to claim only about half of the £300 due him annually.

Dryden was still under contract to the King's Company. In 1677 he gave them his *All for Love,* an adaptation of Shakespeare's *Antony and Cleopatra.* Although its reception was not enthusiastic, it is generally regarded as his finest dramatic achievement. Its lack of acclaim may have been due in part to the deterioration of the King's Company, which was in financial distress. Subsequently Dryden shifted his activities to the Duke's Theatre, where his comedy *Limberham,* his adaptation of *Troilus and Cressida,* and his tragedy *Oedipus* (written in collaboration with Nathaniel Lee) were performed in 1678.

The Satires

Shortly after joining the Duke's Company, Dryden attacked the dullness of his fellow playwright Thomas Shadwell in *MacFlecknoe.* The attack seems to have been unprovoked, and the bitterness aroused by this unsolicited lampoon was heightened by political differences between the two playwrights. Dryden was a royalist; Shadwell was a Whig and a supporter of the Earl of Shaftesbury, who was scheming among the Whigs to

The actress Nell Gwyn, later mistress to King Charles II, appeared in many of Dryden's plays. This engraving by Gerard Valck is after a portrait by Sir Peter Lely. (National Portrait Gallery, London)

have Charles II's brother, the Catholic Duke of York, excluded from succession to the throne. Dryden was apparently commissioned by the King to expose the treason of the Whig sedition and the presumption of Shaftesbury, and he produced two of the finest political satires in English—*Absalom and Achitophel* (1681) and *The Medal* (1682). His next poem, *Religio laici* (1682), while nominally a defense of the authority of the English Church, was in effect also a satire on the unreason of all who dissented.

When Charles II died in 1685, Dryden was reappointed laureate by James II. At this time Dryden became a Catholic and in 1687 wrote a public apology for his new religion, *The Hind and the Panther.* Although his enemies accused him of accommodating his faith to that of his king in order to secure preferment, there is no evidence that James influenced Dryden's conversion. His adherence to his new faith after 1688 cost him the laureateship. During James's short reign Dryden was occupied primarily with poetry. He translated selections from Latin poets such as Virgil, Horace, and Lucretius. He also wrote several fine lyric odes: "Threnodia Augustalis," in memory of Charles II, "To the Memory of Anne Killigrew," and "A Song for St. Cecilia's Day."

In 1688, when William III appointed Shadwell poet laureate, Dryden was forced to return to the theater to earn a living. He produced a number of plays—*Don Sebastian* (1689), *Amphitryon* (1690), and *Cleomenes* (1690)—none of which was notably successful. He then turned to translating, which proved more profitable. His greatest translations were probably the *Satires of Juvenal and Persius* (1692), the *Works of Virgil* (1697), and the *Fables* (1700), a collection of tales from Ovid, Giovanni Boccaccio, and Geoffrey Chaucer. He was the first English author to earn his living by his writing. Dryden died on May 1, 1700.

Further Reading

John Dryden is listed in the Literature study guide (II, E, 1, d; II, E, 2, d; II, E, 3, b). The principles of neoclassicism are especially evident in the works of Dryden and Alexander POPE.

The standard biography of Dryden is Charles E. Ward, *The Life of John Dryden* (1961). Sir Walter Scott's account in *The Works of John Dryden* (18 vols., 1808; revised and edited by George Saintsbury, 1882–1893) is also excellent. The best critical study of Dryden's poetry is Earl Miner, *Dryden's Poetry* (1967). Two recent studies of the heroic plays are Arthur C. Kirsch, *Dryden's Heroic Drama* (1965), and Selma Zebouni, *Dryden: A Study in Heroic Characterization* (1965).

DRYSDALE / By R. M. Younger

The Australian painter Sir George Russell Drysdale (born 1912) gave his countrymen a changed vision of their continent through his landscape paintings of Australia's rural frontier.

Russell Drysdale was born on Feb. 7, 1912, at Bognor Regis, Sussex, in England. The family moved to Australia, and Russell attended Geelong Grammar School in Victoria. He intended to take up farming but developed a strong interest in art and in 1935 began studying painting in Melbourne, continuing at the Grosvenor School in London and La Grande Chaumière in Paris during 1938–1939.

Returning to Melbourne, Drysdale found a strong resistance to acceptance of the newer art forms. He decided to move to Sydney, where the art world was awakening to European influences, and he immediately found himself at home. In 1941 he traveled through the remoter sections of the hinterland; *Man Feeding His Dogs* and *Moody's Pub* capture the region's emptiness.

Painter of the Backcountry

From the early 1940s, when he began interpreting the life of Australia's rural frontier in a new and highly personalized style, Drysdale turned aside from the established Australian school. Australian impressionism had become something of a stereotype, and Sir Arthur Streeton and other landscapists had painted coastal areas and

Russell Drysdale in 1961. An unfinished painting, Billy the Lurk, *is on the easel. (Australia House, London)*

well-grassed pastoral lands accessible to the main cities. Drysdale took for his settings the wide, dry, ocher-hued heartland of the continent, where he sensed the essence of the Australian experience. He used a warm, deep-toned palette to present somber and astringent views of desolate "heartbreak" landscapes typical of the back-country and to show how the emptiness and monotony affected those who made their lives in this environment.

Drysdale created pictorial enigmas that preserve something of the land's mystical quality and of the special response of people to it. As critic James Gleeson pointed out (1969): "Man is not shown by Drysdale as protagonist at grips with ruthless nature; rather he is drawn as a malleable creature upon whom the external forces have imposed the stamp of their authority."

Drysdale's first exhibition, in Sydney in 1942, established him as the leading exponent of a new kind of national painting. The dramatic interpretations of a rigorous and monotonous environment are compelling, evocative, and clearly Australian; yet for all their starkness the paintings reveal Drysdale's respect for the basic subtleties of classical art and his discerning awareness of the European tradition in all its richness.

Drysdale captured wartime themes in *Albury Platform* and *Home Town* (both 1942). In 1944 he did a striking series of illustrations showing soil erosion in the western region of New South Wales; published in leading newspapers, the drawings brought home the awful reality of one of the nation's severest droughts. The *Drover's Wife* (1945) and the *Cricketers* (1948) are examples of the artist's ability to place human subjects in vast settings without negating them. *Old Larsen* (1953) is an outstanding example of his character portraiture.

Prizes and Exhibitions

In 1947 Drysdale won the Wynne Prize, Australia's principal landscape award. He was selected for the Twelve Australian Artists Exhibition sponsored by the Arts Council of Great Britain (1953) and for the Venice Biennale (1954).

In 1959 Drysdale did a series of drawings to illustrate newspaper articles by A. S. Marshall on the continent's northwest frontier lands; subsequently these appeared in Marshall's *Journey among Men* (1962). Following this series, Drysdale painted aborigines of the tropical regions, showing them as symbolic figures sometimes barely distinguishable from the totems, trees, and rocks of their tribal land.

A retrospective exhibition of Drysdale's paintings was held in Sydney in 1960. He was knighted in 1969.

Further Reading

Sir Russell Drysdale is listed in the Australia and New Zealand study guide (II, G). His approach to the painting of Australian landscape was as distinctive and vital as the approach to portraiture introduced by Sir William DOBELL. Other Australian painters were Sir Arthur STREETON and Sidney NOLAN.

A useful reference is the publication by the National

Art Gallery of South Wales, Sydney, *Russell Drysdale: A Retrospective Exhibition of Paintings from 1937 to 1960;* Drysdale's views on the artist's role are included. Drysdale is discussed in relation to Australian art in Bernard Smith, *Australian Painting, 1788–1960* (1962). Drysdale's outlook and his place in the contemporary art scene are explored in James Gleeson's elaborately illustrated review *Masterpieces of Australian Art* (1969).

DUANE / By Lewis C. Perry

The American journalist William Duane (1760–1835) was an effective advocate of Jeffersonian democracy. He and his son William John Duane, a prominent lawyer, were embroiled in the political controversies of the time.

William Duane, engraved after the portrait done by Saint-Mémin in 1802. (Library of Congress)

William Duane came from a family of Irish patriots. Born near Lake Champlain, N.Y., he was taken by his mother to Ireland when he was 5. Disinherited for marrying a Protestant, he became a printer and went to Calcutta, India. He prospered until he was deported for printing attacks against the governmental officials of the East India Company. Vain attempts to seek justice in London deepened his hatred of England. In 1796 he went to America, where bitter partisan conflict was spreading and other Irish immigrants were already bringing a special radical fervor to the experimental republican government.

Duane assisted Benjamin Franklin Bache in editing the *Aurora,* the leading journal of the Jeffersonian party. When Bache died in 1798, his widow, Margaret, continued publication; Duane, himself a widower, married her 2 years later. He also intensified the paper's vehement, often sarcastic advocacy of the Jeffersonian cause. An eloquent writer and a clever editor, he was hated by the Federalists.

John Adams's administration never succeeded in jailing or silencing Duane. But he was constantly in danger, was once attacked by armed men, and in 1799 was charged with sedition in both state and national courts. Safety came only with the election of Thomas Jefferson in 1800. To Jefferson, Duane was more than a partisan editor; he was a trusted adviser and a good printer and bookseller.

When the capital was moved from Philadelphia to Washington, Duane moved too; but he never received the patronage in printing he had expected from the Jeffersonians, and he became increasingly disillusioned with them. An unswerving Democrat, he wrote *An Epitome of Arts and Science* (1811), which attempted to make useful knowledge available to those who lacked wealth and leisure. The *Aurora* ceased publication in 1822. Duane died on Nov. 24, 1835.

Toward the end of his life Duane had joined the opposition to the National Bank. That institution, with its vast powers seemingly uncontrolled by the government, represented a new form of tyranny to many Democrats. One of Duane's five children, William John Duane (1780–1865), was a central figure in the resulting controversies. Through his state offices and through a series of publications, he became a noted opponent of banking monopolies.

President Andrew Jackson, at war with the National Bank, decided to remove the government's deposits and place them in state banks. On June 1, 1833, he appointed William J. Duane secretary of the Treasury. The Jacksonians apparently assumed that Duane, a well-known opponent of the National Bank, would carry out their wishes. He refused, and on September 23 he was dismissed. His opposition to the National Bank was actually a suspicion of all banks. He felt that Federal deposits should be where close watch was possible. More careful and astute than many other Jacksonians, Duane saw the dangers in reckless state banking that would lead to the Panic of 1837.

Further Reading

William Duane is listed in the American History study guide (IV, G, 4). The poet Philip FRENEAU was a contemporary journalist.

Duane's place in the development of American newspapers is noted in Frank Luther Mott, *American Journalism: A History, 1690–1960* (3d ed. 1962). He also figures prominently in James Morton Smith's authoritative study of the Alien and Sedition Laws, *Freedom's Fetters: The Alien and Sedition Laws and American Civil Liberties* (1956). See also Eugene Perry Link, *Democratic-Repub-*

lican Societies, 1790–1800 (1942), for Duane and his party; Harry Tinkcom, *The Republicans and Federalists in Pennsylvania* (1950), for Duane and his home state; and Nathan Schachner, *The Founding Fathers* (1954), for Duane and national politics. For the controversies in which the younger Duane was involved see Arthur Schlesinger, Jr., *The Age of Jackson* (1945), and Bray Hammond, *Banks and Politics in America, from the Revolution to the Civil War* (1957).

* * *

DUBČEK / By T. C. W. Blanning

The Czechoslovak politician Alexander Dubček (born 1921) served briefly as head of his country's Communist party. His attempts to liberalize political life led to the occupation of Czechoslovakia by the Soviet army and his dismissal from office.

Alexander Dubček (pronounced doob′chĕk) was born on Nov. 27, 1921, the son of a cabinetmaker who had just returned from the United States. His family lived in the U.S.S.R. from 1925 to 1938, and it was

Alexander Dubček. (*Keystone Press, London*)

there that he received his education. During World War II he was an active member of the underground resistance to the Germans in Slovakia.

After the war Dubček made his career as a functionary of the Communist party. He was elected to the Presidium of the Slovakian and then of the Czechoslovakian Communist party in 1962, and in the following year he became first secretary of the Slovakian party's Central Committee. Yet when he succeeded Antonin Novotny in January 1968 as first secretary of the Czechoslovakian Communist party, he was not well known in his own country and was hardly known at all outside it.

Pressure for the relaxation of the rigid orthodoxy prevailing in political life had been mounting in Czechoslovakia for a considerable time and had been strengthened by economic discontent. Dubček became the personification of this movement and promised to introduce "socialism with a human face." After his accession to power, censorship was relaxed and plans were made for a new federal constitution, for new legislation to provide for a greater degree of civil liberty, and for a new electoral law to give greater freedom to non-Communist parties.

The Soviet government became increasingly alarmed by these developments and throughout the spring and summer of 1968 issued a series of warnings to Dubček and his colleagues. Dubček had attempted to steer a middle course between liberal and conservative extremes, and at a midsummer confrontation with the Soviet leaders he stood firm against their demands for a reversal of his policies.

It was thought that Dubček had won his point on this occasion, but on August 20 armies of the U.S.S.R. and the other Warsaw Pact countries occupied Czechoslovakia. Mass demonstrations of support for Dubček kept him in power for the time being, but his liberal political program was abandoned.

Over the next 2 years Dubček was gradually removed from power. In April 1969 he resigned as first secretary of the party, in September he was dismissed from the Presidium, and in January 1970 from the Central Committee. In December 1969 he was sent to Turkey as ambassador. The final blow came on June 27, 1970, when he was expelled from the Communist party, and shortly afterward he was dismissed from his ambassadorial post.

Further Reading

Alexander Dubček is listed in the European History study guide (XII, H, 1). Nicolae CEAUSESCU of Romania and TITO of Yugoslavia were more successful in minimizing Soviet influence in their countries.

The best biography of Dubček, and a successful attempt to relate his career to developments within Czechoslovakia as a whole, is William Shawcross, *Dubček* (1971). The best book on the 1968 crisis itself is Philip Windsor and Adam Roberts, *Czechoslovakia, 1968* (1969). Valuable background is provided by Edward Taborsky, *Communism in Czechoslovakia, 1948–1960* (1961).

* * *

DUBE / By Albert S. Gérard

John Langalibalele Dube (1870–1949) was a South African writer and propagandist for Zulu culture. He was one of the first writers in an African language.

John L. Dube (pronounced dōō′bā) was born on Feb. 11, 1870, at Inanda, Natal. His father was one of the first African ministers ordained by American missionaries. Dube studied at Oberlin College (1888–1890) and later at the Union Missionary Training Institute in Brooklyn.

On his return to Natal in 1901, his admiration for such Negro leaders as Booker T. Washington drove him to found the first native-owned educational institution in South Africa, the Zulu Christian Industrial School, at Ohlange. Its purpose was to teach the Christian religion and modern skills while encouraging the development of Zulu culture. During the first decade of the 20th century, while writing articles in English for the *Missionary Review of the World,* Dube also launched the first Zulu newspaper, *Ilanga laseNatal* (The Sun of Natal), in the hope that it would provide useful training ground for future Zulu writers, as indeed it did.

In 1912, when the threat of racialist Boer supremacy in the newly formed Dominion of South Africa awoke African intellectuals to the need for unified all-black action, John Dube was elected the first president of the South African National Congress and was sent with a delegation to gain support in Great Britain. This was of no avail, and as a result of this failure, of personal quarrels among black leaders, and of financial troubles in the organization, Dube withdrew from the Congress in 1917 and dedicated himself to running his institute and his journal, to advising the Zulu royal house, and to writing *Isitha somuntu nguye uqobo lwakhe* (1922; The Black Man Is His Own Worst Enemy), in which he preached the gospel of self-help and inner change.

This was one of the first books in Zulu by a native author. But Dube's chief contribution to the growth of vernacular creative writing was *Insila kaTshaka* (1930), a semihistorical, ethnographical novel, which was later (1951) translated into English as *Jeqe, the Bodyservant of King Tshaka* and which recalls the power and the glory of the Zulu empire in the first half of the 19th century while stressing the bloodthirsty cruelty that was associated with it. Dube may be considered the founder of the Zulu novel: it was as a result of his example that the first Zulu novelist of note, R. R. R. Dhlomo (born 1901), gave up his awkward attempts at writing in English and turned to his native tongue. *Insila kaTshaka* was Dube's only venture in prose fiction: he later turned back to straight didactic writing, especially a biography of Isaiah Shembe, a Zulu prophet and founder of a dissident church, who died in 1935 after composing the earliest original hymns in the language.

But Dube had not given up politics altogether. While disappointment had caused him to renege his earlier radicalism, he had become the leader of the Natal Native Congress, which was considered eminently reliable by the South African authorities. In 1937 he was elected as Natal's delegate at the Natives' Representative Council, and he became the first African to be awarded an honorary doctorate by the University of South Africa. He died on Feb. 11, 1949.

Further Reading

John L. Dube is listed in the Africa study guide (IX, B, 11). His successor to the Natives' Representative Council was Albert LUTHULI. Dube belonged to the same generation as Thomas MOFOLO, Samuel MQHAYI, and Sol T. PLAATJE.

There is no biography of Dube. George Shepperson and Thomas Price, *Independent African* (1958), a study of the Nyasaland movement of 1915, contains numerous references to Dube and his activities. For general background on the area see Donald L. Wiedner, *A History of Africa South of the Sahara* (1962), and Eric A. Walker, *A History of Southern Africa* (1964).

DU BELLAY / By Donald Stone, Jr.

The French poet Joachim du Bellay (ca. 1522–1560) was second only to Ronsard in his mastery of 16th-century poetic forms and showed an arresting talent for satire and simplicity.

Joachim du Bellay (pronounced dü bĕ-lā′) was born at the Château de la Turmelière in Anjou, probably in 1522. When he was about 23, he began to study law at Poitiers, but the lure of poetry was stronger and Du Bellay soon left for Paris to study along with Pierre Ronsard and Jean Antoine de Baïf under the great Jean Dorat, who taught Latin and Greek literature at the Collège de Coqueret.

In 1549 Dorat's students published the *Deffence et illustration de la langue française,* written by Du Bellay. It defended French against Latin and proposed ways by which French writers could elevate their language and literature to the perfection of the classics. The work specifically singled out the Italian sonnet, the ode, the elegy, the epic, and tragedy and comedy as practiced by the ancients as fitting genres to replace the traditional medieval forms. With the *Deffence* Du Bellay published the first major sonnet cycle in France, the *Olive.*

Du Bellay's major works, the *Regrets,* the *Divers jeux rustiques, Le Premier livre des antiquitez de Rome,* and the *Poemata* (all published in 1558), owe a large part of their inspiration to his stay in Rome, where he went with his relative Cardinal Jean du Bellay in 1553. However, with the passage of time his enthusiasm for Rome gave way to bitter disappointment in both the city and

Joachim du Bellay. (French Cultural Services of the French Embassy)

the Church, and in August 1557 he returned to Paris.

These four works of 1558 are quite diverse. The *Poemata* contains only Latin verse. The *Jeux rustiques*, in French, is mainly a collection of light works in the tradition of Navagero and Secundus. The *Antiquitez* and the *Regrets* offer Du Bellay's most brilliant French poetry in a serious vein. The former work contrasts Rome's past glory with the decay that Du Bellay discovered. The *Regrets* can be divided into three parts. The first relates Du Bellay's unhappiness in Rome and his longing for France and includes his famous sonnet *Heureux qui comme Ulysse*. The second part is a biting satire on Rome and the Holy See, and the third treats his return to the French court.

More personal than the *Antiquitez*, the *Regrets* reveals Du Bellay as a versatile master of the sonnet form. He was derivative, like all the poets of his time, but was particularly skillful in conveying a sense of private anguish or scorn. The young poet died of a stroke on New Year's Day 1560.

Further Reading

Joachim du Bellay is listed in the Literature study guide (III, E, 2). He and Pierre RONSARD were members of a group of poets known as the Pléiade.

H. W. Lawton's anthology of Joachim du Bellay's *Po-*

ems (1961) includes a discussion of the poet's life and works. Useful for an understanding of Du Bellay's Roman poems is Gladys Dickinson, *Du Bellay in Rome* (1960).

DUBINSKY / By Melvyn Dubofsky

David Dubinsky (born 1892) was an outstanding American trade union official. His leadership of the International Ladies' Garment Workers' Union demonstrated his ability to combine the more mundane attributes of the labor movement with the broader social vision of a reformer.

Together with such men as John L. Lewis, Sidney Hillman, and Philip Murray, David Dubinsky built the American labor movement as it now functions. During the Great Depression and the New Deal of the 1930s, through the creation of industrial unions (as opposed to craft unions) in the mass-production industries, these leaders brought trade unionism into a position of power whereby labor influenced big business and national politics.

Dubinsky (originally Dobnievski) was born in Brest-Litovsk in Russian Poland on Feb. 22, 1892, the youngest of six children in a poor Jewish family. His father moved the family to Lodz, where he operated a bakery. At the age of 11 David went to work for his father. By 14 he was a master baker and a member of the Bakers' Union, an affiliate of the Polish Bund, a revolutionary organization of Jewish workers.

Membership in the Bund led to Dubinsky's arrest in 1907 during a wave of Czarist repression following the abortive 1905 Russian Revolution. After a short jail term he returned to union activity, leading a strike by bakers in Lodz, which resulted in another arrest and expulsion to Brest-Litovsk. Dubinsky, however, returned illegally to Lodz and to union affairs, only to be arrested in 1908 and this time sentenced to exile in Siberia.

He was too young to be sent to Siberia, so Dubinsky was jailed in Lodz for a year and a half, until he was old enough to be transported there. On the way to Siberia he escaped and, convinced he had no future within the Russian Empire, decided to emigrate to the New World. In 1911 Dubinsky arrived in the United States.

Early Union Career

Within 2 weeks Dubinsky took out his first papers, joined the Socialist party, and enrolled in night school. He soon became a garment cutter (the most skilled craft in the garment industry) and a member of Local 10, International Ladies' Garment Workers' Union (ILGWU), the union which represented the trade's skilled-labor "aristocrats." At first Dubinsky devoted his time to Socialist party activities and to the Cooperative movement, but after his marriage to Emma Goldberg in 1914 he began to concentrate upon his craft and to take more interest in local union affairs.

Dubinsky spoke for the more recent immigrants in the union, whose increasing numbers assisted his rise to union power. In 1918 he was elected to Local 10's executive board and a year later was vice president. Elected president in 1920, the following year Dubinsky also became general manager, a full-time, well-paid position that allowed him to leave the cutter's bench. By 1924 he added to his offices the secretary-treasurership of the local, thus becoming the most powerful figure within the New York locals that dominated the ILGWU.

A born pragmatist whose Socialist dreams had died, and eager to rise in the union hierarchy, Dubinsky joined the anti-Communist faction of the ILGWU during the 1920s in the internal war that almost tore the organization apart. With the aid of Dubinsky's powerful Local 10, the anti-Communists triumphed, but the union was wrecked and nearly bankrupt.

New Deal

A member of the ILGWU's general executive board since 1923, Dubinsky was elected secretary-treasurer in 1929, allowing him to run the union since its president was desperately sick. In 1932 the president died, and Dubinsky replaced him, still retaining his secretary-treasurer's office. Until 1959 he held both positions.

Franklin Roosevelt's election to the U.S. presidency in 1932 offered Dubinsky true opportunity. Taking advantage of New Deal labor legislation, Dubinsky had increased his union's membership to over 200,000 by the end of the next year.

Elected to the American Federation of Labor (AFL) executive council in 1934, Dubinsky supported the industrial unionists' effort to organize mass-production workers. When the AFL refused its assistance, Dubinsky in 1936 resigned from the executive council. He assisted in forming the Committee on Industrial Organization (CIO). Always a firm believer in labor unity, however, when the CIO became a permanent, second national labor federation in 1938, Dubinsky took the ILGWU out. He returned his union to the AFL in 1940 and 5 years later was reelected to the AFL executive council.

Political Activities

During the 1930s Dubinsky broke with socialism, becoming a fervent supporter of Roosevelt's New Deal. He declared, "Trade unionism needs capitalism like a fish needs water." Because New York City's Jewish workers looked with suspicion upon the local Democratic machine, Dubinsky helped create the American Labor party to capture former Socialist voters for the New Deal. When he thought that Communists had taken over the American Labor party, he helped found the Liberal party. By the mid-1940s he was one of the nationally respected leaders of the pro–New Deal, rabidly anti-Communist wing of the American labor movement.

At his retirement from union office in 1966, Dubinsky left a thriving labor organization, though it was no longer committed to the establishment of a cooperative society.

Dubinsky's heritage to the labor movement was a belief in militant economic action, a trust in reform politics, and a faith in the justice of a socially conscious capitalism.

Further Reading

David Dubinsky is listed in the American History study guide (IX, B, 3). Sidney HILLMAN was another union organizer in the garment industry. The administration of Franklin ROOSEVELT boosted the efforts of industrial unionists.

The World of David Dubinsky (1957) is a complete but uncritical biography by Max D. Danish, who worked for Dubinsky. Another glowing tribute to Dubinsky is the general history of the ILGWU and the needle trades by Benjamin Stolberg, *Tailor's Progress: The Story of a Famous Union and the Men Who Made It* (1944). Two books by Irving Bernstein offer the most objective ac-

David Dubinsky. (Library of Congress)

count of Dubinsky's union activities in the 1920s and 1930s: *The Lean Years: A History of the American Worker, 1920–1933* (1960) and *Turbulent Years: A History of the American Worker, 1933–1941* (1969). A short but excellent general introduction to the garment industry and its unions is Joel Seidman, *The Needle Trades* (1942).

✳   ✳   ✳

DUBNOV / By Ezri Atzmon

The Jewish historian, journalist, and political activist Simon Dubnov (1860–1941) was one of the founders of historical autonomism, a method of interpreting history in terms of national self-determination.

Simon Dubnov (pronounced do͞ob′nôf) was born in Mstislav, in the district of Mohilov, in Latvia. He received a traditional Jewish education at his grandfather's home, but in his youth he turned away from Jewish tradition. He read widely and was deeply impressed by the writings of Enlightenment authors. In 1874 he started attending a Jewish state school, but soon transferred to a non-Jewish one. After graduation he attempted several times to get admitted to a teachers' seminary, but he failed in the entrance examinations.

In 1880 Dubnov moved to St. Petersburg, where he lived with his older brother. Four years later he returned to his native town, but in 1890 he moved to Odessa and began his research on eastern European Jewry. Between 1903 and 1906 he stayed in Vilnius, where he fought for the establishment of Jewish national schools. After the pogrom of Kishinev in 1903, he demanded that Jewish self-defense be organized. In 1906 he accepted the chair of Jewish history at the Institute of Natural Sciences in St. Petersburg.

Opposing the Soviet regime, in 1922 Dubnov moved to Berlin, where he resided until Hitler's accession to power in 1933. With the Nazi occupation of Riga in 1941, the entire Jewish population was expelled and exterminated. When the sick and feverish Dubnov was being loaded on a bus, a drunk Latvian policeman shot the old man in the neck and killed him. He was buried in the community grave in the old cemetery of the Riga ghetto.

His Thought

Dubnov devoted his life to Jewish historical research and to the sociological interpretation of Jewish history. He started with an evaluation of Jewish personalities in the periodicals *Razsviet, Voskhod, Pardess,* and *Hashiloakh* (1881–1901). In the years 1893–1895 he published a series of documentary studies on the history of eastern European Jewry. His central idea was that Jewish life in the Diaspora was basically the history of centers of Jewry which, with the passage of time, moved from one country to another. His sociological conception of Jewish history found its full expression in his *General History of the Jewish People.* He saw the Jewish people in the Diaspora as one that had lost some of the factors usually sustaining a nation; the Jewish people had therefore developed a unique social regime and climate which enabled it to survive as a nation in the midst of foreign communities.

Further Reading

Simon Dubnov is listed in the Religion study guide (II, F, 1, a). Leopold ZUNZ was another noted Jewish historian.

Dubnov's *Nationalism and History: Essays on Old and New Judaism* (1958) has an excellent introductory essay on the author by Koppel S. Pinson, the editor. See also Aron Steinberg, ed., *Simon Dubnov, the Man and His Work: A Memorial Volume on the Occasion of the Centenary of His Birth, 1860–1960* (1963).

✳   ✳   ✳

Simon Dubnov. (YIVO Institute for Jewish Research)

DU BOIS / By John H. Bracey, Jr.

William Edward Burghardt Du Bois (1868–1963) was a major black American

scholar, an early leader in the 20th-century black protest movement, and an advocate of pan-Africanism.

On Feb. 23, 1868, W. E. B. Du Bois was born in Great Barrington, Mass., where he grew up. During his youth he did some newspaper reporting. In 1884 he graduated as valedictorian from high school. He got his bachelor of arts from Fisk University in Nashville, Tenn., in 1888, having spent summers teaching in black schools in Nashville's rural areas. In 1888 he entered Harvard University as a junior, took a bachelor of arts *cum laude* in 1890, and was one of six commencement speakers. From 1892 to 1894 he pursued graduate studies in history and economics at the University of Berlin on a Slater Fund fellowship. He served for 2 years as professor of Greek and Latin at Wilberforce University in Ohio.

In 1891 Du Bois got his master of arts and in 1895 his doctorate in history from Harvard. His dissertation, *The Suppression of the African Slave Trade to the United States of America, 1638–1870,* was published as No. 1 in the Harvard Historical Series. This important work has yet to be surpassed. In 1896 he married Nina Gomer, and they had two children.

In 1896–1897 Du Bois became assistant instructor in sociology at the University of Pennsylvania. There he conducted the pioneering sociological study of an urban community, published as *The Philadelphia Negro: A Social Study* (1899). These first two works assured Du Bois's place among America's leading scholars.

Du Bois's life and work were an inseparable mixture of scholarship, protest activity, and polemics. All of his efforts were geared toward gaining equal treatment for black people in a world dominated by whites and toward marshaling and presenting evidence to refute the myths of the racial inferiority of Negroes.

As Racial Activist

In 1905 Du Bois was a founder and general secretary of the Niagara movement, an all-Negro protest group of scholars and professionals. Du Bois founded and edited the *Moon* (1906) and the *Horizon* (1907–1910) as organs for the Niagara movement. In 1909 Du Bois was among the founders of the National Association for the Advancement of Colored People (NAACP) and from 1910 to 1934 served it as director of publicity and research, a member of the board of directors, and editor of the *Crisis,* its monthly magazine.

In the *Crisis,* Du Bois directed a constant stream of agitation—often bitter and sarcastic—at white Americans while serving as a source of information and pride to black Americans. The magazine always published young black writers. Racial protest during the decade following World War I focused on securing antilynching legislation. During this period the NAACP was the leading protest organization and Du Bois its leading figure.

In 1934 Du Bois resigned from the NAACP board and from the *Crisis* because of his new advocacy of a black

W. E. B. Du Bois in his office at the Crisis. *(The* Crisis, *New York)*

nationalist strategy: black-controlled institutions, schools, and economic cooperatives. This approach opposed the NAACP's commitment to integration. However, he returned to the NAACP as director of special research from 1944 to 1948. During this period he was active in placing the grievances of black Americans before the United Nations, serving as a consultant to the UN founding convention (1945) and writing the famous "An Appeal to the World" (1947).

Du Bois was a member of the Socialist party from 1910 to 1912 and always considered himself a Socialist. In 1948 he was cochairman of the Council on African Affairs; in 1949 he attended the New York, Paris, and Moscow peace congresses; in 1950 he served as chairman of the Peace Information Center and ran for the U.S. Senate on the American Labor party ticket in New York. In 1950–1951 Du Bois was tried and acquitted as an agent of a foreign power in one of the most ludicrous actions ever taken by the American government. Du Bois traveled widely throughout Russia and China in 1958–1959 and in 1961 joined the Communist party of the United States. He also took up residence in Ghana, Africa, in 1961.

Pan-Africanism

Du Bois was also active in behalf of pan-Africanism and concerned with the conditions of black people wherever they lived. In 1900 he attended the First Pan-African Conference held in London, was elected a vice president, and wrote the "Address to the Nations of the

World." The Niagara movement included a "pan-African department." In 1911 Du Bois attended the First Universal Races Congress in London along with black intellectuals from Africa and the West Indies.

Du Bois organized a series of pan-African congresses around the world, in 1919, 1921, 1923, and 1927. The delegations comprised intellectuals from Africa, the West Indies, and the United States. Though resolutions condemning colonialism and calling for alleviation of the oppression of Africans were passed, little concrete action was taken. The Fifth Congress (1945, Manchester, England) elected Du Bois as chairman, but the power was clearly in the hands of younger activists, such as George Padmore and Kwame Nkrumah, who later became significant in the independence movements of their respective countries. Du Bois's final pan-African gesture was to take up citizenship in Ghana in 1961 at the request of President Kwame Nkrumah and to begin work as director of the *Encyclopedia Africana*.

As Scholar

Du Bois's most lasting contribution is his writing. As poet, playwright, novelist, essayist, sociologist, historian, and journalist, he wrote 21 books, edited 15 more, and published over 100 essays and articles. Only a few of his most significant works will be mentioned here.

From 1897 to 1910 Du Bois served as professor of economics and history at Atlanta University, where he organized conferences titled the Atlanta University Studies of the Negro Problem and edited or coedited 16 of the annual publications, on such topics as *The Negro in Business* (1899), *The Negro Artisan* (1902), *The Negro Church* (1903), *Economic Cooperation among Negro Americans* (1907), and *The Negro American Family* (1908). Other significant publications were *The Souls of Black Folk: Essays and Sketches* (1903), one of the outstanding collections of essays in American letters, and *John Brown* (1909), a sympathetic portrayal published in the American Crisis Biographies series.

Du Bois also wrote two novels, *The Quest of the Silver Fleece* (1911) and *Dark Princess: A Romance* (1928); a book of essays and poetry, *Darkwater: Voices from within the Veil* (1920); and two histories of black people, *The Negro* (1915) and *The Gift of Black Folk: Negroes in the Making of America* (1924).

From 1934 to 1944 Du Bois was chairman of the department of sociology at Atlanta University. In 1940 he founded *Phylon*, a social science quarterly. *Black Reconstruction in America, 1860–1880* (1935), perhaps his most significant historical work, details the role of black people in American society, specifically during the Reconstruction period. The book was criticized for its use of Marxist concepts and for its attacks on the racist character of much of American historiography. However, it remains the best single source on its subject.

Black Folk, Then and Now (1939) is an elaboration of the history of black people in Africa and the New World. *Color and Democracy: Colonies and Peace* (1945) is a brief call for the granting of independence to Africans, and *The World and Africa: An Inquiry into the Part*

Which Africa Has Played in World History (1947; enlarged ed. 1965) is a major work anticipating many later scholarly conclusions regarding the significance and complexity of African history and culture. A trilogy of novels, collectively entitled *The Black Flame* (1957, 1959, 1961), and a selection of his writings, *An ABC of Color* (1963), are also worthy.

Du Bois received many honorary degrees, was a fellow and life member of the American Association for the Advancement of Science, and a member of the National Institute of Arts and Letters. He was the outstanding black intellectual of his period in America.

Du Bois died in Ghana on Aug. 27, 1963, on the eve of the civil rights march in Washington, D.C. He was given a state funeral, at which Kwame Nkrumah remarked that he was "a phenomenon."

Further Reading

W. E. B. Du Bois is listed in the American History study guide (VIII, E, 3, b; VIII, F, 3) and the Africa study guide (IX, A, 1). Marcus GARVEY shared his sense of black nationalism. Du Bois became a citizen of Ghana at the invitation of President Kwame NKRUMAH.

Indispensable starting points for an understanding of Du Bois's life are his autobiographical writings (the dates are of the most recent editions): *The Autobiography of W. E. B. Du Bois: A Soliloquy on Viewing My Life from the Last Decades of Its First Century* (1968); *Dusk of Dawn: An Essay toward an Autobiography of a Race Concept* (1968); *Darkwater: Voices from within the Veil* (1969); and *The Souls of Black Folk* (1969). Two critical biographies are Francis L. Broderick, *W. E. B. Du Bois: Negro Leader in a Time of Crisis* (1959), and Elliott M. Rudwick, *W. E. B. Du Bois: A Study of Minority Group Leadership* (1960; 1968). Also of importance is the W. E. B. Du Bois memorial issue of *Freedomways* magazine (vol. 5, no. 1, 1965). This was expanded and published in book form as *Black Titan: W. E. B. Du Bois* (1970). Arna Bontemps, *100 Years of Negro Freedom* (1963), has a biographical sketch. Meyer Weinberg, Walter Wilson, Julius Lester, and Andrew G. Paschal edited Du Bois readers. Philip S. Foner edited *W. E. B. Du Bois Speaks* (1970), two volumes of speeches and addresses.

✳   ✳   ✳

DU BOIS-REYMOND
/ By Clifford Mawdsley

The German physiologist Emil Du Bois-Reymond (1818–1896) made important discoveries about the modes of action of nerves and muscles and was the founder of modern electrophysiology.

Emil Du Bois-Reymond (pronounced dü bwä′ rā-môN′) was born in Berlin on Nov. 7, 1818. His early education was gained partly at the French College in Berlin and later at the College of Neuchâtel. At the age of 18 he entered the faculty of philosophy at the University of Berlin. He once described himself (in 1875) as having "intellectual leanings impelling me in almost equal degree in various directions of natural knowledge." His eclectic tastes were reflected in his early years at the university when he studied philosophy, theology, mathematics, physics, and chemistry. In 1841 he became assistant to Johannes Müller, who suggested that he study some of the electrical properties of muscle and thus guided Du Bois-Reymond into a field of study which was to engross him for the next half century.

Succeeding Müller as professor of physiology in Berlin in 1858, Du Bois-Reymond agitated for a new, well-equipped department. Because of his influence with the German emperor, who much admired him, a new physiological institute was built on the Wilhelmstrasse, and it opened on Nov. 6, 1877. It served as a model for the design of physiological laboratories until the end of the 19th century. The main lecture theater contained the unusual feature of a private box for visiting royalty, which, surprisingly, was occasionally occupied by Du Bois-Reymond's imperial patron.

Du Bois-Reymond's honors and appointments were legion. In 1867 he was appointed perpetual secretary of the Berlin Academy of Sciences. Between 1859 and 1877 he was joint editor of *Müllers Archiv,* and afterward, until his death, he edited *Archiv für Physiologie.* He served as president of both the Physical and the Physiological societies of Germany and was elected a foreign fellow of the Royal Society of London.

Many physiologists during the 19th century were attracted to "vitalism." Müller himself was a protagonist of this philosophy, which held that a vital force, present in living things, could alter physical and chemical laws. It was suggested that the organism functioned as a whole and that experimentation on its separate functions was invalid. Du Bois-Reymond rejected this indeterminate theory. He was a "materialist" and believed in the cogency of scientific analysis of the components of living processes. He was attracted to the materialistic philosophers and wrote memoirs of some of them, including Voltaire and Denis Diderot. His own philosophical views were outlined in two collections of essays, *The Limits of Natural Science* (1872) and *Seven World Riddles* (1880). His writings encompassed other nonscientific topics; among them were essays on university organization (1870) and on the relationship between natural history and natural science (1878).

Du Bois-Reymond died at Berlin on Dec. 26, 1896.

Contributions to Neurophysiology

Luigi Galvani late in the 18th century discovered that muscle has electrical properties. During the same period Alessandro Volta showed that muscles can be made to contract continuously by rapidly repeated electrical stimulation. Volta was describing tetanic contraction, though this label was introduced much later, in 1838, by Carlo Matteucci. Matteucci determined that a difference of potential exists between a nerve and its damaged muscle. Du Bois-Reymond defined the phenomenon of

Emil Du Bois-Reymond. *(Bildarchiv)*

tetanization and first repeated Matteucci's experiments and then went on to augment them.

Du Bois-Reymond introduced the technique of stimulating nerve and muscle by means of a short-duration (faradic) current from the modified induction coil which he devised and which bears his name. He was the first to demonstrate that muscular contraction is accompanied by chemical changes in the muscle, and he also confirmed that the cut surface of a muscle exhibits a difference in electrical potential from that of its intact surface. Further, he suggested that muscles and nerves contain electromotive molecules. In 1843 he demonstrated that ions are formed within a nerve when it is stimulated by a current from a nonpolarizable electrode; this phenomenon he called electrotonus. He discovered that there is a negative change in potential from the resting state when nerves or muscles are stimulated (1843–1848). Using his induction coil, he formulated his "law of stimulation," which postulated that nerve and muscle are not excited by a constant current, no matter what its strength, but that they are very responsive to sudden changes in current intensity.

The summary of Du Bois-Reymond's hypotheses was a postulation that all the electrical phenomena accompanying neural and muscular activity depend on electromotive molecules, arranged end to end, along cylinders of tissue. He believed that electrophysiological stimulation was simply a form of electrolysis.

Du Bois-Reymond rarely published discoveries in separate papers. The bulk of his work appeared collectively in his most famous book, *Untersuchungen über Thierische Elektricitat* (Researches on Animal Electricity). The first volume appeared in 1848, the first part of the second volume in the following year. Eccentrically, the latter book ends in the middle of a sentence, which remained incomplete until the rest of the second volume was published 35 years later (1884).

Most of Du Bois-Reymond's observations were correct and have since been confirmed, but his theoretical inferences often proved to be wrong. He was, however, a pioneer in the study of neuromuscular physiology and its electrical correlates and indicated the method and the direction of future experiments. His ideas, though wrong in detail, contain in embryo form part of the modern concept of neurophysiology that nerve and muscle conduction is mediated by the passage of an electrical wave whose generation depends on a flux of ions across the tissue membrane.

Further Reading

Emil Du Bois-Reymond is listed in the Science study guide (VI, F, 2). He was a pupil of Johannes MÜLLER, one of the great physiologists of the century, and joined a distinguished group of Müller's disciples, which included Hermann von HELMHOLTZ and Rudolf VIRCHOW.

A biography of Du Bois-Reymond and an authoritative survey of his work are given in the obituary by A. D. Waller in *Proceedings of the Royal Society*, vol. 75 (1905). A short account of his life and work is in Fielding H. Garrison, *An Introduction to the History of Medicine* (1913; 4th ed. 1929). See also Charles J. Singer, *A Short History of Medicine* (1928; 2d. ed., with E. Ashworth Underwood, 1962), and Arturo Castiglioni, *A History of Medicine* (trans. 1941; 2d ed. 1947).

DUBOS / By George Basalla

René Jules Dubos (born 1901), the French-born American microbiologist, pioneered in the development of antibiotics and was an important writer on humanitarian and ecological subjects.

René Dubos was born on Feb. 20, 1901, at Saint-Brice, France. After receiving a scientific education, he went to Rome in 1922, where he was on the staff of the International Institute of Agriculture. Within 2 years he left to attend Rutgers University in New Jersey, from which he received his doctorate in microbiology in 1927. Dubos immediately began his long and distinguished association with the department of pathology and bacteriology at the Rockefeller Institute for Medical Research in New York City. Except for 2 years as a professor of medicine at Harvard Medical School

René Dubos. (United Press International Photo)

(1942–1944) he was continuously involved in research at the institute from 1927.

Dubos was a pioneer in the development of antibiotic drugs. Shortly after joining the Rockefeller Institute, he began searching for an antibacterial substance that would destroy the microorganism causing pneumonia. In the 1930s he discovered a soil-dwelling bacterium that produced a chemical substance capable of weakening the outer capsule of pneumonia bacteria so that they would be vulnerable to the body's natural defenses. He later showed that this substance, the antibiotic tyrothricin, was composed of two chemicals—tyrocidin and gramicidin. His work paved the way for the eventual discovery of streptomycin. Upon completing his investigation of tyrothricin he turned to tuberculosis research and won new recognition in that field.

In the 1950s Dubos began writing books on scientific subjects for a more general audience. In these he touched upon the philosophical foundations and social implications of science, warned against the naive utopianism of many medical thinkers, and argued for a study of the effect of the *total* environment upon man. His wisdom, humanitarian outlook, and lucid writing made Dubos one of the most perceptive and popular contemporary science writers. He produced over 200 scientific papers and more than a dozen books, including *Louis Pasteur: Free Lance of Science* (1950), *The White Plague: Tuberculosis, Man, and Society* (1952), *The Mirage of Health* (1959), *The Dreams of Reason* (1961),

The Unseen World (1962), *The Torch of Life* (1962), *So Human an Animal* (1968), *Man, Medicine, and Environment* (1968), and *Reason Awake* (1970).

In his dual role as scientist and author, Dubos accumulated numerous honors, including honorary degrees from European and American universities, awards from scientific and medical organizations, membership in the National Academy of Sciences, the Arches of Sciences Award for the popularization of science, and the Pulitzer Prize in letters (1969). In 1970 he became director of environmental studies at the State University of New York at Purchase, N.Y.

Further Reading

René Dubos is listed in the Science study guide (VII, G, 4). He was inspired by the experiments of Louis PASTEUR with soil bacteria as antimicrobial agents. Élie METCHNIKOFF observed the phenomenon of microbial antibiotic action. Alexander FLEMING discovered penicillin. Streptomycin was discovered by Selman A. WAKSMAN.

George Washington Corner, *A History of the Rockefeller Institute, 1901–1953: Origins and Growth* (1965), recounts in detail Dubos's life and work. Dubos's place in the development of microbiology can be reviewed in Hubert A. Lechevalier and Morris Solotorovsky, *Three Centuries of Microbiology* (1965).

DUBUFFET / By Sara McGrath

The French painter Jean Dubuffet (born 1901) explored the possibilities of materials and surfaces in works that depict commonplace subjects. Throughout his career he reacted against conventional ideas of beauty and remained apart from artistic movements.

Jean Dubuffet (pronounced dü-bü-fě′) was born on July 31, 1901, in Le Havre, the son of a wine merchant. He began attending art classes when he was 15 years old, and in 1918 he went to Paris to study painting at the Académie Julian. Six months later he left school to paint on his own.

Questioning the value of art and of culture, Dubuffet stopped painting in 1923. In 1930 he began a wine business in Paris which he subsequently gave up to resume painting. He returned again to the wine business, but from 1942 on he devoted himself exclusively to painting.

Dubuffet had his first exhibition in 1944 in Paris. With a crudeness reminiscent of the *art brut* (naive, unprofessional art) he so much admired, Dubuffet portrayed such ordinary subjects as people riding the Paris subway and a girl milking a cow. He was attempting "to bring all disparaged values into the limelight." These early paintings display the interest in texture, earth colors, and ironic humor that is characteristic of all Dubuffet's work.

When Dubuffet's second major show took place in Paris in 1946, the popular response was one of outrage. Strongly influenced by graffiti, Dubuffet had broken all accepted visual conventions by his choice of subject and technique.

Spurred by his interest in naive art, Dubuffet made his first visit to North Africa in 1947. He made two subsequent visits to the Sahara between 1947 and 1949, and he responded to his experience by creating works in which landscape and texture became increasingly important.

In 1950 Dubuffet began a series of paintings of female nudes which he called *Corps de Dames*. The formless, grotesque, and often humorous figures represent the direct antithesis to classical proportion and beauty. Dubuffet wrote extensively about his rejection of esthetic conventions, which was a current running through all his work.

Because of his wife's ill health Dubuffet moved to Vence in the south of France in 1955. He was increasingly preoccupied with creating a new kind of landscape painting. With an inventiveness that is typical of his approach to his work, he tried out new methods, which included scattering sand on the painting, scratching it with a fork, and assembling pictures out of butterfly wings. From the new techniques and materials arose a rich variety of works, among them a cycle called *Texturologies*. These pictures, which celebrate the ground

Jean Dubuffet in his studio in April 1967, a photograph by Luc Joubert, Paris. (Pace Gallery, N.Y.)

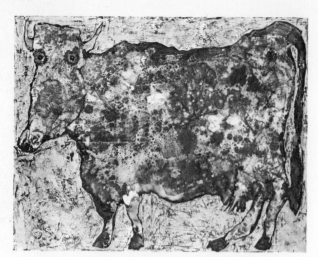

The Cow with the Subtile Nose, *painted in 1954 by Dubuffet. (Collection, The Museum of Modern Art, New York, Benjamin Scharps and David Scharps Fund)*

and contain no figures, appear to be nonrepresentational, but Dubuffet's works, however abstract they may appear, are always about something. The *Texturologies* are about matter, and by using the same thick impasto that he used to depict figures he suggests the oneness of nature and man.

When Dubuffet returned to Paris in 1961, he again took to depicting people and their environment. The bright colors and subject matter of these works recall the panoramas of city life he painted in 1943–1944. This return to an earlier style and subject matter was characteristic of Dubuffet; there was in his work a fundamental consistency in its dedication to "disparaged values" and in its aim of removing the boundaries between man and nature.

In 1962 Dubuffet moved to Le Touquet. At this time he began his longest series, entitled *L'Hourloupe* (a word he invented), which possess a decorative quality that is not evident in his earlier work. He also continued to paint everyday subjects, concentrating on inanimate objects such as typewriters, scissors, and clocks. In spite of their stylistic departure, these paintings are consistent with Dubuffet's entire output in their humor and naiveté.

Further Reading

Jean Dubuffet is listed in the Art study guide (III, L, 1). He was influenced by Paul KLEE and Max ERNST. The series of "Woman" paintings by Willem DE KOONING correspond to the kind of work Dubuffet did in his *Corps de Dames* series.

The best book on Dubuffet is Peter Selz, *The Work of Jean Dubuffet* (1962). It is a thorough commentary on his life and work and includes translations of many of his writings. Alan Bowness's introduction in *Jean Dubuffet: Paintings* (1966), the catalog for his Tate Gallery retrospective, is very useful. An indispensable book for placing Dubuffet in the context of his century is Werner Haft-

mann, *Painting in the Twentieth Century* (1954; trans., 2 vols., 1961; rev. ed. 1965).

DUCCIO / By Edmund Eglinski

The Italian painter Duccio di Buoninsegna (1255/1260–1318/1319) was the first great master of the Sienese school. His art represented the culmination of the Italo-Byzantine style in Siena and created the foundation for Sienese Gothic art.

Little is known about the life of Duccio (pronounced dōōt′chō). It is thought that he was born in the 1250s, probably toward the end of the decade. The first documentary reference which has come down to us is dated 1278. Thereafter several documents give us some hints about the artist's personality. He was, for instance, frequently in debt, as receipts of payment indicate. He was fined several times for petty offenses such as blocking the street and once for refusing to join the militia fighting in Maremma. From these fragmentary references we might conclude that Duccio was one of the first bohemian artists. A document of 1319 indicates that he was dead.

Duccio's role in the development of early Sienese painting may be equated roughly with the roles of both Cimabue and Giotto in the development of Florentine painting. Like Cimabue, Duccio represented the culmination of the Italo-Byzantine style of the 13th century in Siena. Duccio and Cimabue, however, stamped their most Byzantine works with the marks of their personalities so that both helped to establish the character of their respective schools of painting. There was in Duccio's style an anticipation of the linear rhythmic movements and patterns that later evolved into the 14th-century Gothic style that equates him with Giotto. The somewhat younger Giotto, however, actually achieved a fully developed Gothic style, whereas Duccio's art merely advanced to its threshold. After Duccio, Sienese painting became wholeheartedly Gothic in the work of Simone Martini and the Lorenzetti brothers.

The "Rucellai Madonna"

Our understanding of Duccio's style depends on two documented works: the *Madonna Enthroned*, called the *Rucellai Madonna*, and the *Maestà*. The *Rucellai Madonna* was commissioned on April 15, 1285, by the Confraternity of the Laudesi of S. Maria Novella in Florence. The contract was discovered in the 18th century and led to the correction of Giorgio Vasari's attribution

(Opposite) Duccio's Madonna Enthroned, *known as the* Rucellai Madonna, *in the Uffizi, Florence. (Kodansha)*

of the *Rucellai Madonna* to Cimabue. Despite this documentary evidence and the discrepancy in style between the *Rucellai Madonna* and other authentic works by Cimabue, some scholars still cling to Vasari's attribution. Others, aware of the stylistic differences but reluctant to accept the *Rucellai Madonna* as a work by Duccio, have invented a third artist, the "Master of the Rucellai Madonna." The consensus of opinion, however, gives the painting to Duccio. There is nothing in the style of the *Rucellai Madonna* that makes its attribution to Duccio implausible. This fact plus the contract of 1285 certainly makes such an attribution acceptable.

In stylistic terms, the *Rucellai Madonna* remains within the Byzantine conventions. It shows a concern for coloristic design uncommon in the late 13th century. In the dress of the six angels flanking the throne, for instance, Duccio abandoned the strict symmetry and deep colors of the more traditional Byzantine works and substituted cool, silvery lilacs, pinks, and light blues, which give the painting a softer and more decorative appearance than was common. This decorativeness is further accentuated by the dancing gold line that traces the hem and opening of the Virgin's mantle.

The "Maestà"

The *Maestà*, Duccio's masterpiece, is fully documented. It was commissioned on Oct. 9, 1308, for the main altar of the Cathedral in Siena and was carried in triumph from Duccio's studio to the Cathedral on June 9, 1311. Between these dates there are several documents of payment and admonitions to the artist to work faster. The *Maestà* is painted on both sides. The front depicts the Madonna enthroned in majesty with saints and angels. In the predella, spandrels, and pinnacles are scenes from

"The Three Marys at the Tomb," one of the panels of the back of Duccio's Maestà. *The work is in the Museo dell'Opera del Duomo, Siena. (Alinari-Anderson)*

the life of the Virgin and portraits of the Prophets. The back is decorated with small panels depicting the life and Passion of Christ.

The *Maestà* is splendid with gold leaf and rich colors. The design of the front is conventional, with the Madonna enthroned, flanked by regular ranks of saints and angels. Duccio did, however, substitute a solid blue mantle for the gold-feathered mantle of the typical Byzantine Madonna and painted a marble Cosmatesque throne in place of the Byzantine wooden throne. As in the *Rucellai Madonna,* the hem and opening of the Virgin's mantle are traced with a sinuously moving gold line. In the narrative scenes on both front and back, Duccio evolved a remarkably accurate figure-setting relationship which created convincing environments for the figures to move through.

Other Works

Other paintings generally attributed to Duccio include a half-length *Madonna and Child* for S. Cecilia in Crevole. This work, which is totally within the Byzantine style, is usually dated before the *Rucellai Madonna,* that is, before 1285, and is therefore Duccio's earliest extant work. The *Madonna and Franciscans,* dating from between the *Rucellai Madonna* and the *Maestà,* perhaps about 1300, is a charming small panel with many of the stylistic characteristics found in Duccio's larger pictures. A *Madonna Enthroned* in Bern dates from the same period as the *Madonna and Franciscans.* Other works include a half-length *Madonna* in Brussels, a half-length *Madonna* in Perugia, and a triptych in London. A polyptych with the half-length Madonna flanked by saints in Siena may be wholly or partly painted by Duccio. Duccio's pupils and followers adhered closely to his style, a fact that has created unusual difficulty for connoisseurs.

Further Reading

Duccio is listed in the Art study guide (III, A, 1). The masters of Sienese Gothic painting were Simone MARTINI and Pietro and Ambrogio LORENZETTI. In Florence, CIMABUE opened the way for the fully developed Gothic style of GIOTTO.

The best available monograph on Duccio is in Italian, Cesare Brandi, *Duccio* (1951). There is nothing comparable in English. Enzo Carli's book for the Astra Aréngarium Series, *Duccio* (1952), is available in English and includes a remarkable amount of information; the reproductions are poor. Evelyn Sandburg-Vavalà's chapters on Duccio and his school in *Sienese Studies: The Development of the School of Painting of Siena* (1953) are excellent for an understanding and appreciation of Duccio's art.

DUCHAMP / By Moira Roth

The French painter Marcel Duchamp (1887–1968) asked questions about the importance and nature of art and the artist and challenged conventional ideas of originality. He was a major influence on 20th-century art.

Marcel Duchamp (pronounced dü-shäN′) was born on July 28, 1887, the son of a notary of Rouen. One of Marcel's brothers, Gaston, known as Jacques Villon, was a painter; another brother, Raymond Duchamp-Villon, was a sculptor. Duchamp moved to Paris at the age of 17 and began to paint. By 1911 he was responding in his painting to cubism, but his subjects were unusually personal and psychologically complex compared to the typical cubist ones.

Scandal of the Armory Show

In his famous *Nude Descending a Staircase, No. 2* (1912) Duchamp used a limited cubist palette and faceting of forms but completely contradicted the cubist esthetic in his choice of an ironic title and stress on actual movement. When this painting was exhibited at the Armory Show in New York City in 1913, it created an uproar and was the focal point for derogatory criticism of the show (one critic described the work as "an explosion in a shingle factory").

In 1912–1913 a radical change took place in both Duchamp's life and art. Together with the writer Guillaume Apollinaire and the painter Francis Picabia, he began working out a highly original and mocking concept of art. Duchamp sought out methods of making art in

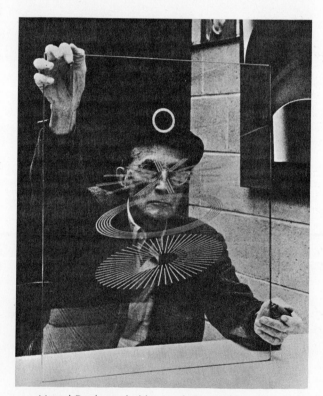

Marcel Duchamp holds a study for a section of the Bride Stripped Bare by Her Bachelors, Even (the Large Glass), executed 1915–1923. The section shown is entitled "Oculist Witnesses." (Library of Congress, Photo by Petersburg Press, London)

which the artist's hand would not be stressed (using chance and mechanical methods of drawing and painting). Increasingly language and the nonvisual side of art became important to him. As he later said: "I am interested in ideas—not merely the visual products. I want to put painting once again to the service of the mind."

Inventor of Ready-Mades

In 1913 Duchamp created his first "ready-made," the *Bicycle Wheel*. This was the first of a limited number of everyday objects which Duchamp chose (sometimes making minor additions), rather than made by hand. In these he questioned conventional ideas about the artist's role in the creation of art and about original and unique artistic products, and he brought up issues as to the value of art, the art market, and the art gallery. In the next few years he turned out a small number of ready-mades; the most famous was his *Fountain*, which shocked the American public in 1917 when they saw an ordinary urinal displayed in an art exhibition.

About 1915 Duchamp began work on a construction on glass, the *Bride Stripped Bare by Her Bachelors, Even*, commonly called the *Large Glass*. It was left incomplete in 1923, and the glass was cracked in 1926. Duchamp used many original and complex processes in its physical creation. The strange mechanical forms in it make up an intricate machine whose workings express his autobiographical experiences and views on sexual and emotional relations and contain many occult references, including alchemist symbolism.

In 1915 Duchamp went to America, where he immediately became part of the New York artistic scene. After World War I he divided his time between New York and Europe. He mixed briefly with the Dadaists in Paris but increasingly withdrew from actual artistic production. By 1923 he was preoccupied with chess. Occasionally he would experiment in kinetic art or create a new ready-made.

His Influence

For many years Duchamp had an underground reputation, with few exhibitions of his works. The leader of the surrealists, André Breton, and others made him into a legendary hero whose life and character were as important as his actual artistic productions. Duchamp lived an apparently contented private life, with a happy second marriage in 1954, and he maintained amicable if slightly ironic contacts with many contemporary artists. Only in the 1960s did he become internationally famous on a public level, when many American artists sought him out in New York and studied his works and ideas, because for them he was a far more important figure, with more contemporary relevance, than Pablo Picasso.

Further Reading

Marcel Duchamp is listed in the Art study guide (III, J, 1, e). He was affiliated with the Dada and surrealist movements, although he cannot be classified under either. Artists who belonged to both groups were Max ERNST, Jean ARP, and Man RAY. Duchamp's brother was Raymond DUCHAMP-VILLON.

Nude Descending a Staircase, No. 2 *(1912) by Duchamp. The artist called the work, executed in watercolor, ink, crayon, and pastel, on a photographic base, a "chromatography." (Philadelphia Museum of Art, Louise and Walter Arensberg Collection)*

There are a number of brilliant earlier articles on Duchamp, but the first long study is Robert Lebel, *Marcel Duchamp* (trans. 1959). It is a moving, somewhat fragmentary, and poetic account of Duchamp, written by a longtime friend. More readable, though less thoughtful, is a succinct chapter on Duchamp in Calvin Tomkins, *The Bride and the Bachelors: The Heretical Courtship in Modern Art* (1965). Arturo Schwarz, *The Complete Works of Marcel Duchamp* (1969), is a lavishly illustrated study by Duchamp's Milanese dealer and friend.

DUCHAMP-VILLON / By Robert Reiff

The French sculptor Raymond Duchamp-Villon (1876–1918) was one of the pioneers of the modern movement in sculpture.

Raymond Duchamp-Villon (pronounced dü-shäN′ vē-yôN′) was born on Nov. 5, 1876, the second of the six children of a notary in Rouen. Christened Raymond Duchamp, he changed his name to distinguish himself from his artist brothers: Gaston, who took the name of Jacques Villon, and Marcel Duchamp. Their father encouraged them to follow careers of their own choosing. All were drawn to art, and each was given a small stipend for support.

Duchamp-Villon went to Paris to study medicine, but by 1898 he had turned to sculpture. He was essentially self-taught. His first work, which showed the influence of Auguste Rodin, was of such high quality that he was admitted to the Salon of the prestigious Societé Nationale des Beaux-Arts in 1901. His sculpture then changed, away from Rodin's earthy humanitarianism toward a neoclassicism in the manner of Aristide Maillol and Charles Despiau. In 1911 Duchamp-Villon executed a head, *Baudelaire*, that owed nothing to Rodin and was far more stylized than anything by Maillol or Despiau. Forms are faceted and simplified and yet without any loss of likeness. The severity of the contours, indeed the conception as a whole, recalls ancient Egyptian portrait busts, except with the *Baudelaire* there is an intensity of expression. Equally laconic, bare, and compact is Duchamp-Villon's bust *Maggy* (1912). His *Lovers* (1913), a plaster relief with a conventional theme, reveals further trends toward abstraction.

About this time Duchamp-Villon embraced cubism as an expression of the avant-garde rather than for its post-Cézanne constructivism. His bronze *Seated Woman* (1914) indicates his concern with increasing abstraction. The bronze *Horse* (1914) shows a radical new approach. This sculpture, despite its title, resembles a turbine or some other power-producing machine. In this respect it is closer in spirit to Italian futurism than to cubism. Duchamp-Villon knew the futurist artist Umberto Boccioni personally and was probably influenced by him. *Horse*, built on a spirallike composition, suggests involuted layers, which gather into a concentration of dynamic, aggressive energy.

Duchamp-Villon served in the army during World War I. He contracted blood poisoning and died at a military hospital in Cannes on Oct. 17, 1918.

Further Reading

Raymond Duchamp-Villon is listed in the Art study guide (III, K, 1, a). He was influenced by Auguste RODIN, Aristide MAILLOL, and Umberto BOCCIONI. Other cubist sculptors were Jacques LIPCHITZ and Alexander ARCHIPENKO. Duchamp-Villon's brother was Marcel DUCHAMP.

The most recent work on Duchamp-Villon is William C. Agee, *Raymond Duchamp-Villon, 1876–1918* (1968), the catalog for an exhibition held at Knoedler's; it contains an excellent bibliography. The Solomon R. Guggenheim Museum published *Jacques Villon, Raymond Duchamp-Villon, Marcel Duchamp* (1956), an exhibition catalog with a short text by James Johnson Sweeney. Discussions of Duchamp-Villon's work can be found in Carola Giedion-Welcker, *Contemporary Sculpture: An*

Raymond Duchamp-Villon, a painting by his brother Jacques Villon, in the Musée National d'Art Moderne, Paris. (Giraudon)

Evolution in Volume and Space (1955; 2d ed. 1961); Jean Selz, *Modern Sculpture: Origins and Evolution* (trans. 1963); and Eduard Trier, *Form and Space: The Sculpture of the Twentieth Century* (trans. 1961).

DUDLEY / By Carl E. Prince

Thomas Dudley (1576–1653), a Puritan leader of the Massachusetts Bay Colony in America, was four times elected governor of the colony.

Thomas Dudley was born in England. Little is known about his formative years except that he was an orphan and was befriended by people who saw that he was educated and placed in service to the English nobility. He rose to the post of steward to the Earl of Lincoln and took pride for having recouped the earl's diminishing fortune by raising tenant rents.

Dudley, converted to the Puritan belief by John Cotton, his pastor in England, came into contact with other emergent Puritans. By 1629 he was one of the small group who founded the Massachusetts Bay Company. Along with John Winthrop and other "persons of worth and qualitie," he became one of the eight shareholders in the company who arrived in the New World in 1630.

Dudley was second only to Winthrop among the leaders who made the crossing; once arrived, they assumed control of the new society. The former steward was now one of the "first magistrates of the Bay Company." Persecuted in the Old World, perhaps Dudley, more than the other oligarchs, became righteous and narrow in the New. "In Calvinism," historian Bernard Bailyn notes, men like Dudley "found doctrines that might be applied to every aspect of life."

For Dudley, at least, this proved all too true. He hoarded corn and lent it to his neighbors with the understanding that he would receive 10 bushels for every 7 1/2 lent; John Winthrop considered Dudley's practices usurious. Historian Edmund Morgan notes that "Dudley was a rigid, literal minded type, ready to exact his pound of flesh whenever he thought it due him." Yet, Dudley had his place in the development of the colony. He was 13 times deputy governor and was elected governor on 4 different occasions.

As might be expected, Dudley was no less rigid and fanatical in religious matters than in matters political and economic. The notorious expulsion of Roger Williams in 1635 was Dudley's most celebrated effort to thwart what he considered to be Winthrop's leniency in religious matters. Dudley also figured prominently in the persecution of Anne Hutchinson, who followed Williams into exile largely because of Dudley's allegations of her heresy. A strong believer in the political power of the oligarchy, and to his dying day (July 31, 1653) almost paranoid on the question of religious heresy, he was nevertheless a remarkable man, part of that first generation of New World Puritans who alone were able to keep the faith.

Further Reading

Thomas Dudley is listed in the American History study guide (II, B, 1, b). John COTTON and John WINTHROP were also leaders of the Massachusetts Bay Colony.

There is an excellent analysis of Dudley in Edmund S. Morgan, *The Puritan Dilemma: The Story of John Winthrop*, edited by Oscar Handlin (1958). James Truslow Adams, *The Founding of New England* (1921), remains useful in placing Dudley in his colonial setting.

✳ ✳ ✳

DUFAY / By Tom R. Ward

The works of the Netherlandish composer Guillaume Dufay (ca. 1400–1474) marked the beginning of the Renaissance and influenced the course of music during the 15th and 16th centuries.

Born probably in the province of Hainaut in what is now Belgium, Guillaume Dufay (pronounced dü-fā′) received his musical training at the cathedral school of Cambrai under Nicholas Malin and Richard

Loqueville (1409–ca. 1419). One of Loqueville's three-voice works is preserved in a four-voice arrangement by Dufay. Cambrai was famous for its cathedral school and for its bishop, Pierre d'Ailly, one of the more influential figures in the Church at this time, who was also chancellor of the University of Paris. Dufay may have been in his retinue during the bishop's stay at the Council of Constance (1414–1418).

This gathering of churchmen from all over Europe may have been the occasion of Dufay's introduction to his first Italian patrons, the Malatesta family. He was in Rimini at the court of the Malatestas in 1419/1420; the works he wrote for members of the family date from this time until 1426.

Between 1426 and 1428 Dufay was in Cambrai. A chanson, *Adieu ces bon vins de Lannoys*, dated 1426 in a contemporary manuscript, may indicate a stay in Laon, a city in which he would hold two benefices in 1430. In 1428 he went to Italy to become a member of the papal chapel, where he remained until 1433. After 2 years in Savoy and Cambrai, Dufay returned to serve in the papal chapel until 1437. During this period his name moves from ninth to first position in the lists of singers.

In his remaining years Dufay's activities can be traced only with difficulty. He is known to have spent much of this time in Cambrai, especially after 1445. According to his will, he also spent at least 5 more years at the court of Savoy. The duchy of Savoy under Louis and his wife, Anne of Cyprus, boasted one of the best chapels in Europe. It appears that during Dufay's later stay in Savoy he received a degree in law from the University of Turin.

Guillaume Dufay (left) with Gilles Binchois, a miniature from the 15th-century manuscript of Martin le Franc's Le Champion des dames *in the Bibliothèque Nationale, Paris. (Giraudon)*

An incomplete motet, *Juvenis qui puellam,* jokingly portrays the disputation required of a degree candidate.

Dufay became a canon at St. Waltrudis in Mons in 1446, having also received a canonicate in Cambrai in 1436. At St. Waltrudis he met the composer Gilles Binchois, who was a canon there. Dufay also had some connection with the Burgundian court in this period since he is named as a member of the chapel of the Duke of Burgundy in a document that is not, however, from that court. The title may have been an honorary one since Dufay's presence there cannot be documented.

The last 30 years of Dufay's life were centered on the Cathedral at Cambrai. Archival documents from the Cathedral contain references to the copying of his music and, on at least one occasion, to the payment to him of 60 écus for having enriched the services with his music. His fame was widespread; for example, in 1458 he was invited to Besançon to arbitrate a dispute over the mode of an antiphon, and later Piero de' Medici referred to Dufay as the ornament of his age. He died in Cambrai on Nov. 27, 1474.

Dufay's will, which is preserved, indicates that he achieved considerable material success in life. He made bequests of artworks, music books, and money to various individuals and institutions, including the bequest of four music books to Charles the Bold of Burgundy. He also requested the performance of some of his own music in his last hour and for his last rites. The motet he specified, *Ave Regina caelorum,* is preserved and has, in addition to the traditional text, a plea for "mercy on thy dying Dufay," indicating that he probably composed it for this purpose. The Requiem Mass he asked to have performed is the earliest polyphonic setting of this service; it has not been preserved.

Dufay achieved a synthesis of the different national styles of the early 15th century. His earliest works are naturally French in nature, but those written in the 1420s show the strong impression the flowing vocal lines of Italian music made on the young composer. This is especially true in his setting of Petrarch's *Vergine bella.* The works of the late 1420s and 1430s give evidence of possible contact with English music and its "sweet sound" of thirds, sixths, and full triads. This mature style is the beginning of the international style of the Renaissance, and it is the music that the theorist Johannes Tinctoris (ca. 1476) calls the "new art . . . whose fount and origin is held to be among the English, of whom Dunstable stood forth as chief. Contemporary with him in France were Dufay and Binchois, to whom directly succeeded the moderns Ockeghem, Busnois, Regis and Caron." The poet Martin le Franc in his *Le Champion des dames* (1441–1442) writes that Dufay "has taken the English countenance and follows Dunstable."

More than 200 compositions by Dufay have been preserved. These include all genres common at the time: Mass Ordinaries, both individual movements and cycles, Mass Propers, motets, and minor liturgical works, as well as French chansons and settings of Italian texts. He used the older isorhythmic technique, but only for festival motets where this older technique would carry a certain connotation suitable to the occasion. He was among the earliest Continental composers to compose cyclic Mass Ordinaries and one of the first to use a secular *cantus firmus* (in the Mass *Se la face ay pale*). He also composed a cycle of hymns for the Church year. In these works one finds the "sweet sound" of thirds, sixths, and full triads and classic examples of fauxbourdon. His chansons, datable in all periods of his creative life, show the changes in style taking place in the 15th century; changes in conception of melody, harmony, and metric flow gradually occur from the earliest to the latest of these works. His style, a fusion of features of French, Italian, and English music of the 1420s, becomes the starting point for composers whose line extends into the 16th century.

Further Reading

Guillaume Dufay is listed in the Music study guide (I, B, 2). He and John DUNSTABLE were the last great masters of the isorhythmic motet. Johannes OCKEGHEM wrote a Mass *Caput* inspired by Dufay's cycle on the same tune.

The best treatment of Dufay's life and work and his position in history is in Gustave Reese, *Music in the Renaissance* (1954; rev. ed. 1959).

DUFF / By Hans Hoekendijk

The Scottish Presbyterian missionary Alexander Duff (1806–1878) was a pioneer of Christian education in India and a foremost leader of the world missionary movement of his day.

Alexander Duff was born in Moulin on April 25, 1806, into a pious family. He was a brilliant student at St. Andrews University. He was ordained in 1829 and immediately volunteered for missionary service in India. The first foreign missionary of the Church of Scotland, Duff stayed in India until 1863, although his term of service was twice interrupted by long furloughs (1834–1839) and 1850–1855) necessitated by overwork and ill health. During his stays in Scotland, he organized the home base and tried to lay a firm foundation for the work overseas.

Duff was firmly convinced that education was the key to responsible missionary work and nation building. Without minimizing the vital importance of a whole network of vernacular primary schools, he focused his attention on higher education in English. When the time came to present the Gospel to the Indian people, Duff chose to work with the upper caste (Brahmin) because he planned for the creation of an Indian Christian elite who would be well versed in Eastern philosophy, Western science, and the Christian faith. Eventually a small group of high quality was expected to become the source of the evangelization of the Indian subcontinent.

Alexander Duff at age 30. (Library of Congress)

Duff called this the "downward filter theory." It was also intended to be one of the creative forces toward the modernization of Indian community life. Duff had the support of the best-known early Indian reformer, Raja Ram Mohun Roy, and was influential in the educational reforms of the British colonial government (1833 and 1854).

As a missionary, Duff hoped that this new style of education might "undermine" Hindu society. For him, non-Christian religion was, before anything else, a matter of ignorance. His method did not produce large numbers of converts, but the 33 who were converted during his work in India became founders of outstanding Christian families. Also as a result of his work, a number of Protestant colleges were founded in India.

After returning to Scotland, Duff continued to work out "a grand strategy of the Kingdom of God." He called for the establishment of chairs of missions in theological schools and in 1867 became the first professor of missions in a Protestant institution (New College, Edinburgh). He also planned a training institute for missionaries and a scientific journal for dealing with all aspects of the Christian world task. He died on Feb. 12, 1878, having won wide acclaim for his work.

Further Reading

Alexander Duff is listed in the Religion study guide (I, P, 1, i). Thomas CHALMERS, who taught Duff at St. Andrews University, exerted a great influence on him. William CAREY was an earlier Protestant missionary to India.

The standard biography of Duff remains George Smith, *Life of Alexander Duff* (1879). For his missionary policy see Duff's *India and Indian Missions* (1839).

DUGDALE / By Richard C. Clark

The English-born American sociologist Richard Louis Dugdale (1841–1883), one of the first investigators to study familial feeblemindedness and criminality, is chiefly known as the author of "The Jukes."

Richard Dugdale was born in Paris of English parentage. He came to New York City with his parents in 1851, where he attended the public schools until, at the age of 14, having shown some ability in drawing, he was employed briefly as a sculptor. At the age of 17 he went with his parents to live on a farm in Indiana. Unable to perform manual labor because of heart trouble, Dugdale learned shorthand. In 1860 he obtained employment as a stenographer in New York City.

Dugdale attended night school at Cooper Union. He developed an overriding interest in sociological questions and was determined to be a social investigator. Since he lacked the academic degrees necessary for a university position, he entered business to accumulate enough money to allow him to pursue such a career.

In 1868 Dugdale became a member of the executive committee of the Prison Association of New York and 6 years later was appointed a committee of one to investigate 13 county jails. Struck by the consanguinity of many of the criminals, he used private funds to make a detailed study of one large family connection, "the Jukes," a fictitious name for a real family. The results of the research were published in 1875 as a Prison Association report, entitled *The Jukes: A Study in Crime, Pauperism, Disease, and Heredity*. The publication created a popular uproar, especially in the press. It was republished in 1877, together with his *Further Studies of Criminals*.

Dugdale believed that the results of his research indicated that heredity was of more importance than environment as a limiting factor in determining character and behavior, although at the same time he tried to give proper emphasis to environment. As evidence, he cited statistics relating to "the Jukes family." He discovered that of 709 persons (540 of "Jukes" blood and 169 of other strains connected to the family by marriage or cohabitation) 180 had been in the poorhouse or received relief for a total of 800 years, 140 had been convicted of criminal offenses, 60 had been habitual thieves, 7 had been murdered, 50 had been common prostitutes, 40 women venereally diseased had infected at least 440 persons, and there had been 30 prosecutions over bastardy. All this had cost the state a minimum of $1,308,-000.

Most of Dugdale's assumptions and conclusions about

hereditary degeneracy are no longer accepted. What Dugdale had discerned is today known as "the poverty cycle" or "culture of poverty," and is believed to be the result of environment, not heredity. The value of his work was that it greatly stimulated discussion and controversy in areas which were much in need of investigation, and on which no unanimous agreement is yet in sight.

In 1880 Dugdale became the first secretary of the Society for Political Education. He was also a member of many sociological and civic organizations, wrote for scholarly reviews, and addressed leading scientific associations, particularly on criminology. The discovery of Dugdale's original manuscript in 1911, revealing the true names of the family, enabled Arthur H. Estabrook to make his comparative study, *The Jukes in 1915* (1916).

Further Reading

Richard Dugdale is listed in the Social Sciences study guide (VI, D, 3). The sociologist Franklin GIDDINGS wrote the introduction for the 1900 edition of *The Jukes*.
Arthur H. Estabrook, *The Jukes in 1915* (1916), contains a memoir of Dugdale and his work. See also George Haven Putnam, *Memories of a Publisher, 1865–1915* (1915; 2d ed. 1916).

✳   ✳   ✳

DUHEM / By Fredric Cheyette

The French physicist, chemist, and historian of science Pierre Maurice Marie Duhem (1861–1916) published work in thermodynamics, physical chemistry, hydrodynamics, elasticity, electricity and magnetism, and the history and philosophy of science.

Pierre Duhem (pronounced dü-ĕm′) was born on June 9, 1861, in Paris. He entered the École Normale in 1882 and qualified for a teaching certificate in 1885. His first published paper on physical chemistry appeared in 1884. That year he also presented a doctoral dissertation in physics, which attacked the "maximum-work principle" of Marcelin Berthelot, a powerful figure in the French academic world. Berthelot succeeded in having the thesis rejected and is reported to have said that Duhem would never teach in Paris. The prediction came true.

Duhem stayed at the École Normale for another 2 years and in 1888 presented a doctorate in mathematics on the theory of magnetism. Meanwhile he published his first thesis and 30 articles on physics and chemistry. In 1887 he was named lecturer at Lille, but in 1893, after a fight with the dean of the faculty, he was transferred to Rennes and in 1894 to Bordeaux. There he remained for the rest of his life, deprived of the position at the

Science Faculty in Paris to which his work would seem to have entitled him. He died at Cabrespine on Sept. 14, 1916.

Duhem believed that physical theories describe, condense, and classify experimental results rather than explain them. He also believed that physical theories evolve by successive changes to conform to experiment and thus gradually approach a "natural classification" that somehow reflects underlying reality. These philosophical ideas led him after 1895 to investigate the history of science, especially in the Middle Ages and Renaissance. His *Studies on Leonardo da Vinci* (3 vols., 1906–1909) revealed the works of medieval scholastics in physics and astronomy that Leonardo had used. He explored these works in *The System of the World* (10 vols., 1913–1959). Although Duhem approached his subject almost exclusively from the point of view of the ancient and medieval contribution to modern science, this history ranks him as the rediscoverer of medieval science.

As a chemist, Duhem contributed to the Gibbs-Duhem equation, which describes the relation between variations of chemical potentials. From 1884 until 1900 and after 1913 his work was predominantly concerned with thermodynamics and electromagnetism; from 1900 to 1906 he concentrated on hydrodynamics and elasticity. Trained before the discovery of radioactivity, Duhem opposed those scientists who sought a mechanical explanation of the universe through the use of atomic and

Pierre Duhem.

molecular models. He believed that classical mechanics was a special case of a more general continuum theory and spent much of his career working on a generalized thermodynamics that would serve as a descriptive theory for all of physics and chemistry. He expressed his views most fully in his *Treatise on Energetics* (2 vols., 1911).

Further Reading

Pierre Duhem is listed in the Social Sciences study guide (VII, A, 2). His views on the nature of physical theories are similar to those of Henri POINCARÉ.

A study by Stanley L. Jaki of Duhem's life and work appears as the introductory essay to Duhem's *To Save the Phenomena: An Essay on the Idea of Physical Theory from Plato to Galileo* (trans. 1969). Armand Lowinger, *The Methodology of Pierre Duhem* (1941), is a full-length study of Duhem's work.

*　　*　　*

DUKE / By James I. Robertson, Jr.

James Buchanan Duke (1856–1925), American industrialist and philanthropist, was the first giant of finance to emerge in the post–Civil War South.

James B. Duke. (Duke University)

James B. Duke was born on Dec. 23, 1856, on a small farm near Durham, N.C., the younger son of Washington Duke. Union troops during the Civil War so ravaged their farm that at war's end, when Washington Duke returned from service in the Confederate Army, the family had to begin anew with total assets of 50 cents and two blind mules. The discovery of a small load of tobacco that had somehow escaped capture by Union forces triggered their rise to wealth. This supply sold so quickly that the Dukes began production and distribution on a large scale. By 1872, at the height of the South's impoverishment, the family was selling 125,000 pounds of tobacco annually.

When, in 1881, the Dukes began to manufacture cigarettes, business boomed. Three years later, with James in control, the company moved its executive offices to New Jersey to take advantage of that state's liberal corporation laws and to exploit the virgin markets of the North and West. Thereafter, the business grew into an international combine as Duke pursued monopolistic methods. Rebates, discrimination, a nationwide secret service, bulldozer tactics against competitors, and price manipulations marked the long "Tobacco War," by which Duke gained complete ascendancy over all rivals.

By 1904 Duke's American Tobacco Company controlled 90 percent of the national market and at least 50 percent of the foreign trade in tobacco. With unlimited power and a capitalization of over $500,000,000, the Duke trust was so powerful that a 1911 Supreme Court decree ordering their monopoly be dissolved had little effect on the company's prosperity.

Duke also developed an interest in the potential of electrical power. In 1905 he organized the Southern (now Duke) Power and Light Company. Within 25 years this utility was "capable of producing more energy than all the slaves of the Old South."

Duke contributed large sums to hospitals and churches. His last notable act was the establishment of the Duke Endowment on behalf of a small Methodist school, Trinity College. He donated more than $60,000,000 toward the creation of a new campus characterized by large buildings of Gothic design. The school was renamed Duke University.

The tall, rugged, redheaded industrialist died on Oct. 10, 1925. Once asked the secret of his success, Duke replied simply, "I had confidence in myself."

Further Reading

James B. Duke is listed in the American History study guide (VIII, D, 2). Other major industrialists of the period included Harvey FIRESTONE and Henry FORD.

John W. Jenkins, *James B. Duke, Master Builder* (1927), and John K. Winkler, *Tobacco Tycoon: The Story of James Buchanan Duke* (1942), give sympathetic treatments of Duke. See also Meyer Jacobstein, *The Tobacco Industry in the United States* (1907), and Nannie May Tilley, *The Bright-Tobacco Industry, 1860–1929* (1948).

*　　*　　*

DULLES / By Dexter Perkins

John Foster Dulles (1888–1959), American diplomat, was secretary of state under Eisenhower. He strove to create a United States policy of "containing" communism.

John Foster Dulles was born in Washington, D.C., on Feb. 25, 1888. His grandfather, John W. Foster, had been secretary of state under Benjamin Harrison, and his uncle, Robert Lansing, had been secretary of state under Woodrow Wilson. Educated at Princeton and the law school of George Washington University, Dulles joined the international law firm of Sullivan and Cromwell in 1911, became a partner in 1920, and was head of the firm in 1927. He was eminent in his field.

Dulles's interest in foreign affairs was of long standing; at the age of 31, he had attended the 1919 Paris Peace Conference as legal counsel to the American delegation. In 1945 he was appointed legal adviser to the United States delegation at the San Francisco conference which drew up the Charter of the United Nations.

A Republican, Dulles served in the U.S. Senate in 1949–1950. In 1951, as ambassador-at-large, he negotiated a peace treaty with Japan, acquitting himself brilliantly in overcoming Soviet opposition and other difficulties.

In 1952 Dulles was an ardent partisan of Dwight D. Eisenhower for president and was rewarded the next year

John Foster Dulles, photographed in 1957. (U.S. Navy Department)

with the office of secretary of state, which he held until his death. In his first months in office Dulles brought about an armistice in the Korean War, probably by the threat of the resumption of the war if the negotiations did not succeed. Less successful was his effort to roll back the Iron Curtain: in the East German revolt of 1953 and the Hungarian revolt of 1956 the United States was unable to offer any support to the rebels.

Dulles was a firm supporter of the North Atlantic Treaty Organization and supported the proposal for an international defense force in Europe. This project failed, however, and it was Anthony Eden, rather than Dulles, who played the leading role in forging a new treaty that invigorated the European alliance and admitted Germany to full membership.

In 1955 came the Big Four Conference at Geneva, attended by the four heads of government—Eden of England, Edgar Faure of France, N. A. Bulganin of the U.S.S.R., and Eisenhower of the United States—with a view to bettering understanding with the Soviet Union. Dulles had a part in the proceedings, but little was accomplished. As a matter of fact, from the outset the secretary of state had regarded the project with pessimism.

In 1956 came one of the most serious crises of Dulles's career. In the summer of that year Gamal Abdel Nasser, the Egyptian dictator, seized and nationalized the Suez Canal, creating great resentment in France and Britain. Dulles labored manfully to find a peaceful solution of the problem, but in December the British and the French, using an Israeli attack on Egypt as a pretext, landed forces in the canal zone. With great courage Dulles protested this violation of the peace and brought the situation before the United Nations. As a result, the invaders were compelled to withdraw.

Dulles's activities were by no means confined to Europe. The United States played a part in the overthrow of a Communist regime in Guatemala. In the Far East, Dulles played a leading role in the formation of the Southeast Asia Treaty Organization, an alliance of the United States, Britain, France, Australia, New Zealand, the Philippines, Thailand, and Pakistan. This alliance did not explicitly call for armed action, but it bound the signatories to consult whenever the integrity of any country in Southeast Asia was menaced. Importantly, it marked the extension of United States commitments in this area. Dulles also signed a defense treaty with the Chinese Nationalist government on Taiwan (Formosa) and twice thwarted hostile attacks by the (Communist) Chinese People's Republic on the Nationalists' island of Quemoy. Dulles's attempt to bring together some of the countries of the Middle East in opposition to communism resulted in an alliance that soon disintegrated.

A believer in keeping firm opposition to the Communist menace, Dulles based his diplomacy on strong ideology. He was ready to use force or the threat of force (as in the Formosa Strait) when he believed that such action would balk aggression. His diplomacy was highly personal. He was not a great administrator, but he was a dedicated public servant. In the last year of his life he suffered from cancer, which he bore with real heroism. He died on May 24, 1959.

Further Reading

John Foster Dulles is listed in the American History study guide (X, A, 2 and 7). He was secretary of state under Dwight EISENHOWER. Other diplomats of the period included Dean ACHESON and Adlai STEVENSON.

Louis L. Gerson, *John Foster Dulles*, vol. 17 in Samuel F. Bemis and Robert H. Ferrell, eds., *The American Secretaries of State and Their Diplomacy* (1967), is recommended. See also John Robinson Beal, *John Foster Dulles* (1957); Roscoe Drummond and Gaston Coblentz, *Duel at the Brink: John Foster Dulles' Command of American Power* (1960); and Richard Goold-Adams, *John Foster Dulles: A Reappraisal* (1962).

✳ ✳ ✳

A. DUMAS / By Neal Oxenhandler

Alexandre Dumas (1803–1870), the prolific French author of plays, popular romances, and historical novels, wrote "The Three Musketeers" and "The Count of Monte Cristo."

Alexandre Dumas, a portrait by François Bellay in the château at Versailles. (Giraudon)

Alexandre Dumas (pronounced dü-mà′) is generally called Dumas *père* to distinguish him from his illustrious son Alexandre (known as Dumas *fils*), who was also a dramatist and novelist. The son of a Creole general of the French Revolutionary armies, Dumas was brought up by his mother in straitened circumstances after his father's death. While still young, he began to write "vaudeville" plays (light musical comedies) and then historical plays in collaboration with a friend, Adolphe de Leuven. Historical themes, as well as the use of a collaborator, were to be permanent aspects of Dumas's style throughout his career.

After reading William Shakespeare, Sir Walter Scott, Friedrich von Schiller, and Lord Byron and while employed as a secretary to the Duke of Orléans (later King Louis Philippe), Dumas wrote his first plays in 1825 and 1826. Others followed, with *Henri III et sa cour* (1829) bringing him great success and recognition. It seemed to the theatergoers of Dumas's time that here at last was serious theater which presented an alternative to effete neoclassical drama.

The Revolution of 1830 temporarily diverted Dumas from his writing, and he became an ardent supporter of the Marquis de Lafayette. His liberal activities were viewed unfavorably by the new king, his former employer, and he traveled for a time outside France. A series of amusing travel books resulted from this period of exile.

His Fiction

When Dumas returned to Paris, a new series of historical plays flowed from his pen. By 1851 he had written alone or in collaboration more than 20 plays, among the most outstanding of which are *Richard Darlington* (1831), *La Tour de Nesle* (1832), *Mademoiselle de Belle-Isle* (1839), and *La Reine Margot* (1845). He also began writing fiction at this time, first composing short stories and then novels. In collaboration with Auguste Maquet he wrote the trilogy: *Les Trois Mousquetaires* (1844; *The Three Musketeers*), *Vingt Ans après* (1845; *Twenty Years After*), and *Le Vicomte de Bragelonne* (1850). *Le Comte de Monte-Cristo* (1846; *The Count of Monte Cristo*) was also a product of this period.

Dumas had many collaborators (Auguste Maquet, Paul Lacroix, Paul Bocage, and P. A. Fiorentino, to name only a few), but it was undoubtedly with Maquet that he produced his best novels. He had assistants who supplied him with the outlines of romances whose original form he had already drawn up; then he wrote the work himself. The scale of his "fiction factory" has often been exaggerated. Although at least a thousand works were published under his own name, most were due to his own industry and the amazing fertility of his imagination. Dumas grasped at any possible subject; he borrowed plots and material from all periods and all countries, then transformed them with ingenuity. The historian Jules Michelet once wrote admiringly to him, "You are like a force of elemental nature."

Dumas does not penetrate deeply into the psychology of his characters; he is content to identify them by characteristic tags (the lean acerbity of Athos, the spunk of D'Artagnan) and hurl them into a thicket of wild and improbable adventures where, after heroic efforts, they will at last succumb to noble and romantic deaths. His heroes and heroines, strong-willed and courageous beings with sonorous names, are carried along in the rapid movement of the dramas, in the flow of adventure and suspenseful plots. Dumas adhered to no literary theory, except to write as the spirit moved him, which it did often.

Dumas's works were received with enthusiasm by his loyal readers, and he amassed a considerable fortune. It was not sufficient, however, to meet the demands of his extravagant way of life. Among his follies was his estate of Monte-Cristo in Saint-Germain-en-Laye, a Renaissance house with a Gothic pavilion, situated in an English garden. This estate housed a horde of parasitical guests and lady admirers who lived at the author's expense.

Later Life

Dumas, who had never changed his republican opinions, greeted the Revolution of 1848 with enthusiasm and even ran as a candidate for the Assembly. In 1850 the Théâtre-Historique, which he had founded to present his plays, failed. After the coup d'état in 1851 and the seizure of power by Napoleon III, Dumas went to Brussels, where his secretary managed to restore some semblance of order to his affairs; here he continued to write prodigiously.

In 1853 Dumas returned to Paris and began the daily paper *Le Mousquetaire*. It was devoted to art and literature, and in it he first published his *Mémoires*. The paper survived until 1857, and Dumas then published the weekly paper *Monte-Cristo*. This in turn folded after 3 years.

In 1858 Dumas traveled to Russia. He then joined Giuseppe Garibaldi in Sicily, and in 1860 Garibaldi named him keeper of museums in Naples. After remaining there for 4 years, he returned to Paris, where he found himself deep in debt and at the mercy of a host of creditors. His affairs were not helped by a succession of parasitical mistresses who expected—and received—lavish gifts from Dumas.

Working compulsively to pay his debts, Dumas produced a number of rather contrived works, among them *Madame de Chamblay* (1863) and *Les Mohicans de Paris* (1864), which were not received with great enthusiasm. His last years were softened by the presence of his son, Alexandre, and his devoted daughter, Madame Petel. He died in comparative poverty and obscurity on Dec. 5, 1870.

Further Reading

Alexandre Dumas is listed in the Literature study guide (III, G, 1). He was influenced by the historical novels of Sir Walter SCOTT.

A good introduction to the Dumas dynasty is André Maurois, *The Titans: A Three Generation Biography of the Dumas*, translated by Gerard Hopkins (1957). A. Craig Bell, *Alexandre Dumas: A Biography and Study* (1950), is a more serious and complete work. In a lighter vein is Herbert S. Gorman, *The Incredible Marquis: Alexandre Dumas* (1929). For a direct look at the source material, Jules E. Goodman, ed., *The Road to Monte-*

Cristo: A Condensation from the Memoirs of Alexandre Dumas (1956), is recommended.

J. B. DUMAS / By Robert F. Erickson

The French chemist Jean Baptiste André Dumas (1800–1884) worked in the field of organic chemistry and developed the "type" theory of organic structure.

On July 14, 1800, Jean Baptiste Dumas was born at Alais. In his youth he was apprenticed to an apothecary. In 1816 he moved to Geneva and studied physiological chemistry in the laboratory of A. Le Royer. In Geneva, Dumas met the famous scientist Alexander von Humboldt, who persuaded Dumas to move to Paris, where he would find greater scientific opportunities. This he did in 1823, and he was engaged as a lecture assistant in chemistry at the École Polytechnique; he became professor of chemistry in 1835. During this period Dumas began to work on his major book, *Treatise on Chemistry,* and he also participated in the founding of the Central School for Arts and Manufactures.

In 1830 Dumas challenged the so-called dualistic theory of the great Swedish chemist Jöns Jacob Berzelius. The dualistic theory stated that all compounds could be divided into positive and negative parts. Dumas presented instead a unitary theory which held that atoms of oppo-

Jean Baptiste Dumas. (Library of Congress)

site charges could be substituted in compounds without causing much alteration in the basic properties of the compound. This theory was related to his belief in families of organic compounds, in which substitutions could be made with the fundamental characteristics of the family remaining unchanged. At this time Berzelius was at the height of his eminence and would accept no affront to his authority; such was the strength of his attack on Dumas that the latter did not continue the dispute. Later researches proved Dumas to have been more correct in his theories than was the Swedish master.

Dumas isolated various essences and oils from coal tar; developed a method for measuring the amount of nitrogen in organic compounds, which made quantitative organic analysis possible; and developed a new method of determining vapor densities. He also concerned himself with determining the atomic weights of such elements as carbon and oxygen and published a new list of the weights of some 30 elements in 1858–1860.

In addition to his scientific achievements, Dumas led an active public life during the reign of Napoleon III. He was minister of agriculture and commerce and then minister of education. He was also a senator, master of the French mint, and president of the municipal council of Paris. His public life ended with the downfall of the Second Empire in 1871. Dumas died in 1884 in Paris.

Further Reading

Jean Baptiste Dumas is listed in the Science study guide (VI, D, 2). Other 19th-century European chemists were Jöns Jacob BERZELIUS, Louis PASTEUR, and Marie CURIE.

There is a chapter on Dumas by Georges Urbain, "Jean-Baptiste Dumas and Charles-Adolphe Wurtz," in Eduard Farber, ed., *Great Chemists* (1961). Particularly useful is James R. Partington's monumental four-volume *History of Chemistry* (1962–1969). The life and work of Dumas are discussed in Aaron J. Ihde, *The Development of Modern Chemistry* (1964), and Isaac Asimov, *A Short History of Chemistry* (1965).

P. L. DUNBAR / By Saunders Redding

Paul Laurence Dunbar (1872–1906), American poet and novelist, was the first black author to gain national recognition and a wide popular audience.

Born the son of a former slave in Dayton, Ohio, Paul Laurence Dunbar achieved a formal education through high school, graduating in 1891. He had served as editor of the school paper and as class poet. Unable to go to college, Dunbar worked as an elevator operator. He published his first book of poems, *Oak and Ivy*, in 1893 at his own expense, and his second, *Majors and Minors*, 2 years later. Seeing the sec-

Paul Laurence Dunbar. (Library of Congress)

ond book, William Dean Howells, then one of America's most distinguished literary critics, urged the young poet to concentrate on dialect verse.

With the publication of *Lyrics of Lowly Life*, for which Howells wrote a laudatory preface, Dunbar's professional career got an auspicious start. Demand for his work was soon sufficient to enable him to earn his living as a writer. He took Howell's advice to study the "moods and traits of his own race in its own accents of our English," so that his art was best shown in those "pieces which . . . described the range between appetite and emotion . . . which is the range of the race." (This was Howells's limited view of the Negro range.)

Dunbar wanted to satisfy the popular taste for the light, romantic, comic, and sentimental. His short stories, which began appearing in popular magazines in the 1890s, usually depict Negro folk characters, Southern scenes, and humorous situations. His first novel, *The Uncalled* (1898), like two of the three that followed—*The Love of Landry* (1900) and *The Fanatics* (1901)—is a sentimental tale about white people. These novels are competent but undistinguished. His last long fiction, *The Sport of the Gods* (1902), is notable only for his failure to realize the potential in the story of an agrarian black family's urbanization.

In 1898 Dunbar married Alice Moore; the marriage was unhappy, and the couple separated in 1901, when Dunbar went to Washington, D.C., as a consultant to the Library of Congress. He was unhappy with his writing too. At about this time he confided to a friend, "I see now very clearly that Mr. Howells has done me irrevocable harm in the dictum he laid down regarding my dialect verse."

Dunbar had contracted tuberculosis and tried all the "cures"; alcohol brought temporary relief, and he became addicted. He continued to turn out short stories and poems. Sick, and discouraged by the lukewarm reception of *The Heart of Happy Hollow* (1904), a collection of short stories, and of *Lyrics of Love and Sunshine* (1905), which contains some of his best verses in pure English, he returned to Dayton, where he died on Feb. 9, 1906. The *Complete Poems of Paul Laurence Dunbar* (1913; still in print) shows how well he succeeded in capturing many aspects of black life.

Further Reading

Paul Laurence Dunbar is listed in the Literature study guide (I, E, 1, b). Richard WRIGHT and Countee CULLEN were black writers of the next generation.

Two full-length biographies of Dunbar are Benjamin Brawley, *Paul Laurence Dunbar: Poet of His People* (1936), and the better-balanced *Paul Laurence Dunbar and His Song* (1947) by Virginia Cunningham. Jean Gould, *That Dunbar Boy* (1958), is for children. Dunbar gets brief treatment in Sterling A. Brown, Arthur P. Davis, and Ulysses Lee, *Negro Caravan* (1941); Hugh M. Gloster, *Negro Voices in American Fiction* (1948); and James A. Emanuel and Theodore L. Gross, *Dark Symphony* (1968).

✳   ✳   ✳

WILLIAM DUNBAR
/ By D. W. Robertson, Jr.

The Scottish poet and courtier William Dunbar (ca. 1460–ca. 1520) wrote satirical, occasional, and devotional works. Although he is conventionally numbered among the Scottish Chaucerians, he owed a great deal to the traditions of French poetry.

V ery little is known about William Dunbar's family or early life. He received a master of arts degree from St. Andrews University in 1479. In 1500 he was granted an annual pension of £10 by James IV, most likely in recognition for his services as a court poet. Dunbar was probably in England during the winter of 1501 in connection with the negotiations for the marriage between King James and Princess Margaret.

Dunbar's most famous poem is perhaps "The Thistle and the Rose," an allegory in the Chaucerian manner, probably written in 1502 to celebrate the impending marriage between James and Margaret. The poet took holy orders in 1504 and may have written "In May as that Aurora did upspring" at about this time. This poem, which is in the form of a debate between a merle and a

nightingale, celebrates love for God. The following years produced a number of occasional poems—one on the birth of Margaret's first child, petitions to the King for increased aid, and a satire on a court physician and alchemist.

In 1507 Dunbar's pension was increased to £20 and in 1510 to the substantial sum of £80. There is no record of the poet after the Battle of Flodden (1513), and he probably died a few years after that disaster for the Scottish court. During his last years he may have written his devotional poems, some of which, like the Christmas poem "Rorate celi desuper" and the aureate hymn to the Blessed Virgin "Hale, sterne superne, hale in eterne," are extremely effective.

Among Dunbar's more famous longer pieces is the satire *The Tretis of the Tua Mariit Wemen and the Wedo*. The poet overhears a nocturnal conversation among three attractive ladies whose tongues have been loosened by wine. The two married women describe the shortcomings of their husbands in very frank language, and the widow, who bears some resemblance to Chaucer's Wife of Bath, reveals her wiles. One of the more attractive moral pieces attributed to Dunbar, reminiscent of Chaucer's "Truth," is "Without glaidnes avalis no tresure," in which the poet assures his readers that if they are just and joyful, Truth will make them strong.

Further Reading

William Dunbar is listed in the Literature study guide (II, C, 1, b). His work shows the influence of Geoffrey CHAUCER.

The most useful editions of Dunbar's poems are *The Poems of William Dunbar,* edited by John Small (3 vols., 1884–1893), and *The Poems of William Dunbar,* edited by W. Mackay Mackenzie (1932). A volume of selected poems was edited by James Kinsley (1958). A careful biographical account of Dunbar based on the scanty evidence that survives is J. W. Baxter, *William Dunbar* (1952). The study by Tom Scott, *Dunbar: A Critical Exposition of the Poems* (1966), is stimulating but untrustworthy.

✳   ✳   ✳

WILLIAM DUNBAR / By Monte A. Calvert

William Dunbar (1749–1810), Scottish-born American scientist and planter, wrote the first topographical description of the Southwest.

W illiam Dunbar was born in Morayshire, Scotland, son of Sir Archibald Dunbar. After study at Glasgow he did advanced work in mathematics and astronomy in London until ill health forced him to seek a warmer climate. In 1771 he went to America and established a plantation in British West Florida with a partner. Plagued by misfortunes—a slave insurrection in 1775 and later plundering by Continental Army

William Dunbar. (Library of Congress)

soldiers—they moved in 1792 to what is now Mississippi to start a new plantation. Applying the principles of scientific agriculture, chemical treatment of the soil, improved models of plows and harrows, and special machinery for pressing and baling cotton, Dunbar made such a success of the venture that he bought out his partner and was able to devote much of his time to scientific investigation.

Like many 18th-century gentleman amateur scientists, Dunbar's interests included astronomy, botany, zoology, ethnology, and meteorology. Appointed surveyor general of the District of Natchez in 1798, he represented the Spanish government in determining the boundaries between Spanish and United States possessions in that area. Immediately thereafter he became a United States citizen and began making the first meteorological observations in the Mississippi Valley. Dunbar attracted the attention of Thomas Jefferson, with whom he corresponded and who secured his admission to the American Philosophical Society. In 1804 President Jefferson commissioned Dunbar to explore the Ouachita River country. In 1805 Dunbar was appointed to conduct similar explorations in the Red River valley.

Among Dunbar's scientific concerns were investigations of Indian sign language, fossil mammoth bones, and plant and animal life. On his plantation he operated an observatory equipped with the latest European astronomical instruments. His particular concern was the observation of rainbows, and he was the first to study the

elliptical type. One of his practical contributions was a method for finding longitude by a single observer, without knowledge of the time. His meteorological speculations included the theory that a region of calm exists within the vortex of a cyclone.

Dunbar corresponded with American and European scientists. He also served as chief justice on the Court of Quarter Sessions and as a member of the Mississippi territorial legislature. His most important writing was the first topographical description of the little-known southwestern territory. He died at his plantation in October 1810.

Further Reading

William Dunbar is listed in the Science study guide (VI, B, 3). Younger scientific contemporaries were Benjamin SILLIMAN and Nathaniel BOWDITCH.

The only biography of Dunbar is Frank L. Riley, *Sir William Dunbar: The Pioneer Scientist of Mississippi* (1899). Additional material on his life can be found in Eron Rowland, *Life, Letters and Papers of William Dunbar* (1930).

DUNCAN / By Stuart Samuels

The American dancer and teacher Isadora Duncan (1878–1927) is considered one of the founders of modern dance.

Isadora Duncan was born Dora Angela Duncan on May 27, 1878, in San Francisco. By the age of 6 Isadora was teaching neighborhood children to wave their arms, and by 10 she had developed a new "system" of dance with her sister Elizabeth, based on improvisation and interpretation. With her mother as accompanist and her sister as partner, Isadora taught dance and performed for the San Francisco aristocracy.

The Duncans went to Chicago and New York to advance their dancing careers. Disheartened by their reception in eastern drawing rooms, they departed for London. In Europe, Miss Duncan won recognition. She shocked, surprised, and excited her audience and became a member of the European intellectual avantgarde, returning triumphantly to America in 1908.

Miss Duncan attacked the system of classical ballet, which was based on movement through convention, and rejected popular theatrical dance for its superficiality. She encouraged all movement that was natural, expressive, and spontaneous. Conventional dance costumes were discarded in favor of scanty Greek tunics and no shoes to allow the greatest possible freedom of movement.

Experimenting with body movements, she concluded that all movements were derived from running, skipping, jumping, and standing. Dance was the "movement of the human body in harmony with the movements of the

Isadora Duncan, a photograph by Genthe. (Library of Congress)

earth." Inspired by Greek art, the paintings of Sandro Botticelli, Walt Whitman's poems, the instinctual movements of children and animals, and great classical music, she did not dance *to* the music as much as she danced *the* music. For her, the body expressed thoughts and feelings; each dance was unique, each movement created out of the dancer's innermost feelings. Her dances were exclusively female, celebrating the beauty and holiness of the female body and reflecting the emergence of the "new woman" of this period.

After World War I Miss Duncan traveled throughout Europe. Her first school (in Berlin, before the war) had collapsed for lack of funds. In 1921 she accepted the Soviet government's offer to establish a school in Moscow. But financial problems continued. Meanwhile, she married the poet Sergei Yesenin, 17 years her junior. When the couple came to America in 1924 at the height of the "Red scare," Miss Duncan was criticized for her "Bolshevik" dances. Returning to Russia, her husband committed suicide.

By 1925 Miss Duncan's life had been filled with tragedy. In 1913 her two illegitimate children had been accidently drowned; she had had a stillbirth; she now became disillusioned with the Soviet Union. She was famous but penniless, and the once beautiful dancer had become indolent and flabby. In 1927, while riding in an open sports car, her scarf caught in a wheel and she was strangled.

Isadora Duncan's death was mourned by many. She left no work that could be performed again, no school or teaching method, and few pupils, but with her new view of movement she had revolutionized dance.

Further Reading

Isadora Duncan is listed in the American History study guide (VIII, F, 6). Ruth ST. DENIS was another dance innovator.

There is no balanced assessment of Isadora Duncan's life. The best introduction is her own passionate and sensitive autobiography, *My Life* (1927). She has been eulogized by friends—see Mary Desti, *The Untold Story: The Life of Isadora Duncan, 1921–1927* (1929)—exposed by enemies, and sometimes appreciated by scholars. A scholarly but badly written biography is Ilya Schneider, *Isadora Duncan: The Russian Years* (1969). Recent, more dispassionate accounts are Allan Ross Macdougall, *Isadora: A Revolutionary in Art and Love* (1960), and Walter Terry, *Isadora Duncan: Her Life, Her Art, Her Legacy* (1964).

DUNMORE / By Hugh Rankin

John Murray, 4th Earl of Dunmore (1732–1809), was the British colonial governor of Virginia during the dramatic years preceding the American Revolution.

John Murray, descended from the French line of Stuarts, succeeded to his father's title in 1765. He also held the titles of Viscount Fincastle, Baron of Blair, Baron of Moulin, and Baron of Tillymount. In 1768 he married Lady Charlotte Stewart, daughter of the Earl of Galloway. Elected in 1761 as one of the 16 Scottish peers to sit in the British Parliament, he was reelected in 1768.

Lord Dunmore was appointed governor of New York in 1770 by Lord Hillsborough, British secretary of state for the Colonies. In 1771 he was promoted to governor of Virginia. He was well liked there, as he had been in New York. His newborn daughter was adopted by the Virginia colony, and two new counties, Fincastle and Dunmore, were named for him. His popularity began to wane in 1773, when he dissolved the House of Burgesses, which had proposed a procolonial committee of correspondence; he repeated that action the following year when the legislature proposed a day of fasting and prayer because of the new Boston Port Bill.

While visiting Virginia's northwest frontier, Dunmore constructed Ft. Dunmore at the forks of the Ohio. In 1774 he led the Virginians in what is often called Dunmore's War. When the Shawnee Indians went on the warpath, the southwest Virginia militia, under Col. Andrew Lewis, advanced down the Kanawha River, while Dunmore himself led another force from Ft. Dunmore. After Lewis defeated Chief Cornstalk, Dunmore negotiated a treaty with the Indians at Scioto. Generally applauded at the time, the governor was later accused of inciting the Indians to warfare and attempting to lead the militia into a trap.

As the colonial revolutionary movement gathered momentum, Dunmore lost what remained of his popularity. To forestall rebels, he removed the powder from the Williamsburg magazine in April 1774, but this action incited so much antagonism that he paid for the powder. In June threats on his life forced him to retreat to the frigate *Fowey*. In November he declared martial law and called upon slaves to desert their masters and join his "Royal Ethiopian" Regiment in return for their freedom.

On Dec. 9, 1775, Dunmore's loyalist troops were defeated by the colonials at Great Bridge. Retiring to his ships, Dunmore bombarded and burned Norfolk. In July 1776, after a conflict on Gwynn's Island, he returned to England.

Once again Dunmore was returned to Parliament as a Scottish representative. From 1787 to 1796 he served as governor of the Bahamas. He died on March 5, 1809, at Ramsgate, England.

Further Reading

Lord Dunmore is listed in the American History study guide (II, B, 3, b). Other colonial governors were Robert DINWIDDIE and Sir William BERKELEY.

There is no biography of Dunmore, although R. G. Thwaites and L. P. Kellog, *Documentary History of Dunmore's War* (1905), contains a good biographical sketch. Dunmore's American career is well covered in Thomas J. Wertenbaker, *Give Me Liberty: The Struggle*

Lord Dunmore. (Library of Congress)

for *Self-government in Virginia* (1958), and Clifford Dowdey, *The Golden Age: A Climate for Greatness—Virginia, 1732–1775* (1970).

DUNNE / By Robert Regan

> Finley Peter Dunne (1867–1936) was an American journalist. He is noted for his humorous sketches in which an Irish saloonkeeper named Mr. Dooley commented on current events.

Peter Dunne was born July 10, 1867, in Chicago, the fifth of seven children of an orthodox Catholic immigrant couple from Ireland. Peter (at 19 he added Finley to his name) graduated from high school in 1884. He covered sports and police courts for several newspapers, then became city editor of the *Chicago Times* when he was 21. Responsible positions on other papers followed. On the staff of the *Evening Post* in 1892, he met Mary Ives Abbott, a cultivated book reviewer for the *Post,* who recognized Dunne's promise and began to guide him. She introduced him to Chicago's select society.

In 1892 Dunne published his first sketch in Irish dialect in the *Post.* His protagonist, modeled upon a taciturn but witty saloonkeeper named James McGarry, was called Colonel McNerry. When the real saloonkeeper complained to Dunne's editor that McNerry sounded too much like McGarry, Dunne changed his character's name to Mr. Martin Dooley. Dunne's unsigned columns satirizing politics and society made Mr. Dooley a Chicago institution, and his fame spread to other cities. In 1898 one much-reprinted column turned Mr. Dooley into a national sensation. When Commodore George Dewey took Manila, Mr. Dooley celebrated the accomplishment of his "Cousin George"—"Dewey or Dooley, 'tis all th' same." In this piece Dunne caught the jubilant mood of victorious America, but subsequently he turned to critical satire when United States imperialism, showing its true colors, began the systematic subjugation of the Philippines. To the Filipinos, Dunne's imperialist says: "We'll treat ye th' way a father shud treat his childher if we have to break ivry bone in ye'er bodies. So come to our arms."

Publication of collections of Dooley sketches in book form began in 1898 with *Mr. Dooley in Peace and War* and continued roughly at the rate of one volume every 2 years for 2 decades.

In 1900 Dunne moved to New York. In 1902 he married Mrs. Abbott's daughter Margaret; they had four children. Dunne became associated with Lincoln Steffens and other "muckrakers" on the *American Magazine,* and he wrote for *Collier's* and several other magazines, but the articles in which he put Mr. Dooley aside and spoke in his own voice were never markedly successful. He died of cancer in New York City on April 24, 1936.

Finley Peter Dunne. (Wide World Photos)

Further Reading

Finley Peter Dunne is listed in the Literature study guide (I, D, 5). An earlier American humorist was Artemus WARD; James Russell LOWELL also wrote some witty dialect pieces.

Elmer Ellis, *Mr. Dooley's America: A Life of Finley Peter Dunne* (1941), contains Dunne's unfinished memoirs. For Dunne's place in the history of American humor see Walter Blair, *Horse Sense in American Humor* (1942). *The Autobiography of Lincoln Steffens* (1931) contains a contemporary sketch of Dunne.

DUNNING / By Robert C. Harris

The American historian, author, and educator William Archibald Dunning (1857–1922) was an authority on the Civil War and Reconstruction periods and an influential teacher.

Born in Plainfield, N.J., on May 12, 1857, William Dunning experienced as a young boy the tragic years of the Civil War, which had a profound effect on his career. For the rest of his life he devoted his energies to researching and training students in this watershed period of history.

Although he studied at Dartmouth College and the University of Berlin, Dunning received all of his degrees from Columbia University. In 1888 he married Charlotte E. Loomis of Brooklyn, who died June 13, 1917. Following completion of his doctorate in 1885, Dunning remained at Columbia, reaching the rank of full professor in 1893. In 1904 he was selected to be the first Lieber professor of history and political science.

Dunning possessed the rare talent of being both a distinguished teacher and a brilliant scholar. A perusal of his writings is impressive. After publishing his doctoral dissertation, *The Constitution of the United States in Civil War and Reconstruction, 1860–1867* (1885), he produced two other books in the same area: *Essays on the Civil War and Reconstruction and Related Topics* (1898), a scientific and scholarly investigation of the period; and *Reconstruction, Political and Economic, 1865–1877* (1907), a volume in the first "American Nation Series," which although partly refuted by revisionists, remains the best summary of the politics of the era.

Dunning was an equally competent political writer. His *A History of Political Theories: Ancient and Medieval, from Luther to Montesquieu* (1905) and *From Rousseau to Spencer* (1920) discuss the development of political theories from ancient to modern times. He also wrote *The British Empire and the United States* (1914), which analyzes the hundred years of diplomatic relations between the two powers starting with the Treaty of Ghent, and he collaborated with Frederick Bancroft on "A Sketch of Carl Schurz's Political Career" in *The Reminiscences of Carl Schurz*, vol. 3 (1908). He also wrote many articles and reviews for the *American Historical Review, Educational Review,* and the *Political Science Quarterly* and was editor of the last from 1894 to 1903.

The "Dunning school" in Civil War and Reconstruction historiography interpreted the events of the period in a manner more favorable to the South. They defended the planters of the antebellum period, blamed the abolitionists for bringing on the war, and vehemently criticized the Radical Republicans for using Lincoln's death to enhance their political ambitions and economic interests by reducing the South to colonial status.

Dunning was one of the founders of the American Historical Association, serving several years on its council and as its president in 1913. He was president of the American Political Science Association at the time of his death.

In 1914 sixteen former students published *Studies in Southern History and Politics,* and 10 years later another group published the commemorative volume *A History of Political Theories, Recent Times.* Dunning died on Aug. 15, 1922.

Further Reading

William Dunning is listed in the Social Sciences study guide (VII, A, 3). Although he did not direct their dissertations, Charles A. BEARD and Carl BECKER were certainly influenced by Dunning's brilliance and scholarship at Columbia.

There is no single volume on the life of Dunning. For a

William Dunning. (Columbia University Libraries)

discussion of Dunning's role in Civil War and Reconstruction historiography see Thomas J. Pressly, *Americans Interpret Their Civil War* (1954; rev. ed. 1962), and Kenneth M. Stampp, *The Era of Reconstruction, 1865–1877* (1965).

DUNS SCOTUS
/ By William J. Courtenay

The Scottish philosopher and theologian John Duns Scotus (1265/1266–1308) contributed to the development of a metaphysical system that was compatible with Christian doctrine, an epistemology that altered the 13th-century understanding of human knowledge, and a theology that stressed both divine and human will.

The century from 1250 to 1350 can be considered the high point of the scholastic movement in philosophy and theology. During that period a number of important developments took place which influenced European thought in subsequent centuries. The first of these developments was the attempt to construct a metaphysical system that would remove or reduce apparent conflicts between natural reason and the truths of revelation, allowing each a specific domain with a certain number of truths in common. This development is often termed the "synthesis of faith and reason" and is consid-

ered one of the major achievements of medieval philosophy. A second development was the perfection of an empirical approach to knowledge and the perfection of the critical tools of logic and scientific inquiry, a movement with important long-range results for the history of modern thought. The third development was the creation of a theological system that would protect the Christian conception of the omnipotence and freedom of God while upholding a practical system in which salvation would be granted to any man who earnestly sought it. In each of these developments Duns Scotus made an important contribution.

His Life

John Duns Scotus was born into a landowning family in the southeastern corner of Scotland, an area strongly influenced by the social, political, and religious institutions of England. According to one tradition, his father was Ninian Duns, who held an estate near Maxton in Roxburghshire. After receiving his early education, possibly at Haddington, John Duns entered the Franciscan convent at Dumfries about 1277–1280 and received instruction there from his paternal uncle, Elias Duns.

Shortly before 1290 John Duns was sent to Oxford, probably to continue his study in the liberal arts. It may have been at Oxford that he received the nickname "Scotus" or "the Scot." While at Oxford he was ordained to the priesthood on March 17, 1291, by Oliver Sutton, Bishop of Northampton.

Scotus, as he eventually came to be called, seems to have completed his study in the arts before 1293, for in that year he began his study for the higher degree of theology at Paris under Gonsalvo of Balboa. Returning to Oxford in 1296, Scotus continued his study of theology and commented on the *Book of Sentences* by Peter Lombard, a standard requirement of any theological faculty in a medieval university and an activity which made the candidate a "bachelor of the *Sentences*." Having read the *Sentences* at Oxford (and possibly also at Cambridge), Scotus returned to Paris in 1302 and in that year read the *Sentences* for the second or third time.

Because of his opposition to King Philip IV's call for a general council against Pope Boniface VIII, Scotus was exiled from France in 1303 and probably returned to Oxford for a year. In 1304, however, Scotus returned to Paris and completed the requirements for the degree of master of theology in 1305. For the next 2 years he held the chair of theology at the Franciscan convent in Paris, debating with other theologians and increasing his reputation. One of his most important works, *Quaestiones quodlibetales,* contains Scotus's version of many debates in which he engaged during this period.

Scotus was transferred in 1307 to the Franciscan house of study at Cologne, Germany, where he lectured until his death the following year on November 8. He was buried in the chapel of the convent.

Relation between Philosophy and Theology

Under the impact of the revival of Aristotle in the 13th century, several theologians attempted to argue for the "scientific" nature of theology. This movement was short-lived, and by the end of the 13th century the scientific quality of theology had been rejected on the grounds that theology did not possess the same type of evidence nor was its method demonstrative in the same sense as mathematics or Euclidean geometry.

Scotus contributed to a more exact understanding of the relation between philosophy and theology. He emphasized the practical and affective nature of theology, denying to it the rigorous demonstrative quality of the Aristotelian sciences. Scotus, however, shared with St. Thomas Aquinas the belief that truth was one and that theology and philosophy do not contradict each other but represent two different approaches to the same truth.

The relation of philosophy and theology, for Scotus, was based on the nature of their respective sources: reason and revelation. Scotus's formulation of this problem followed the pattern established by St. Thomas Aquinas, although Scotus restricted the number of theological truths that could be established by natural reason, unaided by revelation.

Metaphysical Beliefs

Scotus understood metaphysics as that aspect of philosophy that studies the nature of *being* itself rather than any particular object possessing being that exists in external reality. Being, understood in this way, was a concept common to God and man. Moreover, certain disjunctive attributes or antinomies could be applied to

John Duns Scotus. (Radio Times Hulton Picture Library)

being, such as "infinite-finite" or "necessary-contingent." On the basis of his belief that the term "being" applied to God and man in the same sense and that one part of a disjunctive requires the other part, Scotus established a proof for God's existence based on the nature of being. The existence of finite, contingent beings requires the existence of an infinite, necessary being, namely God.

Epistemology and Empiricism

Scotus shared with St. Thomas Aquinas a strong belief in the primacy of sense experience in the process of human knowledge. Scotus, however, gave the intellect of man a more active role in cognition than was customary in the late 13th century. In opposition to the more common Aristotelian epistemology, he argued that the intellect could come into direct contact with the object to be known. Scotus therefore played a very important role in the transformation of medieval epistemology from a conception of the intellect as a passive receptacle that knows only universal concepts to a view of the intellect as an active mind that knows individual things.

Theological Beliefs

The main feature of Scotus's theology is the importance he gives to the primacy of the will in both God and man. In contrast to St. Thomas Aquinas, who tended to emphasize the intellect or reason, Scotus stressed the freedom of the divine will and the freedom of the human will within an order freely chosen by God.

The freedom of God, for Scotus, means first of all that creation was not necessary. God not only chose the *type* of world He wished to create; He chose to create. Having once chosen, however, it is the nature of God to abide by His decisions. Although He always retains the power to do otherwise, He never arbitrarily reverses His decisions.

The second area where God's freedom is evidenced is in man's salvation. God, for Scotus, predestines those He wishes to save apart from any foreseen merits. Moreover, God retains His freedom to accept or reject the Christian who fulfils the divine commandments.

This absolute power of God is limited by His own free decision to allow man freedom and to award eternal life on the basis of human merit. Man, for Scotus, is also primarily will and is united to God through love more than through reason. Man has the freedom to fulfil God's demands and thus obtain salvation.

Marian Doctor

The last important area of Scotus's thought concerns his teaching on Mary, the mother of Jesus. Duns Scotus is known as the Marian doctor because of the high status he accords to Mary. Scotus taught that Mary was born without the stain of original sin, a doctrine known as the Immaculate Conception and eventually recognized as dogma in the Roman Catholic Church. The support of Scotus's teaching by many within the Franciscan order facilitated the development and final acceptance of that doctrine.

Further Reading

John Duns Scotus is listed in the Philosophy study guide (II, C, 2). He and his fellow Franciscan St. BONAVENTURE opposed the philosophy of St. THOMAS AQUINAS.

The best biographical sketch of Duns Scotus can be found in Alfred B. Emden, *A Biographical Register of the University of Oxford to A.D. 1500,* vol. 1 (1957). Among the many histories of medieval philosophy that include the thought of Scotus, the clearest description can be found in Frederick Copleston, *A History of Philosophy,* vol. 2 (1950). There are several more detailed studies in English of various aspects of Scotus's thought. Two excellent studies of Scotus's metaphysics are Cyril L. Shircel, *The Univocity of the Concept of Being in the Philosophy of John Duns Scotus* (1942), and Allan Wolter, *The Transcendentals and Their Function in the Metaphysics of Duns Scotus* (1946). The best study of Scotus's epistemology is Sebastian Day, *Intuitive Cognition: A Key to the Significance of the Later Scholastics* (1947). A more general evaluation of Scotus's thought and his impact on modern philosophy is provided in J. F. Boler, *Charles Peirce and Scholastic Realism: A Study of Peirce's Relation to John Duns Scotus* (1963).

DUNSTABLE / By Charles Hamm

John Dunstable (ca. 1390–1453) was the most celebrated English composer of the entire 15th century. His works were known and imitated all over western Europe.

Contemporary documentation of John Dunstable's life is sparse. From his tombstone, which was in St. Stephen Walbrook, London, until it was destroyed in the Great Fire, it is known that he died on Dec. 24, 1453, and that he was also a mathematician and astronomer. Several tracts on astronomy once in his possession are in various English libraries, and from one of these it is known that he was in the service of John, Duke of Bedford, brother of Henry V. John became regent of France in 1422 and maintained a chapel in that country until his death in 1435; thus it is likely that Dunstable was on the Continent for some years. He is mentioned by several contemporary and slightly later theorists. Other information must be deduced from his music and the manuscript sources that preserve it.

Almost all of Dunstable's known works are sacred. There are 20-odd settings of items of the Mass Ordinary (single sections, Gloria-Credo or Sanctus-Agnus pairs, and complete cyclic Masses), 12 isorhythmic motets, some 20 motets and polyphonic settings of liturgical melodies, and 2 secular pieces.

Most of Dunstable's compositions are found in nonin-

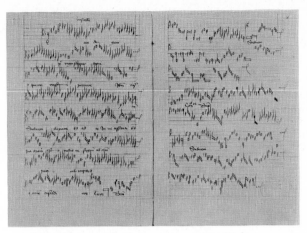

Pages from a 15th-century manuscript of John Dunstable's motet Beata Dei Genitrix. (Bayerische Staatsbibliothek, Munich)

sular sources. Almost all of his motets are in a manuscript in Modena (probably copied in Ferrara); some of these motets and most of his Mass music are in sources in Trent and Aosta. Other works are in Bologna, Florence, Berlin, El Escorial, Paris, and Seville. Only a handful of English sources of his music have survived, and many of these are fragmentary. The destruction of musical manuscripts (and instruments) for religious and political reasons at a later time created a situation whereby no major sources of polyphonic music remain in England for roughly the middle years of the 15th century. It is fortunate that English music was so widely admired and copied on the Continent.

Lack of biographical information and precise datings for manuscripts makes a chronology of Dunstable's works very difficult. In a general way, the isorhythmic motets, with their rigidly structured formal frameworks and general harmonic style, look back to techniques popular in the 14th century, and such harmonizations of liturgical melodies as the *Magnificat secundi toni* and *Ave Regina celorum* are clear descendants of late-14th-century English descant settings. On the other hand, the *Missa Rex seculorum* and *Missa Da gaudierum premia,* cyclic Masses with each section built over a common tenor, are innovative works, early examples of a species of composition that was to be a cornerstone of Mass composition for the next century, and some of the non-isorhythmic—and probably later—motets, such as *Quam pulchra es* and *Salve Regina mater mire,* anticipate the motet style of the generation of Josquin des Prez with their careful declamatory settings of the text, fuller harmonic style, and independence of the individual voices.

Stylistic features of English music were known to and imitated by such Continental masters as Guillaume Dufay and Gilles Binchois. This can be seen in their music, in the incorporation of a harmonic style more dependent on thirds and sixths and their taking up of such structural devices as the tenor, or *cantus firmus,* Mass. It is also attested to by writers of the time. Martin le Franc, in his lengthy poem *Le Champion des dames* (1441–1442), speaks of Dufay and Binchois as having found a new way in music, based on the English style of Dunstable. And Johannes Tinctoris in his *Proportionales musices* (ca. 1476) maintains that a fundamental change took place in music in the early 15th century, that it originated with Dunstable, and that not only Dufay and Binchois but also such men as Johannes Ockeghem, Anthoine Busnois, and their contemporaries were affected by this new style.

This statement may be exaggerated. The English influence came not only from Dunstable but also from his contemporaries, particularly Leonel Power. But a good case can be made for the suggestion that the diffusion, popularity, and influence of English music were never so great as during the first half of the 15th century, and Dunstable stands at the head of this school.

Further Reading

John Dunstable is listed in the Music study guide (I, B, 1). His motets foreshadowed those of JOSQUIN DES PREZ. Dunstable's English style influenced Guillaume DUFAY and Johannes OCKEGHEM.

Stylistic and biographical commentary on Dunstable are in the following standard works: Gustave Reese, *Music in the Middle Ages* (1940); Manfred F. Bukofzer, *Studies in Medieval and Renaissance Music* (1950); Frank Llewellyn Harrison, *Music in Medieval Britain* (1958); and Donald Jay Grout, *A History of Western Music* (1960).

St. Dunstan, a medieval illumination. (Radio Times Hulton Picture Library)

ST. **DUNSTAN** / By Gerard A. Vanderhaar

The English monk and archbishop St. Dunstan (ca. 909–988) was a counselor of kings and a respected churchman. He made the English monasteries into centers of religion and culture.

Dunstan was born into an important family near Glastonbury in Somerset. As a young man, he lived for a time in the household of King Athelstan but incurred the displeasure of some of the officials by his love of singing and reading. Accused of black magic and pressured into leaving the court, Dunstan lived for a short time with the bishop of Winchester, who persuaded him to become a monk.

As a hermit near Glastonbury, Dunstan disciplined himself through prayer and penance. He worked as a silversmith and copied manuscripts. The next king, Edmund, called Dunstan back to court as one of his counselors and eventually made him abbot of Glastonbury. Under Edmund's successor, Edred, Dunstan practically ran the kingdom. But his luck changed when Edwy succeeded to the throne in 955. Dunstan's outspoken criticism of the King's loose conduct earned him a sentence of exile. For 2 years Dunstan lived on the Continent, near Ghent in Flanders, with a group of monks guided by the strict rule of St. Benedict. In 957 some of King Edwy's subjects rebelled and set up a separate kingdom. Their leader, Edgar, called Dunstan back from Flanders and appointed him bishop first of Worcester and then of London. When Edwy died 2 years later, Edgar became sole king of England. He made Dunstan archbishop of Canterbury, head of the entire Church in England.

For almost 30 years, seen by some as a golden age, Dunstan and King Edgar cooperated closely, Dunstan preaching respect for the King's law and the King giving money to help build churches and monasteries. Dunstan was as strict with his clergy as he was with himself. His experiences in Flanders taught him that monks should live in an atmosphere of self-sacrifice. He enforced the law of celibacy wherever possible. He forbade the selling of Church offices (simony) and the appointing of relatives to positions of authority (nepotism). He encouraged his people to fast and preached the ideal of justice for all. Once he refused to say Mass until some counterfeiters had paid the penalty decreed by the magistrate. Their hands were chopped off.

By his forceful preaching and administrative ability, his friendship with the King, and his personal example, Dunstan succeeded in reforming the Church in England. The monasteries he influenced became sources of genuine religious spirit for the people and provided many bishops for England as well as missionaries for northern

Europe. He was accepted as a saint by the English people soon after his death on May 19, 988.

Further Reading

St. Dunstan is listed in the Religion study guide (I, C, 4). He was influenced by the rule of St. BENEDICT.

The most recent biography of St. Dunstan is Eleanor S. Duckett, *Saint Dunstan of Canterbury* (1955), a clearly written historical sketch. David Knowles, *The Monastic Orders in England* (1940; 2d ed. 1963), details St. Dunstan's important contributions. For his place in the perspective of English history see G. O. Sayles, *The Medieval Foundations of England* (1948; 2d ed. 1950).

Harvard College during Henry Dunster's time, a conjectural drawing by Harold R. Shurtleff, showing the "old college" from Harvard Yard. (Harvard University Archives)

DUNSTER / By Winfred E. A. Bernhard

Henry Dunster (ca. 1609–1659), an English-born American clergyman, was distinguished as the innovative and forceful first president of Harvard College.

Henry Dunster was born in Bury, Lancashire, England, the fifth child of a yeoman farmer. At 17 he entered Magdalene College at Cambridge University and, upon completion of requirements, received a bachelor of arts degree. He returned to Bury as a teacher and curate, studied Oriental languages, and in 1634 was granted a master of arts degree from Cambridge. Under spiritual stress, Dunster gravitated to Puritanism and emigrated to New England.

Although relatively unknown, Dunster was chosen president of Harvard College upon his arrival in Boston in 1640. He revived an institution that was virtually defunct, reuniting the scattered student body and establishing degree requirements. With Cambridge and Oxford as models, he was determined to put Harvard on secure foundations. The college laws were first codified in 1646, a charter obtained in 1650, and the holdings of the library increased through gifts. Dunster and Thomas Shepard, the eminent Puritan and theologian, petitioned the New England Confederation for contributions from the inhabitants, obtaining £250 in gifts of wheat by 1653. Dunster advocated 4 years' residence for the bachelor of arts degree, and although protesting students refused to pay commencement fees, he successfully instituted the change. Edward Johnson in his *Wonder Working Providence* (1654) observed that "the learned reverend, and judicious Mr. Henry Dunster [was] fitted from the Lord for the work."

In 1641 Dunster married Elizabeth, the widow of Jose Glover. Marriage brought President Dunster financial security and also Glover's printing press. Operated for years in Dunster's house, this press was the first one in the Colonies and was later acquired by Harvard. Elizabeth Dunster's death in 1643 led to conflict between her children and Dunster over the estate. In 1644 he chose a second wife, Elizabeth Atkinson, who outlived him.

While a member of the Cambridge church, Dunster refused to have an infant son baptized. Public hostility to his Baptist views led to demands for his resignation from Harvard. On Oct. 24, 1654, he resigned, later becoming a minister at Scituate in Plymouth Colony. He died there in 1659.

Further Reading

Henry Dunster is listed in the Social Sciences study guide (IV, C, 3). James BLAIR and John WITHERSPOON were also instrumental in establishing an American college system.

Jeremiah Chaplin, *Life of Henry Dunster: First President of Harvard College* (1872), is the standard biography. Samuel Eliot Morison, *The Founding of Harvard College* (1935), gives an excellent account of Dunster's presidency. Two informative background works are Morison's *Builders of the Bay Colony* (1930; rev. ed. 1958) and Louis B. Wright, *The Cultural Life of the American Colonies, 1607–1763* (1957).

DUPLEIX / By Martin Blumenson

The French colonial administrator Joseph François, Marquis Dupleix (1697–1763), sought to establish a French empire in India but was frustrated by indifference at home and by growing British power.

Joseph François Dupleix (pronounced dü-plĕks′) was born in Landrecies on Jan. 1, 1697, into a wealthy family. After making several voyages to America and India, in 1721 he was named a member of the superior council at Pondicherry, India, of the Com-

Marquis Dupleix. (Bulloz)

pagnie des Indes—the French counterpart of the English East India Company. In addition to his official duties he engaged, as was the custom, in private business ventures and gained a fortune. In 1731 he became governor or superintendent of French affairs in Chandernagor, where he administered his office with great competence and established a fruitful trade with China.

In 1742 Dupleix was appointed governor general of the company with authority over French investments in India. Ambitious to found a great French colony at a time when native governments were in a state of political dissolution and when commercial advantages were open to European nations, Dupleix found himself opposed by British designs. He was also hampered by a bitter jealousy on the part of the Comte de La Bourdonnais, governor of the isle of Bourbon, and by a lack of understanding among the company officials in France.

The War of the Austrian Succession permitted Dupleix partially to realize his aims. The capitulation of Madras to the French in 1746 fostered his purpose, but restoration of the city to British control blocked him. He sent an expedition against Fort St. David in 1747, but it was defeated by the nawab of Arcot, who was allied with the British. When the British besieged Pondicherry in 1748, Dupleix conducted a brilliant defense, but news of the peace of Aix-la-Chapelle arrived during the operations and halted further military activities.

Dupleix sought to subjugate southern India and use military forces to safeguard commercial advantages. He sent troops to aid sovereign claimants to the Carnatic and the Deccan, who were opposed by British-supported rivals. In the end, Dupleix was unable to match the British aspirations and activities directed by Robert Clive,

and French influence declined as British power increased.

In 1754 the French government, wishing to avoid further conflict with the British in India, sent a special commissioner, Charles Robert Godeheu, to replace Dupleix, who returned to France that year. Although he had expended his personal fortune to support his public policy, he found that the Compagnie des Indes was unwilling to reimburse him and that the French government would do nothing to help him. Regarded at the time as an ambitious and self-serving adventurer, he died in obscurity, neglect, and poverty in Paris on Nov. 10, 1763. He was, however, one of the greatest French colonial administrators of the 18th century, but his country's lack of interest defeated him.

Further Reading

The Marquis Dupleix is listed in the European History study guide (VI, B, 2) and the Asia study guide (II, A, 5, b). His great rival was Robert CLIVE.

For information on Dupleix see G. B. Malleson, *Dupleix* (1895), and Henry Dodwell, *Dupleix and Clive: The Beginning of Empire* (1920).

E. I. DU PONT / By Richard T. Farrell

Éleuthère Irénée du Pont (1771–1834), a French-born American manufacturer, founded the gunpowder mill which became the basis of E. I. du Pont de Nemours and Company.

Born in Paris on June 24, 1771, E. I. du Pont was the son of Pierre Samuel du Pont de Nemours, a leading economist of the physiocratic school. Irénée demonstrated little interest in school, and in 1788 he went to work for Antoine Lavoisier, the noted French chemist who was chief of the royal powder works. He became Lavoisier's first assistant in 1791.

Following the French Revolution, Irénée's father found he could not cooperate with the new government and decided the family should emigrate to the United States. The decision was undoubtedly influenced by the elder Du Pont's friend Thomas Jefferson, with whom he had become acquainted when Jefferson was serving as minister to France. Thirteen members of the family, including Irénée, his wife, and three children, sailed for the United States and arrived in Newport, R.I., on New Year's Day 1800.

On a hunting trip with Col. Louis de Toussard, an American military officer, Irénée du Pont discovered that American gunpowder was not only poor in quality but high in price. They made a study of the powder industry in America and concluded that the construction of a powder mill might be a profitable venture. Du Pont and his brother Victor returned to France to seek the assistance of former associates. He obtained designs for machinery and the equipment he would need, plus pledges of financial support. Upon his return he purchased a farm 4 miles from Wilmington, Del., as the site for his factory. In 1803 the small mill began processing saltpeter for the government, and eventually the company produced the first powder for sale.

During the next few years the company increased its production and sales, but not without problems. Stockholders grew tired of Du Pont's continuous expansion and demanded their share of the profits. Two explosions, one in 1815 and another in 1818, resulted in 49 deaths and considerable financial loss. Orders from the U.S. government during the War of 1812, however, made Du Pont the major powder producer in America.

Du Pont had other interests besides gunpowder. In 1811, with his brother Victor and Peter Baudy, he opened a woolen mill on the Brandywine River. Du Pont helped establish a cotton mill and a tannery. In 1822 he became a director of the Bank of the United States. He died on Oct. 31, 1834, in Philadelphia.

Further Reading

E. I. du Pont is listed in the American History study guide (IV, E, 3). Moses BROWN and Francis Cabot LOWELL were among the first to establish factories in the United States. Du Pont's son, Pierre Samuel DU PONT, continued building the family business.

Bessie Gardner du Pont edited and translated *Life of*

E. I. du Pont. (H. Roger-Viollet)

Éleuthère Irénée du Pont (12 vols., 1923–1927), which is largely a collection of Du Pont's correspondence. His life in the United States is included in her *E. I. du Pont de Nemours & Co.: A History, 1802–1902* (1920). Max Dorian, *The Du Ponts: From Gunpowder to Nylon* (1961; trans. 1962), contains extensive references to Irénée du Pont, as does William S. Dutton, *Du Pont: One Hundred and Forty Years* (1942).

P. S. **DU PONT** / By Saul Engelbourg

The American industrialist Pierre Samuel du Pont (1870–1954), as chairman of the board of E. I. du Pont de Nemours and Company, was among those responsible for its phenomenal success in the 20th century.

Pierre Samuel du Pont was born in Wilmington, Del., on Jan. 15, 1870. After receiving a bachelor of science degree from the Massachusetts Institute of Technology in 1890, he became a chemist in the family firm. He pursued a variety of business activities until 1902, when he and two cousins purchased and reorganized the family company. He became president of the firm in 1915, an office he held until he became chairman of the board in 1919. He remained in the latter post until 1940.

Du Pont guided the company through its enormous expansion during World War I and its later product diversification program outside the explosives industry. He emphasized competence rather than family membership: the company made a successful transition from a family operation to one run by professional managers. The new company structure stressed division of authority between central management and the operating departments; the former concentrated on long-run policy decision making while the latter focused on day-to-day problems. In adapting his company's organizational structure to its new marketing strategy, Du Pont was an industrial and administrative innovator.

The company first invested in the General Motors Company in 1917, with massive investment 3 years later. In 1920 William C. Durant, president of General Motors, found himself in financial difficulty. Because possible failure of General Motors might have jeopardized Du Pont's investment, a Du Pont syndicate rescued Durant, but the price was his holdings in General Motors. Reluctantly, Pierre du Pont became president of General Motors and occupied that office until 1923, when Alfred P. Sloan, Jr., replaced him.

Du Pont was also active in public affairs. He held numerous offices in the state government of Delaware, including tax commissioner. Initially a supporter of Franklin D. Roosevelt, Du Pont strongly opposed governmental intervention in business affairs and so opposed Roosevelt's reelection in 1936. He was one of the founders of

Pierre Samuel du Pont. (Library of Congress)

the American Liberty League, which unsuccessfully appealed to voters to defeat the New Deal because it seemed to represent an infringement on individual liberties.

Du Pont died in Wilmington on April 5, 1954. As much as any other man, he can be credited with the success of the Du Pont Company in the 20th century.

Further Reading

Pierre Samuel du Pont is listed in the American History study guide (VIII, D, 2). The family firm was founded by E. I. DU PONT. James B. DUKE and Harvey FIRESTONE were other leading 20th-century industrialists.

The key source concerning Du Pont is Alfred D. Chandler and Stephen Salsbury, *Pierre S. du Pont and the Making of the Modern Corporation* (1971). Various aspects of his life and career are treated in the histories of the family and its enterprise: William S. Dutton, *Du Pont: One Hundred and Forty Years* (1942); Max Dorian, *The Du Ponts: From Gunpowder to Nylon* (1961; trans. 1962); and William H. A. Carr, *The Du Ponts of Delaware* (1964). Du Pont's years at General Motors receive extensive comment in the chapter on that firm in Alfred D. Chandler, Jr., *Strategy and Structure: Chapters in the History of the Industrial Enterprise* (1962). George Wolfskill recounts the story of the leading right-wing organization of the 1930s in *The Revolt of the*

Conservatives: A History of the American Liberty League, 1934–1940 (1962).

DU PONT DE NEMOURS
/ **By Paul G. Dobson**

The French political economist, public administrator, and reformer Pierre Samuel du Pont de Nemours (1739–1817) expounded the economic doctrines of the physiocrats.

Born in Paris on Sept. 14, 1739, Pierre Samuel du Pont (later, de Nemours; pronounced dü pôn′ də nə-mōōr′) was the son of Samuel du Pont, a master watchmaker, and Anne Alexandrine de Montchanin, member of a derogated noble family. After becoming a watchmaker and dabbling in medicine, he turned to letters as a means of attaining recognition. In 1763 he was introduced to François Quesnay, whose physiocratic thought greatly influenced him.

In Du Pont's early works—*Of the Exportation and Importation of Grains* (1763), *Physiocracy* (1767), and *Of the Origin and the Progress of a New Science* (1767)—he stated the core ideas of his thinking. He believed in a presocial natural order in which man had rights and duties based on the physical necessities of life. Man had propertorial rights over his life and possessions; his duties were to supply his own and others' needs and to respect others' rights and property. From these assumptions followed the belief that the natural source of wealth was land, and the labor and commerce associated with agriculture. All other forms of industry were secondary and related to luxury, which detracted from the expansion of agriculture and the accumulation of wealth. Du Pont believed that society should discourage nonproductive industries and free agriculture from all unnatural restraints. Good government, therefore, should work to eliminate custom barriers and excessive and unproductive taxation, which inhibited the growth of agriculture and trade. He also held that only hereditary monarchy could ensure the proper use of natural resources.

In 1774 Du Pont was appointed inspector general of commerce under his close friend A. R. J. Turgot, whom he served primarily as private secretary. With the fall of Turgot in 1775, Du Pont went into retirement at his estates near Nemours. There he finished drawing up Turgot's *Memoir on Municipalities* (1776), which in modified form served as the basis for some of the reform proposals of later ministers. Since there is no way of knowing how much of the *Memoir* was actually the work of Du Pont, there may be some justification in his claim that the bulk of later reform proposals were actually based on his ideas. It is known, however, that his role in the commercial treaties of 1783 and 1786 was considerable.

During the Assembly of the Notables (1787), Du Pont served as second secretary of the meetings—a privilege he was granted because he had been ennobled in 1783 for his services to the Crown. With the failure of the Notables, he became active in the Revolutionary movement and in 1789 was elected to represent the Third Estate from Nemours. As a member of the Constituent Assembly, he served on 11 economic committees. Du Pont was a moderate Revolutionary who believed reform should go no further than was absolutely necessary to ensure the realization of physiocratic principles. He advocated the separation of powers in government, a bicameral legislature, and a strong monarchy.

His views earned him the disfavor of most of the leaders of the Revolution, and Du Pont retired from public life in 1791. Chosen to sit in the Council of Elders in 1795, he was in constant opposition to the policies of the Directory and was proscribed in 1797, being suspected of royalism. He then resigned from the Elders and turned his thoughts to America, which he considered "the only asylum where persecuted men can find safety." He traveled to America in 1799 to introduce physiocratic ideas into the young republic.

On his return to France in 1802, Du Pont played an intermediary role in the Louisiana Purchase and was later elected to the Paris Chamber of Commerce. He did not, however, find favor with Napoleon, and his ambition of election to the Imperial Senate was never realized. In 1814 he supported the restored Bourbon monarchy, viewing the Charter of 1814 as similar to his own proposals of 1789. Napoleon's return from exile prompted Du Pont to flee to America, where he spent the last years of his life in retirement at his son's powder plant in Delaware. He died on Aug. 7, 1817, after a brief illness.

Pierre Samuel du Pont de Nemours.
(Photo-Hachette)

Further Reading

Pierre Samuel du Pont de Nemours is listed in the European History study guide (VI, B, 3) and the Social Sciences study guide (V, B, 2). Closely associated with A. R. J. TURGOT, he devoted his literary and public career to popularizing the physiocratic doctrines of François QUESNAY. His son E. I. DU PONT was an early American industrialist.

A full-length study is Ambrose Saricks, *Pierre Samuel du Pont de Nemours* (1965). A profile of Du Pont is the older, but useful work by Henry Higgs, *The Physiocrats: Six Lectures on the French Économistes of the 18th Century* (1896; repr. 1963). For general background see Peter Gay, *The Enlightenment* (2 vols., 1966–1969).

DURAND / By Frederick A. Sweet

The American painter and engraver Asher Brown Durand (1796–1886) was a prominent figure in the first generation of the Hudson River school of painters.

Asher Durand was born on Aug. 21, 1796, in Jefferson Village, N.J., of a French Huguenot family. His first training was with his father, John Durand, a watchmaker. At 17 Asher was apprenticed to the engraver Peter Maverick and showed such facility that after 5 years they became partners. Durand also attended the American Academy of Fine Arts. When John Trumbull, who ran the academy, engaged Durand to engrave his painting *The Declaration of Independence,* Maverick, jealous of his former pupil, dissolved the partnership. Durand then set up his own establishment and was soon America's leading engraver. He engraved many portraits and book illustrations and executed a fine engraving of John Vanderlyn's *Ariadne.*

Although Durand had occasionally done some painting, he did not give up engraving in favor of painting until about 1834, when Luman Reed, a wealthy New York collector, commissioned him to do portraits of the early American presidents. In 1840 Durand traveled to Europe, where he admired the work of the 17th-century Dutch masters as well as Salvator Rosa and Claude Lorrain. Durand succeeded Samuel F. B. Morse as president of the National Academy of Design, New York, in 1846 and held the office until 1862, when he resigned.

Because Durand had been trained as an engraver, his earlier paintings are hard in texture and meticulous in detail, and his color is pale in tone. However, he soon developed a freer style and a richness of color. Two notable canvases, the *Morning of Life* and the *Evening of Life,* are allegories of the ages of man and depict imaginary landscapes in a rich and luxurious manner. But he was also a very factual painter. While most artists of the Hudson River school made sketches on the spot from

Asher Durand, a self-portrait. (Courtesy of The New-York Historical Society, New York City)

Railroad, was a major force behind the first transcontinental railroad.

Thomas C. Durant was born in Lee, Mass., on Feb. 6, 1820, the son of well-to-do parents. Although he graduated from Albany Medical College, he left medicine for his uncle's firm, which exported flour and grain. Durant later moved to New York City to open a branch office and became widely known in financial circles because of his activities in stocks.

Railroads were a popular investment in the 1850s, and Durant joined with Henry Farnam in building the Michigan Southern, the Chicago, Rock Island, and Pacific, and the Mississippi and Missouri. In 1862 the Federal government designated the Central Pacific and Union Pacific railroads to construct the first transcontinental line. Durant claimed that he influenced President Abraham Lincoln to select Omaha as the line's eastern terminus, although most authorities give the credit to Grenville M. Dodge. The Union Pacific ran into early financial difficulty, and Durant, vice president of the company, persuaded Congress to double the land grant and also to allow the road to issue bonds equal to those issued by the government, which was the transcontinental's major financial backer.

When the Union Pacific ran into difficulty selling its securities at par value as was required by the charter, Durant devised a scheme whereby a group of company executives formed a construction company called the Crédit Mobilier of America. This firm was awarded the construction contracts and accepted the securities as payment. To protect the firm against loss, the contracts

which they worked up paintings in the studio, he was a pioneer in making actual paintings out of doors. As a result, his color is more true to nature than that used by his contemporaries. His *Monument Mountain, Berkshires* and numerous scenes done in the Catskills are remarkably fresh interpretations of the natural world.

In memory of his friend and fellow painter Thomas Cole, who died in 1848, Durand painted *Kindred Spirits,* showing Cole and the poet William Cullen Bryant standing on a cliff overlooking a Catskill stream. If overliterary in content, the painting does show the close association between writers and painters during the American romantic period.

Further Reading

Asher Durand is listed in the Art study guide (IV, C, 1, a). Other Hudson River school painters were Thomas COLE and Frederick Edwin CHURCH.

Durand is discussed in Frederick A. Sweet, *The Hudson River School and the Early American Landscape Tradition* (1945), and E. P. Richardson, *Painting in America* (1956). See also Oliver Larkin, *Art and Life in America* (1949; rev. ed. 1960).

✳ ✳ ✳

T. C. **DURANT** / By Thomas B. Brewer

The American Thomas Clark Durant (1820–1885), an executive of the Union Pacific

Thomas C. Durant. (Library of Congress)

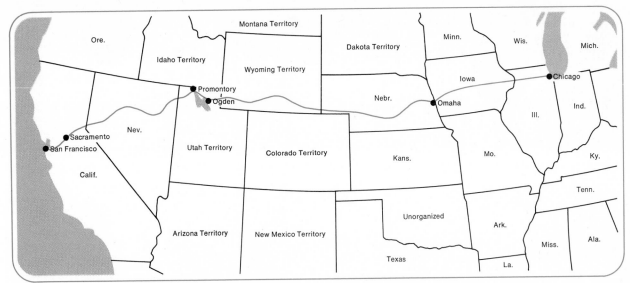

Route of the transcontinental railroad. The Union Pacific Railroad, building westward from Omaha, and the Central Pacific, building eastward from Sacramento, met at Promontory, Utah. There a golden spike joined the two lines in a single transcontinental system.

were high enough to offset the sale of the securities below par. Regardless of the corrupt nature of the operation, money was secured and construction continued.

In 1865 Oakes and Oliver Ames, Massachusetts manufacturers, entered the Crédit Mobilier and began a battle for control with Durant. For 2 years the rival factions, known as the "Boston Crowd" and the "New York Crowd," contended for supremacy. At stake in the struggle was not only the construction company but the entire Union Pacific. Durant was forced out of the Crédit Mobilier in 1867, but efforts to sever him from the railroad failed. An agreement then followed between the two groups for construction of some 667 miles of track; the agreement proved profitable to the Crédit Mobilier, but the Union Pacific was left with a shoddily built line and heavy overcapitalization. Losing control to the Ames brothers, Durant held on just long enough to help Leland Stanford drive in the golden spike to complete the nation's first transcontinental railroad on May 10, 1869. On May 25 Durant was dropped from the board of directors of the Union Pacific.

Durant was married and the father of a son and daughter. His last years passed uneventfully in the Adirondacks.

Further Reading

Thomas C. Durant is listed in the American History study guide (VII, E, 2). He was one of a number of vigorous and immensely prosperous railroad builders, such as E. H. HARRIMAN and James J. HILL.

No full-length study of Durant exists. For his role in the Union Pacific see Nelson Trottman, *History of the Union Pacific: A Financial and Economic Survey* (1923), and a popular work, Wesley S. Griswold, *A Work of Giants: Building the First Transcontinental Railroad* (1962).

W. C. DURANT / By Saul Engelbourg

The American industrialist William Crapo Durant (1861–1947) was the founder of General Motors, an automobile manufacturing company.

William C. Durant was born in Boston, Mass., on Dec. 8, 1861. He grew up in Flint, Mich., where he became a leading carriage manufacturer. In 1886 he organized the Durant-Dort Company and helped to make Flint the carriage capital of the nation.

Durant acquired control of the Buick Motor Car Company in 1904 and revived it; by 1908 Buick was one of the four leading automobile companies. Durant had a vision of the boundless possibilities of the automobile, particularly the moderate-priced car, and attempted to capitalize on these possibilities by establishing a large-scale enterprise based on volume production. He intended that his company would be well financed, market a variety of automobiles, and produce many of its own parts.

After an attempt to buy Ford Motor Company in 1907 failed because Henry Ford wanted to be paid in cash, Durant established the General Motors Company the next year. He began with the Buick and added Cadillac, Oldsmobile, Oakland (Pontiac), and other lesser companies. Durant overextended himself, and by 1910 General Motors needed the intervention of a bankers' syndicate to lift the burden of debt. Durant returned to the automobile business in 1911 with the Chevrolet car. In 1916, with the backing of the Du Pont family, he recovered control of General Motors.

In 1919 General Motors was one of the largest American industrial enterprises, but Durant exercised little control over its operation; General Motors was too decentralized to be effective. When the Panic of 1920 occurred, Durant was overcommitted in the stock market. He tried unsuccessfully to support the price of General Motors stock; he was forced out of the company in 1920 by the Du Ponts, who wanted to protect their sizable investment.

The remainder of Durant's life was anticlimactic. In 1921 he started Durant Motors, which failed to become a major automobile producer. Durant Motors was already shaky when the 1929 crash occurred; the Depression then sharply reduced automobile sales and resulted in 1933 in dissolution of the firm. Durant was bankrupt by 1935. During his remaining years he engaged in a variety of business enterprises but without marked success. He died in New York City on March 18, 1947.

Durant was a pioneer in the automotive industry, and his most notable creation, General Motors, has dominated the automobile market since. Some of his chance ideas, such as the entry of General Motors into the manufacture of refrigerators, were highly successful. However, Durant never succeeded in organizing an administrative structure adequate for the giant enterprise he founded, and the task of converting General Motors into an enduring monument was left to his successors.

Further Reading

William C. Durant is listed in the American History study guide (VIII, D, 2). Later presidents of General Mo-

William C. Durant. (United Press International Photo)

tors were Pierre Samuel DU PONT and Alfred P. SLOAN, Jr.

There is no good biography of Durant. John B. Rae, *The American Automobile: A Brief History* (1965), places Durant in the context of his times and industry. Alfred D. Chandler, Jr., *Strategy and Structure: Chapters in the History of the Industrial Enterprise* (1962), has a chapter which analyzes Durant's administrative strategy. Carl Crow, *The City of Flint Grows Up: The Success Story of an American Community* (1945), includes a brief account of Durant's early years.

DÜRER / By Jan Białostocki

The German painter and graphic artist Albrecht Dürer (1471–1528) introduced the achievements of the Italian Renaissance into northern European art. His prints diffused his new style, a fusion of the German realistic tradition with the Italian ideal of beauty.

Until the end of the 15th century late medieval realism in the north and the art of the Renaissance in Italy developed more or less independently of each other. While Italian artists invented rules of perspective and proportion to govern their representations of man in his natural environment, the German and early Netherlandish painters perfected their observation and depiction of individual natural phenomena without, however, establishing a correct perspectival space within which to contain the multiplicity of detail. Albrecht Dürer (pronounced dü′rər) was, in effect, the first non-Italian artist to associate the humanistic disciplines with the esthetic pursuits of art.

Albrecht Dürer was born on May 21, 1471, in Nuremberg. His father, Albrecht the Elder, was a Hungarian goldsmith who went to Nuremberg in 1455, where he married Barbara Holper, daughter of a goldsmith. The young Dürer received his first training in his father's workshop as an engraver. He executed his first self-portrait, a drawing in silverpoint, at the age of 13.

His Apprenticeship

From 1486 to 1490 Dürer was apprenticed to the Nuremberg painter and woodcut illustrator Michael Wolgemut, following which he went on his bachelor's journey, the route of which is not known but which presumably led him to the Rhineland and to the Netherlands, since influences of early Netherlandish art are traceable in his works. He arrived in Colmar in 1492, soon after the death of the prominent German graphic artist Martin Schongauer in 1491, and continued on to Basel, where he stayed until late 1493 working extensively as a woodcut designer.

There is a difference of scholarly opinion in regard to Dürer's work in Basel, mostly woodcuts in books illustrat-

Albrecht Dürer, a self-portrait in the Uffizi, Florence. (Alinari)

Return to Nuremberg

In 1498 Dürer published a series of 15 woodcuts, the *Apocalypse,* which represents the highest achievement of German graphic art in that medium and which had a dramatic message to impart on the eve of the Protestant Reformation. The series is a tour de force in giving shape, in a realistic framework, to the fantastic images conjured up in the Book of Revelation. Each of the woodcuts represents a homogeneous action but at the same time contributes to create a powerful unity of the whole series. In the *Apocalypse* series as well as in the later series of prints representing the Passion of Christ (the *Great Passion,* begun before 1500 and published in 1511; the *Small Passion,* 1509–1511, repeated in copper engravings in 1507–1513; and the *Life of the Virgin,* 1500–1511), Dürer interpreted the Gospel in a new, human, and understandable language, organically fusing northern realism with the ideal beauty of Italy.

In Dürer's painting, another self-portrait (1498; Madrid) marked the turning point of his art. He represented himself as a humanist scholar and an elegant young man without the attributes of his profession. In this way he opposed the concept of art as craft current outside of Italy. "There were many talented youths in our German countries who were taught the art of painting but without fundamentals and with daily practice only. They therefore grew up unconscious as a wild uncut tree," he wrote. He wanted to be different and to change his followers: "Since geometry is the right foundation of all painting, I have decided to teach its rudiments and principles to all youngsters eager for art. . . ."

In his altarpieces Dürer revealed his interest in perspective, as in the *Paumgartner Altarpiece* (1502–1504). His portraits, such as *Oswolt Krell* (1499), were characterized by sharp psychological insight. Dürer depicted mythological and allegorical subjects in engravings on metal, for example, the *Dream of the Doctor* (after 1497) and *Sea Monster* (ca. 1498), and he also used that technique for one of his most popular prints, the *Prodigal Son* (ca. 1496). Dürer represented the hero in a novel way, the scene chosen being neither the prodigal son's sinful life nor the happy ending of his return to his father, but the moment in which the hero becomes cognizant of his sinful life and begins his repentance. In the print *Nemesis* (1501–1502) Dürer's study of human proportion is manifested, together with his taste for complicated humanistic allegory, which appears in several of his prints of that period.

Second Trip to Italy

In 1505 Dürer went to Venice again. Records of that stay abound in his letters to his humanist friend Willibald Pirckheimer. There is no mention of a visit to Rome. The assumption that Dürer visited Rome has been a subject much discussed by art historians. It was only quite recently that the inscription "Romae 1506" was discovered on his painting *Christ among the Doctors* (Lugano), which seems to argue favorably for the assumption that he did go to Rome. Until recently scholars knew only

ed by several artists. The works generally ascribed to him show he was an extremely lively and many-faceted artist, interested in the representation of various aspects of daily life. The prints and drawings he executed at that period were influenced by Schongauer and the Housebook Master, the two major representatives of Rhenish graphic art.

In 1493 Dürer painted a self-portrait (Paris) in which he represented himself in a lyrical, romantic vein and inscribed above his head, "My affairs will go as ordained in Heaven." In May 1494 he returned to Nuremberg, and 2 months later he married Agnes Frey.

First Trip to Italy

In the fall Dürer journeyed to Venice, Padua, and Mantua. He copied works by the leading contemporary Italian masters, and it is apparent in his drawings that he soon learned how to impart to his figures perfection of anatomy, classical pathos, and harmony. It was at this time that Dürer began to be interested in the art of the ancients, although he probably had access to the classical works largely through Italian copies and interpretations. In the process of assimilating the spirit of classical art, he became aware of the necessity of art theory, to which he later devoted much of his time. Dürer's travels not only opened his eyes to the marvels of ancient art but also to the variety to be found in nature, which he captured in his excellent landscape drawings and watercolors of Alpine views.

Melencolia I *was engraved by Dürer in 1514.*
Melencolia; Knight, Death, and the Devil; *and* St.
Jerome in His Study *constitute Dürer's so-called*
Master Engravings. (The Metropolitan Museum of
Art, Rogers Fund, 1919)

that he went as far as Bologna, but even if he really visited Rome his stay there must have been rather short as it left no visible traces in his drawings.

It was the art of Venice that profoundly influenced Dürer's work. He was on good terms there with artists, humanists, and noblemen. He wrote Pirckheimer that the painter Giovanni Bellini was his friend and wanted Dürer to paint a picture for him. It seems, however, that it was Dürer's prints rather than his paintings which established his reputation.

In 1506 Dürer painted for the church of the German merchants in Venice, S. Bartolommeo, his most Italian picture—in composition as in color: the *Feast of the Rose Garlands.* Even today, in spite of its damaged condition, "a solemn splendor of the southern town rests upon the picture," according to M. J. Friedländer. Dürer's portraits done at this time excel by nature of their soft subtlety of chiaroscuro, compositional simplicity, and lyrical mood, for example, *Portrait of a Young Girl* (1505; Vienna). The same freedom of touch, subtle and flexible, characterizes his drawings of nudes, done during and after the Italian journey.

Nuremberg Altarpieces

The large altarpieces executed when Dürer returned to Nuremberg show a mixture of colorful Italianisms with the traditional northern style. One of them is the *Heller*

Altarpiece (1507–1509). The central panel was destroyed by fire in 1729 and is known only through a copy by Jobst Harrich. The wings were painted by Dürer's assistants, and four panels were executed by Mathias Grünewald.

The other two important altarpieces of that period are the *Adoration of the Trinity* (1511) and the *Martyrdom of the Ten Thousand* (1508), in which Dürer's placement of little figures in vast landscapes was a return to his early style, based on the traditions of northern painting. Dürer was also returning to his personal heritage in that he once again took up the engraver's burin as his main tool.

Melancholy and Humanism

Perhaps Dürer's most important works of the period from 1513 to 1520 were his engravings. In them his humanistic interests appear, developed through his friendships with distinguished German scholars, especially Pirckheimer. Through Pirckheimer, Dürer became acquainted with contemporary Italian thought as well as with classical philosophy and its recent revival known as Neoplatonism. The three so-called Master Engravings *Knight, Death, and the Devil* (1513), *St. Jerome in His Study* (1514), and *Melencolia I* (1514) are the climax of Dürer's graphic style and also express his thoughts on life, man, and art.

These engravings are allegories of the three kinds of virtue associated with the three spheres of human activity: in *Knight* the active sphere is depicted; in *St. Jerome,* the contemplative sphere; and in *Melencolia I,* the intellectual sphere, which Erwin Panofsky describes as an allegory of "the life of the secular genius in the rational and imaginative worlds of science and art." The three prints excel not only in transmitting their complicated allegorical messages but also in conveying a powerful expression of mood: heroic in *Knight,* intellectually concentrated but serene in *St. Jerome,* and dramatic and gloomy in *Melencolia.* At the same time they show the greatest virtuosity in the handling of the medium; their silvery, vibrant surfaces contain both graphic and pictorial effects. It is possible that *Melencolia* was connected with a difficult moment in the development of Dürer's theoretical concepts, which he formulated at that time, although it was only later that his theoretical works were published.

Dürer was equally interested in a direct depiction of observed data. Throughout his life he drew and engraved simple motifs studied from life, as in the dramatic drawing of his old mother, emaciated and ill (1514).

Until 1519 Dürer worked for Emperor Maximilian I, taking part in the execution of various artistic projects of allegorical and decorative character, mostly in graphic media (the *Triumphal Arch* and the *Triumphal Procession of Maximilian I)* but also in miniature (drawings in the *Maximilian I Prayer Book,* 1515).

Last Period

In July 1520 Dürer left for the Netherlands in order to receive from Charles V, Maximilian I's successor, the reconfirmation of his yearly salary of 100 florins that Maximilian had allotted him. This trip was a triumph for the artist and proved the esteem with which he was regarded. In his travel journal Dürer left a moving day-by-day record of his stay in Antwerp and of his visits to various Dutch, Belgian, and German towns. He met princes, rich merchants, and great artists. He drew portraits, landscapes, townscapes, and curiosities in his sketchbook. He met Erasmus of Rotterdam, whom he greatly admired and of whom he made a portrait drawing, which he later engraved (1526).

Dürer's last years were difficult. The Reformation was creating great religious and social changes. Dürer supported Martin Luther, whose teachings were heralded by Dürer's *Apocalypse*. In his last drawings, such as the *Oblong Passion* (10 drawings, 1520–1524), he expressed his powerful religious feelings, but held in check by a severe composition.

Dürer's last great work was the so-called *Four Apostles* (1526). The monumental, sculpturesque figures towering in their shallow space represent Saints John and Peter (left panel) and Saints Mark and Paul (right panel). The two paintings were probably intended as the wings of a triptych, the central panel of which was not executed. He gave the panels to the Town Council of Nuremberg. In the panels he included quotations from the writings of the saints represented, which contained accusations against "false prophets." Dürer's work proclaimed the unity of the new faith against the different sects arising at that time.

In 1525 Dürer published his book concerning perspective (*Instruction in Measurement*), and in 1527 his treatise on fortifications appeared. He died on April 6, 1528, a few months before his last and most important theoretical work, *The Four Books on Proportions*, was published. Excellent painter, engraver, and draftsman, Dürer was also a learned theorist. Active in art and science, he was the first true Renaissance artist outside of Italy and in his diversity a typical Renaissance man.

Dürer's Influence

Dürer's influence was greater than that of any artist of northern Europe of his time and was most widely felt through his woodcuts and engravings. He created a language of visual forms that furnished his contemporaries and followers with modern tools adapted to their needs: his art was a translation of the Italian Renaissance vocabulary into a dialect understandable north of the Alps. Dürer was beloved by the German romantic artists and writers of the 19th century, for whom he represented the quintessential German artist.

Further Reading

Albrecht Dürer is listed in the Art study guide (III, E, 1, b). He was influenced by Giovanni BELLINI, Andrea MANTEGNA, and Martin SCHONGAUER. Part of the *Heller Altarpiece* was painted by Mathias GRÜNE-WALD. Albrecht ALTDORFER, Lucas CRANACH THE ELDER, LUCAS VAN LEYDEN, and PONTORMO were influenced by Dürer's engravings.

An English edition of Dürer's writings is William Martin Conway, *Literary Remains of Albrecht Dürer* (1889; rev. ed. 1958). A selection of his writings is included in Wolfgang Stechow, ed., *Northern Renaissance Art, 1400–1600: Sources and Documents* (1966). There are several works on Dürer in English, all overshadowed by the magisterial monograph of the foremost Dürer scholar, Erwin Panofsky, *The Life and Art of Albrecht Dürer* (2 vols., 1943; paperback ed., 1 vol., 1971). Old but good is William Martin Conway, *The Art of Albrecht Dürer* (1910). Wilhelm Waetzoldt, *Dürer and His Times* (1935; trans. 1950), written for a general audience, stresses the cultural background. For a study of Dürer's drawings see *Dürer: Drawings and Water Colours*, selected and with an introduction by Edmund Schilling (trans. 1949); and for the prints see Arthur M. Hind, *Albrecht Dürer: His Engravings and Woodcuts* (1911). The humanistic background and the symbolism of the *Melencolia I* print are discussed in Raymond Klibansky, Erwin Panofsky, and Fritz Saxl, *Saturn and Melancholy* (1964).

DURHAM / By Robin Higham

John George Lambton, 1st Earl of Durham (1792–1840), was the tactless and energetic English statesman best known for his report on Canada, which laid the basis for the country's Dominion status.

John George Lambton was born in London on April 12, 1792. After attending Eton College, he joined the dragoons in 1809 but resigned in 1811. From 1813 to 1828 he was a member of Parliament. In 1830 he was made a privy councilor, created a baron, and appointed lord privy seal, and he also entered the House of Lords. He had a hand in preparing the First Reform Bill of 1832. In the same year he was made ambassador extraordinary in succession to St. Petersburg, Vienna, and Berlin, and he was rewarded for his service by being created viscount the following year. For the next 2 years Lord Durham led the advanced Whigs but in 1835 went once again to St. Petersburg as ambassador to Russia.

In 1837 Lord Durham returned home and in the next year was appointed high commissioner to Upper and Lower Canada and governor general of the British provinces in North America. Revolts in both Upper and Lower Canada in 1837–1838 had warned the British government that the Canadians were demanding responsible government and that the situation could not be ignored. Durham spent 6 months in Canada. He sent political prisoners to Bermuda—with which step he exceeded his orders—and it caused his fall.

But upon his return to Britain, Lord Durham published his famous *Report on the Affairs of British North America*. In it he enunciated the principle that the ex-

*Lord Durham, a painting by Thomas Phillips.
(National Portrait Gallery, London)*

ed. 1962), and C. E. Carrington, *The British Overseas* (1950; 2d ed. 1968).

DURKHEIM / By Fredric Cheyette

The French philosopher and sociologist Émile Durkheim (1858–1917) was one of the founders of 20th-century sociology.

Émile Durkheim (pronounced dür-kĕm′) was born at Épinal, Lorraine, on April 15, 1858. Following a long family tradition, he began as a young man to prepare himself for the rabbinate. While still in secondary school, however, he discovered his vocation for teaching and left Épinal for Paris to prepare for the École Normale, which he entered in 1879. Although Durkheim found the literary nature of instruction there a great disappointment, he was lastingly inspired by two of his teachers: the classicist Numa Denis Fustel de Coulanges and the philosopher Émile Boutroux. From Fustel he learned the importance of religion in the formation of social institutions and discovered that the sacred could be studied rationally and objectively. From Boutroux he learned that atomism, the reduction of phenomena to their smallest constituent parts, was a fallacious methodological procedure and that each science must explain phenomena in terms of its own specific principles. These ideas eventually formed the philosophical foundations of Durkheim's sociological method.

From 1882 to 1885 Durkheim taught philosophy in several provincial lycées. A leave of absence in 1885–1886 allowed him to study under the psychologist Wilhelm Wundt in Germany. In 1887 he was named lecturer in education and sociology at the University of Bordeaux, a position raised to a professorship in 1896, the first professorship of sociology in France.

On his return from Germany, Durkheim had begun to prepare review articles for the *Revue philosophique* on current work in sociology. In 1896, realizing that the task was too much for a single person to do adequately, he founded the *Année sociologique*. His purpose, he announced, was to bring the social sciences together, to promote specialization within the field of sociology, and to make evident that sociology was a collective, not a personal, enterprise. In 1902 Durkheim was named to a professorship in sociology and education at the Sorbonne. There he remained for the rest of his career.

Achieving Consensus

The Division of Labor, Durkheim's doctoral thesis, appeared in 1893. The theme of the book was how individuals achieve the prerequisite of all social existence: consensus. Durkheim began by distinguishing two types of "solidarities," mechanical and organic. In the first, individuals differ little from each other; they harbor the same emotions, hold the same values, and believe the

ecutive branch in Canada would have to make its peace with local interests by instituting a system of responsible government, revising the land ownership laws, fostering immigration, and providing a system of municipal government. He also urged that Upper and Lower Canada be united so as to outnumber the French Canadians. Durham died shortly after his report was completed, in Cowes, Isle of Wight, on July 28, 1840.

Energetic, vain, and high-spirited, Durham tried to keep the Canadian issue nonpartisan in British politics. It is arguable that it was not so much the tactless Durham who created responsible government as the able colonial secretaries and governors who followed him and implemented it.

Further Reading

Lord Durham is listed in the Canada study guide (III, A, 2). The rebellion of William Lyon MACKENZIE and Louis-Joseph PAPINEAU was one of the principal reasons for the issuing of the Durham report.

The best biography of Durham is Leonard Cooper, *Radical Jack: The Life of John George Lambton, First Earl of Durham* (1959). The older works are Stuart J. Reid, *Life and Letters of the First Earl of Durham, 1792–1840* (2 vols., 1906), and Chester W. New, *Lord Durham: A Biography of John George Lambton, First Earl of Durham* (1929). For the place of the Durham report in the development of the British Empire see E. L. Woodward, *The Age of Reform, 1815–1870* (1938; 2d same religion. Society draws its coherence from this similarity. In the second, coherence is achieved by differentiation. Free individuals pursuing different functions are united by their complementary roles. For Durkheim these were both conceptual and historical distinctions. Primitive societies and European society in earlier periods were mechanical solidarities; modern European society was organic. In analyzing the nature of contractual relationships, however, Durkheim came to realize that organic solidarity could be maintained only if certain aspects of mechanical solidarity remained, only if the members of society held certain beliefs and sentiments in common. Without such collective beliefs, he argued, no contractual relationship based purely on self-interest could have any force.

Collective Beliefs

At the end of the 19th century, social theory was dominated by methodological individualism, the belief that all social phenomena should be reduced to individual psychological or biological phenomena in order to be explained. Durkheim therefore had to explain and justify his emphasis on collective beliefs, on "collective consciousness" and "collective representations." This he did theoretically in *The Rules of Sociological Method* (1895) and empirically in *Suicide* (1897). In the first, he argued that the social environment was a reality and therefore an object of study in its own right. "Sociological method," he wrote, "rests wholly on the basic principle that social facts must be studied as things; that is, as realities external to the individual." The central methodological problem was therefore the nature of these realities and their relationship to the individuals who compose society.

In *Suicide* Durkheim demonstrated his sociological method by applying it to a phenomenon that appeared quintessentially individual. How does society cause individuals to commit suicide? To answer this question, he analyzed statistical data on suicide rates, comparing them to religious beliefs, age, sex, marital status, and economic changes, and then sought to explain the systematic differences he had discovered. The suicide rate, he argued, depends upon the social context. More frequently than others, those who are ill-integrated into social groups and those whose individuality has disappeared in the social group will kill themselves. Likewise, when social values break down, when men find themselves without norms, in a state of "anomie" as Durkheim called it, suicide increases.

From what source do collective beliefs draw their force? In *The Elementary Forms of Religious Life* (1912) Durkheim argued that the binding character of the social bond, indeed the very categories of the human mind, are to be found in religion. Behind religion, however, is society itself, for religion is communal participation, and its authority is the authority of society intensified by being endowed with sacredness. It is the transcendent image of the collective consciousness.

During his lifetime Durkheim was severely criticized for claiming that social facts were irreducible, that they had a reality of their own. His ideas, however, are now accepted as the common foundations for empirical work in sociology. His concept of the collective consciousness, renamed "culture," has become part of the theoretical foundations of modern ethnography. His voice was one of the most powerful in breaking the hold of Enlightenment ideas of individualism on modern social sciences.

Durkheim died in Paris on Nov. 15, 1917.

Further Reading

Émile Durkheim is listed in the Social Sciences study guide (VII, D, 2). He was influenced by Numa Denis FUSTEL DE COULANGES. Durkheim's nephew was the anthropologist Marcel MAUSS.

Robert A. Nisbet presents a comprehensive analysis of Durkheim's ideas in *Émile Durkheim* (1965). A collection of essays on various aspects of Durkheim's work appears in Kurt Wolff, ed., *Émile Durkheim, 1858–1917: A Collection of Essays with Translations and a Bibliography* (1960). See also Charles Elmer Gehlke, *Émile Durkheim's Contribution to Sociological Theory* (1915), and Harry Alpert, *Émile Durkheim and His Sociology* (1939). A more general study is Talcott Parsons, *The Structure of Social Action: A Study in Social Theory with Special Reference to a Group of Recent European Writers* (1937; 2d ed. 1964).

Émile Durkheim. (Library of Congress)

DÜRRENMATT

/ By Frederick R. Benson and Monica Stoll

The works of the Swiss playwright Friedrich Dürrenmatt (born 1921) combine surface realism with an absurd and almost surreal artistic vision, expressed in an abundance of oppressive, distorted, often ironic detail.

The son of a Protestant minister, Friedrich Dürrenmatt (pronounced dü′rən-mät) was born near Bern. He studied theology and philosophy at the universities of Bern and Zurich with the intention of becoming a teacher. But he began to write and entered the field of graphic design in order to support himself. During the late 1940s, while residing in Basel, he composed his first two serious plays, *It Is Written* (1946) and *The Blind* (1948).

Dürrenmatt's first success on the postwar German stage was *Romulus the Great* (1949), an "unhistorical historical comedy" about the fall of the Roman Empire. In this commentary on the absurdity of human values—with contemporary satirical implications—the last Roman emperor, more interested in breeding chickens than in politics, stoically accepts the inevitable course of history and hands his crown to the barbarian invader. The dramatist was later to write, "The world, for me, stands as something monstrous, an enigma of calamity that has to be accepted but to which there must be no surrender."

With his two succeeding works, *The Marriage of Mr. Mississippi* (1950), a grotesque "dance of death" mocking ideology as a solution to man's predicament, and *An Angel Goes to Babylon* (1953), an obscure, fragmentary drama challenging "God's injustice," Dürrenmatt's reputation was established in Europe. *The Visit* (1955), however, extended the author's impact. Caught in a struggle between moral and material values, the dramatic protagonist of this work is an entire community which slowly succumbs to the temptation of murdering one of its members for the sake of a promised fortune.

Dürrenmatt's nondramatic prose also explores "black comic" elements with penetrating irony. Among the radio scripts prepared during this period are *The Vega Enterprise* (1956), a science-fiction thriller which ends with the atomic bombing of the last humane sanctuary in a corrupt universe, and *A Nocturnal Conversation with a Despised Man* (1957), which contains a dialogue between the secret executioner and the idealist on the futility of self-sacrifice and the art of dying. Many of his shorter efforts can be termed detective mysteries; in fact, Dürrenmatt wrote, "How is the artist to survive in a 'world of *educated* people, of literates?' . . . Perhaps best by writing crime stories, by creating art where nobody suspects art." His full-length novel *Greek Youth Seeks a Greek Maid* (1955), however, does offer some genuine comic relief from the oppressive quality of the author's world view, but *The Deadly Game* (1956) is yet another study of the subconscious guilt which undermines the basis of existence.

Three years after *The Visit* Dürrenmatt returned to the theater with *Frank V,* a poorly received musical drama. *The Physicists* (1961), his first classically constructed work, restored the playwright to favor. In an interview shortly after *The Meteor* opened in 1966, Dürrenmatt stated, "Theatre has to be sensuous. A play isn't so much constructed as composed, almost musically; resonances, relationships, opposites, reversals determine its structure." Thus the tragic quality of his plays, a sense of alienation created by irony and the bizarre, never detracts from his intelligent mastery of his craft.

Dürrenmatt preferred to term his plays "comedies," and in *Problems of the Theatre* (1955) he expressed the belief that tragedy could no longer be written because the modern age, lacking a well-ordered world—with established standards of guilt and retribution—is not suited for it. Dürrenmatt did not want to be regarded as the spokesman for any particular movement or point of view in theater, and he wrote, "The stage is not a battlefield for theories, philosophies and manifestoes, but rather an instrument whose possibilities I seek to know by playing with it."

Further Reading

Friedrich Dürrenmatt is listed in the Literature study guide (III, J, 2, b). His contemporary Max FRISCH also contributed to the German avant-garde theater.

The Playwrights Speak, edited by Walter Wager (1967), includes a chapter by Dürrenmatt on his theory of theater. Murray B. Peppard, *Friedrich Dürrenmatt* (1970), contains a discussion of Dürrenmatt's writings as well as biographical details. Several critical surveys of drama devote sections to the playwright: see Hugh F. Garten, *Modern German Drama* (1959).

Friedrich Dürrenmatt. (Süddeutscher Verlag, Rohnert)

DUVALIER / By Bleecker Dee

François Duvalier (1907–1971) was Haitian president for life. Trained as a physician and known to his people as "Papa Doc," Duvalier dominated his country and its institutions as no other Haitian chief executive.

Little is known of the origins of François Duvalier (pronounced dü-vå-lyä′). Though some of his ancestors came from Martinique, his parents were Haitians, and he was born in Petit-Goâve in southern Haiti. An early Haitian Africanist, he was one of the founders of the Haitian intellectual Griot movement of the 1930s, and he built a reputation as a scholar, ethnologist, and folklorist.

Duvalier graduated in 1934 from the Haitian National University Medical School. He was active in the U.S. Army–directed sanitary programs initiated in Haiti during World War II. In 1944–1945 he studied at the University of Michigan. After returning to Haiti, Duvalier became minister of health and labor in President Dumarsais Estimé's government. After opposing Paul Magloire's coup d'etat in 1950, Duvalier returned to the practice of medicine, especially the anti-yaws and malaria campaigns. In 1954 he abandoned medicine and went into hiding in the Haitian backcountry, until a Magloire amnesty granted to all political opponents in 1956 enabled him to emerge from hiding. He immediately declared his candidacy for the next elections.

Accession to Power

Duvalier had a solid base of support in the countryside and, like the campaigns of the other candidates, his was based on national reconciliation and reconstruction. He made various tactical alliances with one or more of the other candidates, won the army to his cause, and finally overwhelmed Louis Déjoie, his main opponent, in what turned out to be the quietest and most accurate election in Haiti's history.

In spite of this auspicious start, Duvalier's government was dogged by problems. The defeated candidates refused to cooperate with him and, from hiding, encouraged violence and disobedience. After Fidel Castro came to power, Cuba began to harbor various Haitian refugees, who had escaped the increasingly harsh Duvalier regime. Furthermore, Gen. Rafael Trujillo, dictator of the Dominican Republic and archfoe of Castro, feared a Cuban invasion through Haiti, and this concern led to Dominican meddling in Haitian affairs.

It was during this period that Duvalier created an organization directly responsible to him, the *tonton-macoutes* (TTM), the Haitian version of a secret police. Through the late 1950s to the middle 1960s this force continued to grow and through brutality and terrorism helped to reduce elements which might oppose Duvalier.

In the 1961 Assembly elections Duvalier had his name placed on the top of the ballots. After the "election" he interpreted this impromptu act as a further mandate of 6 years. In the words of the *New York Times* of May 13, 1961, "Latin America has witnessed many fraudulent elections . . . but none will have been more outrageous than the one which has just taken place in Haiti."

After the 1961 elections the American government

François Duvalier. (Organization of American States)

made it clear that the United States regarded those elections as fraudulent and that Duvalier's legal term should end in 1963. During 1962 the American AID Mission was withdrawn from Haiti, and by April 1963 an American fleet maneuvered close to Port-au-Prince. On May 15, to show its disapproval of Duvalier's continued presence, the United States suspended diplomatic relations. At the same time, with Haitian-Dominican relations at a low ebb, Duvalier's pledged ideological enemy, President Juan Bosch of the Dominican Republic, was threatening to invade Haiti. Even the Organization of the American States (OAS) became involved, sending a fact-finding mission to Haiti. However, Duvalier remained firmly in control, the Dominicans backed down, and a few days later the American ambassador was withdrawn.

President for Life

After the election of 1961 and the "continuation" of 1963, it was only a matter of time before Duvalier moved to have himself installed for life as Haitian president. "Responding" to just such a request, Duvalier consented on April 1, 1964. Duvalier's rubber-stamp Legislative Chamber rewrote the 1957 Constitution, specifically altering Article 197 so that he could be declared president for life. A "referendum" was held, and on June 22, 1964, Duvalier was formally invested.

After that time Haitian political life was relatively anticlimactic. Having dominated his country and in the process thwarted the United States, the OAS, and the Dominican Republic, Duvalier was in complete control.

During the 1960s he survived several disastrous hurricanes and several *opéra-bouffe* "invasions." A small, gray-haired, crew-cut, dark-skinned Negro, Duvalier was suffering from chronic heart disease and diabetes. In January 1971 he induced the National Assembly to change the constitution to allow his son, Jean Claude Duvalier, to succeed him. Duvalier died on April 21, 1971, and his son succeeded him without difficulty.

Further Reading

François Duvalier is listed in the Latin America study guide (IV, J, 2). Earlier presidents were Jean Pierre BOYER and Henri CHRISTOPHE.

Recent and useful works on Duvalier and his government include Leslie F. Manigat, *Haiti of the Sixties* (1964); Jean-Pierre O. Gingras, *Duvalier: Caribbean Cyclone* (1967); Al Burt and Bernard Diederich, *Papa Doc* (1969); and Robert I. Rotberg and Christopher K. Clague, *Haiti: The Politics of Squalor* (1971).

Among the several excellent background books on Haiti are Melville J. Herskovits's classic sociological study *Life in a Haitian Valley* (1937); Rayford W. Logan, *The Diplomatic Relations of the United States with Haiti, 1776–1891* (1941); Hugh B. Cave's delightful travelog, *Haiti: Highroad to Adventure* (1952); Seldon Rodman, *Haiti: The Black Republic* (1954; rev. ed. 1961); and James H. McCroklin's monographic work on the U.S. Marine occupation period, *Garde d'Haiti, 1915–1934* (1956). An excellent source of information on anything Haitian is James G. Leyburn, *The Haitian People* (1941; rev. ed. 1966). This classic scholarly work presents an interpretive overview of the history, culture, and society of Haiti and is brought up to date with a new foreword by Sidney W. Mintz.

DVOŘÁK / By Philip Friedheim

> Antonín Dvořák (1841–1904), one of the greatest Czech composers, is most noted for his attractive and apparently effortless melodic gifts and the unfailing brilliance of his orchestration.

Antonín Dvořák (pronounced dvôr′zhäk) was a nationalistic musician, basing his style on melodic and rhythmic patterns found in the folk music of his own country. At the same time he was not excessively concerned with program music, and he worked most successfully in instrumental forms utilizing traditional classical structures, such as symphonies and chamber works. Even those compositions which contain programmatic titles tend toward a general atmosphere rather than a musical structure that follows a preconceived literary outline.

Born on Sept. 8, 1841, in a small town near Prague into a moderately poor worker's family, Dvořák showed considerable interest in music as a child. When he was 16 he moved to Prague to continue his education, studying at

Antonín Dvořák. (Music Division, The New York Public Library)

the Prague Organ School from 1857 to 1859. He received not only a thorough musical training that introduced him to the works of the great masters of the past, but also one that exposed him to the more "advanced" composers like Robert Schumann and Richard Wagner.

In 1861 Dvořák joined the orchestra of the National Theater in Prague as a violist, where he remained for 10 years, performing for a while under the leadership of Bedřich Smetana. During this time Dvořák wrote numerous compositions, but not until 1873, with a performance of his grand patriotic work *Hymnus* for chorus and orchestra, did he achieve some renown. His compositions attracted the attention of Johannes Brahms, who prevailed upon his publisher to print some of Dvořák's works. The two composers became close friends.

Always composing an apparently effortless output of music, including the popular *Slavonic Dances* (1878), Dvořák soon became a professor of composition at the Prague Conservatory. In 1884 he made the first of a series of trips to London to conduct his own music. There he earned a commission to compose a choral work, *The Spectre's Bride*. He received an honorary doctorate degree from Cambridge University in 1891, the same year he composed his popular *Carnival* overture.

After successful tours of Russia and Germany, Dvořák accepted an invitation in 1892 to become the director of the National Conservatory of Music in New York City. While in the United States he wrote what is probably his most famous work, the Symphony in E Minor, *From the New World* (1893). There has always been some confusion as to the extent to which Dvořák either imitated or directly borrowed melodic material from American folk music. All the music is original, however, and despite the fact that the theme of the second movement has been made into the song "Goin' Home," it is not a Negro spiritual but a melodic invention by Dvořák. Perhaps the greatest problem presented by the *New World* Symphony is that it tends to blind audiences to the merits of some of his other symphonies. One in G major (1889) and another in D minor (1885) are certainly its equal in musical quality. In 1893 he also wrote his *American String Quartet,* the best-known of his 13 quartets, and a charming sonatina for violin and piano, a masterpiece in miniature.

In 1895 Dvořák returned to the Prague Conservatory, completing his cello concerto, probably the most outstanding concerto ever written for that instrument, and a perennial concert favorite. From this point on he concentrated on symphonic poems and operas. *Rusalka,* the ninth of his 10 operas, completed in 1900, was his last major work. Very popular in Czechoslovakia although rarely performed outside the country, *Rusalka* is a stunning lyric fantasy, an evocative retelling of the familiar story of the water nymph who fell in love with an all-too-human prince. In 1901 Dvořák became the director of the Prague Conservatory. He died on May 1, 1904.

Further Reading

Antonín Dvořák is listed in the Music study guide (I, H, 2). The founding father of Czech nationalistic music was Bedřich SMETANA.

Two major studies of Dvořák are John Clapham, *Antonín Dvořák: Musician and Craftsman* (1966), which deals mainly with the music, and Gervase Hughes, *Dvořák: His Life and Music* (1967), which treats the biographical data and the works in chronological order. An earlier but still useful work is Alec Robertson, *Dvořák* (1945). Good background studies are Gerald Abraham, *A Hundred Years of Music* (1938; 3d ed. 1964); Rosa Newmarch, *The Music of Czechoslovakia* (1942); and Alfred Einstein, *Music in the Romantic Era* (1947).

DWIGHT / By James Axtell

Timothy Dwight (1752–1817), an American Congregational minister, was president of Yale College and New England's leading religious politician.

Timothy Dwight was born in Northhampton, Mass., into one of New England's most extraordinary families on May 14, 1752. His maternal grandfather was the famed theologian Jonathan Edwards. His mother, a woman of great intellect, educated him according to her own ideas. A child prodigy, Timothy was ready for college at 8, but Yale did not enroll him until he was 13. Studying 14 hours a day, he earned highest honors at graduation in 1769 but also developed an eye ailment that plagued him all his life.

Dwight assumed the headship of the Hopkins Grammar School in New Haven, Conn., for 2 years before returning to Yale as a tutor. There he joined the brilliant "Connecticut Wits," John Trumbull and Joseph Howe, who were patriotic belles-lettrists ambitious to make America "the first in letters as the first in arms." When Yale's aging president was forced to resign in 1777,

Dwight, only 25, was pushed by some for the presidency. But the Yale Corporation had other opinions of the witty young man and called for his resignation instead. Before he left, Dwight married Mary Woolsey on March 3, 1777.

The following October the U.S. Congress appointed Dwight chaplain of the Connecticut Continental Brigade. A year later, on his father's death, he returned to his family in Northampton. He spent 5 vigorous years running two farms, preaching, sitting in the Massachusetts Legislature in 1781 and 1782, and founding a coeducational academy in 1779 to teach modern subjects as well as Latin and Greek. He left the school for the pulpit of Greenfield Hill, Conn., on July 20, 1783, where he established another school.

Dwight's journalistic assault against Yale started in 1783 in the *Connecticut Courant;* he used the pen name Parnassus. But when Yale's president Ezra Stiles prevented any legislative "intermeddling in college affairs," Dwight returned to the writing that had earned him prominence among the Connecticut Wits. *The Conquest of Canaan,* written earlier but published in 1785, was the first epic poem produced in America.

On June 25, 1795, Dwight accepted the presidency of Yale, a few weeks after the death of Stiles. For almost 22 years "Pope Dwight" (as the unregenerate called him) administered the college with great ability, ushering it into its modern era. No scholar himself, he had the vision to appoint men who were or would become scholars, and he allowed greater faculty participation in col-

Timothy Dwight, a portrait by John Trumbull, presented to Yale College by members of the class of 1817. (Yale University Art Gallery)

lege government, traditionally the monopoly of the Yale Corporation and the president. Student relations were significantly improved, though Dwight held autocratic sway. Besides administering an exuberant college and giving counsel of weight in the affairs of state to visiting dignitaries, he taught the moral philosophy course to the seniors, supplied the college pulpit twice a Sabbath, and served as professor of divinity.

On Jan. 11, 1817, Dwight ceased to reign. His stormy life had personified the contradictions and strengths of New England Puritanism wedded to Federalism.

Further Reading

Timothy Dwight is listed in the Religion study guide (I, O, 1, q) and the Social Sciences study guide (VI, G, 3). Tapping REEVE and Noah WEBSTER were also American educators.

The definitive biography of Dwight is Charles E. Cunningham, *Timothy Dwight, 1752–1817* (1942). Kenneth Silverman, *Timothy Dwight* (1969), is a recent scholarly study. See also Leon Howard, *The Connecticut Wits* (1943). Ralph Henry Gabriel, *Religion and Learning at Yale: The Church of Christ in the College and University, 1757–1957* (1958), contains a chapter on Dwight and American Protestantism.

DZERZHINSKY / By Don Karl Rowney

The Soviet politician Felix Edmundovich Dzerzhinsky (1877–1926) participated in the Polish and Russian revolutionary movements. He was the organizer and first administrator of the Soviet internal security apparatus.

F elix Dzerzhinsky (pronounced dyər-zhēn′skĭ) was born in Poland of a landholding family. While still a student, he became involved in antigovernment politics, and on completion of his secondary education he embarked upon a career as a revolutionary political leader. Between 1897 and 1917 he was arrested and imprisoned or exiled five times. Although most of his actual political work was in Poland, he became more deeply involved with the Russian Social Democratic party than with the Social Democratic party of Poland and Lithuania; he was ultimately identified with the Leninist (Bolshevik) faction of the Russian revolutionary movement.

It was only after the Bolshevik seizure of power in 1917 that Dzerzhinsky's talents began to be fully exploited. In December 1917 he accepted appointment as chairman of the All Russian Extraordinary Commission, subsequently known by its Russian initials, Cheka. This organization was responsible for enforcing obedience to party and state decisions during the early days of the Revolution. The Cheka is generally regarded as the principal instrument of "Red terror" during the course of the

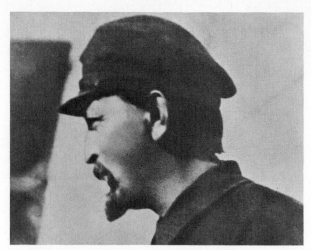

Felix Dzerzhinsky. (Novosti from Sovfoto)

civil war.

Although his opinions on policy frequently varied from those of Lenin, Dzerzhinsky's obedience to established policy seems to have been complete, and he held a large number and range of offices during the unsettled postrevolutionary days. In the summer of 1920 he was appointed head of the People's Commissariat for Internal Affairs (NKVD); the following spring he became commissar of the Peoples' Commissariat of Ways and Communications; and in February 1924 he was named president of the Supreme Council of National Economy (Vesenkha).

Throughout this period Dzerzhinsky supported the stated policy of the party with increasing vigor, while rejecting all alternative views. In particular he stood on the side of centralization as the Central Control Commission, originally founded to ensure that the center reflected the wishes of the party rank and file, became an agency for placing supporters of Stalin's policies in positions of power.

After the death of Lenin in 1924, the struggle for power between Stalin and his opponents sharpened, and Dzerzhinsky increasingly played the role of an apologist of both party unity and Stalin. During a particularly acute Central Committee confrontation in 1926 Dzerzhinsky, vigorously defending Stalin, suffered a fatal heart attack.

Further Reading

Felix Dzerzhinsky is listed in the European History study guide (X, C, 2; XI, O, 1). He strongly supported Joseph STALIN.

There is a translation of Dzerzhinsky's early work in his *Prison Diary and Letters* (1959). Although there is an extensive literature on Dzerzhinsky in periodicals, there are few full-length works. The best known of these in English are B. Jaxa-Ronikier, *The Red Executioner Dzierjinski* (trans. 1935), and Bernard Bromage, *Man of Terror: Dzherzhynski* (1956). Background material on the police apparatus can be found in Simon Wolin and Robert Slusser, eds., *The Soviet Secret Police* (1957).

Eads E Enver Pasha

EADS / By Abram Foster

James Buchanan Eads (1820–1887), an American engineer and inventor, developed ironclad ships during the Civil War and designed the world's first steel-arch bridge.

James B. Eads was born in Lawrenceburg, Ind., on May 23, 1820. His father moved his family often, and James attended various public schools until the age of 13. After 5 years as a dry-goods clerk in St. Louis, he became a purser on a Mississippi River steamboat and a self-taught expert in river navigation and hydrography.

Eads patented a diving bell in 1841 and used it on specially designed craft to salvage wrecked riverboats. After a brief, debt-ridden interval, he returned to salvaging, which proved very lucrative after 1848. He amassed a fortune and lived in semiretirement from 1857 to 1861.

In 1861 President Abraham Lincoln summoned Eads for advice on how to use western rivers for military purposes. Eads proposed a fleet of armor-plated, steam-driven gunboats and contracted to build seven 600-ton vessels. Ironclads became the mainstays of the Army's Western Flotilla and from Oct. 1, 1862, the nucleus of the Navy's Mississippi Squadron.

During the Civil War, Eads built 14 armored gunboats, 6 of them turreted; their 11- and 15-inch guns, worked by steam, could fire every 45 seconds. He converted and armed at least 11 others. These boats were indispensable in defeating the Confederacy.

In 1865 Congress authorized construction of the first bridge across the Mississippi at St. Louis, although it was

James B. Eads. (Library of Congress)

declared impractical by leading civil engineers. Eads was selected to build it. The bridge, with three arches, each over 500 feet, and a roadway 50 feet above the water, was the world's first steel-arch railroad bridge. Finished in 1874 after 6 years of building, it brought Eads international fame. For many years the only bridge spanning the Mississippi, it was vital in opening the transcontinental railroad system.

Among engineers Eads received even greater recognition for his work on the lower Mississippi channel. Congress approved his proposal to open the river's mouth and maintain the channel at his own risk, and the job was completed in 1879. Eads's ingenious jetties redirected and accelerated the current; sediment was deposited at sea, and the channel, deepened to 30 feet, made New Orleans an ocean port.

Eads became a technical adviser on river control for many American and foreign port cities. His plan for deepening the Mississippi northward to the mouth of the Ohio later proved practicable. In 1884 he became the first American to receive England's coveted Albert Medal of the Society of Arts. Later he was the first engineer to be voted into America's Hall of Fame. He died on March 8, 1887, in Nassau, Bahamas.

Further Reading

James B. Eads is listed in the Science study guide (VI, H, 3). Another 19th-century bridge builder was John ROEBLING.

Florence L. Dorsey, *Road to the Sea: The Story of James B. Eads and the Mississippi River* (1947), supersedes earlier biographies by Louis How (1900) and W. Sherwood Stuyvesant (1930).

EAKINS / By Lloyd Goodrich

Thomas Eakins (1844–1916) was the most powerful figure painter and portrait painter of his time in America. He was a leading naturalist and one of the era's strongest painters of the current scene.

Thomas Eakins was born on July 25, 1844, in Philadelphia. After his graduation from Central High School, he studied for 5 years at the Pennsylvania Academy of the Fine Arts, where he drew chiefly from casts. To make up for his lack of study of living models, he entered Jefferson Medical College and took the regular courses in anatomy, including dissecting cadavers and observing operations.

In 1866 Eakins left for Paris, where he went through 3 years of rigorous academic training at the École des Beaux-Arts under Jean Léon Gérôme. He also traveled in Italy and Germany. In December 1869 he went to Spain. In Madrid's Prado Museum his discovery of 17th-century Spanish painting, especially the work of Diego Ve-

Thomas Eakins in his studio. (The Metropolitan Museum of Art, Gift of Charles Bregler, 1941)

lázquez and Jusepe de Ribera, came as a revelation after the insipidity of the French Salons. After a winter in Seville, Eakins went back to Paris. In July 1870 he returned to Philadelphia, where he would live for the rest of his life, never going abroad again.

The Realist

Eakins now took for subjects the life of his place and period, Philadelphia of the 1870s; and with uncompromising realism he built his art out of this. His first American paintings were scenes of outdoor life in and around the city—rowing on the Schuylkill River, sailing and fishing on the Delaware River, hunting in the New Jersey marshes—and domestic genre picturing his family and friends in their homes. These works revealed utter honesty, a sure grasp of character, and an unsentimental but deep emotional attachment to his community and its people. From the first, they had the strong construction, the sense of form and of three-dimensional design, and the complete clarity of vision that were to mark Eakins's style thenceforth. The most important work of this period was the *Gross Clinic* (1875), portraying the great surgeon Samuel D. Gross operating before his students in Jefferson Medical College. The painting shocked the public and critics but established Eakins's reputation as a leader of American naturalism.

Scientific Interests

Eakins had an unusual combination of artistic and scientific gifts. Anatomy, higher mathematics, and the science of perspective were major interests to him and played an essential part in his painting. As early as 1880, he was using photography as an aid to painting, as a means of studying the body and its actions, and as an independent form of pictorial expression. In 1884 he collaborated with the pioneer photographer Eadweard Muybridge in photographing the motion of men and animals, but Eakins improved on Muybridge's method of employing a battery of cameras by using a single camera.

Another of Eakins's interests was sculpture. Sometimes he made small models for figures in his paintings, and he produced several full-scale anatomical casts. In the 1880s and early 1890s he executed eight original pieces. All of them were in relief, some in very high relief, almost in the round. Although he did not try to make sculpture his major medium, the strength and skill of his few pieces indicate that he might have achieved results as substantial as in painting.

The Teacher

A natural teacher, in 1876 Eakins began instructing at the Pennsylvania Academy and in 1879 became acting head of the school. Discarding old-fashioned methods, he subordinated drawing from casts to painting from the model, and based instruction on thorough study of the human body, including anatomy courses and dissection —innovations that were to revolutionize art education in

America. But his stubborn insistence on the nude, particularly the completely nude male model in lectures on anatomy, scandalized the academy trustees and the more proper women students, and he was forced to resign in 1886. Most of his men students seceded from the academy and started the Art Students' League of Philadelphia, which continued for about 7 years, with Eakins as its unpaid head.

Until his early 40s Eakins had painted varied aspects of contemporary life, outdoors and indoors, as well as many portraits. But the academy affair and the lack of popular success for his paintings (at 36 he had sold only nine pictures for a total of a little over $2,000) probably explain why in the middle 1880s he abandoned his picturing of the broader American scene, except occasionally, and concentrated on portraiture.

His Portraiture

In this more restricted field Eakins displayed growing mastery. Those who sat for his portraits were not the wealthy and fashionable, but his friends and students and individuals who attracted him by their qualities of mind —scientists, physicians, fellow artists, musicians, the Catholic clergy. They were pictured without a trace of flattery but with a profound sense of their identity as individuals. Eakins's sure grasp of character, his thorough

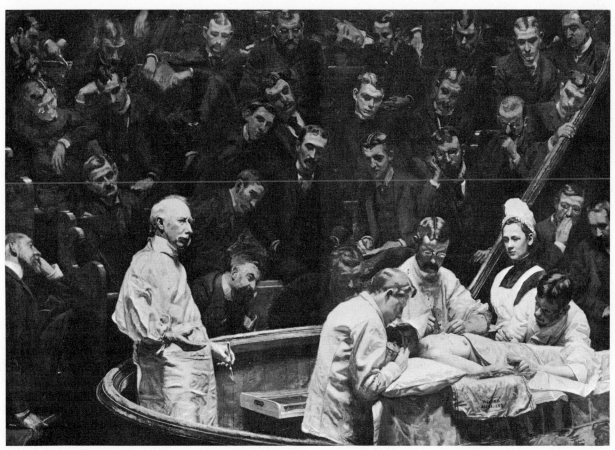

Agnew Clinic, painted by Eakins in 1889. (University of Pennsylvania)

knowledge of the human body, and his psychological penetration gave his portraits intense vitality. His paintings of women, in contrast to the bodiless idealism of his academic contemporaries, had a flesh-and-blood reality and sense of sex. Eakins's portraiture forms the most mature pictorial record of the American people of his time, equal to John Singleton Copley's record of colonial Americans.

But none of these qualities made for worldly success. Commissions were rare. Usually Eakins asked sitters to pose, then gave them the paintings. Even so, his sitters often did not bother to take their portraits, so that he was left with a studio full of them. After the 1880s he suffered increasing neglect from the academic art world—or actual opposition, as when they refused to exhibit the masterpiece of his mature years, the *Agnew Clinic* (1889). In spite of this lack of recognition, he continued to work in the same uncompromisingly realistic style, and some of his strongest works were painted during the 1900s. Finally, in old age, he received a small shower of honors.

In 1884 Eakins had married Susan Hannah Macdowell, a former pupil and a gifted painter. They had no children but many students and friends. Fortunately he had a modest income from his father, and they lived in the family home, where he had lived since childhood. It was there that he died on June 25, 1916.

Eakins's work had a vitality, substance, and sculptural form greater than that of any other American painter of his generation. His figure compositions, particularly the relatively few based on the nude or seminude figure, achieved plastic design of a high order. The prudish limitations of his environment, combined with his own intransigent realism, thwarted full expression of his healthy sensuousness and his potentialities in design. But with all these reservations, Eakins's art was a monumental achievement. He was the first major painter of his period to accept completely the realities of contemporary American life and to create out of them a strong and profound art.

Further Reading

Thomas Eakins is listed in the Art study guide (IV, D, 1, b). With Winslow HOMER he was the American representative of the new naturalism in 19th-century painting. Eakins's sense of his subject's inner life is reminiscent of the powerful portraiture of colonial painter John Singleton COPLEY.

The first monograph on Eakins, and still the most complete, is Lloyd Goodrich, *Thomas Eakins: His Life and Work* (1933). Margaret McHenry, *Thomas Eakins Who Painted* (1946), adds personal material about the artist and his sitters and friends. Roland McKinney, *Thomas Eakins* (1942), and Fairfield Porter, *Thomas Eakins* (1959), are shorter biographical and critical accounts, with numerous illustrations. Sylvan Schendler, *Eakins* (1967), is a full-length study of Eakins and his art in relation to American society and culture of his period and includes 158 illustrations.

EARL / By Abraham A. Davidson

Ralph Earl (1751–1801) was an American painter whose work recalls the archaisms of 17th-century colonial limners. He was one of America's earliest landscape artists.

Ralph Earl was born in rural Connecticut. Nothing is known of his early training. In 1775, working in New Haven, he and the engraver Amos Doolittle visited the recent battle scenes of the American Revolution at Lexington and Concord. Earl's four painted battle pictures, engraved by Doolittle, were among the earliest such scenes done in America. The forms are sharply drawn with little modeling and take on the look of flat paper cutouts.

Earl's father was a colonel in the Revolutionary Army, but Earl's own sentiments lay with the loyalists. Refusing to fight the King's troops and fearing for his safety, he fled to England in 1778, where he remained for 7 years. He left behind him Sarah Gates Earl, his wife and cousin. Later Earl married again (never having divorced his first wife) and also later left his second wife. He seems to have been a man of unstable temperament. William Dunlap's history of American art published in 1834 observed that Earl "prevented improvement and destroyed himself by habitual intemperance."

Ralph Earl's portrait Roger Sherman, *painted about 1777. (Yale University Art Gallery, Gift of Roger Sherman White)*

Only a handful of Earl's paintings from the period prior to his English trip still exist. The best is the portrait *Roger Sherman* (ca. 1777), in which Earl's roughhewn, laborious, but direct approach brings inner qualities of the sitter into full relief. Sherman was a slow, tenacious type who rose from humble origins through his own efforts to become lawyer, judge, and prominent civic leader. Earl painted him in browns and blacks, against a bare backdrop, seated in a plain Windsor chair, looking doggedly ahead.

When Earl returned to America, he tried to settle in New York but could not make a go of it and became an itinerant painter in Connecticut. His colors grew brighter and his figures more supple, but his paintings still had the primitive, 17th-century limner look, which was not uncommon for itinerant painters of the time. His paintings were uneven in quality. Among the best are the portrait *Daniel Boardman* (1789), in which a lovely, grassy landscape with soft mists falling over the hills stretches behind the figure; and the portrait *Mrs. William Mosley and Son Charles* (1791). His Connecticut hillscapes of the 1790s are precise and factual, yet manage to catch the personality of the place.

Earl's clumsy power was representative of the work of itinerant Connecticut painters in the late 18th and early 19th centuries.

Further Reading

Ralph Earl is listed in the Art study guide (IV, B, 1, d). His contemporary Gilbert STUART specialized in portraiture.

Laurence B. Goodrich, *Ralph Earl: Recorder for an Era* (1967), offers a lively account of his career. William Sawitzky, *Ralph Earl, 1751–1801* (1945), is a catalog of an exhibition of Earl's works at the Whitney Museum of American Art, New York, and the Worcester Art Museum, Mass.

* * *

Edward M. East. (Keystone)

EAST / By George H. Daniels

Edward Murray East (1879–1938), an American plant geneticist whose experiments led to the development of hybrid corn, also made distinguished contributions to genetic theory.

Edward M. East was born on Oct. 4, 1879, at Du Quoin, Ill. After high school he worked in a machine shop and in 1897 entered the Case School of Applied Science in Cleveland, Ohio. A year later he transferred to the University of Illinois, graduating with a bachelor of science degree in 1901. In 1903 he married Mary Lawrence Boggs.

East became interested in the new field of genetics. As assistant at the Illinois Agricultural Experiment Station, he analyzed the protein and fat content of Indian corn grown under an experimental breeding program. After receiving his master of science degree at Illinois in 1904, he became an agronomist at the Connecticut Agricultural Experiment Station at New Haven for 4 years. He worked mainly with corn and tobacco but continued his earlier studies with the potato, incorporating these in his doctoral thesis for the University of Illinois in 1907.

Continued experiments on the effects of inbreeding in corn, together with independent work at the nearby Carnegie Institution for Experimental Evolution, finally led East to the development of hybrid corn. This new method of seed production revolutionized corn growing throughout the world.

In 1909 East joined the faculty of the Bussey Institution of Harvard University (later reorganized as a graduate school of applied biology). He continued his corn and tobacco experimentation at the Connecticut Agricultural Experiment Station but also began more theoretical work. He discovered (independently of a Swedish plant breeder) the phenomenon later known as "multiple factors" which provides a Mendelian interpretation for "blending inheritance," previously thought outside of Gregor Mendel's laws. East also made distinguished studies of self- and cross-incompatibility, heterosis, cytoplasmic heredity, and hybridization.

East's work during World War I with the National Research Council and the U.S. Food Administration aroused his interest in the implications of biology for world problems and human affairs. He wrote two popular books warning of impending disaster if the exponential increase in world population was not quickly halted.

East served as president of the American Society of Naturalists (1919) and of the Genetics Society of America (1937). He was a member of the American Philosophical Society and the National Academy of Sciences. He died on Nov. 9, 1938, in Boston.

Further Reading

Edward M. East is listed in the American History study guide (VIII, D, 4). In genetics Hermann J. MULLER found methods for artificially inducing mutations, and Thomas Hunt MORGAN described the phenomena of linkage and crossing-over. In agriculture Henry A. WALLACE developed several strains of hybrid corn, and Luther BURBANK bred many new varieties of plants.

The only source for East's biography is the sketch by Donald F. Jones in the National Academy of Sciences, *Biographical Memoirs*, vol. 23 (1945), which contains a complete list of East's publications.

✳   ✳   ✳

EASTMAN / By Abram Foster

By mass-producing his inventions, the American inventor and industrialist George Eastman (1854–1932) promoted photography as a popular hobby. He was also a benefactor of educational institutions.

George Eastman was born in Waterville, N.Y., on July 12, 1854, and educated in Rochester public schools. He advanced from messenger to bookkeeper in the Rochester Savings Bank by 1877. Frugal with money—his only extravagance amateur photography—he spent his savings on cameras and supplies and went to Mackinac Island. When photographic chemicals ruined his packed clothes, he became disgusted with the wet-plate process.

In the 1870s American photography was still slow, difficult, and expensive. Equipment included a huge camera, strong tripod, large plateholder, dark tent, chemicals, water container, and heavy glass plates. Eastman experimented with dry-plate techniques. He was the first American to contribute to photographic technology by coating glass plates with gelatin and silver bromide. In 1879 his coating machine was patented in England, in 1880 in America. He sold his English patent and opened a shop to manufacture photographic plates in Rochester. To eliminate glass plates, Eastman coated paper with gelatin and photographic emulsion. The developed film was stripped from the paper to make a negative. This film was rolled on spools. Eastman and William Walker devised a lightweight roll holder to fit any camera.

Amateurs could develop pictures after Eastman substituted transparent film for the paper in 1884. Flexible

George Eastman. (Courtesy of The New-York Historical Society, New York City)

film was created by Hannibal Goodwin of New York and a young Eastman chemist, Henry Reichenback. The long patent dispute between Goodwin and Eastman was the most important legal controversy in photographic history. A Federal court decision on Aug. 14, 1913, favored Goodwin. Goodwin's heirs and Ansco Company, owners of his patent, received $5,000,000 from Eastman in 1914.

In 1888 Eastman designed a simple camera, the Kodak (Eastman's coined word, without meaning), which was easy to carry and eliminated focusing and lighting. With a 100-exposure roll of celluloid film, it sold for $25.00. After taking the pictures and sending the camera and $10 to the Rochester factory, the photographer received his prints and reloaded camera. Eastman's slogan, "You press the button, we do the rest," was well known.

Anticipating photography's increased popularity, in 1892 Eastman incorporated the Eastman Kodak Company. This was one of the first American firms to mass-produce standardized products and to maintain a chemical laboratory. By 1900 his factories at Rochester and at Harrow, England, employed over 3,000 people and by 1920 more than 15,000. Eastman, at first treasurer and general manager, later became president and finally board chairman.

Daylight-loading film and cameras eliminated returning them to the factory. To Eastman's old slogan was added "or you can do it yourself." A pocket Kodak was marketed in 1897, a folding Kodak in 1898, noncurling film in 1903, and color film in 1928. Eastman film was indispensable to Thomas Edison's motion pictures; Edison's incandescent bulb was used by Eastman and by photographers specializing in "portraits taken by electric light."

Eastman's staff worked on abstract problems of molecular structure and relativity, as well as on photographic improvements. During World War I his laboratory helped make America's chemical industry independent of Germany, and finally the world leader.

Concerned with employee welfare, Eastman was the first American businessman to grant workers dividends and profit sharing. He systematically gave away his huge fortune to the University of Rochester (especially the medical school and Eastman School of Music), Massachusetts Institute of Technology, Hampton Institute, Tuskegee Institute, Rochester Dental Dispensary, and European dental clinics.

After a long illness the lonely, retiring bachelor committed suicide on March 14, 1932, in Rochester. He had written to friends, "My work is done. Why wait?"

Further Reading

George Eastman is listed in the Science study guide (VI, H, 3). Another famous inventor of the period was Thomas EDISON.

The best biography of Eastman is Carl W. Ackerman, *George Eastman* (1930). Robert Taft, *Photography and the American Scene: A Social History, 1839–1889* (1938), places Eastman in perspective in the evolution of photography. Mitchell Wilson, *American Science and Invention: A Pictorial History* (1954), is also helpful.

＊ ＊ ＊

EATON / By Thomas H. Baker

> Dorman Bridgman Eaton (1823–1899), American lawyer and author, was a strong advocate of civil service reform and wrote the draft on which the Civil Service Act of 1883 was based.

Dorman Eaton was born in Hardwick, Vt., on June 27, 1823. After graduation from the University of Vermont and Harvard Law School, he practiced law in New York City. He distinguished himself as a legal scholar by editing a new edition of James Kent's *Commentaries* and other works, and as a practicing attorney, especially as counsel for the Erie Railroad. In connection with some of the bitter controversies involving the railroad, he was attacked and seriously injured by unidentified assailants.

Meanwhile, Eaton began his lifelong interest in governmental reform, assisting in the creation of a New York City municipal board of health and a professional fire department and in the reorganization of the police courts. In 1856 he married Annie Foster.

In 1870 Eaton gave up his private practice to devote full time to the cause of national civil service reform.

George William Curtis, Carl Schurz, and Eaton were among the earliest advocates of ending the spoils system in national politics. Under President U. S. Grant, Eaton succeeded Curtis as chairman of the first civil service commission, serving from 1873 to 1875, when the commission became ineffectual after Congress cut off its funds.

In the early 1870s Eaton had toured Europe to study civil service reform, and in the late 1870s, at the request of President Rutherford B. Hayes, he revisited England to make a formal report on its merit system. The result, published as *The Civil Service in Great Britain: A History of Abuses and Reforms and Their Bearing upon American Politics* (1880), was influential in the movement for reform in the United States. In the meantime, the New York Civil Service Reform Association, the nucleus of the powerful National Civil Service Reform League, had been founded in Eaton's home.

The assassination of President James Garfield in 1881 by a disappointed office seeker gave impetus to the reform movement, which culminated in the passage of the Pendleton Civil Service Act of 1883. The final bill was based on Eaton's draft. President Chester A. Arthur appointed Eaton chairman of the three-man Civil Service Commission established under the new law, a post he held until his resignation in 1886.

Renewing his interest in city government, Eaton wrote *The Government of Municipalities* (1899), one of the first such studies. He died on Dec. 23, 1899. In his will he endowed chairs at Columbia and Harvard universities to continue the study of national and municipal government.

Further Reading

Dorman Eaton is listed in the American History study guide (VII, G, 4, a). Other activists for civil reform were George William CURTIS and Carl SCHURZ. Senator George PENDLETON sponsored the civil service legislation of 1883 in Congress.

The work of Eaton and his fellow reformers is covered in Frank Mann Stewart, *The National Civil Service Re-*

Dorman Eaton. (Library of Congress)

form League (1929); Paul P. Van Riper, *History of the United States Civil Service, 1789–1957* (1958); and Leonard D. White, *The Republican Era, 1869–1901: A Study in Administrative History* (1958).

✳   ✳   ✳

EBBINGHAUS / By David Shakow

The German psychologist Hermann Ebbinghaus (1850–1909) is best known for his innovative contribution to the study of memory through nonsense syllables.

Hermann Ebbinghaus (pronounced ĕb′ĭng-hous) was born on Jan. 24, 1850, near Bonn. In 1867 he went to the University of Bonn and somewhat later attended the universities of Berlin and Halle. After the Franco-Prussian War he continued his philosophical studies at Bonn, completing a dissertation on Eduard von Hartmann's *Philosophy of the Unconscious,* and received his doctorate in 1873.

Ebbinghaus's goal was to establish psychology on a quantitative and experimental basis. While professor at Berlin, he founded a psychological laboratory, and in 1890 he founded the journal *Zeitschrift für Psychologie und Physiologie der Sinnesorgane.* He became full professor in Breslau in 1894, where he also founded a laboratory. In 1905 he moved to Halle, where he died on Feb. 26, 1909.

In psychology Ebbinghaus found his own way. None of his instructors determined in any marked way the direction of his thinking. A major influence, however, was the combination of philosophical and scientific points of view he found in Gustav Theodor Fechner. He acknowledged his debt in the systematic treatise *Die Grundzüge der Psychologie,* which he dedicated to Fechner.

Ebbinghaus was an unusually good lecturer. His buoyancy and humor, together with the unusual clarity and ease of his presentation, assured him of large audiences. Another valuable trait was his Jamesian tolerance, which led him as editor to publish widely diverse opinions—a policy vital to a young science.

Ebbinghaus himself published relatively little. No records exist of the work he did before he published *Memory* (1885). In the introduction to this work, in the section on nonsense syllables, he says only, "I have hit upon the following method," and goes on to discuss the nature and mechanics of nonsense syllables. Memory, a fundamental central function, was thereby subjected to experimental investigation.

In 1894 William Dilthey claimed that the new psychology could never be more than descriptive and that attempts to make it explanatory and constructive were wrong in principle, leading to nothing but confusion of opinion and fact. Since this amounted to an attack on the very keystone of Ebbinghaus's faith, he undertook, despite his reluctance for controversy, to defend psychology as he understood it. In an article in the *Zeitschrift für Psychologie* for 1896, he justified the use of hypothesis and causal explanation in psychology.

When Ebbinghaus died, the *Grundzüge* that he had begun early in the 1890s was only a little more than half completed; a colleague, Ernst Dürr, finished it. The major virtues of these volumes lie in their readableness and convenient format rather than in any radical approach to psychology, but these qualities, together with their comprehensiveness and minor innovations, were sufficient to produce an enthusiastic reception. Ebbinghaus's *Abriss der Psychologie* (1908), an elementary textbook of psychology, also achieved considerable success.

Ebbinghaus's influence on psychology, great as it was, has been mostly indirect. *Memory,* undoubtedly his outstanding contribution, was the starting point for practically all of the studies that have followed in this field.

Further Reading

Hermann Ebbinghaus is listed in the Social Sciences study guide (VI, F, 2). The history of general experimental psychology has passed through three successive phases, and Ebbinghaus's *Über des Gedächtnis* (1885) stands as the middle-phase landmark, between those of Gustav Theodor FECHNER and Sigmund FREUD.

Ebbinghaus's *Memory: A Contribution to Experimental Psychology* was reissued with a new introduction by Ernest R. Hilgard (1964). There is no biographical work on Ebbinghaus. The most complete picture of him is in Edwin G. Boring, *A History of Experimental Psychology* (1929; 2d ed. 1950). See also Gardner Murphy, *Historical Introduction to Modern Psychology* (1929; rev ed. 1948).

✳   ✳   ✳

EBERT / By Diethelm Prowe

The German Social Democratic leader Friedrich Ebert (1871–1925) served as the first president of Germany.

Friedrich Ebert (pronounced ā′bərt) was born in Heidelberg on Feb. 4, 1871, the son of a master tailor. Trained as a saddler, he turned to socialism at the age of 18 under the influence of an uncle. Although the anti-Socialist law was repealed that same year (1889), political harassment forced the young journeyman to change jobs and residences several times until he settled in Bremen in May 1891. Elected head of the local saddlers' union shortly after his arrival, he devoted his time increasingly to politics. He left his job and joined the Social Democratic organ *Bremer Buerger-Zeitung,* becoming editor in March 1893.

A tireless agitator, popular campaigner, and able organizer, Ebert quickly rose in the Bremen Social Democratic party (SPD). In 1900 he was elected to the City Parliament and became secretary of the local consolidated un-

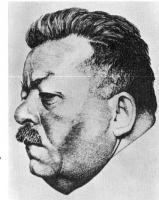

Friedrich Ebert. (German Information Center, New York)

ion organization. From his dominant position in the Bremen labor movement he entered the national party hierarchy in 1905 as secretary of the Party Executive Committee and in 1912 was elected to the Reichstag (Imperial Diet). Here his reputation as a mediator between the right and left wings of the party brought his election to the SPD Executive in 1913; in 1916 he became party floor leader in the Reichstag.

A vigorous advocate of peace and an opponent of annexations during World War I, Ebert was the man to whom the defeated monarchist leadership turned in the face of threatening revolution and chaos in 1918. Initially opposed to the proclamation of the republic, he organized a provisional People's Commission of Social Democrats and Independent Socialists on Nov. 9, 1918. This government signed the armistice with the Western Powers (Nov. 11, 1918), dealt with revolutionary threats from left and right (chiefly through an agreement with the army, the "Ebert-Groener Deal"), and made preparations for the election of a Constitutional Assembly (January 1919). On Feb. 11, 1919, the National Assembly elected Ebert provisional president of the new German Republic; he was reelected by the Reichstag in October 1922.

Ebert gave the presidential office a special dignity through his honesty, simplicity, strong convictions, and concern for the common man. Continually striving to maintain government stability, he promoted strong coalitions of the moderate forces of the Reichstag in order to combat the numerous antirepublican threats from right and left and to strengthen a foreign policy of reconciliation. He was, however, virulently attacked by the nationalist press, and his health finally broke in a bitter struggle against a malicious accusation of high treason (December 1924) which was upheld by a reactionary court. He died in Berlin on Feb. 28, 1925.

Further Reading

Friedrich Ebert is listed in the European History study guide (X, D, 1; XI, D, 1, a). He was influenced by the socialistic thought of Ferdinand LASSALLE. Ebert's policies were opposed by Wolfgang KAPP.

There is no biography of Ebert in English. For general information see Erich Eyck, *A History of the Weimar Republic* (2 vols., 1954–1956; trans., 2 vols., 1962–1963), and Carl E. Schorske, *German Social Democracy, 1905–1917* (1955).

* * *

EBOUÉ / By Edouard Bustin

Adolphe Felix Sylvestre Eboué (1885–1944) was a governor of French Equatorial Africa. As a successful and apparently well-adjusted black Frenchman, he represented the epitome of French assimilationist policy.

Felix Eboué (pronounced ĕ-bwā′) was born in Cayenne, French Guiana, on Dec. 26, 1885, the son of a gold washer and of a comparatively well-educated mother. In 1901 he traveled to France on a scholarship to complete his secondary education at Bordeaux, where he also picked up an adolescent interest in the political ideas of French Socialist leader Jean Jaurès as well as a lifelong penchant for sport. Between 1904 and 1908 he pursued twin courses of study at the Paris Law School and at the École Coloniale.

Early Civil Service

Upon graduating from the École Coloniale in 1908, Eboué asked to be assigned to the French Congo (modern Republic of Congo), an area which had just acquired considerable notoriousness as a result of widespread

Felix Eboué. (H. Roger-Viollet)

abuses committed against the African population. He was sent to the remote and undesirable district of Ubangi-Shari (modern Central African Republic), where he labored tenaciously against administrative inertia and covert racial prejudice, making slow but steady progress on the civil service ladder and collecting anthropological material, which he later published in book form: *Les Peuples de l'Oubangui-Chari* (1931; The People of Ubangi-Shari) and *La Clef musicale des langages tambourinés et sifflés* (1935; The Musical Key to Drum and Whistle Languages).

Eboué's liberal views, his Masonic affiliations, and his friendship with West Indian novelist René Maran, whose prize-winning novel *Batouala* (1921) painted an unflattering picture of French Equatorial Africa, appear to have caused some official annoyance with Eboué during the 1920s. But Eboué was no anticolonialist and seems to have taken a dim view—at least initially—of the criticism leveled against French rule by such men as novelist André Gide and journalist Albert Londres.

In 1932, having finally been promoted to a senior grade in the colonial civil service, Eboué was dispatched to Martinique, then served as secretary general of French Sudan (modern Mali) from 1934 to 1936. With the coming to power of the left-of-center Popular Front coalition in 1936, however, Eboué received his first gubernatorial appointment in Guadeloupe, and although political influences resulted in his recall from that West Indian island after 2 years, he was given a key post in 1938 as governor of Chad.

The appointment of a black governor by a Jewish minister (Georges Mandel) took on additional significance against the ominous backdrop provided by the rise of German and Italian fascism. Also, Chad had a considerable strategic value in view of Mussolini's expansionist policies in Africa. Eboué stepped up military preparedness by developing military roads through northern Chad, which were later used by the Free French forces in their victorious advance into Libya.

Free French Leader in Africa

When France fell in 1940, Eboué refused to follow the Vichy government's orders to break all relations with Great Britain and on Aug. 26, 1940, became the first governor in Africa to rally to De Gaulle, a move that was emulated within a few days by the governors of French Congo and Ubangi-Shari. French Equatorial Africa thus became the first bastion of the Free French government. On Nov. 12, 1940, Eboué was appointed governor general of all Equatorial Africa, and in December, Free French forces, using Chad as a base, began military operations against the Italians.

Eboué's main efforts during the next 3 years were devoted to the pursuit of the war effort, but he also found time to introduce some of the reforms he had advocated as a junior official, such as the development of secondary education and the protection of African values and institutions. At the same time, however, his opposition to any kind of nationalist movement was similar to that of any high official: during his incumbency the Amica-

liste movement in the Congo was severely repressed, and its leader, André Matswa, died in jail in 1942. Eboué's last public action was his participation in the 1944 Brazzaville conference which laid down the principles of postwar French colonial policy. On May 27, 1944, while on leave from his post, he died of pneumonia in Cairo.

Further Reading

Felix Eboué is listed in the Africa study guide (IX, C, 11). Léopold SENGHOR was also prominent in French-speaking Africa.

A biography of Eboué is Brian Weinstein, *Eboué* (1972). Satisfactory histories of Equatorial Africa are scarce. A survey of African history in which Eboué is mentioned is Roland Oliver and J. D. Fage, *A Short History of Africa* (1964). See also Basil Davidson and Adenekan Ademola, eds., *The New West Africa* (1953). A longer study that combines history, sociology, and anthropology is Virginia Thompson and Richard Adloff, *The Emerging States of French Equatorial Africa* (1960).

ECCLES / By Stephen W. Kuffler

The Australian neurophysiologist Sir John Carew Eccles (born 1903) made a series of original contributions to the knowledge of how nerve cells communicate with each other.

John Eccles was born in Melbourne on Jan. 27, 1903. He graduated from medical school in 1925. A Rhodes scholar, he went to Oxford University to work with Charles Scott Sherrington, probably the greatest student of the physiology of the nervous system in the 20th century. Eccles carried on and developed further his teacher's scientific and philosophical ideas. He spent his formative scientific years at Oxford (1925–1937), later worked in Australia and New Zealand, and in 1966 moved to the United States.

During the early 1930s Eccles became interested in the nature of synaptic transmission, particularly in the fundamental question of how signals are transferred from one nerve cell to another. For the next 30 years he pursued this theme in his characteristic style, which was different from that of most scientists. He generally proposed a hypothesis, made it as precise as possible, and championed it with enthusiasm and energy until eventually it was either found to be false or was greatly modified by new experimental data. While many workers feel it is a sign of failure if a pet hypothesis has to be abandoned, Eccles took pleasure in this and was stimulated into a new formulation. The approach of espousing hypotheses and attempting to falsify them by new data Eccles owed to the philosopher of science Karl Popper.

In 1937 Eccles moved to Sydney, where he headed a small, isolated research institute attached to a local hos-

John Eccles. (Australian News & Information Bureau)

pital. With several younger colleagues, including Bernard Katz, who influenced him greatly, he studied the transmission of impulses from nerve to muscle. At that time Eccles held strongly to the view that transmission of signals between cells was "electrical"; that is, information between cells was transferred by current flow. His collaborators favored the view that it was "chemical"; that is, it was mediated by a chemical agent which was secreted by one cell and then spread to a neighboring one. Some years later, largely through Eccles's own experiments, the chemical hypothesis was shown to be the correct one, and as a result he became a proponent of chemical transmission. He carried out studies of synaptic transmission in the mammalian nervous system by making electrical recordings from the interior of individual nerve cells and analyzing in great detail the processes of excitation, as well as inhibition, at cell junctions. For this work he was awarded the Nobel Prize in physiology or medicine in 1963.

Eccles's investigations covered additional areas of the nervous system, as his aim was always an understanding of the working of the entire brain. He explored the functional interconnections in the cerebellum, summarizing his results in *The Cerebellum as a Neuronal Machine* (1967).

Eccles's influence extended beyond his immediate scientific circle. In Australia he was a founder and president of the Academy of Sciences. He published in numerous scientific journals, gave many public lectures, and wrote a series of books which had wide circulation,

including *Physiology of Nerve Cells* (1957) and *Physiology of Synapses* (1964). He also edited *Brain and Conscious Experience* (1966).

Further Reading

John Eccles is listed in the Science study guide (VII, F, 2). England became a flourishing center of neurophysiology, with such eminent men as Charles Scott SHERRINGTON, Lord ADRIAN, and Henry DALE establishing active groups from which emerged the leaders of the neurophysiological sciences.

A sketch of Eccles's life is in Theodore L. Sourkes, *Nobel Prize Winners in Medicine and Physiology, 1901–1965* (rev. ed. 1967). His work is discussed in Alan Lloyd Hodgkin, *The Conduction of the Nervous Impulse* (1964), and in much greater detail in Ragnar Granit, *Charles Scott Sherrington: An Appraisal* (1967).

ECHEVERRÍA / By Donald A. Yates

The Argentine author, poet, and political theorist José Estéban Echeverría (1805–1851) pioneered the romantic mood in literature in the New World and also formulated the political ideals of a secret group combating the dictatorial regime of Rosas.

José Estéban Echeverría (pronounced ā-chā-věr-rē′ä) was born on Sept. 2, 1805, in Buenos Aires. His father died shortly thereafter, and the boy was raised by his mother and several doting aunts. For reasons unexplained and apparently beyond his control, he left school to take a job as a customshouse clerk.

Out of this reflective period came a determination to seek a fuller education than Echeverría's young country could provide. In 1826 Echeverría settled in Paris and resumed his formal studies, most significantly, political science from a sociological perspective. His reading broadened to include writers cultivating a new and exciting mode: Goethe, Schiller, and especially Byron. From these readings developed a growing sense of self-identification with romantic expression and ideas.

By 1830, Echeverría was back in Buenos Aires. His early romantic poems, including "Elvira, or the Bride of the Plate" (1832), attracted little interest. His volume of verses entitled *Consolations* (1834) had considerable public success, owing no doubt to its dominant themes of patriotism and romantic love. In *Rhymes* (1837) he included a long narrative poem called *The Captive Woman*, in which his poetic genius is wedded to national themes. In this poem, with striking descriptions of the Pampa, the Indian tribes of the area, and the romantic adventures of two young lovers, he accomplished his aim of "Americanizing" Argentine literature.

In 1838 Echeverría was instrumental in founding the Association of May, a secret society whose goal was to

José Estéban Echeverría. (Archivo General de la Nacion, Buenos Aires)

return Argentina to democratic rule. Its credo, composed by Echeverría and published in 1846 under the title *The Socialist Dogma,* was an idealistic work of democratic propaganda. The dictator Juan Manuel de Rosas eventually obliged many of the association members, including Echeverría, to flee to Uruguay.

During the years remaining before his death in exile on Jan. 19, 1851, Echeverría wrote some relatively unsuccessful verse—"The Guitar" (1842) and its continuation "The Fallen Angel" (1846)—which dealt with the Don Juan theme. But it was a prose sketch, "The Slaughterhouse," found among his papers and published in 1871 that secured his literary reputation. This starkly realistic anecdote, which recounts the death of a young opponent of the Rosas regime at the hands of Rosas supporters employed at the Buenos Aires slaughterhouse, is one of the most powerful and memorable prose narratives ever written in Spanish America.

Further Reading

José Estéban Echeverría is listed in the Latin America study guide (IV, A, 2, a). Other well-known Argentine writers were Ricardo GÜIRÁLDEZ, José HERNÁNDEZ, and Bartolomé MITRE.

There is no book-length study of Echeverría's work in English. For general background see Alfred Coester, *The Literary History of Spanish America* (1916); Arturo Torres-Ríoseco, *The Epic of Latin American Literature* (1942); Pedro Henriquez-Ureña, *Literary Currents in*

Hispanic America (1945) and A Concise History of Latin American Culture (1947; trans. 1966); Enrique Anderson-Imbert, *Spanish-American Literature: A History,* vol. 1 (trans. 1963; rev. ed. 1969); and Jean Franco, *An Introduction to Spanish-American Literature* (1969). Consult also the Instituto Internacional de Literatura Iberoamericana, *An Outline History of Spanish-America,* edited by John Englekirk and others (1941; 3d ed. 1965).

ECK / By Edward M. Peters

The German theologian Johann Maier von Eck (1486–1543) was a leading Roman Catholic opponent of Luther.

Johann Eck (pronounced ĕk) was born at Eck in Swabia, and like Martin Luther was of peasant stock. He studied at Heidelberg and other universities before becoming a doctor of theology in 1510. Eck taught at the University of Freiburg and after 1510 at the University of Ingolstadt. His academic career was early marked by a taste for humanist scholarship and intense criticism of ecclesiastical abuses, and he soon was widely known and respected as a scholar and orthodox churchman.

In 1517, when Luther, a professor of theology at the University of Wittenberg, published his 95 theses criticizing certain religious practices, Eck responded with a set of countertheses, which he called "Obelisks" and circulated privately. Karlstadt, a supporter of Luther's, obtained a copy of Eck's work and responded publicly with a collection of 400 theses. In 1518 Eck arranged for a debate with Luther and Karlstadt at Leipzig in the following year. At the debate Eck quickly disposed of Karlstadt and then took on Luther himself, skillfully drawing the reformer into extremely heretical positions and achieving a personal triumph.

When academic recognition was slow in coming, Eck took his case to Rome and elicited a papal bull from Leo X excommunicating Luther and condemning his position. Eck then brought the bull back to Germany and urged Emperor Charles V to apply force to Luther. Following Luther's condemnation, Eck remained the defender of Catholicism against him. Since Luther, however, refused to respond to his challenges, Eck turned his attention to other reformers and in a number of works condemned various theological errors. His career as the champion of orthodoxy culminated in his Confutation of the Protestant Augsburg Confession in 1530.

Because of his opposition to the Reformation, Eck has been criticized as a scholar and as a man, both by his contemporary opponents and by many historians since the 16th century. Although he was indeed given to excessive self-praise and could be extremely insulting to his enemies, he was a distinguished scholar, a practical

Johann Eck, an engraving published in 1572. (Bildarchiv)

administrator, and a man very much aware of and sympathetic to the various intellectual currents of his time.

Further Reading

Johann Eck is listed in the Religion study guide (I, H, 2). Among those he opposed were KARLSTADT and Martin LUTHER.

The standard biography of Eck is in German; there is no biography of him in English. The interested reader should consult modern general accounts of the Reformation such as *The New Cambridge Modern History*, vol. 2: G. R. Elton, ed., *The Reformation, 1520–1599* (1958); A. G. Dickens, *Reformation and Society in Sixteenth-Century Europe* (1966); and H. G. Koenigsberger and George L. Mosse, *Europe in the Sixteenth Century* (1968). Another source of information on Eck is the scholarship on Martin Luther; for example, good short accounts are in Roland H. Bainton, *Here I Stand: A Life of Martin Luther* (1950), and Robert Herndon Fife, Jr., *The Revolt of Martin Luther* (1957).

ECKHART / By Edwin H. Zeydel

The German Dominican Johann Eckhart (ca. 1260–ca. 1327), called Meister Eckhart,

founded German mysticism. A theologian and preacher, he represented God as dwelling in man's soul.

Born near Gotha in Thuringia, Johann Eckhart (pronounced ĕk′härt) joined the Dominican order and studied in Strassburg and Cologne. In Paris he received a master's degree in theology in 1302. He became provincial in 1303, later vicar, in Bohemia. In 1311-1313 he was again in Paris as a teacher and then was professor of theology in Strassburg until 1323. Finally, he taught and preached as regent in Cologne.

Eckhart was twice involved in ecclesiastical conflicts. He favored the Pope in the struggle between Louis IV of Bavaria and the papacy over the imperial election. He was later a victim of the displeasure of Archbishop Henry II of Cologne, who was determined to destroy the Dominican order. Cited before a hostile tribunal, Eckhart was accused of heresy on 100 counts. He appealed to Pope John XXII in Avignon and was received there but returned to Cologne because of illness. He died soon after and was posthumously condemned, or suspected, of heresy on over 20 counts.

His Thought

Eckhart's doctrine of the "little spark in man's soul" (*Seelenfünklein*) afforded direct confrontation with God. To him God is not an aloof personal deity in whose image man was created, but a shapeless, incommensurable being ever unchanged and immanent in all matter and creatures. Once man sheds the dross of personal assertiveness and selfish drives, he can merge with God, becoming one with Him, like Christ. Eckhart was deemed heretical for denying a difference between the essence of God and that of creatures and for negating the temporal nature of the world. He was not, however, a pantheist.

Eckhart ranged far in his studies. He was beholden to Aristotle, St. Albertus Magnus, and St. Thomas Aquinas, but also to the Neoplatonism of the Spanish rabbi Maimonides and the Moslem philosopher Averroës. As a preacher and prolific writer, he addressed the people in the vernacular and his fellow clerics in Latin. He coined many German philosophical terms, and scholasticism received a fresh stimulus as he preached of emotions welling from his heart and emerging from everyday life. He influenced two other mystics: Johannes Tauler of Strassburg (died 1361) and the Swiss Heinrich Seuse, or Suso (died 1366).

Further Reading

Meister Eckhart is listed in the Religion study guide (I, F, 5), the Philosophy study guide (II, D, 2), and the Literature study guide (III, C, 3). He developed a new form of "layman's piety," reminiscent of WOLFRAM VON ESCHENBACH. A great 14th-century Flemish mystic was Jan van RUYSBROECK.

Claud H. Field translated *Meister Eckhart's Sermons*

Strassburg is still confined in its medieval walls in this 17th-century view. From 1313 to 1323 Meister Eckhart was professor of theology at Strassburg, probably at the Dominican studium. (Bibliothèque Nationale, Paris)

(1931). *Meister Eckhart: An Introduction to the Study of His Works, with an Anthology of His Sermons* was selected, translated, and annotated by James M. Clark (1957). An excellent background study that discusses Eckhart is Clark's *The Great German Mystics: Eckhart, Tauler, and Suso* (1949).

EDDINGTON / By Roger H. Stuewer

The English astronomer Sir Arthur Stanley Eddington (1882–1944) greatly advanced theoretical astrophysics as a consequence of his original contributions to the theory of relativity and his studies on the internal constitution of stars.

Arthur S. Eddington was born on Dec. 28, 1882, at Kendal, Westmorland. His father was the headmaster and proprietor of a school where John Dalton once taught. Arthur was a precocious child, and by his own account had mastered the 24 x 24 multiplication table before he could read. He received his bachelor's degree in 1902 from Owens College, Manchester, and immediately proceeded to Trinity College, Cambridge. At Cambridge he placed first in the mathematical tripos examination in his second year, an unprecedented achievement. In 1905 he took his bachelor's degree from Cambridge University; in 1907 he became Smith's Prize winner and was elected a fellow of Trinity College; and in 1909 he obtained his master's degree.

In 1906 Eddington was appointed chief assistant at the Royal Observatory at Greenwich. He remained there for 7 years, gaining much practical astronomical experience. While there he initiated a program for determining latitude variation of stars which, with modifications, is still in force today, and engaged in theoretical researches on the systematic motions and distributions of the stars recorded in the Groombridge Catalog. These last studies formed the basis of his Smith's Prize essay and culminated in his book *Stellar Movements and the Structure of the Universe* (1914). One important result was that he confirmed Jacobus Kapteyn's 1904 conclusion that there are two star streams in the Milky Way.

In 1913 Eddington was appointed Plumian professor of astronomy at Cambridge; a year later he became director of the Cambridge Observatory and was elected a fellow of the Royal Society. During World War I he began studies on Albert Einstein's general theory of relativity and on stellar structure. As secretary of the Royal Astronomical Society, Eddington received for publication a copy of Einstein's paper of 1915, the only one to reach England during the war. By the end of the war Eddington had become one of the few men to master Einstein's general theory, had made original contributions to it, and had written the first account of it in English.

In 1919 Eddington led the famous solar eclipse expedition to West Africa and proved, as Einstein's theory demanded, that starlight is deflected in passing close to a massive body such as the sun. Later, Eddington generalized H. Weyl's theory of the electromagnetic field, and in 1925 W. S. Adams spectroscopically verified Eddington's 1924 prediction of a large gravitational red shift of

Arthur S. Eddington, a portrait by W. Rothenstein. (National Portrait Gallery, London)

the light emitted by Sirius's white dwarf companion. In 1930 Eddington proved that an Einstein universe is unstable, thereby lending support to the concept of an expanding universe.

In 1915 Eddington also began studying the internal constitution of stars, a subject largely of his own creation. During the ensuing years he demonstrated, for example, the importance of radiation pressure in helping thermal pressure maintain a star's stability against gravitational collapse. He, as well as Harlow Shapley, showed that variable stars change their brightness because they pulsate. He also derived his famous mass-luminosity law, which shows that the more massive a star, the brighter it is.

Eddington was a master of popular science writing, a talent which he exploited especially after 1927. He also increasingly expounded his controversial philosophical and theological convictions. Moreover, spurred on by Paul Dirac's 1928 discovery of the relativistic wave equation for the electron, Eddington during the last 16 years of his life attempted to wed relativity to quantum theory in what came to be called his fundamental theory. Undisturbed by the criticism that this elegant but speculative theory evoked, Eddington pursued it to the end. Few today accept it, but its positive elements may one day be reborn in different form.

Eddington was knighted in 1930 and received numerous honors throughout his life, including the coveted Order of Merit in 1938. He remained a bachelor and died in Cambridge on Nov. 22, 1944.

Further Reading

Arthur S. Eddington is listed in the Science study guide (VII, B, 1). In his theoretical studies he drew upon the works of Albert EINSTEIN, Edwin HUBBLE, and Paul

DIRAC. One of Eddington's students was the French astronomer Georges LEMAÎTRE.

A full-length biography of Eddington is Allie Vibert Douglas, *The Life of Arthur Stanley Eddington* (1956). For a shorter biographical sketch see H. C. Plummer's obituary notice in the *Biographical Memoirs of the Fellows of the Royal Society*, vol. 5 (1945–1948). See also John W. Yolton, *The Philosophy of A. S. Eddington* (1960).

EDDY / By Donald K. Gorrell

The American founder of the Christian Science Church, Mary Baker Eddy (1821–1910) showed a unique understanding of the relationship between religion and health, which resulted in one of the era's most influential religious books, "Science and Health."

Mary Baker was born July 16, 1821, at Bow, N.H. A delicate and nervous temperament led to long periods of sickness in her early years, and chronic ill health made her weak and infirm during much of her adult life. In 1843 she married George Washington Glover, but he soon died and she returned home, where she bore her only child. She married Daniel Patterson, a traveling dentist, in 1853; however, his frequent trips and her invalidism led to a separation by 1866 and a divorce several years later. In 1877 she married Asa Gilbert Eddy.

In her quest for health, Mary Baker had visited Dr.

Mary Baker Eddy. (Library of Congress)

Phineas P. Quimby of Portland, Maine, in 1862, and found that his nonmedical principles cured her. She absorbed his system and became a disciple. In 1866 she claimed to have been completely cured of injuries suffered in a fall by what she called "Christian science." By 1870 she was teaching her new-found science in collaboration with practitioners who did the healing. Her key ideas were published in *Science and Health with Key to the Scriptures* (1875).

This book and Mary Baker Eddy's forceful personality attracted numerous followers, and on Aug. 23, 1879, the Church of Christ, Scientist, was chartered. Asa Eddy helped organize the movement. Mrs. Eddy chartered the Massachusetts Metaphysical College in 1881, where she taught her beliefs. Asa Eddy died in 1882, and the next year Mrs. Eddy began to publish the *Journal of Christian Science*.

Her fame spread, support grew, and Mrs. Eddy became wealthy. But dissensions divided the Church, and in 1889 "Mother Eddy" moved to Concord, N.H., apparently withdrawing from leadership. In seclusion, however, she restructured the Church organization: the First Church of Christ, Scientist, in Boston was established on Sept. 23, 1892, as the mother church. Mrs. Eddy was its head, and all other churches were subject to its jurisdiction. Though internal quarrels diminished, they continued to the end of her life. Partly to guarantee a trustworthy newspaper for the movement, Mrs. Eddy began publishing the *Christian Science Monitor* in 1908. That year she moved to Chestnut Hill near Boston, where she died on Dec. 3, 1910.

Further Reading

Mary Baker Eddy is listed in the Religion study guide (I, Q, 1, i). A contemporary founder of another new religion was Felix ADLER.

Science and Health with Key to the Scriptures (1875 and later editions) is the most important of Mrs. Eddy's writings. Sibyl Wilbur, *The Life of Mary Baker Eddy* (1908), is the laudatory official biography. A friendly but more scholarly study is Robert Peel, *Mary Baker Eddy* (2 vols., 1966–1971). Critical accounts are Edwin F. Dakin, *Mrs. Eddy: The Biography of a Virginal Mind* (1929), and Ernest S. Bates and John V. Dittemore, *Mary Baker Eddy: The Truth and the Tradition* (1932).

* * *

EDEN / By Eileen and Stephen Yeo

The English statesman Anthony Eden (born 1897) served as prime minister during the disastrous British invasion of Suez in 1956.

From a wealthy and privileged background, Anthony Eden was born on June 12, 1897, the son of Sir William Eden, and was educated at Eton. He interrupted his schooling to fight in the King's Royal Rifle

Anthony Eden, photographed in 1957. (United Press International Photo)

Corps during World War I and then attended Christ Church, Oxford, gaining first-class honors in Oriental languages in 1922. In 1923, as a Conservative, he won the seat he was to hold during the rest of his parliamentary career, Warwick and Leamington. So revealing of the peculiarities of British politics, his first opponent was the Socialist the Countess of Warwick, who was also his sister's mother-in-law. In 1923 he also married Beatrice, the daughter of Sir Gervase Beckett; this union was dissolved in 1950.

Eden's political ascent was steady, as he moved through a series of government posts mainly dealing with foreign affairs. In 1938, as foreign secretary under Neville Chamberlain, he staunchly opposed the "appeasement" policy toward dictators like Hitler and Mussolini, and he resigned from the Cabinet. His book *Foreign Affairs* (1939) reflects his views in this period. When Winston Churchill replaced Chamberlain, he immediately recalled Eden to the Cabinet, seeing him as a trustworthy ally since they shared the same view of the German threat. Besides giving him the posts of secretary for dominion affairs (1939–1940), secretary for war (1940), foreign secretary (1940–1945), and leadership of the House of Commons (1942–1945), Churchill primed him to take over the leadership of the Conservative party. This succession was further cemented when Eden married Clarissa Spencer Churchill in 1952.

Deputy leader of the opposition from 1945 to 1951, Eden became deputy prime minister and foreign secretary when a Tory government was returned in 1951 and became prime minister when Churchill retired in April 1955. In 1956 the Suez crisis broke. Egyptian president Gamal Abdel Nasser nationalized the Suez Canal, which had been jointly owned by the British and French governments and individual shareholders. It was not an unusual nationalistic expropriation, but Eden likened the situation to that of 1938 and overreacted. Largely on his own initiative, he dispatched an Anglo-French military force but withdrew them in the face of hostile world opinion. This action led, however, to severe strain in Anglo-Arab relations. Eden resigned in January 1957 on the grounds of illness; he then retired from the political scene and worked on his *Memoirs*. He was created Earl of Avon in 1961.

Further Reading

Anthony Eden is listed in the European History study guide (XI, A, 1; XII, A, 1) and the International Law study guide (V, A, 1, a). He succeeded Sir Winston CHURCHILL as prime minister and was succeeded by Harold MAC-MILLAN.

Although there are biographies available, such as Alan Campbell-Johnson, *Anthony Eden: A Biography* (1955), the most fascinating sources for Eden's career are his own *Memoirs,* which provide splendid insight into his character: *Facing the Dictators* (1962); *The Reckoning* (1965); and *Full Circle* (1960), which includes his account of Suez.

✳   ✳   ✳

EDGEWORTH / By Anne Fremantle

The British author Maria Edgeworth (1767–1849) wrote novels that are characterized by clear, vivid style, good humor, and lively dialogue.

Maria Edgeworth was born on Jan. 1, 1767, the second of the 21 children (by four wives) of Richard Edgeworth, whose family supposedly came from Edgeware, England, to Edgeworthtown, Ireland, about 1573. Richard Edgeworth was a model landlord, living on his estates and improving them. Maria's mother died when she was 6, and within a few months her father married again. Maria was happy with all her stepmothers, the last being 20 years her junior, and spent her whole life surrounded by her family, never even having a room of her own. She worked in the living room at a desk her father made for her, writing on folio sheets she sewed together in chapters.

When she was 16, Maria became her father's secretary and accountant. Edgeworth was devoted to J. J. Rousseau's ideas and brought up his children on Thomas Day's *Sandford and Merton,* a didactic educational book. Richard encouraged Maria to write, and together they produced *Practical Education,* which advised parents to deliver short sermons, to instruct gradually, and to teach mainly by conversation. Maria's own first book was *The Parents' Assistant* (1796), a delightful collection of short stories, of which the most famous is "Two Strings to His Bow." The same year appeared her *Letters from Literary Ladies.*

In 1800 Miss Edgeworth published *Castle Rackrent,* of which Irish author Padraic Colum wrote, "One can read it in an hour. Then one knows why the whole force of England could not break the Irish people." She was the first to depict Irish peasants as human beings. Miss Edgeworth's *The Absentee* (1812) was written as a play, but Richard Sheridan, who wanted to produce it, found the censor would not allow public discussion of the spending of Irish rents in England. The Russian Ivan Turgenev declared he got a revelation from Maria Edgeworth's sto-

ries, and the word "absenteeism" occurs on the first page of his *Smoke.* Sir Walter Scott said that he hoped "in some distant degree to emulate the admirable Irish portraits of Miss Edgeworth" and that she had shown him his path; in fact, *Waverley* has been called a Scots *Castle Rackrent.* Jeanie Deans, in Scott's *Heart of Midlothian,* may have been modeled on Maria Edgeworth.

Later novels by Miss Edgeworth were *Belinda* (1801), *Ormond* (1817), *Frank* (1822), and *Harry and Lucy* (1825). Sir Walter Scott stated that "in natural appearance she is quite the fairy Whipity of our nursery tale . . . who came flying in through the window to work all sort of marvels. Maria writes while she reads, speaks, eats, drinks and no doubt while she sleeps." Calm, cheerful, and unselfish, she was small and slight, with bright, very blue eyes and tiny hands and feet.

In 1802 Miss Edgeworth went with her father, stepmother, and a small sister to Paris, where she met Madame de Genlis, one of whose books she had translated, and J. A. de Ségur, who had translated her *Belinda.* Her father, to whom she submitted and who corrected all her writing, was thought by all to be a pompous bore. Miss Edgeworth was so modest that Lord Byron wrote, "No one would have suspected she could write her name"; he added, "Her father thought nothing except his own name worth writing." After her father's death Miss Edgeworth took two of her sisters abroad, spending more than a year in France and Switzerland. She was proposed to by the Chevalier Edencrantz, confidential secretary to the king of Sweden, but she would not leave her family, or he his monarch.

In 1823 Miss Edgeworth spent 2 weeks with Sir Walter

Maria Edgeworth. (Radio Times Hulton Picture Library)

Scott at Abbotsford, and in 1825 Scott visited her at Edgeworthtown, which had become a shrine at which all visitors to Ireland paid homage. In 1844 she was made a member of the Royal Irish Academy. At 70 she learned Spanish. During the potato famine of 1847, she worked among the starving. She died on May 22, 1849. Asked during her lifetime to furnish biographical details, she replied that "as a woman" her life had been "wholly domestic and could be of no interest to the public." Her stepmother wrote after Miss Edgeworth's death that "her whole life of eighty-three years, has been an aspiration after good."

Further Reading

Maria Edgeworth is listed in the Literature study guide (II, F, 1, c). Her works were admired by Sir Walter SCOTT.

Two recent works on Maria Edgeworth are Isabel C. Clarke, *Maria Edgeworth, Her Family and Friends* (1950), and Elizabeth Inglis-Jones, *The Great Maria* (1959). An older work is Emily Lawless, *Maria Edgeworth* (1904).

* * *

EDISON / By Abram Foster

The American inventor Thomas Alva Edison (1847–1931) held hundreds of patents, most for electrical devices and electric light and power. Although the phonograph and incandescent lamp are best known, perhaps his greatest invention was organized research.

Thomas Edison was born in Milan, Ohio, on Feb. 11, 1847; his father was a jack-of-all-trades, his mother a former teacher. Edison spent 3 months in school, then was taught by his mother. At the age of 12 he sold fruit, candy, and papers on the Grand Trunk Railroad. In 1862, using his small handpress in a baggage car, he wrote and printed the *Grand Trunk Herald,* which was circulated to 400 railroad employees. That year he became a telegraph operator, taught by the father of a child whose life Edison had saved. Exempt from military service because of deafness, he was a tramp telegrapher until he joined Western Union Telegraph Company in Boston in 1868.

Early Inventions

Probably Edison's first invention was an automatic telegraph repeater (1864). His first patent was for an electric vote recorder. In 1869, as a partner in a New York electrical firm, he perfected the stock ticker and sold it. This money, in addition to that from his share of the partnership, provided funds for his own factory in Newark, N.J. Edison hired technicians to collaborate on inventions; he wanted an "invention factory." As many as 80 "earnest men," including chemists, physicists, and mathemati-

cians, were on his staff. "Invention to order" became very profitable.

From 1870 to 1875 Edison invented many telegraphic improvements: transmitters; receivers; the duplex, quadruplex, and sextuplex systems; and automatic printers and tape. He worked with Christopher Sholes, "father of the typewriter," in 1871 to improve the typing machine. Edison claimed he made 12 typewriters at Newark about 1870. The Remington Company bought his interests.

In 1876 Edison's carbon telegraph transmitter for Western Union marked a real advance toward making the Bell telephone practical. (Later, Émile Berliner's transmitter was granted patent priority by the courts.) With the money Edison received from Western Union for his transmitter, he established a factory in Menlo Park, N.J. Again he pooled scientific talent, and within 6 years he had more than 300 patents. The electric pen (1877) produced stencils to make copies. (The A. B. Dick Company licensed Edison's patent and manufactured the mimeograph machine.)

The Phonograph

Edison's most original and lucrative invention, the phonograph, was patented in 1877. From a manually operated instrument making impressions on metal foil and replaying sounds, it became a motor-driven machine playing cylindrical wax records by 1887. By 1890 he had more than 80 patents on it. The Victor Company developed from his patents. (Alexander Graham Bell impressed sound tracks on cylindrical shellac records; Berliner invented disk records. Edison's later dictating machine, the Ediphone, used disks.)

Incandescent Lamp

To research incandescence, Edison and others, including J. P. Morgan, organized the Edison Electric Light Company in 1878. (Later it became the General Electric Company.) Edison made the first practical incandescent lamp in 1879, and it was patented the following year. After months of testing metal filaments, Edison and his staff examined 6,000 organic fibers from around the world and decided that Japanese bamboo was best. Mass production soon made the lamps, although low-priced, profitable.

First Central Electric-Light Power Plant

Prior to Edison's central power station, each user of electricity needed a dynamo (generator), which was inconvenient and expensive. Edison opened the first commercial electric station in London in 1882; in September the Pearl Street Station in New York City marked the beginning of America's electrical age. Within 4 months the station was lighting more than 5,000 lamps for 230 customers, and the demand for lamps exceeded supply. By 1890 it supplied current to 20,000 lamps, mainly in office buildings, and to motors, fans, printing presses, and heating appliances. Many towns and cities installed central stations.

Increased use of electricity led to Edison-base sockets, junction boxes, safety fuses, underground conduits, me-

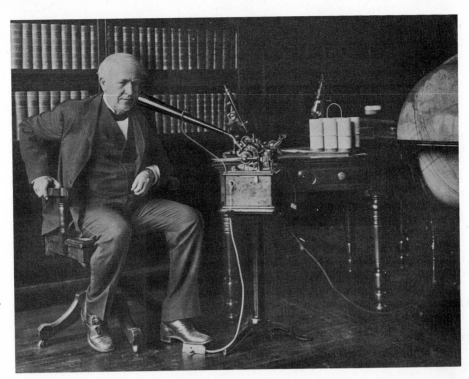

Thomas Edison. (Courtesy of The New-York Historical Society, New York City)

ters, and the three-wire system. Jumbo dynamos, with drum-wound armatures, could maintain 110 volts with 90 percent efficiency. The three-wire system, first installed in Sunbury, Pa., in 1883, superseded the parallel circuit, used 110 volts, and necessitated high-resistance lamp filaments (metal alloys were later used).

In 1883 Edison made a significant discovery in pure science, the Edison effect—electrons flowed from incandescent filaments. With a metal-plate insert, the lamp could serve as a valve, admitting only negative electricity. Although "etheric force" had been recognized in 1875 and the Edison effect was patented in 1883, the phenomenon was little known outside the Edison laboratory. (At this time existence of electrons was not generally accepted.) This "force" underlies radio broadcasting, long-distance telephony, sound pictures, television, electric eyes, x-rays, high-frequency surgery, and electronic musical instruments. In 1885 Edison patented a method to transmit telegraphic "aerial" signals, which worked over short distances, and later sold this "wireless" patent to Guglielmo Marconi.

Creating the Modern Research Laboratory

The vast West Orange, N.J., factory, which Edison directed from 1887 to 1931, was the world's most complete research laboratory, an antecedent of modern research and development laboratories, with teams of workers systematically investigating problems. Various inventions included a method to make plate glass, a magnetic ore separator, compressing dies, composition brick, a cement process, an all-concrete house, an electric locomotive (patented 1893), a fluoroscope, a nickel-iron battery, and motion pictures. Edison refused to patent the fluoroscope, so that doctors could use it freely;

but he patented the first fluorescent lamp in 1896.

The Edison battery, finally perfected in 1910, was a superior storage battery with an alkaline electrolyte. After 8000 trials Edison remarked, "Well, at least we know 8000 things that don't work." In 1902 he improved the copper oxide battery, which resembled modern dry cells.

Edison's motion picture camera, the kinetograph, could photograph action on 50-foot strips of film, 16 images per foot. A young assistant, in order to make the first Edison movies, in 1893 built a small laboratory called the "Black Maria,"—a shed, painted black inside and out, that revolved on a base to follow the sun and kept the actors illuminated. The kinetoscope projector of 1893 showed the films. The first commercial movie theater, a peepshow, opened in New York in 1884. A coin put into a slot activated the kinetoscope inside the box. Acquiring and improving the projector of Thomas Armat in 1895, Edison marketed it as the Vitascope.

Movie Production

The Edison Company produced over 1,700 movies. Synchronizing movies with the phonograph in 1904, Edison laid the basis for talking pictures. In 1908 his cinemaphone appeared, adjusting film speed to phonograph speed. In 1913 his kinetophone projected talking pictures: the phonograph, behind the screen, was synchronized by ropes and pulleys with the projector. Edison produced several "talkies."

Meanwhile, among other inventions, the universal motor, which used alternating or direct current, appeared in 1907; and the electric safety lantern, patented in 1914, greatly reduced casualties among miners. That year Edison invented the telescribe, which combined features of the telephone and dictating phonograph.

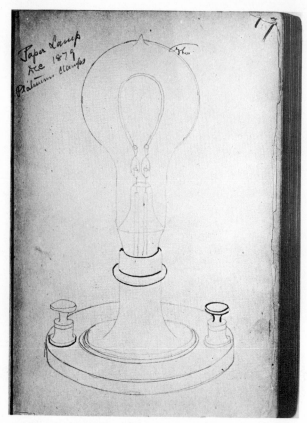

A page from Edison's notebooks showing a sketch of an incandescent lamp, which he invented in 1879. (Edison National Historic Site, West Orange, N.J.)

Work for the Government

During World War I Edison headed the U.S. Navy Consulting Board and contributed 45 inventions, including substitutes for previously imported chemicals (especially carbolic acid, or phenol), defensive instruments against U-boats, a ship-telephone system, an underwater searchlight, smoke screen machines, antitorpedo nets, turbine projectile heads, collision mats, navigating equipment, and methods of aiming and firing naval guns. After the war he established the Naval Research Laboratory, the only American institution for organized weapons research until World War II.

Synthetic Rubber

With Henry Ford and the Firestone Company, Edison organized the Edison Botanic Research Company in 1927 to discover or develop a domestic source of rubber. Some 17,000 different botanical specimens were examined over 4 years—an indication of Edison's tenaciousness. By crossbreeding goldenrod, he developed a strain yielding 12 percent latex, and in 1930 he received his last patent, for this process.

The Man Himself

To raise money, Edison dramatized himself by careless dress, clowning for reporters, and playing the role of homespun sage with aphorisms like "Genius is 1 percent inspiration and 99 percent perspiration" and "Discovery is not invention." He scoffed at formal education, thought 4 hours' sleep a night enough, and often worked 40 or 50 hours straight. As a world symbol of Yankee ingenuity, he looked and acted the part. George Bernard Shaw, briefly an Edison employee in 1879, put an Edison-type hero into his novel *The Irrational Knot:* free-souled, sensitive, cheerful, and profane.

Edison had more than 10,000 books at home and masses of printed materials at the laboratory. When launching a new project, he wished to avoid others' mistakes and to know everything about a subject. Some 25,-000 notebooks contained his research records, ideas, hunches, and mistakes. Supposedly, his great shortcoming was lack of interest in anything not utilitarian; yet he loved to read Shakespeare and Thomas Paine.

Edison died in West Orange, N.J., on Oct. 18, 1931. The laboratory buildings and equipment associated with his career are preserved in Greenfield Village, Detroit, Mich., thanks to Henry Ford's interest and friendship.

Further Reading

Thomas Edison is listed in the Science study guide (VI, H, 3; VII, H, 3). He made the telephone of Alexander Graham BELL practical. Edison used the film of George EASTMAN in his movie-camera inventions.

The most recent biography of Edison, filled with human interest, is Matthew Josephson, *Edison: A Biography* (1959). Biographies emphasizing his inventions include William Adams Simonds, *Edison: His Life, His Work, His Genius* (1934), and H. Gordon Garbedian, *Thomas Alva Edison: Builder of Civilization* (1947). There is more emphasis on industry in John Winthrop Hammond, *Men and Volts: The Story of General Electric*, edited by Arthur Pound (1941). See also Charles Singer and others, eds., *A History of Technology*, vol. 5: *The Late Nineteenth Century* (1958).

EDWARD I / By M. C. Rosenfield

Edward I (1239–1307), known as the "Greatest of the Plantagenets," was king of England from 1272 to 1307. His reign witnessed the growth of parliamentary power, the enactment of extensive reforms, and the spread of English control over Scotland and Wales.

The eldest son of Henry III and Eleanor of Provence, Edward was born on June 17/18, 1239. In October 1254, at the age of 15, he married Eleanor of Castile, by whom he had 10 children. She died in 1290, and in September 1299 Edward married Margaret of France, by whom he had three children.

Soon after Edward's first marriage, Henry III gave him Gascony, Ireland, Bristol, and the march between the Dee and the Conway rivers. In the latter area, as the Earl of Chester, he gained experience in warfare with the Welsh. His attempt to introduce the English system of counties and hundreds provoked Llewelyn ap Gruffydd, Prince of Wales. During the Parliament of Oxford in 1258, Edward sided with his father, but in the following year he became a leader of the "Bachelorhood of England" in support of Simon de Montfort and the Provisions of Westminster. Again in support of his father, Edward attacked the Welsh who were supporting the rebellious barons, and in 1264 he attacked the barons at Northampton. Edward caused his father's defeat and his own capture at the Battle of Lewes. After his escape Edward led the victory over the barons at Evesham, and in the next years, as he received the submission of the barons, Edward became an advocate of a policy of healing.

Edward was made the steward of England in 1268 as well as warden of the city and the Tower of London. He gained popularity by abolishing the levy of customs and by urging laws against the Jewish moneylenders. He left for the Crusades in 1271 and fought bravely at Acre and Haifa. While Edward was on the way home, his father died, and he succeeded to the crown on Nov. 20, 1272.

Domestic and Foreign Policies

After his coronation on Aug. 19, 1274, Edward initiated an active legislative program to overthrow feudalism and to develop the parliamentary system of government. He earned the name of "English Justinian" as a flood of legislation was passed. The first important reform was the Statute of Westminster I, passed in 1275 to amend the evils of the earlier civil war. It was followed by the Statute of Gloucester (1278), which reformed territorial jurisdiction; the Statute of *Mortmain* (1279), which reformed ecclesiastical landholding; the Statute of *Quia Emptores* (1290), which enabled land sales; the Statute of Westminster II, which reformed legal rights; and the Statute of Winchester, which reformed the national military force.

Edward was also busily engaged in the first years of his reign in his attempts to control Wales. Prince Llewelyn at first refused to attend Parliament but submitted to the English in 1276. This submission did not last long, however, and Edward was forced to take up arms, killing Llewelyn in 1282 and bringing his brother, David, to trial in 1283. This victory over the Welsh rebels resulted in the Statute of Wales, which brought the English pattern of administration to Wales.

By 1292 Edward was also involved in Scotland, where 13 claimants sought the throne. After the Scotch asked for arbitration by the English, Edward placed John Balliol (the third son of the founder of Balliol College, Oxford) on the Scottish throne. Balliol was forced to surrender Scotland in 1296, and a second expedition was made in 1300, when the Scottish lords asked that Balliol be allowed to reign. Edward defeated the Scottish rebels under William Wallace at Linlithgow Heath in 1298 and eventually executed Wallace in London.

In addition to attempting to control Scotland and Wales, Edward was active in holding his possessions on the Continent. From 1286 to 1289 he spent much time in France and Gascony. After the loss of Gascony to Philip IV in 1294, he was able to receive support for military activities from a Parliament of all three estates in 1295, and he received financial help from the clergy in 1297. Although the barons opposed the campaign to Gascony, Edward sailed for Bruges to help the Count of Flanders against the French. The following year, at the persuasion of Boniface VIII, he deserted his ally to make a truce with France in order to recover the lost territory.

The last years of Edward's reign were spent in conflict with his barons, who were against his military activities both at home and abroad. To obtain their support, he was forced to reissue the Great Charter in 1299. While traveling north to deal with the threat of Robert Bruce, the new leader of the Scottish rebels, he died at Burgh-on-Sands on July 7, 1307. His burial took place at Westminster Abbey on October 27.

Further Reading

Edward I is listed in the European History study guide (II, D, 1, d; II, F). He succeeded HENRY III of England and was succeeded by EDWARD II. He supported Simon de MONTFORT. As king, Edward opposed LLEWELYN AP GRUFFYDD and ROBERT I.

The most recent biography of Edward I is E. L. G. Stones, *Edward I* (1968). For Edward's early life see F. M.

King Edward I of England meets with his bishops in this illumination from a 14th-century manuscript. (Department of Manuscripts, British Museum)

Harlech Castle, built by Edward I in 1285, in Harlech, Merioneth, Wales. (Ministry of Public Buildings and Works)

Powicke, *King Henry III and the Lord Edward* (2 vols., 1947). Various aspects of the reign are covered in John E. Morris, *The Welsh Wars of Edward I* (1901), and in two works by T. F. T. Plucknett, *Legislation of Edward I* (1949) and *Edward I and Criminal Law* (1960). General histories of the period include Sir James H. Ramsay, *The Dawn of the Constitution* (1908), and F. M. Powicke, *The Thirteenth Century, 1216–1307* (1953; 2d ed. 1962).

EDWARD II /By M. C. Rosenfield

Edward II of Carnarvon (1284–1327) was king of England from 1307 to 1327. His reign witnessed the decline of royal power and the rise of baronial opposition.

Edward II was born on April 25, 1284, the fourth son of Edward I and Eleanor of Castile. He acted as regent during his father's absence in Flanders in 1297–1298, signing the Confirmatio Cartarum. He was created Prince of Wales and Earl of Chester in 1301.

One of his first acts upon succeeding to the crown on July 8, 1307, was to recall his favorite, Piers Gaveston, who had been banished by Edward I, and to make him Earl of Cornwall on August 6. He also appointed Gaveston regent of Ireland and custos of the realm. In January 1308 Edward married Isabella, the daughter of Philip IV of France. These two acts aroused such baronial opposition that 21 "lords ordainers" were appointed to administer the country.

Under the pretense of attacking the Scottish rebels, Edward marched north in 1310. His real aim, however, was to avoid the ordainers and Thomas of Lancaster, the leader of the barons. Civil war broke out. The strife ended with the murder of Gaveston by the Earl of Warwick on June 19, 1312. The following year an amnesty was granted.

Hoping to win popular support, Edward resumed the war against the Scots. His sound defeat by Robert Bruce at Bannockburn in 1314 caused him to lose what little remaining influence he had. Edward's high-handed treatment of the Mortimers and other nobles alienated many of the nobility.

Edward offended his wife by his fondness for the younger Hugh le Despenser. After sending Isabella to France to negotiate a dispute between himself and her brother, he had to deal with her attempt to dethrone him when she returned in 1326 with troops and the support of Roger Mortimer. Unable to count on the support of his barons, whom he had offended by his unwillingness to consult with them, Edward fled to the west and was captured on Nov. 16, 1326, at Neath in Glamorgan. On June 20, 1327, he was forced to resign the throne. Imprisoned in Berkeley Castle, Edward was poorly treated. He was murdered on Sept. 21, 1327, and then buried at Gloucester Abbey.

Further Reading

Edward II is listed in the European History study guide (III, D, 1, a; III, E, 1, a). He succeeded EDWARD I and was succeeded by EDWARD III. He was defeated by ROBERT I.

Edward II's early life is the subject of Hilda Johnson, *Edward of Carnarvon* (1946). Harold F. Hutchison, *Ed-*

ward II (1972), emphasizes the King's political life. The basic study of his reign is T. F. Tout, *The Place of the Reign of Edward II in English History* (1913; 2d rev. ed. 1936). The constitutional history of his reign is treated in J. Conway Davies, *The Baronial Opposition to Edward II* (1918), and the relations with Scotland in W. Mackay Mackenzie's works, including *The Battle of Bannockburn* (1913). A basic general work on the period is May McKisack, *The Fourteenth Century, 1307–1399* (1959).

* * *

EDWARD III / By M. C. Rosenfield

Edward III (1312–1377) was king of England from 1327 to 1377. The Hundred Years War between England and France began during his reign.

King Edward II of England, an electrotype from the effigy in Westminster Abbey. (National Portrait Gallery, London)

The eldest son of Edward II and Isabella of France, Edward III was born on Nov. 13, 1312, at Windsor. He was created Earl of Chester 11 days after his birth; he was made Count of Ponthieu and Montreuil on Sept. 2, 1325, and Duke of Aquitaine a week later. In October 1326 Edward was named guardian of the kingdom, and he succeeded to the throne on Jan. 25, 1327.

For the first 4 years of his reign, Edward III was a figurehead for the rule of his mother and Roger Mortimer, with a regency during his minority in the hands of Henry of Lancaster. On Jan. 24, 1328, Edward married Philippa of Hainaut, by whom he had seven sons and five daughters. Later in 1328 Edward was forced to give up all claims to Scotland by the Treaty of Northampton. This treaty caused Mortimer's unpopularity to grow. In November 1330 Edward was sufficiently strong to have Mortimer executed and to confine his mother for the rest of her life at Castle Rising.

With the government in his own hands, Edward resumed the conflict with Scotland, and by 1332 he had established Edward de Balliol on the Scottish throne. Soon Balliol was ousted, and Edward again invaded Scotland, defeating the Scots in July 1333 at Halidon Hill and conquering southern Scotland and the area north of the Forth.

Edward also concerned himself with the economic interests of the country. In 1332 he encouraged Flemish weavers to come to England and teach their skills. In 1337 he prepared for war against the French, who were hoping to cut into the Flemish wool trade with England. With the support of James van Artevelde of Ghent, Edward made an alliance with Ghent, Ypres, Bruges, and Cassel, as well as a treaty with Emperor Louis V for the hiring of troops. In July 1338 Edward went to Flanders, and the following year he laid siege to Cambrai.

Conflict with France

In order to retain Flemish support, Edward took the title of king of France in January 1340, thus reviving a claim that was to last throughout the medieval period and into the reign of George III. He returned to England for supplies, and that same year the English defeated the French in the naval battle at Sluis, the traditional beginning of the Hundred Years War. Edward returned to France in 1342, landing at Brest with the aim of securing Brittany, and laid siege to Tournai.

The following year plans were made at Sainte-Madeleine for a 3-year truce, but Edward claimed that Philip VI of France broke the truce and sent an English force to sack Harfleur, Saint-Lô, and Caen. Through a flanking movement, the English were able to destroy the French army at the Battle of Crécy near Abbeville on Aug. 6, 1346. After a year-long blockade and siege, Calais surrendered. Lacking supplies to continue the war, Edward returned to England in 1347.

Edward's activities in France had stripped England of troops, giving King David II of Scotland an opportunity to rise in revolt. Encouraged by Philip of France, Scottish troops crossed the border, raiding as far south as the Tyne, and conducted a drive to force the English out of Scotland. This attempt was foiled at the Battle of Neville's Cross in 1346. David was captured and the English recovered much of southern Scotland.

While war with France continued, with a Spanish fleet fighting for France being defeated off Winchelsea in 1350, Edward devoted his attention to internal matters. He founded the Order of the Garter, the senior British

King Edward III of England, electrotype of an effigy in Westminster Abbey. (National Portrait Gallery, London)

order of chivalry, probably in 1348. As a result of an outbreak of the plague, the Statute of Laborers was enacted in 1351 in an attempt to stabilize wages. To control the Church, the Statute of Provisors was enacted the same year and that of Praemunari 2 years later.

By the mid-1350s the war with France had been resumed, but the King now relied on his eldest son, Edward the Black Prince, who led the English to victory at the Battle of Poitiers (Sept. 19, 1356) over King John II of France. The following year, on May 8, Edward III gained vast lands and ransom at the Treaty of Bretigny in return for a promise to abandon his claim to the French throne. This promise was not carried out, and warfare continued.

In 1362 Edward reorganized Gascony and Aquitaine in an attempt to control his French holdings. The following year a plan for the union of England and Scotland was agreed upon by King David but was defeated by the Scottish Parliament. The same period saw the rise of strong English nationalism. The use of French in the law courts ended in 1362, and the payment of Peter's Pence to the papacy was discontinued in 1366. The enactment of the Statute of Kilkenny in 1367 was an attempt to check English colonists in Ireland from adopting Irish customs.

Foreign military commitments continued. In 1367 the Black Prince was sent to help Pedro of Castile regain the throne of Spain, which had been usurped by his half brother, Henry of Trastamare, with the help of the French. Major fighting broke out in France again 2 years later as a result of English "free companies"; the Black Prince seized Limoges and killed all its inhabitants. Desultory warfare occurred in Poitou and Touraine, causing the French to burn Portsmouth in 1369 in retaliation.

Later Reign

Old before his time, Edward took a mistress, Alice Perrers, after the death of his queen in 1369. He allowed the government to be administered by John of Gaunt. He remained passive in the struggles between the barons and the Church, though he attached Church lands in 1371 to raise money for the continuation of the French war. In the struggle between the reforming members of Parliament led by the Black Prince and the Lancastrians led by Henry of Lancaster, his chief minister, Edward was almost a spectator. After the death of the Black Prince in 1376, Edward appears to have been almost deserted. He died the following year on June 21.

During the early years of his reign, Edward was an enlightened king. He made a strong effort to maintain economic ties with Flanders, and his interest in building a navy caused Parliament to call him "king of the sea." However, the military exploits of his reign in the conflict with France were of no lasting benefit to the nation. His victories were due more to superior manpower and supplies rather than to any great military or tactical skill on his part. His financial management had kept the country always in debt, and by the time of his death most of the fruits of his victories had vanished, especially with the loss of Aquitaine in 1374. During the last years of his reign, Edward was unable to cope with either constitutional or social crises.

Edward III and his court watch two jousting knights at a tournament in this illumination from a medieval manuscript. (Bodleian Library, Oxford)

Further Reading

Edward III is listed in the European History study guide (III, A, 1, a; III, D, 1, a). He succeeded EDWARD II and was succeeded by RICHARD II. Among his sons were EDWARD THE BLACK PRINCE and JOHN OF GAUNT. Edward fought the French under PHILIP VI, JOHN II, and CHARLES V.

There is no modern biography of Edward III. For the general background of his reign see Sir James H. Ramsey, *Genesis of Lancaster, 1307–1399* (2 vols., 1913), and May McKisack, *The Fourteenth Century, 1307–1399* (1959). The conflicts with Scotland are treated in E. W. M. Balfour-Melville, *Edward III and David II* (1954), and Ronald Nicholson, *Edward III and the Scots, 1327–1335* (1965). The causes of the French conflict are treated in Henry Stephen Lucas, *The Low Countries and the Hundred Years' War, 1326–1347* (1929). For the war itself see Edouard Perroy, *The Hundred Years War* (1945; trans. 1951); Alfred H. Burne's more detailed *The Crécy War* (1955); and H. J. Hewitt, *The Black Prince's Expedition of 1355–1357* (1958). Foreign relations are dealt with in P. E. Russell, *The English Intervention in Spain and Portugal in the Time of Edward III and Richard II* (1955); religious matters in William Abel Pantin, *The English Church in the Fourteenth Century* (1955);

legal development in B. Wilkinson, *The Chancery under Edward III* (1929); and economic matters in George Unwin, ed., *Finance and Trade under Edward III* (1918). For information on the last years of Edward's life see F. George Kay's account of Edward's mistress, *Lady of the Sun: The Life and Times of Alice Perrers* (1966).

EDWARD IV / By K. Fred Gillum

Edward IV (1442–1483) was the first Yorkist king of England. His reforms and innovations invigorated 15th-century English government.

Born at Rouen on April 28, 1442, Edward IV was the son of Richard, Duke of York, and Cecily Neville. He took part in the Wars of the Roses from the first battle at St. Albans (1455), and in 1460 he accompanied Richard Neville, Earl of Warwick (the "Kingmaker"), and the Calais garrison when Warwick invaded England and raised rebels in Kent and in the north demanding "good government." The success of this uprising established Richard of York as regent and heir of

King Edward IV of England, painted by an unknown artist. (National Portrait Gallery, London)

the ineffective Henry VI of Lancaster, but Henry's queen, Margaret of Anjou, did not accept this political disinheritance of their son, Prince Edward of Lancaster. Her Army of the North defeated and killed Richard of York at Wakefield (Dec. 30, 1460). Margaret's success in liberating Henry VI and her failure to attack London simplified Edward's position. The 6-foot teenager entered the capital and claimed the crown.

Edward's popular election by crowds at St. John's Field (March 1, 1461) and at St. Paul's, Westminster Hall, and the Abbey (March 4, 1461) was a constitutional novelty. Of at least equal importance was the march north and the 10-hour battle at Towton (March 29, 1461), which left the Lancastrians scattered fugitives. The June 28 coronation followed a Parliament that voted attainders but no funds, and it reminded the new king of his promise of better government.

Early Reign

In 1461 Edward's government was more Neville than Yorkist. The 33-year-old Warwick ruled the north, installed his brother George as chancellor, and corresponded with foreign rulers as a national spokesman. However, Edward's 1464 marriage to Elizabeth Woodville, widow of John Grey of Groby, crossed Warwick's plan for the King to marry Bona of Savoy, sister-in-law of Louis XI of France. The numerous Woodvilles advanced rapidly, and inevitably they quarreled with the Nevilles. In 1467 Edward sent Warwick to parley with the diplomats of Burgundy, France, and Brittany. Then he struck his own bargain with Burgundy, dismissed George Neville as

chancellor, and crowned the effect by marrying Warwick's wealthy 79-year-old aunt to a 19-year-old Woodville.

Warwick retaliated forcefully. With Edward's brother George of Clarence as his new candidate, the Kingmaker used the Calais garrison to capture Edward in 1469. However, this time the earl's "good government" slogans failed to win broad support, and Edward regained power. Driving Warwick and Clarence to France was a doubtful success for Edward, for with the help of Louis XI and in the cause of "Lancaster and the Old Families" they returned in 1470. Unarmed and unsupported, Edward fled to Burgundy, and Henry VI was restored.

With help and soldiers from Burgundy, Edward returned to England in 1471. Warwick was slain at Barnet (April 14), Prince Edward was killed at Tewkesbury (May 4), Margaret of Anjou was captured, and Henry VI died the night of the army's return to London (May 21). The lack of a standing army had made the English crown the prize of foreign-sponsored expeditions.

Invasion of France

Alliance with Burgundy and hostility to France was Edward's policy from 1471 to 1475, but it was difficult to coordinate a body as slow as Parliament with a man as unstable as Charles the Bold against an intriguer as seasoned as Louis XI. In 1473 Parliament voted funds for a campaign, but by the time Edward had transported his army to Europe, Charles was distracted by imperial ambitions. Edward conducted his own invasion but only for a price. At Picquigny on Aug. 29, 1475, Edward agreed to give up the expedition and Margaret of Anjou. Louis agreed to pay Edward 75,000 crowns within 15 days and thereafter a secret pension totaling 50,000 crowns per year.

Financially, this settlement turned the tide for Edward. He paid his debts and amassed a comfortable fortune, thus indirectly relieving the pressure on his government's Exchequer. However, even the public form of this treaty was unpopular in England as marking an "inglorious" episode. Edward may have considered England well out of the rivalry that Louis waged against Charles until the latter's death in battle against the Swiss in 1477. Yet the French king's diplomatic net extended to Edward's family, finding a ready dupe in George of Clarence. Edward's patience with his brother's repeated betrayals was exhausted when George reportedly gossiped about the legitimacy of Edward and his children. Clarence was attainted in Parliament and executed in 1478.

Louis's 1482 publication of the secret pension seems to have alarmed Edward into searching for new diplomatic alternatives at the time of his sudden illness and death at Westminster on April 9, 1483. Edward's 12-year-old son was proclaimed Edward V, with his uncle, Richard of Gloucester, as regent.

Further Reading

Edward IV is listed in the European History study guide (III, E, 1, c). His younger brother later ruled as RICHARD III. Edward was allied with CHARLES THE BOLD against LOUIS XI.

The siege of a walled city, an illumination from a Flemish manuscript made for King Edward IV of England. (Trustees of the British Museum)

Cora Scofield, *The Life and Reign of Edward the Fourth* (2 vols., 1923), is a comprehensive biography. Useful background information is supplied in E. F. Jacob, *The Fifteenth Century, 1399–1485* (1961); S. B. Chrimes, *Lancastrians, Yorkists, and Henry VII* (1964; 2d ed. 1966); and J. R. Lander, *The Wars of the Roses* (1965). On constitutional developments of the period, S. B. Chrimes, *English Constitutional Ideas in the Fifteenth Century* (1936), presents a useful commentary, while B. Wilkinson, *Constitutional History of England in the Fifteenth Century, 1399–1485* (1964), excerpts documents and chronicles on major events.

EDWARD VI / By Melvin J. Tucker

Edward VI (1537–1553) was king of England and Ireland from 1547 to 1553. His short reign witnessed the introduction of the English Prayer Book and the Forty-two Articles, and thus this period was important in the development of English Protestantism.

The son of Henry VIII and his third wife, Jane Seymour, Edward VI was born on Oct. 12, 1537. His mother died 12 days after his birth. Edward spent most of his childhood at Hampton Court, where he pursued a rigorous educational regimen. He learned Latin, Greek, and French and studied the Bible and the works of Cato, Aesop, Cicero, Aristotle, Thucydides, and the Church Fathers. Roger Ascham, the author of *The Schoolmaster,* was a sometime tutor of his penmanship, and Sir John Cheke of Cambridge instructed him in classical subjects. Philip van Wilder taught him the lute. Edward knew a little astronomy and occasionally jousted. When lost in his studies, he was cheerful.

Since Edward was only 9 years old when he became king in 1547 on the death of his father, a group of councilors stipulated in Henry VIII's will ruled the kingdom in his name. His council elected his uncle Edward Seymour, the Earl of Hertford, as lord protector, and Hertford soon was created Duke of Somerset.

Somerset's Protestantism and his interest in solving the government's financial difficulties set England on a course of religious and economic change. Thomas Cranmer, the archbishop of Canterbury, given liberty to indulge his Protestant tendencies, pushed through the repeal of Henry VIII's Six Articles (1547), dissolved the chantries (1547), and through the Act of Uniformity (1549) endorsed an English Prayer Book that prescribed a new religious service. This Prayer Book was subsequently revised in 1553 (Second Act of Uniformity). All Englishmen were forced to use it and to adopt the Protestant form of worship. Reaction to the first Prayer Book stimulated an uprising, the Western Rebellion in Cornwall in 1549, which was quelled at Exeter. The Forty-two Articles of religious belief adopted by Parliament in 1551 demonstrated further movement toward Protestant doctrine and were eventually made the basis of Elizabeth's Thirty-nine Articles.

Edward had a consuming interest in religion. No study delighted him more than that of the Holy Scriptures. He daily read 12 biblical chapters, and he encouraged preachers with strong Protestant views. For example, Nicholas Ridley and Hugh Latimer, both later executed for their beliefs by Queen Mary I, were regular preachers. Even the Scottish reformer John Knox delivered a few sermons. John Calvin, the Geneva reformer, wrote to him.

Resistance to a new tax on sheep (1548) and an inquiry into enclosure led to a Norfolk rising called Ket's Rebellion (1549), which was instrumental in precipitating Somerset's fall. The rebellion fueled the antagonism of John Dudley, Earl of Warwick, who thought Somerset too lenient in dealing with the rebels. Warwick became Edward's chief minister and was created Duke of Northumberland. He had, however, little time in which to practice his authority. Edward contracted measles and smallpox in April 1552 and was never well thereafter. He was still too young for marriage. A contract made in 1543 for his marriage to Mary, Queen of Scots, had been abandoned in 1550. In 1551 a contract had been drawn for the hand of Elizabeth, the daughter of Henry II of France. But on July 6, 1553, Edward died of tuberculosis.

A priggish, austere boy, Edward had little sympathy for his uncle Somerset and almost no friends. He was short for his age and fair-complected and had weak eyes. His death at 15 left the English Protestant cause without its principal defender and caused Northumberland hastily and unlawfully to place his daughter-in-law, Lady Jane Grey, on the throne. Though Edward's reign was brief, it marks an important milestone in the development of English Protestantism.

Further Reading

Edward VI is listed in the European History study guide (IV, A, 1, b) and the Religion study guide (I, J, 1). He succeeded HENRY VIII and was succeeded by MARY I. The Duke of SOMERSET and Thomas CRANMER served under Edward.

The best biography of Edward VI is Hester W. Chapman's scholarly and well-written *The Last Tudor King* (1958), which underscores personal detail. See also the older, less objective study by Sir Clements R. Markham, *King Edward VI: An Appreciation* (1907). For background on the religious change consult Jasper Ridley, *Thomas Cranmer* (1962), and A. G. Dickens, *The English Reformation* (1964; rev. ed. 1967).

EDWARD VII / By Barry McGill

Edward VII (1841–1910) was king of Great Britain and Ireland from 1901 to 1910. His short reign was marked by peace and prosperity.

Born on Nov. 9, 1841, at Buckingham Palace, Edward VII was the eldest son of Victoria and Albert. Bertie, as he was nicknamed, proved unresponsive to the elaborate educational scheme his parents imposed. He gained command of German and French, some skill in public speaking, and little else. Beginning in 1859, he attended Christ Church, Oxford, for four terms, interrupted by an American tour in 1860. Formal schooling ended in 1861 at Trinity College, Cambridge.

Dismayed by what Queen Victoria called "Bertie's fall," which occurred with an actress in Ireland in 1861, his parents considered travel and an early marriage the best remedy. Discussion of Princess Alexandra, whose father was heir to the Danish throne, as a suitable bride preceded the Prince Consort's death in 1861. After a trip to the Holy Land, Edward married Alexandra at Windsor on March 10, 1863.

Despite Victoria's early determination to initiate Ed-

King Edward VII of England. (Queens Borough Public Library, Picture Collection)

ward into affairs of state, she withheld the key to Foreign Office boxes during his long tenure as Prince of Wales because of his indiscretion. Edward's imprudence persisted during his exclusion from apprenticeship: he had to testify in the Mordaunt divorce case (1870); he was deeply involved in the Aylesford scandal (1876); and the Tranby Croft affair (1891) brought him to court again, this time as a witness to cheating at baccarat. Understandably, the tone of the prince's set alarmed the Queen and offended nonconformist consciences. But his hearty self-indulgence had an appeal transcending classes. As a winner at the racecourse and as an arbiter of taste, the prince was genuinely popular. The European web of dynastic marriages familiarized Edward with other royalties. He relished the spectacular state visits required by British diplomacy, but he did not make foreign policy.

When he succeeded to the throne on the death of Victoria in 1901, Edward was a portly, balding, bearded figure. He created the Order of Merit and introduced automobiles as royal transport. Edward supported Lord Fisher's naval reforms and Lord Haldane's reorganization of the army, but he was not as close to any ministers as Queen Victoria had been to Lord Melbourne and Benjamin Disraeli. The great constitutional crisis of his reign—whether to promise the Liberal ministry a creation of

(Opposite) Edward VI as a child, a painting by Hans Holbein the Younger, in the National Gallery, Washington, D.C. (Kodansha)

PARVVLE PATRISSA, PATRIÆ VIRTVTIS ET HÆRES
ESTO, NIHIL MAIVS MAXIMVS ORBIS HABET.
GNATVM VIX POSSVNT COELVM ET NATVRA DEDISSE,
HVIVS QVEM PATRIS, VICTVS HONORET HONOS.
ÆQVATO TANTVM, TANTI TV FACTA PARENTIS,
VOTA HOMINVM, VIX QVO PROGREDIANTVR, HABENT
VINCITO, VICISTI. QVOT REGES PRISCVS ADORAT
ORBIS, NEC TE QVI VINCERE POSSIT, ERIT.

peers sufficient to overcome the Tory majority in the House of Lords, and, if so, on what conditions—was unresolved at his death. Edward VII died of bronchitis followed by heart attacks on May 6, 1910, and he was interred at Windsor.

Further Reading

Edward VII is listed in the European History study guide (IX, A, 1, b). He succeeded VICTORIA and was succeeded by GEORGE V. Lord BALFOUR and Lord ASQUITH served under Edward.

Sir Sidney Lee, *King Edward VII: A Biography* (2 vols., 1925–1927), may be supplemented by Philip Magnus, *King Edward the Seventh* (1964). For the flavor of Edward's reign see S. Nowell-Smith, ed., *Edwardian England, 1901–1914* (1964).

EDWARD THE BLACK PRINCE

/ **By M. C. Rosenfield**

The English soldier-statesman Edward the Black Prince (1330–1376) was heir apparent to the English throne. Active in the military affairs of the period, particularly in the English conflict with France, he earned fame as a skillful and valorous fighter.

Born on June 15, 1330, Edward the Black Prince, also known as Edward of Woodstock (after his place of birth), as Prince of Wales, and sometimes as Edward IV, was the eldest son of Edward III and Philippa of Hainaut. On March 18, 1333, shortly before his third birthday, he was created Earl of Chester, and he was made Duke of Cornwall on March 3, 1337. During the next few years he was guardian of the kingdom while his father was absent on the Continent, and on May 12, 1343, Edward was created Prince of Wales. At the age of 15 he was knighted by his father at La Hogue, and the following year Edward took an active role in the winning of the Battle of Crécy against the French. It was at this battle that he obtained the name of "the Black Prince," possibly because he wore black armor.

In the following years Edward was active in the military expeditions of his father, taking part in the expedition to Calais in 1349. By 1355 he was the King's lieutenant in Gascony and leader of an army in Aquitaine that was invading southeastern France. In 1356 he was outflanked in battle by King John. After a failure to negotiate a peace, Edward defeated the French and captured their king at the Battle of Poitiers (September 19).

In October 1361 Edward married the 33-year-old Joan, Countess of Kent, who was the widow of Sir Thomas Holland. As an orphan, she had been brought up in the household of Edward III along with Edward. Known as the "Fair Maid of Kent," Joan had two sons by the Black Prince.

Edward continued to play an active role in the govern-

ment and in military matters. On July 19, 1362, he was created prince of Aquitaine and Gascony, and during the next years he was busy in France, attempting to check the "free companies" that continued to war against the French. In 1367 he undertook an expedition into Spain to assist Don Pedro of Castile, who had been deprived of his throne by Henry of Trastamare with French aid. With an army of 30,000 men Edward crossed the Pyrenees and won a third great battle at Navarrete. Due to illness, he was forced to return to his holdings in France. When war broke out with Charles V of France in 1369, Edward laid siege to Limoges. Upon its capture all its inhabitants were put to death.

Ill health caused Edward to return to England in 1371, and in the following year he resigned his principality and began to take an active part in English internal politics. He became the champion of the constitutional policy of the Commons against the corrupt court and the party of the Lancastrians. Edward was active in the reform plans as set forth in the "Good Parliament" of 1376, but his

Edward the Black Prince, electrotype of an effigy in Canterbury Cathedral. (National Portrait Gallery, London)

death caused much of this work to remain undone. He died on June 8, 1376, a month before the Parliament was dissolved.

Although he is known to history as a great soldier, the Black Prince's victories were due more to superior numbers than to great skill on his part. His greater contribution was his attempt to deal with the political situation in England.

Further Reading

Edward the Black Prince is listed in the European History study guide (III, A, 1, a: III, D, 1, a). He was the son of EDWARD III and the brother of JOHN OF GAUNT. His son reigned as RICHARD II.

The primary sources on the Black Prince are Jean Froissart, *The Chronicle of Froissart*, translated by Sir John Bourchier (6 vols., 1901–1903; repr. 1967); *The Life of the Black Prince by the Herald of Sir John Chandos*, edited by Mildred K. Pope and Eleanor C. Lodge (1910); and *The Register of Edward, the Black Prince* (4 vols., 1930–1933). There is no recent comprehensive biography of Edward, although a recent short study by Dorothy Mills, *Edward, the Black Prince* (1963), is of value. Older works are G. P. R. James, *A History of the Life of Edward the Black Prince* (2 vols., 1836); R. P. Dunn-Pattison, *The Black Prince* (1910); and Marjorie Coryn, *The Black Prince* (1934). Edward's military activities are related in H. J. Hewitt, *The Black Prince's Expedition of 1355–57* (1958), and his burial in Sir James Mann, *The Funeral Achievements of Edward the Black Prince* (1950). For historical background on the period see May McKisack, *The Fourteenth Century, 1307–1399* (1959), and Arthur Bryant, *The Atlantic Saga*, vol. 2: *The Age of Chivalry* (1964).

✳   ✳   ✳

EDWARD THE CONFESSOR

/ **By Robert W. Hanning**

Edward the Confessor (died 1066), the last king of the house of Wessex, ruled England from 1042 to 1066. Attracted to religion and to Norman culture, he was not a vigorous leader. He gained a reputation, not fully deserved, for sanctity and was eventually canonized.

The youngest son of Ethelred the Unready and his Norman wife, Emma, Edward was born sometime after 1002. When Ethelred's authority crumbled in the face of Danish invasions and dissensions among the English nobility, Emma and her children took refuge in 1013 at the court of Richard II, Duke of Normandy. Ethelred died in 1016, and Edward's eldest brother, Edmund Ironsides, succeeded him but died later the same year. Cnut of Denmark was in possession of England, and Edward and his remaining brother Alfred were in exile in Normandy. As he grew up, Edward became thoroughly imbued with Norman manners.

After Cnut's death in 1035, England experienced several years of factional strife, during which Edward's brother Alfred returned to England and was murdered by a powerful earl, Godwin of Wessex. In 1041 Cnut's last surviving son designated Edward his successor, and the following year Edward, with widespread popular support, became king of England.

The first half of Edward's reign was full of uncertainties. Until 1047 England was threatened by a possible invasion by King Magnus of Norway, who claimed the English throne because of an agreement made with Cnut's son. Meanwhile, internal difficulties sprang from the rivalries of the great earls Godwin, Leofric, and Siward (formerly Cnut's councilors) and their ambitious descendants. Godwin, murderer of Edward's brother, was especially troublesome, but Edward, lacking the power to confront him, pacified him for several years. Edward married his daughter Edith in 1045. The match was childless, inspiring a later legend that Edward, in his saintliness, had never consummated it. Edward also met opposition from his mother, whose lands he confiscated in 1043. To counteract his lack of trusted English councilors, Edward invited to his court a number of Norman and Breton knights and clerics, whose presence angered the English magnates.

In 1051 Edward, using as an excuse Godwin's refusal to obey an order, moved against his great rival. He exiled Godwin, banished Edith from the court, designated William, Duke of Normandy, as heir to the throne of England, and arranged that a Norman, Robert of Jumièges, become archbishop of Canterbury. The following year the situation reversed itself. Godwin returned with a large fleet, and he and Edward were officially reconciled to prevent a civil war and resultant Norse invasion. The archbishop and most of the Norman courtiers were banished. Godwin died soon after, in 1053, but his son Harold became Earl of Wessex and Edward's most powerful adviser.

For the rest of his reign Edward, by choice or necessity, did not exercise dominant control over affairs of state, leaving to Harold, to Godwin's other son Tostig (from 1055 to 1065 Earl of Northumbria), and to other powerful nobles the prosecution of wars against the revived power of Wales and the settling of domestic policies. In 1057 Edward's nephew, since 1016 an exile in Hungary, came to visit him but died soon after his arrival in mysterious circumstances. His death made it clear that Edward's successor would be either William of Normandy or the popular Harold of Wessex.

Edward became increasingly interested in religious matters, devoting much of his attention in his later years to the founding of Westminster Abbey. He also loved hunting and was less inclined to ascetic and pious practices than his posthumous reputation, based on a miracle-laden hagiographical biography written soon after his death, suggests. Edward died on Jan. 5, 1066. Harold was quickly chosen his successor, but by the end of the year William of Normandy (known as the "Conqueror") had been crowned at Westminster in the abbey whose construction Edward had supervised with such loving care.

Edward the Confessor gives his instructions to Harold in a scene from the Bayeux Tapestry. This 11th-century tapestry, once attributed to Queen Mathilde, wife of William the Conqueror, depicts the Norman conquest of England and hangs in the Musée de l'Ancien Évêché, Bayeux. (Giraudon)

Further Reading

Edward the Confessor is listed in the European History study guide (I, F, 1). A son of ETHELRED, he was succeeded by WILLIAM I of England.

The main historical source for Edward's life and reign is *The Anglo-Saxon Chronicle,* edited and translated by G. N. Garmonsway (1953). A modern full-length study is Frank Barlow, *Edward the Confessor* (1970). The hagiographical *The Life of King Edward,* edited and translated by Frank Barlow (1962), is not a historical record but testifies to the growth of the cult of Edward after his death. See also F. M. Stenton, *Anglo-Saxon England* (1943; 2d ed. 1947), and C. N. L. Brooke, *The Saxon and Norman Kings* (1963).

EDWARD THE ELDER
By Robert W. Hanning

Son and successor of Alfred the Great, the Anglo-Saxon king Edward the Elder (died 924) continued his father's spirited defense of Anglo-Saxon domains against Danish invaders. He also greatly increased the power of the West Saxon monarchy.

Nothing of importance is known of Edward before his succession to the West Saxon kingship in 899, on the death of his father, Alfred. At that time Wessex and its dependent kingdoms were in no immediate danger of invasion by the Danes, who had harassed England for over a century and whom Alfred had twice beaten off decisively. Nonetheless, the colonies established by the Danes in northern and eastern England were a constant threat to the Anglo-Saxons, and Edward fought occasional, inconclusive battles with the colonists during the first decade of his reign. On one occasion, shortly after his accession, his cousin Ethelwold, frustrated in his attempt to claim the rule of Wessex for himself, raised an army in Danish England and attacked Edward's lands. Edward raided East Anglia in retaliation and killed Ethelwold.

In 909 Edward sent an army to attack the Northumbrian Danes. When they retaliated the following year, the Danes were so conclusively defeated that they ceased to be a factor in the Anglo-Danish wars for some years. Edward then began a systematic campaign to subdue East Anglia and the Danish midlands with the help of his sister, Ethelfleda (Aethelflaed), Lady of the Mercians, widow of a Mercian king dependent upon Wessex. Her chain of fortresses constructed throughout northern Mercia and Edward's intelligent use of the militia system created by Alfred enabled the King to consolidate his annual gains against the Danes and to turn the chronic disunity of the colonists against themselves.

Edward the Elder as depicted on a contemporary coin. (Bibliothèque Nationale, Paris)

When Ethelfleda died in 918, Edward assumed closer control over Mercia. In the same year several of the princes of western Wales accepted Edward as their lord. By the end of 918 the last Danish strongholds had surrendered. Now all England south of the Humber was under Edward's authority.

In the later years of his reign Edward fought battles against new adversaries—Viking raiders stationed in Ireland who attacked the western coast of Mercia. In 920 Edward campaigned against the raiders, and at the end of the summer all the kings of Britain acknowledged his overlordship. Thereafter, Edward remodeled the administrative structure of Mercia, creating several new shires. His last battle was fought against a rebellious force of allied Mercians and Welshmen—two groups traditionally restless under West Saxon domination.

Edward died on July 17, 924, and was succeeded by his son Athelstan, who consolidated his father's considerable military and political achievements.

Further Reading

Edward the Elder is listed in the European History study guide (I, F, 1, b). He succeeded ALFRED as king of the Anglo-Saxons.

The known facts of Edward's life and reign are preserved in *The Anglo-Saxon Chronicle*, edited and translated by G. N. Garmonsway (1953). F. M. Stenton, *Anglo-Saxon England* (1943; 2d ed. 1947), provides the most lucid and thorough modern commentary. For other useful background see the chapter on Aethelflaed, Lady of the Mercians, in Peter Cleomoes, ed., *The Anglo-Saxons* (1959).

EDWARDS / By Jesper Rosenmeier

Jonathan Edwards (1703–1758), colonial New England minister and missionary, was one of the greatest preachers and theologians in American history.

At the close of the 17th century, the science of Isaac Newton and the philosophy of John Locke had significantly changed man's view of his relationship to God. Man's natural ability to discover the laws of creation seemed to demonstrate that supernatural revelation was not a necessary prelude to understanding creation and the creator. God was no longer mysterious; He had endowed men with the power to comprehend His nature and with a will free to choose between good and evil.

It was Jonathan Edwards's genius that he could make full use of Locke's philosophy and Newton's discoveries to reinterpret man's relationship to God in such a way that the experience of supernatural grace became available to people living in an intellectual and cultural climate very different from that of 17th-century England. In so doing, Edwards helped transmit to later generations the richest aspect of American Puritanism: the individual heart's experience of spiritual and emotional rebirth. Further, by his leadership in the religious revivals of the early 18th century, Edwards helped make the experience an integral part of American life for his own time and for the following century.

Jonathan Edwards was born on Oct. 5, 1703, in East Windsor, Conn., where his father was a minister. Jonathan's grandfather was pastor to the church in Northampton, Mass. Jonathan was the only boy in the family; he had 10 sisters. He graduated from Yale College in 1720, staying on there as a theology student until 1722, when, though not yet 19 years old, he was called as minister to a church in New York. Edwards served there for 8 months. In 1723, though called to a church in Connecticut, he decided to try teaching. He taught at Yale from 1724 to 1726.

Early Writings

At an early age Edwards showed a talent for science. At Yale he studied Newton's new science and read Locke with more interest "than the most greedy miser" gathering up "handfuls of silver and gold, from some newly discovered treasure." During these years he also began recording his meditations on the Bible and his observations of the natural world. Edwards's central purpose was not to become a scientist but to lead a life of intense holiness.

Edwards's "Personal Narrative" (written ca. 1740) and his letters and diaries show a young man whose religious experience was of great power and beauty. As Edwards tells it, after several "seasons of awakenings," at the age of 17 he had a profound religious experience in which "there came into my mind so sweet a sense of the glorious *majesty* and *grace* of God, that I know not how to express. I seemed to see them both in a sweet conjunction; majesty and meekness joined together; it was a sweet, and gentle, and holy majesty; and also a majestic meekness; an awful sweetness; a high, and great, and holy gentleness." Adapting Locke's philosophy to his own purposes, Edwards interpreted the "sweet" sense of God's majesty and grace as a sixth and new sense, created supernaturally by the Holy Spirit. As he wrote later in *A Treatise of Religious Affections* (1746), the new sense is not "a new faculty of understanding, but it is a new foundation laid in the nature of the soul, for a new kind of exercises of the same faculty of understanding."

Edwards's perception of ultimate reality as supernatural is further evidenced in his statement that "the world is . . . an ideal one." He wrote in his youthful "Notes on the Mind": "The secret lies here: That, which truly is the Substance of all Bodies, is the infinitely exact, and precise, and perfectly stable Idea, in God's mind, together with his stable Will, that the same shall gradually be communicated to us, and to other minds, according to certain fixed and exact Methods and Laws."

In 1726 Edwards was called from Yale to the Northampton church to assist his grandfather; when his grandfather died in 1729, Edwards became pastor of the church. In 1727 he married the beautiful and remarkable Sarah Pierrepont of New Haven.

Early Revivals

Religious revivals had been spreading through New England for 100 years. In his youth Edwards had seen "awakenings" of his father's congregation, and his grandfather's revivals had made his Northampton church second only to Boston. In early New England Congregationalism, church membership had been open only to those who could give public profession of their experience of grace. The Halfway Covenant of 1662 modified this policy, but when Edwards's grandfather allowed all to partake of the Sacraments (including those who could not give profession of conversion), he greatly increased the number of communicants at the Lord's Supper.

Edwards's first revival took place in 1734–1735. Beginning as prayer meetings among the young in Northampton, the revivals soon spread to other towns, and Edwards's reputation as a preacher of extraordinary power grew. Standing before his congregation in his ministerial robe, he was an imposing figure, 6 feet tall, with a high forehead and intense eyes. A contemporary wrote that Edwards had "the power of presenting an important Truth before an audience, with overwhelming weight of argument, and with such intenseness of feeling, that the whole soul of the speaker is thrown into every part of the conception and delivery. . . . Mr. Edwards was the most eloquent man I ever heard speak."

Edwards endeavored to convey as directly as possible the meaning of Christ's Crucifixion and Resurrection. His words, he hoped, would lead his listeners to a conviction of their sinful state and then through the infusion of divine grace to a profound experience of joy, freedom, and beauty. Edwards's *A Faithful Narrative of the Surprising Work of God in the Conversion of Many Hundred Souls in Northampton, and the Neighboring Towns and Villages* (1737) relates the history of the 1734–1735 revival and includes careful analyses of the conversions of a 4-year old child and an adolescent girl.

Edwards's preaching and writings about the nature and process of the religious experience created powerful enemies. In western Massachusetts the opposition to Edwards was led by his relatives Israel and Solomon Williams, who maintained that a man's assurance of salvation does not lie in a direct and overpowering experience of the infusion of grace and that he may judge himself saved when he obeys the biblical injunctions to lead a virtuous life. Edwards too believed that a Christian expresses the new life within him in virtuous behavior, but he denied that a man is in a state of salvation simply because he behaves virtuously. For him, good works without the experience of grace brought neither freedom nor joy.

In 1739 Edwards preached sermons on the history of redemption. He clearly thought the biblical promises of Christ's kingdom on earth would be fulfilled soon. His interest in the history of redemption is further evidenced in the many notes he made on the prophecies he found in the Bible and in natural events.

Great Awakening

In 1740 the arrival in America of George Whitefield, the famous English revivalist, touched off the Great Awakening. Revivals now swept through the Colonies, and thousands of people experienced the infusion of

Jonathan Edwards, a portrait by Joseph Badger. (Yale University Art Gallery, Bequest of Eugene Phelps Edwards, 1938)

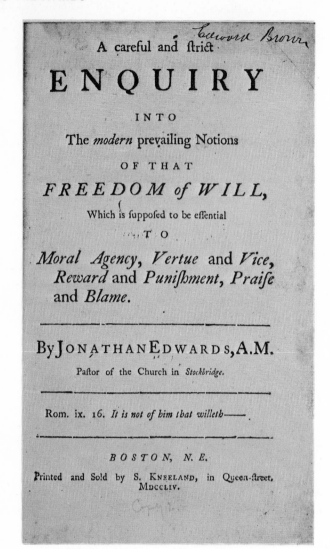

A careful and ſtrict · *Edward Brown*

ENQUIRY

INTO

The *modern* prevailing Notions

OF THAT

FREEDOM of WILL,

Which is ſuppoſed to be eſſential

TO

Moral Agency, Vertue and *Vice,
Reward* and *Puniſhment, Praiſe*
and *Blame.*

By Jonathan Edwards, A.M.

Paſtor of the Church in *Stockbridge.*

Rom. ix. 16. *It is not of him that willeth*——

BOSTON, N. E.

Printed and Sold by S. Kneeland, in Queen-ſtreet.
MDCCLIV.

Title page of the first edition of Jonathan Edwards's treatise A Careful and Strict Enquiry into the Modern Prevailing Notions of That Freedom of Will . . ., *published in Boston in 1754. (Library of Congress)*

grace. The emotional intensity of the revivals soon brought attacks from ministers who believed that White-field, Edwards, and other "evangelical" preachers were stirring up religious fanaticism. The most famous attack was made by Charles Chauncy in *Seasonable Thoughts on the State of Religion in New England* (1743).

Edwards defended the Great Awakening in several books. He acknowledged that there had been emotional excesses, but on the whole he believed the revivals were remarkable outpourings of the Holy Spirit. His works of defense include *The Distinguishing Marks of a Work of the Spirit of God* (1741), *Some Thoughts Concerning the Present Revival of Religion in New England* (1742), and *A Treatise Concerning Religious Affections* (1746), the last a classic in religious psychology. He also wrote a biography of his daughter's fiancé, the Indian missionary David Brainer.

The Great Awakening intensified Edwards's expecta-

tions of Christ's kingdom. With English and Scottish ministers, he began a Concert of United Prayer for the Coming of Christ's Kingdom. To engage people in the concert, he wrote *An Humble Attempt to Promote Visible Union of God's People in Extraordinary Prayer for the Revival of Religion* (1747).

Edwards's Dismissal

The troubles that culminated in Edwards's dismissal from Northampton began in the 1740s. Considerable opposition to Edwards had remained from his revivals. Animosity between him and members of his congregation was increased by an embarrassing salary dispute and an incident in 1744 when Edwards discovered that some children had been secretly reading a book on midwifery. Many children of influential families were implicated; Edwards's reading of their names publicly from the pulpit was resented. But the most important factor in Edwards's dismissal was his decision, announced in 1748, that henceforth only those who publicly professed their conversion experience would be admitted to the Lord's Supper. His decision reversed his grandfather's policy, which Edwards himself had been following for 20 years.

Edwards was denied the privilege of explaining his views from the pulpit, and his written defense, *An Humble Inquiry into the Rules of the Word of God, Concerning the Qualifications Requisite to a Complete Standing and Full Communion with the Visible Christian Church* (1749), went largely unread. After a bitter struggle, the church voted 200 to 23 against Edwards, and on July 1, 1750, he preached his farewell sermon.

Late Works

In August 1751 Edwards and his large family went to Stockbridge, Mass., where he had been called as pastor to the church and missionary to the Indians. As a missionary, he defended the Indians against the greed and mismanagement of a local merchant. These struggles consumed much of his time, but he still managed to write extensively. Among the most important works are *A Careful and Strict Enquiry into the Modern Prevailing Notions of That Freedom of Will . . .* (1754) and *The Great Christian Doctrine of Original Sin Defended* (1758). In the first, he asserted that a man has freedom to choose but freedom of choice is not the same as freedom of will. The power which decides what a man will choose—his willing—is in the hands of God and beyond his personal control. In *Original Sin* Edwards maintained that all men live in the same unregenerate state as Adam after the fall.

Two other works show that Edwards had not become embittered by his dismissal. In *The Nature of True Virtue* (1756) he defines virtue as benevolence to "being" in general. *Concerning the End for Which God Created the World* (1756) is a prose poem, a praise to God Who is love, and Whose universe is the expression of God's desire to glorify Himself.

In January 1758 Edwards became president of the College of New Jersey (now Princeton). Two months later he died of fever resulting from a smallpox inoculation. He was buried in Princeton.

Further Reading

Jonathan Edwards is listed in the Religion study guide (I, O, 1, n). Other leaders of the Great Awakening were George WHITEFIELD and Gilbert TENNENT.

A new edition of Edwards's *Works* is in preparation by the Yale University Press; two volumes, edited by Perry Miller, have appeared (1957). The major biography remains Samuel Hopkins, *Life of the Rev. J. Edwards* (1833), reprinted in *Jonathan Edwards: A Profile,* edited by David Levin (1969). The most important study of Edwards's thought is Perry Miller, *Jonathan Edwards* (1949). Other important studies are Ola E. Winslow, *Jonathan Edwards, 1703–1758* (1940); Douglas Elwood, *Philosophical Theology of Jonathan Edwards* (1960); and James Carse, *Jonathan Edwards and the Visibility of God* (1967). For background see Perry Miller, *The New England Mind: From Colony to Province* (1953), and Alan E. Heimert, *Religion and the American Mind* (1967).

EGGLESTON / By Walter Blair

Edward Eggleston (1837–1902) was an American minister and historian. He was also Indiana's leading writer of local-color fiction.

Born in Vevay, Ind., Edward Eggleston, too frail to attend school regularly, was taught by his father to read in several languages. His religious training was intensified after his parents' conversion to Methodism and then, after his father's death in 1846, by his mother's marriage 4 years later to a Methodist minister.

Edward Eggleston, photographed in his library in 1902. (Library of Congress)

Ordained as a minister himself in 1856, Eggleston served as a circuit rider, Bible agent, and minister. He was a Methodist preacher in Minnesota churches in 1858, when he married Lizzie Snyder, who bore him four children. Beginning in 1866 Eggleston edited and wrote for Sunday school and juvenile periodicals. By 1874 he had abandoned Methodism; in Brooklyn, N.Y., he founded the Church of Christian Endeavor, serving as its pastor until 1879. Meanwhile he had begun to publish adult fiction serially in the magazine *House and Home,* of which he was editor.

Eggleston's *The Hoosier School-Master* (1871), much admired by subscribers and later by the public, was based on the experiences of his brother George and influenced by James Russell Lowell's dialect poems and southwestern humorous works. This realistic account of life in backwoods Indiana helped launch the local-color movement that flourished in America for 3 decades. Eggleston's reputation was furthered by *The End of the World* (1872), about the Millerite religious sect in pioneer Indiana, and *The Circuit Rider* (1872), based on personal experiences. *Roxy* (1878) portrays a river town much like Vevay. Eggleton's final noteworthy novel, *The Graysons* (1888), is a historical romance in which the young Lincoln is a character.

Eggleston had long considered his fiction a kind of history. Between 1878 and 1888 he published several biographies and histories for children. In accordance with a view he expressed in 1900 as president of the American Historical Association, he planned a comprehensive account of the growth of American civilization. His belief —much more novel then than it was later—was that the best history is a record of a people's culture, not of its politics and wars. *The Beginners of a Nation,* subtitled "A History of the Source and Rise of the Earliest English Settlements in America with Special Reference to the Life and Character of the People," appeared in 1896, and in 1901 he published *The Transit of Civilization from England to America in the Seventeenth Century.* These were the only volumes Eggleston completed before a stroke partially disabled him in 1899; a second stroke led to his death on Sept. 2, 1902, at Lake George, N.Y. The two social histories, which Carl Van Doren called "erudite, humane, and graceful," were pioneering achievements. Eggleston was survived by his second wife, whom he had married in 1891.

Further Reading

Edward Eggleston is listed in the Literature study guide (I, D, 1, a). Other local-color writers were Bret HARTE and the master of the genre, Mark TWAIN. Eggleston was influenced by the dialect material of James Russell LOWELL.

George Cary Eggleston, Edward's brother and also a successful writer, provides an intimate memoir, *The First of the Hoosiers* (1903). William Randel wrote a superior biography, *Edward Eggleston: Author of the Hoosier School-Master* (1946). Randel is also the author of an excellent critical study, *Edward Eggleston* (1963).

EHRENBURG / By Elliott D. Mossman

The Soviet author Ilya Grigorievich Ehrenburg (1891–1967) is best known for his role as a man of letters throughout the first 50 years of Soviet history. He wrote more than 100 books and pamphlets, which range from lyric verse, to fiction, to journalism.

Ilya Ehrenburg (pronounced ĕr′ən-bŏŏrg) was born on Jan. 27, 1891, in Kiev. He came from a middle-class Jewish family, and his father worked in a brewery. The rampant anti-Semitism of Kievan life at the turn of the century made a deep impression on young Ehrenburg. Throughout his life he engaged in the fight against racism. In 1896 Ehrenburg's family moved to Moscow, where Ilya entered the First Moscow Gymnasium. Although he was a poor student, he drew inspiration from Moscow life. Leo Tolstoy kept a townhouse next to the Ehrenburg home, and Maxim Gorky lived for a short while in the Ehrenburg house.

Ehrenburg's formal education ended in 1907, when he was expelled from the gymnasium for leading an anti-czarist strike. He had been exposed at school to ideas of revolution and early leaned toward the Bolshevik ideology. Ehrenburg was arrested several times in 1907 and 1908 for radical writings, and he was finally exiled in 1908. His exile brought him to Paris in 1909, where he settled down in the émigré artists' colony.

The experiences of Ehrenburg in Paris from 1909 to 1917 and from 1924 to 1940 left an indelible impression on his life and art. His acquaintance with Pablo Picasso and Diego Rivera introduced him to the avant-garde in the arts. His contacts among Russian émigrés led him to reflect on the problems of Russia's historical destiny in the context of European civilization. During the 1910s Ehrenburg led the life of a literary bohemian, attending lectures at the Haute École des Études Sociales, working as a tourist guide and stevedore, and testing his talent as a writer. His first literary work was poetry, and he published a book of poems entitled *Paris* at his own expense in 1910. Ehrenburg spent much of World War I working as a correspondent for various Russian newspapers.

Ehrenburg had deep reservations about the Russian Revolution. He returned to Russia in 1917 after the February Revolution, working at various literary and journalistic jobs until 1921. Ehrenburg married in 1919, and he and his family left the Soviet Union in 1921, traveling about Europe until 1924, when they settled in Paris. In 1921 in Belgium, Ehrenburg wrote his most successful novel, *The Extraordinary Adventures of Julio Jurenito and His Disciples*. This satirical novel portrays the comical adventures of a Mexican as he confronts the absurdities of capitalist and socialist life in Europe and the Soviet Union.

From 1924 until his return to Moscow in 1940, Ehrenburg lived the life of a journalist and free-lance writer throughout Europe. Although he came to accept the role of the Soviet Union in world affairs and to praise the Soviet Union's opposition to fascism, Ehrenburg was hesitant about committing himself to life in the Soviet Union. In 1932 he became a regular correspondent for the Soviet newspaper *Izvestia*. His duties as journalist took him to Spain in the 1930s, where he wrote about the Spanish Civil War. In 1940 he was again in Paris, then occupied by German troops. His book *The Fall of Paris* (1942) presents an excellent account of the Occupation.

Ehrenburg returned to Moscow in 1940 with a worldwide reputation. He worked as a war correspondent for the Soviet newspaper *Pravda* throughout World War II. Ehrenburg's attitudes toward the unreasonable strictures placed on the Soviet writer by socialist realism were ambivalent until after the death of Stalin. In 1954, however,

Ilya Ehrenburg. (Sovfoto)

Ehrenburg published *The Thaw,* depicting the harm done to Soviet writing by the heavy hand of the Soviet bureaucracy. The title of this novel became the name of the liberal decade of the 1950s in Soviet literature. Ehrenburg further contributed to the thaw in Soviet literary policy with his memoirs, *People, Years, Life,* published in the late 1950s and early 1960s. Ehrenburg's memoirs are a valuable source of information for students of Soviet literature.

Ehrenburg was an urbane man, an extremely prolific writer, and a protector of the arts. He died in Moscow on Sept. 1, 1967.

Further Reading

Ilya Ehrenburg is listed in the Literature study guide (III, J, 7, a). Among his friends were Anna AKHMATOVA, Isaac BABEL, Boris PASTERNAK, and Mikhail SHOLO-KHOV.

The best source on Ehrenburg's life is his autobiography. For critical appraisals of his writings see Max Eastman, *Artists in Uniform: A Study of Literature and Bureaucratism* (1934), and Vera Alexandrova, *A History of Soviet Literature* (1963).

EHRLICH / By Carl H. Browning

The German bacteriologist Paul Ehrlich (1854–1915) advanced the science and practice of medicine by applying the fast-growing achievements of organic chemistry to the problems of disease. He is known for his discovery of Salvarsan.

Paul Ehrlich (pronounced ār′lǐKH) was born on March 14, 1854, at Strehlen, Upper Silesia. While still at school he took a great interest in chemical experiments and even got the local druggist to compound throat lozenges according to his original prescription.

Preparatory Work

At first Ehrlich attended Breslau University but found it dull and uninteresting because it lacked biology and organic chemistry, his favorite subjects. Accordingly, he passed on to the new University of Strasbourg, where he experimented with histological staining, but he returned to Breslau in his third term. In 1878 he graduated in medicine at Leipzig. His thesis was a contribution on the theory and practice of histological staining—the conception of the processes in their chemical, technological, and histological aspects—in which his idea of a chemical binding of heterogeneous substances to protoplasm was first expressed. Already in 1876, he had discovered the "mast" cell by its basophilic granules.

Early in his student career Ehrlich started investigations which in spite of their apparent diversity converged on a

Paul Ehrlich. (New York Academy of Medicine Library)

common principle: the action of drugs as a manifestation of their specific affinity for particular constituents of cells. According to Ehrlich, substances which affect bodily functions do so by virtue of combining with particular components of the animal. In chemical idiom, certain atom groups (side chains) of the drug combine with receptor atom groups of the cellular protoplasm and lead to the action. This was his famous "side-chain theory."

Ehrlich spent several years in Egypt recovering from a severe case of phthisis. On his return to Germany, Robert Koch, from whom Ehrlich had received an understanding of the modern discipline of cellular pathology and also the relation of bacteriology to disease processes, offered him a place in his new Institute for Infectious Diseases. Here Ehrlich perfected methods of preparing and standardizing diphtheria antitoxin from horses. Meanwhile he was appointed director of the State Institute for Serum Research and Serum Control at Steglitz near Berlin. Work on tumors and immunological studies occupied the forefront of his research until about 1909. In 1908 Ehrlich received the Nobel Prize in medicine for his studies on immunity.

Science of Chemotherapy

The Speyer-Ellissen family of Frankfurt offered to endow a research institute for Ehrlich's work on chemotherapy. The institute, named George Speyer-Haus, was built, and in 1906 Ehrlich became director. The methods of chemotheraphy, that is, treating infections with synthetic compounds antagonistic to pathogenic agents without seriously damaging the host, had arisen in 1891, when it was observed that methylene blue exercises a curative action on human malaria. Before the founding of the institute, Ehrlich had conducted work on an experimental scale with a small staff, and this resulted in a veritable miracle: the cure of a trypanosome infection that was invariably fatal in mice in 3–4 days. Cure followed one subcutaneous injection of a synthetic dye, trypan red, administered within 24 hours of the anticipated time of death. Other drugs were found to possess a degree of therapeutic effect, and certain organic arsenical compounds, "atoxyl" derivatives, also proved to be trypanocidal. From these the drug Salvarsan was derived, which Ehrlich found to be the most efficient curative agent for human syphilis then known, although it was sometimes liable to produce toxic effects. The science of chemotherapy was thus born.

Ehrlich's tremendous achievements were the outcome of a life of unremitting scientific preoccupation to which almost everything was sacrificed. The furor of Salvarsan made him one of the celebrities of his time, both in science and commerce. He died in Bad Homburg, Hesse, on Aug. 20, 1915.

Further Reading

Paul Ehrlich is listed in the Science study guide (VI, G, 2). He shared the Nobel Prize in 1908 with the Russian bacteriologist Élie METCHNIKOFF.

For Ehrlich's own writings see F. Himmelweit, ed., *The Collected Papers of Paul Ehrlich* (1956). Accounts of Ehrlich's life and work are Herman Goodman, *Paul Ehrlich: A Man of Genius and an Inspiration to Humanitarians* (1924), and Martha Marquardt, *Paul Ehrlich* (1951). A sketch of his life is in Theodore L. Sourkes, *Nobel Prize Winners in Medicine and Physiology, 1901–1965* (1953; rev. ed. 1966).

* * *

EIFFEL / By Lawrence Wodehouse

The French engineer Alexandre Gustave Eiffel (1832–1923) is best known for the Eiffel Tower, which he built in Paris in 1889.

Born in Dijon, Gustave Eiffel (pronounced ī′fəl) studied at the École Polytechnique and the École Centrale in Paris. He designed numerous bridges, the first in 1858 in Bordeaux, viaducts, and exhibition buildings; the ultimate in exhibition architecture came in 1889, when he built his famous tower in Paris. Throughout his life he was concerned with innovative structures and especially with the effects of wind loading on plane surfaces. He built an air tunnel in his laboratory at Auteuil for experimental purposes.

Eiffel's most famous bridge, the Maria Pia over the Douro at Oporto, Portugal (1876), spans 500 feet by a single arch, 200 feet above high-water level, which with additional side pylons supports the horizontal superstructure. Also during that year Eiffel collaborated with the architect L. A. Boileau the Younger on the Bon Marché Department Store in Paris, the first glass and cast-iron department store. A glass wall along all three street facades, with circular pavilions at the corners, enclosed a store comprising open courts covered by skylights to an extent of 30,000 square feet. Slender columns supported balconies, bridges, and the glazed roof. The store still stands, although it has a masonry skin added in the 1920s.

Eiffel's Garabit viaduct over the Truyère near Ruines, France, is 1,625 feet long and 400 feet high and has a central span of 210 feet. Other works by Eiffel include a revolving cupola for the Nice Observatory, and the structure that supports F. A. Bartholdi's Statue of Liberty in New York City (1886).

An associate engineer on the Garabit viaduct, Maurice Koechlin, encouraged Eiffel in his design for the Paris exhibition tower of 1889. It was the factory-made components, fitted together on the site for the viaduct, that made the 984-foot-high Eiffel Tower possible.

Each of the 12,000 different component parts of the tower was designed to counteract wind pressures, and 2,500,000 rivets were used to create a continuous structure. Four main piers, each with a slight curve, anchored to separate foundations incorporated elevators; two acted on a combined principle of pistons and chains, and the two American Otis elevators acted on a hydraulic piston system. Other hydraulic elevator systems linked the first level to the second one and the second level to the third.

Further Reading

Gustave Eiffel is listed in the Art study guide (III, I, 2, a). His tower and the two libraries Henri LABROUSTE built in Paris are important examples of 19th-century metal construction.

Jean Prévost, *Eiffel* (1929), the only monograph on Eiffel, is brief and in French. Two publications in English on the Eiffel Tower are Gaston Tissandier, *The Eiffel Tower* (1889), and Robert M. Vogel, *Elevator Systems of the*

Gustave Eiffel. (French Embassy Press and Information Service)

Eiffel Tower, 1889 (1961). Siegfried Giedion, *Space, Time, and Architecture: The Growth of a New Tradition* (1941; 5th ed. 1967), connects Eiffel with the development of structural techniques of the 19th century.

EIJKMAN / By Robert G. Colodny

The Dutch physician and biologist Christian Eijkman (1858–1930) was a pioneer in the study of the biochemical basis of health and in the recognition and study of vitamins.

C hristian Eijkman (pronounced ĭk′män) was born to a schoolteacher in Nijkerk on Aug. 11, 1858. He took his degree in medicine at Amsterdam in 1883 and then trained as medical officer for the army of the Dutch East Indies. His first official position was as assistant to the Dutch commission to study the scourge of beriberi in Batavia. The commission returned to Europe in 1887, but Eijkman remained as director from 1885 to 1896. In 1898 he was called to the chair of hygiene and forensic medicine at Utrecht. He became a member of the Royal Academy of Sciences of the Netherlands in 1907.

Eijkman arrived in Batavia at a time when there had been many severe outbreaks of beriberi. Beriberi is characterized by ascending paralysis and cardiac symptoms and edema, and it carried a frightful 80 percent mortality in some outbreaks. The epidemic nature of the disease seemed to be strong evidence that it was spread by a pathogen. As director of the civilian research laboratory, Eijkman, having been unable to isolate a causative organism, began to study the laboratory chickens which had been struck by the disease. None of the refined autopsy techniques indicated that the disease was infectious. Then fate revealed the clue to the puzzle: the chickens were being fed polished white rice, but when whole rice grain was given instead, the animals recovered. Eijkman also demonstrated that the disease could be produced at will by feeding the chickens only polished rice and that the husks removed by polishing would cure the disease if given with the polished rice.

Eijkman's work led to investigations of prisons where beriberi was rampant. It was found that men fed primarily on polished rice were stricken, while those who consumed crudely crushed whole grain rice remained healthy. Eijkman drew the conclusion that the disease was linked to the mode of rice preparation, but he incorrectly assumed that the husks contained an antidote to a toxic substance in the grain.

In 1896 ill health brought Eijkman back to Holland. Meanwhile his collaborators in Java, particularly Gerrit Grijns, continued to explore the beriberi problem and eventually demonstrated conclusively that the disease was caused by a dietary deficiency, not a poison. In 1911 the Polish chemist Casimir Funk separated a substance from grain polishings which could cure the disease. He

Christian Eijkman. (Rijksmuseum, Amsterdam)

named it Vitamine; it is now known as vitamin B_1 (thiamine). The world was a giant step closer to understanding the biochemical nature of nutrition.

Eijkman won the Nobel Prize in medicine in 1929. He died on Nov. 5, 1930.

Further Reading

Christian Eijkman is listed in the Science study guide (VII, G, 2). He shared the Nobel Prize with F. Gowland HOPKINS, another pioneer in the study of the biochemical basis of health.

Biographical sketches of Eijkman can be found in Sarah R. Riedman and Elton T. Gustofson, *Portraits of Nobel Laureates in Medicine and Physiology* (1963) and *Nobel Lectures, Physiology and Medicine: Including Presentation Speeches and Laureates' Biographies, 1922–1941* (1965). Useful general works include T. R. Parsons, *The Materials of Life: A General Presentation of Biochemistry* (1930), and F. R. Jevons, *The Biochemical Approach to Life* (1964; 2d ed. 1968).

EINSTEIN / By Roger H. Stuewer

The German-born American physicist Albert Einstein (1879–1955) revolutionized the science of physics. He is best known for his theory of relativity.

In the history of the exact sciences, only a handful of men—men like Nicolaus Copernicus and Isaac Newton—share the honor that was Albert Einstein's: the initiation of a revolution in scientific thought. His insights into the nature of the physical world made it impossible for physicists and philosophers to view that world as they had before. When describing the achievements of other physicists, the tendency is to enumerate their major discoveries; when describing the achievements of Einstein, it is possible to say, simply, that he revolutionized physics.

Albert Einstein was born on March 14, 1879, in Ulm, but he grew up and obtained his early education in Munich. He was not a child prodigy; in fact, he was unable to speak fluently at age 9. Finding profound joy, liberation, and security in contemplating the laws of nature, already at age 5 he had experienced a deep feeling of wonder when puzzling over the invisible, yet definite, force directing the needle of a compass. Seven years later he experienced a different kind of wonder: the deep emotional stirring that accompanied his discovery of Euclidean geometry, with its lucid and certain proofs. Einstein mastered differential and integral calculus by age 16.

Education in Zurich

Einstein's formal secondary education was abruptly terminated at 16. He found life in school intolerable, and just as he was scheming to find a way to leave without

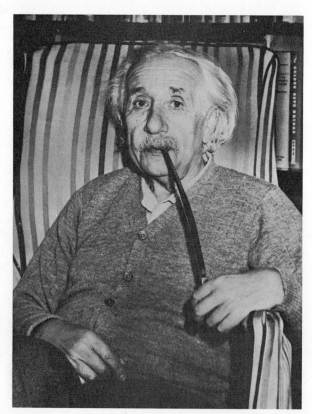

Albert Einstein. (National Archives, Washington, D.C.)

impairing his chances for entering the university, his teacher expelled him for the negative effects his rebellious attitude was having on the morale of his classmates. Einstein tried to enter the Federal Institute of Technology (FIT) in Zurich, Switzerland, but his knowledge of nonmathematical disciplines was not equal to that of mathematics and he failed the entrance examination. On the advice of the principal, he thereupon first obtained his diploma at the Cantonal School in Aarau, and in 1896 he was automatically admitted into the FIT. There he came to realize that his deepest interest and facility lay in physics, both experimental and theoretical, rather than in mathematics.

Einstein passed his diploma examination at the FIT in 1900, but due to the opposition of one of his professors he was unable to subsequently obtain the usual university assistantship. In 1902 he was engaged as a technical expert, third-class, in the patent office in Bern, Switzerland. Six months later he married Mileva Maric, a former classmate in Zurich. They had two sons. It was in Bern, too, that Einstein, at 26, completed the requirements for his doctoral degree and wrote the first of his revolutionary scientific papers.

Academic Career

These papers made Einstein famous, and universities soon began competing for his services. In 1909, after serving as a lecturer at the University of Bern, Einstein was called as an associate professor to the University of Zurich. Two years later he was appointed a full professor at the German University in Prague. Within another year and a half Einstein became a full professor at the FIT. Finally, in 1913 the well-known scientists Max Planck and Walter Nernst traveled to Zurich to persuade Einstein to accept a lucrative research professorship at the University of Berlin, as well as full membership in the Prussian Academy of Science. He accepted their offer in 1914, quipping: "The Germans are gambling on me as they would on a prize hen. I do not really know myself whether I shall ever really lay another egg." When he went to Berlin, his wife remained behind in Zurich with their two sons; after their divorce he married his cousin Elsa in 1917.

In 1920 Einstein was appointed to a lifelong honorary visiting professorship at the University of Leiden. During 1921–1922 Einstein, accompanied by Chaim Weizmann, the future president of the state of Israel, undertook extensive worldwide travels in the cause of Zionism. In Germany the attacks on Einstein began. Philipp Lenard and Johannes Stark, both Nobel Prize–winning physicists, began characterizing Einstein's theory of relativity as "Jewish physics." This callousness and brutality increased until Einstein resigned from the Prussian Academy of Science in 1933. (He was, however, expelled from the Bavarian Academy of Science.)

Career in America

On several occasions Einstein had visited the California Institute of Technology, and on his last trip to the United States Abraham Flexner offered Einstein—on Einstein's terms—a position in the newly conceived and funded Institute for Advanced Studies in Princeton. He went there in 1933.

Einstein played a key role (1939) in mobilizing the resources necessary to construct the atomic bomb by signing a famous letter to President Franklin D. Roosevelt which had been drafted by Leo Szilard and E. P. Wigner. When Einstein's famous equation $E = mc^2$ was finally demonstrated in the most awesome and terrifying way by using the bomb to destroy Hiroshima in 1945, Einstein, the pacifist and humanitarian, was deeply shocked and distressed; for a long time he could only utter "Horrible, horrible." On April 18, 1955, Einstein died in Princeton.

Theory of Brownian Motion

From numerous references in Einstein's writings it is evident that, of all areas in physics, thermodynamics made the deepest impression on him. During 1902–1904 Einstein reworked the foundations of thermodynamics and statistical mechanics; this work formed the immediate background to his revolutionary papers of 1905, one of which was on Brownian motion.

In Brownian motion (first observed in 1827 by the Scottish botanist Robert Brown), small particles suspended in a viscous liquid such as water undergo a rapid, irregular motion. Einstein, unaware of Brown's earlier observations, concluded from his theoretical studies that such a motion must exist. Guided by the thought that if the liquid in which the particles are suspended consists of atoms or molecules they should collide with the particles and set them into motion, he found that while the particle's motion is irregular, fluctuating back and forth, it will in time nevertheless experience a net forward displacement. Einstein proved that this net forward displacement of the suspended particles is directly related to the number of molecules per gram atomic weight. This point created a good deal of skepticism toward Einstein's theory at the time he developed it (1905–1906), but when it was fully confirmed many of the skeptics were converted. Brownian motion is to this day regarded as one of the most direct proofs of the existence of atoms.

Light Quanta and Wave-Particle Duality

The most common misconceptions concerning Einstein's introduction of his revolutionary light quantum (light particle) hypothesis in 1905 are that he simply applied Planck's quantum hypothesis of 1900 to radiation and that he introduced light quanta to "explain" the photoelectric effect discovered in 1887 by Heinrich Hertz and thoroughly investigated in 1902 by Philipp Lenard. Neither of these assertions is accurate. Einstein's arguments for his light quantum hypothesis—that under certain circumstances radiant energy (light) behaves as if it consists not of waves but of particles of energy proportional to their frequencies—were absolutely fundamental and, as in the case of his theory of Brownian motion, based on his own insights into the foundations of thermodynamics and statistical mechanics. Furthermore, it

was only after presenting strong arguments for the necessity of his light quantum hypothesis that Einstein pursued its experimental consequences. One of several such consequences was the photoelectric effect, the experiment in which high-frequency ultraviolet light is used to eject electrons from thin metal plates. In particular, Einstein assumed that a single quantum of light transfers its entire energy to a single electron in the metal plate. The famous equation he derived was fully consistent with Lenard's observation that the energy of the ejected electrons depends only on the frequency of the ultraviolet light and not on its intensity. Einstein was not disturbed by the fact that this apparently contradicts James Clerk Maxwell's classic electromagnetic wave theory of light, because he realized that there were good reasons to doubt the universal validity of Maxwell's theory.

Although Einstein's famous equation for the photoelectric effect—for which he won the Nobel Prize of 1921—appears so natural today, it was an extremely bold prediction in 1905. Not until a decade later did R. A. Millikan finally succeed in experimentally verifying it to everyone's satisfaction. But while Einstein's equation was bold, his light quantum hypothesis was revolutionary: it amounted to reviving Newton's centuries-old idea that light consists of particles.

No one tried harder than Einstein to overcome opposition to this hypothesis. Thus, in 1907 he proved the fruitfulness of the entire quantum hypothesis by showing it could at least qualitatively account for the low-temperature behavior of the specific heats of solids. Two years later he proved that Planck's radiation law of 1900 demands the *coexistence* of particles and waves in blackbody radiation, a proof that represents the birth of the wave-particle duality. In 1917 Einstein presented a very simple and very important derivation of Planck's radiation law (the modern laser, for example, is based on the concepts Einstein introduced here), and he also proved that light quanta must carry momentum as well as energy.

Meanwhile, Einstein had become involved in another series of researches having a direct bearing on the wave-particle duality. In mid-1924 S. N. Bose produced a very insightful derivation of Planck's radiation law—the origin of Bose-Einstein statistics—which Einstein soon developed into his famous quantum theory of an ideal gas. Shortly thereafter, he became acquainted with Louis de Broglie's revolutionary new idea that ordinary material *particles,* such as electrons and gas molecules, should under certain circumstances exhibit *wave* behavior. Einstein saw immediately that De Broglie's idea was intimately related to the Bose-Einstein statistics: both indicate that material particles can at times behave like waves. Einstein told Erwin Schrödinger of De Broglie's work, and in 1926 Schrödinger made the extraordinarily important discovery of wave mechanics. Schrödinger (as well as C. Eckart) then proved that Schrödinger's wave mechanics and Werner Heisenberg's matrix mechanics are mathematically equivalent: they are now collectively known as quantum mechanics, one of the two most fruitful physical theories of the 20th century. Since Ein-

Einstein (center) with two other noted 20th-century physicists: A. A. Michelson (left), who measured the speed of light, and R. A. Millikan, discoverer of cosmic rays. (Photo by Underwood & Underwood)

stein's insights formed much of the background to both Schrödinger's and Heisenberg's discoveries, the debt quantum physicists owe to Einstein can hardly be exaggerated.

Theory of Relativity

The second of the two most fruitful physical theories of the 20th century is the theory of relativity, which to scientists and laymen alike is synonymous with the name of Einstein. Once again, there is a common misconception concerning the origin of this theory, namely, that Einstein advanced it in 1905 to "explain" the famous Michelson-Morley experiment (1887), which failed to detect a relative motion of the earth with respect to the ether, the medium through which light was assumed to propagate. In fact, it is not even certain that Einstein was aware of this experiment in 1905; nor was he familiar with H. A. Lorentz's elegant 1904 paper in which Lorentz applied the transformation equations which bear his name to electrodynamic phenomena. Rather, Einstein consciously searched for a general principle of nature that would hold the key to the explanation of a paradox that had occurred to him when he was 16: if, on the one hand, one runs at, say, 4 miles per hour alongside a train moving at 4 miles per hour, the train appears to be at rest; if, on the other hand, it were possible to run alongside a ray of light, neither experiment nor theory suggests that the ray of light—an oscillating electromagnetic wave—would appear to be at rest. Einstein eventually saw that he could *postulate* that no matter what the velocity of the observer, he must always observe the same velocity c for the velocity of light: roughly 186,000 miles per second. He also saw that this postulate was

consistent with a second postulate: if an observer at rest and an observer moving at constant velocity carry out the same kind of experiment, they must get the same result. These are Einstein's two postulates of his special theory of relativity. Also in 1905 Einstein proved that his theory predicted that energy E and mass m are entirely interconvertible according to his famous equation, $E = mc^2$.

For observational confirmation of his general theory of relativity, Einstein boldly predicted the gravitational red shift and the deflection of starlight (an amended value), as well as the quantitative explanation of U. J. J. Leverrier's long-unexplained observation that the perihelion of the planet Mercury precesses about the sun at the rate of 43 seconds of arc per century. In addition, Einstein in 1916 predicted the existence of gravitational waves, which have only recently been detected. Turning to cosmological problems the following year, Einstein found a solution to his field equations consistent with the picture (the Einstein universe) that the universe is static, approximately uniformly filled with a finite amount of matter, and finite but unbounded (in the same sense that the surface area of a smooth globe is finite but has no beginning or end).

The Man and His Philosophy

Fellow physicists were always struck with Einstein's uncanny ability to penetrate to the heart of a complex problem, to instantly see the physical significance of a complex mathematical result. Both in his scientific and in his personal life, he was utterly independent, a trait that manifested itself in his approach to scientific problems, in his unconventional dress, in his relationships with family and friends, and in his aloofness from university and governmental politics (in spite of his intense social consciousness). Einstein loved to discuss scientific problems with friends, but he was, fundamentally a "horse for single harness."

Einstein's belief in strict causality was closely related to his profound belief in the harmony of nature. That nature can be understood rationally, in mathematical terms, never ceased to evoke a deep—one might say, religious—feeling of admiration in him. "The most incomprehensible thing about the world," he once wrote, "is that it is comprehensible." How do we discover the basic laws and concepts of nature? Einstein argued that while we learn certain features of the world from experience, the free inventive capacity of the human mind is required to formulate physical theories. There is no logical link between the world of experience and the world of theory. Once a theory has been formulated, however, it must be "simple" (or, perhaps, "esthetically pleasing") and agree with experiment. One such esthetically pleasing and fully confirmed theory is the special theory of relativity. When Einstein was informed of D. C. Miller's experiments, which seemed to contradict the special theory by demanding the reinstatement of the ether, he expressed his belief in the spuriousness of Miller's results—and therefore in the harmoniousness of nature—with another of his famous aphorisms, "God is subtle, but he is not malicious."

This frequent use of God's name in Einstein's speeches and writings provides us with a feeling for his religious convictions. He once stated explicitly, "I believe in Spinoza's God who reveals himself in the harmony of all being, not in a God who concerns himself with the fate and actions of men." It is not difficult to see that this credo is consistent with his statement that the "less knowledge a scholar possesses, the farther he feels from God. But the greater his knowledge, the nearer is his approach to God." Since Einstein's God manifested Himself in the harmony of the universe, there could be no conflict between religion and science for Einstein.

To enumerate at this point the many honors that were bestowed upon Einstein during his lifetime would be to devote space to the kind of public acclamation that mattered so little to Einstein himself. How, indeed, can other human beings sufficiently honor one of their number who revolutionized their conception of the physical world, and who lived his life in the conviction that "the only life worth living is a life spent in the service of others"? When Einstein lay dying he could truly utter, as he did, "Here on earth I have done my job." It would be difficult to find a more suitable epitaph than the words Einstein himself used in characterizing his life: "God is inexorable in the way He has allotted His gifts. He gave me the stubbornness of a mule and nothing else; really, He also gave me a keen scent."

Further Reading

Albert Einstein is listed in the Science study guide (VII, C, 2). One of the ways in which his independence in scientific matters manifested itself after 1926 was in his opposition to the Copenhagen interpretation of quantum mechanics, expounded by Niels BOHR, Werner HEISENBERG, and Max BORN.

Numerous biographies of Einstein have been written. Three of the best are Philipp Frank, *Einstein: His Life and Times,* translated by George Rosen (1947); Carl Seelig, *Albert Einstein: A Documentary Biography,* translated by Mervyn Savill (1956); and Ronald W. Clark, *Einstein: The Life and Times* (1971). Einstein's illuminating "Autobiographical Notes" and bibliographies of his scientific and nonscientific writings can be found in P. A. Schilpp, ed., *Albert Einstein: Philosopher-Scientist* (1949; 2d ed. 1951). See also Max Born, *Einstein's Theory of Relativity* (trans. 1922; rev. ed. 1962); Leopold Infeld, *Albert Einstein: His Work and Its Influence on Our World* (1950); and Max Jammer, *The Conceptual Development of Quantum Mechanics* (1966).

EISAI / By E. Dale Saunders

The Japanese Buddhist monk Eisai (1141–1215) introduced the Zen Buddhist Rinzai sect to Japan, and under him Zen first became acknowledged as an independent school of Buddhism. He is also responsible for popularizing the cultivation of tea in Japan.

Also known by his honorific title of Zenko *kokushi* (national teacher), Eisai (pronounced ā-sī) came from a family of Shinto priests in the district of Okayama. Like many famous priests in his period, he studied at the great Tendai center on Mt. Hiei. In 1168 he made his first trip to China, where he visited Zen centers, especially those flourishing on Mt. T'ien-t'ai. He was much impressed by what he saw and felt with growing conviction that Zen could greatly contribute to a reawakening of Buddhist faith in Japan.

In 1187 he undertook a second trip to the continent for the purpose of tracing the origins of Buddhism to India. The authorities, however, refused him permission to go beyond Chinese borders. He studied on Mt. T'ien-t'ai until 1191, where he was ordained in the Rinzai (Chinese, Lin-ch'i) sect and returned to Japan. He constructed the first Rinzai temple, the Shofukuji, at Hakata in Kyushu.

Eisai proclaimed the superiority of Zen meditation over other Buddhist disciplines, thus provoking the ire of the Tendai monks who sought to outlaw the new sect. However, Eisai enjoyed the protection of the shogun Minamoto Yoriie, and in 1202 he was given the direction of the Kenninji in Kyoto. Like Saicho, and particularly Nichiren, Eisai associated his type of Buddhism with national welfare and promoted Zen by publishing a tract entitled *Kozen Gokoku Ron* (The Propagation of Zen for the Protection of the Country).

But Eisai was constantly obliged to face Tendai and Shingon opposition. As a compromise, Eisai conducted

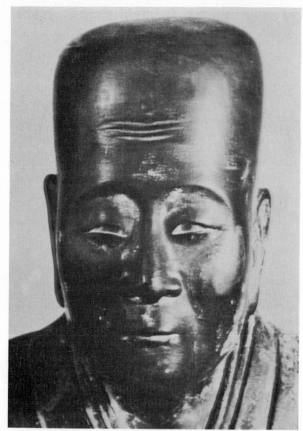

Eisai. (International Society for Educational Information, Tokyo, Inc.)

the Kenninji not as a purely Zen establishment but also with places for Tendai and Shingon worship. Indeed, he continued to recite Shingon magic formulas. Shortly before his death, Eisai established by government order the third Zen monastery at Kamakura, the Jufukuji, and the close relationship of Zen with the military caste dates from this time.

Introduction of Tea

Although tea had been introduced to Japan about 800 by Buddhist monks who had gone to China, its cultivation and consumption were not widespread before Eisai's time. Eisai, returning from China in 1191, brought tea seeds with him and planted them near Kyoto. In 1214 he composed the *Kissa Yojoki* (Drink Tea to Improve Health and Prolong Life), in which he set forth the hygienic and curative value of tea. Tea was considered an important adjunct to Zen meditation, for it acted as a mild stimulant against sleepiness.

Further Reading

Eisai is listed in the Asia study guide (III, B, 4, b). Earlier religious innovators were KUKAI and SAICHO of the Heian period.

A discussion of Eisai and excerpts from his writings may be found in Ryusaku Tsunoda and others, eds., *Sources of the Japanese Tradition* (1958). A good book

on the history of Zen is Heinrich Dumoulin, *A History of Zen Buddhism* (trans. 1963).

EISENHOWER /By Dexter Perkins

Dwight David Eisenhower (1890–1969) was leader of the Allied forces in Europe in World War II, commander of NATO, and thirty-fourth president of the United States.

Dwight Eisenhower was born in Denison, Tex., on Oct. 14, 1890, one of seven sons. The family soon moved to Abilene, Kans. The family was poor, and Eisenhower early learned the virtue of hard work. He graduated from West Point Military Academy in 1915. He was remarkable for his buoyant temperament and his capacity to inspire affection.

Eisenhower married Mamie Doud in 1916. One of the couple's two sons died in infancy; the other, John, followed in his father's footsteps and went to West Point, later resigning from the Army to assist in preparing his father's memoirs.

Army Career

Eisenhower's career in the Army was marked by a slow rise to distinction. He graduated first in his class in 1926 from the Army's Command and General Staff School. Following graduation from the Army War College he served in the office of the chief of staff under Gen. Douglas MacArthur. He became MacArthur's distinguished aid in the Philippines. Returning to the United States in 1939, Eisenhower became chief of staff to the 3d Army. He attracted the attention of Gen. George C. Marshall, U.S. Chief of Staff, by his brilliant conduct of war operations in Louisiana in 1941. When World War II began, Eisenhower became assistant chief of the War Plans Division of the Army General Staff. He assisted in the preparations for carrying the war to Europe and in May of 1942 was made supreme commander of European operations, arriving in London in this capacity in June.

Supreme Commander in Europe

Eisenhower's personal qualities were precisely right for the situation in the months that followed. He had to deal with British generals whose war experience exceeded his own and with a prime minister, Winston Churchill, whose strength and determination were of the first order. Eisenhower's post called for a combination of tact and resolution, for an ability to get along with people and yet maintain his own position as the leader of the Allied forces. In addition to his capacity to command respect and affection, Eisenhower showed high executive quality in his selection of subordinates.

In London, Eisenhower paved the way for the Novem-

Dwight Eisenhower's arrival in New York City in June 1945, following the Allied victory in Europe, was the occasion for a triumphant ticker tape parade. (U.S. Army Photograph)

ber 1942 invasion of North Africa. Against powerful British reluctance he prepared for the June 1944 invasion of Europe. He chose precisely the day on which massive troop landings in Normandy were feasible, and once the bridgehead was established, he swept forward triumphantly—with one short interruption—to defeat the German armies. By spring 1945, with powerful support from the Russian forces advancing from the east, the war in Europe was ended. Eisenhower became one of the best-known men in the United States, and there was talk of a possible political career.

Columbia University and NATO

Eisenhower disavowed any political ambitions, however, and in 1948 he retired from military service to become president of Columbia University. It cannot be said that he filled this role with distinction. Nothing in his training suggested a special capacity to deal with university problems. Yet it was only because of a strong sense of duty that he accepted President Harry Truman's

appeal to become the first commander of the newly formed North Atlantic Treaty Organization (NATO) in December 1950. Here Eisenhower's truly remarkable gifts in dealing with men of various views and strong will were again fully exhibited.

Eisenhower's political views had never been clearly defined. But Republican leaders in the eastern United States found him a highly acceptable candidate for the presidency, perhaps all the more so because he was not identified with any particular wing of the party. After a bitter convention fight against Robert Taft, Eisenhower emerged victorious. In the election he defeated the Democratic candidate, Adlai Stevenson, by a tremendous margin.

Eisenhower repeated this achievement in 1956. In 1955 he had suffered a serious stroke, and in 1956 he underwent an operation for ileitis. Behaving with great dignity and making it clear that he would stand for a second term only if he felt he could perform his duties to the full, he accepted renomination and won the election

President Eisenhower signs the historic civil rights bill of the 85th Congress on Sept. 9, 1957. (Dwight D. Eisenhower Library)

with 477 of the 531 electoral votes and a popular majority of over 9 million.

The President

Eisenhower's strength as a political leader rested almost entirely upon his disinterestedness and his integrity. He had little taste for political maneuvers and was never a strong partisan. His party, which attained a majority in both houses of Congress in 1952, lost control in 1954, and for 6 of 8 years in office the President was compelled to rely upon both Democrats and Republicans. His personal qualities, however, made this easier than it might have been.

Eisenhower did not conceive of the presidency as a positive executiveship, as has been the view of most of the great U.S. presidents. His personal philosophy was never very clearly defined. He was not a dynamic leader; he took a position in the center and drew his strength from that. In domestic affairs he was influenced by his strong and able secretary of the Treasury, George Humphrey. In foreign affairs he leaned heavily upon his secretary of state, John Foster Dulles. He delegated wide powers to those he trusted; in domestic affairs his personal assistant, Sherman Adams, exercised great influence. In a sense, Eisenhower's stance above the "battle" no doubt made him stronger.

Domestic Policies

To attempt to classify Eisenhower as liberal or conservative is difficult. He was undoubtedly sympathetic to business interests and had widespread support from them. He had austere views as to fiscal matters and was not generally in favor of enlarging the role of government in economic affairs. Yet he favored measures such as a far-reaching extension of social security, he signed a law fixing a minimum wage, and he recommended the formation of the Department of Health, Education and Welfare. After an initial error, he appointed to this post Marion B. Folsom, an outstanding administrator who had been a pioneer in the movement for social security in the 1930s.

Civil Rights

But the most significant development in domestic policy came through the Supreme Court. The President appointed Earl Warren to the post of chief justice. In 1954 the Warren Court handed down a unanimous decision declaring segregation in the schools unconstitutional, giving a new impetus to the civil rights movement.

Eisenhower was extremely cautious in implementing this decision. He saw that it was enforced in the District of Columbia, but in his heart he did not believe in it and thought that it was for the states rather than the Federal government to take appropriate action. Nonetheless, he was compelled to move in 1957 when Arkansas governor Orval Faubus attempted to defy the desegregation decision by using national guardsmen to bar Negroes from entering the schools of Little Rock. The President's stand was unequivocal; he made it clear that he would enforce the law. When Faubus proved obdurate, the President enjoined him and forced the removal of the national guard. When the Negroes admitted were forced by an armed mob to withdraw, the President sent Federal troops to Little Rock and federalized the national guard.

A month later the Federal troops were withdrawn. But it was a long time before the situation was completely stabilized.

The President's second term saw further progress in civil rights. In 1957 he signed a measure providing further personnel for the attorney general's office for enforcing the law and barring interference with voting rights. In 1960 he signed legislation strengthening the measure and making resistance to desegregation a Federal offense.

Foreign Policies

In foreign affairs Eisenhower encouraged the strengthening of NATO, at the same time seeking an understanding with the Soviet Union. In 1955 the U.S.S.R. agreed to evacuate Austria, then under four-power occupation, but a Geneva meeting of the powers (Britain, France, the U.S.S.R., and the United States) made little progress on the problem of divided Germany. A new effort at understanding came in 1959, when the Russian leader Nikita Khrushchev visited the United States. In friendly discussions it was agreed to hold a new international conference in Paris. When that time arrived, however, the Russians had just captured an American plane engaged in spying operations over the Soviet Union (the Gary Powers incident). Khrushchev flew into a tantrum and broke up the conference. When Eisenhower's term ended, relations with the Kremlin were still unhappy.

In the Orient the President negotiated an armistice with the North Koreans to terminate the Korean War begun in 1950. It appears that Eisenhower brought the North Koreans and their Chinese Communist allies to terms by threatening to enlarge the war. He supported the Chinese Nationalists. Dulles negotiated the treaty that created SEATO (Southeast Asia Treaty Organization) and pledged the United States to consult with the other signatories and to meet any threat of peace in that region "in accordance with their constitutional practices. . . ." This treaty was of special significance with regard to Vietnam, where the French had been battling against a movement for independence. In 1954 Vietnam was divided, the North coming under Communist control, the South (anti-Communist) increasingly supported by the United States.

In the Near East, Eisenhower faced a very difficult situation. In 1956 the Egyptian dictator Gamal Abdel Nasser nationalized the Suez Canal. The government of Israel, probably encouraged by France and Great Britain,

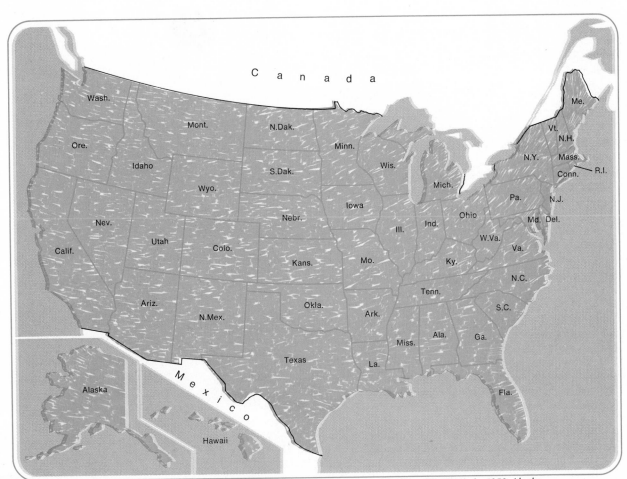

The United States at the close of the Eisenhower administration (Jan. 20, 1961). In 1959 Alaska and Hawaii were admitted to the Union as the forty-ninth and fiftieth states.

launched a preventive war, soon joined by the two great powers. The President and the secretary of state condemned this breach of the peace within the deliberations framework of the United Nations, and the three powers were obliged to sign an armistice. These events occurred at a particularly inauspicious time for the United States, since a popular revolt against the Soviet Union had broken out in Hungary. The hands of the American government were tied, though perhaps in no case could the United States have acted effectively in preventing Soviet suppression of the revolt.

In the Latin American sphere the President was confronted with events of great importance in Cuba. Cuba was ruled by an increasingly brutal and tyrannical president, Fulgencio Batista. In 1958, to mark its displeasure, the American government withdrew military support from the Batista regime. There followed a collapse of the government, and the Cuban leftist leader, Fidel Castro, installed himself in power. Almost from the beginning Castro began a flirtation with the Soviet Union, and relations between Havana and Washington were severed in January 1960.

In the meantime the United States had embarked upon a course which was to cause great embarrassment to Eisenhower's successor. It had encouraged and assisted anti-Castro Cubans to prepare to invade the island and overthrow the Castro regime. Though these plans had not crystallized when Eisenhower left office in 1961, it proved difficult to reverse them, and the result for the John F. Kennedy administration was the fiasco of the Bay of Pigs.

Assessing His Career

It will be difficult for future historians to assess Eisenhower's foreign policy objectively. Ending the Korean War was a substantial achievement. The support of NATO was most certainly in line with American opinion. In the Far East the extension of American commitments can be variously judged. It is fair to Eisenhower to say that only the first steps to the eventual deep involvement in Vietnam were taken during his presidency.

One other aspect of the Eisenhower years must be noted. The President's intention to reduce the military budget at first succeeded. But during his first term the American position with the Soviets deteriorated. Then came the Soviet launching of the Sputnik space probe in 1957—a grisly suggestion of what nuclear weapons might be like in the future. In response, United States policy was altered, and the missile gap had been closed by the time the President left office. Unhappily, the arms race was not ended but attained new intensity in the post-Eisenhower years.

Few presidents have enjoyed greater popularity than Eisenhower or left office as solidly entrenched in public opinion as when they entered it. Eisenhower was not a great orator and did not conceive of the presidency as a post of political leadership. But at the end of his administration, admiration for his integrity, modesty, and strength was undiminished among the mass of the American people.

Eisenhower played at times the role of an elder statesman in Republican politics. His death on March 26, 1969, was the occasion for national mourning and for worldwide recognition of his important role in the events of his time.

Further Reading

Dwight Eisenhower is listed in the American History study guide (IX, E, 2, b; X, A, 2). During the cold war he tried to advance American-Soviet understanding by meeting with Soviet premier Nikita KHRUSHCHEV. John Foster DULLES was Eisenhower's much trusted secretary of state.

Works written by Eisenhower are *Crusade in Europe* (1948) and his account of the presidency, *Mandate for Change, 1953–1956: The White House Years* (1963) and *Waging Peace, 1956–1961: The White House Years* (1965). For a brief summary of Eisenhower's early career see Marquis W. Childs, *Eisenhower, Captive Hero: A Critical Study of the General and the President* (1958). For the war years see W. B. Smith, *Eisenhower's Six Great Decisions* (1950). Eisenhower's election to the presidency is covered in Arthur M. Schlesinger, Jr., ed., *History of American Presidential Elections* (4 vols., 1971). Very important is Sherman Adams, *Firsthand Report: The Story of the Eisenhower Administration* (1961). The most illuminating discussion of the President is Emmett John Hughes, *The Ordeal of Power: A Political Memoir of the Eisenhower Years* (1963). See also Robert J. Donovan, *Eisenhower: The Inside Story* (1956), and Merlo J. Pusey, *Eisenhower the President* (1956).

✷   ✷   ✷

EISENSTEIN /By Frederick R. Benson and David Lissandrello

The Soviet film director and cinema theoretician Sergei Mikhailovich Eisenstein (1898–1948) achieved fame for his emotionally inflammatory political epics of the Russian Revolution.

Born in Riga, the son of a wealthy shipbuilder, Sergei Eisenstein (pronounced ) went as a young man to St. Petersburg, where he studied architecture and engineering. During the Russian Revolution he constructed trenches and also acted in plays for the Bolshevik army. Shortly after the civil war, he managed a carnival and a small workers' theater in Moscow. Following service with the engineering corps during World War I, Eisenstein was appointed assistant director and chief dramatist for the Proletcult Theater. His most celebrated avant-garde productions included a dramatization of Jack London's story, *Mexicalia*, of A. N. Ostrovsky's *Much Simplicity in Every Wise Man*, and an experimental play, *Anti-Jesus*.

First Films

Frustrated by the stage's inability to achieve total realism, Eisenstein abandoned theater for the incipient Soviet film industry, directing his first motion picture, *Strike,* in 1924. With *Potemkin* (1925) the director was able to exploit effectively his sadistic fantasies, culminating in the apocalyptic violence of the Odessa steps scene.

Ten Days That Shook the World (1927), based on John Reed's classic account of the early days of the Russian Revolution, proved ineffective both as cinema art and as political propaganda. Critics later raised serious doubts about the historical reliability of the film and justifiable questions regarding the character of its creator. The scene in *Ten Days That Shook the World* in which a student is attacked by vicious aristocratic women and subsequently murdered, his body lying on the waterfront, his neck lacerated, his torso exposed, appeared to have more erotic than political significance for its creator. Eisenstein was not criticized so much for his homosexuality as for the frequently disconcerting emotional excesses and moral obliquities it invariably produced in his work.

Activities Abroad

Eisenstein's final revolutionary epic, *The General Line* (1929), was a leisurely and often evocative ode to the joys of agricultural collectivism. It found favor with Stalin, and that year Eisenstein was granted permission for an extended tour abroad. After a brief teaching assignment at the Sorbonne in Paris, the director went to Hollywood, intending to undertake an American production. Under contract to Paramount studio he composed a script, *Sutter's Gold,* subsequently rejected by the studio as morally indecent. Next he began intensive work on a film adaptation of Theodore Dreiser's *An American Tragedy.* His decision to present the novel in the form of an interior monologue, in opposition to the commercial ideas of the producers, resulted in his peremptory dismissal from the project.

Sergei Eisenstein. (Sovfoto)

Eisenstein then attempted to write and direct a film on location in Mexico. He was intoxicated by the warm sensuality and primitive spontaneity of Mexican life. *Que Viva Mexico* took shape, sections of the complex scenario being composed for each day's shooting. Eisenstein was unwilling to conclude the picture after its allotted budget had been expended. The film was confiscated and turned over to a Hollywood editor who divided the footage into three separate pieces. On the basis of the hypnotic beauty and visionary power evident in several sequences from the mutilated epic (released in the United States as *Time in the Sun, Thunder over Mexico,* and *Day of Death*), it can be said that had Eisenstein been permitted to complete the production the result would have possessed considerable poetry and depth.

Later Career

Upon returning to the Soviet Union in 1932, Eisenstein was confronted with a restrictive philistinism even more oppressive than the lack of understanding he had encountered in the United States. His nearly completed film *Bezhin Meadow,* based on Ivan Turgenev's tale of peasant life, was condemned and suppressed for its religious mysticism and "formalistic excesses." Also disparaged was Eisenstein's theory of montage. Eisenstein responded by publishing an article, "The Mistakes of *Bezhin Meadow,*" in which he repudiated his former esthetic commitments, vowing to "create films of high quality, worthy of the Stalinist epoch." The result, *Alexander Nevsky,* was a simpleminded and vapid historical pageant depicting the heroic overthrow by the Russian people of their 12th-century Teutonic oppressors. Although the film was praised at first for its patriotism and its anti-German virulence, the treaty signed by the Soviet Union with Nazi Germany in 1939 necessitated its immediate withdrawal from circulation.

In 1940 Eisenstein wrote his finest study of film esthetics, *Film Form,* which contains a brilliant analysis of parallels between cinematic and novelistic techniques. The same year Eisenstein began composing the scenario for *Ivan the Terrible,* a massive historical epic with contemporary overtones; although subtler and richer in psychological nuances than his previous work, this biographical parable of Russia's first dictator-despot possesses a claustrophobic opacity that is at times physically intolerable.

While attending a party celebrating the premiere of *Ivan the Terrible* (Part I) the director collapsed from a heart attack. During his early convalescence Eisenstein was informed that the already filmed Part II of *Ivan the Terrible* would not be shown in the U.S.S.R. Ravaged by physical deterioration and the emotional torments of a lifetime, Eisenstein spent his remaining months preparing a second theoretical study, *Film Sense,* and teaching classes in cinema technique at the Soviet Cinema Institute.

Further Reading

Sergei Eisenstein is listed in the European History study guide (XI, O, 6). He was strongly influenced by D. W. GRIFFITH.

The authorized biography is Marie Seton, *Sergei M. Eisenstein* (1952). Other valuable biographical sources are Vladimir Nizhniy, *Lessons with Eisenstein* (1962), and Ivor Montagu, *With Eisenstein* (1968). Intelligent critical analyses of his work can be found in Robert Warshow, *The Immediate Experience: Movies, Comics, Theatre and Other Aspects of Popular Culture* (1962); James Agee, *Agee on Film* (1964); Eric Rhode, *Tower of Babel: Speculations on the Cinema* (1966); and Dwight Macdonald, *Dwight Macdonald on Movies* (1969). For perceptive discussions of Eisenstein's film theory see Rudolf Arnheim, *Film as Art* (1957), and André Bazin, *What Is Cinema?*, essays selected and translated by Hugh Gray (1967).

* * *

EITOKU / By Hugo Munsterberg

Kano Eitoku (1543–1590) was a Japanese painter of the Momoyama period. Working in the bold, colorful style typical of the decorative screen painting of the 16th century, he was the leading artist of his day and one of the most influential Japanese painters.

A member of the illustrious Kano family, Eitoku (pronounced ā-tō-kōō) was born in Kyoto. He received his training under his father, Kano Shoei, and his grandfather, Kano Motonobu, who was the leading painter of the first half of the 16th century. Eitoku's first major work was the decoration of the Jukoin sanctuary at Daitokuji, a famous Kyoto Zen temple, a task he undertook with his father in 1566. Eitoku's fame soon spread, and he became the favorite artist of Oda Nobunaga, the military dictator of Japan, who gave him several commissions. Among those were a set of screens depicting the city of Kyoto and the decoration of Nobunaga's splendid castle at Azuchi on Lake Biwa.

After Nobunaga died in 1582, his successor, Toyotomi Hideyoshi, continued to patronize Eitoku. Among the many outstanding works he produced for Hideyoshi, the most ambitious were the paintings for the castle in Osaka and the Juraku palace in Kyoto, which Eitoku undertook in 1587. Assisted by a large team of collaborators, he produced hundreds of wall paintings, sliding screens, and folding screens, which for sheer magnificence surpassed anything seen in Japan up to that time.

None of the castles and palaces built by Nobunaga and Hideyoshi has survived, so that the works which made Eitoku famous have largely perished. However, there are several sets of screens which give a good idea of his style. Among the most remarkable are a six-fold screen representing a kind of Japanese cedar called *hinoki* (National Museum, Tokyo), a huge screen depicting lions (Imperial collection), and a pair of six-part screens showing hawks and pines (Tokyo University of Arts). All these pictures are painted in the same bold style, using powerful brushstrokes, large forms, brilliant colors, and gold leaf, and emphasizing flat decorative patterns rather than realistic representation. It is this type of painting for which Eitoku is famous and which is the most characteristic expression of the Momoyama period.

While works of this type were generally displayed in the public rooms of the palaces and castles, monochrome ink painting continued to be used for the private apartments. Good examples of Eitoku's work in this medium are the 16 sliding screen paintings, or *fusuma*, which the artist executed early in his career for the Jukoin in Kyoto. The subjects represented—such as birds and flowers in a landscape setting and the "Four Accomplishments"—are Chinese in origin, and the monochrome ink style is derived from Chinese sources through his grandfather, Kano Motonobu. Yet the way in which Eitoku handled his brush with broad, vigorous strokes, stressing pattern rather than space, is very different from the earlier painting of either the Chinese or the Japanese, showing the artist's originality.

Further Reading

Kano Eitoku is listed in the Asia study guide (III, B, 5,

Hawk on a Pine Tree, a six-panel screen by Kano Eitoku. (Tokyo University of Arts Library, Photo by Takayasu Chino)

b). The Japanese painter SESSHU was an earlier master of monochrome ink painting.

Although there is no monograph on Kano Eitoku in English, his work is discussed in *Pageant of Japanese Art,* vol. 2: *Painting* (1952), edited by staff members of the Tokyo National Museum; Robert Treat Paine and Alexander Soper, *The Art and Architecture of Japan* (1955; rev. ed. 1960); and Terukazu Akiyama, *Japanese Painting* (1961).

✻　　✻　　✻

EKWENSI / By Harry A. Gailey

Cyprian Ekwensi (born 1921) was a Nigerian writer who stressed description of the locale and whose episodic style was particularly well suited to the short story.

Cyprian Ekwensi.

Cyprian Ekwensi (pronounced āk-wān′sē) was born at Minna in Northern Nigeria and later lived in Onitsha in the Eastern area. He was educated at Achimota College, in Ibadan, the Gold Coast, and at the Chelsea School of Pharmacy of London University. He lectured in pharmacy at Lagos and was employed as a pharmacist by the Nigerian Medical Corporation.

After favorable reception of his early writing, he joined the Nigerian Ministry for Information and had risen to be the director of that agency by the time of the first military coup in 1966. After the continuing disturbances in the Western and Northern regions in the summer of 1966, Ekwensi gave up his position and relocated his family at Enugu. He became chairman of the Bureau for External Publicity in Biafra and an adviser to the head of state, Col. Odumegwu Ojukwu.

Ekwensi began his writing career as a pamphleteer, and this perhaps explains the episodic nature of his novels and general lack of plot development. These tendencies are well illustrated by *People of the City* (1954), in which Ekwensi gave a vibrant portrait of life in a West African city. It was the first major novel to be published by a Nigerian. Two novellas for children appeared in 1960; both *The Drummer Boy* and *The Passport of Mallam Ilia* were exercises in blending traditional themes with undisguised romanticism.

Ekwensi's most widely read novel, *Jagua Nana,* appeared in 1961. It was a return to the locale of *People of the City* but boasted a much more cohesive plot centered on the character of Jagua, a courtesan who had a love for the expensive. Even her name was a corruption of the expensive English auto. Her life personalized the conflict between the old traditional and modern urban Africa.

Burning Grass (1961) is basically a collection of vignettes concerning a Fulani family. Its major contribution is the insight it presents into the life of this pastoral people. Ekwensi based the novel and the characters on a real

family with whom he had previously lived. Between 1961 and 1966 Ekwensi published at least one major work every year. The most important of these were the novels, *Beautiful Feathers* (1963) and *Iska* (1966), and two collections of short stories, *Rainmaker* (1965) and *Lokotown* (1966).

Further Reading

Cyprian Ekwensi is listed in the Africa study guide (IX, B, 4). Other literary figures of Nigeria were Wole SOYINKA and Amos TUTUOLA.

Among the studies in which Ekwensi's work and life are discussed are Ulli Beier, ed., *Introduction to African Literature* (1967); Ezekiel Mphahlele, ed., *African Writing Today* (1967); Oladele Taiwo, *An Introduction to West African Literature* (1967); Martin Tucker, *Africa in Modern Literature: A Survey of Contemporary Writing in English* (1967); and Margaret Laurence, *Long Drums and Cannons: Nigerian Dramatists and Novelists, 1952–1966* (1968).

✻　　✻　　✻

ELEANOR OF AQUITAINE
/ By Mary Cheney

Eleanor of Aquitaine (ca. 1122–1204) was queen of France from 1137 to 1152 and queen *of England from 1154 to 1204. Her second marriage, which brought southwestern France to the English king, affected the relations of France and England for almost 300 years.*

Eleanor was the elder daughter of William X, Duke of Aquitaine, and Aenor (Eleanor) of Châtellerault. William died on April 9, 1137. The marriage of his heiress was of great importance because Aquitaine was one of the largest fiefs of France. Probably in accord with her father's wish, Eleanor married Louis, son of King Louis VI (July 25, 1137); they were installed as rulers of Aquitaine at Poitiers (August 8) and crowned king and queen of France at Bourges on Christmas, Louis VI having died. The young king seems to have been fond of his beautiful wife, but Eleanor is said to have complained that she had married a monk and not a king.

In June 1147 Louis and Eleanor set out on a crusade, arriving at Antioch in March 1148. Here they quarreled, and the validity of their marriage was questioned. However, she and Louis reached home together. On March 21, 1152, their marriage was annulled on grounds of consanguinity. The King's wish for a male heir—Eleanor having borne two daughters—was probably the decisive reason.

Less than 2 months later Eleanor married Henry Plantagenet, Duke of Normandy, Count of Anjou, and soon to be king of England. They were crowned at Westminster on Dec. 19, 1154. Henry II was 11 years younger than his wife. Their marriage was a political match; he wanted her lands, and she needed a protector. Eleanor and Henry had eight children: William (1153–1156); Henry the "young king" (1155–1183); Matilda (1156–1189), who married Henry the Lion, Duke of Saxony; Richard (1157–1199); Geoffrey, Duke of Brittany (1158–1186); Eleanor (1162–1214), who married Alfonso, King of Castile; Joanna (1165–1199), who married William II, King of Sicily, and later Raymond, Count of Toulouse; and John (1167–1216).

Richard was regarded from an early age as heir to his mother's duchy. In 1168 she brought him to live there, maintaining a court centered at Poitiers. Though Richard was given the ducal title, Eleanor had both power and responsibility. Now she also had full opportunity to give patronage to poets and authors. This relatively happy period ended abruptly in 1173. Eleanor, goaded perhaps by Henry's unfaithfulness, allied with the king of France against him. Her young sons joined her; indeed, as the young Henry was already 18, he may have instigated the plot. King Henry crushed the rebels and forgave his sons but kept his wife in semi-imprisonment until he died.

With the accession to the English throne of her favorite son, Richard (called the "Lion-Hearted"), on Sept. 3, 1189, Eleanor resumed her royal position and regained control of her property. She arranged his coronation, and in the winter of 1190/1191 she traveled to Navarre to fetch his future wife, Berengaria, and escorted her to Sicily to join Richard before he left for Palestine. During his absence she worked with the Council of Regency in

Eleanor of Aquitaine (left) and her second husband, King Henry II of England, are portrayed on a column from the 12th-century Church of Notre Dame du Bourg at Langon, France. (The Metropolitan Museum of Art, The Cloisters Collections, 1934)

England, and she had the unpleasant task of helping to thwart the treachery of John, her youngest son. She received Richard's letters about his captivity and organized the collection of his ransom.

On Richard's sudden death (April 6, 1199), Eleanor supported John's claim to succeed to the English throne against that of her grandson Arthur of Brittany. She herself did homage to King Philip of France for Aquitaine, and she formally took control of the duchy.

In July 1202, when John and Philip were at war, Eleanor was besieged in the castle of Mirabeau by John's enemies, nominally led by her grandson Arthur. John defeated the besiegers and captured his nephew. His mother was able to spend her last months in freedom. She died on April 1, 1204, and was buried at the abbey of Fontevrault, where her effigy remains.

Further Reading

Eleanor of Aquitaine is listed in the European History study guide (II, C, 1, a; II, D, 1, c). She was the wife of LOUIS VII and then of HENRY II and the mother of RICHARD I and JOHN.

The best biography of Eleanor is Amy Ruth Kelly, *Eleanor of Aquitaine and the Four Kings* (1950). There are also Régine Pernoud's shorter and more romantic *Eleanor of Aquitaine,* translated by Peter Wiles (1967), and Curtis Howe Walker, *Eleanor of Aquitaine* (1950). These works must be used with caution because the sources do not reveal Eleanor's motives and opinions.

✳ ✳ ✳

ELGAR/ By Peter S. Hansen

The works of the English composer Sir Edward Elgar (1857–1934) ushered in the modern flowering of English music. His work is characterized by brilliant orchestration and impressive craftsmanship.

Edward Elgar was born on June 2, 1857, in Worcester. His father played the organ and directed the choir in St. George's Catholic Church, was a violinist in local orchestras, and ran a music store. This musical ambience was school and conservatory for Edward, who received no formal musical education except for a few violin lessons. He served his apprenticeship as a church organist, choirmaster, and director of amateur orchestras and the band of the county lunatic asylum. The focus of musical activity was the annual choir festival, when distinguished conductors and soloists performed oratorios by George Frederick Handel and Felix Mendelssohn, as well as newly commissioned works, with the local choir.

Elgar's earliest works were for his church choir, and in later years his most important compositions were large oratorios commissioned for choir festivals. Through these performances he became known throughout England. His first important orchestral piece was the *Enigma Variations* (1899). The "enigma" refers to the theme on which the variations are written, a countertheme to an unnamed and unplayed melody. There have been many conjectures about the mysterious theme, but its identity has never been determined. Each of the variations is labeled with the initials or nickname of friends of the composer, and each variation is a musical character sketch. The piece is beautifully orchestrated and written.

Elgar's choral masterpiece is *The Dream of Gerontius* (1900). Written to a religious poem by Cardinal Newman,

it is perhaps the finest English composition of the Victorian era. It is Wagnerian in its use of leitmotivs characterizing the protagonists and situations, the rich, chromatic harmony, and the masterful orchestral writing.

Other important works by Elgar are the Violin Concerto (1910) and two overtures, *Cockaigne* (1901) and *Falstaff* (1913). His best-known piece is *Pomp and Circumstance No. 1* (1901), a concert march from which the patriotic hymn "Land of Hope and Glory" was written. Its honest, brilliant tunes epitomize the optimism of Edwardian England.

Elgar was knighted in 1904 and named master of the king's music in 1924. By the time of his death on Feb. 23, 1934, in Worcester, the younger 20th-century composers had made his music seem old-fashioned. Later evaluations, however, have been more generous, and Elgar's place in music seems once again assured.

Further Reading

Sir Edward Elgar is listed in the Music study guide (I, I, 4). The following generation of English composers is represented by Gustav HOLST and Sir Ralph VAUGHAN WILLIAMS.

The best works on Elgar are W. H. Reed, *Elgar* (1939), which includes analyses of three major works; Diana McVeagh, *Edward Elgar: His Life and Music* (1955); Percy Marshall Young, *Elgar, O. M.: A Study of a Musician* (1955), a biography which emphasizes his music; and Michael Kennedy, *Portrait of Elgar* (1968), a study of his character. A good background study which discusses Elgar's work is Joseph Machlis, *Introduction to Contemporary Music* (1961).

ELGIN/ By D. M. L. Farr

James Bruce, 8th Earl of Elgin (1811–1863), was the governor general of Canada who implemented the principle of "responsible government" in colonial administration and paved the way for the development of a Commonwealth comprising autonomous nations.

The son of the 7th Earl of Elgin, who collected the Elgin Marbles for the British Museum, James Bruce was born in London on July 20, 1811. He studied at Eton and Oxford, where he graduated in 1833. For a short time he was a Conservative member of Parliament for Southampton, but on the death of his father in 1841 he succeeded to the peerage and was thus denied a career in the House of Commons.

Elgin received a colonial appointment as governor of Jamaica in 1842 and 4 years later was given the more important post of governor general of Canada. Arriving in Canada in January 1847, he brought with him clear instructions from the Whig colonial secretary, Lord Grey, to concede "responsible government" to Canada by ac-

Sir Edward Elgar (left) with tenor John McCormick. (Music Division, New York Public Library)

Lord Elgin. (Library of Congress)

relationships with four ministries during his term of office, Elgin left Canada amidst general regret. He went on two diplomatic missions to China in later years and served briefly in Lord Palmerston's Cabinet in 1859–1860 as postmaster general. In 1862 he was appointed to the highest post in Britain's overseas service, the position of viceroy of India, but he died suddenly in India on Nov. 20, 1863, at the beginning of his term.

Further Reading

Lord Elgin is listed in the Canada study guide (III, A, 3). Robert BALDWIN and Sir Louis-Hippolyte LAFONTAINE were staunch supporters of the idea of self-government for Canada.

There are a number of biographies of Elgin, mostly emphasizing his Canadian experience. One of the first was Sir John Bourinot, *Lord Elgin* (1903), in "The Makers of Canada" series. This was followed by W. P. M. Kennedy, *Lord Elgin,* in the 1926 edition of the series, which used new material. There is also a biography by J. L. Morison, *The Eighth Earl of Elgin* (1928). Elgin's correspondence on Canadian affairs with Lord Grey was published as *The Elgin-Grey Papers, 1846–1852,* edited by Sir Arthur G. Doughty (4 vols., 1937).

ELIJAH BEN SOLOMON
/ By Paul Reich

The Jewish scholar Elijah ben Solomon (1720–1797) was the greatest authority on classical Judaism in modern times. Known for his mental acumen and personal piety, he was given the exalted titles of Gaon (excellency) and Hasid (saint).

cepting the advice of ministers who could command the confidence of a majority in the legislature.

Acting upon these directions, Elgin called to office in March 1848 a group of reformers from Canada West and Canada East headed by Robert Baldwin and Louis-Hippolyte Lafontaine. The next year he accepted the recommendation of these ministers by signing the Rebellion Losses Bill, even though he was personally unhappy over its provision to pay compensation to the victims of the rebellion of 1837. For this act of political wisdom Elgin was subjected to personal abuse from the English Tory population of Canada East, who felt outraged by what appeared to be a payment to "traitors." Elgin's far-seeing action in this crisis marked the ultimate test of "responsible government" in the senior colony of the British Empire and paved the way for the extension of the principle to other settlement colonies.

Before he left Canada in 1854, Elgin was responsible for the negotiation of a reciprocity treaty with William L. Marcy, United States Secretary of State. This provided for the free admission of natural products between the British North American colonies and the United States, and it gave a considerable spur to the economic life of the colonies before it was abrogated in 1866.

A popular governor general, who built up harmonious

E lijah ben Solomon (pronounced ĭ-lī′jə bĕn sŏl′ə-mən) was born and died in Vilna, Poland. He displayed a prodigious intellect as a child, and at the age of 10 he insisted that he study by himself because he refused to be influenced by any special school of thought or methodology. Complete independence of thought characterized his profound scholarship. He remained in Vilna all of his life, except for a short period of voluntary exile that many scholars imposed upon themselves as an act of penance. His pilgrimage to Palestine was aborted, and he returned to his native city, where he dedicated his life to study. The community wished to designate him as their rabbi, but he refused. Out of deference they voted him a small stipend which often proved inadequate, and he had to rely upon his wife to manage the family's financial affairs. His modesty did not prevent his fame from becoming universal, and even as a young man many queries were addressed to him from the greatest scholars and authorities.

Elijah searched for truth wherever it could be found. His intellectual horizons were very broad, and he insisted that all disciplines—mathematics, astronomy, philology, and grammar—could assist in the true understanding of the basic works of classical Judaism. He mastered these subjects and wrote treatises on them.

The number of Elijah's works is said to exceed 70. Many of them have been published, others are in manuscript, and some are lost. He wrote commentaries on a number of biblical books, on the tractates of the Mishna, and on portions of the Jerusalem Talmud. His glosses to the entire Talmud (Babylonian and Jerusalem) display great linguistic insights, and his suggested textual emendations have been confirmed by later examination of manuscripts. He wrote a commentary on Joseph Caro's *Shulhan Aruk*. He also composed a treatise on Hebrew grammar, which the traditional scholars sought to overlook. Another area in which he did pioneer work was that of the early Tannaitic Midrashim, which precede the Talmud and which provide the first stratum of Jewish legal development.

Elijah's interest in classical Talmudic studies did not deter him from study of the Cabala, or Jewish mysticism, and he wrote a commentary on the *Zohar*, the magnum opus of Cabala, which is generally considered to be the work of Moses de Leon.

While Elijah strenuously avoided involvement in communal affairs, he did emerge from his isolation by twice issuing bans of excommunication against the Hasidim (Pietists), whose deprecation of scholarly pursuits as deterrents to genuine spiritual immersion was considered by him as a serious danger to the classical Jewish tradition. Elijah Gaon has been acclaimed as the last great theologian of classical rabbinism whose writings closed one great period of Jewish history but whose personal example has been an endless inspiration to subsequent generations.

Further Reading

Elijah ben Solomon is listed in the Religion study guide (II, E, 5). He wrote commentaries on the works of Joseph CARO and Moses de LEON. He opposed the doctrines of Hasidism, which were taught by his contemporary BAAL SHEM TOV.

Detailed biographical studies of Elijah ben Solomon are in Leo Jung, ed., *The Jewish Library*, vol 6: *Jewish Leaders* (1953), and Simon Noveck, ed., *Great Jewish Personalities in Ancient and Medieval Times* (1959). See also Louis Ginzberg, *Students, Scholars and Saints* (1928).

C. W. **ELIOT** / By Milton Berman

The American educator Charles William Eliot (1834–1926) was president of Harvard from 1869 to 1909 and transformed the college into a modern university.

Born in Boston on March 20, 1834, of a distinguished New England family, Charles W. Eliot graduated from Harvard in 1853. He taught mathematics and chemistry there (1854–1863). He toured Europe (1863–1865), studying chemistry and advanced methods of instruction, and returned to become a professor at the Massachusetts Institute of Technology. In 1869, having attracted favorable attention by several articles on educational reform, he was chosen president of Harvard.

Eliot's 40-year tenure permitted him to press slowly but consistently for change. The effect of his innovations was revolutionary and thoroughly altered Harvard. He drew ideas from his European experience, and he later paid tribute to the stimulating effect of the innovations undertaken at Johns Hopkins University under Daniel Coit Gilman.

Eliot developed an organized 3-year program in the law school, using the case system of instruction based on studying actual court decisions rather than abstract principles. In the medical school he introduced laboratory work and written examinations in all subjects, and he gradually made available clinical instruction in Boston hospitals. In 1872 the university began to grant doctoral

Elijah ben Solomon. (Library of Congress)

Charles W. Eliot. (Library of Congress)

degrees, and the Graduate School of Arts and Sciences was formally organized in 1890, taught by the same faculty that served the undergraduate college.

Eliot's best-known reform was the elective system. Undergraduates could choose from a wide variety of courses in each field rather than follow a prescribed curriculum. By offering many advanced courses to undergraduates, Eliot was able to employ in the college outstanding scholars who divided their time between undergraduate and graduate schools. Harvard became a leading center for graduate study and research and by the 1890s had earned an international reputation for academic excellence.

Always interested in secondary education, Eliot was active in the National Education Association (NEA), becoming president in 1903. He strongly influenced the 1892 report of the NEA "Committee of Ten" that led to the standardization of college preparation and admissions, and he helped found the College Entrance Examination Board in 1906. In 1910 he edited *The Harvard Classics*, a "five-foot shelf" of outstanding books through which those unable to attend college might acquire a liberal education. He retired in 1909 and died at Northeast Harbor, Maine, on Aug. 22, 1926.

Further Reading

Charles W. Eliot is listed in the Social Sciences study guide (VI, G, 3). Two other outstanding presidents of Harvard were Abbott Lawrence LOWELL and James CONANT.

Henry James, *Charles W. Eliot: President of Harvard University, 1869–1909* (2 vols., 1930), is the best and most complete biography. Samuel Eliot Morison's two books, *The Development of Harvard University since the Inauguration of President Eliot, 1869–1929* (1930)

and *Three Centuries of Harvard: 1636–1936* (1936), are invaluable on Eliot's work at Harvard. Eliot's view of his profession may be found in his *Educational Reform: Essays and Addresses* (1898) and *University Administration* (1908). *Charles W. Eliot: The Man and His Beliefs*, edited by William Allan Nielsen (2 vols., 1926), is a collection of Eliot's best essays and addresses on a variety of topics.

G. ELIOT / By Avrom Fleishman

> George Eliot was the pen name used by the English novelist Mary Ann Evans (1819–1880), one of the most important writers of European fiction. Her masterpiece, "Middlemarch," is not only a major social document but also one of the greatest novels in the history of fiction.

Mary Ann Evans was born in Warwickshire, the daughter of an estate agent or manager. Her education was a conventional one, dominated by Christian teachings and touched by the enthusiasm generated by the Evangelical movement of church reform. In her 20s she came into contact with a circle of freethinkers and underwent a radical transformation of her beliefs. Influenced by the so-called Higher Criticism —a largely German school of biblical scholarship that attempted to treat sacred writings as human and historical documents—she devoted herself to translating its findings for the English public. She published her translation of David Strauss's *Life of Jesus* in 1846 and her translation of Ludwig Andreas Feuerbach's *Essence of Christianity* in 1854.

In 1851 Mary Ann Evans became an editor of the *Westminster Review*, a rationalist and reformist journal. In that capacity she came into contact with the leading intellectuals of the day, among them a group known as the positivists. They were followers of the doctrines of the French philosopher Auguste Comte, who were interested in applying scientific knowledge to the problems of society. One of these men was George Henry Lewes, a brilliant philosopher, psychologist, and literary critic, with whom she formed a lasting relationship. As he was separated from his wife but unable to obtain a divorce, their relationship challenged Victorian ideas of respectability. Nevertheless, the obvious devotion and permanence of their union came to be respected.

"Adam Bede"

In the same period Miss Evans turned her powerful mind from scholarly and critical writing to creative work. In 1857 she published a short story, "Amos Barton," and took the pen name "George Eliot" in order to obviate the special aura then attached to lady novelists. After collecting her short stories in *Scenes of Clerical Life* (2 vols., 1858), Eliot published her first novel, *Adam Bede*

(1859). The plot was drawn from a reminiscence of Eliot's aunt, a Methodist preacher, whom she idealized as a character in the novel. The story concerns the seduction of a stupid peasant girl by a selfish young squire, and it follows the stages of the girl's pregnancy, mental disorder, conviction for child murder, and transportation to the colonies. A greater interest develops, however, in the growing love of the lady preacher and a village artisan, Adam Bede. The religious inspiration and moral elevation of their life stand in contrast to the mental limitations and selfishness that govern the personal relations of the other couple.

Eliot's next novel, *The Mill on the Floss* (1860), shows even stronger traces of her childhood and youth in small-town and rural England. It follows the development of a bright and attractive heroine, Maggie Tulliver, among the narrow-minded provincials who surround her. Through the adversities that follow her father's bankruptcy, Maggie acquires a faith in Christian humility, fostered by her reading of Thomas à Kempis. But events become more complex than her ascetic way of life can respond to, and the final pages of the novel show the heroine reaching toward a "religion of humanity," which it was George Eliot's aim to instill in her readers.

"Silas Marner"

In 1861 Eliot published a short novel, *Silas Marner*, which through use as a school textbook is unfortunately her best-known work. It concerns the redemption from misanthropy of the lonely, long-suffering Silas Marner by

George Eliot, a painting by J. Burton. (Library of Congress)

a child who comes accidentally to his door and whom he adopts. The fairy-tale qualities of the plot are relieved by the realism with which Eliot invested the rural setting and by the psychological penetration with which she portrayed her somewhat grotesque characters.

In 1860 and 1861 Eliot lived abroad in Florence and studied Renaissance history and culture. She wrote a historical novel, *Romola* (published 1862–1863), set in Renaissance Florence. This work has never won a place among the author's major achievements, yet it stands as a major example of historical fiction. The story follows the broad outlines of *The Mill on the Floss*—a young woman's spiritual development amid the limitations of the world around her—but the surroundings of Florentine history are considerably more complex than those of provincial English life. Romola experiences Renaissance humanism, Machiavellian politics, and Savonarola's religious revival movement. She moves beyond them all to a "religion of humanity" expressed in social service.

Despite some lapses into doctrinaire writing, George Eliot always aimed at creating conviction in her readers by her honesty in describing human beings, refraining from the tendency to make them illustrations of her ideas. In her next novel, *Felix Holt* (1866), she came as close as she ever did to setting up her fiction in order to convey her doctrines. In this work, however, it is not her ethical but her political thought that is most in evidence, as she addressed herself to the social questions that were then disturbing England. The hero of the novel is a young reformer who carries George Eliot's message to the working class. This message is that their advancement beyond widespread misery could be made by the inner development of their intellectual and moral capacities and not alone through political reforms or union activities. In contrast to Holt, the conventional progressive politician is shown to be tainted by political corruption and insincere in his identification with the working class. The heroine validates this political lesson by choosing the genuine, but poor, reformer rather than the opportunist of her own class.

"Middlemarch"

George Eliot did not publish any novel for some years after *Felix Holt*, and it might have appeared that her creative vein was exhausted. After traveling in Spain in 1867, she produced a dramatic poem, *The Spanish Gipsy*, in the following year, but neither this poem nor the other poems of the period are on a par with her prose. Then in 1871–1872 Eliot published her masterpiece, *Middlemarch*, a comprehensive vision of human life, with the breadth and profundity of Leo Tolstoy's *War and Peace*. The main strand of its complex plot is the familiar Eliot tale of a girl's awakening to the complexities of life and her formulation of a humanistic substitute for religion as a guide for her conduct. But the heroine, Dorothea Brooke, is here surrounded by other "seekers in life's ways," a man of science and a political reformer, whose struggles and discoveries command almost equal attention. Moreover, the social setting in which the heroes' challenges are presented is not merely sketched in or worked up from historical notes but rendered with a comprehensiveness and subtlety that makes *Middlemarch* a major social document as well as a work of art. The title—drawn from the name of the fictional town in which most of the action occurs—and the subtitle, *A Study of Provincial Life,* suggest that the art of fiction here develops a grasp of the life of human communities, as well as that of individuals.

George Eliot's last novel was *Daniel Deronda* (1874–1876). It is perhaps her least-read work, although recent critical attention has revealed its high merits in at least one half of its plot, while raising still unanswered questions about its less successful half. The novel contrasts and interweaves two stories. One is a marriage for personal advantages by a young woman of keen intelligence who discovers that she has given herself to a scoundrel. The other story is the discovery by a young British gentleman that he is of Jewish origin and his subsequent dedication to the Jewish community by espousal of the Zionist resettlement of Palestine. The ethical relationship of these widely divergent situations and characters is one of the chief interests of the author, but although her intention is clear, her literary success is less so.

In 1880, after the death of Lewes, George Eliot married a friend of long standing, John Walter Cross. She died in the same year, having reached an influence on many of her contemporaries amounting almost to the position of a prophetic teacher.

Further Reading

George Eliot is listed in the Literature study guide (II, H, 1, b). Charles DICKENS and William Makepeace THACKERAY were other major English novelists of this period.

Gordon S. Haight edited the comprehensive edition of *The George Eliot Letters* (7 vols., 1954–1955). Haight's *George Eliot* (1968) is likely to become the standard biography of Eliot, although the "official" biography by her husband, J. W. Cross, ed., *George Eliot's Life as Related in Her Letters and Journals* (3 vols., 1885), is still useful. Two preeminent critical studies of Eliot's novels are Barbara Hardy, *The Novels of George Eliot: A Study in Form* (1959; rev. ed. 1963), and W. J. Harvey, *The Art of George Eliot* (1961). For a discussion of the intellectual currents underlying her works see Bernard J. Paris, *Experiments in Life: George Eliot's Quest for Values* (1965).

* * *

J. **ELIOT**/ By Ola Elizabeth Winslow

John Eliot (1604–1690), English-born clergyman of the first New England generation and missionary to the Massachusetts Indians, translated the Bible and other books into the Algonquian tongue.

John Eliot's baptismal record, dated Aug. 5, 1604, is preserved in the church of St. John the Baptist in Widford, Hertfordshire. His father had extensive landholdings in Hertford and Essex counties. When John was a child, his parents moved to Nazeing. Just before his fourteenth birthday he matriculated at Jesus College, Cambridge, where he prepared for the ministry. He took his bachelor of arts degree in 1622. In 1629–1630 he lived with Thomas Hooker and his family in Little Baddow, Essex. After the Separatist Hooker escaped to Holland, Eliot, who as a Nonconformist minister was also unsafe, decided to emigrate to New England, as many other young ministers were doing.

To the New World

Eliot arrived in Boston on Nov. 3, 1631, when the settlement was barely a year old. While John Wilson, pastor of Boston's first church society, was absent, Eliot was asked to occupy the pulpit. On Wilson's return Eliot was invited to remain as teacher. He refused, having promised Nazeing friends who were intending to emigrate that if he was not permanently engaged when they arrived he would be their pastor. The Nazeing group settled in Roxbury, Mass., and Eliot was ordained immediately as their teacher and later as pastor.

Pastor at Roxbury

Eliot stayed at Roxbury for the remainder of his years. The pleasure of his life was increased by the arrival of two sisters and, later, two brothers. Hanna Mumford, to whom he was engaged, had also come with this group.

John Eliot. (*Library of Congress*)

Their wedding, in October 1632, is the first marriage on the town record.

For his first 40 years in Roxbury, Eliot preached in the 20- by 30-foot meetinghouse with thatched roof and unplastered walls that stood on Meetinghouse Hill. The church grew with the town, and Eliot's long ministry was marked by imaginative leadership both within and without the membership circle. His share in founding the Roxbury Grammar School and his efforts to keep it independent and prosperous were only part of his contribution to the community. In addition to preaching and the care of his people, he also had the traditional share of a first-generation minister in various religious and civil affairs.

"Apostle to the Indians"

These numerous and valuable local services, however, did not give John Eliot the place he holds in American history. That place is described by his unofficial title, "Apostle to the Indians," for whose benefit he gave thought, time, and unstinted energy for over half a century. He was not sent to them as a missionary by church, town, or colony but went voluntarily in fulfillment of his duty to share in Christianizing the Indian, which, according to the original Massachusetts charter, was expected of every settler and was "the principal end of this plantation." Long before either church or civil leaders realized that Christianization was an English wish rather than an Indian one, they had puzzled over ways of proceeding. Individual ministers had tried unsuccessfully to bring Indians to the meetinghouse.

Learning the Indian Language

The chief barrier between European and Indian was communication. Sign language and a jargon of pidgin English and Indian would do for barter but not for sermons. The Algonquian language, spoken by the various tribes of Massachusetts Indians, presented a formidable problem to those trained in classical and European languages; further, there were no written texts, dictionaries, or grammars. Eliot learned the language by taking into his home an Indian boy, a captive in the Pequot War, who had learned to speak and understand everyday English and also to read it; he could not write. The boy's pronunciation was very distinct. As Eliot listened, he made word lists which revealed inflexional endings, differentiated nouns from verbs and singulars from plurals, and gave many hints of language behavior to Eliot, who had a distinct gift for such understanding. The process of mastering this strange tongue well enough to use it for expressing his own thought was arduous, but Eliot persisted, and on Oct. 28, 1646, preached his first sermon in Algonquian to a small group of Indians gathered at the wigwam of a chieftain at Nonantum (now Newton). The Indians understood well enough to question him. They felt his friendliness and invited him to preach again.

First Indian Bible

A detailed report of the first four of these woodland

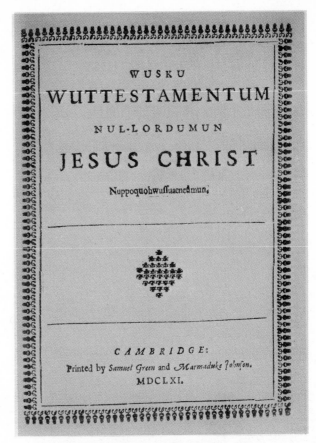

The title page of Eliot's translation of the New Testament into Natick, an Algonquian Indian language. Eliot's translation of the complete Bible was issued in 1661–1663 and was the first Bible to be printed in the American colonies.

meetings, taken down by another minister, was given to Edward Winslow, newly appointed agent of the colony. It was immediately printed in London under the title "The Day-Breaking, if not the Sun-Rising of the Gospell with the Indians in New England." Winslow drafted a bill which led to Parliament's chartering the Society for the Propagation of the Gospel among the Indians of New England. Throughout England and Wales funds were solicited. With this money Eliot bought school supplies, carpenter and farm tools, cloth, spinning wheels, and other articles needed in the work of education and civilization to which, in addition to his Roxbury parish, he devoted the remainder of his life. The first edition of his translation of the Bible into Algonquian (1661–1663) was the first Bible printed in the Colonies.

This story has many chapters. Fourteen self-governing Indian towns were founded, native teachers and preachers trained, and new skills learned and practiced. But King Philip's War (1675–1676) destroyed the Indian towns; only four were rebuilt. The "Praying Indians," exiled to Deer Island, suffered lamentably. John Eliot died in 1690, before restoration of the villages had really begun. But he had lived to see the second edition of his

Indian Bible. With this book he had written the beginnings of a pioneering story in race relations for his own day. His feat of translation is still a marvel to scholars.

Further Reading

John Eliot is listed in the Religion study guide (I, M, 2, a; I, O, 1, m). Samuel KIRKLAND was also a missionary to the American Indians during this period.

A recent full-length study of Eliot is Ola Elizabeth Winslow, *John Eliot, "Apostle to the Indians"* (1968). He is also discussed in Walter Eliot Thwing, *History of the First Church in Roxbury* (1908); Samuel Eliot Morison, *Builders of the Bay Colony* (1930); and William Kellaway, *The New England Company, 1649–1776* (1961).

T. S. ELIOT / By Francis Warlow

Thomas Stearns Eliot (1888–1965), American-English author, was one of the most influential poets writing in English in the 20th century, one of the most seminal critics, an interesting playwright, and an editor and publisher.

T. S. Eliot. (Radio Times Hulton Picture Library)

On Sept. 26, 1888, T. S. Eliot was born in St. Louis, Mo., a member of the third generation of a New England family that had come to St. Louis in 1834. Eliot's grandfather, William Greenleaf Eliot, Unitarian minister and founder of schools, a university, a learned society, and charities, was the family patriarch. While carrying on a tradition of public service, the Eliots never forgot their New England ties. T. S. Eliot claimed that he was a child of both the Southwest and New England. In Massachusetts he missed Missouri's dark river, cardinal birds, and lush vegetation. In Missouri he missed the fir trees, song sparrows, red granite shores, and blue sea of Massachusetts.

Eliot Family

Henry Ware Eliot, the father of T. S. Eliot, became chairman of the board of a brick company and served the cultural institutions his father had helped found, as well as others. He married an intellectual New Englander, Charlotte Champ. After bearing six children, she turned her energies to education and legal safeguards for the young. She also wrote a biography, some religious poems, and a dramatic poem (1926), with a preface by her already widely respected youngest child, Thomas.

Eliot grew up within the family's tradition of service to religion, community, and education. Years later he declared, "Missouri and the Mississippi have made a deeper impression on me than any part of the world." The Eliots also spent summers on Cape Ann, Mass. These places appear in Eliot's early poetry, but in the *Four*

Quartets of his maturity his affection for them is most explicit.

Education of a Poet

In St. Louis young Eliot received a classical education privately and at Smith Academy, originally named Eliot Academy. He composed and read the valedictory poem for his graduation in 1905. After a year at Milton Academy in Massachusetts, he went to Harvard in 1906. He was shy, correct in dress, and intellectually independent. He studied under such versatile men as William James, George Santayana, Josiah Royce, and Irving Babbitt. He discovered Dante and heard talk of reviving poetic drama. Among such student personalities as Walter Lippmann, Heywood Broun, Conrad Aiken, and E. E. Cummings, Eliot made a modest impression as a contributor and editor of the *Harvard Advocate*. He was quietly completing his bachelor of arts degree in 3 years and was hard on the track of a new poetic voice. In 1908 he discovered Arthur Symons's *The Symbolist Movement in Literature,* and through it the French poet Jules Laforgue. From the example of Laforgue, other French symbolists, and late Elizabethan dramatists, he began to develop the offhand eloquence, the pastiches and discordant juxtapositions, the rhythmic versatility, and the concern masked by evasive irony and wit that would soon dominate the American-British renascence in poetry.

Eliot's stay at Harvard to earn a master of arts in philosophy was interrupted by a year at the Sorbonne. He returned to Harvard in 1911 but in 1914 he went abroad again on a Harvard fellowship to study in Germany. When World War I broke out, he transferred to Merton College, Oxford, and studied with a disciple of F. H. Bradley, who became the subject of Eliot's dissertation. Ezra Pound, the young American poet, discovered Eliot at Oxford. Though they were quite different, they shared a devotion to learning and poetry. After Oxford, Eliot decided to stay in England and in 1915 married a vivacious Englishwoman, Vivienne Haigh Haigh-Wood. He taught at Highgate Junior School for boys near London (1915–1916) and then worked for Lloyd's Bank. While teaching, he completed his dissertation, *Knowledge and Experience in the Philosophy of F. H. Bradley.* The dissertation was accepted, but Eliot did not return to America to defend it so as to receive his doctorate. His study of Bradley, however, contributed to his thought and prose style.

Early Poetry

When the United States entered World War I in 1917, Eliot tried to join the U.S. Navy but was rejected for physical reasons. That year his first volume of verse, *Prufrock and Other Observations,* appeared and almost immediately became the focus for discussion and controversy. Eliot's abruptly varied rhythms and his mixtures of precision and discontinuity, contemporary references and echoes of the past, and immediate experience and haunting leitmotifs spoke to the distraction and alienation that World War I had intensified in Western civilization. This quality was most effective in the ironically titled poem "The Love Song of J. Alfred Prufrock," in which the Victorian dramatic monologue is turned inward and wedded to witty disillusion and psychic privacies to present a dilettante character fearful of disturbing or being disturbed by anything in the universe. Prufrock moves through a dehumanized city of dispirited common men on an empty round of elegant but uncommunicative chitchat. The many voices within him, speaking in approximations of blank verse and in catchy couplets, contribute to what Hugh Kenner, the American critic, called an "eloquence of inadequacy."

Critic and Editor

As literary editor of the *Egoist,* a feminist little magazine, from 1917 to 1919, Eliot began the editorial and critical careers that would continue until his death. The back pages of the *Egoist* were entrusted to a succession of young poet-editors, and here, with the aid of Ezra Pound, the new poetry and criticism got a hearing. Eliot was also writing anonymous reviews for the *London Times* and publishing essays that announced the appearance of a sometimes pontifical but illuminating critic. In 1919 two of his most influential pieces appeared. "Tradition and the Individual Talent" advocated the "depersonalization" of poetry and a redirection of interest away from the poet's personality to the poem, the process, and the tradition to which the poem belonged. "Hamlet and His Problems" defined "objective correlative," a term soon to achieve wide currency, as a particular object, act, sequence, or situation which the poet infuses

with a particular feeling in order to be able to call it up economically by mere mention of the thing or event. In this essay Eliot demonstrated the need to cut through received opinion to the literary work itself. He declared that the "primary problem" in *Hamlet* is not the character but the play, because the character has to bear the burden of an "inexpressible" emotion "in excess of the facts as they appear."

In his early critical essays, collected as *The Sacred Wood* (1920), *Homage to John Dryden* (1924), *Selected Essays: 1917–1932* (1932), and *The Use of Poetry and the Use of Criticism* (1933), Eliot pointed to the poets, critics, and cultural figures who had been helpful to him and might assist others in adjusting 20th-century experience to literary and cultural tradition. Eliot was drawn to precision and concreteness in language, seeking "to purify the dialect of the tribe," as he later put it. He called attention to thematic or muscial structure for communicating complex psychological experience, to past mergers of thought and feeling that could counteract the modern "dissociation of sensibility," and to the "mythical method" of James Joyce's novel *Ulysses* and of his own poetry—a method that contrasts the balance and sanity of masterpieces and the ages that produced them with the contemporary deracination that isolates individuals culturally and psychologically. With learned understatement he also assessed critics from Aristotle to his Harvard teacher Irving Babbitt. He found creative guides in 19th-century French symbolists; the 17th-century man of letters John Dryden and his predecessor John Donne; the Jacobean dramatists; and beyond them Dante, a bitter exile who created a serene masterpiece.

A rising poet and critic, Eliot made his way into elite British circles. The Bloomsbury group led by Leonard and Virginia Woolf welcomed him; as a somewhat British American, both conservative and liberal leaders could accept him; and young writers on both sides of the Atlantic offered respect and affection. When restless Pound left London for Paris in 1920, Eliot quietly assumed the leadership of England's young intelligentsia.

In "Gerontion" (1920) Eliot offered a shorter, less fragmented perspective on Prufrock's unfocused world, resorting again to the interior monologue, this time spoken by a despairing old man who did not believe or act passionately in youth and now regrets the spiritual waste of his life.

"The Waste Land"

While convalescing from exhaustion in 1921, Eliot advanced his diagnosis of war-enervated, spiritually moribund Europe with a draft of *The Waste Land.* This was to become, after publication in 1922, the most influential and controversial poem of the century. Eliot corresponded with Pound about the poem, and Pound's drastic editing compressed it, no doubt unifying and sharpening it. Eliot acknowledged Pound's help by dedicating the poem to him in Dante's words as "il miglior fabbro," the better maker.

In *The Waste Land* Eliot defines alienation and also

A scene from Murder in the Cathedral, *a play by T. S. Eliot. (Library of Congress)*

indicates a remedy. Voices such as Prufrock's and Geron-tion's are still heard, but Eliot's spokesman is now a mild Jeremiah, a lonely prophet or pilgrim who seeks spiritual regeneration in person and in thought throughout a corrupt city and across a disoriented continent. Spring is no longer the joyous season of renewal: "April is the cruelest month," for it calls unwilling people to physical and spiritual regeneration, to leave off unsacramental sex and materialistic busyness. Eliot had intensified and extended the varied rhythms and montages of his earlier interior monologues and now organized them in a five-part structure deriving from Beethoven's late quartets. While sordid and distracted images still abound, hopeful ones have increased, and a greater tension exists between the two. Social disintegration is equated with a shattered wasteland, but the poem's central consciousness is nevertheless alert to the possibility of recreating personal and communal wholes out of the present and the past, of fertility rites, Christianity, Indian philosophy, and Western literature and art: "These fragments I have shored against my ruin."

Also in 1922 Eliot founded the *Criterion,* an influential little magazine that appeared until 1939, when he discontinued its publication. In it he stressed learning, discipline, and the constant renewal of tradition in literature. The magazine also reflected his growing religiousness and his devotion to the idea of a culture stratified by class and unified by Christianity.

As author of *The Waste Land* and editor of the *Criterion,* Eliot assumed a dominant role in literature in America and in Great Britain. He left Lloyd's Bank in 1925 and joined Faber and Faber, Ltd., a publisher, eventually rising to a directorship there.

Meanwhile Eliot was crossing a divide in his career. He ended his preoccupation with one kind of alienation in "The Hollow Men" (1925), where the will-less subjects of the poem cluster in a dead land, waiting like effigies for a galvanic revelation that does not come. They comment on their lot in a spastic chorus that includes a children's game song, a fragment of the Lord's Prayer, and a parody of "world without end" and other expressions from the Bible and the Book of Common Prayer.

"The Hollow Men," "Gerontion," and *The Waste Land* compose a triptych that delineates the estrangement of the self in a society fallen into secularism, with the central panel, *The Waste Land,* suggesting the possibility of salvaging the self by reconstituting culture out of its scattered parts.

Religious and Cultural Views

In 1927 Eliot became an Anglo-Catholic and a British citizen. With the heightened social consciousness of the worldwide economic depression, a reaction set in against his conservatism. It grew more difficult to explain away on literary grounds the anti-Semitic references in several of his poems. In *After Strange Gods* (1934) Eliot took the literary ideas of his "Tradition and the Individual Talent" and made them apply to culture. He also declared that too many freethinking Jews would be a detriment to the kind of organic Christian culture he proposed. This work, along with *The Idea of a Christian Society* (1939) and *Notes toward a Definition of Culture* (1948), indicated Eliot's stand against the pluralistic society of most Western democracies. Without a reconstruction of Christendom, the alternative, he felt, was paganism.

With *Ash Wednesday* (1930), while the literary tide was flowing Leftward, Eliot emerged as the sole orthodox Christian among important Anglo-American poets. The title of this six-part poem refers to the beginning of Lent, the most intense season of penitence and self-denial in the Christian year. The poem's central consciousness is an aging penitent closer to the convert Eliot than his spokesman in any previous major poem. Like his antecedents, the penitent is alienated—but from God, not from society or nature; and following the precedents of Dante and St. John of the Cross, the 16th-century Spanish mystic, he sets out to draw near the divine presence. The poem is his interior monologue narrating his progress and praying for guidance. The tone of unbroken sincerity and passionate yearning, of anxiety and some joy is new for Eliot. The penitent desires to abandon ambition, his fading powers of expression, the enticements of the world, and all that may prevent his mounting the turning stairs toward salvation. Though his longing for the vision of God known in childhood is not fulfilled, he progresses toward it, and he will persist. American critic F. O. Matthiessen remarked how Eliot with "paradoxical precision in vagueness" used wonderfully concrete images to convey the mystery of a spiritual experience.

In 1934 Eliot published *After Strange Gods* and also brought his religious and dramatic interests together in *The Rock.* This pageant mingles narrative prose with poetic dialogue and choruses as part of a campaign to raise funds to restore London's churches. Eliot's speakers ask for visible gathering places, where the "Invisible Light" can do its work.

In 1935 *Murder in the Cathedral,* perhaps Eliot's best play, was produced at Canterbury Cathedral. It has to do with Archbishop Thomas Becket, who was assassinated before the altar there in 1170. Its theme is the historical competition between church and state for the allegiance of the individual. Its poetry suggests blank verse with deviations. Becket prepares, like the penitent in *Ash Wednesday*, to accept God's will, knowing that "humanity cannot bear much reality." After his death, the chorus, speaking for humanity, confesses that "in life there is not time to grieve long," even for a martyr.

"Four Quartets"

In 1936 Eliot concluded his *Poems 1909–1935* with "Burnt Norton," the first of what became the *Four Quartets*, an extended work that proved to be his poetic viaticum. "Burnt Norton," in which Eliot makes vivid use of his recurring rose-garden symbolism, grew out of a visit to a deserted Gloucestershire mansion. This poem engendered three others, each associated with a place. "East Coker" (1940) is set in the village of Eliot's Massachusetts ancestors. The last two quartets appeared with the publication of *Four Quartets* (1943). The third, "The Dry Salvages," named for three small islands off the Massachusetts coast where Eliot vacationed in his youth, draws on his American experiences; and the fourth, "Little Gidding," derives from a visit to the site of a religious community, now an Anglican shrine, where the British king Charles I paused before he surrendered and went to his death. Here Eliot asks forgiveness for a lifetime of mistakes, which no doubt includes his possible anti-Semitism of the years before the war. Each of the quartets is a separate whole but related to the others. All employ the thematic structure of music and the five movements of *The Waste Land*. The theme, developed differently, is the same in each: a penitential Eliot seeks the eternal in and through the temporal, the still dynamic center of the turning world. One may seek or wait in any place at any time, for God is in all places at all times. The theme and method continue those of *Ash Wednesday*, but the feeling in *Four Quartets* is less passionately personal, more compassionate and reconciled. The verse is serene, poised, and sparsely graceful.

Midway in his composition of *Four Quartets*, Eliot published *Old Possum's Book of Practical Cats* (1939). Here Eliot the fabulist appeared, and the humorist and wit resurfaced.

The Playwright

The Family Reunion, the first of Eliot's four plays for the professional stage, appeared in 1939. He later observed that its hero was a prig but its poetry the best in any of his plays. This play, like the other three, employs the familiar conventions of drawing-room comedy to encase religious matters. *The Family Reunion* and *The Cocktail Party* (1940) both involve analogs with classical Greek dramas. *The Confidential Clerk* (1954) and *The Elder Statesman* (1959) even employ potentially melodramatic situations, although they are not developed popularly, for Eliot is preoccupied with individual religiousness and the self-revelations and mutual understandings it effects within families. In fact, *The Elder Statesman*, the last and simplest of his plays, contending that true love is beyond verbal expression, is dedicated to his second wife, Valerie.

The most successful of these plays, *The Cocktail Party*, enjoyed respectable runs and revivals in London and New York. It puts the tension between the temporal and the eternal in more effective dramatic terms than do the other plays. By means of the familiar, a cocktail party, Eliot involves the audience in the unbelievable, a modern martyrdom. He contrasts lives oriented to the natural with that of a martyred missionary devoted to the supernatural. At the same time he parallels a Greek drama more subtly than he did in *The Family Reunion*.

Eliot's drawing-room plays, however, have only a limited appeal. The poetry in the last three is unobtrusively effective, carried by voices moving naturally along the hazy border between poetry and prose. They are not so much powerful plays as suggestive ones.

Honor and Old Age

Following World War II there were important changes in Eliot's life and literary activities. In 1947 his first wife died. Suffering from nervous debilities, she had been institutionalized for years, and Eliot had visited her every Sunday and kept his suffering and deprivation private. In 1948 he received the Nobel Prize and the British Order of Merit, and the list of his honors continued to grow. Publishing no important poetry after the *Four Quartets*, he devoted himself to the poetic drama, the revitalization of culture, some new criticism in *On Poetry and Poets* (1957), the readjustment of earlier critical judgments, and the editing of collections of his poetry and plays. In 1957 he married his private secretary, Valerie Fischer, and enjoyed a felicitous marriage until he died on Jan. 4, 1965, in London. In accordance with earlier arrangements his ashes were deposited in St. Michael's Church, East Coker, his ancestral village, on April 17, 1965.

Many poets and artists paid final tribute to Eliot—Pound: "A grand poet and brotherly friend"; W. H. Auden: "A great poet and a great man"; Allen Tate: "Mr. Eliot was the greatest poet in English of the 20th century"; Robert Lowell: "He was a dear personal friend. Our American literature has had no greater poet or critic"; Robert Penn Warren: "He is the key figure of our century in America and England, the most powerful single influence." Avowedly Christian in a secular age, Eliot tried to revitalize the religious roots of Western culture. His career recalls the versatile man of letters of the 18th century.

Further Reading

T. S. Eliot is listed in the Literature study guide (I, E, 2, b). He had early contact with Ezra POUND, was influenced by the philosophy of F. H. BRADLEY, and paid homage to English metaphysical poets such as John DRYDEN and John DONNE.

A recent edition of Eliot's work is *The Complete Poems and Plays of T. S. Eliot* (1969). Donald C. Gallup, *T. S. Eliot: A Bibliography* (1952), lists Eliot's writings through 1951.

The literature on Eliot is extensive. Herbert Howarth, *Notes on Some Figures behind T. S. Eliot* (1964), provides biographical information. Hugh Kenner, *The Invisi-*

ble Poet: T. S. Eliot (1959), is probably the standard work on Eliot. Francis O. Matthiessen, *The Achievement of T. S. Eliot* (1935; 3d ed. 1958), provides a balanced introduction. Russell H. Robbins, *The T. S. Eliot Myth* (1951), primarily because of Eliot's conservatism, offers a negative view. Other studies include Elizabeth A. Drew, *T. S. Eliot: The Design of His Poetry* (1949); Helen L. Gardner, *The Art of T. S. Eliot* (1949); and D. E. S. Maxwell, *The Poetry of T. S. Eliot* (1952). George Williamson, *A Reader's Guide to T. S. Eliot: A Poem-by-Poem Analysis* (1953; 2d ed. 1966), is a helpful reference work.

Collections of critical estimates of Eliot are Balachandra Rajan, ed., *T. S. Eliot: A Study of His Writings by Several Hands* (1947); Richard March and M. J. Tambimuttu, eds., *T. S. Eliot: A Symposium* (1948); Leonard Unger, ed., *T. S. Eliot: A Selected Critique* (1948); and Neville Braybrooke, ed., *T. S. Eliot: A Symposium for His Seventieth Birthday* (1958). Studies of particular works include Raymond Preston, *"Four Quartets" Rehearsed* (1946), and Robert E. Knoll, ed., *Storm over the Waste Land* (1964).

ELIZABETH / By Sidney Harcave

The Russian empress Elizabeth Petrovna (1709–1761) ruled from 1741 to 1761. Her reign was marked by Russia's continuing Westernization and growth as a great power.

Born in Moscow on Dec. 18, 1709, Elizabeth was the daughter of Peter I and Catherine Alekseyevna. Her education, emphasizing French, German, and the social graces, was designed to prepare her for marriage to a member of European royalty. However, all efforts to provide a suitable husband, including her father's attempt to arrange a marriage between her and Louis XV of France, failed. The beautiful and vivacious Elizabeth was forced to accept a life of spinsterhood but not one of chastity. Over the years she had many lovers, chief among them Alexis Razumovsky.

Elizabeth spent the first 3 decades of her life in political obscurity during which time the Russian throne passed, after the death of Peter I, to a succession of her relatives: her mother, as Catherine I; a nephew, as Peter II; a cousin, as Empress Anna; and finally her young cousin Ivan VI, whose mother, Anna Leopoldovna, served as regent.

That obscurity was lifted in 1741, when a movement began to remove the allegedly pro-German regent and her son Ivan VI and to install Elizabeth as empress. In November of that year, supported by Alexis Razumovsky, Elizabeth accepted the role of legitimate claimant to the throne. She led a detachment of guardsmen to seize the regent and her son and then dramatically proclaimed herself empress of Russia.

An intellectually limited and sensual person, Elizabeth

Empress Elizabeth of Russia. (Giraudon)

gave little attention to the day-to-day business of government. She was shrewd enough, however, to see the importance of some political matters, particularly those that personally concerned her. To protect her position, she dealt harshly with any who might become threats, among them the family of the former regent, whom she kept imprisoned. Although Elizabeth made neither domestic nor foreign policies, she influenced both through her choice of officials and her response to their counsel.

Some notable domestic changes occurred during Elizabeth's reign. The number of Germans in the government was reduced. The privileges of the landed nobility were enhanced at the expense of the serfs. The process of Westernization was accelerated by the introduction of structural improvements in St. Petersburg; the opening of the first Russian university, in Moscow, in 1755; and the establishment of the Academy of Arts in 1757.

Elizabeth took pride in the advance of her country as a great power during her 20 years as empress. In the latter part of her reign, when Russia was at war with Prussia, she followed the battle reports closely. With victory almost in sight, Empress Elizabeth died on Dec. 25, 1761.

Further Reading

Elizabeth is listed in the European History study guide (VI, I, 1). She was the daughter of PETER I. Her reign was closely followed by that of CATHERINE THE GREAT.

Robert Nisbet Bain, *The Daughter of Peter the Great* (1899), is both readable and useful. A more recent work is Tamara Talbot Rice, *Elizabeth, Empress of Russia*

(1970). See also Herbert Harold Kaplan, *Russia and the Outbreak of the Seven Years' War* (1968).

ELIZABETH I / By Roger Howell, Jr.

Elizabeth I (1533–1603) was queen of England and Ireland from 1558 to 1603. She preserved stability in a nation rent by political and religious dissension and maintained the authority of the Crown against the growing pressures of Parliament.

Born at Greenwich, on Sept. 7, 1533, Elizabeth I was the daughter of Henry VIII and his second wife, Anne Boleyn. Because of her father's continuing search for a male heir, Elizabeth's early life was precarious. In May 1536 her mother was beheaded to clear the way for Henry's third marriage, and on July 1 Parliament declared that Elizabeth and her older sister, Mary, the daughter of Henry's first queen, were illegitimate and that the succession should pass to the issue of his third wife, Jane Seymour. Jane did produce a male heir, Edward, but even though Elizabeth had been declared illegitimate, she was brought up in the royal household. She received an excellent education and was reputed to be remarkably precocious, notably in languages (of which she learned Latin, French, and Italian) and music.

Edward VI and Mary

During the short reign of her brother, Edward VI, Elizabeth survived precariously, especially in 1549 when the principal persons in her household were arrested and she was to all practical purposes a prisoner at Hatfield. In this period she experienced ill health but pursued her studies under her tutor, Roger Ascham.

In 1553, following the death of Edward VI, her sister Mary I came to the throne with the intention of leading the country back to Catholicism. The young Elizabeth found herself involved in the complicated intrigue that accompanied these changes. Without her knowledge the Protestant Sir Thomas Wyatt plotted to put her on the throne by overthrowing Mary. The rebellion failed, and though Elizabeth maintained her innocence, she was sent to the Tower. After 2 months she was released against the wishes of Mary's advisers and was removed to an old royal palace at Woodstock. In 1555 she was brought to Hampton Court, still in custody, but on October 18 was allowed to take up residence at Hatfield, where she resumed her studies with Ascham.

On Nov. 17, 1558, Mary died, and Elizabeth succeeded to the throne. Elizabeth's reign was to be looked back on as a golden age, when England began to assert itself internationally through the mastery of sea power. The condition of the country seemed far different, however, when she came to the throne. A contemporary noted:

"The Queen poor. The realm exhausted. The nobility poor and decayed. Want of good captains and soldiers. The people out of order. Justice not executed." Both internationally and internally, the condition of the country was far from stable.

At the age of 25 Elizabeth was a rather tall and well-poised woman; what she lacked in feminine warmth, she made up for in the worldly wisdom she had gained from a difficult and unhappy youth. It is significant that one of her first actions as queen was to appoint Sir William Cecil (later Lord Burghley) as her chief secretary. Cecil was to remain her closest adviser; like Elizabeth, he was a political pragmatist, cautious and essentially conservative. They both appreciated England's limited position in the face of France and Spain, and both knew that the key to England's success lay in balancing the two great Continental powers off against each other, so that neither could bring its full force to bear against England.

The Succession

Since Elizabeth was unmarried, the question of the succession and the actions of other claimants to the throne bulked large. She toyed with a large number

Queen Elizabeth I of England, portrait by an unknown artist. (National Portrait Gallery, London)

of suitors, including Philip II of Spain; Eric of Sweden; Adolphus, Duke of Holstein; and the Archduke Charles. From her first Parliament she received a petition concerning her marriage. Her answer was, in effect, her final one: "This shall be for me sufficient, that a marble stone shall declare that a Queen, having reigned such a time died a virgin." But it would be many years before the search for a suitable husband ended, and the Parliament

Above, Queen Elizabeth's troops at Tilbury await the Spanish invasion in 1588, while fire and storms destroy the Invincible Armada. Below, the Queen (rear, center) gives thanks in St. Paul's Cathedral for England's deliverance from the Armada. (The Mansell Collection, London)

reconciled itself to the fact that the Queen would not marry.

Elizabeth maintained what many thought were dangerously close relations with her favorite, Robert Dudley, whom she raised to the earldom of Leicester. She abandoned this flirtation when scandal arising from the mysterious death of Dudley's wife in 1560 made the connection politically disadvantageous. In the late 1570s and early 1580s she was courted in turn by the French Duke of Anjou and the Duke of Alençon. But by the mid-1580s it was clear she would not marry.

Many have praised Elizabeth for her skillful handling of the courtships. To be sure, her hand was perhaps her greatest diplomatic weapon, and any one of the proposed marriages, if carried out, would have had strong repercussions on English foreign relations. By refusing to marry, Elizabeth could further her general policy of balancing the Continental powers. Against this must be set the realization that it was a very dangerous policy. Had Elizabeth succumbed to illness, as she nearly did early in her reign, or had any one of the many assassination plots against her succeeded, the country would have been plunged into the chaos of a disputed succession. That the accession of James I on her death was peaceful was due as much to the luck of her survival as it was to the wisdom of her policy.

Religious Settlement

England had experienced both a sharp swing to Protestantism under Edward VI and a Catholic reaction under Mary. The question of the nature of the Church needed to be settled immediately, and it was hammered out in Elizabeth's first Parliament in 1559. A retention of Catholicism was not politically feasible, as the events of Mary's reign showed, but the settlement achieved in 1559 represented something more of a Puritan victory than the Queen desired. The settlement enshrined in the Acts of Supremacy and Conformity may in the long run have worked out as a compromise, but in 1559 it indicated to Elizabeth that her control of Parliament was not complete.

Though the settlement achieved in 1559 remained essentially unchanged throughout Elizabeth's reign, the conflict over religion was not stilled. The Church of England, of which Elizabeth stood as supreme governor, was attacked by both Catholics and Puritans. Estimates of Catholic strength in Elizabethan England are difficult to make, but it is clear that a number of Englishmen remained at least residual Catholics. Because of the danger of a Catholic rising against the Crown on behalf of the rival claimant, Mary, Queen of Scots, who was in custody in England from 1568 until her execution in 1587, Parliament pressed the Queen repeatedly for harsher legislation to control the recusants. It is apparent that the Queen resisted, on the whole successfully, these pressures for political repression of the English Catholics. While the legislation against the Catholics did become progressively sterner, the Queen was able to mitigate the severity of its enforcement and retain the patriotic loyalty of many Englishmen who were Catholic in sympathy.

For their part the Puritans waged a long battle in the Church, in Parliament, and in the country at large to make the religious settlement more radical. Under the influence of leaders like Thomas Cartwright and John Field, and supported in Parliament by the brothers Paul and Peter Wentworth, the Puritans subjected the Elizabethan religious settlement to great stress.

The Queen found that she could control Parliament through the agency of her privy councilors and the force of her own personality. It was, however, some time before she could control the Church and the countryside as effectively. It was only with the promotion of John Whitgift to the archbishopric of Canterbury that she found her most effective clerical weapon against the Puritans. With apparent royal support but some criticism from Burghley, Whitgift was able to use the machinery of the Church courts to curb the Puritans. By the 1590s the Puritan movement was in some considerable disarray. Many of its prominent patrons were dead, and by the publication of the bitterly satirical *Marprelate Tracts*, some Puritan leaders brought the movement into general disfavor.

Foreign Relations

At Elizabeth's accession England was not strong enough, either in men or money, to oppose vigorously either of the Continental powers, France or Spain. England was, however, at war with France. Elizabeth quickly brought this conflict to a close on more favorable terms than might have been expected.

Throughout the early years of the reign, France appeared to be the chief foreign threat to England because of the French connections of Mary, Queen of Scots. By the Treaty of Edinburgh in 1560, Elizabeth was able to close off a good part of the French threat as posed through Scotland. The internal religious disorders of France also aided the English cause. Equally crucial was the fact that Philip II of Spain was not anxious to further the Catholic cause in England so long as its chief beneficiary would be Mary, Queen of Scots, and through her, his own French rivals.

In the 1580s Spain emerged as the chief threat to England. The years from 1570 to 1585 were ones of neither war nor peace, but Elizabeth found herself under increasing pressure from Protestant activists to take a firmer line against Catholic Spain. Increasingly she connived in privateering voyages against Spanish shipping; her decision in 1585 to intervene on behalf of the Netherlands in its revolt against Spain by sending an expeditionary force under the Earl of Leicester meant the temporary end of the Queen's policy of balance and peace.

The struggle against Spain culminated in the defeat of the Spanish Armada in 1588. The Queen showed a considerable ability to rally the people around herself. At Tilbury, where the English army massed in preparation for the threatened invasion, the Queen herself appeared to deliver one of her most stirring speeches: "I am come amongst you . . . resolved in the midst and heat of battle, to live and die amongst you all. . . . I know I have the body but of a weak and feeble woman, but I have the heart and stomach of a king and of a King of England too."

That the Armada was dispersed owed as much to luck and Spanish incapacity as it did to English skill. In some ways it marked the high point of Elizabeth's reign, for the years which followed have properly been called "the darker years." The Spanish threat did not immediately subside, and English counteroffensives proved ineffectual because of poor leadership and insufficient funds. Under the strain of war expenditure, the country suffered in the 1590s prolonged economic crisis. Moreover, the atmosphere of the court seemed to decline in the closing stages of the reign; evident corruption and sordid struggling for patronage became more common.

Difficulties in Ireland

The latter years of Elizabeth's reign were marked by increasing difficulties in Ireland. The English had never effectively controlled Ireland, and under Elizabeth the situation became acute. Given Ireland's position on England's flank and its potential use by the Spanish, it seemed essential for England to control the island. It was no easy task; four major rebellions (the rebellion of Shane O'Neill, 1559–1566; the Fitzmaurice confederacy, 1569–1572; the Desmond rebellion, 1579–1583; and Tyrone's rebellion, 1594–1603) tell the story of Ireland in this period. Fortunately, the Spaniards were slow to take advantage of Tyrone's rebellion. The 2d Earl of Essex was incapable of coping with this revolt and returned to England to lead a futile rebellion against the Queen (1601). But Lord Mountjoy, one of the few great Elizabethan land commanders, was able to break the back of the rising and bring peace in the same month in which the Queen died (March, 1603).

Internal Decline

The latter years of Elizabeth also saw tensions emerge in domestic politics. The long-term dominance of the house of Cecil, perpetuated after Burghley's death by his son, Sir Robert Cecil, was strongly contested by others, like the Earl of Essex, who sought the Queen's patronage. The Parliament of 1601 saw Elizabeth involved in a considerable fight over the granting of monopolies. Elizabeth was able to head off the conflict by promising that she herself would institute reforms. Her famous "Golden Speech" delivered to this, her last Parliament, indicated that even in old age she had the power to win her people to her side: "Though God hath raised me high, yet this I count the glory of my crown, that I have reigned with your loves. . . . It is my desire to live nor reign no longer than my life and reign shall be for your good. And though you have had, and may have, many princes more mighty and wise sitting in this seat, yet you never had, nor shall have, any that will be more careful and loving."

The words concealed the reality of the end of Elizabeth's reign. It is apparent, on retrospect, that severe tensions existed. The finances of the Crown, exhausted by war since the 1580s, were in sorry condition; the economic plight of the country was not much better. The Parliament was already sensing its power to contest issues with the monarchy, though they now held back, perhaps out of respect for their elderly queen. Religious tensions were hidden rather than removed. For all the greatness of her reign, the reign that witnessed the naval feats of Sir Francis Drake and Sir John Hawkins and the literary accomplishments of Sir Philip Sidney, Edmund Spenser, William Shakespeare, and Christopher Marlowe, it was a shaky inheritance that Elizabeth would pass on to her successor, the son of her rival claimant, Mary, Queen of Scots. On March 24, 1603, the Queen died; as one contemporary noted, she "departed this life, mildly like a lamb, easily like a ripe apple from the tree."

Further Reading

Elizabeth I is listed in the European History study guide (IV, A, 1, c). A daughter of HENRY VIII, she succeeded MARY I and was succeeded by JAMES I. Her rival claimant for the throne was MARY, QUEEN OF SCOTS. Lord ESSEX, Lord LEICESTER, Sir Francis DRAKE, Sir John HAWKINS, and Sir Walter RALEIGH served under Elizabeth.

The standard biography of Elizabeth is J. E. Neale, *Queen Elizabeth* (1934), which is sometimes eulogistic. Neville Williams, *Elizabeth, Queen of England* (1967), although interesting, is not likely to replace Neale. Elizabeth Jenkins, *Elizabeth the Great* (1958), has been highly praised but contains little new information. B. W. Beckinsale, *Elizabeth I* (1963), is a useful study that indicates a cautious break from the traditional Neale view. Hilaire Belloc's well-known *Elizabeth: Creature of Circumstance* (1942) is a biased study written from the Catholic viewpoint.

Frederick Chamberlin, *The Private Character of Queen Elizabeth* (1922), is useful in some respects, such as the queen's medical history, but should be used with caution. More useful on Elizabeth's medical history is Arthur S. MacNalty, *Elizabeth Tudor: The Lonely Queen* (1954). Mandell Creighton, *Queen Elizabeth* (1899; repr. 1966), though dated, repays careful study for its assessment of the Queen. Joel Hurstfield, *Elizabeth I and the Unity of England* (1960), is a highly compressed, valuable study stressing Elizabeth's concern to achieve unity in England. Joseph M. Levine, ed., *Elizabeth I* (1969), is an able compilation of writings on Elizabeth by her contemporaries; Levine contributes an introduction, a chronology of the life of Elizabeth I, and a bibliographical note.

Important studies of aspects of Elizabeth's reign include J. E. Neale, *Elizabeth I and Her Parliaments, 1559–1581* (1952) and *Elizabeth I and Her Parliaments, 1584–1601* (1957), the best works on parliamentary politics and the role of the Queen in government; Conyers Read, *Mr. Secretary Cecil and Queen Elizabeth* (1955) and *Lord Burghley and Queen Elizabeth* (1960), which is useful on diplomacy as well as the partnership with Burghley; Mortimer Levine, *The Early Elizabethan Succession Question, 1558–1568* (1966); and Wallace MacCaffrey, *The Shaping of the Elizabethan Regime* (1968), a major new study of the early years of the reign.

Elizabeth figures prominently in many of the surviving documents of the period and in nearly all secondary ac-

counts. Two useful bibliographies are Conyers Read, ed., *Bibliography of British History: Tudor Period, 1485–1603* (2d ed. 1959), and Mortimer Levine, *Tudor England, 1485–1603* (1968).

Recommended for general historical background are J. B. Black, *The Reign of Elizabeth, 1558–1603* (1936; 2d ed. 1959); S. T. Bindoff, *Tudor England* (1951); A. L. Rowse, *The England of Elizabeth: The Structure of Society* (1951) and *The Expansion of Elizabethan England* (1955); James A. Williamson, *The Tudor Age* (1953); and G. R. Elton, *England under the Tudors* (1955; repr. with a new bibliography, 1962).

✳   ✳   ✳

ELIZABETH II / By Eileen and Stephen Yeo

Elizabeth II (born 1926) became queen of Great Britain and Northern Ireland in 1952. She maintained the prestige of the monarchy in an age of egalitarian rhetoric and mass communication.

Elizabeth was born on April 21, 1926; her uncle, not her father, was heir to the English throne. Her father, George VI, became king when her uncle, Edward VIII, abdicated in order to marry Wallis Simpson.

Queen Elizabeth II of England, photographed in 1956. (Radio Times Hulton Picture Library)

The new royal family speedily won affection, especially during World War II, through their willingness to share the sufferings and austerity of the nation. Princess Elizabeth and her sister, Princess Margaret, pitched into the war work. Princess Elizabeth married Prince Phillip of Greece in 1947. She was crowned queen on Feb. 6, 1952.

Elizabeth had no political power (although the prime minister made a weekly report to her), and her role as head of state was symbolic and ceremonial. Her duties were wide and included, in addition to constitutional work such as opening Parliament, entertainment of foreign dignitaries and tours of Britain and the Commonwealth. Although she received "salary" for public duties from the Civil List (£475,000 in 1952), her wealth derived from her vast personal fortune.

Elizabeth was criticized for failing to present herself effectively as the symbol of a multiracial and democratic Commonwealth. Despite the fact that she ended the practice of receiving debutantes at court, her retention of the myriad of court offices and her staffing them mainly from the aristocracy prompted a peer to remark on "the social lopsidedness to which the monarchy is still prone."

Educated by private tutors, Elizabeth sent her two eldest children, Prince Charles (born 1948) and Princess Anne (born 1950), to Gordonstoun and Benenden, respectively, both public schools (that is, private boarding schools), in order to enable them to mix with a wider social range of people. But these schools draw their students largely from the affluent middle and upper classes. To critics like Lord Altrincham, the monarchy will not play a useful 20th-century role until it has created "a truly classless and Commonwealth court."

Further Reading

Elizabeth II is listed in the European History study guide (XII, A, 1). She succeeded GEORGE VI. Sir Winston CHURCHILL, Anthony EDEN, Harold MACMILLAN, and Harold WILSON served under Elizabeth.

There are numerous hagiographic works about Elizabeth II which are of little use to the serious student. More interesting are the recent works which try to evaluate the role and relevance of the monarchy. These include Lord Altrincham and others, *Is the Monarchy Perfect?* (1958), a collection of essays by critics who wish to retain the monarchy; Dermot Morrah, *The Work of the Queen* (1958), and Sir Charles Petrie, *The Modern British Monarchy* (1961), both by monarchists; and Kingsley Martin, *The Crown and the Establishment* (1962), written by a Socialist with republican leanings.

✳   ✳   ✳

ELLINGTON / By Albert McCarthy

Edward Kennedy "Duke" Ellington (born 1899), certainly America's most brilliant jazz composer, was considered by many to be one of the great composers of the 20th century, irrespective of categories.

On April 29, 1899, Edward Ellington, known universally as "Duke," was born in Washington, D.C. He divided his studies between music and commercial art, by 1918 establishing a reputation as a bandleader and agent. In 1923 he went to New York City and soon became a successful bandleader. In 1927 he secured an important engagement at the Cotton Club in Harlem, remaining there (aside from occasional tours) until 1932.

Ellington's band made its first European trip in 1932; after World War II it toured Europe regularly, with excursions to South America, the Far East, and Australia. One peak period for the band was from 1939 to 1942, when many critics considered its performances unrivaled by any other jazz ensemble.

As a composer, Ellington was responsible for numerous works that achieved popular success, some written in collaboration with his band members and with his coarranger Billy Strayhorn. The Duke's most significant music was written specifically for his own band and soloists. Always sensitive to the nuances of tone of his solo-

Duke Ellington, photographed in 1943. (Library of Congress)

ists, Ellington wrote features for individual sidemen and used his knowledge of their characteristic sounds when composing other works. His arrangements achieved a remarkable blend of individual and ensemble contributions. However, because most of his works were written for his own band, interpretations by others have seldom been satisfactory.

With *Creole Rhapsody* (1931) and *Reminiscing in Tempo* (1935) Ellington was the first jazz composer to break the 3-minute time limitation of the 78-rpm record. After the 1940s he concentrated more on longer works, including several suites built around a central theme, frequently an aspect of American Negro life. Always a fine orchestral pianist, with a style influenced by the Harlem stylists of the 1920s, Ellington remained in the background on most of his early recordings; after the 1950s he emerged as a highly imaginative piano soloist.

Ellington was nominated for the Pulitzer Prize in 1964. The City of New York gave him a prize and Yale University awarded him a doctor of music degree in 1967; Morgan State and Washington universities also gave him honorary degrees that year. On his seventieth birthday Ellington was honored by President Richard Nixon at a White House ceremony and given the Medal of Freedom. In 1970 he was elected to the National Institute of Arts and Letters.

Further Reading

Duke Ellington is listed in the Music study guide (II, D, 3). He was a contemporary of jazz soloists Louis ARMSTRONG and Charlie PARKER.

There is no satisfactory biography of Ellington. Peter Gammond, ed., *Duke Ellington: His Life and Music* (1958), contains some first-rate essays on Ellington. See also Barry Ulanov, *Duke Ellington* (1946), and George E. Lambert, *Duke Ellington* (1961). Gunther Schuller, *The History of Jazz* (1968), includes the most perspicacious and scholarly study of Ellington's recordings of the 1920s.

ELLISON / By Richard M. Ludwig

American author Ralph Waldo Ellison (born 1914) wrote "Invisible Man," a classic 20th-century American novel. He was an early spokesman among black Americans for the need for racial identity.

Ralph Ellison was born in Oklahoma City on March 1, 1914. His father, a construction worker, died when Ellison was 3, and his mother stretched a meager income as a domestic worker to support her son. He studied music at Tuskegee Institute from 1933 to 1936. He worked on the New York City Federal Writers Project, contributed stories, reviews, and essays to *New Masses*, the *Antioch Review*, and other journals (these

writings have not yet been collected); and in 1942 became editor of the *Negro Quarterly*. He met Richard Wright and Langston Hughes during these years; both had a major influence on his work, along with T. S. Eliot, Ernest Hemingway, and the Russian novelists.

After brief duty in the U.S. Merchant Marine during World War II, Ellison won a Rosenwald fellowship to work on the novel which brought him instant recognition and the National Book Award, *Invisible Man* (1952). The story of a young man's growing up, first in the South and then in Harlem, it is sensational, brutally honest, and graphic in the humiliating, often violent treatment the nameless hero suffers at the hands of the Southern white men who "educate" him and the Northern black men who "use" him. But Ellison reminds the reader that he "didn't select the surrealism, the distortion, the intensity as an experimental technique but because reality is surreal." When, at the end of the novel, the hero creeps into an empty Harlem cellar to escape from the world, it is only the last of his many bouts with "invisibility." The life of a black American has always been relentlessly unreal, and his search for identity endless. But what Ellison's novel illuminates is the common plight of all human beings in the confrontations between dream and reality, light against darkness, idealism smothered by disillusion, injured psyche, adopted personae. In 1965, in a poll of 200 writers and critics, they voted *Invisible Man* the most distinguished novel published between 1945 and 1965 in America.

Ellison's *Shadow and Act* (1964) is a collection of 20 essays and 2 interviews. He contributed to *The Living*

Ralph Ellison. (Bibliothèque Nationale, Paris)

Novel (Granville Hicks, ed., 1957), *The Angry Black* (John A. Williams, ed., 1963), and *Soon One Morning* (Herbert Hill, ed., 1963) and to numerous literary journals. He lectured at the Salzburg Seminar in 1954; taught Russian and American literature at Bard College from 1958 to 1961; was visiting professor at the University of Chicago in 1961 and visiting professor of writing at Rutgers University from 1962 to 1964; and in 1964, became visiting fellow in American studies at Yale University.

Further Reading

Ralph Ellison is listed in the Literature study guide (I, E, 3). He was influenced by Richard WRIGHT and Langston HUGHES.

Perceptive critical comment on Ellison is available in Robert Bone, *The Negro Novel in America* (1958; rev. ed. 1965); Ihab Hassan, *Radical Innocence: Studies in the Contemporary American Novel* (1961); Marcus Klein, *After Alienation: American Novels in Mid-century* (1964); Jonathan Baumbach, *The Landscape of Nightmare* (1965); and Seymour L. Gross and John Edward Hardy, eds., *Images of the Negro in American Literature* (1966).

Lincoln Ellsworth in 1926. (Library of Congress)

ELLSWORTH / By Ralph D. Gray

Lincoln Ellsworth (1880–1951), American adventurer and explorer, became the first man to cross both the Arctic and the Antarctic by air.

The son of a wealthy businessman and financier, Lincoln Ellsworth was born in Chicago on May 12, 1880. Graduating from preparatory school in 1900, he briefly attended Yale and Columbia universities, but his real interest was in outdoor life. He traveled extensively, working in Canada and Alaska as a railroad surveyor and mining engineer. He then formally studied practical astronomy and surveying in preparation for realizing his lifelong ambition—polar exploration.

A true adventurer, Ellsworth participated in the Canadian government's buffalo hunt of 1911, prospected for gold, spent 3 years with the U.S. Biological Survey on the Pacific coast, and volunteered for service in World War I, training as a pilot in France. Following the war and a protracted illness, Ellsworth in 1924 joined a geological expedition to Peru.

The following year Ellsworth joined and largely financed the expedition with Roald Amundsen, the Norwegian explorer, that initiated Arctic exploration by air. Flying from Spitsbergen for the North Pole in two planes, the party of six reached 87°44'N before being forced down with engine trouble. One plane was badly damaged during the landing, and it took 3 weeks to get the other plane off the polar ice pack. They returned to Spitsbergen to announce that no land existed on the

European side of the pole. In 1926 Amundsen and Ellsworth returned to the Arctic, this time with a semirigid airship, the *Norge*.

Ellsworth concentrated on geologic work in the American Southwest for several years, although in 1931 he represented the American Geographic Society on the Arctic flight of the *Graf Zeppelin*. He undertook the exploration of Antarctica by air in 1933. In 1935, on his third attempt, Ellsworth and his pilot crossed Antarctica, landing 16 miles short of Richard Byrd's abandoned camp at Little America, where they were rescued. On this and a subsequent flight in 1939 Ellsworth discovered and claimed for the United States 377,000 square miles of land.

Ellsworth was a bold, imaginative, superbly conditioned man. He died in New York City on May 26, 1951.

Further Reading

Lincoln Ellsworth is listed in the Geography and Exploration study guide (VII, A, 1). A contemporary polar explorer was Richard E. BYRD.

The only books dealing with Ellsworth's life were written by the explorer himself: *The Last Wild Buffalo Hunt* (1919); two books written with Roald Amundsen, *Our Polar Flight* (1925) and *First Crossing of the Polar Sea* (1927); *Exploring Today* (1935); and the autobiographical *Search* (1932) and *Beyond Horizons* (1937). *Air Pioneering in the Arctic*, edited by Ellsworth (1929), is a collection of articles on his expeditions.

ELSASSER / By Sydney Chapman

The American physicist Walter Maurice Elsasser (born 1904) made original contributions to geophysics and to the discussion of the physical foundations of biology.

Walter Elsasser was born in Germany on March 20, 1904. After university studies at Heidelberg and Munich he gained a doctoral degree in physics at Göttingen in 1927. His subsequent employments were diverse, in many institutions and in three countries. At the Technische Hochschule, Berlin (1928–1930); at Frankfurt University (1930–1933); and while research fellow and guest lecturer at the Sorbonne (1933–1936), his main work was in atomic physics. He went to the United States in 1936 and was naturalized in 1940. In 1937 he married Margaret Trahey, and they had a daughter and a son. In 1964 he married Susanne Rosenfeld.

Elsasser's first appointments in the United States were in meteorology at the California Institute of Technology (1936–1941) and then at the Blue Hill Observatory, Harvard (1941–1942). During World War II he was employed at the Signal Corps Laboratories in New Jersey, where his researches dealt with the atmospheric transmission of radio and radar waves. Following the war, he engaged in industrial research for a short time at the New Jersey Laboratories of the Radio Corporation of America. After that he held professorial posts at several universities, including Pennsylvania (1947–1950), Utah (1950–1956), California at La Jolla (1956–1962), New Mexico at Albuquerque (1960–1961), and Maryland (from 1968). In 1958 he published a book, *The Physical Foundation of Biology,* an important and highly original work concerned with broad philosophical, physical, and biological matters, strikingly different from his main researches. A sequel appeared in 1966, *Atom and Organism.*

Calculations of wind systems led Elsasser by 1938 to consider the possibility that convection motion might exist within the earth's metallic core and might obey certain laws of cosmic magnetohydrodynamics. He first studied the phenomenon of "secular variation" and demonstrated that his formulation of the magnetohydrodynamics of a spherical conductor provided quantitative results in agreement with the observed phenomenon. Elsasser also explained how eddies within the circulation of the earth's core can account for the secular variation, whose distribution is regional and whose time scale, a few centuries, differs greatly from that of surface geological changes.

Being interested in the origin of the earth's permanent geomagnetic field, Elsasser first proposed a thermoelectric origin, but this did not account for the self-sustaining nature of the permanent field, and he abandoned it in favor of a dynamo theory. According to this model, the presence of a magnetic field in the core results in motion of matter perpendicular to the field, which in turn gives rise to a field producing motion, and so on in self-sustaining action.

Elsasser was elected to the National Academy of Sciences in 1957 and awarded the Bowie Medal of the American Geophysical Union in 1959. He received the Fleming Medal of the AGU in 1971. In his late research, Elsasser concentrated his efforts on the study of the earth's upper mantle.

Further Reading

Walter Elsasser is listed in the Science study guide (VII, E, 3). Other 20th-century geophysicists are Sydney CHAPMAN, Maurice EWING, and Arthur HOLMES.

Elsasser's work in quantum physics is briefly discussed in William H. Cropper, *The Quantum Physicists and an Introduction to Their Physics* (1970). See also David Robert Bates, ed., *The Planet Earth* (1957; rev. ed. 1964).

✳   ✳   ✳

Walter Elsasser. (Courtesy S. Chapman and W. Elsasser)

EMERSON / By Carl Bode

Ralph Waldo Emerson (1803–1882) was the most thought-provoking American cultural leader of the mid-19th century. In his unorthodox ideas and actions he represented a minority of Americans, but by the end of his life he was considered a sage.

Though Ralph Waldo Emerson's origins were promising, his path to eminence was by no means easy. He was born in Boston on May 25, 1803, of a fairly well-known New England family. His father was a prominent Boston minister. However, young Emerson was only 8 when his father died and left the family to face hard times. The genteel poverty which the Emerson family endured did not prevent it from sending the promising boy to the Boston Latin School, where he received the best basic education of his day. At 14 he enrolled in Harvard College. As a scholarship boy, he studied more and relaxed less than some of his classmates. He won several minor prizes for his writing. When he was 17, he started keeping a journal and continued it for over half a century.

Unitarian Minister

Emerson was slow in finding himself. After graduation from Harvard he taught at the school of his brother William. Gradually he moved toward the ministry. He undertook studies at the Harvard Divinity School, meanwhile continuing his journal and other writing. In 1826 he began his career as a Unitarian minister. Appropriately, Unitarianism was the creed of the questioner; in particular it questioned the divine nature of the Trinity. Emerson received several offers before an unusually attractive one presented itself: the junior pastorship at Boston's noted Second Church, with the promise that it would quickly become the senior pastorship. His reputation spread swiftly. Soon he was chosen chaplain of the Massachusetts Senate, and he was elected to the Boston School Committee.

Emerson's personal life flowered even more than his professional one, for he fell in love, deeply in love, for the only time in his life. He wooed and won a charming New Hampshire girl named Ellen Tucker. Their wedding, in September 1829, marked the start of an idyllic marriage. But it was all too short, for Ellen died a year and a half later, leaving Emerson desolate. Though he tried to find consolation in his religion, he was unsuccessful. As a result, his religious doubts developed. Even the permissive creed of Unitarianism seemed to him to be a shackle. In September 1832 he resigned his pastorate; according to his farewell sermon he could no longer believe in celebrating Holy Communion.

Emerson's decision to leave the ministry was the more difficult because it left him with no other work to do. After months of floundering and even sickness, he scraped together enough money to take a 10-month tour of Europe. He hoped that his travels would give him the perspective he needed. They did, but only to the extent of confirming what he did not want rather than what he wanted.

Professional Lecturer

However, the times were on Emerson's side, for he found on his return to America that a new institution was emerging that held unique promise for him. This was the lyceum, a system of lecturing which started in the late 1820s, established itself in the 1830s, and rose to great popularity during the next 2 decades. The local lecture clubs that sprang up discovered that they had to pay for the best lecturers, Emerson among them. Emerson turned the lyceum into his unofficial pulpit and in the process earned at least a modest stipend. He spoke to his audi-

Ralph Waldo Emerson. (Courtesy of the American Museum of Natural History)

ences with great, if unorthodox, effectiveness. They saw before them a tall, thin Yankee with slightly aquiline features whose words sometimes baffled but often uplifted them. After a few seasons he organized his own lecture courses as a supplement to his lyceum lectures. For example, during the winter of 1837–1838 he offered the Boston public a group of 10 lectures on "human culture" and earned more than $500. Equally to the point, his lectures grew into essays and books, and these he published from the early 1840s on.

Emerson's Creed

As a transcendentalist, Emerson spoke out against materialism, formal religion, and Negro slavery. He could not have found targets better designed to offend the mass of Americans, most of whom considered making money a major purpose in life and church and churchgoing a mainstay and, until they faced the hard fact of the Civil War, either supported slavery or were willing to let it alone. But Emerson spoke of slavery in the context of the Fugitive Slave Law (1850), saying, in one of his rare bursts of profanity, "I will not obey it, by God."

Emerson, however, was not merely *against* certain things; he both preached and exemplified a positive doctrine. He became America's leading transcendentalist; that is, he believed in a reality and a knowledge that transcended the everyday reality Americans were accustomed to. He believed in the integrity of the individual: "Trust thyself," he urged in one of his famous phrases.

He believed in a spiritual universe governed by a mystic Over-soul with which each individual soul should try to harmonize. Touchingly enough, he believed in America. Though he ranked as his country's most searching critic, he helped as much as anyone to establish the "American identity." He not only called out for a genuinely American literature but also helped inaugurate it through his own writings. In addition, he espoused the cause of American music and American art; as a matter of fact, his grand purpose was to assist in the creation of an indigenous American national culture.

Publishing His Ideas

His first two books were brilliant. He had published a pamphlet, *Nature*, in 1836, which excited his fellow transcendentalists; but now he issued two volumes of essays for a broader public, *Essays*, First Series, in 1841 and *Essays*, Second Series, in 1844. Their overarching subjects were man, nature, and God. In such pieces as "Self-reliance," "Spiritual Laws," "Nature," "The Poet," and "The Over-soul," Emerson expounded on the innate nobility of man, the joys of nature and their spiritual significance, and the sort of deity omnipresent in the universe. The tone of the essays was optimistic, but Emerson did not neglect the gritty realities of life. In such essays as "Compensation" and "Experience," he tried to suggest how to deal with human losses and failings.

Whether he wrote prose or verse, Emerson was a poet with a poet's gift of metaphor. Both his lectures and his published works were filled from the first with telling phrases, with wisdom startlingly expressed. His next book, after the second series of essays, was a volume of his poems. They proved to be irregular in form and movingly individual in expression. After that came more than one remarkable volume of prose. In *Representative Men: Seven Lectures* (1850) Emerson pondered the uses of great men, devoting individual essays to half a dozen figures, including Plato, Shakespeare, and Goethe. *English Traits* (1856) resulted from an extended visit to Great Britain. In this volume Emerson anatomized the English people and their culture. His approach was impressionistic, but the result was the best book by an American on the subject up to that time.

Meanwhile, Emerson had been immersed—sometimes willingly, sometimes not—in things other than literature. He had found a second wife, pale and serene, in Lydia Jackson of Plymouth. He had married her in 1835 and got from her the comfort of love, if not its passion. They had four children, one of whom, Waldo, died when he was a little boy; the others outlived their eminent father. As Emerson's family life expanded, so did his friendships. After leaving his pastorate in Boston, he had moved to nearby Concord, where he stayed the rest of his life. In Concord he met a prickly young Harvard graduate who became his disciple, friend, and occasional adversary: Henry David Thoreau. Emerson added others to his circle, becoming as he did so the nexus of the transcendentalist movement. Among his close friends were Bronson Alcott, George Ripley, and Theodore Parker.

Emerson's public life also expanded. During the 1850s he was drawn deeply into the struggle against slavery.

Though he found some of the abolitionists almost as distasteful as the slaveholders, he knew where his place had to be. The apolitical Emerson became a Republican, voting for Abraham Lincoln. When Lincoln signed the Emancipation Proclamation (Jan. 1, 1863), Emerson counted it a momentous day for the United States; when Lincoln was killed, Emerson considered him a martyr.

Last Years

After the Civil War, Emerson continued to lecture and write. Though he had nothing really new to say anymore, audiences continued to throng his lectures and many readers bought his books. The best of the final books were *Society and Solitude* (1870) and *Letters and Social Aims* (1876). However, he was losing his memory and needed more and more help from others, especially his daughter Ellen. He was nearly 79 when he died on April 27, 1882.

America mourned Emerson's passing, as did much of the rest of the Western world. In the general judgment, he had been both a great writer and a great man. Certainly he had been America's leading essayist for half a century. And he had been not only one of the most wise but one of the most sincere of men. He had shown his countrymen the possibilities of the human spirit, and he had done so without a trace of sanctimony or pomposity. The *Chicago Tribune*, for instance, exclaimed, "How rare he was; how original in thought; how true in character!" Some of the eulogizing was extravagant, but in general the verdict at the time of Emerson's death has been upheld.

Further Reading

Ralph Waldo Emerson is listed in the Literature study guide (I, C, 2). Other transcendentalists were Henry David THOREAU, Theodore PARKER, and Bronson ALCOTT.

Emerson's *Journals* were reedited with care by William Gilman and others (7 vols., 1960–1969). Also valuable are *The Letters of Ralph Waldo Emerson*, edited by Ralph L. Rusk (6 vols., 1939). The best biography is still Rusk's *The Life of Ralph Waldo Emerson* (1949). The best critical study of Emerson's writing is Sherman Paul, *Emerson's Angle of Vision: Man and Nature in American Experience* (1952), which concentrates on Emerson's principle of "correspondence." Stephen E. Whicher, *Freedom and Fate* (1953), is also valuable; it is called an "inner life" of Emerson and concentrates on the 1830s. The only treatment of Emerson's mind and art as they relate to the transcendentalist movement is Francis O. Matthiessen's superb *American Renaissance: Art and Expression in the Age of Emerson and Whitman* (1941).

* * *

EMINESCU / By Zoe Dumitrescu Buşulenga

The Romanian poet Mihail Eminescu (1850–1889) inaugurated modern sensitiveness and expression in Romanian poetry through his achievements in content and craftsmanship.

Mihail Eminescu (pronounced ĕ-mĕ-nĕ′skōō) was born at Ipotesti in northern Moldavia on Jan. 15, 1850, into a family of country gentry. He spent his first years like a peasant child in the midst of nature and under the influence of folklore. His adolescence was agitated by conflicts with his family. He interrupted his studies several times, going on tours with theatrical companies. He made his literary debut at 16 in the Romanian review *Familia* (The Family), published in Budapest.

Eminescu studied philosophy in Vienna from 1869 to 1872 and in Berlin from 1872 to 1874. Returning to Romania in 1874, he held several minor jobs in Iaşi (custodian of the university library, inspector of schools, subeditor of an obscure newspaper). There, and after leaving Iaşi, he found himself under the influence of the political and esthetic literary circle Junimea ("Youth"). In 1877 Eminescu went to Bucharest to work on the staff of the newspaper *Timpul* (Time). Eminescu's steady journalistic activity filled the years from 1877 to 1883. Struck by insanity in 1883, he lived until 1889 in a dramatic alternation between lucidity and madness.

Eminescu concentrated in his work the entire evolution of Romanian national poetry. The most illustrative poems of his early years (1866–1873) are "The Dissolute Youth," "The Epigones," "Mortua Est," "Angel and Demon," and "Emperor and Proletarian." The overwhelming influences on his poetry of this period were from Shakespeare and Lord Byron.

The ever deeper influence of Romanian folklore, his close contact with German philosophy and romanticism in the years 1872 to 1874 when he was preparing for a doctor's degree in philosophy in Berlin, and the evolution of his own creative powers carried Eminescu toward a new vision of the world. His poetical universe shifted to the spheres of magical transparencies offered by folklore as ideal and possible grounds for a love that was both a dream and a transfiguration. His poetical expression became increasingly inward, simplified, and sweetened. His poetry began to show rare strength and beauty, involving a universe in which a demiurgical eye and hand seemed to have conferred a new order upon the elements and to have infused them with infinite freshness and power.

In "The Blue Flower" Eminescu offered a new interpretation of the aspiration in the fulfillment of love. The most important poem written during this period was "Călin" ("Leaves from a Fairy Tale"), a synthesis of the epical and the lyrical, with a description of the Romanian landscape.

After 1876 the sphere of Eminescu's inner experience deepened. The poetry of his maturity reached all human dimensions, from the sensitive, emotional ones to the intellectual, spiritual ones. Until 1883 his poetry was an uninterrupted meditation on the human condition in which the artist always stood on the summits of human thinking and feeling. The most important works of his

Mihail Eminescu. (Editura Enciclopedică Română, Bucharest)

last period are "A Dacian's Prayer," "Ode in the Ancient Meter," and the "Epistles." His masterpiece is "The Evening Star" (1883), a version of the Hyperion myth. Ideas and meaning, expressed in symbols, are manifold, profoundly ambiguous, and discernible in an esthetic achievement of supreme simplicity and expressiveness. In *Barren Genius*, a posthumously published novel of romantic trend, and especially in "Poor Dyonis," a fantastic, philosophical short story, Eminescu added some demiurgical features to his romantic hero.

Further Reading

Mihail Eminescu is listed in the Literature study guide (III, I, 6). Eugene IONESCO was a later Romanian-born author.

Eminescu's poems were translated by Sylvia Pankhurst and I. O. Stefanovici as *Poems of Mihail Eminescu* (1930). Eminescu is treated in E. D. Tappe, *Rumanian Prose and Verse* (1956).

*　　*　　*

EMMET / By Lawrence J. McCaffrey

The Irish nationalist Robert Emmet (1778–1803) was executed after leading an unsuccessful revolution against British rule. His youth, passionate oratory, and courage in the face of death have made him a permanent symbol of romantic, revolutionary, Irish nationalism.

R obert Emmet was the youngest of 18 children born to a prominent Anglo-Irish Protestant family. His father, Dr. Robert Emmet, was state physician of Ireland. In 1793 Emmet enrolled at Trinity College, Dublin. He excelled in his studies and won a reputation as a fiery orator. Emmet was influenced by the liberal views of the Enlightenment and the conduct of an older brother who was a member of the Society of United Irishmen. In 1796 Emmet joined the radical group.

Inspired by the examples of the American and French revolutions, the United Irishmen demanded an Ireland free of English influence and governed by a reformed Parliament representing both Protestant and Catholic opinion, elected by a democratic franchise. Frightened by the increasing militancy of the United Irishmen, the intensity of Catholic discontent, and the threat of internal insurrection supported by French invasion, the Irish government adopted measures restricting civil liberties. The Earl of Clare, Lord Chancellor of Ireland, began to investigate student opinion at Trinity, and in 1798 Emmet was forced to leave the college.

Emmet maintained United Irishmen connections but apparently did not participate in the 1798 revolution. After the Irish and British parliaments passed the Act of Union, creating the United Kingdom of Great Britain and Ireland (1800) and completely destroying the legal existence of the Irish nation, Emmet and his friends considered revolution even more imperative. He left for the Continent to confer with Irish exiles. Napoleon and other French leaders expressed a willingness to assist an Irish revolution. In 1802 Emmet returned to Dublin to create an army of liberation, hoping for French assistance.

Emmet used his own funds to buy weapons, mostly pikes. He asked the Dublin proletariat to strike a blow for liberty. Unfortunately, he failed to establish effective communications with United Irishmen outside the metropolitan area and was unaware that the government had infiltrated his organization. When authorities discovered a cache of arms, Emmet decided to raise the standard of revolt. On July 23, 1803, he issued a proclamation establishing a provisional government for an Irish Republic; he put on a general's uniform of green and white with gold epaulets and led his band of about 80 men out to battle. No help arrived and the revolt was crushed by British soldiers. Emmet managed to escape but refused to leave for America, insisting on remaining close to his fiancée, Sarah Curran, daughter of the famous barrister, John Philpot Curran. On August 25 British soldiers captured Emmet.

On Sept. 19, 1803, the government brought Emmet to trial. Sadistic Lord Norbury was the judge, and Leonard MacNally, an informer, was defense counsel. The jury delivered a guilty verdict. Before sentencing, Emmet brilliantly defended his nationalism. He said that he was prepared to die for the future of Irish freedom, closing with the words: "Let no man write my epitaph. . . .

When my country takes her place among the nations of the earth, then, and not till then, let my epitaph be written." On September 20 he was hanged.

Emmet's image among Irish nationalists far exceeds the merits of his performance as revolutionary. He was naive, impractical, flamboyant, excessively talkative, and a poor organizer. British vengeance, however, converted a pathetic effort into a triumph of martydom. Thomas Moore's poems about Emmet enhanced the image of noble and tragic martyr. Irish exiles in America were particularly loyal to Emmet's memory, learning the words of his speech and naming their children and patriotic organizations after him. Emmet's example of blood sacrifice watered Irish nationalism, motivating Fenians and the men of the Easter Rebellion of 1916 and the Anglo-Irish war.

Further Reading

Robert Emmet is listed in the European History study guide (VII, A, 1). Michael COLLINS and Patrick H. PEARSE were later Irish revolutionary leaders.

Helen Landreth, *The Pursuit of Robert Emmet* (1948), claims that British government spies and informers acted as agents provoking revolt to further William Pitt the Younger's Irish policy and that Emmet was an unknowing victim of British duplicity and tyranny. Owen Dudley Edwards in "Ireland" in *Celtic Nationalism* (1968) recognizes Emmet's contribution to the romantic myths of revolutionary nationalism but compares his total impact unfavorably when measured against Wolfe Tone's. See also Leon O'Broin, *The Unfortunate Robert Emmet* (1958), and R. Jacobs, *The Rise of the United Irishmen* (1937).

EMPEDOCLES / By Donald A. Ross

The Greek philosopher, poet, and scientist Empedocles (ca. 493–ca. 444 B.C.) propounded a pluralist cosmological scheme in which fire, air, water, and earth mingled and separated under the compulsion of love and strife.

E mpedocles (pronounced ĕm-pĕd′ō-klēz) was born of a noble family in the Sicilian city of Acragas (modern Agrigento). He is said to have studied under Xenophanes or Parmenides. His work shows familiarity with Pythagoreanism, although stories about his banishment from the sect, like many of the legends that grew up around him, may be discounted as misinterpretations of statements in his writings. It is certain that he had a profound interest in natural science and in certain religious ideas, and although there is no hint in the surviving portion of his writings that he took an interest in political affairs, the Sicilian historian Timaeus tells of his efforts to establish a democracy in Acragas. Aristotle says that Empedocles was offered the kingship but refused it. Accounts of his death are so con-

An ancient coin of Selinus, Sicily, showing the local river-god sacrificing at the altar of Asclepius, the Greek god of medicine (represented by the cock). The coin commemorates the terminating of a malaria epidemic by Empedocles, who diverted one river to clear another river which had become stagnant. (Trustees of The British Museum)

fused as to make it impossible to determine either the date or the place, although Aristotle noted that he did not live past the age of 60.

Of his two poems, *On Nature* and *Purifications*, which totaled some 5,000 verses, fewer than 500 lines survive. *On Nature* presents Empedocles's philosophical system. Fire, air, water, and earth, the four roots or elements of which everything is made, are eternal and move through the cosmos with a swirling motion. The problem of change is solved by positing the existence of love and strife as the two forces which affect the four basic elements. Depending on which of these two principles holds sway at a given moment, the universe is either in a state of happy unity or of warring disunity, with possible gradations between the extremes.

Purifications was an extended poem dealing with the human soul and espousing the Orphic and Pythagorean tenets of immortality and metempsychosis, which were widespread in the Greek West in the 5th century B.C. Empedocles asserted that he had been boy, girl, bush, fowl, and fish in earlier lives, and he speaks of his present life as punishment for past sins.

Empedocles is less well known as the father of Sicilian rhetoric (Aristotle called him the inventor of rhetoric) and as an important contributor to medical science.

Further Reading

Empedocles is listed in the Philosophy study guide (I, A, 3). Other Pre-Socratic philosophers who believed that the physical world is composed of matter, which is not infinitely subdivisible, and that the movement of matter is local were ANAXAGORAS and DEMOCRITUS.

Selected fragments of Empedocles's two poems, with English translation and full analysis, are found in G. S. Kirk and J. E. Raven, *The Presocratic Philosophers: A Critical History with a Selection of Texts* (1962). Useful discussions are found in John Burnet, *Early Greek Philosophy* (1892; 4th ed. 1930), and Kathleen Freeman, *The Presocratic Philosophers: A Companion to Diels, Fragmente der Vorsokratiker* (1946; 2d ed. 1959).

ENCINA / By Juan Bautista Avalle-Arce

Juan del Encina (1468–1529?) is called the father of Spanish drama. He was also the foremost Spanish musical composer of his time.

The original name of Juan del Encina (pronounced än-thē′nä) was Fermoselle, but he adopted the name of his probable birthplace, a small village in the province of Salamanca. In all likelihood Encina studied at the University of Salamanca under Antonio de Nebrija, the foremost Spanish humanist of his time. He then entered the service of the Duke of Alba, in whose palace of Alba de Tormes he discharged the multiple functions of playwright, poet, composer, and musician for 7 years. Encina published his *Cancionero* (a collection of plays and *villancicos*, or polyphonic songs) in Salamanca in 1496; other works were added to this collection in later editions.

Encina went to Rome in 1498, where he entered the papal chapel and eventually became singer to Leo X. During this time Encina continued to write plays. While in Rome he obtained several ecclesiastical benefices in Spain, and in 1510 and 1513 he was in Málaga as archdeacon and canon. He had obtained, however, papal dispensation to collect his benefices without discharging his duties.

In 1519, aged 50, Encina took holy orders and went on a pilgrimage to the Holy Land, which he described in his poem *La Trivagia*. He celebrated his first Mass in Jerusalem. Encina returned to Spain as prior of León, where he resided from 1523 until his death.

As a poet, Encina was most successful in brief, lyrical pieces, which he set to music himself; his romances were also more lyrical than narrative. His great popularity as a composer is attested to by the fact that 61 of his *villancicos* were collected in the *Cancionero musical de Palacio* (ca. 1500). As a playwright, Encina brought to their final development the theatrical forms derived from medieval liturgical drama. He inaugurated Renaissance drama in Spain. His early dramas (such as *Egloga de las grandes lluvias*) were Nativity plays, with rustic shepherds as protagonists. His later plays (such as *Egloga de Plácida y Vitoriano*) were Italianate in spirit, much longer, and complicated in form. His shepherds were now of classical inspiration. The joy of life he sang about in his later plays was almost neopagan in its exuberance.

Further Reading

Juan del Encina is listed in the Literature study guide (III, D, 5) and the Music study guide (I, B, 4). The Portuguese dramatist and poet Gil VICENTE was influenced by Encina. The Spanish composer Luis MILÁN wrote *villancicos* that are outstanding for their grace and refinement.

The best interpretation in English of the literary works of Encina is James R. Andrews, *Juan del Encina: Prometheus in Search of Prestige* (1959). A good appreciation of his musical works is in Gilbert Chase, *The Music of*

The frontispiece from a 1507 edition of the works of Juan del Encina. (Bibliothèque Nationale, Paris)

Salem, Mass., in September 1628. Under his directorship Salem became a Puritan beachhead in New England. He sent two brothers who continued using the Anglican Prayer Book back to England as undesirable colonists, and he chopped down Thomas Morton's frivolous maypole at Merrimount. Both actions indicated his impulsiveness and partisanship. He later had the cross of St. George removed from Salem's militia flag because of its papal connotation and was reprimanded by the legislature for his political indiscretion.

In 1629 the New England Company was reorganized as the Massachusetts Bay Company, and when Governor John Winthrop arrived in 1630 Endecott relinquished his leadership, although he remained among the colony's public servants. Endecott's lack of restraint was demonstrated again in 1637, when he led an expedition against the Pequot Indians to avenge the murder of a trader. After destroying one Indian settlement, Endecott and his men went to another. Ignoring pleas for caution by Connecticut settlers, Endecott continued to destroy Indian canoes and villages until, satisfied, he returned to the safety of Boston and Salem, leaving Connecticut to suffer the reprisals of the Indians in the Pequot War. Later, as governor of Massachusetts during the Quaker intrusions of the 1650s, he bore much of the responsibility for the inhuman treatment of the Quakers—ranging from imprisonment and banishment to execution. King Charles II eventually rebuked Massachusetts and Governor Endecott for their cruelty.

Despite his strictness and narrowness, Endecott served the colony as best he could. His election to colonial of-

Spain (1941), and Gustave Reese, *Music in the Renaissance* (1959). The early chapters in N. D. Shergold, *A History of the Spanish Stage: From Medieval Times until the End of the Seventeenth Century* (1967), contain valuable background information.

* * *

ENDECOTT / By H. Roger King

John Endecott (1588–1655) was one of the English founders of the Massachusetts Bay Colony and later its governor. He often used harsh measures against the colony's enemies.

Born in Devon, John Endecott may have seen some military service. He early became interested in colonization through the influence of John White, a Puritan clergyman. Endecott was included among the six patentees of the New England Company because he was willing to emigrate as the director of the Cape Ann settlement.

Appointed "chief-in-command" and commissioned to prepare the way for more colonists, Endecott arrived at

John Endecott. (Library of Congress)

fices attests to his honesty and willingness to serve the common good. In addition to minor posts, he served 5 yearly terms as deputy governor and 15 as governor, filling the governorship longer than anyone else. If he was overzealous in defending the truth as he saw it, he was like many others in an overzealous age.

Further Reading

John Endecott is listed in the American History study guide (II, B, 1, b). John WINTHROP was the other important governor of Massachusetts Bay Colony.

The only recent biography of Endecott is Lawrence S. Mayo, *John Endecott: A Biography* (1936). Background material can be found in Herbert L. Osgood, *The American Colonies in the Seventeenth Century* (3 vols., 1904–1907); James Truslow Adams, *The Founding of New England* (1921); Frances Rose-Troup, *The Massachusetts Bay Company and Its Predecessors* (1930); and Charles M. Andrews, *The Colonial Period of American History* (4 vols., 1934–1938).

ENDERS / By Joseph L. Melnick

> The American virologist John Franklin Enders (born 1897), a leader in modern virology, cultivated poliovirus in tissue cultures of human cells and developed an attenuated live vaccine for measles.

John Enders was born on Feb. 10, 1897, in West Hartford, Conn. After completing his undergraduate degree at Yale University he earned a master's degree in English at Harvard University. But before completing doctoral work he became attracted to the study of bacteriology under Hans Zinsser, and in 1930 he received his doctorate in this field. He then embarked upon a remarkable and productive career as a member of the faculty of Harvard Medical School. He became head of the Research Division of Infectious Diseases of Children's Hospital, Boston, in 1947.

In the late 1930s Enders focused on virologic problems. His first major breakthrough was the development of techniques for detection of antibodies to mumps virus; he and others subsequently showed that the virus could be grown in chick embryos and tissue culture. On the basis of this work the immunology and epidemiology of mumps infection could be studied, a skin test was developed, and it was shown that the infection frequently was inapparent. Finally, the studies provided the basis for the development of preventive measures against the disease, which now include an attenuated live-virus vaccine.

While Enders and his colleagues were continuing the study of mumps and chicken-pox viruses, various types of human cells in culture were being used. Enders suggested that some of the cultures be inoculated with po-

John Enders. (National Library of Medicine, Bethesda, Md.)

liovirus, which at that time could be studied only with difficulty in a few species of expensive experimental animals. The poliovirus did propagate in one type of culture made up of cells which were not from the nervous system. This discovery, and the studies which it made possible, opened the way to a new era in poliovirus research, the most dramatic aspect of which was the possibility for development of poliovirus vaccines. For this work Enders was awarded the Nobel Prize in 1954.

Enders began studies with another disease, measles. In 1954 he reported success in growing the virus in tissue culture and followed this by a model series of investigations that resulted in a measles vaccine. Turning his concern to cancer-related viruses in later years, he made important contributions to this field, particularly to studies of fusion of cells from different species as a means of altering cell susceptibility to viruses.

His significant contributions to many areas of virology brought him honors from all over the world, but Enders continued to devote himself to his laboratory and his students. Because of the breadth and incisiveness of his thought, many of his contributions were conceptual and definitive, representing major steps opening up whole new areas for further experimentation and extension of knowledge. But, while achieving wide recognition and public acclaim, John Enders remained a "virologists' virologist."

Further Reading

John Enders is listed in the Science study guide (VII, G, 4). His work laid the foundation for the development of a poliomyelitis vaccine by Jonas SALK.

A recent tribute to Enders can be found in the foreword to *Perspectives in Virology VI* (1968), which was dedicated to him. The foreword was written by Frederick C. Robbins, one of Enders's colleagues, with whom he shared the Nobel Prize. Theodore L. Sourkes, *Nobel Prize Winners in Medicine and Physiology, 1901–1965* (1953; rev. ed. 1967), includes a biography of Enders and a description of his work. A biography is also in the Nobel Foundation, *Physiology or Medicine: Nobel Lectures, Including Presentation Speeches and Laureates' Biographies* (3 vols., 1964–1967). Information on his work is in any review of the literature of medical virology and in virology textbooks.

ENGELS / By Saul K. Padover

The German revolutionist and social theorist Friedrich Engels (1820–1895) was the cofounder with Karl Marx of modern socialism.

Friedrich Engels (pronounced ĕng′əls) was born on Nov. 28, 1820, in Barmen, Rhenish Prussia, a small industrial town in the Wupper valley. He was the oldest of the six children of Friedrich and Elisabeth Franziska Mauritia Engels. The senior Engels, a textile manufacturer, was a Christian Pietist and religious fanatic. After attending elementary school at Barmen, young Friedrich entered the gymnasium in nearby Elberfeld at the age of 14, but he left it 3 years later. Although he became one of the most learned men of his time, he had no further formal schooling.

Under pressure from his tyrannical father, Friedrich became a business apprentice in Barmen and Bremen, but he soon called it a "dog's life." He left business at the age of 20, in rebellion against both his joyless home and the "penny-pinching" world of commerce. Henceforth, Engels was a lifelong enemy of organized religion and of capitalism, although he was again forced into business for a number of years.

While doing his one-year compulsory military service (artillery) in Berlin, Engels came into contact with the radical Young Hegelians and embraced their ideas, particularly the materialist philosophy of Ludwig Feuerbach. After some free-lance journalism, part of it under the pseudonym of F. Oswald, in November 1842 Engels went to Manchester, England, to work in the office of Engels and Ermens, a spinning factory in which his father was a partner. In Manchester, the manufacturing center of the world's foremost capitalist country, Engels had the opportunity of observing capitalism's operations—and its distressing effects on the workers—at first hand. He also studied the leading economic writers, among them Adam Smith, David Ricardo, and Robert Owen in English, and Jean Baptiste Say, Charles Fourier, and Pierre Joseph Proudhon in French. He left Manchester in August 1844.

On his way back to Germany, Engels stopped in Paris, where he met Karl Marx for a second time. On this occasion a lifelong intellectual rapport was established between them. Finding they were of the same opinion about nearly everything, Marx and Engels decided to collaborate on their writing.

Engels spent the next 5 years in Germany, Belgium, and France, writing and participating in revolutionary activities. He fought in the 1849 revolutionary uprising in Baden and the Palatinate, seeing action in four military engagements. After the defeat of the revolution, he escaped to Switzerland. In October 1849, using the sea route via Genoa, he sailed to England, which became his permanent home.

In November 1850, unable to make a living as a writer in London and anxious to help support the penniless Marx, Engels reluctantly returned to his father's business in Manchester. In 1864, after his father's death, he became a partner in the firm, and by early 1869 he felt that he had enough capital to support himself and to provide Marx with a regular annuity of £350. On July 1, 1869, Engels sold his share of the business to his partner. He exulted in a letter to Marx: "Hurrah! Today I finished with sweet commerce, and I am a free man!" Marx's daughter, Eleanor, who saw Engels on that day, wrote: "I shall never forget the triumphant 'For the last time,' which he shouted as he drew on his top-boots in the morning to make his last journey to business. Some hours later, when we were standing at the door waiting for him, we saw him coming across the little field opposite his home. He was flourishing his walking stick in the air and singing, and laughing all over his face."

In September 1870 Engels moved to London, settling near the home of Marx, whom he saw daily. A generous friend and gay host, the fun-loving Engels spent the remaining 25 years of his life in London, enjoying good food, good wine, and good company. He also worked hard, doing the things he loved: writing, maintaining contact and a voluminous correspondence with radicals everywhere, and—after Marx's death in 1883—laboring over the latter's notes and manuscripts, bringing out volumes 2 and 3 of *Das Kapital* in 1885 and 1894, respectively. Engels died of cancer on Aug. 5, 1895. Following his instructions, his body was cremated and his ashes strewn over the ocean at Eastbourne, his favorite holiday resort.

Personality and Character

Engels was medium-height, slender, and athletic. His body was disciplined by swimming, fencing, and riding. He dressed and acted like an elegant English gentleman. In Manchester, where he maintained two homes—one for appearances, as befitted a member of the local stock exchange, and another for his Irish mistress—he rode to hounds with the English gentry, whom he despised as capitalists but by whose antic behavior he was sardonically amused.

Engels had a brilliant mind and was quick, sharp, and unerring in his judgments. His versatility was astonishing. A successful businessman, he also had a grasp of virtually every branch of the natural sciences, biology, chemistry, botany, and physics. He was a widely respected specialist on military affairs. He mastered numerous languages, including all the Slavic ones, on which he planned to write a comparative grammar. He also knew Gothic, Old Nordic, and Old Saxon, studied Arabic, and in 3 weeks learned Persian, which he said was "mere child's play." His English, both spoken and written, was impeccable. It was said of him that he "stutters in 20 languages."

Engels apparently never married. He loved, and lived with successively, two Irish sisters, Mary (who died in

1863) and Lydia (Lizzy) Burns (1827–1878). After he moved to London, he referred to Lizzy as "my wife." The Burns sisters, ardent Irish patriots, stirred in Engels a deep sympathy for the Irish cause. He said of Lizzy Burns: "She came of real Irish proletarian stock, and the passionate feeling for her class, which was instinctive with her, was worth more to me than all the blue-stockinged elegance of 'educated' and 'sensitive' bourgeois girls."

His Writings

Engels published hundreds of articles, a number of prefaces (mostly to Marx's works), and about half a dozen books during his lifetime. His first important book, written when he was 24 years old, was *The Condition of the Working Class in England in 1844*, based on observations made when he lived in Manchester. It was published in German in 1845 and in English in 1892. His next publication was the *Manifesto of the Communist Party* (*Communist Manifesto*), which he wrote in collaboration with Marx between December 1847 and January 1848, and which was published in London in German a month later. An anonymous English edition came out in London in 1850.

Engels also collaborated with Marx on *The Holy Family*, an attack on the Young Hegelian philosopher Bruno Bauer, which was published in Germany in 1845. Another collaboration with Marx, *The German Ideology*, was written in 1845–1846, but it was not published in full until 1932.

In 1870 Engels published *The Peasant War in Germany*, which consisted of a number of articles he had written in 1850; an English translation appeared in 1956. In 1878 he published perhaps his most important book, *Herr Eugen Dühring's Revolution in Science*, known in an English translation as *Anti-Dühring* (1959). This work ranks, together with Marx's *Das Kapital*, as the most comprehensive study of socialist (Marxist) theory. In it, Engels wrote, he treated "every possible subject, from the concepts of time and space to bimetallism; from the eternity of matter and motion to the perishable nature of moral ideas; from Darwin's natural selection to the education of youth in a future society."

Engels's *Development of Socialism from Utopia to Science* was published in German in 1882 and in English, under the title *Socialism, Utopian and Scientific*, in 1892. In 1884 he brought out *The Origins of the Family, Private Property and the State*, an indispensable work for understanding Marxist political theory. His last work, published in 1888, was *Ludwig Feuerbach and the End of Classical German Philosophy*. Both of these last books are available in English. Two works by Engels were published posthumously: *Germany: Revolution and Counter-Revolution* (German, 1896; English, 1933) and *Dialectics of Nature*, begun in 1895 but never completed, of which an English translation appeared in 1964.

Engels's Ideas

In his articles and books Engels elaborated and developed, both historically and logically, basic ideas that go under the name of Marxism. His work was not an imitation of Marx but constituted a consistent philosophy at

Friedrich Engels. (Bildarchiv)

which both men had arrived independently and had shared in common. Engels refined the concept of dialectical materialism, which Marx had never fully worked out, to include not only matter but also form. He stressed that the materialist conception takes into consideration the whole cultural process, including tradition, religion, and ideology, which goes through constant historical evolution. Each stage of development, containing also what Engels called "thought material," builds upon the totality of previous developments. Thus every man is a product both of his own time and of the past. Similarly, he elaborated his view of the state, which he regarded as "nothing less than a machine for the oppression of one class by another," as evolving, through class struggles, into the "dictatorship of the proletariat."

Further Reading

Friedrich Engels is listed in the Social Sciences study guide (VI, B, 2; VI, C, 1 and 2). His contributions to modern socialist and communist theory were second only to those of Karl MARX.

Although Engels's writings are available in English, there is no good biography of him in English. Some biographical information can be found in Gustav Mayer, *Friedrich Engels: A Biography* (1934; trans. 1936), a dated and incomplete work; Grace Carlton, *Friedrich Engels: The Shadow Prophet* (1965), a superficial biography not based on original sources; and Oscar J. Hammen, *The Red 48'ers: Karl Marx and Friedrich Engels* (1969). Good general works which discuss Engels are Edmund

Wilson, *To the Finland Station: A Study in the Writing and Acting of History* (1940); George Lichtheim, *Marxism: An Historical and Critical Study* (1961); and Bertram D. Wolfe, *Marxism: One Hundred Years in the Life of a Doctrine* (1965).

✳ ✳ ✳

ENGLAND / By Donald K. Gorrell

The Irish churchman John England (1786–1842) was a controversial figure in Ireland and America. The first Roman Catholic bishop of Charleston, S.C., he founded the first American Catholic newspaper.

Born in Cork on Sept. 23, 1786, John England was educated in a Protestant school, where he was ridiculed as the only "papist." He trained for the priesthood at the College of St. Patrick. Ordained at Cork in 1808, he served there until 1817. His labors as chaplain, educator, preacher, and writer earned favorable attention, but his political agitation displeased leaders of both Church and state. Finally, in what seemed an attempt to get him out of the way, he was appointed bishop of the new diocese of Charleston, S.C.

Arriving in America in 1820, England discovered among the disorganized flock of Catholics spread throughout the Carolinas and Georgia a strong element of "trusteeism"—that is, laymen preferred to select their own priests. He proposed to correct this by creating a democratic constitution for the diocese that would provide for conventions of priests and laity but abolish parish trustees. Though his people accepted this compromise, it was viewed unfavorably by northern bishops. In Philadelphia and New York, England attracted Irish Catholic loyalties; this was regarded by local bishops as meddling and increased England's unpopularity with the hierarchy.

During 1822 England created a seminary, where he did much of the training of priests himself. He also started publishing the *United States Catholic Miscellany* (1822–1861), the first distinctly Catholic paper in America, which sought to defend the faith against outside attacks, explain Catholic doctrine, and convey internal Church news. It stands as his greatest achievement, even though episcopal jealousies kept it from becoming a national journal.

Through the *Miscellany* and his numerous controversies, and as a preacher and speaker, England became nationally famous. In 1826, as the first Catholic to address a joint session of the U.S. Congress, he spoke for 2 hours on Catholic beliefs. Yet his anticipated appointment to a more prestigious diocese never materialized. Meanwhile, partly because of his extended absences from the diocese, his constituency failed to enlarge. A steady burden of debts and growing fatigue led to prolonged illness; he died on April 11, 1842.

Further Reading

John England is listed in the Religion study guide (I, Q, 2, a). Others involved in developing American Catholicism included John CARROLL and John HUGHES.

The standard source is a critical edition of England's works, *The Works of the Right Reverend John England, First Bishop of Charleston*, edited by Sebastian G. Messmer, Archbishop of Milwaukee (7 vols., 1908). Peter Guilday, *The Life and Times of John England, First Bishop of Charleston, 1786–1842* (2 vols., 1927), remains the authoritative biography. See also Dorothy Grant, *John England* (1949). For background see Thomas T. McAvoy, *A History of the Catholic Church in the United States* (1969).

✳ ✳ ✳

John England, a portrait by J. M. Fontaine. (Bulloz)

ENNIN / By John Kie-chiang Oh

Ennin (794–864) was a Japanese monk who founded the Sammon branch of the Tendai sect. He studied Esoteric Buddhism in T'ang China.

The family name of Ennin (pronounced ĕn-nēn) was Mibu, and he was born in the Tsuga district of Shimotsuke Province (modern Tochigi Prefecture). Becoming a disciple of Saicho, the founder of the Tendai sect in Japan, Ennin led a rather colorless life as a monk and teacher at the Enryakuji (another name for this

Ennin. (International Society for Educational Information, Tokyo, Inc.)

temple was Sammon). He was sent to China for study in 838. His *Nyuto Gubo Junreiki* (Record of the Pilgrimage to China in Search of the Holy Law) is full of fascinating details of his adventures, from the time he sailed from Japan until his return in 847.

At first unable to obtain the necessary Chinese authorization to visit either of China's two most important Buddhist centers on Mt. Wu-t'ai and Mt. T'ien-t'ai, Ennin later managed to secure the help of an influential general to reach Mt. Wu-t'ai and other holy sites. Ennin returned to Japan after extensive study with the masters of each of the Tendai disciplines.

Upon his return to Mt. Hiei, the Emperor conferred upon Ennin the rank of *daihosshi* (great monk). Ennin then organized study of the two Mandalas, initiated Esoteric baptism, and promoted other branches of Esoteric learning. He taught the invocation of Buddha's name (*nembutsu*), which he had heard on Mt. Wu-t'ai and which was to become in some of the popular sects an all-sufficient means of gaining salvation, though for Ennin it appeared to be of less importance than Esoteric learning.

Ennin stayed on Mt. Hiei as *zasu* (chief abbot) for more than 20 years, and during his ministry he founded the monastery called Onjoji (more usually known as Miidera) at the foot of Mt. Hiei on the shore of Lake Biwa. A measure of Ennin's success is the fact that the bestowal by the court in 866 of the posthumous title of

Jikaku Daishi on him and that of Dengyo Daishi on his master Saicho marks the beginning of the custom of posthumous titles in Japan.

Further Reading

Ennin is listed in the Asia study guide (III, B, 3, b). The founders of Esoteric Buddhism in Japan were KUKAI and SAICHO.

There is a brief discussion of Ennin's diary describing the hazards of his trip to T'ang China and the introduction of Esoteric cults to Japan in Edwin O. Reischauer and John K. Fairbank, *East Asia: The Great Tradition* (1960). A cogent discussion of the spread of Esoteric Buddhism in Japan is in Ryusaku Tsunoda and others, *Sources of Japanese Tradition* (1958). For a brief discussion of Ennin's role in the development of the Heian Society see George B. Sansom, *A History of Japan* (3 vols., 1958–1963).

ENNIUS / By Michael Simpson

> Quintus Ennius (239–169 B.C.) was a Roman poet. Called the father of Latin poetry, he is most famous for his "Annales," a narrative poem relating the history of Rome.

Ennius (pronounced ĕn′ĭ-əs) was born at Rudiae in Calabria. He knew three languages or had, as he said, "three hearts": Oscan, his native tongue; Greek, in which he was educated, possibly at Tarentum; and Latin, which he learned as a centurion in the Roman army. While stationed at Sardinia during the Second Punic War, he met Cato the Elder, whom he taught Greek. Cato took him to Rome in 204 B.C.

At Rome, Ennius lived frugally on the Aventine. He supported himself at first by teaching Greek, then turned to adapting Greek tragedies and some comedies for the Roman stage, and he wrote poetry as well. He was a friend of prominent Romans of that time, especially Scipio Africanus and Marcus Fulvius Nobilior and his son Quintus, who gained for him Roman citizenship. Ennius knew the comic poet Caecilius Statius, and Pacuvius, the Roman dramatist, was his nephew.

Ennius was a very versatile poet although, according to Ovid, he possessed more genius than art. The remains of Ennius's works are fragmentary. Of the *Annales*, the most important part, some 600 lines or about one-fiftieth of the whole, remains. Some fragments are as long as 20 lines.

Naevius had written a historical epic before Ennius, but the special claim to greatness of his *Annales* is its meter, the hexameter. Henceforth, much of the greatest Latin poetry would use this meter. The poet's hexameters seem crude and clumsy beside Virgil's, often being heavily spondaic, ignoring caesuras and elisions, and carrying alliteration and assonance to extremes. Neverthe-

Ennius, an ancient portrait. (Vatican Museums, Rome)

less, they can at times rise to a rugged and powerful dignity.

Euripides was a favorite model for Ennius in his adaptations of Greek tragedy. Of the 22 titles of plays known to be his, 3 are from extant tragedies of Euripides. Fragments of his tragedies number about 400 lines.

As a writer of comedy, Ennius was evidently less successful, for only two titles are known. Lesser works include *Satires* (Latin *satura*, medley), a work in varying meters on different topics, including criticism of morals and politics, and the first work of its kind; *Epigrams*; *Hedyphagetica*, or *The Art of Dining*; *Epicharmus*, a didactic poem on nature; and *Euhemerus*, a rationalization of Greek mythology.

Ennius's contribution to Roman culture was twofold. First, by adapting Greek tragedies he made Greek ideas current at Rome; and second, he had a direct influence on subsequent writers.

Ennius was of a convivial nature if Horace, who said he always composed in his cups, and Jerome, who said he died of gout, can be believed. He was writing until his death, and his version of the play *Thyestes* was produced the year he died.

Further Reading

Ennius is listed in the Literature study guide (III, A, 2,

a). He influenced LUCRETIUS and VIRGIL in didactic and epic poetry. CICERO quoted Ennius frequently.

A new standard reference work on Ennius is *The Tragedies of Ennius: The Fragments*, edited by H. D. Jocelyn (1967), a comprehensive volume with a Latin text, full explanatory introduction, and extensive interpretative commentary. For more information on Ennius and his place in Latin literature see H. J. Rose, *A Handbook of Latin Literature* (1936; 3d ed. with a new bibliography, 1961), and Moses Hadas, *A History of Latin Literature* (1952).

ENSOR / By Reinhold A. Heller

The Belgian painter and graphic artist James Ensor (1860–1949) populated his works with masks, skeletons, and grotesque images of humanity. A sense of existential anxiety dominates his fantastic personal visions.

I was born at Ostend, on Friday, April 13, 1860, the day of Venus. At my birth Venus came toward me, smiling, and we looked into each other's eyes. She smelled pleasantly of salt water." In this imaginative recollection of his birth, James Ensor (pronounced ĕn′sôr) also described the duality of his art:

James Ensor's Self-portrait in the Flowered Hat *(1883), in the Musée des Beaux Arts, Ostend. (Giraudon)*

Entry of Christ into Brussels, an 1888 painting by Ensor, in the L. Franck Collection, London. (Lauros-Giraudon)

on the one hand, the fantasies of a humanistically inclined imagination; on the other, the pleasures and terrors observed as a child living in a somber Belgian town whose existence was threatened by the same sea which was its source of life. Before beginning art studies at the Brussels Academy in 1877, Ensor painted the landscape surrounding Ostend—small houses isolated in vast light-flooded spaces. At the academy he began painting imaginative, rhetorical themes; under the influence of Dutch baroque painting and French impressionism he started using a free, divided brushstroke.

After 3 years of study Ensor returned to Ostend to the attic studio above his parents' souvenir shop; he spent the remainder of his uneventful life in Ostend. Using heavy, impasto pigments, he depicted the middle-class interiors in which his family lived. A somber, disquieting air of mystery surrounds the isolated figures as they drink tea, listen to piano music, or sit in melancholy introspection.

In 1883 Ensor became a founding member of the Belgian avant-garde artists' group Les XX, which brought works by contemporary French artists to Brussels and fought for increased artistic freedom from the dictates of official taste. From 1883 until 1887 Ensor painted little but evolved the overtly fantastic images with which his art is generally associated. The carnival masks of Ostend surrounding him in his studio made their appearance in *Scandalized Masks* (1883) and *Haunted Furniture* (1885; destroyed) and were joined by numerous skeletons bringing psychotic horror and terror into the bourgeois interiors. The life and temptations of Christ, de-

picted with the features of the artist, became the subject matter of numerous drawings in 1886; he developed these motifs in his first etchings that year. He created 133 prints, most of them during 1885, 1889, and 1895–1899.

In the etching *The Cathedral* (1886) Ensor first explored the theme of a mocking, destructive, roving mob. His most noted painting, the *Entry of Christ into Brussels* (1888), depicts raucous carnival crowds escorting Christ-Ensor into the city, which is decorated with Socialist banners and advertisements for mustard. The massive canvas is a caustic commentary on contemporary Belgian political, artistic, and social values. Even Les XX refused to exhibit it, and during the following years this group continued to reject his controversial work.

Probably Ensor's unique use of Christian imagery rather than his unorthodox painting technique with its impasto surfaces, slashing brushstrokes, and depersonalized images caused his works to be disclaimed by academic and "free" artists as well as by critics. By identifying himself with Christ, Ensor transformed accepted biblical imagery into personal observations on the universal conflicts of innocence and evil, as well as private attacks on his critics; opposition to his own symbolic art thereby became equated with the tortures of Christ's Passion.

Ensor's sole contact with the world around him was through the medium of his art, which reflected the imagery of his eccentric, morose broodings. Even still-life paintings and landscapes appear strangely menacing, imbued with the erotic, sadistic, and self-tormenting qualities of Ensor's narrative paintings. In the smaller and more private scale of his prints and drawings, his morbid demonology attained an even greater psychotic intensity as he condemned humanity and himself to the visual torments of his private inferno.

After 1900 Ensor's imagery became tamer, more a parody than a condemnation of society, perhaps a reflection of the esteem he finally gained in official art circles. To his achievements as a painter, he added those of a writer of essays and plays, reflecting the world of his paintings and prints. A greatly respected and honored citizen of Ostend, Ensor died on Nov. 19, 1949.

Further Reading

James Ensor is listed in the Art study guide (III, H, 4). Other artists who depicted a heightened and distorted actuality were Vincent VAN GOGH, Ferdinand HODLER, and Edvard MUNCH.

The most perceptive analysis of Ensor's work is Libby Tannenbaum, *James Ensor* (1951). A more subjective approach is by the poet Paul Haesaerts, *James Ensor* (1957; trans. 1959), which offers numerous color reproductions. For background information see Bernard S. Meyers, *The German Expressionists: A Generation in Revolt* (1957; concise ed. 1963), and Peter Selz, *German Expressionist Painting* (1957).

ENVER PASHA / By Janet E. Ragatz

The Turkish soldier Enver Pasha (1881–1922) was the dominant member of the Young Turk triumvirate ruling the Ottoman Empire during World War I.

Enver Pasha. (Radio Times Hulton Picture Library)

On Nov. 23, 1881, Enver Pasha (pronounced ən-vĕr′ pä-shä′) was born of a Turkish father, a bridge keeper in the Black Sea town of Apana, and an Albanian mother. Joining the military, he was posted as a subaltern to Salonika, where he joined a secret antigovernment group. He rose rapidly in the public eye when, in the spring of 1908, he defied Sultan Abdul Hamid II and fled with fellow rebel officers into the Macedonian hills. Their demand was for restoration of the 1876 Constitution, suspended since 1877. Always action-minded, always alert to the dramatic, he enjoyed his activities as a member of the liberal Committee of Union and Progress, the "Young Turks," particularly after the 3d Army Corps threatened to march on Istanbul in July and forced Abdul Hamid to restore the constitution.

The Young Turks established a government under Mahmud Shevket but were nearly overthrown on April 14, 1909. Enver participated in both movements and then returned to Berlin, where he had been serving as military attaché. He was awed by Prussian militarism and left in 1911 to join in the Turkish defense of Benghazi against the Italians. He detailed this experience in *Tripoli* (1918).

Returning to Istanbul, Enver became chief of staff of the 10th Army Corps, which he led into the Second Balkan War in a futile landing attempt on the Gallipoli Peninsula in February 1913; in July, Enver reoccupied Edirne.

Between the wars Enver participated in the shooting of the war minister, Nazim Pasha, and the ouster of the pro-British grand vizier, Kiamil Pasha. In January 1913 the Young Turks resumed control of the government. The assassination of their premier, Mahmud Shevket, in June intensified their aggressiveness. A major purge followed, with Enver dismissing over 1,200 officers in one day alone. By Jan. 13, 1914, Enver had made himself minister of war, a strategic position from which he influenced his associates into an alliance with Germany signed secretly on August 2. Subsequently he approved the German bombardment of Odessa and Sevastopol, which precipitated the Ottoman Empire's entry into World War I.

During the winter of 1914/1915 Enver Pasha, leading a Turkish army in the Caucasus, suffered a disastrous defeat. He compounded this bloody record with acquiescence in the forced deportation and consequent death of innumerable Armenians evacuated from the frontier area.

Enver subsequently became the dominant personality in the government, but his aloofness and vanity alienated him from other Young Turks. When the Ottoman Empire collapsed, he fled to Germany and later to Russia. Condemned to death in Istanbul, he died leading an anti-Bolshevik insurrection among the Central Asian Turks around Bukhara on Aug. 4, 1922.

Further Reading

Enver Pasha is listed in the Asia study guide (I, E, 2). Many of his efforts paved the way for the reforms of Kemal ATATÜRK.

Ernest E. Ramsaur, *The Young Turks: Prelude to the Revolution of 1908* (1957), is an excellent source on Enver Pasha. Enver Pasha's later career is recounted in detail in Ulrich Trumpener, *Germany and the Ottoman Empire, 1914–1918* (1968). Also useful is Frank G. Weber, *Eagles on the Crescent: Germany, Austria, and the Diplomacy of the Turkish Alliance, 1914–1918* (1970).

✳   ✳   ✳